A 3

Enterprise in Oil

Enterprise in Oil

A HISTORY OF SHELL
IN THE UNITED STATES

by

KENDALL BEATON

New York

APPLETON-CENTURY-CROFTS, INC.

1957

About This Book

T HIS BOOK is an attempt to present, within the confines of a single
volume, the story of the origin and growth of the Shell Oil Company and its predecessor and subsidiary companies in the United States.

In preparing it, the author, a member of the company's staff, has had
full access to all company records and has been assisted by company
personnel in every way possible. The resulting book is "official" only in
that the company willingly sat for its portrait and paid the painter's fee;
it does not necessarily endorse the result.

In the history of an enterprise begun as recently as 1912, many events
are still too near for judicious appraisal. For this reason, the author has
tried to stick to facts and avoid unnecessary historical judgments and
other expressions of opinion. Despite this attempt, his own views have, of
course, crept in; in these cases, it should be borne in mind that opinions
are the author's and not the company's.

The author feels especially fortunate in having had the benefit of the
combined recollections of the men who helped found and build the Shell
Oil Company. Acknowledgment of his indebtedness to them individually,
and to the many others who helped with this book, is made in the pages
immediately following the text.

Many aspects of the history of any company are too specialized or too
detailed to interest the general reader. To remove this material from the
text and yet preserve it for those who are interested, a chronology, a
listing of officers of the chief Shell subsidiaries, and tables showing the
company's main financial and operating statistics have been arranged as
appendices at the back of the book.

The present volume will amply fulfill its purpose if it can assist some
future historian, twenty-five or fifty years hence, in arriving at a better
appraisal of the Shell companies and their place on the American scene.

Contents

Maps and Illustrations

Enterprise in Oil

CHAPTER I

Big Moment of the Nineteenth Century

THE Shell oil companies in America are of recent origin and rapid growth. It was only a little more than forty years ago that they started from two small concerns, one in Seattle, the other in Tulsa. The growth of these small companies in four decades has been impressive—from nothing in 1912 to the present nation-wide organization whose yearly sales and total assets now regularly pass the billion-dollar mark to place Shell well up in the ranks of America's top twenty companies. In their rapid development the American Shell companies have hardly been alone. Their rise has reflected the steady growth of the American oil business, an industry which has itself come a long way in forty years. A century ago it did not exist.

Of the world's large and essential industries, petroleum is one of the newest. Not quite a century ago, kerosene made from newly discovered American crude oil vaulted into world-wide use, banishing the after-sunset darkness to which the average man, through the centuries, had been accustomed. This new oil was put to use to manufacture lubricants for the mechanical wheels which powered the great second industrial revolution of the 1870's and 1880's. As a fuel, petroleum replaced coal on the seas, giving a longer cruising range to the trading and naval fleets of the world. In the form of gasoline, petroleum made possible the invention and development of two brand-new forms of transport: the automobile and the airplane. All this since E. L. Drake brought in his first oil well at Titusville, Pennsylvania, on an August afternoon in 1859.

And yet, petroleum, and the industry which has made it an almost universal article of commerce, are only in a sense "new." It would, perhaps, be more accurate to say that Drake's well signalized the rediscovery by the Western World of the usefulness of petroleum.

In 1859, this very same "rock oil" was one of the substances longest known to man—known, in fact, since the dawn of recorded history some six thousand years ago.

In that area of the Near East between the Tigris and Euphrates rivers which is generally conceded to be the first known home of man, there were, and still are, surface evidences of hard asphalt, fluid asphalt, and asphaltic oil deposits. To the north, on the Caspian Sea, was the area of Baku and its rich oil deposits, where gas escaping through crevices gave rise in prehistoric times to sects of fire-worshippers. Even today the temples of one of these sects, the Parsees, may be found there.[1] * Farther west in Palestine, the Dead Sea, which apparently has seepages in its bed, has had asphalt floating on the surface of the water as far back as people can remember. This famous "asphalt fishery" furnished bitumen to the ancient Egyptians who used it, first to impregnate cerements in which they wrapped their dead, and later on, in actual mummification.[2]

The Old Testament is full of references to asphalt which modern readers do not usually recognize because the English translators of the King James Version, themselves not knowing the product, translated the Greek word *asphaltos* as *slime* or *pitch*. Noah, building his Ark, used natural asphalt as a caulking agent. The builders of the Tower of Babel used it for mortar. And Moses' mother, making him a cradle of bulrushes, "daubed it with slime and with pitch, and put the child therein."[3]

The word "petroleum," from the Greek words meaning "rock oil," did not appear in Medieval Latin until around 1000 A.D. In ancient times, the words used to designate both crude oil and its products were *naphtha, asphaltos (um), bitumen,* and *maltha*. In the common parlance, it was "rock oil," "mineral oil," "earth oil," "earth balsam," "earth wax," and many other similar terms. And there were numberless nicknames denoting the area in which a particular petroleum was found: Persian naphtha, Jew's pitch, Rangoon oil, Trinidad bitumen, Barbados tar, Seneca oil, and so on. The first three of these names—naphtha, asphalt, and bitumen—survive in modern usage, but now are applied to petroleum fractions of definite specification.[4]

Other ancient peoples of the Tigris-Euphrates area knew of asphalt

---

* Numbered footnotes are citations of sources which are gathered in the back of the book, beginning on page 705; the casual reader probably will not find it necessary to consult them. Explanatory footnotes are indicated by symbols and appear at the bottom of the pages.

and used it widely as an adhesive and waterproofing agent. In lower Mesopotamia, part of the present-day country of Iraq, excavations have unearthed ornaments and statuary of the ancient Sumerians dating back to 3500 B.C. in which asphalt, perfectly preserved, acted as the adhesive element. The Sumerians' successors, the Babylonians, put asphalt to much more widespread use in paving, wall-building, and waterproofing. They are credited with using bituminous mortar as early as 2200 B.C. Its use in succeeding dynasties led to public building projects, each more impressive than the one which had preceded it—temples, palaces, public buildings, the famous hanging gardens of Babylon (one of the Seven Wonders of the Ancient World), roadways, sewers, retaining walls to keep back the river Euphrates, bridges to cross it, and even a tunnel under it. In all these, asphalt, much of it intact today, served as the bonding agent. By the time of the fall of Babylon in the sixth century before Christ, mortar made with lime was coming into use, and continued in use throughout the ensuing Persian empire. It is interesting to note the effect of this change upon the permanence of public building; many Babylonian works still exist while those of the later-day Persians have completely passed away. Unaffected by time, asphalt mortar contemporary with the Tower of Babel still can be found joining together blocks of stone which have long since turned to dust.[5]

Nor were petroleum deposits confined to the Near East. In India, modern excavators have discovered, in the remains of an ancient, unknown, pre-Aryan civilization which flourished there about 3000 B.C., baths made of brick in which asphalt was used as a waterproofing liner. As early as 200 B.C., when the young and virile Roman Republic was still fighting Carthage in the Punic Wars, the Chinese had already developed oil-drilling methods, using the same principles as those employed by Drake. They went as deep as 3,500 feet, using bamboo poles and crude brass bits.[6]

Beside their early prowess at drilling for oil, the Chinese also put natural gas to use. Early European travellers visiting China found that each well-to-do Chinese attempted, if possible, to have his own "fire well." The gas was conducted away in hollow bamboo poles to desired locations where it was burned to provide both heat and light. A porcelain orifice placed in the end of the bamboo pole kept it from catching fire.[7] But advanced as the Chinese methods were, they were of scant use to the Western World which did not hear of them until nearly 2,000 years later.

We also know now, although the world of the ancients did not, that in almost every quarter of the globe surface petroleum deposits were to be found, dating from antiquity. Such proved to be the case, to mention only a few instances, in Burma and the East Indies; in Romania and Galicia; in California; in the Gulf area of Texas and Mexico; in the Allegheny Mountain region of Pennsylvania and New York; in the Caribbean—Cuba, Trinidad, Venezuela.

Petroleum was also early put to medicinal and agricultural uses, probably most intelligently by the Romans. As medicine it was, of course, a component of strange preparations which would today excite ridicule. But it is noteworthy that Roman writers such as Varro described the disinfecting qualities of petroleum and oil vapors. Perhaps even more remarkable, Varro employed it to fight various diseases which were caused, he insisted, by invisible, tiny creatures. Uses of oil in agriculture, described in the *Geoponica* of the third and fourth centuries A.D., included the burning of petroleum as a fumigant beneath bushes and trees to kill caterpillars; daubing exposed portions of trees with a tar-like mixture of asphalt and oil; painting rings of a bituminous agglutinant around tree trunks to keep ants away—not to mention rubbing hens with a mixture of bitumen, resin, and sulphur to make them lay bigger eggs! [8]

And in war, petroleum early assumed tremendous importance as a chief ingredient of "Greek Fire," a mixture of finely divided quicklime and petroleum which would ignite spontaneously upon contact with moisture. Although the principle seems known in the days of the early Roman Empire, it remained for the later-day Eastern Roman (Byzantine) Empire to introduce the Western World's first explosive weapon and make it the terror of the Middle Ages. Spurting from pumps mounted on the prows of Byzantine vessels, or thrown in hand grenades that closely resembled modern grenades, Greek Fire was the atomic bomb of its day (a period of nearly a thousand years) and the secret of its manufacture was just as carefully guarded. Possession of this destructive weapon in an age of hand-to-hand fighting helped account for the supremacy of the Byzantine empire during medieval times, and it was not until the introduction of gunpowder that Constantinople finally fell in 1453.[9]

While most of the early uses of petroleum centered about asphalt, petroleum did, to a limited extent, find some use among the ancients in the applications for which it was later to become famous: as a source of heat and light. There is considerable evidence for believing that the ancient peoples of the Tigris-Euphrates area burned crude oil for heat and light, although probably on a limited scale. Except as just mentioned, petroleum found little use in the Roman and Greek empires, for the very good reason that neither of these peoples had abundant supplies of oil in their own homelands. The Arab culture of the Middle Ages did, however, keep alive and spread its knowledge of petroleum. We have extensive evidence that Arabs of this period refined and sold oil, chiefly from Persia, on a substantial scale. By the early 900's the Sultan's guards at Cairo were burning a petroleum distillate in their torches; and tradition tells us that the great Cairo fire of 1077 destroyed some 1,400 barrels (equivalent to nearly eight railroad tank cars) of naphtha and crude oil.[10]

In the Baku area, there was a considerable petroleum industry at an early date. Marco Polo, visiting the area in 1272, reported "in the neighborhood no other [oil] is used in their lamps and people come from distant parts to procure it." [11] The first British ambassadors to Burma in the late 1700's found a flourishing petroleum industry in existence there, one estimate declaring that there were in excess of 500 hand-dug wells in operation supplying burning oil for upwards of seven million customers.[12] And in many areas of Europe small local petroleum seepages were worked, and the oil sold nearby for burning and for axle grease.

The reader may wonder that oil had not, as late as 1850, been put to use in Western Europe as a source of heat and light. It was a question of the economics of distribution. Most of the sources of supply were in far-off places, difficult or impossible to reach by existing transportation. The Burmese fields were located far up the Irrawaddy River, half a world away; the fields of Persia and Meso-potamia were in the middle of a vast desert; the Baku field faced the landlocked Caspian Sea, completely cut off from the West by the Caucasus Mountain range. Had large oil deposits been located on the outskirts of London, Paris, or Rome, there is no doubt that the petroleum industry would have developed centuries sooner.

In the end, the modern petroleum industry was inaugurated by the discovery of oil in western Pennsylvania, an area traversed by, or near to, four large railway systems. And this discovery was preceded by three decades of persistent searching for new illuminants, resulting in the development of a new trade devoted to marketing patent lamps and oils to go with them.

Kerosene and Coal Oil

SINCE the dawn of history, the world had literally been waiting for the sunrise, for it provided the only practical source of light. True—lamps, candles, torches, braziers, tapers, and other sources of artificial light had been known for centuries, but only the wealthy could afford to use them regularly. The poor man sat by an open fire when he wanted light; otherwise he went to bed. Cheap, artificial illuminants brought a tremendous change to the life-after-dark of the average man, and in a very short time.

The beginnings of this tremendous change started with improvements in the lamp. For centuries, the "classical" lamp made of clay, stone, terra cotta, china, or metal had been in use in almost every place where animal and vegetable oils were burned to produce light. This lamp was nothing more than a shallow vessel with a handle on one side and a spigot for the wick on the opposite side. The wick, made of fibers, was solid like a piece of rope; to increase the size of the flame the size of the wick could be enlarged up to a point. When the wick was made too large, imperfect combustion at the center of the wick caused excessive smoking and diminished rather than increased the amount of light.

A milestone in the improvement of the lamp was set forth in a patent of 1784 by Aimé Argand, a physician and chemist of Geneva, Switzerland. Argand got around the problem of incomplete combustion at the center of the wick by devising a circular wick, such as is used in oil stoves today. This introduced an updraft through the center and allowed the wick to burn evenly on both sides, all the way around.[13] With a glass chimney added, the Argand lamp gave off a clear bright light, and was immediately put to use throughout Europe and America to burn sperm oil, made from the head of the sperm whale.†

---

† It would be a mistake to infer that only the Argand lamp was used with whale oil. Almost any shallow vessel with a wick would work after a fashion. The whale-oil lamp common in America was a small glass jar with a wick in the center and no chimney, quite similar to the alcohol lamp still used by chemists. Also in widespread use in humbler homes, from colonial times up to about 1850, were the "Phoebe" and "Betty" lamps, generally hung from the ceiling. They burned any kind of animal or vegetable fat, and used a piece of twisted rag for a wick. A discussion of candles, which date back many centuries, is here omitted because candles have been in every age a more expensive source of light than lamps.[14]

Sperm oil, and a secondary grade called merely "whale oil," were the most popular illuminants then available. Dutch fishermen had introduced whale oil to modern Europe about 1650, but soon exhausted the supply of whales in nearby waters. During the 1700's, the business of whale fishing shifted to America and centered about the Massachusetts ports of Gloucester, New Bedford, and Nantucket. The American whale fishermen, like their Dutch counterparts, soon killed off all the nearby whales, and undertook progressively longer trips in their search for whale oil. First it was to Brazil and the South Atlantic, then around the Horn to the Pacific. Since whaling vessels did not return home until they had full cargoes of oil, voyages got longer in both distance and time, until some vessels were going as far as the Japan Sea, staying out of port two or more years and prying into every nook and cranny of the world which might hide a whale. In the face of the increased cost of such voyages, the price of whale oil went higher and higher, until by the mid-1850's, sperm oil was bringing between $2 and $2.50 per gallon, a large amount in a day when the average head of a family earned only a few dollars a week.

With rising prices, substitutes for whale oil were offered. In the 1780's, the idea of burning a naphtha distilled from coal tar had been proposed in a patent by the Earl of Dundonald.[15] About 1820, Karl von Reichenbach of Stuttgart, Germany, distilled from wood tar and coal tar a wax which he called paraffin.[16] In France, Belgium, Holland, and Germany, considerable interest was displayed in colza oil, pressed from the seeds of a cabbage-family plant grown in those countries. In Scotland, a fish oil was produced and sold. And in Western Europe and America, a new oil, camphene, made its appearance. Because it was distilled from turpentine and then mixed with alcohol, camphene had a disturbing tendency to explode. None of these illuminants was as satisfactory as sperm oil. The light they gave off was dim, and their price, while lower than that of the whale oils, was still not cheap.

Then, within little more than five years, a new and much more satisfactory illuminant was produced, by several men working independently of each other, each trying to produce an oil which would give as much light as whale oil but sell at a lower price.

One of the first to succeed was Dr. Abraham Gesner, a Canadian physician and geologist, who in August 1846 demonstrated at a lecture on Prince Edward Island an illuminating oil which he had made from Trinidad bitumen.[17] A few years later, in 1849, he discovered Albertite, or Albert "coal" as it was incorrectly called, a natural asphalt occurring in Albert County, New Brunswick.[18] From Albert coal, Gesner distilled a satisfactory illuminating oil, and in 1853 he came to the United States to take out patents on his process and on the name he had given to the product, Kerosene.‡ His patents, issued in June 1854, were transferred to a group of New York businessmen who organized the North American Kerosene Gas Light Company of New York, and that year built a refinery on Newtown Creek, Queens, and began the manufacture of kerosene, or "coal oil." The company's first sales agents were John H. and George W. Austen of New York, who introduced to America the "Vienna burner," a flat-wick variation of the Argand lamp which was cheap to manufacture and was soon widely copied throughout the country.[20]

Gesner had, however, been preceded to the patent office by James Young, an able Scotch manufacturing chemist with a keen appreciation of the value of patents. Late in 1847, Young had been approached by a mine owner of Derbyshire, England, who had discovered modest amounts of petroleum in one of his coal mines. Its inflammable nature made its disposal a nuisance, and the mine owner wondered if Young could make something useful from it. In the fall of 1848, Young, his lawyer, and the mine owner formed a partnership to build a small refinery to refine this petroleum into lubricating oils and paraffin § by means of processes evolved by Young.[22] Because the supply of petroleum available to him was small, Young soon turned his attention to coal,[23] and in the fall of 1850 received a British patent covering the manufacture of paraffin and an intermediate crude oil from bituminous coals.* Two years later a similar patent was granted to him in the United States. With his partners, Young set up a works at Bathgate, Scotland, where they at first manufactured naphtha and lubricating oils and, after 1856, "paraffin oil" for illumination and

‡ Derived from the Greek words *keros*, wax and *elaion*, oil. A Gesner relative, who was in the room at the time the name was being chosen, recalled thirty years later that "at that time, camphene, a compound of alcohol and spirits of turpentine, was in use as an illuminator, and it was decided to adopt its termination, the public being familiar with it, and accordingly 'Kerosene', instead of 'Keroselain' was decided upon." [19]

§ Although Young is credited by many writers with having produced an illuminating oil in 1847, there is no indication that he did so until 1856. [21]

* Actually a misnomer, as was the term "coal oil" which grew out of it. Some of these "coals," like Gesner's albertite, were asphaltic substances; others, like Young's "Bathgate Coal," were a variety of oil-bearing shale.

solid paraffin for candle-making. Young was vigorous in protecting his patent claims and did not hesitate to bring infringement suits, with the result that prospective refiners generally licensed his process. In America alone, there were, in 1858, twenty-three licensees of Young's process.[24]

Conspicuous among these American licensees was Samuel Downer, Jr., of Boston, who had been in the whale oil and sperm candle business for twenty years and had amassed a considerable fortune. In 1854, he purchased a small firm at Waltham, Massachusetts, which was making lubricating oils from the coal tar residue left over as a by-product of city-gas manufacture. A partner in this concern, a skilled chemist named Luther Atwood, and its sales agent, Joshua Merrill, continued in Downer's employ. In 1856 they went to Glasgow to build a plant for a Scotch licensee of their process, Geo. Miller & Company. While in Glasgow, Atwood saw some of Young's "Bathgate naphtha," a dark, brownish liquid which the Miller company was buying for use as a rubber solvent; by experimentation Atwood distilled a fine illuminating oil from it. When Young saw this lamp oil, he at once undertook to make it himself, and it was an almost immediate success. Atwood and Merrill returned to America full of enthusiasm and persuaded Downer to undertake the manufacture of "coal oil." At first they experimented with Trinidad asphalt, but soon gave it up, licensed Young's process, imported Albert coal from New Brunswick, and by 1858 were engaged in the manufacture of coal oil on a large scale.[25]

The achievements of these pioneers were sizeable. Gesner's accomplishment is unconsciously recalled thousands of times each day when customers all over the world ask for the lamp oil which he first called kerosene. Young, a distinguished practical chemist of his day, is remembered today as the father of the Scotch shale oil industry. Downer and his associates were responsible for technical developments such as new treating methods and a commercial cracking process; and the large size of their business enabled them to become substantial exporters of American kerosene. Downer accepted the price of rapid technological change without complaint: well entrenched in the whale oil business, he did not hesitate to invest a fortune in the new "coal oil" industry, and he was later to adopt the new Pennsylvania petroleum equally quickly and build the largest of the early petroleum refineries. While the development of the coal oil industry was due in great part to the efforts of these three groups of men, it is well, in attempting to apportion credit, to keep in mind Gesner's generous statement on the subject: "The progress in this case has been gradual. It has been carried on by the labors not of one mind, but of many, so as to render it difficult to discover to whom the greatest credit is due." [26]

By today's standards, the prices charged for the new coal oil were exorbitantly high. Young sold his product for $1.25 to $1.50 a gallon, Downer for $1.35 to $1.40, and prices of $1.50 a gallon were the general thing in country stores of 1859.[27] It is no great wonder, then, with such good profits to be made and an eager market waiting to buy, that a considerable number of businessmen undertook to refine coal oil. By the end of 1859 there were fifty-three of these refineries in operation in the United States alone. The installations of Gesner's and Downer's companies were large, staffed by men of considerable technical ability. For the most part, the other refineries in America consisted of a boiler still, condensing worm, and a few vats; they were operated by "practical men" without technical education.[28]

One such was Samuel M. Kier, of Pittsburgh, who used for raw material not coal but crude petroleum which he obtained from his father's salt wells; he also sold crude oil as patent medicine. By 1851, he was producing from a one-gallon still an untreated distillate which he called Carbon Oil. It had some success when sold locally as an illuminant, and from 1857 onwards was distributed in quantity by A. C. Ferris, a lamp oil merchant of New York.[29] In later years, Kier's neighbors in western Pennsylvania mistakenly claimed for him the distinction of having been the first man to distill petroleum. While he cannot be accorded this honor, his efforts were nevertheless important, if only for the part one of his advertising circulars played in getting the new petroleum industry under way.

3

The Drake Well

ONE hot summer day in 1856, so the oft-told story goes, George H. Bissell stopped for a moment to mop his brow in the shade of a drug-store awning on lower Broadway, New York City. Looking into the store window, he saw one of the circulars which Kier was putting out to advertise his medicinal crude oil. It was in the form of a bogus bank note, emphasizing that "Kier's Petroleum, or Rock Oil, the Celebrated Natural Remedy" came from a well on "The Bank of the Allegheny" more than 400 feet below the earth's surface. The illustrations showed salt-well drilling equipment which had been in common use for many years to drill brine wells and artesian water wells. For two years now, Bissell had been associated with an oil enterprise, and seeing this illustration, he is supposed to have said to himself, "Here is the solution of our problem. Instead of digging for oil, we can drill!" [30]

Like many other good stories, this one is probably not true, for ten years later in making a statement to a government commission covering his part in these early developments, Bissell did not mention the incident, or even claim the credit for the idea of drilling.[31] Just what did happen is still largely a matter of conjecture. Most of the early historians of oil were incurable romantics, and the firsthand accounts left by individual participants in this first enterprise are a morass of contradiction. Weeding and sifting and making allowances for personal prejudices and bad memories, the modern reader can, however, piece together a fairly reasonable chain of events.

It starts with Bissell, a young man who had been teaching school at New Orleans, returning in the fall of 1853 to his alma mater, Dartmouth College, and calling on one of his old friends, Dr. Dixi Crosby of the medical school. In Dr. Crosby's office he saw a bottle of Pennsylvania petroleum which had been left there only a few months before by another Dartmouth man whom Bissell knew well, Dr. Francis B. Brewer of Titusville, Pennsylvania. Brewer had taken this sample of "Seneca Oil" from an "oil spring" on his father's farm on the banks of Oil Creek, a stream named for oil seepages found there by the first white men. The previous year, Brewer reported, he had made a partnership arrangement with J. D. Angier of Titusville to work the spring by digging trenches and collecting the oil produced, some three or four gallons in a day.[32]

Albert H. Crosby, the young son of Dr. Crosby, immediately became enthusiastic over the prospect of petroleum as a large and substantial business, furnishing the raw material for the manufacture of lamp oil. He induced Bissell to pay his expenses to Titusville in the summer of 1854. He came back highly impressed, more enthusiastic than ever, and with Brewer's promise to sell a hundred-acre tract embracing the chief spring, provided Bissell would organize a company to exploit the land.[33]

As Bissell and his partner in New York, Jonathan G. Eveleth, were at the time engaged in promoting a stock issue of the American & Foreign Iron Pavement Company and the Safety Railway Switch Company, promotion of a third company was a very natural thing for them to undertake. In November 1854, Brewer deeded the land to Eveleth and Bissell for $5,000 to be paid later, and the partners at once set out to market $250,000 worth of stock in the Pennsylvania Rock Oil Company which they had organized.[34]

Interested with them in this new enterprise was a group of New Haven businessmen headed by James M. Townsend, one of that city's leading bankers. Townsend pointed out to them how little the investor knew of oil and its value, and how useful in stock promotion an expert's report would be, especially a report from a respected scientist such as Prof. Benjamin Silliman, Jr., head of the chemistry department at Yale, and one of the leading scientific men of his day.

Like his father, who in 1833 had been the first scientific man to investigate the oil spring at Cuba, New York, and render a report on it, the younger Silliman was deeply interested in petroleum. Samples were promptly shipped to him from Pennsylvania and he began a methodical, scientific examination of petroleum and the uses to which it could be put. Silliman's report, completed in April 1855, accurately forecast the products which would be the backbone of the oil business for the next fifty years.[35]

Silliman said he had distilled lamp oils from this petroleum and had burned them in several types of lamps, making photometric calculations as to the amount of light which a petroleum illuminating oil would produce. In the camphene lamp, he found, the oil would burn successfully, and large yields of it could be distilled at a reasonable cost. The residue could, with almost no waste, be distilled into lubricants and into paraffin for the manufacture of candles. Besides its fine qualities as an illuminant, ". . . the oil does not gum or become acid," Silliman pointed out; it did not turn rancid or deteriorate on exposure; and remained liquid in extreme cold, giving it "important qualities for a lubricator." "It appears to me," he concluded, "that there is much ground for encouragement in the belief that your Company have in their possession a raw material from which, by simple and not expensive process, they may manufacture very valuable products." [36]

Silliman's report endorsed the findings of Luther Atwood, of Boston, who had also been asked to make an analysis. The favorable pronouncements of these two chemists helped overcome objections, and stock in the proposed enterprise was sold to several New Haven men. As a result of this New Haven interest, the company was soon reincorporated in Connecticut, capitalized at $300,000, with Professor Silliman as president and New Haven as headquarters. The new arrangement was not without its drawbacks. A series of petty bickerings developed between the New York and New Haven interests, eventually bringing matters to a point where no more money could be raised for the treasury. Even the services of Angier, who had meanwhile continued to collect small amounts of oil from the springs, had to be dispensed with, and the company's affairs came to a complete standstill.

And thus affairs languished for many months, until Bissell, according to the story, received his inspiration to drill, and interest flared up anew. The company had no funds, so Bissell induced a New York real estate firm, Lyman & Havens, to drill a well on the property. Lyman & Havens were to pay the company a royalty of 12 cents a gallon on all oil produced. But before they could commence operations, they were overwhelmed by the Panic of 1857, and affairs returned to their former impasse. At this juncture, Townsend came to the rescue. He proposed that he and a few New Haven friends would inspect the land, and if they still thought it worth while, undertake to drill.

This brings into the story Edwin L. Drake, a restless Vermont jack-of-all-trades, who had gone west in his early years and returned to take jobs as a clerk, express agent, and finally conductor on the New Haven railroad. In 1854 his wife had died, and with his small daughter Drake had moved into the same hotel where Townsend lived, and the two had subsequently become acquainted. During the summer of 1857, Drake fell ill and had to take a leave of absence from his conductor's job. By December, he was feeling better, so he consented to go to Pennsylvania for Townsend, primarily to get some papers signed which would clear up a minor defect in the company's title to the Brewer land. So, chiefly because he was idle and had access to a free railroad pass, Drake was selected for the honor of becoming the father of the modern petroleum industry.

But once again history proved, in Drake, that although selection may be, and often is, haphazard, it takes more than the mere circumstance of being selected to make a man and his ventures successful.

From the minute of his arrival in Pennsylvania,† Drake conducted himself in a manner to win the approbation of all. He immediately made up his mind that oil could be obtained in large quantities "by Boreing as for Salt Water."[37] He tried to find out all he could about salt-well drilling, and went to Tarentum, Pennsylvania, near Pittsburgh, to look at Kier's wells there.‡ He inquired about salt drillers to ascertain what manner of men they might be (very temperamental, he found out, and always thirsty for whisky).

Like young Crosby (who had been obliged to drop out soon after the company had been organized because he lacked the money to buy stock), Drake returned from the oil regions, bubbling over with enthusiasm. On the strength of his report, a lease was taken from the Pennsylvania Rock Oil Company which provided that the lessees would bear the expense of the drilling, in return for delivering to the Pennsylvania Rock Oil Company one-eighth of all the oil produced. The Seneca Oil Company was organized by Townsend to do the drilling, and Drake was elected president. The amount of royalty to be paid on their very first lease set a precedent which has since been broken only in years of fast-and-furious oil development, and then usually to the operators' sorrow. Eveleth and Bissell raised a row when they heard what had been done, Bissell even threatening court action to prevent the work from going ahead. To keep peace, Drake and his associates executed a supplementary lease agreeing to pay the company 12 cents a gallon royalty, the same amount as had been proposed by Lyman & Havens, instead of one-eighth.

Seneca Oil Company was to pay Drake $1,000 a year and to allow him another $1,000 to drill for oil. With his new wife, Drake arrived in Titusville, May 1858, and started to work the diggings left by Angier. He arranged a pump, actuated by the water power of the nearby river, and by June had the diggings producing about ten gallons a day. Then he went again to Tarentum to observe the drilling of salt wells a little more closely, hired a salt driller to come and drill for him, and went back to Titusville to build the derrick which was finished by mid-August. As money to buy the boiler for drilling did not arrive from Connecticut, Drake had to put the driller off, while he earnestly beseeched his backers to send him more money, pointing

† To impress the Titusville villagers, Townsend had sent the legal papers ahead addressed to "Colonel" E. L. Drake, a title which stuck to Drake the rest of his life.

‡ Since Drake visited this area in 1857, it may be that the New Haven group got its idea of drilling for oil from his observations.

out that "I have got as far with five hundred dollars as any other company have with five thousand, and further than some have with ten thousand dollars." [38]

It was now too late to start in 1858, but early in 1859 Drake went to Tarentum again and hired another driller who failed to appear. Downright discouraged, and about ready to quit, Drake got a letter from Lewis Peterson, Jr., one of the pioneer salt-well oil men at Tarentum, recommending a blacksmith, W. A. (Uncle Billy) Smith. Though he had never drilled a salt well, Smith had worked around the salt-drilling country and had made salt-drilling tools for both Kier and Peterson. Uncle Billy was willing to drill Drake's well for him, and to make the drilling tools, and would charge for his own services, and those of his half-grown son thrown in, $2.50 a day. Uncle Billy made the tools in his shop, at a cost of $76, and arrived in Titusville to put them to use in the middle of May.[39]

By February 1859, the original $1,000 had been spent, and in April, the Connecticut group sent $500 more, after which the stockholders refused to advance any more money. Drake borrowed $500 locally on his own promissory note, and Townsend continued to advance sums from his own pocket. Finally even Townsend became discouraged and sent Drake a last remittance with which to pay all bills and return to New Haven.[40] His letter fortunately did not arrive in Titusville until Monday, August 29, 1859, when it was hardly noticed, for the whole town was on fire with the news that Drake and Uncle Billy had struck oil.

They had, indeed, struck oil. On Saturday when the well was closed down for the weekend, they had drilled to 69½ feet. When Uncle Billy dropped by on Sunday to look in on the well, he found it filled with oil up to the top.[41] People who came next day to see if the news was true found that Drake and Uncle Billy had already rigged up the pump previously used in Angier's diggings by fastening its handle to the walking beam of the derrick, and were pumping America's first real oil well at the rate of eight to ten barrels a day.

In New York, Bissell, who had arranged for the news to be telegraphed, immediately bought all the stock of the Pennsylvania Rock Oil Company that he could lay hands on, and took off for Titusville where he enlarged his interests by taking options on a great many nearby properties. He was not alone; the scoffers, whatever else may be said of them, were not slow to realize the value of the Pennsylvania oil lands, once someone had shown them how to get at the oil.

Townsend and his New Haven associates, who had done so much to sponsor the first well, were soon undone by the high royalty—$5.04 a barrel—which they had agreed to pay when oil was worth $20 a barrel. As other wells were drilled, the price of crude oil dropped to less than the amount the Seneca company was obliged to pay in royalties. Under these circumstances, operation of Drake's first oil well was only intermittent, and finally, in 1864, the Seneca company closed out its business and sold its property. Townsend and his associates, far from making money on the discovery, rescued only the amount of their original investment. Bissell, on the other hand, with his promoter's instinct had hustled to Titusville to acquire lands which were to make him rich and famous as the "discoverer" of oil. Townsend would hardly have been human had he not resented in later years, as it is said he did, Bissell's refusal to speak to his former friend when they met on the street.[42]

For Drake, Fate had reserved the pathetic end which seems to await so many pioneers. With his well completed, he showed no especial eagerness to join the oil land scramble, and in the ensuing months drilled a total of only two more wells. His New Haven associates, with vague mutterings about "inefficiency," ousted him as president in March 1860.[43] The Titusville townspeople elected him justice of the peace, and from this position he derived some $3,000 a year in fees because of the great number of land transactions caused by the oil boom. He also acted as purchasing agent for Schieffelin & Company, the New York drug house, who bought much of the oil for resale to kerosene manufacturers. This netted him an estimated $5,000 a year additional. In 1863, taking some fifteen to twenty thousand dollars with him, Drake left the Oil Regions, went to New York, and lost it all in a brokerage house in which he became partner.[44] He returned to Vermont, broke, and there developed arthritis which became progressively worse until he was completely crippled. On his doctor's advice, he later moved to Chapel Hill, New Jersey, to be near the sea.

One day in 1869, while he was still able to walk, Drake was in New York and there on the street ran into an old friend Zebulon Martin, proprietor of a Titusville hotel. Martin was shocked to see Drake in the same coat he had worn nine years previously, and to learn that he had only 60 cents in his pocket. Martin hurried back to the Oil Regions in the hope of raising a considerable fund from the men who had benefited so much from Drake's discovery. There was great talk of building him a fine home and providing him with a trust fund; but after fifteen months less than $5,000 had been collected. The disappointed friends next proceeded to Harrisburg where in 1873 they lobbied through the legislature a pension of $1,500 a year. It was as a pensioner of the State of Pennsylvania that Drake died in obscurity in 1880.[45]

Although Drake made no money from his oil well and died a poor man, it was he who almost singlehanded had brought about the completion of the project. Bissell, the father of the Pennsylvania Rock Oil Company, was never sufficiently interested to drop his promotional schemes and go drill a well; neither was banker Townsend, who refused at first to let his name be associated publicly with so shaky an enterprise; Peterson and Kier, who actually owned oil-producing salt wells and knew the value of petroleum, did not think of deliberately drilling for oil; and Professor Silliman, whose foresight proved so great in other matters, confessed in later years that the production of crude petroleum by drilling would never have occurred to him. It was Drake who kept on, amid the ill-concealed ridicule of the villagers, on inadequate advances sent from Connecticut, to complete America's first successfully drilled oil well, marking the birth of the modern oil industry—a big moment of the Nineteenth Century.

4

After Drake

DRAKE, like Columbus, was not the first in his field. There were many Leif Ericsons of the oil business. But Drake's discovery, like that of Columbus, came at a time when the world was ready for it.§ In the

§ Drake's part in the establishment of the modern oil industry has been very well summed up in Max Ball's lively book *This Fascinating Oil Business:* "The Drake well was not the first to produce oil; oil had been produced from hand-dug wells for several thousand years, as we have seen. It was not the first drilled well to produce oil, for many wells drilled for salt had produced oil, both in the United States and China. It was not even the first well drilled for the specific purpose of obtaining oil, for the Chinese probably drilled wells for that purpose before the time of Christ. What then was unique about the well drilled on Watsons Flat by E. L. Drake, erstwhile railroad conductor, 'Colonel' by courtesy, field superintendent for the Seneca Oil Company? Simply this: It was the first well drilled for the specific purpose of obtaining oil, in a prolifically oil-bearing region, at a time when the lamps and machinery of a rapidly-industralizing world were in need of a cheap source of illuminants, fuels, and lubricants." [46] If we add "and at a location where it could be reached by the relatively cheap transportation of the new railroads," this would be an adequate appraisal of Drake's contribution.

vicinity of Titusville everyone seemed to know of the success of the well almost instantly, and in the next few months excitement reached a fever pitch, described by witnesses of both events as exceeding that of the California gold rush ten years before. Leasing of lands, both by individuals and joint stock companies, proceeded at a brisk rate and drilling operations were begun without delay.

In the face of such activity, available supplies of crude oil increased many-fold, and prices declined commensurately. The first oil from Drake's well brought $20 a barrel; the next year, 1860, a half million barrels were produced, bringing an average of $9.60 a barrel to the producers. By 1861, new fields had been opened in West Virginia and Ontario; and "fountain wells," or gushers, further increased the supply. As a result, crude oil took a nose-dive during 1861 from $9.60 to 52 cents a barrel.[47]

This more abundant supply of oil convinced many kerosene refiners that they could now safely give up their coal-oil processes and shift to the new raw material. In November 1860 there were fifteen new refineries in the United States using petroleum only, and 56 others which still based their processes on the oil-bearing minerals commonly miscalled "coal." [48] In the Oil Regions of Pennsylvania, new refineries were built rapidly and not quite five years after the completion of Drake's first well, there were some sixty refineries in Pennsylvania alone.[49] Farther west, in Ohio, another large refining center developed around Cleveland, and there in 1863 John D. Rockefeller and his partners started the business which developed rapidly into the giant Standard Oil Company.

Meanwhile a market, not just in western Pennsylvania, but a world market, was being built. American consuls in Europe, proud of their country's new industry, became the best salesmen the oil business had. In five years, the value of America's petroleum exports rose from zero in 1860 to more than $15,000,000 in 1865—ranking the new industry sixth in American exports, with Britain the best customer.

European oil regions, some of which had been worked by hand for centuries, got into production using the techniques demonstrated by Drake. In 1872, the Russian government cancelled its monopoly of the Baku field, and soon after, the first American-style oil wells were drilled there. Ten years later, the drilling method was introduced to the oil fields of Galicia and Romania, and in all three areas, refineries were erected to supply kerosene to nearby markets.[50]

But for the next thirty years, America, which had a head start in the business as well as superior transportation facilities for distribution of its product, was to be the dominant supplier. The older illuminants—sperm oil, whale oil, colza oil, camphene, coal oil, beeswax, fish oil, tallow, lard, olive oil—were all falling by the wayside, as a new product, produced cheaply and in abundance, was giving light to the world and to America a new industry of unsuspected size and importance.

CHAPTER II

Other Beginnings, Ten Thousand Miles Away

IF WE have dwelt on the details of events leading up to the drilling of Drake's well, it was for a reason. The same delays, the same disbeliefs, the same crippling timorousness which delayed the completion of the Drake well were, twenty years later, to be repeated with variations half way around the world.

Our scene shifts from the oil fields of Pennsylvania and the financial circles of New York and New Haven to the island of Sumatra, in the Dutch East Indies, across the Straits of Malacca from Singapore. The financial circles become those of the Indies' capital, Batavia, Java, and of the mother country, Holland.[1] Eveleth and Bissell, the promoters, and Drake, the operating man, are all united in the person of Aeilco Janz Zijlker. The part of Uncle Billy Smith, whose technical knowledge made drilling of the first well possible, is to be played here by Dutch Government mining engineers. James M. Townsend, the encouraging New Haven financier, is to find a counterpart in G. A. de Lange and associates of Batavia, and later in N. P. van den Berg. The pattern of many of the early tribulations of the Pennsylvania Rock Oil Company is visible in events leading to the founding of the Royal Dutch Company. Other events, naturally, are to differ; for, after all, this is a new and different story.

During the year 1880, Aeilco Janz Zijlker,* superintendent of a Dutch tobacco-planting company, was making the rounds of his company's plantation in Langkat on the Sumatra East Coast when a tropical storm came up and forced him and his guide to take shelter in a tobacco barn. When it was dark, the guide lighted a torch; for brilliance and clearness of flame it surpassed any torch Zijlker had seen. Thinking it might be made of some exotic resinous wood unknown to Europeans, he inquired of the guide, who assured him that

* The combination *ij* in Dutch is equivalent to *y* in English.

it had been made in quite the regular way, except for rubbing it with "earthwax," a substance obtained from skimming pools of water in the neighborhood. "Earthwax" had been used for torches, the guide said, as far back as anyone in that part of Sumatra could remember.†
The next day, Zijlker had the native take him to one of the pools where instantly he recognized the familiar odor of kerosene, a product which by 1880 was reaching the Indies from America in quantity.

He took a sample and hurried with it to Batavia. It would, a chemist said, make a very fine lamp oil, with a yield of about 60%. Heartened by this news and further encouraged, no doubt, by reports which had reached even the East Indies jungle of the phenomenal success of an American, Rockefeller, in the lamp oil business, Zijlker lost no time in going to see the Sultan of Langkat, who, under Dutch sovereignty, ruled over the area near the "earthwax" springs. The Sultan readily granted him a lease to explore for and produce petroleum.

Back in Batavia again, Zijlker tried to peddle his concession. But, as is usual in such circumstances, he encountered the skeptics. How did he know there was oil there? And if there was, how much? True, most listeners had to concede Zijlker's major contention: that an oil company operating here, in the center of the East Indian market, eliminating the long haul from New York and Philadelphia, should certainly be able to make and sell kerosene cheaper than the Standard Oil Company and still make a profit.

It is to their credit that two Batavia banking houses, Tiedeman & Van Kerchem and the Netherlands Indies Trading Bank, advanced several thousand guilders to Zijlker against stock in the Preliminary Sumatra Petroleum Company. The money was to be used for the exploratory drilling necessary to determine the extent of Zijlker's petroleum deposits. If promising, Zijlker's holdings would later be organized into an operating oil company. Zijlker recognized the value of being adequately financed at the start, so with the blessings of the Batavia houses, he went to Holland in 1882 in an attempt to secure more capital.

Bankers in Holland were, to put it politely, incredulous. Besides doubting the existence of oil, they also indicated that they didn't like the nature of the title which Zijlker had secured from the Sultan;

---

† Oil from seepages had been known and used locally in the East Indies for centuries, and from time to time small quantities of crude petroleum for medicinal purposes had been shipped to Holland. Zijlker's contribution was the establishment of the first oil-producing and refining company in Sumatra.

and anyhow, even if there was oil in Sumatra, how were they to know whether or not it could be made into kerosene cheaply enough to compete with that being sold in the Far East by Rockefeller? Seeing that he was wasting his time, Zijlker went back to the Indies where he set about overcoming one of the bankers' objections. In August 1883, he obtained from the Sultan of Langkat a "genuine mining concession," to run for 75 years, embracing most of his original tract, called Telaga Said.

Next, he had to get some drilling done. With what funds he himself had and with the amounts advanced by the Batavia firms, he had about $10,000 for the exploratory drilling; enough, certainly, for a few shallow wells. A bigger problem was: Who should drill them? The nearest Pennsylvania driller was more than ten thousand miles away. Zijlker made the further disheartening discovery that drilling of wells in the Indies had been reserved as a government prerogative by the Department of Mines. This bad news was made more bearable when he learned that there was at the moment a group of government engineers in the Indies, who were prepared to drill water wells for private persons for a fee. He approached them on the matter of drilling for oil, and they agreed.

Zijlker furnished the department with the necessary drilling rig, and on July 4, 1884, they began to drill the first oil well in Sumatra. This first well was inconclusive. The second, called Telaga Toenggal No. 1, was brought in at 22 meters (about 72 feet, a yard deeper than Drake's well) in June 1885. At this depth, it produced slightly more than five barrels a day (about half the production of Drake's well), but when it was drilled deeper, production fell off to less than a barrel a day. Leaving Telaga Toenggal, they proceeded to drill other wells, none of them very successful.

Adriaan Stoop, a young geologist of the Department of Mines who had been placed in charge of the operation, feared making a bad name for himself this early in life. He prevailed upon the Dutch governor-general to send him to Pennsylvania so that he could see firsthand how drilling was done. Stoop's trip was approved on condition that it take no longer than 100 days, and he arrived in Pennsylvania in August 1886. Considering the natural reluctance of the Pennsylvania men to hand over useful information to a potential competitor, the amount of material which Stoop collected and took back with him is remarkable. He looked into the methods then in use for finding oil, for drilling wells, for capping gushers, and for installing oilfield pumps; he investigated the American manner of refining kerosene and lubricating oil; assembled information on the transportation of crude oil by pipe line and tank car; looked into the manufacture of barrels and tins; noted ways in which by-products were burned for fuel; got figures on the cost of the finished product; and even made a digest of state and local laws relating to the transportation, storage, and refining of petroleum. It is small wonder that such a comprehensive survey should have served as the cornerstone of the Indies petroleum industry, and have had as much effect on its development as the Silliman report did on the beginnings of the industry in America.

The drilling done by Zijlker and the Department of Mines had continued unsuccessfully during Stoop's absence. Then, Nature herself seemed to take a hand. Telaga Toenggal No. 1, the second well drilled, had originally produced about five barrels a day, and finally declined to less than a barrel a day. In 1887, two years later, it was gauged again, and found to be producing 144 barrels a day! Thereafter a careful watch of it was kept; by 1889 production from this early well had increased by another 20 barrels a day.‡ These 164 barrels of oil a day were the bright spot in an otherwise depressing picture. Zijlker's funds were now exhausted. The Department of Mines ordered its men to stop drilling. Tired, lonely, dejected, with nothing to show for nearly ten years' work, Zijlker booked passage for Holland, with little left except a prayerful hope that somehow he might raise money enough to carry on.

It was a happy fate that placed on board this same ship N. P. van den Berg, whose mood offered a distinct contrast to Zijlker's. Van den Berg was returning to Holland after sixteen successful years in the Indies, during which time he had headed the Java Bank and had built it into a successful financial institution, prominent, sound, and greatly respected. Always alert to prospects of new enterprises for the Indies, he had been watching Zijlker's Preliminary Sumatra Petroleum Company since its inception. When Zijlker mentioned the operating company he wanted to form, Van den Berg said he was impressed with the chances for the venture's success and consented to become its chairman. Thus, at one stroke, the first round was won. For, like the bank he had built, Van den Berg was prominent, sound, and greatly respected. With his backing, there would be little difficulty in raising capital.

‡ This well was still producing fifty-seven years later when the Japanese invaded Sumatra early in 1942.[2]

Back in Holland, Van den Berg and Zijlker proceeded at once to the organization of a new company. Van den Berg's interest made it possible to get together for the new board a group of men whose names would inspire confidence in even the most conservative circles. By early spring the board had been chosen, the prospectus issued, and a president elected. And just to give an added measure of confidence, application was made to King William III for permission to use the word *Koninklijke* (Royal) in the name of the new firm, which was granted "on condition, however, that this will be taken as proof only of His Majesty's moral support." [3]

Indeed, quite enough confidence was created, for on May 8, 1890, when the 1,100 shares at 1,000 guilders each [4] were offered to the public, Dutch investors oversubscribed the issue four and one-half times, and shares had to be assigned them in proportion to the amounts they had subscribed. Zijlker turned over his concession to the new company for $68,400 cash and 200 paid-up shares of stock worth $50,000, most of which he distributed to the Batavia interests who had had faith enough to advance the original exploratory capital. Thus equipped with oil lands and money in the bank, the new company came into legal existence on June 16, 1890. Its full name was Naamlooze Vennootschap Koninklijke Nederlandsche Maatschappij tot Exploitatie van Petroleumbronnen in Nederlandsch-Indië, but everybody called it "Koninklijke," or in English, "Royal Dutch." §

2

The Royal Dutch

ZIJLKER, the patient pioneer who, alone, had been responsible for the ten-year chain of events which led to the founding of the Royal Dutch Company, was to be denied the satisfaction of seeing his child grow and prosper. Scarcely six months after the incorporation of the new company, he died suddenly at Singapore, on December 27, 1890.

§ Literally, "Royal Dutch Company for the Working of Petroleum Wells in Netherlands India." "Naamlooze Vennootschap" signifies joint-stock company, is equivalent to the "S. A." (Anonymous Society) used in the names of French, Spanish, Italian, and Romanian corporations. This rather cumbersome corporate title was shortened on February 14, 1949, to N. V. Koninklijke Nederlandsche Petroleum Maatschappij, or Royal Dutch Petroleum Company.

Zijlker's role as a pioneer, when we consider it, probably exceeds in scope that of any single one of the early Pennsylvania men. Drake, after all, only drilled the well. Eveleth and Bissell had organized the company. And they had not found the oil-bearing land; it had been brought to their attention by Dr. Brewer. In Sumatra, Zijlker combined the roles of all four, and more besides. He had found the oil, he had obtained a long-term lease, he had arranged to drill wells to prove the existence of oil in commercial quantities, he had organized a company. But most of all, he had the foresight to see, as no oil pioneer before him had, that the oil business of the future would be not a sprawling collection of producers, refiners, and marketers. The oil trade of the future, he foresaw, would go to the companies who produced and refined their oil near the point of sale. This was, after all, only a logical development, but not until Zijlker had anyone proposed such a development for the Far Eastern market. The company of his creation was, therefore, unique—a modern, integrated, "well-to-wick" concern, operating near its chief market.

Considering Zijlker's untimely death, it is fortunate that he was not the first president of the company, for had he been, the lapse in leadership at this point might have proved too much for the new organization. The directors had selected for president J. A. de Gelder, an energetic and respected young naval engineer, who had already spent some time in the Indies. He had been a chief mover in improving Batavia's harbor, and had been elected a member of the influential Council of the Indies. De Gelder was back in Holland early in 1890, when Zijlker and Van den Berg, forming their company, asked him to become president. The engineering experience of the new president was put to immediate use for there were many things to be done.

Paramount, of course, was the design and construction of a refinery. Pangkalan Brandan, on the Babalan River near the Telaga Said concession, was chosen as the location, and plans for the refinery were drawn up by De Gelder, who had never seen one, from descriptions given in Stoop's report. Tankage and a bridge for the river (they had to build a railroad) were ordered from Belgium; the agitator and a major part of the construction tools from Germany; rails and rolling stock for the train from France; tin, sheet iron, and other metals from England; only the boilers could be made in Holland.

Not trusting Stoop's report in the matter of the all-important drilling equipment, De Gelder sent two young Delft graduates (the first of a long procession of Delft engineers that still continues) to Bradford, Pa., then the heart of oil production, to observe drilling, purchase a drilling rig, and hire drillers and stillmen. Through the Oil Well Supply Company, they hired four Pennsylvania oil men: W. B. Montgomery, driller; T. E. Bradish, tool dresser, rig builder and stillman; and D. Muir and H. Johnson, stillmen. The next year the same company sent out three more men, H. H. Beers, oil treater; J. Keefe, stillman; and W. M. Montgomery, tool dresser and rig builder.[5] At Pittsburgh, De Gelder's emissaries bought refining equipment, and at New York can-making machinery and machinery to manufacture the wooden cases. They arranged for their purchases to be shipped all on one ship, which arrived in Sumatra in the fall of 1890.

In the Indies, things did not proceed so rapidly. When this equipment arrived, the actual site of the refinery had not yet been determined; it was not finally selected until December. Bickering at home prevented the sending out of a construction superintendent until mid-1891, six months after the work was under way, so that a year after materials had first begun to arrive, construction had barely started. Impatient, De Gelder asked for another man, who would have authority almost equal to his, to go to Sumatra and manage affairs. It was thus that J. B. August Kessler, formerly a partner of Tiedeman & Van Kerchem in Batavia but now back in Holland, was chosen "assistant president" and dispatched to Sumatra, arriving in September 1891. From this point on until his death, Kessler was to be the mainspring of activity, planner, builder, and administrator of the Royal Dutch Company. His decision and his action were to build a refinery in the tropical jungle and to put it in operation; his determination and courage were to see the struggling young company through its first, most perilous years.

A man of energy, Kessler "took hold" at once. Construction proceeded on the refinery, despite tropical storms and inexperienced labor. Drilling of a second well, to supplement the production of Telaga Toenggal No. 1, was started. A brickyard and the narrow-gauge railway were built. Finally, on February 28, 1892, the first still was completed and distillation of crude oil started. This first Royal Dutch refinery, modeled on its contemporary American counterparts, had three horizontal stills each of 600 barrels capacity; a condensation system which utilized river water; tanks and an agitator for treating the finished product; and a case and can factory. The kerosene was packed in two five-gallon tins in a wooden case. At full capacity, the refinery could turn out 1,600 cans a day (300 barrels) of kerosene,

BIRTHPLACE OF THE ROYAL DUTCH COMPANY

for which it was necessary to process between 800 and 900 barrels of crude oil.[6]

Early in April, Kessler took a few cases of the new "Crown Oil," as it had been christened, and went to Penang, an important business center of the Straits Settlements. There on April 9, 1892, he launched the Royal Dutch Company's commercial career with a publicity stunt. A group of local luminaries, including the editor of the *Penang Gazette,* was invited. Tests were devised to determine the relative burning qualities of the American, Russian, and Sumatra oils. The light produced, the amount of carbon formed, smoking, odor of the oil, and other burning qualities were noted. Crown Oil won hands down over its Russian and American competitors. A careful description of the tests was drawn up, and those present signed their names, in the manner of sportsmen attesting a new record. The *Gazette's* editor was enthusiastic, and in his article ventured to prophesy:

> With a greater and more constant brightness, little or no smoke, the least possible quantity of carbon on the wick or mantle, clear, transparent white in color and almost without odor, the Langkat oil is, in our opinion, headed for a great future. If we consider furthermore that it is produced here in the vicinity and that the transportation costs are consequently lower than those incurred by the other oils, it must be admitted that this oil, if matters are managed right, is in a position to dominate the local market and the markets of the Far East.

This rather rosy statement, and its qualifying "if," quite accurately summarized the outlook for the infant Royal Dutch in the spring of 1892. Kessler arranged at once for agents to handle Crown Oil at Penang and Singapore in the Straits Settlements and at Medan in Sumatra. But before the company would receive the initial returns from the agents' sales, a process which took several months, there was grave danger that it would run completely out of funds and die a-borning. Kessler must see that "matters are managed right" during this crucial period.

Applications for a loan (it would have been difficult at such a moment to float an additional stock issue) were made to several banks without success. Kessler then called on Hendrik Deterding, the young Penang sub-agent of the Netherlands Trading Society. Deterding had been present at the "Crown Oil" tests on April 9, and now took it upon himself, as his bank's agent at Penang, to enter into a contract agreeing that the Netherlands Trading Society would advance the Royal Dutch Company one florin per case against each ten-gallon case of lamp oil manufactured and put into storage. Funds were thus made available; the company could proceed on a less perilous basis; and Kessler could go home to collect his reward.

In May 1892, he returned to Holland; in November, De Gelder resigned and Kessler succeeded him as the Royal Dutch Company's chief executive officer. In the Indies, a Scot, James Waddell, succeeded Kessler as manager. The initial troubles were not entirely over, however, for the financial market took a dip, ushering in a period of depression and low prices which lasted, with little intermission, until 1897. Nearness to the Far Eastern market at such a time was not without its drawbacks for the Royal Dutch Company had to realize its entire income from the sale of kerosene. There was no market in the Orient for industrial products, such as lubricants, benzine, or paraffin, and the European market for these products could be supplied more cheaply by companies nearer to Europe.

By late 1892, things were so bad that poor Waddell was writing to Holland that "the only alternative (or at least the best one so far as I can see) is to sell the enterprise and sell it at once as a going concern, before we are forced to stop. We could go on for one month, or for two months, only with the greatest of good luck and at a risk which is altogether too great. A fall in prices (and they are falling now), a fall in the rate of exchange (which also seems probable), the loss of a ship, the failure of an agent, the locking up of a few thousand cases for a few weeks, the breakdown of our case-manufacturing machine, any of these things and many others that can easily happen, would stop our supply of cash at once, with no means to pay the personnel or to send them home." The situation, which had looked rosy only a few months before, was now, in a word, desperately black.

Confronted with this situation, there seemed but one solution: Kessler went back to the Indies as manager, in May 1893. No sooner had he got there, than there began an attack of the ferocious Atjeh natives. The refinery was in a state of siege for several days, the climax coming the night of May 31, when considerable property was destroyed and three workmen killed. Luckily the attackers retreated without setting fire to the refinery, or the Royal Dutch Company's history would have ended then and there. Lacking $4,800 to pay the premium, the company had allowed its fire insurance policy to lapse.

The attack of the Atjehs marked the low point. Soon after, things began to get better. Kessler at once saw the fallacy under which Waddell had been operating. When he had been losing twelve cents a case on a daily production of 700 cases, Waddell had reasoned "it is but clear as day that on a production of 1,400 cases I would lose twice as much." Gradual increases in output during the rest of the year disproved this theory, and by the end of 1893 the company's finances had improved enough so that a small dividend (2%) could have been paid. Kessler advised against it, however, lest holders of adjoining concessions should be seized with the idea that the business was extremely profitable and start developing properties which the Royal Dutch hoped to acquire for itself.

The year 1894 brought better times, and once again Kessler prepared to return to Holland. To replace him in the Indies, the directors sent Hugo Loudon, son of a Dutch governor. In addition to acquaintance in governmental circles, Loudon had acquired a great deal of practical engineering experience. Kessler stayed with Loudon for a period of several months, returning to Holland early in 1895.* There he overwhelmed the directors with good news: oil production was up, refinery output was up, the company was making a profit, and would be able on 1894 operations to pay its first dividend, 8%. And the future now seemed assured, for Crown Oil was finding increasing sale in the Netherlands Indies, the Straits Settlements, Burma, Siam, French Indo-China, and Hong Kong.

The annual report for 1894 hadn't been out long before it became plain that it looked good to persons other than Royal Dutch stockholders. In June 1895, W. H. Libby, representative of the Standard Oil Company in Europe, opened negotiations with Kessler with a view to acquiring the Royal Dutch's Sumatra properties. In July, Kessler and Libby met in Paris and discussed the matter at length, but without result. Two years later, in the summer of 1897, Libby made a much stronger bid. His proposal amounted, in brief, to this: Royal Dutch would increase its capital from 3 to 12 million shares, with the new shares to be purchased by Standard. With this 75% interest in hand, Standard would then operate the Royal Dutch Company as a producing, refining, and marketing subsidiary East of Suez. The proposal was unattractive to the Royal Dutch shareholders—in part, at least, because Standard offered only 750 florins per share for assets which the company itself valued at 4,500 florins per share. More important was the directors' realization that in the long run Standard, far from its source of supply, would have a hard time in the Far East competitive battle. The proposal was unanimously rejected.

During the later part of 1897, Royal Dutch shares fell to half their value on the Amsterdam market and it was discovered that Standard

---

* Loudon remained in the Indies until 1902, when he returned to Holland to become a managing director of the Royal Dutch Company; he retired from this position in 1920 and was elected a member of the board of directors in 1921, serving as chairman of the board from 1929 until his death in 1941. His son, J. H. Loudon, is current general managing director of the Royal Dutch Company.

was quietly buying them up. In alarm, measures were taken to prevent this Standard "infiltration." New by-laws were adopted in April 1898 authorizing the issue of 1,500 shares of preferred stock which would carry sole voting control, could not be transferred without the approval of the other holders of this stock, and could be issued only to Netherlands citizens, or Netherlands corporations whose officers were predominantly Netherlands citizens. The success of this maneuver marked the first victory of the small Royal Dutch Company in the competitive struggle with the much larger Standard Oil Company. It marked, too, the joining of a battle whose outcome would eventually be decided in other parts of the world.

With some of the initial difficulties of production and refining on their way to a successful solution, another problem began to assume serious proportions. The first lots of the new Crown Oil had been shipped as regular cargo and sold through agents. But as output mounted, it was apparent to Kessler that more efficient transportation had to be organized and that thoughtful attention should be directed to the many subjects associated with distribution. Would company-owned transport, for instance, be more economical than paying freight? Would a sales force working directly for the company be more effective than agents? By this time, too, it was clear that the original intention of having one man in the Indies responsible for production, refining, distribution, and sales was asking a little too much of that one man. "I need," Kessler wrote back to Holland, "a 'pushing fellow,' with long experience and keen business insight. The salary will have to be high, of course. He will have to be in the company's service and will not be allowed to have other interests or business."

From the descriptive phrase he used, it is not hard to guess whom Kessler had in mind. He had known Hendrik Deterding when the young sub-agent of the Netherlands Trading Society was growing up in Holland. From the first, Deterding had taken a deep interest in the new company; he had attended the tests at Penang in April 1892 at which Crown Oil was launched; he had helped, materially, a few weeks later by negotiating with Kessler the inventory mortgage arrangement which provided the Royal Dutch with badly needed operating funds. Kessler had noted Deterding's interest in the oil market, had recognized his outstanding ability and knowledge of Oriental trade. For some time now, he had made it a practice to consult Deterding when he was hunting for personnel or planning important moves. With Kessler's mind now made up on having both a technical manager and a commercial manager in the Indies, what better choice could there be than Deterding?

Deterding, still extremely young for one whose experience and capabilities were so widely respected, could look forward to a fine future with the Netherlands Trading Company. But for a man of Deterding's ambition and resourcefulness, it was not the most appealing of futures —always to work for others, with little connection between what he made for the company and what he himself earned, and to be trapped in a spot where advancement depended for the most part on retirement of seniors. It is not surprising that he was pleased when Kessler, leaving for Holland early in 1895, stopped off at Penang to ask him if he would consider taking the job. Terms offered were a contract for three years at $1,000 a month (Straits Settlements dollars, equal to about $500 in American money) plus a further increment to be determined by the results of the sales efforts.

For his part, Deterding saw the opportunity and seized it. But the directors, Kessler found on his arrival in Holland, weren't quite as excited about the proposition. Ruefully, he wrote Deterding, "I had forgotten that in Holland people live longer and there is therefore more time for everything." The approval needed to engage Deterding hung fire for more than a year. Finally, another post was offered to Deterding by the trading company, and he cabled Kessler to let the matter drop. Fortunately for the future of the Royal Dutch, his cable crossed one from Kessler saying that the appointment would soon be on its way. By a hair's breadth the situation was saved; and Deterding, the man who more than any other single person was to change the course of the company's history, came to work for the Royal Dutch on July 13, 1896. Deterding was then thirty years old, energetic and so obviously ambitious that Kessler, to put the directors' minds at ease, had promised to "withhold any high-sounding title from him." He went to work as "our salesman."

With the vigor for which he was to become famous, Deterding plunged into the problems of his new job. Agents, who usually carried competing brands as well, were being employed to handle the sale of Crown Oil in Far Eastern ports. Deterding objected to this arrangement. "The first step I want to take is replacing the Straits agents by private employees . . . I am thinking of a larger and better-regulated sale."

The second step Deterding had in mind was the conversion of his company's operations to bulk shipments. The bulk shipping method had been introduced to the Orient in the summer of 1892 by M. Samuel & Co., of London, who had also introduced the complement to the tanker, the large tank installation ashore, able to receive all, or a large part, of a tanker's cargo. In its first years, the Royal Dutch had neither the volume of trade nor the money necessary to install a system of bulk distribution. Now things were different.

Starting in August 1896, a month after he was hired, Deterding began an extensive tour of India and the Straits Settlements, picking out sites for tank installations. Kessler did the same in China. By early 1897, their labors began to show results. That year, the Royal Dutch adopted bulk shipments, a revolutionary revision in its transportation and distributing arrangements. In March and April 1897, two small tank steamers which had been built in Europe arrived and were put in service; in April the Royal Dutch's first tank installation was put in operation at Hong Kong; by the end of May the Singapore installation was ready. The next year and a half brought other tank installations along the China Coast at Swatow, Fu Tsjau, Amoy, Tientsin, Hankow, and Chin-Kiang (near Shanghai); and at Calcutta, Madras, Bombay, and Karachi in India. In October and November, the company acquired two more tank ships, the *Halaban* and *Babalan*, slightly larger and seaworthy enough for trips through the Bay of Bengal and the South China Sea. In addition to these vessels, the company chartered two other tankers, making six in all. These revisions in transportation and distribution occupied a large part of Deterding's time for the ensuing five years and brought a large increase in sales and an equally large reduction in selling expenses.

Such foundations laid in a period of general financial distress were in better times to prove doubly sound. The end of 1897 found the new company after five years of operation in extremely healthy condition, organized to distribute and market its product in the most efficient manner, and able to pay a handsome dividend of 52%. Presaging events which were to come, the headquarters of the commercial manager were at Deterding's instance moved from Singapore to The Hague. Up to now the people who had organized Royal Dutch and operated it through its early years had thought of the company as an Indies concern. Deterding, with visions of a larger enterprise, wanted to be nearer the centers of world trade.

Early in 1900, Kessler went out to the Indies on what was to be his last trip. Upon his arrival he was already ill, and soon after he headed homeward, but, like Zijlker, he was destined to die en route. On

December 14, 1900, he passed away at Naples, forty-seven years old, "killed by overwork," as Deterding was to write later.[7]

Kessler's death marked the end of the infancy of the company. Like Zijlker, who had died ten years before him, he was one of the company's true pioneers. Zijlker's dogged stubbornness had hung on for a decade to result finally in the establishment of the company. For another decade, Kessler's indomitable drive had met and overcome obstacles before which lesser men might have given way. To Zijlker goes the credit for founding the company; to Kessler the distinction of actually establishing it, of creating something where nothing was before, of laying foundations so sound and durable that his successor could build on them a great and powerful world-wide company, in the record-breaking time of thirteen years.

At the end of this first period of its history, the Royal Dutch was a full-grown concern. Because of its remote location, it had been forced to organize the exploration, production, refining, transportation, storage, and sales of its product. In less than eight years this "integrated company," half way around the world from the other major oil-producing areas, had met with such success that its name was heard in oil circles everywhere. In Kessler's own words, "the company enjoys a prosperous condition and is completely armed for a successful battle against its competitors."

3

Deterding

THE general of the battle was to be Deterding. The directors, early in 1901, elected him to the chief executive position of the company, in accordance with Kessler's last wish, expressed just as he embarked for his final trip to the Indies. For the next thirty-five years Deterding was to guide the destinies of this ever-growing group of companies with a sagacity that proved Kessler's confidence. Deterding's accomplishments for the Royal Dutch can be quickly summarized by repeating the oft-quoted opinion that he did for the oil industry of the Old World what Rockefeller did for that of the New. To attempt an estimate of his character and personality is not so easy.

Hendrik Wilhelm August Deterding, like his American counterpart, came from a humble family; both men were as children subjected to the sobering influence of a fatherless bringing-up—Rockefeller [8] because his father, an itinerant doctor, was absent from home almost constantly; Deterding because his father, a master mariner, died when young Hendrik was only six. Both attended high school and left, adults ahead of their time, to go to work at an early age. Bookkeeping was the first job of each, Rockefeller in a small Cleveland office, Deterding in one of Holland's largest banks. Both had an abiding interest in and an unusual grasp of figures which made them superb judges of value, a trait to which each man was many times in later years to attribute his success. Both, by tireless energy, rose from book-keepers to heads of international oil companies which they built. But here the parallel ends.

In 1901, when Deterding was elected to Kessler's position, Rockefeller was already sixty-two years old and had relinquished his active role in the Standard management. His company and his fortune had been built in the days when "oil" generally meant one product, kerosene. Deterding was to build in a new petroleum industry with many products, and to work in a corporate set-up where, although he would wield great power, he would never be in absolute control. During the trust-building days of the Nineteenth Century, the prevailing philosophy had said, in effect, "We'll buy out our competitors; if they won't sell, we'll run them out of business." The object—total control of a given field of trade—did not permit leaving competitors in the field. Deterding early saw that such thinking could lead only to one disastrous trade war after another; that it would require tremendous cash resources of each combatant; that this fighting would use up precious energy which could be more usefully employed. He was fond of the Dutch proverb *"Eendracht maakt macht"* (pulling together makes power), and evolved a less harsh philosophy.

This philosophy, backed by action, was to lead to a group of companies, allied instead of wholly owned, and managed by common consent along lines agreed to by their owners. Such a corporate structure admitted of no one solitary boss. Consequently, Deterding, during his thirty-five years at the helm of the Royal Dutch-Shell Group, was never a law unto himself. Always there stood above him to counsel and advise, and to act as a brake when they thought him too exuberant, the boards of the Royal Dutch and Shell companies, as well as the voices of a variety of smaller interests whose part ownership in one or more enterprises made it necessary to consult them regularly. Deterding was, as is the modern corporation executive, a "hired hand," selected for his intelligence and ability to carry out the day-to-day management of a large jointly owned enterprise.

Against such a background it is apparent that the most valuable single quality which he could possess would be an incisive clarity of mind, an ability to see in a maze of detail the fundamentals of a situation. Such clarity of mind, or "simpleness," as he preferred to call it, Deterding had in abundant degree. "Hard Work," he was to say in his memoirs thirty years later, "plus just a little Vision provides better ignition-fuel than wizardry for carrying a man to the top. I believe that the master-key to Success—no matter whether it be Success in the temporal or spiritual sphere—is in the hands of every one of us at the start. . . . Its name is Simplicity. Simplicity, I mean, in the sense of . . . reducing to the simplest possible terms every problem which besets us, no matter in what human relationship. . . .

"For my own part I got the best and most useful lesson life ever taught me by stumbling across the value of Simplicity accidentally as a very young man; in fact, way back in the eighties, when up against my first job of any real responsibility. Then it was that I learnt the great fundamental truth, and have held fast to it ever since, that anything which is complicated is wrong. Simplicity rules everything worth while, and whenever I have been up against a business proposition which, after taking thought, I could not reduce to simplicity, I have realised it was hopelessly wrong and I have let it alone.

"That first responsible job of mine wasn't easy, but then, no worthwhile job is ever easy in its beginning. My first business years were spent in an Amsterdam bank, and at length, when I could see no prospect of promotion ahead . . . I decided, like so many other young Dutchmen, both then and now, to go to the Dutch East Indies in the employ of the Netherlands Trading Society. . . . Now came my chance. On my arrival at Medun, I was told by the Society's agent that the bookkeeping at Deli, a more remote branch, had become distinctly indifferent; I must go there to put things straight. A task more easily said than done. Indeed, when I tried to settle down to it, although I have a natural bent for accountancy, I doubted whether it could be done at all.

"Here was a set of books so hopelessly muddled that it was hard to know where to begin and where to end in my attempt at reducing chaos to order. These books had been balanced monthly, but no balance as struck was correct. Where then could I start? Any trained bookkeeper will appreciate the fix I was in. The first examination completely non-plussed me. 'Will you be able to stick it out?' the sub-agent, Mr. Cruys, asked me not unsympathetically on the Saturday morning of my first week on the job. 'I'll let you know Monday morning,' I told him.

"For the next forty-eight hours I applied myself to what for me even to this day has always proven an unfailing aid to hard thinking— a strenuous bout of outdoor physical exercise.

"Walking was the only form in which such exercise could be taken by a young stranger without money in a strange town, and particularly in a town so strange as a typical town of the Far East. During the whole of that week-end I walked, walked, walked—cudgelling my wits, meanwhile. And when I went back to work on Monday, I felt that I could see at least a ray of light in the darkness. But this did not break through into anything like sunshine until the following Thursday, when, by dint of sticking at it unceasingly for four solid days, I managed to arm myself with a very definite clue as just where to begin and where to end in the straightening out of the mess.

"Eventually, after still more browsing, I found the way out. The muddle extended over eighteen months. In order to strike an absolutely true basis from which to start, I had to begin by checking the daily inventory from the day of my start and then work backwards in the books on each day's record for the whole of that period. Meantime, side by side with this tedious work, I installed a new set of books so that at any rate from the date of my arrival the bookkeeping was correct. I put all in apple-pie order within four months, which my employers considered to be a record, and they increased my salary by seventy-five per cent. Never since then have I received so big a raise.

"But what a ridiculously simple solution! you may think. Any fool could have thought of that! And maybe, you will be right. All solutions are simple when once you arrive at them. The trouble with the fool is that he lets go of his problem too lightly—usually as soon as he has found that it is a problem at all; or else, he commits the still worse blunder of hanging on it too long and wastes his energies in trying to solve something which is really insoluble. The wise man never lets go of a problem, which it is his duty to solve, until he has analysed it through and knows in his heart that it cannot be solved. Then, if he can't cut the dead wood away from it, he cuts the whole thing for ever clean out of his life.

"Had I let that tough bookkeeping job at Deli master me, instead of my mastering it, my whole life would have been different. A minor bookkeeper I then was and a minor bookkeeper I should probably still be, if I had not grappled with, and finally throttled that hydra-headed monster in the shape of the jumbled, confused mass of figures I had then to unravel. The supreme advantage to me of unravelling those figures was that it gave me the unravelling habit.

"Ever since, when anything in my working-life has baffled me, I have never rested till I have unravelled it, if it could be unravelled. . . . Simplicity, when you think of it, is the hall-mark of almost every man who achieves. Only a small man has time to be complex. The big men, it seems to me, are nearly all simpletons—not simpletons, of course, in the general acceptance of the word as a term of derision, but what I would call 'the Higher Simpletons,' meaning that it comes to them by instinct to conform to this gospel of Higher Simplicity by which I set so much store."[9]

This story in Deterding's own words gives a fairly accurate picture of the man. Forceful, direct, not easily discouraged, self-confident, determined, and tenacious. But most important were his open-mindedness, his lack of preconceived ideas, and, as he abundantly points out, his gift of seeing even the most intricate matters simply. This gift in later years was to shine during negotiations, as it enabled him with remarkable speed and accuracy to reduce a welter of figures to their simplest terms—the difference between cost price and selling price. And it was this ability to see something besides figures in a balance sheet that Deterding later insisted upon when he picked subordinates for key spots in the companies he built.

4

Shell of London

By 1901, The "Shell" Transport & Trading Company, Limited, of London, was in a competitive position in the Indies similar to, but larger in size than, the Royal Dutch Company. Like the Royal Dutch, it had been in the oil business only since the early Nineties, but unlike the Royal Dutch, its experience as an Oriental trading concern stretched back some sixty years.

The firm from which The "Shell" Transport & Trading Company

evolved had its start in 1830 when Marcus Samuel established a modest East End, London, trading concern to deal with the Orient.[10] Among the articles he imported were polished sea shells, useless items to be sure, but very dear to the hearts of Victorian ladies who decorated screens, boxes, and other knick-knack items with them; commercially, shells were used to manufacture mother-of-pearl for buttons and knife handles. These sea shells, ancestors of the most widely known trademark in the oil business, were by no means the only merchandise in which M. Samuel & Company dealt. Every type of manufactured goods, from cloth to pins and pianos, was taken by them to the East, sold, and the proceeds used to buy return cargoes of tea, jute, rice, and commodities such as copra (dried split coconut) for the soap factories of England.

By early becoming an expert on transport, Samuel made money, and his business grew rapidly during the middle years of the Nineteenth Century. He established offices in the principal ports of the Far East and proceeded to acquire the agency for several shipping lines running to Japan. Then, when the company was more than forty years old, and prospering, something happened to change its history. Commodore Matthew Perry's celebrated landing in forbidden Japan in 1853 and the subsequent opening up of the traffic with the Western World brought about in the short space of twenty-five years a major upheaval in Japanese life. By the 1880's, Japan's business and trade, modeled on that of Europe and America, was developing with astonishing rapidity. Samuel's two sons, Marcus and Samuel, who had taken over the business after his death in 1874, saw that the old method of trading was in for a drastic revision, for they could no longer plan on purchasing raw materials from an undeveloped country in exchange for the finished products it needed. Confronted with this crisis in trade, the Samuel firm looked for and found a manufactured product which was not at that time produced in Japan—kerosene.

In his search for supplies, it was only natural that Samuel should turn to Russian oil; for while small quantities of kerosene from that source were being shipped to the Orient, the trade was by no means large. In 1890, Marcus Samuel traveled to Baku to have a look at the oil industry there. He found the Swedish Nobel Brothers already entrenched as leading refiners, transporters, and marketers, not only of kerosene but also of fuel oil, a product as yet little used in other areas.

Robert and Ludvig Nobel, older brothers of the more famous Alfred, had come to Baku in the early 1870's. Oil had been known to the region since prehistoric times and a semblance of an oil industry was already in existence there, but it remained for the industrious Nobels to organize it into a thriving enterprise. Baku, located on the land-locked Caspian Sea, had no outlet to the outside world so the Nobels transported their product up the Volga River and sold it in the interior of Russia. But the treeless lower Volga country around Baku presented a problem. In America, where wood was cheap and plentiful, refiners could afford to pack and ship their kerosene in barrels; the cost of a barrel in Baku made other means of transportation imperative. Oil had already been transported in tanks placed inside the holds of ships, but it remained for the Nobels to design the first modern tanker, in which the hull of the vessel did double duty as the walls of a tank, and the engine works were placed in the rear of the ship to minimize the fire hazard. As there was no shipyard on the Caspian Sea capable of building such a vessel, the keel of this first real tanker, the *Zoroaster,* was laid in Sweden in 1877. When completed, the vessel was taken in sections through the inland waterways of Russia and reassembled on the Caspian, where it was put into service.

Because it was landlocked, Baku had no access to the ocean transportation needed to get its oil to the world market. During the early 1880's construction was started on the Transcaucasian & Black Sea Railroad to connect Baku with Batum on the Black Sea and thereby with the outside world. The railroad's builders ran out of money before the tracks were completed and the Paris Rothschilds came to the rescue, advancing the capital necessary to finish the line and gaining control of it. Taking advantage of their position, the Rothschilds organized an oil company, the Société Commerciale et Industrielle de Naphte Caspienne et de la Mer Noire (called ''Bnito'' for short), and built a large refinery at Batum. With the completion of the railroad in 1883, they soon were selling kerosene in continental Europe and in England and sending occasional cargoes to the Far East, as well.

Samuel, a true shipping man at heart, saw the Nobel tankers and was much taken by the economies of operation which this method offered. If he had a tanker to provide cheap bulk transportation, a source of supply as near as Batum, and if he could take the tanker through the new Suez Canal instead of around the Cape, then he most certainly could compete against the Standard, even if they dropped the price. Would the Rothschild company, he asked, sell him kerosene? It would, of course, be inviting competition to do so; but the

East was not Rothschild's main market, so the Bnito agreed to supply Samuel with lamp oil on condition that he sell it East of Suez.

With a contract for supplies in hand, Samuel promptly set about building a tanker. He didn't have enough money for the venture but found that William Gray & Sons of West Hartlepool were willing to finance his tanker as well as build it. Construction was started in 1891 and the new ship, the *Murex*, the first of a fleet which later would number several hundred vessels, was launched in May 1892. Permission to transport kerosene in bulk through the Suez Canal was finally wrested from the Canal authorities† and the 4,200-ton *Murex*, loaded with Russian kerosene, made its appearance in Eastern waters during the summer of 1892. Its arrival signalled a new day for the Oriental oil business. No longer would the small commission agent dominate the distributing end of the business; from now on the advantage would go to the man who could ship in bulk.

With energy and with an understanding of shipping born of sixty years of dealing with the Orient, the Samuel firm at once set about organizing a new system of supply and distribution. Instead of expensive shipment in the hold of a steamer as regular freight, lamp oil would henceforth be transported to the Far East by tanker and unloaded into large tank installations located at seaports throughout India, Malaya, and the China coasts. From these points, kerosene could be shipped, still in bulk, by railroad tank car or barge to bulk depots in the interior. The depots, in turn, would put the kerosene in drums and ship them to individual dealers who would dispense kerosene from the drum into the customer's own container. The storekeeper would return the empty drum to the depot for refilling. The bulk system, as the Nobels had proven in Russia, was more efficient, less wasteful of materials, and, most important, permitted utilization of the cheapest form of shipping.

Building of tank installations, it was planned, would be handled by local businessmen with sufficient capital to finance the large investment required. Such men were available, and building of tanks went

---

† The prohibition against shipments of bulk oil through the Canal was at least understandable. The Canal authorities were only reflecting the general opinion of the time in regarding bulk oil in approximately the same category as dynamite. Even the eminent petroleum chemist Sir Boverton Redwood vigorously supported this view.[11] It is little wonder, then, that Samuel always regarded this first shipment as one of his major triumphs; it is, in fact, the chief business accomplishment he mentioned in his biographical sketch in the British *Who's Who*.

forward rapidly. But Samuel and his wholesalers, called collectively the Tank Syndicate, hit an unexpected snag. Standard Oil's five-gallon kerosene can had become a part of Oriental life! Almost indispensable, it was put to every sort of use. Household utensils made elsewhere from iron or copper were in the East fashioned from an empty kerosene can. Naturally, the Oriental customer resented the threatened disappearance of an article which had become so large an item in his way of living. The Tank Syndicate floundered for a while, but finally came up with the right answer: instead of packing the kerosene in drums, the depots would erect can-filling plants and package the kerosene near the point of sale in bright new cans made in the East. The can would not be rusty when it reached the customer, as it would have travelled only a few miles, instead of all the way from Brooklyn or Philadelphia; it would also cost less, having been made in the Orient with cheaper labor.

At this point, in the mid-1890's, disturbing news began to come from Russia. The Russian government, which had reserved the oil industry to itself as a government monopoly from 1806 to 1872,[12] was once again thinking monopolistic thoughts and had just decreed that no oil could be transported from Batum to Vladivostok, except in Russian ships. It might be, Samuel feared, that Russia was preparing to take over its oil business. If such a government monopoly came into being, what assurance had Samuel that it would sell to him? Or would the monopoly step in behind his back and take his customers, the owners of the tank installations?

To help allay this fear of insecure supplies, as well as to acquire a source nearer their market, the Samuels established themselves as producers in the Indies in 1896 by acquiring, for £2,500 (then about $12,000) and a royalty, the three concessions held at that time by J. H. Menten on the wild shores of Koetei, a province of East Borneo.[13] A Dutch company, called Nederlandsch Indische Industrie en Handel Maatschappij (Netherlands Indies Manufacturing & Trading Company) was organized by the Samuels in 1898 to operate the concession and the refinery which they planned to erect at Balik Papan.

To guard against the possibility that the Russians might organize an export company and establish relations with the Samuels' agents, leaving no agents, no tanks, no Russian oil, and a mortgaged fleet of tankers for which no cargoes could be found, the Samuels proposed that the oil interests of M. Samuel & Company be separated from the rest of their operations and that a new company be organized, having as its property the Samuel producing leases and the projected refinery in the Indies, the tanker fleet, and the agents' tank installations and sub-depots. The Samuels would thus be assured of a market and the agents of steady supplies, with an additional opportunity to share in whatever profits the over-all enterprise should make. This proposal was accept-able to all concerned and on October 18, 1897, The "Shell" Transport & Trading Company, Ltd., was organized, taking its name from the brand name of the kerosene the Samuels had been selling.‡ Each par-ticipant received stock in the new organization in proportion to the assets he had contributed; as the Samuel firm had contributed the lion's share of the property, the stock issued to them enabled them to retain control of the enterprise.

Drilling of the Borneo oil field proved somewhat of a disappoint-ment, as far as the light fractions were concerned. The oil was heavy, and could be refined into a saleable kerosene only by mixing with it lighter kerosene from another source. It was, however, excellent for fuel, and for that purpose it could be used unrefined. Samuel thus became one of the pioneer promoters of the use of oil fuel, especially in the marine field. Being a good shipping man, he saw the immense advantage of liquid fuel over coal, and saying "we have nothing to overcome but prejudice," [15] promptly began using it in his own ships and urging both private shipowners and the British Admiralty to adopt it. His argument that a vessel using fuel oil could carry a larger amount of fuel energy in the same space was hard to answer and even-

---

‡ There are a number of fanciful stories in circulation in this country concerning the origin of the Shell name. The one most frequently heard (it also has been printed in company house organs at various times) tells how the Samuel children, presumably the late Lord Bearsted and his brother Samuel, were playing on the beach with sea shells, and decorated the family picnic basket with them. Their father, so the story goes, was promptly inspired to make and sell baskets decorated with shells and his business was at once successful. Like most "inspirational" stories, this account has little basis in fact. The family business as "Dealer in Foreign Shells" is known to date back at least to 1830, and probably earlier; Marcus Samuel (Lord Bearsted) and his brother Samuel, whose childish play is supposed to have furnished the inspiration, were not born until 1853 and 1855, respectively, by which time the business had been going some twenty years. The Hon. Peter Samuel, in a letter on June 8, 1950, confirmed that he had never heard this story told within the family.[14] The company's business did originally revolve around the shell trade, of course, and this motif has been preserved in the brand name "Shell," in the names of the Shell tankers, and in the nomenclature of the company's lubricating oils, the latter two being christened after the various genera of sea shells.

tually the prejudice against oil fuel was overcome. A major portion of
the credit for converting British vessels to the new fuel § is generally
accorded Samuel.[17]

The Balik Papan refinery proceeded slowly, beset with the same
kind of delays that the Royal Dutch had encountered at Pangkalan
Brandan, and it was not until late in 1899 that it was finally placed in
operation. Meantime, in 1898, Samuel contracted with the Moeara
Enim, one of the new Dutch oil companies which had been established
in southern Sumatra since 1890, to purchase its entire output. This
kerosene the Shell planned to market in the Orient, using Shell tankers
for transportation.

Then, in January 1901, a prolific new source of oil was discovered
in the New World. Previously, Pennsylvania and Ohio had produced
the bulk of American oil reaching the outside world; by controlling
transportation between these fields and the Atlantic seaports, Rockefeller had been able to control most of the oil business of his day.
However, about 1890, a decline in Pennsylvania production set in and
this growing shortage, as has always been true in the history of the
industry, brought a rash of exploratory drilling and the subsequent
discovery of oil in a new area, the Texas Gulf Coast. There the Lucas
Well, on Spindletop, a salt dome just outside Beaumont, Texas, was
brought in on January 11, 1901. The sea was nearby; the production
of a well could be piped right to a ship; it was impossible for any one
company to get and hold control.

Promptly, Samuel took advantage of the availability of the new
Spindletop oil and five months later, in June 1901, made a long-term
contract for supplies with the J. M. Guffey Petroleum Company. His
Bnito contract forbade him to take Russian oil to Europe; the Indies
oil was too far away and could be sold on the spot, anyhow; but with
supplies from this new field in Texas, Samuel was in a position to
enter the European market. Thus assured of supply, Samuel began
construction of four large tankers to be put in service on the trans-
Atlantic run.

The Shell had had a truly remarkable growth. From one tanker and
a contract with Bnito only eight years before, it had grown by 1900 to
one of the largest of the world's oil companies with 30 ocean-going

§ This was only a partial victory in Samuel's eyes. He was opposed to burning
oil under boilers on the grounds that it was "a waste of the world's resources." He
took an early lead in encouraging the adoption of the Diesel engine, and was
instrumental in the Shell Group's building a Diesel-powered tanker long before the
First World War.[16]

tankers, 31 ocean depots throughout the East and eleven more planned, 320 subsidiary depots in towns through the Orient,[18] an oil field in Borneo and a newly completed refinery there; and contracts for supply with Moeara Enim in Sumatra, Bnito in Batum, and Guffey in Beaumont. No other oil company, not even Standard, had sources of supply as well distributed over the globe. Shell's position seemed secure and the future bright indeed.

By the turn of the century, the Shell company had, working from an opposite starting point, arrived at the same type of organization that Royal Dutch had—a completely integrated company. Royal Dutch had found themselves with crude oil on their hands. To get rid of it, they refined it; to get the refined product to market, they chartered and later built tank steamers; to sell the product after it was there, they entered directly into the building and operation of tank installations. Shell had come at it the other way. They needed something to sell; kerosene looked good. To compete, they needed cheap transportation, so they built tankers. With large investments in tankers, it became prudent to acquire constant supplies of product; hence, the purchase of producing properties and the building of a refinery.

The marketing installations of both companies were by 1900 duplicated in most of the cities of India and China; they were both gaining in sales volume almost daily, but their American competitor was still a controlling factor in the market. Together, they might surpass him; they both had Indies production, tanker fleets, and tank installations, things which even the Standard did not have in the East. True, they lacked Standard's tremendous pool of operating capital built up through thirty-five years of highly profitable operation, but both Shell and Royal Dutch did have able, energetic leadership, a thorough knowledge of transportation and finance, and, most important, sources of crude oil and finished products completely removed from Standard's sphere of influence. If they must fight Standard, why not do it now, on a rising market, rather than wait for the next fall in prices?

Royal Dutch-Shell

LOOKING back in 1934, Deterding gave Standard Oil credit for an indirect assist. If that company "and one or two more had not gone on hitting us by price-cutting, and hitting us with such vim around that early period," he wrote, "the Royal Dutch might quite conceivably have been a small company, almost unheard of today. But when an opponent, bigger and stronger than yourself, keeps on belabouring you with blows, and dealing them out at you good and hard, you are bound to see the obvious, if you can see anything at all. And in our case, the obvious once more was simply that *to survive these price-cutting onslaughts, we just had to hit back*. Equally obvious was it, also, that if we hit back alone, we would be knocked clean out of the fighting ring." [19]

Samuel's Shell Transport & Trading Company, because of its prominence, was the most logical ally. There were others, too, in the Oriental market—the Rothschilds, who still shipped some case oil from Batum, but had neither tankers nor tank installations; the Nobels who did likewise, on a smaller scale; and two East Indies concerns, the "Sumpal" (Sumatra Palembang Petroleum Company), which had been organized in the late 1890's by Kessler's brother, D. A. J. Kessler, its output from the start going under contract to the Royal Dutch; and The Dordrecht Petroleum Company, established on Java in 1887 by Adriaan Stoop and his brother, selling its entire output in the home country, Java.

To fight Standard, Deterding had come to realize, it was necessary, first, to unite in one enterprise every competitor who could be prevailed upon to join, and, second, to try to cancel out one of Standard's great competitive advantages by moving into areas where up to now Standard had been free to raise or lower its prices to make up for losses in areas where it might for the moment be selling at rock-bottom prices. Deterding's energy, his directness, and his ability can be seen in the manner in which he moved, swiftly and confidently, to accomplish these objectives.

With the realism so typical of him, Deterding appreciated that his company was but a very small David ranged against a bigger-than-average Goliath. First, he proceeded to get the other Dutch East Indies companies arrayed squarely behind him in a producers' association. Thus fortified, he tackled a much bigger proposition: a joint enterprise to effect a union of Shell and Royal Dutch operations. This project presented difficulties, for it was not easy to talk of combination to a firm which was larger, better known, and headed by the current Lord Mayor of London.

Not that such a union had never before entered anyone's head. Various types of working arrangements, usually providing for the sale to Shell of Royal Dutch's output, had been proposed during the early days of both companies, but these negotiations had always wound up in an impasse. Then, during 1901, reports began to reach Deterding that all might not be well with Samuel. The long and expensive delay in building the refinery at Balik Papan had deprived the Shell of badly needed product; when at last the refinery had got into operation, it ran into trouble with the crude; and Shell's shortage of product was not eased by the Moeara Enim contract: in 1901, that company had asked for more time to fulfill its obligations. These difficulties were reflected in the Shell company's dividends for 1901—a bare 2½%, in sharp contrast to the 24% dividend that the prospering Royal Dutch paid its shareholders that year.

For negotiating with Samuel, Deterding needed an intermediary. Such a man was found in the person of Frederick Lane, of Lane & Macandrew, a calm, patient, tactful, English businessman who had started in the business of chartering out tank ships. This had brought him in contact with the Paris Rothschilds, for whom he had become London representative. In his capacity as the Rothschilds' representative, Lane had frequent contact with the Samuel firm and enjoyed their full confidence. During 1901, Deterding became acquainted with Lane and was so impressed by Lane's all-around ability that thirty years later, he would still remark, "Frederick Lane was the cleverest man I have ever known in all my experience." [20] Lane, although a much older man, listened to young Deterding's scheme for uniting the Royal Dutch, Shell, and others who cared to join in an organization strong enough to stand up to Standard. He made endless good suggestions, acted as mediary between Deterding and Sir Marcus Samuel (who had been knighted in 1898) and, equally important, brought Deterding's accomplishments and ability to the attention of the Rothschilds, whose support in financial matters Deterding greatly desired.

The Shell, for the time at least, was in a much stronger bargaining position; and as Deterding did not wish to see his company submerged and become merely the Far East branch of a London concern, nego-

tiations ground to a halt several times during the ensuing months. Had
it not been for Lane's skill as a diplomat, plus an unfortunate turn of
circumstances that made Samuel less sure that he could go it alone, the
proposed union might never have come about.

Samuel's Shell Transport & Trading Company had made spectacular advances in a short time, but was in an insecure position, vulnerable in case of prolonged reverses. Its tanker fleet, certainly the most
extensive in the Old World, had been built on borrowed money, on
which interest and principal payments had to be made. To do this, all
tankers had to be kept fully employed. Spindletop was not proving to
be the hoped-for bonanza; production had declined and the Guffey
company was not able to deliver Shell as much oil as it had promised.*
The fortunes of war also dealt a blow. In 1900, the Boxer Rebellion in
China brought the capture of Tientsin and destruction of Shell property there and at other points in China. In 1901, Shell had also listened
to offers of purchase from the Standard Oil Company, but had finally
declined Standard's offers. The refusal of these offers only brought
nearer the threat of a decisive struggle with Standard.[22]

In this mood, negotiations proceeded in greater earnest; the only
major question remaining was who should have charge. Samuel was
respected in business both at home and abroad, was head of a substantial enterprise, and had been honored by his countrymen by election
to the office of Lord Mayor of the City of London. He could hardly
be expected to take an inferior position, but Deterding, who wrote of
himself, "mine is a personality which does not readily submerge itself," [23] could not be expected to take a back seat, either. Finally, Deterding went to London, and there in a face-to-face meeting, he and
Samuel quite unexpectedly worked out a solution. Samuel would become chairman of the new company, have a voice in major decisions,
and always have the power of veto; Deterding would be entrusted
with the actual day-to-day management. Now the major obstacles

---

* It is greatly to Samuel's credit that he did not choose to exact a "pound of
flesh" at a time when he could legally have done so, much to his own benefit.
On June 28, 1901, when it looked as though the Spindletop wells would never stop
gushing, Guffey had signed a contract agreeing to deliver Shell 4½ million barrels
of oil over a twenty-year period at 25 cents per barrel. By 1902, output was declining
rapidly and in August of that year, Guffey's Spindletop wells stopped flowing. The
Pittsburgh Mellons, who had recently floated a $5,000,000 bond issue for the Guffey
company, stepped in to salvage what they could of the business. The contract with
Shell could not be filled except at a loss to them, so Andrew Mellon went to London
in the summer of 1903 to ask Sir Marcus Samuel if he would consent to cancelling
it. Samuel agreed, and the Guffey company (later to become Gulf Oil Corporation)
was saved from almost certain bankruptcy.[21]

A. J. Zijlker (1840–1890) spent a decade patiently laying foundations for the Royal Dutch Company, organized at The Hague in June 1890.

J. B. August Kessler (1853–1900) took up where Zijlker left off, with energy and vision launched and built the new company's business.

The first refinery of the Royal Dutch Company, at Pangkalan Brandan in the jungles of northern Sumatra, looked like this in 1892, the first year of operation.

Hugo Loudon (1860–1941) followed Kessler in the Indies, became Royal Dutch managing director (1902–1921) and board chairman (1929–1941).

Zijlker's first well, Telaga Toenggal No. 1, brought in in June 1885, was the foundation of the Royal Dutch Co. It produced oil as late as 1942.

Distilling section of the Pangkalan Brandan refinery, 1893–1896. Roofs over the stills provided protection against heavy tropical rains.

The "Shell" Transport & Trading Company, Ltd., grew out of the Oriental trading business of M. Samuel & Co., of London. The Samuels had acquired a Borneo oil field and, when the oil proved too heavy for refining, they became pioneer salesmen of oil fuel. This demonstration installation, set up in the 1890's at the Yokohama depot, helped convert Japan to oil fuel.

Early photo of Yokohama distributing installation, selling kerosene furnished by the Samuels' tankers.

Sir Marcus Samuel, first Viscount Bearsted (1853–1927), founded The "Shell" Transport & Trading Company, of which he was lifelong chairman. He had a thorough knowledge of shipping, was the first to ship oil through the Suez Canal, and pioneered the introduction of oil fuel for m e r c h a n t and naval vessels.

More than any other man, H. W. A. Deterding (1866–1939) was responsible for the rapid rise of the Royal Dutch-Shell Group of companies. He was general managing director of the Shell Group companies from their formation in 1907 until his retirement in 1936. This picture, snapped by a ships' news photographer in New York Harbor in the Twenties, shows Sir Henri at the height of his career.

European

were removed. Union without sacrifice of sovereignty could be a reality.

The Rothschilds, whose ownership of "Bnito" made them important in the Far Eastern oil trade, would also come in; their support and their name, eminently respected in financial circles, would be more than welcome. Lane, from his position as intermediary, had seen what an attractive proposal the new arrangement would offer the Rothschilds and had convinced them of it.

On June 27, 1902, a three-party agreement was signed by Shell, the Rothschilds, and the Royal Dutch. They agreed to set up a new marketing company to act as sole selling agent for all three interests in the Far East. It would be named, in honor of the region, The Asiatic Petroleum Company, Ltd. Samuel was to be chairman; Deterding, managing director.† Capital was set at £2,000,000 and shares were subscribed one-third by each participant. Asiatic also became the sole selling agent throughout the world for the Indies producers (Royal Dutch and other East Indies companies allied with it), but both Samuel and the Rothschilds retained for themselves the markets they already had in Europe. Deterding promptly opened an office in London where for the rest of his business career his chief headquarters were to be. The next year was spent in preparations, and on July 2, 1903, Asiatic officially began operation.

The new company, uniting the selling efforts of Standard's three main competitors in the Far East, was an oil deal of major significance. Although no particular note was taken of it in America outside of oil circles, it was in Europe recognized as a major accomplishment and a triumph for young Deterding, still in his mid-thirties. The companies forming Asiatic had, in effect, agreed to stop fighting each other and concentrate on Standard. No actual amalgamation of their properties took place; Asiatic rented its tankers from Shell and Royal Dutch for a ten-year period; tank installations and railroad tank cars were likewise rented from those who owned them. Royal Dutch, Shell, and Bnito all retained their producing and refining functions, surrendering to the new company only their Oriental sales activities; agreements which each had in force with other parties were not upset. The new

† A position equivalent to president of an American corporation. Neither Deterding nor Samuel made large personal fortunes. Deterding's estate came to some £2,000,000; that of Samuel, who had a much larger proprietary interest in the business, to £4,000,000, both small amounts compared to Rockefeller's wealth. In 1913, after Rockefeller had set up his famous Foundation, the value of his investments still exceeded $900,000,000.[24]

creation was, as it were, a "trial marriage." If it worked, fine; if not, there was very little that the participants could lose.

The new alliance could, and would, give the Standard a "run for its money." But for the time being, at least, that company still remained the big power in the oil business. It would require something fundamental—a revolution in the nature of the oil business itself—to tip the scales in favor of the newcomer. Just such a revolution had been brewing and was to take place with the emergence of gasoline as the oil companies' major product.

Not that gasoline was a new product. It had been the plague of the refiner since the beginning of the industry. Too explosive to be burned as boiler fuel and a dangerous contaminant if much of it were included in kerosene, it was usually led away to pits some distance from the refinery and there burned in the open air.

Oil as it comes from the well in its crude state is a mixture of hydrogen and carbon compounds. At the top of the scale are the gases which come from the well as natural, or casinghead, gas; at the bottom of the scale are the residues of refining, the heavy sludge-like materials such as those which go into asphalt. In between these two extremes lie all the common products of the oil industry. In the early years of the petroleum industry, only the heavier part of the light liquid fraction, kerosene, was desired for use as lamp oil; later refiners distilled lubricating oils from the bottom fractions, if there was sufficient demand, and, if there was demand, made paraffin for use in candle-making. This was about the extent of the oil industry's manufacturing processes until the turn of the century, except in a few areas where the heavier fractions were sold locally for fuel.

During the years of the foundation and early growth of the Shell and Royal Dutch companies, a new vehicle, the automobile, was being developed by European and American inventors. The year 1883, which saw the opening up of Baku's trade with the outside world, and the granting of Zijlker's concession in the Indies, also saw Gottlieb Daimler, of Mannheim, Germany, perfect his new hot-tube system of ignition. Two years later, when Zijlker was bringing in his first good producing well, Daimler had built his first motorcycle; the same year another German, Karl Benz, completed a successful, gasoline-driven motorcar. By the 1890's, European manufacturers were turning out automobiles in considerable number (all handmade, of course) and some of the new vehicles were finding their way to America, chiefly as playthings of the socialites of the Gay Nineties.[25]

The bicycle was then at the height of its popularity. In the natural course of events, dozens of resourceful bicycle mechanics all over the country began to turn their attention to building gas buggies for themselves. This wave of back-yard tinkering produced some remarkable results. Charles E. Duryea and his brother Frank, of Chicopee Falls, Massachusetts, produced the first American-made car in 1892, and by 1895 had organized a factory in Springfield to manufacture the "Duryea Buggyaut." Elwood Haynes, field superintendent of a natural gas company in Kokomo, Indiana, and a mechanic, Elmer Apperson, built an automobile which they drove in the Kokomo Fourth-of-July parade in 1894. During these same years, Henry Ford, an engineer in the powerhouse of the Detroit Edison Company, spent his evenings in a back-yard garage evolving the vehicle which would later make him famous. In 1897, R. E. Olds started production of his first Oldsmobile at Lansing, Michigan; and three years later moved to Detroit to establish the Olds Motor Works, the first factory to produce automobiles in quantity. Olds made 2,000 cars in the next two years, sold them for $650 each, and paid his stockholders a cash dividend of 105%—proving that quantity production of automobiles was not only possible but profitable. Finally, in 1903, the same year that saw the founding of Asiatic, the Ford Motor Company was organized in Detroit.

A new age in transportation was on its way and the petroleum industry was to fuel it. In 1895, there had been 300 automobiles in America; ten years later there were 78,000; by 1910 there would be 459,000; and by 1914, more than 1,700,000.[26] The demand for gasoline, as a result, increased by leaps and bounds. It could, happily, be more than met by Asiatic. From the Royal Dutch fields in Sumatra, rich in high-gravity crude, came a fine motor fuel which could be shipped to Europe almost without cost, for tankers bringing out Russian lamp oil from Batum could return loaded with the Sumatra gasoline. As the Asiatic was merely a selling company, collecting a commission from each of the participants, the Royal Dutch, as chief supplier of gasoline to Asiatic, profited greatly during this period, paying its stockholders in the years 1903–1906 dividends of 65%, 50%, 50%, and 73%, or nearly 240% in four years. These handsome dividends contrasted sadly with those of Samuel's Shell company which, during the same period, was able to pay its shareholders only about 5% each year.

The reason for this wide disparity in earnings was the unforunate

position in which the Shell people found themselves. No one had foreseen the great upsurge in gasoline demand, a demand so great that
even the Standard Oil Company could not meet its commitments and
in 1903 contracted with Asiatic to take all of the latter's gasoline surpluses. Standard, to meet its greatly increased gasoline demand at
home, upped its refining operations; kerosene, until now the prime
product of oil refiners, became a by-product of gasoline manufacture
almost overnight. As gasoline manufacture increased, more and more
by-product kerosene became available. Standard, unable to dispose of
its kerosene production at home, dumped it on the European market
for whatever it would bring. In this demoralized kerosene market,
Samuel was hurt badly because, at the time of the formation of
Asiatic, Shell had kept its European markets for itself. As a result,
Shell lost money on much of its European marketing. In 1904, for instance, Shell sold 110,000 tons (about 35,000,000 gallons) of kerosene
in Europe at a net loss of £112,000 ($545,440).[27] Already spread
pretty thin, the Shell company could not stand continued losses of
this dimension and withdrew completely from the German market in
1906. The falling off of crude oil production in the Spindletop field
was a further blow, for Shell had arranged long-term contracts for the
purchase of Spindletop oil and had built on mortgage four large new
tankers to handle this commerce.

Now Deterding's dream of a permanent alliance between Royal
Dutch and Shell became more attractive to Samuel. Certainly the
combined size of the two companies would serve as security against
encroachment by competitors, and the operating economies which
such a merger could effect would bring a substantial saving. No longer
in a position to ask even a fifty-fifty share in such a merger, Samuel
contented himself with making the most he could of his position.

By April 1906, Samuel and Deterding were discussing the arrangements. The Shell would not lose its identity; instead two new companies, one British, the other Dutch, would be formed, and to them
would be transferred all the properties now owned by both Shell and
Royal Dutch. The profits would be divided in accordance with the
degree of participation upon which Samuel and Deterding had determined: 60% to the Royal Dutch, 40% to the Shell. Only one question
remained in Samuel's mind. With his company in the minority, how
could he be sure that Deterding would manage the new concerns so
that results would not be prejudicial to Shell's interest?

Here Deterding's industrial statesmanship shone. He proposed that Shell sell a large block of its shares, say 25%, to the Royal Dutch. Then Samuel could rest assured that the management would earnestly attempt to make money in equal degree for both companies. No one could demur further; in the face of such fairness Samuel quickly gave in and the directors and stockholders approved the principles of the proposed agreement.‡ This insight into Deterding's essential fairness is important, for it was on that foundation-stone that a large group of companies was to be built in mutual trust, without the bickering and undercover struggles that have marred the histories of many large corporations.

"Unlike some of our past rivals," Deterding pointed out in his memoirs, "it could never be said of us that we grew to mammoth size by gobbling up competitors after beating them into helplessness. . . . To crush a rival is to make an enemy. To buy out a competitor at too cheap a rate is like employing a good man at too low a rate. . . . No party to an amalgamation should be left with the idea that he has made a bad bargain; instead of squeezing him out, take him in as a partner in the amalgamation; in short, make him your friend instead of your foe." [30] Deterding was always to maintain that the experience of others is the cheapest experience we buy; in this concept of amalgamation he certainly shows that he had learned from the experience of Rockefeller not to aim at too large a degree of control and court disaster by running afoul of hostile public opinion.

‡ The continuing importance of the Shell company under the new arrangement was not immediately apparent to outside observers at the time. In September 1906, shortly after the merger had been announced, the editor of *The Petroleum Review,* London, bade Samuel a premature farewell in a long editorial paying tribute to his accomplishments. It concluded, "Personally and on behalf of many members of the petroleum industry, I am bound to say that we all regret that as a result of the new arrangement, the interest of Sir Marcus Samuel in the oil trade will, perhaps to some extent lapse, but should this be so, we shall all look to him as one who has so ably represented the petroleum industry for the past 15 years. His name will always be associated with the carriage of oil in bulk to the Far East, with the employment of tank steamers for general cargoes, with the remarkable development of the Borneo oil fields, and the yeoman service he has rendered in the cause of liquid fuel, while last but not least his successful importation of benzine in bulk to this country, which has given so great an impetus to the motor-car industry." [28] Royal Dutch continued to hold its large block of Shell shares for several years; however, after Deterding's good faith had thus been established, it became pointless to retain so large a holding. Over the years, much of this block of stock has been disposed of, the largest amount, 11¼ million shares, being sold to the public in June 1922. By the end of 1951, the original 25% interest had been reduced to a nominal holding of one share.[29]

In 1951, Sir Robert Waley Cohen, who had then been associated with the Shell Transport & Trading for a half century, attested how harmoniously the Royal Dutch-Shell amalgamation worked out in practice: "As far as I can remember, no vote has ever had to be taken at a combined Board meeting. All our decisions have been unanimous and our interests have been identical in every way." [31]

In April 1907, the stockholders of each company approved the merging of Royal Dutch and Shell properties. In the summer of that year, the proposed new companies were set up. N. V. De Bataafsche Petroleum Maatschappij (The Batavian Petroleum Company), with headquarters at The Hague, was organized to own and manage all of the oil lands and refineries belonging to Royal Dutch and Shell Transport & Trading. The Anglo-Saxon Petroleum Company, Ltd., located in London, was created to take over the tankers, tank installations, and other distributing facilities. Both these new companies were owned 60% by the Royal Dutch, 40% by Shell, and their directors allotted, in proportion to ownership, two from the Shell to three from the Royal Dutch. The Asiatic, in which the Rothschild interest continued until the 1930's, remained the marketing company for the new combination, with the Royal Dutch-Shell ownership in it being placed on the same 60-40 basis. By these arrangements of 1907, both Royal Dutch and Shell divested themselves of all properties except securities and became thenceforth purely holding companies.

These three companies, Asiatic, Bataafsche, and Anglo-Saxon, owned jointly by the Royal Dutch and the Shell thus became the nucleus of a growing oil empire called for convenience the Royal Dutch-Shell Group.§ As this Royal Dutch-Shell Group was not a corporate entity, it presented an organizational problem—aside from sitting in the middle of the North Sea, where could the top management make its headquarters? A sensible compromise, typical of the harmonious relations within the Group, settled what might have been a serious problem for some concerns. The head offices in London and at The Hague were both retained. Top executives divided their time between the two cities. London, the undisputed financial center of Europe, became headquarters for commercial affairs of the Group and

§ The Asiatic name, despite the company's world-wide scope, remained unchanged for forty years; finally it was altered to The Shell Petroleum Company, Ltd., early in 1946. Anglo-Saxon functioned for nearly half a century; in 1955, as the result of corporate simplification, Anglo-Saxon's business was transferred to Shell Petroleum, and the Group's main operating companies reduced to two—Shell Petroleum and Bataafsche.

The Hague world headquarters for the technical side of the business—exploration, production, refining, research, and, later on, chemical manufacture.

The new arrangement was enormously successful. Applying the same formula of fairness, the Group soon acquired allies throughout the world. Some retained almost complete independence, selling only their products under long-term contracts; some sold their crude oil; some retained ownership but let the Group manage their companies; some sold a minority interest, some a majority, some their whole companies. There was no set rule. Had the principle of 100% ownership been applied, it is doubtful whether the Royal Dutch-Shell Group would have had such a meteoric rise in so short a space of time, for outright acquisition requires staggering amounts of cash.

By 1913, the year before World War I, the two concerns, which ten years before had been of no more than medium size, had together, and combined with others, vaulted into a foremost place among the world's oil companies. A controlling interest in the large Astra Romana in Romania made the Group that country's largest single oil company. Rothschild's Bnito had been purchased, and the Group had made large-scale arrangements with producing organizations in the Russian oil fields. Producing companies had been started in Iraq and Egypt. Large acquisitions had been made in Venezuela, where the Group was to play the role of pioneer. In Mexico, good beginnings were being laid for an important future stake in that country's oil business. And in America, two new companies, the American Gasoline Company on the Pacific Coast and the Roxana Petroleum Company of Oklahoma, were already in operation.

CHAPTER III

Sumatra to Seattle

1912–1920

O N SEPTEMBER 16, 1912, an Anglo-Saxon tanker, the S.S. *Romany*, pulled into Richmond Beach, a secluded cove on Puget Sound twelve miles north of Seattle, and discharged into the tanks of a brand-new water terminal a cargo of more than a million gallons of Sumatra gasoline. A few days later, on October 4, 1912, an 8,000-gallon shipment was dispatched in a brand-new Shell tank car to Chehalis, Washington, and the sale of Shell gasoline in America got under way.[1]

Having already entered the markets of Europe, Asia, Australia, and parts of Africa, the Royal Dutch-Shell companies could be expected in the natural course of events to extend their operations to the Americas—especially North America where the number of automobiles, increasing by leaps and bounds, offered a fine new market for anyone with gasoline to sell. There was also a desire to "operate in the Standard's back-yard" so as to make sure that this competitor would not be able to offset losses from price wars abroad by charging high prices at home. This latter motive was not, however, as important as a much more everyday consideration: how to replace a substantial market that had just been lost.

As noted in the preceding chapter, Standard had been unable to meet its market requirements for gasoline and in 1903 had contracted to take from Asiatic any surplus gasoline which the Group had to offer. On the Pacific Coast this had resulted in imports by the Standard Oil Company of California of three or four cargoes (5,000,000 to 8,000,000 gallons) of gasoline a year.[2] Then, Standard of California had built its own refinery and begun buying large amounts of crude oil from two British firms, California Oilfields, Ltd., at Coalinga, California, and Lobitos Oilfields, Ltd., of Peru. With product coming from its own refinery, Standard was not as dependent upon Asiatic for supplies of gasoline. In 1910, Standard notified Deterding that the cargoes formerly purchased from Asiatic would no longer be needed.[3] Where could Deterding dispose of these five to eight million gallons of gasoline which had been going to the Pacific Coast? Why not, indeed, in the same area?

There certainly was nothing wrong with the West Coast as a market. It was newly settled country, a country of long distances and high hills. Once the automobile had made its appearance there, it was welcomed and rapidly adopted as a leading means of transportation. Then, too, the West Coast was nearer to Sumatra than any other spot in the country, and it could be reached by cheap water transportation without long hauls overland afterward.

Back in 1904, Deterding had tried importing gasoline into America, with sufficient success to know that it would work. That year a tanker had been on its way from the East Indies to Germany when Standard reduced the price of gasoline on the German market. With characteristic vigor, Deterding had diverted the vessel to Philadelphia * where the cargo had been sold at a profit, causing considerable concern in the Standard ranks.[5]

Then, in 1910, price wars between Standard and the Royal Dutch-Shell had started up again both in the Far East and Europe, causing Deterding to point out "that although the price of Crude Oil was on the increase, our great competitor (The Standard Oil Co.) reduced the price of Refined Products on the market. This has been still more marked in the course of 1911, and has strengthened us in our conviction that the price reduction had no other object than to hamper us as much as possible in the development of our business. . . . A curious fact, which in our opinion is characteristic of the intentions of our competitors, is that the prices of Kerosene were reduced most and quickest in the Netherlands India, whilst in Holland, where we sell no Kerosene, but only Benzine, the benzine prices were reduced most." [6] This hit where it hurt, in the annual earnings statements. In 1911 the Group's receipts for kerosene alone were $3,750,000 less than the year before.[7]

To offset Standard's advantage at home, Deterding had long thought of entering America. Its vast distances were lending tremendous impetus to development of the motorcar industry; the Group

---

* It is interesting that Ida Tarbell took note of this transaction in her *History of the Standard Oil Company*, published the same year, and predicted: "It is a sign of what well may happen in the future—the Standard's domestic market invaded." [4]

companies had surpluses of gasoline; a contract for sale of part of
those surpluses had just been cancelled; and the price battle with
Standard had started again. Every consideration indicated that the
time to act was here. "When our business grew to such international
dimensions," he remarked later, "we obviously had to dig ourselves in as traders on American soil; otherwise we would have lost
our foothold everywhere else. Until we started trading in America,
our American competitors controlled world prices—because, as previously explained, they could always charge up their losses in underselling us in other countries against business at home where they
had a monopoly." [8]

With his mind made up to enter America, Deterding received a
chance caller at his office in London one day late in the summer of
1910.[9] The visitor was Richmond Levering, president of the Indian
Refining Company, of Lawrenceville, Illinois, who was faced on a
smaller scale with the same stiff competition from Standard. He had
come to Europe primarily to seek out new markets for the Havoline
motor oil which his company made. Deterding and Levering got on
well; soon they had laid aside motor oil for something much more
grandiose—a joint marketing arrangement for the entire "Atlantic
market," consisting of Western Europe and the east coast of the
Americas.

For these countries Deterding and Levering devised a plan which
anticipated that Indian and the Shell Group would form joint companies for each of three main areas into which they had boldly divided
the whole of Western Europe and the Atlantic coastline from Canada
to Cape Horn. The Group would supply the gasoline, Indian the
kerosene and lubricating oils. In Canada, where the Group already
had been selling some gasoline to the British American Oil Company,
Shell would organize the company. Along the Atlantic Seaboard and
in Central and South America, Indian would organize the new companies. In Europe, the management would be divided: the Scandinavian
countries to be covered by Indian, the rest by existing Shell marketing
organizations. Equally important, Levering was to do his best to bring
into the new venture some of the outstanding independent oil companies, such as Gulf Oil, controlled by the Mellons of Pittsburgh. [10]

In the eastern part of the United States, Indian would handle the
business, selling cargoes of gasoline brought in by Group tankers. To
make headway against the hard competition which they expected to
encounter in Standard's home territory, costs would have to be kept

as low as possible. This Deterding thought they could do, if Indian could assemble cargoes of American kerosene for export. With the tankers carrying full cargoes in both directions, the cost of transportation would thus be cut to the lowest possible figure.

On the Pacific Coast, where Indian had no representation, Shell would make its own arrangement, although Levering tried to insist on a joint arrangement there.[11] The big deal between Indian and Shell did not come off, as we shall soon see; but during the months that followed, Levering and Deterding remained friendly and Levering materially assisted the Group in getting the West Coast installations under way and in lining up for purchase producing properties in Oklahoma.

In May 1911, the U. S. Supreme Court ordered the Standard Oil Company broken up into 33 separate organizations, but this development did not have as much effect on Deterding's plans as the casual observer might assume. In the first place, he had already resolved to enter America; it only remained to decide where and how. More important, Deterding regarded the dissolution of Standard Oil as merely a clever legal trick to confuse the American public;[12] the Standard companies, he felt, still continued to act in concert. And, indeed, one of the most diligent students of Rockefeller and his companies reports that they continued to respect each other's traditional territories and spheres of activity for at least a decade longer.[13]

2

The American Gasoline Company

FROM the beginning of 1911, then, Deterding was planning constantly for that day nearly two years later when the first Shell gasoline would be sold in America. Some who have not known this fact, including a number of the company's own employees, have in the years since 1912 jumped to the romantic conclusion that these first plans were made and executed in secrecy, and that the opening of the Richmond Beach terminal came as a surprise and a shock to the oil world. However good a story it may make, this was not the case.

Deterding, among modern business leaders, had many outstanding characteristics. One of these was an almost unbelievable frankness and openness concerning business matters and plans for the future. From the first, the annual reports he wrote for the Royal Dutch Company were models of lucidity and candor. In sharp contrast to the perfunctory annual statements of American companies of the period, his reports often ran to as many as forty pages. "Of one thing I am certain . . . ," he wrote in later years, "Our Royal Dutch-Shell operations would never have succeeded as they did if we had tried to keep any part of our general working policy a secret. Year after year, in our annual reports to our shareholders published broadcast in the newspapers, I have always taken great care to explain each stage in our development and also to announce just where we were expanding in many different parts of the world. With the growth of our interests, we had inevitably to increase our capital, and there is no better way of winning the confidence of your shareholders than to make them understand as you go along every possible detail of just how any business, into which they have put their money, has been run." [14]

To such a man, it was only natural that any plans for entering America should be announced in advance, as indeed they were, a year and a half before that first-day sale. On April 12, 1911, the *Oil & Gas Journal* announced, "The Petroleum World, London, is authority for the statement that the Royal Dutch-Shell combine has decided to establish an office at San Francisco. The management will be entrusted to a member of the London staff of the Asiatic Petroleum Company, one of the Royal Dutch-Shell combine's subsidiaries." During the balance of 1911 alone, the same journal carried eight more articles on the subject, all of them longer than this first announcement. One, on July 13, 1911, shows clearly how widespread was the publicity given the contemplated move; it quoted Sir Marcus Samuel before the annual meeting of The Shell Transport & Trading Company: "As I anticipated, the splendid quality of 'Shell' spirit has so established itself that we are now erecting installations in Canada and the United States for its regular supply." The news, clearly, was given out; but to only a few did it mean anything.

The "member of the London staff of the Asiatic Petroleum Company" to whom the *Oil & Gas Journal* referred was F. P. S. Harris, manager of the gasoline department of Asiatic. In January 1911, while Levering and Deterding were still attempting to settle the details of their proposed partnership by trans-Atlantic correspondence, Deterding sent out two emissaries from London to get things under way. Harris, who was in charge, was accompanied by a pleasant young Dutchman, J. C. van Panthaleon, Baron van Eck, scion of a respected Dutch family and law graduate of the University of Utrecht. In 1908,

Van Eck had been hired by Hugo Loudon, had served a period of apprenticeship in various departments at The Hague and in London, mastering shorthand by evening study and soon after becoming Deterding's secretary. Harris, as head of the Asiatic gasoline department, was concerned chiefly with making arrangements to dispose, through new channels, of the cargoes which Standard had formerly purchased. Van Eck was to stay behind and run the marketing operation if they found it necessary to go into the business of distributing gasoline themselves.[15]

They arrived in New York in January 1911, and as a first order of business acquired property for an ocean terminal at Montreal and got construction under way, for Deterding had decided to go into business in Canada in any case. Levering sent one of his engineers, H. H. Beers,† to assist with the design of the depot and the letting of the contracts for its construction. Altogether, about a month was spent on these arrangements. Late in February, Harris and Van Eck left for California.[16]

They went first to Los Angeles where they called at the main office of the Union Oil Company, chief competitor in California of the Standard. Union had since 1909 been importing gasoline from Texas and the Mid-Continent, so it was reasonable to suppose that they might be interested in purchasing some of this high-grade, light-gravity Sumatra gasoline. Union made Harris an offer for the cargoes formerly sold to Standard, and Harris cabled the offer to Deterding in London. Deterding wanted about a quarter of a cent a gallon more, so he instructed Harris and Van Eck to proceed with the formation of a marketing company.

Prior to this, Levering, who was eager to participate in the West Coast arrangement, had sent Julius W. Copmann, an old Standard Oil man now associated with Indian, to the Pacific Coast; there Copmann had hired H. R. Gallagher and Donnell G. Fisher to set up an organization to be called the Indian Refining Company of California. Gallagher, a vigorous young Canadian who had been in San Francisco for some years with the real estate department of the Southern Pacific Railroad, was to be general manager; and Fisher, who had been a fuel oil salesman for the Associated Oil Company, was to have charge of sales. Gallagher opened a small office in San Francisco, and began a

† The same Beers who had been employed as an oil treater during the early days of the Royal Dutch Company's first refinery at Pangkalan Brandan. See page 26.

preliminary survey of sales possibilities. The gasoline market west of the Rockies, he recalled 40 years later, amounted to some 25,000,000 gallons yearly in 1910 and was dominated by Standard.[17]

Harris and Van Eck went to San Francisco where they talked the possibilities over with Gallagher and Fisher. California, where all of the West Coast's oil was produced, had Standard, Union, Associated, and other companies such as the smaller Puente in Los Angeles. In the booming Pacific Northwest—Oregon, Washington, and British Columbia—there were fewer companies offering gasoline for sale and the price was also higher by about two cents a gallon, for allowance had to be made for transportation from the refineries in California. As Shell's gasoline had to come from Sumatra, about equidistant from Seattle and San Francisco, the Pacific Northwest seemed the better market, provided it had consumption enough to support another oil company.

So, through Thomas H. Breeze, a San Francisco attorney who was a close friend of the lawyer Levering had employed in New York, inquiries were made as to the volume of gasoline sales in the Northwest. For the state of Washington, Breeze wrote a lawyer friend in Seattle, Winlock W. Miller, who obtained the gasoline sales figures for 1910 from the state government in Olympia. The figures which he sent to San Francisco must have looked good to Van Eck and Harris, for they decided to build ocean terminals at Seattle, Portland, and Vancouver, British Columbia. A fourth terminal was contemplated for the San Francisco area. During the summer of 1911, Harris, accompanied by Van Eck and Gallagher, selected the sites for the Seattle, Portland, and San Francisco installations.[18]

Through George V. Kittinger,‡ a prominent Seattle real estate man, acquisition of the Seattle terminal site was arranged. It was a strip of sand, backed by railroad tracks, at Richmond Beach, twelve miles north of Seattle on Puget Sound. Beers, who by now had the Montreal terminal well under way, came west to draw up designs for these new terminals.[19] Within a few months, the last attempts at a joint Shell-Indian venture petered out, and Beers, Gallagher, and Fisher all came over onto the Shell payroll.

On the first of April 1912, Fisher was sent to Seattle to be responsible for the sales effort in the Pacific Northwest. For offices he rented two rooms in the Northern Bank Building (now the Seaboard Build-

‡ Father of L. T. Kittinger, many years later a vice president of Shell Oil Company.

SHELL LOCATIONS ON THE PACIFIC COAST, 1912–1920

ing) in Seattle, and a month or so later hired a Seattle lad, Howard Tuckett, as general factotum. Located in the same building were Reitze, Storey & Duffy, architects and engineers, who were called in to help Beers with his designs and blueprints.§ For several months, Fisher and Tuckett comprised the whole office force in Seattle, with Van Eck spending much of his time there during 1912. As a company had not yet been organized, expenditures were made from the "J. C. van Eck Loan Account," money which the Group had advanced to Van Eck personally. Fisher's salary was a personal check from Van Eck; Tuckett got cash from his pocket. Understandably, young Tuckett found it hard to believe that he was working for one of the world's largest oil companies.[20]

Priority in construction was given the Seattle terminal. Later on there would be, according to plans, terminals at Vancouver in British Columbia and Portland in Oregon, but, for the initial months, the Seattle terminal could serve both points by railroad tank car. As soon as the Richmond Beach site had been selected, Van Eck, Gallagher, and Fisher set out to purchase property for sub-depots. Eleven such places were chosen and the depots built and put into operation as rapidly as they could be completed, some in 1912, the rest in 1913.

For a distributing sub-depot in the Seattle area, property was purchased at Westlake Avenue and Highland Drive along the shores of Lake Union, at that time the outskirts of town. The location had a railroad siding, and the lake would make it possible eventually to bring supplies in by barge. Here tankage and a small office were built.[21] Company-operated depots were also planned for Tacoma, Spokane, Portland, and Vancouver, B. C. In the latter two cities, sub-depots were merely temporary measures until water terminals could be built. With all this construction under way, it was time to organize a company.*

The choice of a name for the new company was not as easy as one would expect. On their arrival in Los Angeles in March 1911, Harris and Van Eck were disturbed to discover that only a few months be-

§ J. C. Storey, one of the partners of this firm, built many of the early Shell service stations in the Northwest and later joined Shell's marketing department. For several years prior to his death, he was general purchasing agent for the Shell Oil Company in San Francisco.

* When Van Eck began to buy real estate in the Northwest, the Washington Refining Company had been organized March 27, 1912, to hold real estate in the State of Washington, since laws of that state, aimed primarily at Orientals, placed restrictions upon ownership of real property by aliens. This company remained in existence until the end of 1953, when it was dissolved; its properties, previously leased to Shell Oil, were conveyed to that company.

fore, in December 1910, a Shell Petroleum Company had been organized there by William Nelson Shell and his brothers. The Shells had taken a lease on 80 acres in the old Newhall field and were attempting to sell $25,000 worth of stock to finance drilling.[22] After considering possible legal complications, Harris decided to go ahead and organize the "Shell Company of California," as he had originally intended.[23] However, Levering, still hopeful that the Indian name might be adopted, protested that "the name of the company should be associated with an American institution." [24] Thus matters stood for more than a year, until finally a "neutral" name, neither Shell nor Indian, was selected. The new firm was christened American Gasoline Company, and was organized under the laws of the state of New York on September 3, 1912.[25]

In addition to the five depots which the American Gasoline Company planned to operate for its own account, there would also be a number of agents. The smaller cities, it was felt, would not have enough gasoline business at the start to make operation of a salaried depot profitable. In towns such as Eugene, Salem, and Medford, Oregon, and Bellingham, Yakima, and Walla Walla, Washington, men with going businesses were willing to take on gasoline as a side line if the company would furnish them with the necessary equipment. Such arrangements were not new. Coal dealers whose businesses were slack in summer quite generally took on ice as a side line to keep their men and their teams busy—an important consideration, for the horses never stopped eating. Hay and grain dealers and many others operated dual businesses. It was quite natural that gasoline, which for the northern climate of Washington and Oregon was still a summer product, should be distributed by part-time agents in the small communities. So, while construction of the tankage for company depots was still under way, Fisher also made arrangements for agents in Washington and Oregon to distribute the new Shell Motor Spirit.[26]

Under these arrangements, the company agreed to supply the agent with the tankage he would need, hand-operated pumps to unload the tank cars, and a horse-drawn tank wagon. As the agent was already in business, he had the necessary horses and driver. He operated on a commission usually of about two cents a gallon, cheaper than the same volume of trade could be handled by company personnel. The agent, thus constituted, was to be an important factor in the Shell distributing organization in the Northwest during the early years, and he still plays an important role in the company's business in less populous areas all over the country.

The ocean terminal at Richmond Beach was completed by September 1912, and in the middle of the month the S.S. *Romany* came steaming down Puget Sound with the first shipment of Shell gasoline for the new American marketing organization. William Warner, a former Anglo-Saxon engineer who had sailed on the *Romany* for many years, had been made superintendent of the new terminal and was there to welcome his old ship. In an Anglo-Saxon work book still extant, he recorded the unloading of a cargo of 1,791,508 gallons of gasoline, most all of it good Sumatra gasoline of .720 specific gravity (65° A.P.I.). His book also records that the first reshipment of product was made on October 4, 1912, to an agent, the Western Oil Company, of Chehalis, Washington, and consisted of a railroad tank car holding 8,115 gallons.

On October 23, another shipment went to the American Gasoline Company's own depot at Tacoma; on October 26, a third tank-car load was dispatched, this time to the company's depot at Spokane. Other shipments show how rapidly new depots were opened in the ensuing weeks—November 1, to the company's depot at Portland; November 2, to the Westlake Ave. and Highland Drive depot in Seattle; November 30, to S. A. Manning & Co., agents at Salem, Oregon. The following year saw five other new depots in the Northwest come into operation: that of the American Gasoline Company at Fifth Avenue and Carolina Street, Vancouver, B.C., which got its first shipment in February 1913; and agents at North Yakima, Walla Walla, and Bellingham, in Washington, and Eugene, in Oregon. During all this period of opening depots the total number of Shell people in the area was very small, the total payroll for November 1912 numbering only twenty-four, exclusive of Fisher and Tuckett.[27]

The *J. B. Aug. Kessler* brought more gasoline in June 1913, but only a small amount (some 180,000 gallons) was unloaded at Seattle; the vessel took most of its cargo to Martinez, California, where a new terminal to serve the San Francisco Bay area was just opening. Further supplies arrived on the S.S. *Cowrie* in August and again in December 1913; on the S.S. *Bulysses* in August 1914 and the S.S. *Eburna* in December 1914. In all, about ten million gallons were brought in. The European war, and the demand for gasoline it created, stopped further shipments. No cargoes arrived after December 1914, and during the ensuing year five of the company's twenty-four depots had to be closed for lack of product.

The new company sold gasoline almost exclusively. Havoline motor oil was handled, but in insignificant quantities.[28] For the most part, the business of the new company consisted of receiving tanker cargoes, reshipping them by railway tank car to sub-depots, and from these points distributing the gasoline in horse-drawn tank wagons to garages, stores, and other retailers who owned their own dispensing equipment. As the primary purpose of the new company was merely to provide a market for cargoes which had formerly been sold to Standard, American Gasoline Company's operations were small in size during these early years, 1912-1914.

3

Wider Horizons

ALTHOUGH, as we have seen, the first sales of Shell Motor Spirit took place in the Northwest, the direction which resulted in the establishment of a terminal and sub-depots in that part of the country had come from San Francisco. Harris and Van Eck in 1911 had set up shop in the quarters which Gallagher and Fisher had already rented, five rooms in the Kohl Building on Montgomery Street. This office remained small during 1911 and 1912, for it was still a conjecture as to whether or not the new venture would pay off. At the end of a year (October 1912) the total staff was only six persons: Van Eck, and his secretary, Miss Kell; Eustace de Gray Birch, secretary of the new company; his secretary, Miss Akin; Gallagher, in charge of sales; and George E. Gordon, hired a month before as the company's bookkeeper. Harris actually held no office in the new company and continued to handle his regular job in London, alternating between that city and San Francisco.[29]

The new "Shell Motor Spirit," as it was called to take advantage of the name which the Group had adopted abroad, met with ready acceptance. Its high gravity made it a quick-starting fuel. It was in fact such a radical improvement over the gasoline then being made from California oil that to burn it properly a car's carburetor needed readjusting. The new company realized the difficulty of undertaking an educational campaign at this juncture, and blended the light Sumatra with heavier gasolines. Its odor, too, was pleasing, compared to the other gasolines on the market, with the result that many customers expressed an immediate preference for the Shell "spirit."

That this was so was all to the good, for even before the first cargo had been landed, Van Eck had pointed out in a report to London that the two main premises upon which the new business was being founded were false. The idea that a surplus of gasoline existed in the Indies was rapidly dispelled when it became known that the production of the Shanghai-Langkat Company in Sumatra, which was to supply the West Coast, had fallen by more than 50% in 1911. During 1911, the production of California crude oil continued upward, with a resultant decrease in the price of both crude and product. This development demolished the thesis that gasoline was scarce enough to bring an unusually good price on the Pacific Coast.[30]

For nearly two years, Van Eck and his sales department were able to stand up to this situation, for the degree of acceptance which their gasoline enjoyed enabled them to ask, and get, a 2¢-per-gallon premium over going prices. But its sale could not continue long at prices higher than Standard's. In the San Francisco area, gasoline had been selling from sixteen to eighteen cents a gallon (there were no taxes in those days) when Shell motor spirit appeared on the scene. Beginning to find itself with an oversupply, Standard of California reduced the price to ten cents.[31]

However, despite the premium price and the popularity of its product, the American Gasoline Company came out $27,000 in the red for 1912, after only three months of operation; and for 1913 it showed a deficit of about the same amount.[32] Asiatic for a time underwrote a portion of the losses in the form of refunds,[33] but after a point was reluctant to continue its losses. On one occasion, the anticipated net return looked so small that Asiatic declined to ship another cargo. Threatened with complete exhaustion of supplies, Van Eck sent urgent cables to London. He eventually received a cargo of mixed Burmese and Persian gasoline of poor color and worse odor. This gasoline put an end to the premium price, and in addition had an adverse effect on the new company's trade, especially in the Portland area.[34]

All this was making it pretty plain that American Gasoline could not long stay in business, buying and transporting half way around the world gasoline that could be produced abundantly right there in California. It also put an end to any hopes Levering might still be entertaining for a joint Shell-Indian venture on the West Coast.†

† The joint marketing arrangement for the Atlantic area had petered out in mid-1911. In making his original proposals to Deterding, Levering had counted on obtaining the support of other large independents to establish a marketing company in the Eastern states in opposition to Standard. Most of these independents declined to join the venture, and Indian was not strong enough to attempt it alone.

Early in 1913, Harris returned to San Francisco with a new set of instructions. It was now time, Deterding had decided, for the Group to buy producing properties in California. And, whether Deterding knew it or not (one suspects he did), the time was auspicious for such a move. The flurry of demand for gasoline and fuel oil at the turn of the century and the resulting high price of crude oil had brought about the discovery of important new fields in California. Most of the oil they produced was sold for fuel, and with the completion of the Panama Canal still in the future, the fuel market was limited to California and nearby points. Transported around the Horn, California oil could not hope to compete with Gulf Coast and Oklahoma fuel, and the Orient could be amply supplied from oil fields much nearer. Consequently, substantial amounts of California oil were being put into storage and in some cases wells were being closed in.

It was into this atmosphere of depressed oil prices that B. H. van der Linden came in the spring of 1913. Van der Linden was a mining engineer, graduated from Delft, who had spent five years with the Group in the oil fields of North and South Sumatra and East Borneo. Once Deterding had decided to purchase properties, he dispatched Van der Linden to California. Harris was to let it be known that he was in the market for producing properties,‡ and as fast as any were offered, Van der Linden went at once to appraise them. Such offers to sell were not hard to come by; in fact, the reverse was true. From the time of his arrival and all during the spring and early summer months of 1913, Van der Linden "scurried like a wild In-

---

‡ This he did through many channels, including statements to the oil press. The following extract from *The Oil Age*, a West Coast trade paper, is a fair sample of the many candid announcements which company officials made during this period: "Some wild and ridiculous rumors have been going the rounds to the effect that these interests [Shell and Royal Dutch] contemplate starting a fight with the Standard Oil Company for the control of the American markets, and these rumors and statements of the press are still afloat, as they make good reading for the sensationally inclined . . . the press is full of the impending fight with Standard.

"Speaking on this subject recently, F. P. S. Harris, prominently identified with the Asiatic Petroleum Company (one of the Shell-Royal Dutch affiliations) who is now in California is quoted as having said:

" 'We have always been willing to admit our intention of entering this field, and yet as soon as an effort on our part is begun, reports are scattered that we have come in with the intention of fighting the Standard Oil Company. Nothing could be farther from the truth. We are here, it is true, to meet the Standard in open competition, but we have no desire to fight them save in a business manner. Our purpose here is to secure business, not to ruin our competitors.

" 'Every report so far published has made another error. It has appeared that we have attempted to envelop our plans in mystery. On the other hand, it has been an open secret that my company has long been seeking an entry into California. Now we are on the eve of securing holdings here, and in two or three months an announcement of our purchases may be expected.' " [35]

dian" [36] from one California oil field to another, examining properties of operators who were anxious to sell. Most of these trips were futile. The attractive properties available were too few and too distant from each other; the rest were offerings of little promise.

Then, on August 6, 1913, came the big break, a cable from Deterding with instructions for Van der Linden to contact the San Francisco office of Balfour, Guthrie & Company, the American branch of the London firm of Balfour, Williamson & Company. Through Balfour's he was to arrange to go to Coalinga to evaluate the properties of California Oilfields, Ltd., a company which Balfour's had organized and managed for the past ten years. The report to Deterding must be back in London by Monday morning, August 11, for Balfour Williamson's offer was to expire at 1 P.M. that day.

Now was a time for secrecy. If Standard, or another competitor, should get wind of the impending deal, they might start bidding against Shell. In frantic haste, under heavy disguise, and even using an assumed name ("G. Warner"), Van der Linden sped away to Coalinga, to confer with Arthur T. Beazley, manager of the California Oilfields, Ltd. The wisdom of the secrecy was attested a few hours after Van der Linden's arrival at Coalinga. The superintendent of the adjoining Standard properties came and inquired of Beazley, "Have you seen some Dutch fellow who is supposed to be snooping around here?"

Even though the company lacked the kind of geological records which Van der Linden would have preferred to find, he completed the appraisal in two days and hurried back to San Francisco, where Harris and Van Eck were waiting for him in the office on Sunday morning. He prepared and they read over a five-page report which was cabled to Deterding. It said, in effect, that the Limited property could safely be counted on to produce 4,000,000 barrels of oil a year for the next ten years, after which production would gradually decline. The short time available made a closer approximation of total reserves difficult. Relying on Van der Linden's judgment, Deterding went ahead. Late Monday afternoon, August 11, 1913, the San Francisco office received a cable that the deal had gone through.[37]

Coalinga

Now at last, Shell was really under way on the Pacific Slope. At one stroke it had acquired one of California's largest oil-producing companies, a company which in 1913 accounted for 4,400,000 of California's total production of 97,788,000 barrels, 4½% of the production of the nation's largest oil-producing state.

For this rich new property ("the Limited," as it was usually called by Shell people in California), approximately $13,000,000 was paid, only about $3,000,000 of it in cash. The Limited had outstanding 400,000 shares of stock of £1 par value. For each share of this stock, the Group offered one share of Shell Transport & Trading common and £1½ in cash. The inducement to exchange shares was excellent, for Shell stock was then selling for about £5 a share. California Oilfields shareholders received in cash one and a half times the amount they had originally paid for their stock, and in addition were given Shell stock worth five times that amount. Shell Transport & Trading took the shares it needed for the deal from unissued treasury stock, the Royal Dutch took the number it needed from its 500,000 shares of Shell T. & T. which had been purchased at the time of the amalgamation in 1907.[38]

California Oilfields stockholders had also received liberal compensation in dividends, for by 1913, Coalinga had behind it a decade of profitable operation. In 1898, the Home Oil Company had brought in its famous Blue Goose gusher, opening up the Coalinga area as a commercial producer.[39] Among the oil hunters who had come to Coalinga at this time was a competent and widely experienced oil man from Pennsylvania, William M. Graham. He thought he saw potential oil production in the lands of the Coalinga East Side field, as yet undeveloped. Graham had knowledge of the business, experience, and courage to go ahead—all he lacked was the money.

Early in 1901, he enlisted the support of Balfour, Guthrie & Company, the San Francisco branch of an astute and enterprising London concern, Balfour, Williamson & Company. Balfour's represented Scottish capital invested all over the world, not in securities, but in going businesses which they managed. Such a group had a variety of interests: they acted as ships' agents, importers, and exporters, the world over; owned and managed businesses of every description, even farms and orchards; and were willing to undertake any venture which gave promise of making an honest penny. Balfour's were new to the oil business; it is to their credit that they saw the merit of Graham's proposition and recommended to their London office that they enter the oil business in Coalinga.

It was thus that California Oilfields, Ltd., came into being as a British corporation organized in London. The stock was offered to the public, with Balfour's buying a substantial holding and Balfour, Guthrie & Company being appointed managing agents of the new company. For his services in getting the enterprise under way, Graham was given a stock interest and made general manager of the Oilfields property.[40]

To staff the new operation, Bill Graham chose men he knew and trusted from the older Pennsylvania, West Virginia, and Ohio fields. His brother Jake, the practical oil man of the family, took actual charge of the drilling and producing operation; and after Bill Graham resigned in 1909, another brother, Al, succeeded him. His cousins, the Jennings brothers, were also prominent in field operations.[41]

Graham's and Balfour's faith in Coalinga was justified; from the first the Limited was a profitable property. In 1903, at the end of the second year of operation, a dividend of 10% was paid; in 1904, 20%; for 1905 and 1906, it doubled again, with a cash payment of more than 50% each year.[42]

These earnings did not go solely for the enrichment of stockholders. Bill Graham was a man who believed that money was made to be spent. Backed by Balfour's, he set about building a model oil town, at first known as Balfour and later as Oilfields. The village of Coalinga was eight miles away, so the company was obliged to make some provision for its men to stay nearer by, and besides the village was a wide-open, roaring boom town, with few physical comforts. (One village sign read: "Bath, 25¢; seconds, 15¢."[43]) The Limited could have followed the style of the day, thrown up a few tar-paper shacks which would be glorified by the name "bunkhouse," hired a contract outfit to do the cooking at so much per head, and let it go at that. Such a camp wouldn't have been any better, or any worse, than what others were offering.§

But Graham didn't believe in that kind of business, as is attested by the affectionate regard with which he is still recalled a half century

§ It was general practice in California at this time for a company to drill its own wells, in contrast to the Mid-Continent practice of hiring contract drillers.

later. And neither did Balfour's. In fifty years of world-wide business operations, they had become accustomed to stationing men in all sorts of uncomfortable spots. Experience had taught them that it was good business to make such places attractive by offering good pay and decent living quarters.

So, by spending a little more money than others might have, Bill Graham and the Balfour management built an oilfield camp which in America has probably never been surpassed for completeness and attention to the comfort of those for whom it was built. The bunkhouses for ordinary laborers were roomy and well built, and as an oil writer of 1908 marvelled, "boast every modern convenience, bathrooms, sinks, running water, and other pleasurable luxuries so seldom found in oil camps." [44] The foremen's bunkhouse was larger and better appointed. For married employees there were comfortable company houses at low rentals.

But the crowning glory of the camp was "The Bungalow," a large H-shaped, one-story building on the crest of a small hill overlooking the rest of the camp. It had been designed for the unmarried white-collar, or "staff," employees. The center section of the bungalow contained luxurious living, library, and dining rooms; the wings were given over to ample private rooms, each with connecting bath. Mrs. Graham, a Santa Barbara socialite, was asked to furnish the bungalow, which she did, sparing no expense. To top it off, she staffed the bungalow with a Scotch gardener and Japanese houseboys. Some style for 1908 for an oil camp in semi-desert country!

The village of Oilfields was a complete, self-contained, almost wholly self-sufficient community. Like most oil camps removed from civilization, it had its own tool shops where many drilling tools were made, as well as a great variety of "fishing" tools designed by the Graham boys and their colleagues from the Eastern fields. There was a tank shop which, starting from flat sheet metal, could corrugate and fashion it into oil storage tanks; a tin shop made a variety of tinware; there was a wood-planing plant, which worked from raw lumber, planing it and cutting it into the sizes of timbers desired for rig-building; there was even a brickyard, staffed by Chinese, to manufacture on the spot the bricks needed for the brickwork under the boilers. The community had its own utilities: a water-condensing plant to provide drinking water; an ice plant; a steam plant to furnish heat to the bunkhouses; and an electric generating plant which furnished current for the shops, offices, living quarters, and drilling rigs.

There were large storehouses where all sorts of raw materials and supplies were warehoused. Oilfields had its own transportation system in "Big Betsy," a large Best steam tractor with wide steel wheels which pulled a train of trackless cars the eight miles from Coalinga station, loaded with rough lumber, billet steel, and other heavy materials. The men were fed from a farming operation which produced vegetables, milk, butter, fresh eggs, poultry, hams, pork, and beef for the table. In time the village even had a nonprofit, cooperative store, where the men were able to buy most necessities at wholesale prices, plus a small fee to cover hire of the store manager. The community had its own post office and, during the early Balfour days, even a salaried minister to conduct services on Sunday.[45]

In common with oilfield workers of the day everywhere, the men at the Limited worked long hours. Drilling crews put in twelve hours a day, seven days a week; day-shift maintenance and construction gangs ten hours. But the hard work and long hours were, according to everybody who ever worked there, more than amply compensated for by the spirit of fun and good fellowship which pervaded the entire camp.

An oilfield worker of those days was often little more than a well-paid drifter; he would work in one field as long as he could stand the location and the loneliness, then quit, always to wander on to another camp. In time, he was possessed by a wanderlust not unlike that which has such a hold on sailors—no place was good enough, he would stay a month, or a year, then drift on. But at Oilfields life was comfortable. The men stayed longer than at the last place, they got to know their fellows and like them. With over three hundred men at all times, and often more, there were enough for all kinds of sports. Oilfields had excellent tennis courts, a sports field, and later on even a golf course and swimming pool. There were Oilfields teams in baseball, basketball, soccer, tennis, many of them famous for miles around. There were evening entertainments—amateur theatricals organized by the men, a glee club, weekly motion picture shows, and the Oilfields Club where an evening could be pleasurably whiled away. Because a majority of the men were unmarried, they had plenty of time for practical jokes, foolishness, and horseplay—a partial account of which would be a book in itself. They were, to use the words of one of them, "grown men acting like boys."[46]

Shell bought a fine producing oil property when it purchased the Limited in 1913, but it also acquired gratis a wonderful legacy of keen, high-spirited men, brought up in an atmosphere of enlightened management. This investment in personnel was to yield returns for many years to come. A surprisingly large number of Coalinga field men, storekeepers, engineers and white-collar personnel would continue for the next three or four decades to advance within the expanding Shell organization: David Heggie, who later became office manager of Shell's new Martinez refinery and eventually vice president and treasurer of Shell of California; John M. Peat, another Scot, destined to head Shell's stores department on the Pacific Coast; Roy S. Fine, who would be first office manager of the Wilmington refinery; Stanley W. Duhig, who later became vice president, treasurer, and director of the Shell holding company in New York. The young engineers, whom Van der Linden was to hire and train in the wholesome atmosphere of Oilfields, would later be the core of the company's production department on the Pacific Coast. The intelligent view of labor-management relations which these men trained at Oilfields took away with them was, in its own way, as valuable as forty million barrels of oil.

From the first, the Limited had sold its crude oil. A crude oil purchase contract was arranged on an annual basis with the Standard Oil Company of California, and for a number of years the Limited supplied about half of Standard's light oil needs. Then starting about 1910, with new fields coming in and the oil market gradually falling, Balfour's annual negotiations with Standard became increasingly difficult. The Standard men would intimate, "but you don't understand the problems of the refiner." So, in 1907, primarily to supply themselves with ammunition for these annual negotiations, Balfour's bought a small, antiquated refinery at the foot of 64th Street, Emeryville, across the bay from San Francisco. A tank car a day of crude oil was shipped from Coalinga and tests were run in the Capitol plant to provide Balfour's with some idea of refining costs. The products produced in the operation, chiefly kerosene, were sold in job lots to large users by Balfour salesmen and a warehouse for storage was maintained at Willbridge, just outside Portland, Oregon. For some years before 1913, Capitol Refining Company had been operated as a subsidiary of the Limited, its accounts kept separately in Balfour's San Francisco office.[47]

The deal was a bargain for both parties: the stockholders of the Limited got back their original investment, plus a very handsome profit in the form of Shell shares, and withdrew successfully from a falling oil market. The Group, in turn, acquired a real foothold in

America: enough crude oil production to supply a refinery, for a cash outlay of slightly more than $3,000,000. In 1901, when Graham had interested Balfour's in Coalinga, there had been wiseacres aplenty who saw a local boy taking gullible foreigners for what they were worth; so it was again in 1913, with even some of the Balfour Guthrie men feeling sorry for Shell.[48] But the *Oil & Gas Journal*'s representative commented on the sale a little more shrewdly: "In the discovery of good bargains it is not easy to beat the Dutch." [49]

5

The Shell Company of California

DURING the same summer that Harris was receiving offers of properties and Van der Linden was scurrying around California to look at them, Van Eck, as the actual operating head of the American Gasoline Company, was getting a marketing operation under way in the San Francisco Bay area.

Two years earlier land for an ocean terminal had been purchased at Martinez, some twenty-five miles northeast of San Francisco on Suisun Bay, an arm of San Francisco Bay. Like Richmond Beach, Martinez was quite far removed from the area it was intended to serve, but it did adjoin the tracks of two railroads, as well as offering a splendid location for dockage facilities. A depot to serve the city of San Francisco by tank wagon was built at Third and Army Streets, the site of the old Arctic Oil Works, which years before had refined lubricants from Alaskan whale oil.[50] E. H. Madge, a Britisher, was placed in charge of the terminal at Martinez, and James Brice in charge of the depot in the city. The first load of gasoline arrived on the *J. B. Aug. Kessler*, in June 1913. Shortly after, more came on the *Cowrie*.*

* A fundamental neighborliness has always existed among oil companies, and even when a vigorous competitor is overtaken by disaster, the others come to his aid. Such an incident of good sportsmanship occurred in connection with the *Cowrie*, and was recalled by H. R. Gallagher just before his death in 1949: "The tanker *Cowrie* went aground on a bar in San Francisco harbor. Standard of California generously came to our aid, sending their chief of transportation and tugs which were able to beach the tanker in Oakland harbor. Here the tanker was lightened sufficiently to allow her to be towed to Martinez. This emergency occurred on a weekend and Standard did the only thing that could have saved our tanker." [51]

But the new company did not find it clear sailing at first. Both the Standard Oil Company and Union Oil Company had provided more intensive coverage of the San Francisco area, the largest metropolitan region of the Coast, than they had of the vast Pacific Northwest. There were at the time only 34,000 automobiles in the entire state of California, and Standard and Union had most of the garages in the area under contract.[52] "Filling" stations, small businesses operated solely for the purpose of selling gasoline direct to the motorist, were just then being introduced. Since the San Francisco area had about all the garages it could support, Shell was faced with the alternatives of (1) waiting for new garages to open up and obtaining their business, or (2) going after the business of existing garages by means of lowered prices, which the company could not afford to offer, or (3) going after the business of the ultimate consumer by opening filling stations.

This last was the only sensible alternative, but desirable as it might be, it was also risky—or at least so it was thought at the time. The other companies were not doing it, and although for the moment Van Eck and Gallagher were interested in service stations only in the San Francisco area, they could look ahead a few years and see that they would soon be selling in less populous areas. In these areas, it would probably be feasible, as in the Northwest, to use agents as distributors and garage dealers for the retail outlets. What kind of fix would the new company be in, then, if it sold direct to the customer in San Francisco, and a few miles away attempted to make sales through garages? One could hear a competitor's salesman saying to a Shell dealer, "Come on, sign up with our company, *we* don't attempt to compete with you."

To avoid possible ill will from garage owners, arrangements were made with Franklin A. Oehm, a San Francisco garage man, to operate Shell's new stations, and the Omen Oil Company was formed for this purpose. It had some twelve or thirteen stations which, although they did not make money, did serve to introduce the new Shell motor spirit to San Francisco. The Omen company lost $15,000 during 1914, and at the end of that year Shell bought up its contract with Oehm for another $15,000. The expected animosity from garage owners had not materialized, and anyhow the competition's hold on existing garages had not slackened, so it was apparent that Shell would have to strike out as its own retailer, in the more populous areas at least.[53]

In 1915, when the Panama-Pacific International Exposition was in full swing at San Francisco to celebrate the opening of the new canal,

Shell obtained the parking-lot concession for the fair and built two big, showy, red-and-yellow stations at the gates of the exposition grounds. It was here that most motorists—indeed, all motorists who came from regions other than the San Francisco area or the Pacific Northwest—first saw the gaudy yellow "cracker-box" station which ten years later would be a familiar sight not only all over the Pacific Slope, but throughout much of the area east of the Rocky Mountains.

By 1915, the company had also opened retail outlets in the Northwest. Early in 1914, Fisher purchased the first curbside pump for use in the area, and throughout 1914 the old account books show a great many payments to S. F. Bowser & Company for "one sidewalk pump and tank." The spring of 1915 witnessed a flurry of filling-station building in Seattle and Portland, and the company entered the motoring season that year with 25 stations of its own in the Northwest.[54]

During these years, the company also bought its first automotive equipment. It may seem odd that a company in the business of catering to motorists should itself "get a horse," but it seems less strange when one realizes that the first gasoline truck in America had been built as recently as 1900[55] and that for the next decade they were considered hazardous and unreliable. It was not until January 1914, that Fisher bought the first tank truck for the Northwest operation, and a little over a year later the first automobiles for company use.[56] Once the new "auto trucks" had been adopted, however, the company's conversion to them was rapid, for Shell did not, like its competitors, have a large investment in horse-drawn equipment.

At Portland, Shell inherited the Capitol Refining Company's warehouse at Willbridge, on the western edge of town. It was decided that this property could be used for a deep-water terminal and in the spring of 1915 the American Gasoline Company's small bulk depot at Stockdale, east of Portland, was closed and its two tanks moved to the Willbridge location. Arrangements were made with the Portland Gas & Coke Company, which had deep-water wharf property about a mile and a half away on the Willamette River, to run a small pipe line from the gas company's dock back to the Willbridge property. This gave Shell an ocean terminal for the Portland area at a very small expenditure.[57]

Through the Capitol Refining Company acquisition, Harris and Gallagher had their attention called to a company in Seattle, one of Capitol's largest customers, the Seaboard Oil Company, operated by Mark J. David. It was a small and highly respected firm which blended lubricating oils and made greases from stocks purchased chiefly from Capitol. The physical property was small, consisting of a rented warehouse, used for the manufacture and storage of product, and inventories of lubricants valued at $40,000. Shell bought Seaboard's inventory, and paid for customer good will and other intangible assets a bonus of $35,000.† It was a good investment, for Seaboard had a string of excellent brand names respected throughout the Northwest, particularly in the lumber business. One of them, remembered even today, was Old Economy Steam Cylinder oil which Shell for many years afterward made and sold in that area, adding only the Shell trade-mark to the old label.[58]

So far, Harris was proceeding rapidly with what he had come to do. Once California Oilfields, Ltd., had been acquired, he set out to determine the location best suited for the refinery they intended to build, and, as soon as that had been decided, to build a pipe line to connect it with Coalinga.

E. R. (Barney) Farley, who later became the company's fuel oil manager, was at the time a young man sitting in the corner of Harris' office. "My boy Farley," as Harris called him, was in a position to remember well the various locations considered for the refinery. Monterey was talked of, and San Luis Obispo, where the *Oil & Gas Journal* incorrectly reported that Shell had purchased a going refinery.[59] But a few figures proved the desirability of the San Francisco area, with its splendid harbor facilities equidistant from Alaska and South America. Martinez filled the bill. All that would be necessary would be to buy more property adjoining the water terminal where a dock and tankage had already been built.

The company was now something more than a vendor of imported gasoline. To indicate its new status, the name was changed in July 1914 to Shell Company of California, Inc. A few months before, in the spring of 1914, the offices had been moved from the small quarters in the Kohl Building to the Security Building,‡ 343 Sansome Street, San Francisco, where two floors (soon enlarged to

† The elder David retired from the oil business at the time of the purchase, but his nephew, L. E. David, continued with Shell, holding several positions of importance in the West Coast sales organization. At the time of his retirement in 1947, he was general manager of Shell Oil Company's marketing department in San Francisco.

‡ Now extensively remodeled, the Security Building is known as the Crown Zellerbach Building.

three and a half) were engaged.[60] Harris' mission was now complete;
in August 1914 he returned to London.

Succeeding him as the new president was William Meischke-Smith,
who had recently been in charge of a part of the Group's operations
in China. Van Eck, as vice president, continued as he had under
Harris, to manage actual day-to-day operations. Harris had bought
properties, let contracts, started things on their way; under Meischke-
Smith, these beginnings were to be brought to completion and the
company launched. It would be an integrated oil company, engaged
in all phases of the business. For this company, a new corporate
organization was created under California law, called the Shell Company of California (without the "Inc."). At the end of 1915, the
properties of Shell Company of California, Inc., California Oilfields,
Ltd., and the Turner and W. K. oil companies, smaller producing
companies at Coalinga which meanwhile had been purchased, were
all transferred to the new Shell Company of California, whose name
would be well known all over the Pacific Slope before another decade
had gone by.

6

The Valley Pipe Line

PURCHASE of California Oilfields, Ltd., was the big turning point in
the early history of Shell in California. "It was," Van Eck recalled
forty years later, "a momentous decision for our group working in
San Francisco and it meant preparing a program with the utmost
speed. Of tremendous importance was the fact that California Oilfields had a contract with the Standard Oil Company of California
for delivery of its crude oil production which had, if I remember
correctly, less than a year to run, a period too short to expect the
completion of plans to take care of the production ourselves.

"But a program was drawn up and it called for decisions on these
points: (1) to select a site for the refinery . . . (2) to build a pipe
line to the refinery site from Coalinga, (3) to expand the distribution
system to take care of the increased volume, (4) to proceed with
proper organization for these requirements (it was for this reason
that Meischke-Smith was sent out to replace Harris whose experience

Start of Shell's business in the Northwest. The time is September 1912; the place the new American Gasoline Company's water terminal at Richmond Beach, just above Seattle. The S.S. *Romany* has just discharged a cargo of about 1,800,000 gallons of Sumatra and Burma gasolines. Other cargoes, totalling in all about 10,000,000 gallons, were brought in during the next two years before the new company began to supply its own requirements from its own California oil fields and its new refinery at Martinez.

Another view of Richmond Beach, taken about 1915.

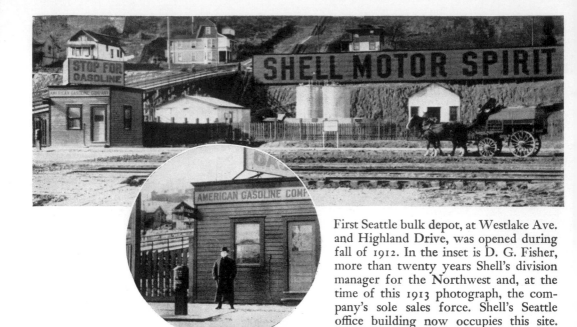

First Seattle bulk depot, at Westlake Ave. and Highland Drive, was opened during fall of 1912. In the inset is D. G. Fisher, more than twenty years Shell's division manager for the Northwest and, at the time of this 1913 photograph, the company's sole sales force. Shell's Seattle office building now occupies this site.

"Tank wagon" meant just that in 1913. This photo was taken shortly after the opening of the Oakland, Calif., depot.

First advertisements: The ad on the left appeared in the Washington and British Columbia Official A. A. A. Blue Book, for 1913–14; the first newspaper ad, *right*, was published in the Seattle *Post-Intelligencer* on June 15, 1913.

Courtesy Peter Gallagher

J. C. van Eck started Shell on the Pacific Coast, later headed Shell Union in New York, still later was a managing director of the Shell Group.

Herbert R. Gallagher (1883–1949) headed Shell's Pacific Coast marketing for twenty years, was later president of Sinclair's holding company.

This 1915 photograph shows the style of station erected in the San Francisco area by the Shell Company of California (American Gasoline's new name). The general plan of Shell's West Coast service stations remained almost unchanged for the next fifteen years. Fuel oil truck was a Kelly-Springfield with 1260-gallon tank.

Shell of California obtained the parking concession for the 1915 San Francisco World's Fair and erected two red-and-yellow stations at the gates of the exposition grounds. This was many motorists' first glimpse of a Shell service station.

A salesman was expected to stock and deliver the less bulky petroleum products such as packaged greases and motor oils. This was a 1921 salesman's car.

was more exclusively confined to sales), (5) to erect storage at Oil-fields to take care of production until completion of the pipe line (The erection of steel tanks at Oilfields was an uneconomic operation but it was necessary) . . . and (6) to reduce the production of crude oil until the newly built refinery could handle it all . . . a ticklish question much debated because nobody could guarantee that, when once closed down for a fairly long period, the wells would come back to their old production when opened up again." [61]

These projects growing out of the Limited purchase were a big order for a small company. The two most urgent projects were the pipe line and refinery, and it was to them that Shell of California's small but highly competent staff turned every attention. Up to now the Limited had delivered its production at Coalinga to the pipe lines of the Standard Oil Company of California, which pumped the oil to the Standard refinery at Point Richmond on San Francisco Bay, some 175 miles to the north. Although there were railroads available to do the hauling, it would have been very poor management even to consider paying freight on the Limited's 1914 production of 12,000 barrels a day, an amount of oil which would have filled 63 railroad tank cars.

By 1914, the pipe line was well established as a means of oil transport. In California, the Pacific Coast Oil Company had built a short, 2-inch line at Newhall north of Los Angeles in 1879–1880 and in 1886 the pioneer Puente Oil Company had constructed a pipe line in the Los Angeles Basin. But it was not until after the turn of the century that California got its first long-distance pipe line, an 8-inch pipe running 280 miles from the Kern River field to the Standard Oil Company's Point Richmond refinery, with a branch to the Coalinga field. The engineers who built this Standard line realized that heavy Kern River oil (13° to 16° A.P.I.) would be difficult to pump; consequently, they located the pumping stations at intervals of twenty-eight to thirty miles apart, instead of the forty-mile interval usual in the East. Construction of the line was finished in 1905, but it required several years of operating experience to overcome the difficulties of pumping heavy oil. In the years between 1905 and 1914, a dozen more lines of substantial length had been laid in California by Associated, Union, and other concerns. [62]

The most recent of these pipe lines had been completed in 1913 for General Petroleum, 212 miles from Maricopa in the Midway field to G.P.'s refinery at Vernon, a suburb of Los Angeles. This line had attracted considerable attention at the time because the pipe climbed the 4,200-foot Tejon Pass, a feat which the experts had declared impossible.[63] Sanderson & Porter, an engineering and construction firm hitherto known chiefly for work in the hydroelectric field, had designed the G.P. line; it was to them that Harris turned. In January 1914, he commissioned Sanderson & Porter to make a preliminary survey of the Coalinga-to-Martinez route, and they reported favorably upon it.

Soon after this report was presented, Shell organized a new company, the Valley Pipe Line Company, on April 16, 1914. Early in June, a contract for surveying, engineering, and building the line was awarded to Sanderson & Porter. The Valley Pipe Line Company was to pay Sanderson & Porter their costs, plus a fee of $250,000. Work got under way at once. The summer of 1914 was spent in surveying and purchasing the right-of-way; actual construction started in October.[64]

In its design and construction the Valley pipe line embodied several innovations, pioneer achievements in pipelining which were reflected in the line's outstanding operating efficiency and modest construction cost. The oil, it was decided, would have to be heated in the manner of previous California pipe lines; otherwise it would be too viscous to flow. Eleven pumping stations embodying heating units were planned, one for every fifteen miles. In addition, a new scheme of pipe arrangement was adopted. Heated oil emerging from the pump station flowed along satisfactorily until it started to cool; at that point Sanderson & Porter decided it would be a good idea to introduce a larger size of pipe. Accordingly, the line was planned as a combination of 8- and 10-inch pipe. Oil would leave the pump station in 8-inch pipe, then at the point where it started to cool and become more viscous (about two-thirds of the distance to the next station), it would go into 10-inch pipe. The 10-inch pipe, by providing half again as much space for the same volume of oil, reduced internal pressure and surface friction. The arrangement worked like a charm, and this combination of two sizes of pipe thereafter became standard practice in building California pipe lines designed to carry heavy oil.[65]

In building the Valley line, Sanderson & Porter also introduced labor-saving machinery on a large scale. Trenches for previous lines had usually been dug by hand, the pipe screwed together with hand tongs, the pipe coated (if it was coated at all) by hand, and the trench backfilled by hand. On the Valley line, trenching machinery was employed, except for twenty miles over the rough terrain of Mt. Diablo. The pipe was screwed together by machinery for the entire length of the line, an accomplishment which made it possible greatly to reduce the number of men required, and to proceed with more speed than formerly. The pipe was cleaned by machinery; a priming coat and a coat of bitumastic enamel applied by machinery; and, excepting again the Mt. Diablo section, the filling of the trench was also done by machinery.[66]

The pipe, weighing 15,000 tons, was fabricated by the Youngstown Sheet & Tube Company in Ohio, and shipped by rail to Boston and New York and thence by water to San Francisco on some of the very first vessels to pass through the brand-new Panama Canal. Except for the pipe, most of the other pieces of equipment installed—boilers, pumps, oil heaters, and storage tanks—were fabricated on the Pacific Coast, either in Los Angeles or San Francisco. The most difficult items to handle, because of their size, were the boilers which weighed thirteen and one-half tons apiece and the oil heaters which weighed thirteen tons. They were shipped by rail to the point nearest the pumping station in which they were to be installed and hauled the remaining distance, sometimes as much as twenty miles, by mule team. The big boilers required a fifty-mule team.

To supervise the purchase of all this material, Sanderson & Porter hired an engineer who had worked for them before, G. C. Noble. Superintendent of construction was another engineer, Fred B. Simms. Both men proved their abilities, and at the termination of the job were asked to come on permanently with Shell; Simms as general superintendent of the pipe line, and Noble as purchasing agent and, later, land manager and secretary of the Shell Company of California. Their cases were typical of how the young and growing Shell company constantly reached out through every contact for able men to add to its staff, men who would be responsible for the company's growth and success in later years.

A large amount of tankage was built at the Coalinga end of the line (twenty 55,000-barrel tanks) and at ten of the pumping stations (a total of twenty 37,500-barrel tanks, two at each station), some 1,850,000 barrels of storage in all, as it was expected that oil from the Limited would have to be stored prior to completion of the Martinez refinery. In addition, a 750,000-barrel concrete reservoir built at Coalinga earlier was reconditioned and readied for service, and at the Martinez end a large battery of steel tanks was erected—

altogether total storage capacity of some 4,000,000 barrels, almost enough to hold an entire year's production of crude oil.

The new line proceeded rapidly through desert country, with time out for about a month during the winter rains of 1914–1915. The eleven pumping stations were built and equipped with reciprocating steam pumps, the steam ends made by Allis-Chalmers, the oil ends by the Dow Pump & Diesel Engine Company of San Francisco. Later, as Shell drilled up the property at Coalinga, a higher proportion of lighter-gravity crude became available. By 1919, it was possible, by blending the lighter with the heavier crudes, to reduce the viscosity of the oil to a point where less pumping energy was required. In 1920, every other station was closed down; the equipment of four stations was moved to Mexico and the fifth to Long Beach. (The remaining pumps still continue to lead useful lives. In 1936 when Shell built a new parallel line in the San Joaquin Valley, these old-timers were connected to the new line and today are operating as efficiently as when installed in 1915. The original pipe is also still in service, carrying greater quantities of oil, at higher pressures, than was originally intended.) Thus superbly equipped, the Valley pipe line was finished in the summer of 1915. The first oil flowed from the Martinez end on August 11, 1915. The Valley line cost less than $3,000,000, one of the best and cheapest pipe lines ever built in California.[67]

7

Martinez

So FAR the moves of the new Shell company in America had, by intention or accident or a combination of both, been admirably well-timed. The new company had entered the market with gasoline at a time when demand for that product was increasing; it had bought one of California's most important oil-producing companies for a bargain figure during a period of low prices; it was building a new pipe line of good materials and top-notch efficiency. The times were also right for the construction of a modern, efficient refinery, for many new technological developments were waiting to be embodied in a refinery.

If Shell had arrived only a few years earlier, this would not have been so. For in 1914, surprising as it may seem today, American refineries were in a relatively primitive state of development, many of them differing hardly at all from the first refineries built in the Oil Regions of Pennsylvania in the years immediately following Drake. The monopoly of the refining end of the business which Rockefeller and his companies had held since the late 1870's was no doubt partly responsible for this lack of technical competition, but the chief reason for this lag was the generally undeveloped state of American technology, particularly the technology of chemical processing.

These early refineries were all pretty much alike. The crude oil was introduced into a horizontal cylindrical steel vessel supported by brickwork (this was the so-called "shell still") and under it a fire, usually of coal, was built. The heat would soon bring the lighter hydrocarbon elements to a boil and give them off as vapors, just as steam is generated by water boiling. These vapors were led away by an overhead pipe and passed through a coil cooled by water. This operation condensed the vapors into a light liquid, called by the general term "naphtha." When the stillman by taking specific gravity tests had determined that all the naphtha fraction had been boiled off, the heat would be increased by adding more fuel to the fire, and a second range of hydrocarbon compounds composing the chief saleable product, lamp oil, would come to a boil. These vapors were also led off, condensed, and run into another storage tank. The fires were then extinguished and the still allowed to cool. When it was cool enough to handle, the residue was drawn off and the still cleaned out for another charge of crude oil.

The refiner's object was to keep the total yield of lamp oil from a barrel of crude oil high, for there was little call for the other petroleum fractions. When they could be sold for cleaning fluids and similar uses, the light parts of naphtha fraction were refined further; and parts of the heavy residue were likewise refined into lubricating oil and tar. Gradually, uses were found for other products of the petroleum refiner. The residue, it was discovered, made excellent boiler fuel, once the difficulties of providing a proper burner had been solved; and gasoline, with the advent of the automobile, became a product of prime importance.

Despite new uses for the refiner's products, this same old, clumsy, batch method of refining continued in use. Its drawbacks were many. As the industry developed and the original small refineries were faced with the necessity of expanding their output, more and more shell stills were added and the size of individual stills became larger. By the end of the Nineteenth Century, stills of 500 to 600 barrels charging capacity were normal, and stills of 1,000 barrels capacity (14 feet in diameter and 42 feet long) and even larger were not uncommon. These stills were not provided with rectifying or fractionating equipment, so it was necessary, in order to obtain quality products, to redistill (rerun) a large quantity of intermediate products and this necessitated an even larger number of stills. As a result, some refineries had an astonishing amount of equipment: one of the largest American refineries, which in 1896 was processing between 30,000 and 35,000 barrels a day of crude oil, had 100 stills of 600-barrel capacity, 21 stills of 500-barrel capacity, and 56 others of smaller sizes.[68]

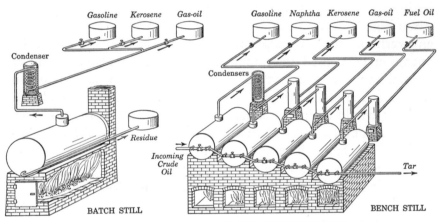

OLD-FASHIONED BATCH AND BENCH STILLS

Batch still, left, raised crude oil to boiling temperature of gasoline, distilled that off, then raised temperature for next product. Bench still, right, passed crude oil over progressively hotter fires, each still in the series separating one fraction.

In fuel consumption, these batch stills were highly uneconomical. After a still had been heated to the highest temperature required at the end of a run, it had to be cooled down so that it could be cleaned out. Moreover, this cleaning of the still after each distillation took it out of operation several hours each day.

At an early date, attention was given to working out a continuous system of distillation that would be more efficient than this batch method. Two patents for such systems were taken out in America between 1860 and 1870. Samuel van Syckel, also noted as the builder of America's first successful oil pipe line, in 1877 built and operated a continuous battery of steam stills for some time, but nothing much was done in this country with his innovation. The continuous still bench was first put to use on a large scale in Russia, where the enterprising Nobel Brothers, using findings of scientists like Mendelejeff, Engler, and Ragousine, built large refineries at Baku using a system that was eventually emulated by other large refineries all over the world.[69]

In this continuous bench-still system, a series of shell stills were arranged side by side in a stepwise order of descending elevation, each still on brickwork lower than the preceding one. Crude oil was charged in a continuous stream to the first still. There it was raised to a temperature sufficient to distill off the lightest fractions. The remaining oil, already partly heated, then passed by gravity flow to the next still where a higher fire raised the temperature further, and distilled off a heavier fraction. The oil remaining in this second still then flowed by gravity to a third still, where an even heavier fraction was distilled off, and so on, each succeeding still producing a heavier fraction. The hot residuum of the final still flowed into a tall tank through which passed pipes containing incoming cold crude oil, making it possible for the heat in the residuum to be used to pre-heat incoming cold oil.

The bench stills used in Russian refineries had 12 to 18 separate stills and produced a corresponding number of distillate fractions, which were then combined to produce the desired products. In operation, each still in the bench was kept at constant heat and often ran for months without a shutdown for cleaning. Bench stills were more efficient in two directions: they saved fuel and they gave a larger production of refined products for the same investment in equipment.

It wasn't until after 1885 that the continuous system was installed in America to any great extent. The larger refineries, most all of which belonged to the Standard Oil group, installed bench stills during the next thirty years; but most of the smaller refiners, no doubt because of the larger investment which such a system required, continued to use the batch method. The Capitol Refining Company in Emeryville was a typical example with its one 250-barrel shell still.

These distilling units, still in general use among American oil refiners as late as 1910, were far inferior to the more efficient distillation processes which the European alcohol industry had known and used for nearly a century. In Europe, some of the alcohol distiller's equipment, such as the Heckmann column, had been adapted to oil refining with the result that European oil refineries were, in general, ahead of their American counterparts in the years following the turn of the century.[70] It was during these very years that a series of developments took place in California and eventually brought about a radical new improvement in the distillation processes of American refineries.

To treat California oil, much of which came out of the ground mixed with water ("in emulsion"), various boiling devices were built, some of them modelled after the water-tube boiler used in the generation of steam. One of the first of these was built from secondhand parts on the Columbia Oil Producing Company's Olinda lease, near the Puente field, by Mr. Clark, the superintendent.[71] Pipe stills had been used in coal-tar distillation since 1890,[72] but it is doubtful if these California pioneers were aware of it. By 1909, Jesse A. Dubbs was operating a small pipe-still dehydrating plant in Santa Barbara County, California, to boil the water out of badly emulsified crude oil.[73]

Up until this time (about 1908), most California crude oils were heavy and contained few of the lighter, more volatile hydrocarbons. As a result, they could be used for locomotive fuel without danger of explosion. But with large production of lighter oil from the Santa Maria, Midway, and Fullerton fields, new devices to remove the inflammable light "tops," from oil that was destined for fuel, started to make their appearance. During 1910–1912, A. F. L. Bell, I. W. Fuqua, E. I. Dyer, A. B. Brown, and Milon J. Trumble designed and built topping plants to produce fuel oil. Bell's process employed conventional shell stills, the rest used some sort of pipe-still arrangement.[74]

In general, these early pipe stills were unsatisfactory because the oil, passing through the heated pipes, had a tendency to leave carbon deposits ("coke") which very soon clogged the pipes. Trumble succeeded in producing a more workable pipe still by the simple device of making the pipes some twelve and a half inches in diameter— so large that they might almost be called small shell stills.[75] Although this introduction of a workable pipe still to the petroleum industry was Trumble's most important contribution, he also developed a complete "system of refining" centered about a chimney-like tower which he called an "evaporator." It was that piece of equipment upon which he applied for a patent in April 1910. The patent was granted in July of the following year, by which time Trumble's first commercial unit was built and in operation, producing fuel for the Santa Fe Railroad, at Fellows, in Kern County, California.[76]

It is interesting to note that Trumble had the idea of fractionally condensing saleable light products (gasoline and kerosene) out of the "tops" removed, while other operators concentrated only on producing fuel oil, and were content to rerun the "tops" through conventional stills to produce gasoline, kerosene, and engine distillate. General Petroleum Corporation in 1912 contracted for a Trumble unit to be built at its new Vernon refinery, and this unit went into operation in May 1913.[77] By this time, Capt. John Barneson, head of General Petroleum, had become interested in the process and had joined with Trumble to organize the Trumble Refining Company to own and license the process patents and construct Trumble units for others.

During these same years, California refiners were also adopting the heat exchanger, which has since become an important feature of every modern distillation unit. Like many other improvements in distillation practice, the principle of heat exchange had been known and used in Europe. As far back as 1780, Argand, inventor of the Argand lamp, is known to have installed heat exchangers in a French distillery; they later became common in European alcohol distilleries, and by the early 1900's, oil refineries in Romania and Russia commonly made use of heat-exchange apparatus.[78] In America, where nature was more bountiful, little thought was given to saving fuel in oil refining. In fact, as long as the batch system prevailed, it was quite impossible, for the process required that the still be allowed to cool and the residue drawn off.

With the advent of continuous refining, it became possible to consider heating arrangements by which the heat of the outgoing residue could be transferred to the incoming cold crude oil to help heat it before it entered the still. In California, refiners did not have the abundant cheap coal common in Eastern refining centers; and perhaps equally important, neither did they have inexhaustible supplies of water for cooling. Pressed by nature from two directions, California refiners began to develop heat-exchange apparatus in which incoming cold crude oil would absorb heat from the outgoing vapor and residue lines. By removing as much heat as possible from the vapors, less water for cooling was required; and the crude oil, now partly warmed, required less fuel to bring it to a boil.

It was at this juncture of the industry, then, that Shell decided to build its new refinery. In December 1914, 368 acres of land adjoining the American Gasoline Company's water terminal at Martinez were purchased for a refinery site at a cost of $144,000.[79] H. H. Beers, of the Indian Refining Company, who after designing the Montreal depot had come west to build the installations in Washington and Oregon, had by now come over to the Shell Company of California as chief engineer. Asked to provide designs for the new refinery, Beers was already at work in the fall of 1914 when Daniel Pyzel, a Dutch engineer of whom the company was to hear much more, appeared on the scene.

Pyzel, graduated from the Technical University at Delft in 1897, had gone to work the same year for the Dordtsche Petroleum Maatschappij, who had sent him to Galicia for a year before dispatching him to Java in 1898. He had later joined the Royal Dutch Company as one of its first technical men, and in 1907 had been sent out to Balik Papan in East Borneo to build a paraffin wax and lubricating plant at the Shell company's refinery there. In 1911, he had returned to The Hague where he was put in charge of the Royal Dutch Company's refineries; in this capacity he had undertaken a world-wide inspection trip of Group refineries, a trip which eventually brought him to San Francisco where he intended to remain a few days to inspect Beers' designs and possibly make some suggestions. The "few days" stretched on into nine months, for Pyzel soon saw that more than minor suggestions would be necessary.

In the first place, the site, though desirable in that it provided dockage and storage tanks, was otherwise a dreadful handicap. It was traversed by hills, some of them quite steep, making impossible an orderly layout of roadways and piping. And the designs looked woefully antiquated to a technologist of Pyzel's training and experience. Not that Beers was at fault; he was merely following the accepted principles of American refining technology in 1914. With P. A. L. Engelbregt to help him, Pyzel revised the plans as completely as possible.

The site was bought and paid for; they would have to use it. This disadvantage was in part offset by the fact that they had a new process to incorporate in the designs for Martinez. Just a few weeks earlier, a contract had been signed with the Trumble Refining Company for the use of the Trumble process by Shell Group refineries. The agreement provided that Shell refineries the world over would become licensees of the Trumble process, that the "Trumble system of refining" would be used by the Group "to the exclusion of all others"; that any improvements in or additions to the process by Shell would become the property of Trumble for purposes of licensing to others; and that a royalty of one and one-half cents per barrel would be paid to Trumble for each barrel of oil processed in a Trumble unit. Under this arrangement, the building of the first Trumble unit at Martinez was started, with Charles Keefe and I. M. Hemphill being sent by Trumble to superintend erection of the unit.[80]

Before they had finished building this new unit, Shell made arrangements in April 1915 to buy out the Trumble Refining Company for $1,000,000 cash.[81] ("The first time I had ever seen a check for anything like that," said Van Eck, thirty-three years later.) This was a lot of money to pay for a patent in 1914 in an industry which was just awakening to the value of technology, and occasioned some eyebrow-lifting in circles that knew of the transaction. But the reasons behind the purchase were sound.

Pyzel had realized when he first saw Trumble's system that it would work better if the "evaporator" were built as a separator for residuum and vapors, and the vapors thereafter fractionated in a series of dephlegmators (short distillation columns) of the type Pyzel had first used in Borneo and later installed in other Shell refineries. Yet he was reluctant to make the change, if the ownership of this improvement was to revert to the Trumble company. And the "to the exclusion of all others" phrase in the contract would, it seemed to Pyzel, seriously handicap Shell's future choice of processes and equipment. There was also the matter of expense; the amount paid in royalties would mount as the Group's refinery throughput mounted. The contract Shell had signed with Trumble had a nuisance value rivalling the value of the process. On top of these considerations, the Group was interested in being as agreeable as possible to Captain Barneson, whose company (and its option on the Union Oil Company of California) they were hopeful of purchasing at the time.[82]

With the Trumble patents safe in the fold, Meischke-Smith, who had negotiated the purchase, organized the Simplex Refining Company to hold and license them. He was its president, Charles F. Cramer was general manager, and N. W. (Skip) Thompson, who had been chief engineer of the Trumble company, came over to Simplex in the same capacity. When Keefe and Hemphill finished installing the unit at Martinez, Keefe went with Simplex and was sent to Miri,

Sarawak; Hemphill went with the manufacturing department of the Shell Company of California, and before his retirement in 1948 served many years as manager of the Martinez refinery.

The first Trumble unit had brought the lighter oil fractions to a boil in the pipe still. The whole, vapor and unboiled liquid, then entered the top of the evaporator where, in addition to the extra vaporization which was supposed to occur, the vapors were separated from the liquid and the liquid residue drawn off to be used later for fuel oil or as stock for the manufacture of lubricating oil. The vapors were separated into three rough fractions (gasoline, engine distillate, fuel oil), and if more accurate fractionation was desired, these fractions had to be put through conventional rerun stills. The point of the Trumble process as its inventor saw it was the evaporator § where, he maintained, a substantial portion of the still-liquid oil was converted into vapor. This Pyzel finally disproved by installing thermometers which showed that the mixture of vapors and liquid entering the evaporator was hotter than the flue gases which "heated" the evaporator! Trumble's exaggerated idea of the amount of evaporation which went on inside his tower led Pyzel to a deathless comment applicable not only to Trumble, but to many a man possessed of an idea: "He's perfectly honest—but you can't believe a word he says."[83]

The purchase of the patents gave Pyzel a free hand. The plan of the second Trumble unit at Martinez incorporated a series of dephlegmators, similar to, but much larger than, the equipment Pyzel had used in the Dutch East Indies. Used with the pipe still, the series of dephlegmators (or fractionating columns, as they are now more commonly called) made a very good combination. In place of the old method of separating oil into saleable products by progressively increasing the heat and condensing each fraction as it boiled off, the pipe still and dephlegmator made possible a complete reversal of the process. In the pipe still, the oil was heated at once to the boiling point of the heaviest fraction desired and the vapors were then led off all together and separated by progressive cooling in a battery of dephlegmators. The first dephlegmator in the battery (cooled by circulating water or cold crude oil) was kept at a temperature at which the heaviest product condensed out. The same operation was then repeated in the next dephlegmator, each dephlegmator cooler than the last, until at last in a final condenser the remaining vapor, light

§ The evaporator was, in fact, the crux of the Trumble patents. The pipe still was not prominent in his patents.

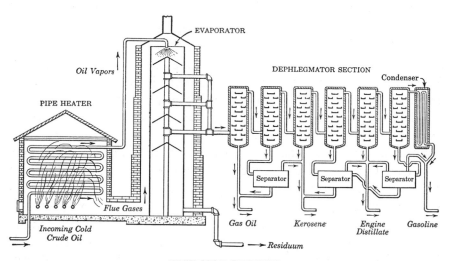

EVAPORATOR

Oil Vapors

PIPE HEATER

DEPHLEGMATOR SECTION

Condenser

Separator   Separator   Separator

Flue Gases

Incoming Cold
Crude Oil

Gas Oil   Kerosene   Engine   Gasoline
                               Distillate

→ Residuum

TRUMBLE PROCESS

*Crude oil was raised in pipe heater to temperature of heaviest product desired,
the vapors and liquid separated in the evaporator, and the vapors fractionated
by progressive cooling into gas oil, kerosene, engine distillate, and gasoline.*

gasoline, became liquid. The pipe still was not new, as we have seen, and a fractionating column had been patented in France as early as 1813 and had in ensuing years come into wide use in alcohol distillation. But it remained for Pyzel, building on Trumble's patents, to combine the two, and introduce a new method of refinery distillation.

The Trumble process, as this arrangement was called, made possible very substantial economies. First of all, because the oil was confined in pipes, it was possible to put a pump on it, speeding up the rate of flow and thereby greatly increasing the volume which a single still could handle in a day. The first two units at Martinez had a designed capacity of 5,000 barrels a day, but it was soon apparent that they were capable of handling 10,000 to 12,000 barrels a day[84]—quite a departure from Capitol Refining Company's one 250-barrel still! To achieve a daily throughput equalling that of the two Trumble units, a large number of cumbersome shell stills, occupying acres of ground and costing far more money to build, would have been necessary. And danger from fire was less with the new units, for although a tube might burst, it would release into the firebox only a few barrels of oil, compared to the much larger volume which was let loose when something went wrong with an old-fashioned shell still.

And so, Shell started off with America's first modern refinery, employing the pipe-still and fractionating-column combination which has since come into universal use in petroleum refining, because it is safe, efficient, and cheaper to construct. Martinez could with a few Trumble units handle the Valley Pipe Line's daily capacity of 28,000 barrels. Trumble unit No. 1 began test runs in the fall of 1915; the second and improved unit started operation in March 1916.

This marked the beginning of permanent refinery operation, but for some months previously the Shell Company of California had been refining its own products. When it had become evident that the pipe line would be completed before the Martinez refinery, Van Eck had made arrangements to rent refining facilities so that the sales department might continue to be supplied.

One was only a few hundred yards away from the Martinez refinery site, on a point called Bull's Head, and belonged to the American Oriental Company, controlled by the Dibble family of San Francisco. Typical of its day, the Amorco refinery was equipped with the old-style shell stills and was profitable to operate only during periods of relatively high product prices. It had closed down in January 1915.* Shell leased it; ran an extension pipe line to Bull's Head; and converted the stills to continuous operation. The operation was put under the supervision of Charles M. Adams, an old-time refiner. This rented refinery was the site of Shell's first laboratory in America; it was headed by Dr. A. W. Jurrissen and had a staff that included Ralph R. Mathews, Ralph Frizzell, Ralph Ahern, and Erle P. Severns.[86]

At Rodeo, nine miles west of Martinez on San Pablo Bay, similar arrangements were made to lease an inactive refinery to which lubricating oil stocks were shipped. There lubricants were made under the supervision of H. L. Burleson, an old-time refiner who had represented Indian Refining on the Pacific Coast after Gallagher left to join the Shell organization.[87] The Capitol Refining Company at Emeryville continued under C. J. Christeen the manufacture of petroleum products, primarily kerosene, spray oils, and asphalt.[88]

At Coalinga, the company built a small refinery on Section 36, property adjoining the Limited which had been purchased for its water wells. There a Trumble unit was erected and put into operation in December 1915. For many years, this small refinery ran at its initial

---

* Superintendent of the American Oriental installation had been young W. S. S. Rodgers, who in November 1915 joined The Texas Company, of which he eventually became president and later board chairman.[85]

rate of about 2,000 barrels a day,† supplying gasoline, kerosene, and fuel oil to the Coalinga and Bakersfield areas.[89]

Early in 1916, a still for manufacturing lubricating oils was built and put into operation at Martinez and a compounding house for blending oils and making greases was completed during the summer of 1916. By August 1916, it was possible to close down the Rodeo refinery and the old Capitol installation at Emeryville; the American Oriental plant had been vacated at the end of March.[90]

The operating crews from these installations moved into Martinez, creating for the moment a hodge-podge of autonomous departments. The job of organizing these departments into a smoothly operating refinery staff was assigned to G. H. van Senden, a Dutch technologist who had been sent to Martinez in 1915 to install the Edeleanu process for treating kerosene. This process, invented in 1907 by Dr. L. Edeleanu, a Romanian chemist and petroleum technologist, was a radically different method of removing the impurities from kerosene. Undesirable aromatic compounds were extracted by use of liquid sulphur dioxide, eliminating the time-honored but less efficient acid-soda treating method. The Group had at once recognized the superiority of the Edeleanu process and installed it successfully in the Group refinery at Ploesti, Romania.[91] Van Senden was familiar with the Edeleanu process and had been sent to Martinez to install a similar unit there. Because of the war then on, it was impossible to obtain from the German manufacturers who normally supplied this equipment the kind of compressors, welded vessels, and fittings which were needed for an Edeleanu plant. It was hoped that the equipment could be fabricated in America, but after running into a great many difficulties the idea was given up.‡

Van Senden was asked to remain at Martinez as assistant superintendent and soon afterward was made superintendent. His job at the start was not small. Besides having to knit independent departments together, he was faced with the more important task of providing the refinery with an operating staff. Construction personnel who had evinced an interest in the oil business were offered the opportunity to learn refining and most of them responded with a will. Some early Martinez employees of whom the company would hear more as the years went by were P. E. Foster, twenty years a Shell refinery man-

† The Coalinga refinery was running at the rate of 6,700 barrels a day in 1946; it was shut down in May 1947.

‡ An Edeleanu plant was not finally installed at Martinez until 1927.

ager, who began his career by working his way on a tramp steamer from New England to California, where he counted himself lucky to get a job twelve hours a day, seven days a week, on the loading racks at Martinez for $90 a month; R. C. Roberts, who went to work as a stillman and later managed three Shell refineries in the Mid-Continent which, in 1916, were yet to be built; and Jan Noorduyn, assistant superintendent, who would later go to the Group's largest refinery at Curaçao (still under construction in 1916) and before his retirement head the Group's Curaçao company.[92]

From the first, Martinez made a complete line of the products refined from petroleum in that day. A record available from early 1917 shows that Martinez regularly manufactured gasoline (one grade), engine distillate (a cross between gasoline and kerosene used in heavy automobile and truck engines of those days), domestic and export kerosene (the export grade for the Orient required less treating), stove oil (heavy kerosene), and residue. Part of the residue was then put through the bench still to get gas oil,§ light lubricating oil, light machine oil, medium machine oil, motor oil, road oil, and asphalt. In the compounding house, other lubricating oils to meet specialized conditions were made by blending the four different lubricating oils in varying proportions. Greases were also made in the compounding house. This complete range of products was adequate to supply the needs of the Shell company's growing marketing organization, and the high quality of these products—in great part a result of Van Senden's insistence on high standards of manufacture—made fast friends of Shell's new customers.

The gasoline and lubricating oils were sold in Shell filling stations, which up to 1920 were limited to the Pacific Northwest and the San Francisco Bay area. The sale of fuel oil (actually 18°-19° crude oil from Coalinga) got under way even before the completion of the Martinez refinery. E. R. Farley, who was in charge of fuel sales until his retirement in 1947, remembers executing the first contract for Coalinga fuel oil in 1914.

In 1915, as the refinery neared completion, Farley hired a solicitor and set him walking the railroad tracks in nearby industrial areas; wherever there was a smokestack, the solicitor tried to make a sale. Because the refinery's storage for fuel was limited, it was necessary to keep its fuel production moving out to customers. To do this Shell

§ A distillate oil formerly used to make illuminating gas, hence the name; now used chiefly as fuel for Diesel engines and domestic oil burners.

The village of Oilfields, located in the heart of Shell's Coalinga properties, as it looked about 1920. Out of sight at left are company shops.

Here is the famous Bungalow. Located on a hill overlooking the village of Oilfields, it provided palatial accommodations for unmarried staff employees.

Well-appointed billiard room in The Bungalow. Photo taken 1910.

This attractive table suggests one reason why The Bungalow is so fondly remembered by all who ever lived in it. Photo taken 1910.

Some Bungalow notables of 1910: *left to right*, Stanley W. Duhig, who became vice president and treasurer of the Shell holding company in New York; David Heggie, destined to hold similar office with Shell Oil in San Francisco; Stanley Fine; Roy Fine (*standing*), first office manager, Wilmington refinery; P. S. Turnbull; Edward Blake, veteran of Shell T. & T.'s Sanga Sanga field in Borneo; John M. Peat, later manager of stores department, San Francisco; and A. M. Dickie.

This is "Big Betsy," a steam-driven Best tractor with a train of trackless cars. It made twice-a-week trips the eight miles to Coalinga station to pick up timbers, sheet metal, billet steel, and other heavy oilfield materials.

Inside view of cable-tool drilling, Coalinga, 1911.

Part of Shell's Coalinga oil field in 1919.

was willing to underbid competitors by 2½¢ a barrel, until the company had under contract the amount of fuel business it wanted. These early customers were all businesses who bought fuel in tank car lots; the day of the domestic oil burner was still in the future. In San Francisco, fuel sales were made in less-than-carload lots to hotels, apartment houses, and institutional buildings; for delivering this oil, the company bought two Pierce Arrow tank trucks in 1915. These early fuel oil sales were all confined to California.[93]

In addition to gasoline, the company sold engine distillate on a considerable scale in the San Francisco area. Because the Edeleanu plant had not been installed, the kerosene sold on the Pacific Coast was treated by the traditional acid-soda process. A large part of Martinez' kerosene was purchased by Asiatic for resale in the Orient, where kerosene specifications were less exacting. This export business continued for a number of years.[94]

8

Ships at Sea

WHILE the Valley Pipe Line was still under construction, arrangements were going forward to supply another type of transportation—tankers. In 1914, Anglo-Saxon, in charge of the Group's ocean transport, sent its superintendent to the United States where he arranged with the Harlan & Hollingsworth shipyards at Wilmington, Delaware, to build three ocean tankers to be named the *Silver Shell*, *Gold Shell*, and *Pearl Shell*. The new vessels were intended primarily to carry products from the Martinez refinery to the ocean terminals at Portland, Seattle, and Vancouver. Surplus carrying capacity, if any, could be put into trans-Pacific or trans-Atlantic service.

Each vessel was of 8,500 tons carrying capacity (about 2,500,000 gallons of gasoline), half the size of the "T-2" tankers which were standard in World War II. The new ships were documented as American Flag vessels, to be operated by the Shell Company of California. During 1915, Shell of California organized three subsidiary companies, one for each vessel. They were named the Silver Shell Steamship Company, the Gold Shell Steamship Company, and the Pearl Shell Steamship Company, and each had a capitalization of $650,000, which represented almost exactly the cost of the construction.[95]

The three "Shell" vessels were hard-luck ships from the start. Launched all about the same time (late 1915 and early 1916, with the *Silver Shell* first, the *Gold Shell* next, and the *Pearl Shell* last), two of them met with accidents within six months. Early in 1916, the *Silver Shell* suffered a collision with a Japanese steamer, and in July of that year the *Gold Shell* ran onto a mine.[96] Hardly had they had time for repairs before a really crippling blow struck—a restrictive American law.

To give every advantage to American intercoastal shipping, Congress passed the Shipping Act of 1916 (the Jones-White Act) which became a law on September 7 of that year. The act provided, under penalty of seizure, that no vessel other than one classed as an "American vessel" might carry cargo or passengers between two American ports. "American vessel" was defined to mean a ship built and documented in the United States and owned by a United States citizen; if the "citizen" were a corporation, it must be a company organized in the United States, with at least three-quarters of its stock held by American citizens, and Americans as its chief executive officers. There was some question in the minds of lawyers as to whether or not this law applied to the three Shell steamship companies, for they were owned 100% by an American corporation, the Shell Company of California.

However, all such doubts were resolved, although only temporarily, by America's entry into World War I. The Federal government, which was taking over most forms of transport, including railroads and pipe lines, requisitioned the new vessels. The *Silver Shell* and *Pearl Shell* were operated by the Group under charter from the War Shipping Board; the *Gold Shell* * was taken over by the Navy on a bare-boat basis. The ships were restored to the company early in 1919, and were kept busy during most of 1920, until the government indicated that it considered their operation by the owner companies a violation of the law. Permission to sell the vessels to Anglo-Saxon was then applied for; it was denied by the War Shipping Board in 1920 and application again in 1921 brought a similar denial of permission. Meanwhile, the companies appointed Anglo-Saxon their managing agents for ports other than United States, and the vessels, although not used for the purpose for which they were built, were kept busy in the China trade. The legal tangle continued through most of the

---

* It figures in John Dos Passos' novel, *1919*.

Twenties, with Shell regularly applying for permission to sell the vessels and the government just as regularly denying it. Finally in 1928, the government gave its consent and the vessels were sold, not to Anglo-Saxon, but to Bataafsche's tanker affiliate, the Nederlandsch-Indische Tank-Stoomboot Maatschappij.[97]

9

The War Years

WITH America's entry into the First World War, the whole petroleum industry rolled up its sleeves and went to work as never before. Here was the world's first really mechanized war, requiring millions of gallons of liquid fuels to keep its machinery going. On the land, motor trucks for the first time were being used in large numbers; on the battlefield a new motorized weapon, the tank, made its appearance; in the air, airplanes were given their first military trial; and on the sea, not only merchant vessels but large naval fleets such as that of Great Britain had been converted to oil fuel. To supply all these needs —gasoline for trucks and tanks and an even better grade of it for airplanes, fuel oil for merchant and naval shipping, and lubricants for all of them—was a large order for the petroleum industry of that day. Hotly competing rival firms, who had previously had as little as possible to do with each other, banded together in the national interest to cooperate with the Oil Administration set up by the Federal government. From this close association there arose for the first time a genuine feeling of mutual respect and friendliness among oil men, which paved the way for the organization of the American Petroleum Institute in 1920.

At Martinez, new equipment was installed to make a special cut of high-grade gasoline for airplanes; a third and then a fourth Trumble unit were erected to bring the refinery's daily average throughput up to 24,000 barrels a day; the capacity of the lubricating oil plant was increased by 50%. The Valley pipe line upped its pumping rate from 5,267,000 barrels in 1916 to 6,400,000 in 1917 and 7,664,000 in 1918. The Martinez docks were jammed, as loading operations went on around the clock. Not only sleek new tankers but stodgy old steamers and even sailing vessels lined up to carry their share of the cargo.[98]

By 1917, the war was, of course, no new thing to the Group. The Shell companies abroad had been in the thick of things since 1914.† For the first three years of the war, Group companies had supplied all the gasoline used by the Allied air force; they had furnished a good part of the motor fuel for the services; and, a far cry from their pioneering days in fuel oil, were hard pressed to supply all the fuel oil that was needed for merchant and naval vessels. Shell Group technical people were freely lent to the Allied armies and navies to assist in the efficient organization of gasoline distribution on the land and of fuel oil at sea.

In addition to turning over to the British government its entire fleet of 75 tankers, twelve of which were torpedoed and sunk,‡ the Shell Group helped the Allies convert old ships into oil carriers. In 1915, Cornelius Zulver of the Group's marine department came up with the most spectacular transport idea of the war—utilizing the space between the double bottoms of cargo ships to carry fuel oil. This trick made it possible to ship more than 7,000,000 barrels of fuel in space which would otherwise have been wasted.[99]

But the accomplishment of which the Group itself was probably the proudest was its record-breaking manufacture of toluene. A shortage of toluene, a vital ingredient of T.N.T. and until this point produced only from coal tar, threatened disaster for the Allies in the spring of 1915. The Shell Group had a process for extracting it from Borneo gasoline, and an extraction plant already built near Rotterdam.§ This plant was pulled down, secretly loaded on a large vessel, and under cover of night transported to England where it was re-erected and put into production less than six weeks from the time the venture was undertaken. It became a model for two more plants which the Group built for the British government and staffed with trained technical people, mostly from Holland. These petroleum sources of toluene, hastily erected though they were, were able during the

---

† It was primarily for their services in connection with Shell's war effort that both Deterding and Samuel received British honors in the years following the war. Deterding was created a Knight of the British Empire in 1920, and adopted thenceforth the French spelling of his first name. Samuel, knighted originally in 1898 and created a baronet in 1903, was raised to the peerage in 1921 with the title of Baron Bearsted; he was made Viscount Bearsted in 1925.

‡ Among them the S.S. *Romany*, which had brought the first gasoline to Seattle, and Samuel's first tanker, the *Murex*.

§ See pages 504-505.

war period to match the entire toluene output of the coal tar industry.[100]

At Martinez, the refinery laboratory investigated the toluene content of the California crude oils available to it. A pilot-plant fractionating column was constructed and an attempt made to produce a toluene fraction; the attempt was not successful because California crude oils did not have as high a toluene content as Borneo oils. In Mexico the Group produced a heavy crude oil so rich in asphalt that it was unsaleable when refined into fuel, so during the war period the Mexican operations received a large amount of attention from the Simplex people on the Coast. Pyzel tried to devise a method for light cracking, or viscosity-breaking, of this heavy Mexican fuel by use of the Trumble "converter," a piece of cracking equipment acquired along with the original Trumble patents. The experiments were carried on at Martinez, and, although they showed some promise, were productive chiefly of local excitement two or three times a week when the converter caught on fire.[101]

The Simplex Refining Company was never busier. Under Thompson as chief engineer, Simplex undertook the design of Trumble units for Group refineries all over the world, let contracts for their manufacture, and shipped the completed units, along with an engineer to supervise their assembly, to Curaçao, Mexico, Egypt, and the East Indies. In addition to Trumble units, Simplex designed three complete refineries to be built in the American Mid-Continent. Once the new refineries got into operation, they built up their own engineering departments, eliminating need for further assistance from Simplex. As a result, Simplex had by the late Twenties become merely a patent-licensing company and its name was changed late in 1926 to Shell Development Company. But these early days of design activity in the Simplex office in San Francisco made a lasting contribution: they served to introduce good engineering practice into the building of refinery equipment in America. The manufacturers of refinery equipment, not slow to see the advantages of improved practice, rapidly built up their own engineering staffs.[102]

The years of World War I also witnessed the start of personnel department activities. In October 1918, Van Senden set up a personnel department (at the time called service and employment department) at the Martinez refinery, a department with advanced ideas for its day. Van Senden's thought was to create a department which would do more than merely hire new hands (the starting point, historically, of almost every personnel department); it should also attempt to see that the man already working got a square deal on the job and had ample opportunity to advance.

Van Senden was concerned in particular with the man who feels he is on a "dead-end street"—his boss perhaps thinks the man a mediocre workman, or, as is more rarely the case, actually harbors ill will toward him. How, Van Senden wondered, could such a man ever get ahead? If he were mentioned for promotion, his boss would almost surely fail to recommend him; if he actively tried to get out and into another department he might, even if he were successful in the maneuver, incur enmity that would last the rest of his days with the company.

Here, then, back in the early days of personnel departments, Van Senden introduced a workable and intelligent system: let every vacancy be filled not by private discussion among a few bosses, but by open "advertising" for the job. A description of the vacancy would be posted on refinery bulletin boards along with information about qualifications required and the rate of pay. The notice would invite any man who thought himself qualified to fill out a form stating his qualifications for the job and forward it, not to his boss who would be allowed no voice in the matter, but to the refinery personnel department. The personnel department and the head of the department having the vacancy would examine the applications and make selections, thus eliminating favoritism and giving a man with experience and a good record the opportunity to move from one department to another, if he chose. This plan worked out well in practice, and in later years was extended, at the request of the union representing them, to workers in the production department as well. From the start, unsuccessful applicants were urged to come in and find out why they had failed and how they might make the grade next time.[103]

Myron Burr was manager of this first personnel department started at Martinez; Charles S. Jobe succeeded him shortly afterwards; and Frank Coats, who held the job until his retirement in 1954, came in 1921. The work of this department, as was pointed out in a report compiled in 1921, was not undertaken out of sentimentality: "There is absolutely no desire to force any kindnesses, welfare work, community singing, or things of that kind on the men. It is simply a business proposition between the company and the men, for in order to work together we must adjust ourselves to each other and the sooner that is done the better, and the basis of the adjustment is fair play."[104]

The war years also had their effect upon Oilfields. At the outbreak of the World War in 1914, Arthur T. Beazley, who had been general superintendent of the Limited, went home to serve in the British Army.* Temporarily, David Heggie, the oldest and most experienced staff member, was placed in charge, but Heggie was a commercial and accounting man (he later became vice president and treasurer of Shell on the West Coast), so an effort was made to find someone trained in the drilling end of the business. Not long before, Van der Linden had met W. C. McDuffie, the young superintendent of a small producing company in the Taft field; soon after, McDuffie had a falling out with his company over labor policy; Van der Linden was delighted to find him available and in April 1914 persuaded the Shell management to hire him as Beazley's successor, even though McDuffie was only twenty-eight at the time.[105]

Under McDuffie, a born leader of men, Oilfields was converted from standard cable-tool drilling to the more modern, faster rotary drilling method. This called for overcoming the prejudices and "it-can't-be-done" attitude of many old-timers; such work, despite his tender years, McDuffie was admirably equipped to do, for he possessed strong leadership qualities and a limitless store of tact. Although not a technical man, McDuffie was quick to grasp the importance of technological improvements; he encouraged and gave every support to able young technical men working under him. This ability to direct a technical enterprise was to carry McDuffie far; only nine years later, in 1924, he would be placed in world-wide charge of production for the Royal Dutch-Shell Group.

McDuffie did everything possible to continue and enhance the favorable labor relations which he found at Oilfields as his heritage from the enlightened policies of Bill Graham and Balfour, Guthrie & Co. As more and more Oilfields men were called to the colors during the war years, it became necessary to consider replacing with women those who had held clerical and stenographic positions. This, at Oilfields, necessitated the building of new living quarters to accommodate the young ladies who were recruited largely from the San Francisco Bay area. Like most McDuffie experiments, the young ladies were a great success in the business; and after the war, nearly all, including the nurse, married Oilfields men. Another experiment of this period, interesting chiefly as a demonstration of open-minded management, was

---

* Beazley did not stay with Shell after the war, but went on to become general manager of the Lobitos Oilfields, Ltd., in Peru.

McDuffie's retention of a University of California psychologist to give
the men the Army "Alpha" (intelligence) test in an attempt to uncover unsuspected ability; these tests, however, pointed to the same
men who were already distinguishing themselves by other means.[106]

In wartime labor negotiation, Shell of California joined with other
West Coast oil companies. In July 1918, the government's War Petroleum Board called a meeting of the Pacific Coast petroleum industry
at Santa Barbara to help avert a strike which the Petroleum Board felt
imminent. The companies, meeting with representatives of their own
employees, agreed upon a general wage structure for the petroleum
industry for a period of one year. Wage scales were drawn up for each
job, and workmen's committees were established to handle grievances.
This agreement was renewed annually until 1921, when the other
members of the industry withdrew.[107] Largely at the instance of
McDuffie and Van Senden, Shell continued these arrangements with
its own employees. Annual Santa Barbara meetings were held all during the Twenties and into the Thirties, and the famous M.O.T.'s
(Memorandum of Terms) which resulted from these friendly meetings with employees set a standard for wages and hours for the production, pipe line, and refining ends of the business.

10

Van der Linden and Ventura

THE original concern of Shell on the Pacific Coast had been to market
imported gasoline. Then the company had acquired substantial crude
oil production at Coalinga and its efforts were next turned to laying a
pipe line, building a refinery, and constructing tankers. With these
major moves completed, attention was once more directed to crude
oil.

During 1914, as already noted, options which California Oilfields,
Ltd., had previously acquired were exercised and Shell bought the
neighboring W. K. and Turner oil companies at Coalinga for a total
of $1,760,000. The Guardian Oil Company, 280 acres of neighboring
property, was acquired early in 1916.[108]

By 1916, with two Trumble units operating at Martinez and the rest of the refinery rapidly nearing completion, there was demand for more oil. Coalinga, the Shell company's only source on the Coast, produced 4,800,000 barrels of crude that year and in 1917 increased drilling raised Coalinga production to 6,350,000 barrels. The village of Oilfields was at its busiest; as many as twenty wells were being drilled at once and more than 600 men were on the payroll.

During these years Van der Linden was introducing production engineering practices into the Limited's operations. Beazley had set up an engineering department shortly after his arrival, but the methods in use at Coalinga seemed inadequate to Van der Linden. He wanted cross-section and contour maps of the Coalinga property and studies of subjects such as underground waters, all of which would be needed if the drilling and production field work were to be guided by scientific principles. Very few oil companies in those years had done anything to put production field work on a scientific footing. In rare instances where work was being done, it was performed in the companies' main offices far from the actual scene of operations. Van der Linden proceeded to build up a staff of qualified engineers who would be on the spot to observe the daily drilling, keep a close check on the formations encountered, and work up an accurate picture of underground conditions so that future drilling might be guided by knowledge rather than guesswork.[109]

Through the offices of his assistant, J. E. (Brick) Elliott, a Stanford alumnus, Van der Linden got acquainted with the geology and engineering departments of that institution and engaged his first production engineering staff as young men, some of whom were still in school. Many of them worked summers at first, coming with Shell as soon as they had finished their college courses. From this source came many able geologists and engineers. A. W. (Pete) Ambrose in 1914 became Shell's first resident exploitation engineer at Coalinga, and probably one of the first production engineers in the modern sense of the word. Later Ambrose joined the Bureau of Mines experiment station at Bartlesville, Okla., and still later he became president of the Cities Service Oil Company. Others of similar background included F. E. Rehm, twenty-five years later a Shell vice president, and T. E. Swigart, who became a Shell production vice president and later president of Shell Pipe Line Corporation.

Van der Linden's production engineers at once proved their worth in dollars and cents. During the First World War, they successfully demonstrated to the California State Mining Bureau that wells could be drilled on Section 27 at Coalinga with one instead of three strings of casing to shut off the upper oilfield waters. In addition to saving time and precious casing, which was scarce because of wartime short-ages, this innovation meant a money saving of approximately $10,000 in the cost of drilling each well.[110]

Shell of California's production efforts were still confined to the Coalinga area when Van der Linden set out to find more oil. Then, on April 1, 1916, at Ventura, California, he met Ralph B. Lloyd, setting in motion a chain of events which were to cause much grief, lead Van der Linden into endless battles, cost his company two and one-half million dollars before commercial results, bring him a sizeable demo-tion, and, eventually, open up one of California's most prolific oil fields. For when Van der Linden met Lloyd, he was tackling Ventura, a region which had behind it half a century of disappointed oil pros-pectors.

The area of Ventura, earlier called San Buenaventura, had looked promising to oil hunters ever since the very beginning of the oil busi-ness in California. George S. Gilbert, formerly in the whale oil busi-ness in Brooklyn, New York, had gone west in Gold Rush days; by 1861, he was successfully refining oil from seepages, and moved his operations to some oil springs on the Ojai Ranch north of the town of Ventura.[111] Gilbert made lubricants and sold them to local vineyard-ists and was thus engaged in 1864 when who should appear on the scene but Professor Benjamin Silliman, Jr., of Yale University, the very same Silliman who ten years before had rendered the report that started the Pennsylvania oil industry on its way.

Silliman knew oil when he saw it, and he saw plenty in Ventura County. "The oil is struggling to the surface at every available point and is running away down the rivers for miles," he wrote enthusiastic-ally to Colonel Thomas A. Scott, vice president of the Pennsylvania Railroad and Assistant Secretary of War in Lincoln's cabinet. Colonel Scott was a bright and energetic man. Three years before, he had had his first taste of oil money, when he, his secretary (a young man named Andrew Carnegie), and the Pennsylvania's president, J. Edgar Thomson, had joined to buy the Story farm on Oil Creek for $40,000. Within a year they had taken out more than a million dollars; and the value of the stock of the company they had formed soon rose to five million dollars. Impressed by the profit possibilities of the oil business,

Scott heeded the voice of a recognized expert such as Silliman. He formed three oil companies in the East and the following year they acquired seven large ranchos in what is now Ventura County, plus a large part of the town, together with other holdings totalling in all some 277,000 acres, one-third the area of the state of Rhode Island. Drilling machinery of the type used in Pennsylvania was shipped to California and in the summer of 1865 drilling was started at a spot five miles up the river from the village of Ventura. They found small quantities of oil, but not enough for commercial production.[112]

Other pioneers also took a flier at Ventura. The Stanford Brothers (two brothers of the more famous Leland) went into Ventura County coincident with the start of Scott's ventures there. They had the idea, natural enough in a mining country, of tunnelling for oil. By 1866 they had completed an 80-foot up-sloping tunnel into the side of Sulphur Mountain north of Ventura. As the area was rich in seepages, some oil would flow by gravity down the inclined floor of the tunnel. Production by this method gave one to twenty barrels a day, and although not a sensational success, tunnelling was continued off and on for the next twenty-five years, thirty-one tunnels in all being dug into the sides of Sulphur Mountain, the longest 1,600 feet. The oil was used chiefly for refining into lubricating oil for the new Central Pacific Railroad, in which Leland Stanford was a chief mover.[113]

The next big try at the Ventura area was made by a local boy, Ralph B. Lloyd, the man whom Van der Linden met that April day in 1916. As a boy, Lloyd had noticed in the region several manifestations of what Van der Linden later was to call, very aptly indeed, "gas from the grass roots down." A. B. Barnard, whose property now comprises the Barnard lease of General Petroleum in the Ventura Avenue field, in 1885 drilled a water well which, much to his disgust, turned out to be a geyser of salt and water. Another rancher, Hartman, whose property now produces oil for Tidewater, dug a water well which tasted salty, so he put a cover over it. A few days later Hartman removed the cover and lit a match to look inside and see what was causing that smell; fortunately, he was not injured by the explosion.[114]

Determined to succeed where others had failed, young Lloyd returned home from college in 1898 and promptly set out to map the Ventura anticline. A few years later, he succeeded in interesting Joseph Dabney with him, and together they leased up all the possible oil-bearing land, with the exception of the Barnard land already mentioned, and a 100-acre plot belonging to the Southern California Edison Company.† To drill their first well, Lloyd and Dabney formed the State Consolidated Oil Company, in which E. J. Miley also invested. They started drilling in 1914. But the savage pressure of the gas took its toll. "After four years of bitter disappointment," Lloyd wrote in a newspaper account many years later, "and the expenditure of several hundred thousand dollars, we had nothing to show but craters blown out of the earth by gas, strings of wrecked casing deep in the earth, and a few puddles of oily salt water. The gas and the salt water seemed to overpower any efforts of man and machinery to get at the oil." As he sat there that day in 1916 "almost dead beat physically and financially" talking to Van der Linden, it is doubtful whether Lloyd painted quite such a gloomy picture. But he and his partners had endured to the limit of their finances and were willing to have someone else take over.[116]

Van der Linden had previously visited the Ventura region and studied its formations at some length. When Lloyd showed him the rugged east end of the anticline with an imposing outcropping of oil layers, Van der Linden promptly became as enthusiastic as Professor Silliman or Ralph Lloyd had ever been. Because Lloyd held such a large part of the field under lease, he was in a commanding position; Meischke-Smith and Van der Linden negotiated through May and June and finally reached an agreement with Lloyd and associates on June 12, 1916. Under its terms Shell took over the leases intact, getting at one stroke the whole Ventura field with the exception of the two parcels already noted. It was a fair deal: the landowners would get their one-eighth royalty, which Lloyd and his associates had bound themselves to pay; and Lloyd and his partners were to receive an additional royalty determined by the going price of crude oil. If oil were $1.00 a barrel or less, they would get nothing; if it were $2.50 a barrel or more, they would get one-eighth; if it were in between—say, $1.75—they would get half of one-eighth, or one-sixteenth. Further, Shell was given the option of buying out this overriding royalty in the future at a cost of $750 per acre for the best acreage, $250 an acre for the balance. The total area involved in the transaction was 13,000 acres, divided among four big leases, the Taylor, the Gosnell, the

† Its predecessor, the Ventura County Light & Power Company, with the idea of supplying gas for light and heat had, in 1903, drilled nine wells to about 400 feet. These wells had been abandoned because of the difficulty of drilling with cable tools and the large amounts of water encountered.[115]

Hartman, and the McGonigle, plus a fifth lease on a parcel of Lloyd family property called the Ventura Land and Water Co.[117]

Drilling got under way almost immediately, with drillers and equipment sent from Coalinga. C. C. Kifer, who had been at the Limited since 1908, arrived to be drilling foreman and remained on the job through all the headaches which were to come. The first well was "spudded in" in August 1916, on the Taylor lease, and during the next year a well apiece on the other three leases was begun.[118]

From the first, difficulties were encountered. To begin with, the geologists did not (nor would they for some years) understand the nature of the underground structure—there were faults, cross-faults, dying out of faults, and, most confusing of all, repetition of a given structure a few hundred feet farther down. And the drillers were just as baffled. Never had they hit anything like this. Drilling would proceed only a few feet before a gas pocket at shallow depths would be encountered. If they were lucky, the gas would blow out only the string of drilling tools; if they weren't so lucky the tools, casing, rig, and all, would go vaulting into the air, a geyser of water and gas would blow for a few days, and then after patiently rebuilding the rig, they would start all over again.[119]

The well on the McGonigle lease was perhaps the most expensive; certainly it was the most picturesque. The McGonigle tract of land was quite far back from the road and completely removed from the rest of Shell's operations at Ventura. A high ridge separated it from the convenient roads; the only way to get into the well site would be to build a long, expensive road. So, it was decided to use another means of reaching the McGonigle property. An aerial tramway a mile and an eighth long was built over this rocky ridge to connect it with the road on the nearest lease. Then began the annoying operation of ferrying every board and timber and piece of drilling equipment to the other side. Transporting a heavy steam boiler to provide power was out of the question—the cable couldn't carry that much weight. It was decided, instead, to use electricity which would also eliminate the problem of hauling fuel. As a result, the McGonigle well was one of the first California wells to be drilled entirely by electricity.[120]

Progress was slow. Cable tools were used on all four wells, and when the sides of the holes showed a tendency to cave in there was nothing to stop them. So they drilled "carrying casing." This meant that a pipe, or casing, small enough to fit in the hole and yet larger in diameter than the string of tools, was suspended around the drilling string and lowered with the drill as the hole got deeper. Mud was pumped under pressure into the top of the casing. As soon as it encountered gas underground, the mud would become light and frothy. More and heavier mud would be hurriedly mixed and pumped down to prevent the well from blowing out.[121]

All the way the field was a freak. The drillers would hit high-pressure gas at shallow depths. If it could be controlled, it meant many hours lost in mixing and circulating heavier mud; if it couldn't be controlled, a blow-out ensued. Then they would run into high-pressure water, also at shallow depths, when they tried to cement the topmost pieces of casing in order to shut off water veins. Such high-pressure water often made it almost impossible for the cement to set. A third, and frightening, occurrence was continual loss of mud circulation. A sudden drop in mud pressure usually meant that high-pressure gas had been encountered, that the mud would soon turn to froth; if more and heavier mud were not pumped down at once, a blow-out would ensue. Just to make things extra confusing, this was not always the case at Ventura. Sometimes the mud didn't encounter gas but would go wandering off through an underground fissure created by one of the field's many cross-faults. Once, after pumping mud frantically for hours, the men discovered a small stream of mud issuing from a surface outcrop a quarter of a mile away.[122] On a much later occasion, in 1940, one of the dry holes drilled by Lloyd & Dabney, 1914–1916, started flowing of its own accord and was plugged up again for safety's sake.[123] Such occurrences were enough to make drillers believe in jinxes and demons; fortunately, they didn't.

Time means money, and lost time means lost money. Nowhere is that better illustrated than in the drilling of oil wells. For every few feet of hole the men succeeded in drilling at Ventura, they lost hours and days in other pursuits, usually in mixing and circulating mud or in trying, against odds, to set casing where there was high-pressure water. Charles Hansen, who was still at Ventura thirty years later, was a young man working on the McGonigle well when he left to go into the army in 1917. The United States entered, fought, and helped win a war. Hansen was discharged and returned to find his crew still drilling away at the same old stand, not much deeper than when he had left.[124]

The Hartman and Taylor wells were still drilling, too, with no results in sight. The well on the Gosnell lease came in in March 1919, producing 120 barrels of oil a day, but with some 500 barrels of salt water mixed with it. Thus encouraged, the company started a second well on the Gosnell property in July 1919. But before they got very far with that, the No. 1 Gosnell gassed up and choked off its small daily production.‡ In four years of drilling, Shell had laid out about two and a half million dollars in the Ventura Avenue field, as it was officially called. That was big money in a day when most oil wells cost only a few thousand dollars to drill. To those less optimistic than Van der Linden, it began to look as if Ventura were a poor bargain indeed. In October 1919, drilling of the unsuccessful McGonigle well was finally abandoned and, late the same year, Shell surrendered the McGonigle lease.[126]

During the early Twenties, rotary rigs were put to work at Ventura; and Gosnell No. 3, drilled partly with a rotary drill and finished with cable tools, came in producing 900 barrels a day of clean oil, in March 1922. At Van der Linden's urging, Shell promptly bought out Lloyd's overriding royalty interest in the Gosnell lease for $80,000, as provided for in the option—an undoubted bargain in the light of later developments.§ But the promise of this Gosnell well was not fulfilled by other immediate successes. For many long months, there were few Ventura enthusiasts aside from Van der Linden.* The company, flushed with the phenomenal success of new fields farther to the south, in 1924 seriously considered selling out its entire Ventura holdings to Associated for $3,000,000. Wiser heads did at least prevent this near-tragedy; but the Hartman lease was surrendered in 1925, later to be leased to Associated who made a success of both it and the McGonigle property.[127]

Van der Linden was recalled to Holland and shortly thereafter re-assigned to the Royal Dutch's first oil field in North Sumatra. He was later to rise to become world-wide head of the Royal Dutch-Shell production activities, but for the moment he was beaten by Ventura,

‡ L. L. Carter, a mechanical engineer, devised a small plant to prevent this emulsifying which was, he contended, caused by the water and oil being forced under high pressure through the small orifice at the well head. His device yielded water, oil, and gas separately. It was improved upon by William Marker, an exploitation engineer, and William Allen, the superintendent, and became the so-called "gun barrel" which is now used by the Shell Group world-wide to prevent emulsifying.[125] The Gosnell No. 1 well produced more than 250,000 barrels before it was finally abandoned in 1951.

§ The overriding interest in the Taylor lease was purchased in 1925 for $1,200,000.

* Ample evidence of this pessimism is the valuation the company placed on its Ventura properties when they were assessed in 1921 for purposes of the Shell-Union deal. Despite the much larger amount Shell had already spent there, the company's own assessors put Ventura down for only $1,000,000.

the same region which had defeated other successful men—Tom
Scott of the Pennsylvania Railroad, the Stanford Brothers, and Ralph
B. Lloyd, later to be numbered among California's wealthiest royalty
owners.

The expensive "failure" at Ventura was not a failure at all. It was
merely an instance of tackling a difficult job before technology was
ready. Very soon afterward heavier drilling equipment and a more
extensive understanding of drilling muds were available. Armed with
these new tools, Shell was able, later in the Twenties, to make Ventura
one of the company's most profitable oil fields.

In its main outlines, this is the story of the early years of the Shell
companies on the Pacific Coast, from their start in 1912 up to 1920. It
is time now to consider the area east of the Rockies where other new
Shell companies were being established during the same years.

Martinez's first Trumble unit under construction, June 1915.

G. H. van Senden, first manager of Martinez refinery,
deep in construction mud,
1915.

Corner of Martinez refinery site, with Bull's Head refinery
of American Oriental Company in middle distance. White
Shell tanks in foreground were part of American Gasoline
Company's Martinez water terminal. Refinery crude oil
storage tanks are on hill, *right*. Photo taken about 1915.

Mule teams hauled equipment for the Valley Pipe Line from the nearest railroad stations. This is a 15-ton oil-heater for one of the pumping stations.

Loading a tanker at Martinez during the First World War.

The S.S. *Silver Shell*, first of three identical tankers built 1915–16 by Shell of California. The two other vessels were named *Gold Shell* and *Pearl Shell*.

Daniel Pyzel, *left*, and N. W. (Skip) Thompson are photographed looking at patent of the old Trumble converter, in San Francisco office of Shell Development Company, 1947. The safe in which the patents were stored was one of the few remaining relics of the old American Gasoline Company. During their Shell careers, both men were active in process development. Thompson invented a hot oil pump which made possible great operating improvements in both the Trumble and Dubbs processes. Pyzel directed Shell's refinery design activities and was a chief mover in establishing the Shell Development and Shell Chemical companies.

Photo by C. E. Crompton

Martinez refinery laboratory, pilot plants and all. This 1916 photograph shows the small laboratory building and, in front of it, experimental stills and agitators.

Drilling crew of Gosnell No. 1, Ventura, Calif., field, about 1919.

B. H. van der Linden, *right*, responsible for Shell's discovery of the Ventura field, is photographed at a luncheon in his honor, Ventura, 1950. At left is E. W. Masters of Shell's Los Angeles production office.

Central section of Ventura Avenue field, May 1925. There are steep hills to left, as well as right. Lemon grove in foreground is reminder of valley's earlier economy.

CHAPTER IV

An Investment in Oklahoma

1912–1920

A T THE very moment that Fisher and his small staff in Seattle were making their first shipment of gasoline in the Pacific Northwest, another group of men in Tulsa, Oklahoma, 2,000 miles away, were getting another new Shell company under way—the Roxana Petroleum Company of Oklahoma, organized October 1, 1912. On the Pacific Coast, Shell had gone into the marketing end of the business; in Oklahoma, the company was entering the opposite end of the business and becoming a producer of crude oil. On the West Coast it had taken nearly two years to get under way; in Oklahoma, it had taken even longer, for Deterding had had his eye on the area since 1909.

For a full decade prior to 1912, Oklahoma had been the scene of a succession of oil excitements. In 1897, the state's first commercially productive well had been drilled at Bartlesville, in the old "Indian Territory." It had not, however, been an immediate success. The area was still frontier country, ten full years to statehood. The development of oil properties in Indian Territory was complicated by the fact that the Indians were wards of the U. S. Government, and the Secretary of the Interior, the Indians' official guardian, refused to grant oil leases on Indian lands. And so that first well, the Nellie Johnstone No. 1, was plugged up but not forgotten.[1]

Then in 1901, the news of tremendous gushers at Spindletop, near Beaumont on the Texas Gulf Coast, electrified the whole country and interest in Oklahoma oil at once revived. In June of that year, a small discovery well was drilled at Red Fork, near the present city of Tulsa. Because this well was a gusher, it brought a rush to the Red Fork area out of all proportion to the actual find.

In a matter of weeks, hundreds of oil prospectors descended on the Tulsa area and promptly located other small, shallow fields not too far away. Equally important for the future of Oklahoma, these newly arrived prospectors generated such pressure for leasing of the Indian lands that the government revised its policy and, in 1902, the Secretary of the Interior began to approve oil leases on Indian lands. This was the signal for opening up the area around Bartlesville and, although the size of the wells in this area in no way compared with the tremendous production of the Spindletop field, there were enough individual wells drilled in the ensuing months to make it profitable for the Prairie Oil & Gas Company to run a pipe line into Bartlesville late in 1904. From that moment onward, Oklahoma was in the oil business.

In July 1904, production was discovered at Cleveland, northwest of Tulsa. Then, late in 1905, came the discovery of Oklahoma's first really big field, the Glenn Pool, ten miles south of Tulsa. Here production of the individual wells was much higher: some of the Glenn Pool wells had initial productions as large as 3,000 barrels a day. It was an excellent paraffin-base oil, of 32° to 38° gravity; it was at shallow depths and could be reached by relatively inexpensive drilling; and there was sufficient gas pressure to raise the oil without pumping. At such news, the oil fraternity the world around pricked up its ears. Prairie (a subsidiary of the old Standard Oil) ran a pipe line into the Glenn Pool in August 1906, and the following year both the Gulf and Texas companies built lines from the Beaumont area into the Glenn Pool. These three lines shipped nearly 3,500,000 barrels a month of Glenn Pool crude during 1907—an indication, if one were needed, that oil was to be had in Oklahoma in highly profitable quantities.[2]

A small group of men in Holland realized the possibilities of the Glenn Pool, and through them the Royal Dutch-Shell Group made its first contact with the Oklahoma oil business. J. Deen and D. A. J. Kessler,* both of whom had already made considerable fortunes as independent producers in Sumatra, and S. F. van Oss, a newspaperman who later founded The Hague *Post,* joined forces in 1907 to buy two producing companies in the Glenn Pool and organize them into the Oklahoma Petroleum Company. The success of their first venture led this Dutch group to start a second company, The Union Petroleum Company, in 1909; and a few months later, a third, the Tulsa Petroleum Company. These new companies proved to be more than they could finance so, during the summer of 1909, Deen and his associates offered to sell out to the Royal Dutch.[3]

---

* Brother of J. B. Aug. Kessler, the early managing director of the Royal Dutch. For more about D. A. J. Kessler, see page 46.

SHELL IN THE MID-CONTINENT, 1912-1925

The basis of the sale was to be so much per barrel for each barrel of "settled production," a standard method of selling producing properties in the Mid-Continent. Buying "settled production" was a handy way to trade oil properties, but it was also highly dangerous for the novice, particularly in Oklahoma where the oil-bearing sands were extremely thin and oil fields customarily played out rapidly. To get an expert's opinion on the estimated life of these properties was therefore essential, and the Royal Dutch sent Pieter Kruisheer, one of its geological assistants, to Oklahoma in the summer of 1909. Kruisheer carefully surveyed the potentialities of the three companies offered for sale and, back in The Hague, rendered a report in November 1909 advising against the purchase.[4]

The average production per well of one of these companies had been 370 barrels a day early in 1908, Kruisheer found. A year later, that figure had dropped to 100 barrels a day and, at the time of his visit six months later, it had fallen to 70 barrels a day. "Settled" production in this case, Kruisheer concluded, meant a decrease of one-half each year, a rate so rapid that he predicted Deen's companies would very soon be in financial difficulties.

Plans to purchase the Deen properties were therefore abandoned, but Kruisheer's visit had served to notify Oklahoma oil men that the Royal Dutch-Shell was a potential customer for producing properties. As a result, several offers reached London and The Hague during the next few months. In the spring of 1910, through Deen's banking friends in Paris, who had bought the Oklahoma properties, an offer reached Deterding which sounded attractive—if for no reason other than its size. The properties offered were more than a million acres of leases in Oklahoma, Illinois, and Indiana belonging to T. N. Barnsdall, an old-time oil man who had started his career in Titusville, Pa. Deterding sent Dr. H. Hirschi, a Swiss geologist, to investigate. Much of the Barnsdall acreage was, of course, still undeveloped, but the point that most depressed Hirschi in his report (Pittsburgh, September 23-25, 1910) was the low price then being paid for Oklahoma oil: "In Oklahoma, the different pipe line companies pay 40¢ a barrel; this price is shockingly low and does not leave the producers any profit. The crude oil from Oklahoma, which is of very good quality, should bring a much higher price." Hirschi went on to say that the venture could be attractive financially, if 15,000 barrels a day of production were obtained—enough to operate a pipe line to the Gulf—for on the Gulf Coast the same oil was worth $1.00 a barrel.

Deterding declined to go on with the Barnsdall deal because of the large amount of money required (the deal anticipated formation of a new company with $100,000,000 capital) but he did get from Hirschi's report an idea which was to become the basis for Shell's eventual entry into the Mid-Continent. It was quite simple: to acquire producing properties capable of yielding 15,000 barrels a day at a purchase price which would average out to approximately 40¢ a barrel, after depreciation and lifting costs had been deducted. If this could be accomplished, any projected Shell company would be on a cost footing equal to that of its competitors and could well afford to lay a pipe line to the Gulf, where Group tankers could load the oil. This was the plan that finally resulted in a new Shell company in the Oklahoma oil fields. As we shall see, the plan was not adhered to in any aspect but it did provide the all-important starting point.

The "catalyst" that finally got Deterding into action was Richmond Levering, whose bold plans and boundless promotional imagination were well-nigh irresistible.† Settled production? Levering knew where there was lots of it. He made an offer of properties in the Bridgeport field of southern Illinois. Total production, he said, was 14,000 barrels a day, and the price would be $400 per barrel. Deterding dispatched Dr. J. Th. Erb, head geologist of the Group at The Hague,‡ to Illinois to investigate Levering's offer. He found that production was indeed 14,600 barrels a day as represented. It came, however, from 995 wells, producing an average of only 14.7 barrels a day,[7] and this made lifting costs proportionately high. Erb estimated that, after the purchase price had been depreciated over the estimated life of these fields and the lifting expense paid, the cost per barrel of oil would be 41.75¢. This was about right for cost, but his answer as to how long the current rate of production could be maintained was just as discouraging as Kruisheer's.

All these reports served only to exasperate Deterding, for he had his heart set on entering the Mid-Continent area. Uncertainty over the

---

† E. DeGolyer, who was kind enough to read the manuscript of this chapter, writes: "Levering was a man of the most remarkable personal magnetism. I had to clean up after him in a deal where his imagination had run riot and he had paid no particular attention to details. When I met him, I was all prepared to dislike him thoroughly, but such was his charm that I would have been willing to invest my few remaining pennies in one of his enterprises." [5]

‡ Dr. Erb, one of the first geologists the Group ever had, became head of the Central Geological Department at The Hague when it was set up in 1913; later he was managing director of the Royal Dutch, 1921–1928, and a member of the board, from 1929 until his death in October 1934.[6]

productive life of each of the fields thus far examined had made it impossible for him to recommend any of the proposed ventures to his board of directors. But he felt in his heart that if he could only persuade the directors to enter the producing business in America, even if the deal appeared unsound at the outset, everything would turn out all right in the end. At this juncture, his old favorite bogeyman, the Standard Oil Company, came to his rescue. On April 11, 1912, Standard through a subsidiary organized the N. V. Koloniale Petroleum Maatschappij to acquire and operate oil fields in South Sumatra. This gave Deterding the ammunition he needed. Next day he gave the board of directors a report of the Indies situation, and with their consent—given, no doubt, half in reluctance, half in alarm—he set off to form a syndicate of £1,000,000 capitalization to buy oil properties in Illinois and Oklahoma. The fact that the directors proposed to share the risk with others indicates that they were not entirely convinced of the soundness of the project.

The syndicate was at first informal, but on June 20, 1912, it was organized into a company called The 's-Gravenhage Association.§ Since it was to purchase American properties, the capitalization of The 's-Gravenhage was fixed in dollars: $4,400,000, the equivalent of £1,000,000. Some 85% of this amount was subscribed at the outset, 51% by the Group, the balance by fifteen of its financial friends, chiefly London and Paris banking houses. The largest minority share (9.4%) was held by the Paris Rothschilds. Three individuals also participated in the syndicate; one of them was C. S. Gulbenkian, who held 1.7%, and was elected a director. The other directors were Frederick Lane and Deterding. The prospectus of this company indicated clearly just what its plans were. The new company's funds would be spent to purchase approximately 10,000 barrels a day of settled production in Illinois and Oklahoma: 368 wells producing 3,500 barrels a day in Illinois, and 341 Oklahoma wells producing 6,920 barrels a day.[8]

Selection of these properties and the taking of options on them was left to Richmond Levering and his associates. Kruisheer, who had made the original survey of the Deen properties in Oklahoma in 1909, was sent to New York early in June 1912 with instructions to buy up to 10,000 barrels a day of settled production at $400 a barrel. Two weeks later, the directors of The 's-Gravenhage Association decided at a meeting that they had perhaps acted too hastily. If, for instance,

§ 's-Gravenhage is the Dutch name for The Hague.

all the properties offered them by Levering were accepted subject only to verification of the production, what assurance would they have that the properties were sufficiently near each other to make the anticipated pipe line feasible? Kruisheer's instructions were accordingly altered—and just as well, for he had meanwhile discovered that the real and offered production differed considerably and that options which Levering was supposed to have in hand had in a great many cases not yet materialized. The future of the properties, particularly those in Illinois, was, Kruisheer felt, so dim that he "could not recommend these transactions either as agent or expert." [9] When one reflects that the Illinois wells were yielding on the average less than ten barrels a day, and the wells in Oklahoma only slightly more than 20 barrels per day, it is easy to see the validity of Kruisheer's conclusion.

The original instructions, ordering Kruisheer to take all production offered by Levering, were now modified to permit him to pick and choose and take into account the location of the wells and the condition in which he found them. At the same time Deterding was impatient to conclude a bargain of some sort, and remonstrated, "Of course some fields decline in production, but others increase; one has to start at the bottom in a new country and it is not always possible to get twenty shillings for the pound." [10]

In his anxiety to get things moving, Deterding decided to send out another agent, a commercial man to be senior in rank to Kruisheer but guided by the latter's technical knowledge. The new representative was Marcus Samuel Abrahams, a Samuel relative who had been along on the original trip to Baku in 1891 and who had in the years since been entrusted with many responsible missions. Abrahams was just back from Egypt where he had organized and launched the Group's new company there, Anglo-Egyptian Oilfields, Ltd.

2

The Roxana

ABRAHAMS, accompanied by his wife, arrived in New York in mid-July 1912. He promptly got in touch with John H. Harvey, a young man of twenty-five, who was vacationing at his home in Petrolea, Ontario. Harvey had grown up in the oil fields of southwestern Ontario where his father and uncle were producers and drilling contractors; he had gone to Egypt in 1910 to work for one of the companies there which had recently been acquired by the Shell Group, and had in this manner become acquainted with Abrahams. When Abrahams returned to England in 1912, Harvey had gone with him and was in Canada when he received word from Abrahams to meet him in New York. There their party was further increased by the addition of A. W. Lauer, an Oklahoma-born geologist connected with the new Shell company in Mexico, and H. B. Woodward,*a statistician formerly with Standard Oil, who had been engaged by Indian Refining Company. Kruisheer had, of course, been on hand to meet the Abrahamses when they arrived.

It was this small party which proceeded to Tulsa, arriving there late in July 1912. Expecting only the crudities of a jerry-built oil boom town, Abrahams and Harvey had been prepared for the worst. They took their own typewriter, in the event that Tulsa did not have such niceties, and Harvey even packed $2,500 in a money belt in case they couldn't find a reputable bank. They were, of course, pleasantly surprised by the Tulsa they found. For while some of the neighboring towns had been indifferent to accommodating the new industry, Tulsans had early set out to make their city the "Oil Capital of the World." They had built one hotel, then another, paved the streets, installed traction lines. Abrahams and his party put up at W. N. Robinson's new Tulsa Hotel, and these quarters (a few hotel rooms with the beds removed) for the next few months served as office space.[11]

All idea of buying the Illinois properties had been dropped by now. Abrahams had correctly interpreted Deterding's instructions to mean "buy in any case." He proceeded rapidly to examine the Oklahoma properties which Levering, who met him in Tulsa, and his scout, Chester J. Copmann,† had lined up. Kruisheer was still of the opinion that the prices asked were considerably more than the true value of the properties. As soon as he had arrived in Tulsa, Abrahams wrote Deterding, July 28, 1912:

> On my arrival in New York I was met by Mr. Kruisheer and we went thoroughly into the work before us, and he was not at all pleased at your having sent me and made up his mind to return to

* Woodward stayed in Tulsa, serving as head statistician of the new Roxana company until 1919.

† Son of Julius W. Copmann, mentioned in the last chapter. The younger Copmann served as head scout of the new Roxana company until 1919, when he entered the producing business on his own account.

Europe; but as I was aware that you wished to have his services in assisting me I did my best, and ultimately succeeded in inducing him to stay on and come with me down here.

I must say that although he is opposed to any oil concession in Oklahoma at the prices you have agreed upon he is doing all he can to help me bring matters to a conclusion.

As I wired you, we have got an option on the Bell properties having paid option money to the extent of $10,000 instead of $15,000 as they at first wanted. The net production is given as 2,500 barrels and the gross at about 3,300 barrels. We propose testing on Monday all the fields simultaneously and to do this Mr. Kruisheer will have to engage a proper independent staff and we have now secured a number of men he wants. These we have got through the Indian Refining Company's agent here who is doing all he can to help us.

I take it that if the production comes up to the stipulated one we will have to close with them, for a sum not exceeding $1,025,000. Of course we will try to pull this figure down.

Mr. Kruisheer has made up his mind that the price of $400 is far too much and I am afraid that I will never get him to agree with me that the properties are worth this amount. But as you have agreed in London that if the properties give the production that is stated by the owners and everything else in order, we are compelled to close the deal. As you told me before I left that we had to take some risk, we will see that the risk is as small as possible and in the event of losing on the "swings we will try to gain on the roundabouts." [12]

Levering, who was urging the purchase of the properties at the $400 price, took a far less charitable view of Kruisheer's objections, and secretly cabled Deterding: "Again I cannot too strongly urge upon you recall Kruisheer. He has antagonized everyone, is not supporting Abrahams, and his reports are not correct. . . . Standard oppose us violently, Indian Refining Company also attacked. I write you full particulars." [13]

Despite the marked differences of opinion, Abrahams went steadfastly ahead to carry out what he interpreted as being Deterding's wishes. In August, he bought the Bell properties mentioned in his letter, the purchase contract dated back to July 22. These were all small companies with scattered properties in the shallow-well fields near Bartlesville and Nowata. They were owned or controlled by John A. Bell, a prominent Pittsburgh coal man and banker, with whom the purchase was negotiated. The Bell companies were six in number: the Standard Oil & Gas Company of Oklahoma, the Signal Oil Company, the Kingbell Oil Company, the Parris Oil Company, the Minnehoff Oil Company, and the Tad Oil Company. Together they embraced about 12,500 acres of leases and had a total daily production when tested of 2,910 barrels.[14] Abrahams agreed to a purchase price of $1,-025,000, as he had mentioned in his letter, plus a further consideration of $50,000 to be paid when the titles were proved. The total price was, therefore, more than the maximum mentioned, but on the basis of reported production it was a little less than $400 per barrel.

On September 4, Abrahams purchased another set of producing properties from Louis C. Sands, vice president and general manager of the Oil Well Supply Company, Pittsburgh. The Sands properties consisted of the Paova and Helmick oil companies (660 and 80 acres, respectively) in the Cleveland field, the Quintuple Oil Company with 960 acres in the Bird Creek field, and 630 acres of property in the Dewey district, near Bartlesville, belonging to the Clephane Oil Company. The Paova acreage was the best, yielding 1,335 barrels a day when gauged; the Helmick produced 750 barrels. Both these companies operated in the Cleveland field, where production by 1912 was declining rapidly. The Quintuple produced only 95 barrels a day, and Clephane 13 barrels. Accordingly, the total price paid was not large—$700,000, plus a commission of $14,000. The money Abrahams used to pay for these two sets of properties was remitted from London.[15]

The next step was to organize a company to hold these new acquisitions. Before he had left New York, Abrahams had visited the Group's attorneys there, the Cravath firm. They had discussed in general how the companies should be set up, and on leaving he had asked for recommendations as to whom he should engage as attorneys in Tulsa. Cravath's had intended to refer him to Herbert Mason of Tulsa, but by mistake Abrahams was given the name of Rice & Lyons.[16] As a result, Rice & Lyons received "over the transom" a new client of whom they had never even heard. Lyons, in a magazine article many years later, said that Richmond Levering proceeded to enlighten the partners as to the identity of their new client. He also went on to tell how the new company was named:

> It was decided that we should proceed to organize an Oklahoma corporation, to take the assignments. The question of the name of the corporation delayed the matter for two or three days, and finally we accepted an invitation to visit the hotel suite, and had the pleasure of having tea with our clients and of meeting the wife of Marcus S. Abrahams. It developed that the invitation really proceeded from the desire of the lady to interview us as to the name of the new corporation. When we told her that practically the only limitation

on the selection of a name was the matter of the use of the same name by a corporation which had already been organized, she immediately showed signs of pleasure and animation. She then stated that she had been given the privilege of naming the new corporation, and she desired the name to be "Roxana", informing us that this was the name of the wife of Alexander the Great. We proceeded to call the office of the Secretary of State, on long distance, and immediately secured the information that the name had not been used for an Oklahoma corporation, and that night articles of incorporation duly signed went forward, providing "that the name of this corporation shall be Roxana Petroleum Company."[17]

"This must be quite a relief to the boys in the office in the Robinson Hotel Building," commented *National Petroleum News*, "as they have been called anything from the Asiatic Petroleum Company to the Arabian Petroleum Company." [18] The new Roxana Petroleum Company of Oklahoma held its first meeting and election of officers in the offices of Rice & Lyons, at Tulsa, on the afternoon of October 1, 1912. Temporarily, Rice was elected president and Lyons, vice president. Harvey, whom Abrahams had brought along to handle the details of day-to-day affairs, was made secretary and treasurer.

In New York, the Cravath firm had proceeded to organize, at Abrahams' instructions, the Roxana Petroleum Company (New York) which received its certificate of incorporation on September 12, 1912, and held its first meeting on September 28. Abrahams became president of the Roxana of New York, which was set up as a holding company for Roxana of Oklahoma. Vice president of the New York company was N. G. M. Luykx, who had meanwhile arrived to open up a one-room office for the new company at 81 Fulton Street, New York. Luykx had held responsible positions with the Group in the Orient and when Abrahams returned to England in November 1912 with his mission completed, Luykx succeeded him as president of the Roxana of New York.

In Oklahoma, both Rice and Lyons resigned their positions in the Roxana of Oklahoma as soon as the organizational preliminaries were over, and Clinton D. Martin, who had been with Waters-Pierce Oil Company in Mexico and made the acquaintance of Shell men there, was chosen president of the new Oklahoma company.‡ Benjamin F. Rice, of Rice & Lyons, was made vice president, a

‡ Waters-Pierce had been part of the old Standard Oil Company until the dissolution of 1911, after which time it operated as an independent company. The selection of Martin gave rise to all sorts of reports in the oil trade papers of 1912–1913, the most frequent of them to the effect that Shell had secretly purchased Waters-Pierce.[19]

position which he held for the next five years. Harvey, as secretary and treasurer, continued to bear most of the responsibility for the new concern until Luykx arrived in Tulsa in March 1913 to take over as president of Roxana of Oklahoma, succeeding Martin.

Meanwhile, the consolidation of the companies that had been purchased could not take place as rapidly as had been hoped, as the legal status of many of them was far from perfect. The Sands companies (Paova, Helmick, Quintuple, Clephane) were taken over by the new Roxana of Oklahoma; but the Bell companies continued to be operated under their former names until the spring of 1913, when their tangled affairs were finally straightened out and Roxana could at last consolidate them into a single organization.

The late Robert T. Swaine, senior partner of the Cravath firm at the time of his death, gives in his history of the Cravath firm some idea of the extent of this legal snarl:

> Abrahams came to the Cravath office for assistance in carrying out the acquisitions. . . . Most of the properties covered by the contracts were held by many small corporations organized under the laws of various states with scant regard for statutory formalities; and the vendors expected, irrespective of the formal provisions of the contracts, to consummate the sales and get their money by transferring the stocks of these corporations. . . . For several months after Abrahams' visit, there was an almost continuous snarl with the different vendors, who had no patience with the "technicalities" that were being raised and were delaying payment of the purchase prices. Abrahams, however, was understanding, particularly when it appeared that the titles of many substantial properties were incurably defective and that in many cases the vendors' interests in so-called "departmental leases" exceeded the 4,800-acre limit imposed by Federal statute.
> Much of the richest oil land in Oklahoma was in the old Indian Territory, and the oil rights were represented by leases made by the Indian Bureau of the Department of the Interior, as guardian for the Indian owners. To prevent monopolization of the leases, and with Standard Oil particularly in mind, Congress had prohibited anyone from owning any interest in more than 4,800 acres of Indian leases. The law was literally construed by the Interior Department, with complete disregard of corporate entities, so that a single stockholder owning a small fraction of the stock of a corporation which itself owned Indian leases covering 4,800 acres disqualified every other corporation in which he had any stock interest from lawfully owning such leases. The problems presented by this legislation and the regulations under it created almost hopeless difficulties in the titles of the

properties being acquired by the Royal Dutch-Shell Group, and required disposal of all Indian leases in the acquired properties in excess of the 4,800-acre limit.

It soon became clear that the primary concern of the Department of the Interior was whether the firm's clients were dummies for the Standard Oil companies; the Secretary was assured that they were not. As a result of the firm's efforts, some of the absurdities of the Department's interpretation of the Federal statutes affecting departmental leases were relaxed, but the statutes and regulations under them continued to be a serious problem.[20]

With these difficulties finally out of the way,§ Roxana of Oklahoma settled down to the life of an oil producer—drilling new wells on the properties acquired, maintaining field properties, producing and selling crude oil. The crude went wherever it would bring the best price: to the big pipe line companies, or to the smaller independent refiners who were often willing to pay a premium. The National Refining Company was one of Roxana's best customers.

Modest offices (six rooms) were rented in the Robinson Arcade Building, Tulsa, and there Harvey, W. H. Mainwaring, the office manager, and their young assistant, C. B. Singleton, attended to the routine of recording the amount of oil sold, collecting payment for it, and meeting the payroll. Harvey acted as liaison between this small office and the superintendents in the field; actual management of individual properties was left pretty much to the superintendents, who had a good deal of discretionary authority. Since the company did not at the moment undertake any ambitious expansion program, it had sizeable net balances from the sale of oil; these sums were remitted to London in the form of dividends.[22]

These profits did not entirely disprove Kruisheer's adverse predictions. Roxana's production of crude oil was 443,000 barrels for the last three months of 1912, with a resulting net profit of $144,000.

§ The Parris, Kingbell, Standard Oil & Gas of Oklahoma, and Signal companies (total cost $1,075,000) were turned over to Roxana of Oklahoma in October 1913 for $950,000 worth of the latter's stock. Assignment of the departmental leases was approved by the Secretary of the Interior on May 6, 1914, and soon after attorneys were instructed to file dissolution proceedings for these companies. Roxana of Oklahoma capital stock, then owned (except for directors' qualifying shares) entirely by Roxana of New York, amounted at this time to $1,000,000 par value—the balance of $50,000 worth of stock having been issued to Abrahams in exchange for the Sands properties which cost him $714,000. Roxana of New York's stock was owned by The 's-Gravenhage Association. The Shell Group in 1913 arranged to buy out the minority shareholders in The 's-Gravenhage Association, giving them Shell Transport & Trading shares in exchange, and ownership of The 's-Gravenhage was thereafter vested in Anglo-Saxon.[21]

During 1913, production totalled 723,000 barrels and yielded a profit of $261,000. But in 1914, a sizeable drop was noticeable—505,000 barrels and net profit down to $88,000. This small return on the sale of half a million barrels of oil is in part accounted for by the fact that the Oklahoma oil market fell apart during 1914, the result of the tremendous production of the new Cushing field. The average price for Oklahoma oil, $1.03 a barrel in 1913, dropped to 55¢ a barrel in 1914. By late 1914, as we shall soon see, the company was bestirring itself to remedy this unfavorable position.

When Mrs. Abrahams and Harvey had been discussing the proposed name of the new company, they had been delighted to find in the back of a dictionary that the name Roxana signified from its early Persian origin "Dawn of a New Day." [23] And indeed it was. Even though the "Old Properties" were later sold because they proved uneconomic to operate, they had provided the much-needed starting point. What is probably the correct view of the purchases was supplied by Deterding in a jubilant letter to Loudon in December 1912, just after Abrahams' return: "At last we *are* in America! Let us hope that this will be the start of a business as good as that in Rumania and the other places." [24]

3

A New Day Dawns: Cushing, Healdton, Yale

Up to 1912, few of the larger oil companies had entered the producing business in Oklahoma. For the most part, they had contented themselves with watching developments and running in pipe lines to buy crude from the independent producers. Shell's active entry through the foundation of the new Roxana company was, therefore, welcomed by most of the independent oil men. The Roxana was a guarantee of increased competition against the Standard companies, but even more important from the Oklahoma oil man's point of view, Roxana was a prospective customer for producing properties. As for being "foreigners," the Roxana men were little different from their neighbors in the Oklahoma oil business. From every corner of the United States and most of the countries of Europe, thousands of men of all kinds had streamed in, attracted by that great magnet responsible for all boom towns—a chance to get rich. Carl Barker, who had gone to Oklahoma during the early days of oil development and joined the Roxana in 1916, recalled thirty years later, "We were all foreigners. Everybody there was from Alabama (as I was), or New England, Oregon, Ohio, Pennsylvania—places which in those days of slower travel made us almost as far from home, and just as 'foreign' to Oklahoma ways, as men who came from across the ocean." [25]

The necessity for reporting to a head office nearly 6,000 miles away was, however, a distinct disadvantage to the early Roxana organization. Particularly was this true when it came to taking leases or purchasing new properties. Deterding took a keen interest in all that went on, and quite understandably wanted an opportunity to approve or disapprove every major move before it was made. Even though he was accustomed to moving rapidly, he did not at the outset have any conception of the speed with which leases changed hands in Oklahoma. There, bidding for leases was a highly competitive, market-place affair wholly unlike anything the Group had encountered in the Indies, Mexico, Venezuela, Egypt, or the Near East, where oil lands (in common with other mining enterprises) were considered public property and permits to work them were obtained in much more leisurely fashion, generally by the grant of a concession from some public authority. Eventually, of course, Deterding came to have a clearer understanding of the radically different situation in Oklahoma, but meanwhile the necessity for obtaining advance approval from London cost the young company a great deal in delay and forfeited opportunity and became a constant source of frustration to Luykx and his lieutenants. [26]

In general, the new Roxana company was well received in American oil circles. Warren Platt's *National Petroleum News*, originally founded to espouse the cause of the "independents," treated the newcomer with fairness and even cordiality. So did other papers concerned with the oil trade. Patrick C. Boyle's publications offered the chief exception to this generally friendly reception. Boyle, long a partisan of the old Standard Oil companies, apparently was undecided as to whether he should welcome or scold the new Roxana company in his daily Oil City, Pa., *Derrick* and his weekly *Oil & Gas Journal*, published at Tulsa. The result was a bewildering series of articles and editorials in these papers. In one issue, the Roxana and the whole Royal Dutch-Shell Group would be dismissed with a contemptuous laugh, "There would be the difference between them [Standard, *et al.*] and the Dutch-Shell that exists between a real merchant and a sutler." [27] Another article, sometimes in the very same issue, might be a welcome which had about it every appearance of sincerity: "Its presence here is welcome, and will be still more so if it can assist in making marketing conditions for the producer better." [28] In yet a third vein, lead editorials denounced "The Foreign Petroleum Menace." [29] This was, perhaps only coincidentally, the attitude which the Standard companies adopted towards the Roxana, an attitude which still baffled Deterding as late as 1919: "It seems to me that amongst their other peculiarities the Standard Oil Company possess one of inconsistency. They intimate in one instance, to you or to the world at large, that the Roxana is asleep and a 'dead horse', and in another instance that they consider the presence of the Roxana and their activities in the United States as an invasion of what they like to call their hunting grounds." [30]

So, with a generally favorable reception and only an occasional catcall from the balcony, the Roxana set about the business of becoming a leading Mid-Continent oil producer. Clearly, the small production which Abrahams had bought in 1912 was only a start. What the company was ready for, and now needed, was a large purchase that would do for Roxana what the acquisition of California Oilfields, Ltd., had done for the Shell Company of California.

When, late in 1910 and early in 1911, Deterding and Levering had been laying their ambitious plans for a joint company for the United States, Levering had been quick to mention the possibility of their being joined by the Gulf company. As we saw, the Pittsburgh Mellons, who controlled Gulf, declined to have any part of that venture. But they had indicated that they were willing to sell out. From the past history of their oil ventures, this was reasonable to expect, for the Mellons had formed an oil company in Pennsylvania and operated it from 1889 to 1895, selling out to Standard when they saw a chance to make a good profit.[31] They had taken control of the Gulf properties, started as the J. M. Guffey Petroleum Company, solely because it seemed the only course by which they could salvage the large loans they had made to Guffey. By 1912, the Mellons had put a decade of hard work and many millions of dollars into the Gulf company. The affairs of this concern had as a result taken a marked turn for the better, although in 1912 Gulf had not yet paid a dividend.

Ever since their dealings with Samuel in 1903, the Mellons had been on friendly terms with the Shell Group and it was on this friendly basis that proposals were made early in 1913 to acquire the Mellon properties. Deterding suggested that a $60,000,000 syndicate, headed by Kuhn, Loeb & Co., be formed in New York to acquire the Gulf properties, Roxana, and La Corona (the Group's new company in Mexico). The Royal Dutch, he proposed, would subscribe $10,000,000 of preferred stock and would undertake management of the new company in return for 10% of the profits.

There were immediate objections to this deal from both sides. The Royal Dutch directorate, somewhat appalled at the very rapid rate of the company's expansion during the past five years, wondered if this might not perhaps be the straw which would break the camel's back—if Gulf's production had declined so rapidly once before, what assurance did they have now that the same thing would not happen again? For their part, the Mellons objected to giving Deterding full control of the new enterprise, since he had indicated that the Group would be willing to subscribe only one-sixth of the total capital. The Mellons were willing to sell, they said, but instead of a syndicate arrangement they wanted "a clean deal for the outright purchase of the company." [32]

Then, during 1913, the sound management of the Mellons began to show results. The Gulf company had a production that year of 10½ million barrels of crude oil, and refined almost 2,000,000 barrels more; it built retail marketing facilities; had assets of some $42,-500,000; and declared its first dividend of $2.50 a share. With each passing month thereafter, it became apparent to the Mellons that their Gulf company was increasing in value. Then, with the onset of the war, oil prices looked up. The deal was off, but even two years later Deterding could not help mourning: "As regards the Gulf Company, we would have made an arrangement with them long ago, but unfortunately, as I told Mr. Mellon some time since, they suffer from knowing too much of oil. . . ." [33]

Gulf was about the only Mid-Continent company which seemed susceptible to selling out. With the acquisition of Gulf no longer a serious possibility, Roxana in 1914 set about the slower, more painstaking method of buying smaller producing properties piece by piece. And, as soon as a proper staff could be assembled, it would also embark on the more hazardous business of hunting for oil fields instead of buying them.

First of all, Roxana needed a competent head geologist who knew the Mid-Continent area. Richard A. Conkling, a young man who had just taken an advanced geology degree at the University of Chicago and had signed on with the Barber Asphalt Co., the Group's partner in Venezuela, was hired and sent to The Hague for six months. He arrived in Tulsa on January 1, 1915, to organize a geological department for Roxana.[34]

Geologists were just then beginning to be accepted gingerly in the Oklahoma oil fields. Up until then prospecting and drilling had been almost entirely in the hands of "practical" men, old-time wildcatters who had little use and less respect for the men they dubbed "rock hounds." Their skepticism, it must be admitted, was not entirely unfounded, for surface geology methods could indicate only where oil might be found. The final test was still the drill. The practical man asked why waste all this time—why not drill in the first place? As long as producing depths were shallow and a well could be drilled for $3,000 to $5,000, the old-timer had a point. While the scientific man was still investigating, the practical man could lease land and drill a well for very little more than the cost of maintaining a geological party in the field. Geologists came into their own with the advent of the larger companies into the business of exploring for oil. Unlike the independent wildcatter, the big companies felt less inclined to put their trust in guesswork.

Cushing

A new field which Roxana's geologists could not ignore was near Cushing and had been brought in by Tom B. Slick, a wildcatter, in March 1912. Because of the substantial production of individual wells (the first produced at the rate of 400 barrels a day), the high quality of the oil, and the ease of getting at it (it was only about 2,300 feet below the surface), a major oil boom got under way in the Cushing area during 1913. Late in November of that year, the boom gained new impetus when Prairie Oil & Gas put down a well and found the much more prolific Bartlesville sand at 2,600 feet. This brought on a period of large gushers and tremendous production. Wells were drilled in frantic haste, faster than tankage could be built to hold their production, and much faster than pipe lines could be extended into the booming new field.

The result was heartbreaking. The year 1913 had seen the price for Oklahoma oil improve greatly, reaching an average of $1.03 a barrel. But with their tremendous local "overproduction," the Cushing operators succeeded in literally breaking the market. By September

1914, the price of oil in the field had dropped to 55¢ and it kept falling until a low of 40¢ was reached in February 1915. "Every gallon of storage in the field is filled and the tanks are slopping over," said a report in the *Wall Street Journal* in the spring of 1914, "and from 3,000 to 5,000 barrels are going to waste daily." In addition to the wasted oil, Cushing was a prolific producer of gas, and billions of cubic feet of it were blown into the air—an irreparable loss, to say nothing of the danger caused by gas collecting in hollows in damp weather to become a serious source of fires and explosions.[35] To prevent some of this waste of gas and oil, and to try to save the Cushing producers from the ruinous results of their own actions, the Oklahoma Corporation Commission intervened—not too successfully—in one of the first attempts at legalized proration.*

In January 1915, still deeper production was found in the northern part of the Cushing field, the effect of which was felt by April when Cushing's production reached its all-time peak, estimated at between 300,000 and 330,000 barrels a day. That year, Cushing produced 49,000,000 barrels of oil, 17% of the total world production for 1915.[37]

It was into this atmosphere that a tall, genial, Dutch geologist with the impressive name of W. A. J. M. van Waterschoot van der Gracht came in the spring of 1915. The Group had at last decided to take the plunge and investigate other Oklahoma properties with the idea of purchasing them. Van der Gracht, then in his early forties, was a graduate lawyer, geologist, and mining engineer; he had headed the Netherlands Geological Service and acquired an excellent reputation as a scientific prospector for minerals. In Oklahoma, he was to be the Group's observer. Some of the reports which he made survive and give an excellent impression of his intelligence, thoroughness, keen powers of observation, and gifts as a writer.

Van der Gracht had been in Oklahoma only a very short time,

---

* The U. S. Bureau of Mines estimated that during 1913 no less than 300 million cubic feet of gas a day were blown into the air at Cushing, a total of 100 billion cubic feet for the year, enough to have supplied New York City's entire domestic fuel requirements. At market rates then current this wasted gas was worth $75,000 a day, while the oil produced was valued at only $25,000.[36] Oil men today wince at the recollection of such happenings. The chief villains were not men but laws. The "rule of capture," which made oil the property of those who first got it above ground, placed a premium on speed and enabled a single operator to call the tune in the development of a whole field. Anti-trust laws forbade action "in concert," even for commendable purposes, and thus helped provide a kind of competition which was hardly in the public interest. It was to take two decades of agitation and public education to bring about the legal changes necessary for intelligent conservation measures.

when, on May 15, 1915, Roxana acquired the Yarhola leases at Cushing from the Devonian Oil Company and Robert E. Fuller. Fuller had taken these leases, amounting in total to 320 acres, from two Creek Indian girls named Linda and Maley Yarhola in February 1912. Not having the money to drill, he made an agreement with Devonian to drill a well for a half interest in the acreage; this share was later increased from one-half to five-sixths as Devonian continued to advance money for subsequent development work.[38]

The first well drilled was on the Maley Yarhola lease (it produced, in general, better than the Linda Yarhola) and came in at 1,360 feet, with a daily production of 75 barrels. Deepened to the Jones sand, it made 5,000,000 cubic feet of gas daily; and deepened still further to the Wheeler sand (2,090 feet) it made 22,000,000 cubic feet of gas a day. The gas production was so large that it was decided to complete the well as a gas producer and for almost one entire winter this single well furnished Oklahoma City with gas. By September 1914, 13 wells had been drilled by Devonian on the two Yarhola leases, and were producing 8,200 barrels daily. At the time of Roxana's purchase of the Yarhola leases in May 1915, there were 36 wells, 28 in the Bartlesville sand and 8 in the less prolific Layton formation, producing a total of 8,500 barrels a day. With 36 wells producing little more than 13 had six months earlier, it is not difficult to see why the owners thought it an auspicious time to sell. It looked as if the decline of the Cushing field, prematurely announced on two other occasions, was at last under way.[39]

For a total purchase price of $1,823,750 Roxana acquired the stock of The Fuller Company, which Fuller had organized to hold his one-sixth interest in the Yarhola leases; Devonian's five-sixths interest (but not the Devonian company); and the Yarhola Pipe Line Company, a 4-inch line about 25 miles long connecting the tank farm (nineteen 55,000-barrel tanks) with a loading rack on the Santa Fe railroad.† The purchase money was supplied from abroad: $840,000 by the Royal Dutch Company; $560,000 by The Shell Transport & Trading Company; $400,000 by Anglo-Saxon Petroleum Company; and $23,750 by The 's-Gravenhage Association.[40]

The transfer of the properties could not take place immediately, for the owners, Linda and Maley Yarhola, were wards of the government, necessitating approval of the transaction by the Department of the

---

† The Fuller Company was dissolved as soon as transfer of title to the property was completed but the Yarhola Pipe Line Company was kept alive and became the ancestor of the present Shell Pipe Line Corporation.

Interior's Bureau of Indian Affairs. The purchase contract had specified that the vendors were to be allowed two months to procure approval for the transfer; if title were not delivered in that time, the deal was off. The Indian agent at Muskogee raised objections, advised the Interior Department against approving the assignments, and "insisted on individual affidavits of all the shareholders of the Royal Dutch-Shell combine!" [41] To account for these queer proceedings, Van der Gracht mentioned that "we have strong circumstantial evidence that the persistent rumors are true, and that the Devonian people received a more attractive offer from the Gulf Company and therefore would not be sorry to have our deal fall through." [42]

Thomas D. Lyons, of Rice & Lyons, went to Washington "to 'pep up' the proceedings" [43] and the necessary approval was finally secured on July 13, just two days before the deadline set in the contract. Immediately Roxana took possession of its new Cushing property and began to clean out wells, install pumps, and take other measures to increase the production which had fallen sadly since it had been gauged May 7, just prior to the sale. Production had in fact fallen so markedly that it was suspected that the sellers had "shot" the wells just prior to the gauge, in order to make them produce temporarily at a much greater rate. Word went around that Roxana had been "hooked" again. [44]

If this were so,‡ it was Roxana's turn to have the last laugh, for

---

‡ A feeling that the company had a poor bargain was no doubt heightened by the knowledge that it could have had a much greater tract in the Cushing field, earlier and for less money. In August 1913, when the Cushing field was still in its first flush of development, Tom B. Slick, an early lessor, offered Roxana 1,700 acres, his Cushing property, for $5,000,000. Deterding countered with an offer of $1,500,000. Slick then offered to sell the part then actually producing (about 1,000 acres) for $3,000,000. Luykx, who had succeeded in getting an option on the Slick properties, recommended that the company pay $4,000,000 for Slick's entire interest. This was not done, and the option was allowed to expire on August 3. On September 1, Slick made another proposal. He would (1) sell the whole of his proven acreage (1,725 acres) for $2,000,000, or (2) all of it except two leases for $1,800,000, or (3) all his proven acreage, plus some 15,000 acres of wildcat acreage, for $2,500,000. Luykx pressed for a quick decision, but Deterding replied that obligations in California (they had just purchased California Oilfields, Ltd.) were heavy and that no money would be available for the Slick proposition. But on October 15, he authorized Luykx to offer Slick $1,750,000 for all his properties. Two months later all of the Shell people were congratulating themselves on not having bought, for "according to the Oklahoma Geological Report, production is now only 1,000 b/d." The wisdom of not buying seemed confirmed, when late in December 1913, Slick's attempt to sell his acreage to Carter Oil Company, a Standard of New Jersey subsidiary, for $1,500,000 fell through, and he then invited Roxana to make him an offer. [45] Unable to find a buyer, Slick was obliged to hold onto these properties which became the basis of the Slick oil fortune. These negotiations show better than a million generalities the extreme difficulty of deciding whether or not to buy in a new field.

Cushing was the field of many producing horizons. In addition to the Layton, Wheeler, and Bartlesville sands already mentioned, two other less productive layers, the Jones and Skinner sands, had been found. Late in 1915, the Gypsy Oil Company, whose properties were near the Yarhola leases, brought in a well in the Tucker sand below the level of the Bartlesville sand, opening another new producing horizon at Cushing. During 1916, Roxana deepened most of its Bartlesville sand wells to the Tucker sand, and the flagging production, 5,000–6,000 barrels a day, rose to considerably more than 10,000 barrels daily at the height of the Tucker "flush." [46]

Best of all, prices improved. In July 1915, crude was still selling for 40¢ a barrel; in August, the posted price advanced to 65¢; in September it was 80¢; in November it hit $1.00; and by the end of December, Cushing oil was bringing $1.20 a barrel, three times what it had been selling for when Roxana purchased the Yarhola leases. The Yarhola leases produced three million barrels for Roxana during the next three years and a total of 5,336,000 barrels before they were traded to Sinclair in 1939.

Healdton

In the midst of the excitement over Cushing, the Healdton field, near Ardmore in south central Oklahoma, went almost unnoticed by the world at large. Healdton was located some two hundred miles south and west of the Tulsa area where the other major Oklahoma oil discoveries had thus far occurred. This remoteness from the rest of the Oklahoma oil fraternity was probably in some measure responsible for Healdton's slow start. An oil prospector named Palmer is supposed to have drilled the first well in the Healdton field, back before the turn of the century when no policy for leasing Indian lands had yet been adopted. As he could not obtain a valid lease, Palmer plugged up his well,§ kept his secret, and died before he could obtain a lease. [47]

Then, in 1907, a young man named Roy M. Johnson moved to nearby Ardmore and started a newspaper there. One of the townsmen, Captain Francis B. Cooke, a retired sea captain, interested Johnson in inspecting seepages he had found. In company with a young man named Edward Galt and his relative, A. T. McGhee, Johnson formed a partnership for the purpose of securing leases. In their lease buying,

§ The location, it is said, is what was later known as the McClure lease. This was part of the acreage acquired by Roxana.

which was always handicapped by lack of funds, they soon ran into two Ardmore real estate men, Sam A. Apple and Wirt Franklin, who had already leased a sizeable block of acreage.

The five joined forces and organized the Plains Development Company. They were unable to do any drilling, for it was only with the greatest of difficulty that they kept their lease rentals paid. Their chances for attracting outside capital were not improved when the Santa Fe railroad drilled a small well near Ardmore and found oil of low gravity, fit only for fuel, and not considered "refinery crude" by Mid-Continent refining standards of the day. Finally, in January 1913 they signed a contract with J. M. Critchlow of Titusville, Pennsylvania, who owned a drilling rig and agreed to drill a well in exchange for one-half the acreage they had assembled.[48]

The property was "checkerboarded," with every other parcel being given to Critchlow, who organized the Red River Oil Company to take title to his holding. His first well, completed in August 1913 at a depth of 950 feet, had an initial daily production of 25 to 75 barrels.* It was the small cost of drilling, rather than the high production of the early wells or the outstanding quality of the oil, that brought outside operators into the Healdton field during 1913 and 1914. Cushing wells were costing $15,000 to $20,000 to drill, but a well at Healdton rarely cost more than $4,000. As drilling went forward at Healdton, bigger wells were encountered, some with initial productions of as high as 4,000 and 5,000 barrels a day, and at this news, operators of greater substance put in an appearance.[49]

Among the first of these was Alexander Mackay, of Dundee, Scotland, head of Mackay, Irons & Company, a firm of chartered accountants. Mackay was also a substantial investor in other ventures. In 1882, he and a number of Scottish associates had organized the Matador Land & Cattle Company which held more than a million acres of ranching land in Texas and had what was reputed to be the largest herd of Herefords in the world. Mackay had further investments in Canada, and citrus and cattle ranches in Florida. Another oil investor attracted to the Healdton scene was R. Leicester Harmsworth, who with his elder brothers, Lord Northcliffe and Lord Rothermere, had made a fortune from England's first mass-circulation newspapers. Harmsworth had dabbled in the oil business before, and had held a

---

* This vagueness of production records was typical not only of the first but of most of subsequent Healdton wells. Production figures through 1915 should be regarded only as indicative.

large interest in two of the companies which went into the Group's
Anglo-Egyptian Oilfields, Ltd., when it was organized in 1911.[50]

Critchlow needed money to carry on the drilling of his wells and,
more important, to build tankage in which to store the oil being
produced. Low prices prevailed in 1914 for all Oklahoma oil as a
result of the overproduction at Cushing, so it was only prudent to
put crude in storage rather than sell it at ridiculously low prices.
Mackay and Harmsworth advanced new working capital to Critchlow's Red River company, and were given in return a 49% interest
in the Dundee Petroleum Company, a new corporation, organized
with Critchlow as president, to be successor to the Red River Oil
Company. During 1914, two other companies with holdings in the
Healdton field were organized by Mackay and Harmsworth, the
Samoset Petroleum Company and the Alma Oil Company.

Yet another partner to these interests made his appearance during
1914—Robert Watchorn, who had started life as a Derbyshire coal
miner, emigrated to America, where he had become, successively, the
first secretary of the United Mine Workers of America, a Pennsylvania politician, and then United States Commissioner of Immigra-
tion. In 1909, he went to California where he was made treasurer of
the Union Oil Company, a job he resigned in 1913. Coming to Oklahoma, he had become interested in the Healdton properties, and spent
some $150,000 buying up the interests of some of the older stock-
holders. Mackay and Harmsworth, who owned two-thirds of the
Samoset company, in the fall of 1914 gave Watchorn a five-year
contract to manage it and made him president. By the spring of 1915,
Watchorn owned, or was in a position to buy, 51% of the Dundee,
50% of the Alma, and one-third of the Samoset. It was at this point,
on March 18, 1915, that Watchorn, Mackay, and Harmsworth agreed
to sell out their Healdton holdings to the Royal Dutch-Shell Group.[51]

By this time, the Healdton field had become famous for the complicated trades and agreements which had transpired there, but it is
doubtful whether there had been any agreement with terms as complicated and confusing as the one which was finally concluded
between these principals and the Royal Dutch-Shell Group on
September 9, 1915, six months after the original contract was supposed
to have been in force. The deal which had been negotiated with
Watchorn, Mackay, and Harmsworth in March 1915, with Dr. Erb
acting as chief negotiator for the Shell Group, called for sale of half
the Healdton assets of the Dundee, Samoset, and Alma companies

to the Group, plus a half interest in some 12,000 acres of wildcat leases, for the sum of $1,500,000 cash, the proceeds to go 50% to Mackay and Harmsworth and 50% to Watchorn. The other half of these companies' assets were to be assigned to a new company not yet organized, which would be capitalized at $3,000,000, one-half the capital stock to go to the Shell Group, a quarter to Mackay and Harmsworth, and a quarter to Watchorn.[52] But neither the Group nor the Mackay-Harmsworth interests were entirely satisfied with the bargain they had made. The Shell Group representatives did not like the complicated nature of the deal. They would have liked to see it simplified, and also, of course, the purchase price reduced some-what. For their part, Mackay and Harmsworth were apprehensive lest they receive less than the fair value of their properties; each week that passed brought successful new wells which increased the potential value of the Healdton field.

Not long after the March deal, Dr. Erb and Van der Gracht went to see Watchorn, and came away with a new proposal: Watchorn would sell out his entire interest for $1,100,000 cash and eliminate himself from participation in the proposed new company. Mackay, on the other hand, was much more interested in stock than cash, for he wanted to be assured of a share in any increase in value of the Healdton properties, should they turn out to be, as he expected, of greater value than had been assumed early in 1915.

To discuss these new proposals Watchorn went to London in June, where Mackay and Harmsworth, apparently with the Group's con-currence, made the proposal that *they* buy out Watchorn's interest in the three companies. Back again in the United States, Watchorn and Van der Gracht spent a fruitless month of negotiation. It is pointless to bewilder the reader with details of further proposals, which by this time had several of the principals confused. Watchorn and Van der Gracht were carrying on discussions in Oklahoma; the Shell Group, Mackay, and Harmsworth in London. By the end of July, Van der Gracht, who was in charge of the negotiations on the American end, was so thoroughly confused himself that he made up a memorandum, still in the company files, in which he attempted to clarify the matter in his own mind.

Finally Watchorn broke the log jam by suggesting that they return to the original March deal, with the modification that he would be bought out entirely. His asking price was reduced to $915,000 cash, and it was on this basis that a contract was at last executed on September 9, 1915, retroactive to March 18. It provided that Watchorn would sell to Roxana his stockholdings in the Alma, Samoset, and Dundee companies. These shares were to be turned over to Mackay and Harmsworth, who would then have 100% of the stock of each company and could proceed to sell these companies' properties to Roxana in exchange for Roxana stock.

This new stock was issued late in 1915. On December 27 of that year, Roxana's capitalization was increased from $1,000,000 to $5,000,-000, a figure which more accurately reflected the value of the company's holdings. The new stock thus created (together with shares already held) was issued so as to give the Group a total holding in Roxana of 73%, and Mackay, Harmsworth, and their associates 27%.

As a result of this complicated trading, Roxana acquired 840 acres of producing property in the heart of the Healdton field with 59 wells and a daily production of about 10,000 barrels. Money to finance Roxana's share of the purchase and to pay for the development work going forward at the time was supplied by the Group, which remitted some $2,500,000 to the Oklahoma company during the summer of 1915.

The Healdton field was then in the period of its most active development. "It is," wrote Van der Gracht in November 1915, "the busiest spot in Oklahoma oildom, due to the activity in drilling, in the construction of steel tankage, and in the building of pipe lines. About 50 strings of tools are running in the field, and the potential production is now exceeding 100,000 barrels from about 425 wells." [53] At Healdton, Roxana had done what it had failed to at Cushing; it had got in in time to share in the full tide of the field's flush production. Healdton was never as big a field as Cushing, but at the end of 1950 it had produced a total of 213 million barrels of oil to place it 26th in all-time rank among the nation's oil fields. Shell's share of the production had during this time come to 33.7 million barrels, about one-sixth of the total. The peak of the Healdton flush production came during the years 1916–1918; in each of these years, the field accounted for more than 4% of America's total crude oil production. And because it did not decline as rapidly as some other of the Oklahoma fields, Healdton served as a nucleus of Roxana's production in the years ahead.

By the end of 1915, Deterding could finally report that the goal he had set himself in 1912—15,000 barrels a day of Mid-Continent production—had not only been achieved, but exceeded. Roxana's daily crude oil output was then in the neighborhood of 18,000 barrels. The work of the geological staff in its search for new oil-producing areas was also under way in earnest. By 1916 the company had nearly 30,000 acres of exploratory leases in Oklahoma, Kansas, and Texas.[54] That year saw two million-dollar leasing deals.

The first was the acquisition from Watchorn of 1,720 acres of unproven leases (called the Otoe leases, in Pawnee County) on a "no oil, no pay" basis. If oil were found, promissory notes for $1,000,-000 which had been placed in escrow were to be delivered over to Watchorn; if a total of 10,000,000 barrels of oil were recovered from these properties he was to receive a further $1,000,000. But if the test wells proved unsuccessful, Roxana could abandon the Otoe leases and the notes would be cancelled.[55] The Bert Diamond well, Roxana's first to be drilled by the rotary method,[56] was a failure and the leases were returned to Watchorn. Oil production was later discovered in the area, and the nearest town is today called Watchorn, Oklahoma.

The other million-dollar deal turned out better. In July 1916, the company acquired for $1,000,000 cash 480 acres of leases near Yale, about ten miles north of Cushing, from the Fortuna Oil Company which had recently been organized by Frank Buttram and D. W. Ohern, two young Oklahoma Geological Survey geologists who were entering the oil business on their own. Buttram and Ohern had drilled one rather inconclusive well. Luykx was not enthusiastic about the Yale property, but Van der Gracht was convinced by the geological indications and prevailed upon Deterding to make the purchase. Van der Gracht's judgment was vindicated when further production was found at Yale in November of that year; but the difference of opinion between himself and Luykx over the deal was the beginning of a permanent rift between the two men. The Yale property, modest enough at first, was in the end highly profitable, for five producing horizons were eventually discovered. And the million dollars purchase money gave Buttram and Ohern the financial push they needed to start them on careers as successful oil producers.[57]

By the end of 1915, the thought, money, and trained personnel which the Shell Group had lavished on its Mid-Continent organization were beginning to produce visible results. As a result primarily of the Cushing and Healdton purchases, Roxana's crude oil production, which had totalled just a little more than 500,000 barrels in 1914, amounted during 1915 to 2,600,000 barrels. Crude oil prices improved simultaneously; Oklahoma oil was bringing $1.20 a barrel by December 1915. With this double improvement, Roxana's earnings climbed sharply: $502,000 in 1915, compared to $88,000 the year before.

But the investment in Oklahoma also continued to mount. In six months of 1915 the Group pumped $6,000,000 into Roxana's production activities. Profitable utilization of this oil, in place of mere sale on the open market, would help materially to recover this large investment. The original plan had been to pipe the company's production to a Gulf Coast port and there load it aboard Group tankers.

In June 1915, Roxana entered into a partnership agreement with the Cushing producers, White & Sinclair, predecessors of the present Sinclair Oil Corporation. Roxana and Sinclair planned to build a pipe line to the Gulf, erect a refinery at some deep-water port there, and set up a marketing organization to sell the refined products on the Atlantic Seaboard. A great deal of local resistance to this plan developed in Oklahoma, inspired chiefly by the crude oil purchasing companies. As a result, Deterding abandoned the idea.[58]

One may be sure, however, that he had no intention of allowing his new company, established at considerable cost in money and effort, to become merely a source of crude oil for competitors' refineries. The year 1916 would see a series of new decisions that would set Roxana on the track to becoming a fully integrated oil company, producing, transporting, refining, and selling in the American Mid-Continent.

4

The Refineries: Cushing, Wood River, New Orleans

JUST as the arrival of the geologists early in 1915 had presaged the company's acquisition of more crude oil, so now, a year later, two new arrivals indicated that Roxana was ready to begin refining. In January 1916, Deterding sent out Richard Airey, a salesman and commercial man, with instructions to acquire a site on the Mississippi River near New Orleans for the construction of a loading terminal, dockage, and eventually a refinery; to look into the erection of a small refinery at, or near, Cushing; and to see to the building of a crude oil pipe line to connect it with the Healdton field. In May, Pyzel, who had been in Holland for some months, returned to America to supervise design of these new refining facilities in the Mid-Continent.[59]

Airey went first to New Orleans, and late in April 1916 bought 366 acres of river-front property in St. Charles Parish, twenty-four miles above New Orleans, for $21,000. The property was part of the old Good Hope plantation, one of the many sugar cane plantations formerly common in that area. The plan was to use this location as a Gulf Coast shipping port for Roxana, and later on perhaps, as a port for importing Mexican oil. Because of this latter plan, Airey proposed to vest title to the Louisiana property in La Corona Petroleum Maatschappij, the Group's company in Mexico, but before long it was decided that it would be more convenient to organize a separate company. Accordingly the New Orleans Refining Company was organized in June 1916; its first meeting was held in Roxana's office at Tulsa on June 24. Airey, Luykx, and Van der Gracht were the directors, and Airey was elected president.[60]

Although the new installation was referred to as the New Orleans refinery from the first, the immediate intention was to erect a tank farm for storing products and a wharf for loading them. Products would be shipped in by tank car from the Mid-Continent, and Airey arranged for two railroads to build sidings to the new location. By the end of 1916, the wharf was built, six 37,000-barrel tanks had been completed, and the finishing touches were being put on the boilerhouse needed to provide steam to operate the loading pumps and generate electricity for lighting this isolated outpost. For the balance of the war years, Sellers, as the location was called in honor of the owner of an adjoining plantation,[61] became a valuable assembly point. There cargoes of aviation and motor gasoline, kerosene, and the all-important fuel oil were collected for loading aboard tankers destined for the embattled Allies abroad.

Before plans were even drawn up for the Cushing refinery, it was realized that the St. Louis area, with its greater proximity to markets, was the logical location for Roxana's permanent refinery. But with the war on, there was a pressing demand for petroleum products of every description, particularly fuel oil, for the Shell companies abroad had sizeable commitments to the British Navy. To wait until some 500 miles of pipe could be manufactured and laid to the St. Louis area would consume too much precious time. It was decided, as a war measure, to build a simple refining installation at Cushing, designed primarily for the production of fuel oil.[62]

Sanderson & Porter, who had built the Valley Pipe Line for Shell in California, were commissioned in May 1916 to construct 126 miles of 6-inch pipe line with a capacity of 5,500 barrels a day to connect this Cushing location with Healdton. The cost was to be more than a million dollars.[63]

Engelbregt, who had superintended the construction of the Martinez refinery, came east to take charge of building the Cushing plant. Work was started in August 1916 and proceeded at a brisk pace; by March 1917 the refinery was ready, and on March 27 it received its first charge of crude oil. During the remainder of 1917, it processed 5,000 to 6,000 barrels a day of crude oil, yielding 13% gasoline, 17% kerosene, 3% gas oil, and 66% fuel oil. The Trumble units, which had reached a fairly satisfactory state of operation in California, developed new "bugs" in Oklahoma, chiefly because of the lighter composition of the crude oils being processed. These difficulties were gradually overcome, and the experience proved valuable in designing units for the permanent refinery in the St. Louis area.[64]

Less than a month after the Cushing refinery had been completed, America entered the war. The new refinery, along with the other Shell facilities in this country, were placed at the disposal of the government in Washington. Since the company was already bending all its energies towards supplying the overseas forces of the United States and its Allies, few rearrangements had to be made in its operating plans. The New Orleans installation served as assembly point for gasoline shipped to American units in France, and did duty as a chief shipping point for the steady stream of products which Cushing turned out until the end of the war.[65]

In addition to his Shell responsibilities, Airey was named Admiralty adviser in New York for purchase of oil supplies for the British fleet. Over and above the shipments from Sellers, La., he arranged for some 1,500,000 barrels of fuel oil (much of it purchased from other companies) to be shipped, a trainload at a time, from Cushing to Shell's Montreal terminal, which had become a collecting and bunkering station for the Admiralty. In all, some 200 of these special tank car trains travelled overland the 2,000 miles from Cushing to Montreal.[66]

Cushing operated full tilt from the time it went on stream in March 1917 until the end of the war late in 1918. By this time, Roxana's permanent refinery at "South Wood River" had begun operation.

Superintendent at Cushing during the first year of operation was John R. Barrott, an old-time practical refiner. When Barrott resigned in May 1918, he was succeeded temporarily by C. J. M. Milo, a Group refinery man from the Indies then on his way home to Holland via the United States.

As soon as the location of the New Orleans and Cushing installations had been determined, Airey had gone on to St. Louis to look at prospective refinery sites in that area. In his search he met Clem Laessig and Harry Grenner of the Automobile Gasoline Company, two former Standard Oil men who in 1905 had started in St. Louis what is now generally acknowledged to have been the first drive-in filling station in America. Laessig accompanied Airey on a tour of possible sites and it was no doubt he who suggested Wood River, Illinois, 12 miles north of St. Louis on the eastern bank of the river.[67] Wood River was near the main railroad lines, near to water transportation (although this was probably not a consideration at the time), and its value as a refinery town was already demonstrated, for Standard Oil of Indiana had erected a refinery there some years earlier. Airey took an option on a site near Wood River.

With the Cushing construction now finished, Engelbregt came north to Wood River to take charge of building the refinery. As he did not expect to be able to stay to see the job through to completion, he brought with him R. B. High, a young University of California mining and geology graduate who had gone to work for Shell at Oilfields late in 1913. High had spent most of the years since 1913 as an inspector of the refinery materials which Simplex was having fabricated in California for shipment overseas. Engelbregt and High arrived at Alton, Illinois, the nearest town with a hotel, in March 1917. They inspected and rejected the site on which Airey had taken an option because it was on land which had been too often flooded in the past. Instead, they purchased a new site, some 172 acres of farm land three miles below the village of Wood River, for $200 an acre.† There in April 1917, construction got under way.[68]

The building of the Wood River refinery was not destined to

---

† Ensuing generations of Shell men were to curse the small area of this site and wonder why more land had not been purchased at the time, particularly as it was known that almost immediate expansion was planned. It is however no mystery to anyone who has read Deterding's correspondence of this period, for nearly every letter ended with an exhortation to keep capital costs low. An easy way to save money was to buy only such land as was immediately needed. This failure to acquire adequate expansion room was to plague almost every Shell refinery, and was particularly troublesome in the case of Wilmington.

proceed as smoothly and rapidly as had Cushing. Although the plans called for little more than a duplication of Cushing, this construction was to take nearly three times as long. The reasons for the delay were all by-products of the war: wartime shortages of practically everything needed to build a refinery, an acute shortage of freight-car space for shipping, and labor unrest set off by the spiralling cost of living. Materials that were available came in off-sizes and were often below quality specifications. The railroad freight congestion of late 1917 made it next to impossible to get anything even if it were available. And in the labor field, a legitimate need for increased wages offered a field day to union organizers from whom the highly industrialized Alton-Wood River area was by no means exempt. By September 1917, Airey was reporting that labor troubles were interfering with the construction of the tank farm and that carpenters and mechanics were refusing to come to work. No sooner had these troubles been patched up than a particularly annoying strike broke out among the bricklayers and completely stopped work on the boilerhouse; it was settled only when Engelbregt went to Indianapolis and negotiated in person with the union's International officers. By late September, Engelbregt was reluctantly reporting that the new plant "will not be ready by the time the pipe line is ready, namely February 28, and it looks as if April or May will be reached before the plant is ready for work." [69]

But if the refinery was falling behind schedule, so was the new 428-mile pipe line to connect Cushing with Wood River. It had been started in July 1916, when Sanderson & Porter had submitted the first cost estimates for such a line. They had been instructed to go ahead, assuming full responsibility for the entire job including location of the line, design and equipment of the stations, and purchase of all the materials. The line was to be of 10-inch diameter, with a minimum throughput of 11,000 barrels a day and a maximum capacity of 24,000 barrels. In the design of the pumping stations, Sanderson & Porter introduced Diesel engines as motive power for the pumps. Diesels were new to America, and this represented a departure in pipe line design.[70]

The Diesel engines and pumps were ordered from Allis-Chalmers, who had supplied part of the pumping equipment for the Valley line in California, and the order for 450 miles of 10-inch pipe was placed with Youngstown Sheet & Tube Company. The first shipment was received at Cushing in March 1917, at which time work on

Marcus S. Abrahams
Founder
Roxana Petroleum Co. of Oklahoma
1912

N. G. M. Luykx
President
Roxana Petroleum Co. of Oklahoma
1913–1917

W. N. Robinson's Tulsa Hotel where Roxana's first offices were located—hotel r o o m s with the b e d s removed.

Main Street, Drumright, Oklahoma, at height of the Cushing field boom.

W. A. J. M. van Waterschoot
van der Gracht
President
Roxana Petroleum Corporation
1917–1922

Richard Airey served as vice president of Roxana and its successors, 1917–1935. He was also president of Asiatic Petroleum Company (New York) and New Orleans Refining Company.

Drilling in the Cushing field, near Drumright, about 1916.

Dr. F. W. L. Tydeman

Roxana's Healdton field office on Wirt Franklin lease, Healdton, 1918.

Dr. F. W. L. Tydeman

Cable-tool drilling on Roxana's Wirt Franklin lease, Healdton field, 1918.

Dr. J. Th. Erb, head of the Group's geological department
at The Hague; Louis Roark, Roxana geologist; R. A.
Conkling, chief geologist; and Van der Gracht, on a trip
from Healdton to Waurika, Okla., 1918.

This patriotic lady, Mrs.
Martha Lair, worked as a
pumper on Roxana's Mullen
lease, in the Healdton field,
during World War I.

Roxana absorption plant, Yarhola lease, Cushing
field, 1921. Tower, *right*, absorbed natural-gas liquids
from oil-well gas; Trumble unit, *left*, separated natural gasoline from absorption oil.

Roxana's Cushing, Okla., refinery, 1918.

Office staff, Cushing refinery, 1917. *Left to right*, C. C. Martin, chief clerk; James Adams, head treater; John R. Barrott, refinery superintendent. Young lady holding service flag is unidentified, as is gentleman to her rear. Wearing striped pants and sleeve protectors is shipping clerk C. E. (Gene) Davis, later Shell manufacturing vice president; Ralph R. Mathews, chief chemist, at right.

The most modern machinery available was used in construction of the 10-inch Cushing-to-Wood River pipe line in 1918.

Wood River, Ill., refinery, February 1920. Third Trumble unit, *center*, was under construction.

An early Roxana advertisement, Alton, Ill., *Evening Telegraph*, January 21, 1921.

P. A. L. Engelbregt superintended construction of Wood River, Cushing, and Martinez refineries.

Dephlegmators of Trumble Unit No. 1, Wood River refinery, 1920.

the line got under way in earnest. From California, Sanderson & Porter brought the same kind of ditch-digging, pipe-screwing, pipe-wrapping and trench-filling machinery used to build the Valley line— as well as several hundred mules who had worked on the Valley line. Even with labor-saving machinery, a tremendous labor force still had to be engaged. The new line from Cushing to Wood River was nearly three times as long as the Valley line in California, and there were difficulties to be overcome such as crossing two major rivers, the Arkansas and Mississippi. At the height of construction activity, as many as 2,000 men were employed in laying the line, building the five pumping stations and dwelling houses for future employees of the pipe line, necessary because most of the stations were in isolated spots where company housing had to be provided. At the same time a telephone and telegraph line was also erected along the pipe line right-of-way.[71]

The nation-wide freight tie-up of late 1917 slowed up deliveries of pipe and several times brought work on the line to a complete standstill; even the Healdton-to-Cushing line was far behind schedule. To push the progress of the line when pipe was available, construction crews worked from several points simultaneously. The arduous crossing of the Mississippi was made without undue event during late October and early November 1917 while much of the line was still incomplete.

Finally, early in July 1918, the line was in shape to begin pumping oil into the Oklahoma end. Soon after, a break was discovered in the Mississippi crossing before oil had yet reached that spot. Nearly a month was lost in grappling for, taking up, and relaying the pipe. On August 23, the Mississippi crossing was finally mended and pumping of oil into the Cushing end of the line was resumed. On August 31, at ten minutes of three in the morning, the first Oklahoma crude issued from the Wood River end of the line.[72]

As a pipe line operator, Roxana could now be said to have arrived. Counting the 6-inch Cushing–Healdton line, the company now had 554 miles of trunk pipe line through the heart of the Mid-Continent, capable of delivering 24,000 barrels of oil a day. The Yarhola Pipe Line Company, which Roxana had acquired in the Cushing purchase, had been kept alive and was made the company's pipe line subsidiary. To manage it, Roxana followed the example of the Shell company on the West Coast and hired an able Sanderson & Porter engineer who had worked on the construction, R. P. Bascom. The new Yarhola line was a common carrier and at once set about fulfilling this function by contracting to carry oil for Standard of Indiana and thus turn to account some of the line's spare capacity. During the balance of 1918, more than a million barrels were transported for outside concerns and more than double this amount was handled for third parties during 1919 and 1920.[73]

By the time crude oil had started to flow from the northern end of the Yarhola pipe line, the Wood River refinery despite the many delays was nearly ready for operation. Two Trumble units had been built, the boilerhouse was ready, the large wooden water cooler, the loading racks, and crude oil and products storage tanks were all finished. Engelbregt had left to take charge of refinery construction abroad early in 1918, and High had succeeded him as superintendent of construction. To assemble a permanent staff to operate the refinery, Dr. F. W. L. Tydeman, a young Dutch chemical engineer and physician who had for a short time been assistant superintendent of the Cushing plant, arrived in April. Tydeman drew most of the key people he would need from the Cushing refinery, which, it had been agreed, would be closed down just as soon as it was no longer needed. Wood River began operations with a permanent staff of about 175. The two Trumble units were filled with oil and fired up, and on September 23, 1918, turned out their first products.[74]

In equipment, the new Wood River refinery was much like Cushing and Martinez, except that the designers of the Trumble units here had had the benefit of experience at the two earlier refineries to guide them in making improvements. The Wood River refinery differed from Martinez and Cushing in that its main heating units used coal for fuel. In the early stages of planning, Engelbregt had made calculations to show that soft coal mined in nearby southern Illinois would be cheaper to burn than oil piped all the way from Oklahoma. An exception to this was made in the case of the Trumble units. There, for safety's sake, it was considered prudent to use oil, for in the event of a leak into the firebox, the oil fuel could be quickly cut off and the fire extinguished. The Trumble units were each designed for a capacity of 5,000 barrels a day, although during the first few months of operation both units together averaged only a little more than 5,000 barrels daily.

During the first year of operation Wood River ran some 2,200,000 barrels of Healdton crude and manufactured fuel oil (66 million gallons), gasoline (11 million gallons), and kerosene distillate (13 million). It had for the moment no facilities such as those at Martinez for turning out a complete range of products, and a plant to make lubricating oils was not added until Roxana began retail marketing in the 1920's. At the start, Wood River's products were sold in bulk on the wholesale market. Eleven tank cars of fuel oil were the first product shipped from the new refinery early in October 1918, and the first tank car of gasoline went to Airey's friends, the Automobile Gasoline Company in St. Louis.[75]

Construction at Wood River did not cease with the start of operations, for an up-and-coming refinery, like a big city, is never finished. The construction crew, 2,000 strong at its height, dwindled to a smaller number, but High and many of his men remained until the spring of 1919, building an additional Trumble unit, workshops, more tankage, company-owned dwellings, and auxiliary facilities such as the shops ‡ for repairing and reconditioning the 550 railroad tank cars which Roxana had purchased. The addition to Wood River's capacity, begun in 1919 and completed in 1920, was designed to bring throughput up to 16,000 barrels a day, although this level of operation was not attained immediately. With Wood River safely in operation, the Cushing refinery was closed down early in 1919 and some of the construction crew were dispatched to Oklahoma to dismantle it. Tanks and part of the apparatus were shipped to Wood River and there reassembled and installed; the remaining equipment which was still usable went to Sellers, La., where the New Orleans Refining Company had at last started to erect a refinery.[77]

In accordance with the original plans, the Good Hope Refinery, as it was called in 1919, was built to process heavy Mexican crude. Mexican oil contained a high percentage of heavy "bottoms" which rendered unsaleable fuel oil produced from it by ordinary refining methods. Airey's plan was to remove the heavy "bottoms" and blend the fuel fractions thus produced with light Mid-Continent fuel oils so as to obtain a product that would meet specifications. Since by-product asphalt and by-product gasoline and kerosene would also

‡ Built in spite of Deterding's advice to the contrary: "I feel in general that we should confine our energies as closely as possible to the petroleum business and not wander into all sorts of subsidiary undertakings . . . at which we are not experts." [76] As a theory of management his view has prevailed in recent years, with most major oil companies abolishing or selling operations not directly related to their main business.

be produced in this operation, facilities for making and treating these products were installed. Asphalt, formerly made in batch stills, was here first produced by means of a pipe still.[78]

The Good Hope refinery (soon to become known as Norco) began operations on May 8, 1920, § with an initial capacity of about 5,000 barrels a day. High, who had built the refinery, became the first operating superintendent. Because the Norco installation operated on imported oil, exported its products, and was owned by a separately constituted company, it had little occasion to cross Roxana's path for the next decade. We shall however hear more of it after 1929, when it became part of the Shell operating organization in the Mid-Continent.

5

Formative Years: Roxana in Tulsa

BY EARLY 1917, the face of Roxana's operations had begun to change. With one refinery nearly complete, a pipe line under construction, and building of a second refinery soon to start, the company was no longer the small oil-producing concern it had once been. Growth and expansion brought a greatly enlarged staff, new offices, and new faces in the executive ranks.

The first major executive change occurred late in 1916 with the departure of John Harvey who had held the office of secretary or treasurer, or both, most of the time since 1912.* Not long after, on March 1, 1917, Luykx tendered his resignation as president and went to join the Sinclair company.† Harvey's place was taken by Thomas F. Lydon, a native of Ireland who had emigrated to St. Louis at seventeen, gone to work in the accounting department of the Missouri Pacific Railroad, and had later become comptroller of the Waters-

§ This anniversary is annually commemorated as "Plant Day" at the Norco refinery.

* Still active in the oil business, Mr. Harvey has for many years been associated with the Keener Oil Company of Tulsa, and was of invaluable assistance in providing material for this book.

† Luykx joined the Sinclair Gulf Corporation and was made a director in June 1917. For the remainder of his career, he was concerned chiefly with Sinclair's marketing and refining activities in the Gulf, Mexico, Cuba, and Central America. He died in 1930, "much to the regret of Mr. Sinclair and his entire organization." [79]

Pierce Oil Company in Mexico where he had become acquainted with Shell men.[80]

Luykx had been filling two jobs. The main one was in Tulsa, where he headed the Roxana Petroleum Company of Oklahoma. But the Roxana Petroleum Company (New York) was still legally alive, although quiescent since July 1914 when its only holding, the shares of Roxana of Oklahoma, had been transferred to the parent company, The 's-Gravenhage Association. In addition to his responsibilities at Tulsa, Luykx had been president of the New York Roxana company and responsible for the New York office which was developing into a valuable supply organization for the Shell Group abroad.

With a war on, many materials could be most readily purchased in America. It was this office, operated not as Roxana but "The Office of N. G. M. Luykx," that handled such matters, and in addition arranged, in the capacity of broker, for the purchase of ever-increasing quantities of petroleum products for shipment abroad. With Luykx's departure, his dual function was split into two jobs. Van der Gracht became president of the Tulsa company, Airey of the New York company, and each a vice president of the other's organization. Henceforth, although Airey kept an office in Tulsa, his main concern was operation of the New York office, which included arranging for the sale of products from Roxana's refineries. After the end of the war, Airey's time was increasingly occupied by the New Orleans Refining Company which he continued to head. The Roxana company began to find markets nearer home, with the quite natural result that the New York and Tulsa offices began to grow apart. In the spring of 1920, the dormant Roxana of New York was revived and its name changed to Asiatic Petroleum Company (New York), Ltd. It became henceforth chiefly a supplier of materials and oils to Group companies outside the United States.‡

At Tulsa, Van der Gracht proved to be an extremely popular chief executive. The handicap of a formidable name was offset by

‡ After the original office at 81 Fulton Street had been outgrown, the New York office moved to 50 Broad Street. Soon after Airey's arrival, he engaged space at 94 Fulton Street and in the new Woolworth Building, 233 Broadway. A few years later, the New York offices were consolidated at 65 Broadway where they remained until the early Thirties when new quarters were taken at 80 Broad Street. Here the offices remained until they were moved uptown to the new R.C.A. Building, 50 West 50th Street, in April 1934. From its formation in 1922 onward, Shell Union Oil Corporation had offices in the same New York quarters. The Asiatic Petroleum Company (New York) was succeeded by a new corporation, the Asiatic Petroleum Corporation (Delaware), in the late 1920's.

an engaging candor and lack of pretense which at once endeared him to the rank and file of employees. It was fortunate that this was so, for Roxana's staff was growing by leaps and bounds, and Van der Gracht's fair treatment did much to knit the many new arrivals into "a happy, loyal, hardworking, well disciplined . . . bunch, proud of its reputation and its company." [81]

The offices at Tulsa grew at a rapid rate. By February 1915, the six rooms in the Robinson Building, at Third and Main Streets, were too small; at that time larger quarters were taken in the Unity Building, at Fourth and Boulder Streets. In the ensuing eighteen months, the company spread out through that building and took additional space off the premises. It was ready to move again and, in August 1917, began to occupy the still unfinished Mayo Building. This move, interrupted by fire and the slow progress of construction, was finally completed a year later.

In August 1918, at the time of the completion of the move into the Mayo Building, the work of departmentalizing 200 office employees had been accomplished. There were at that time thirteen departments: geological, scouting, land, field (now called production), gas, technical (forerunner of the present manufacturing department), traffic, purchasing, tax and claims, accounting, insurance, statistical, and sales. The sales department had been set up upon the completion of the Cushing refinery; in order to be near the center of the wholesale tank car market it had been located not in Tulsa but Chicago and W. O. Andrus, the first sales manager, reported for all practical purposes not to Van der Gracht but to Airey. Andrus died suddenly in December 1918 and A. F. Garrett, the assistant sales manager, was made manager, being succeeded in the fall of 1919 by G. G. Woodruff. This sales department remained relatively small until Roxana entered the retail business in 1923.[82]

Among the heads of the other departments were several of whom more was to be heard. The geological department was headed by Conkling, scouting by Copmann, production by J. W. Bates, who had been engaged for the job by Van der Linden in California. Bates left at the end of 1925, the others before him. Among those who stayed on were P. R. Chenoweth, head of accounting, who later became secretary of the company; C. B. Singleton, who served as purchasing agent for more than 25 years; Edward Hepner, head of the technical department, who was secretary of the Shell Chemical and Shell Development companies for nearly 15 years prior to his retirement in 1943; and Carl Barker, manager of insurance, who retired in 1953. For most of his career, Barker was head of the old insurance, tax, and claims department. The relative youth of Shell's executives, compared to those of other businesses, often occasions comment today. Such comments must have been even more prevalent in Tulsa in 1918, for none of the men mentioned here was more than in his mid-thirties at the time and several were younger.

Operated as another department, although actually a separate company, was the Tret-O-lite Corporation which had a brief existence during 1918. It is interesting not for any lasting importance it had on the company's future but simply as a demonstration of the wide-awake disposition of the young Roxana company. The Tret-O-lite venture was an attempt to make saleable oil from heavy tank bottoms which not only had no commercial value, but represented a disposal problem as well. A process for treating crude oil emulsions involving the use of chemicals had been invented by William S. Barnickel of St. Louis, who had begun manufacture of the treating chemical which he called Tret-O-lite. The process was working with enough success on crude oil emulsions to prompt young Rolland M. Hunter, Roxana's assistant production manager, to try it on tank bottoms which were a particular problem for Roxana at Healdton where the oil was heavy.[83] The trials encouraged the Roxana management not only to undertake the process for their own account, but to form a company to treat similar oil for others.

In the spring of 1918, a six months' license under Barnickel's patents and an option to buy his company at the end of that period were obtained by Roxana for a cash payment of $50,000. The Tret-O-lite Corporation was organized to conduct this venture, with Hunter as vice president and general manager. The first operations, particularly at Healdton, were encouraging; recovery of oil from the bottom settlings of tanks cost about 63¢ a barrel, obviously a profitable venture with oil selling for more than $2.00 a barrel. In other oil fields, the Tret-O-lite process was less rewarding, for the collection of tank-bottom sludge at a reasonable cost from widely separated tank farms proved to be an almost insuperable obstacle. (The collection problem has been the downfall of a hundred other schemes, before and since, for recovering usable oil.) The Tret-O-lite business had been largely Hunter's idea; it received a mortal blow when he died in December 1918, a victim of the 1918–1919 influenza epidemic. The time for exercising the option, which would have required an additional $200,000 in cash and $750,000 worth of Tret-O-lite Corporation stock, was at hand. Roxana elected instead to abandon the enterprise, and by the end of 1918 most of its Tret-O-lite plants had been closed down and dismantled; in July 1919 the company was dissolved. Barnickel's Tret-O-lite Company (as distinguished from the Tret-O-lite Corporation) is still in business today, manufacturing chemicals for desalting and dehydrating crude oil. The Shell companies have continued to buy these Tret-O-lite chemicals for the treatment of their own emulsified crude oil and tank bottoms.[84]

Employee Relations in World War I

The years in Tulsa were formative ones for Roxana. Not only was the company growing, but a complete transformation was under way in the American oil business. Consumption of petroleum products was reaching levels thought impossible a few years before. The technical man had started coming into his own, whether he was an oil field geologist, a refinery engineer, or simply an eager young man like Hunter trying to salvage oil that was formerly wasted. No less important a transformation was taking place in wages and working conditions.

By the calendar, "prewar" meant only five years in the past, but reckoned in terms of wages and hours of work it was a generation ago. During the First World War the drillers' old two-shift, twelve-hour day, standard since the beginning of the industry in Pennsylvania, began to give way to a three-shift, eight-hour working day. Along with these decreased hours of work came better pay. By 1919, a driller was earning 38% more than he had in 1914, while putting in 13% fewer hours; on pipe lines, shift engineers earned 52% more in 18% less time; and in the refineries, the stillmen took home 65% more every week and worked 28% fewer hours.[85]

No doubt a few lagged behind as is usual in such cases, but the majority of the companies were glad to see the improvement in their business transformed into improved working conditions for their employees. Roxana took the lead in providing good wages and good working conditions. By 1918, rising living costs were beginning to pinch most employees; during that year the company increased all salaries by 10%, as a temporary cost-of-living bonus. This addition was made permanent in 1919. But more important than immediate compensation was Roxana's introduction, early in 1917, of the

Provident Fund, a savings plan which forty years later was still one of the most outstanding in American industry.

The Provident Fund, one of Deterding's finest creations, was set up in October 1912 in Holland, having as its object the accumulation "for each member of a certain capital to provide for them when they will have to retire from the service of our companies, or in case of death, for their families." [86] The general plan of the fund was to allow each qualified member (qualifications determined by the individual companies) to contribute 10% of his salary annually to the fund. The Shell company which employed him would then match the employee's contribution, and the whole would be put away at interest, not to be drawn upon until retirement or resignation from the company. Once started, the payments were made by means of automatic salary deductions which continued as long as the employee remained on a Shell payroll. Moreover, the original plan contemplated that when the employing company had enjoyed a good year it would contribute a bonus percentage over and above its matching contribution. Some of Roxana's "staff" (i.e., salaried) employees had been admitted early in 1917, a year in which the company paid a 15% bonus contribution in addition to its matching contribution of 10%. This meant that, with the employee's own contribution, those who were fortunate enough to be members of the Provident Fund accumulated 35% of their total salaries § during 1917, at a cost to themselves of only 10%.[87]

The Provident Fund regulations left it to the employing company to establish standards for admission to the fund. Generally, most companies—like Shell of California, which had introduced the Provident Fund three years earlier—chose to limit participation to salaried employees of a year's service with the company. Since there was no set rule, Van der Gracht announced the plan to employees generally in November 1918, soon after Wood River had started up. It was his idea that all who had been on the payroll three months should be allowed to join, but this "letting down the bars" to admit hourly paid ("operating") employees in addition to salaried people met with little favor from the other Shell companies who were admitting only

§ The plan as announced to employees generally in November 1918 specified $480 as the limit which any one employee might contribute in a year. This would have had a limiting effect only on the highest salaries, as the average employee earned considerably less than $400 a month in 1918.

staff people. In the face of their opposition, Van der Gracht was forced to drop his plan; a quarter century later, all operating personnel were admitted to participation in a new Provident Fund.

The employees who had left their jobs to join the colors were very much on Van der Gracht's mind, and to provide them with a "letter from home," he started *Roxoleum*, a lively company magazine, in January 1918. He took a personal interest in the magazine's contents, contributing signed articles on several occasions; his brother, Theodore van der Gracht, provided illustrations, art work, and colored covers; and Rolland Hunter, assistant field (production) manager, volunteered to edit it. The result was a highly readable house organ, and the copies which have survived give a good idea of the high morale of the Roxana organization of those years.*

As a further demonstration of the company's feeling of responsibility toward the 265 employees [88] who had left, or were soon to leave, for military service, the Roxana management early in 1918 had a statement printed outlining the company's military service policy. Single employees who volunteered and had no dependents were to receive encouragement, occasional packages, and the *Roxoleum* which had been started for their express benefit; if they should be so unfortunate as to become prisoners of war, regular shipments of scarce commodities would be made to them. Men with families would be assisted financially should the need arise, in an amount to suit the needs of the individual case (generally, the difference between a man's former income and his military pay, but in a few cases, more); and substantial assistance would be available to help alleviate distress in the families of any who were killed or returned from service permanently disabled. All employees, married or single, were assured of a job on their return, regardless of their physical condition, and all who were members of the Provident Fund had their monthly contributions to the fund paid for them by the company.[89] Generosity such as this was not usual in American industry of that day. Formulation of such policies and their announcement in an intelligent manner did much to enhance Roxana's reputation with its employees and all who knew them.

---

* A file of *Roxoleum* was made available to the author through the kindness of Dr. F. W. L. Tydeman, who had preserved the complete set. The issues ran from January 1918 through December 1920, at which time the magazine was discontinued. The Shell Company of California also launched the short-lived *Shell Beacon* in August 1918; it was purely for the company's men in service and was discontinued with the end of the war.

The Big Oil Hunt Begins

DEMAND for petroleum products mounted enormously in the years 1916–1920. Part of this increase represented wartime demand, but the great bulk of new demand came from the amazing growth of the automobile. In this five-year period, the number of automobiles in service in the United States increased threefold: 1916, 3½ million; 1917, 5 million; 1918, 6 million; 1919, 7½ million; and in 1920 more than 9 million cars on the road. To meet this demand, the Mid-Continent oil industry drew on its great reservoirs of crude at Cushing and Healdton, for meanwhile no new discoveries of comparable size were being made. This high demand and absence of sizeable new fields brought a sharp increase in the crude oil market. The price of Oklahoma oil, which had climbed by the end of 1916 to $1.40 a barrel, continued upward. It went to $2.00 before 1917 was out, to $2.25 in 1918, $2.75 in 1919, and finally hit its highest price ever, $3.50 a barrel, in 1920. In the face of such prices, it is not surprising that these years were a period of intense exploratory activity. Geologists, scouts, and land men swarmed over the western prairies from the Gulf of Mexico to the Canadian border and drilling crews to put down exploratory wells followed close behind. The total cost of this exploratory effort was tremendous, but as the rewards for success were great, men, money, and materials were poured without stint into the big hunt for oil.

The Roxana organization had two additional reasons for joining the hunt. The first was that its pipe line and refinery capacity were in excess of its daily crude oil production. Van der Gracht had, in fact, counselled against building the refinery until the company should have a larger amount of oil at its disposal; but Deterding had been, as usual, anxious to get going: "I quite agree with your policy that we would rather have built a refinery when we were certain of a permanent production of crude behind it, but we may have to wait rather too long for that position." [90] The other compelling reason for acquiring new oil reserves was that Roxana's current high level of production was only temporary. In 1916 the company produced 4,084,000 barrels, most all of it from Cushing and Healdton. Late that year, Cushing production fell off sharply with the result that total production for 1917 was a full million barrels less. This meant higher unit costs for production expense and overhead, for the total outlay had to be divided by a smaller production. Coupled to rising labor costs this gave an adverse picture for 1917: production costs which had been 13.4 cents per barrel in 1916 rose to 26.6 cents per barrel in 1917,[91] and net profit for the company, $1,850,000 in 1916, fell to $126,000 in 1917.

During 1917, Roxana's big oil hunt got under way. By January 1, 1918, the company had acquired several new properties in Oklahoma, and leased land for exploratory drilling in North Texas, North Central Texas, the Texas Gulf Coast, Kansas, and Wyoming.

As yet, however, all of Roxana's actual production of crude oil was still in Oklahoma. At the beginning of 1918, there were the "Old Properties" which Abrahams had purchased in 1912: the Bartlesville district with an office at Dewey; the Adair pool of northeastern Oklahoma with an office at Nowata; and the Cleveland field along the Arkansas River some forty miles west of Tulsa. The Cleveland production was holding up well, but the other two fields were by 1918 becoming expensive to operate, and in August 1919, they were sold to the Harvey Crude Oil Company.[92]

The Cushing properties were now past their peak. By early 1918, they had a daily production of some 1,100 barrels, only about one-eighth the volume of three years earlier. An office for the Cushing field was maintained in the village of Drumright, which was nearer to the field than Cushing. The Healdton properties (office at Wirt, Okla.) were responsible for the lion's share of Roxana's production. The Yale venture, started nearly two years earlier, was still proceeding slowly, although by late 1919, Roxana's Yale production would rise to 1,000 barrels a day.[93]

Located on land belonging to the Osage nation, some fifteen miles northwest of Bartlesville and just south of the Kansas border (nearest town Elgin, Kansas) were the Belmont properties which Roxana had acquired in April 1917 for $1,000,000, half in cash and the balance to be paid from future profits. These properties consisted of 3,520 acres of proven lands with 20 wells yielding a daily total of only 250 barrels.[94] They were remote from other Roxana properties and the pipe line; consequently, as in the case of the Old Properties, the company was on the lookout for a purchaser.†

---

† During 1921, Roxana drilled several 1,800-foot wells (all unsuccessful) in an attempt to locate deeper production on the Belmont leases before they expired in March 1922.[95]

At a point some hundred miles due west of Tulsa, half way between the towns of Covington and Garber, Roxana had acquired in May and July 1916 two leases of 160 acres each which early in 1918 were being developed into successful oil-producing property. Roxana had acquired these leases before Sinclair had drilled the discovery well in September 1916. The initial production at Covington was not large, but the oil was of excellent quality and at a depth of only 1,130 feet. Roxana's first well was completed on the Schroeder lease, February 1, 1918. Two others came in soon after, and by the fall of 1918 the company had three rigs drilling, two on the Schroeder and one on the Wolfe lease. At the end of the year, nine wells had been completed, yielding a total of about 150 barrels a day. A year later, Roxana's Covington production was 800 barrels a day, and it continued to increase during 1920 when the oil brought $5.00 a barrel because of its premium quality. The best days of the Covington field (or Garber field as it was more often called) were to come in the middle Twenties, with production from deeper and more prolific sands. From the Schroeder lease alone, the company during the next thirty years would realize net earnings of some $13,000,000.[96]

Roxana geologists, scouts, land men, and drilling crews were all over Oklahoma in the years 1918–1920, attempting, generally in vain, to bring in successful wildcat wells. Late in 1917, drilling was started at Bessie, in Washita County, in the extreme west of Oklahoma about 35 miles east of the present Elk City field. The well was unsuccessful and in May 1919 was finally abandoned. During 1918, an exploratory well was drilled at Lucien, a few miles east of Covington, and abandoned in January 1919. During 1920, the company's wildcat drilling in Oklahoma was increased, several areas west of Healdton being investigated without result. These numerous failures in Oklahoma were accompanied by one success: in 1919 acreage was secured near Jennings, a few miles northeast of Yale, and there by early 1920 the company had production of 6,000 barrels a day.[97]

Casinghead Gasoline

In addition to hunting for new oil in Oklahoma, Roxana also tried to get the maximum yield from its existing fields by conservation measures such as the installation of casinghead (or "natural") gasoline plants. Roxana's first such plant was built on the Maley Yarhola lease at Cushing, work starting in September 1916 and the plant going into operation in April 1917. The conventional casinghead gasoline plant in the Mid-Continent was a compressor plant in which the gas was compressed and chilled to condense out of it light gasoline components, in much the same way as water is condensed out of steam.

Pyzel was asked to prepare plans for the plant on the Yarhola lease, and it was only natural that he should decide on an absorption plant following the general design of the Group's first casinghead gasoline plant which he had built in Sumatra some years earlier. For the Sumatra plant he had adopted the absorption towers which had been in common use for many years for "scrubbing" gas in the European coal gas and shale oil industries. An absorption tower was filled with wooden grids, ceramic or metal rings, or other material offering a very large surface area. Incoming cold absorption oil entered the top of the absorption column and flowed down over these obstacles, spreading out in a thin film. "Wet" gas from an oil well, more or less saturated with light gasoline vapors, rose inside the tower, coming in intimate contact with the downward flow of the thin film of oil which absorbed the light gasoline vapors from the "wet" gas. The gas passed out of the top of the tower relatively free of liquids, or "dry."

The mixture of absorption oil and light gasoline fractions was then put through a simple distillation process to distill out the light fractions from the heavy absorption oil. The absorption oil was in this manner used over and over. The natural gasoline,‡ as it is most commonly called today, was sold for blending with heavy naphthas to make motor fuel. Where local sale was not convenient, the natural gasoline was (beginning at a somewhat later period) mixed with the crude oil stream on its way via pipe line to the refinery.

The Yarhola absorption plant, designed to process 5,000,000 cubic feet of gas daily,[98] was the first in the Cushing field to use this absorption method in place of the more common compression process. As a result, it attracted a good deal of attention among local oil men. Construction cost of such a plant was less than that of a comparable compressor plant, chiefly because of the elimination of costly compressors. The absorption process could in addition work on gas less rich in liquid hydrocarbons; this meant that it could profitably recover gasoline in fields where the compression method was uneconomic.

‡ The terms "casinghead gasoline" and "natural-gas gasoline" are also used. "Casinghead gasoline," heard much more frequently thirty years ago, meant, strictly speaking, only the gasoline which was recovered from casinghead (i.e., oil well) gas; "natural-gas gasoline" embraces all liquids recovered from natural gas. It has become shortened in use to the present-day term "natural gasoline."

Lower operating and maintenance costs were also claimed for the absorption process, although at first the operating costs of the Yarhola plant were considerably higher than anticipated.

As soon as sufficient production of gas was encountered in the Yale field, Roxana built a casinghead gasoline plant there during the winter of 1917–1918; it started operation in March 1918. A similar plant was completed and put into operation at Covington in December 1919. These were both compressor plants. From the first, the Shell companies were keenly aware of the value of the liquid hydrocarbons in gas. They made every attempt to recover these liquids, and by the early Twenties had become leading producers of casinghead gasoline.

Dry Holes in Texas

In no less vigorous fashion, but with less successful results, the vast area of Texas was subjected to an intensive exploratory program, 1917–1920. As early as 1915, Van der Gracht had spotted favorable indications on the Sabine Uplift, near Kilgore, in what is now the heart of the East Texas field. Leases were taken, and a few years later an exploratory well was drilled, but it proved to be a dry hole.[99]

Roxana's entry into the Texas oil fields came early in 1917. In February, Conkling and F. B. Plummer made a preliminary survey of the prospects of North and North Central Texas and soon after several geological parties were sent out. Their first lease was taken at Cross Plains, in Callahan County, some 40 miles southeast of Abilene. In May, active geological work began, not only in North Central Texas, but along the Gulf Coast as well. Parties under Sam Wells, John G. Burtt, C. H. Hammill, C. E. Hyde, and Angus McLeod were established in Texas; Plummer, in charge of the Texas work, opened an office at Houston. Leases were taken at Stratton Ridge, near Velasco, about 50 miles south of Houston on the Gulf Coast, and drilling was commenced there under the supervision of John R. Suman, a mining engineer and classmate of R. B. High at the University of California. Roxana drilled four wells on the Seaburn lease at Stratton Ridge, before finally abandoning the property in the spring of 1919. Later, in 1922, Stratton Ridge developed into an oil field, although such a small one that Roxana would have profited little even if the drilling had been successful.[100]

Meanwhile, North Texas and North Central Texas were a beehive of activity. The company established an office at Mineral Wells in April 1917 and geologists, scouts, and land men fanned out through the neighboring counties to lease fourteen blocks of wildcat acreage, each block 3,000 to 6,000 acres. By the end of 1917, three exploratory wells were being drilled in this area, one each at Graford and Brad in Palo Pinto County and at South Bend in Young County.[101]

The Houston office was retained until the spring of 1919, but most of its personnel, including Plummer, head geologist, Suman, § technical superintendent, and G. E. Bates, manager of the land department, had long before moved to Mineral Wells. The South Bend well was successfully brought in for 50 barrels a day from 1,880 feet in November 1919, the discovery well of the field. Other drilling around Cisco in Eastland County resulted in "a good pumper" early in 1920. By February 1920, the company had 12 wells drilling in Texas, most of them in this area, although a solitary well was being drilled over in Rusk County, in East Texas.[102]

In July 1918, a well completed on the Burkburnett townsite in North Texas yielded 2,200 barrels a day, precipitating a rush to that area. Within three weeks, Burkburnett was a boom town with nearly 60 wells in the process of drilling. Roxana dispatched scouts and land men to the area from the Mineral Wells office, but the boom spirit then abroad throughout North Texas made the price of even wildcat acreage prohibitive.

Despite the hard work and large amount of money lavished on the North Central Texas area, it was apparent by the spring of 1920 that results were going to be far below expectation. Some production had been obtained near South Bend, but it was not large enough to warrant the accolade of complete success; the other wildcat wells were either dry holes or had failed to yield oil in paying quantities. The staff at the Mineral Wells office was now dwindling rapidly; it was soon closed and the few who remained transferred to a small office at Graham, near the South Bend field. In this instance at least, it could not be said that the company had hesitated to drill; but the drilling seemed to bring only continued disappointment. By the time the five-year leases on these fourteen blocks of acreage in North Central Texas expired early in the Twenties, twelve of the fourteen had either been sold or farmed out to others.[103]

In fairness to Roxana's geologists, it should be remarked that the company's disappointments in the North Central Texas area were

§ Suman left Roxana in July 1919 to become vice president and general manager of the Rio Bravo and East Coast oil companies. A quarter century later, he was director and vice president of Standard Oil Company (New Jersey).

no greater than those of most other companies. Oil hunting activity in this area was especially feverish, for the rush to the area came at a time when war had driven crude prices sky-high and operators, large and small, spent large sums willingly. It is doubtful if the amounts spent on leasing and wildcat drilling were ever recovered from oil discovered in the North Central Texas area.

Haynesville

From the Mineral Wells office, some of the land men and geologists had gone on to northern Louisiana, where oil had been discovered near Homer, in the northwestern corner of the state, in September 1918. In August 1919, a large gusher was brought in in the Homer field. As usual, it caught the attention of the oil fraternity and soon the area around Shreveport was the scene of busy leasing activity. Roxana in August 1919 acquired a half interest in a large block of leases, about 25,000 acres near Haynesville, fifteen miles north of Homer, and soon after opened a land and leasing office in Shreveport. For this acreage, the company paid $40,000 and agreed to drill two test wells about 3,000 feet deep.[104]

These wells drilled at Haynesville were particularly exasperating for they were followed by the discovery of a new field, but not by Roxana. The company drilled the two wells it had agreed to, plus two more for good measure. Taylor No. 1 was abandoned in November 1919, at 1,085 feet; Taylor No. 2 at 2,950 feet in May 1920. A third well, Meadows No. 1, was abandoned at 2,904 feet on August 21, 1920; and the fourth well, Sayles No. 1, started in March, was abandoned in October 1920. With each successive failure, Roxana surrendered parts of its acreage, and after the failure of the third well it had sold all but about 500 acres to its partner, the brothers J. E. and C. B. Smitherman of Shreveport, for $7,500. Oil "shows" had been encountered at about 2,200 feet during the drilling of the second Taylor well, so the Smithermans decided to rework it. They gave it up as impractical in December 1920, and started drilling a new well close by. On March 30, 1921, this well blew in at 2,850 feet, making about 8,000 barrels a day of light oil. It was the discovery of the Haynesville field.[105]

This was indeed one of the "big ones that got away." During the remaining months of 1921, Haynesville produced 3,000,000 barrels of oil and in its peak year, 1922, nearly 20,000,000 barrels. It was an instance of missing the producing horizon by drilling right through it, a misfortune from which oil hunters are still not exempt. Realization of the true extent of the new field and the news that the Smithermans had resold Roxana's former interest for $3,375,000 brought a determined attempt within the company to fix the blame for the Haynesville failure. Van der Gracht magnanimously shouldered the entire responsibility, pointing out that he should have recognized the danger of using rotary tools, particularly when employing contractors who drill at so much per foot and therefore depend on speed for their profit. Apparently the plastering action of the drilling mud sealed off oil shows which might have been noticed under other circumstances.[106]

It was almost as if a malignant fate stood jeering at Roxana's elbow. In Kansas, starting as early as 1916, the company had undertaken a number of wildcat wells from which it got nothing except a reputation for hard luck—a reputation which, it was later claimed, became so widespread that superstitious old-time drillers refused to drill alongside "the jinxed Roxana boys." [107]

Matador

During these same years, Roxana had another exploratory group, far removed from the oil excitements of the Mid-Continent and Gulf Coast, examining the possibilities of the Rocky Mountain area. Max W. Ball, a young engineer and geologist with the U. S. Bureau of Mines, was engaged to head up the Rocky Mountain venture. In June 1917, Herman Witkamp, a B.P.M. geologist from the Indies, and Ball went to Cheyenne, Wyoming, and set up temporary headquarters at the Plains Hotel, while lining up office space and hiring the rudiments of a staff. Ball hired a Bureau of Mines compatriot, Robert G. Porter, to be office manager; two geologists, a scout, and a land man were sent up from Tulsa; two women "office geologists" were engaged; and soon after, Alvin T. Schwennesen was hired from the U. S. Geological Survey and made head geologist of the Rocky Mountain division and acting manager in Ball's absence. Witkamp returned to the Indies in April 1918.[108]

Oil was not new in Wyoming. The state had producing fields before Texas and Oklahoma came into prominence as oil states, but unscrupulous stock promotions had given Wyoming a bad name in oil-investing circles and there were no nearby markets of consequence. In face of these obstacles the Wyoming oil business had developed slowly; then in 1917, under the stimulus of higher prices, the state's production jumped by one-third. Early in 1917, Van der Gracht had sent in geological parties and their report had given rise to the Rocky Mountain venture.[109]

Late in the summer of 1917, the first option was taken for a lease on the Rex Lake structure in the Laramie Basin. This option was not taken up, however, as the depth to which the geologists estimated it was necessary to drill, 3,200 feet, was considered too deep and expensive for a wildcat. Next came leases on the Chicago and Colony Creek structures. Several wells were drilled on this latter structure, with portable rigs being used to help keep the cost low. In the spring of 1919, Ball's geologists also started looking for favorable prospects in northern Montana, and this increased work raised the size of the Roxana staff in the area to about forty-five in late 1919, when the offices had to be enlarged to thirteen rooms in the Annex Building and the Cheyenne correspondent of *Roxoleum* boasted that "the Roxana is credited with having brought to Cheyenne a greater working force and more families than any other oil company." [110]

In February 1920, the Roxana crew began drilling a test well on the Quealy structure in the Laramie Basin. A little later the Roxana geologists found favorable indications in Utah, in territory normally considered Shell of California's province. As further extensions of the Rocky Mountain operations would more than likely involve other similar territory, it was decided to organize the Rocky Mountain venture into a new concern, to be owned one-half by Roxana and one-half by Shell of California. This new organization, called the Matador Petroleum Company, was incorporated in May 1920, with Van der Gracht as president and Ball as general manager.

The peak of Shell activity in the Rocky Mountain region was almost coincident with the organization of this new company. The operations which it took over, including the drilling of the Quealy well, were slow and expensive. Freezing weather brought continued delays; drilling was constantly being "closed down for the winter"; and here, as at Ventura, delay meant high costs with little visible return. Deterding, knowing little of geology, but impressed by practical considerations such as the distance of the Rocky Mountain area from refining and marketing centers, had opposed the venture from the first.[111] Without some sort of success to report, the days of the Rocky Mountain venture were numbered. In the spring of 1921, the breakup came.

Ball had committed Matador to participation in a test well to be drilled on the Duchesne structure in Utah. The cost of this well promised to be high; executives of Matador's parent companies had already authorized nearly $200,000 for the Quealy well, which was still drilling without success. To them, this fresh expenditure in a new and unknown area looked like a proposal to throw good money after bad. They declined to back Ball, and in April 1921 he resigned. Several other members of the Matador staff left at this time. Soon after, the Duchesne acreage was surrendered to the Ute Petroleum Company, an independent concern organized by Denver interests, with Ball as president. The test well which this new group drilled on the Duchesne structure later in 1921 was a failure.[112]

Meanwhile, the lease which Matador had obtained on the Colony structure from the State of Wyoming had to be surrendered in May 1921, by reason of the company's failure to fulfill drilling requirements. In July of the same year, management of Matador was transferred from Roxana to Shell of California, and on January 21, 1922, the Cheyenne office was closed and its furniture, office equipment, and records shipped to San Francisco. The staff, except for the drilling crew on the Quealy well, was disbanded.[113] For all practical purposes, the Rocky Mountain venture was dead.*

For the men involved in Roxana's first big oil hunt, the over-all results, contrasted with the money and effort expended, were discouraging. For geological work, wildcat acreage, and exploratory drilling, the company spent more than $1,500,000 in 1920 alone. True, there were three new oil fields, Covington and Jennings in Oklahoma and South Bend in Texas. But they could not help remembering the disappointing near-miss at Haynesville and the score and more of outright failures on the Gulf Coast, in North Central Texas, in southern and western Oklahoma, in Kansas, and in the Rocky Mountain area—failures which, unfortunately, tended to obscure Van der Gracht's very real abilities as one of the outstanding oil geologists of his time.[115]

The fault was certainly not with the number of geologists available, for during these years Roxana had some sixty well-trained men roaming the Gulf and Mid-Continent, not counting Ball's men in the Rocky Mountain area. Nor was it with the quality of the geologists,

---

* Matador was revived briefly during 1924 when Schwennesen opened a small office in Denver under the old name. His assignment was to look over known structures and tell the company whether they seemed sufficiently promising to warrant active entry into the area. Late the same year he rendered an unfavorable report and closed up the Denver office.[114] During 1925, the Matador company was formally dissolved.

for their number included men of high professional calibre—Van der Gracht, Ball, Schwennesen, Plummer, Conkling, Suman—each of whom would later distinguish himself in his chosen field. And working with them were many others who would later become the backbone of Shell's geological organization in the United States.†

Nor was there a lack of interest on Van der Gracht's part. During these years he was literally a "travelling salesman" president, abroad in all kinds of weather, in every season, visiting each area under consideration to see at first hand the progress of the work, to advise, and to encourage. He travelled by automobile through endless quagmires of muddy roads, by horseback, by airplane, and (on a trip he took with Erb and Conkling in 1920) even by covered wagon and railroad boxcar.[116]

Nor was it a failure to follow up the geologists' findings by drilling test wells, expensive as they were. No geologist of course is ever completely satisfied with the number of wildcat wells his company is drilling; "just one more" before a lease is abandoned might turn the trick, or perhaps the same well should be drilled deeper. During these years, 1917–1920, Roxana had slight hope of acquiring new crude reserves in any manner except by discovery, for the price of oil was so high that producing properties were for sale only at exorbitant prices. Deterding was, accordingly, reconciled to spending large sums for exploratory drilling, and although an additional well here and there would in some cases have meant the difference between success and failure, it was not possible for any except clairvoyants to say just where this additional money should have been spent.

The real trouble lay deeper. It was with geology itself. Only a few years before, surface geology had been the last word in scientific exploration. Now it was rapidly becoming less effective as an oil-prospecting tool, for most of the easily discovered oil-bearing formations of the Gulf and Mid-Continent had by this time been found. The recommendations of the surface geologists were therefore becoming more and more speculative and the drill was once again on its way to becoming the sole exploration tool, as the large number of dry holes drilled by the oil industry in 1920 (7,356, an increase of almost 50% over the previous year) amply attests. A new exploration method was needed, something which would enable the geologist

† A list of others not mentioned here reads like a Who's Who of Oil Hunting. Several were charter members of the American Association of Petroleum Geologists, and almost to a man they later became well known for their abilities, either as independent consultants or as members of the geological staffs of other oil companies.

to "see" beneath the surface; and Shell geologists were shortly to play an important part in introducing the first of these new geophysical tools in the early 1920's.

And last, but by no means least, Lady Luck had failed to do her part for the Roxana prospectors. Luck is hardly scientific but even Everette DeGolyer, one of the most successful exponents of scientific oil-hunting, has written: "It takes luck to discover oil. Prospecting is like gin rummy. Luck enough will win but not skill alone. Best of all are luck and skill in proper proportion, but don't ask what the proportion should be. In case of doubt, weight mine with luck." [117]

For the Shell organization in America, this was merely the end of the first chapter in the Big Oil Hunt: in some of the ensuing ones, Luck would smile more kindly.

7

A New Roxana—and St. Louis

THE amount of money which the Roxana needed for construction of two refineries and 550 miles of trunk pipe line could not come from the earnings of a small company which was at the same time paying for a large exploratory program in the Gulf Coast, Mid-Continent, and Rocky Mountain areas. The Cushing refinery had cost $750,000, the original Wood River refinery double that amount, the purchase of railroad tank cars about $1,800,000. This capital expenditure had, therefore, to be provided from outside. For the Royal Dutch and Shell companies to supply all of these funds from abroad, even had they so desired, was not easy to do in the middle of a war when all sorts of exchange regulations restricted the flow of capital, particularly from England.‡ To help provide dollars in the United States for the use of Roxana, the Royal Dutch Company

‡ Indeed, there had been a period at the beginning of the war when all remittances to the new Shell company in San Francisco had been blocked because of exchange regulations. The company then had construction work on the refinery and pipe line in full swing, with large payrolls to be met. Hat in hand, Meischke-Smith solicited the company's bankers, the Bank of California, for a loan with which to meet payrolls and other pressing bills, only to be refused. Finally, he obtained temporary assistance from the Fleischhackers of the Anglo & London Paris (now Crocker-Anglo) National Bank. Soon afterwards, restrictions were lifted and the remittances resumed.[118]

late in 1916 arranged through the New York brokerage house of Kuhn, Loeb & Co. to sell 74,000 Royal Dutch sub-shares on the American market. §

The receipts of the company from this stock issue, after deducting the underwriters' commissions, totalled between $12,000,000 and $13,000,000, but not all of this money was available for the Roxana's use. Among other things, the Group was then purchasing materials in the United States for shipment abroad to refineries then under construction in Egypt, Venezuela and Curaçao; and in addition, sizeable sums in U. S. dollars were needed for the purchase of petroleum products on the American market for shipment to the Allies. To obtain the funds it needed, the Roxana also negotiated loans with American banks, generally the American Exchange National Bank of New York (predecessor of the present Irving Trust Company) from whom it borrowed as much as $800,000 in 1917.

The most dependable source of money, however, and the one upon which Roxana came increasingly to rely was the prospering Shell Company of California, from whom it borrowed more than $11,000,000 in the three years ending mid-1919. Some index of the Roxana's activity may be had by noticing the amounts of money it owed affiliates, chiefly Shell of California, at the end of each of the following years: 1916, $4,120,000; 1917, $8,767,000; 1918, $13,867,000. There was little immediate prospect of liquidating such large loans; and yet to continue paying interest on them would cost Roxana upwards of a million dollars annually. The obvious solution was to enlarge the capitalization of the company, issuing stock to the largest creditors in exchange for the amounts Roxana owed them.

The $5,000,000 capitalization of the Roxana Petroleum Company

§ The original Royal Dutch Co. shares were in the value of 1,000 florins, more than $400 each, and because they were selling in Europe for about five times par, some $2,000 a share, the company had for some time been offering sub-shares of one-tenth face value. Kuhn, Loeb & Co. placed certificates for 74,000 of these sub-shares in trust with the Equitable Trust Company (a predecessor of the present Chase Manhattan Bank), who issued three Royal Dutch "American Shares" for each Amsterdam sub-share on deposit, or a total of 222,000 American shares. This stock was marketed by Kuhn, Loeb & Co. and traded on the New York Stock Exchange until the 1930's, after which it was traded "over the counter." Three American shares could be exchanged in Amsterdam for a 100-florin Amsterdam sub-share, and some of the American shares were over the years redeemed in this manner, although in 1945 some 170,000 American shares were still outstanding. In 1954, the Royal Dutch Co. placed a new issue of 50-florin shares on the New York Stock Exchange; these new shares were freely convertible into shares of other denominations and holders of the 1916 American shares had the option of exchanging their holdings for the new 50-florin stock, on the basis of three of the 1916 shares for two of the 1954 shares.[119]

of Oklahoma was now well below the corporation's actual value.
The obvious course was to increase capitalization so as to reflect more
accurately the true value of the company's assets. The additional stock
thus created could be issued to Roxana's creditors in exchange for
the cash advances they had made. Since no one could foresee exactly
the future earning power of this stock, it was proposed as an inducement that it be issued at a discount. This could not be done under
Oklahoma law, for the state constitution provided that stock of an
Oklahoma corporation must be issued for a consideration equal to
the full value of the stock. Another disadvantage of Oklahoma
incorporation was that a majority of the directors had to be residents
of the state, a requirement which made it necessary to include on
the board a number of *pro-forma* directors whose chief qualification
was residence in the state of Oklahoma. Also, the "of Oklahoma"
on the end of the Roxana company's name, once needed to prevent
confusion, was no longer necessary and was becoming less desirable
as Roxana expanded its operations into other states. All of these
considerations suggested expansion of the company's capitalization
and reincorporation in another state.

Accordingly, a new company, the Roxana Petroleum Corporation,
was chartered in Virginia on March 8, 1917. The intention was to
transfer to this new company, as soon as possible, all the business and
assets of the Roxana of Oklahoma. The Shell Company of California
would receive for its claims preferred stock in the new company
and also in the new pipe line company which had yet to be organized.
The increase in common shares would be distributed among existing
stockholders, the bulk going to the Royal Dutch-Shell Group.
Alexander Mackay and his associates agreed to reduce their holding
in the new company slightly, from 27% to 25.1%, in recognition of
the fact that they had not advanced any new money. Again, legal
difficulties held up the proceedings. The Cravath firm, the company's
New York attorneys, pointed out that, under the interpretation of
Internal Revenue law then prevailing, the proposed stock dividend
could be taxed as income. A case testing this ruling was then in the
lower courts, so it was decided to await its outcome. The Roxana
of Oklahoma continued for nearly three years longer to be the
active company; the newly organized Roxana Petroleum Corporation
was during this period little more than a name.

Finally, in February 1920, unwilling to wait for a court decision
any longer, the company went ahead.[120] Roxana of Oklahoma's assets

were transferred to the new Roxana Petroleum Corporation, using as capitalization the same amount as the old company.* In March, the Supreme Court ruled that stock dividends were not income. In October 1920, the capitalization of the new company was expanded by $35,000,000, and the new stock thus created was distributed as a stock dividend.

The Yarhola Pipe Line Company had, as we have seen, taken title to the pipe lines as they were built. Its money was provided largely by loans from the Shell Company of California to Roxana, which re-lent the money to Yarhola. By October 1919, this debt amounted to some $8,225,000. On October 7, 1919, a new organization, the Ozark Pipe Line Corporation, was chartered in Maryland; three days later it took over all the assets of Yarhola Pipe Line as of October 1. The capitalization of the Ozark company was $10,400,000: 200,000 shares of common at $2 each and $10,000,000 worth of preferred stock bearing 7% interest. Some $8½ million of this stock was issued to Roxana at 77½% of par in settlement of $6,133,000 of Yarhola's indebtedness to Roxana; these shares were turned over by Roxana to Shell of California. The 200,000 shares of Ozark common stock were issued at a substantial discount, 25.1% going to Mackay and his associates, the balance to the Group. In October 1920, Ozark's common stock was increased to $20,000,000, and the new $18,000,000 worth of shares were distributed as a stock dividend. At the same time, par value of the shares was raised to $100 each.

Along with changes in the names of the companies, came another important shift: a change in the location of the company's main office.

In February 1919, Van der Gracht and Lydon had gone to London for important discussions with the Group's directors. Many things had to be considered, now that Roxana was a producing and refining company with products to be sold. One of the first points discussed, and one on which there was universal agreement, was that the Tulsa head office would be more conveniently located in St. Louis. It would be nearer to the company's chief market, in a larger city with more numerous railway connections, nearer to New York, and—a point apparently considered important—it "would remove the whole office right away from the oil field excitement." [121]

---

* The old Roxana Petroleum Company of Oklahoma could not be dissolved immediately because it was involved in litigation; the formal certificate of dissolution under the laws of Oklahoma was not issued until September 20, 1929.

As soon as they returned, Van der Gracht and Lydon lost no time in finding new office space in St. Louis. In the April 1919 issue of *Roxoleum*, Van der Gracht announced the impending move, adding, "We are sorry, indeed, to leave Tulsa, where we have made such friendly business connections during the six and a half years of our operations."

The production and scouting departments were left behind in Tulsa intact. Towards the end of June, all the other departments began the trek to St. Louis, where they moved into the fourteenth floor of the yet-unfinished Arcade Building, on the southeast corner of 8th and Olive Streets. The Chicago sales department also moved to St. Louis, leaving behind in Chicago only a small local sales office. For the next two decades Roxana was to call St. Louis home, and a whole generation of Shell management would, as a result, be prominently sprinkled with St. Louisans.

The move to St. Louis marks clearly and sharply the end of the first chapter in Roxana's history. The company now had more than 2,000 employees, and its annual sales surpassed $9,000,000. Gone were the days of the small, growing organization with the close associations and friendly spirit of the small town. Roxana was fast on its way to becoming a big company, and it was time for it to leave the scenes of its birth and early growth and head for the big city.

The Shell Company of California, too, had emerged from its initial period, and like Roxana was ready for bigger things. At this point, their stories merge and can be told from here on in a single narrative.

CHAPTER V

A Springboard to Prominence

1920–1925

D ETERDING was never one to discount the future, and in consequence he had an optimistic idea of the turn the oil business
would take following the war. In 1916, we find him writing
to Van der Gracht in Tulsa, "This is a century of travel and the
restlessness which has been created by the war will make the desire
for travel still greater." [1] The desire for automobiles in postwar
America was, indeed, so great that the demand could not immediately
be met; for several months, secondhand cars sold at prices above
what they had cost new two or three years earlier. Then in 1920,
nearly two million new cars rolled off the production lines, a number
four times that of 1914; and the registered motor vehicles on the
road that year rose to ten million.

The sharp increase in the number of customers produced a demand
for gasoline so great that during 1919–1920 temporary gasoline
shortages developed in several areas of the country. This brisk demand
was only a portent of what lay ahead: the number of automobiles
would continue to multiply all through the Twenties. By 1925, for
example, more than 4½ million new cars and trucks would come
from the factories in a single year and total vehicles on the road
would pass the 20-million mark.

To keep up with its voracious customer, the oil business had to
expand in every department. More oil must be found, more pipe lines
laid, more refineries built, more service stations erected. Into the
hustle of this booming market, the young American Shell companies
jumped eagerly. Here was their chance not only to make money,
but to broaden operations until the American Shell companies would
at last be counted among the country's leading oil enterprises.

The Shell companies could not sell products they did not have. To
manufacture sufficient gasoline, they needed sizeable new supplies

of crude oil and a refining process which would extract a larger percentage of gasoline from each barrel of oil. That both these things were forthcoming at this time proved a decisive factor in the companies' history. Had Shell of California and Roxana failed to acquire in quick succession a large number of prolific new oil fields, or had they failed to adopt and develop an efficient new cracking process, their subsequent careers would have been quite different. As it was, however, the physical and technological resources of both companies increased tremendously. By 1925, their combined production of crude oil was 275% greater than it had been in 1920 (contrasted with an industry-wide increase of 72% during the same period) and the amount of gasoline they were able to turn out had risen 660%.

This 1920–1925 period, then, was of outstanding importance, for it witnessed the Shell companies' rise, in a brief five years, to a position of national prominence.

2

Bonanza Days in California

For five years past, the Shell Company of California and Roxana had been absorbed in expensive and near-futile exploration efforts. By the end of 1921, Shell of California had spent five years and three million dollars in an attempt, thus far unsuccessful, to bring in commercial production at Ventura. Roxana's failures during the same period were spread over a much wider area: the Louisiana and Texas Gulf coasts, North Central and East Texas, western Oklahoma, Kansas, Utah, and Wyoming. Then, suddenly, in 1921, the hard-luck prospecting of the 1916–1921 period came to an abrupt end with the beginning of a series of oil discoveries.

The most spectacular of these new strikes occurred on the Pacific Coast where Shell of California's exploratory budget had been devoted almost entirely to Ventura. The company had a substantial reserve of crude oil at Coalinga and during the war years had supplied its requirements by drilling up the old Limited property, which was thus enabled to provide some six million barrels a year to the Martinez refinery. In 1918, Van der Linden, who had been charged with the responsibility for the company's exploratory and production

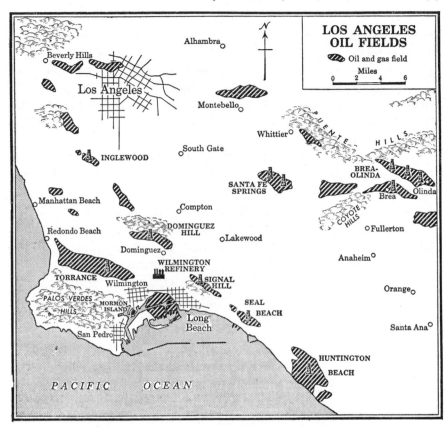

LOS ANGELES BASIN OIL FIELDS

efforts, was joined by Dr. W. van Holst Pellekaan, a Dutch geologist who had previously served with the Group in the Indies. Van Holst Pellekaan was given the exploratory end of the California company's business, while Van der Linden continued to direct production. Shell of California began a new hunt for oil production, utilizing surface geology, the only method then practical for West Coast operations.[2]

For twenty years, the dominant fields in the California oil business had been those located in the San Joaquin Valley—Coalinga, Midway-Sunset, McKittrick. In the vicinity of Los Angeles and at Santa Maria farther north on the coast, there were older fields but their production was small compared to the prolific fields of the Central Valley. In the years following World War I, oil men once again turned their attention to the Los Angeles area, for geologists had begun to suspect that some of the long, low hills of that area might cover deep-seated, oil-bearing anticlinal domes. During 1918–1921, geologists from a number of oil companies examined these elongated structures. In 1919, a well drilled by Union Oil of California on one of these structures at Santa Fe Springs, a few miles south of Pasadena and east of the Los Angeles city limits, encountered oil, although in too small a quantity to make it immediately a commercial field. This discovery did, however, provide encouragement to those who were prospecting nearby.[3]

In May of 1920, Standard Oil of California brought in a small well at Huntington Beach, twenty miles southeast of Los Angeles. This well was followed in November of that year by a large well making more than 2,000 barrels a day. At once, a rush to the region was on. Huntington Beach had earlier been laid out into town building lots, and most of them at the time of the discovery well had already been sold. Because of this widely dispersed ownership and the smallness of individual holdings, Huntington Beach became the scene of wasteful "town-lot" drilling which in California reached new heights of extravagance. The town-lot drilling boom at Huntington Beach was just approaching its height in June 1921, when Shell brought in a 600-barrel well on Signal Hill behind Long Beach, between Huntington Beach and Los Angeles. This well, called Alamitos No. 1, began producing on June 25, 1921, opening one of the most exciting chapters in Shell's production history.

Signal Hill

Behind the then-small city of Long Beach, Signal Hill rose sharply, its 365 feet of elevation making it a prominent feature of the local landscape. In Indian days, it was said, the local red men had used its pinnacle as a point for signalling their brethren on Catalina Island, some 35 miles out to sea. Later, in Spanish times, the hill had occasionally served as a beacon for ships. The whole of Signal Hill and much of the surrounding territory had for two centuries been included in two Spanish ranchos, Los Cerritos and Los Alamitos, both of which had continued as cattle ranches through most of the Nineteenth Century. In the late 1880's, a settlement called Long Beach was started on a part of this land; but in 1920 it was still a relatively small city. Several of the more arable parts of the hill had been given over to truck farming, and then in the building boom following World War I, an ambitious residential real estate development had been laid out and a great many small lots on the scenic front side of the hill had been sold.

Late in 1919, Dr. van Holst Pellekaan went to Peru and Ecuador to undertake an extended geological reconnaissance of those countries for the Group. To replace him in his absence, Alvin T. Schwennesen, head geologist of the Matador in Cheyenne, was sent west, arriving in San Francisco late in November 1919. Schwennesen immediately set about familiarizing himself with the Los Angeles area, and under his direction Shell began mapping some of the more promising structures. D. H. Thornburg, a Shell geologist who had grown up in Long Beach and who remembered having seen marine fossils and tilted beds when he had played on Signal Hill as a boy, mapped the Hill. His surface geology confirmed the findings of earlier workers who had suspected that Signal Hill was the crest of a large, possibly oil-bearing anticline. Whether or not the underlying formations contained oil, and at depths which could be reached by drilling methods of that time, could be determined only by drilling a wildcat well. This the company decided to do, going as deep as 5,000 feet if necessary. Following this decision, Shell of California spent $60,000 to lease 240 acres on Signal Hill. Much of it was a single large tract which had not yet been subdivided, leased from the Alamitos Land Company. Not long before (1917), Union Oil Company had drilled an unsuccessful well on Signal Hill at what is now the junction of Wardlow Road and American Avenue. For Shell's well location, Thornburg and J. W. Paulsen, another Shell geologist, selected a site just back of the brow of the hill, on the edge of a tract belonging to the Alamitos Land Company.[4]

Following the practice then current, the Alamitos No. 1 well was drilled with rotary tools to a depth at which good oil showings were obtained. Then, lest the action of the rotary drill and its circulating mud seal off the oil-producing sands, the well was finished with old-fashioned cable tools. On March 23, a Shell rotary crew from Oilfields moved in and started drilling. By May 2, they had reached 2,765 feet and a core was taken, revealing oil sand. Cheered by this news, Shell of California appropriated another $50,000 to lease additional acreage. A casing to shut off upper waters was run to the bottom of the hole and cemented, and then a cable-tool crew arrived to finish the well. On May 23, while making a test for water shut-off, the cable-tool crew found 70 feet of oil standing in the hole, along with a substantial amount of gas. This good news got around Long

Beach in no time and, during the final month of drilling, the crew spent much of their time keeping interested sightseers off the derrick platform.[5]

Drilling had proceeded to 3,114 feet by June 23, when oil blew out over the crown block 114 feet in the air. The well soon choked up and stopped flowing. During the two days ensuing, crews worked around the clock to get the hole cleaned out and the well into production. Excitement ran high and when the clean-out job was finally finished and oil from Alamitos No. 1 started flowing to tanks at four o'clock in the morning on June 25, 1921, five hundred spectators were gathered to witness the sight. During its first twenty-four hours, the new well made 590 barrels of 22° gravity oil, and soon after production increased to 1,200 barrels a day.

From the moment of the completion of the Alamitos well early that June morning, Signal Hill became an uproar of activity, activity which increased with ever-mounting intensity for the next two years. Only a few houses, such as the one belonging to Andrew Pala on the crest of Signal Hill, had actually been built; but most of the more desirable lots had been sold. These individual landowners naturally wished to join in the bonanza resulting from Shell's discovery well, and they were to be helped in this desire by the usual boom-town aggregation which overnight descended on Long Beach: speculators, promoters, and a large selection of reputable and experienced oil men. They came in such numbers, and the excitement was so intense, that soon the bidding for leases forced royalty percentages up well beyond customary levels.

Established operators with capital and equipment could offer a landowner the advantage of being able to begin drilling immediately. The speculators and lease-hounds were, of course, unable to make such commitments, but they could offer increased royalty rates. Even established operators, such as Shell, had begun by offering royalty rates of one-sixth rather than the conventional one-eighth prevalent in most other oilfield areas. In the face of the competition generated by the lease traders, this one-sixth rate soon jumped to one-quarter, one-third, and a few months later several landowners in the western part of the field obtained the fantastic royalty of one-half. It goes without saying that cash "bonuses for signing" also reached high levels. In other cases promoters offered to buy the landowner's royalty interest outright, for cash sums so large that they were difficult to refuse.

The concerns who offered the high royalty fractions were ones

Shell's Alamitos No. 1, discovery well of the Signal Hill, Calif., field, brought in on June 25, 1921. Signal Hill was a turning point for Shell, supplying oil for new refineries and large-scale marketing expansion.

Courtesy W. E. Feistner

Shell's Andrews No. 3 at Signal Hill blew in, March 1923, and was brought under control without mishap. By this time, Shell's Signal Hill crews were experts at capping gushers and extinguishing fires. This is how the rear of Signal Hill looked in the year of its peak production.

Courtesy E. E. Tiffany

Shell's Nesa No. 1 at Signal Hill caught fire early September 2, 1921, and burned for two days before it was finally put out by dint of heroic measures and much ingenuity.

Courtesy W. E. Feistner

The Nesa fire was extinguished by smothering it with mud and steam. Just before this operation began, W. E. Feistner donned an asbestos suit to inspect the well-hole.

Courtesy C. C. Kifer

Shell crews became so expert at emergency operations that they were often called on by competitors. Picture shows geyser of oil issuing from Petroleum Midway's Ryder No. 1, late in February 1923. A crew of ten Shell foremen undertook to cap this gusher and earned $1,000 apiece for four hours' work. The photographer printed their names on the tank.

The large number of derricks in this picture, taken during the second Signal Hill boom of the late Twenties, gives some idea of the bustle that attended development of Signal Hill.

Before Shell discovered oil on Signal Hill, most of the front side of the hill had been subdivided into building lots and sold. The result of this widely dispersed ownership of small tracts of land was a tremendous number of wells, with the feet of one derrick often interlocking the feet of another. This excessive drilling would doubtless have been unprofitable, except for one thing: Signal Hill proved to be the world's richest oil deposit in terms of barrels produced per acre. The bristling derricks shown here, once Signal Hill's trademark, are now rapidly disappearing.

who, while in no position to begin drilling immediately, knew that they would have little difficulty in raising the necessary capital once they had in hand a signed lease covering acreage near producing property. The stock promoters on the other hand were only remotely interested in drilling for oil. Generally, they would buy the land-owner's royalty interest and then capitalize it as a company with thousands of shares of stock which could be sold to a gullible public unfamiliar with oil royalties but eager to "get in on something big." The promoters ran free bus trips from Los Angeles to Signal Hill, set up eating tents where they served free lunches to their guests and followed that with a lecture by a so-called expert and a trip to look at Shell's new well, the only thing of interest which could be shown the prospective investor. There is no record of just what the pro-moters told these would-be shareholders, but it is a safe bet that the purchaser usually came away thinking he had bought a lot more than one five-hundred-thousandth of a one-sixth interest in an oil well which had yet to be drilled. For some the story had a happy ending, after all; the field proved so prolific that many of these intended victims actually profited from their highly unlikely invest-ments.[6]

Keeping the guests of the promoters and the other swarms of the curious off the derrick platform, where they might be injured or cause injury, was a full-time job in the early weeks of the Alamitos well. The men who worked on it remember many a weekend when they were forced to brandish axe handles to drive the spectators back out of harm's way. These interruptions became so annoying that eventually the crew built a high barbed-wire fence all the way around the well site.[7]

With all this fever-pitch excitement and confusion, with high cash bonuses and high royalty percentages being offered, with dozens upon dozens of small plots overlying the probable area of the new oil field, it was clear to the Shell men on the spot that they were headed straight into a period of intensive town-lot drilling, which might very well be more hotly competitive than anything seen up to that time. Shell held about one-quarter of the new field, and would therefore be obliged to join in this fast-and-furious activity if it hoped to recover its proportionate share of the oil. The company had the initial advantage: it was there first, with drilling equipment and a few crews of men.

McDuffie, who by 1921 had become general production superintendent, lost no time in following up this initial advantage. He had arrived during the days when the Alamitos well was still drilling. With its successful completion, he laid out plans for moving in drilling crews, rigs, materials, and supplies as rapidly as possible. Clearly foreseeing the break-neck drilling race ahead, McDuffie outlined a drilling program under which Shell immediately undertook to drill three more wells on the outer boundaries of its leases. The second well started was Nesa No. 1 on the crest of the hill some 800 feet east of Cherry Avenue; the third was Horsch No. 1 farther back on the hill and just east of Cherry Avenue; and the fourth, Stakemiller No. 1, was down the face of the hill from the Alamitos well. For drillers, crew members, and roustabouts, McDuffie drew on the ready-made labor force at Coalinga and men arrived from Oilfields at the rate of about thirty a day, day after day, all during the summer of 1921.[8]

This excellent staff from Coalinga now had a chance to show its mettle under conditions completely different from the leisured, orderly manner in which the Limited's fee property had been developed. O. P. (Happy) Yowell became drilling superintendent; J. R. (Jack) Gignoux was engineer to plan construction; W. E. Feistner, as superintendent of construction, had to round up materials and get the job done; E. E. (Gene) Tiffany was put in charge of transportation, always a first-class headache in any newly opened oil field. W. A. (Art) Trout, master mechanic at Oilfields, came to Signal Hill bringing with him some of the best Oilfields mechanics and even some of the heavy machinery from the Oilfields shops. W. C. (Brick) Nidever, head gauger, came to measure, analyze, and attempt to store in highly inadequate tankage the oil which gushed from Shell's new wells on Signal Hill. Stanley Duhig, already an Oilfields "old-timer" of more than fifteen years' experience, arrived to organize the office, account for the oil on which lessors were already clamoring for royalties, meet the payrolls, and pay the bills for equipment and supplies which were pouring in pell-mell from every side. Wildcat wells such as the one Shell was drilling at El Monte were forthwith discontinued, so that the company might have the services of men like Charles Butler and S. R. (Pinkie) Robinson for the more important drilling campaign on Signal Hill.[9]

Each man had his work cut out for him. In the shortest possible time, it was necessary to build derricks, offices, shops, garages, tool sheds, tank farms, pipe lines; to construct roads; to supply the trucks, teams, and drivers to do the hauling of a vast amount of equipment and supplies; and last (or rather first) to acquire these materials.

In particular, lumber for rig-building was always at a premium whenever an oil boom broke out in a new and unexpected place. Early in July, Shell bought enough lumber to build eleven rigs. It came streaming in by railroad car, followed closely by shipments of pipe, oil tools, drilling rigs, and boilers from Oilfields. Lacking a place to unload, Tiffany's men took this avalanche of materials off the flatcars and piled it on the ground adjoining the tracks. Hard pressed for help, Tiffany and Feistner hired on the spot the drivers who came to deliver lumber, cement, and other building materials. Soon they had 150 horses and mules, 50 trucks, and 127 drivers hard at work transporting the hundred and one items needed in a booming oil field.[10]

In an atmosphere reminiscent of fighting a fire, men still managed to keep their heads and get their work done amidst frenzied hurry and "never enough"—never enough material, never enough labor, never enough room (some of the office force operated without desks for months), never enough drilling mud (Tiffany's drivers went miles away to dig it from abandoned sumps), and never, of course, enough time. Crews often worked around the clock as a well neared completion, and foremen and field superintendents lost all track of time as they sped hither and yon, overseeing a dozen jobs at once. Work proceeded with such alacrity that there were a great many humorous incidents, as might be expected, such as foremen appearing on the scene and bawling out a drilling or construction crew, only to realize next day that the crew belonged to a competitor.[11]

In October, the Horsch well drilled by Shell just east of Cherry Avenue came in a producer, and resulted in the scene of intense activity being shifted from the southeast to the northwest of the field. Soon after, General Petroleum's Black & Drake No. 1, some 1,500 feet west of the Horsch well, blew in out of control, giving the first indication of the really prolific production which lay beneath Signal Hill. It was then that royalties rose as high as one-half. Because of these steep prices and because of its heavy commitments in the eastern end of the field, Shell did not join in the lease "play" in the western part of the field. The company did, however, own a half-dozen leases in that section which had been taken earlier. Possibly it might have taken more, even at high prices, had it not been for

Dr. van Holst Pellekaan's conviction, based on surface "dips" exposed on the back of Signal Hill, that "there is no oil west of Cherry Avenue." This area west of Cherry Avenue has proved to be the major part of the Signal Hill, or Long Beach field, as it now is called.[12]

By the end of April 1922, ten months after Shell's Alamitos No. 1 had first gone into regular production, there were 108 completed oil wells on Signal Hill with a daily production of 14,000 barrels divided among 37 competing companies. Of this number, Shell of California had 28 wells, or approximately 25%, of the total and 6,000 barrels a day, or about 42%, of the total production.[13]

This was just the beginning. Signal Hill was already crowded with derricks but by the time another year had passed it would be literally bristling with them, some built so close together that their feet interlocked. The hill itself on windless days was shrouded in a fog of steam issuing from the boilers that drove the drilling rigs. All during 1922, drilling kept on at an ever-mounting pace, with the peak of activity coming in July 1923, when there were 270 drilling rigs * all running at once. This resulted in the field's reaching a peak production of more than 7,500,000 barrels during the month of October 1923. In the rush, the "combination" style of drilling—part of the way with rotary, part with cable tools—was discarded as being too time-consuming, and thus it was on Signal Hill that the rotary first came into its own in California fields.[15]

With all this hurry and the carelessness which haste brings, with so many men working at such close quarters, with open fires blazing in more than 200 boilers, it is a marvel (and one which continues to impress most of the men who lived through it) that Signal Hill did not become the scene of calamitous accidents. There were, to be sure, several accidents in the course of the first two years which might have developed into first-class tragedies. Fortunately, they did not. Most of these accidents involved fires; probably the most spectacular was the first, on Shell's Nesa No. 1.

The Nesa well had been drilled as far as it was scheduled to be drilled with the rotary tools, the casing had been run and cemented, and after the cement had hardened the cable-tool drillers had started late in the day of September 1, 1921, to drill through the cement

---

* About 75 of the 270 rigs were Shell's. Some idea of Shell activity on the Hill at that time may be had from the fact that during 1923 the company's stores department at Long Beach turned loose into the field $9,000,000 worth of drilling equipment and oilfield supplies.[14]

plug at the bottom of the casing.[16] During the two weeks the cement had been hardening, a pocket of gas had collected. When the drill penetrated the cement plug, a jet of gas shot upwards with a roar and soon afterward caught fire. This roaring torch, 125 feet high, could be seen twelve miles away by land and thirty miles out to sea. It burned two days before McDuffie, Yowell, and their men could bring enough equipment into place to attempt to extinguish it.

They brought into position a large number of boilers, Shell's and competitors', and prepared to extinguish the flame by smothering it with streams of mud and steam poured in from every side. These preparations were too interesting and dramatic not to draw a tremendous crowd, and Feistner became hero of the day by donning an asbestos suit and going in as far as he could to see whether drilling machinery lay over the burning hole (*see photo, following page 176*). It didn't; so the jets of mud and steam were applied, and the blazing torch snuffed out, although the escaping gas continued to roar. It was at this juncture that the fire-fighters looked up to see one of their spectators calmly smoking a cigarette only a few feet away—an illustration, if one were needed, of the necessity for keeping sightseers away. The Nesa well was completed shortly afterwards and thirty years later was still producing.[17]

Within the next six months three other Shell wells on Signal Hill—Martin No. 1, Andrews No. 3, and Wilbur No. 1—blew in out of control, took fire, and were successfully extinguished by Yowell and his crew who soon acquired an enviable reputation as fire-fighters and well-cappers. A crew consisting of Yowell and nine drilling foremen set a record in February 1923 when they successfully capped a competitor's gusher in four hours, and were paid $10,000 for the job, $1,000 per man. (*Photo following page 176.*) A chief cause of these accidents had been lack of sufficiently heavy drilling mud. When new and heavier mud made its appearance, along with improved blow-out preventers (large valves under the drilling platform anchored in concrete), accidents such as these blow-outs and fires were largely eliminated.

Signal Hill would have been a memorable oil field on the basis of the tremendous activity of 1921–1923. But there was still more to come. No sooner had the production of some of the original wells begun to decline than a new area in the northwest part of the field, called Los Cerritos, opened up in 1925. This was but the first of several extensions which followed during the 1920's and 1930's; some were extensions in area, others were extensions through discovery of deeper horizons in the old parts of the field. Because of these extensions, production at Signal Hill was remarkably sustained in spite of town-lot drilling: the operators were sitting on one of the most productive fields in the world. By the end of 1950, the Long Beach field, as it is now generally called, had produced more than 750,-000,000 barrels of oil—more than half a million barrels per acre—making it the richest field in terms of production per acre that the world had ever seen. And in all-time rank, it stood third among American oil fields, exceeded in total production only by the East Texas and Midway-Sunset fields. With about 25% of the total acreage, Shell had between 20% and 25% of the total number of wells and the same percentage of the total production.

Some of Shell's 270 wells proved spectacularly good producers. Shell No. 5, on a piece of fee property, had by the end of 1950 produced in excess of 2½ million barrels. Babb & Tucker No. 4 had yielded considerably more than 2 million barrels. The discovery well, Alamitos No. 1, had nearly reached the 700,000-barrel mark.[18] For Shell, this splendid find could not have come at a more opportune moment. It gave the company, hitherto unrepresented in Southern California, the local production it needed to enable it to build a refinery and begin the retail sale of gasoline and other petroleum products in the West Coast's largest consuming area.

Santa Fe Springs

Union Oil Company had brought in a producing well at Santa Fe Springs in October 1919, as already noted, but its production was too small to bring on an immediate rash of activity. Then in November 1921, Union completed another well for 2,588 barrels of oil during the first day. This success at Santa Fe Springs touched off an intensive drilling campaign of proportions almost equal to Signal Hill, and it came at almost exactly the same time. Despite keen competition, Shell obtained leases in this new field, and although acquisition costs were high, these leases proved extremely profitable.

Santa Fe Springs was unlike Signal Hill in that it was a "flush" field, producing during its initial stages tremendous quantities of oil and then falling off rapidly thereafter. The peak production of Santa Fe Springs came in August 1923, when the field produced 322,500 barrels of oil a day. This tremendous production almost coincided with the peak production of Signal Hill only two months later. The result was that the Los Angeles Basin, in 1920 an insignificant producer compared to the Central Valley of California, was three years later literally flooded with oil. During the year 1923, the amount of oil produced by Signal Hill, Santa Fe Springs, Huntington Beach, and the other smaller fields in the Los Angeles Basin was so great that this relatively small area that year accounted for 20%, or one-fifth, of the world's total production of crude oil.

Los Angeles Basin

Such a large production of oil in one small area would have undoubtedly brought, as it had so often in the past, completely demoralized markets and financial ruin to many of the operators concerned, had it not been for unusually favorable factors which helped to offset the normal consequences of overproduction. The demand for gasoline continued to mount at almost break-neck speed. The new supplies of crude in the Los Angeles area were much higher in gasoline content (and therefore in greater demand) than most of the oils previously encountered in California. The Los Angeles area fields were adjacent to deep-water transportation, so that the newly produced oil could be moved out into world markets immediately without the delay or the expense of building long pipe lines. Even with all these favorable factors in attendance, the price of crude oil dropped sharply in the Los Angeles Basin as production continued to mount. The oil from the original Alamitos discovery well at Signal Hill had brought $1.50 a barrel in June 1921; a year later the market price for 27° gravity oil at Signal Hill had slipped to $1.15; and by the end of 1923 it was down to 68 cents.[19]

The low price had the advantage of making Los Angeles oil attractive to offshore buyers, with the result that many Atlantic Coast refiners found it feasible to supply part or all of their crude requirements from Los Angeles via the Panama Canal. Production of Mexican crude dropped sharply during 1922–1923 and continued to decline throughout the Twenties, so that many refiners who had formerly drawn supplies from that source were obliged to turn to California. Continuing demand, a low but not profitless price, and accessibility to world markets thus saved the Los Angeles producers from disaster. After the peak production of 1923 slacked off, prices once again improved, going to $1.16 a barrel by the end of 1924 and $1.34 by the end of 1925.

Pending construction of a refinery in the area, Shell of California was confronted with the serious problem of what to do with the large stocks of crude oil which it was accumulating. The initial production of the Alamitos well was sold to the Wilshire Oil Company of Los Angeles who hauled it away by tank truck. As soon as possible, three 55,000-barrel tanks were shipped in from Coalinga and erected, but with other wells coming in, these few tanks were far from adequate. During these critical weeks, Nidever excited the admiration of his fellow workers by ingenious juggling of crude runs and available tankage so that Shell's new wells on Signal Hill did not once have to be shut in.[20]

Soon after, an arrangement was made with Union Oil of California to connect Shell's tanks with Union's loading pipe line, and load Shell's Signal Hill oil aboard Union tankers for shipment to Martinez. Meanwhile, on the back side of Signal Hill, work went forward on a Shell tank farm that would later be used in conjunction with a new Shell refinery in nearby Wilmington. Production continued to mount at such a rapid rate that the company made additional arrangements with Union to permit the new tank farm to be connected to the Union line, and Union agreed to continue transporting oil in its tankers to the Shell refinery at Martinez.

Standard Oil of California, already heavily interested in the Huntington Beach field, did not wish to become involved in another town-lot drilling proposition, so it elected to stay out of the Signal Hill field entirely. Standard did, however, run a line into Signal Hill so that it might become a purchaser of crude oil there. Until Shell's permanent facilities were ready, Shell sold some of its Signal Hill crude to Standard. Standard's tankers were also engaged to transport crude to Martinez for Shell, although Union and General Petroleum vessels did the bulk of the company's contract carrying. The tanker carriage charge ran between 8 and 10 cents per barrel.[21]

Oil production of the three new Los Angeles Basin fields had risen to such giddy heights, so quickly, that every producing company was hard pressed to provide sufficient storage. In the emergency, the large producers and purchasers adopted the expedient of building concrete-lined earthen reservoirs in addition to conventional steel tanks. By July 1923, some $40 million was being spent on storage tanks and reservoirs, not counting the storage which had been completed in the Los Angeles area during the previous twelve months— 14½ million barrels of steel tankage and 21½ million barrels of reservoirs, excluding other millions of barrels of storage capacity represented by smaller tanks on the well sites. During the summer of 1923, Shell alone had 5 million barrels of storage building and had just acquired acreage for reservoirs to hold 4 million barrels more. Building of even more storage was obviated only by the execution of temporary crude sales contracts with companies such as Union and Associated.[22]

Curtailment at Coalinga

Faced with this acute storage problem and with a large current production from highly competitive fields, Shell of California decided to close down its Coalinga property as far as feasible. Late in 1922, 305 wells at Oilfields capable of producing 16,000 barrels a day were shut in. In their constant search for storage space, the hard-pressed Shell men conceived the idea of reversing the direction of flow of the Coalinga-to-Martinez pipe line, and using the 1,100,000-barrel tank farm at Coalinga and the 1,500,000 barrels of steel tankage along the pipe line for storing Signal Hill oil. The 750,000-barrel concrete reservoir which had been built at Coalinga in Balfour Guthrie days was reconditioned and pressed into service. Many who were at Martinez at the time remember seeing tankers lined up at the Martinez wharf, often as many as four or five, waiting to discharge their oil into the northern end of the Martinez-to-Coalinga line.[23]

During 1921–1922, production at Coalinga was gradually cut back, as soon as it became apparent that the Los Angeles area could be counted upon to furnish all of Shell of California's crude requirements. Finally, in December 1922, with the prospect of the peak year 1923 just ahead, the company shut in the Coalinga production except for a small trickle from offset wells around the borders of the property. Obviously, the sensible course was to keep the fully owned Coalinga property as a reserve for the future; and as more and more fields came in in the Los Angeles area during the Twenties, Coalinga continued shut in. Except for the opening of a few wells to obtain special grades of crude needed in lubricants manufacture and for the drilling of a second row of offset wells around the property boundaries in 1925, the old Limited property ceased activity until 1932 when it began gradually to be put back into production.[24]

This gradual closing down of Coalinga solved another problem. It enabled the company to send a steady stream of highly trained production men from Coalinga to Shell's new Los Angeles Basin fields, thus helping to alleviate what would otherwise have been a critical shortage of skilled men. It was, as well, the beginning of a fortunate dispersal of Coalinga men throughout the Shell production organization—fortunate because a great many of these men would soon rise to high positions in the company's management, taking with them the liberal training in human relations which they had received at Oilfields.

Dominguez Hill

Once the prolific oil-bearing nature of these long, low hills in the Los Angeles Basin had been demonstrated, geologists and drillers of exploratory wells began to go over the whole region with a fine-tooth comb. The result, as might be expected, was the discovery of other fields close on the heels of Huntington Beach, Signal Hill, and Santa Fe Springs. Most of these new discoveries were of sufficient size and productivity to have become famous in their own right, as no doubt would have been the case had they not been overshadowed by such tremendous neighbors.

Dominguez Hill (now called Dominguez), inland some three or four miles from Long Beach, was discovered by Union Oil in September 1923. Since most of the acreage belonged to three landowners, instead of hundreds, it was possible for Union and Shell, who were the chief operators at Dominguez, to develop the field more sensibly, without the undue haste and excessive drilling that had been features of Huntington Beach, Signal Hill, and Santa Fe Springs. Shell started drilling its first well at Dominguez on the Reyes lease in December 1923. The Dominguez field † reached its peak production during 1925, that year netting the company more than 4,000,000 barrels of oil.[26]

Torrance

The Torrance field, west of Dominguez Hill, was discovered in June 1922. Shell held 195 acres, and began its first well at Torrance

---

† Dominguez was the scene of an interesting freak accident in the early summer of 1925. Shell's Reyes No. 27 had been drilled to the top of the producing formation, the casing run and cemented. While the cement was setting, high-pressure gas collected below and blew the head off the well. A geyser of sand, water, pine cones, and pieces of petrified wood spouted from Reyes 27 for two weeks. Fred Knief and his crew finally succeeded in getting a gate valve on the well-head, and had just finished when a subterranean roar caused them all to take to their heels, not a minute too soon. With a deafening crash the ground gave way and boiler, rig, draw-works, platform, and derrick all disappeared into the ground, with only the top few feet of the derrick remaining visible. The geyser of sand, pine cones, etc., had hollowed out a large underground chamber and the overlying earth could no longer support the weight upon it. The cavity was left for a dumping place, and during World War II yielded large amounts of scrap iron for salvage drives.[25]

(or Redondo, as it was then called) in August 1922, completed in May 1923 for 146 barrels a day at 3,600 feet. It was a low-gravity, asphaltic oil and initial development was slow until larger wells were brought in. Then came another town-lot boom. Torrance reached its peak during May 1924; Shell shared in the boom by drilling some 65 wells during 1924 and 1925. Torrance was, however, a flush field and production subsequently fell to a point where several Shell wells became unprofitable to operate. During 1929, the company began abandonment of its Torrance leases, restoring the ground to its original condition as specified in the lease terms. The Torrance venture, as a result of its early end, cost Shell a long-term net loss of about $4,000,000.[27]

Seal Beach

Another discouraging development in a period otherwise distinguished for successes was Seal Beach, a swampy location three miles east of Signal Hill. Here Shell of California early took leases, and began drilling its first well, Bryant No. 1, in December 1922. Four wells were drilled on the Bryant lease, the first and second yielding about 50 barrels of oil daily accompanied by 2,000 barrels, and more, of water. The third well, inconclusive, was abandoned in November 1925 after having been drilled to 7,000 feet—a considerable depth for the time. The No. 4 Bryant well, also unproductive, was abandoned in April 1926. A fifth well drilled on the nearby Fred Bixby lease encountered enormous quantities of warm salt water and was also abandoned. Because of the large amount of money which had been spent with almost negligible results, the company decided to surrender its Seal Beach acreage ‡ in May 1926.[28]

The Marland Oil Company soon after leased part of the Bixby property and only three months later, in August 1926, brought in a 1,240-barrel well at 4,400 feet. Because it was of commercial proportions, the Marland well is considered the discovery well of the Seal Beach field. The Seal Beach miss was almost as disappointing as Roxana's failure at Haynesville, Louisiana, a few years earlier. Shell did not return to the field until nearly twenty years later in 1944. At that time, the company took a new lease on Bryant property at the edge

‡ Old-timers love to recall how this decision embarrassed the accountants in the Long Beach office. A large amount of lumber had been used to build a backstop and bleachers for the Shell ball diamond at Signal Hill; in anticipation of further drilling, the lumber had been charged on the books to "Bixby No. 2," which was, of course, never drilled.

of the Seal Beach field and drilled Bryant No. 5 which, along with a number of subsequent wells, yielded satisfactory production.[29]

Inglewood

Another Los Angeles Basin field in which Shell was active during this period was Inglewood, near the site of the present Los Angeles Airport. It was discovered by Standard Oil of California in September 1924 and, although at its peak Inglewood production was only a third that of Signal Hill, it was nevertheless an extremely profitable field for Shell and helped make up for disappointments such as Torrance and Seal Beach. The Inglewood field covered 885 acres and all but 22 of these acres were held by five companies, with the result that wasteful town-lot drilling was avoided. Shell completed its first well at Inglewood, Rindge No. 1, for 2,000 barrels a day in May 1925 and in July discovered a second producing zone with its Rindge No. 9. By Christmas 1925, the company had realized more than 1,800,000 barrels of oil from Inglewood, enough to pay for the year's expenses and leave a cash balance of more than a million dollars in the bank. Inglewood was, in this respect, one of the most profitable of Shell's fields in California. Later on, in the early 1930's, the company increased its holdings at Inglewood by purchase.[30]

Casinghead Gasoline

Along with the large-scale oil production of the Los Angeles Basin during these years, there was an accompanying large production of oil-well or "casinghead" gas—the gas that occurs with oil in nature and provides the pressure to lift the oil of a flowing well to the surface. In some of the earlier fields, such as Cushing in Oklahoma, the wastage of gas during the period of flush production had been tremendous, and for several reasons: the ratio of gas to oil was very high; the populous gas-consuming centers were far away, requiring large investments in pipe lines to connect the field with a profitable market; even the demand for casinghead gasoline, which could be extracted from the gas, was not great because the automobile then was still in its infancy.

But on the Pacific Coast in the 1920's it was a somewhat different story. The amount of gas produced in proportion to oil was smaller, and intelligent efforts were made to utilize it. At Signal Hill, where production first reached sizeable proportions in the spring of 1922, plans got under way at once to build an absorption plant for the manufacture of casinghead gasoline. Before it could be completed, a second compressor unit was added, the two of them going into operation in September 1922. Thereafter oil and gas production from Shell's properties on Signal Hill rose so rapidly that the gasoline department had difficulty in building enough new plant capacity to process the steadily increasing stream of gas. Three months later at the end of December 1922, the plant had twelve compressor units and by the spring of 1923 it had sixteen.[31]

The merits of casinghead gasoline as a blending agent in motor fuel were by now fully appreciated, with the result that prices for casinghead gasoline (or natural gasoline, as it is called today) rose to 16 cents a gallon wholesale. This made it possible to pay off the capital construction costs of one of these plants in only sixty days.[32]

A further inducement to full utilization of casinghead gas was the fact that there was a market for the "dry," or residue, gas left over after the gasoline plants had removed the saleable liquids. California had neither wood nor coal in quantities that were large enough, and the booming city of Los Angeles and its thriving suburbs early came to rely on natural gas not only as a fuel for cooking and home-heating, but for industrial use as well. Large amounts of Shell's Signal Hill gas were sold to public utility companies in the area. Taking full advantage of this favorable market situation, Shell of California missed few opportunities for building casinghead gasoline plants. At one time during the Twenties, the company accounted for 25% of the total casinghead gasoline manufactured in California.

Ventura

With all this activity in the Los Angeles area, it was only natural that development work at Ventura should proceed rather slowly during the years 1920–1925. Shell's Gosnell No. 3 came in for 940 barrels a day of 29° oil in March 1922, and because it was the first well to give indication of commercially feasible production, it has since been classed as the field's discovery well—although in the light of later knowledge it was possible to go back and complete some of the earlier "unsuccessful" wells as commercial producers.§ In October 1922, Associated Oil Company, which had acquired Lloyd's State Consolidated properties, brought in Lloyd No. 5 for 1,900 barrels a day. During the next two years the cable-tool rigs which had done

§ For earlier history of Ventura, see pages 106-112.

the original drilling at Ventura gave way to combination rigs, and finally the rotary method was adopted entirely. The new and heavier rotary rigs, using weighted drilling mud, were able to withstand the high underground pressures which had been so troublesome to the company's early drilling efforts at Ventura.

By 1925 it was possible to reach depths between 5,000 and 6,000 feet at Ventura, and in that year Associated completed its Lloyd No. 9A at 5,150 feet for an initial production of 4,870 barrels a day. With the completion of this large well, active development work got under way and has proceeded at an orderly pace from that time to the present. Most of the Ventura leases were large in area and in the hands of a relatively few companies, thus precluding a town-lot drilling scramble. Twenty-five years later, California refiners would be thankful that this had been so, for Ventura's tremendous potential production was thus saved for a future time when floods of oil would no longer be issuing from the Los Angeles Basin.[33]

San Joaquin Valley

During these years between 1920 and 1925, Shell of California also prospected other areas in its territory. At Albuquerque, New Mexico, an exploration office was opened under Dr. E. F. Davis early in 1920; at the same time other prospecting crews were at work in Utah. In 1922, there was some small-scale wildcatting in the San Joaquin Valley, in the Buttonwillow district and at Belridge and an unsuccessful well was put down near the Sargent field, one of California's oldest and smallest oil fields just east of Watsonville on the coast. None of these ventures yielded any returns, except for a helium well in Utah which had to be turned over to the government.[34]

More productive of eventual results was the entry of Shell of California into the Bakersfield area of the San Joaquin Valley in the spring of 1924, when a small office was set up at Bakersfield under A. R. May. The first major project of this Bakersfield group was the valuation of property of the Belridge Oil Company in the North and South Belridge fields, near which Shell had drilled an unsuccessful wildcat the year before. May recommended outright purchase of these developed properties, together with undeveloped lands totalling some 30,000 acres, all owned in fee, for $8,000,000—a bargain in the light of later developments. Extensions of productive areas and discovery of deeper horizons in both the North and South Belridge fields in ensuing years made the Belridge Oil Company a valuable property indeed. (In the thirty years following 1924, the Belridge company paid out some $19,000,000 in dividends and in 1953 had an indicated book value of more than $35,000,000.) Shell decided, however, to pass up the Belridge properties. Their cost seemed too great, at a time when sizeable fields were being discovered in the Los Angeles area for a much smaller outlay of cash.[35]

As a matter of fact, the bonanza years which the California oil hunters had enjoyed since 1921 were beginning to have a cautionary effect upon California oil companies. Inventories of oil above ground, especially in the Los Angeles area, were large and still growing. When, in July 1926, May's group at Bakersfield discovered the Mt. Poso field, the customary rapid development did not follow. Mt. Poso and other Shell discoveries and acquisitions in the San Joaquin Valley were put by, as a sort of insurance policy, and were not actively developed until the mid-Thirties. Even so, Shell of California's production jumped more than 300% in the five years between 1920 and 1925— from 6,000,000 to 19,500,000 barrels.

3

A Change of Luck for Roxana

THIS same five-year period saw an almost equal improvement in Roxana's production picture. That company's crude oil output more than doubled, from 3,000,000 barrels in 1920 to 7,800,000 in 1925. It was not Roxana's good fortune to discover a field of major importance during these years, as Shell of California had done at Signal Hill. The bulk of Roxana's new production came from judicious purchases of semi-proven acreage—lands near known fields with a better-than-average chance of producing oil.

Because of the high price of crude oil and the resulting high price of proven and semi-proven oil lands, Roxana had felt obliged to confine its activities to pure wildcatting in the late years of the war and the immediate postwar period. But with the onset of a temporary depression in 1920–1921, the price of Mid-Continent crude dropped from $3.50 to $1.00 a barrel during the first six months of 1921. Once again the purchase of semi-proven lands became feasible. In the spring of 1921 the Roxana management modified a policy of five years' standing, and began to look around for attractive buys. In their new search for proven and semi-proven properties, Van der Gracht and his associates were fortunate in making the acquaintance of a spectacularly successful Oklahoma wildcatter, Ernest W. Marland.

Burbank

By 1921, Marland's star was approaching its zenith. In 1908, he had come to Oklahoma from Pittsburgh to get a fresh start, after having already made and lost a million-dollar fortune in the gas fields of Hancock, West Virginia. Marland turned his attention to Kay County, in northern Oklahoma west of the Osage Nation, an area where little successful drilling had been done up to then. With some Pittsburgh associates (W. H. McFadden, a former executive of Carnegie Steel Corporation; J. H. McCaskey, a salesman of Duchess County sauerkraut; and Lew H. Wentz, an ex-Pittsburgh politician and professional baseball player), Marland finally succeeded in 1911, bringing in the Ponca field, the first promising discovery west of the Osage Nation. By 1917, McCaskey and Wentz had withdrawn from the venture and gone into the producing business on their own. That year, Marland organized the Marland Refining Company to build and operate a refinery at nearby Ponca City.[36]

Then began a series of fortuitous discoveries which were soon to place Marland's name in the fore of Oklahoma oil producers. In December 1916, he brought in the North Newkirk field in northern Kay County. It was a gas field, and became the basis for another Marland enterprise, the Kay County Gas Company, which for the next three years supplied several nearby cities with their entire gas requirements. In 1918, the Blackwell field, where Marland and Wentz had drilled a number of gas wells in 1912, became a substantial oil producer through the discovery of deeper horizons.

Late in 1918 the Bureau of Indian Affairs, which had thus far kept the western part of the Osage Nation's property off the market, announced its intention of granting 160-acre leases in that area. The terms were high: one-sixth royalty to the tribe (raised to one-fifth when the wells averaged more than 100 barrels a day in any month) plus a cash bonus to be determined by public auction at Pawhuska, seat of the Osage Council. Because of highly favorable geologic indications and the fact that oil in varying amounts had already been found north, south, east, and west of the Osage territory, Marland and hundreds of others, from major companies to the smallest producers, hurried off to the Pawhuska auctions and attempted to buy as many leases as they could pay for. It was with leases thus acquired that Marland made his first really big strike at Burbank, where he brought in the 780-barrel discovery well in May 1920. As leasing and drilling progressed, it became apparent that Burbank was the biggest and richest Oklahoma oil field since Cushing.

In common with most wildcatters, Marland was in constant need of money to develop his successful strikes. His long run of successful discoveries had necessitated plowing back all available resources into oil-field development work. He was, in addition, not averse to paying large prices for leases. And coupled to these was the added drain of his own personal expenditures, on a scale so lavish that in Oklahoma the Marland name had become synonymous with prodigality. To meet these heavy obligations, Marland often found it necessary to sell off part of his leases in a new field.

The slump of 1920–1921 brought a sharp drop in prices and all oil companies found themselves with smaller profits and assets of greatly reduced value. The Marland Oil Company with assets valued at $100,000,000 [37] found itself with a net profit during the first half of 1921 of only $347,000—and this without any allowance for depreciation, depletion, amortization, inventory shrinkage, or Federal income taxes.[38] With a deficit impending, Marland was finding it harder than usual to raise money; he was, in fact, hunting for a prospective partner to share in the expense of developing his proven Burbank holdings. Since Roxana was receptive to acquiring semi-proven acreage, it was only natural that the two companies should get together.

On February 26, 1921, Roxana signed an agreement with Marland to take over an undivided half interest in three of Marland's 160-acre leases in the Burbank field, on which four wells, including the discovery well, had been drilled. Roxana was to pay a total purchase price of $1,500,000—$1,000,000 of it in cash and the balance in oil as produced. Management of the properties was given to Roxana, and Marland's Kay County Gas Company agreed to deliver Roxana's share of the oil to the Ozark line at Yale by means of a pipe line which the Marland company owned running from Quay, near Yale, to Ponca City. It was a good buy for Roxana and, as Marland had paid only $15,000 for this acreage at a Pawhuska auction in February 1919, it was also a profitable deal for him. During ensuing months, Roxana acquired interests in other Burbank leases and eventually its holdings in the field were larger than Marland's.[39]

Burbank was developed rapidly during the next two years. The peak production of the field, some 122,000 barrels a day, was reached in July 1923. Surrounding towns, in typical boom fashion, mushroomed overnight. Burbank (today a village of less than 300 inhabitants) boasted a population of 2,500 to 3,000; had a thriving business center, equipment houses, a bank, and 250 teams of horses to haul the familiar heavy oilfield equipment.[40] Particularly well remembered by Roxana old-timers (although with no great affection) was "Whizzbang," an oilfield camp near the company's DeNoya lease, teeming with the usual retinue of gamblers, bootleggers, and their hangers-on —a real, old-fashioned, wide-open boom town. "Whizzbang" disappeared with the passing of peak drilling activity and long ago became the quiet village of DeNoya, Oklahoma.[41]

With the northwest extension which went beyond the limits of the Osage Nation and into the eastern part of Kay County, the Burbank field eventually covered 23,000 acres. Its production by the end of 1950 had passed 230 million barrels. The lion's share of the Burbank production went to Phillips Petroleum and Carter Oil, companies which had put up staggering amounts of cash to purchase large blocks of acreage at the Pawhuska auctions. Roxana, with a total original investment of only $1,500,000, percentage-wise probably fared best of the three, for its over-all share of the Burbank field * was next to that of Phillips and Carter.[43]

Tonkawa

Burbank was only one of the plums dropped in Roxana's lap by Ernest Marland. At Tonkawa, about 35 miles west of Burbank, the Marland company completed another wildcat on June 29, 1921, only four days after Signal Hill had come in. Its production from only 2,660 feet was twice that of the Signal Hill discovery well. The Humphreys Petroleum Company, which held substantial acreage in the area, had given Marland a quarter-section (160-acre) lease on the proviso that he drill a well to test the formation. Enlisting the assistance of others interested in the area, Marland got Prairie Oil & Gas to put up $2,500 "dry hole money" and his own Kay County Gas Company furnished $5,000. Finally, by offering half his acreage to Cosden

* The Burbank properties (which later included acreage acquired through the Union of Delaware, Wolverine, and Comar deals) continued to produce for Shell through 1938. At the end of that year, they were traded to Phillips in exchange for Phillips leases at Churchill and Udall, Kansas, and Avant, Oklahoma.[42]

Oil & Gas, Marland persuaded that company to join the venture as an equal partner. These arrangements illustrate the difficulty Marland often had in obtaining money for wildcat drilling, especially in areas which had failed to excite the geologists.

There was no immediate rush to the Tonkawa area even after this first well had come in for a thousand barrels a day. Marland, as usual, started hunting for a partner with ready cash to help him develop the acreage adjoining his Tonkawa discovery well. The land on which the Marland-Cosden well had come in was a full section (640 acres); each company owned a half interest in the lease. Marland, in addition, owned an adjoining 240-acre lease outright. Soon after completion of the discovery well, he offered Carter Oil Company a half interest in these 560 acres for $1,000,000 and was turned down.[44]

A few weeks later, Marland went to London hoping to convince Deterding that Roxana should participate in the Tonkawa venture by purchasing an interest in a new company, named Comar Oil Company, which Marland had organized under Delaware law on July 11, 1921. As a result of Marland's representations, Roxana agreed to acquire a half interest in Comar and early in September a contract was signed. It provided that Marland would turn over his holdings in the Tonkawa field to the new Comar company and that Roxana would put up $2,000,000—one million in cash immediately, the second million when it was needed for development work. Comar was to be owned thenceforth in equal shares by Marland and Roxana and the management of the company vested in Roxana. The affairs of the new company were handled by an office set up in Ponca City.

This agreement between Marland and Roxana went into effect September 19, 1921. Almost immediately, the new Comar company's first well came in for 3,300 barrels a day, an inkling of the kind of production which would be encountered at Tonkawa. Other wells completed soon afterward produced as much as 5,000 barrels a day initially, and three main productive sands were encountered from the outset. (The field as a result was often called Three Sands, and the nearby boom town was so named.)

Tonkawa oil was of 43° gravity, extremely light and therefore highly desirable for refining into gasoline. By straight-run distillation, it yielded 46% gasoline. For this reason, many refining companies were anxious to obtain Tonkawa oil and ran lines into the field. Their eagerness resulted in a rare circumstance: a surplus of pipe line capacity in a flush field. On May 1, 1923, when Tonkawa hit its peak production of 111,000 barrels a day, there were fifteen pipe lines already connected to the field and eleven more building—altogether a total carrying capacity of 185,000 barrels a day. For once, in a new field, there was no temporary local "overproduction" and lowered prices as a result of a shortage in transportation facilities.[45]

Comar added to the 580 acres it held in Tonkawa field. In 1922, when the field was extended northward, Comar acquired much of the new acreage. Then, late that same year, Comar purchased the Alcorn Oil Company's Tonkawa leases for $3,000,000 in cash and oil and the Wrightsman Petroleum Company's leases for $1,000,000. By late 1925, this joint Roxana-Marland company held some 1,900 acres of producing leases at Tonkawa, yielding about 50% of the field's total production. The bulk of the field's output was flush production and came during the 1920's, but it was large enough to place Tonkawa among the memorable fields of Oklahoma oildom.[46]

North and South Braman

Tonkawa was the most productive of Comar's holdings, but the company was also active in a few other areas. The chief of these were the North and South Braman fields in the extreme northern part of Kay County, adjoining the Kansas line, where Marland had earlier done promising core-drilling. Because of these favorable indications, Comar spent some half-million dollars to acquire leases covering the whole of these two fields, except a quarter-section and a small tract of two acres near Braman townsite. The discovery wells of the North and South Braman fields which came in during the spring of 1924 seemed to indicate another field of tremendous potentials, as big as Burbank or Tonkawa, but later development failed to fulfill these hopes. Comar in 1923 developed acreage in the northwest extension of Burbank, and also had minor holdings in a few other Osage and Kay County fields.[47]

Comar was active in the production of casinghead gasoline, for there were large quantities of gas in the Tonkawa field. In June 1922, the Comar Gasoline Company was organized as a subsidiary of Comar, owned 75% by Comar and 25% by Marland and managed by Marland. This subsidiary eventually built three gasoline plants in the Tonkawa field with a total capacity of 34,000 gallons a day. Another joint-venture gasoline plant was that of the Romarti Gasoline Company, organized in March 1922 as a three-way partnership of Roxana, Marland, and Tidal Refining, a Tide Water subsidiary.

Romarti owned and operated a casinghead plant of 12,000 gallons per day capacity in the Burbank field.[48]

Despite the fact that the Tonkawa field did not have the long life of Signal Hill, Tonkawa and the Comar venture were as much the making of Roxana as Signal Hill was of the Shell company on the Coast. From Comar issued a golden stream of dividends all during the Twenties, reaching a peak of $19,000,000—one-half of which was Roxana's—in 1926. Altogether, the $2,000,000 investment in Comar had yielded Roxana $30,540,000 in dividends by the end of the Twenties. Better still was the high-grade oil, 30 million barrels of it, which comprised a very substantial share of Roxana's increased crude output during this period.

Kansas, Texas, Louisiana

The properties which Roxana acquired in conjunction with Marland were not the whole story of the company's production effort in the years between 1920 and 1925. As we shall see shortly, Roxana fell heir to several worth-while properties as a result of the Shell-Union merger of 1922 and also participated in new oilfield developments in Kansas, Oklahoma, Texas, Arkansas, and Louisiana.

The Kansas work, as in the preceding period, yielded little by way of actual results: in 1922 the company had only one well in the state, producing only 333 barrels through the whole year; in 1923, two wells in Kansas had a total production of 4,105 barrels; in 1924, the company drilled a successful well, proving up a part of the southwest portion of Winfield field. By the end of 1925, Roxana had a mere six wells in Kansas with a total production for the year of 103,000 barrels.

In North Central Texas, drilling continued on the wildcat properties that had been leased in the late years of the war. In the South Bend and Crystal Falls areas, some small production was obtained. Roxana had 40 wells in that area in 1922, yielding a total for the year of only 287,000 barrels. In 1923, 61 wells yielded 962,000 barrels with little change during the ensuing year. These low-producing, high-cost properties were located too far from the company's pipe line to make their continued operation feasible, and a few years later they were relinquished.[49]

In the summer of 1921, the company sent geologists into the Navarro County area of East Texas, with the result that Roxana had some 350 acres under lease in the area when the Powell field, near Corsicana, came in in January 1923. Roxana drilled twelve wells in that field. The production of the Powell field reached its peak of 355,000 barrels a day in November 1923, held up fairly well throughout 1924, and then declined. As late as 1923–1924, Roxana had only 60 wells in Texas with a total annual production of about 900,000 barrels. More wells were drilled during 1925, but they did not increase the total output perceptibly.[50]

During 1924, a headquarters staff of exploration, land, and production men was gathered at Dallas under Dr. van Holst Pellekaan, who had come east from California. This office had charge of Roxana's three exploration and production divisions: the Central division, located at Dallas and covering North Texas, North Central Texas, East Texas, northern Louisiana, Arkansas, and West Texas; the Gulf Coast division, office at Houston, covering the Texas and Louisiana Gulf Coast; and the Mid-Continent division, located in the company's old office space in the Mayo Building, Tulsa, with responsibility for Oklahoma and Kansas.[51]

In Louisiana, where Roxana had gradually abandoned most of its acreage in the Haynesville area following the initial unsuccessful venture, the company was able to regain some of its lost ground. About 500 acres of the original holdings in the Haynesville area had been retained and in May 1921, two months after the discovery well had been completed, the company bought another 320 acres of leases, in June another 40 acres, in July 40 acres more, and in August another 60 acres. Late in 1921 offset wells were begun on this acreage and by the end of 1922 Roxana had drilled 28 wells at Haynesville which produced that year some 633,000 barrels of oil. This was the year of Haynesville's peak production. In later years, the company's take from the field dropped sharply: 265,000 barrels in 1923; 124,000 barrels in 1924; 84,000 barrels in 1925.[52]

Smackover

Early in 1921, oil was discovered at El Dorado in southern Arkansas, near the Louisiana border. The price of leases immediately rose to high levels, making the acquisition of acreage there unattractive, especially in view of the low gravity of the oil (18° to 23°). Many oil companies began prospecting the nearby area, and Roxana was holding acreage in April 1922 when a prolific new field was brought in at Smackover, Arkansas, not far away. During the remainder of 1922, Roxana drilled seven wells at Smackover for a total production of 187,000 barrels and in 1923 completed 27 more. The yield of these 34 wells during 1923 was 1,102,000 barrels, a daily average production of about 90 barrels per well.[53]

Smackover was a typical boom field. Transportation was poor, storage could not be built fast enough to keep up with well completions, and much of the crude was as a result stored in earthen reservoirs or behind earthen dams. O. D. Story, who was there at the time as a young supply clerk, remembered seeing reservoirs so large that they were literally lakes, with men in boats rowing over the surface taking soundings to help them gauge the amount of oil in "storage." [54]

Heavy oil, similar to that encountered at El Dorado, was found at Smackover; but from another horizon the field yielded a light oil of premium quality. Roxana drilled ten more wells at Smackover during 1924, and produced that year 951,000 barrels of Smackover crude. In 1925, the field's peak year, the company had 77 wells at Smackover which yielded 2,189,000 barrels of oil. Much of it was shipped by tank car to Wood River and used for the manufacture of lubricating oils. The field declined rapidly after the peak of 1925 had passed. But for a few short years, Smackover was one of the country's large oil fields and, at the end of 1950, it still ranked in all-time eighth place among U. S. oil fields.[55]

In Oklahoma, most of Roxana's new production during the years 1920–1925 came from its joint efforts with Marland or from properties acquired in the Shell-Union deal. Roxana's wholly owned wells in Oklahoma at the end of 1925 numbered 563, an increase of only 51 over 1922. They produced 4,875,000 barrels of oil in contrast to Roxana's share of the Comar production, 5,902,000 barrels, and production from one of the largest of the properties received in the Shell-Union merger, 1,223,000 barrels. The old stand-bys, Cushing and Healdton, continued to decline during the Twenties; but Covington (or Garber, as it was more commonly called) got a fresh lease on life during 1925, when deep production at 4,200 feet was encountered. This was high-quality oil of 42° gravity and brought a premium price.[56]

In the Okmulgee County district, due south of the old Glenn Pool, several fields were active in the early 1920's, with Roxana holding considerable acreage in two of them, the Slick district to the west and the Beggs district to the south. In southwestern Oklahoma, some 60 miles west of the Healdton field, two new pools called North Duncan and West Duncan were developed in the early Twenties; Roxana had productive acreage in each. It also acquired several blocks of acreage in the Hewitt field, near Healdton.

The Beginnings of Geophysics

All during the Twenties, Roxana geologists and geophysicists were hard at work attempting to locate new oil deposits, and in their search they made use of the most modern of scientific techniques. In later years, when Ernest Marland spoke of the formation of Comar, he said, "I made the contract which founded this company after studying the exploration and development methods of the Royal Dutch Shell Company in Mexico and South America, and after coming to the conclusion that their scientific advancement was away ahead of any American oil company." [57] Marland was a devout believer in the value of the scientific approach in oil-hunting and he knew from observation that the Shell Group and the people associated with it had in great measure been responsible for introducing to the American oil industry its first geophysical tools. E. L. DeGolyer, himself a pioneer of the first rank in this field, gives credit to the Royal Dutch-Shell Group for several of these important innovations. [58]

The first improvement over surface geology as a method of hunting for oil was the introduction of the diamond core-drill, previously used in the United States for mineral prospecting of other kinds. Van der Gracht had used the core drill hunting for oil in Romania during 1914, the year before he had come to the United States to join Roxana. During Roxana's big exploratory campaign, he introduced the core drill to American oil fields, 1918–1919. The taking of cores, as the reader may surmise, gave positive information on the nature of the formations below the surface. To the oil geologist, such information was valuable because it was often possible, in shallow holes, to get evidence of favorable geologic structure (or lack of it) without the expense of deep test wells. The first notable success for core drilling was the discovery of the northern extension (the most prolific part) of the Tonkawa field in the summer of 1922. [59]

Then, in 1922, came the introduction to the Gulf Coast of the torsion balance, an instrument for measuring fluctuations in gravity. The torsion balance had been developed as a field version of the Coulomb balance, a century-old laboratory instrument, by the Hungarian physicist Baron Roland Eötvös, head of the physics department at the University of Budapest. Eötvös built his first instrument in 1890, and had improved it substantially when the first field investigations were undertaken with it in Hungary in 1901. In 1915–1916, he undertook to survey an oil field near Vienna and, during 1917–1918, the Germans put it to use in Romania for oil-hunting purposes. Dr. J. Th. Erb, head of the Group's geological department at The Hague, was quick to grasp the importance of the new instrument for locating anticlines that might prove to be oil-bearing. In the years right after the war, Erb arranged to have some of these instruments manufactured for the Group.[60]

Torsion balance observations, made at various points over a given area, provided data from which changes in the pull of gravity could be computed. By correlating these gravity data with available geological information, it was possible to obtain some idea of the subsurface structure of the area. Such information was helpful in areas such as the flatlands of the Texas and Louisiana Gulf Coast, where the usefulness of surface geology was limited in the search for buried salt domes. Salt domes were by no means certain indicators of oil, but they provided valuable clues to its possible whereabouts.

In the years immediately following the war, Dr. Erb got the Group to try the Eötvös balance in several locations—in the Hurghada field of Egypt, in Seria (Northwest Borneo), and in Mexico. During 1921, F. B. Plummer, who had been Roxana's chief geologist in previous wildcatting operations in North Central Texas and northern Louisiana, spent several months in Europe familiarizing himself with this new geophysical instrument. In the spring of 1922, he returned to the Gulf Coast of Texas and Louisiana as head of a special unit which was to try to get a production foothold in that area—by discovery, purchase, or the promotion of partnership deals. Plummer was accompanied by a draftsman, F. W. J. Haas, and was instructed, largely for reasons of secrecy, to draw money and other assistance from the chairman of the New Orleans Refining Company. Plummer opened a small office in Houston, and hired Walle Merritt to handle land-leasing. L. G. Christie, who was sent from the Shell Company of California to join them in May 1923, recalls that the office at that time consisted only of Plummer, Merritt, Haas, and two stenographers.[61]

Late in 1922, the first torsion balance crew, under W. H. Terrell, got under way in the field and a second, under A. van Weelden, started operating early in 1923. After the passage of several months, further efforts at secrecy (undertaken in the hope of obtaining leases unobtrusively and cheaply) were dropped, and this separate group under Plummer came under the Roxana exploration and production headquarters office newly set up in Dallas. The Houston unit continued its prospecting work and by the end of 1925 had 119,000 acres in Louisiana and 625,000 acres in Texas under lease for exploration with geophysical tools.[62]

The Eötvös torsion balance was put to work to find hidden salt domes, for almost all the domes covered by hills and other protuberances had already been located by surface geology methods. The torsion balance work went slowly. The instrument was delicate, several hours were required to set it up and record the data, and a large number of individual observations had to be taken in each area under survey. The balance consisted of a hair-like torsion wire from which a light metal beam was suspended; on each of the beams there were equal weights placed at unequal heights. A shaft of reflected light traced a pattern on photographic paper, producing a record of the instrument's measurements. Thirty years later, DeGolyer would write, "Although I was partly responsible for its introduction, I might as well admit that I have never understood the functioning of that delicate instrument well enough to explain it." [63]

Almost coincident with the introduction of the Eötvös balance came another geophysical tool, the seismograph, successfully introduced to America by Marland Oil Company, early in 1924.† Originally used to record earthquake tremors, seismic recording instruments had been put to more immediately practical uses during World War I by the Germans who had found adaptations of the seismograph useful in locating enemy artillery emplacements. These seismic methods were adapted to oil-hunting by Dr. L. Mintrop of Germany. In 1920, he made a seismic survey for oil at Neuen Gamme, near Hamburg, and later the same year surveyed an oil-bearing salt dome in the north German plain. The first large-scale trial of the seismograph as an oil-hunting tool came in Mexico when in 1923 the Group's Mexican company hired Mintrop to make a seismic survey which proved unsuccessful. The same year Marland put Mintrop's seismograph crew to work, also unsuccessfully, in the Powell district of East Texas. Early in 1924, Marland began working the salt-dome region of the Gulf Coast, an area which was expected to respond much more readily to this type of exploration. Soon after, the Gulf Production

† The guiding spirit behind this development was no doubt Van der Gracht, who was a top-notch petroleum geologist. At this time (1922–1928) he was vice president in charge of exploration of the Marland companies.

Company and Roxana also began using the seismograph in the Gulf Coast area.[64]

This was the so-called refraction seismograph. A shock was created by setting off a charge of dynamite on or near the surface. The energy waves emanating from the explosion were picked up by a series of seismometers, or listening ears, placed on the surface of the ground at various points several miles from the explosion point. These listening ears, hooked to a central recording point by electrical wires, picked up the arrival of the first of the energy waves, making possible an accurate record of their travel time from the point of the explosion. Through soft formations, such as beds of sand and shale, these energy waves travelled in underground arcs with known velocity between the explosion point and the seismometer. A compact formation, such as the hard plug of a buried salt dome, would transmit the energy waves at a much faster rate, in effect refracting them much as a prism refracts a light ray. Waves thus refracted would arrive at the seismometer in an abnormally short time. By setting off and recording explosions at different points in the same area, it was possible to outline areas through which the waves passed faster than normal, and thus locate salt domes of the kind common on the Gulf Coast.

During 1924, three of these hidden salt domes were located on the Gulf Coast by means of the refraction seismograph. The success of this new method touched off a wave of seismic exploratory activity, by several companies, along the Texas and Louisiana coasts. This activity lasted through the Twenties and in six years cost an estimated $25,000,000. The German organization set up by Dr. Mintrop supplied most of the equipment and crews during this period.[65]

In May 1925, Amerada Petroleum Corporation, which had been organized by Lord Cowdray, the Group's partner in Mexico, set up the Geophysical Research Corporation in Tulsa. Under the direction of J. C. Karcher, this research group was responsible for adding refinements which helped make the refraction method so useful along the Gulf: the radio time-break and electrical recording. More important, Karcher's group developed and in 1929 introduced the reflection seismograph, a new method which reflected the energy waves off hard underground beds and measured the time periods required for the waves to travel from the surface to the reflecting beds and back to the surface again. With a series of these readings and a knowledge of the velocities of the waves in the formations penetrated, it was possible to plot with a fair degree of accuracy the shape and depth of the reflecting layers. The reflection method permitted the extension of seismic work to areas other than the salt-dome fields of the Gulf Coast, at that time the only region where the refraction seismograph had yielded worth-while results. After 1930, the new reflection method rapidly displaced the earlier refraction seismograph and became one of the most widely used exploration tools.[66]

The seismograph had two important advantages over the torsion balance. Refraction seismic work was faster for locating salt domes and the reflection seismograph permitted direct mapping of underground structures. With the torsion balance, the underground struc-

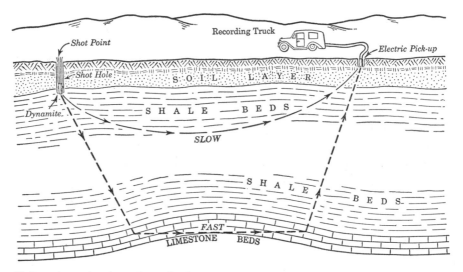

Refraction seismograph took advantage of fact that energy waves travel more quickly through hard formations, such as limestone, than they do through less compact layers near the surface. Recordings over a wide arc pin-pointed location of hard formations, such as buried salt domes.

ture had to be inferred from extensive interpretation of data. Even so, Roxana did not discard the torsion balance immediately, nor did other companies which had it in use. Roxana put the refraction seismograph to work in 1924–1925, but in the next few years continued to use both the torsion balance and the seismograph. In 1927, the company had as many as 28 torsion balances at work at one time. Eventually, in the 1930's, a new, much simpler, and more rapid gravity instrument, the gravity meter, was developed; it still continues in use. On the West Coast, the Eötvös balance did not prove successful and in 1927 Shell of California abandoned further trial of the method.[67]

In 1925, Roxana located the Allen and Clemens domes in Brazoria

County, Texas, by means of the torsion balance. During the next few years, the company lavished a great deal of time and large sums of money on a thorough attempt to prove these two domes as oil producers. The Allen dome yielded one 11-barrel-a-day well which produced a total of 80,000 barrels of oil in twelve years, but was otherwise unproductive despite nine deep wells drilled on it. Eleven deep wells in the Clemens dome yielded nothing at all. This dome was not a total failure, however; later it was developed by others for the sulphur it contained.[68]

Another geophysical tool introduced in the late Twenties was the

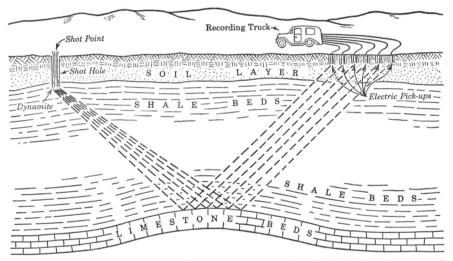

Reflection seismograph recorded energy waves reflected off hard underground formations, revealing both presence and shape of possible oil-bearing formations and permitting direct mapping. Refraction method had been suitable for Gulf Coast only; reflection method was put to widespread use.

magnetometer, an instrument that measures changes in the vertical component of the earth's magnetic field. The magnetic pull of rocks and minerals below the earth's surface varies in accordance with the magnetic mineral content of these rocks and minerals and their depths. With the magnetometer, networks of observations could be taken over a given area much in the fashion of gravity surveys. The data obtained, when properly analyzed, gave some suggestion of subsurface structures. Magnetometer results were highly variable, and hence undependable, when confined to a small area. But the instrument was less fragile than gravity instruments, was simple to set up, and could survey a widespread area quite rapidly. During the late Twenties, Roxana used the magnetometer extensively in the Texas Panhandle, West Texas, Oklahoma, and Kansas. As an instrument for locating drilling prospects, the magnetometer was not much used by Roxana after 1929. It is, however, still used for over-all surveys of unexplored areas and when so used is commonly carried by airplane over the terrain under survey.[69]

Still another technique tried by Roxana on the Gulf Coast in the late Twenties, but without success, was an electrical exploration system devised by the brothers Conrad and Marcel Schlumberger, of Paris. Schlumberger electrical exploration crews working at De Quincy, Kinder, and Lake Charles, Louisiana, and Laredo, Texas, were finally instructed to abandon their work and return home in July 1927. The Shell Company of California, which also tried the Schlumberger exploration method, obtained more encouraging results and continued the experiments through the 1920's, although they were in the end inconclusive. The Schlumbergers later became famous in the American oil business for their electrical well-logging method which, under sponsorship of the Shell companies, was introduced into Venezuela and the United States in 1932.[70]

4

The Shell-Union Deal

For a long time Deterding had wanted to organize a larger and more powerful Shell company in the United States. He had, in addition, clearly realized the desirability of enlisting American capital in the venture so that the American investing public might be favorably disposed towards the American Shell companies.[71]

As early as February 1916, we find Deterding writing to Van der Gracht in Tulsa, "It is, of course, always galling (apart from political considerations) in any country to see an enterprise doing well without local people being interested. It is contrary to human nature, however well a concern like that may be directed, or however much it may have the interest of the people at heart, not to anticipate there will be a kind of jealous feeling against such a company." [72] During the war years, Deterding on occasion put out feelers to see how such a company might be organized.

He was thoroughly shocked to discover that American investment bankers of the day expected a considerable share of any new enterprise in exchange for selling its stock. "Of all the grasping individuals I have ever met," he exclaimed in a letter, "the American bankers, who take up such issues, absolutely take the cake. . . . The proposal was that a certain amount of preference stock should be issued to the public and that the bankers should get as their commission no less than 40% ordinary capital. Now, if this 40% were going to be a permanent holding of the bankers, much as it is, still there might be some excuse for it, the bankers seeing that through their influence and on their moral responsibility the public takes all the preference capital. But what is really the case? No sooner has the American public swallowed the preference shares than the bankers start about, by means of press campaigns and all sorts of leaflets, to 'boom' the company. . . . After these ordinary shares have been launched on the public, the bubble bursts and back go the shares, down goes the credit of the company, down go the preference shares, and the company stands convicted of having 'landed' the American public. It would be a real 'let in,' or 'take in,' and no good would be derived from it . . . the Americans would hate us for having let them lose money." [73]

The Shell-Union deal with which we are to be concerned here was of far-reaching importance in this connection, for it made possible the achievement of these long-term objectives without the speculative pitfalls which Deterding was so anxious to avoid. At the same time, it added several valuable new properties to Shell's holdings in California and Oklahoma.

It all began nearly ten years earlier, when Robert Watchorn,‡ at the time treasurer of the Union Oil Company of California, induced Lyman Stewart, founder and head of that company, to give him an option to purchase the Stewart holdings in Union for $150 a share. For $1,000,000, Watchorn sold this option to Eugene de Sabla, president of Esperanza Consolidated Oil Co., which shortly afterwards became General Petroleum Corporation. General Petroleum held this option a short time, during which period Shell flirted with the idea of buying it. Unable to exercise the option for lack of funds, General Petroleum assigned it to the Mercantile Trust Company, of San Francisco. The San Francisco bank sold the option to a British group headed by Andrew Weir (later Lord Inverforth) and J. Tilden Smith.[74]

‡ See pages 136-138.

Because Union of California stock was selling well below the $150-a-share price called for in the option, the London group did not exercise the option, and it expired in April 1914. However, the same month that this option expired, Union signed a new contract with Weir and Smith to replace the expired option. It provided that they would purchase 150,000 shares of Union Oil's treasury stock for $100 a share. To carry out this plan, the London group in June 1914 organized the British Union Oil Company, Ltd., and made a first payment of $2,500,000. They were not able to make the second payment, due in August 1914, because of exchange restrictions arising from the First World War which had just broken out. Weir and Smith were granted a year's extension, but to no avail; in March 1915, the deal was called off. In return for the $2½ million already paid over, British Union received 25,000 shares of stock in Union of California.[75]

Nothing further was heard of this block of stock until the years immediately following the war. Then, in the spring of 1919, a group of New York financiers was organized for the purpose of securing a large (if possible, a controlling) interest in Union of California. The nucleus of this group had been drawn together by their mutual interest in the Baldwin Locomotive Works, of Eddystone, Pennsylvania. Chief of them was Percy A. Rockefeller (1878–1934), a nephew of John D. Rockefeller and son of William, the Rockefeller brother who had served as president of the Standard Oil Company of New York, from its organization in 1882 until 1911.

Through his father and elder brother, who served as directors of numerous railroads, Percy Rockefeller was well acquainted in railroading circles. He was also interested in a number of mining companies and through this connection had met Henry Lockhart, Jr., a promoter who had operated in mining and banking circles for the past two decades. They were both acquainted with Charles H. Schlacks, a former executive of the Denver & Rio Grande, Colorado Midland, and Western Pacific railroads, who had during the war years been general manager of the Eddystone Rifle Plant, a subsidiary of Baldwin Locomotive. A chief mover in the Eddystone enterprise was Samuel F. Pryor, head of Remington Arms, director of Baldwin Locomotive, and a close associate of both Percy Rockefeller and his father. Drawn together by common interests, urged on by Lockhart's promotional zeal, and backed by Percy Rockefeller's fortune, this group set off on the ambitious enterprise of obtaining control of Union Oil of California and building overnight a substantial operating

Frederick Godber was president of Roxana 1922–1928; is now chairman of Shell Transport & Trading. He was knighted in 1942 and created Baron Godber early in 1956.

George Legh-Jones was president of the San Francisco company from 1923 to 1934. He is now a managing director of Shell Transport & Trading, was knighted in 1952.

Oilfield village of Three Sands, Okla., in Tonkawa field, taken in July 1925.

Hewitt, Okla., field of Wolverine Petroleum Corporation, in 1922.

First licensed Dubbs cracking unit shown on its completion at Wood River, March 1921.

Right, the same plant after it was wrecked by explosion, December 1921, killing two men and badly burning several others. The unit which was built to replace it was a complete success, and Shell became one of the pioneer users of Dubbs cracking.

Courtesy P. E. Fost

Four Wood River Dubbs plants in May 1925. The fractionating units were on high towers to permit gravity feed-back. This arrangement was later eliminated by introduction of a successful hot oil pump, a Shell contribution.

oil company. In this project they were joined by a number of men prominent in New York financial circles who, along with the Percy Rockefeller group, subscribed the capital of the syndicate.[76]

Forsyth Wickes, a corporation lawyer, was retained as counsel. To handle the actual purchases, the syndicate in the summer of 1919 sent Lockhart and Wickes to California where a $15,000,000 credit had been arranged for them with a Los Angeles bank. Union Oil of California needed money. In April 1919, its board had voted to increase the company's capitalization from $50 to $100 million. Lockhart and Wickes negotiated with Lyman Stewart for the purchase of $20 million worth of this new treasury stock, and in addition bought such shares as they could from private investors. In this manner, and by purchase of the British Union block of shares which then numbered some 27,000 shares, the syndicate by September 20, 1919, acquired 102,764 shares of Union of California stock plus options to purchase an additional 19,516 shares.§ Not counting expenses connected with the acquisition, these shares of stock and subscription rights cost the syndicate $16½ million cash. As soon as the stock was in hand, it was assigned to a new company which had been organized for the purpose earlier that month.[78]

While these purchases were in progress, a separate syndicate managed by W. D. Ticknor and J. W. R. Crawford, and also backed by Percy Rockefeller, purchased some 1,700,000 shares of the Columbia Oil Producing Company, an old, respected Los Angeles firm, and executed agreements for the purchase of another 1½ million shares. For these Columbia shares, they paid $2,582,000 and deposited $500,-000 for the shares still to be acquired. These shares were also assigned to the new company.[79]

The new holding company, organized under the laws of Delaware, was christened simply Union Oil Company. To raise funds to pay for its stock acquisitions and to provide money for working capital, Union of Delaware sold $34,000,000 worth of common stock. After the Union of California and Columbia stock purchases had been paid for, this left some $15,000,000 in the treasury as working capital.[80]

Schlacks, who had no previous experience with the oil business, was elected president of the new company, and the Union of Delaware board, drawn largely from New York financial circles, was impressive

§ In August 1919, Union offered its shareholders the right to subscribe for 14¾ shares of new stock for each 100 shares held. These subscription rights were transferable, and the syndicate offered to purchase them at the rate of $60 a share.[77]

for the number of well-known names it included. Representing Percy Rockefeller's interest were W. E. S. Griswold, Samuel F. Pryor, and later on, J. W. R. Crawford, all men who had been associated with him in other enterprises; Charles Hayden, of Hayden, Stone & Company, now widely remembered for the bequest which built the Hayden Planetarium; Gates W. McGarrah, of the Chase National Bank, who later became president of the Bank for International Settlements in Basle; James H. Perkins, president of the Farmers Loan & Trust Company, and later chairman of the National City Bank and president of the New York Clearing House; Charles H. Sabin, president of the Mechanics & Metals National Bank, and soon to be chairman of the Guaranty Trust Company; Bayard Dominick, partner in the brokerage firm of Dominick & Dominick; Francis H. Swift, head of the Boston financial house, F. H. Swift & Company; Samuel M. Vauclain, president of the Baldwin Locomotive Works; W. L. Stewart, president of Union Oil Company of California, and E. W. Clark, vice president and general manager of that firm; T. W. Phillips, Jr., a prominent Pittsburgh oil man and member of Congress; Schlacks and Lockhart. Of this group, Lockhart, Griswold, Crawford, Sabin, Perkins, and Phillips were the most active in Union of Delaware affairs.[81]

With a directorate of such capabilities, fifteen million dollars in the bank, and large holdings of dividend-paying stock, the new company should have been a success. Its staff was small, consisting only of the president, treasurer, secretary, a legal department, and a publicity man to get favorable notices in the newspapers and assist the sale of stock, together with the necessary clerks and stenographers—some thirty people in all. Seven rooms in the Equitable Building at 120 Broadway were sufficient for office space.[82] But a staff not operating on sound principles, even if small in numbers, can do irreparable damage.

"It is lavish expenditure and costly mistakes at the outset which cripple so many oil companies," Deterding constantly lectured his own executives.[83] He could have used the Union of Delaware as an example to illustrate his text. Perhaps the most glaring mistake was made at the beginning, when the directors failed to select a seasoned oil man to head up the management. However competent they may have been in their own fields, the company's executives were experienced not in oil but in railroading and finance.

A second liability was the "promotion-minded" philosophy of some of the company's chief backers, particularly Henry Lockhart who had a large voice in Union's affairs. A natural-born promoter, Lockhart envisioned a large oil company operating in every branch of the business, from coast to coast, and speedily set about building it. There was nothing unsound in such an idea, and Lockhart might have succeeded if he had not embarked upon this venture at a time when the price of oil and of oil properties was at an all-time high, with really good properties not for sale at any price. The more prudent Shell companies, as we have seen, felt that prices (1917–1921) were too high to acquire producing properties by purchase, and had accordingly restricted their activities to wildcatting.

The promotional genius is, however, not deterred by pessimistic considerations. Backed by Percy Rockefeller, Lockhart promoted a company called Commonwealth Petroleum Corporation, a holding company which bought stock control of three small California oil-producing companies, all of them located in old fields. Commonwealth also acquired the stock of an old-time California drilling contracting firm, the W. D. Head Drilling Company, which at the time of the purchase had almost no tangible assets and a large hidden debt. The new Union of Delaware was only a month old when it voted to buy the Commonwealth concern, exchanging 1⅕ shares of Union of Delaware for each share of Commonwealth.[84]

Soon after, in December 1919, the company ordered four tankers constructed, two of 12,500 deadweight tons each and two of 10,000 d.w.t. It is unlikely that an experienced oil man would have committed his company to such a venture, for Union had no oil to transport. The producing companies just acquired either sold their oil locally as refined products or were tied up by long-term crude sales contracts. Schlacks hoped to resell the vessels upon completion at higher prices, but it was a poor speculation, for the shipbuilding market was then at an all-time high. Union hired a vice president to take charge of this tanker construction, which became during the next few months one of the chief enterprises of the Union office at 120 Broadway.

Early in 1920, two new companies joined the growing list of Union of Delaware subsidiaries. National Exploration Company was organized by the Rockefeller-Lockhart interests, with J. W. R. Crawford as president and separate offices at 522 Fifth Avenue. The object of this company was to explore for oil and buy leases. Union subscribed 26% of National's stock and agreed to pay it an annual fee for geological information.

In January 1920, the Eddystone Oil Company was organized as a wholly owned subsidiary of Union and soon after was given title to the Wayland Oil & Gas Company properties in West Virginia which Union purchased in March 1920 for $1,700,000. The Wayland properties amounted to a total of 15,000 acres with a total daily production of only 260 barrels. During the next year, Union lent Eddystone more than three million dollars to buy other high-cost, low-volume properties.[85]

In July 1920, Union spent $5,250,000 cash to buy from The Texas Company its interest in a contract with the Central Petroleum Company, a small Oklahoma producing concern. This contract covered management of Central, the right to purchase all of its crude oil production, and an option to purchase two-thirds of the Central common stock before April 1923.[86]

Thus, in the short space of nine months following the organization of the company, Union of Delaware dissipated its cash resources in the purchase of new properties, some of them of dubious value and all of them purchased at a time when the price of producing properties was at an all-time high. Not only was the $15,000,000 working capital gone; Union had, to finance operations of some of its newly acquired subsidiaries, borrowed from those with cash to spare and lent to those in need of funds, setting up a complicated tangle of intercompany debts. In addition, Union was obligated to pay up to $9,-000,000 for the four tankers then on the ways in shipyards.

The 1920–1921 depression, which hit during the second half of 1920, found Union of Delaware greatly over-extended and in need of stringent economies. James H. Brookmire, operator of *Brookmire's Investors' Service*, a stock market newsletter, was brought in and made vice president in charge of finance. He set about cutting down staff, particularly the excessive number of vice presidents who had been inherited from companies acquired during the previous year, and began looking for purchasers for the tankers. The two 12,500-ton tankers were sold to Pan American Petroleum & Transport Company early in 1921 and a profit of $280,000 was realized on the sale. In November 1920, Union nearly succeeded in selling its holding (9%) in the highly unprofitable Manhattan Oil Products Company to Indian Refining Company (in which Lockhart was also active), but the deal fell through. Subsequently Indian took over management of Manhattan with an option to buy Union's interest in exchange for Indian shares.[87]

Union was not without its successes, but they came at a time when they only added to the financial burden. During the summer of 1920, National Exploration was successful bidder on leases in the Burbank field, paying more than half a million dollars cash for them. Money was needed for this payment and for the subsequent drilling which had to be done. Union went to the banks early in 1921 and borrowed some $3,000,000. Then, in April 1921, another subsidiary encountered good production at Huntington Beach, California, necessitating the raising of additional development money.

It was at this juncture, in April 1921, with the money gone, more needed, and Percy Rockefeller unwilling to supply it, that Lockhart asked for and obtained from the Union of Delaware directors permission to approach the Royal Dutch-Shell Group to see if the Group would be agreeable to an amalgamation of the Shell and Union interests in the United States. Early in May, the Union of Delaware directorate appointed a formal committee and six months of protracted negotiation got under way.[88]

Lockhart had met Deterding the previous summer and from their talk had gained the impression that the Group could be interested in acquiring the Union of Delaware properties, the most attractive of which was the large shareholding in Union of California. Lockhart went to London and, as a result of his trip, Union of Delaware and the Shell Group agreed to make a detailed valuation of their own and each other's properties, as a starting point for negotiations.[89]

The Shell Group stipulated in advance that certain of their assets in the United States would be excluded—Asiatic Petroleum Company in New York, because it was not engaged in the domestic oil business and had become primarily an organization supplying materials and oils to the Shell companies abroad; the Simplex Refining Company which held the Trumble patents used by the Group world-wide; the New Orleans Refining Company, operated by Asiatic of New York and engaged in foreign rather than domestic trade; and the three disputed Shell tankers, the *Gold Shell*, *Pearl Shell*, and *Silver Shell*. All the assets of the Shell Company of California, the Roxana Petroleum Corporation, the Ozark Pipe Line Corporation, and the Matador Petroleum Company would be included in the proposed amalgamation.

For the evaluation work which would precede negotiations, two appraisal teams were appointed. The Group's team was headed by Dr. F. A. A. van Gogh, chief geologist and head of the production department at The Hague; the Union of Delaware team was headed by Paul

Paine, a Los Angeles independent oil man who represented Union of Delaware on Union Oil of California's board.* The two teams travelled throughout the United States during May and June 1921, appraising their own and each other's property as of May 31, 1921, the date which had been agreed upon as closing date for purposes of the deal. Where their appraisals differed, members of the two teams got together for frequent conferences. Agreement between the two groups upon the value of a given piece of property generally removed it from further discussion; in this manner, the two appraisal teams handled much of the preliminary negotiation.

The appraisals of both groups were completed by midsummer, and in August a Union of Delaware deputation consisting of Schlacks, Brookmire, Forsyth Wickes, Ernest Tracy, Paul Paine, and two accountants sailed to join Lockhart in London. There the entire month of September was given over to negotiation, with Waley Cohen, Hendrikus Colijn, the younger Kessler,† Frederick Godber, Adrian Corbett, and occasionally Deterding, sitting in to represent the Shell Group.[91]

The happy thought of an amalgamation instead of an outright sale of the Union assets had been in mind from the beginning. This idea had been proposed by Lockhart and Rockefeller who felt that Union stockholders who might object to outright sale would be much more amenable to a merger. From Shell's viewpoint this arrangement was advantageous, for it eliminated the necessity of putting up the large amount of cash which an outright purchase would have required. Instead, the Group would turn over Shell of California, Roxana, Matador, and Ozark Pipe Line to the new amalgamated company and receive stock in the new company commensurate with these assets.

The chief concern of the negotiators was how large a percentage of the amalgamated company to allot to Union and how large a share to assign to Shell. Union's most valuable asset was its stock interest in the Union Oil Company of California, which on May 31, 1921, stood at

---

* Union of California allowed the Delaware company representation on the Union of California board in proportion to the Delaware company's holding. On March 1, 1921, five new Union of California directors had thus been elected. In addition to Paine, they were Schlacks, president of Union of Delaware; J. E. Fishburn, president of the Merchants National Bank, Los Angeles; Harry Chandler, publisher of the Los Angeles *Times;* and H. W. O'Melveny, Los Angeles attorney.[90]

† Son and namesake of J. B. August Kessler, who played so important a role in the early history of the Royal Dutch Company, the younger Kessler followed in his father's footsteps. In 1924, he was made a managing director of the Royal Dutch and in 1948 he was elected chairman of the Royal Dutch board of directors.

130,869 shares, or 26.17%, of Union of California's outstanding common stock. It had cost Union of Delaware $20,440,000 in cash, or an average of $156.20 a share against its current market value of $130.[92]

The oil-producing properties which Union of Delaware controlled through its subsidiaries were of inconsequential value by comparison. Of these, the Central Petroleum and Columbia Oil Producing properties were the most valuable. Many of the others were of little worth, and Van Gogh's appraisal recommended definite exclusion of Union's Kentucky and West Virginia producing properties which had a low yield, were expensive to operate, and were far removed from any Shell refinery. The Manhattan Oil Products Company, then insolvent and loaded with debt, was also recommended for exclusion. The tankers which Union owned would, of course, be of no value to the American Shell companies who found it legally impossible to operate the tankers they already owned.

Sharp differences of opinion between the two groups over the value of the Union assets considerably slowed the progress of negotiations, as did the presence in London of Ernest Marland. At that time, the Marland company was owned about 20% by Marland personally; the next largest stockholder was Percy Rockefeller who held about 4%. Marland's recent rash of discoveries was keeping him on the constant lookout for development money. Part of the reason for his being in London at this time was to complete the arrangements covering Roxana's participation in Comar. It was not unnatural that at the same time he should propose a more extensive alliance with the Group. Marland had a high opinion of the Group and the chief executive officers of the Group were, in their turn, very favorably impressed by him.[93]

Two deals were proposed: an all-inclusive company which would take in the Shell, Union, and Marland properties; or, in the event that this fell through, a merger of the Roxana and Marland interests in the Mid-Continent. Officials of the Group were willing to make Marland president of the new American company.[94] Late in September, an appraisal of the Roxana and Marland properties was instituted, covering also the New Orleans refinery which Marland wanted to include in the deal. Meanwhile, talks with the Union of Delaware people continued, and by the first week of October an agreement with them was reached. Discussions with Marland continued sporadically through the first half of 1922, with the subject being raised again by Kessler on a visit to America in May 1922.[95] These talks were eventually broken off, however, for Marland's favorable reserve position led him to place too high a value upon his company.‡

On October 8, the Union delegation in London cabled to their board of directors in New York that they had agreed to a division of the stock in the new amalgamated company on the basis of 72% to the Royal Dutch-Shell Group and 28% to Union of Delaware. This latter percentage was to be increased to one-third, if within a year control of Union Oil Company of California were obtained either by purchase of more of that company's stock or by agreement with its management. Both Union and Shell were to pay all the outstanding indebtedness of the companies they turned over, which meant that Union of Delaware would have to raise an additional five million dollars.

The Union of Delaware delegation which signed the cable told its directors that "every possible point has been fought out and these terms best obtainable," adding that Percy Rockefeller had "strongly approved these terms before sailing." [97] At a meeting of the Union directors five days later, the terms were approved; and immediately thereafter Wickes proceeded to draw up a formal contract which was completed and signed in London on October 19, 1921.

This agreement provided, among other things, that a new company would be organized under the laws of the State of Delaware with 10,000,000 shares of no-par-value common stock. Of this number, 8,000,000 shares were to be issued immediately, 5,760,000 shares to Anglo-Saxon which owned the capital stocks of Shell of California, Roxana, Matador, and Ozark Pipe Line; the remaining 2,240,000 shares to Union of Delaware. Anglo-Saxon also agreed to pay Union $386,000 in cash and to assume $777,777 of Union's indebtedness to New York banks. [98]

The cash which the Group had agreed to pay, plus receipts from sale of Union assets not turned over to the new company, would, it was planned, liquidate Union of Delaware's debts amounting to some $5,000,000. The stock which Union received in the new company would be distributed among the Union shareholders, along

‡ He was also naturally reluctant to surrender the control which his large stock ownership gave him. It undoubtedly would have been to the long-run advantage of both parties if this proposed deal had gone through, for Marland soon lost his company, anyhow. In 1923 he turned to J. P. Morgan & Company in his search for money, and by 1928 the Morgans had become so heavily involved that they removed Marland as president of his company, installed a new management, and merged it with the much smaller Continental Oil Company. Marland tried to make a fresh start, but was stopped by the depression. He was elected to Congress, 1932-1934, and served as governor of Oklahoma, 1935-1939. He died in 1941. [96]

with any cash left over. The new company was organized early in 1922, and thereafter Union of Delaware transacted no further business, except to liquidate its remaining assets. Shares of the new company were distributed to the Union stockholders in December 1922, but sale of the remaining assets proceeded slowly, and it was not until December 1929 that Union Oil Company (Delaware), its assets sold and bills paid, was finally dissolved.[99]

5

Shell Union Oil Corporation

THE new company which was organized as a result of the amalgamation of the Shell and Union properties was chartered under the laws of Delaware on February 7, 1922, and named, appropriately enough, Shell Union Oil Corporation. Its first officers § were Union of Delaware men—W. H. Allen, president, and J. H. Brookmire, secretary and treasurer. Adrian Corbett, an executive of the Shell Group in London who had taken a prominent part in the Shell-Union negotiations and who was on his way to St. Louis to become an officer of the Roxana, was instead elected vice president of the new Shell Union.[100]

In November of the same year Deterding assumed the presidency of the Shell Union and Van Eck, who had served as president of the Shell Company of California since Meischke-Smith's departure in 1919, came east to take on the job of vice president and chief New York executive of Shell Union. In May 1924, Deterding moved up to chairman of the board and Van Eck became president of Shell Union.

At this juncture it would probably be well to take note of changes in executive personnel of the other American Shell companies in the years between 1921 and 1923. In January 1923, Van Eck was succeeded as president of the Shell Company of California by George Legh-Jones, a young Englishman who had previously managed the

§ Officers for purposes of organization (a three-month period) were General Avery D. Andrews, president, and Alexander Fraser, secretary and treasurer, both associated at that time with Asiatic Petroleum of New York. They resigned in May 1922.

liquid fuel department of Asiatic in London. Not long before this, a similar important change had taken place in Roxana. Frederick Godber, another young executive from Shell Group in London, had come to St. Louis late in 1919 and soon after had been made a vice president. Early in 1922, he was elected president of Roxana. Van der Gracht, recalled to The Hague, chose instead to resign; he joined Marland Oil Company as vice president in charge of exploration and in this capacity was responsible for several of Marland's innovations in the fields of geology and geophysics.* Godber's position as a Roxana vice president was filled by a young Dutchman, R. G. A. van der Woude, who served until early 1924.

Shortly after the end of the war, Deterding had demonstrated his awareness of the need for an American chief executive. Late in 1919, General Avery D. Andrews had been installed in New York to serve as chairman and chief legal advisor of the Shell companies in the United States. General Andrews, then fifty-five, had already enjoyed a distinguished career. Graduated from West Point in the Class of 1886, he had subsequently qualified for the bar and practiced law in New York, where he had served along with Theodore Roosevelt as a member of the New York Police Commission during the famous clean-up drive of 1895–1898. As a result of his law practice, Andrews later became chief counsel and vice president of the General (Barber) Asphalt Company of Philadelphia. Through a subsidiary, the Caribbean Petroleum Company, organized in New Jersey in 1911, the Barber people held large undeveloped oil concessions in Venezuela. They tried to interest American capital in becoming partners with them in this Venezuelan venture. Unsuccessful, General Asphalt had sent Andrews to London where he had enlisted the participation of the Shell Group. The Group agreed to furnish the necessary technicians and put up the development money, with the Barber people contributing their concessions. Stock ownership in the Caribbean company was realigned: from early 1913, the Group held 75% of the stock of Caribbean Petroleum Company, the remaining 25% was owned by General Asphalt, and the company managed by the latter

---

* Dr. van der Gracht later served as officer or director of numerous Marland affiliates; in common with most other Marland executives, he left with the advent of the Morgan management in 1928. His later career in Holland was that of a distinguished scientific man; he wrote extensively for scientific periodicals and was inspector-general of the Netherlands Government Mines at the time of his retirement in 1940. He died in Holland, August 12, 1943, at the age of seventy.[101]

under the direction of Andrews. Caribbean brought in the discovery well of the Mene Grande field in February 1914, opening up Venezuela as an oil-producing country.† During the World War, Andrews had returned to the Army and become assistant chief of staff to Pershing in France.[102]

Deterding, knowing Andrews from past association in the Caribbean venture, considered his background and eminence ideal for the position of chairman and chief legal advisor of the American Shell companies, and early in 1919 asked Andrews if he would serve, with duties "similar to those of the Chairman of an English company." [103] Andrews accepted, making his offices with Richard Airey's Asiatic company in New York. He brought with him, to serve as corporate secretary of these companies, Alexander Fraser, a young Scot who had advanced from a General Asphalt bookkeeper in Trinidad to the position of Andrews' assistant and who had during the war been secretary of the Inter-Allied Petroleum Council in London. Andrews concerned himself with broad general policy; operational matters continued to be under the direction of the presidents of the companies concerned. An important part of Andrews' activities covered relations with governmental bodies. He served in this capacity until his retirement at the end of 1930.‡

The contract providing for the creation of Shell Union had stipulated that it should have a board comprised of not more than nineteen members; of these, the Shell interests would be entitled to elect fourteen and Union of Delaware five. The total number permissible was increased during 1922 and at the end of that year Shell Union had twenty-one directors—nine of them men who had been directors of Union of Delaware: Frederic W. Allen (a partner in Lee, Higginson & Company), James H. Brookmire, Bayard Dominick, Charles Hayden, Samuel F. Pryor, Charles H. Sabin, Samuel M. Vauclain, E. P. Whitcomb, and Henry Lockhart, Jr. The executive committee,

† In 1923, the Group purchased the Barber people's minority interest in Caribbean, allowing them to retain a one-eighth royalty interest. In October 1946, this remaining interest was purchased by the Shell Group for $25,000,000 cash. Two years later, the company was renamed Shell Caribbean Petroleum Company. It still retains its original charter, granted November 27, 1911, under the laws of the State of New Jersey.

‡ It is pleasant to record that retirement has agreed with General Andrews. He was at the time of this writing (1956) well into his ninety-third year, hale, hearty, and keen of memory. His reminiscences were of material assistance in preparing several sections of this volume.

numbering six, included two former Union men, Allen and Lockhart; the other four were Deterding, Van Eck, Airey, and Godber.

Alexander Mackay was also included on the new board. It will be recalled that he and his associates, organized as the Dundee Corporation, owned some 25.1% of Roxana's capital stock. The Shell-Union deal made it necessary for 100% of Roxana's stock to be turned over to the new Shell Union company, so the Group arranged to buy out Dundee's minority participation in Roxana in exchange for 505,383 shares, or 6.3%, of the new Shell Union stock. These shares were taken from the Shell Group's 72%, reducing the Group's total holding in Shell Union to 65.7%. The Mackay interest remained for several years one of the most important minority blocks of stock, and Mackay served as a Shell Union director for the rest of his life.

The Columbia and Puente Properties

The agreement creating Shell Union contemplated that Union's properties on the West Coast would be assigned to and become a part of the Shell Company of California, and that Union's Oklahoma properties would in a like manner be turned over to Roxana. The work of taking over these properties and making them a part of the Shell operating organization was accomplished rapidly.

The most valuable of the California properties were those of the Columbia Oil Producing Company which had producing leases in fields located a few miles east of the Los Angeles city limits—the Montebello, Puente, and Brea-Olinda fields.* The Puente field was noteworthy in many respects, particularly for its great age as oil fields go. Drilling there had been started early in the 1880's; a well brought in in January 1886 for about 11 barrels a day was one of the first commercially profitable oil ventures in Southern California.[104] W. R. Rowland, a cattle rancher who had inherited Rancho El Puente from his father, owned the land and had as his partner in the venture William Lacy, a Los Angeles steel maker.[105]

Under W. E. Youle, a famous old-time driller, some thirty wells were drilled for Rowland & Lacy in the Puente field during the next ten years. The wells were not large producers, but their production held up well and Rowland & Lacy were able to organize their prop-

---

* Brea-Olinda is the officially recognized name for the two areas, one of which was (and still is, colloquially) called Brea Canyon and the other Olinda (or sometimes Columbia Olinda).

erty into the successful Puente Oil Company. In 1886, Puente built a 2-inch pipe line to nearby railroad loading racks, the first pipe line in the Los Angeles area. In 1895, Puente erected a small refinery at Chino, north of the Puente Hills, to supply fuel oil to the adjoining refinery of the American Beet Sugar Company. Later on, when there was a demand for gasoline, Puente bought a depot site on North Alameda Street, Los Angeles, and began selling gasoline in Los Angeles through its own company-owned retail stations.[106]

About 1900, the Rowland and Lacy interests participated in the organization of the Columbia Oil Producing Company. Puente's producing properties were turned over to Columbia, and Puente became thenceforth the marketing and refining subsidiary of the new company. At the time Shell of California took Columbia over in 1922, Columbia's Montebello field properties were making 580 barrels a day and the Brea-Olinda properties 3,425 barrels daily. Shell was not at the time overly impressed with the potential value of these properties. In the long run, however, they proved worth having. The Puente sales department provided a start for Shell's marketing organization in Southern California, and even the antiquated 1,000-barrel Chino refinery was of brief use. The old Puente field is still producing small amounts of oil; and the Brea Canyon section of the Brea-Olinda field, drilled deeper as recently as 1950, produced 876,000 barrels of oil that year.[107]

Eddystone Oil Company, another Union of Delaware subsidiary, held the Ashton and Davenport leases at Huntington Beach. These leases were making about 1,300 barrels a day when Shell took over; eventually they produced some 6,000,000 barrels of oil for Shell before they were given up as unprofitable in the middle Twenties. Both Eddystone and National Exploration Company turned over substantial amounts of wildcat acreage to Shell, but these lands were poorly located and were soon relinquished.[108]

In the Midway field, other Union of Delaware subsidiaries, the Dunlop Oil Company and United Western Consolidated Oil Company, between them held three leases and one piece of fee property with a combined daily production of 230 barrels; these Shell took over and operated. United Western Consolidated also had an 80-acre lease with six wells in the McKittrick field, with only one well producing (5 barrels a day) in 1922; this property was sold. Commonwealth Petroleum Company had non-producing acreage at Gardena

Heights and a lease in the Rosecrans field with an abandoned well on it and two more drilling; both these properties were given up.[109]

Western Union

The other Union of Delaware property in California was the Western Union Oil Company which held the Careaga and Harris leases in the Santa Maria field, an isolated oil field in northern Santa Barbara County which had been brought in on the Careaga lease in August 1901. The Western Union company was originally a California-owned producing company selling its crude under long-term contract to Associated Oil Company. The Careaga lease, its largest and most productive, had been drilled up in the decade following 1901.

The Careaga lease was scheduled to lapse at the end of twenty years; pumping rights were guaranteed, but not the right to drill new wells. Union of Delaware had undertaken to increase Western Union's production by drilling twenty new wells and had spent $2,000,000 in two years of drilling. The increase in production was not up to expectations (in 1921 a total of about 1,400 barrels a day), but Shell nevertheless renegotiated the lease with the Careaga heirs and continued to develop the property on a less ambitious scale. Because of its remote location, the Santa Maria field (now officially called Orcutt) never became an integral part of Shell operations. The crude production of ensuing years was sold, generally to Union of California. In 1950, the Santa Maria was still producing oil for Shell, but it averaged only 256 barrels a day, or a total for the year of 93,258 barrels.[110]

All told, the California properties taken over from Union of Delaware had produced by the end of 1950 more than 52,400,000 barrels of crude oil for Shell—enough certainly to have justified Shell's participation in the Shell-Union deal.

The Los Angeles Office

An incidental by-product of taking over Union of Delaware's California properties was the creation of the office of vice president in charge of production. The Union of Delaware men on the new Shell Union board felt that they should have some representation in Shell of California's executive group. Paul Paine was asked if he would take the job; he agreed with the stipulation that he serve one year only. Quite to everyone's surprise, he meant what he said; in

June 1923, exactly one year later, Paine resigned. He was succeeded as production vice president by W. C. McDuffie.§

Union of Delaware's old offices in the Higgins Building at Second and Main Streets, Los Angeles, were taken over and became head-quarters for Shell's production department hitherto located in San Francisco. James Mainland, formerly with the Union of Delaware's auditing firm in Los Angeles, was made office manager; Stanley Duhig, who had been managing the Signal Hill office functions, became assistant office manager.

Wolverine

Union of Delaware's properties in the Mid-Continent were much more scattered and miscellaneous. Union's high-cost, low-producing wells in Kentucky, Ohio, and West Virginia had been excluded from the Shell-Union deal because they probably would have been un-profitable to operate even if Shell had had pipe line connections to that area.

Commonwealth Petroleum's Mid-Continent holdings were for the most part useless to Roxana. Of the Commonwealth properties, Roxana chose to keep only one lease in Texas and seven in Oklahoma. National Exploration also owned a good deal of worthless property; its Kansas leases were surrendered forthwith, along with eight in Oklahoma. National did, however, have an undeveloped lease at Depew, Oklahoma, then producing about 25 barrels a day; and a few other Oklahoma leases including one at Duncan. National's most valuable holdings were three Osage Nation tracts in the Burbank field on which it had brought in wells with initial productions as high as 3,450 barrels a day. These properties were easily connected by pipe line with Roxana properties in the same area.[111]

The most important of Union of Delaware's Oklahoma properties was the Central Petroleum Company, upon which Union had pur-chased an option during the summer of 1920. Central was a holding company, organized originally in 1910 as the Central Fuel Oil Com-pany, a Delaware corporation, to hold the stock of twenty-three small oil-producing firms. Most of these twenty-three firms had

§ Later in the Twenties, McDuffie went to The Hague, where he was put in world-wide charge of the Group's production activities. He was succeeded as vice president in California by William Reinhardt, who resigned in March 1931 to head the new Kettleman North Dome Association. J. U. Stair, manager of Union of Delaware's oil operations in California at the time these properties were taken over by Shell, succeeded Reinhardt and served until his death in 1939.

been among the pioneers of Oklahoma oildom, organized during the early boom years, 1903–1907. An enterprising railroad man, Edwin B. Foster, had in March 1896 obtained a ten-year lease of the Osage Nation. Foster died soon afterward and the lease passed to his brother, who organized the Indian Territory Illuminating Oil Company. Rather than drill itself, the I.T.I.O. chose to divide its holding into small parcels which it sublet to others, retaining an overriding royalty interest. This was one of the reasons for the astonishingly large number of producing companies in this section of Oklahoma during the early days of the business. The Foster lease, upon its expiration in 1906, was renewed for an additional ten years.[112]

The Central Fuel Oil Company ran into financial difficulties not long after its organization. As a result of defaulting on the first sinking fund payment due on its $6,000,000 bond issue, the company passed into receivership late in 1911. After extensive negotiations, it was reorganized as the Central Petroleum Company under the laws of the State of Maine in August 1913. The $6,000,000 worth of bonds were replaced by an equal amount of preferred stock in the new company and The Texas Company, which had a contract to purchase all of Central's crude oil production, agreed to guarantee the interest on this preferred stock for the next ten years. In exchange for assuming this liability, Texaco was given a contract to manage the new Central company together with voting control of two-thirds of the new company's common shares, which were placed in escrow pending fulfillment of the agreement. At the end of the ten-year period The Texas Company under its contract had the option of relinquishing its control of Central or of purchasing, at face value, the $6,000,000 of preferred stock. In the latter event, Texaco would also become outright owner of two-thirds of Central's common stock. It was this contract with its rights and obligations that Union of Delaware purchased in July 1920 for a cash payment of $5,250,000.[113]

Upon Roxana's falling heir to the various Union of Delaware properties in the Mid-Continent, it was left to Godber to decide whether or not Shell Union should exercise this option to acquire control of Central Petroleum. He arranged for Van der Linden to come east from California and make an evaluation of Central's properties. At the same time, the St. Louis office of Price, Waterhouse & Company was instructed to undertake a detailed audit of Central's operations, primarily to discover the amount of back income taxes which might be due. Van Gogh, in his appraisal of Union of Delaware's assets in the summer of 1921, had not been particularly impressed with the value of Central Petroleum; he was further discouraged to discover that Central had been the ultimate purchaser of a number of the "Old Properties" which Roxana had disposed of in 1919.

Central's chief producing asset was a holding in the relatively new Hewitt field. Roxana was already an operator in the Hewitt field, and could therefore tie in to its own operations properties it might acquire from others in the area. On the strength of the Hewitt holding, which was still largely undeveloped, Van der Linden recommended the purchase. Central's treasury contained current assets of some $2,000,-000 so Godber calculated that, in effect, the purchase of Central's preferred stock would represent a net outlay of about $3,750,000. Van der Linden felt that Central's Hewitt holdings alone were worth this amount. Meanwhile, Tide Water, which owned about one-sixth of Central's common stock, offered Godber $4,000,000 for the option on Central. But Godber felt strongly that "if we are in the oil business, we should not dabble in sales of part of our assets." Acting upon this recommendation, Shell Union in October 1922 gave notice of its intention to exercise the option. The deal was completed by August 1923.[114]

In the years following 1916, Central's original twenty-three subsidiary companies had dwindled through the expiration of leases to five companies, the chief of which was Wolverine Oil Company. By the time Shell took title to its Central holdings, the remaining subsidiaries had been consolidated into a single company. Upon accession of the Shell management, Central's name was changed to Wolverine Petroleum Corporation to prevent confusion with other Oklahoma oil companies of similar name.[115] Godber was elected president of Wolverine, Van Eck and Lydon were made vice presidents, L. E. Beszelzen became secretary and treasurer. Thenceforth, Wolverine made its headquarters in St. Louis with the Roxana organization. Because one-third of the common stock remained outstanding, it was necessary to keep separate accounts, with Roxana paying going market rates for all crude oil it obtained from Wolverine. Profits from these crude oil sales enabled Wolverine in the years between 1924 and 1926 to retire the $6,000,000 preferred stock issue. With the preferred stock out of the way, dividend payments were begun on the common stock in the latter year and during the life of the company Shell's share in these dividends amounted to $4,630,000.* The purchase of control in Wolverine was not a spectacular bargain, but it made available to Roxana during the next fifteen years some 12,500,000 barrels of crude oil, repaid the investment, and yielded a conservative profit.

Such, then, was the "inheritance" of producing properties which Shell of California and Roxana received from the Shell-Union deal. These properties had at the time of the deal been regarded as secondary in importance to the primary goal—a controlling interest in the Union Oil Company of California. But, as matters turned out, the producing properties were to prove a sort of grand consolation prize, for the effort to secure control of Union of California was to end in failure.

6

"A Kind of Jealous Feeling"

DETERDING had never been more correct than when he had ventured to predict that the American Shell companies, if successful, would engender by their success "a kind of jealous feeling." [116] His suggested antidote for this unfavorable public opinion—the formation of a new Shell company in America with outside capital—would perhaps have been successful in forestalling this ill-feeling had it been carried through when the suggestion was first made. However, the organization of Shell Union some six years later came at a time when it only served to heighten a wave of anti-Shell sentiment that was giving executives of the American Shell companies many uneasy moments during the early Twenties.

The center of the disturbance was Los Angeles, where the Stewart family had fallen into the unfortunate habit of airing their business disagreements in the local courts and newspapers. (Lyman Stewart, one of the founders of Union Oil of California and now chairman of that company, often publicly opposed the policies of his son, W. L. Stewart, who was president of Union.) As early as May 26, 1921, news of the then-impending Shell-Union deal had leaked out and been published in the Los Angeles *Express*, causing consterna-

* For later history of Wolverine, see page 493.

tion in the ranks of the Stewart family and their business associates. Because of the large amounts of new common stock which had been issued in the years 1910–1920, the Stewarts had lost their position as majority owners of Union of California but still managed to retain operating control of the company. If the rumors of a merger of Union of Delaware with the Shell interests were true, their control of Union would be threatened, for the Delaware company's 26% holding in Union of California was the largest single block of common stock outstanding.[117]

As soon as it was ascertained that these rumors were indeed true, the Stewarts and their friends sprang into action. On October 17, 1921, two days before the contract between Anglo-Saxon and Union of Delaware was even signed, a group of twenty Los Angeles businessmen (including the Stewarts and most of the chief executives of Union of California) sent a circular letter to that company's shareholders. They proposed that the small shareholders assign their Union of California stock to a voting trust which, it was hoped, would secure assignment to it of shares representing 51% or more of the total stock outstanding. These shares could then be voted as a unit by trustees friendly to the current management.

The letter addressed itself, in most exhortatory terms, to Californians' local pride: "Your company is one of the great institutions of California. It was created and developed by Californians. Its properties are largely in California. A large majority of its shares are owned in California. A very great majority of its stockholders live in California. . . . Why should we Californians, owners collectively of a majority interest, really remain in the minority?"[118] This language was calm indeed beside that of the Los Angeles press which willingly joined the "crusade." "Every stockholder owes it to his pocketbook, to California, and to the nation to keep the American flag flying over California's oil fields," cried the Los Angeles *Express* in an editorial[119] which was representative of that paper's continuing barrage of alarmist stories.

The Shell executives did not allow themselves to be drawn into this public battle. They were aware that their company's success thus far owed much to favorable reception by the general public. They held fast to the 130,869 Union of California shares which had come to Shell Union from Union of Delaware, but they did not attempt to increase this holding. At prevailing prices it would have required at least $20 million to buy shares enough to ensure control. The scramble for Union of California stock was nevertheless intense during the early months of 1922, for in addition to the Union of California management, a San Francisco group had entered the market and was attempting to corral enough shares to become the deciding factor. Under this stimulus, the price of Union of California common reached 197⅜ on the New York Stock Exchange early in 1922.[120]

By the end of March 1922, the group associated with the Union of California management had been successful in assembling 273,833 shares, or 54.7%, of the stock outstanding—enough to assure them control. On March 25, 1922, they organized the Union Oil Associates, a corporation to own and control this stock. Small shareholders who had promised to turn over Union of California stock received shares in Union Oil Associates entitling them to dividends. Voting of their stock was thenceforth done *en bloc* by the directors of the new voting-trust holding company.

Up against a stone wall such as this, the Shell management accepted defeat gracefully. For the remainder of 1922, hope was still entertained in Shell circles that Shell could come to some kind of an agreement [121] with the Union of California management—an agreement which might, perhaps, allow Union to continue as an independent company representing the Shell interests in Southern California on a partnership basis. Shell Union's chief concern in attempting to acquire control of Union was to avoid making the heavy outlay necessary to build refineries and a marketing organization for Shell of California in the southern part of the state, an area where Shell was thus far represented only in the producing end of the business. When these attempts at control came to naught, Shell Union abandoned the effort and began keeping an eye out for a possible purchaser for its large block of Union of California stock.

A stock dividend of 80% was meanwhile declared by Union of California in December 1922. This increased Shell Union's holding by 104,000 shares, so that the company's total number of Union of California shares now came to 235,564. In the spring of 1924, Shell Union made arrangements to sell this entire holding to the New York brokerage firm of Dillon, Read & Company for $112 a share. This brought a total of $26,383,168, or $5,590,000 more than the original cost price at which the shares were carried on Shell Union's books. Meanwhile, the company had also collected more than $4,000,-000 in dividends—a total cash return in two years of some $10,000,000 on its Union of California holdings. This 50% return in two years made the failure to acquire control of Union quite palatable. Far more discomforting was a by-product of the Union fracas—a Federal Trade Commission investigation into Shell's affairs, undertaken at the direction of the United States Senate.

Partly as a result of newspaper stories concerning Union of California, Senator William H. King of Utah in September 1921 introduced in the Senate a resolution calling upon the Federal Trade Commission to "investigate and report to the Senate respecting the ownership by persons who are not citizens of the United States" of shares of Union of Delaware, Union of California, and Shell of California "and their subsidiary and affiliated companies; the acreage of oil lands which has been acquired by said corporations or any of them, within the last year; and what measures are being pursued by said corporations to further extend their holdings of oil lands within the United States." The F.T.C. was also asked to determine whether or not Great Britain, the British Dominions, Holland, Romania, "or other countries having oil lands" discriminated against American companies who wished to acquire and develop oil leases.[122] This resolution was passed by the Senate on June 29, 1922. It was not, as can be seen from its contents, inspired purely by what had recently transpired in Los Angeles. It was, rather, the product of several diverse influences.

One of these influences, wholly extraneous in that it had nothing whatever to do with Shell or the oil business, was the quite widespread anti-British feeling of the immediate postwar years. This bad feeling would have had little effect upon the American Shell companies had it not been for eager demagogues. During the war they had been quick to infer German connections from the quite innocuous name "Dutch-Shell." Now, equally quickly, they switched to branding it "the British Shell company." In fact, no less a gentleman than Senator Henry Cabot Lodge of Massachusetts declared upon the Senate floor, April 12, 1921, that "the British Government actually controls 'Royal-Dutch Shell.'" He was supplied with these "facts," he said, by Secretary of the Interior Albert B. Fall whose information came from "our geologists and other entirely reliable sources." [123]

General Andrews promptly prepared a detailed letter refuting each of Fall's main arguments with specific information, and Lodge by way of apology had the letter printed in the *Congressional Record* of April 27. Andrews had the letter reprinted in pamphlet form and sent it to the principal daily newspapers, leading brokerage houses, every member of Congress, and a large number of government officials in the hope † that it would "put an end, once and for all, to the persistently repeated allegation of British Government control of our Group." [124]

Another influence, much less disinterested, was the pressure brought to bear on the U. S. State Department by American oil companies who were having difficulty in securing oil concessions abroad. They claimed that they were being discriminated against by foreign governments, in some cases to the advantage of the Royal Dutch-Shell Group.

Added to all these factors was the "kind of jealous feeling" which Deterding had predicted, an uneasy apprehension on the part of some of Shell's American competitors who felt no doubt that Roxana and Shell of California were growing at a rate too fast for comfort.

Faced with the Federal Trade Commission inquiry, General Andrews took the only sensible and honorable course he could have taken. He cooperated fully with the commission's investigators, answering their questions in detail and with full information. The result was a 152-page "Report of the Federal Trade Commission on Foreign Ownership in the Petroleum Industry," published by the Government Printing Office in Washington on February 12, 1923, with a note of thanks in the opening pages to Andrews for his "material assistance." The report gave a full picture of the world-wide scope of the Group's operations and an up-to-date account of the Shell companies in this country. Senator King, who had introduced the resolution calling for the report, was apparently satisfied, as were others who had voted for the investigation—proof, if proof were needed, that a full, prompt, and truthful answer will silence almost any critic.

It did not silence Secretary Fall, but in retrospect it is easy to see why. The first public inkling of the Teapot Dome and Elk Hills

---

† This hope was, however, not completely justified. A real whopper like this is hard to kill. It was reprinted repeatedly during the Twenties by newspapers hostile to the company, and may occasionally still be heard today in uninformed circles. Another piece of misinformation, quite similar to the "British ownership" story, made its appearance on the scene slightly later. This story had it that the Dutch royal family (or, more generally, Queen Wilhelmina) owned control of the Royal Dutch Company. Considerable research has failed to unearth the origin of this report, but a reasonable guess would be that it is tied to the word "Royal" in the company's name. Royal Dutch stock is as widely held in Holland as is American Telephone & Telegraph in this country, and by the same type of people: small investors who put their money into a steady-dividend, "blue-chip" stock.

leases had come to light in the spring of 1922, and the Senate soon afterward had authorized an investigation into the propriety of Fall's making these leases. Senator Thomas J. Walsh of the investigating committee had labored quietly through the fall and winter of 1922–1923, amassing the pile of evidence which was later to send Secretary Fall to jail. At this juncture (February 1923), no detail of what was soon to be known as the Teapot Dome Scandal had yet been made public; but enough of Senator Walsh's findings were known in Washington circles to make it impossible for Fall to continue in office.[125] He resigned on March 4, 1923, creating as he left a diversion that may have been designed to take the minds of the curious off the reasons behind his resignation.

Roxana was at the time waiting for the Interior Department, the Indians' legal guardian, to approve the terms of three leases which the company had taken in the normal course of business on Indian land in Oklahoma. Two of the leases were on Creek land in Okmulgee, Okfuskee, and Seminole counties; the third lease, in Washington county, belonged to a Cherokee Indian. These leases provided Fall with what looked like a ready-made issue. On March 3, his last day in office, he refused to give Departmental consent to these three leases, on the ground that to do so would be a violation of regulations which he had promulgated a year earlier. These regulations forbade Interior Department Indian agents to approve the lease of Indian land, or the renewal of leases already in force, to "aliens or persons not citizens of the United States." [126]

The story of this action was published in the New York *Times* of March 7, 1923, although little note of it was taken elsewhere. Fall, now out of office, began a steady bombardment of the Shell companies in a series of special articles which appeared three days running in the *Times*, twice on the front page.‡

On Sunday, March 18, the *Times* carried on its front page a long story treating in greater detail the reasons behind Fall's action in refusing the Roxana leases, including a column-length quotation from the ex-Secretary. In this account, Fall made much of the Federal Land Leasing Act of 1920, which forbade the lease of Federal public lands to persons or corporations not citizens of the United States,

---

‡ Curiously enough, none of the other leading New York papers of the time printed a word of these stories. Why the *Sun, World, Tribune, Herald, Daily News*, and *American* for these dates ignored an item which the *Times* considered front-page news is a mystery.

unless the countries of which they were nationals granted similar privileges to Americans. As evidence of discrimination against American companies, Fall mentioned the recently published F.T.C. report which, he said, showed discrimination in almost every country including several of the British and Dutch dominions.[127]

The next day, Monday, March 19, the *Times'* front-page story ran to nearly five columns: it quoted Fall again, but was mainly a digest of the F.T.C. report. On Tuesday, March 20, Fall appeared with his wildest charges yet, in a lurid story (this time relegated to page 23) headlined "Stronger Oil Trust at Work, Fall Says." The Royal Dutch-Shell Group was, he said, "part of a gigantic movement, international in its nature, and charged by the French writer Delaisi and others to be carried on with the aid and assistance of certain foreign governments, to exhaust the oil supplies of the United States while denying our explorers the right to prospect for oil elsewhere. . . . It is a trust plan modeled on the original plan of Standard Oil but increased to world magnitude. It is being carried on more ruthlessly than any operation of Standard Oil and is aimed directly at the United States. . . . In accordance with the publicly-made boasts of its promoters, the United States will pay to Great Britain during the next few years many times more than the entire British refunded debt to us." [128]

This irresponsible attack was the last of Fall's blasts. The next day the *Times* carried the news that the new Secretary of the Interior, Hubert Work, had granted Roxana's request for a hearing on the Indian leases, to be held at Washington starting April 16. Attorneys for Roxana, Shell Union, and the Indian lessors appeared at the hearing to argue that Fall's action in refusing to approve the leases was "an arbitrary perversion of the powers of the Department of the Interior as guardian of the Indians." [129]

A month later, on May 16, 1923, Secretary Work handed down his decision and it was published in full in a front-page story in the *Times*.[130] He agreed with the arguments of the Shell lawyers, and upheld them on every point. The Indians' land was, he held, private property. Congress had assigned the Interior Department power to approve leases solely for the purpose of seeing that the Indians were not cheated. The Federal Land Leasing Act of 1920 applied, by express terms of that Act, only to lands "owned by the United States." Fall had exceeded his authority when he promulgated regulations denying Indian leases to aliens. Secretary Work therefore revoked Fall's regulations and approved the lease of Indian lands to Roxana.§

The Shell management had had no doubt that this would be the outcome, once the matter was laid before a fair-minded man. Commenting on this fracas, the Royal Dutch annual report said: "Some of our competitors have endeavoured to create difficulties for us by invoking political action based on propaganda in which, as is usual in these cases, the facts have been falsely represented. This movement does not cause us any undue anxiety, because we have confidence that the truth will eventually prevail and when that takes place public opinion in America will frustrate these efforts." [132]

This is exactly what happened, although the process was gradual. Fall dropped out of the picture almost at once, thoroughly discredited by the Teapot Dome investigation which started soon afterward. The Shell companies continued during most of the Twenties to receive unfriendly notices from the sensational press, and writers like Arthur Brisbane, a leading columnist for the Hearst papers, were particularly annoying in their deliberate repetition of statements which had repeatedly been shown to be false.* The company took the position that "you can't argue with a nut" and did not dignify this vilification with an answer. Eventually the attackers tired of their sport and went off to worry someone else.

As far as the general public was concerned, the obvious malice of these attacks undermined their effectiveness. If the attacks had been calculated to harm the Shell companies' business, they were a miserable failure. It was during these very same years that the American Shell companies entered upon their period of greatest marketing

§ This decision settled the company's rights only as they pertained to Indian lands. Secretary Fall had in 1922 denied the Shell Company of California a lease on Federal lands in the Woodside oil dome of Wyoming, unless the company could prove to his satisfaction, within 60 days, that American oil companies were not discriminated against in any of the British or Dutch domains, an impossible task, of course. As a result of the company's inability to satisfy such requests the right of Shell of California and Roxana to take leases on Federal land remained in doubt for the next six years, and was not resolved until late in 1928 when the question was settled in Shell's favor. As matters turned out, this disability was not of great importance, for Federal lands available for lease during these years were not particularly attractive. The disability was removed in time to allow Shell of California to get in on the Kettleman Hills field in 1929.[131]

* Despite the detailed and conclusive evidence to the contrary, which was easily available in the F.T.C. report or obtainable from any bank or broker, Brisbane continued all during the Twenties to refer to "the Shell Oil Company, largely owned by the British Government." [133]

expansion, with Shell products finding a ready acceptance with the motoring public everywhere.

Perhaps the American public shared the sentiments of the *Petroleum Times*. In 1924, when the oil scandals were at their height and heads of half a dozen American oil companies stood accused of dishonesty, that publication felt moved to comment: "While, like all other large concerns of this character, the Royal Dutch-Shell has not escaped bitter criticism and misrepresentation, on the whole its affairs have been singularly free from anything in the nature of scandal. The names of the leading personalities associated with the organization have always stood high in the estimation of the industrial world, and any unprejudiced person must admit that the affairs of the combination have been conducted both with great ability and a high degree of probity." [134]

7

Shell Bets on the Dubbs Process

DURING the years immediately preceding and following 1920, the American oil refining industry was in a ferment as a new process with important commercial implications was being developed. This new development was "cracking"—the breaking apart of heavier petroleum molecules, such as those found in the kerosene, gas oil, and fuel oil fractions, to make more of the saleable light products such as gasoline.

Now, cracking was far from a new thing—although several patent holders and litigants of the 1920's found it convenient to forget this fact. In his report made for Eveleth & Bissell, five years before Drake's first oil well had been drilled, Professor Silliman had noted the cracking phenomenon: "The question forces itself upon us, whether these several oils are to be regarded as *educts* (i.e., bodies previously existing, and simply separated by the process of distillation) or whether they are not rather produced by the heat and the chemical change in the process of distillation. The continued application of an elevated temperature alone is sufficient to effect changes in the constitution of many organic products, evolving new bodies not before existing in the original substance." [135]

Attempting to answer the question he had propounded, Silliman conducted extensive experiments during the winter of 1854–1855 and found that, in general, when the temperature was raised above 300° C. (572° F.), a more viscous, yellowish oil of greater density was obtained, having what Silliman called "a strong empyreumatic odor." [136] It was, in fact, a sample of this cracked oil which Silliman used for the photometric experiments that convinced Eveleth & Bissell that a satisfactory lamp oil of sufficient brilliance could be made from petroleum.

Luther Atwood of Boston, a well-known practical chemist of the early coal oil business, undertook experiments about 1857 to see if he could make a lamp oil from the heavy residues left over after the distilling operation had been completed. He was successful, and in 1860 was granted a patent for a method of increasing the yields of illuminants by cracking at atmospheric pressure. Atwood's method was practiced widely in the early American oil refineries with the result that all but 6% or 7% of the heavy residue from Pennsylvania oils was cracked into saleable kerosene. [137]

James Young, the Scotch shale oil pioneer, also developed a cracking process; he used pressure to increase the cracking temperature. In 1865, Young obtained a patent on his method.

G. L. Benton, of Titusville, Pennsylvania, obtained a U. S. Patent in 1886 for a method of cracking oil to produce kerosene, using high temperatures (700° F.) and high pressures (500 lbs. per sq. in.). James Dewar and Boverton Redwood, prominent British chemists of their day, in 1889 patented a method of cracking and condensing the product, both operations being conducted under pressure. Two Russians, V. Schukhow and S. Gavrilow, obtained a Russian patent in 1891 for an extremely advanced method of producing kerosene by cracking. These are only a few of the more outstanding cracking patents issued in the years before 1900. [138]

That there should be such a large number of early patents and processes in this field is really not surprising, for it is almost impossible to distill heavy oils at temperatures high enough to vaporize them without some of the heavy molecules being cracked apart to form new molecules of lighter petroleum substances. There is even evidence to show that in the Arab world of 1000 A.D. a rude cracking process was known and practiced, enabling the Arabs to break up asphalt into a lighter, more volatile oil which they called "naphtha" and used as an illuminant. [139] An invariable result of cracking, as a molecule of oil breaks apart, is the formation not only of lighter molecules, but also of heavier ones, some of them nearly pure carbon. That a great deal of cracking took place in the old-fashioned shell stills we now realize. When the distilling operation in one of the stills was allowed to continue for any length of time, the bottom of the still became coated with a hard layer of coke which had to be scraped out periodically.

Barring coke deposits, the development of the art of cracking would have been a relatively simple matter. As it was, however, "coking up" was the bane of the refiner's existence. These carbonaceous deposits clogged pipes and gradually formed thick layers on the bottom of the old-fashioned shell stills, layers which quickly became so thick that they acted as effective insulation against the heat from the firebox below. Then, if the fire were increased sufficiently to overcome the insulating effect of the coke deposit, the still bottom would become glowing red and "burn out." Or, even worse, it might burn through and drop the oil into the firebox, causing a dangerous conflagration.

The length of time it took for the oil industry to develop effective cracking methods is a good illustration of a cardinal point of practical technology, a point the impatient will do well to keep in mind: a chemical reaction may be thoroughly understood, but to translate it into a commercially profitable operation is quite another matter. Eventual success must be preceded by years of expensive trial and error; often there must be improvements in collateral fields, such as (in this case) the steelmaker's and welder's arts; and always there must be the economic incentive to make the venture attractive.

Cracking to make kerosene had been carried on when all the world was crying for kerosene. Then, with the development of a substantial fuel oil market around the turn of the century and a simultaneous drop in kerosene demand, the economic incentive to make kerosene at the expense of fuel oil disappeared. With this development, the art of cracking fell into temporary disuse. To make gasoline by a similar process was still in the future, for up until World War I most refiners could manufacture all of their gasoline requirements by simple distillation. It remained for a company unusually situated by a peculiar set of circumstances to acquire the economic incentive to crack heavy oils and produce more gasoline.

That company was the Standard Oil Company of Indiana, a refining and marketing unit of the old Standard Oil combine. When Standard Oil was broken up into separate companies by the Supreme Court in 1911, Standard of Indiana found itself with the world's largest refinery, situated at Whiting, Indiana, just east of Chicago, and a marketing organization blanketing eleven states of the Midwest. The company did not have (and was not to have for another twenty years) its own crude oil production, so it was forced to get as much as possible from its purchased raw materials. Located in the heart of the American Midwest, an area well supplied with cheap coal and far removed from ocean transport, the Indiana company found itself unable either to sell its fuel production locally or to move it into world markets at a reasonable cost. Fuel oil in Indiana's territory was literally a drug on the market. The company was bound to see the advantage of cracking its cheap fuel to produce gasoline.

The Burton Process

About 1910, Dr. W. M. Burton, head of Standard of Indiana's manufacturing activities, and his associate, Dr. R. E. Humphreys, began experimental work to see if they could successfully produce gasoline by cracking the heavier oils. In their first attempts, they turned to the most logical of the heavy oils—the so-called residual fuel, the part left over after all the desired lighter products have been removed by straight-run distillation. They soon gave up residual fuel as a raw material, however, for they were convinced that the heavy residual oil would cause rapid coking of the cracking still and make any cracking process impracticable.[140] Next they turned to gas oil, the so-called "distillate fuel," heaviest of the fractions produced by straight-run distillation. By subjecting gas oil to pressures of about 75 pounds and holding it at temperatures between 700° and 750° F., Burton and Humphreys were able to get considerable quantities of a yellowish, smelly, light oil quite similar in its general characteristics to gasoline.

In the summer of 1912, the Indiana company built a full-scale experimental still, and applied for a patent covering the process. The patent, issued January 7, 1913, in the name of Dr. Burton, became the basis of what was soon known as "the Burton process." On March 1, 1913, Standard of Indiana cautiously announced the new "motor spirit" made by its cracking process. The new fuel would be marketed on a trial basis, the announcement said, for a period of one year. It was not intended for automotive engines but for stationary engines and heavy trucks, and would be sold for 3 cents a gallon below the prevailing price of gasoline.[141]

The Burton still took a gas oil charge of slightly less than 200 barrels, raised it carefully to cracking temperature, and produced an average of 3 barrels of cracked gasoline per hour. At the end of the run (24 to 30 hours), it had to be closed down, cooled, and cleaned out. Burton asked his company for an appropriation of $1,000,000 to build 60 of these 200-barrel cracking stills, and after considerable debate received the funds he needed to build the first

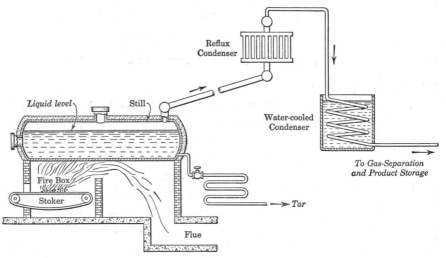

EARLY BURTON PROCESS

Early Burton process resembled the old batch still, took a 200-barrel charge of oil, raised it to 700°–750° F., and produced about 3 barrels of gasoline per hour for 24–30 hours. It was then closed down for cleaning.

commercially successful gasoline cracking plant. Ten years later, Standard of Indiana had built 800 of these stills to achieve a total gross charging capacity of just under 200,000 barrels.[142] The physical size of these plants would be staggering to a person familiar only with the much more compact equipment of a modern refinery. That the Indiana company could make money cracking gasoline with this elaborate, low-volume equipment was attributable chiefly to the low price of the charging stock rather than to any efficiency of the Burton process. The Burton process was, after all, merely another modification of the shell still. Like all shell still processes, it was a batch operation and required a tremendous investment in equipment in order to achieve any kind of manufacturing volume.

Competitors did not have access to figures to show whether or not Burton's process was profitable, but the very fact that Standard of Indiana was willing to spend the immense sums required for this large plant construction was silent testimony to the success of commercial-scale cracking. In the years between 1915 and 1920 a rash of new cracking processes, each trying to improve on Burton's method without infringing his patent, burst upon the oil refining industry. Some of them were unworkable "paper patents," little more than the idle dreams or hopeful imaginings of eager inventors. Others were workable, but prohibitive in their operating costs. A much smaller number had genuine merit and were destined shortly to replace the Burton process, just as surely as the Trumble pipe still and the fractionating column had been destined to replace the older methods of distillation.

With the enormous increase in demand for gasoline during World War I, prices rose and stimulated the inventors still further. Almost every large refiner began either to do experimental work in the hope of developing a cracking process of his own or, failing that, to purchase patent rights from some independent inventor who had a process for sale. Standard Oil of Indiana announced its willingness to license the Burton process on a royalty basis, but only to refiners who would agree not to sell gasoline made by the process in the eleven Midwestern states constituting "Indiana territory." [143] Since the Midwest was the chief area of cracking activity, this was an insuperable obstacle for refiners operating in that region. There were, of course, additional considerations: the cost of building Burton units was high, and no refiner relished the prospect of paying royalty to a competitor if there were any hope of developing a process of his own. Moreover, most refinery operating men did not like the combination of pressure and overheated bottom plates inherent in the Burton cracking still. These features, along with the unreliable hammer-welded construction then common, had caused disastrous fires and explosions.

Other Cracking Processes

So, beginning in 1916–1917, most of the large refiners started seriously to search for a cracking process the patent rights of which they could control—a process which would, they hoped, be cheaper to build and operate and which would avoid the dangerous features of the Burton stills.

In 1918, The Texas Company under Ralph C. Holmes and Frederick C. Manley began construction of a commercial cracking unit at Port Arthur, Texas. For this purpose, Texaco purchased a series of patents which had been granted earlier to Joseph H. Adams, and some nickel-catalyst vapor-phase patents from William A. Hall. By 1920 they had completed and placed in operation the first unit of what became known as the Holmes-Manley process.[144]

Standard Oil of New Jersey likewise began experimental work on cracking in 1918. In 1921, it purchased a series of patents from Carleton Ellis, a well-known chemist, and used them as the basis of Jersey's so-called "Tube-and-Tank" process which began operating on a small scale that year.

Meanwhile, Pyzel in California was not idle. The Trumble patents purchased in 1914 had included a patent for the so-called "Trumble converter," a primitive cracking unit. One of the Group's pressing refinery problems at the time was the need for upgrading the heavy asphaltic fuel oil produced in Mexico—oil so heavy that it barely met fuel buyers' specifications. With the idea of developing a method to crack this Mexican heavy fuel into a lighter, more acceptable fuel oil, Pyzel had a semi-commercial-size Trumble converter built at Martinez in 1916. Experimental runs on this unit went on for several years, but it was evident well before 1920 that the Trumble converter was ill-adapted to gasoline manufacture. This Trumble converter was eventually developed into a successful cracking unit called a "viscosity breaker," and units were built and shipped to Trinidad, Curaçao, and Suez.[145]

While the Trumble converter never successfully made cracked gasoline, it was in many respects a step forward over the Burton process. It worked on a continuous basis, rather than employing the batch method of Burton's first cracking stills, and it introduced the so-called "closed ring" principle (U. S. Patent 1,281,884) which later played an important part in cracking patent litigation. In the course of the process, a portion of the unvaporized heavy oil was continuously withdrawn and replaced by an equal amount of fresh oil: this was the closed-ring principle.

In addition to experimental work at Martinez, the Shell men went to look at every new cracking process which appeared on the horizon, in the hope that one of them might be the answer. During 1917–1919, Pyzel, Edward Hepner (head of Roxana's technical department in Tulsa), and Tydeman (then Hepner's assistant, and shortly afterwards manager of the new Wood River refinery) were forever setting out to view some new process, regardless of how good or bad it sounded. These processes were almost endless. Thirty years later Tydeman recalled having inspected and reported on installations of the Rittman, Greenstreet, Parker, D'Yarmett, Gomory, Hansen, Wade, Waxler, Sherman, Jenkins, and Coast processes.[146] In this search for a winner, Pyzel finally met Hiram J. Halle, president of the Universal Oil Products Company of Chicago. Thus began an association which was to launch the Dubbs process on a commercial scale and completely change the complexion of cracking technology.

The Dubbs Process

The beginning of the Dubbs process went back to 1909, when Jesse A. Dubbs, a California oil refiner, had applied for a patent on a method he had devised for de-emulsifying California crude oil. (Trumble's work with refinery processing equipment, it will be remembered, had begun in an attempt to solve this same problem.) Dubbs' patent application hung fire for more than five years; finally on January 5, 1915, a patent for "Treating Oil" was issued to him. It described a method of heating emulsified oil in tubes under self-generated pressure. Dubbs did not have cracking in mind when he originally applied for his patent; but before it had been issued, the success of the Burton process had prompted him to amend the application to include cracking.[147]

Shortly before his patent was issued, Dubbs and his son, who had the incredible name of Carbon Petroleum Dubbs, had come in contact with a group of enterprises managed by Hiram J. Halle for his financial backer, J. Ogden Armour. Armour, son of Philip D. Armour, the founder of Armour & Company, was interested in a variety of businesses besides meat-packing. One of them was the Standard Asphalt & Rubber Company of Independence, Kansas, an ailing concern which Armour had given to Halle to manage. In 1913, the younger Dubbs had gone to work for this firm. As a condition of his employment, Standard Asphalt had agreed to buy the senior Dubbs' patent when issued.[148]

Armour had a great interest in fundamental research, no matter what the field, and Halle had little difficulty in persuading him to form a new company, the National Hydrocarbon Company,† to

† Organized under the laws of South Dakota in 1914; later it changed its name to Universal Oil Products Company.

purchase the Dubbs patent and do development work on it. After the Independence refinery was sold in 1916, a laboratory was built by the Armour interests nearby and there experimental work in cracking was carried on. Carbon Petroleum Dubbs also did research work on his own, in a small laboratory attached to his home in Wilmette, a Chicago suburb. The younger Dubbs' work resulted in a long series of patents, the first of them granted in 1917.[149]

With unfailing faith in Halle, Armour put up large sums of money for research. In 1917, Universal Oil Products Company (National Hydrocarbon's new name) hired Dr. Gustav Egloff to direct its research. In 1921, it began the erection of a half-million-dollar laboratory at Riverside, a Chicago suburb—all this before a penny had been collected in royalties. Pyzel, when he first met the U.O.P. people, was greatly impressed by their willingness to spend big money on research.

"Clean Circulation"

On March 19, 1919, C. P. Dubbs filed a patent application for his "clean circulation" idea.‡ It was a logical further development of Trumble's "closed ring" principle. This "clean circulation" idea had been embodied in an experimental Dubbs plant built at the Standard Asphalt refinery in Independence, Kansas. The charging stock, gas oil, was heated to cracking temperatures in a pipe still consisting of ten 4-inch pipes, twenty feet each in length. The heated oil then passed into an unheated but well-insulated "cracking chamber," made up of four 10-inch pipes of the same length. Here the cracking reaction continued.

The products of this cracking reaction were oil vapors, gases, heavy unvaporized oil, and coke. Most of the coke settled in the cracking chamber, from which it had to be removed at the end of the run. The heavy, black unvaporized oil was continuously drawn off from the last of the 10-inch pipes which formed the cracking chamber. Thus the heavy oil, rich in heavy carbon elements that caused coke deposits, was removed from the process at this point. The oil vapors and gases, freed of this heavy material, were then carried through an upward-sloping vapor line to an air-cooled "aerial condenser." Here the heaviest vapor, practically freed of gasoline elements, was condensed, to be returned ("recycled") to this heating still, along with incoming fresh charge stock.

‡ Issued as U. S. Patent No. 1,392,626, October 4, 1921.

The remaining vapors passed into a water-cooled coil, where they were condensed into a liquid, called "pressure distillate," which contained about 60% gasoline. This pressure distillate, together with uncondensable gas, flowed into a pressure tank from which the distillate and gas were drawn off by means of separate pressure-regulating valves.

The heavy, black unvaporized oil, which had been drawn off at an early stage in the process, contained most of the coke-forming materials. Its removal from the process at an early stage was a major forward advance in cracking-unit design and made it possible to operate a Dubbs unit not for a matter of mere hours, but for several days before it became necessary to close down and clean out the unit. The yield of gasoline was slightly less by this method, but the savings in shut-down time and clean-out expense more than compensated for the reduced yield. Pyzel at once grasped the importance of this "clean circulation" feature of the Dubbs process, and tried to obtain a license under this patent alone.

By the summer of 1919, the backers of the Dubbs process felt that it was far enough developed to be shown to the industry. Halle invited the Western Petroleum Refiners Association and the National Petroleum Association (an organization of Pennsylvania refiners) to send committees of their members to witness a full-scale trial run of the experimental Dubbs plant at Independence. Pyzel, after seeing this plant in operation, sent Tydeman and Sverre Petersen, of Roxana's Technical department, to report on it.

The trial run lasted from July 19 through July 27, 1919, processed 2,700 gallons of charging stock and recovered 1,374 gallons of gasoline, a gasoline yield of 50½%. The charge stock was recirculated approximately ten times through the unit during the period of the run, with relatively little coking. The visiting refiners were encouraged by Halle's assurance that it would be Universal's policy to license the Dubbs process freely to all comers without restriction; that Universal would provide the technical assistance necessary to build and start up each new unit; that Universal would guarantee a minimum gasoline recovery of 30% of 400-endpoint gasoline (failing which the licensee would not be obliged to accept the unit); and that Universal would defend and "hold harmless" its licensees against any infringement suits which might be brought by owners of other patents. Best of all was the announcement that, although the test had been conducted on gas oil charge stock, the Dubbs process could operate on residual fuel.[150]

The Shell people had been impressed from the start with the ability of the Dubbs unit to charge residual fuel in place of the scarcer and more expensive gas oil. This feature, Pyzel remembers, was heartening to Deterding, who had maintained all along that it was foolish to look for processes to crack gas oil. Deterding felt that in the near future the market price for gas oil would make it too expensive to be used as charging stock, an estimate of the situation which turned out to be correct.[151]

It was, however, mainly Pyzel's doing that Shell finally abandoned attempts to develop a process of its own. With statesmanship rare for a man who had been the chief mover in the development of the Trumble converter, Pyzel wrote in October 1919, "It is of course more or less disagreeable for me to say so, but I am convinced that even if we should finally develop our converter into a gasoline plant (which, by the way we have not yet accomplished), the Dubbs process will always have the value of greater simplicity . . . and greater simplicity means, especially in apparatus of this character, diminished risk of breakdowns or failures, reduced cost of installation and of upkeep and repair. Therefore, I can only say that, as far as the cracking of gas oil into gasoline is concerned, we are already beaten in advance, and I think it is better to acknowledge this, than to hang onto a lost cause for the sake of personal or 'company' pride." [152]

Late in 1919, Shell became the first licensee of the new Dubbs process. On December 12, Roxana signed a contract with Universal Oil Products, agreeing to erect a commercial-scale Dubbs unit at Wood River and pay Universal a royalty of 15 cents a barrel for all oil processed. Universal, for its part, provided guarantees of minimum gasoline yield, using 32° to 36° gas oil as charging stock. The unit, to be designed by Universal, would make continuous runs for about ten days. Then it would be closed down for cleaning and twenty-four hours after it had been shut down, Universal promised, the unit would be back "on stream" again. Remembering the onerous contract which Shell of California had signed with the Trumble Refining Company some years earlier, Pyzel specified that all improvements in the process made by Shell would remain Shell property.[153]

Construction of this first unit got under way at Wood River in March 1920. It had an intake capacity of 250 barrels of gas oil a day, and was ready for its first runs in March 1921. Like the first Trumble unit at Martinez, the Wood River Dubbs unit was designed by the inventor's engineering staff; their uncontrollable "aerial condenser" for separating the gasoline vapors and returning the heavy "reflux" to the heating unit was, however, replaced by "circulating dephlegmators" of Pyzel's design. In subsequent units, Pyzel and other members of the Simplex staff made several important additions and changes which contributed materially to the success of the Dubbs process.[154]

The 24-hour clean-out guarantee which Universal had made was destined to be a source of trouble. Try as they would (and Carbon Petroleum Dubbs was right on the job living in a Wood River refin-

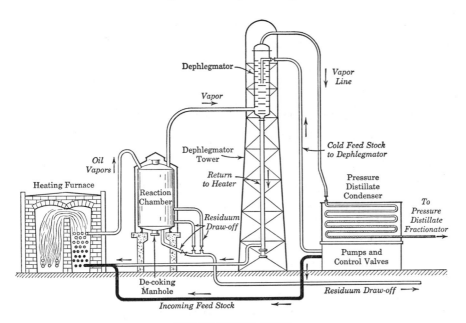

EARLY DUBBS UNIT

Residuum draw-off from cracking chamber provided important "clean circulation" feature of Dubbs process. Cold feed-stock entered by way of dephlegmator tower, and also directly by pump. The product, cracked gasoline (or "pressure distillate") was later redistilled.

ery staff house), the U.O.P. people found it difficult to shut down the unit, cool it enough to allow it to be cleaned, clean it, test it, and get it back on stream, all in twenty-four hours. The balance of 1921 was spent in test runs. One of these, in December 1921, resulted in disaster. In their haste to get the unit back into production within the guaranteed time, the Dubbs staff were accustomed to fire up before all of the air (used to test for leaks) was out of the system. For some reason, never satisfactorily explained, this practice caused a severe explosion which wrecked the unit, killed two men and badly burned several others, including Dubbs and P. E. Foster, at the time head stillman at Wood River.[155]

The destroyed unit was replaced by a modified one. In addition, it was decided to build another unit incorporating new features which had meanwhile suggested themselves. This new design was developed in part by the Simplex staff in San Francisco and in part by Universal. The contribution of Pyzel, Engelbregt, and others of the Simplex staff was a new pipe-still furnace which had a single tube-coil in place of the three parallel coils of Universal's first design. Universal proposed that the 10-inch horizontal pipes which had served as a cracking chamber in the original unit be replaced by a single, large, well-insulated chamber, 10 feet in diameter and 10 feet high. In later units, the size of this cracking chamber would be gradually increased until it was 30 and even 40 feet high.

The object of these changes was to enlarge the interiors so as to permit cracking of residual fuel, which was cheaper and more abundant than the gas oil charge-stock used by the first unit. Residual fuel was heavier than gas oil and contained such high percentages of coke-forming elements that it was impractical as feed-stock for the original unit because of rapid coking. However, with the enlarged interiors, Shell at last had a cracking process that would do what other processes of the day could not do: crack residual fuel.

The Cross Process

So well had the Dubbs process proved itself in Shell's eyes that late in 1922 construction was started at Wood River on six additional Dubbs units. Lest any good bets be ignored, Roxana early in 1922 also undertook to build two units employing the Cross process. This experimentation with the Cross process, undertaken chiefly as a "hedge" against failure of the Dubbs process, was strongly supported by Dr. W. C. de Leeuw,§ who did not always see eye to eye with Pyzel in technical matters.[156]

The Cross process was the work of the brothers W. M. Cross and Roy Cross of Kansas City. Their first sizeable experimental unit had been erected at Rosedale, Kansas, before 1916 and the first patents covering their process had been issued in that year. In 1920, a licensed,

§ Dr. de Leeuw, who had previously headed the Amsterdam laboratory for nearly ten years, arrived early in the Twenties to assist Pyzel, and made his headquarters in St. Louis.

commercial Cross unit was erected at the Indian Refining Company's plant in Lawrenceville, Illinois.[157]

The Cross process heated clean gas oil to high temperatures (875° to 950° F.) under extremely high pressures (approximately 600 pounds per square inch) to produce a re-formed oil, which the inventors called "synthetic crude." This "synthetic crude" was high in gasoline content and was next subjected to straight-run distillation to obtain gasoline, kerosene, and the other normal petroleum fractions. In this manner, the gas oil charged to these first Cross units yielded 30-40% gasoline, 50-55% recycle stock, 5-10% residuum, and about 5% gas. It was a promising process, and in 1921 a group called the Gasoline Products Company was organized to buy the Cross patents.[158]

Later in the 1920's, Cross cracking would become a formidable competitor to the Dubbs process, after equipment had been added to accomplish fractionation without rerunning the "synthetic crude." But at the time these early Cross units were installed at Wood River, the process still had several disadvantages. Its extremely high operating pressure (more than four times that of the Dubbs process, and nearly ten times that of the Burton process) presented many construction difficulties. The reaction chambers of the original units were, in fact, heavy one-piece steel forgings made in Germany by the famous Krupp munitions works. High temperatures also made the Cross process expensive to operate. But most important from Shell's point of view, the Cross process could not use residual fuel for charge stock, but only the lighter, more expensive gas oil. Before abandoning Cross cracking entirely, Roxana built two more Cross units at Wood River.[159]

The Fleming Process

Meanwhile, other cracking experiments had been going forward at Martinez. Anxious not to miss any promising process, Pyzel arranged for Shell of California to install the Fleming cracking process on a trial basis. Richard Fleming, a former Standard Oil man, had conceived the idea of eliminating coking by placing a cylindrical shell still, 10 feet in diameter and 30 feet tall, in an upright position, surrounding it with a chimney-like affair of brickwork, and applying heat evenly all around the sidewalls while leaving the bottom unheated. He reasoned that carbon particles would have a lesser tendency to adhere to the vertical sidewalls and form coke, and would settle instead to the unheated bottom of the still.

Fleming obtained a patent in December 1919 and his first unit was built by Shell at Martinez, where it went into operation during the summer of 1920. The trial operations of the Fleming unit were quite satisfactory, but in December 1920 a fire broke out, leading to the discovery that the still had developed a large bulge because of a defective weld, so it was closed down to avoid a more serious accident. The fabricators, M. W. Kellogg Company of Jersey City, shipped a new still to Martinez in March 1921, and regular runs of the Fleming still were resumed in May.[160]

Fleming's still took an initial charge of about 360 barrels of gas oil, and operated "on the feed," i.e., a stream of gas oil was fed into the still, corresponding in volume to the quantity of "pressure distillate" drawn off (about 200 barrels a day). This "feeding" kept the oil at an even level inside the unit. After a run of 40 to 60 hours, it had to be closed down so that the coke, which had formed meanwhile, could be removed from the still bottom. Gasoline yield was approximately one-third the volume of oil charged. By late 1922, the tremendous new flood of crude oil from Shell's Long Beach field had Martinez so hard pressed for storage space that the Fleming still was closed down for want of tankage to store its products. Fleming had a weak patent position which he later acknowledged by taking a license under the Burton process. His process was a distinct improvement upon Burton's but it was nevertheless a batch process not susceptible to clean circulation, and it required gas oil for charging stock. Several successful Fleming installations were built, the largest at Marland's Ponca City refinery. By mid-1920's, the more highly developed Dubbs and Cross processes had made the Fleming process obsolete.[161]

The Hot Oil Pump

California refiners were in general behind the Mid-Continent in adopting cracking processes. The scarcity of coal on the West Coast gave California refineries a better market for their fuel oil, as did the proximity of ocean transportation. The heavier California crude oils also presented coking problems that were more difficult to overcome. It was 1925–1926 before cracking plants began operation on a serious scale in California refineries.

In May 1922, Shell decided to build a commercial-size Dubbs plant for experimental purposes at Martinez. This plant was completed and put in operation during March of the following year.[162] Later that year, this plant had to be shut down because of the extreme shortage of tankage at Martinez; later on, it successfully resumed operation.

It was on this experimental Dubbs plant at Martinez that the first hot oil circulating pump was installed—a motor-driven centrifugal pump, designed by Pyzel and Engelbregt in cooperation with the Byron Jackson Pump Manufacturing Company. It was capable of handling very hot oil under high pressure. Until the advent of the hot oil pump, Dubbs plants had pumped fresh charging stock to the top of the dephlegmators, along with a large quantity of "reflux" (oil for recycling). This mixture of fresh oil and reflux flowed by gravity through the pipes of the cracking coil, whence it was discharged into the top of the reaction chamber. The pressure to force this large volume of oil through the pipe coil and into the reaction chamber came entirely from placing the dephlegmator upon higher and ever higher steel towers. This gravity-feed arrangement had operational drawbacks, as well as entailing extra construction expense. The hot oil pump at once removed the operating difficulties, doubled the throughput of the plant, and eliminated the need for the ungainly dephlegmator towers. The Byron Jackson pump was presently replaced by a simpler steam-driven duplex hot oil pump, developed earlier by N. W. Thompson for use on the Trumble converter. Thompson's pump was ideal for Dubbs units, since it performed well under hard service and reduced construction expense.[163]

Universal lost no time in adopting this improvement. In exchange for this and earlier contributions which had been made to the Dubbs process by Shell, and in consideration of Shell's assigning to Universal such Trumble patents as were applicable to cracking, Universal agreed to grant Shell a 25% reduction in royalty payments.

Low-Level Operation

When the Dubbs process was finally adopted by Shell refineries on the West Coast, they put into practice a much superior method of operation—a method which greatly increased the efficiency, profitability, and general attractiveness of the Dubbs process. This was the so-called "low-level operation," a technique suggested by experimental operations at Martinez during 1925 and developed into full-scale operation at the new Wilmington-Dominguez refineries during 1927–1928. Like the original development of cracking, low-level operation was evolved in response to the pressure of economics.

There were at this time two usual methods of Dubbs operation: cracking intensively, which eventually filled the cracking chamber with petroleum coke, or cracking less intensively and producing some coke along with a residual fuel oil containing 30% to 35% sludge. Cracking to coke was the method generally followed in the Midwest, because it produced a higher yield of gasoline and the coke, once it had been dug out of the cracking chamber, found a ready market. But on the Pacific Coast, where natural gas had been in use for some years as a domestic and industrial fuel, there was no demand for coke. Nearness to ports, on the other hand, suggested that a substantial market could be found for marine fuel oil. For this reason, Dubbs units were operated to crack less intensively. The only saleable product from this kind of operation was the gasoline, because of the lack of a market for coke and the extremely high sludge content of the fuel oil.

These twin problems received the attention of Dr. A. W. Jurrissen and his small staff at the Martinez refinery laboratory. They tried first to prevent carbon formation by use of a stirring apparatus inside the cracking chamber. This apparatus worked more easily when the chamber was not filled to capacity, and carbon deposition, it was noted, fell off. By March 1925, they felt confident enough to try a commercial-scale trial run of the "Jurrissen method" on a Dubbs unit at Martinez. A charge of 2,000 barrels, consisting half of Dubbs residue and half of pressure distillate, yielded gasoline, some coke, and a cracked residue that contained only 2½% sludge, as against a previous sludge content at least ten times greater.[164] Subsequent trials were not as successful; practical application of Jurrissen's experimental discoveries awaited opening of the new Dominguez refinery with its large batteries of cracking units.

Dominguez, planned for eventual expansion to 96 Dubbs cracking units, went on stream with eight units late in 1927. During the following year, the operating staff at Dominguez, composed of such men as A. E. Lacomblé, assistant superintendent of the Wilmington-Dominguez refineries, J. F. M. Taylor, operating head at Dominguez, D. M. Day, assistant superintendent at Wilmington, W. E. Mullemeister, head of the cracking department, A. H. Calderwood, maintenance foreman, and A. B. Cox, master mechanic, worked hard to put Jurrissen's idea into practical operation. They dispensed with the stirring apparatus altogether, reasoning that the liquid in the cracking chamber, if its level were low enough, could be kept in a state of turbulence by the incoming cracking charge.[165]

One of these eight new units was put on experimental runs at the low level. When it was temporarily closed down one day, Calderwood climbed to the top of the chamber and looked down a manhole to see what was going on. He saw a thick, asphaltic fog above the liquid. As it slowly condensed, this fog formed stalactites of asphalt on the cables that had been installed inside the chamber for the purpose of breaking out the coke. But the walls of the vessel, down which a thin film of condensed vapor was slowly flowing, did not coke as badly because of the washing action of the downward-flowing condensed vapor. From this observation came a remodeled cracking chamber which proved the practicality of low-level cracking.

Lacomblé, then a young assistant superintendent, took the responsibility in his boss's absence for giving orders to strip from the cracking chamber the cable, cable racks, and other protuberances around which coke might form. A trial run of the stripped unit proved successful beyond their highest expectations. Twenty years later, both Lacomblé and Calderwood remembered the excitement they experienced at the finish of the run when they removed the manholes, looked into a clean cracking chamber, and realized the significance of their success. To intensify the wall-washing action responsible for this success, the Dominguez team developed a flange to distribute the wall-washing film evenly and a level indicator, useful during the early days of operation, although it was later discarded. With these refinements, low-level cracking was a full-blown reality. Before the summer of 1928 was out, all of Shell's Dubbs units on the Pacific Coast had been converted to low-level operation.[166]

The differences which this new operating technique brought were tremendous. Formerly the cycle of operation had been four to five days; then the units had to be closed down, cooled, and the rock-hard coke removed with considerable difficulty. With low-level operation, cracking time was reduced, the amount of cracking was less, and, in consequence, coke formation was cut materially. Because of these much smaller coke deposits, low-level operating cycles could be extended to sixteen and even nineteen days before it became necessary to close down the units for cleaning. And the coke from low-level cracking was easily removed for it was soft and mealy, more nearly resembling heavy sludge.

The new method eliminated most of the unsaleable coke, greatly decreased operating expenses, and, best of all, produced a residual oil containing less than 2% sludge. A little blending would bring this

fuel up to sales specifications. With Dubbs residue now saleable as residual fuel, Shell was able to turn a former liability to immediate
profit. True, the reduced cracking time of low-level operation meant
a slightly smaller gasoline yield. However, the savings from longer
operating cycles and the profit from the now-saleable residue more
than offset the drop in gasoline production. Before long, even this reduction in yield of gasoline was cancelled out by the greatly increased
daily throughput possible with the new method of operation. Low-
level operation soon spread to other refineries, and in 1929, the U.O.P.
people, who were entitled by agreement to this improvement, applied
for a patent covering low-level operation.[167]

Licking the Corrosion Problem

Corrosion was another problem connected with Dubbs operation.
At Norco, the main vapor line of one of the early units exploded
without warning and the whole contents of the unit blew out in one
tremendous torch—happily without hurting anybody. This vapor
pipe, it developed on inspection, had corroded to a point where it was
too thin to withstand pressure. Immediately, measuring the thick-
nesses of the pipes and reaction chamber walls became a part of the
procedure of each close-down, lengthening the time a unit was out of
production and therefore adding to operating expense.[168]

Even more costly, of course, was the destructive effect of corrosion
upon expensive cracking equipment. At Wilmington, where Dubbs
units had been started up in May 1926, it was found just one year
later that chambers of these units had become seriously weakened. In
an effort to halt corrosion, many expedients were tried. At Martinez,
Pyzel set up a chromium-plating plant and had the insides of several
chambers chromium-plated. But the plating was very expensive, and
did not hold more than a few months.

Cheaper solutions were developed at Wood River. There, injecting
lime into the oil vapors to help neutralize corrosive action was tried
with a fair degree of success.* John Turner, head stillman of cracking
plants at Wood River, suggested coating the interiors of the chambers
with cement to protect the metal against the corrosive acids and phe-
nols of the hot oil vapors. Although a better method was found some
years later, Turner's method worked well at the time; during 1928 the

---

* Lime-injection was covered by the Jenkins cracking patents, so Shell had to
arrange to pay the Jenkins Process Company royalties for the use of this method,
a practice which continued until fairly recent times.[169]

interiors of most of the Shell Dubbs units were coated with cement applied by spray gun.[170]

At Wilmington, where pipes became paper-thin and gave way due to very rapid corrosion, Calderwood started keeping a careful set of records of each variable which might be hastening corrosion. In this manner, it was soon determined that the sulphur compounds in oil had their most corrosive effects between the temperatures of 750° and 775°. By removing insulation where it was keeping the oil at this critical temperature, and by adding insulation at other spots in order to boost temperatures beyond the critical range, the Wilmington refinery licked the worst of its line corrosion problems.[171]

By the late 1920's, Shell technologists, working sometimes with the Universal people but often alone, had successfully solved most of the major problems connected with operating Dubbs units. Their contributions were important, for Shell was at the time by far the biggest user of the Dubbs method. Under the terms of agreement with U.O.P., free use of all these improvements was given to Universal for its own use and for licensing to others. Shell's Dubbs royalties continued at the rate of 15 cents a barrel (subject to the 25% discount which Pyzel had negotiated) until the spring of 1926, when he and Halle worked out a supplementary arrangement. Thereafter, Shell's Dubbs royalties were further reduced in recognition of the large amounts of oil being processed. The schedule of royalties in effect at the beginning of 1929 was 15¢ a barrel to Universal for the first million barrels of intake, 14¢ for the second million, and so on down to 4¢ a barrel for quantities over 79½ million barrels. These quantities were calculated on a calendar-year basis, included all refineries owned by the Shell Group of companies world-wide, and were subject to the 25% discount.[172] The discount was enjoyed 22½% by the royalty-paying company; 2½% was paid over to Simplex Refining Company in exchange for Simplex's design and engineering services. Even with these discounts, Shell's royalty payments to Universal were large: by 1930 they exceeded $3,000,000 a year.[173] The Dubbs process, thanks to Shell's early support, was forging ahead steadily. Soon it would overshadow its earlier competitors.

The Cracking Patent Litigation

As the reader has no doubt suspected, most of the cracking patents were bound to conflict with each other. The thousands of cracking patents which issued from the Patent Office in the ten years following

Burton's 1913 patent were probably more troublesome than all the technical problems incident to developing a successful cracking process.

Faced with thousands of applications from hundreds of applicants, covering an involved and highly technical process of which very little was as yet understood even by the inventors, the patent examiners approved the issuance of scores of patents that were so similar that men highly skilled in the art of cracking could note little difference among them.

There was also the highly important matter of "prior art," as it is called in patent law. Hadn't Burton's patent (and all those following it) been anticipated by earlier patents, such as that of Dewar and Redwood? Here again the patent office was up against some hard questions, not as easy to answer as they might at first seem. Frank Howard, president of Standard of New Jersey's research company, writing in 1922, spoke sympathetically of the difficulties which confronted the patent examiners.[174]

> It is almost universally the case that an invention consists of a combination of something that is new with something that is old. In the art of cracking oil, the patents, without exception so far as we know, do not even purport to cover fundamentally the operation known as "cracking". They obviously could not do so, for this operation, under the same or another name, is at least one hundred years old. What the patents do cover, each of them, is some particular combination of steps, or pieces of equipment arranged for use in some definite fashion. Perhaps no single one of the pieces of equipment or the steps of procedure will be new in itself; perhaps the novelty will consist only in its application in that particular combination.
>
> In other cases, the novelty may consist in the addition of some single new step or piece of equipment to an apparatus or process which was *in toto* old with the exception of the new part. For example, in the cracking art, probably two-thirds of the patents which have been issued relate to improvements in the same general method used in the Burton process, i.e., distillation of the heavy oil under pressure. . . .
>
> It follows . . . that almost all of the patented cracking methods . . . are themselves infringements of some one or more other patents.

The result of this patent confusion was a dilemma of the first order. Nearly every holder of a cracking patent, if he could afford the expense, brought infringement suits against any refiner who seemed to be infringing his process in some manner. Probably the most famous of these suits—certainly the longest—was a suit filed in 1916 by Universal Oil Products against Standard of Indiana for infringement of Jesse Dubbs' patent No. 1,123,502, filed in 1909 and issued in 1915. The Dubbs patent, while admittedly for the de-emulsification of crude oil, did mention the treating of oil by heat under self-generated pressure. Burton's basic patent (applied for 1912, issued 1913) also utilized self-generated pressure; but since Dubbs' application antedated Burton's, Universal filed suit claiming infringement.

A special master was appointed by the Federal court to hear testimony, as it was obvious that the suit would be very lengthy and highly technical. Testimony taken at various points around the country dragged on all through the 1920's. This case, with its long parade of experts, is still remembered as one of the lengthiest civil cases on record. By 1931, when it was finally settled out of court, the testimony amounted to more than 22,000 pages. A high spot which attracted attention outside the industry was the testimony of U.O.P.'s director of research, Dr. Gustav Egloff (known in the trade as "Gasoline Gus"). He testified for several months late in 1927 and early 1928 at a hearing in St. Louis. On February 16, 1928, the St. Louis *Post-Dispatch* felt moved to comment editorially:

> We are lost in admiration of Doctor Egloff, oil expert of the Universal Oil Products Company of Chicago. In the dim, dead days of last November, he took the witness stand in a suit of his company against the Standard Oil Company. No matter what the suit is about, Dr. Egloff today is still on the stand and still talking. The workaday world has saluted the Armistice colors, waxed fat on Thanksgiving turkey, dressed a Christmas tree, observed the New Year's saturnalia, and paid court to its lady love on the day of St. Valentine—and Doctor Egloff is still testifying. How does he do it? Well, one day an unwary attorney asked him to define *emulsion*. Snapping into the subject, Doctor Egloff answered him in seven calendar days of four hours each. . . . We repeat we admire him, but—remembering the seven-day answer to the emulsion question—we would never be so incautious, especially if we were in a hurry, to ask him what time it is.[175]

While this protracted suit was dragging on through the 1920's, owners of some of the other cracking processes had entered into cross-licensing agreements. By 1923, Standard of Indiana (Burton process), Standard of New Jersey (Tube-and-Tank process), Texaco (Holmes-Manley process), and the Gasoline Products Company (Cross process) had executed a series of cross-licenses making it possible for each of these four companies to use the cracking patents of the other three without payment of royalty. Thenceforth, these "Patent Club" companies, as they had been nicknamed, could drop all litigation among themselves † and concentrate on fighting owners of "outside" processes, the chief of which was Universal with its Dubbs process.

In September 1923, Standard of Indiana brought suit against Universal charging that the Dubbs process infringed the Burton patents; and in 1924, The Texas Company brought suit against Warner-Quinlan (a refining and marketing company in the New York area later purchased by Cities Service) charging that this company's operation of a Dubbs unit constituted an infringement of Texaco's Adams patents. Universal participated directly in the Warner-Quinlan case because of Halle's policy of defending licensees. Universal was at the same time vigorously bringing infringement suits against any refiner who licensed a process from the "Patent Club" group of companies.

The result was that a refiner proposing to license any of the five leading cracking processes could be sure of an infringement suit, brought either by Universal or by one of the "Patent Club" companies. In addition to being a great inconvenience to prospective patent licensees, this state of affairs was also bad for the patent-owning companies who were obliged to spend hundreds of thousands of dollars for legal fees and court costs. By 1931, Universal had spent $1,-800,000 on its suit against Standard of Indiana, to say nothing of the large sums it had laid out to defend its licensees in individual infringement suits.[177] Halle and the Universal people were anxious to put an end to this large expense and during 1930 Pyzel took the lead in helping them work out a solution which came to be known in patent circles as the "Peace of 1931."

The "Peace of 1931"

Briefly, this settlement involved the purchase of U.O.P. by Shell Union and Standard of California, the two largest licensees of the Dubbs process. The other four companies would then, according to the plan, license the Universal patents and Universal's suits against them would be dropped.

† In 1924, the government filed suit against the "Patent Club" companies, charging that their cross-licensing agreements were a conspiracy in restraint of trade and that a long list of their patents (including the original Burton patent) were invalid on grounds of prior art. This case was five years in the lower courts, and was not definitely settled until the Supreme Court in April 1931 found in favor of the defendant companies on every point, and dismissed the government's case. This decision validated the Burton patent about which there had been so much dispute, but the validating decision came after the patent had expired.[176]

The details of this settlement had been worked out and approved by the parties concerned late in 1930. The sole obstacle remaining was the Warner-Quinlan suit, and a decision in that case was expected momentarily. If the court found for The Texas Company, Universal's patent position would be seriously impaired. A group composed of legal counsel and executives of some of the companies concerned gathered in Halle's office in Chicago on January 6, 1931, anxiously awaiting telephoned word of the outcome of the suit. They soon received it. The court found for Warner-Quinlan, holding that Texaco's Adams patents were invalid. Upon receipt of this news, the papers necessary to formalize the patent agreement were signed, and U.O.P.'s fifteen-year-long suit against Standard of Indiana was dropped.[178]

Shell and Standard Oil of California organized a new company, the United Gasoline Corporation, to carry out the purchase. The agreements signed on January 6 provided that United Gasoline would buy Universal Oil Products Company for $25,000,000. Forty per cent of this purchase price, or $10,000,000, was cash. This sum was provided $7,500,000 by Shell and $2,500,000 by Standard Oil of California. These two companies received stock in United Gasoline in proportion to the amounts of money they furnished; but to assure Standard of California that it had no idea of attempting to acquire control, Shell proposed that a small amount of voting stock be authorized and issued in equal amounts to both companies. The remaining $15,000,000 of purchase money was raised by selling United Gasoline serial notes in the amount of $3,000,000 to five companies—Shell, Standard of California, Standard of Indiana, Standard of New Jersey, and Texaco. In return for subscribing these notes, each of the five companies was granted a paid-up license under the Universal cracking patents.[179]

The purchase money which transferred ownership of Universal to the oil companies went to individuals who had held U.O.P. stock through good times and bad. It is pleasant to record that Armour's widow thus received more than $8,000,000 in cash at a time when it helped materially to repair the family fortunes. C. P. Dubbs, who had had faith enough in his own inventions to take stock in payment, was also rewarded handsomely, receiving more than $3,500,000 cash. The Universal organization was left untouched. Halle and C. P. Dubbs ‡ continued on in their former capacities, and Egloff continued to direct

‡ Dubbs headed Universal's research and development department until 1930, was thereafter an unpaid consultant.[180]

the company's research. Even the Universal name was preserved. As soon as organizational formalities were over, United Gasoline changed its name to Universal Oil Products Company, and the old South Dakota corporation of similar name was dissolved.

In 1937, a further agreement, which was a logical sequel to the 1931 arrangements, eliminated at last all contention between Universal and the Patent Club group. On December 1, 1937, The Texas Company, Standard of Indiana, Standard of New Jersey, and three companies hitherto not parties to these agreements—Atlantic Refining Company, Gulf Oil Corporation, and Gasoline Products Company (owner of the Cross process)—granted Universal licensing rights to all cracking patents owned by them.[181] Atlantic and Gulf each subscribed to $3,000,000 worth of Universal serial notes and received licenses under the Universal patents, as the other oil companies had done six years earlier. This move, dubbed by some of the lawyers the "Treaty of 1937," brought tranquillity to the business of licensing thermal cracking patents. Now U.O.P. could issue a blanket license under all the main processes and a refiner with a license could be reasonably sure that he would be safe from suits and counter-suits.

Universal continued to develop and improve the Dubbs process at its now-famous Riverside laboratory. It also offered the small refiner a complete engineering and refinery design advisory service—all without charge if he were a licensee. Large continuing expenditures for research kept U.O.P. in a leading position, with the result that many refiners came to look upon Universal as a sort of refinery architect and to hold its counsel in high esteem. One small refiner remarked to Pyzel, "Even if I couldn't use the Dubbs process, the royalty I pay them would be worth it. They give me the benefit of having a big company's engineering department."[182] This royalty was reduced during 1932 from the standard 15 cents to 10 cents a barrel.§

§ It will probably be well to discuss Universal's subsequent history at this point. In 1944, a suit which U.O.P. had brought against the Globe Oil & Refining Company for infringement of C. P. Dubbs' "clean circulation" patent and Egloff's "selective cracking" patent reached the Supreme Court. The High Court held both patents invalid. Although the clean circulation patent had expired by the time of the decision, this decision virtually destroyed Universal's thermal cracking patent position. That year the oil company owners of Universal made an outright gift of their interest in U.O.P. to the American Chemical Society which now owns it. All of the more important thermal cracking patents owned by Universal have since expired. That it still continues to do a profitable business is proof of the value of the company's engineering, research, and design services, as well as testimony to the alertness of its management which has kept abreast of refinery technology by developing and patenting many new oil refining processes.

Cracked Gasoline Gives Improved Performance

Just as the cracking processes underwent tremendous improvement all during the Twenties, so did the reputation of cracked gasoline.

Burton's original "spirit" was, as we have seen, regarded as a distinctly inferior product and sold for 3 cents under regular gasoline price. This unsavory reputation lingered through the early 1920's. The reasons were not hard to find: cracked gasoline was heavier at a time when the lighter, quick-starting gasolines were thought best; it contained a large number of unsaturated hydrocarbon compounds and these tended to make it unstable, causing discoloration and gumming. Worst of all from the customer's viewpoint were the large number of sulphur compounds in the cracked product, giving it a foul odor.

Tydeman, manager of Wood River at the time Dubbs cracking was installed there, many years later recalled the difficulty refiners had in making cracked gasoline pass muster: "As to quality: cracked gasoline had to be suitable for blending with straight-run, and therefore have the accepted endpoint of 437° to 450° F.; it must be reasonably stable so as not to discolor and gum before it was used; and it must not stink any more than the next fellow's, and if possible less. Accordingly, the pressure distillate from the cracking stills was treated, usually with sulphuric acid, to polymerize the gum- and color-forming components and oxidize some of the 'skunk' (mercaptans); it was then re-distilled so as to leave the polymers in the bottoms. Then it was blended with straight-run and went to market while everybody kept his fingers crossed. Of course always some stuff would get backed up in a tank corner and gum and color and the distributor would yell; or he would sell it anyhow and the customer screamed, and then we had the Sales Department on our neck. So the treating of pressure distillate, or cracked gasoline, was an everlasting research problem in those days." [183]

Then, the widespread research being carried on during this 1920–1925 period by people such as Dr. Thomas Midgeley and Sir Harry Ricardo into the subject of detonation, or engine "knocking," pointed to a new motor fuel. Ricardo was the first to notice that cracked gasoline, because of the "undesirable" aromatics it contained, was high in anti-knock value. This meant that in engines of proper compression ratio cracked gasoline could be a knockless fuel. In 1926 a widely circulated booklet, "Now the Truth About Cracked Gasoline Can Be

Told," helped to give the cracked product a new respectability among refiners.[184]

With this development, cracked gasoline, once produced to supplement supplies of the straight-run product, began to displace it. Before the 1930's were out, straight-run gasoline for automotive purposes would be completely off the market. Cracking, and particularly Dubbs cracking, had won a place for itself larger than the most optimistic had foreseen.

8

New Refineries: Wilmington, Arkansas City

THE new sources of crude oil which Shell of California and Roxana acquired during the first half of the Twenties were substantial. In 1920, these companies together had accounted for 2.2% of the nation's crude oil production; by 1925, their percentage had risen to 5.5%. This increased production made possible the erection of new refineries, the enlargement of existing ones, and expansion of the marketing territories of both companies.

In Southern California this expansion seemed almost instantaneous. As a result of new discoveries such as Signal Hill and Santa Fe Springs, Shell of California emerged overnight as a big producer in the Los Angeles Basin. Its position in that area was further enhanced by the Shell-Union deal, which gave the company a number of substantial properties.

In themselves, these former Union of Delaware properties would have been enough to warrant setting up a Shell organization in Southern California. Columbia Oil Producing Company, with its refining and marketing subsidiary, Puente Oil Company, came to Shell as a going concern. The management of Shell of California wisely decided to build its sales department in Southern California around the Puente organization. H. S. Botsford, fifteen years general manager of Puente, was made manager of Shell's newly created Southern marketing division.* Puente had only a small, antiquated refinery at Chino and about

---

* The exploration and production end of the company, although under different management, occupied common quarters with the sales department. The Higgins Building, with occasional extensions of space, remained Shell's Los Angeles headquarters until 1931, when the practically new main office of the defunct Union Insurance Company, at 1008 West Sixth Street, was purchased and remodeled.

a dozen and a half service stations in the Los Angeles area, but the favorable reputation of this little company was out of all proportion to its size.[185]

The Chino refinery, operating by old-fashioned methods, skimmed off only the lightest part of the gasoline fraction and blended it with casinghead gasoline. The result was a motor fuel of superior quick-starting properties, so popular and sought-after that the company had a waiting list of some 300 prospective dealers who hoped some day to handle Puente gasoline. Shell decided to take advantage of this high degree of public acceptance by making the conversion to the Shell brand gradual. For a year and a half, Puente's green colors were continued, as was its trademark, a muscular arm and clenched fist—"The Gasoline with the Punch."

A new refinery to process the Shell production in the Los Angeles area was a first order of business. Union Oil of California already had a considerable plant at Wilmington, and hopes that Shell might acquire control of this company, or come to some sort of arrangement with it, delayed construction of a new Shell refinery in the area. Meanwhile, Puente's small Chino refinery continued to be Shell's sole source of supply for the Los Angeles area.

Erle Severns and Frank Esterlin of the Martinez laboratory were sent to Chino to see what they could do inexpensively to modify the equipment and increase throughput. They found five batch stills of the most old-fashioned type. By the exercise of much ingenuity, they devised a scheme for tapping these stills at different levels and connecting them in series to form a sort of jerry-built bench still capable of operating on a continuous basis. Simplex designed and sent a dephlegmenator to be used in connection with this impromptu still arrangement. Thus re-equipped, the daily capacity of the Chino refinery was raised to about 2,000 barrels a day, yielding 25-30% gasoline. It was not thought wise to spend any large amount of money at Chino, for the company intended to operate the plant only through 1923.† At the end of this time, it was expected, a new Shell refinery would be in operation in the Los Angeles area.[187]

Wilmington

By late 1922, it was apparent that the Union of California would continue its way independently, so in January 1923 Shell bought 243

---

† The Chino refinery was shut down for good early in April 1924. Its equipment was junked and its tankage and the fourteen acres of land on which it had stood became, for a time, a depot for Shell's sales department. Eventually the land was sold to the city of Los Angeles for city stables and a dump.[186]

acres of land for a refinery site near Wilmington, just outside the Los Angeles city limits and not far from Signal Hill. At the same time, the company arranged with the city of Los Angeles to lease a portion of Mormon Island in Los Angeles-Long Beach harbor and there it built a marine loading station to handle both refined products and crude oil.

By March, work on the new refinery was well under way. Meanwhile, the flood of crude oil from Signal Hill and Santa Fe Springs continued to pour in on the incomplete refinery. To store it, seven concrete-lined earthen reservoirs were begun, most of them capable of holding a million barrels apiece, and one huge reservoir, 3½ million barrels. Before the summer of 1923 was out, all of the reservoirs were finished and nearly all of them were full. (These reservoirs had an unfortunate side effect: they gobbled up much of the 243-acre tract that had been purchased for the refinery site.) By late September, two of Wilmington's three Trumble units had been completed, and on September 25, 1923, they began operation. Superintendent during the construction had been W. C. (Mike) Little, who was succeeded by William Cameron when the refinery began actual operations.[188]

Because of the large volumes of crude oil available for processing in the Los Angeles area, Wilmington was destined to become a large-volume producer of a relatively few products. Where Martinez made a full range of products, including such "fussy" refining jobs as the manufacture of grease and the blending of spray oils, Wilmington's attention was directed chiefly to producing gasoline, kerosene, and fuel oil in large quantities. Early in 1926, a fourth Trumble unit was built at Wilmington to rerun cracked gasoline from the newly built cracking units. By the end of 1926, the new refinery was averaging a crude oil intake of 30,000 barrels a day, the rate at which it would continue to operate for several years to come.

The Mormon Island terminal, completed in 1923, all during the Twenties played a part in Shell's Pacific Coast operations that was out of all proportion to its size. From Mormon Island, during these years, were shipped most of the products exported by Shell of California and most of the crude oil that Asiatic, acting for Group companies abroad, bought from Los Angeles Basin producers during the years of booming production.[189]

Arkansas City

Just as Shell of California's new production from its rich Signal Hill holdings had necessitated a new refinery nearby, so also did Roxana's bonanza, the Tonkawa field. The decision to build a second Shell refinery in the Mid-Continent came early in 1923. The energetic Arkansas City, Kansas, Chamber of Commerce induced Roxana to locate its new refinery there by the gift of what was in effect a free site. Roxana paid the Chamber of Commerce $20,000, which probably little more than covered the Chamber's incidental expenses in connection with the acquisition of the land, and in exchange agreed to build a plant that would cost at least $3,000,000.[190]

Like many another gift horse, this free refinery site was never wholly satisfactory. It lay at the junction of the Arkansas and Walnut rivers and flood waters regularly inundated it. The first of these floods came in June 1923, when construction had been under way only six weeks. Most of the preliminary work was ruined by the flood waters. Not discouraged, the company built a combination dike and railroad grading all the way around the site. Thus protected, work got under way again.

The Arkansas City refinery had at the start four Trumble topping units and six Dubbs cracking units. The first of the Trumbles was completed and put on stream December 15, 1923. By the middle of March all four Trumbles were in operation, along with the first of the Dubbs units. The new refinery's initial capacity ran between 12,-000 and 14,000 barrels a day. A little later, more Dubbs units were added, and by 1926 "Ark City," as the refinery was called inside the Shell organization, was running 20,000 barrels a day, the rate at which it continued to operate thereafter. Dr. R. H. Waser was the refinery's first superintendent and R. C. Roberts was assistant superintendent.

Like Wilmington, the Arkansas City refinery became a volume producer of a relatively few products: gasoline, kerosene, gas oil, residual fuel, coke. It was located on several main railroads—the Santa Fe, Missouri Pacific, and Midland Valley—enabling it to become Roxana's source of supply for the whole tier of states between the Mississippi River and the Rockies, from North and South Dakota to Oklahoma.

To keep pace with the company's increased supplies of crude, the capacity of Roxana's Wood River refinery was also considerably extended. During 1922 and 1923, five new Trumble units were built and put into operation, in addition to the Dubbs and Cross cracking plants already mentioned. These same years also saw the installation of two lubricating oil plants. The first, in 1924, was a conventional plant. The second, built to supersede it the following year, cost half a million dollars and incorporated the brand-new Schulze process, a high-vacuum distilling method which Shell was among the first to adopt. With the completion of these facilities, Roxana was equipped to supply its customers a range of products almost as complete as that made by Shell of California at Martinez.

It was, then, hardly surprising that Roxana should begin looking for a broader market than the one offered it by the wholesalers who up to now had sold the company's products. How Roxana established and built its own wholesale and retail organization throughout the Midwest, and how Shell of California expanded its sales activities over the entire Pacific Slope will be the story of the next chapter.

CHAPTER VI

The Golden Era of Volume

1925–1930

I T IS safe to predict that the American Twenties will within a very short time (if, indeed, they have not already) become in the minds of all who lived through them a wonderful memory of golden, exciting, carefree years, recalled with as much fondness and nostalgia as were The Gay Nineties a generation ago. It is not strange that this should be so. For America, the Twenties were a last gay fling before discarding adolescent ways and settling down to the serious business of becoming a responsible world power.

This fling manifested itself in many ways. Few previous periods of American history had seen so much general prosperity, or held such sanguine hopes for the economic future. For once in his life, the average American (largely because of increased productivity) had enough money left over after paying for the rent and groceries to indulge himself in a few extras. Sociologists and popular historians have made much of the speak-easy and stock market speculation as symbols of the Twenties. But throughout the land, the great symbol of the Twenties was, for the average American, the automobile and the new way of life it brought.

By the early 1920's, automobiles had become more dependable and easier to start and operate. Dirt roads, with their mudholes, were gradually giving way to paved highways that greatly increased the distance a man could travel in one day and still return home at night. Best of all, standardization, mass production, and large sales were bringing the price of new cars down within the reach of almost everyone. (The 1926 Ford sedan, for instance, sold for less than $500.) The number of automobiles on the road increased at an incredible rate all during the Twenties: 6¾ million passenger cars were in service in 1919; ten years later there were more than 23 million, to say nothing of 3½ million trucks and buses.

The day of the automobile had indeed arrived. "And as it came," wrote Frederick Lewis Allen in *Only Yesterday*, "it changed the face of America. Villages which had once prospered because they were 'on the railroad' languished with economic anaemia; villages on Route 61 bloomed with garages, filling stations, hot-dog stands, chicken-dinner restaurants, tearooms, tourists' rests, camping sites. . . . In thousands of towns, at the beginning of the decade a single traffic officer at the junction of Main Street and Central Street had been sufficient for the control of traffic. By the end of the decade, what a difference!—red and green lights, blinkers, one-way streets, boulevard stops, stringent and yet more stringent parking ordinances—and still a flow of traffic that backed up for blocks along Main Street every Saturday and Sunday afternoon. Slowly but surely the age of steam was yielding to the gasoline age." [1]

This gasoline age brought sweeping changes in the private life of the individual motorist. Just as surely, it brought a whole new method of doing business to the oil companies that supplied his gasoline. The greatly enlarged gasoline volume of the Twenties made little companies into big ones, almost overnight. Equally important, the hope of establishing a profitable business brought scores of newcomers into the field, intensifying the competitive spirit in gasoline marketing far more than any act of Congress or anti-trust prosecution could ever hope to do. Established companies continued to expand their businesses, but the inroads of the newcomers considerably reduced the entrenched companies' "share" of the market. Standard of California, for instance, had some 54% of the Pacific Coast gasoline business in 1919;[2] by the late 1920's, despite a large increase in the volume of its sales, Standard's share of the market had been whittled down to a little more than 20%. It was the Twenties, with their rapidly growing markets and furious competition, which saw the development of the present pattern of major companies in the American oil industry. It was during the Twenties that Texaco, Cities Service, Gulf, Sun, Phillips, Richfield, Sinclair, Skelly—to name only a few—assumed their present positions of importance in the industry. And many of the old Standard companies, broken up in 1911, were by the mid-Twenties well on their way to outstripping their former parent in size.

For the young and vigorous Shell companies, this was a period of enormous growth. In 1920, Shell-branded gasoline was being sold only in three Pacific Coast states and British Columbia; in the Mid-Continent, Roxana's small sales were on the "spot," or wholesale tank car, market. Within five years, this state of affairs underwent a drastic change. By 1925, the Shell Union companies were accounting for some 5¼% of the total national gasoline sales,[3] thus establishing the market position which they were to hold for the next quarter of a century.

All of American business was, in these years, caught up in a period of exciting expansion. Business generally could say, in paraphrase of Dr. Coué, "every day, in every way, we're getting bigger and bigger." It was a time of unbridled optimism, an era of golden volume, golden hopes, golden dreams, and, sometimes, golden profits. Lords of all were the salesman and his helpmeet, the advertising man. Under them, salesmanship became scientific insofar as anything dealing with imponderable, unpredictable human nature can ever be said to be "scientific." For the first time, business generally dropped the old hit-and-miss salesmanship in favor of "the scientific approach"—consumer surveys, market research, applied psychology, and carefully planned advertising campaigns, all of which have since become distinctive features of American selling.

Above all, the new salesmanship was enthusiastic. Fred F. French, the New York real estate man, in a talk to his salesmen summed up the spirit of the whole decade: "There is no such thing as a reason why not." [4] In many instances to be sure, this spirit was carried, in extravagant excesses of zeal, to extremes that now seem amusing. But should we condemn, or even laugh? Who, of those who lived through those wonderful Twenties, does not even now feel a secret tug at his heartstrings when he recalls the golden, exciting, carefree years when the sky was the limit and vigorous young enthusiasm had not yet experienced the cruel disillusionment of deficit, depression, and retrenchment?

Salesmanship by the late 1920's had become more than mere peddling, more than a business. It was an art and, to some of its most avid practitioners, almost a religion. Smile, if you will, but then for a moment imagine that you are back in 1928 listening to Bruce Barton, one of the most fervid of the new salesmanship's exponents, as he addressed himself to American oil men. His little talk, entitled "The Magic of Gasoline," epitomizes the spirit that was abroad in the business world:[5]

> Stand for an hour beside one of your filling stations. Talk to the people who come in to buy gas. Discover for yourself what magic a dollar's worth of gasoline a week has worked in their lives.
> My friends, it is the juice of the fountain of eternal youth that you are selling. It is health. It is comfort. It is success. And you have sold

merely a bad smelling liquid at so many cents per gallon. You have never lifted it out of the category of a hated expense. It is an item for father to grumble about in the family budget. It is something for mother to economize on, though she has to drive five miles out of her way to save a cent a gallon.

There is a magnificent place for imagination in your business, but you must get it on the other side of the pump. You must put yourself in the place of the man and woman in whose lives your gasoline has worked miracles.

In the light of that superior wisdom which always seems to come twenty-five years too late, we can now look back and see that this flurry of high-powered salesmanship had deep-seated economic causes. Rapidly mounting productivity in every line of business was producing a total of more goods and services than could readily be sold. To help market this excess, the super-salesman appeared. In the oil business super-salesmanship manifested itself in a constant struggle to widen the market by extending territories and opening an ever-larger number of outlets. For a time at least, these efforts were successful to a high degree. But pressed from the rear by uncontrolled, ever-mounting production of crude oil, refiners and marketers found themselves during the last three years of the Twenties with more gasoline than even their big, new markets could absorb. A persuasive salesman might, perhaps, sell a man more suits of clothes than he could wear, or more automobiles than he could drive, but no amount of salesmanship could make him buy more gasoline than he could use. To increase sales, some of the oil companies began to offer better gasolines and new and better services, in the hope of wooing away their competitors' customers. When these devices proved successful, competitors retaliated by bettering their own products and services, often cutting prices at the same time. Thus began the competitive race called gasoline marketing, a race that, happily for the motorist, still continues.

The great period of Shell marketing expansion, with which this chapter is chiefly concerned, occurred during the second half of the Twenties. Properly to tell this story, however, we must reach back into the early years of the decade. It was during those years that Shell of California began in earnest to build an organization capable of selling its entire output on the Pacific Slope; and the same period saw Roxana lay the foundations for its great spurt of expansion during the late Twenties.

The Golden Age in California

THE beginning of the Twenties found Shell of California's sales department little changed from the organization set up in the early years of the company. Shell's chief gasoline sales areas were still the Pacific Northwest and the San Francisco Bay region. Even so, the company was in 1920 considered one of the West Coast's four major marketers of gasoline, but it was a very poor fourth to the other three. Standard of California enjoyed some 54½% of the total Pacific Coast gasoline market, Union Oil of California about 20%, Associated slightly more than 10%, Shell barely 4%.[6] During 1921, the year Shell of California began to expand its sales capacity by building new depots and service stations, the company manufactured for sale some 60 million gallons of gasoline. By 1929, this figure was more than 630 million gallons, a tenfold increase in eight years. Shell of California was by the end of the Twenties no longer a weak fourth, but in very strong second place, its total sales exceeded only by the long-entrenched Standard Oil Company of California.

Confronted by this remarkable record achieved in so short a time, the reader will have little difficulty in understanding why, in the memories of Shell men everywhere, the sales activity of the Shell Company of California during the Twenties typifies a golden era which can never again be duplicated. It was a time of fast-moving expansion and uninhibited selling carried on by a young and vigorous sales force who believed literally that there was "no such thing as a reason why not."

The reasons behind Shell's spectacular success on the West Coast in the Twenties were several. First of all, the demand for gasoline was good. The state of California, by far the largest consumer on the Coast, saw its motor vehicle registration rise 250% during the decade, a rate of growth more rapid than the national increase of 175%. A second consideration was California's very substantial increase in crude oil production during these years, an increase in which Shell shared fully. These increases provided a stimulus for stepping up sales commensurately. A third factor in this success was a top-notch sales organization, whose youth and vigor, intelligence and ambition, made them as competent a team of oil marketers as any company could ever hope to have.

Van Eck, under whose presidency the big expansion program started, had the happy faculty of delegating responsibility to qualified lieutenants, once the main lines of policy had been established. The resultant feeling of individual responsibility by men throughout the organization made it possible for a relatively small sales department to do a big job. Legh-Jones, who succeeded Van Eck, wisely adhered to this policy.

Herbert Gallagher, who had headed Shell sales on the West Coast from the start, had been made a vice president as early as 1914, and served in this capacity for twenty years under the presidencies of Harris, Meischke-Smith, Van Eck, and Legh-Jones. Because of his continuity in the job and his wide business and social acquaintance, Gallagher, probably more than any of the men under whom he served, was "Mr. Shell" in the minds of the Pacific Coast business world. An able executive, he concerned himself with the larger aspects of sales, leaving the execution of particular programs in the hands of the men under him.

The key men under Gallagher were the division managers. The Northern division, which took in British Columbia, Washington, Oregon and, later in the Twenties, Idaho, Montana, and a part of Wyoming, had its headquarters in Seattle in a company-owned building built on the property which had been Shell's first depot in that city. Manager of the Northern division was Donnell G. Fisher, who had built the organization man by man, starting from a sales force of one (himself) in 1912. Fisher was able, intelligent, and hard-working, an executive who knew how to instill in his men an appreciation of these qualities in their own work.

A southern corner of Oregon, northern and central California as far south as Bakersfield, and, later, Utah and Nevada, and a corner of Wyoming comprised the Central division with offices located in the company's head office in San Francisco. The Central division's manager was genial, kindhearted, easygoing E. P. Christie, "Pop" to all his "boys." Christie had a considerable hand in developing Shell's distinctive service stations, particularly those of the San Francisco Bay area.

Shell's marketing in Southern California and, later, Arizona and western New Mexico, was organized as the Southern division which started in Los Angeles in 1922 around the nucleus of the Puente properties which Shell had taken over in the Shell-Union deal. Its manager at the start was H. S. Botsford, a veteran oil marketer who was general manager of Puente at the time and who had previously been sales manager of Union Oil of California for several years. He was succeeded a few years later by J. C. Wheeler.

Although the company's sales activities developed rapidly during the Twenties these three divisions remained the chief administrative units of the Shell of California sales department. To handle the company's greatly extended sales coverage, a sort of subsidiary division, the district sales office, was developed during the late Twenties. These district offices were miniature division offices, having responsibility for as many as twenty depots. The depot was in turn a miniature district with the depot manager responsible for all sales of product made from his depot, including the operation of company-owned service stations in his area. A typical depot had one or two trucks, a warehouse, and employed a clerk and a yardman, in addition to the truck drivers. Fiscal functions, except for billing and collections, were handled by the three division offices.[7]

As these sales organizations grew during the Twenties, they promoted to positions of responsibility scores of alert and energetic young men, most of whom had started as service station operators or attendants and learned the business from the ground up. Shell of California's sales department thus unconsciously became a training ground for some of the best of the company's future sales executives. Later they would be scattered broadcast throughout the Shell sales organization and have upon Shell marketing the same leavening effect that the men from Coalinga had had upon the company's production department.

The big expansion began during the second half of 1921. That year the company built seven new depots, and acquired 200 new retail outlets, ten of them stations owned and operated by the company.* During 1922, the acquisition of the Puente properties in Los Angeles served as a nucleus for the new Southern California distributing organization and expansion got under way in earnest. Thirty-eight new

---

* The terms *station*, *depot*, and *terminal* are employed widely in the oil industry and do not always mean the same thing. In Shell parlance *station*, or more fully *service station*, refers to the retail outlet patronized by the motorist; *depot*, or *bulk depot*, is the wholesale distribution point which receives and stores gasoline and other products and makes deliveries to service stations. *Terminals*, much fewer in number, are very large tank installations generally located on deep water; their chief function is to receive products in large quantity and transship them in smaller lots to the bulk depots.

depots (an increase of 100%) and more than 300 new service stations, 101 of them company-operated stations, were added that year; in May, Van Eck recorded with pardonable pride, in his monthly report to the board of directors, that Shell of California's gasoline sales had passed the million-gallon-per-week mark.[8]

With the completion of the Wilmington refinery and extensions to Martinez during 1923, roughly twice as much product was available for the sales department to sell. That year, 79 new depots were put into operation (a further increase of more than 100%) and 343 new Shell retail outlets went into service. Six more depots were added in 1924, another 39 in 1925, and by the end of that year 2,913 stations were pumping Shell gasoline on the Pacific Coast.

One of them was Shell Company of California Station No. 27, at the corner of Fell and Stanyan Streets, San Francisco, which was the following May adjudged "The Ideal Filling Station" in a contest sponsored by *The Oil Trade*. Not all of Shell's California stations were as outstanding, but the average of them would rate surprisingly high, even by today's standards. Perhaps it would be instructive at this point to inquire briefly into the nature of these California stations of the mid-Twenties.

Development of the Service Station

The first chain of drive-in service stations in the country can, without doubt, be credited to Harry Grenner and Clem Laessig of St. Louis, who organized the Automobile Gasoline Company and in 1905 built the first of their small chain of drive-in stations in that city.[9] It remained, however, for California, and particularly the Los Angeles area, which had the greatest number of automobiles in the state, to develop the type of service station familiar to the present-day motorist.

In Los Angeles, chains of service stations operating on uniform principles and dispensing numerous free services made their appearance in large numbers well before 1920. One of the earliest operators there was Earl Anthony whose business, the National Supply Company, was purchased by Standard Oil of California in 1914, to become the nucleus of that company's chain of owned and operated stations. Another pioneer operator was the Puente Oil Company, which despite its small size was, like many another Los Angeles concern, a completely integrated oil company, producing from its own wells,

Beginnings of the Service Station

Early garages dispensed gasoline from these portable "buggies"; many early Shell dealers used similar equipment.

Automobile Gasoline Co., St. Louis, in 1905 opened first "drive-in" station with gravity tank and garden hose.

Automobile Gasoline Company's experiment proved a success. Here is one of its later stations at 12th and Pine Streets, St. Louis. The company had about forty outlets, plus a depot, when it was purchased by Shell in September 1929.

This San Franscisco service station was typical of Shell's company-operated outlets on the West Coast during the late 1920's. Note separate "California-style" rest rooms.

This interior is a sample of the spotless cleanliness for which company-operated service stations were justly famous in California. Photo taken about 1928.

Much care was lavished on flowers and shrubs to improve the service station's appearance. This San Francisco area station of the mid-Twenties was typical.

Shell tried to adapt its units to low-volume areas. This "Junior" station, *right*, at San Jose in 1926, is one of two such stations that the company built before abandoning the idea as impractical.

As the Twenties wore on and service station expansion continued unabated, Shell of California looked for new ways to finance construction. One method was for a landowner to build a station, lease it to Shell on long-term lease; Shell in turn sublet the station to a dealer. Photo shows first of Shell's "3-party lease" stations, Eureka, Calif., about 1928.

This 1928 photo of the service station on Roxana's Indianapolis bulk depot property shows that the "California style" station had moved east practically intact.

Although Midwestern service station standards in the Twenties were in general not up to those of California, there were exceptions, as the photograph on the right shows. It is *part* of the lounge of the ladies' rest room in a Western Oil Refining Company station, Indianapolis.

This same Western Oil Refining firm, which Shell purchased in 1929, built solidly and well. The station below is typical of its Indianapolis outlets, built of brick and masonry in a day when the average station was of wood or metal.

Photos courtesy B. A. Gwynn

refining in its own small refinery, and selling its gasoline through company stations direct to the retail purchaser.†

Gallagher and Christie also very early took a lively interest in company-operated stations in the San Francisco area, where the sale of gasoline through garages had hitherto been the usual thing. They had two stations at the San Francisco World's Fair in 1915, stations which in appearance and construction were prototypes of the average Shell station of the Twenties. Because Shell was a late-comer to the San Francisco market and found most of the garages there already handling competitors' products, it was only natural that this new form of direct selling should have a strong appeal to the Shell sales department.

In 1920, though, the company-operated station was still a relatively small factor in the total market. Standard that year had 220 company-operated stations, Associated 85, Shell 77, and Union 32.[11] The bulk of retail sales was still made by dealers—garages, general stores, auto accessory stores, hardware and paint stores. Shortly after 1920, the company-operated station rapidly began to increase in importance. Van Eck, in testimony given to a Senate subcommittee in 1923, revealed the extent of this changed state of affairs. His company, he said, had 204 company-owned stations in operation during the first six months of 1922 and they accounted for 44% of Shell of California's total gasoline sales during that time.[12] This was a trend of undeniable importance, for the stations which thus accounted for 44% of sales represented in numbers only 11% of the 1,841 retail outlets selling Shell gasoline on the Coast that year. Company stations

† An interesting difference between the Pacific Coast and Eastern oil markets is the much greater prevalence of integrated companies on the Coast. In the Los Angeles area, where the oil fields were very near, often within, the city limits of California's chief oil-consuming city, a small producer could without undue expense build his own refining and sales organization. By the second quarter of 1928, the State of California reported 19 companies, each selling more than 1,000,000 gallons of gasoline during that period. Most all of them were integrated companies, although not all were major companies by any means. In the Mid-Continent, by contrast, where the small producer was far removed from major centers of consumption, he very frequently sold his oil to a nearby independent refiner who refined it into products that were shipped by rail in tank car lots to independent jobbers in more populous areas. The prices these jobbers were willing to pay the independent refiners for their products determined the wholesale tank car, or "spot," market. In California, chiefly because of the more fortuitous location of oil fields in respect to markets, the role of the middleman, as represented by the independent refiner and jobber, has been of small importance.[10] The competitive battle there has been waged at the retail level, which has of course been greatly to the customer's advantage.

were becoming the big-volume outlets, the show-places, the pace-
setters for the dealers to follow. Development of this company-
operated station can best be viewed in California, for the oil industry
east of the Rocky Mountains did not take to widespread operation
of company stations until later in the Twenties, generally adopting
insofar as applicable the design and practice of California stations.

The years from 1914 to 1920 were a formative period for the
company-operated station in California, witnessing the gradual evolution and development of the company station so familiar during the
Twenties. It was during these years that the name "service" station
was adopted in California and put into general use. This nomenclature
spoke volumes of the companies' attitude toward the customer, and
was in marked contrast to the area east of the Rockies where "filling
station" was still the term used within the industry as late as 1930.

Free services offered by the California stations had their beginnings
in this formative period before 1920. It is worth remarking that they
originated not with dealers but with company-operated stations,
often with the company stations of the smaller Los Angeles chains,
for the "big fellows" had no monopoly on ingenuity.

Fred M. Dull, who was operating a Puente company station on
Wilshire Boulevard, Los Angeles, in 1916, has provided a good
description of his station and the services it rendered.[13] His station
was a wooden building, some 10 feet wide by 30 feet deep, with
double canopies projecting from the front. A sales room occupied
the front two-thirds of the building, and the back portion was given
over to a storeroom. The gasoline pumps were located, as at present,
on an "island," with driveways for cars on either side. The pumps,
brand-new at the time, could deliver up to five gallons, a distinct
improvement over the old, single-stroke, one-gallon pumps hitherto
in general use. In addition to one grade of gasoline, the station sold
two grades of motor oil (Pennsylvania and Western) and grease in
1-, 5-, and 10-pound tins. There were no facilities for lubrication.
The motorist usually went to a garage for this service; or, if he was
economy-minded, bought the materials and did the job in his own
back yard. Motor oil was stored in "highboys" (small square tanks
with attached pumps on top) and delivered to the car in flexible-
spout measures. The average oil sale was one to two quarts at a
time. The station did not "change oil" as a regular practice, but
occasionally an attendant would drain a customer's crankcase in the

interest of increasing sales. The company service station of this period usually sold only petroleum products, but Dull's station, a little ahead of its time, stocked a few accessories—tire "boots," tubes, patching materials, extra valves, and valve caps.

Free services were then becoming common in Los Angeles company stations. Dull's customers in 1916 could expect to have their oil and water checked, the windshield wiped, and the tires inflated, if necessary. However, these services were free only in that the company made no charge for them. The motorist customarily tipped the attendant for his trouble: the passing motorist, ten cents to a quarter, depending on the service rendered, and the regular customer $5 or $10 at Christmas.

The cleanliness for which California stations were soon to become famous was already very much in evidence. In part it was accidental. The day was long, the men ambitious, and the intervals between cars often lengthy in those days of light traffic. To keep busy during his free time, the operator (and his assistant, if he had one) cleaned the station. Dull recalls that "every nook and cranny of that station was dusted, cleaned, scoured, or painted, as the occasion demanded. The general effect was always one of sparkling cleanliness and thorough-going neatness. Our packaged products at first had paper labels, but the company soon switched to painted labels, for our house-cleaning was so vigorous that paper labels were scrubbed off in the process." Personal cleanliness went with a clean station. The operators wore sparkling white uniforms with black bow ties.

The operator and his assistant usually composed the entire staff. The operator would open the station at seven in the morning, put in ten hours, and be relieved at five in the afternoon by his assistant, who would keep the station open until 10 P.M., or a little later in some localities. Both men worked seven days a week, with one day off in fourteen; salary for the operator was $80 a month, and $50–$55 for his assistant. Stations such as this one pumped 16,000 to 18,000 gallons a month, much more than they would a few years later after the period of intense competition had arrived.

George P. Thomson, who joined the Shell Company of California in 1916 as a service station operator in the San Francisco Bay area, recalled similar experiences, with some variations.[14] For $75 a month and a 5% commission on the station's motor oil sales, Thomson worked ten hours a day, six days a week, and supplied his own khaki-colored uniform.‡ His first "station" was a curbside pump in front of a general store in Oakland. The storekeeper supplied the location, the Shell company furnished the equipment and operator. Because it was located on "automobile row," this station sold as much as 500 gallons a day through a one-gallon curbside pump. Soon after, Thomson was moved to a larger company station, also in Oakland, where Shell had thirteen company-operated stations at the time.

In addition to gasoline, Thomson's station sold engine distillate, a heavier, cheaper fuel, between gasoline and kerosene in its characteristics. Distillate could be burned in the engines of trucks and large cars, provided a pre-heating device had been installed. Because cars of the day were "oil hogs," motor oil sales were comparatively high and the 5% commission on oil sales, which the service station operator generally shared with his assistants, amounted to $5 to $7.50 a month per man. As in Los Angeles, the station was kept in immaculate condition, the cleaning being done by the operator in his spare time. No auto accessories aside from Schrader valves and valve caps were carried, for the primary purpose of the company was to push the sale of its own products. To this end, there were displays in the salesroom of packaged motor oil and greases.

It is easy to see that the concept of thorough-going free service originated in the Los Angeles area, for in Thomson's Oakland station the service given the motorist was confined to dispensing gasoline and motor oil, and perhaps wiping the windshield. Operators were cautioned not to inflate the customer's tires. In 1916, the cord tire had not yet come into general use. The high-pressure fabric tire of that day, held in place by a metal bead inserted between the wheel and tire rim, was dangerous to inflate because at pressures of 55 to 60 pounds the tire frequently blew out, sending the metal bead flying through the air. Even so, a good tipper could get his tires inflated. Tipping was an accepted custom, and on a good Saturday, the three men at Thomson's station could expect to divide $12–$14 in tips. Holidays were not frequent: from the very first, Thomson's station kept open all day Sunday; Thanksgiving and Christmas were about the only days in the year that the station did not open for business.

Al Hind, who went to work as an attendant in a Shell company station at Burlingame in 1917, remembers a common problem of the day was to acquaint the new attendant with the various makes of

‡ By the early Twenties, Shell of California had adopted white uniforms for all of its company stations, a standard that remained in effect for nearly thirty years.

cars. Most of the young men who went to work in service stations in those days did not own cars, and were therefore generally unfamiliar with them. A new man had to be taught the rudiments of the automobile. He had to familiarize himself with the dozens of makes and models then on the road, far less standardized than today. Manufacturers seemed to take pride in building cars which were unlike all others, including their own previous models. Even such simple features as the location of the gasoline tank varied greatly from car to car. The new man had to master these differences during his first few days on the job. It was also helpful if he could learn some housewifely bits of lore about the idiosyncrasies and peculiarities of each make of automobile, so that he could offer helpful advice in a variety of emergencies which have happily disappeared with the development of more dependable automobiles.[15]

Two service station operating manuals which have survived are interesting evidence of the evolution of Shell service station procedure in California between 1920 and 1927.[16] The 1920 manual sets forth policy toward air and water service and tipping, which was apparently becoming a nuisance: "Air and water service is a gratuity which you are expected to render the public, showing no distinction as to whether the individual is a Shell customer or not. Gratuities must not be accepted at any time and when offered, make proper explanation to the customer." By 1927, no injunction against tipping was necessary, and the attendant, now called a "service station salesman," was expected to ask the customer, "Can I check the tires for you?"

Late in 1920, the company began to furnish service station uniforms free and pay for up to three launderings per week. Reading of magazines and newspapers while on duty was forbidden under penalty of ten days' suspension, although "attendants desirous of keeping up with the oil business or improving themselves" could apply for approved reading matter which would be furnished by the company. Most of a man's spare time would obviously be devoted to cleaning the station, for approved cleaning procedures for various parts of the station occupied many pages of the 1920 book.

There was great emphasis on safety precautions. Employees were forbidden to smoke, and forbidden to fill a customer's gasoline tank while the engine of his car was running; if the customer demurred, an understandable reaction in those days of hard-to-start cars, the attendant was authorized to refuse to make the sale. Rest rooms had not yet appeared in 1920, and the only excuse for an attendant leaving his station was "to take advantage of toilet facilities."

By 1927, operating procedures reflected the growth of intensified competition. Uniforms were no longer free, and suggested sales procedure was as rigidly prescribed as the movements of a square dance. The "service station salesman" was told where to stand, what to say and do, and how to push company products that were the most profitable (Western motor oil, for instance, instead of Golden Shell, a Pennsylvania-style oil that Shell did not manufacture). The touring service, which in 1920 had consisted of Shell "traffic booklets" and lists of Shell stations, now featured "our road map and mileage chart."

Station cleanliness was still of paramount importance and was enforced by division office inspectors who, like bank examiners, swooped down on a station unannounced. They graded a station "B" (Bad Odor), "F" (Fair), "G" (Good), "E" (Excellent), or "P" (Premium). A "P" rating was worth $5 a month in extra pay, divided between the two "salesmen" in charge of the station; a "B" classification had to be removed before the inspectors' next visit. If it were not, all station employees were downgraded to a beginner's salary, and on third offense were automatically dismissed. A tipster warning of an impending inspection visit could also expect automatic suspension or dismissal.

Terms and conditions of sale also changed in the years between 1920 and 1927. In 1920, attendants were urged to sell coupon books, but credit was also available, controlled by an "authorized list" issued for the purpose. Coupon books were of three kinds: gallonage books good for 50 or 100 gallons; script books, representing money values of $5 and $10; and motor oil books containing 20 coupons each good for a quart of oil. Commercial customers were generally allowed the privilege of credit and were billed at a lower rate; certain other customers were issued Shell identification cards which, upon presentation, enabled them to buy gasoline at 1¢ off regular price. By 1927, the coupon books good for gallons of gasoline and quarts of motor oil had been discontinued, but script books of $10 and $20 value were being pushed for sale to "private persons desiring the convenience of paying at infrequent intervals." Charge accounts, except for commercial accounts, were discouraged although credit cards, issued yearly or quarterly in accordance with the customer's credit rating, were being issued by all three division offices.

The 1927 manual also laid down company policy on discrimination among customers: "Salesmen should be careful in their attendance upon Oriental and Latin classes of customers § and refrain from using broken English in conversation with them. The Shell Company will not tolerate or retain in its employ any salesmen who allows his personal opinions and prejudices to result in his being discourteous or negligent in rendering gratuitous service to a customer."

So much for the evolution of service station operating procedures in California. Of equal interest is the standardized Shell station which became almost a company trade-mark to the West Coast motorist of the Twenties. This was the so-called "A" station, or as the men of the Shell sales department branded it with good-humored accuracy, the "cracker box."

The "Cracker-Box" Station

In concept and in architecture, the cracker-box station was simplicity itself. It was primarily a roof, some 32 feet long by 16 feet wide. Underneath the roof, occupying half the space, was a 16-foot-square enclosure made of the small glass windowpanes known in the building trade as "factory sash." The other half of the space beneath the roof was left open, supported at the end by two posts, to form the canopy that had become customary in California stations. At the edge of the canopy, alongside the supporting posts, were the gasoline pumps, generally two in number. Stations like this, built of wood, were used by the Shell Company of California at the San Francisco World's Fair in 1915. They were destined to be the standard design for the next fifteen years.*

By 1920, the wooden building, which met with objections from fire commissioners in some cities, had given way to one made entirely of steel. With this improvement, Shell had a building that was a veritable Model "T" of service stations. It was hot in summer and cold in winter, but it did provide shelter for the operator when it was raining, and storage and display space adequate for the needs of the day. And it was economical. It came from the manufacturer as a complete package. The necessary panels, framework, window sashes, doors, bolts and nuts were all packed in a couple of crates

§ California had no appreciable Negro population at this time.

* Exceptions were made in a few areas such as Berkeley and Palo Alto, where Spanish Mission and Southern Mediterranean styles were adopted to harmonize with the architecture of neighboring real estate developments.

which could be stored 15 or 20 at a time in warehouses and drawn
upon by the sales department as needed. The parts could be assembled in a few days by inexperienced help. Exclusive of the glass for
the factory sash, the "A" station package cost $700; the complete
station, provided with pumps, tanks, pumping equipment, a graded
yard and concrete driveways, cost [17] on the average about $3,500.†
It might not be handsome, but then, as soon as the station had been
erected, it was given a coat of bright yellow paint with bright red
trim and this effectively put an end to aesthetic considerations.

Since it was useless to try to prettify the "cracker-box" station, the
sales department, particularly in Christie's Central division, very
wisely concentrated on beautifying the grounds. In this, they were
eminently successful. Shrubbery and trees to improve the looks of
the service station grounds were planted at all company stations in
the Central division, and portions of the plot not actually needed
for driveways were given over to lawn.

The result was a station surprisingly pleasant to the eye—green
grass, shrubs, hedges, even beds of flowers at the more pretentious
stations. At one time during the Twenties, the company had a head
gardener and three assistants in the San Francisco area; they kept
busy mowing lawns, trimming hedges, and planting flowers. Away
from the metropolitan centers, there was a regular allowance of
$250 for the purchase of trees and shrubs for each new company
station.[19] During this period of the early Twenties, with each
company trying to outdo the other in free service, rest rooms became
a competitive necessity in the urban areas of California. Hundreds
of stations were already built, so the new rest room facilities were
housed in a separate "convenience building," located in a back corner
of the service station plot, the entrances discreetly screened by lattice-
work up which morning glories and rambler roses often grew.

It is no wonder, then, that despite its high utility and essential
ugliness, a station such as Shell Company of California's No. 27 could
be adjudged "America's Finest Filling Station." Photographs and
ground plans of it published in The Oil Trade,[20] which awarded the
prize, show that it had a dozen or so small trees, banks of flowering
shrubs, a handsome fountain filled with water plants, and in front
a bed of red and yellow flowers spelling out SHELL. The attendants
in immaculate white uniforms and the two Shell house-flags fluttering

† Later in the Twenties, the addition of rest rooms together with the general rise
in cost of labor and materials brought this average cost up to $5,000.[18]

in the breeze completed an attractive picture. The imagination and ingenuity of Christie and his men had made a potential eyesore into a very pleasant spot, a credit not only to their civic-mindedness but also to their realization that an attractive station was a fine advertisement and a good business-getter.

Shell of California moved fast in those days of the early Twenties. Once the amount to be spent on new facilities had been determined, Van Eck and Gallagher let the men under them proceed with a minimum of interference. Speed was the watchword, for by hurrying the Shell sales organization could move into a new territory before competitors could guess what they were up to. The men actually on the job were allowed to use their own judgment in all but the most major matters. They grabbed off for Shell any area which looked good to them, picking their own service station sites and slapping up cracker-box stations in a week to ten days. The break-neck speed at which the sales department moved in those days has given rise to a great many stories, many of them no doubt literally true.

E. H. Sanders, who was assistant division manager of the Central division at the time, loves to tell how they invaded the San Jose-to-Santa Barbara territory, building eight depots and a hundred service stations all in a matter of six weeks. Sanders and Claude Donaldson, the Central division's traffic manager, first rode the 260-mile stretch of road between the two towns and picked likely sites for depots and stations. They were followed closely by real estate men who, to save time and expense, leased rather than bought most of the desired sites. Then came the construction crews in relays. First, crews to dig holes in the proposed service station lots and bury the underground storage tanks the station would need. Next, crews to pour the concrete foundation for the station, leaving bolt studs sticking out of the concrete. Meanwhile the crates containing the complete "A" station would be delivered. As soon as the concrete had hardened, a crew arrived to install the pumps and bolt the station in place, anchoring it to the foundation by means of the stud bolts protruding from the concrete. Then came the paint crew to apply a coat of red and yellow, and the station, once its storage tanks had been filled from the new depot, was in business—about ten days from start to finish. In some instances, Sanders recalls, they moved so fast that stations were actually built and in operation before the legal papers covering lease of the land had reached San Francisco for signature by an officer of the company.

Another story illustrative of the dizzy speed at which the marketing department moved in those days was Shell's entry into Eureka, California. Until that time, Eureka and the surrounding territory had been largely served by Standard Oil of California dealers. Then, perhaps without considering the effect it would have upon these dealers, Standard built a company station in the area. Dismayed and angered at competition from their supplying company, the dealers decided to give their business to someone else. Early one morning one of them telephoned Shell's San Francisco office. Would Shell supply them? You bet! And right away! Tank car loads of gasoline which had just left the Martinez refinery were rerouted to Eureka. Sanders and Donaldson jumped in a car and headed north and Thomson (who was by now in charge of service station real estate) got aboard the train with the tank cars of gasoline. Shell's Santa Rosa depot, 225 miles from Eureka, was the nearest. A phone call to Santa Rosa sent their tank trucks and painting crews on the way to Eureka. By the end of the next day, the Standard dealers in Eureka had been painted red and yellow, the tank cars had arrived and been shunted to a lumberyard siding where they were unloaded by siphons into the tank trucks from Santa Rosa, and before nightfall 50,000 gallons of Shell gasoline had been delivered.[21]

This was the kind of pace which the energetic young salesmen of the Shell Company of California set for themselves in the early years of the Twenties. That pace was to continue with hardly a pause for breath until the summer of 1930.

Beginnings of Advertising

In this rapid expansion campaign the company's hustling young sales organization demonstrated that it had mastered one of the most important aspects of marketing—the elusive art of attracting and holding public attention. Although at times Shell of California's promotional campaigns were so high-spirited that they had a carnival atmosphere about them, there was, nevertheless, planning and efficient organization behind them and they were carried out with a minimum of expense. In fact, for much of the Twenties the company had no advertising budget at all.

Shell's attention-getting campaign had begun early, with the blazing, bright yellow paint which was lavished on the company's service stations, depots, trucks, railroad tank cars, and highway signs.

In the exuberant spirit of the Twenties, Shell paint jobs were offered without stint to Shell dealers, whether they sold 500 or 5,000 gallons a month. Shell painting crews were not stingy with the company's paint; they applied a bright yellow coat to the dealer's pumps, his store front, his fences, his curbstones, even the trunks of his trees, and punctuated their work with a trim of dazzling red. At this rate it wasn't long before the Pacific Coast motorist began to believe that Shell was literally everywhere. No matter what some might think of red and yellow as a color combination, all had to admit one thing— you could see it.

Some of the sales promotion schemes devised to keep the motorist coming into Shell stations were as uninhibited as the Shell colors. Christmas-theme exhibits installed at key service stations for children (and their gasoline-buying parents) greatly increased sales during the dullest season of the year. Despite their mounting cost as they grew more elaborate with the passing years, the Shell "Christmas Shows" were good business and more than paid for themselves in increased sales. In 1929, one of these stations equipped with a Christmas display sold 12,000 gallons of gasoline in a single day,[22] a good month's business for most stations. The Shell "Treasure Hunts" made a game of the universal longing to dig for buried treasure, the "treasure" being certificates for merchandise prizes of every description. Each summer thousands of shell-shaped roadside signs were converted to forest-fire prevention posters, and drew so much favorable comment that the company was still continuing this public service advertising on billboards thirty years later.

For the motorist's windshield, there were attractive shell-shaped stickers, available as souvenirs of national parks and of all the larger cities. And in the fall, there were free shell-decorated football pennants. With the advent of radio, the company embraced the new advertising medium enthusiastically. There was an hour's "Symphonette" on a Monday evening network, and a six-day-a-week, hour-long, morning radio show, "Shell Happytime with Dobbsie," that became one of the phenomenal successes of early radio.

A different kind of advertising got under way in 1928 with the establishment of a regular advertising department headed by Sanders, who had been responsible for most of the company's promotional ideas. The J. Walter Thompson Company was engaged as Shell's advertising agency that year, and attention-getting "trick" adver-

tising was laid aside for more lasting campaigns which would present
the motorist with reasons for buying Shell products.‡

Nevada and Arizona

The second half of the Twenties saw Shell extend its territory and
intensify its coverage of the markets where the company was already
represented. During 1925, the company went into two states, Nevada
and Arizona, where it had previously sold only tank car lots of
products, chiefly fuel oil for the mining and smelting industries.
Nevada became part of the Central division's territory, the chief
retail areas there being Reno and Las Vegas. Arizona was handled by
the Southern division, and a separate corporation, the Shell Oil Company of Arizona, was organized to take title to the new Shell properties there. These properties were at the start nine depots, with the
necessary drums, delivery trucks, and salesmen's autos, the whole
outlay coming to $283,000.[23] Soon after, a similar corporation, Shell
Oil Company (Nevada), was organized for that state.

Depot Operation Changes

Depot operation began to change somewhat at this time, a direct
result of better roads, better trucks, and better tires. The early
delivery trucks all had solid rubber tires, because the fabric-wall
pneumatic tires of the time were not strong enough to carry the
load of a truck. These solid rubber tires were poor shock absorbers.
Driven too fast, a truck with solid rubber tires would literally shake
itself to pieces. To prevent this, Shell tank trucks were equipped with
governors which kept speeds below 12 miles an hour.[24]

Such slow speeds meant that a truck could not go very far in a
day. This necessitated numerous small depots, many of them so small
that they were operated on a "lock-up" basis § from the start. By
the mid-Twenties, low-pressure pneumatic tires strong enough for
truck use were available, making possible an increase in the driving
radius of a truck. The result was that some of the "lock-ups" could
be closed and dismantled. This trend was noticeable in Shell of Cali-

‡ Three years later, in 1931, the St. Louis and New York Shell companies designated the Thompson company to handle their advertising and since that time Shell's
national product advertising has been in the hands of the Thompson agency. Henry
M. Stevens of that firm, delegated to handle the Shell account in San Francisco late
in 1928, continued as account executive until his death in 1953.

§ The driver, or drivers, who operated out of such a depot were its only staff;
when not there, they locked it up.

fornia's figures for 1926. The year saw an unusual amount of market expansion activity, with some $1,500,000 budgeted for expansion, and gasoline sales up 25 million gallons over the previous year. Yet despite this large increase and the opening of 350 new Shell stations, the total number of depots actually declined by two.

Importance of the Dealer

Company-operated stations were increasing in importance, but dealers still continued to play a large part in Shell's total gasoline sales. Particularly in low-volume areas, a dealer could operate more cheaply. He could cut corners on service, and in general he did not attempt to compete with company stations in details such as rest rooms and landscaping. Often, too, he derived considerable income from the sale of non-petroleum merchandise.

At the beginning of the Twenties on the Coast, Associated was generally considered the "big dealer company." [25] It had adopted the practice of making equipment available to dealers, either on loan or on low-cost lease, in exchange for a contract in which the dealer agreed to handle Associated products exclusively. In 1920, Associated had some 750 dealers operating on these exclusive contracts; Union, the only other company having the exclusive-dealing contract at the time, had 48 dealers under contract.[26]

Standard and Shell, largely for reasons of cost, did not look with favor on this plan, and in general refrained from giving equipment to dealers on what amounted to a gratis basis. Occasionally, when hard pressed by competing offers, Shell would break over and lend a dealer a pump, or rent it to him for $1 a year. In these rare instances, the company did not require an exclusive contract, but only the dealer's assurance that he would not use this free equipment to sell a competitor's product. Dealers of this period often carried several brands of gasoline, much as grocery stores stocked competing brands of breakfast foods.

The dealer's margin, i.e., the difference between the retail price and the price he paid, was generally thought to be 2¢, a differential announced by Standard, the "market leader," back in 1914. Actually, the dealer margin varied from dealer to dealer; a company trying hard to get a dealer's business often raised the margin to 3¢ or even 4¢ a gallon. In common with most of the majors except Standard, Shell was by the early Twenties pretty generally granting dealer margins of 3¢, although the company's officially announced dealer margin was still 2¢ a gallon. In August 1922, Standard took note of the fiction of this 2-cent margin, and increased it to 3¢. From this point on through the Twenties, the dealer's margin was to be a problem of mounting seriousness, and would lead the companies and the dealers through all sorts of commercial vicissitudes.

Larger Margins and Price Wars

The plain truth of the matter was that retail markets were weakening, although nobody wanted to admit it. The tremendous new supplies of crude oil were more than even a booming economy could absorb. By 1925, the actual state of affairs in the oil market was a far cry from the hysterical conclusion of Senator LaFollette's investigating subcommittee * only two years before: "If a few great oil companies are permitted to manipulate the prices for the next few years, as they have been doing since January 1920, the people of this country must be prepared before long to pay at least $1 a gallon for gasoline." [27]

As the market continued to weaken, the result of oversupply and intense competition at the retail level, oil companies all up and down the West Coast tried to offset their smaller per-unit profit by increasing volume. This was one of the most potent incentives to the tremendous marketing expansion of the Twenties. In this drive for greater volume, the companies not only built new retail stations of their own, but tried to sign up more dealers, generally by means of granting larger margins. In this way, margins went from 3¢ to 4¢ to 5¢, until by 1928, many dealers enjoyed margins as large as 6¢ and even 7¢ per gallon.

But by this time, these margins were largely theoretical. The dealer, in his struggle to get more business at the retail level, began sacrificing part of his margin in the form of discounts, at first to commercial customers and other large users, then to his regular customers, and finally to all comers in the form of an open price reduction. Whenever this latter state of affairs became general, a price war was on,

---

* A hearing conducted during the early months of 1923 by the so-called "LaFollette Committee," a subcommittee of the Senate Committee on Manufacture. Senator Robert M. LaFollette of Wisconsin was chairman of the subcommittee, and his son Robert M., Jr., who later became a senator himself, was the subcommittee's secretary. They heard several hundred pages of testimony, published later in two thick volumes. The title of these volumes, *The High Cost of Gasoline and Other Petroleum Products*, is indicative of the complete lack of impartiality that characterized the hearings.

with each dealer trying to cut below the advertised price of his nearest competitors.

In September 1926, a really serious price war of this nature broke out in the Los Angeles area.[28] It continued through the fall of 1926 and the spring months of 1927, spreading through most of the Pacific Coast area. By the end of April 1927, the retail price of gasoline had tumbled to 13¢ in the San Francisco area, 10½¢ in Los Angeles.

Early in May 1927, there was a temporary halt in the gasoline war, with a return to March 1st prices and restoration of dealer margins to some semblance of order. Shell dealers taking tank wagon deliveries were given 4¢ off the retail price; those taking railroad tank car lots, 5¢ off retail. More than a few dealers, however, continued to enjoy margins as large as 6¢ under contracts they had signed during the price war. The retail price used as a starting point for these contracts was the price charged in company service stations.

The chances for profit during the remaining months of 1927 seemed so slim, even with the market temporarily stable, that the Shell Company of California in June 1927 decided to halt all expenditures for marketing expansion until prices improved and to "cut expenses to an absolute minimum consistent with the conduct of the business." [29] As a result, only one market extension of any note was made during the remainder of that year. In May 1927, Shell opened a new bulk station at Honolulu and began doing business in the Hawaiian islands.

Hawaii

Entry into this new market came primarily as a result of a contract which Shell of California had just signed with the Honolulu Consolidated Oil Company, a subsidiary of the Matson Navigation Company. Honolulu Consolidated was a California producing concern which the Matson people had started in the years before the First World War to assure themselves of a steady supply of fuel oil for their steamships. By 1927, Honolulu Consolidated's production had grown until it was far in excess of Matson's needs. Shell contracted to buy a substantial part of this production and remit to the Honolulu company the amounts realized from the sale of products manufactured from this oil, less refining and marketing expenses and a certain amount for profit. As a corollary to the agreement, Shell contracted to supply the Matson Line with fuel at each of its main ports, of which Honolulu was, of course, a most important one.[30] The

Hawaiian business established as a result of this contract has continued a small but profitable adjunct of Shell's West Coast marketing activity.

The weak markets of 1927, which prevailed to a greater or lesser degree through the rest of the Twenties, were a direct result of too much crude oil on the Pacific Coast market. This fact some failed to realize or refused to acknowledge. The Shell management, however, was under no illusions on this score. In the Shell Union annual report for 1926, Van Eck wrote:

> The unfavourable gasoline situation has been aggravated by the increase in crude oil production to a figure far beyond the current needs of the industry. In the opinion of your directors the remedies for the present state of affairs are twofold. In the first place, the output of crude oil should be reduced, thereby conserving the oil for the time when its production will be essential to meet the needs of the world. This policy has been and is being followed by your Company as far as is practicable without causing injury to the Company's interests, but as is well known, the conservation of crude oil in competitive fields can only be accomplished by the agreement of all concerned, so that the results so far have been disappointing.
>
> In the second place, the oil companies should continue and extend the movement towards the marketing of an improved quality of gasoline by lowering the final boiling point. Such a step is clearly in the general interest in that it provides the motoring public with a better and more efficient gasoline and tends to check the existing over-production, due largely to the inclusion in gasoline of the high boiling fractions which are not suitable for use in automobiles as they cause knocking and dilution of the lubricating oil. The Shell Company of California took the lead in introducing a better quality of gasoline on the West Coast.

The measures that were eventually taken in an attempt to combat some of the disastrous effects of this overproduction of crude oil are discussed in some detail in Chapter VII. Marketing of an improved gasoline, which Van Eck here referred to, started in the fall of 1925.

On November 24 of that year, Shell of California began sale of its "61° gravity" gasoline, 3° lighter than the 58° gravity motor fuel then prevalent on the West Coast. Assisted by a vigorous promotion effort, sales jumped at once, and by mid-January 1926, the new gasoline was running 35% ahead of the previous year's sales.[31] Next came a reduction in the end boiling point, which had the effect of excluding some of the heavier hydrocarbons. Shell of California's product was some 37° below the accepted Pacific Coast endpoint of 437° F., and during 1927 "Shell 400—the Dry Gas" began to be extensively advertised on the Coast, a campaign which continued for the remainder of the Twenties.†

Even with the expanding domestic market it enjoyed during the Twenties, Shell, in common with most California refiners, continued to sell on the export market—a term used in California to designate all sales not destined for Pacific Coast points. During 1927, Shell of California turned increasingly to this offshore market, selling substantial quantities of gasoline and kerosene to Atlantic Seaboard refining and marketing companies such as Standard of New Jersey, Socony, Sun, Amoco, Atlantic Refining, and others who were taking advantage of the low prices then prevalent in California. Asiatic also bought cargoes for shipment abroad.

At the outset of 1928, lower prices then prevalent in the Gulf of Mexico seemed to make the export market less attractive, so Shell of California resolved to spend nearly a million dollars that year on new marketing facilities. In April 1928, 78 new sub-depots were projected, 50 for the Central division and 28 for the Northern division. Together with new rolling stock, they were to cost some $556,000 and were expected to increase the company's sales by 10,-000,000 gallons during the year. Other new facilities, including new dockage at Portland and a new terminal at Oakland, increased the outlay by another $250,000.[32] In addition to these major items of expansion, Shell of California also extended its marketing activities to a great many less populous rural areas during 1928. The result was a sharp increase in the number of the depots. At the end of 1928, Shell of California had 414 depots, contrasted with 221 only twelve months before, and its retail outlets had increased by 500 to a new total of 4,012. Despite earlier expectations to the contrary, the export market remained strong during 1928 and Shell of California sold as much gasoline offshore as it did on the Pacific Coast market.

During the last quarter of 1927, Shell of California picked up one-half of the total increase in gasoline sales in California, so that at the end of the year it was accounting for 18% of the state's total gasoline business.[33] During the early months of 1928, the company continued to add to this impressive lead. In the second quarter of

† The development of gasoline specifications during this period is discussed in Chapter VII.

1928, for instance, the sales of the state's largest gasoline marketers were on this order:

CALIFORNIA GASOLINE SALES (GALLONS), SECOND QUARTER, 1928 [34]

Standard of California	65,300,058
Shell of California	42,225,778
Richfield Oil Company	31,838,253
Union Oil Company	28,740,062
Associated Oil Company	25,346,150
The Texas Company	16,947,503
Pan-American Petroleum Corp.‡	16,605,765
General Petroleum Corp.‡	14,420,848

This tabulation shows, better than words, how much Shell of California had increased its business, by dint of energetic expansion, in the short space of a very few years. The company's profits for August 1928 were $2,500,000, a record high for any month since its establishment, and double the figure of a year before.[35]

Compared to the chaotic conditions of the fall and winter of 1926–1927, marketing conditions of the 1928 season were relatively stable. Dealer margins, however, continued to be an annoying source of trouble. In May of 1928, most of the California majors had engaged in a battle for dealers, which, although brief, had the effect of increasing all dealer margins to 5¢ a gallon.[36] As always, these "long" margins were a warning of trouble ahead. Dealers had shown themselves able to operate a profitable business on 2 to 3 cents a gallon. Whenever the oil companies started to bid against each other for dealers and increase the dealer margin above this level, they could expect to see the dealer start sacrificing part of his extra margin in the form of price cuts, open or secret, as he attempted to get a larger share of the public's business for himself. During the fall months of 1928, price-cutting activity started up again, led off by those favored dealers who had managed to wangle 6-cent margins from their suppliers.

In these price-cutting campaigns, company-owned stations were the heaviest losers. If they instituted cuts, it did not alter the competitive situation since the dealer's price was tied to the retail price charged at company stations. Accordingly, company stations tried to hold the line on prices, and emphasize service and cleanliness in an attempt to offset the attraction of gasoline 2¢ to 3¢ a gallon

‡ Shortly after this, Pan-American's stations were taken over by Richfield, and General Petroleum was purchased by Socony, to become that company's Pacific Coast affiliate.

cheaper. Income from new services, such as lubrication (which Shell had begun on a modest scale in Los Angeles in 1927[37]) could help make up for some of the loss of revenue resulting from decreased volume. But there was no gainsaying the fact that when a price war of any consequence was on, company stations lost a serious amount of business. Only the most spendthrift motorist would continue to pay two, three, and even four cents a gallon more for the same brand of gasoline, merely to enjoy the extras that went with company-station service.

To free themselves of the service station price which was the basis of their dealer contracts, the supplying companies could, as the Associated Oil Company had been doing for some two or three years,[38] lease out their company-owned stations, generally to the former salaried manager, grant him a margin as large as that enjoyed by any of their dealers, and hope that he could absorb out of this margin some of the price cuts necessary to meet competition.

During the late months of 1928, with dealer price-cutting starting up again, most of the major suppliers, including Standard, began to lease their stations to dealers. Legh-Jones resisted this trend as long as he could, for Shell was now operating 559 service stations on the Pacific Coast, more than any of its competitors. Much of Shell's favorable reputation with the motorist was due to these attractive, well-run company stations which would not, in all probability, be operated on the same high standards by dealers. However, by December 1928, these company stations were, because of reduced volume, barely breaking even and some were actually losing money. Some move in the direction of leased stations obviously had to be made. The method of leasing which Legh-Jones finally selected had the virtue of assuring Shell some degree of quality control over the appearance of its stations while allowing all the advantages of lease operation.[39]

Van Fleet & Durkee

Two energetic marketing men from General Petroleum Corporation, W. C. Van Fleet, former Northwest division manager for G.P., and W. P. Durkee, Jr., also of the G.P. sales department, had resigned shortly after that company had been purchased by Socony in 1928.[40] Legh-Jones decided to lease a number of Shell stations to them *en bloc*, leaving the details of operation to Van Fleet and Durkee. They organized a new company, Van Fleet-Durkee, Inc., early in January 1929, and to this new company Shell of California leased 220 of its company-owned stations in the Los Angeles area.[41] Van Fleet & Durkee promptly sublet each individual station to a dealer, generally the same man who had been the station's salaried manager. From now on, the dealer was in business on his own. He had a 6¢-a-gallon margin from which must be deducted rent and operating expenses. These items generally came to about 2¢ a gallon, and sometimes less, leaving the dealer three or four cents to use in cutting prices to meet the competition and regain the station's former volume.[42]

Shell kept title to the real estate it leased Van Fleet & Durkee. Van Fleet & Durkee agreed to assume all responsibility for the stations while under their operation, and in turn were to receive any operating profit they might be able to make. Shell agreed in addition to pay them a portion of the operational savings and increased volume which they might be able to effect. The V. & D. subleases to individual dealers contained clauses making the continuance of the lease contingent upon the dealer keeping up reasonable standards of service and cleanliness. This gave Shell some assurance that reasonably good standards would be maintained.[43]

Some of the advantages of this new type of operation became evident at once. First of all, the former manager was now on his own; whatever he made above expenses was his to keep. With this incentive, he worked even harder than before; and Van Fleet & Durkee, who were vigorous merchandisers, stood at his elbow with suggestions on how to go out and get new business. A second advantage of dealer operation, it soon developed, was that fewer men were needed to operate the same station. With the dealer paying their salaries, he saw to it that the men kept busy. He also began to make a few common-sense decisions as to the amount of free service that should be rendered, for by the late Twenties free service in many California stations was being carried to unnecessary extremes. When the motorist realized that these services were coming out of the dealer's pocket, he didn't, the dealer discovered, expect quite as much "for free." A third important saving in time and effort came by removing such items as credit, collections, commercial and other discounts, from the realm of oil company policy. Now such matters were up to each dealer individually, and he could do as he wished about them. And fourth was a situation of which Van Fleet & Durkee took advantage to the full—the dealer could now sell all manner of accessories which the oil companies had been reluctant to install in their own stations for fear of offending garage owners, who were an important segment of most companies' dealer organization.

V. B. Guthrie, managing editor of *National Petroleum News*, made a trip to Los Angeles in March 1929 to report on the progress of this new type of station operation. "Van Fleet & Durkee," he wrote, "have already arranged with a wholesale accessory house to put in the Shell stations a carefully selected line of accessories . . . lamp bulbs, fan belts, valve stems, dressing and polishes and so on. The accessory company stocks the station and replenishes the stock. They sell the stock to the operator, giving him time enough to pay for it so that it is not a burden on him. They [V. & D.] are arranging for the sale of tires and plan to install lubricating service at the stations also." [44]

Theirs was, indeed, an almost ideal set-up. Shell owned the stations, the individual dealers paid the rent, the suppliers of accessories warehoused and delivered their goods in their own trucks, and generally on consignment. Van Fleet & Durkee had little invested in the business besides enthusiasm, but they had plenty of that. From their office in the American Bank Building, Los Angeles, came a constant stream of pep talks. Through their monthly, *The V. & D. Message*, their dealers were urged, wheedled, exhorted, and prodded to sell, sell, sell; to get customers to mention them favorably; to get friends to send in business; to leave the station and go out and ring doorbells. Van Fleet & Durkee attempted to convert the service station operator, accustomed only to dispensing the gasoline and oil for which the customer had come in, into an aggressive salesman who would actively push a large selection of automotive accessories (V. & D. insisted they be called "necessities"), as well as the quite comprehensive line of Shell specialty products which were just then being put on the market.

E. C. (Ed) Harrison, who was a division manager of the Van Fleet & Durkee organization at the time, recalled that "regular monthly contests were inaugurated throughout the chain to keep dealers competing with each other. They were urged to go off the premises after business, and at least one dealer organized a crew of boys during the summer months to make door-to-door calls with kits of Shell specialty items such as dry cleaner, furniture polish, fly spray, and lighter fluid. New automotive 'necessities' were added almost daily to the merchandise line, and supervisors travelled in cars filled with stocks of small items. Besides 'beating the bushes' for business himself, one enterprising dealer even enrolled as salesmen people who owed him money, paying them a commission on what they sold to help liquidate their debts." V. & D. dealers washed cars, repaired flat tires, did "scientific" lubrication in accordance with "The V. & D. System," offered (in Los Angeles) a brake-testing and wheel-alignment service, and even dispensed touring information from a big, fat "Ask Van Durk" book furnished to all V. & D. operators.[45]

Legh-Jones was highly pleased with Van Fleet & Durkee's operation of Shell's former company stations. In July 1929, V. & D. were given 90 more Shell stations in northern California around the San Francisco area. By November, they had under lease some 600 Shell stations, all that the company owned except for a few stations in each locality that were continued under Shell operation for the purpose of establishing the "service station price" called for in contracts.§

The reader must not imagine that this new type of operation put an immediate end to price wars. Far from it. When the independent dealers who had started the price cutting saw a number of well-located company stations in a position to meet their competition, many of them became panicky and began to slash prices openly. As a result, January and February and the early part of March 1929 witnessed the worst gasoline price war that the Pacific Coast had yet seen. The war was not confined to metropolitan areas where such disturbances had usually started in the past, but spread throughout the entire Pacific Coast territory. With the exception only of Arizona and British Columbia, the posted retail price of gasoline was reduced 4¢ through all of this area during February 1929. In the real centers of price cutting, prices dropped to fantastic lows. Refining companies sold to dealers for less than their cost of manufacture. Dealers sold to the public at, and in some instances below, the prices they had paid the oil company truck which delivered the gasoline. For upwards

§ The later history of V. & D. falls in the 1930's. They changed their corporate name in March 1931 to Shell Service, Inc., and a year later Shell bought them out, paying $50,000 for good will and $25,000 for the "Ask Van Durk" travel book. Shell Service, Inc., continued to be operated a short while after the purchase, first with Van Fleet as president and then, after his resignation, with J. W. (Wynn) Miller as president.[46] The stations did not again become company-operated units, and most of the old V. & D. dealers were retained in the change-over. Durkee became manager of Shell's Southern division in 1932, and in October 1933 was elected a vice president of Shell Union in New York. He later returned to San Francisco to serve as vice president in charge of marketing from November 1934 until May 1938. He died in 1945.

of six weeks San Francisco garages sold at cost, and in Los Angeles the retail price of gasoline, state tax included, dropped below 10¢ a gallon.[47]

None of the participants, no matter how large their resources, could keep this up for long. Shell of California's profits for March 1929 were barely 10% of what they had been a year before; and for the four-month period December 1928 to March 1929 earnings were less than half what they had been twelve months earlier, in spite of a 20% increase in the volume of gasoline sold. On March 19, Standard raised the retail price 6¢ a gallon; other companies soon followed suit. Everybody, apparently, had had enough, for they let the increase stand, except in Los Angeles where sporadic underselling continued, but on a much smaller scale.[48]

By the end of April 1929, major company prices were fairly firm at 17¢ in San Francisco (16½¢ in Los Angeles), and they remained at approximately this level for the rest of the year. During the spring months, most of the larger suppliers busied themselves writing new dealer contracts—this time on a basis not of service station price but of the "tank wagon," or delivered, price to the dealer. By midsummer most dealers had signed new contracts which gave them 4¢ off tank wagon price, with tank wagon price defined as 3¢ below service station price. These contracts were still unrealistic in that they allowed a theoretical 7-cent margin, but they were at least a start in the right direction.

Shell had been reluctant to enter into the cut-throat competition of the preceding months, and early in April 1929 issued a policy statement underlining that fact. After explaining the course of the recent price war, the statement concluded: "In all this disturbance, Shell has endeavored to follow rather than take the lead . . . at no time has it taken the lead in price reductions. Shell regrets the present unsettled condition of the retail market particularly as it affects the dealers. We consider the dealer, as we always have in the past, the most important unit in the marketing of our products to the consuming public. And the biggest problem before us today is to again place the dealer in a position where he can enjoy a fair profit on his investment and his personal efforts." [49]

With the passing of this severe price war, it began to look as though fairly stable markets could be expected during the remaining months of 1929. The increased volume which the company had picked up during the price war yielded a handsome half-million-dollar increase in profits during May 1929, $1,907,000 against $1,460,000 the year before. Once again, the company began to turn its attention to marketing expansion, this time with the idea of building eastward until Shell of California would run into the territory served by Roxana.

Utah

Sales in Nevada, where Shell was already represented, were increased during 1929 by entering eastern Nevada, an area the company had not previously served. During the spring and early summer months, Shell entered Utah, buying and building. A Shell district marketing office was opened at Salt Lake City on April 1, 1929, and distribution of gasoline began immediately through the purchased facilities of three small chains of service stations, Rich Oil Company, Gray Service Stations, and Service Oil Company. Each had a small depot, and the three of them together owned a total of twenty stations. At the same time, Shell began construction of six depots, the largest of them at Salt Lake City and Ogden. By the end of the year, the company had, in addition, eight jobbers in Utah and through them and its own installations was supplying about 20% of the state's total oil requirements.[50]

Here it was that the West Coast and Mid-Continent companies could be said at last to have joined hands. The Utah territory abutted Colorado, where a Roxana jobber had for some months been selling Shell-branded gasoline. Theoretically at least, a motorist could now drive from coast to coast and buy Shell gasoline all the way.

Idaho, Montana, Wyoming

In Idaho, where the company had for some years been making sales through jobbers, the amount of this coverage was stepped up during 1929. Montana, where Shell had not been represented, was entered during 1929 by the construction of eight depots, the easternmost at Billings. These Montana depots were selling gasoline at the rate of 800,000 gallons a month by the end of 1929.

This is the logical place to mention the purchase of the Southern Idaho Oil Company, of Boise, in April 1930, for it really was a delayed part of the 1929 expansion program. For several years this company, owned by the Morrison-Knudsen interests, had been supplied by Shell. By late 1929, it was distributing some 2,000,000 gallons a year of Shell gasoline, along with a complete line of Shell motor oils and greases. It owned seven depots, well located through southern Idaho, operated a substantial chain of service stations, and in addition supplied a large number of dealers both in Idaho and western Wyoming. It was one of the few occasions when Shell of California's sales department expanded by purchase rather than by building. For Southern Idaho Oil, the company paid Morrison-Knudsen $400,000 * cash.[51]

The year 1929 also saw entry into western Wyoming on a modest scale, thus giving the Shell company representation in all of the Pacific Coast and Intermountain states.

Gasco Motor Fuels

In Portland late in the summer of 1929 Shell bought the Gasco Motor Fuel business of the Portland Gas & Coke Company, the concern from whom Shell had earlier leased dockage for its Willbridge depot. As a by-product of its gas manufacture, the Portland company produced benzol which, blended with a low-endpoint gasoline, gave a motor fuel of excellent anti-knock characteristics. Production of the Gasco fuel was limited by the Portland Gas & Coke Company's output of benzol. Even so, the business had by 1929 grown to a point where they were buying some 3,000,000 gallons of gasoline a year for blending purposes. Chiefly to insure this volume to itself, Shell bought the Gasco business for $36,000 and, beginning in September 1929, started selling Gasco through Shell stations † in the Portland area.[52]

Shell Oil Company of British Columbia

In its own small way, the business begun in 1913 in the Vancouver area had continued to expand. In July 1929 it was organized into a new and separate corporation called Shell Oil Company of British Columbia, Ltd. The stock of this new company was wholly owned

* It is interesting to speculate what effect this purchase money may have had in building several successful careers. Morrison and Knudsen were already well-known in their area as earth-moving contractors; their oil distributorship had, in fact, been developed as a side line of this business. At the time they sold their oil company to Shell, they were getting ready to bid on the tremendous job of building Hoover Dam. This enterprise, too big for a single contractor, was bid off by a syndicate called The Six Companies, Inc. A prime mover in organizing this syndicate was young Henry J. Kaiser, and Shell men who negotiated the deal remember Kaiser was often present, evincing an anxious interest, for each of the six companies needed every cent of cash they could lay their hands on.

† Gasco, organized as the Gasco Motor Fuel Company, Limited, was continued as a small but profitable part of Shell's Portland business until after World War II.

by Shell of California. That company's chief executive served as president of Shell of British Columbia. Actual head of operations was Fisher, who as vice president of Shell of British Columbia continued to run the Vancouver operation as part of his Northern division.[53]

All this expansion meant a happy increase in Shell of California's volume during 1929. At the end of that year it had 469 depots, was supplying 4,366 retail outlets, and had sold 347,962,000 gallons of gasoline, an increase of 87,250,000 gallons, or a full one-third, over 1928. Shell service was now literally everywhere west of the Rockies. Not long after this, a young man in San Francisco, signing himself "H. S. M. B.," sent the following lighthearted news item to *The Shell Magazine* in London: [54]

> Driving across the Great American Desert in Western Utah last August, Mr. Legh-Jones, President of the Shell Oil Company, was alarmed to hear his motor sputter and finally die. Out of fuel! And in a desolate country, the nearest gasoline station many miles away.
>
> In this parched, barren prairie, Shell service seemed at the other end of the world. Yet hardly had Mr. Legh-Jones begun to bemoan the circumstances when a speck appeared far across the sands. It grew larger, then took on the contour of a truck—a yellow and red Shell truck! And it was laden with the Shell Gasoline that Mr. Legh-Jones' 16-cylinder Cadillac likes best.
>
> No matter where you are, you'll run across Shell service or it will run across you!

3

Selling Shell in the Midwest

For a time in the early Twenties, it looked as though Roxana would acquire a full-blown sales department by the outright purchase of a going concern. When the Shell-Union negotiations were under way in London in the fall of 1921, Henry Lockhart had proposed to Deterding that the Indian Refining Company be made part of the deal and incorporated into the contemplated new company. Richmond Levering, who had helped Indian to such a spectacular rise a decade before, had lost control of the company at the time of the First World War and had died soon afterwards, early in 1921. The Indian company, floundering in financial difficulties which were a result of both the 1920–1921 depression and of Indian's own over-extended position, had come under the control of a New York group which included Lockhart. Through him, they offered the Indian organization to Shell for $18,354,000.[55]

At the time, Indian owned its own refinery at Lawrenceville, Illinois, the newly purchased Central Refining Company adjoining it, some 2,000 barrels a day of crude oil production in the old fields of Illinois and Indiana, and a small pipe line system. It was buying 15,000 barrels a day of crude in order to meet its refinery requirements of 17,000 barrels a day. Indian had for many years been engaged in marketing and by 1921 had nearly 1,900 railroad tank cars, some 166 company-owned service stations, and a world-famous motor oil brand, Havoline.

Nothing came of this proposal in 1921, but during the summer months of 1922 interest flared up anew. Roxana had Price, Waterhouse & Company make an audit of Indian's financial condition, and Van Senden and Van der Linden were brought east from California to appraise the company's refining and producing properties. All were discouraged by what they saw. Financially, Indian was, and had been, operating at a loss. Its refineries were hopelessly antiquated, expensive to operate, and would need almost complete renewal immediately. Its oil-producing properties furnished only a small fraction of the refineries' requirements, and were scattered through low-yield, high-cost fields then in their decline. Indian's most attractive asset was its sales department with its company-owned retail outlets and good customer acceptance for its products. "If we can get it at the right price," Godber wrote to Van Eck, "it will give Roxana the distributing organization it needs." But Lockhart and his associates had now raised their price to $26,000,000, a figure which precluded further serious consideration of the proposed purchase.[56]

Roxana's 1922 budget had provided a sum of $1,000,000 for "creation of a distributing organization"[57] but by the time the Indian deal had been fully explored,‡ it was too late to do anything that season except to begin negotiations with the Lilly White Oil Company of Lima, Ohio.

It was obvious that Roxana was determined to get into marketing. The company had, it is true, operated profitably for a decade. Half

‡ Indian struggled on through the Twenties and finally, unable even to meet its payrolls, was purchased by The Texas Company in 1931. Texaco has preserved the Havoline brand name.

of this period it had not even owned a refinery, and since the opening of the temporary refinery at Cushing in 1917, followed by the Wood River refinery in 1918, the company had maintained a small sales force to sell on the wholesale tank car market the relatively few products turned out by the refinery. A. P. Ruether, who came to work in the St. Louis sales department in April 1920, remembers that this tank car sales department consisted at the time of G. G. Woodruff, sales manager; J. A. Strong, assistant to Woodruff; G. A. Burns, chief clerk and credit manager; Mr. Wentworth, who handled statistics; and Ruether, who kept track of shipments. The chief products handled were gasoline, kerosene, fuel and road oils, all in tank car lots. There were sales representatives stationed in Chicago and Cleveland, plus one or two travelling representatives who worked out of St. Louis. A small road-oil department disposed of the company's entire output in the states of Illinois and Indiana.[58]

In the early Twenties, the trend of the future seemed to be in the direction of company-owned, company-operated distributing facilities. Roxana's sister company in California was showing a substantial profit from its marketing operations, or at least it was making more money than Roxana. Now, Roxana's large new supplies of crude oil from Tonkawa gave the company the economic stimulus it needed to enter the distributing field where it might enjoy some of the wholesaler's and retailer's profit, and at the same time be less at the mercy of the vagaries of the wholesale market.

For five years, the company had been selling the products of the Wood River refinery in tank car lots to jobbers, distributors, and brokers. Of these sales, a substantial part was made under contract; but, even so, prices received under these contracts were uncertain, for they generally were based upon the daily "spot" market. This was the price which jobbers and brokers, bidding against each other, established as the going wholesale price of unbranded gasoline, f.o.b. the refinery gate, as of a given day. This price could fluctuate quite violently within a twelve-month period, as it did, for instance, in 1923. On March 19 of that year, gasoline in the Wood River area was bringing 14¢ a gallon at the refinery gate. This figure dropped rapidly during the spring and summer months and, by November 19, the same gasoline was bringing only 6⅛¢ a gallon.[59]

In addition to uncertain prices, the wholesale market had another very undesirable feature from Roxana's point of view: its gasoline was anonymous. A few small jobbers, it is true, sold under the brand name "Roxana," but the great majority of them had their own brands. Godber felt, justifiably, that Roxana should get away from this anonymous marketing and begin to enjoy the better prices which a branded "Shell" gasoline could command.[60]

And so it was, that early in 1923 a program of rapid entry into the Midwestern market got under way. By the end of the year it had made astonishing strides; by the end of 1930, Roxana would have more depots than the Shell company on the Coast and the number of its retail outlets would be more than double the number of the California company. The reader has seen the fast-and-furious pace at which the expanding West Coast Shell organization moved during the Twenties; it will be left to him to visualize the speed with which the Roxana organization had to move to accomplish what it did in the short space of seven years.

R. G. A. van der Woude, Roxana vice president from 1922 to 1924, was designated to oversee the beginning of this marketing expansion, with Woodruff, the sales manager, in direct charge. Company-owned depots and service stations were to be built or acquired by purchase. To oversee them, a distributing department was set up in the St. Louis office under J. A. Strong, "under whom the organization had to be built from the ground up." [61]

Godber had correctly foreseen the need of a seasoned sales organization. For the next half-dozen years, the demand for experienced men constantly ran ahead of the supply. To help make up this deficiency, Roxana always tried in the case of purchases to take over the purchased company's employees. In some cases, men who had sold their businesses immediately assumed executive positions in the Roxana sales organization. In other cases, the purchase of a jobbing firm would be made contingent upon the owner's coming into the Roxana organization, at least for a specified minimum period, in order that the newly acquired facilities might be under the direction of a man of demonstrated ability acquainted with the territory. But despite such constant recruitment, there was still plenty of room in Roxana's sales department: any number of accountants, clerks, and others with experience in a dozen different fields were gladly hired and put to work.

The company's expansion activities got under way with a bang during 1923. The year 1923 was, indeed, Roxana's *annus mirabilis*. Crude production at Tonkawa was at its height, providing Roxana with a steady stream of cash dividends to be used in the expansion and a steady flow of crude oil for refining into products. To supply more products, a new refinery was erected at Arkansas City and at Wood River a plant to make lubricating oil, hitherto not needed. E. C. Peet, later to become chief fiscal officer of the Royal Dutch-Shell Group, was at the time a young man in the treasury department of the St. Louis office. "The year 1923," he recalled many years later, "was the start of six years of phenomenal growth, chiefly in the Mississippi Valley and adjacent territory. We hired green help and learned marketing by trial and error. Locations for some of the early bulk depots were picked by a method no more scientific than standing in the St. Louis office and sticking pins into a map at what looked like convenient intervals." [62]

That the company had ambitious expansion plans in mind for 1923 we may gather from the minutes of the directors, who early that year authorized company officers to qualify Roxana to do business in the states of Indiana, Michigan, Ohio, Wisconsin, Iowa, Kentucky, Nebraska, Minnesota, and North and South Dakota, as soon as it might be convenient to do so. Add to this the states in which Roxana was already doing business by virtue of its producing, refining, and pipe line operations—Oklahoma, Missouri, Illinois, Kansas, Arkansas, Louisiana, and Texas—and it will be seen that the company was setting up ambitious goals for itself. During 1923, it qualified in the states of Indiana, Ohio, Michigan, Minnesota, Iowa, Nebraska, and Wisconsin. [63]

Lilly White

The first major move in this marketing expansion program was the completion of negotiations, February 12, 1923, for the purchase of the Lilly White Oil Company, a sizeable jobbing organization selling 8,700,000 gallons of gasoline a year in seventeen counties of northwest Ohio. This company had been started as the Townsend Oil Products Company, of Leipsic, Ohio, in 1915, and in 1918 had expanded and moved its main office to Lima, Ohio. The same year it signed a contract for supplies with the new Roxana refinery at Wood River and had ever since taken its gasoline from Roxana, selling it under the "Lilly White" brand name. Early in 1923, Roxana acquired approximately 94% of Lilly White's common stock for $578,000 cash. Lilly White's assets at the time consisted of 17 bulk depots, 20 service stations, automotive equipment, a general office in Lima, and a list of some 300 dealers, most of them general stores and garages.

Later that year, Roxana organized a new company bearing the same Lilly White name to take over this purchase.[64]

For the next few years, the Lilly White organization continued, as a subsidiary of Roxana, to operate pretty much as it had before. At the beginning of 1924, the brand name of its gasoline was changed to "Shell," and in April 1926 the company was rechristened Roxana Petroleum Corporation (Delaware). It was not until July 1929 that this subsidiary was finally dissolved and its operations incorporated into the Roxana organization as the Lima division. It was, however, far from static in the intervening years: its sales volume by 1929 was nearly 35,000,000 gallons, quadruple that of six years before.[65]

Illinois Division

Roxana's first marketing divisions were two in number and were set up almost simultaneously in April 1923. The first by a few hours was the Illinois division, J. C. Munro, manager. Its early operations were centered about the purchase of a single filling station owned by Lincoln Bancroft, of Vandalia, Illinois, and of the Mur-Du Oil Company which operated bulk depots at Murphysboro and DuQuoin in southern Illinois. Later the same year, the Crystal Oil Company of Decatur, Illinois, was purchased and the Illinois division office was moved from St. Louis to Decatur, and placed under the management of T. T. Roberts, former owner of Crystal.[66]

St. Louis Division

The second division was St. Louis. Here company-owned depots started operation in the spring of 1923, accompanied by the creation of a St. Louis division under the managership of Dan E. Lavin. In general, Roxana built, rather than purchased, its facilities in the St. Louis area. The first company owned and operated station in the area was at Palm and Farrar Streets, St. Louis, opened in July 1923.[67]

Chicago Division

Later in April 1923, the first delivery of Shell-branded gasoline in Chicago was made from a temporary bulk plant located at 26th Street and Blue Island Avenue. The first company-operated station in the area was at 130th and Carondolet Streets in the Hegewisch suburb of Chicago. There had, of course, been a Roxana sales office in Chicago ever since the company had started refining and selling products in 1917. In June 1923, this tank car sales office was enlarged into the Chicago division, and J. F. Tillotson was made manager. In 1924, the territory of the Chicago division was enlarged by the purchase of Commercial Oil & Supply Company, a Gary, Indiana, jobber with one bulk plant. Rapid acquisition of dozens of filling stations and depots in the area of Metropolitan Chicago during the next few years provided adequate outlets for a full-scale division.[68]

Northern Division

The area outside Metropolitan Chicago, plus Indiana and Michigan where Shell representation was acquired on a small scale during 1923, was assigned to a new Northern division, set up in Chicago in September 1923 coincident with the moving of the Illinois division from St. Louis to Decatur. Munro, who had been manager of the Illinois division, became manager of the new Northern division at Chicago.

From this bare outline, the reader can see that the hastily built Roxana sales organization moved rapidly during 1923. By the end of the year the company had four marketing division offices—one each at St. Louis and Decatur, two in Chicago, and the Lilly White organization in Lima. The company owned and was operating 58 bulk depots, 106 tank trucks, 52 company service stations, and had 1,017 dealers under contract in the states of Missouri, Illinois, Indiana, Michigan, Kansas, and Ohio, to say nothing of "open dealers" who sold Shell products but were not under contract.[69]

ROXANA MARKETING EXPANSION, 1923–1925 [70]

	Bulk Depots	Tank Trucks	Company Stations	Contract Dealers	Gasoline Sales in Dollars
1923	58	106	52	1,017	$14,462,000
1924	85	279	124	1,444	25,763,000
1925	108	330	162	2,316	39,536,000

Indiana Division

Marketing divisions continued to grow and multiply. On April 1, 1923, Roxana had purchased the property of the Tri-States Oil Company, of Seymour, Indiana, a small jobber having a single depot and one service station. This station, which had the distinction of being the first to sell the Shell brand east of the Rocky Mountains, served as the nucleus of a considerable number of Shell outlets which were established in Indiana during 1924–1925. The small office which had

Parades and festivals were the delight of California Chambers of Commerce in the 1920's. Shell spent heavily on floats like this one for Fresno's 1924 "Raisin Day."

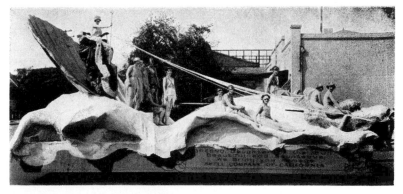

The universal yen to dig for buried treasure inspired Shell of California's famous "Treasure Hunts," extremely popular events in the mid-Twenties. The eager diggers, *left*, are waiting for the "go" signal in Seattle's 1927 "Treasure Hunt."

Digging for buried wealth (certificates good for merchandise prizes, enclosed in plaster-of-Paris shells) at San Jose's Treasure Hunt, 1927.

Company stations tied in with the Treasure Hunts, giving out "clew slips" to the motorists. This 1927 photo taken in Seattle shows a company station completely decked out for the occasion, and the attendants dressed as pirates.

Christmas displays were used by Shell of California to boost flagging gasoline sales in the winter months. An early Christmas exhibit, *above*, at Fell and Stanyan Streets, San Francisco, 1925, was a snow-clad representation of Mt. Shasta. Each year, the Christmas displays became more elaborate, reaching a climax in the block-long 1930 "Toytown," *below*, installed at Fell and Baker Streets, San Francisco, at a cost of $40,000. Despite high cost, Christmas displays paid for themselves in increased business. During a single day of the 1929 Holiday season, the Fell and Baker Street station sold 12,000 gallons of gasoline. Year-round business, as recorded on the graph, *right*, also showed a marked improvement.

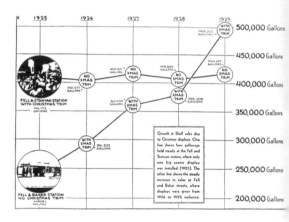

And then there was "Dobbsie" (Hugh Barrett Dobbs) whose hour-long morning program was one of the phenomenal successes of early radio. A blend of inspiration, soothing syrup, and community singing, it was broadcast over an extensive West Coast network and had an enormous appeal at the time. Shell made the most of Dobbsie's enthusiastic followers. When they chartered buses to go see him at the 1929 Sacramento State Fair, *above*, Shell's advertising department thoughtfully provided decorations for the buses. When the Matson Line's S.S. *Malalo* announced a "Shell Ship of Joy" cruise to Hawaii, *left*, every berth was booked in the depression year 1931. Dobbsie's broadcasts from movie theatres were pioneer "live-audience" shows, like the one, *below*, at Salt Lake City. Dobbs, at center, is wearing the four-stripe naval uniform.

All photos courtesy E. H. Sanders

Opposition to roadside signs led Shell of California to convert its shell-shaped billboards to the cause of forest-fire prevention in 1924, a move which won the company many new friends. Thirty years later, Shell still devoted its West Coast billboards to the forest-fire theme one month every year.

Shell-shaped billboards were designed for the approaches of many West Coast cities. These signs, *below*, reproduced as windshield stickers and given out at service stations, were highly popular travel souvenirs in the late 1920's.

Modern-style advertising started in 1928, when Shell of California set up an advertising department and began its first large-scale use of newspaper space.

been opened in Indianapolis in 1923 became a division office in January 1925, when A. F. H. Payne was made division manager. During the next five years, the facilities of several Indiana jobbers, totalling 23 bulk plants and 44 service stations, were purchased and incorporated into the Indianapolis division. These companies were the Knox Oil Company of Vincennes; Interstate Petroleum Products Company, Huntington; Anderson Oil Company, Anderson; Dixie Service Station, Inc., Bedford; Cooksey Oil Company, Brookville; and Williams Oil Company, Muncie. All were small jobbers except the Interstate concern which owned 13 bulk plants and 22 service stations.[71]

The Indiana division took in not only the area adjoining Indianapolis but also included Roxana operations in Michigan, formerly a part of the territory of the Northern division in Chicago. What was left of the Northern division was moved to Moline, Illinois, where Roxana had recently bought the Tri-Cities Oil Company and Moline Oil Company. The Northern division subsequently began acquiring jobbers in Minnesota and Wisconsin, and during the next few years bought the Trilling Oil Company, Sheboygan; Northern Oil Company, Rice Lake, Wisconsin; Menomonie Oil Company, Menomonie, Wisconsin; Rochester Oil Company, Rochester, Minnesota; and Penn-American Oil Company, Redwood Falls, Minnesota. All were small concerns, except Penn-American which had thirteen bulk plants.

Minnesota Division

In October 1927 Roxana acquired two jobbers in the Twin Cities area. The Eagle Oil Company, a St. Paul distributor, owned a depot and six service stations; the Jennison-Rollins Oil Company, Inc., of Minneapolis, had one depot and twenty service stations. Because owners of these companies wanted to retain an interest in the business, a new company for the Twin Cities area was organized, the Eagle Oil Company (Delaware), of which Roxana held 60% and the sellers the balance. This company, rechristened the Minnesota Shell Corporation shortly afterwards, was managed by J. E. Grininger of the Eagle interests and John C. Jennison and Carl I. Rollins of Jennison-Rollins. They retained their 40% of the new company until June 1929, when they sold out to Roxana. On July 1, 1929, a marketing division office was opened in Minneapolis to handle the business of this area.[72]

Shortly thereafter, late in 1929, a Wisconsin division office was opened in Milwaukee. The Northern division lost part of its territory at this time, and was renamed the Iowa division.

Western Division

In February 1927, the Shell trade-mark at last moved into Oklahoma, the state which had witnessed Roxana's start fifteen years earlier. The company purchased the Tulsa Independent Oil Company, owner of one bulk plant and three service stations in Tulsa, and publicly announced its intention of buying other jobbers and service stations that might be for sale in the area. By the end of 1927, Roxana owned 14 depots and 17 filling stations in Oklahoma, had 77 dealers under contract and had set up a Western division with offices in Tulsa. The company's entry into Colorado was made at one stroke. A single jobber, the Navy Gas & Supply Company, of Denver, contracted to handle sales of Shell products throughout the state of Colorado.[73]

Shell American

The northwest corner of Indiana did not become the Indiana division's territory. In October 1926, Roxana bought a half interest in a Kokomo jobber, the Great American Gasoline Company. This company had started business in 1921 and had purchased its gasoline from Roxana from the start, reselling it under the brand name "Hot Spot." By 1926, Great American had built up a sizeable business, with 10 bulk depots, 22 company-operated service stations, and annual sales of 9 to 10 million gallons. The men who had built this profitable business, Robert L. Tudor, of Kokomo, and his partners, Mark A. Brown, a Chicago banker, and Earl B. Barnes, an Indianapolis lawyer, wished to keep a continuing interest in it. A partnership arrangement was proposed and Roxana accepted, happy to be associated with men who had proven their capabilities. Roxana on the one hand and Tudor, Brown, and Barnes on the other agreed henceforth to be equal partners.

The company's name was changed in February 1927 to Shell American Petroleum Company, and Roxana's nominees were elected to the chief offices. Actual management of the company remained in the hands of the men who had built it. Tudor continued to direct Shell American until he retired late in 1929 in favor of one of his younger men, P. H. (Bull) Durham, who managed Shell American for the next twenty-five years.§ By agreement, Shell American was assigned the northwest corner of Indiana. In ensuing months, it traded its facilities at Greencastle, North Manchester, and Rockville for Roxana facilities at Plymouth, South Bend, La Porte, and Michigan City. During the next few years Shell American purchased three jobbers in its own area: the Houston Oil Company, of Rensselaer, 1926; Wabash Valley Oil Company, Logansport, 1927; and Mutual Service Oil Company, Knox, 1931.[74]

The purchases of marketing property made by the St. Louis management had thus far, despite their rapidity, been on a fairly orderly basis. But with the arrival of 1929, the whole Roxana organization became infected with "expansion-itis." It was a common enough malady that year. All but the most stodgy of companies (and few could have called Shell that) seemed to be riding high on a wave of optimism.

Behind this seeming optimism were some hard economic facts. Unit profit was dropping sharply; only by increasing total sales volume could sales managers hope to equal their previous year's profits. This pressure to increase sales volume brought on a multiplication of retail outlets that had by 1929 become a serious problem. On more than one occasion during 1929, the Shell management pointed with pride to the fact that their companies' most recent expansion had "followed the policy of purchasing existing facilities, which has avoided duplication and, we believe, has helped to strengthen the market." [75]

But Shell was not in business merely to strengthen the market. Like its competitors, it was reaching out for greater sales volume. The quickest way to achieve volume was to buy going businesses. This also solved the important collateral problem of how to provide and train an adequate staff. The year 1929 saw Roxana branch out even more than most of its competitors. Purchases were made north, south, east, and west, and a half-dozen new division sales offices were set up to operate the company's booming business. "During 1929 and early 1930," Peet recalls, "some thirty-five marketing companies were purchased by Shell Petroleum, and the memos announcing purchases and personnel changes passed through Head Office so fast that only a man with a very good memory could keep up with them all." The Shell Union companies that year spent well in excess of

§ Shell purchased Shell American's outstanding stock in 1955; during 1956, the Shell American operation was absorbed into Shell Oil's marketing organization.

$40,000,000 for marketing expansion, a large part of it in the Mid-Continent.[76]

Cleveland Division

In Ohio a number of jobbers were bought out in rapid succession: Home Oil Company, Wilmington, Ohio, purchased in April 1929; Accurate Measure Oil Company, Columbus, May 1929; Gerkins Oil Company, Dayton, August 1929; Columbus Oil Company, Columbus, September 1929. The Columbus Oil Company was a sizeable distributing organization, owning 22 bulk depots and 64 service stations. With its purchase, September 1, 1929, a new marketing division was set up at Cleveland to handle the increased business in eastern Ohio. In October 1929 the Peerless Oil Company of Elyria, Ohio, was purchased and in December the Akron Oil Company, of Akron. Continuing this Ohio expansion, the Kentucky-Independent Oil Company, of Cincinnati, was bought out in April 1930; the Portsmouth Oil Company, Portsmouth, in May 1930; and the Tiona Oil Company, Warren, Ohio, in November of that year. The Lima and Cleveland divisions were combined at Cleveland in July 1930. By this time the Ohio divisions had 70 depots and were selling 50½ million gallons of gasoline annually.[77]

Western Oil Refining Company

The Columbus purchase was part of Shell's biggest deal to date. The Columbus Oil Company was a subsidiary of the Western Oil Refining Company, of Indianapolis, which had been organized in 1910 by J. H. Trimble, who with his sons owned Western at the time of sale to Shell. Western Oil Refining had 24 bulk plants and 131 service stations in Indiana, including 56 in the city of Indianapolis. Together, Western and its Columbus subsidiary were selling some 40,000,000 gallons of gasoline a year through a total of 46 depots and 195 service stations. These Western and Columbus stations were in the main well located and all were of very good construction. Most of them were large, roomy brick buildings with tile roofs—far more expensive structures than Roxana or its major competitors were in the habit of putting up. The Trimbles had built Western and its subsidiary into one of the largest jobbing organizations in the Midwest. To buy them out, Roxana had to pay big money, $6,600,000 cash.[78]

But even by the inflated standards of 1929, the Roxana appraisers felt unable to place a valuation of more than $4,400,000 on the Western properties. The balance, $2,200,000, a full one-third of the total purchase price, was put down on the books to "good will." Large as this figure for "good will" was, it might have been justifiable if Roxana had cashed in on the good reputation of the Western outlets and their "Silver Flash" brand of gasoline. But in changing these stations over to the Shell brand, the Roxana sales department provided an excellent illustration of how an inexperienced sales force learns by trial and error.

In Los Angeles seven years earlier, the Shell Company of California had been at great pains to keep the customers of the Puente company by making the change-over to the Shell brand so gradual as to be almost imperceptible. But the Roxana sales department, for reasons that now seem inconsequential, decided that a quick change-over would be a feather in its cap. Western operated its stations through Saturday, August 31. Immediately after closing time that night, the Roxana sales department moved in with all the help it could press into service. Salesmen, bookkeepers, and office boys, as well as the regular paint and maintenance crews, worked right through Labor Day weekend to paint the Western stations red and yellow, erect Shell signs, and install the familiar shell-shaped globes on the gasoline pumps. In a matter of hours, all trace of Western's green and white colors, the Silver Flash name, and 2¼ million dollars' worth of good will had vanished. Former Silver Flash customers, far from being pleased and surprised, were shocked and dismayed. Their dismay ripened into resentment and cost the stations' new owner a considerable amount of gallonage * in the months that followed.[79]

Michigan Division

On this same day, September 1, 1929, two new division offices were opened. One, already mentioned, was at Cleveland; the other was at Detroit. During the six years since 1923, Roxana had enlarged its company-owned facilities in the Michigan area only slightly. For the most part it had funnelled its increased distribution in Michigan through the plants of jobbers. Then, during the summer of 1929, two of the company's largest jobbers in the area had been snatched away by competitors. The Shell jobber for the city of Detroit, the

---

* It should also be mentioned that Shell did not continue Western's liberal discount policies, and this no doubt did cost the company the business of price-minded customers.

Wayco Oil Company which was selling about 30,000,000 gallons of gasoline annually, had been purchased by Paragon Oil Company (later acquired by Gulf); Mutual Oil Company, selling some 12,000,-000 gallons of gasoline a year at other Michigan locations, was acquired by Cities Service. To make up for this sizeable loss, Roxana's sales department decided to concentrate on building and buying new facilities in that area.[80]

The new Michigan division, set up in Detroit with Dan E. Lavin as division manager, was given jurisdiction over four company depots in Michigan which formerly had been under the Indiana division. These old depots at Benton Harbor, Battle Creek, Kalamazoo, and Niles served as the nucleus of the new division. At the same time, the company spent $258,000 to acquire the Dittmar-Raths Oil Company of Saginaw, a jobber with one depot and six service stations. With this start, Lavin's group speedily bought suitable sites in and around Detroit, and during the fall and winter months of 1929–1930 were hard at work building new stations. So great was their haste that they put up canvas awnings and tents so that construction might proceed in spite of snow and rain. Depots were erected at the same time and on January 1, 1930, the first delivery of product was made from the new Detroit depot. During 1930, two more Michigan jobbers were purchased, the Western Oil & Gas Company of Ludington, two depots and four stations (July 1930); and the Oakland Oil & Gas Company of Pontiac, one depot and nine stations, in September.[81] The company did not, however, rely wholly on its own distribution in Michigan. In the northern parts of the state, jobbers still continued to play an important role.

Automobile Gasoline Company

It was also during September 1929 that the St. Louis division, which had hitherto built most of its own facilities, increased its distribution in that city by buying the pioneer Automobile Gasoline Company from Clem Laessig who had founded it in 1905. At the time of the purchase (September 9, 1929) the business consisted of a depot, ten company-operated stations, and some thirty additional outlets. Many of them had changed little in appearance from the first gravity tank and garden hose arrangements of a quarter century before. Laessig's company was doing a good business under its "Powerite" trade-mark and had, in addition, a substantial trade in fuel oil.[82]

Southern Division

During 1928, ambitious plans were laid for capturing the two remaining major markets in which the company did not as yet operate, the Atlantic Seaboard and the Gulf-South. As early as June 1927, proposals were being made that the New Orleans Refining Company might serve as the nucleus for a third Shell company in the United States, a company which would produce, refine, and market petroleum products in the area south of the Ohio, and east of the Mississippi. This plan was extensively considered during 1928 and a tentative name, Southern Shell Company, was selected. New Orleans was picked for the headquarters, and some consideration was even given to selection of executives for the new company.[83]

However, the New Orleans Refining Company had never engaged in retail marketing. Its sales, almost all in the export trade, were generally in cargo lots and its sales force was a total of three men. Since the St. Louis company would be called upon to furnish the bulk of the staff, why not let that company supervise the entire operation? The idea for a separate Southern Shell Company was abandoned early in 1929, and entry into marketing in the Gulf Coast area got under way under the aegis of the Roxana organization. J. C. Munro, division manager at Moline, was sent to New Orleans to become manager of the new Southern division which opened at New Orleans in February 1929 in the old New Orleans Refining Company offices.

Beginning with the purchase in March of the Empire Oil Company, a small jobber at Sylacauga, Alabama, the company fanned out rapidly through the Gulf Coast states during the next few months. It bought several jobbers, among them the People's Oil Company, New Orleans; Superior Oil Company, Biloxi; Brown Oil Company, Birmingham; Muscle Shoals Oil Company, Florence, Alabama; Palm Oil Company, Mobile; Independent Oil Company, Crowley, Louisiana; Southern Petroleum Corporation, Memphis; and the Independent Oil Company, of Corinth, Mississippi. The Brown company of Birmingham, with six bulk plants, was the largest of the purchases. Roxana's service stations in the Gulf-South states were for the most part built by the company, with the exception of a small number picked up through the purchase of jobbing organizations.[84]

Marketing coverage of Texas and the eastern part of New Mexico also came under the New Orleans office. In these two states, the company endeavored to serve dealers from company depots and operate company stations only in the areas of Houston, Galveston, and Beaumont. Distribution of Shell products in the rest of Texas and New Mexico was handled by jobbers.[85]

Florida Division

The other Gulf Coast state, Florida, and its neighbor Georgia, were constituted a separate division, and a division office opened at Jacksonville in March 1929 with Carl D. Crites, formerly at Lima, as division manager. A sizeable ocean terminal costing some $286,000 had just been completed at Tampa in anticipation of the company's marketing in Florida. Another larger terminal, costing $735,000, was nearing completion at Jacksonville.† In Florida, depots at Tampa, Lakeland, Winter Haven, Deland, and Gainesville were purchased. Georgia was well provided with jobbers willing to handle Shell products, so with the exception of a depot purchased at Savannah, the company elected to distribute its products through jobber organizations in that state.[86]

Buying up existing jobbers provided a method for acquiring ready-made sales organizations, as we have seen. It must not be presumed, however, that the Roxana organization of the Twenties made no use of the jobber per se. If a jobber sold his gasoline under the Shell brand name and if he seemed reasonably likely to remain a Shell customer, there was no particular point in buying his business. Throughout the Twenties, the Roxana sales department devoted a good deal of effort to convincing jobbers that they should sell under the Shell brand, with the result that there were by 1929 a considerable number of "Shell-franchise" jobbers. In marginal territory having few cities or large towns, Shell-franchise jobbers were utilized almost exclusively; and in four states—North and South Dakota, New Mexico, and Colorado—Roxana did not attempt to establish its own distribution.

Roxana's retail service stations and company-operated bulk depots were under the supervision of the marketing division offices. By early 1930 these offices were thirteen in number: Minneapolis, Milwaukee, Moline, Decatur, Chicago, St. Louis, Indianapolis, Lima, Cleveland, Detroit, New Orleans, Tulsa, and Jacksonville. The number of division offices was large, because unlike their Pacific Coast counter-

† These two terminals were built by Asiatic of New York. When completed, they were purchased by Shell Union and turned over to Roxana.

parts the Mid-Continent division offices had no district offices under them. The division managers reported to Strong and his distribution department in the St. Louis head office. Woodruff, the sales manager, was concerned chiefly with sales of gasoline in tank car lots, for despite the company's enormous expansion in the field of retail marketing, more than half of Roxana's total gasoline sales were still being made on the wholesale market as late as 1930.[87]

The "Filling Station"

It might be well at this point to comment briefly upon Roxana's service stations of the Twenties for they presented a marked contrast to those of the Shell Company of California. In the first place, Roxana's stations were, strictly speaking, "filling stations." The Mid-Continent, slower to adopt the company-operated station, had not yet reached the excesses of free service which had by the late Twenties become almost standard on the West Coast. In the second place, the physical appearance of the stations would soon differ considerably, although when Roxana started building its first stations, the "California style" building was adopted as a model.[88]

In Roxana's case, it was only natural that the company should build, for its first stations, metal "cracker boxes" of the kind its sister company in California was employing so profitably. These stations were Stefco steel buildings, manufactured in Michigan City, Indiana. They did not offer much protection against the rigors of a midwestern winter and eventually were discarded in favor of more substantial buildings of wood or masonry. However, during most of the Twenties, Roxana continued to put up these cracker-box buildings.[89]

Roxana's purchase of distributing companies all during the Twenties brought it a collection of stations as impressive for their diversity as Shell of California's were for uniformity. Some of these outlets, such as those acquired from the Western Oil Refining Company, were veritable palaces of petroleum marketing. At the opposite end of the scale were others little better than shacks. All were united, however, in one thing: they were covered with a coat of dazzling yellow paint with bright red trim, and they stood out from the landscape every bit as much as Shell of California's stations. J. G. Sinclair, one of the early Mid-Continent division managers, remarked twenty-five years later, "With that paint, we didn't *need* advertising." [90]

Shell advertising in the Mid-Continent got started during 1926, using the conventional media: large road signs, billboards, newspaper space, and the radio. Shell customers in the Midwest witnessed no such spectacular stunts as the Treasure Hunts and Christmas Shows staged on the West Coast. But Stanley Wilson, the first Roxana advertising manager, with the help of Strong, the distribution manager, did develop and introduce the Shell-shaped globe which soon became a fixture on Shell pumps throughout the United States and in many countries abroad.[91]

Another contribution to Shell marketing practice introduced by the Roxana organization during these years was the salesmen's school at Wood River. Sporadic attempts had been made earlier, by both Shell of California and Roxana, to see that company salesmen had some understanding of the manufacture and technical properties of the products they were selling. With its sales force growing by leaps and bounds, Roxana found large-scale instruction imperative. Beginning with a session in June 1928, the company conducted a very creditable salesmen's school at the Wood River refinery. The course of instruction covered the complete range of refinery operations, with particular emphasis being placed upon the oils and greases about which the Shell industrial salesmen needed to know more. The course was of a month's duration and even employed such modern teaching techniques as instructional movies.[92] A similar school was started at the Martinez refinery a year later.‡

4

Coast to Coast: Shell Eastern

ON APRIL 19, 1929, a group of Boston business and civic leaders gathered for luncheon at the Hotel Statler. It was an important occasion in the history of their host, a newly organized company called Shell Eastern Petroleum Products, Inc. After luncheon, the guests adjourned to a service station at the corner of Church and Stuart Streets, and there watched Shell Eastern's president inaugurate the

‡ Both efforts were discontinued in the early Thirties, victims of economy drives then current. Dr. G. P. Koch, who had taught the Martinez school, began a travelling school in 1937; classes were held at various locations on the Pacific Coast and Atlantic Seaboard until stopped by the war in 1942. In 1947, the Shell marketing school was revived and placed under the direction of Dr. Koch until his retirement at the end of 1950.[93]

sale of Shell gasoline in the East by pumping a tankful into the car of Frank F. Fahey, president of the New England Council.[94] Thus began the last lap in the American Shell companies' effort to secure nation-wide marketing coverage. Before the year was out they would be selling Shell in all forty-eight states, Hawaii, and the District of Columbia.

It is doubtful if anyone in the Shell organization had foreseen growth this rapid. And in all probability few, if any, had anticipated the speed with which this newest Shell company would accomplish its job. It had taken nearly twenty years to build the Shell marketing organization on the Pacific Coast. Roxana had cut that time to half a dozen years. Now, the new Shell Eastern company would spread itself up and down the Atlantic Seaboard in a matter not of years but months.

The dramatic swiftness with which the new company moved is attributable in part to the fact that the idea of a Shell company in the East was not new. For nearly five years entry into this inviting market had been considered in one form or another, and the actual start of business in February 1929 came after nearly two years of preparations and negotiations. This information will no doubt be a disappointment to the romantically inclined who liked at the time to view the entry of Shell Eastern into the Atlantic Seaboard market as a giant move on an international chessboard. In this instance, Shell's appearance on the Eastern Seaboard was supposed to be a retaliatory move against the Standard Oil Company of New York.

This story—believed, incidentally, by many Shell people—had its rise as a consequence of the Russian revolution. The Shell Group, one of the largest oil producers in Russia, had lost all its properties to the Communists, who had seized them without payment. Determined that the Russians should not sell oil from these properties in international trade without remitting at least a part of the proceeds to the former owners, Deterding had during most of the Twenties successfully prevailed upon his major competitors not to buy Russian oil. Then, in 1927–1928, Socony began buying Russian kerosene for resale in India. Deterding's protests were loud, vigorous, and widely publicized. The story got started that Deterding had invaded Socony's "territory" (New York State and New England) to get even. It is easy to see now that denials of any such intent, which were made by Shell officials at the time, served only to strengthen the story in the minds of those intent on believing it.[95] Exciting and interesting as such stories are, they are almost never true. Once again we are brought up against the unexciting truism that business considerations rather than individual passions govern the conduct of successful businesses.

As early as the summer of 1925, two years before the Socony ruckus, Shell of California was giving serious thought to entering the Atlantic Seaboard market in order to dispose of impending surpluses of gasoline. Corbett in London, Van Eck and Airey in New York, Godber in St. Louis, and Legh-Jones in San Francisco all exchanged considerable correspondence on the subject. Airey had suggested the creation of a new corporation, the Shell Company of New York, to be owned half by his Asiatic company and half by Shell Union. Godber,§ however, correctly predicted that the anticipated surpluses would fail to materialize. When this proved to be the case, the matter was dropped for that season.[96]

By the fall of 1926, the California market was again showing signs of developing serious surpluses, and this time Shell of California went much more thoroughly into the matter of creating an East Coast outlet. Gallagher was sent east to go into the matter thoroughly with Airey; together they made a survey of the Atlantic market. The report, which Gallagher wrote, outlined three ways in which Shell of California might go about selling its gasoline on the Eastern Seaboard.[97]

The simplest and cheapest method, since it required no supervision and no investment, would be to engage the services of one or more distributors, concerns that owned marine terminals and assumed complete responsibility for making sales to jobbers, even to guaranteeing the jobbers' accounts. For their services, these distributors normally charged the supplying companies ¼ ¢ a gallon.

A second method would be for Shell to build its own marine installation and set up a small tank car sales organization, similar to the Roxana sales force before 1923. Either alternative would return the California company about the same net proceeds for its gasoline. The second plan had the advantage of giving the supplying company control over the sales force and selling policy. Both methods had the disadvantage of selling Shell gasoline unbranded.

The third course open was to enter the Atlantic Seaboard as Roxana was then entering the Midwest market, establishing company depots

§ From late 1925, Roxana had a jobber in western New York State selling under the Shell brand.

and service stations and selling under the Shell brand name. If this method were adopted, the most desirable markets at the start would be the highly populous areas adjacent to New York Harbor. Next, in order of their apparent profitability, were Baltimore, Boston, Philadelphia, Jacksonville, and Portland, Maine.

The distributor plan required no investment at all. Establishment of a tank car sales organization would require a marine terminal, but for the moment the new organization could use a new terminal just erected at Bayonne, New Jersey, by Asiatic of New York for use in the latter's bunkering business. Direct operation in the New York area would, Gallagher estimated, cost in the neighborhood of $6,000,000 to start—five barge depots at a cost of $4,000,000; five show-place stations on main highways at $150,000 each; a hundred less pretentious stations at an average of $40,000 each; plus the necessary trucks and automotive equipment. Not counting depreciation, the company could expect to realize from direct operation about the same as by the other two methods, a net of $9\frac{1}{2}$¢ a gallon. The cargo buyers of gasoline in California were at the moment offering this much, so once again the project of an Eastern Seaboard marketing company was allowed to lapse.

But not for long. During 1927 and 1928, the Group's refinery at Curaçao was substantially expanded, increasing the quantities of product available for sale on the Atlantic market. For the American side of the Atlantic, Richard Airey, head of Asiatic of New York, acted as the Group's chief agent. It was from him that the next suggestions came.

The developments which finally led to the establishment of a Shell company on the Atlantic Seaboard were the result of a quite casual luncheon conversation one day in 1927 between Alexander Fraser, at the time secretary of Asiatic (New York), and John F. Riddell, Jr., a New York oil broker dealing in cargoes of petroleum products. Riddell mentioned to Fraser that a Mr. Carter, president of a Boston firm of refiners and marketers, was in New York looking to buy crude oil. Thinking to do some business for the Group companies in Venezuela, Fraser expressed interest, and later that day Riddell took him around to meet Carter at the latter's hotel.[98]

Soon discussions between Carter and Airey were under way. Airey asked if Carter's company might not be interested in a contract for supplies of product instead of crude oil. When Carter did not say no, Airey inquired if he might perhaps be interested in something a little more permanent, such as handling the sale of Shell products on the Atlantic Seaboard. Airey got in touch with Adrian Corbett, and soon Carter received an invitation to go to London for further talks. This he did in January 1928. It could have hardly been a happier meeting as far as Carter was concerned, for not long before he had reluctantly concluded that the only hope for his concern was to sell it as a going business.[99]

The New England Oil Refining Company, for that was its name, had a short and sorry history. Started ten years before on the crest of the postwar boom, it had been poorly managed, saddled with debt, and since 1923 had been on the verge of bankruptcy. Like Union of Delaware, it had behind it a number of men prominent in financial circles; like Union, it had failed to put a man familiar with the oil business at the head of the company; and again like Union, it had run into trouble during the 1920–1921 depression. On top of all this, the New England company had the further disadvantage of being built on an unlikely foundation. For most refining companies, fuel oil was at best a profitable side line; but the New England Oil Refining Company had been organized specifically to refine and market fuel oil.

The years immediately following World War I brought a coal shortage which was particularly acute in New England. During the shortage, mill owners in Massachusetts and Rhode Island converted to fuel oil and were willing to pay good prices for it. In Mexico, the Panuco field was then reaching the height of its production of heavy, asphaltic crude, good for little else save boiler fuel. A group prominent in Boston business and financial circles, many of them owners or managers of mills, proposed to bring Mexican crude to Massachusetts, refine it, and sell it as industrial fuel.[100] The venture was made doubly attractive by government assistance at the outset. The Navy Department, in a contract negotiated by its assistant secretary, Franklin D. Roosevelt, agreed to advance the Boston group $3,000,000 in cash and provide transportation for 5,000,000 barrels of crude oil from Mexico to Fall River, where it had been decided to build the refinery. In exchange for its assistance, the Navy was to receive 3,000,000 barrels of Navy "A" fuel oil and 200,000 barrels of gasoline.[101]

The refinery, built on a 20-acre point of land just north of Fall River, betrayed the bankers' lack of interest in technology. It consisted of old-fashioned bench stills, cumbersome, expensive, and entirely unsuited to a "topping" operation such as the new company proposed to conduct. The initial capacity of the refinery was 20,000 barrels a day, later increased to 27,000 barrels, making it the largest refinery in New England.

The crude oil was to come wholly from Mexico, where, at the time the enterprise had been conceived, serious overproduction prevailed with resultant low prices. One of New England Refining's contracts made during this period called for 18,000,000 barrels of Panuco crude, at 12¢ a barrel loaded in Tampico harbor.[102] To transport this oil from Mexico to Fall River, Swiftsure Oil Transport, Inc., was set up by some of the same interests to buy seven 12,500-ton tankers. These vessels were later transferred to the New England Oil Steamship Company, a subsidiary of the refining company, and a mortgage given for the unpaid balance on the tankers. Four miles up the Taunton River, some 200 additional acres of land were purchased to provide space for the eventual erection of a large tank farm to be connected to the refinery by pipe line. This property was organized as the Assonet Oil Storage Company, another subsidiary.

Then, with the New England company barely started, its misfortunes began. During 1921, Mexican crude production dropped sharply, which meant that the company could not hope for fulfillment of the wonderfully cheap crude supply contracts upon which its whole business had been founded. In a search for cheap crude, the New England company turned to Venezuela and secured a quarter of a million acres of concessions, some of them in the Mene Grande field. Here wells were drilled, but without success.[103]

Without a stable source of crude, the company led a hand-to-mouth existence, and in its best years barely met its depreciation and interest charges. Matters were not improved by a series of reorganizations during the first half of the Twenties that added greatly to the complexity of the company's already muddled affairs. A holding company and several additional subsidiaries were created, chiefly for the purpose of issuing additional securities in a desperate attempt to stave off insolvency. By early 1923, New England had come to the end of its financial rope; it lacked the money to meet even its day-to-day expenses. The Boston banks who were the most heavily involved lent the company $3,000,000 for working capital in the form of a so-called "revolving fund," secured by a mortgage on inventories and open accounts receivable. This was a humiliating arrangement for the company and its employees, for all receipts had to be turned over to the banks and all tanks of products were padlocked and hung with signs warning that the contents must not be removed without permission of the banks.[104]

As if to compound these misfortunes, the first of a series of interminable lawsuits began. They were brought by minority stockholders who claimed that the recent reorganizations had been accompanied by irregularities which, in effect, constituted fraud. These lawsuits, extremely involved and difficult to understand, dragged on for five years and raised serious doubts about the competence of the company's management.* A group of creditor banks, fearful that their money would be totally lost, in 1925 asked Andrew F. Carter, a former Navy commander who was at the time vice president of The Russell Company, a Boston management firm, to see if something couldn't be salvaged. Carter found that the New England group of companies was almost hopelessly in debt. There were two bond issues. The first, for $3,750,000, was secured by a first mortgage on the refinery; the second issue, amounting to $5,000,000, was backed by a general mortgage on the rest of the company's properties. Interest on both issues was at the high rate of 8%. There were $7,000,000 worth of tanker notes at 7%, $1,500,000 of 7% gold notes which had been issued by the Venezuelan subsidiary, and preferred stock on which dividends were required to be paid regularly. The bonds were in default, both as to principal and interest; the preferred stock dividends were not being paid; the interest on the revolving fund was the only obligation the company was meeting.[106]

---

* To explain the long and confused court cases that grew out of the shuffling of securities between the holding company, New England Oil Corporation, and its subsidiaries, would require more space than can be justified in a Shell history. The original suit rose from charges by Ernest W. Wiltsee that he was entitled to a 10% promoter's profit in connection with the financing of some of the Venezuelan lands. During a corporate reorganization, Wiltsee along with other noteholders had been asked to exchange his notes for common stock in the holding company. Because of other securities issued by other New England subsidiaries at the same time, Wiltsee claimed that the exchange of notes for stock did not constitute valid payment. The U. S. Circuit Court of Appeals in Boston agreed with Wiltsee, and in January 1925 awarded him a $176,000 judgment against the company. Following Wiltsee's lead, the company's receivers brought similar action against the noteholders' committee, which included the presidents of Boston's three most prominent banks as well as most of the other interests originally associated with the company. In May 1926, the court found this noteholders' committee guilty of fraud and awarded the company a judgment of $3,327,740 against them. This development thoroughly discredited the company's early backers, and a petition asking severance of the noteholders' committee from the company was filed in the same court soon after. Wiltsee's judgment against the company was later reversed by a higher court; this reversal was upheld by the U. S. Supreme Court in November 1927, when it refused to review the case. In July 1928, the U. S. District Court in Boston which had been hearing the "New England Oil Cases" since April 1927, dismissed the remaining litigation.[105]

On top of this distressing financial situation, there was an inefficient muddle of marketing subsidiaries. Not intending originally to go into the marketing of gasoline, New England had at first sold its gasoline output to Socony. But in the years following 1920 it had gradually bought all, or parts of, a hodgepodge of gasoline-distributing and filling-station companies. In some of these companies, such as the Mayflower Oil Company, New England held a majority interest, but more often its ownership was fractional, which meant that the companies could not be controlled and operated along uniform principles. Carter recommended acquiring control of as many of these companies as possible, disposing of the rest, and consolidating the whole operation in the interest of economy. But these were at best minor economies. Things looked so bad that when the interests who had asked for the report requested Carter to step in and attempt to put some of his recommendations into effect, he agreed only on condition that he not be asked to assume a legally responsible office. Later on, after some of the litigation had been settled in the company's favor, Carter accepted office in the company, and at the time of his trip to London early in 1928 he was chairman of the board, president, treasurer, and general manager of the New England Oil Refining Company.[107]

By enforcing strict economy, eliminating duplication, and consolidating some of the subsidiaries, Carter managed to keep the company in business, but he could do little to alter its fundamental difficulties. He made arrangements with Standard of California and Gulf to drill New England's Venezuelan properties; they, too, failed to find oil. The company was forced to turn to its competitors in California, the Gulf Coast, and Venezuela for cargoes of crude oil to keep operating. With New England Refining always dependent upon others for supplies, results could not help but be bad, as Carter pointed out to the stockholders late in 1926: "The company is now forced to purchase a large part of its crude oil from competitors, in uncertain amounts and at fluctuating prices. This situation has prevented the company from entering into long-term contracts for the sale of its refined products and has subjected it to all the disadvantages of a fluctuating market."[108] He could not hope to raise more money, for the bonds and notes already outstanding far exceeded the company's assets, leaving the preferred and common shares worthless. Clearly, a sale or, better yet, an advantageous merger, was the company's chief hope, for it offered the only means by which the stockholders could ever hope to recover anything on their investment.

From Shell's point of view, the New England Refining company was of value chiefly as a nucleus around which to build an Eastern marketing organization. The refinery with its antiquated equipment and 20-acre site was "more of a liability than an asset"; the existing equipment would have to be scrapped and the small size of the site precluded building a new refinery on it. The dockage and tanks would make it useful as a terminal, but hardly worth the $4,326,000 which an independent engineer had reported as its "reproduction value."[109]

The properties which most interested Shell were the depots and service stations. There was a marine terminal at New Bedford and bulk depots, located on both water and rail, at Fall River, Bridgeport, Bangor, and New London, and rail depots at Wellesley and Lowell, Massachusetts. Mayflower Oil Company, which owned and operated 40 filling stations, had a rail and water depot at New Haven, a leased depot at Plymouth, and rail depots at Salem and Braintree, Massachusetts. In addition, Mayflower owned a half interest in the Holden Oil Company of Manchester, New Hampshire, a company with a depot and two stations in that city. In 1926, New England had bought control of Metropolitan Filling Stations, Inc., a chain of 43 stations in Greater Boston served by a water and rail depot at Chelsea. Lacking funds to make the purchase outright, New England had purchased one-third of Metropolitan's stock and arranged for the balance to be purchased by men friendly to the company. Some $650,000 would be necessary, it was estimated, to acquire this remaining outstanding interest. Together these marketing companies sold about 13,890,000 gallons of gasoline yearly, half of it through company-operated stations.[110]

The bulk of the Fall River refinery's gasoline output was, however, sold in tank car lots on the wholesale market: in 1928 some 46,000,000 gallons. As the company did not manufacture lubricants, it had contracted to handle the Marland brands. New England had a fleet of 500 railroad tank cars, on which $220,000 was still due, some small ships and barges used to supply its depots, about 75 motor trucks, the six tankers (one of the original seven had been lost at sea), and miscellaneous foreign properties, the chief of which were the Venezuelan lands and 2,000 acres of worthless leases in Mexico.[111]

The discussions in London between Carter, Corbett, and Sir Robert

Waley Cohen in January 1928 were of an exploratory nature and resulted in a memorandum in which the Shell Group proposed formation of a new company, to be controlled by Shell, and issue of new securities to replace those outstanding. Carter sailed for New York February 1, 1928, a copy of the memorandum in his pocket along with the draft of a supply contract under which Asiatic proposed to supply New England with such products as it did not make itself.

The London executives were impressed by Carter's ability and integrity.[112] In February, Waley Cohen wrote him a more definite offer. However, Carter could do little except sound out his various creditor groups. Litigation still dragged on in the courts, and until it was settled the New England company would not be free to dispose of any of its assets. Fairly certain of an eventual deal and anxious to get on with the necessary expansion of New England's sales outlets, Asiatic in March 1928 agreed to advance up to $1,000,000 for the purchase of new marketing properties. These would remain in Asiatic's name but be operated by New England until such time as a deal could be consummated. Under this arrangement, Asiatic of New York purchased for $810,000 cash Yankee Filling Stations, Inc., Municipal Filling Stations of Bridgeport, Inc., and Yankee Filling Stations of New Haven, Inc., a chain of some 65 stations in western Massachusetts and Connecticut, owned by D. T. (Dixie) Smith.[113]

Late in June, Carter, accompanied by a representative of the Boston banks, made a second trip to London, and this time he returned with a concrete proposal. Asiatic in a written offer to the New England company proposed that a new joint company be formed to take over the Fall River refinery and the Assonet land, the service stations, depots and equipment, the trucks, and the railroad tank cars. Since majority control of the new company was to be given to the Shell Group, the new company would not be able under existing laws to own or operate the tankers; they were therefore left out of the deal, but the Group did agree to give the Swiftsure vessels preference whenever it chartered tankers. Preferred stock in the new company was to be given to the bondholders, in exchange for the securities they held, and to the Shell interests in exchange for $3,500,000 of new working capital which the Shell Group would provide. The Group would receive 51% of the new company's common stock; the balance of the common stock would be left for distribution to some of the remaining creditor groups. Carter was to be president of the new company, and he and two others to be nominated by the Group would form the company's executive committee. The new company would draw its supplies from the Group, in accordance with a contract to be negotiated annually.[114]

Just prior to the receipt of Asiatic's offer, the Federal District Court in Boston dismissed the remaining litigation and New England's creditor groups were at last free to discuss the Group's offer. Considering the shape the New England company was in, Carter felt he had bargained well for his company. With the exception of the tankers which the Shell Group could not legally own and the Venezuelan land which would be given to noteholders who had a prior claim on it, Carter had succeeded in getting the Shell interests to take all of the New England Oil Refining Company's properties. In his negotiations with Shell people, he had convinced them of the desirability of purchasing all of the New England assets so that the new company might start off with the good wishes of all the New England creditor groups.

The proposed purchase of the refinery was certainly an example of Shell's willingness to take over the whole organization. From the first the Shell people in on the deal had planned to shut down and dismantle the refinery if they did purchase it. A terminal could be built for a million dollars; so the refinery storage facilities could not be considered as really worth the $3,000,000 of preferred stock which Shell had agreed to pay the owners of refinery mortgage bonds. It was, however, from this source that trouble now came. Holders of the mortgage bonds on the refinery were unfortunately influenced by an engineer's appraisal which put the "replacement value" of the refinery at $4,300,000, an entirely fallacious figure, for who would seriously consider replacing a refinery that had been obsolete the day it was built? The holders of the $3,750,000 bond issue were not deterred by such arguments; they expected to recover their investment in full, and accordingly refused Shell's offer. Without unanimity, negotiations ground to a halt. The New England company was declared bankrupt early in October 1928; the receivers in bankruptcy appointed by the court were Carter and Robert Proctor, a Boston attorney.

Airey and Corbett, who had been active in negotiating the deal on behalf of Shell, late in October 1928 concluded that there was no prospect of coming to any agreement with the bondholders who owned the refinery. The other creditor groups were willing to sell their interest, but without the terminalling facilities provided by the Fall River and New Bedford installations (both owned in essence by the holders of the refinery mortgage), the marketing properties were by themselves much less attractive. Discouraged, Airey proposed forgetting the whole thing and considering instead purchase of the Beacon Oil Company, a substantial refining and marketing company in the same area, which was known to be for sale.[115]

At about this point it was decided that Shell Union should own and operate any new Atlantic Seaboard marketing company which might be formed. Van Eck took over the negotiations, and proposed that instead of stock the refinery mortgage holders be offered cash. This met with favor, and appraisers from Roxana in St. Louis were called in to look over the New England company. Carl Barker, manager of Roxana's insurance, tax, and claims department, prepared a valuation report; J. A. Strong, distribution manager, surveyed New England's sales policies, potentialities, and personnel; W. F. Jones, accounting manager, examined the company's systems and accounting methods. Van Eck disliked the idea of the proposed company with an outside interest in it; the annual supply contract for such a company would, he anticipated, be a certain source of future disagreement. He proposed that the new company be wholly owned by Shell Union and that those who had already agreed to take preferred stock be given Shell Union shares instead.

Early in December in 1928, Shell Union offered $2,250,000 cash for the refinery and $2,310,000 for the marketing properties. A brief delay was caused by Beacon Oil Company (which had meanwhile been quietly purchased by Standard of New Jersey) asking for permission to bid. Beacon's offer was not up to Shell's, so a few days before Christmas 1928, the court finally approved sale of New England's assets to Shell Union.

It would, it was expected, take several weeks to close the deal. Meanwhile the new company, Shell Eastern Petroleum Products, Inc., was organized under the laws of Delaware on January 22, 1929, with a head office at 141 Milk Street, Boston, the same building in which the old New England offices were located.† Inspection of titles and foreclosure of the refinery mortgage by the bondholders took some weeks, and it was not until February 4, 1929, that New England's marketing properties—the Mayflower Oil Company's four

---

† These remained Shell Eastern's offices for the next year. Early in 1930, the company moved its headquarters to the new Chanin Building, on East 42nd Street in midtown New York.

bulk depots and 40 filling stations, Metropolitan's 43 stations and depot, and Holden Oil Company's two stations and depot—were transferred to the new company. For these properties, Shell paid $2,310,000 in Shell Union shares valued at $32 a share, plus $607,000 in cash needed to buy up the outside interest in Metropolitan Filling Stations.‡ The next day, February 5, a foreclosure sale was held to dispose of the refinery; for it and the New Bedford terminal Shell paid $2,250,000 cash. In addition Shell paid the banks $1,000,000 for the inventories secured by the revolving fund mortgage.[116]

As soon as the property transfer had been made, Carter resigned as a receiver of the New England company and was elected president of the new Shell Eastern. The new company's vice president in charge of marketing was W. J. Filer, who had been assistant sales manager of Roxana in St. Louis since 1923. U. F. O'Brien, who had been chief fiscal officer of the New England company, became vice president and treasurer of Shell Eastern. T. S. Marshall, a member of the Roxana advertising department, was made advertising manager of the new company. For the most part, the rest of Shell Eastern's employees and executive staff were former employees of the New England Oil Refining Company.

The months that lay ahead were busy ones for the new company. Filling stations and depots had to be repainted, and Shell signs and pump globes installed. New trucks were purchased and a fleet of automobiles for the salesmen, all painted Shell's vivid red and yellow colors. During this interim period the inventories which had been purchased were disposed of, so that by the time the new company was ready to make its first sale of Shell-brand gasoline late in April, it had a product which was "Shell" both in name and quality.

The Fall River refinery was shut down for good, and its stills and other refining equipment scrapped. The docks and tanks remaining at the Fall River refinery site eventually became Shell Eastern's largest terminal in New England, the point from which gasoline was transshipped by barge to smaller water depots throughout New England.

Farther south, the new company also acquired other terminal properties. At Wagners Point, near Baltimore, Asiatic had under construction a terminal similar to the two it had built in Florida.

‡ In order to simplify the Metropolitan transaction, creditor groups headed by J. P. Cotton and M. G. Chace organized the King Phillip Oil Company which took title to these properties, paid the balance due on them, and transferred them to Shell free of encumbrances.

This Baltimore terminal was purchased by Shell Eastern, as was also a tract of land in New York Harbor acquired not long before by Asiatic. This property was at Boynton Beach (or Sewaren), New Jersey, a small summer-resort community just north of Perth Amboy. Here the new Shell Eastern proposed to build a New York terminal along with a plant to refine lubricating oils.[117]

Early in the year, on January 12, 1929, before the company had been organized officially, a purchase contract was negotiated to buy Bang Service Stations, Inc., a chain of 18 stations extending from the Bronx along Long Island Sound up into southern Connecticut, supplied from a bulk plant at Mt. Vernon, New York, convenient to water transportation. This company, owned chiefly by its supplier, the Galena-Signal Oil Company, was doing about 3,000,000 gallons annually through its eighteen stations;[118] Shell paid $637,000 for its business and properties. The Baltimore terminal, the property at Sewaren, the Bang stations in New York, the Yankee stations in Connecticut, and the properties purchased from the New England organization were the physical assets with which the new Shell Eastern set up in business. Excluding the payment for product inventories, these purchases totalled just under $7,000,000 in cash and Shell Union shares.§

This new Shell Eastern organization, hastily put together as it had been, got off to a flying start and continued to expand throughout 1929 and 1930, spending before the end of 1930 nearly $25,000,000 on new facilities. Chiefly, these new facilities were depots, strings of service stations, and the necessary tank trucks and automobiles.[119]

R. M. Clough, who had been sent to St. Louis in January 1929 to consult with the St. Louis sales organization and order from Roxana's suppliers paint enough to last the year out, remembers that new outlets were acquired at a rate so rapid that a year's supply of red and yellow lasted the booming new Shell Eastern only five months. By the end of April, the repainting and change-over to the Shell brand in the Boston area had been completed. In New York, a temporary district office was opened in a single room at 25 Broad Street. In the Baltimore area, the first cargoes were delivered in mid-April.[120]

Early in April, Shell Union let its stockholders know by means of a circular the tremendous expansion plans which were afoot within the American Shell companies that year, all across the continent.

§ In cash some $4,740,000; in Shell Union common stock, about $2,210,000.

Soon, the circular said, Shell gasoline would be on sale in every state except Texas. Already there were some 27,850 Shell pumps in the United States—12,000 on the Pacific Coast, 15,000 in the Mid-Continent, and 850 in New England—and there would be more before the year was out.[121]

A sample of the expansion that came through purchases may be had in the New York area. The nucleus which had been provided by the Bang stations was soon added to by the purchase of Sierks, Lane & Sierks, a chain of stations with a depot at Inwood, Long Island, and the Paragon Oil Company's filling stations in Manhattan. For a depot to supply Manhattan Island, the company purchased the waterfront plant of the Forrest Box & Lumber Company, on Newtown Creek, Brooklyn, and there installed the necessary tankage—underground, because of city fire laws. Early the following year arrangements were made to permit Shell to use the terminalling facilities of the Lewis Coal & Oil Company at Port Washington, Long Island, and shortly after a contract was made with Underwood Coal & Oil Company of Patchogue, Long Island, to permit Shell to build a depot on its property. All of these New York area depots had the advantage of being accessible by water, thus allowing products unloaded by tanker at the Sewaren deep-sea terminal to be transshipped to the depots by barge.[122]

In the Baltimore area, the Wagners Point terminal was completed in July, giving the company access by water to that region. Late in the year, marketing facilities in Washington, D.C., were purchased, giving Shell representation in the District of Columbia, the last link in its coast-to-coast coverage. (Marketing in Texas had meanwhile started in October.) The Carolinas were served by a terminal at Wilmington, North Carolina, which Shell operated under contract for five years and finally purchased from the National Oil Company. From the start, the new company did a good business in the Carolinas; the Wood River refinery shipped an entire trainload, twenty-six tank cars, of motor oil to North Carolina in April 1930.[123]

Throughout Shell Eastern's territory, from the Canadian border to the Georgia-South Carolina boundary, the company continued to purchase small jobbers and chains of service stations during 1929 and 1930. Such purchases became so common that a regular procedure was developed complete with printed forms. The sales offices kept their eyes open for likely buys and this information was passed along to the head office. Real estate men were then sent out promptly, generally with power to conclude a deal on the spot. Next, a "take-over day" was appointed, when the seller surrendered his business to the purchasers. On that day, a crew of company auditors would arrive to place a book value upon the new property and inventory. A standardized set of printed forms covered each aspect of the purchase. The last form was a memorandum sent to all departments, notifying them that the business formerly operated by (blank) and located at (blank address) had become a part of the Shell Eastern organization as of (blank date).

Shell Eastern, as did its sister company in the Mid-Continent, tried in most cases to obtain the services of the former owner of the business. This was of considerable importance, for the new company was faced with the necessity of building a sales department in an even shorter time than had Roxana. The case of George L. Switzer, of Rochester, New York, is illustrative. Switzer had started a parking and service garage in Rochester in 1920 and built it into a chain of garages by 1929. In 1924 he had established Seneca Stations, Inc., a chain of service stations which by 1929 numbered 17 units. In October of that year he sold out to Shell Eastern, but Shell made the purchase contingent upon Switzer's coming with the new company for a period of at least two years. Switzer balked at the idea of going to work for a salary, so Shell Eastern offered him instead an over-riding commission on all Shell sales made in Rochester for the two-year period.* By means such as this, Carter and Filer recruited a sales force in record time.[124]

But purchases alone could hardly have accounted for Shell Eastern's spectacularly rapid expansion. The bulk of Shell Eastern's retail outlets were not owned by the company but were the property of independent dealers. A large measure of the credit for the company's phenomenal success in signing up dealers must be given to Carter. While operating the Mayflower stations, he had experimented with granting territorial franchises to dealers, agreeing that the company would neither open a station of its own near a franchised dealer nor sell to another dealer in the immediate area. The big marketers in New England had no such policy. Standard Oil of New York, the oldest and largest marketer in the area, often opened a company station near one of its Socony dealers, or sold in tank car lots (and therefore at a lower price) to another dealer located nearby. In either

---

* Switzer continued with Shell, became the company's merchandising manager and, later, retail manager, which position he held until his retirement in 1954.

case the long-established dealer felt that his own supplying company was competing with him, directly in the case of a company-operated station, pricewise in the case of a tank car dealer. The same general situation prevailed in Metropolitan New York and New Jersey, where the largest marketers were Socony and Standard of New Jersey. Carter persuaded the Shell management to allow him to try the dealer franchise. The results were ahead of even his expectations.[125]

The local Shell Eastern salesman would make a list of a dozen or two desirable dealers in each town, and these dealers would be invited to a dinner at the leading local hotel. After dinner, Carter would address them briefly and explain what Shell Eastern had to offer. Then he would depart, often to hurry on to another such gathering in a neighboring city, leaving the salesmen to sign up dealers for Shell Eastern. Enough to blanket the city could usually be signed up in an hour. "It was like shooting fish in a barrel," Carter recalled twenty years later.

Up to this time, a large proportion of dealers in New England and other parts of the Atlantic Seaboard had carried two, three, and even more brands of gasoline. Shell Eastern asked that its dealers sell Shell exclusively in return for the promise of exclusive territory. This happy state of affairs "with dealers practically begging to be taken on" lasted throughout 1929–1930.[126] By the end of the latter year, Shell Eastern had some 11,250 pumps in service along the Atlantic Seaboard—a fine record for so short a time and rivalling the 12,000 Shell pumps on the Pacific Coast and 15,000 in the Mid-Continent.[127]

5

Feeding the Big Expansion

THE most conspicuous aspect of Shell's activities during the second half of the Twenties was the tremendous expansion of its sales organization. Less obvious but equally important was the development of new sources of supply. New oil fields were discovered, new pipe lines laid, and new refineries erected.

Even so, production from these new oil fields and the supplies of products from the new refineries lagged behind the rapid increase in the company's over-all sales. Particularly was this true east of the

Rocky Mountains. As far back as 1917, when Roxana's temporary refinery at Cushing started up, the company had begun purchasing crude oil on a small scale to make up the differences between Roxana's own production and its refinery capacity. These purchases were never discontinued and with the passing years they continued to grow in size. In 1925, for instance, when the Tonkawa production was at its peak, Roxana still purchased from outside sources some 3¼ million additional barrels of crude.† Even that did not make up the deficit in supplies, and Roxana that year bought nearly 12,000,000 gallons of finished gasoline from other refiners.[128]

During the second half of the Twenties the gap between the company's actual supplies and its marketing requirements continued to widen, until by 1929 it reached serious proportions. By this time, the California company had also become a heavy purchaser of crude.‡ Production of Shell of California in 1929 was 23,702,000 barrels and its purchases that year amounted to 11,809,000 barrels. Roxana's production was 21,020,000 barrels and it purchased 13,026,000 barrels. Later on, in the Thirties, these disproportionately large purchases were to lead to the uncomfortable conclusion that the company had expanded its selling organization too rapidly. But at the moment, crude oil purchases caused little concern. The Shell companies were enjoying a satisfactory refining profit on the oil they processed, and there was always the chance that they might suddenly find themselves by virtue of discovery with all the crude they could use.

At no time in the Twenties did such a happy turn of events seem improbable. The early Twenties were, as we have seen, full of good fortune for Shell of California, and, to a slightly lesser extent, for Roxana. During the second half of the Twenties, the California company continued to develop the fields which had come to prominence

† This represents net purchases from outside sources. Roxana's total purchases of crude oil in 1925 came to nearly 10¼ million barrels, including the oil purchased from royalty owners and from Comar and Wolverine.

‡ About half of Shell of California's purchases were through two large contracts. One agreement, negotiated in 1927 with J. Paul Getty, provided that Shell would take about 2,500 barrels a day of Getty's production for three years at Standard of California's posted price. The second contract, negotiated with the Honolulu Consolidated Oil Company in June 1927, provided that Shell would take at least 10,000 barrels a day of Honolulu's crude production for a ten-year period; payment was to be made according to a schedule which was designed to yield Honolulu the proceeds received from the products made from this crude, less Shell's charges for transportation, refining, marketing, and 5% profit. During these same years, the company negotiated several one-time purchase contracts, chiefly with independent producers in the Los Angeles Basin, for quantities as large as 500,000 and 1,000,000 barrels.[129]

earlier in the decade. Signal Hill production had begun to taper off when a deeper, equally prolific new horizon was discovered during 1927. During the fall of that year and the early months of 1928, drilling activity at Signal Hill matched in intensity that of five years earlier; some 350 wells were drilling during May 1928. Inspired by the success at Signal Hill, operators in the Santa Fe Springs field began deep drilling during the summer of 1928, and for the next twelve months Santa Fe Springs was the scene of activity reminiscent of its earlier days. The production of both fields jumped sharply in consequence. In the Bakersfield area, several new fields were discovered, although development of most of them was held up, pending the day when the oil would actually be needed.[130]

At Ventura, where the early Twenties had seen only meager results, deeper drilling brought better yields and by the second half of the Twenties oilfield development work at Ventura was in full swing. During 1927, Edison No. 19 at Ventura was brought in at 7,100 feet for 1,600 barrels a day, the deepest well in the world producing oil in any quantity.

Along the Gulf Coast, the geophysical work begun early in the Twenties continued. On the Gulf Coast of Louisiana, oil-bearing salt domes were located by Roxana at White Castle and Black Bayou. Discovery wells on both structures were drilled by Roxana during 1929. Both fields eventually developed into good producers. Black Bayou, marshy land in Calcasieu Parish, Louisiana, for which Roxana had paid $15,000 in 1923, presented a special problem in logistics. It was low-lying country miles away from railroads and highways, and the immediate surroundings were too soggy for construction of an overland route. Instead, canals were dredged to Black Bayou, where a special oil camp was built with bunkhouses for unmarried employees and small cottages for men with families. Motorboats furnished all the transportation. Mail and groceries were delivered daily by boat from Orange, Texas, the nearest sizeable town, and children of school age were transported to and from their classrooms by the same unique method.[131]

In Kansas, Roxana obtained substantial acreage in the South Udall pool, in the Oxford district, and during 1929 Roxana discovered new pools at Benton and Elyria. Like most Kansas and northern Oklahoma fields, these fields were flush producers from thin formations and soon dwindled into insignificance. In Oklahoma in 1927, the company discovered the Lovell pool and a new pool in the Marshall district.[132]

West Texas

West Texas, an area hitherto largely untapped, was the scene of the really big discoveries of the late Twenties. Roxana had up to that time been pretty much of a hard-luck prospector. Under Van Holst Pellekaan, the company began to "buy protection," a method of oil prospecting which experience has shown to be very productive of results in the long run. To "buy protection" means simply that the company undertakes to lease, while land is still cheap, likely-looking acreage in likely-looking areas. The idea is to avoid drilling and instead pay such rental fees as are necessary to hold the acreage against the day when someone else may bring in a well and prove the value of the territory. Since hundreds of thousands, even millions, of dollars can be spent on a few unsuccessful wildcat wells, "buying protection" has much to recommend it. The difficulty is that there are a tremendous number of likely-looking unproved areas. To adopt such a policy widely in the vast Mid-Continent area would have required a long purse indeed. With the financial resources at the disposal of Roxana, it was advisable to purchase protective acreage only in areas where land was plentiful and cheap. Such an area was West Texas, and there protective acreage bought cheaply yielded very good results.

Early in 1924, the company established an exploration and land district office at San Angelo [133] and began to lease acreage in the vast area of West Texas and eastern New Mexico known as the Permian Basin, equal in extent to two or three normal-sized states. Geophysical tools such as the torsion balance were used to supplement the findings of surface geologists, and scouts kept an active tab on wells that were drilled by others in order that subsurface information might be correlated with other findings. Even so, buying leases in an area where wells were still so far removed from each other remained in the realm of guesswork. A company intent upon acquiring protective acreage normally bought a "spread," a checkerboard of leases throughout an area where prospects were considered good. Since in "checkerboarding" only part of the land was leased, the cost was much less than the outlay for a solid block of leases. A much wider spread of leases could therefore be purchased for the same amount of money. Furthermore, in checkerboarding large amounts of land were left unleased and there was always a chance that a competitor might lease some of this acreage and drill a successful well, which would be to the benefit of the holder of the surrounding checkerboard.

The first commercial production discovered in the West Texas area was the Westbrook field in Mitchell County in 1921. In May 1923, the Big Lake field in Reagan County had come in, and in August of the same year the Artesia field of Eddy County, New Mexico. The Big Lake field was the first to tap production in the Permian limestone, a formation at the relatively shallow depth of 2,900 feet. Permian crude was "sour," i.e., high in sulphur content, and presented special problems to the refiner. However, further drilling showed that the Big Lake field was of substantial proportions and Roxana entered the area. In May 1925, the World-Powell field in Crockett County, southwest of San Angelo, came in. Here Roxana held acreage, and completed its first West Texas well, a 50-barrel pumper, on May 19, 1926. Although this and subsequent wells in the field were small, they encouraged the company to intensify activity in the West Texas area.

McCamey

In September 1925, the discovery well of the McCamey field was brought in. Here Roxana held substantial protective acreage, purchased a year earlier for $1.25 an acre. The producing formation was at a shallow depth (2,000 feet) and the extent of the McCamey field large. Drilling proceeded rapidly and a year later the company had 41 wells and daily production of about 2,000 barrels in the McCamey field. It was, and still is, hot, dry, dusty, desert country. Water supply was an acute problem all during the early years, and drinking water at McCamey had to be imported at a cost of $2 a barrel, nearly double the price of oil, which was selling for $1.25.

Hendricks

Other discoveries in West Texas followed during the early months of 1926. In July 1926, the Hendricks field in sparsely settled Winkler County came in, the biggest West Texas find yet. Roxana land men obtained large tracts in the vicinity of the discovery well and also purchased a half interest in an independent operator's acreage there. Hendricks wells were large producers in comparison to other fields in West Texas. Roxana's first well in the field, completed in October 1927, had a daily production of 1,860 barrels; another well drilled shortly after produced 3,300 barrels a day. And they were at the shallow depth of 2,800 feet. By January 1928, Roxana's production from the Hendricks field alone had risen to more than 20,000 barrels a day. This was a lot of oil, and Roxana from this point onward would be considered one of the large producers in the West Texas area. For this new eminence, the company could thank the judicious purchase of protective acreage.

Yates

Only three months after the discovery of the giant Hendricks field, the discovery well was brought in in the Yates field in Pecos County, 25 miles southeast of McCamey. Here were large quantities of oil at unbelievably shallow depths; and here Roxana had been holding protective leases for nearly a year and a half. Most all of these 2,000 acres of leases eventually proved productive. Like Hendricks, the Yates field was a prolific producer, and the oil was at a depth of little more than 1,000 feet. Many Yates field wells made production history. The biggest, drilled in 1929 to 1,070 feet, produced on test 4,083 barrels of oil in 34 minutes, or 204,680 barrels a day, one of the largest flows of oil ever gauged from a single well.

In November 1927, the Jordan field some thirty-five miles north of McCamey and the Cooper-Jal field in southwestern New Mexico were discovered. In both fields Roxana held substantial amounts of protective acreage. During 1928, seven other new fields were discovered in the West Texas area. On March 1928, came the Tobarg field, a northwest extension of Yates; in July, the Kermit field in Winkler County; in November, the Shipley field, in Ward County; and in December, the important new field at Hobbs, New Mexico, where Roxana once more had a substantial portion of the acreage. By the end of 1928, there were fourteen important producing fields in West Texas and New Mexico; Roxana, by virtue of its policy of buying protective acreage, had holdings in eight of them. In the three largest—Yates, McCamey, and Hendricks—the company had the major share of its total West Texas production, some 30,000 barrels of oil a day from 111 wells.

Shell Pipe Line Corporation

The remoteness of West Texas, the complete absence of local storage facilities and the lack of pipe lines into the area were a serious handicap to the rapid development of Roxana's new fields in the Southwest. The company, with a large program of marketing and refinery expansion then under way, naturally wished to cut its crude purchases as much as it could; construction of a new pipe line got under way promptly. In view of the location of Roxana's refineries, there was little question as to the route the new line should follow. McCamey, where the company already had sizeable production and district headquarters, was chosen as the point of origin. The most obvious course was to connect with the Ozark line at Cushing, 481 miles distant.

In the fall of 1927, during the same months that Roxana was bringing in its first wells in the Yates and Hendricks fields, the Ozark Pipe Line Corporation drew up plans for a 10-inch line with fourteen stations and an initial capacity of 35,000 barrels a day. The capacity of the old line northward from Cushing to Wood River would also have to be increased by nearly this amount. These extensions, the new construction, about 100 miles of gathering lines, and the necessary tank farms cost more than $20,000,000.[134]

To finance this project, and others which the company felt might be necessary soon, the pipe line company on November 1, 1927, sold $30,000,000 of 25-year bonds bearing 5% interest, guaranteed both as to principal and interest by the parent company, Shell Union Oil Corporation. To assist the sale of these securities a name more closely identified with Shell was advisable, so on October 25, 1927, Ozark Pipe Line Corporation changed its name to Shell Pipe Line Corporation. Work on the line was pushed energetically and was finished in March 1928 ahead of schedule, thanks to the energy of R. P. Bascom, general manager of the pipe line, who had been made a vice president of the pipe line company in January 1928.

The Cushing-to-Wood River line was "looped," i.e., a considerable amount of new pipe was laid parallel to the old line to help increase its capacity. At this time, late 1927 and early 1928, the old Cushing–Wood River line, laid ten years before, was pulled up, cleaned, recoated, rewound, and lowered back into the trench.

Pending completion of the new pipe line from McCamey to Cushing, rail transportation was used extensively for West Texas crude. The company built and operated at Monahans a loading rack capable of loading at one time an entire trainload of 60 tank cars; at McCamey a similar loading rack with a capacity of 54 cars was erected. With oil filling steel storage tanks as fast as they could be built, the Roxana production men decided to build concrete-lined earthen reservoirs to supplement the steel tankage. A reservoir of

Typical sub-depot of the mid-1920's.

Courtesy B. A. Gwynn

Selling Shell in the Midwest. B. A. Gwynn, later Shell district manager in Indianapolis, poses beside his 1927 company Chevrolet.

Entrance to Norco, La., refinery, summer 1930, shortly after purchase by Shell Petroleum.

Shell Building, St. Louis
Photo taken in 1933

First sale of Shell gasoline in the East, Church and Stuart Streets, Boston, April 19, 1929. *Left to right,* J. A. Fraser, Shell Eastern's district service station superintendent; H. W. Boynton, Shell Eastern distribution manager; U. F. O'Brien, secretary and treasurer of Shell Eastern; H. A. Browne, Shell Eastern traffic manager; T. S. Marshall, advertising manager; C. F. Mills, vice president, First National Bank of Boston; Edwin C. Johnson, vice president, Boston Chamber of Commerce; W. J. Filer, Shell Eastern marketing vice president; Frank J. Fahey, New England Council, who made first purchase; and A. F. Carter, Shell Eastern president.

Laying cornerstone of San Francisco Shell Building, November 8, 1929. *Left to right*, E. H. Sanders, advertising manager; H. H. Anderson, in charge of the building project; C. L. Harris, credit manager; G. H. van Senden, manufacturing vice president; L. E. David (partially hidden), later general manager, marketing; John Lauder, vice president and treasurer; David Heggie, Lauder's successor a few years later; E. P. Christie, San Francisco division manager; T. D. Peace, insurance manager; President George Legh-Jones (with trowel); A. R. Bradley, secretary and head of legal department; John M. Peat, manager, stores department; J. C. Storey, purchasing agent; Herbert R. Gallagher, marketing vice president; R. S. Milligan, Shellane manager; J. A. Dean, librarian (face partially covered); I. J. Harvey, Jr., later president of The Flintkote Co.; Edward Hepner (right eye covered), secretary, Shell Chemical; R. R. Griffin, later vice president of marine transportation, New York; N. W. Thompson, chief engineer; Harry Fuller, auditor; E. F. James, office manager, San Francisco division; E. A. Franquelin, cashier; D. W. Davisson, automotive mgr.; and C. S. Jobe, personnel mgr.

Legh-Jones and Deterding at opening of San Francisco Shell Building, April 16, 1930.

San Francisco Shell Building
Nightly bathed in golden light

slightly more than 1,000,000 barrels capacity was erected at Mona-hans, and another even larger at McCamey. But the dry, sandy West Texas subsoil proved an unsuitable foundation for leak-proof reservoirs. Both reservoirs had constantly to be repaired, and were abandoned once the period of unrestricted production had passed.[135]

Voluntary Proration

Unrestricted production was by this date beginning to give even the most independent-minded producers pause for thought. It was in West Texas, an area far removed from markets and endowed with seemingly limitless supplies of crude oil, that the first successful production-limitation measures were put into effect. A voluntary proration plan got under way in the Yates field on October 1, 1927. It became the model for a similar plan imposed a year later by the Texas Railroad Commission in the Hendricks field where water encroachment, caused by too-rapid release of the underground gas pressure, had reached serious proportions. Among more enlightened oil men, sentiment from the mid-Twenties onward favored restrictive measures to prevent waste and help preserve some of the newer oil discoveries for a day when they would be needed. The Shell companies, wherever they operated, took a conspicuous role in urging conservation measures.

Gas Conservation

During the second boom of Signal Hill in 1927–1928, Shell of California did its best to see that the flush production of gas from this new zone was not wasted. In the spring of 1928, the company arranged for the Southern California Gas Company, which had been buying gas from Shell in the Dominguez Hill field, to take its supplies from Signal Hill instead. Shell then purchased a gas line belonging to the City of Long Beach, connected it to Shell's gas production at Signal Hill, and piped the excess Signal Hill gas to Dominguez Hill where it was pumped down into the oil sands for storage. This was a highly experimental technique at the time, but it more than justified the company's pioneering faith. The gas was saved for a future time when it could be sold, and it also had an immediate beneficial effect upon oil production in the Dominguez field. Several wells which had ceased to flow of their own accord and had been put on the pump, responded to this increase in underground gas pressure and started to flow again. Lifting expense was thereby lessened and this gas-saving project became feasible for its effect upon oil production alone.

This work could not be carried on without the cooperation of competitors, for a gas storage program increased the production of all wells in the field. Shell obtained the agreement of Union Oil, co-owner with Shell of the Reyes lease where it was proposed to inject the gas, and the cooperation of the landowners was assured by paying them as royalty a share of the injected gas. By midsummer 1928, Shell was putting 9,500,000 cubic feet of gas daily into underground storage at Dominguez, and Union 5,000,000 feet.[136] The project was also to the advantage of the Southern California Gas Company, for it permitted storage of gas during summer months, when demand is less, and withdrawal during the winter period of peak demand. This meant that the gas company, with greater potential supplies at its command, could solicit more business. In recent years, many natural gas pipe line companies have undertaken similar underground storage of gas in order to increase the total capacity of their business.

At Ventura, where the amounts of gas produced were exceptionally high in relation to oil production, the company in 1926 built a casinghead (or natural) gasoline plant of 150,000 gallons a day capacity, at the time the largest in the country. The large production of this plant made it worth while for the company to think of new methods for shipping this unstabilized natural gasoline to the Wilmington refinery, where it was "stabilized" (a process which removed the most volatile of the natural gasoline elements) and later used for blending with finished gasoline. Railroad shipment for this much natural gasoline (20 tank cars a day) was expensive, and evaporation losses which ran anywhere from 5% to 20% made it even more expensive. A pipe line seemed the obvious answer. Several short lines were already transporting natural gasoline in California, one of them a 3-inch line some 30 miles long running from Shell's Brea field to the Wilmington refinery. However, to build a larger and longer line (it was 100 miles from Ventura to Wilmington) and take it over two mountain ranges was a different proposition.

The natural gasoline would need to be pumped under constant high pressure and, because of the length of the pipe line and the nature of the terrain to be traversed, would need at least two pumping stations: one at Ventura where the natural gasoline was put into the line, another at some mid-point. The problem would be to coordinate pumping rates of these two stations. This difficulty was overcome by designing a switch mechanism based on float-levels. This float switch made possible a mid-point pump station at Simi, California, with the operation of the Simi pumps automatically synchronized with those at Ventura. The arrangement also acted as a safeguard in the event of leaks, for shutting down the Ventura station automatically brought the Simi pumps to a halt. This unique line, built of 4- and 6-inch diameter welded pipe, was completed in 33 days and put into operation on April 1, 1927. It cost just under a million dollars, an amount soon repaid in freight savings and evaporation losses, which were cut to less than 1%.[137]

Such conservation-minded measures, which would have seemed strange to the average American oil man only a decade before, were a very interesting sign of the times. Many of the larger companies, accustomed to efficient methods of operation in other departments of their business, were appalled at the waste, chiefly a product of haste, in the producing end of the business. During the second half of the Twenties, sentiment—and in a few instances concrete action— pointed increasingly to the fact that the day was coming when profligacy with a precious natural resource would no longer be tolerated.

East Chicago Refinery

During the second half of the Twenties, Shell kept abreast of its increased crude production and its rapidly growing markets by adding new capacity to existing refineries, and building three new refineries and purchasing a fourth.

The first of the new refineries was in the Chicago area, where Roxana already had created a large market for its products, and needed a nearer source of supply in order to be competitive with Standard of Indiana and Sinclair. Early in 1926, Carl Barker of Roxana's St. Louis office began assembling a suitable refinery site on the shores of Lake Michigan, east of Chicago, partly in East Chicago and partly in Hammond, Indiana. There construction got under way in April 1926. By December, the refinery operating staff was beginning to arrive and in March 1927, using crude oil brought in by tank car, the new East Chicago refinery began to manufacture its first gasoline, although all units were not yet complete. Later that month, a 249-mile 8-inch pipe line, to connect East Chicago with the northern terminus of the main pipe line at Wood River, was finished and put in service. In July, the rest of the processing units were ready to go on stream. The East Chicago refinery had at the start a crude throughput of about 25,000 barrels a day, making it slightly larger than Arkansas City.[138] Dr. R. H. Waser, who had been superintendent at "Ark City" when that refinery started up, was made superintendent of the new East Chicago plant; R. C. Roberts was assistant superintendent.§

For distilling, the Shell companies had since 1915 used Trumble units, a combination of pipe still and dephlegmators which was now becoming outmoded. For the East Chicago refinery, Roxana licensed the new and much more efficient Badger unit, a combination of pipe still and bubble-tray fractionating tower, manufactured by E. B. Badger & Sons Company. Four of these Badger units were built at the start, three for crude oil distillation and a fourth for running "pressure distillate" from the cracking units. For cracking, six Dubbs units were installed at the start. There was a market in the Chicago area for petroleum coke, so the cracking units were designed to "crack to coke." Because of the necessity for cleaning out the coke, each of these Dubbs units was a "double installation," a single furnace with two cracking chambers. One chamber was operated for cracking while the other was closed down to allow removal of the coke, an arrangement which, in theory at least, permitted continuous operation. In July 1929, two more Dubbs units were added at East Chicago, bringing the total to eight, and another Badger unit was installed to provide the necessary additional topping capacity. This raised the refinery's throughput to 30,000 barrels a day, the level at which it was to operate for the next decade. The Wood River–East Chicago pipe line, originally of 15,000 barrels a day capacity, was increased to 27,000 barrels a day by looping during 1927.[139]

From the point of view of transportation, East Chicago was an excellent location. Dockage was built on the lake front and the two lake tankers were kept busy supplying water terminals which Roxana had built meanwhile at Detroit, Cleveland, and Toledo. Even points as far east as Buffalo could be supplied profitably. By-product gases, wasted in many other areas, could here be sold to public utilities for the enrichment of artificial gas. Coke, a bothersome by-product in most refining areas, was readily saleable to the heavy industries nearby. Even supplies such as sulphuric acid could be piped in direct from the adjoining plant of the chemical company which made it.

§ These titles are equivalent to the present titles of manager and superintendent.

Refined products not shipped by water went to markets that were nearby—so near, in fact, that a large portion of East Chicago's output could be delivered by the switching railroad which served the Chicago area. Like Arkansas City, East Chicago concentrated on volume production of a few products: gasoline, kerosene, gas oil, fuel oil, road oil, and asphalt. Lubricants and other small-volume products for Roxana's entire marketing area continued to come from Wood River.[140]

Dominguez Refinery

Late in the summer of 1927, another new refinery started up at Dominguez in southern California. This plant should in reality have been called the cracking division of the Wilmington refinery. Eight Dubbs units had been put into operation at Wilmington early in 1926. By the methods of operation then in use (the low-level method was still to be evolved) these eight units were not adequate. More were needed—but where to put them? When the Wilmington refinery had been erected three years earlier, the company had purchased a 243-acre site, land enough for substantial expansion. Erection of huge crude oil reservoirs had however gobbled up much of the original tract, leaving almost no room for expansion. And now, because of the boom in the Los Angeles area, owners of the adjoining real estate were asking three times as much as in 1923.[141]

The company looked a little farther afield and finally chose a spot some three miles north of Wilmington, in the neighborhood of Dominguez, where Asiatic a few years earlier had erected a 40-acre tank farm to store its crude purchases. Shell of California bought this tank farm and a substantial amount of acreage surrounding it. The site for the contemplated new installation had to be spacious, for plans called for 12 rows of 8 Dubbs units, or 96 units in all. To start, the first row of eight units was erected, together with a Trumble unit to rerun the pressure distillate produced by the Dubbs units. This Trumble unit was ready in late August 1927, and the first of the Dubbs units started operation on September 1. Within the next month, the other seven cracking units and a unit for the continuous treating of products got into operation.[142]

The Dominguez refinery was never really a separate entity. Its cracking plants treated residue which came from the distilling units at Wilmington, pumped through pipes running along a right-of-way which connected the two plants. Other pipes carried steam, water, and products between the two plants; they were, in fact, as intimately connected as if they had been a single refinery. A separate managerial staff was not created. The refinery superintendent and refinery office at Wilmington sufficed for both plants. To supervise Dominguez operations on the spot, a new post was created, "assistant superintendent, Wilmington refinery, in charge of Dominguez refinery." At the time of the start of Dominguez operations, E. H. Schippers was refinery superintendent at Wilmington, A. E. Lacomblé assistant superintendent, and J. F. M. Taylor assistant superintendent in charge of Dominguez. In later years, the company officially designated this dual plant the Wilmington-Dominguez refinery; but in the Twenties, it was, for purposes of statistics, counted as two separate refineries. The 96 Dubbs units were never built. Soon after, the development of low-level cracking made it possible for a few units to do the work of many.

At Martinez, capacity was increased during the Twenties by the installation of additional Trumble units. By the end of 1929, Martinez had six of these units in operation, giving the refinery a crude intake of 42,000 barrels a day. The Edeleanu plant which Van Senden had come from Romania to build in 1915 was finally erected at Martinez in 1927. Soon after, a similar plant was put up at Wilmington. Kerosene purified by the Edeleanu method of solvent extraction was of high quality and met with a good sale. For a time during the late Twenties an "Edeleanu extract" was produced for blending with gasoline to make a premium-grade motor fuel.

With better automobile engines being developed, the need for better motor oils became increasingly apparent. The company could buy Pennsylvania oils and resell them under its own brand, or—a much more promising course—try to improve the motor oils it was making from the asphaltic-base California crude oils. Here the Edeleanu process once more proved its value. A chief shortcoming of California lubricants was that they were too viscous at low temperatures and not sufficiently viscous at high temperatures. This viscosity trouble could be corrected by removing some of the compounds responsible. The Edeleanu process, it was found, could remove 15% to 20% of these objectionable compounds.[143]

Meanwhile, experiments went forward at Martinez under G. A. Kramer, who had been hired to set up a motor laboratory. Kramer's work on improving motor oil properties led to the development of a high-vacuum distillation process which was patented under his name. To test the relative merits of the Kramer process on California crude oils, the company decided to build two high-vacuum lube oil distilling plants at Martinez, one to embody Kramer's process, the other to use the Schulze process which had recently been installed at Wood River. These plants went into operation late in 1925, and, although both were eventually supplanted by newer and better processes, at the time they made possible distinct improvements in the motor oils Shell manufactured in California.

Houston Refinery

Roxana's booming new West Texas fields required an outlet and the new marketing operations on the Atlantic Seaboard needed product. The result was Roxana's fourth refinery, located at Deer Park on the new Houston Ship Channel, some 18 miles east of the city of Houston. Here, on a square mile of land, the company during 1928 began construction of a modern, well-designed refinery. For once, the site was big enough; that it paid to buy sufficient land at the outset will not be questioned by anyone who has compared the clean, orderly layout of the Houston refinery with some of the older refineries built on inadequate plots.

R. B. High, who had superintended construction of Wood River and Norco, was placed in charge of construction at Houston, and when the refinery was finished, became its first superintendent.

Like Wilmington, Arkansas City, and East Chicago, Houston was a volume refinery, producing a relatively few products in quantity. Accordingly, its equipment was simple: three Badger topping units, similar to those at East Chicago, and six Dubbs cracking units. Two of the cracking units were designed for operation at low level, the other four for cracking to coke. The Houston refinery had at the start a capacity of 20,000 barrels a day.

To supply the Houston refinery, a 446-mile, 10-inch pipe line having nine stations and a capacity of 33,000 barrels a day was built from McCamey in West Texas to the refinery, and completed in April 1929. The first topping unit began operation on August 13, 1929. Other units were completed and put into operation soon after. Since it drew its crude supplies exclusively from the "sour" oils of West Texas, the Houston refinery was compelled to learn the intricacies of refining oil that was high in sulphur content. The special acid-resisting alloys required for the refining units and the additional labor and chemicals needed for the treatment of the products added to both the capital expense and operating costs.

Most of the Houston refinery's products were shipped out of the Gulf Coast area, either to the Atlantic Seaboard or to Group companies abroad. The remaining products (not a large amount) went to the Roxana sales department which began the sale of Shell gasoline in several areas of Texas in the fall of 1929 as soon as the refinery was completed.

Norco

The other "new" refinery of this period was the ten-year-old refinery of the New Orleans Refining Company, which Roxana acquired by purchase early in 1929. This refinery, some 24 miles up the Mississippi from New Orleans, had been completed in 1920 and High, who had built it, remained to manage it for most of the Twenties. During this period, Norco (as it was called from the initials of the company) had for the most part imported heavy Mexican crude, topped it to remove gasoline and kerosene, and blended the fuel cut with light distillates purchased and shipped in by tank car from the Mid-Continent. The heavy "bottoms" produced in the course of refining Mexican crude were converted into asphalt. Some of this asphalt found its way to the American market, chiefly through the Roxana organization, but the rest of Norco's products were shipped by tanker to Group companies abroad. As long as this arrangement lasted, it was only logical to have the operation under Asiatic's supervision. But by the late Twenties, the Group's requirements could be met by the newly enlarged Curaçao refinery and Mexican crude production, Norco's source of supply, had fallen sharply. The New Orleans refinery was beginning to draw a large proportion of its supplies from Gulf Coast sources.

At this point, with consideration being given to Shell's entry into the Gulf-South market, Shell executives entertained the idea of establishing a new southern Shell company, using the New Orleans Refining Company as a nucleus. This idea was discarded, as we have seen, but the idea of taking over the Norco refinery was not. Roxana's recent oil discoveries in Louisiana made a nearby refinery desirable, and the company's expanding sales activities throughout the South could absorb all the products that Norco made. By 1928, the refinery was processing about 15,000 barrels of crude a day and producing gasoline, kerosene, fuel oil, and asphalt. Asphalt production and sales were a unique and important part of the New Orleans Refining Company's activity.

In the years when the refinery had been owned by Asiatic, the export nature of its business had made the refinery the scene of two interesting process experiments, one of which was successful. The unsuccessful experiment, carried on at Norco from 1923 to 1926, was an attempt to use silica gel in petroleum refining to replace the conventional acid-soda treatment for removing impurities from kerosene. Mexican crude oil was rich in aromatics, not all of them removable by conventional methods; in consequence, it was difficult to refine it by traditional methods into kerosene of illuminating quality. Silica gel, a dry powder manufactured by the Davison Chemical Company of Baltimore, removed impurities by selective absorption and, unlike sulphuric acid or sulphur dioxide gas, did not have a corrosive effect on refinery equipment. For this reason, and because of its high degree of selectivity, great hopes were entertained for silica gel. The New Orleans Refining Company, and the Shell Group world-wide, contracted for its use. The trial units, all built at Norco, provided one disappointment after another. Operating expense was higher than had been anticipated, and the silica product also proved to have an erosive effect upon the interiors of the refining units. After thousands of dollars of expenditure and much heartbreaking experimental work at Norco, conducted under the supervision of Dr. William C. de Leeuw,* the silica gel process was finally abandoned as a failure. Attempts at Martinez to adapt silica gel to lubricating oil manufacture likewise ended in failure.[144]

Norco's successful experiment was the "stabilizing" of casinghead gasoline for shipment by tanker. In the Mid-Continent, Roxana during the Twenties acted as purchasing agent for Asiatic, buying and shipping to Norco as many as 3,000 tank car loads a month of casinghead gasoline. Here was an excellent example of the extra profit which can sometimes be earned by operating on an international scale. Casinghead, a left-over from the Mid-Continent, could be blended with heavy naphtha from Curaçao, another left-over, to make a saleable motor fuel for a third part of the world, Europe.

Because of the high volatility of "wild" (unstabilized) casinghead, it had never been successfully shipped in tankers. Evaporation caused

---

* Dr. de Leeuw returned to Holland in the late Twenties after the failure of his silica gel work. See also pages 246-247.

large losses, nullifying the profitability of tanker shipment, and vaporization made it dangerous to handle. At Norco, S. C. Carney, F. C. Cutting, and A. B. Culbertson collaborated on the design of a series of "stabilizing" columns, following the De Brey system of pressure rectification patented some years earlier by Bataafsche. A prototype of this system had been installed earlier in the Twenties at the Yarhola absorption plant at Healdton. These stabilizers, built at Norco in 1926, consisted of three pairs of bubble-tray fractionating columns. In operation, they stripped out the propane and butane, which (because they boiled far below room temperatures) were the main cause of casinghead gasoline's instability. The balance of the liquid left after stabilization could be successfully shipped in tankers. Then, in order not to waste the propane and butane which had been removed in the course of the stabilization process, quantities of the Curaçao heavy naphtha were brought to Norco and there blended with these very light products. The resulting mixture was a stable liquid which could also be shipped in tankers. Thus, the whole of the purchased casinghead eventually found its way across the Atlantic.[145]

This blending of gasoline and the manufacture of asphalt had by 1928 become Norco's main business. The physical equipment at the refinery was not extensive. There were four old Trumble units which were worked mainly for the production of asphalt;† one modern Badger unit built during 1928; two small Dubbs cracking units installed in the early years of that process; and three stabilizers for casinghead gasoline.[146] The company had its own small sales staff and offices in the Canal Bank Building, New Orleans, where the vice president and general manager, L. V. F. van Eeghen, made his headquarters.

During the fall of 1928, Roxana concluded arrangements for the outright purchase of the New Orleans Refining Company, as of the end of 1928, for $6,610,000.[147] In March 1929, Norco's business was taken over by Roxana and the refinery designated the "Norco" refinery. The village of Sellers, where the refinery was located, early in 1930 officially changed its name to Norco, Louisiana, serving as a reminder of the New Orleans Refining Company which was officially dissolved on December 30, 1929. P. E. Foster, who was managing the refinery at the time of the take-over, continued as superintendent. The New Orleans Refining Company offices in town

† Some of these units were still operating successfully in 1956.

became the new Southern marketing division of the St. Louis company.[148]

The refinery promptly set to work to install new gasoline manufacturing facilities so that it might serve as a source of supply to the nearby marketing territory. By the end of 1929, two new Badger units had been built at Norco, capable of handling a crude intake of 17,000 barrels a day, and four large new Dubbs units had been built and put into operation. For the moment, most of the refinery's crude oil supplies came from West Texas via pipe line to the Houston Ship Channel and thence by barge. About 15,000 barrels of crude a day were supplied to Norco in this manner during 1929.

For the first years of its operation, Shell Eastern met most of its gasoline requirements by blending naphtha with casinghead gasoline. The naphthas, chiefly from Curaçao, were shipped by ocean tanker to the Fall River, Sewaren, Baltimore, and Wilmington, North Carolina, terminals. At the terminals it was a relatively simple matter to blend naphtha with casinghead gasoline. They were mixed in large tanks and then the contents of the tank were recirculated by pumps to assure a thorough mixture. The casinghead for these operations came from the Mid-Continent, shipped at first in railroad tank cars, a relatively expensive method. Then, as soon as arrangements could be made, casinghead for Shell Eastern was stabilized at Norco and shipped to the East Coast terminals via a chartered tanker, the *General Markham*. Smaller quantities of naphtha also came in by tanker from the Houston and West Coast refineries, and occasionally cargoes of gasoline were purchased from Shell in California. Shell Eastern's kerosene came from the new Edeleanu plants at Martinez and Wilmington; most of its heavy fuels from Curaçao; its lubricating oils were shipped in from Wood River by tank car.[149]

Shell at High Tide

THE new names, the new faces in the executive ranks, the sparkling new office quarters of the Shell companies were all by late 1929 helping to give a public impression of the growth and prosperity of the American Shell Companies.

Both the Pacific Coast and Mid-Continent companies had changed their names late in 1928. These changes, which made little difference within the organization, originated from a desire to associate the companies' names more closely with the brand name of the products they were selling. On the West Coast, members of the San Francisco management had long objected to the absence of any word which would indicate the nature of the company's business in the title Shell Company of California; in addition, Fisher and his sales staff in the Northwest objected to the "of California" and, wherever they could, dropped the offending words completely. For these reasons, late in 1928 the name of the San Francisco company was changed to Shell Oil Company, effective January 1, 1929. In St. Louis, Roxana, with a name not even remotely associated with the brand name of its products, had even more cogent reasons for changing. On October 10, 1928, Roxana issued an announcement that its name had been changed and would thereafter be Shell Petroleum Corporation.[150]

Constant expansion of the American Shell organization, and the maturing of executives who only a few years before had been young and relatively inexperienced men, gave rise to a number of promotions which by late 1929 had appreciably changed the faces in the executive ranks.

First of all, Deterding, who had been president of Shell Union since shortly after its formation in 1922, moved up to the position of chairman of the board in May 1924, allowing Van Eck to assume the presidency of Shell Union. Then, in 1928, almost at the same time that Roxana changed its name to Shell Petroleum, Godber, who had been president of that company for nearly seven years, was called back to London and appointed a managing director of the Group's main operating companies.‡ His successor in St. Louis was

‡ He was knighted in 1942, and with the retirement of the second Lord Bearsted from The "Shell" Transport & Trading Company, Ltd., in 1946, Sir Frederick succeeded him as chairman. Ten years later, in the New Year's Honors List, Sir Frederick was raised to the peerage, and took the title Baron Godber of Mayfield in the County of Sussex.

Ulrick de B. Daly, a young executive who had held positions with the Group in other parts of the world and who had since early 1928 been a vice president of the St. Louis company.

At about this same time, both the Mid-Continent and West Coast companies, in recognition of the increased size of their organizations, began the appointment of vice presidents to head up each of their main operating departments. In March 1928, Dr. W. van Holst Pellekaan, Roxana's chief geologist, was appointed vice president in charge of exploration; George S. Rollin, who had come up through the ranks in the company's production department, became vice president in charge of production; and G. G. Woodruff, who had been sales manager, was made vice president in charge of sales. Later the same year, Dr. F. W. L. Tydeman, who had managed the Wood River refinery since it started operation in 1918, was made manager of a newly created manufacturing department in the St. Louis office and at the end of 1929 was elected vice president in charge of manufacturing.

On the West Coast, William Reinhardt was named vice president in charge of production § at the beginning of 1928, and Dr. E. F. Davis vice president in charge of geology early in 1929. G. H. van Senden, who had managed the Martinez refinery since it went on stream, was in 1928 placed in charge of a newly created manufacturing unit in the San Francisco office and, like his counterpart in St. Louis, was made a vice president at the end of 1929. Herbert Gallagher, who had been Shell of California's vice president in charge of sales since 1914, late in 1928 took over the job of setting up the new Shell Development and Shell Chemical companies, becoming president of both. E. L. Miller, who had been with the company since its early days, was made vice president of marketing in Gallagher's place. In the spring of 1929, Woodruff in St. Louis resigned as sales vice president and Miller was installed as his successor. A few months later, in October 1929, Gallagher resumed his old job as vice president of Shell Oil in San Francisco.

In both companies the treasurer also held the office of vice president, John Lauder at San Francisco from 1920 onwards, T. F. Lydon at St. Louis from 1922. Lauder and Lydon were both men of marked

§ Not a new position on the West Coast. The company had created this position at the time the Union of Delaware properties were taken over in 1922. Paul Paine, formerly associated with Union, served from June 1922 to June 1923, and had been succeeded by W. C. McDuffie who held the job until July 1926.

ability. These abilities brought them vice-presidential titles at an early date, and a decisive voice in their companies' affairs. In both companies, the office of vice president and treasurer was next to the president's in authority. For most of the Twenties, matters such as personnel policy were under the vice president and treasurer, together with other functions that would later be assigned to specialized departments as the companies grew.

The staffs of both companies had grown immensely during the Twenties and both organizations were early confronted with the problem of providing more office space. Roxana's space in the Arcade Building, St. Louis, had been ample at the time of the move from Tulsa in 1919. But the company's offices were already overcrowded in 1923 when the first marketing division offices were set up, and additional space for them had to be engaged in the Republic Building. Overcrowding continued to worsen; the company's staff was still increasing at a rapid rate, and there were no suitable quarters where the entire Roxana organization might be housed. Late in 1924, the company decided to put up its own office building and purchased a desirable corner at 13th and Olive Streets, facing on a small park. There a twelve-story building, quarter-round in shape, having 130,000 square feet of floor space and costing more than a million dollars, was erected during 1925.[151] It was called from the first the Shell Building, or more popularly, "Shell Corner." Roxana moved into this handsome new head office on January 1, 1926.*

In San Francisco, office congestion was no less severe. In 1919, the company had abandoned its quarters in the Security Building, 343 Sansome Street, and taken five floors of the old Standard Oil Building at 200 Bush Street.[152] These quarters, increased by the taking of additional floors, sufficed until the late Twenties. In the spring of 1929, Shell Oil bought a well-located plot, at the junction of Bush, Battery, and Market Streets in downtown San Francisco, and announced its intention of putting up the finest office building in the city, a 29-story Gothic shaft, finished in terra cotta. Legh-Jones placed H. H. Anderson, who had already demonstrated his versatility and capacity for hard work, in full charge of the project. The new Shell building, which cost $4¼ million complete, was finished and occupied in ten months, nearly a month ahead of schedule. It was

---

* Roxana Investment Corporation, a wholly owned subsidiary, was organized in Delaware, November 26, 1924, to build and own the St. Louis Shell Building which cost approximately $1,140,000.

ahead of its time in design: office walls were sectional units which could be taken apart and reassembled overnight; each office had its own thermostat for controlling the heat to suit the occupant; the building was equipped throughout with a pneumatic tube system to eliminate carrying about by hand all but the most bulky mail; and a garage annex was provided with parking space for nearly 200 automobiles.[153]

More than any other physical thing, the Shell Building in San Francisco symbolized the high tide of Shell's affairs in America. The building was—and still is—a prominent feature of the San Francisco skyline, particularly at night with its full length bathed in golden-yellow floodlight. It was more than a physically conspicuous office structure. It spoke eloquently of a company that had been absolutely unknown to America twenty years before and was now a very sizeable factor in the American oil business and one of the country's great industrial enterprises.

Tacit acknowledgement of the Shell companies' new importance was an invitation to Deterding to address the American Petroleum Institute's tenth annual meeting held in Chicago early in December 1929. His speech, called "Common Sense in the Petroleum Industry," was typical of the man, blunt and straightforward and not particularly pleasing to many of his competitors who were having their first look at him.

Then, before returning to Europe, Deterding took a leisurely swing around the United States to see at first hand the remarkable progress the Shell companies had made in the decade now ending. Less than twenty years before, all of it had been only an ambitious dream in the back of his mind. Now he visited three sizeable operating subsidiaries, with oil-producing properties in almost every producing region of the country. That year, they had produced some 47,000,000 barrels of oil, manufactured more than 180,000,000 gallons of casinghead gasoline, and run 290,000 barrels of crude a day through nine refineries to make more than a billion and a quarter gallons of gasoline. Only two long-established companies, Standard of New Jersey and Standard of Indiana, were larger refiners than the American Shell companies.[154] And that was not all—the new Shell companies had their own marketing facilities to sell this gasoline: 1,000 depots, 1,800 trucks, and more than 30,000 Shell pumps scattered through every state of the Union.

Most of all, Deterding was pleased with the Shell employees he met—intelligent, hard-working, energetic Americans, nearly 35,000 strong, proud of their company and proud of the part they had had in building it. He sat down and penned them a New Year's greeting: [155]

> In the short time that I have been here the topic of conversation is the great strides the Shell Union has made not only in production for which great and deserved credit is due to our splendid Production Department but also to the marvelous organization which places Shell products within the easiest reach of everybody in the [United] States. Credit for this can only be due to our splendid staff of salesmen and their organization; it is a fine achievement to rouse competitors to imitation, which is the greatest compliment of your competitor, the man who can judge you better than anybody.
>
> I really feel proud of our great Shell Union and thankful to its personnel for what they have achieved in such a short time against such great odds. Three times hurrah and a hundred times Thanks.
>
> Yours,
>
> DETERDING

CHAPTER VII

Depression and Deficit

1930–1935

O N April 16, 1930, Sir Henri Deterding stood atop the shining new 29-story Shell Building in San Francisco and watched his Lady raise a new flag on a new mast. The band played the Star-Spangled Banner, and Sir Henri led the guests in three cheers.[1] They had opened the new Shell Building. But the new building, although most of the guests didn't realize it, was a monument not to the beginning but to the end of an era. In seventeen years, the Shell organization in America had grown from a few small bulk depots in the Pacific Northwest and a few thousand barrels a day of crude oil production in Oklahoma to a major producer of oil, a sizeable refiner, and one of the nation's leading marketers with service stations everywhere. In fact, Shell Union and The Texas Company were the only oil companies operating in all 48 states. Here was an accomplishment for which Deterding could praise his men, as he had in his New Year's greeting, and for which he himself could have taken (although he didn't) a large measure of credit.

Here, too, was a point in the growth of any corporation where it would be wise to pause for a moment, to analyze and consolidate operations after a decade of hurried expansion. Shell Union had three main operating companies, one each for the West Coast, the Mid-Continent, and the Atlantic Seaboard, in addition to two producing subsidiaries, Comar and Wolverine, in Oklahoma. Logically all should have been one company. The many moves which finally brought about this amalgamation will be the central story of the next two chapters.

It is doubtful whether the Shell officials present at the dedication of the new Shell building thought they would be spending the better part of the decade in modernizing, consolidating, cleaning house, and in general putting their companies on a firmer footing. But if such intentions had been their sole program, they had the times on their side. In the outside world here and abroad, a major economic depression was getting under way and would force them to trim sails whether they would or no.

Not quite six months before, on October 24, 1929, had come the famous Black Thursday of Wall Street, when the roaring, ever-rising big bull market of 1928–1929 slipped, tottered, and with a deafening crash came tumbling to the ground. A foolhardy, extremely contagious wave of public over-optimism had in six months driven stock prices to undreamed-of heights. Now, just as quickly, public sentiment reversed itself. Quickly mounting, panicky pessimism developed overnight and in a matter of days brought an end to the boom, an end to the Golden Twenties, and the beginning of long years of financial distress that would affect every facet of American life from the humblest individual to the largest corporation.

The shock of the spectacular stock market collapse brought to general attention a number of unhealthy economic symptoms that hitherto had been overlooked in the wave of stock market optimism. But to blame the Great Depression upon the crash of 1929 would be to attribute a flood to the giving way of the last weak, water-soaked piece of levee. The causes of the depression lay farther back.[2]

From its earliest days as a nation up until 1914, America had relied on European financial centers for money for new capital investment. Stocks and bonds of American railroads, of new industrial enterprises in the North and Midwest, and bonds of state and municipal governments were subscribed in large part by the financial markets of London, Paris, Amsterdam, and Berlin. These European centers were glad to place their money favorably and to take their interest payments in the form of goods which America had to offer: raw cotton from the South, wheat and other grains from the West. With the outbreak of World War I and the involvement of all the large European nations, America found itself in the unique position of being the chief manufacturing and mercantile nation at peace and able to trade with the whole world. The warring European countries needed large quantities of American manufactures, in addition to the foodstuffs and raw materials they had formerly taken. To pay for these purchases, the belligerent governments forced their nationals to sell the American securities they owned and, when these were gone, other securities which represented much of Europe's investment in South America. In the short space of two to three years the United States paid off its debt to Europe (at discounts of up to 40%), acquired holdings in Latin America, and, still making money, was able to lend some eleven and a half billion dollars to Europe during the last year of the war and the immediate postwar period.

A complete reversal of America's position had taken place. A debtor nation for generations, it had become a creditor, and in so short a time that most Americans failed utterly to comprehend their country's new place in the world. This failure to understand the economic facts of life was, from 1920 onwards, one of the chief factors aggravating the unhappy state of world fiscal affairs.

Everybody agreed that Europe should pay its debts to us but American bankers, in their new-found position of lenders, wanted to place money abroad, increasing all the more the total of foreign debt. The farmers of the West believed they should continue to export their wheat, just as the South was determined to do with cotton. Yet almost everyone favored not only retaining but increasing the already high tariffs. In 1921, egged on by organized labor afraid of competition from "cheap foreign labor" and by businessmen who entertained similar fears of goods manufactured in Europe, Congress passed an "emergency" increase in the tariff rates. The next year, a broad upward revision in the tariff was made.

Unable to pay in goods, as America had been allowed to do during the years when she was a debtor nation, the European countries undertook to meet their obligations by the export of gold to this country, thereby weakening their own currencies. To meet their heavy reparations payments, Austria and Germany even shipped abroad the gold which had served as backing for their currencies, and serious monetary crises resulted during 1922–1923. Both countries suffered so heavily from inflation that their currencies became useless, and new ones had to be substituted. Following this came a movement to get the Western World back on the gold standard. This stabilizing of currencies, desirable though it was, brought a gradual deflation of commodity prices from the mid-Twenties onward.

Meanwhile, America had been in and out of a postwar depression. Following the Armistice, a tremendous inflationary boom started. Prices soared out of sight, and commodities reached extremely high peaks in the spring of 1920. Then came a quick break in prices, and a depression of about a year's duration, from mid-1920 to mid-1921. Business improved during 1922 and soon was booming again, although prices were now more reasonable. The big Twenties boom was now under way. Building, both for business and residential purposes, went forward on an unprecedented scale. Durable goods— machines, machine tools, and consumer goods such as automobiles and radios—were turned out in unprecedented quantities.

The industrial boom of the Twenties was outstanding for its large-scale production. Technological improvements were making it possible for one man to produce more, and thereby lower the unit price of most manufactured goods. At the same time, food prices not only remained stable but actually declined as a result of tremendous farm surpluses. This new combination of decreasing food prices and low prices for manufactured goods, unaccompanied by a reduction in wages, did, in truth, make it seem that a new era had at last arrived. The average man had money to spend for things other than the bare essentials of life. Nowhere was this better reflected than in the purchase of automobiles. During the five years just prior to 1930, nearly 19,000,000 automobiles were made and sold—a number of automobiles equal to the total number on the road in 1925. The year 1929 alone saw 4,587,000 new passenger cars produced, a production record which remained unsurpassed for twenty years.

Then, in 1930, automobile manufacture, a sensitive index of the Twenties' prosperity, dropped by nearly one-half as national income fell sharply. Industrial output in general declined by 28%, and all over the country banks began to fail as a result of the decreased value of their chief holdings, commercial paper and loans on real estate. In 1930 alone, more than a thousand banking institutions closed their doors. How many more would close, how severe the Great Depression would become, no one, mercifully, could foresee.

Money from the American Market

DURING the months of financial stress which lay ahead, the American Shell companies were to find themselves in a vulnerable position. Like many others who had expanded rapidly during the late Twenties, the Shell companies were now faced with reduced markets, sharply reduced prices, high depreciation charges arising from the high prices they had paid for their facilities, and a large amount of long-term debt at relatively high rates of interest. Most corporations financed their expansion programs during the Twenties by issuing stock and borrowing money. In this respect, the Shell companies were no exception. The debt they had thus accumulated was to loom large in the years ahead. It will perhaps be appropriate here to examine briefly the methods that Shell Union, which was responsible for matters such as finance, used to raise the large sums needed by its subsidiaries during the 1920's.

Hardly had Shell Union been organized when new money was needed. Six millions were needed for the purchase of the preferred stock of Central Petroleum Company (Wolverine) under the option which Shell Union had elected to exercise; other millions were needed for new oilfield development and the building of the Wilmington and Arkansas City refineries. In May 1922, not quite three months after organization of the new company, Shell Union sold $20,000,000 of "Series A" preferred stock, bearing 6% interest and callable at 110.* But $20 million was a drop in the bucket to ambitious young companies like Roxana and the Shell Company of California. In 1923, with both Roxana and Shell of California building new refineries and expanding their sales activity, more money was needed. To provide $20,000,000 more for new capital expenditures, the remaining 2,000,000 shares of common stock, authorized but not issued, were that year sold at $10 a share. In 1924, the directors arranged to sell Shell Union's holding of Union Oil of California stock for nearly $30,000,000. In two years, the American financial market thus provided Shell Union with some $70,000,000 of operating capital.

The facilities provided by this new working capital were respon-

---

* The "call price" of a security is the per cent of face value which the issuing company agrees to pay in the event that it elects to redeem, or "call," a long-term issue prior to the scheduled maturity date.

sible for making the next three years the most profitable in Shell Union's brief history. The company showed a profit in 1924 of $24,560,000; of $23,216,000 in 1925; and in 1926, with Tonkawa production at its peak, $36,519,000. During these three years $13,800,-000 was set aside out of net earnings as a special reserve; $44,000,000 was paid out in dividends; and the balance, some $40,000,000, was retained for investment in the business.

By 1927, the industry's success in finding and producing crude oil was beginning to have noticeable effects. Every year since 1922, more crude oil had been produced than could be handled by America's refineries and the products which were refined were in excess of the market demand. As a result, large amounts of unsold crude oil and gasoline began to pile up in storage. This situation continued to worsen and by 1927 had reached really alarming proportions. By the end of that year, crude oil stocks above ground totalled 380,000,000 barrels, more than one-third the year's production, and the gasoline manufactured was 1,437,000,000 gallons in excess of demand. The oil business as a whole was headed for trouble.

Shell's fat profits of 1924–1926 disappeared in 1927. Although the volume of sales made by the Shell Union subsidiaries increased more than 10%, money receipts from these sales dropped from 149 to 140 million dollars, and profit for the year slid from $36,500,000 in 1926 to $11,000,000 for 1927. Dividends were paid at the rate of 1925, but to do so it was necessary to dip into surplus for $3,000,000. New money for expansion obviously was not to be had from retained profits as had been the case during the past three years.

At this point the directors, if they had been at the helm of an organization other than an oil company, would probably have sought to issue additional common stock. But the stock market, bullish about so many other businesses, looked with a jaundiced eye at low-paying oil issues. The average profit of 400 representative industrial companies during 1927 was 9.4% of their net worth; the comparable figure for 24 leading oil companies was 4.9%, or just about half. It was probably for this reason that the stocks of most oil companies did not participate in the big bull market of the late Twenties. While shares of companies in other lines of business doubled, trebled, and even quadrupled in value, demand for oil shares kept a sober course.

Another method of raising funds had to be adopted. In May 1927, Shell Union sold its first debenture bond issue, $50,000,000 worth of 5% twenty-year bonds. Some $16,965,000 was spent out of the receipts of this $50,000,000 issue to redeem the "Series A" preferred stock still outstanding; the remainder went chiefly to finance Roxana's large program of new capital expenditures. Then in November of the same year, Shell Pipe Line Corporation sold $30,000,000 of 5% twenty-five-year bonds, with Shell Union guaranteeing both interest and principal. The proceeds of the Shell Pipe Line issue were used to build the new McCamey–Cushing and Wood River–East Chicago crude oil lines, with some unexpended balance being left over for future construction.

In 1928, construction was started on the new refinery at Houston, negotiations were under way for the purchase of a large share of The Flintkote Company and for the purchase of the New England Oil Refining Company, and the mammoth marketing expansion of the late Twenties continued to roll on. Clearly more money was needed. Oil shares had gone up a bit and were now slightly more in favor. During 1928, 3,000,000 additional shares of common stock were authorized and sold at $10 a share to bring in $30,000,000 of new money. As with the previous issue of additional common shares, stockholders were given the privilege of subscribing for the new shares on a pro-rata basis in accordance with the amounts of stock they already held. In both cases, the Group elected to exercise this option, so that the percentage of its holding in Shell Union remained unchanged.

During 1929, with new expenditures in all departments at a peak, it became evident that still more money was needed. The profit of the previous year had been better than that of 1927, but after dividends were paid only six million dollars were left over. The Shell Union management decided upon a new issue of preferred stock to raise the necessary funds. The speculative market of 1929 favored common stocks. To insure ready sale of $40,000,000 of Shell Union preferred stock, which was issued in June 1929, the terms of the issue provided that each preferred share might be converted to $3\frac{1}{3}$ shares of common stock at $30 any time before July 1, 1932, or 2.85 shares at $35 thereafter until July 1, 1935, when the option expired. This preferred issue bore $5\frac{1}{2}$% interest and was callable at 105.

Then, late in 1929, just as the big financial storm was breaking, the Shell Union directors decided to borrow an additional $50,000,000 by means of a bond issue floated at 5% on October 1, 1929. A concession was made to prospective purchasers by offering the bonds with stock purchase warrants attached, permitting the holder of each $1,000 bond to purchase 25 shares of Shell Union common stock at $35 a share any time within the next ten years.

Here, in summary, are the amounts and sources of new money which went into Shell Union during the 1920's:

SHELL UNION OIL CORPORATION FINANCING, 1922–1929

1922	Series A preferred stock (redeemed in 1927, therefore not counted)		
1923	Additional common stock		$ 20,000,000
1924	Receipts from Union Oil of California stock		30,000,000
1927	Shell Union bonds		50,000,000
1927	Shell Pipe Line bonds		30,000,000
1928	New Common Stock		30,000,000
1929	5½% Preferred Stock		40,000,000
1929	Shell Union bonds		50,000,000
	Profits 1922–1929	$160,066,000	
	Dividends paid 1922–1929	102,758,000	
	Retained and invested in the business		57,308,000
		Total	$307,308,000

This large sum, all raised from the New York financial markets, represented in the main American capital. The chief exception was the case of the new common issues, where the Group was entitled to purchase 65%, or some $32,500,000, of this new stock as it was issued. A number of private European investors also bought bonds in 1927 and 1929 and shares of the 1929 preferred stock, just as they purchased securities of other American companies. But the bulk of this new money, some $265,000,000, was furnished by American investors.

Responsibility for providing finance rested with Van Eck in New York, and credit for Shell Union's astute financial management during this period was due largely to him and his fellow directors, a number of whom were members of New York financial houses. The advice of F. W. Allen, one of these "outside" directors, was especially helpful; and it was Allen's firm, Lee, Higginson & Co., which marketed the company's securities.

In the Red

SHELL entered the depression with an organization built on the crest of a boom at boom prices. In consequence, the company would for the next several years be saddled with high depreciation charges. Much of the money which had paid for this expansion would in itself also prove expensive, for it had been borrowed at bull-market interest rates. In 1930, the company had outstanding some $166,000,-000 in interest-guaranteed securities which that year cost $9,000,000 in bond interest and preferred stock dividends. In the bleak years ahead, Shell would be handicapped by these high depreciation rates and high debt-service charges.

For the first few months of the depression, the momentum of the great expansion year 1929 kept the Shell organization going full tilt. In the Midwest, the marketing department was being enlarged on such a broad front that a halt could not be called abruptly and along the Atlantic Seaboard the job of building the company was still unfinished. In both areas, construction of new service stations and bulk depots continued through the initial months of the depression, and wheels did not begin to grind to a halt until the fall of 1930.[3]

As far as sales went, 1930 was a fairly good year. In spite of the depression, the nation-wide demand for gasoline was up by 800,-000,000 gallons, and Shell with its large number of new outlets had to refine more gasoline than ever before—1,364,000,000 gallons, an increase of 53,000,000 gallons over 1929. But this increased volume of sales brought a much smaller return in dollars. When accounts for 1930 were in, they showed a net deficit of more than five million dollars.

At the prospect of impending deficit, the Shell Union directors voted in mid-1930 to omit dividends on the common stock. Although it hadn't been privileged to enjoy the rising prices of the big bull market, Shell stock thereafter joined the market as it fell. Before 1930 was out, Shell Union common had hit a low of 5¼.† The new preferred stock, issued at 100 less than a year before, dropped to 55 and the three bond issues slumped to between 70% and 80% of their face value.

† Nearly double the low of 2½ during 1931 and 1932.

But 1930 was only an uneasy breeze before the hurricane. Hopeful signs of recovery apparent in late 1930 and early 1931 vanished as the whole financial structure of Central Europe suddenly collapsed in the spring of 1931. This catastrophe, a result largely of the terms imposed upon the defeated nations by the Versailles Treaty, touched off a new wave of financial panic. In the United States, economic conditions quickly worsened, and soon almost every business was in the grip of the worst depression anyone could remember.

On top of all this, the oil business had special problems of its own. With the crude oil market already grievously oversupplied and prices falling rapidly, the tremendous East Texas field was brought in. At once a new oil boom was on, with fearful repercussions. During July 1931, crude oil dropped below 20 cents a barrel throughout the Mid-Continent. With crude at half its 1930 price level, the retail price of gasoline fell by an average of four cents a gallon nationally. In some places, markets collapsed completely and gasoline was sold for less than cost. A new figure, spawn of his times, the "gasoline bootlegger," appeared on the scene. Margins, if there were any, had by now become so narrow that some "tea-kettle" refiners tried to make a profit by deliberate evasion of gasoline taxes, which by 1931 had grown to a figure of four cents a gallon on a national average.‡ During 1931, twenty leading oil companies showed a net deficit of $96,000,000, or minus 1.6% of their net worth, compared to a 2.7% profit that year by the rest of American industry.

In this 1931 debacle, Shell was one of the heaviest losers. That year Shell Union had a net operating deficit of $27,000,000, more than one-quarter of the total deficit run up by the twenty leading oil

‡ Gasoline excise taxes, collected from the motorist by the service station operator, had their origin on the Pacific Coast in the years immediately following World War I. At first, there was little objection to them, for the levies were small and the states which collected such taxes were spending as much, or more, on road construction. During the Twenties this tax spread rapidly and increased in amount; by 1929 all forty-eight states had gasoline taxes. With the advent of the depression, states which did not have laws to prevent such practices began diverting receipts from the gasoline tax to other purposes. In many sections of the country, counties and municipalities also enacted gasoline taxes of their own, and in mid-1932 the Federal government enacted a cent-a-gallon gasoline tax. To resist further encroachment of the taxing authorities, the American Petroleum Institute in 1932 set up a permanent American Petroleum Industries Committee to combat by public education further attempts to tax gasoline. The A.P.I.C. sought to bring home to the public the desirability of tax laws that would prevent diversion of gasoline tax funds to non-highway purposes, a principle which has since gained wide acceptance, although the legislatures of about half the states have yet to write it into law.

companies, and the largest deficit of any of the majors. Why was Shell singled out for losses heavier than those of its competitors? Why were those losses so large, larger than the profits of some of the best years of the Twenties?

An important reason was that the Shell companies in America were relative newcomers. Shell Petroleum had been in the retail field only eight years and Shell Eastern a scant two years. As newcomers during a time of high real estate and building costs, they had paid well for their properties and this now meant overhead and amortization charges much larger than those of competitors who had been longer in the market. In the Midwest, Shell was up against companies like Standard Oil of Ohio, founded in 1870, and Standard of Indiana, in business since 1889, both of them blanketing their territories. In the East, Shell Eastern was confronted by several companies which had been in business long before Royal Dutch or Shell was even thought of: Socony, Standard of New Jersey, and Atlantic Refining Company. Having been in business for a great many years, these companies had already amortized most of their capital investment, which meant that their annual fixed charges consumed a lower percentage of their incomes than Shell's. Again because of long establishment, the older companies generally enjoyed much larger volume and this meant lower unit operating costs.

In the face of these losses, Shell Union resisted the temptation to improve the picture by changing the rules in the middle of the game. It did not, as many of its competitors did, reduce the rate of its depreciation write-offs, or eliminate large items of future depreciation by charging off, in a recapitalization scheme, millions of dollars of capital assets. This adherence to established depreciation policy cost the company millions of dollars in years when it could have cut or eliminated its losses by following the example of competitors.[4]

This insistence upon sticking to established depreciation policy showed markedly in the income statement for 1931. All three Shell companies lost money that year. Shell Oil Company in San Francisco, the best established of the three, was able to report a relatively small loss of $1,750,000. Shell Eastern, still new and doing a comparatively small business, lost $6,275,000. Shell Petroleum in the Mid-Continent reported a really alarming deficit, $33,850,000. Together the operating deficits of the three companies totalled nearly $42 million, a figure which was reduced by Shell Pipe Line's earnings of nearly $15,000,000.§

By dint of much hard work, the whopping deficit of 1931 was turned into a small profit of $660,000 in 1932. But 1933 and 1934 brought continued low prices and further deficits for Shell Union— $4,240,000 in 1933 and $1,353,000 in 1934. Shell Union's net losses for the five years 1930–1934 came to $37,000,000 and would have run much higher had not Shell Pipe Line continued to pay substantial dividends and Shell Oil Company on the Pacific Coast showed a profit from 1932 onwards. The Pacific Coast earnings and the pipe line dividends were extremely important to Shell Union during these years of distress for they helped offset Shell Petroleum's heavy deficits which totalled, during these five years, $104,490,000.

Retrenchment

In every area, plugging the leaks became the order of the day. First, insofar as possible, an end was put to new capital expenditure. In 1929, that amount had approximated $100,000,000; two years later, it had been reduced to $16,605,000. Construction was halted at refineries; the building of more depots and new service stations was stopped; drilling activity, already on the decline in 1929, was sharply curtailed. In this manner, further large expenditures were forestalled; only in crucial cases did construction proceed. Even then, soul-searching inquiry preceded each outlay of cash: Was the expenditure justifiable in times of such cheap oil?

Rather than incur drilling expenses which would eat into the money on hand, leases that had cost $4,000,000 to acquire were surrendered in 1930. During 1931, other leases representing double this amount, $8,043,000, were likewise allowed to lapse. Even so, Shell Petroleum alone found it imperative, because of competitive conditions, to spend almost $6,000,000 that year in developing its producing properties. Where possible, the company attempted to farm out acreage instead of doing the drilling called for in its leases. Under a farm-out arrangement, the company turned its lease over to another operator, retaining for itself only an overriding royalty interest. In the East Texas field, the chief locale of drilling activity in 1931, Shell Petroleum completed 221 wells on its own,

§ Since Shell Pipe Line's earnings were derived largely from Shell Petroleum's patronage, the reader can if he wishes apply these earnings against Shell Petroleum's deficit, which would then be reduced to about $19,000,000.

farmed out another 108. Some large expenditures, however, had to be made in the interest of economy. One of these was the construction of a 191-mile, 10-inch pipe line from the East Texas field to the Houston refinery, completed in 1931.

This period of low crude prices saw a marked increase in the company's purchases of crude oil. The purchases had a thrice-beneficial effect in that they (1) helped bolster crude prices in the industry, (2) provided Shell with crude as cheaply as it could have produced its own, and (3) kept the company's crude oil reserves in storage below ground against the time when prices would be better. Shell's own production in 1930 was only 28% of its estimated potential, and about two-thirds of actual production the year before; by 1931, Shell's own production was only 16% of potential.[5] In 1930, crude purchases exceeded Shell's own production by a million and a half barrels.

The prime interest of Shell Union during this critical period was to conserve cash, even at the expense of passing up attractive opportunities for investment. No one knew how long the depression would last; already it had lasted far longer than anyone had expected. Under Van Eck's prudent management every effort was bent towards maintaining a large bank balance, for axiomatic though it may be, no company can go broke with money in the bank. But without ample fluid assets, large and intrinsically sound concerns may totter in a time of crisis.

Shell Union entered the depression with $58,700,000 cash on hand and in short-term and demand loans, most of it the product of the $50,000,000 bond issue of September 1929. By the end of 1930, with the depression just getting under way, the cash balance had slipped to $25,400,000. During the next year, every effort was made to improve this position, and despite the disastrous events of that year the ready money on hand at the end of 1931 totalled $36,-850,000.*

To achieve this position was costly. A great many of the leases which Shell surrendered rather than drill would no doubt have proved of enormous value, and in one case properties of substantial worth were forfeited in East Texas. Pressed to improve his company's cash

* Preoccupation with maintaining a sound cash position was not confined to Shell Union. During 1931, the Royal Dutch-Shell Group of companies world-wide made every effort to conserve cash. The Royal Dutch Company's annual report for 1931 took the highly unusual step of listing the cash resources of each principal subsidiary, a total of some 343 million florins, equivalent at the time to $137,000,000.

position, Daly, president of the St. Louis company, took the opportunity to sell several hundred acres of leases in East Texas, making a profit on them and eliminating the necessity for meeting drilling obligations. The wisdom of disposing of this potentially valuable acreage soon became a subject of dispute, and Daly resigned in April 1931. With the benefit of hindsight, it is easy to condemn a policy that hoarded cash while passing up bargains in oil-producing properties in a day when bargains could be had. However, it is well to recollect the spirit of the times and remember that large and seemingly prosperous business concerns all over the world were failing for lack of fluid assets. It is also well to remark that this experience made a lasting impression on a whole generation of Shell men, who would without doubt follow a somewhat different course if again faced with similar circumstances.

Besides eliminating new expenditures, current operations had to be trimmed. This was done by a long series of economy committees, who started work almost at the outset of the depression and continued all through the worst of it. The first of these economy committees was set up on the Pacific Coast in June 1930, with Anderson as chairman. Legh-Jones instructed each vice president to examine his department and curtail all non-essential activity and staff. The economy committee was assigned the job of making independent studies of each department and proposing, with the concurrence of the vice president concerned, definite suggestions for rearrangement of work and reduction of staff. As a result, total personnel was reduced 32% by the end of the year, from 11,955 on February 1, 1930, to 8,130 December 31. In the sales department, for instance, it was found that by relieving salesmen of extraneous duties such as managing depots and routing trucks, an increased number of sales could be made with a substantially reduced sales force.[6]

In St. Louis, a Central Economy Committee was set up in October 1930 with Fraser as chairman. In each of the operating and staff departments, subsidiary economy committees were set up to study in detail the operations of the department. The work performed by the department was carefully analyzed, with particular attention being paid to areas where it overlapped the work of other departments. Every effort was directed toward elimination of this duplication and overlapping, either by transferring such work entirely to one department, or, where possible, by consolidating departments. In these analyses, organization charts were prepared which showed the

name and position of each employee, with a full description of his
duties. The departmental committees were asked to recommend all
possible economies, including the simplification and elimination of
work then being done and the reduction of departmental staffs.[7]

With the advent of more serious economic conditions during 1931,
the work of these economy committees was intensified, and the entire
organization from top to bottom was subjected to rigorous self-
examination. As a result, some quite drastic economies were put
into effect.

In exploration, large money savings were realized by the simple
expedient of virtually ceasing operations. With a large overproduction of crude oil plaguing the industry, and daily getting worse instead
of better, the economy committees saw little sense in continuing the
hunt for more oil—especially when the company was being pressed
to conserve every cent of cash. Accordingly, exploratory crews were
laid off wholesale, and for several months during the worst of the
depression only a skeleton of Shell Petroleum's exploration staff remained on the payroll.[8] In the production department, drilling almost
ceased and drilling crews were laid off one after the other. By 1932,
if it had not been for the development of East Texas, there would
have been almost no drilling crews working.

In the refineries, only limited economies were possible, for even
in the expansionist Twenties refinery managers had always paid strict
attention to keeping costs down. The volume of refinery operations
was cut back in the face of declining demand and ever-rising gasoline
stocks. At Wood River half of the Dubbs units were closed by 1932,
and similar cutbacks were made at other refineries. The annual figures
for gasoline output of the Shell Union companies reflect these cuts:

BARRELS OF GASOLINE MANUFACTURED, 1930–1934

1930	32,477,000
1931	30,366,000
1932	29,447,000
1933	28,562,000
1934	28,101,000

The decrease in throughput increased the unit cost of manufacture,
as the economy committees were later to discover. But for the moment, gasoline prices were extremely depressed and it was considered
good business to purchase rather than refine a large part of the

company's requirements. Shell's third-grade gasoline was purchased from independent refiners to a large extent. These purchases, it was hoped, would also have the laudable effect of helping to strengthen the wholesale market, which was at the time completely demoralized.

On the pipe lines, only relatively minor economies were possible, for, like the refineries, the pipe lines had always utilized their manpower in a highly efficient manner. Pipe line unit costs could be lowered chiefly by increasing the volume of oil pumped, not possible when refineries were cutting back their operations.

In marketing, almost everyone could see opportunities for staffcutting, consolidations, and operational economies. All sorts of theories of marketing management had their day in court, with the result that Shell Petroleum in particular went through a constant and bewildering shuffling of marketing division offices all during the early years of the depression.

Shell Petroleum had, at the start of 1930, thirteen marketing divisions. In the summer of 1930, a new regional management plan was adopted and four regional managers appointed. A. F. H. Payne, manager of the Central region with headquarters in St. Louis, had the St. Louis, Moline, Minneapolis, and Tulsa divisions under his supervision; J. C. Munro, division manager at New Orleans, was made manager of the new Southern region which took in the New Orleans and Jacksonville divisions; the Milwaukee, Bloomington, Chicago, and Indianapolis divisions were organized as the Northern region and placed under the managership of G. A. Burns at Chicago; the Eastern region, under Carl Gerteis at Cleveland, had direction of the Detroit, Lima, and Cleveland divisions. Coincident with the institution of this regional plan, the Lima and Cleveland divisions were consolidated at the latter city and the Milwaukee division, only six months old, was closed and most of its territory given to the Minneapolis division.

These arrangements barely lasted the year out. At the beginning of 1931, the regional manager plan was abolished and wholesale consolidation of divisions began. A new Central Division at St. Louis took over the St. Louis, Minneapolis, Moline, and Tulsa divisions, together with the southern half of the Bloomington division's territory. The remainder of the Bloomington territory was assigned to Chicago. In the South, the Jacksonville division was consolidated into the New Orleans division.[9]

These large-scale consolidations, which affected eleven of the

Doolittle and the famous Gee Bee, winners of the Thompson Trophy race in 1931.

Fuelling Fokker monoplane for San Francisco-Los Angeles flight, 1928.

Courtesy W. A. F. Millinger

Remember when you wished the instructor would "LEAVE THAT THROTTLE ALONE"?

THOSE nerve-racking lessons before they let you solo! Just when you yanked back on the stick the instructor would jam the throttle shut and laugh at you—while you tried to wobble her out of a stall.

You know why he did it, of course. You're supposed to be able to pull out of any sort of a hole that engine failure gets you into.

Meanwhile, a lot of people were trying—and still are trying—to make engine failures fewer and farther apart. Some are working on ignition, some on alloys and valves and bearings; sustained flight records show how well they are succeeding.

Others are working on fuels and lubricants. Shell has a group in the chemistry and motor laboratories. They not only seek improvements; every lot of Shell aviation products is tested carefully before it can be sold. Every chance of variation is eliminated. Those nervous moments you spent during your first few hours' flying can be forgotten now, as far as Shell products are concerned.

SHELL
AVIATION GASOLINE
SPECIAL SHELL TRUCKS MAKE RAPID DELIVERIES TO EVERY FLYING FIELD

THAT'S CLIMB!

One of those zooms that stops every pilot, mechanic and lounger on the field—did you ever think what's behind that sky-rocket climb?

Wind tunnels and logarithms, stress tests and streamlining; study, design, invention — engine development, your own tedious hours of training — all those things and one other:

The *propelling force* is in your fuel tanks. Aviation gasoline is a study in itself. At Shell laboratories, aviation gasoline is literally taken apart and put together again — every bit that is refined. Shell Aviation Gasoline has reached an astounding degree of development — just as ships and engines have. Better 5% point, lower 90% point, lower end-point, lower vapor pressure! No other commercial grade can match it — it is even better than government specifications for fighting grade!

SHELL
AVIATION GASOLINE

These 1929–30 Shell aviation advertisements were aimed at the private flyer.

SHELL'S NEW DEAL!

Super SHELL

SHALL I FILL YOUR TANK WITH THE NEW SUPER SHELL, SIR? IT HAS NO THREE CENT PREMIUM, NOW!"

Super SHELL

Never before at less than a 3¢ premium
now at the price of ordinary gas

TODAY, Super Shell gasoline is again on sale at all Shell service stations—and it is even better than ever!

263,792,796 gallons of this famous motor fuel have been bought by motorists—every one of whom paid 2¢ extra per gallon for its premium qualities—a total of $8,513,783.88 above the regular price.

Now, for the first time, Super Shell gasoline is offered at the price of ordinary gasoline.

This is Shell's New Deal.

You Save 3¢ a Gallon Premium You motorists—112,327 of you—have told us, when we asked you in our service stations and in your homes,

that you want gasoline that is economical to purchase and economical to use. A gasoline that gives good mileage . . . power and pick-up, that starts quickly and has a high anti-knock value.

Super Shell has all these qualities. In particular, it gives you good mileage.

By a special precision process of refining Super Shell, the Shell Petroleum Corporation has succeeded in eliminating the waste parts of a gasoline that reduce mileage and increase operating costs.

Super Shell gives you, in concentrated form, only those parts of a gasoline which your engine needs to operate efficiently and economically.

You get the parts to give you real mileage and quick pick-up. You get the quick-starting parts so your engine will start without wasteful choking. You get real anti-knock parts to prevent your engine from knocking on hills and in traffic. For Super Shell has a higher anti-knock rating than any gasoline to which ethyl has not been added.

Change to Super Shell Super Shell is colored golden for your protection. Results will prove its economy for you.

If you prefer an ethylized gasoline, it is obtainable under the name of Super-Shell Ethyl—an improved gasoline with ethyl added. A double premium gasoline at a single premium price.

ALL WASTE PARTS REMOVED

Shell Petroleum's lagging sales in the early depression prompted one of Shell's memorable advertising campaigns. A new Super-Shell gasoline, comparable to the former premium, was introduced at regular gasoline prices on April 8, 1933, backed by vigorous advertising, *left and below.* The new gasoline was an instant success; by June, storage tanks were empty and refinery runs had to be increased.

RUMORS CONFIRMED

In 3 days, Shell will announce a new gasoline of outstanding performance

Announcement

APRIL 8th

SHELL

HAS THIS GASOLINE *What You Want?*

When we asked 112,327 of you motorists, you told us the qualities you wanted in a gasoline.

You'll find these exact qualities in Shell's new gasoline.

You'll see it has

APRIL 8th

SHELL GASOLINE

APRIL 8

TO-MORROW THE NEWS BREAKS

The announcement of Shell's New Gasoline

SHELL

First DIESEL POWERED PASSENGER CAR

CUMMINS DIESEL

To help Diesel fuel sales, the company joined in C. L. Cummins' cross-country Diesel auto test-run in 1935. Cummins made the trip from New York to Los Angeles on $7.63 worth of Shell Diesoline, but Diesel autos have yet to appear.

New and cheaper automatic oil burners and cheaper oil fuel brought an increase in domestic fuel oil consumption during the depression. This 1935 truck was typical of Shell's new fuel oil delivery fleet.

DOMESTIC SHELL FUEL OILS

Mission-style station, to harmonize with Stanford campus, 1932.

Station embodying motif of San Francisco Shell Building, 1931.

L. B. Veeder, one of the developers of Shellubrication, took to lubricating automobiles while dressed in dinner clothes—to prove that lubrication needn't be messy work. St. Louis, 1934.

One of two new stations built in Indianapolis during 1934.

R. G. A. van der Woude was president of Shell Petroleum, St. Louis, 1931–1933, and of the parent Shell Union Oil Corporation, New York, 1933–1947.

Alexander Fraser headed Shell Petroleum, 1933–39, and successor Shell Oil Co., Inc., 1939–47; Shell Union president, 1947–49; executive committee chairman, 1949–51.

The New Team

At the A.P.I. Convention, 1933: Van der Woude, president, Shell Union; Legh-Jones, president, San Francisco; W. Gould, president, Shell Eastern; Van Eck, vice chairman, Shell Union; Fraser, president, St. Louis.

Sidney Belither was president of the San Francisco company, 1934–1939; executive vice president and board chairman, Shell Oil Company, Inc., 1939–1948.

thirteen divisions, were accompanied by large-scale lay-offs. Staff reduction had, in fact, been the motivating reason behind most of them. Large numbers of employees, from junior clerks to division managers, were dismissed.† Employees fortunate enough to be still on the payroll and making more than $200 a month, received a sliding-scale pay cut of 7½% to 20% in October 1931. A year later, on July 1, 1932, a general 10% reduction was made in all salaries; those who had previously received a cut of less than 10% had their salaries adjusted to bring the total cut to that percentage.

By the end of 1931, staffs had been pared to the bone. In the Mid-Continent where the company's losses had been greatest, the reductions in staff were the largest. Shell Petroleum at the end of 1929 had 19,900 employees; in two years this number was reduced to 9,590, a cut of more than 50%. On the Pacific Coast, the payroll dropped from 12,290 to 7,490, or 39%, during the same period. Shell Eastern, still growing, had 3,320 employees early in 1932, an increase of 38% over 1929. Those who had been let out were given first consideration for re-employment, and by the end of 1932 the total number of employees was on the way back up. Attempts were made to spread the work among a larger number of part-time people. It had also been discovered that economy committees in some instances had been too zealous, cutting personnel below the minimum required to keep the business going.

New Faces in Management

With Daly's resignation in 1931 there began a long series of top-level personnel changes, most of them in St. Louis. Daly was replaced as president by R. G. A. van der Woude, who, it will be remembered, had been vice president of Roxana, 1922–1924. During the same year E. L. Miller, who had been marketing vice president since 1929, returned to San Francisco and Van Eeghen, who had managed the New Orleans Refining Company during the Twenties, succeeded him.

Late in 1932, as part of the general economy drive, the St. Louis

---

† For those who had been in the company's service long enough to accumulate a substantial balance, the Provident Fund proved a godsend in this emergency. In his memoirs, written in 1934, Deterding commented: "During the past two years, I confess, I should have felt uneasy if the Provident Fund I established, over twenty years ago . . . had not assured as ample provision as can be reasonably expected for any employee with whose services we have been regretfully obliged to dispense until the coming of better times." [10]

production department staff was decentralized. The Dallas office was closed, and the remaining staff moved to Houston. Production department functions being performed in the St. Louis head office were, in the main, moved either to Tulsa or Houston. Rollin, who had been vice president in charge of production at St. Louis, was moved to Tulsa with the same title; at Houston, T. E. Swigart, who had been assistant field superintendent on the West Coast, was brought east and made vice president in charge of the newly enlarged Houston office. Anderson, who had come to St. Louis from San Francisco a few months earlier, was in charge of this reorganization; he was elected general vice president of Shell Petroleum late in 1932.

Tydeman, manufacturing vice president, was shifted to San Francisco to become assistant to his old friend Pyzel and later a vice president of Shell Development Company. His place at St. Louis was filled by J. F. M. Taylor, a young Englishman who had for several years past been superintendent of the Wilmington Refinery. Taylor was made manager of manufacturing in St. Louis and, not long after, vice president. Thomas F. Lydon, long the company's vice president and treasurer, died suddenly in June 1933; he was succeeded by a West Coast treasury man, John W. Watson.

The years 1933 and 1934 brought other changes which almost completely reconstituted the executive teams of all three operating companies and Shell Union as well. In 1933, Van Eck was made vice chairman of Shell Union's board (Deterding still retained the chairmanship) and chairman of the executive committee. Van der Woude, after two years as president in St. Louis, went east to succeed Van Eck as president of Shell Union. Succeeding Van der Woude in St. Louis was Alexander Fraser, who had since 1930 been a vice president of the St. Louis company, and who would during the next fifteen years play an increasingly large role in the company's affairs.

In New York, Carter, who as president of Shell Eastern had done a spectacular job in getting Eastern operations organized, resigned in 1933 and was succeeded by W. Gould, a Britisher who had been a vice president of the Shell Oil Company in San Francisco for the past year.‡ During the same year P. E. Lakin, recently president of Shell's secondary marketing company in California, came to St.

‡ During the Second World War, the government took good advantage of Carter's combination naval and oil background. For the duration of the war, he served as chairman of the Army-Navy Petroleum Board, the body responsible for supplying military petroleum requirements. In this capacity, he rose to the rank of rear admiral, retiring at the end of 1945.

Louis to assume the position of general sales manager; when Van Eeghen left in 1936, Lakin succeeded him as marketing vice president.

Very soon after coming to New York, Van der Woude began to give serious thought to making Shell Union into a direct operating company that would take over operations then vested in the three Shell operating companies in San Francisco, St. Louis, and New York. To get things under way, vice presidencies for two of the main operating departments, manufacturing and marketing, were created in New York. Van Senden, who was then vice president in charge of manufacturing on the Coast, came east in the fall of 1933 to serve in a similar capacity with Shell Union. To be marketing vice president, Van der Woude picked W. P. Durkee, Jr., formerly of Van Fleet-Durkee, Inc.

A top-level shift in San Francisco during 1934 completed the change of faces. Legh-Jones, who had ably managed Shell operations on the Coast ever since Van Eck had left for New York in 1923, returned to London to become manager of Anglo-Saxon.§ His place in San Francisco was taken by Sidney Belither, an Englishman who had served with the Group in the Far East for many years and who had more lately become a vice president at San Francisco. In 1930, it had been Van Eck in New York at the head of Shell Union, Carter as president of Shell Eastern, Daly in St. Louis, Legh-Jones in San Francisco; in each of these chairs a new man now sat—Van der Woude, Gould, Fraser, Belither. The new team had a lot to do.

Refinancing

In addition to cutting operating expenses and keeping on hand a large cash balance, it was a good idea to attempt to reduce the annual interest payments on Shell Union's bonded indebtedness, to reduce the amount of the indebtedness itself, and to postpone the day when it must be repaid. Because of the bad market conditions in general and the poor earnings of Shell Union in particular, prices of company securities had fallen to low levels during 1931 and 1932. Shell Union common, which had sold at prices between $20 and $40 a share all during the Twenties, now hit $2.50 a share; the preferred

§ In 1937, Legh-Jones was made a managing director of each of the Group's main operating companies. The same year he was appointed to the board of Shell Transport & Trading Company, and in 1944 he was made a managing director of Shell T. & T. He was knighted in 1950. During 1951, Sir George retired from the management of the Group's operating companies, but he continues to serve as a managing director of The Shell Transport & Trading Company, Ltd.

stock issued in 1929 at $100 a share fell as low as $15 in 1931 and $18 in 1932. During 1935, the Shell Union and Shell Pipe Line bond issues of 1927 reached lows of 56⅞% and 47% respectively, and the 1929 bond issue went down to 47% of face value.

Now was the time to use some of the cash Van Eck had so carefully husbanded. Beginning in 1931, when things were so bad that dividends on the preferred stock had to be omitted,* the company took advantage of the low market price of its own securities to buy some $6,330,-000 worth of bonds. In 1932, bonds with a face value of $26,300,000 were bought for a cash outlay of $19,600,000; in 1933, $10,500,000 was spent to buy more bonds; and in 1934, the balance of the 1929 $50,000,000 bond issue was called in and redeemed and $8,500,000 worth of 1927 bonds were purchased. Money for these purchases came from the company's treasury with the exception of $9,000,000 borrowed from banks on short-term loan in 1934.

In five years of depression, Shell Union's indebtedness in the form of preferred stock and bonds was reduced by almost $70,000,000. The reduction was made the hard way and at great sacrifice, for the money spent to buy up company securities might have been used in more profitable ways. Now, however, much of the great load of high-interest debt had been lifted. Of the large oil companies, the three having the largest indebtedness were Standard of New Jersey, Gulf, and Shell; Shell made by far the most progress in debt reduction during these years of the early Thirties.[11]

LONG-TERM DEBT REDUCTION, 1930–1934

	End of 1930		End of 1934		
	Funded Debt	Long-Term Loans	Funded Debt	Long-Term Loans	% of 1930 Debt
Standard Oil (N.J.)	$167,355,000		$102,157,000	$39,304,000	84.5%
Gulf	125,904,000		91,229,000	400,000	72.6%
Shell Union	125,500,000	$9,730,000	47,208,000	6,377,000	39.6%

No night lasts forever. In 1935, receipts from sales increased by $16,000,000. This, in combination with the measures already taken to economize and reduce interest on the debt, finally put Shell

---

* As a protection for holders of the preferred shares, the terms of the issue had provided that preferred shareholders could elect one-third of the directors if at any time four consecutive dividends should be omitted. Under these provisions, the preferred shareholders elected a third of the board on May 18, 1933. No dissension resulted from this move, for several of the new directors had already served on the board and were friendly to the management.

Union back in the black. After all expenses had been paid there was a net profit of $6,800,000 for 1935, not enough to permit the resumption of dividends but an indication at least that Shell was at last out of the financial woods. During late 1935, arrangements were made to float a new $60,000,000 bond issue at 3½%, in place of the 5% paid previously. The details of this issue were completed early in 1936 and the new bonds offered to the public on March 10, 1936. From the proceeds of the new issue, the unredeemed portions of the two 1927 bond issues, now amounting in total to $47,000,000, were called in and paid. The balance was made available for new capital expenditure, badly needed after five years of curtailed operations.

But riding out the storm of the nation's worst depression had several other aspects. In two branches of the oil business, production and marketing, conditions were abnormally disturbed and deserve more detailed attention.

4

Overproduction, Conservation, Proration

"ARE the United States going on producing all they can—more than they can consume—with the result that they are exporting today at a low price what they are likely to be importing later on at a higher price? Are they going on over-producing today when they may be over-consuming in a few years?" Deterding inquired in his talk to the American Petroleum Institute in 1929.[12] Even at this late date such sentiments were far from popular. Happenings of catastrophic proportions had to take place before the oil fraternity and the public in general became convinced of the need for conservation.

Sentiments favoring conservation were not new to Shell men. In 1930, a year when many other businessmen were hunting for a scapegoat, Van Eck had calmly appraised the situation and written in the company's annual report, "The year 1930 was by far the most critical in the history of the industry and, while this to some extent was due to the general business depression, it is unfortunately a fact that it was due to a far greater extent to conditions for which the industry itself is responsible. It is now generally recognized that the basic cause of the industry's troubles is overproduction, and that until this has been corrected no stabilization will be possible. . . . The failure to restrict drilling operations throughout the country, resulting not only in the opening up of new flush fields but in the over-development and ruthless drainage of existing fields, has largely contributed to the ills of the industry." In three sentences, Van Eck told the oil industry what most of its members were at last reluctantly beginning to admit—that they were producing more crude oil than the country could possibly use.

The Rule of Capture

Ever since the start of the oil business in Pennsylvania, the industry had been a victim of these periods of overproduction. This excess production usually ran its course quickly and before long a period of impending scarcity would bring greatly improved prices. This in turn would bring a new flurry of exploratory drilling, accompanied generally by the discovery almost overnight of several prolific new oil fields. The oil from these new fields would once again cause over-production, until the new fields began to taper off. Then the cycle would repeat itself.

The periods of intense drilling almost always brought severe price breaks which, from the first, producers tried to avoid but with little success. A seemingly insuperable obstacle was the nature of the laws governing ownership of oil lands. In the United States, the owner of the land owned the subsurface rights as well. This meant in the case of a coal deposit that the owner could develop it upon discovery or, if he chose, wait until some future time. But the owner of land in a proven oil area could not wait, if his neighbors had chosen to drill. He must either drill at once or run the risk of losing the oil under his land to neighbors with producing wells.

Just what were the property rights of a landowner to the oil under his land? Many legal theories were advanced during the early days of the oil business and finally in 1889 the Pennsylvania Supreme Court arrived at the decision which was to be the basis of American oil and gas law. The court held that oil belonged not to the man whose property it underlay, but to the man who reduced it to possession. This same legal principle had been applied by English courts years earlier to game birds, and was known as the "rule of capture." During the years to come, this rule of capture was to prove the chief obstacle to orderly and rational development of oil fields. Any producer in an oil field was legally entitled to all the oil he could produce, no matter whose land was drained. His neighbors, naturally, were determined to see that this oil did not come from beneath their land.[13]

The resulting scramble was wasteful in every respect. Far more wells were drilled than necessary, and they were produced wide open in an attempt to get as much oil above ground as quickly as possible. In a field of any importance, this overdrilling and wide-open production led to another wasteful consequence. Immense amounts of storage—wooden tanks, steel tanks, and earthen reservoirs—were built, an amount of tankage far greater than would have been necessary if the oil had been produced in smaller quantities over a longer period. Likewise the number and capacity of the pipe lines, both for gathering oil in the field and transporting it to refining centers, usually exceeded actual needs. All of this additional expenditure for superfluous wells, additional storage, and excess pipe line capacity constituted *economic waste*, for it meant that the producers were having to spend much more than they should on these items.

Far more important was the *physical waste* of oil and gas. Gushers in the early days often ran for weeks unchecked until storage could be built to hold the oil they were pouring forth. And with every effort bent towards the building of tanks and pipe lines, little thought was given to the gas, that useful agent whose pressure helped the oil come to the surface. Gas, in staggering quantities, was vented into the air or burned in the field in flares.

This economic and physical wastage in the oil fields was more than enough to condemn the production practices which had resulted from the application of the rule of capture. It was, however, another result of these production practices which loomed largest in the public attention—overproduction. In almost every rapidly developed oil field, there was a period of local overproduction, often not "overproduction" at all when total needs were considered. But these local floods of oil put a premium on available storage and transportation facilities. Those who could not afford to build large amounts of tankage, much less their own pipe lines, had little choice but to sell their crude at distress prices to crude purchasing companies or refiners with pipe line connections. In many cases, as in Oklahoma in the early days, producers received for their oil prices that were little above, or even less than, their actual costs. These low prices hit hardest at the men who could least afford it, the small producers who had spent their whole resources upon a few wells.

The Unit-Operation Plan

All these conditions had long demonstrated to the more thoughtful members of the oil fraternity the need for some sort of control over oilfield development—some method which would reduce both economic and physical waste, which would remove oil producing from the status of a feast-or-famine business, something which would, best of all, improve prices to the producers, for with oil worth more there would be more incentive to prevent waste.

To clamp restrictions on a business as highly competitive as oil producing was no easy job. Before effective controls could be adopted, as they finally were in the mid-Thirties, a multitude of things had to be done. One of the most important was to demonstrate the necessity for physical conservation measures. For this demonstration, the new petroleum engineers, trained and developed by the U. S. Bureau of Mines and a few of the major companies, were largely responsible. In 1913, I. L. Dunn of the U. S. Bureau of Mines station at Marietta, Ohio, successfully showed that production of oil from formations that were nearly depleted could be increased by injecting gas into these formations. The same year, the American Institute of Mining and Metallurgical Engineers set up a Petroleum Committee, and thenceforward the serious thought of a segment of the engineering profession was devoted to the business of oil production.[14]

The success of the "Marietta process" turned the attention of these engineers to the role played by gas energy in the oil reservoir. With study came the realization that the gas was valuable not only as a fuel but also as energy for lifting the oil from the underground reservoir. At about the time Van der Linden set up his first production engineering department at Coalinga,† an able group of

† This was one of the first such departments in an American oil company. Its attention was directed to subsurface problems, and one of Van der Linden's first triumphs was convincing the California State Oil and Gas Supervisor that mud-laden fluid could be successfully used to seal off oil layers which were being bypassed in the process of deeper drilling, a development which made possible a considerable saving in casing pipe during the years of World War I. Two other members of Van der Linden's early department, A. W. Ambrose and T. E. Swigart, later made names for themselves in the Bureau of Mines. Ambrose headed the experiment station which the Bureau set up at Bartlesville, Oklahoma, in 1919, and Swigart continued the studies of J. O. Lewis on the Marietta process. He also did considerable work in the measurement and reduction of gas/oil ratios, and believes he was probably the first to employ this now-standard term. In 1924, Swigart was hired by McDuffie to become production engineer for the Shell Company of California, and was instrumental in putting the Marietta process into operation in that company's Brea Canyon and Dominguez fields during 1927. Another Shell engineer under McDuffie, H. H. Anderson, made pioneer studies into the nature of drilling mud, 1922–1923.[15]

rising young engineers began to pass back and forth from the private companies to the Bureau of Mines, always studying and experimenting, and publishing their findings as Bureau of Mines papers. In the years following 1916, they began to measure gas/oil ratios (i.e., the number of cubic feet of gas produced with a barrel of oil) in an attempt to determine the practicability of cutting down the amount of gas produced in order to prolong the flowing life of the well.

A gas engineer who had founded an oil company, H. L. Doherty of Cities Service, set in motion a series of investigations which by 1926 had definitely proved that gas had another important function. Dissolved in oil, gas lowered the oil's viscosity and surface tension. Oil containing considerable amounts of gas would thus pass more readily through underground formations, with a resultant higher total recovery than from oil reservoirs whose gas had been allowed to escape. All of this new information pointed to a clear conclusion: wells should not be allowed to produce wide open, for too-rapid production dissipated the gas pressure.[16]

Somehow, production must be cut back to reasonable levels in the interest of prolonging the life of a producing field and reducing the wastage of gas. During most of the great production crises of the past, attempts had been made to get producers to agree to cut their daily production. Most of these efforts (the first was as far back as 1866) had as their object the support of prices and, like commodity "pools" the world around, were destined to failure in advance. If successful, they resulted in an increase in price; producers who had pledged themselves to produce only a specified daily quota promptly broke their pledges in order to produce more and take advantage of the higher prices.[17] At the height of the booms in the Cushing and Healdton fields in Oklahoma, the state government intervened. The object was not conservation per se but equitable apportionment of available storage and pipe line facilities. The production crisis of 1923 in California also brought attempts at pro-rata production in the summer of 1924; but here again, the interest was in "ratable takings" by the pipe lines rather than in pure conservation.[18]

Once a field had been seriously overdrilled, the damage was done anyhow. More orderly development of an oil field would be assured if the furious drilling competition could be eliminated. This had been amply proved in fields such as Coalinga East where Shell and Standard of California were the only operators of any consequence, owned the land in fee, and could develop the field without undue haste. But such instances were rare; most fields had dozens of operators, from major companies to the smallest of independents.

What was needed was a plan that would overcome the basic unfairness of the rule of capture. Max Ball, then a young geologist with the Bureau of Mines, as far back as 1916 had suggested increasing the size of oil tracts, either by legal requirement or voluntary action, in order to minimize the destructive effects of competitive drilling. Nothing came of Ball's proposal, but at the annual meeting of the American Petroleum Institute in 1924, Henry L. Doherty startled the industry with a proposal that each new oil field be developed not in hot competition, but as a unit. The boundaries of each new discovery would be developed to outline the limits of the pool. This done, development work could then proceed in an orderly manner, with a single company acting as operator of the unit. Proceeds realized from the oil produced would be divided equitably among the lease owners in the pool, each lease owner receiving a share of the proceeds proportionate to the acreage of his holdings. In a 5,000-acre pool, for example, the holder of 50 acres would participate in the proportion 50/5,000, or 1%, of the total regardless of whether or not his particular tract had a well on it. Royalty owners would participate in royalty payments on the same basis.

Under such an arrangement, the lease and royalty owners in a new field would probably not receive as much money during the first few years of development, but the chances were that they would in the long run receive a much larger total amount. The field would be developed in orderly fashion. Only such wells as were actually needed to recover the oil would be drilled; one system of gathering lines, instead of many competing ones, would be laid; and only such tankage as was needed for field storage would be erected. All this would mean less capital cost, a smaller amount of expense to be charged off against each barrel of oil produced. Gas could be more intelligently utilized: one large casinghead gasoline plant could be built instead of many small ones, thus affording further economies; and the operating company would hold back production until it had made arrangements for profitable sale of the field's gas production, rather than burning the gas in the field as formerly. Best of all to the producer concerned with price, orderly development promised to eliminate most of the temporary local overproduction which had so often in the past forced small operators, who could not afford to build tankage, to sell their oil at distress prices. Such unit-operation plans had, in fact, already proved their worth in several countries where oil deposits belonged to the government and were developed on a concession basis.

This unit plan, it seemed to Doherty, had everything to recommend it. He was quite unprepared for the storm of protest it created. Here, we see yet another of the difficulties which had to be overcome before production control could become a reality: the reconciliation of differences within the industry. The large companies whose interests were spread through most of the country's major oil-producing regions were building for a future ten or more years away. Small operators, with a few acres in one or two fields, were much less inclined to take the long view. Landowners, almost all of them individuals, wanted to see as much oil as possible produced right away, for they collected royalty only on actual production.

Clearly, in most fields a unit plan could be put into successful operation only if it were backed by law. This immediately raised the question of who was to enact the law. Federal control, such as that advocated by Doherty, would be uniform in every state. But would it be legal? The Constitution had made no such grant of power; it had in fact stipulated that powers not granted to the Federal government were expressly reserved to the states.

The Federal Oil Conservation Board, appointed by President Coolidge in December 1924 and consisting of the Secretaries of War, the Navy, the Interior, and Commerce assisted by a small technical staff, made sizeable contributions to the legal aspects of conservation. The Board's first report, rendered in 1926, emphasized that natural gas had an important role in raising oil, and offered the opinion that the states could exercise their police powers "to prevent waste or destruction of a common property by one of the owners." "Gas," the report said, "is more than a commodity of smaller commercial value associated with oil; it is the efficient agent provided by nature for bringing oil within the reach of man. Dissolved in the oil, the gas makes the oil flow more freely to the well and there forces it upward, and the longer the gas is retained in solution the larger is the recovery of oil. Waste of gas is therefore a double waste, and the impairment of gas pressure in an oil sand by one owner may prevent his neighbors from recovering any of the oil beneath their land and himself from securing more than a small part of the oil underlying his own land." Uniform conservation laws throughout the oil-producing states could be secured, the board suggested, by conference among the states concerned, and the finalized agreement could take the form of a compact among the states approved by Congress.[19] This was the genesis of the Interstate Oil Compact, which was not finally adopted until nearly a decade later, after other methods had failed.

Then, in the years beginning with 1927, a complicating factor entered the picture. The permanent imbalance between the country's crude oil production and its capacity to consume oil products began to take on serious proportions. More and more, people in all branches of the oil industry began to suggest plans for limiting production so that oil markets would not be completely ruined. The term *conservation* (prevention of waste) was now heard less than *proration* (reduction of production, with the reduction shared on a pro-rata basis).

Proration

In October 1927, the producers in the Yates Pool in West Texas demonstrated that proration could be successfully practiced on a voluntary basis. With single Yates wells having potential daily productions of more than 100,000 barrels a day, it was evident to all of the operators in the field that some kind of production limitation must be practiced to protect themselves from ruin. A committee was formed to survey the field's potential and assign each company a daily "allowable," calculated on a per-acre rather than a per-well basis. To see that these allowables were adhered to, the operators in the Yates field appointed Roxana's district gauger, Bruce Clardy, as umpire. The plan succeeded. A year later, in October 1928, a total of 72,000 barrels a day was being produced by all of the Yates operators, out of a potential of more than 4,000,000 barrels daily. In May of the following year, the Texas Railroad Commission, the body empowered to enforce that state's oil regulations, put a compulsory proration plan into effect in the Hendricks field of West Texas, using the Yates plan as a model.[20]

From this point onwards, "conservation" became a hopelessly confused term. In the minds of some, it meant prevention of physical waste only; to others it signified prevention of physical *and* economic waste; to a third group it meant proration pure and simple. And the advocates of proration were also confused about their aims. Some were interested chiefly in assuring to the producer equitable use of available transportation and storage facilities; some (the stripper-well producers) in maintaining a market price high enough to permit the

continuance of their high-cost production operations; others in restricting the total output of oil in the hope that decreased production
would bring increased prices. This jumble of motives, singly or in
combination, meant "conservation" in the minds of various members
of the oil industry. It is little wonder that they found difficulty in
agreeing with each other. As if these reasons for disagreement were
not enough, discussions of conservation at this point degenerated into a
battle between the proponents of state control and those who favored
control by the Federal government.

Herbert Hoover, a stout foe of waste in any form and a friend of
proration so long as it was not for the purpose of raising prices, had
been a member of the Federal Oil Conservation Board since its
inception. With his advent to the Presidency, he took steps to reduce
wasteful overproduction by withdrawing from further leasing activity
all Federal oil lands. He attempted to compose the industry's differences by directing his Secretary of the Interior, Dr. Ray Lyman
Wilbur, to call a meeting of the governors of the oil states and the
representatives of the leading oil trade associations at Colorado Springs
in June 1929. The conference was under the chairmanship of Mark
L. Requa, a personal friend of Hoover's and a long-time advocate of
conservation. Secretary Wilbur laid before the meeting a plan calling
for the formation of an interstate oil compact "by which each of the
oil states would agree to set up regulation to repress excessive drilling
and waste in collaboration with the others." [21] President Hoover sent
a message to the conference urging adoption of this plan. However,
a great many of the delegates by now had become enamored of
Federal control, and the Federal government's plan for an interstate
compact was rejected.‡

Voluntary Unitization

This did not mean that the oil companies were unable to cooperate
for conservation on a voluntary basis. Doherty's unit plan was put
into effect by five of the major oil companies (Shell, Sun, Texas,

‡ In the light of later experience, this action seems inexcusable. In justification of
the oil men's stand it should, however, be pointed out that they associated previous
failures in this field with state laws which had proved impossible to enforce. And
"Federal" control in 1929 was not yet synonymous with the New Deal. Mr. Hoover
was still irritated at the oil men's action twenty years later, and wrote in the second
volume of his *Memoirs* (1952): "One of the stupidest actions of big business was
this demand for collectivism by Federal action to pull themselves out of a hole of
overproduction. . . . Then, after this taste of collectivism, the same men who had
led the opposition to my proposal at Colorado Springs themselves advanced the
'Hoover principle' (by name), and it was almost unanimously supported by the
industry—sitting in sackcloth and ashes." [22]

Humble, Pure) in the Van pool of Van Zandt County, Texas, discovered in October 1929. Before development drilling started, these five companies agreed that the discoverer, Pure Oil Company, should handle the entire operation. Thenceforth, development of the Van pool was at an unhurried pace; wells were properly spaced, wasteful duplicate expenditures were eliminated, and the wells were produced "choked back" to reduce the production of gas and save its lifting energy as long as possible.

The success of the Van pool unitization agreement offered a model for a much larger and more important conservation effort, the Kettleman North Dome Association in California. In the Kettleman Hills, east and south of Coalinga, oil had been discovered late in 1928. The first production from the field was crude condensate of 60° gravity, as light as the gasoline then being sold, and so light that it could be sold unrefined from the well for use as motor fuel. Subsequent production yielded a light, highly desirable crude oil, ranging from 34° to 51° gravity. There were tremendous quantities of gas with the Kettleman Hills oil; there was no doubt in any mind that unrestrained production would cause an unparalleled wastage of gas.§ Since much of the field was on government land, the Secretary of the Interior stepped in to prevent waste. Secretary Wilbur dispatched Dr. George Otis Smith, the distinguished director of the United States Geological Survey, to California and Dr. Smith in July 1929 succeeded in negotiating with all of the operators in the field an agreement that they would cease all operations in the area for a period of two years. This was to allow a breathing spell during which, it was hoped, the various interested parties would agree on a suitable conservation plan for developing the huge new field.[24]

The very extent of the Kettleman Hills field, the high grade of its crude oil, the unbalanced production situation in California (where production was running some 60% ahead of requirements) all combined to have a sobering effect upon the Kettleman Hills leaseholders. Under the leadership of Dr. Smith, several interested oil men, including two from Shell, William Reinhardt, production vice president, and his assistant production superintendent, T. E. Swigart, worked hard with representatives of other interested companies to draw up

§ Shell Oil Company's Armstrong No. 1, on a test made July 10, 1929, yielded 205 barrels of 60.7° oil in thirty-three hours, accompanied by gas production at the rate of 5,400,000 cubic feet per day. Standard of California's No. 81-11P, brought in ten days later, produced 834 barrels a day of oil and 18,850,000 cubic feet of gas.[23]

a plan which would find favor with all the landowners and operators, a group much larger than those in the Van pool. As a result of their negotiations, the Kettleman North Dome Association, a legal corporation, was organized during the early months of 1931, and to it each leaseholder transferred all his oil rights in the area. He got in exchange an interest in the total oil in the pool, in proportion to the acreage of his contribution.* Reinhardt resigned his Shell vice presidency to become first general manager of the new association which acted as the operating company for the unitized area.[25]

Both the Van and Kettleman North Dome unit plans worked out as well as their proponents had predicted. Money savings in operations were substantial; oil was produced at the maximum efficient rate, but no faster; and, best of all, gas was kept in the ground in storage for possible sale in the future and for certain use in lifting oil. It is quite possible that these unit plans and the proration arrangements such as those adopted at Yates and McCamey would have sufficed to solve the oilfield conservation problem, had it not been for East Texas. Crude oil production, as the result of increasing voluntary and state-imposed proration, showed a satisfactory decline from mid-1929 through all of 1930. In fact, crude production was below domestic demand from mid-1930 to the end of the year, which meant that the large above-ground stocks of crude were at last being drawn upon.

East Texas and Chaos

Then came East Texas. Never in the history of oil prospecting had a major discovery come at a less auspicious time. A penniless, seventy-year-old wildcatter named Columbus Joiner, on October 3, 1930, after four years of dogged drilling, brought in his Daisy Bradford No. 3 in Rusk County, unleashing the largest flood of oil the world had ever seen. His original well produced some 225 barrels a day from 3,600 feet, so interest in Joiner's discovery was at first only mild. About a month later, the Deep Rock Oil Company and associates completed a 10,000-barrel-a-day gusher and in the ensuing weeks wells drilled by others, often miles apart, all encountered the same producing horizon. From that point onward the history of the East Texas field was written in superlatives.[26]

The new pool, it was soon shown, covered all or parts of five counties, the largest field the industry had ever experienced. Its very

* Shell's interest stood at 8.45049% on December 1, 1950.

area made it a menace, for there was land enough for everyone who wanted to drill, or so it seemed. The fact that the producing horizon was less than 4,000 feet down through easy drilling made it a simple matter for anyone with a few thousand dollars' worth of credit to join the boom. And in the depression year of 1931 there were plenty of unemployed men from other trades who were eager to join any venture. In February of 1931, production from the East Texas field was 25,000 barrels a day; six months later it had climbed, despite proration orders, to 1,000,000 barrels daily! Coming onto an already depressed market, this flood of oil completely demoralized the oil industry. In East Texas, field prices of oil per barrel dropped to 10¢, 6¢, and one lot of 50,000 barrels even sold for 2½¢ a barrel.[27] Here was a crying example of economic waste, for East Texas oil was of good quality and yielded large amounts of gasoline by simple distillation.

The Texas Railroad Commission promulgated proration regulations before the boom was fairly under way but the ease of getting a lease, the cheapness of drilling, the arrival of gasoline bootleggers with their "tea-kettle" refineries, and the determination of thousands of men to get rich quick made attempts at enforcement futile. On top of this, the local courts took a dim view of proration regulations, and any producer who did not wish to abide by the state proration orders could go to court and get an injunction forbidding the state authorities to molest him.

The flood of East Texas oil had widespread repercussions throughout the Mid-Continent. In Oklahoma prices had not yet reached the low levels of East Texas, but the state oil regulatory body was having the same trouble with the courts. Early in August 1931, Governor William H. (Alfalfa Bill) Murray, in an attempt to rid himself of the courts, declared martial law 50 feet around each well in the twenty-nine Oklahoma fields covered by state proration orders. Governor Ross Sterling of Texas, hard pressed by events in East Texas, followed suit on August 17, declaring martial law for Upshur, Gregg, Smith, and Rusk counties (the area of the East Texas Field) on the ground that "a state of insurrection, tumult, riot, and breach of peace" existed there. Some $225,000 worth of natural gasoline and a billion and a half cubic feet of gas were being wasted each day, he said, to produce oil selling for only $105,000.[28] Martial law, while certainly not to be commended, did mark the turning point in conservation. The shock of seeing men with guns in the oil fields woke the public to the reckless waste that was being caused by an irresponsible minority of producers. From this point on, the general public, whether connected with the oil business or not, began to take an active interest in the subject of conservation.

The Interstate Oil Compact

The idea of an interstate compact, though it had been dropped by the Colorado Springs meeting in 1929, was not entirely dead. In the early months of 1931 Governor Murray called a series of meetings of the oil-state governors; this resulted in the organization (March 9, 1932) of the Oil States Advisory Committee. A year of meetings and hearings ensued and in May and June 1932 legislation was introduced in Congress which would have permitted two or more states to compact with each other for the conservation of oil and gas, and for the prevention of exhaustion of domestic sources of supply. Monthly production quotas were to be assigned to each state, and a quota placed on oil imports.

At this point, the question was raised of whether or not a tariff on oil imports † would be necessary if the oil compact legislation were passed. Accordingly, at the instance of the Independent Petroleum Association of America which was pushing for a tariff of $1 a barrel on imported oil, the interstate compact bill was shelved— an unfortunate turn of events for it would have undoubtedly been enacted and obviated a great deal of subsequent trouble. The Oil States Advisory Committee was scheduled to meet for further discussions in Fort Worth in November 1932, when suddenly the Independent Association, a group often prone to adopt the short-term view, withdrew its support and came out in favor of a quota plan under Federal control.[29]

With the advent of the Roosevelt administration in March 1933, new ideas of government and economics appeared on the Washington scene. No longer was production to be regulated merely in the interest of preventing waste. Regulation would be aimed at bettering prices by cutting back production, decreasing refinery runs, and upping prices at the retail level. In such an atmosphere, the advocates of Federal control carried the day—and included in their number were several of the industry's most prominent members. Reviewing the events of this period fifteen years later, the Mineral Section of

† This legislation, and some of the agitation leading up to it, is discussed in the closing pages of this chapter.

the American Bar Association wrote: "The attractiveness of federal regulation for the industry then cannot now be minimized or detracted from by all the speechifying and subsequent repentance indulged in by those of rank and quality in the executive world of the industry. . . . Put mildly, the industry was enthusiastic about the possibilities of using the code device to govern their activities under the protecting wing of . . . the Federal Government. An eagerness existed for activity as contrasted with inactivity; anything seemed better than existing conditions. . . . But the calculation that each side had made (erroneously or not) was that it would run the show. It is to the credit of both participants that neither would let the other get away with the original concepts each possessed of what the code would do for their interests." [30]

The National Industrial Recovery Act, which became law in June 1933 and gave the President through his code-making authority almost unlimited powers over all industry, also contained a special provision known as Section 9(c) of Title I. This section gave the President power to prohibit the transportation in interstate and foreign commerce of petroleum or petroleum products produced or withdrawn from storage at a rate in excess of the amounts prescribed by state regulatory bodies. Violators were subject to a fine of $1,000 or imprisonment of up to six months for each offense. The same month that Congress passed this legislation, the Texas Railroad Commission reduced the East Texas allowables from 850,000 to 550,000 barrels a day. Prices improved immediately. It is a matter of debate whether this was the result of the Federal law, or of the more moderate attitude adopted by the local courts who now refused to grant injunctions.

Section 9(c) did not go long untested. In the Panama Refining case, decided by the Supreme Court on January 7, 1935, this section of the National Industrial Recovery Act was declared unconstitutional on the grounds that regulation of production was a matter expressly reserved to the states. Promptly a new law, the Connally Hot Oil Act, was drafted to replace Section 9(c). "Hot oil" was defined, and its transportation, and the transportation of products made from it, was forbidden in interstate or foreign commerce. Control over shipments under this law was exercised by a Federal Petroleum Board set up with main offices at Kilgore, Texas, in the heart of the East Texas field. The "tender" system inaugurated by this board was effective immediately, and between 60 and 80 of the East Texas refineries processing illegally produced crude folded up in the course of a few months.[31]

Meanwhile, those segments of the industry which had supported Federal control only a few months before were coming to reverse their position. The turning point was the annual meeting of the American Petroleum Institute held at Dallas in November 1934. The main speaker was Secretary of the Interior Harold L. Ickes, who also held the title of Petroleum Administrator. Secretary Ickes called for strong Federal control of the oil industry, and for a declaration holding the industry to be a public utility.[32]

At this juncture, Ernest Marland, who had been elected governor of Oklahoma in November 1934, revived the interstate compact idea.‡ As a result of a series of meetings of the oil-state governors held at Marland's home in Ponca City late in 1934 and early 1935, representatives of Oklahoma, Texas, California, New Mexico, Arkansas, Colorado, Illinois, Michigan, and Kansas on February 15, 1935, adopted "An Interstate Compact to Conserve Oil and Gas," and legislatures of all the signatory states except California ratified it by July. Congress passed the necessary permissive legislation on August 27, 1935.

The Interstate Oil Compact's authority was moral and persuasive, rather than real and coercive. The signatory states, which by 1955 numbered twenty-two,§ compacted to work together within a con-

---

‡ His attitude in the controversy over state vs. Federal controls was typical of the industry's. Only a few months earlier, as a Congressman, Marland had been championing Federal control.

§ Alabama, Arkansas, Colorado, Florida, Illinois, Indiana, Kansas, Kentucky, Louisiana, Michigan, Mississippi, Montana, Nebraska, New Mexico, New York, North Dakota, Ohio, Oklahoma, Pennsylvania, Tennessee, Texas, and West Virginia. California had been a signatory to the original Interstate Compact, and its governor and legislature gave wholehearted support to oil conservation all during the 1930's. The state had (and still has) a law to prevent unreasonable waste of gas, but it had no effective law to control the rate of oil production. In 1932, the California legislature passed, and the governor signed, the Sharkey Bill, which provided measures for regulating crude oil production. California's peculiar referendum laws, which enable voters to pass on almost anything, whether or not they understand it, played into the hands of those who opposed the personal sacrifices which conservation measures would require of them. A hastily created association obtained enough signatures to get the matter put on the ballot. The foes of conservation used as their chief argument against the proposed law a cartoon showing a shark (the Sharkey Bill) eating the consumer. The voters defeated the measure in May 1932. The Atkinson Oil Control Bill, a conservation law in harmony with those recently adopted by other states, was likewise defeated by California voters in November 1939. Of the other oil-producing states, all except Illinois now have effective conservation laws.

stitutionally approved formula to conserve the petroleum wealth of the nation. Each signatory state assumed a moral responsibility to enact and enforce within its own borders laws designed to prevent physical wastage of oil and gas, and to use its police powers to see that maximum ultimate recovery was made from every oil pool within its jurisdiction.

By terms of the compact, a permanent Interstate Oil Compact Commission was created, its members drawn from the regulatory bodies of the states concerned, to act as a fact-finding body to determine the most advantageous methods, practices, and conditions of conservation. This work is accomplished through a series of subcommittees drawn from the best minds in the industry, along with a small permanent staff and executive secretary with offices in the State Capitol building at Oklahoma City. The high calibre, undisputed integrity, and obvious sincerity of the men associated with the Interstate Oil Compact Commission have made it possible for them to exercise an amount of moral suasion which few officers of the law ever seem to enjoy. During its formative period, 1935–1936, E. W. Marland was chairman of the new commission and Col. (later General) E. O. Thompson, chairman of the Texas Railroad Commission, served as chairman 1936–1940. With men of such calibre, the new organization got safely through its initial period. It is pleasant to record that their successors have been equally able and respected.

In the many months leading up to the adoption of the Interstate Oil Compact, a battle had been fought and won for "conservation principles that would eschew the hypnotic effects of price control and its concomitant philosophies." [33] The commission has accordingly devoted its attention to conservation per se. The wholehearted support which the commission has given to prolonging the life of oil fields through producing at the maximum efficient recovery rate has had salutary side effects. This maximum efficient recovery rate for any given field, is, of course, far below the rate of wide-open production; as a consequence, wasteful periods of flush production with resultant low field prices have for the most part been eliminated. This welcome economic effect has, however, been incidental to the main purpose of preventing physical waste of oil and gas and insuring maximum ultimate recovery.

Credit for all these developments is due to this effective agency for self-regulation—created, supported, and administered by the oil states themselves.* The commission has "lived in a glass house" from its inception, and attempted with every means at its disposal to convince the minority elements of the industry, who at one time made conservation measures impossible, that production at the maximum efficient rate, without waste of reservoir energy, is in the long run best for all concerned—the big producers, the small producers, the royalty owners, and the consuming public.

The Shell organization helped to further passage of these laws in every way it could. In the early Twenties, the Royal Dutch Company had begun advocating the unitized operation of oil pools. Deterding had, in his A.P.I. speech and on numerous other occasions, endorsed the principle of cooperation among competitors to reduce waste and bring about a more realistic balance between production and consumption. Late in 1931 and early in 1932, Kessler had made public his own plan for the reduction of production on an international basis, modifying it several times to conform with local conditions and legal requirements in various countries. With legalized conservation at last a reality in America, the Shell Union companies took the lead wherever they could. By 1933, they were participating in nineteen unit operations on the Pacific Coast and in the Mid-Continent, and Shell Petroleum was managing the unitized pool in the new Lucien, Oklahoma, field, where it held 34% of the total acreage.[34]

5

Accent on Sales: Gasoline Wars, the N.R.A., the Iowa Plan

THE depression did not shrink the size of the gasoline market immediately. Over-all gasoline sales during the first two years of the Thirties actually continued on upward: 1930 sales were three-quarters of a billion gallons above 1929, and in 1931 this figure went up another 378 million gallons. This trend could not continue indefi-

* The interested reader may well ask how it is possible, with such Federal laws on the books as the Connally Act, to give credit for the favorable results almost solely to this aggregation of state agencies. The Connally Act's chief value is that it puts the prestige of the Federal government behind the states' conservation efforts by guaranteeing Federal prosecution of any producers or refiners who refuse to abide by the laws of their own state.

nitely. In three years between 1929 and 1932 national income shrank by nearly 50%, and the number of cars on the road soon showed a decline. In 1931, motor vehicle registrations took their first downward turn, falling that year by some 670,000; in 1932, 1,730,000 registrations were not renewed; and in 1933 the number of vehicles in operation declined by another quarter of a million—a total of 2,656,-000 cars and trucks off the road in the short space of three years.

The decline in registrations greatly decreased gasoline consumption—by a billion gallons a year in both 1932 and 1933. There was a furious scramble for the business that was left. With demand down and stocks of gasoline up, the stage was set for a bad drop in prices. The national average of retail gasoline prices (exclusive of tax) dropped from 17.9 cents a gallon in 1929 to 12.4 cents in 1933, or five and a half cents a gallon.

Averages tell only part of the story. Everywhere there were too many gasoline stations and more were being built daily. An article in *Fortune* in October 1932 concluded that "the U. S. oil business has invested $1,000,000,000 in unnecessary marketing facilities with an annual loss of $450,000,000, or about 4 per cent on the entire investment in all branches of the industry." [35]

In such a situation local price cutting assumed fearful proportions. It would start innocently enough with a little "under-the-canopy" price cutting, discounts given secretly by a dealer who did not openly alter his posted prices. In such a situation, it did not take long for the dealers who were losing business to locate the secret price cutter. Then the price cutting was on in earnest. One or more of the other dealers, in an attempt to gain back some of the lost trade, would cut below the former lowest price. The original cutter would lower his price again, openly this time, and the "war" would be on, drawing into it not only all the dealers in the area but their supplying companies as well. All seemed grimly determined to hang on; and as prices went lower and lower, with no one benefiting except the lucky customer, it often seemed that each of the combatants was bent on demonstrating that his bank roll was bigger than the other fellow's.

On the Pacific Coast, Los Angeles, with its dozens of small refining and marketing companies and nearby supplies of crude oil, was the trouble spot where West Coast price wars generally started, as has been noted in the previous chapter. In the Mid-Continent, almost every sizeable metropolitan area had its share of price cutting, touched off generally by the large independent chains of service stations concentrated in the big-city areas. On a national average, gasoline prices dropped by four cents a gallon between 1930 and 1931. There was an improvement in prices during 1932, but by 1933 the levels were again shockingly low.

Just what these low prices meant to Shell Petroleum in its chief markets can be visualized by quoting some of the retail prices, tax included, prevalent at company stations during 1933. That year, Shell Petroleum's retail prices in Chicago for housebrand ("regular") gasoline ranged from 11.1¢ to 13.1¢ a gallon, including 3¢ tax, with Silver Shell, the third-grade gasoline, selling for 2¢ less; in St. Louis where the tax was 3¢ a gallon, service station prices fluctuated between 10.2¢ and 12.2¢; in Detroit, where the tax was 4½¢, retail prices were between 11½¢ and 13½¢. In Indianapolis, with 5½¢ tax, the fluctuation for the year was between 11.7¢ and 13.9¢ a gallon; at Atlanta, where the tax was 7½¢ a gallon, retail prices ran between 13½¢ and 14¢; and in New Orleans, also with a 7½¢ tax, retail prices of housebrand went as low as 8¢ during the year, with Silver Shell selling for 4¢ a gallon less.[36]

Simple arithmetic will show the reader that the amount realized by the company, after tax, was very small—too little to pay for the cost of operating service stations and bulk depots and pay the refinery price for gasoline, which that year averaged between 5¢ and 7½¢ a gallon. And in instances such as New Orleans, where the tax was 7½¢ and prices, tax included, went as low as 4¢, the company was clearly 3½¢ out of pocket before it began to account for its costs. Such cases were by no means isolated: in Portland, Oregon, where the tax was 6½¢ a gallon, retail prices fell during 1933 to 5¢. Such prices gave rise to utterly ridiculous situations. In a number of instances where suppliers had contracted to furnish gasoline at so many cents per gallon below their own service station price, they found themselves in the insane position of shipping carloads of gasoline absolutely gratis—with a check to the customer for the difference accompanying the shipment! [37]

On the Atlantic Seaboard, price wars followed a somewhat different pattern. In the Mid-Continent, price wars were usually started by large chains of independent marketers. In the East, price warfare was generally confined to metropolitan areas and touched off by tank car dealers of the major companies. These dealers bought at a lower price than regular dealers and were therefore in a position to increase their share of the market by price cutting. Under the impetus of such cutting, retail prices on the Atlantic Seaboard often dropped for months at a time to 14¢, 13¢, and even 12¢ a gallon (tax included), but they did not descend to the absurd levels reached in some areas of the Mid-Continent, Gulf Coast, and Far West. Shell Eastern did not have tank car dealers, so it was a sufferer from, but never a starter of, price wars. In common with generally accepted trade practice, it did, however, attempt to "protect" its dealers in a severe price-cutting campaign. This protection generally took the form of guaranteeing the dealer a 2-cent margin. This meant, in the event of a price war, that the dealer with a 4-cent margin would be expected to share price cuts equally with his supplier until his margin had fallen to the guaranteed minimum of 2¢. Thereafter, the company absorbed the full amount of the cuts.[38]

Besides local price wars, there were in almost every area the "cut-rate artists," gasoline marketers who made price their specialty. These operators usually set up shop at railroad sidings, bought naphtha, kerosene, and casinghead gasoline in tank car lots, blended them together, and dispensed the mixture from hastily erected facilities for absurdly low prices. Such an operator was often legitimate, but in a great many cases he was not. In the words of a 1932 *Fortune* article, "This is one of the gasoline war's innumerable guerillas. He is probably evading taxes by smuggling gasoline, which is similar to bootlegging in that it is very often well worth the penalties which may be incurred. . . . His equipment is rickety and he is in for a quick haul and a get-away." [39]

In this jungle of throat-cutting which cannot be dignified by the word competition, the major companies and their dealers stood to lose the most. Theirs were the large investments in depots, service stations, and nationally known brands. Their stations and their dealers had accustomed the motorist to niceties such as rest rooms and to services other than the mere filling of an empty tank. Under the impact of a depression which cut national income in half, the emphasis in gasoline sales shifted overnight from quality to price. To compete with the track-side operator Shell reluctantly followed the lead of other major companies and installed, where it was necessary, a third pump to dispense "fighting gas," usually called "Green Streak" in the Far West, "Silver Shell" in the Mid-Continent and Atlantic Seaboard areas.‡ It sold at prices as low, or nearly as low, as those of the track-side operators; it might be "distress stock" purchased from smaller refiners on the spot market, or low-octane gasoline produced in Shell refineries with a minimum of processing. Since it was "fighting gas," the price of third-grade gasoline was raised or lowered as local conditions demanded; generally it was sold for 2¢ a gallon less than housebrand, but where competition was severe, a third-grade gasoline might be sold for 3 or even 4 cents below housebrand.[40]

On the Pacific Coast, there was another marketing phenomenon: the so-called secondary, or "concubine," companies controlled or operated by major companies and used to compete in markets where price was the primary factor. Such companies usually had their own depots, their own delivery trucks, their own string of service stations, and their own sales personnel. Their supplies came in large part, if not wholly, from the companies that controlled them. With the exception of Union Oil of California and The Texas Company, all of the Pacific Coast majors had a try at operating secondary companies at some time during the Thirties, and several of these organizations still survive.[41] In the opinion of the Shell management, secondary companies were hard to justify, for they caused duplication of facilities in times of extreme low prices. Their main advantage was that they could go after business where price competition was strongest without precipitating an all-around reduction in prices.

Early in 1933, Shell Oil acquired the business of the Independent Petroleum Company which operated in Seattle and Portland and was already engaged in the cut-price field. It was decided to convert it to a secondary company not only for the Northwest, but also for those markets in California where price competition was fiercest— Los Angeles, San Francisco, Sacramento, Fresno. The Guardian Oil Company at Coalinga, purchased some fifteen years before, had never been dissolved, so its name was assigned to the new company. P. E. Lakin, an up-and-coming member of the Shell Oil sales department, was put in charge of the new operation. Guardian was to be completely divorced from Shell, so an old Shell depot in Emeryville, no longer used, was taken over as site for its offices. The new com-

---

‡ The Shell Union annual report for 1932 underscored Shell's reluctance to introduce a third-grade gasoline: "Your subsidiary Companies, much against their judgment and very reluctantly, were compelled to follow the introduction of a third grade gasoline designed to meet the competition of cut-rate gasolines. It has not proved a complete success."

pany had its own colors, its own pumps, trucks, tankage, depots, and sales staff. It sold two brands of gasoline, the first equivalent to Shell housebrand, the second grade equal to Green Streak. Prices were about a cent under comparable grades at Shell stations, but could be lowered in localities where there was a war on. Supplies reached the Guardian depots from Shell terminals and, in a few areas where there were no Guardian depots, through jobbers.

Shell had entered upon the business of operating a secondary company halfheartedly, for it meant selling for the lowest prices gasoline which could have brought a better price at Shell stations. No spectacular successes resulted from the Guardian operation,§ and the N.R.A. code, adopted soon afterwards, set minimum prices below which Guardian could not cut. During 1934, only a year after it had started, the Guardian operation quietly folded up.[43]

The N.R.A.

Then, into the midst of this dog-eat-dog atmosphere came a new administration in Washington, intent on doing something overnight which would help the American economy right itself. Within its first three months in office, the new administration asked for and got dictatorial powers over the currency, sweeping powers to regulate agriculture, and an all-inclusive bill allowing it to regulate commerce and industry in the interests of recovery. With a grim enthusiasm born of desperation, the American business community buckled down to support the new administration's efforts, even though many of the new proposals were shocking to those with a respect for traditional American liberties.

One of these sweeping grants of power, the National Industrial Recovery Act, under which the National Recovery Administration was created, set up new rules for the oil industry, rules which had the effect of calling a moratorium on throat-cutting long enough for some of the more reckless members of the industry to come to their senses. Under the act, members of an industry were to get together and formulate a "code of fair competition" for their business. Upon approval by the President, this code would have all the force of law

§ P. E. Lakin, who was kind enough to read over the manuscript of this section, wrote, "From a direct marketing standpoint this was true. Actually, the experience was of tremendous value in the formation of marketing policies. Yours Truly certainly learned that the way to deal with 'concubines' and 'second-story sluggers' was to build a distribution set-up that was strong enough economically to compete directly with the lower price marketers." [42]

of the land, with violators subject to heavy fines.[44] The oil industry drew up a petroleum code and on August 23, 1933, President Roosevelt signed it. The new Petroleum Code had regulations governing labor, production, refining, and marketing.

To provide more employment, hours of work were set at a maximum of 40 a week, except in service stations where the maximum could be 48. Minimum wages were fixed, according to a sliding scale which varied with different sections of the country, at 45 to 52 cents an hour. Weekly pay of service station attendants was set at $12 to $15 a week, depending upon the population of the town. Hiring of persons under sixteen years of age was prohibited. The right of employees to bargain collectively was guaranteed, and discrimination against individuals for union activity was forbidden.

Most of the production provisions of the N.R.A. have been discussed in the preceding pages on conservation. There was, however, provision concerning crude prices as well as production limitation. As a general yardstick for crude prices, it was made illegal under the code to sell Mid-Continent crude for less than $18\frac{1}{2}$ times the per-gallon tank car price of 60–64 octane gasoline in the same area.

In refining, the country was divided into eight refining districts, and the President was authorized to appoint an agency to "suggest a proper relationship between inventories of gasoline and sales thereof for each district."

For the marketing end of the business, the Petroleum Code was much more explicit. Each retailer of petroleum products was required to post his price, was forbidden to sell below that posted price, and required to maintain each posting for at least 24 hours. No sales could be made below the cost of manufacture plus reasonable distributing expenses. The use of lotteries, prizes, and games of chance in connection with the sale of gasoline was forbidden, as also was the giving away of premiums, trading stamps, or free goods. Fuel oil dealers were forbidden to render burner service unless a charge of at least $10 a year was made for it. Credit terms which suppliers might grant to retailers were rigidly defined, and prices established for dispensing equipment which could no longer be furnished free. Free repairs or paint jobs to dealers' premises were forbidden, except for the painting of pumps. No free equipment of any sort might be furnished dealers, except for advertising signs and pump globes. In addition, suppliers were forbidden to lend money to retailers or to pay them for the privilege of advertising on their premises. For good measure, misleading advertising and filling of tanks with gasoline of other than the brand advertised were also forbidden. In their prohibitions, the code makers offered an interesting catalogue of the low state to which oil marketing had descended.[45]

A national code authority, the Petroleum Administrative Board, was set up in Washington, with Harold L. Ickes, Secretary of the Interior, as administrator. In California, where the voters had successfully defeated earlier attempts to set up a state oil board, there was no agency to carry out the production provisions of the code, so the President set up the Pacific Coast Petroleum Agency to administer the production and other codes. The marketing code on the West Coast differed in that it recognized three types of companies. The so-called "Group A" companies were the seven majors—Associated, General, Richfield, Shell, Standard of California, Texaco, and Union. The "Group B" companies were the "concubine" companies, owned by or affiliated with these majors. The "Group C" companies were bona fide independents, twenty-five in number. Retail prices charged by the "Group A" companies were to be considered "base price." "Group B" companies were to be allowed to sell $\frac{1}{2}$¢ a gallon below this base, and "Group C" companies 1¢ a gallon below.[46]

Soon things started to level out, whether because of the N.R.A. or in spite of it is still an unsettled argument. In 1933, the Century of Progress Exposition at Chicago introduced a new, streamlined car to America; automobile production shot back up to 2,178,000 cars in 1934, the first time it had passed the two million mark since 1930. Registrations, too, increased by a healthy 1,100,000. The demand for motor fuel jumped more than a billion and a quarter gallons. Crude oil in Oklahoma, East Texas, and Signal Hill was back up to a respectable $1 a barrel, and the national average of gasoline prices (exclusive of tax) rose from 12.4¢ to 13.6¢.

Then, in May 1935, the United States Supreme Court held the National Industrial Recovery Act unconstitutional and the Petroleum Code, along with the codes for other industries, promptly fell apart. During the period of the Code, a measure of recovery had come to the oil industry but it is extreme oversimplification to attribute any large part of the improvement to the N.R.A. Gasoline consumption, gasoline prices, automobile prices, automobile production, and motor vehicle registrations all continued to rise and during 1936 reached levels higher than at any time under the code.

National Petroleum News summed up the situation in an editorial:

"The Supreme Court's decision does not require the industry to make a fool of itself, to cut prices and wages, to increase hours of labor, to give away premiums and marketing equipment, to run more crude and make more gasoline than the markets require. While the code sought by law to forbid all these bad things, they were actually eliminated by the voluntary action of the industry." [47]

The Iowa Plan

The demise of the N.R.A. was big news, but the same issue of *NPN* carried an announcement from Standard Oil of Indiana that would have more lasting effect upon the marketing end of the industry than the N.R.A.

All during the depression years, scapegoats were constantly being singled out as *the* thing responsible for hard times. One such scapegoat was the chain store, which had grown rapidly during the late Twenties and in its growth injured just enough local merchants to lend credence to the charges now levelled against it. The retail druggists' and grocers' lobbies were especially active during the winter of 1934–1935, and by February 1935 no fewer than 104 anti-chain-store bills had been introduced in the legislatures of 34 states. Many of them were passed. Almost without exception, they were frankly designed not for revenue-raising purposes but for the purpose of placing a disability on retail outlets that were the members of a chain. The number of units that constituted a chain and the amount of tax assessed varied from state to state. In most, a more or less similar pattern was followed. Less than a half dozen units could go untaxed; for each store over that number there would be an annual tax that rose in amount as the number of units in the chain increased.

Not all these bills passed, and some of those that did pass exempted service stations. But others, such as the Iowa chain store tax, included service stations and made them liable to not one but two types of tax. After July 1, 1935, the Iowa tax law called for a tax on each unit in the chain, running from $5 a station on five to ten units up to $155 per station for every station over fifty. In addition, the Iowa law taxed the chain's gross receipts heavily, beginning at $25 for an annual volume of $50,000 with a graduated levy running up to 10% on annual receipts of $1,000,000 and over. For Standard Oil of Indiana, which had about 850 company-operated outlets in Iowa, a year's tax bill under the new legislation could run to well over a million dollars. [48]

To avoid the penalties of this new Iowa law, the Indiana company announced in May 1935 that its 850 Iowa stations would be leased to their former managers wherever practicable, and otherwise to qualified outsiders. Gasoline would be delivered to the dealer by the company acting in the capacity of wholesaler. Determination of the retail price would be up to the retailer. Theoretically of course that had been the situation before, but where supplying companies also owned and operated retail stations, the retail prices they posted at company stations often had the effect of establishing a ceiling price. The dealer was free, it is true, to raise or lower his retail prices at will; but he could hardly expect to hold or increase his business if he were charging a price much more than the retail price posted at his supplier's company-operated stations. The dealer's freedom in price determination was chiefly freedom to lower prices. In times of price battles, the dealers cut prices first and company stations tried to hold to the higher price as long as they could.*

The existence of company-operated retail outlets had been a source of friction between dealers and their suppliers, so much so that dealers insisted on supply contracts tied to the retail price charged at company stations. Such contracts operated in the dealer's favor in times of low prices, as we have seen, but they were hard on the supplying company during a bad price war. Now the companies operating in the Mid-Continent saw a way to avoid ruinous chain store taxes, realign the basis of their sales contracts with dealers, dispense with the headaches of overseeing far-flung retail operations, and reduce the number of people on their payrolls by getting out of retailing altogether.

Relinquishing company-owned stations to dealers on a large scale was not new. The same plan had, as we have seen, been tried with success by most of the large operators on the Pacific Coast during the late 1920's. However, the motivating reasons in this case had been of a temporary nature; by the early 1930's several Pacific Coast

---

* The subject of price determination is too complicated for an adequate discussion here. Several books have been written on gasoline price, and the voluminous T.N.E.C. hearings and monographs of the late Thirties were devoted in large part to the prices of oil and oil products. The interested reader looking for a shorter account is referred to two excellent and understandable papers: Edmund P. Learned, "Pricing of Gasoline: A Case Study," *Harvard Business Review*, November 1948, pp. 723-756, and Harold Fleming, *Oil Prices and Competition*, New York, American Petroleum Institute, 1953, 62 pages. A recent book-length treatment is Ralph Cassady, Jr., *Price Making and Price Behavior in the Petroleum Industry*, New Haven, Yale University Press, 1954.

companies were once again operating their own stations with salaried personnel. In most instances, Shell continued dealer operation after buying up the Van Fleet-Durkee contract in 1932; but the industry had not followed Shell's lead in California as it now followed Indiana Standard's in Iowa. By July 1, 1935, when the new taxes became effective, every operator of service station chains in the state of Iowa, with the exception of one jobber, had converted to the new "Iowa plan" of operation.[49]

Companies not operating in Iowa watched the Iowa experiment with interest. As soon as it became apparent that its advantages outweighed the disadvantages, there was a rush to convert to the Iowa plan and during the next few years, most of the major-company outlets in the Mid-Continent and along the Atlantic Seaboard were placed in the hands of dealers. (An exception among the majors was Standard of Ohio, marketing only in one state; it continued to operate its company-owned stations.)

In most instances, the Iowa plan was an attractive business proposition, both for the man who ran the station and the company which owned it and supplied the product. The early gasoline retailers all had been dealers, and dealers had remained the backbone of the oil companies' sales organization even when chain operation was at its height.† But up to now the dealer had usually built and furnished his own outlet. When the oil companies had started to build stations, they had operated them, and many companies even leased and operated stations which they did not own.

Because few men work for others as well as they work for themselves, the Iowa plan got off to a good start. With the station his to operate, the former manager, now a dealer, saw new ways to economize. He saw to it that tires, batteries, and other items didn't disappear from the premises without being paid for. He welcomed the opportunity to sell non-petroleum merchandise because it augmented his income from gasoline and motor oil. He saw that friendliness and courtesy, once practiced because they were company policy, were his cheapest and most persuasive form of advertising.

On the companies' side, the Iowa plan was a good deal, too. Besides eliminating liability to chain store taxes in states which had such levies, the Iowa plan left to the dealer such questions as minimum wages,

† In March 1935, just before inauguration of the Iowa plan, integrated companies were making only 14% of their total gasoline sales through company-operated stations.[50]

maximum hours, and unionization of attendants. Payrolls for retail employees were eliminated, and the company was relieved of the details of supervision, money collections, and service station book-keeping. The operator soon discovered that he had indeed had a lot done for him. A dispatch from Des Moines on July 5, 1935, after only five days of the Iowa plan, said that the average dealer (formerly the company's salaried manager) was finding that the extra work of bookkeeping and ordering merchandise was extending his own work week from the 48 hours he had worked under the N.R.A. to a figure more nearly approaching seventy.[51] The man who preferred to work for a stated salary, rather than take his chances as his own boss, didn't look too kindly on the new plan. Fortunately, the average dealer was not of this stamp and jumped at the chance to make more money for himself.

In some other respects, leaving the retail operation in the hands of a dealer wasn't as satisfactory. As many oil men had predicted, the great problems of 100% dealer operation were service and clean-liness. Formerly, even though dealers had vastly outnumbered com-pany stations, company stations had set standards of cleanliness and free service which competition forced the dealer to follow. Now, the pace-setters would have to be leaders among the dealers them-selves. Shell soon began a program of education that still continues, aimed at getting dealers to keep their standards of operation as high as those of former company stations. This was necessary because, working for himself, the dealer was much less likely to spend time doing things that were unproductive of revenue, such as cleaning rest rooms. The oil company salesmen calling on dealer accounts soon found that the hardest part of their jobs was not selling their products but in selling the dealer on the necessity for continuing the high standards which the public had come to expect.

Advertising helps which company stations had received were given to dealers. In fact, oil company dealers as a whole probably get more sales aids and sales suggestions from their suppliers than dealers han-dling most other lines of merchandise. Service stations, unlike grocers, generally carry only one brand of product; the supplier whose sales depend on these outlets is understandably willing to do all he can to help assure their success.

In 1935, the Iowa Plan was adopted as a temporary solution for an immediate problem: it provided a method of operating stations which the company had built with intention of operating. Twenty

years later the Iowa Plan was still with the industry; it had become
an institution for other reasons. Before the days of lubrication and
specialized tools and services, when only a single gasoline and one
motor oil were carried and both in small quantity, the dealer usually
had or could borrow money enough to build and stock his own
station. With the general increase in real estate and construction
costs, with the advent of more elaborate stations whose two rest
rooms cost more than a whole station used to, with a host of special
tools to buy, and with larger inventories of petroleum products and
accessory items to purchase, the dealer now needed several thousand
dollars just to finance his inventory and buy his tools. Increasingly,
he looked to the company to supply the station.

6

Other Markets, Advertising, A New Station

SERVICE stations and automotive gasoline wholly aside for the moment,
there were other new and important markets to which the company
gave an increasing amount of attention in the 1930–1935 period. Chief
among them were domestic fuel oil, aviation gasoline, and specialty
products.

Oil fuel, of course, was nothing new; its sale had been an important
part of the business before the turn of the century. But always it was
burned by ships, factories, or large institutional buildings, for oil
burning required a trained boilerman in attendance. Then, during the
First World War the scarcity of coal, felt especially in New England,
spurred on the burner makers and in the years immediately following
the war, domestic oil burners began to make their appearance.

Development of Domestic Oil Burners

In 1921, some 9,000 oil burners were sold for home installation,
but they were as yet far from perfected. The most common burner
of that day was the so-called "mushroom" burner, fed by gravity
and operated on a natural draft. During the early Twenties this type
of burner, which was often no more than a one-piece iron casting,
sold well at prices approximating $100. But it did not give really
satisfactory service. With imperfect weather conditions, the natural

draft was a liability. The burner would smoke and soot, and the imperfect combustion this created caused oil consumption to mount unduly. The combination of natural draft with gravity feed made the range of regulation narrow: the mushroom burner furnished too much heat in mild weather, not enough in cold weather, and could not be turned down sufficiently at night.[52]

Helped along by these objections, the mechanical-draft burners which had been on the market in 1921 in small numbers made steady progress. Despite its much greater cost, the mechanical burner overtook the natural-draft burner in sales during 1925. Development of the domestic oil burner thereafter was more rapid. In most models of the mechanical burner, the draft was supplied by a motor-driven blower and the oil by an electric pump; such a burner was susceptible of automatic control. The years between 1927 and 1930 saw the development of thermostats; connected to motor-driven burners, they provided steady, automatically controlled temperatures. Here indeed was luxurious home heating: oil, stored in a tank and pumped through pipes, burned automatically in the furnace to provide an even room temperature regardless of the weather. Gone were constant attendance upon the furnace, hand stoking, and laborious removal of ashes. In 1929 alone, more than 100,000 of the new automatic burners were installed in American homes. But they were still luxury heat. The burner installations themselves were expensive and only in a few sections of the country where coal was extremely high in price, could fuel oil compete with coal.

This price barrier was finally removed by depression conditions. The cost of oil burners, because of quantity production and depression prices, was greatly reduced. The distillate fuel oil used by domestic oil burners dropped in price nearly 50% between 1929 and 1931. With cheaper burners and cheaper fuel, oil could now compete with coal in home heating and in a few areas, such as New England, oil fuel could even undersell coal. As a result, the number of domestic oil burners increased sharply in 1935, burner installations passed the million mark, and by the end of the Thirties had nearly doubled.

Shell had been making and selling fuel oil since the days of its first refineries in America. In the San Francisco area as early as 1915 the company had purchased trucks for delivering fuel oil to apartment houses and institutions. During the late Twenties and early

Thirties, the Shell companies began to go after the domestic fuel business. The 1930–1935 period saw the development of fleets of Shell tank trucks equipped with long hoses and automatic metering devices to deliver fuel oil into the tanks of individual users. Similar trucks were put into service by the jobbers who handled the largest share of the company's domestic fuel oil sales.

Kerosene-Burning Appliances

At the same time, kerosene consumption took a sharp swing upward, a result of the new range oil burners which were replacing wood and coal in the kitchen stoves of rural areas. Kerosene-burning hot-water heaters were in the process of being introduced, and many homes without central heating were converting their wood or coal stoves to kerosene, or purchasing one of the new kerosene space heaters. In New England, where range oil burners had developed, there were 590,000 of them in service by 1932.[53] By 1935, kerosene demand hit 47,645,000 barrels, a figure far exceeding consumption during any year of the 1920's. This increased sale was handled by established dealers in kerosene (garages and general stores, for the most part) and by jobbers who used the same kind of trucks they had put into service for fuel oil.

Automotive Diesel Engines

For the moment it also looked as though Diesel-engine fuels might be sold widely to the general public. Hopefully, "Shell Diesoline" was introduced early in the Thirties. However, about the only passenger-car application which Diesel fuel ever saw was a widely publicized cross-country trip made by C. L. Cummins, a Diesel engine manufacturer, in the summer of 1935. Cummins equipped an Auburn automobile with a Diesel engine of his own design and proved that it could be driven from New York to Los Angeles on $7.63 worth of Shell Diesoline. Diesel-powered cars were confidently predicted for the next season, but so far they have failed to appear. The reasons are not far to seek. Engine manufacturers have thus far failed to produce a Diesel engine that, for a given power output, is comparable to the gasoline engine in price. A second stumbling block is that Diesel fuel, because it is much heavier than gasoline or kerosene, evaporates so slowly that its unpleasant odor cannot be dissipated. Such drawbacks have not proved important to operators of trucks and buses; to them operating economy is a paramount consideration.

The Aviation Market

Shell's active entry into the American aviation market during the early Thirties was in reality one of the culminating moves of the great expansion of 1929. Shell "spirit" had fueled Louis Blériot's first flight across the English channel in 1909, and the Shell companies on the Continent had become active sellers of aviation gasoline soon afterward. In 1920, the Group set up a formal aviation department in London to supply gasoline to customers such as the K.L.M. (Royal Dutch Airlines), which started operations that year.[54]

Progress of commercial aviation in America lagged behind that in Europe during the early half of the Twenties, and it was not until late in the decade that demand for aviation gasoline became large enough to warrant a separate organization to handle its sale.‡ By 1929, the American Shell companies were selling some high-quality gasoline for aviation purposes, but a special department to handle aviation sales did not come until late in 1929.

At that time, Shell Oil in San Francisco set up an aviation department and for its manager hired a well-known aviation figure, Capt. John A. Macready. Macready had been a member of the two-man team which made the first non-stop flight across the American Continent in 1923, and he had served as chief test pilot at McCook Field until 1926. His new San Francisco aviation department started officially on January 1, 1930. Soon after, on January 15, 1930, Shell Petroleum in St. Louis hired an equally noted flier, Lt. James H. Doolittle, to manage its aviation department. Three months later, the triumvirate was complete when Major R. G. Ervin was engaged

‡ In May 1920, the new K.L.M. (Royal Dutch Airlines), organized in 1919 by Dr. Albert Plesman, began its first scheduled service between Amsterdam and London. In September 1920, K.L.M. started an Amsterdam-Hamburg-Copenhagen run; and four years later, on October 1, 1924, it began flying from Amsterdam to Batavia, Java. In the United States, airmail service started during the First World War with Army Air Corps planes. This had the effect of retarding the development of American commercial aviation. Late in 1925 the Post Office awarded its first general airmail contracts to five airlines: Varney Air Lines (later merged with others to form United), Robinson Air Lines (contract later transferred to American), Western Air Transport (now Western Air Lines), National Air Transport (another company which merged to form the present United Air Lines), and Colonial Air Transport, a predecessor of the present-day American Airlines. Colonial, which claimed an airmail contract for the Boston–New York run dating back to 1924, was organized by Cornelius V. Whitney, Percy A. Rockefeller (of Union of Delaware fame), William H. Vanderbilt, and Juan Trippe, later president of Pan-American Airways. Reflecting the later development of American aviation is the fact that Standard Oil of New Jersey, generally Shell's chief competitor in fields such as this, did not set up an aviation department until July 1928.

to manage a new aviation department for Shell Eastern in New York. All three men had a common background in that they had been World War I fliers who continued in the Air Corps in peacetime, Doolittle coming directly from that service to Shell, Macready from General Motors where he had been assistant general sales manager of G. M.'s Frigidaire division, Ervin from the Curtiss Flying Service where he had been vice president in charge of New England operations. Because aviation was nation-wide, the three departments were run as a unit almost from the first, with activities coordinated through Doolittle in St. Louis.[55]

The aviation gasoline business presented a much different picture in 1929 than it did a few years later. In 1929, a total of 20½ million gallons of gasoline were sold for aviation purposes, of which less than a third, some 6¼ million gallons, were used in scheduled airline operations. The other 14¼ million gallons were sold at airports to unscheduled airlines and private fliers. In the two years following Lindbergh's sensational flight to Paris in 1927, thousands of Americans had bought and were learning to fly their own airplanes, just as their fathers had bought and learned to drive automobiles a quarter of a century before. Many people thought that the airplane was now about to displace the automobile, just as the auto had displaced the horse. But with the coming of the depression, private flying proved far more dispensable than the automobile had ever been.

In 1930, sales of aviation gasoline to airlines pulled abreast of private plane consumption. Sales to airlines took the lead in 1931 and continued to account for an increasingly large percentage of the total, until by 1935 airlines were using a full two-thirds of the aviation gasoline sold.[56] Airlines had been carrying air mail and passengers since the late years of the Twenties, but commercial aviation got a really big boost in 1933, the same year which saw streamlining come to the automobile industry. The DC-2, a radically new and practical airplane manufactured by the Douglas Aircraft Company, made its appearance that year. Two years later a similar two-engine plane of higher horsepower and larger carrying capacity, the DC-3, replaced it and became an immediate success with nearly all of the world's commercial airlines. Substantial time cuts in airline schedules resulted in increased popularity of flying, and greater popularity brought more frequent flights.

Shell's aviation departments at San Francisco, St. Louis, and New York went after their share of this increased airline business. It was

business for which all the oil companies competed strongly: an airline
offered large volume and bought its gasoline for a year at a time. To
get this business, prices in many cases were shaved to the level of
dubious profitability. Despite the hot competition, Shell during the
first half of the Thirties acquired the accounts of Northwest Airlines,
which was gradually expanding its Chicago–St. Paul mail run westward; of the new Chicago & Southern Air Lines (now Delta-C. & S.),
originally a West Coast concern; and of the burgeoning American
Airlines. By 1933, Shell Petroleum was supplying American with
2½ million gallons of aviation gasoline annually at nineteen airports
in the South and Southwest.[57]

Another quantity buyer of aviation gasoline was the government
and here again the business was fiercely fought for, and for the same
reasons. Shell got some of the contracts on which it bid, but its most
spectacular government sale was the delivery of the first commercial
quantities of iso-octane to the Army Air Corps in 1934, a story
which is told in detail in the chapter on the war years.

In addition to the government services and the airlines, there were
two other major markets for aviation gasoline: the aircraft manufacturers who used large amounts in engine testing, and the airport
operators who sold chiefly to private fliers. The latter two markets,
though smaller in volume, offered more stable commitments, and
Shell concentrated a good deal of sales effort on them. Dating from
these years, many large aircraft manufacturers have been supplied
in whole or in part by Shell. Airport operators sold much smaller
volumes of gasoline, but they were widely scattered which meant
that they could offer the representation which every oil company
felt it should have.

At the creation of the new aviation departments each was provided
with planes: two for San Francisco and another for the salesman in
Los Angeles, one for St. Louis, and one for New York.[58] All three
managers spent a good share of their time making personal calls at
airports in their territories. The Shell Eastern department, for instance, had by 1934 visited every town in its territory having an
airport and had given rides to more than 36,000 Shell dealers, jobbers,
prospective airport dealers, state and municipal officials, and news-
papermen.[59] This attention to the airport market resulted in Shell's
obtaining a considerable share of the airport business. While volume
was not as large, the prices were generally more satisfactory. The
only drawback to the airport dealer business was the necessity for

meeting unrealistic requests for dispensing equipment. For the smaller airports, a fixed station, dispensing gasoline from 55-gallon drums with hand-operated pumps, was a more economical arrangement. But when the new tank trucks with power-operated pumping equipment became available, the small airport dealers immediately began to clamor for them. Such a truck gave the dealer a great deal of mobility, was much easier to operate, and was therefore highly desirable from his viewpoint. But with volume small, an oil company could not afford to furnish such expensive equipment at nominal rentals. Resisting these unrealistic demands for equipment without losing the business soon became the chief headache of the airport salesmen.

By 1935, Shell's aviation departments had signed up some good airline accounts; some excellent manufacturers' accounts; substantial sales to the government, with emphasis on the high-quality products of research; and a large number of airport dealers.[60]

No small amount of prestige was lent to the Shell aviation salesman's efforts by *Shell Aviation News*, an international aviation monthly which the Group issued from London, beginning in July 1931. Unlike most aviation publications then on the market, *Shell Aviation News* made no attempt to espouse a particular cause or viewpoint, with the result that it soon gained world-wide respect in aviation circles as an impartial reporter of the news. It published technical articles by some of the ablest minds in aviation, and a list of its authors over a twenty-year period reads like a Who's Who in international aviation. In addition to the English-language version, a French edition has for some years been issued from Paris.

Specialty Products

Also receiving increased attention were specialty products, a term generally embracing all those items that can be or are produced as by-products but which are not primary petroleum products. A specialty product of the early kerosene refineries, for instance, was paraffin wax and the candles made from it. Shell refineries in America, with the exception of Martinez, were from the first devoted to large-volume manufacture of a comparatively few products. Martinez was equipped to make lubricating oils, greases, spray oils, asphalts, and other low-volume products. Lubricating oil was manufactured by Shell Petroleum at Wood River and asphalt at Norco, but aside from incidental production of naphthas and the manufacture of petroleum coke at Arkansas City and East Chicago, none of the other refineries made what could properly be called specialty products.[61] The reason, of course, was simple: it takes millions of barrels of gasoline, kerosene, and fuel oil to supply the nation for a year; but the country can get by on relatively insignificant volumes of most specialty products.

The manufacture of these smaller-volume products was not new by any means. But it was not until the late Twenties that Shell, with every thought bent towards sales, made an effort to sell specialty and technical products and to develop new ones. By the fall of 1928 the West Coast motorist could buy Shell dry cleaner, auto polish, household lubricant, spring oil, furniture polish, insect spray, and cleaning and lighter fluids. In the Midwest he could buy some of these specialties and, in addition, "Shellane," the company's new "bottled gas" for cookstoves. Paint and varnish manufacturers and dry cleaners were already using Shell naphthas and solvents in their businesses. During 1929, Shellane also became available on the Pacific Coast, and departments to handle these new specialties and technical products were set up by both Shell Oil and Shell Petroleum.[62]

In the early depression years, Shell stations nation-wide began to carry stocks of merchandise to supplement their incomes from gasoline and motor oil. Specialty products became the backbone of this new sales effort. Vigorous promotions, such as one-cent sales, were inaugurated and attempts were made to get Shell specialties into regular retail outlets—department stores, hardware stores, grocery and chain stores. Then the sales department made a sobering discovery: as much money as went into gasoline advertising, or more, would have to be spent to advertise specialty products if their sale in competition to comparable advertised products was to be a success. In stores, the average customer showed a marked preference for a floor wax such as Johnson's, for instance, rather than the unadvertised Shell product. At a service station, it was different. The customer had come to buy at least one Shell product; it was not too difficult to sell him another.

The profitability of packaged specialties became, and continued to be, a matter of argument after the first burst of enthusiasm died away. A satisfactory profit could be shown on paper, but this calculation did not take into account the large amounts of shopworn merchandise which the company regularly took back from its dealers, allowing them full credit because they were valued customers for Shell gasoline—a practice which a specialty wholesaler selling to ordinary retail outlets would not have permitted. In any event, two points could not be disputed: the sale of specialties increased the dealer's net income, and the introduction of a satisfactory Shell specialty into a customer's home left him favorably disposed towards the rest of the Shell line, as well as keeping the company's trademark before him for six months to a year, since polishes, sprays, and handy oil were not used up immediately.[63]

It remained for another branch of the specialty department, the technical products such as mineral spirits, naphthas, and process materials, some seventy-five of them in all, to do the really big volumes. By the end of the 1930–1935 period or shortly thereafter, both specialties and technical products were being sold by all three Shell operating companies, and specialties were being made and packaged at Martinez, Wood River, and the Sewaren, New Jersey, terminal where a small plant had been built. The Shellane operation centered about the East Chicago refinery, principally because of freight advantages.[64]

New Motor Oils

Over the years, as automobile manufacturers increased the compression ratios of their engines, refiners were obliged to devote a good deal of research to methods for making motor oils that would not oxidize and form sludge in the new engines. Most refiners also had a desire to produce from their own crude oils premium-grade lubricants comparable in quality to the Pennsylvania motor oils which most companies still stocked in addition to their own brands, as Shell did with its "Shell-Penn." The virtue of Pennsylvania-grade lubricants was the raw material. Pennsylvania crude oils were simple, paraffin-base oils while the much more abundant crudes of the Mid-Continent, Southwest, and Far West had either asphaltic bases or a mixture of asphaltic and paraffin bases. New refining processes to make possible manufacture of premium-quality oils, comparable to Pennsylvania lubricants, were developed by several companies and put into commercial operation during the early 1930's.

These new processes substituted solvent extraction for traditional distilling methods. Two of the most notable of the solvent extraction processes were furfural extraction and the Duo-Sol process, in both of which Shell had a good patent position because of the Group's long-standing interest in solvent extraction.

Furfural is an oily liquid distilled from bran, oat hulls, and similar substances. An important and early patent covering its use as an extractant in petroleum processing had been taken out in 1923 by Rhenania, the Royal Dutch-Shell affiliate in Germany. In the United States, the Indian Refining Company had developed and put into operation a furfural extraction process for the manufacture of its lubricating oils. This process, along with a solvent dewaxing method, had been chief considerations at the time of Texaco's purchase of Indian Refining in 1931. Texaco, looking to put the process into large-scale manufacture and license it to other refiners as well, discovered Rhenania's patent and approached Pyzel to see if he could arrange a license. This was the first knowledge that the Shell people in this country had of the Rhenania patent, but they used their bargaining position to good advantage. In exchange for a per-barrel royalty, Texaco was licensed to use the Rhenania patent and license it to others, along with the Van Dyck patents mentioned below.

The Duo-Sol process, the development of the Max B. Miller Company, employed two solvents, propane and a phenol-cresol mixture, running in countercurrent to each other. Dr. J. van Dyck of the Group's Amsterdam laboratory had also done a great deal of work on process flow and had taken out basic patents covering the so-called "backwash," or double countercurrent, principle in which a partially processed extract fraction is returned to the tail end of the extraction system to increase the efficiency of the recovery process. When, early in 1933, Shell Petroleum decided to install a Duo-Sol plant at Wood River and approached Miller for a license it was suggested that Miller might like to incorporate this backwash principle in the Duo-Sol process. At about the same time the "JUIK Group" (Jersey, Union, Indiana, and M. W. Kellogg), which held a patent position in phenol extraction and in the use of propane as an extractant, pointed out to Miller the possibility of patent conflicts. Negotiations followed and Shell agreed to turn over to Miller full use of the Van Dyck backwash patents as they applied to the Duo-Sol process, and the JUIK companies in a similar manner agreed to assign Miller rights under their patents. This left Miller free to license the Duo-Sol process without fear of litigation. From royalties collected Miller received a small percentage as management and licensing fee; the remainder was paid 30% to Shell, with Miller and the JUIK group dividing the other 70%.

The Duo-Sol process was capable of producing high-quality lubricants from both distillate and residual charge stocks. Wood River completed a Duo-Sol plant during 1934, and a furfural plant was installed at Martinez at about the same time. The single-solvent methods like furfural extraction were cheaper to operate than the Duo-Sol process which employed two solvents, but the Duo-Sol process remained for many years the only method suitable for working residual oils. Later, a tower de-asphalting process developed by Kellogg made it possible to treat residuals with a single solvent, and this was the process chosen for installation at Shell's Houston refinery in the postwar years.

For their day, both the furfural and Duo-Sol processes were a big step forward in the manufacture of lubricating oil. The new Shell motor oils proved themselves equal to Pennsylvania oils in performance and the company within a few years was able to discontinue carrying Shell-brand Pennsylvania oils. An interesting footnote is that most Pennsylvania refiners have since adopted these or similar solvent extraction processes.[65]

Premium Gasoline

Discussion of Shell marketing in the 1930–1935 period is not complete without mention of improvement in the quality of all grades of gasoline and the program of planned advertising that let the public know about these improvements. Both developments had their roots in the Twenties, and each is to some extent interwoven with the other.

Prior to 1920, almost all gasoline was being made by the straight-run distillation method, with the lightest gasoline generally considered best. In those pre-1920 days, straight-run gasoline averaged 64°–66° gravity but as the pressure to produce more and more gasoline from a barrel of crude mounted, the gravity and the volatility were gradually lowered. In 1922, the U. S. Navy's latest specifications for motor gasoline were adopted by all government procurement agencies. One of the Navy specifications, a final boiling point of 437° F., soon became standard for the refining industry. To this 437° endpoint the refiners added a specification of their own, gravity of 58° to 60°. These dual specifications, 58°–60° gravity and 437° endpoint, described the gasoline called "New Navy" in the wholesale trade; it was a universal standard on the wholesale gasoline market all during the Twenties.[66]

During these same years cracking was increasing and cracked gasoline of roughly the same specifications was blended with the straight-run gasoline. Gravity continued to be the chief measure of gasoline quality. Shell of California plugged its "61-Gravity" gasoline (1925), while in the Mid-Continent, the bustling Phillips company stabilized large amounts of casinghead down to 60° to 70° gravity and marketed it as "Phillips 66." During the second half of the Twenties, Shell in the Mid-Continent went to work on the other specification, the final boiling point, lowering it from the conventional 437° endpoint to 400°. This lowered final boiling had the effect of excluding some of the less volatile fractions.[67]

By 1926, the Wood River refinery was making substantial quantities of 400-endpoint gasoline which Roxana introduced as a premium-priced motor fuel, called briefly "Shell Aviation." Then, in January 1927, Roxana reduced the final boiling point of its premium fuel from 400° to 375° F.[68] This new premium gasoline, put on the market early in 1927, was called "Super-Shell"; it sold for 3¢ a gallon more than the price of regular "Shell" gasoline. Coincident with this improvement, the regular 437-endpoint Shell gasoline was replaced with the 400-endpoint fuel that had been sold as premium gasoline a year earlier.[69]

Shell on the Pacific Coast continued for a time on a one-gasoline basis, and in 1928 a vigorous campaign on behalf of "Shell 400—the 'Dry' Gas" was prepared by the J. Walter Thompson Company's San Francisco office. Immediately upon acquisition of the Shell account, the Thompson agency started *Shelling The Line*, a peppy monthly organ for the sales force to present "facts and ideas to help win sales battles" and launched vigorous campaigns, both for Shell "400" and Shell motor oil.[70]

From 1910 onwards, pioneer research work was being done on the causes of detonation, or "knocking," as it is commonly called—first in England (1910–1912) by H. R. (later Sir Harry) Ricardo and after 1916 in America by Dr. Thomas Midgley, Jr., and T. A. Boyd of General Motors.[71] After the end of World War I, Asiatic in London took on financial sponsorship of Ricardo's work and in the early Twenties he developed the so-called "E-35" engine to test any motor fuel for "Highest Useful Compression Ratio," the point at which knocking began. Midgley and his associates developed a more compact test engine. More important, they discovered that minute quantities of tetraethyl lead (a poisonous metallic compound) would, when added to ordinary gasoline, decrease the gasoline's tendency to knock. In August 1924, General Motors and Standard Oil of New Jersey formed a joint company, the Ethyl Gasoline Corporation, to make and sell this compound which they called

Ethyl fluid. Several companies contracted to use the new additive in a premium-priced, anti-knock gasoline.

Shell, however, did not take immediately to the leading of gasoline. No doubt the company hoped for a time that Ricardo's researches would uncover a comparable anti-knock compound. Little did anyone realize that Midgley and Boyd had had a piece of incredible luck and, out of thousands of possible additives, discovered the best one almost at first try. Also, as in the case of the cracking processes a few years earlier, Shell did not relish the idea of paying royalties to a competitor. Further, in that area of the Midwest covered by Standard of Indiana, the Indiana company had secured from the Ethyl people a five-year exclusive contract [72] which effectively barred Roxana from using Ethyl fluid in the most important part of its marketing area. There was another important deterrent, the dangerous nature of the compound itself. Tetraethyl lead could damage engines when too much was added and its toxic effects had, in a plant where it was made, caused a number of cases of lead poisoning and four deaths. In May 1925, the Ethyl people, in response to public outcry, withdrew their product from the market for a year until studies could be made and adequate safety measures put into effect. [73]

Hard pressed by competition, Shell continued its efforts to find a method of producing gasolines of high anti-knock value without the use of tetraethyl lead. In May 1930, Shell Oil in San Francisco put on the market a new premium fuel, a blend of low-endpoint cracked gasoline with high-boiling Edeleanu extract. It was called Super-Shell, was advertised as containing "eka-benzol," and possessed an H.U.C. value (the rating determined by tests on the Ricardo engine) equal to or better than competing premium fuels containing Ethyl fluid. [74] It sold for 3¢ a gallon more than Shell "400."

For the time being (1927–1930), Shell Petroleum was able to make a satisfactory premium fuel by blending cracked gasoline, which had good anti-knock qualities, with about 10% of straight-run gasoline manufactured from selected crudes. Smackover, Hendricks, Yates (deep zone), Black Bayou, and White Castle crudes were segregated and used to make this premium-grade straight-run product for blending. The main problem was to obtain enough such oils; also the deep cracking employed to produce the cracked components was expensive. C. M. Kellogg, the company's refinery economist, calculated that beyond 73 octane it would be cheaper to employ tetraethyl lead for additional octane increases. During 1930, Shell Petroleum finally concluded that it must in the interest of economics plan on manufacturing a premium gasoline containing tetraethyl lead. The Indiana company's exclusive contract had now expired, so in January 1931 Shell Petroleum launched an Ethyl gasoline called Super-Shell Ethyl to replace Super-Shell as the premium gasoline.§ The segregated crudes formerly used to produce straight-run stock for blending into Super-Shell were thereafter diverted to aviation gasoline. Super-Shell Ethyl was introduced to the Atlantic Seaboard during 1931, and by the following spring Ethyl-blending facilities were in operation on the Pacific Coast.[75]

The New Advertising

Concurrent with the adoption of Super-Shell Ethyl on the West Coast in the spring of 1932, Shell "400" was withdrawn as the regular gasoline.* A new, higher-octane housebrand gasoline containing the cracked components formerly used in Super-Shell was introduced to replace Shell "400" and christened Shell "3-Energy" gasoline. The Thompson agency was called in to do a full-scale advertising job, and about $750,000 was allotted to the campaign on the Coast, more than Shell had previously spent on promotion. Two three-month campaigns were run during 1932 with spectacular success. The company's percentage of the total West Coast business increased and these additional sales paid for the campaign, which had the salutary side effect of thoroughly "energizing" the sales force.[76]

The company's first big sales meetings were held in connection with the "3-Energy" drive. From then on, these "hypodermic campaigns," as they were called in sales management circles, came to be a regular spring feature. They were, of course, the delight of the sales force, for they were a "shot in the arm" that immediately halted declining sales, pepped up the salesmen and dealers, and launched a new product with a new name. But, as with a hypodermic, the effects of such a campaign wore off quickly. And if the campaign were outstandingly successful, it usually brought retaliation from competitors in the form of new campaigns for their gasolines.[77]

In the Mid-Continent, sales had reached new lows by early 1933.

§ The Super-Shell name proved a hardy perennial. It was revived in 1933 for housebrand and used until shortly before the war, when the former housebrand name was restored. While this book was in press (summer 1956), the company announced plans to introduce a new improved premium fuel, using the Super Shell name that had long been a favorite both of motorists and the Shell sales organization.

* Regular gasoline containing tetraethyl lead, at the time called "Q-gasoline" within the trade, was first marketed by Shell in 1938.

Gasoline prices constantly declined despite the general improvement in quality. Shell Petroleum had retired the old name "Super-Shell" with the introduction of Super-Shell Ethyl in 1931–1932. This set of circumstances set the stage for the St. Louis company's first big advertising campaign. Shell Petroleum's regular gasoline at that time had an octane rating of 60 to 62; by blending cracked gasoline with highly aromatic components from the new vapor-phase cracking unit which had just been built at Wood River, the refinery was able to achieve an octane number of 70.[78] This was as good as the octane rating of the old Super-Shell, a name still very much alive in the public memory. The company decided to withdraw its current housebrand, "Shell 400," substitute the new 70-octane fuel, call it Super-Shell, and put behind it the most vigorous promotion to date.

In late March 1933, "teaser" ads began to appear all over the Midwest admonishing motorists to watch for "Shell's New Deal," on Saturday, April 8. On that day the new gasoline was launched— "A premium gasoline at the price of 'regular.'" Parades streamed down city streets on April 8, and stations were decorated until they looked like ship launchings with banners bearing the slogans "Today's New Deal," "New Super-Shell," "No 3¢ Premium." Everyone had expected the campaign to be successful, but the actual degree of success was astonishing. Sales in some places increased by as much as 100% and by June the Wood River refinery, which had held back its cracking capacity since 1931, began scraping tank bottoms.[79]

By July, the *Shell Globe* was running page after page of fine type— names and addresses of dealers who had switched to Shell to take advantage of this effective promotion. The campaign was a turning point in Shell marketing. The anti-knock qualities of both regular and premium grades had now been greatly raised, and the power of effective, planned advertising, even in the midst of serious depression, had proved itself beyond a doubt. During the summer of 1933, Shell Oil in San Francisco scrapped its "3-Energy" campaign in favor of the Super-Shell-at-price-of-regular advertising. From this point onwards, there would be (with the exception of the war and immediate postwar years) gradual yearly improvements in the octane rating and stability of Shell gasolines. And Shell advertising, until then largely a haphazard affair, would be planned carefully on a national basis with the San Francisco, St. Louis, and New York companies working together and the J. Walter Thompson Company handling the account nation-wide through offices in each of the three cities.

To supplement the companies' advertising, house organs for Shell employees and Shell dealers made their appearance during this period. In San Francisco, a new magazine, *Shell Progress*, was launched in January 1930. It was much larger than *Shelling The Line*, had handsome full-color covers, and ran between 30 and 40 pages an issue. Sanders, the San Francisco advertising manager, did not have funds to pay for the new magazine so he financed it by selling advertisements to manufacturers of tires, steel storage tanks, pumps, metal stations, air compressors, and other products having a market with the dealer. Because it had been supplanted, *Shelling The Line* ceased publication with the issue of September 1930. The new *Shell Progress* proved none too hardy in the face of depression; in May 1931, it was suspended, to be revived a year later as a sales tool for the "3-Energy" campaign.

At the start of 1931, two new Shell papers appeared in other parts of the country, *The Shell Globe* in St. Louis and *The Sign of the Shell* in New York. *The Shell Globe*, addressed to the entire employee family, was edited by Shell Petroleum's personnel manager, Walter F. Jones. At the beginning of 1933, a separate employee paper called *Shell News* was started, and in March 1933 *Shell Globe* became the magazine of the Mid-Continent sales department, similar in appeal to the West Coast *Shell Progress*.

In New York, *The Sign of the Shell*, a professional-looking magazine edited by A. F. Maple and later by W. M. Thompson, made its appearance in January 1931. Since Shell Eastern's organization was concerned entirely with marketing, it was a sales paper from the first. By 1936 when L. T. Kittinger came on from California to head up Shell Eastern's marketing, *The Sign of the Shell* had become a substantial and well-edited publication; Kittinger had its name changed in September 1936 to the shorter *Shell Progress*.†

If the house magazines were important in building sales-consciousness internally,‡ the touring services developed during this period

---

† To complete the story of the Shell house organs: another *Shell News* was started on the Pacific Coast in 1938; it was a tabloid-size, monthly employee newspaper edited by C. E. Totten and later by Ozé Van Wyck. With the consolidation of San Francisco and New York offices at the beginning of 1949, the West Coast *Shell Progress* and *Shell News* were discontinued.

‡ Motion pictures were another internal sales aid introduced at this time for sales department meetings. By the summer of 1933, *Shell Globe* was publicizing "a new talking motion picture, 'Super-Shell Comes Through!'" It had been preceded by three other "talkies": "The New Super Shell," "The Sign of the Shell," and "Smashing Records with Shell."

were equally effective in building good will with the general public. Both the San Francisco and St. Louis companies had distributed road maps in the late Twenties. During 1930, Van Fleet & Durkee had started a "Recreation Service" built around the slogan "Tour with Van Durk." "Van Durk," supposed to be any V. & D. dealer, was actually Bert Van Tyler, a Californian who toured all of Shell Oil Company's marketing area and made up an extensive book of travel information. This book, placed in the hands of any V. & D. service station operator, was supposed to make him into "Van Durk," the man who knew where to go, what to see, and how best to get there. The book was mimeographed, and by 1931 had become a bulky 536-page affair, too cumbersome to be really workable. When Van Fleet and Durkee sold out to Shell in the spring of 1932, they got $25,000 for this Van Durk Recreation Service, and R. G. Landis, who had edited the V. & D. house organ, came with Shell to organize a Shell touring service on the Pacific Coast.[80]

Meanwhile, a real touring service had been started in the East. In 1929, while its head office was still in Boston, Shell Eastern had started distributing free maps to its dealers and selling them to jobbers, as Shell Petroleum did, at or below cost. During the summer of 1931, Shell Eastern set up a touring bureau in its New York office to dispense all sorts of travel information by mail. It supplied descriptive leaflets, folders, and maps with made-to-order individual routings. There were metropolitan maps of the large cities, individual road maps of each state, and "Travelaide," a weekly map posted at service stations to show current road construction and detours. By 1932, Shell road maps were being printed in four colors and were available in Shell stations from coast to coast.[81] The advertising departments of all three companies worked hard to make their touring services the best in the business and the next few years saw them grow to substantial size, with bureaus in the Shell buildings at San Francisco, Los Angeles, St. Louis, and the R.C.A. Building in New York, Shell Eastern's new headquarters.

The New Service Station

In addition to new gasolines and new free services, the motorist began to notice a marked change in the physical appearance of the service station during the early Thirties. As far as the Shell organization was concerned, Van Fleet & Durkee had proved beyond dispute the profitability of offering the motorist items other than petroleum products. Many independent dealers had, of course, carried lines of automotive and even non-automotive merchandise long before this; but it was not until the early Thirties that Shell stations generally began selling items such as tires and tubes, head lamps, and gasoline-tank caps, in addition to Shell greases and specialty products. The stocking of such goods marked the beginning of the now-standard TBA (tires, batteries, accessories) line carried by nearly every Shell dealer.

With decreased volume, increased number of outlets, and greatly increased competition, oil marketers everywhere during the early Thirties turned to automotive lubrication, a field in which only a few had been active in the late Twenties. "A grease job," as it was less elegantly called, had been considered too messy and too unremunerative to bother with in the days of high per-station volume. Now, with both volume and prices down, company after company began to offer a lubrication service to help enlarge the dollar volume of its stations.

There were drawbacks of course. Even at depression prices the lift necessary to raise a car from the floor cost $600 or more; the power greasing equipment and multiplicity of wrenches added at least another $250.[82] And most service station operators weren't trained mechanics, even though they did understand the rudiments of car care. This last objection was overcome by developing detailed charts that showed the points at which lubrication should be applied to every make and year of automobile. These simple charts, against which the operator checked his work as he went along, were introduced to Shell stations by Van Fleet & Durkee in 1929–1930 as the "V. & D. System" of lubrication. In 1931, the year which saw the greatest industry-wide increase in specialized lubrication, Shell Petroleum in St. Louis introduced a complete car-upkeep service throughout its marketing territory and called it "Shell Specialized Chassis Lubrication Service," a name which was mercifully shortened three months later to the now-familiar "Shellubrication." During the following summer, Shell Oil Company on the Coast adopted and introduced its "Shell 51-Point Upkeep System" at company-owned stations; from it a simpler system was adapted for outlets of better dealers.[83]

Both developments, the introduction of more merchandise and the start of a lubrication service, necessitated physical changes in the service station building. Some way had to be provided for getting underneath the car, either by installing a lift to raise it, or by digging a pit into which the operator could descend. In less temperate climates, the pits or lifts had to be enclosed. The result was the "lube bay," a built-on room big enough to hold a workbench, the automobile being worked on, the necessary lubricating equipment, and the lift or pit. Because pits were cheaper they were the most common; lifts, however, were preferable since they looked better, were easier to keep clean, and did not present a safety hazard (people could, and did, fall into open pits).

One or two lube bays built on the side of a station radically altered its appearance, not always for the better. So a great deal of attention was directed during the early Thirties to redesigning the whole plan of the Shell station. On the West Coast, between 1932 and 1934, the Shell Oil sales department experimented with several new types of service station building. An architect who had worked on the Shell building was retained to create a series of experimental designs, some plain and simple embodying a motif copied from the Shell building, some as elaborate as the station in Burlingame which was decorated with a $300 granite vase and had several hundred dollars' worth of brass window sash.[84]

On all of the redesigned stations, the old yellow paint with red trim was dropped in favor of a more subdued color scheme. Pastel shades running from buff to near-white were tried, and finally a shade of cream was adopted. The old colors were retained in red and yellow stripes running around the base of the service station building, and in the color scheme of the company's identifying signs. During this period the admirable idea was put forward that each station should be designed to fit its location: utility, appearance, efficiency all would benefit. In practice, though, this idea of providing individualized stations proved far too expensive, so toward the end of the 1930–1935 period two general styles of building began to emerge, one for new construction, the other for "face-lifting" the older stations built during the 1920's. In both, the increased sale of non-petroleum merchandise was apparent. The former service station office was now a greatly enlarged salesroom with large windows affording a good view of the products on display inside. And all the new stations had at least one lubrication bay.

Although it cost money at a time when money was scarce, remodeling service stations and building new ones during this period of low costs was a good investment. A new-looking, up-to-date station attracted passing motorists and generally brought an immediate increase in business; an enlarged station could handle larger dollar volume and make more money; moreover, by the mid-Thirties a great many of the stations built during the Twenties were ready for renewal.

Station Leases and "Promoted Deals"

In spite of the shortness of capital during these years, the Shell Union companies made it a policy to spend on new marketing facilities each year an amount of money at least equal to the amounts they had written off for sales department depreciation.[85] Shell Oil in California, for instance, by this means in 1932 provided a million dollars to be spent on new stations and modernization of existing ones. The company was obliged to make these outlays if it was to hold its market position.

During these years of scarce capital, the Shell sales departments on the West Coast and in the Mid-Continent made increasing use of lease arrangements to provide the new retail outlets they needed. In the late Twenties, Shell and other companies on the West Coast had started using the so-called "paint lease," an arrangement whereby the premises of a dealer handling more than one brand of gasoline were leased, painted with company colors, and leased back to the dealer, with an agreement that he would handle only the supplier's gasoline. In exchange, the dealer usually collected, as the difference between what he was paid for his premises and what he himself paid in rental, an amount equal to 1¢ a gallon on his monthly gasoline sales.

This "paint lease" worked so well in converting "split dealers" into 100% accounts that it soon evolved into the "two-party lease," an arrangement for converting open-account dealers, who were likely to change suppliers overnight, into "controlled outlets" committed for a stated period to the sale of one particular brand of gasoline. A two-party lease worked much the same as a paint lease: the supplier leased a dealer's premises for a stated period, then leased the premises back to the dealer at a lower rental, generally calculated to equal 1¢ a gallon on his business. Both Shell Oil and Shell Petroleum hustled to sign dealers to two-party leases in the early Thirties; during 1931, for instance, Van der Woude was able to report that Shell Petroleum by this means increased the number of its "controlled outlets" from 3,800 to 6,000.[86]

From these relatively simple arrangements, designed originally to pick up and hold gallonage, came another set of arrangements, the so-called "promoted deal" and "three-party lease," designed to enlist the capital of others in the construction of new service stations at a time when the company could not spare the funds to build as many new stations as the sales department felt necessary. In "promoting a deal," the salesman or local manager would pick a desirable corner, find out who owned it, then call upon the owner to see if he would be interested in building a station on his land and leasing it to Shell. If he agreed, the company would furnish him with designs and blueprints, engage a contractor for him, and assist the construction in every way possible. If the property owner lacked the funds, the company tried to find someone who would buy the land from him and build the station and, slightly later, the company undertook to find a bank or private individual willing to lend the necessary money, acting as the landowner's guarantor where required. The owner of a promoted station leased to the company a station that was completely equipped except for inventories of products. Shell undertook to find and install a suitable dealer, and the legal arrangement for the station, signed by the owner, the dealer, and the company, was called a "three-party lease." On the West Coast, Kittinger, then a comer in the sales organization, vigorously pushed these promoted deals with three-party leases; in some areas of California, in the early Thirties, as many as twenty new promoted stations were built to every one that the company erected with its own funds.[87]

By 1935, a great many newly built Shell stations lined the highways and other hundreds had been drastically remodelled. In addition, several hundred new dealers had been signed up, attracted chiefly by the company's vigorous advertising. For the most part, the purchase of distributing companies was now a thing of the past, but two substantial jobbers were acquired during this period, the Arrow Oil Company of Kansas City (1932) and the O'Neil Oil Company of Milwaukee (1934). Ralph H. Erichsen, who had been president of Arrow Oil since 1927, became division manager of Shell Petroleum's new Western marketing division, set up at Kansas City in January 1933. From May 1938 until his resignation late in 1941, he served as the company's general sales manager east of the Rockies. The O'Neil firm in Milwaukee had started as an oil and paint company in 1893. George F. O'Neil, the company's founder, already well advanced in years, did not come with Shell; but J. A. Sheridan, the O'Neil sales manager, became Shell's district manager for Milwaukee, a position he still held in 1956.

Conspicuous among the newly built stations in the Mid-Continent was an elaborate, double-cantilever-canopy station with a tower, located at the junction of Lindell Boulevard, Vandeventer and McPherson Avenues in St. Louis, opened with tremendous fanfare in mid-1934. For the occasion twelve "Shell Girls," dressed in red and yellow riding habits, received visitors and presented orchids to the ladies; Hollywood-style searchlights bathed the station in light; the St. Louis Civic Band played on the roof; and L. B. Veeder, who had had a large hand in developing "Shellubrication," inaugurated his stunt of lubricating a car while dressed in dinner clothes. During the remainder of the year, other stations were opened with similar pomp at Lakewood, Xenia, and Lima, Ohio; Kenosha, Wisconsin; Indianapolis (two); and Detroit.[88]

A sales-minded, aggressive marketing department had worked hard. No one was particularly surprised, then, to note in 1935 that although they had been through five years of far from pleasant financial experiences, the Shell companies had at the end of that period a total of 20,640 retail outlets, as against 13,500 outlets five years before. Nation-wide, the companies had 6.3% of the total gasoline market that year and were exceeded in the volume of their gasoline sales by only three competitors: Socony (8.7%), Standard of Indiana (8.5%), and Texaco (7.5%).[89] The improved efficiency of the whole organization could also be noted. This increase in stations was a full 53% over 1930, but the number of depots had not only not increased proportionately—there were actually twenty fewer than in 1930.

7

Transportation and Tariffs

EVERY period of economic crisis brings forth a flood of suggested palliatives, and one of them is usually protectionism. During the early years of the depression, a small but vocal element in the oil industry raised a cry against imports and, it must be admitted, their position seemed fair enough in a country where local overproduction had already reduced the prices of oil and oil products to absurdly low levels. From 1930 onwards, there was agitation for an oil tariff which was passed finally as part of the Revenue Act of 1932.

This restriction of imports had an effect upon Shell Eastern's operations, for, as already mentioned, it was technically an importing company. Like all East Coast companies, Shell Eastern had to bring its supplies in by water. The Shipping Act of 1916 made it impossible for the company to own its own tankers and Group tankers could not be employed to deliver products from Houston and Norco to Atlantic Coast ports, for this would have constituted coastwise shipping. Tankers belonging to the Group could, however, deliver Curaçao products to any port on the Eastern Seaboard or load cargoes for shipment to points outside the United States, for a foreign-flag vessel is permitted under the law to come in to discharge or pick up a cargo.

It was this peculiarity of American law which had led to Shell Eastern's becoming an importer of motor fuel. By accepting delivery of Curaçao naphtha at any of the Atlantic Coast terminals, and having Shell Petroleum deliver over in exchange equal quantities of products at the docks of the Houston and Norco refineries, it was possible to use Group tankers to transport most of Shell Eastern's requirements. The imports and exports balanced out, and Shell Eastern was not in reality a net importer. Under these arrangements, Shell Eastern during 1929 imported some 168,000,000 gallons of products made at the Curaçao refinery from Venezuelan crude, and during 1930 double this amount.[90]

Some of Shell Eastern's competitors, who had been getting a run for their money from the new company, lost no time in bringing the amounts of Shell Eastern's imports to public attention. Concerned because these disclosures did not present the full facts, Godber, in Chicago for the A.P.I. Convention in November 1930, issued a statement explaining the situation:

> Certain interested parties who have apparently not taken the trouble to analyze the figures in order to secure for themselves the true position are claiming that imports from Venezuela are largely responsible for the present very low prices on the domestic market. We cannot speak for other importing companies, but we do know that these imports, so far as the Shell Union is concerned, have no bearing upon the domestic market.
>
> The facts are that Shell Union has a distributing organization on the East Coast of the United States, which it has built up to provide

an outlet for its production in California and the Gulf Coast. This contemplated, in line with the policy of other American companies, the shipment by sea of supplies to the East Coast so that, in addition to the gasoline marketed on the Pacific Coast and the Midwestern and Gulf markets, its entire sales organization throughout the United States would be supplied with gasoline produced from crude obtained and refined in its entirety within the United States.

Certain freight disadvantages to this plan, however, induced us to ship our California and Gulf supplies to Europe and elsewhere instead of to the East Coast . . . so that, in effect, an exchange gallon for gallon of Venezuelan for American oil took place and the domestic market remained unaffected. This is quite clear because if, as has been suggested, our imports of Venezuelan gasoline were to be diverted to Europe and our California and Gulf supplies shipped to the East Coast, the net quantities marketed by us in this country would remain the same.[91]

In the annual report for 1931, the directors noted that Shell Eastern's imports of gasoline during 1931 had been reduced by 50%, but remarked, "A tariff on imported oil continues to agitate the minds of the oil industry." On July 1, 1932, this tariff went into effect: $2\frac{1}{2}$¢ a gallon on motor fuel, $\frac{1}{2}$¢ a gallon on crude oil, 4¢ a gallon on lubricating oil. At the same time the government placed a cent a gallon tax on all motor fuel.[92]

With margins already small, no company could hope to stay in business while paying an extra $2\frac{1}{2}$¢ a gallon for the privilege of importing Curaçao naphtha. Other means had to be found. During late 1930 and all of 1931, arrangements were made with the Pennsylvania Shipping Company of Philadelphia to deliver from the Gulf Coast a part of Shell Eastern's products. Similar arrangements for the Los Angeles-to-New York run were made with Sun Oil Company. With the start of this activity, Shell Union in May 1931 set up a marine department in New York under R. R. Griffin. For the rest of the 1930–1935 period, Griffin's chartering activities kept the East Coast supplied with gasoline, and later in the Thirties less expensive arrangements were worked out.[93]

The agitation for protective tariffs was not confined to the United States. For some time, Canada had collected a duty on the import of most petroleum products. While these duties placed importing companies such as Shell at a disadvantage, the handicap was not great enough to warrant the expense of constructing a separate refinery in Canada. Then, during the early Thirties, providing local employment became a consideration of the first importance and Canadian policies changed. During the summer of 1932, the Canadian government raised the import duty on finished gasoline to 2½¢ a gallon, with crude remaining duty-free.[94] This made it necessary for Shell Oil to alter its method of doing business in British Columbia.

In Vancouver there had been increasing sentiment late in the Twenties against "foreign" companies.[95] This feeling had encouraged Shell in San Francisco to organize in mid-1929 a separate Shell company for British Columbia, the Shell Oil Company of British Columbia, Limited. The logical source of supply for the Vancouver company was still the Martinez refinery which had shipped products to British Columbia for nearly fifteen years. The volume of the British Columbia business was so small that (even though it was legally possible) it would have been uneconomic to build and operate a tanker to handle it. Shell products for British Columbia were delivered for the most part by Union of California or General Petroleum tankers, for both companies had surplus carrying capacity which they were glad to hire out to others.

With the raising of the Canadian tariff, these arrangements came to an end. Shell had to build facilities for manufacturing gasoline in British Columbia, or else market gasoline at a competitive disadvantage. Although the company grudged this unnecessary expenditure at a time when funds were scarce, it chose to build a small refinery, rather than abandon an area where it had been marketing for twenty years. Waterfront property was purchased at North Burnaby, on Burrard Inlet east of Vancouver, and there in the summer of 1932 construction started on a 2,500-barrel-a-day topping unit which by 1935 had been increased in capacity to 4,000 barrels a day. The new refinery, called Shellburn, received blended crude from Martinez by barge and made gasoline enough to supply the Shell operation in British Columbia. Motor oils and other smaller-volume products continued to come, as before, from California.[96]

CHAPTER VIII

Competitiveness, A New Yardstick

1935–1940

IN THE history of the Shell companies in America, the period from their establishment in 1912 to the onset of the depression in 1930 had been a time of steady growth. The five years of depression from 1930 to 1935 were a time for holding fast and weathering the storm. Now, in the second half of the Thirties, from 1935 to 1940, the Shell companies would make a sharp turn in their course and a sharp break with the past.

As if to signalize this break with the past, Deterding, who had been of the period of the companies' rapid growth and expansion, now retired. He had felt obliged to remain at the helm during the severe part of the financial crisis. Now that this period seemed past, he severed his connections during 1936 with the 400-odd companies he had helped found and build. As a final gesture of appreciation, the Royal Dutch Company elected him to its directorate, a body that acts as watchdog of the shareholders' interests and does not, therefore, include men who are members of the company's management. Deterding's service as a director was destined to be brief. He was suffering from angina pectoris, and on Saturday, February 4, 1939, he died of a heart attack at his home in St. Moritz.[1]

The year of Deterding's retirement saw the passing of other links with Shell Union's past. Alexander Mackay, who had been Roxana's partner in the Healdton deal back in 1915 and who had at the formation of Shell Union come on the board to represent his syndicate, died, as did Charles Hayden, one of the old Union of Delaware directors and a member of the Shell Union board since its formation. Two other highly esteemed directors who had served since the beginning retired: Bayard Dominick, of Dominick & Dominick, who was succeeded by his brother, Gayer; and Richard Airey, head of the New York organization of Asiatic Petroleum Corporation since

the time of the First World War. Van Eck, who had founded the
Shell company on the West Coast and judiciously overseen the American Shell organization ever since, left for London to become one of
the five managing directors who were appointed at the time of
Deterding's retirement.*

Another break with the past during the second half of the Thirties
was in basic business philosophy. Volume, which for many years had
served as the primary measuring stick of performance in the marketing end of the business, was to give way to a new concept, "competitiveness." This new idea—that Shell must in each of its major
markets bring its costs in line with those of its most favorably situated
competitor, or else abandon that market—does not seem very revolutionary at first glance. But to rely on volume as the chief indicator
of success or failure had by 1935 become second nature to a whole
generation of oil marketers.

From the days of the pioneer Woolworth stores thirty years
before, the principle of volume selling had become almost an obsession
in retail merchandising. By the Twenties, the guiding principle in
the retail field had become small profits multiplied by many sales to
yield a large aggregate profit. Businessmen hastened to assemble
chains of cigar stores, drug stores, food markets, service stations,
accessory and other stores. Even department stores, which had represented big volume in another age, joined hands to form nation-wide
chains. In the oil business, there was additional impetus toward volume
selling from two other sources. The first was the millions of automobiles pouring from Detroit and requiring motor oil and gasoline
in large quantity; the second impetus toward volume selling came
from the huge supplies of crude oil which the overproduction of the
Twenties dumped in the oil men's laps, setting off a race for customers
rarely, if ever, equalled in mercantile history.

The volume principle worked well on a rising or stable market.
But when prices started to fall and the small per-unit profit was
converted into a loss, the total of the losses could be staggering, as
Shell and many others had learned. For five years now, during the
rigors of the worst depression and the most highly competitive oil

* These men acted as the management of the three main Group companies: The
Asiatic (now Shell) Petroleum Company, The Anglo-Saxon Petroleum Company,
and Bataafsche Petroleum Maatschappij. The number of these managing directors
has varied over the years; the Royal Dutch Company, because of its 60% ownership
of Group companies, has the privilege of naming a majority of the managing
directors.[2]

market America had ever seen, the Shell management had been busy trimming expenses, plugging holes, and cutting overhead to the bone in a valiant and successful effort to weather the storm. The year 1935 saw improvement and a profit of $6,800,000. During 1936, business in general picked up, the oil business improved, and Shell Union was able to report a profit of $22,000,000, its best showing since the bonanza year of 1926, ten years before. But no one could say for sure that business had taken a permanent turn for the better. Even if it had, the Shell management was determined to put the company on a sounder footing, so that such staggering losses could not again occur.†

Had all oil companies fared as badly during the early Thirties, perhaps the determination of the Shell men would not have been so strong. But such was not the case. In the Mid-Continent, where Shell's largest losses had occurred, many companies had continued to make money during the very worst times. Outstanding was the long-established Standard Oil Company (Indiana) which operated entirely within this area of low prices and severe competition. The reason that the Indiana Standard could make money was that its costs were much lower. It had been in business since the 1890's, and most of its real estate had been purchased and its plant equipment installed at costs far below those which prevailed in the late Twenties. Much of Indiana's investment had long ago been amortized completely, so that the Indiana company was, in effect, having free use of these facilities. Shell, on the other hand, a relative newcomer, was struggling under a crushing load of high annual depreciation charges on properties and equipment acquired at peak prices in the boom market of the Twenties.

Explanations, much as they clarified the matter, still did not change the hard fact that Shell's costs were higher in many areas than those of its most favored competitors. For instance, even in the good year of 1936, Standard of Indiana's profit had been 2.6¢ per gallon of gasoline sold, while the comparable figure for the Shell companies east of the Rockies was 1.0¢. This meant that in the face of a falling

† Shell Union's money-losing subsidiaries managed to keep going during their darkest days by borrowing from the parent company. These loans were tremendous in size, and the hard-pressed subsidiaries had little prospect of repaying them. Between August 1934 and November 1938, Shell Union made a further investment in the stocks of its two money-losing subsidiaries. The investment in Shell Petroleum, representing accumulated debts due Shell Union by Shell Petroleum, came to $141,-542,000; Shell Eastern's debt, expunged in a similar manner, came to $10,097,000—altogether a total of more than $150 million.

market, the Indiana company could lower its price by 2½¢ and still make a tenth of a cent a gallon; Shell, in similar circumstances, would be incurring an outright loss of 1½¢ a gallon.[3] Clearly, it was time to shift the emphasis from volume to profitability.

Early in March 1935, Van Eck who was then still in New York wrote Fraser in St. Louis that it might be wise to undertake a thorough review of Shell Petroleum's marketing "to determine if we should not withdraw from those areas where we are at competitive disadvantages, or where we constantly lose money."[4] A month later, Van der Woude, president of Shell Union, suggested to Fraser that this special scrutiny might be directed toward areas (1) where Shell was at a competitive disadvantage because of transportation costs, or (2) where distribution was thin either because of sparse settlement or small share of the trade, with Shell's supervisory and overhead expenses consequently higher, or (3) areas where a concentration of refineries brought on periodic local price wars. His letter concluded with the first mention of the consideration that was soon to be paramount in Shell's managerial circles: "The essential fact that we must now recognize is that we must be prepared to relinquish gallonage where it is clearly apparent that its retention is affecting our overall performance adversely . . . [and be] prepared to adopt profits rather than gallonage as a measuring stick for market performance."[5]

Soon the first of a long series of studies was to start, studies which would require endless calculation, hard thought, and careful re-examination of ideas which for years had been accepted without question. The conclusions of these studies would often make unpleasant reading, and when it came time to put the suggested remedies into effect a large measure of business courage would be needed.

The physical changes brought about by this search for competitiveness would be far more sweeping than anyone had at first foreseen. Imagine, for a moment, the case of a hypothetical transportation clerk sitting in Shell Petroleum's head office in the Shell building, St. Louis, on a January morning in 1937. He has just finished sending a wire to the Arkansas City refinery requesting the refinery to ship four carloads of gasoline to Lincoln, Nebraska, and to arrange to forward the empty tank cars to the East Chicago refinery. He no doubt would have found it hard to believe that by September 1940 he would be sitting in another head office a thousand miles away, that the Arkansas City refinery would then have been closed down two full years, that Shell would no longer be selling gasoline in Nebraska (and eight other states), that shipping by tank car would in large measure have given way to new "products pipe lines," that the East Chicago refinery, closed down and dismantled, would be a terminal on one of these lines, and—to top it all off—that he would be working for a company called not Shell Petroleum Corporation but Shell Oil Company, Inc.

2

The Salmon Report

In this search for competitiveness, the lion's share of the work and responsibility was to fall to Fraser. The Shell Oil Company on the Pacific Coast had lost money one year and the Shell Eastern organization on the Atlantic Seaboard had lost substantial sums every year except 1935, but the largest losses by far had been sustained in the Mid-Continent by the Shell Petroleum Corporation. The St. Louis company had, in fact, been losing money ever since 1927 and in the nine years 1927–1935 had sustained a total deficit of more than $125,000,000.‡

During the late Twenties these losses, while unpleasant, were not alarming and were put down to the high cost of hurrying. The company was bent on capturing in a few short years markets which would normally take a decade or more to develop. It had to expect some losses. But with the onset of the depression, these losses were soon of staggering proportions. By the enforcement of strict economies and the coincidental improvement of prices during 1935 and 1936, Shell Petroleum finally managed to show a small profit in the latter year. But its position was still precarious. A few months of lowered prices could put it right back into the red, as would be proved two years later.

The chief factor which brought about the big decision that changed the course of Shell's history was the steady increase in demand for petroleum products. All during the depression years, demand for gasoline had continued strong and by 1936 annual U. S. demand for

‡ Shell Petroleum's deficits, 1927–1935, were incurred as follows:

1927–$ 7,810,000	1930–$28,570,000	1933–$13,367,000
1928–$ 4,176,000	1931–$33,852,000	1934–$11,766,000
1929–$ 9,203,000	1932–$16,161,000	1935–$ 1,375,000

gasoline was some 4½ billion gallons above 1929 consumption; and demand for kerosene and fuel oil was mounting at an even faster rate. This increase brought the Shell companies east of the Rockies squarely up against the question of supply. Shell Petroleum needed more crude oil. If it were to be purchased, could these purchases be justified if the oil were to be refined and sold at a loss? Obviously it was sheer folly to buy more oil and increase refining capacity to meet a demand that promised only continued losses. Was the company prepared, as an alternative, not to supply a part of this additional demand and sacrifice thereby its cherished "market position"?

As already noted, a willingness to withdraw from unprofitable areas had been expressed early in 1935. Throughout the ensuing months, there was a good deal of discussion of the topic, obscured always by an almost complete lack of the kind of figures needed. If, for instance, Shell did withdraw from certain unprofitable marketing areas, what assurance was there that this curtailed volume might not bring higher unit costs in refining, thus offsetting the anticipated savings? To supply this lack of reliable figures, Fraser early in 1936 appointed a small committee to go thoroughly into every phase of the situation: "probable increase in consumption of gasolines, fuels, lubricants, Diesel oil, etc.; crude oil supplies, present and expected; pipe line and refinery extensions, and refined product arrangements necessary to accommodate the probable requirements." [6] To head the committee, Fraser appointed J. H. Salmon, an engineer who had spent most of his Shell career working on costs and who was at the time manager of the company's shipping and supplies department. The three other members of the committee were C. M. Kellogg, G. R. Berry, and J. H. Wagner.

The "Salmon committee" labored long and hard all through 1936, and in January 1937 delivered their report to Fraser. It was exhaustive enough to satisfy the most inquisitive: 337 legal-size pages, with 32 charts and 61 maps, bound in two huge volumes. Besides being a monumental work, this "Supply and Demand Survey" was a monument of another sort. Careful studies of isolated aspects of the companies' operations had on occasion been made before; but the Salmon Report was the first to attempt an over-all consideration of Shell's function as an integrated oil company, with all the departments of the business from service stations to exploratory geologists being viewed in their relationship to each other. The report was a monument to the end of managerial thinking in which hunches and guesswork had played so large a part. From this point onward, reliance on these scientific glimpses into the future would become regular Shell practice.

The Salmon Report was a five-year projection of the demand and supply position of Shell Petroleum Corporation. On the "demand" side of the ledger, an effort was made to formulate a careful estimate of the increase which could be expected in demand for petroleum products in the five years ahead. Estimates were assembled of expected increases in population and in the number of motor vehicles, oil burners, and Diesel engines. After careful study, figures representing estimated increase in demand were projected. Deliberately, these estimates were kept on the low side, but even so they showed that by 1941 the oil industry could expect an increase in demand for gasoline of 31% more than 1935, an increase in distillate fuels (used for home heating and Diesel engines) of 62.6% over 1935, and in lubricating oils an increase of 53.6%.§

Then, on the "supply" side of the ledger, the committee "took a look into the cupboard"[7] to see how Shell Petroleum could most profitably meet this increased demand in supplying the necessary crude oil, transporting it, refining it, and in shipping, storing, and marketing the finished products. Already, they pointed out, the company was having difficulty in meeting the mounting demand, for there had been little increase during the depression years in Shell's facilities for turning out more products.

First of all, the company would need more crude oil. Known reserves could provide only a small portion of the foreseen demand. All available money, therefore, should be directed into exploration and production activities and into the purchase of proven oil-producing properties. It was agreed that no new discoveries of consequence could be hoped for in Kansas or Oklahoma, but discoveries or new production could be looked for in West Texas and New Mexico, southwest Texas, East Texas, and the Gulf Coast regions of Texas and Louisiana. As Shell was producing only 15% of the West Texas oil that it was transporting and refining, every effort

§ It is interesting to see how these estimates turned out. The actual demand for gasoline in 1941 was 53% greater than 1935, and distillate fuel demand was up by slightly more than 100%. Part of this discrepancy was due to the conservative nature of the estimates, but wartime demands were no doubt chiefly responsible. The lubricating oil estimate, not so likely to be affected by war, was "on the nose"; actual demand in 1941 was up 53.8% from 1935, as against the committee's estimate of 53.6%.

should be made to buy producing properties near the Shell pipe line in West Texas, paying a slight premium, if necessary.

Next came consideration of facilities for transporting these increased amounts of crude oil. For purposes of discussion, the refineries were divided into two convenient groupings: the northern refineries (Arkansas City, Wood River, East Chicago) serving the Midwestern markets; and the southern refineries (Houston and Norco) supplying the Gulf, the Deep South, and Shell Eastern. The northern refineries would have to continue drawing their supplies from Kansas, Oklahoma, West Texas, and New Mexico, relying more and more, as the years went by, on the West Texas region where prospects were still good for additional discoveries. Shell had been one of the first companies to put into use the discovery that casinghead gasoline, extracted in the oil fields from natural gas, could be added to the crude oil stream in a pipe line to reduce the viscosity of the crude. Thus diluted, the crude could be pumped at a faster rate, increasing the amount a pipe line could handle in a day's time, with no additional capital expenditure for this added capacity and a "free ride" for the casinghead gasoline. For the next few years, the committee said, the existing pipe line from West Texas to Cushing could be made to meet increased demands if diluents were added to reduce the viscosity of the oil.

The segment of pipe line from Cushing on up to Wood River was a different story. That line had to handle crude from the Kansas and Oklahoma oil fields in addition to the oil from Texas. Completing the "loops" in the Cushing-to-Wood River line by laying new pipe and installing new pumping equipment would cost $1,500,000 and raise the daily capacity of the line from 63,000 to 75,000 barrels. The northern refineries would in all likelihood eventually need all of the West Texas production, so it did not seem feasible to contemplate increasing the capacity of the line from West Texas to the Houston refinery. For the moment, Houston could get by with existing pipe line arrangements, although a not-too-distant increase in the capacity of the East Texas–Houston line was recommended. Deficits in crude supply at Houston could be made up by barging oil in from the Gulf Coast fields. Norco, which received all its supplies by water, would continue this arrangement.

In refining, the survey showed that the pinch was already on in the northern refineries' area. Anticipated gasoline sales from these refineries in 1937 would be 630 million gallons, with the refineries able to turn out only 596 million gallons. Some 20 million gallons of casinghead gasoline would be purchased in the Mid-Continent for use as pipe line diluent, so this left 14 million gallons to be purchased on the open market for shipment to Shell customers.

SHELL PETROLEUM CORPORATION REFINERY CAPACITY, 1936

In barrels per day

Wood River	43,000	
Arkansas City	17,000	
East Chicago	29,000	
Total Northern Refineries		89,000
Houston	76,000	
Norco	21,000	
Total Southern Refineries		97,000
Total		186,000

At the moment a large, new cracking unit, Dubbs 17, was being completed at Wood River. Some spare cracking capacity would be available there. With the expenditure of only $17,000 for new topping equipment, Wood River's capacity could be increased by 3,000 barrels a day. This had not been done before because of a lack of storage tanks. The report proposed that $514,000 worth of new storage tanks be erected at Wood River; following this, the refinery's topping capacity could then be increased at an estimated cost of $236,000, making available another 6,000 barrels a day of refinery capacity.

The committee recommended these capacity increases for Wood River because of the spare cracking capacity available there. To raise the daily capacity of the East Chicago refinery by 6,000 barrels would have cost $1,800,000 because no spare cracking capacity was available at East Chicago, and new facilities would have been necessary throughout. Similarly, 8,000 barrels a day of new capacity at Arkansas City would have cost $750,000. This expenditure was definitely not recommended because of the dwindling crude supplies and chaotic market conditions in that area. As for the southern refineries, considerable new capacity had just been added at Houston and would suffice for the time being.

In the matter of product transportation, the Salmon committee had drawn up a proposal which was to have a lasting effect on the future earnings of the company. Everyone knew, in a general way, that transportation of gasoline by pipe line was vastly cheaper than by railroad tank cars, but so far nothing had been done about it in the Shell organization. In every state where the most favored competitor had costs lower than Shell's it was due to lower transportation costs. These lower costs resulted from (1) a refinery located near the main market, with the necessary crude oil supplies being shipped in by pipe line, or (2) shipping finished gasoline into the area by pipe line. Shell could arrange for product transportation through a common-carrier system such as the Great Lakes Pipe Line. But to use the Great Lakes System, Shell would have to ship from the Arkansas City refinery where, as already noted, the future of crude supplies was not good.

Why, then, should Shell not have its own gasoline line originating at Wood River? At first glance this seemed like too expensive a project, but after the profitability figures had been drawn up, they showed that it would be more expensive to continue without one. The committee proposed that a gasoline pipe line be built from Wood River east into Ohio, running through the central parts of Illinois and Indiana, terminating in a split in Ohio, with one branch going south to Columbus and the other north to Toledo. The line would cost $5,440,000, but was expected to pay for itself in transportation savings within five years.

Such a line would place Shell in the position of having costs as low as, or lower than, its most favored competitor in a populous area where the company already had a heavy investment in marketing properties. Further, the proposed line would relieve the pinch on the East Chicago refinery by supplying northern Ohio, which up to now had received its products from East Chicago. Product tankage which was due to be built either at the Wood River or East Chicago refineries could be located along the new line instead.

As for marketing prospects, the committee was not pessimistic. The next five years, they felt, should be good with the exception of some unprofitable and marginal areas. The unprofitable areas were Arkansas, Colorado, and, in Shell Eastern's territory, western New York and western Pennsylvania. In each of these areas, there was competition from local refiners whose costs Shell could not hope to equal. Marginal territory was North and South Dakota, Nebraska, and Oklahoma. In these states, Shell Petroleum realized a small marketing profit, but on a very small volume. The report recommended immediate abandonment of the unprofitable areas and withdrawal from the marginal regions as rapidly as the gallonage then being sold in these areas could be diverted to more profitable markets. The committee opposed further capital expenditures for marketing facilities unless attractive opportunities were discovered in metropolitan areas. Metropolitan areas, despite a host of price-cutters, had generally proved profitable because of high volume and resultant low unit handling costs. In addition to gasoline, the committee recommended that an effort be made to secure a larger share of the lubricating oil business which could be handled without enlarging existing facilities.[8]

Such, in brief, were the recommendations of the Salmon committee study. That these recommendations were not all adopted we shall presently see, but they pointed the way for a frontal attack on costs. Up to this point, costs had been attacked by paring expenses within the existing framework of the organization. Now, Fraser and the able men he had around him—H. Bloemgarten, A. J. Galloway, N. J. McGaw, H. H. Anderson, A. E. Lacomblé, P. E. Lakin, and W. H. Eaton, to mention only a few—went to work in earnest to alter the actual pattern of the organization so that unprofitable situations which had dogged Shell Petroleum for a decade could at last be eliminated, and the foundation laid for a more compact organization built around the arteries of cheap transportation.

3

The Products Pipe Line

NOT every proposal of the Salmon report met with ready acceptance, but on one recommendation there was universal accord: the desirability of building a gasoline pipe line. Even by conservative estimates, the transportation savings which the projected line would make possible could, in a five-year period, more than pay for the construction cost of the line. Shell would be assured costs as low as, or lower than, its most favored competitor in this highly populous area where it already had such a large investment in distributing facilities.

In March 1937, approval was given for the gasoline pipe line, and by May the laying out of the line was well under way. To save time and money, aerial photography was put to use. First, the best maps available were obtained of the region through which the line was to pass and the "ideal" route drawn on the maps. Then, with the maps to guide them, aerial photographers took pictures of the entire route. These photographs, pasted together, provided a composite picture of the proposed line. Natural and man-made obstacles could be spotted in advance and the route of the pipe line altered to bypass them. From these aerial views, maps were then prepared for land-survey parties.

Early in August 1937, Shell Petroleum announced the building of this gasoline pipe line. Soon afterwards, land-survey parties and right-of-way men began the preliminary work necessary to secure easements from the owners of the property through which the line would pass. While this work was going on, the design of the line had been determined and bids let for pipe and pumping equipment, so that actual field construction could be started on the western end of the line by mid-September 1937 before the surveyors and land men had completed their job on the eastern end of the line.

All the work up to this point had been done for Shell Petroleum by the Shell Pipe Line Corporation, since the latter organization had men experienced in all phases of pipe line construction. Then, late in 1937, it was decided that it would be possible for the new pipe line to transport not only gasoline but other products as well—kerosene, fuel oil, naphtha, even aviation gasoline. This decision meant redesigning the line and developing new techniques of operation, quite different from anything the pipe line company had ever built or operated. Accordingly, the responsibility for the design and construction of the line was taken over by Shell Petroleum in January 1938. S. S. Smith, who had earlier earned a reputation for ingenuity as head of the company's natural gasoline department, was put in charge.

For pointers in designing the new pipe line, Smith turned to the existing * gasoline pipe line systems—Tuscarora (owned by Standard of New Jersey), Keystone (Atlantic Refining), Susquehanna (Sun), and the biggest of all, the Great Lakes System, a common carrier owned by several oil companies. None of these lines were at the time handling other than gasoline, although the Keystone line had on

---

* America's first products pipe line was older than most people think. The United States Pipe Line Company in June 1893 completed a line for shipping kerosene from Titusville to Wilkes-Barre, Pennsylvania, later extended it to tidewater, and still later built a parallel line. These lines operated until 1923.[9]

occasion made experimental runs of fuel oil. Keystone had not, however, found a simple and satisfactory dispatching system. For actual
line design, the Susquehanna line, completed in 1936, offered the best
model. Like Shell's Ventura–Wilmington gasoline line built in 1927,
the Susquehanna line was automatic, although attended. Smith
decided to copy this method of operation, simplifying the design
and using different equipment. His dispatching control system was
original.[10]

With the decision to make the new line as nearly automatic as
possible, it was necessary to discard the Diesel-driven reciprocating
pumps which had already been purchased and partially installed.
Instead, electrically powered centrifugal pumps were purchased,
along with other equipment not originally contemplated. With the
new designs accepted and the equipment ordered, construction proceeded at a rapid pace. By January 20, 1938, the 8-inch pipe was laid
as far as Zionsville, Indiana, just east of Indianapolis. Originally, the
line had been scheduled to extend all the way to Toledo. However,
Standard Oil of Ohio already had a 6-inch line from Toledo to
Fostoria, Ohio. McGaw and Eaton approached Standard with a proposal that Standard extend this line from Fostoria to Lima, Ohio.
Renting capacity on the Standard line would permit a saving in construction costs by ending the main line at Lima. There would be a
spur, as originally planned, from Lima to Springfield and Columbus.
By mid-April 1938, the line was in operation as far as Zionsville, and
by mid-June it had been completed all the way to Lima. The spur to
Columbus was finished during 1939.

Counting the spur to Columbus, the total length of the line was 450
miles. It had four pumping stations: Wood River and Casey, Illinois;
Zionsville, Indiana; and Lima, Ohio. There were terminals for the
storage and distribution of products at the Zionsville and Lima stations, and in addition there were four terminals along the line at
Effingham, Illinois; Terre Haute and Muncie, Indiana; and Springfield, Ohio. These terminals were designed and constructed by the
marketing department. The products pipe line department designed a
new terminal for Columbus, Ohio, and redesigned the existing marine
terminal at Toledo. Each terminal could load railroad tank cars as
well as trucks, and the Toledo terminal could load lake tankers and
barges besides.

In operation, the new line combined the best features of existing
gasoline pipe lines and added many new ones of its own, including a

new dispatching system superior in accuracy and simplicity to anything yet devised. Two major problems in dispatching were (1) to keep adequate supplies of each product on hand at each terminal, and (2) to know accurately what products were in the line, and just where they were, at any given time. The first problem was solved by having the transportation and supplies department prepare exact estimates of product requirements at each point, periodically checking the estimates against performance to see that they were accurate. The second problem, keeping track of the product in the line, was not quite so easy of solution. All the existing gasoline pipe lines made laborious calculations using records kept at each station of the number of barrels pumped each hour. Smith's new, simpler, and more accurate system was based on a dispatching board which reproduced the line in miniature. This board was a long table with a shallow slot running its entire length. Along the slot were markers indicating each station and terminal. The distance at which these markers were placed from each other represented, to scale, the exact distance in barrels between each station. To fit the slot, long strips of calibrated paper were printed on which each gradation represented 100 barrels. There was a different color of tape for each product to be shipped.

When a tender of product started its way eastward from Wood River, an appropriately colored strip of paper would be introduced into the slot at the Wood River end of the board and moved once an hour to keep pace with the actual rate of flow. If it were desired to draw off, say, 4,000 barrels at the Effingham terminal, the tape would have cut from it each hour an amount of paper to indicate to scale the exact amount withdrawn from the line at that point during the past hour. Because oil products expand and contract with the rise and fall of temperature, the station markers could be adjusted, again according to scale, either to the right or left to represent the amount of expansion or contraction in volume which had taken place between the stations.

To keep the board functioning accurately, it was necessary to have up-to-the-minute information reported hourly from each station along the line. This information included the rate of pumping at each station, the pressure at which the product was being pumped, the temperature and specific gravity of the product and, if product were being taken off, the rate of the off-take. These figures were recorded by automatic instruments and reported over the teletype sysem which was provided to link the stations together. The dispatching board had to be manned twenty-four hours a day, for pumping continued around the clock. The dispatcher in St. Louis was placed in complete control of all product movement. He told each station by teletype when to start and stop pumps, when to take off product, and how much. So perfectly did this system work in actual operation, that the dispatcher found himself able to predict, within five minutes of absolute accuracy, just when a given tender of product could be expected at any station along the line.

Different products could be pumped through Shell's new line, one after the other, without appreciable mixing—but only if the speed of flow and the pressure within the pipe line were kept at carefully predetermined levels. This necessitated a close attention to the flow and pressure factors and called for a degree of precision hitherto uncommon in the pipe line business. To eliminate as far as possible the chance of human error, the pumping equipment was built so that it could be actuated by automatic pressure controls. As an added safeguard, automatic electrical devices were provided which would shut down the motors when pressures rose or fell beyond pre-set levels, ring an alarm bell, and even turn on a signal light to indicate the source of the trouble. In case of actual breakage of the pipe, block valves installed every ten miles could be turned off to isolate that segment of the line. The station at Casey, Illinois, built only to provide pumping power, was so constructed that two men could supervise it. It was almost completely automatic, and the chief items of its equipment were so constructed that they would start and stop in response to the pressure of pipe line flows.

The capacity of the new products pipe line when it got into regular operation in the summer of 1938 was 16,000 barrels a day when pumping gasoline, 14,000 barrels a day when pumping the heaviest fuel oil.[11] During 1939, the capacity of the line was raised 8,000 barrels a day by adding two new pumping stations, one at Vandalia, Illinois, and the other at Carbon, Indiana. The capacity of the line was materially increased in later years by the installation of more powerful pumping equipment and the erection of new stations, the last four of which, installed in 1950, were fully atomatic and operated by remote control.

To build the pipe line in the state of Indiana, an outside contractor was hired, but all the work in Illinois and Ohio was done by Shell Pipe Line Corporation construction crews. This economy and the arrangements for use of the Standard of Ohio line made possible a substantial saving in construction costs. The original estimate had been for $5,440,000; complete, the new line actually cost $4,785,000.[12] In transportation savings alone, the line more than paid for itself within the first five years. More important, it placed Shell on a thoroughly competitive basis in the heart of its Midwestern marketing territory.

4

North of the Ohio, East of the Mississippi

ALTHOUGH the Salmon report early in 1937 had recommended immediate abandonment of those marketing areas which were unprofitable and gradual withdrawal from marginal territories, execution of this move dragged. Everybody hated to give up territories which had been acquired only recently, and there was always the nagging suspicion that things might improve enough to make such drastic steps unnecessary. Indeed, business did improve during 1935–1936, the improvement continued throughout most of 1937, and Shell Petroleum enjoyed one of its rare intervals of making money. In the fall of 1937, however, the national economy took a sharp downward turn, ushering in the famous "recession." Shell Petroleum started to lose money again immediately. In the month of November, it showed a net loss of nearly a half million dollars and during the following year it once again operated at a deficit.

Late in October 1937, Van Eck wrote Fraser pressing him to undertake studies of the company's marketing territory with the idea of concentrating on the most profitable areas only. Van Eck was concerned about the large amounts of crude oil which Shell Petroleum was purchasing. Shell Petroleum's crude purchases had risen to a point where the company was buying 60 barrels of oil for each 40 barrels of its own production. The company had recently assumed the full job of supplying Shell Eastern (some supplies had until then been coming from California) and in the years just ahead, market demand in Shell Petroleum's own territory promised to increase at a rate faster than the rate at which new additions could be made to the company's crude oil reserves. To help correct this situation, Van Eck asked:[13]

1. Would it not pay you better to reduce your purchases of crude by, say, 50,000 barrels a day, consequently closing down, for instance, Arkansas City refinery and New Orleans refinery and

restricting your markets to the most profitable ones (instead of merely eliminating the unprofitable markets?)

2. Would it not be better to take care of the increased demand by sacrificing part of the less remunerative markets, rather than by expanding everywhere?

To answer these questions, Van Eck suggested a survey by a senior officer not connected with the marketing, supplies, or manufacturing department of Shell Petroleum. Fraser agreed, and proposed that the survey be made by L. G. McLaren, sales manager of Shell Oil Company in San Francisco, and McGaw, who had been spending a year or two in London.

Only a few years before, it would have been unthinkable for a member of the management group to suggest that some of Shell's hard-won territory be abandoned. Equally unthinkable would have been a suggestion that the company not expand its facilities but stand still and pass up its "share" of the new business. Here was the death knell of nation-wide coverage. Nearly ten years of experience had shown that representation in all forty-eight states was no world-beater as a sales argument. Market coverage a "mile wide and an inch deep"[14] had meant high costs and, in all too many cases, no profits. Now the Shell management was willing to abandon nation-wide representation, to sacrifice market position, to stand still for a few years—if these measures would improve the company's profitability.

McGaw and McLaren surveyed Shell Petroleum's territory in two sections: the area served by the so-called northern refineries, and the area served by the southern refineries, which included, of necessity, Shell Eastern's markets. By March 1938, reports on both areas were finished.

Immediate attention was directed to the northern refineries' area. Early in March 1938, Fraser reported that Shell Petroleum had, in effect, decided to vacate the entire area west of the Mississippi River.[15] Some of the territory would be abandoned immediately, the remainder as soon as the gallonage sold there could be absorbed by more profitable markets east of the Mississippi. To be vacated at once were North and South Dakota, western Nebraska, western Kansas, Oklahoma, and Arkansas. This action would not entail a sacrifice of investment for, with the exception of Oklahoma, the company operated through jobbers in these areas. Iowa, eastern Kansas, eastern Nebraska, and western Missouri would be vacated as soon as possible. From these areas withdrawal could not be swift, for here there were a good many company-owned depots and service stations. These properties would have to be sold or exchanged with other companies for facilities located in the area where Shell Petroleum had now decided to concentrate, east of the Mississippi and north of the Ohio rivers.

The eventual role of the Arkansas City refinery was, for the moment, still under study. As alternatives to abandoning it, proposals were made (1) that its capacity be cut and that its products be shipped through the existing Cushing-to-Wood River crude oil pipe line; (2) that the refinery be modernized and a pipe line built to carry its products to Kansas City and Omaha. The first alternative was in reality only postponing the final decision and the second proposal looked too expensive. At a meeting in St. Louis on April 13, 1938, a management committee decided that the only sensible course was to close Arkansas City completely. The refinery had outlived its usefulness. The territory it served was soon to be abandoned, the refinery equipment was nearly obsolete, and the nearby crude oil supplies had dwindled to a trickle. Regretfully, a statement was handed to the newspapers:

> Shell Petroleum Corporation announces that, in furtherance of its policy of gradual withdrawal from marketing activities in the states of Kansas, Oklahoma, Nebraska and the Dakotas, it was decided to close down in the near future its refinery at Arkansas City, Kansas, from which that area receives its supplies. This plant has been in continuous operation since 1923 when constructed. . . .
>
> This decision has been taken in the light of economic conditions affecting the petroleum industry in the Mid-Continent which have resulted in an increased disparity between the price of crude oil and the prices the industry receives for the refined products. . . . The current price of 4¾ cents per gallon for gasoline in Oklahoma is 20 per cent below the price prevailing in the corresponding period of last year. Today's price per barrel for 36° gravity crude is unchanged from a year ago. . . .
>
> The operation of the Arkansas City refinery has been continued on an unprofitable basis for some time in the hope that the situation might change for the better, but there does not appear to be any sign of improvement to justify continued operation.
>
> It is deeply regretted that this action is necessary, particularly because of the employees who will be affected by the shut-down.

And so, after fifteen years of operation, the Arkansas City refinery closed down forever in June 1938. The shutdown was conducted over a three-month period. First the crude stills, then the cracking units, and finally the treating and shipping equipment were closed down. By July, all activity had ceased except for shipping some of the still-remaining products. Desirable equipment was shipped to the other refineries. The remainder of the refinery, including nearly all the tankage, piping, and other fittings, was sold to a junk dealer and the land, which had been a gift, was turned back to the city. The crude oil the refinery had used, though dwindling, was a good grade of "sweet" crude, and could be put to excellent use at Wood River where a large part of the available supplies were high-sulphur ("sour") crudes from West Texas. New jobs were found for many of the operating and maintenance employees on the products pipe line, then just starting; supervisory employees were transferred to the other refineries; and R. C. Roberts, the Arkansas City manager, became the new manager at East Chicago.[16]

By mid-July, the move to vacate marketing territory had made considerable progress. Shell Petroleum had withdrawn almost completely from the states of North and South Dakota, Nebraska, Oklahoma, Arkansas, and Kansas.[17] Despite its haste to complete the evacuation of this area, the company was careful not to run out on any jobber. As soon as the marketing department men knew definitely that a given area was to be vacated, they would notify competitors and, since there was plenty of scrambling for business in 1938, the jobber usually had several prospective suppliers to choose from. Where this was not so, the company continued to supply him, until a competitor could be found who was willing to take on the account.‡ In the vicinity of Omaha, profitable exchange arrangements were made, so six jobbers were retained in that area. In eastern Kansas, the company continued to operate its properties until a purchaser could be found. In other areas, such as Iowa and parts of eastern Nebraska, exchange arrangements had been worked out which temporarily yielded a profit, although the intention was to vacate the area eventually.

The changes in the refining end of the business were not yet at an end. A new possibility, not contemplated when the closing of Arkansas City was first considered, now presented itself. By July 1938, when Roberts went north to become manager of the East Chicago refinery, there was talk that it, too, might soon be closed down. In May 1938, C. E. Davis, of the manufacturing department, was as-

‡ As a result of this policy, Shell Petroleum in October 1940 was still supplying 31 jobbers in South Dakota, Nebraska, Missouri, Iowa, Minnesota, and Oklahoma.

signed to study the feasibility of shutting down the East Chicago refinery and concentrating all of the northern refineries' capacity at Wood River. By early September a preliminary report was ready and in October a detailed study was presented.

The impetus for this study had come from three sources: (1) The crude oil line running from Wood River to East Chicago was already too small to supply East Chicago's needs; (2) the refinery since its construction in 1926–1927 had had very little modernization and now needed, or would soon need, new processing equipment throughout; and (3) new processes using refinery waste gases were coming to the fore, particularly in the manufacture of aviation gasoline. These processes could not be operated economically on small volumes of gas.

The combined capacity of Wood River and East Chicago was at this time 75,000 barrels a day, 60% of it at Wood River, 40% at East Chicago. Davis' assignment was to find out what would be the result if East Chicago were closed completely, the needed new equipment installed at Wood River, and the crude oil pipe line from Wood River converted into a line to carry products north to the Chicago area.

In the first place, his report answered, the pipe line problem would be solved. At the time substantial quantities of oil, in excess of what the Shell line could handle, were being shipped over the facilities of the Texas-Empire pipe line. If East Chicago were to continue in operation, it would be necessary to lay additional pipe to connect it with Wood River. However, if converted to a line for handling products, the existing pipe could without enlargement more than handle the volume of products then being manufactured at East Chicago.

As for the new refinery processing units, there was much to recommend their installation at Wood River instead of East Chicago. Since the Twenties, there had been substantial advances in the design of cracking units. The new cracking plants could handle substantially larger volumes with resultant lower unit costs. Simple economy dictated their adoption. At Wood River one of these new units, Dubbs 17, had been built in 1936. In the design of topping units, there had been similar advances. To save money on operations, it would be logical to install a new 30,000-barrel-a-day topping plant at East Chicago; but from a practical point of view it would be next to impossible, for 100% of the refinery's capacity would then be tied up in one topping unit. This would greatly restrict the refinery's operating flexibility because the supplies of oil available made it necessary for East Chicago to run alternately on sweet and sour crudes. If, on the other hand,

Wood River's capacity were increased to 75,000 barrels a day and this 30,000-barrel unit were erected at Wood River, the desired lower operating costs would result without impairing flexibility of operation. Clearly, the large, new units were setting a trend away from scattered small refineries.[18]

On the third point, making larger supplies of waste gases available at one location, the proposal would be a move in the right direction. With the exception of a small polymerization plant at East Chicago, little was being done to utilize the bulk of the refinery's waste gas; it was sold for fuel to the Northern Indiana Public Service Company. By concentrating East Chicago and Wood River refinery capacity at one point, enough gases would be available to build new units to make products such as aviation gasoline.

Bringing together the capacity of both refineries at one location could be expected to yield, through operating economies and increased value of by-products, direct savings of $1,765,000 annually. The total cost of relocating East Chicago's capacity at Wood River and converting the crude oil line to a products pipe line was estimated at $6,500,000. At the estimated rate of savings, the project would pay for itself in a little less than four years.[19]

Weighing all these advantages, the Shell management decided late in 1938 to close down East Chicago and concentrate the capacity of both refineries at Wood River. The decision could not be put into effect as rapidly as had been the case at Arkansas City because none of East Chicago's markets were to be abandoned. New capacity had first to be built at Wood River, and East Chicago operations transferred to Wood River gradually without interrupting the orderly flow of products to market.

Of the anticipated $6,500,000 expenditure, the largest single amount was for a large cracking unit at Wood River, Dubbs 18, construction of which was begun during 1939. In addition, there was a 30,000-barrel topping unit to be built at Wood River, and extensions to be made to the refinery's boiler plant, water cooling system, absorption plants, and other facilities. It had been decided to salvage the East Chicago reforming unit, so it was dismantled, shipped to Wood River, and re-erected there. To keep the cost of this work as low as possible, it was scheduled over a period of several months throughout 1939 and well into the first half of 1940. Finally, in March 1940, East Chicago began its closing-down operation which was completed by June. Equipment not wanted at Wood River was dismantled and sold.

The East Chicago refinery was lake-front property with dock facilities for loading lake tankers and barges, so the refinery site was converted into the terminus of the new products pipe line. The refinery tankage and buildings were saved for the new terminal, and some of the cracking chambers were converted into storage tanks for propane and butane.[20]

In May 1940, Shell Pipe Line Corporation turned the Wood River–East Chicago crude line over to Shell's products pipe line department. Work began at once to convert it to products operation. In the interest of keeping capital expenditure low, it was decided to use the Diesel-driven reciprocating pumps with which the line was already equipped, even though they precluded the automatic features of electrically driven equipment.§ Even so, considerable new material had to be purchased for the line and new tankage for marketing depots had to be built along the line. This work was completed rapidly and the first shipment of products reached East Chicago through the new line early in June 1940.[21] During the early months of operation, propane was also shipped through the new line, a revolutionary development at the time.

Thus, in little more than two years, the Shell organization in the Mid-Continent was pulled together. Early in 1938 it had been a widely scattered company with three refineries and markets in every Midwestern state. By mid-1940, it was a closely knit organization with one large refinery and a concentration of marketing effort in the most densely populated area. Best of all, this area was now served by cheap transportation. It was completely encircled by waterways: the Great Lakes on the north, the Mississippi River to the west, the Ohio River to the south. Through the heart of the region, where water carriers could not go, there now ran two large arteries of supply—the North products pipe line from Wood River to East Chicago, and the East line from Wood River to Columbus and Toledo. By early 1941, Fraser could say "Ten years ago over 90% of our products were transported by rail throughout the Middle West. Today we are practically off the rails." [22]

The success of this overhauling of operations could be seen in the

§ These pumps were removed and replaced with Diesel-driven centrifugal pumps in 1948 and the 8-inch pipe was replaced with 14-inch pipe in 1953.

earnings figures. In 1931, Shell east of the Rockies (Shell Petroleum and Shell Eastern) had sustained a total net loss of more than $40,000,-000. By 1940, the East-of-the-Rockies companies had eliminated this overwhelming deficit and were able to report a net profit for the year of $2,635,000. This vastly improved showing was not attributable to any great improvement in prices, for in 1940 the average wholesale price of gasoline was still only 4¾¢ a gallon, a bare half cent more than 1931. The big improvement was in the realm of cost cutting.

The concentration of refining capacity at Wood River was to benefit not only Shell but the nation, for it placed the company in a position to produce disproportionately large amounts of war products such as aviation gasolines in the years when they would be so badly needed.

5

Cutting Marketing Overhead

DURING this same period, the second half of the 1930's, detailed attention was given to many other phases of marketing. Actual supervision of the marketing end of the business had since the start been in the hands of division managers, whose authority and responsibility varied in each of the three operating companies. Now, in the late Thirties, careful attention was given by all three companies to increasing the division manager's authority. This increase in authority, it was hoped, would be accompanied by a commensurate increase in the division manager's responsibility for the sales effort under his direction. At this time, a great many accounting and clerical functions formerly performed by the head office were transferred to the marketing divisions. Other changes in marketing policy and procedure during this period were plentiful. New trucks, able to go farther and carry more, made possible the closing down of many depots. Large, new water terminals were built to take advantage of the cheap transportation of inland waterways. Marginal and unprofitable marketing territories outside the Midwestern area were singled out and abandoned.

The decentralization of marketing division management started first on the Pacific Coast. Shortly after Belither had become president there in August 1934, he started planning a redistribution of marketing territory. The West Coast divisions had changed little since the establishment of the company. The Seattle division embraced all of the Pacific Northwest including British Columbia; the San Francisco division covered northern and central California and Nevada; the Los Angeles division took in Southern California, Arizona, and as much of New Mexico as the company attempted to cover. These territories were too large to be supervised closely by offices that in many cases were hundreds of miles away, so district offices, subsidiary to the divisions, had grown up over the years. By 1935, there were 22 of these district offices within the divisions. In addition to the three big divisions, there were also two smaller division offices, one in Honolulu, dating from 1927, and a more recent office established in Salt Lake City during 1933–1934.

Exclusive of Hawaii, this made four division offices and 22 district offices. Belither's reorganization plan, presented in March 1935, proposed that these 26 offices be replaced by twelve offices, all of division rank, at Vancouver, Seattle, Spokane, Salt Lake City, Portland, Oakland, Sacramento, San Francisco, Fresno, Los Angeles, a Southern California division also at Los Angeles, and Phoenix. These new offices were set up during the early summer months of 1935. The two offices in Los Angeles were an experiment. Los Angeles County was the most hotly competitive gasoline market on the Coast, and it was felt that a better job could be done by a separate division management devoting its entire time to that area.

On the Atlantic Seaboard, Shell Eastern had been losing money consistently. The company decided to try "the West Coast touch," and sent for L. T. Kittinger, general manager of marketing at San Francisco. Kittinger arrived late in 1935 and was made sales manager of Shell Eastern at the beginning of 1936. Coming fresh from the atmosphere of decentralization, he decided to give it a trial in the Atlantic Seaboard organization. At the time, Shell Eastern had six marketing divisions: Boston, Syracuse, Brooklyn, Philadelphia, Baltimore, and Charlotte, North Carolina. At the beginning of 1937, this number was increased to ten by the addition of Portland, Maine, Hartford, Albany, and Elizabeth, New Jersey.

In the Mid-Continent, the Shell Petroleum division office set-up, as noted in the last chapter, went through its ups and downs during the early years of the depression. At the finish of the helter-skelter growth of the Twenties, there had been thirteen division offices; by the time the economy committees of the early Thirties had finished swinging their meat-axes, these thirteen divisions had been reduced to six: Chicago, Detroit, Cleveland, Indianapolis, St. Louis, and New Orleans. Retrenchment this severe did not last long. The Jacksonville office was re-opened in 1932; a new division was created at Kansas City early in 1933; the former Minneapolis division, closed briefly, was re-opened at Des Moines; and by the second half of the Thirties a new division had been set up at Nashville, Tennessee, to handle jobber business.[23]

The second half of the McGaw-McLaren report, mentioned earlier, was turned in late in March 1938. It was a survey of the markets supplied by Shell Petroleum's southern refineries, Houston and Norco. This area included, in the territory of Shell Petroleum Corporation, the states of Tennessee, Georgia, Florida, Alabama, Mississippi, Louisiana, and Texas, and all of Shell Eastern's marketing territory. Although losses were being sustained in much of this area, McGaw and McLaren pointed out that many of these losses were of a more temporary nature than those of the Mid-Continent. In view of the large amounts of capital then being spent on exploration and production activity along the Gulf Coast, they warned against "a wholesale elimination of markets unless it can be clearly demonstrated that such markets are unprofitable for fundamental reasons beyond our control." [24] As a yardstick of marketing performance in the southern refineries' area, McGaw and McLaren took the price which the company could have received for gasoline if it had been sold at the refinery (the Gulf cargo price) and contrasted it with the receipts obtained from sales through the company's marketing department. Using this test, they found several areas that were losing money.

Current returns from the Gulf-South states—Texas, Louisiana, Mississippi, Alabama, and Florida—were disappointing to say the least. It was this area particularly that McGaw and McLaren had in mind when they cautioned against "wholesale elimination of markets" because Shell with nearby crude production and refineries was essentially in a sound position. Even so, the current low prices and the generally depressed economy of the region did not promise any immediate improvement. The problems of this area were taken in hand a few months later by F. A. C. Guépin, who became general vice president at St. Louis in the spring of 1939, and Eaton, who had been closely tied in with many of the company's major economy moves. Guépin and Eaton recommended conversion from company depots to jobber operation through most of the Gulf-South states. This move, together with a gradual revival of the region's economy, justified the decision to remain in these states.[25]

In Texas, where operations had never been on a profitable footing outside a small area adjacent to Houston, losses in several places were in excess of 1¢ a gallon. Laredo, San Antonio, and Waco were recommended for immediate abandonment.

In Shell Eastern's territory, Pennsylvania, New Jersey, the western portion of New York and the Hudson Valley, and the Boston area all showed disappointing returns. The worst were Pennsylvania and western New York State. At Buffalo, for instance, the company in the latter half of 1937 hauled gasoline all the way from Houston and realized from its sale in Buffalo 2¢ a gallon less than could have been received at the refinery gate in Houston. In the western New York area, Shell was at a competitive disadvantage in transportation, for most of its competitors either had low-cost water or products pipe line transportation into the area. Volume was low, and the amount of marketing investment high in proportion to volume handled. There was, in addition, considerable competition from locally refined products. McGaw and McLaren recommended that this area be vacated, that the Syracuse division office be closed, and that the volume formerly sold in the region be transferred to the Albany area, where greater volume would help cut that division's unprofitable showing.

Pennsylvania was Shell Eastern's worst market. It had to compete with locally refined products and it had a very small share of the trade, only 1.75% of the total gasoline volume of the state. In Philadelphia, Shell Eastern was realizing nearly 2½¢ a gallon less than the Gulf cargo price, and in all other parts of the state at least 1¢ a gallon less. McGaw and McLaren proposed that marketing in Pennsylvania be abandoned forthwith and the Philadelphia office closed. Because the potential for industrial sales was good, it was agreed that a small staff would be left in Philadelphia exclusively for industrial sales. In addition, the company would attempt to keep service stations in operation along the main north-south highways in eastern Pennsylvania. New Jersey, especially the central and southern portions, was also highly unprofitable, so it was proposed that marketing be discontinued there.

At Boston, two factors conspired to keep operations on an unremunerative basis. One was an abnormal depression in local market prices at the time McGaw and McLaren made their survey, the other was the fact that Shell's Boston terminal was too old and too small to be efficient. At the time, another committee was making a study of how the Boston terminal could best be replaced. Meanwhile, McGaw and McLaren recommended that every measure be taken to cut expense, and suggested that overhead could be trimmed by having two division offices take over the territory then being handled by the Elizabeth, Hartford, and Boston divisions. It was voted to defer this recommendation, however, as the existing arrangement had been in effect less than a year.

During the summer of 1940, the Hartford and Elizabeth division offices were closed and their territory split between the Boston and Metropolitan New York divisions. The latter had moved in 1938 from Newtown Creek, Brooklyn, to new quarters at Jackson Heights, Queens. Also during the summer months of 1940, the Portland, Maine, office was closed and its territory combined with that of the Boston division, and the Charlotte office closed and the territory assigned to Baltimore. With these changes, the Shell marketing organization on the Atlantic Seaboard assumed its present complexion.

In addition to carrying out these recommendations, other changes had been made by the time 1940 rolled around. There was a withdrawal from marketing in northern Louisiana because of low volume, and in 1940 the New Orleans * and Jacksonville division offices were closed and a division to take care of the whole South was set up in Atlanta.[26] In the Midwestern territory from which Shell Petroleum withdrew in 1938, there were division offices at Des Moines and Kansas City. These offices were closed at that time and a new division office opened at Minneapolis where, because of a new water terminal, the company was increasing its marketing effort. Further to reduce overhead in the Mid-Continent area, the Nashville office was finally closed in the spring of 1942.

The Massachusetts Pipe Line

The report on the Boston terminal which McGaw and McLaren had mentioned was submitted late in 1938. Shell's existing terminal in Boston was an inheritance from the old New England Oil Refining Company, and had long since seen its best days. The land and amount of tankage were too small, and the dock was too decrepit to be used. Additional tankage and a dock had to be rented at considerable cost from a competitor who had terminal facilities adjoining. The re-

---

* The New Orleans division was re-established in 1953.

port estimated that buying new waterfront property in Boston and building a terminal there would cost some $1,285,000. The existing large terminal facilities at Fall River on the old New England Oil refinery grounds could be fully utilized by running a short products pipe line north from Fall River into the Boston area. The terminal to supply metropolitan Boston could then be located away from the waterfront, delays from heavy traffic would not be so great, and the purchase price of land would be much less. Total cost of the proposed line, including a terminal at Waltham, a Boston suburb, was estimated at $745,000, about 60% of the cost of a new marine terminal in Boston.[27]

In November 1939, money for the project was authorized, $1,113,-000 in all. This increase in cost over the original estimate was occasioned by a general rise in the cost of materials and labor which had taken place during the preceding twelve months, plus the cost of a spur line to the Worcester area not included in the original calculations.

Construction got under way early in 1940 amid much greater difficulties than pipeliners were accustomed to in the West. The area between Fall River and Boston was thickly settled and of fairly rough terrain, so that high-priced property and natural obstacles were both frequently encountered; where possible, they had to be bypassed. It was January 1941 before the first pumping of product began. Even then, the terminals at Waltham and at West Boylston, near Worcester, were not complete; the West Boylston segment of the line was finally put in operation in September. The added difficulty in construction and the constant rise in prices meanwhile served to bring the cost of the complete job to $1,800,000, but even at this figure the line proved a good investment.[28]

The pipe was 6 inches in diameter, and from Fall River to Waltham measured 58 miles. The spur to West Boylston, which branched off at Sherborn, was slightly more than 24 miles long. The line was not expensive to operate, as it had only a single pumping station located at Fall River. In use, the Massachusetts line enabled Shell to distribute petroleum products cheaply in the thickly settled, heavy-traffic area of Metropolitan Boston. It eliminated the necessity of building an expensive marine terminal; it made possible fuller use of existing land and tankage at Fall River; and it even lowered tanker rates slightly, for incoming tankers no longer had to go all the way to Boston. In later years, other branches were added to the Massachusetts line, making possible additional economies.

Surveys in the Intermountain Area

There were also regions on the Pacific Coast where the Shell Oil Company was at a competitive disadvantage. In the Intermountain region—Montana, Wyoming, Utah—there were local production of crude oil and local refining, making it impossible for the company to bring in products all the way from the Coast and still be on a comparable footing. Utah was a good example. When Shell Oil had entered that state in 1929, the average gasoline price posted by Utah Oil Refining Company, a Standard of Indiana subsidiary, was 4¢ a gallon above average prices on the Pacific Coast. Freight from Shell refineries to Utah points was 4¾¢, just about the amount of the price differential. During the early depression years, Utah Oil, which had a refinery in Salt Lake City, lowered its prices to conform to those on the Coast. At these rates it could still make money but Shell, saddled with a freight charge of nearly 5¢ on every gallon, was hopelessly non-competitive. For a while, the company tried purchase and exchange arrangements but without much success.[29]

With the development of the Turner Valley oil field in Canada, surpluses of Montana crude that had formerly gone across the border remained in Montana. Under the impact of this local crude over-supply, prices dropped 30¢ a barrel during 1938 and the low-cost gasoline made from this oil affected Shell's markets as far west as Spokane. At the time, the company's sales volume in Montana was about 10,000,000 gallons a year, about 9% of the market. In November 1938, John Burtt, Keith Miller, and R. W. McOmie were sent to investigate the Montana situation. They recommended purchase of the Northwest Refining Company, a local concern which controlled 1,800 barrels a day of production in the Cut Bank field and had a small refinery nearby. The proposal was that Shell operate this refinery as a skimming plant, to provide itself with a local supply of gasoline, and sell the remaining refinery fraction to the Great Northern Railway for fuel.[30]

Nothing came of this proposal. A year later, in the fall of 1939, a second deputation, consisting of G. V. Birkinshaw, C. H. Britten, E. W. Masters, F. Simmons, and J. H. White, made a thorough survey of Shell's operations in the Rocky Mountain area. The company's costs through most of the region were so high, they found, that most of its leading competitors could have undersold Shell by several cents and still made a good profit. To overcome this unsound position in the Rocky Mountain area, the committee recommended spending $2,380,000 to acquire two local firms, the Home Oil Company and the Rice Oil Company. These purchases would make Shell competitive in the area, the committee felt, by furnishing local crude reserves, a refinery, and additional marketing properties. However, Shell Petroleum had decided to withdraw from its section of Colorado as early as 1937, and Fraser † took a dim view of expanding in an area where the potential was not high. In a letter to Belither, written shortly after the presentation of this report, Fraser urged the San Francisco company to abandon completely its marketing activity in Utah, Wyoming, and the northwestern corner of Colorado.[31]

Utah operations that year resulted in a net loss, so in March 1940 Shell Oil decided to withdraw from Utah and the sections of Colorado and Wyoming adjoining.[32] Products could be barged up the Columbia River to Spokane, so the company would continue marketing in Idaho and the western portions of Montana. At this time the division office in Salt Lake City was closed and its remaining territory was handed over to the Spokane division. At about the same time, it was also decided to terminate the experiment of two division offices in Los Angeles; they were merged into one Los Angeles division office early in 1940.

While all these moves were taking place to decentralize marketing supervision, there was a simultaneous movement towards centralization of the actual distributing points. In the Mid-Continent area where the company had bought out jobbers in the Twenties, depots of course had come with the deal. Often some of these depots were located near existing facilities already owned by the company, or perhaps yet another jobber would be purchased and he would have depots in the same area as the first jobber. Most of these superfluous depots were weeded out and closed down by the economy committees of the early Thirties. But with rough roads, lumbering trucks, and small deliveries to service stations, a sizeable number of depots were needed to keep an active territory supplied with gasoline.

Now, by the mid-Thirties, the necessity for a multiplicity of depots began to disappear. The old slow trucks with solid rubber tires had given way to sleek new models with larger carrying capacities (3,500 gallons and even more), and they could travel faster and cover more ground in the course of a working day. As far as the Shell organiza-

† By this time, late 1939, the San Francisco and St. Louis companies had merged and Fraser was president of the new company.

tion was concerned, the end of the small depot was foretold one day in 1936, when the Shell Oil Company at Los Angeles put into service the first of its new semi-trailer "Clipper" trucks. The Hollywood depot was closed down and its territory thereafter supplied direct from the Wilmington refinery some 30 miles away.[33]

The Clipper truck and the new terminals along Shell's products pipe line in Illinois, Indiana, and Ohio pointed to further large-scale economies. By the late Thirties, a sweeping program of closing down excess depots was under way. Harry Jacobs, executive assistant to the marketing vice president, and P. W. Engels, assistant operations manager, were almost constantly on the road, recommending that three, four, or even more depots be closed and their territory supplied from a single point. In the state of Ohio, for instance, there had been approximately 120 depots. In a very few years this number was reduced by one-half; even in spite of this reduction, surveys continued to see if a smaller number of depots couldn't be made to do the job.[34]

This centralization of distributing points could be successful only if dealers accepted larger deliveries. So the sales force went to work on an educational campaign to persuade the dealer that it was in his interest, as well as the company's, to receive larger quantities of gasoline at less frequent intervals. Dealers had become accustomed to calling the depot on the telephone to deliver 150 or 200 gallons of gasoline. Now, larger underground storage capacity was provided at the service station and, where necessary, credit arrangements were modified so that the dealer could take larger deliveries. In a short time the sales department was able to show successful results: in some divisions, the average "dump" of gasoline rose from 150 gallons to as much as 600 gallons. With the new, larger trucks, the number of trucks per depot could be cut—in a typical instance, from eleven of the old solid-rubber-tired trucks to as few as three of the new ones, thus further reducing capital investment and annual overhead charges.[35]

The managements of all three Shell operating companies had resolved to spend as little as possible on new service stations because (1) the retail gasoline business was still bad with profits very low, (2) the whole industry was overbuilt with the result that business per unit was small and per-unit operating costs high, and (3) Shell's available capital could be invested to more advantage in new crude oil reserves and more efficient transportation facilities. But, regardless of the desirability of this course of action for Shell, it was not possible to adhere to it entirely. Other companies were building new stations and modernizing old ones in the never-slackening race for customers.

Consequently, the Shell companies found themselves forced by competition to build some new service stations and to remodel and modernize others, even though they would have preferred not to. In the Mid-Continent region, so-called "promoted deals" were for the most part used to finance these new stations. The promoted deal had the disadvantage of all rent-paying propositions, but as a temporary expedient it did provide much-needed new stations without capital outlay. During 1937, Shell Petroleum arranged to have 98 "promoted" stations built; in 1938, 101 more; and 61 during the first nine months of 1939.[36]

On the Pacific Coast, Shell Oil Company continued to build new stations on a small scale from its own funds. Twenty-two new stations were built in 1936, 34 in 1937, 17 in 1938, and 21 during the first half of 1939. In addition, each year saw some 50 or more stations rebuilt and modernized. By mid-1939, it was apparent that holding down service station construction was costing the San Francisco company business. Three years earlier, Shell Oil had sold 15% of the total gasoline in the area; by mid-1939, the company's share of the market had slipped to 13.9%. As a result of this drop in business, Belither and his marketing department decided to spend $1,500,000 during 1940 to build 86 new stations and modernize another 163. These additional outlets, it was estimated, would yield new sales of approximately 12,000,000 gallons yearly.[37]

In advertising, the sales departments of all three companies joined hands during these years to conduct their first really national advertising campaigns. Following successful campaigns in 1937 and 1938, the company embarked on a different sort of advertising in 1939. During the late Thirties, the toll of traffic deaths had risen to appalling proportions and those directly concerned with automobiles became more and more concerned. In 1937, Paul Hoffman, president of Studebaker, organized the Automotive Safety Foundation, supported by his and other automobile companies. In 1939 Shell became the first oil company to contribute to the new foundation, and that year Shell's advertising appropriation was spent in direct support of traffic safety. Across the country, newspapers, magazines, and billboards carried the message of Shell's "Share-the-Road" campaign, a propaganda effort aimed at the "road hog" and careless driver.

The "Share-the-Road" campaign did not directly advertise Shell gasoline, but it created so much good will for the company's product that the same theme was repeated during 1940. Emblems were available at Shell stations for those who signed a pledge to drive carefully and share the road, and during two years motorists affixed millions of these emblems to their license plates. Shell made motion pictures and put travelling marionette shows on the road to get across to future drivers some of the fundamental rules of traffic safety.‡

Back in the Twenties, when the company had first spread across the continent, a chief argument for so doing was that a motorist headed from the Atlantic to the Pacific could buy Shell all the way. With the withdrawal in 1938 from much of the territory between the Rockies and the Mississippi River, Lakin proposed that sales coverage be continued by setting up "tank car dealers" along the main transcontinental highways in areas where territory had been vacated. In practice, this plan did not work out because of high costs and the difficulty of supervising operations without setting up offices. This lack of representation was in some degree offset by arrangements made in 1939 with the Skelly Oil Company, which had stations in nearly all of the states which Shell had recently vacated. Skelly agreed to honor Shell credit cards in certain specified states and Shell reciprocated by honoring Skelly cards in other areas.§

In sum, the years between 1935 and 1940 were ones of great activity in the marketing end of the business—as active, in a wholly different way, as had been the days of the late Twenties, a decade before. The watchword had changed from "Where can we expand?" to "Where can we withdraw and consolidate to improve our chances of making money?"

This change in philosophy had produced striking physical changes. By 1940, the company had 702 miles of product pipe lines where there had been none in 1935; as a corollary to this development, it now owned 1,023 railroad tank cars, some 200 fewer than five years before. The number of its depots had dropped from 1,205 in 1935 to 1,077 in 1940, with some 1,400 tank trucks as against more than 1,700 five years earlier.

‡ The company's active interest in promoting highway safety has continued, through financial grants to the Automotive Safety Foundation and other safety organizations, sponsorship of traffic safety awards, and most recently a new series of institutional advertisements featuring safe-driving tests.

§ This arrangement lasted until early 1950, when it was cancelled and a similar agreement made with the Continental Oil Company.

The total number of service stations was down, too. Part of the decrease was due to vacating large areas of marketing territory; the rest to the adoption of a policy of larger deliveries. Retail outlets that were not really service stations (a pump in front of a general store) were not suited to this program of larger deliveries. Selling only a little gasoline, they could not be expected to take larger deliveries, so their business had to be relinquished. As a result there were, at the end of 1940, approximately 1,400 fewer retail outlets being supplied by Shell east of the Rockies. On the Pacific Coast, though, there were some 400 more, making the net loss about a thousand: 20,369 outlets in 1935; 19,397 at the end of 1940.

Cutting the cost of transporting products from refinery to distributing center, reducing the number of distributing points, using better and fewer trucks, getting dealers to accept larger deliveries, and reducing administrative overhead had all helped. At best, however, it was only a healthy start in the right direction. An intensive study of distribution efficiency would bring still further economies in the years that lay ahead.

6

Cheaper Water Transportation

WITH every form of transportation under study, it was only natural that water transportation should receive a careful re-examination during this period. Here the Shell management had a dual purpose: reduction of the current expense of water transportation, and diversion to water transport products that were still being shipped by more expensive carriers.

In common with its chief competitors, Shell had been using water transportation in the Great Lakes region for many years. The East Chicago refinery had been equipped with loading docks when it was built, and water terminals had been erected at Detroit and Cleveland in 1928 and at Toledo in 1930. During the early Thirties, additional terminal facilities were provided in smaller cities of the Great Lakes area, particularly on the Michigan peninsula where the company built terminals in some cities and in others made arrangements for its products to be handled by jobbers who owned terminals. In 1939,

Shell built a new water terminal at Grand Haven, Michigan, and during 1940 arranged for new terminalling facilities at Kipling, Michigan, and Green Bay, Wisconsin.

The lower Mississippi and Ohio rivers were used for shipping petroleum products, but far too large a volume still moved into this area by rail. In 1936, Shell completed a water terminal on the Ohio River at Paducah, Kentucky, and in 1939 another at Nashville, Tennessee, on the Cumberland River, a tributary of the Ohio. At Louisville, Cincinnati, and Memphis, arrangements were made to lease terminals belonging to others. In 1940, construction was started on a large Mississippi River terminal at Cape Girardeau, Missouri.

But the upper Mississippi, from St. Louis north to Minneapolis and St. Paul, was not used for the transportation of petroleum products. It is to Fraser's credit that Shell Petroleum took advantage of this splendid natural waterway, and became at this late date a pioneer shipper of petroleum products on the upper Mississippi. The river was frozen over part of the year, but that difficulty could be circumvented by building enough storage to carry the terminal through the winter. In 1937, Shell Petroleum built its first terminal on the upper Mississippi, at St. Paul, Minnesota. Later the same year, a second terminal was completed at Bettendorf, Iowa, and in 1940 a third terminal was built at Winona, Wisconsin.

On the Pacific Coast, especially in the Northwest, the business had been built around water terminals from the first, but it was still possible to add a new one here and there. A new terminal was built during 1939 on the Columbia River at Attalia, Washington, and during 1940 a second was completed at Stockton, California, and construction started on a third at Sacramento.

Shell's eastern operation was based entirely on ocean terminals, as all its products were shipped in by deep water. During the late Thirties, steps were taken to divert more products to river, canal, and lake transportation wherever feasible. New inland terminals were built in Shell Eastern's territory, such as the one at Plattsburg, New York, on Lake Champlain, completed late in 1939. Also during 1939, Shell Eastern built a new ocean terminal at Richmond, Virginia.

The terminal building program of the late Thirties made it possible to reach, with cheap water transportation, areas which had hitherto been served by more costly methods. In addition, this building of terminals over an extended period was well suited to Shell's financial resources, for unlike a products pipe line, terminals did not have to be built all at once.

To take advantage of inland water transportation, it was not necessary for Shell to own and operate its own fleet of barges and tugboats. There were a number of concerns in the business of operating oil barges, and generally Shell in the Mid-Continent supplied its transportation needs by "spot charter" from such owners. The rates for these charters fluctuated in accordance with demand. By the mid-1930's, with more companies utilizing the inland waterways, the price of chartering barges began to increase and put Shell at a competitive disadvantage in relation to the companies who owned their own fleets. Shell Petroleum looked around for a solution and in November 1938 signed a long-term contract of affreightment with the National Oil Transport Corporation. This contract gave Shell assurance of reasonable rates over a long period and guaranteed National Oil steady employment for the thirty or so barges and small tankers needed to do the job. Such long-term contracts have since supplied the bulk of the company's barge and lake-tanker transportation in the Midwest.

As was seen in earlier chapters, legal provisions pertaining to coastwise shipping made it impossible for Shell to own and operate ocean tankers between U. S. ports. At first glance, this seemed an insuperable barrier to obtaining ocean transportation anywhere near as cheap as that of competitors who owned and operated their own ships. Until the mid-Thirties, however, Shell's inability to own ocean tankers was not a serious handicap.

On the Pacific Coast, the Northwest had to be supplied by tanker from Martinez and Wilmington. The tanker fleets of competitors such as Union of California and General Petroleum Corporation had spare capacity and were glad to pick up extra revenue by carrying Shell's products. East of the Rockies, there was no need for deepwater transportation until Shell Eastern began operations on the Atlantic Seaboard in 1929. At that time, as recounted in the previous chapter, Shell Eastern's gasoline supplies were provided initially by an exchange agreement with the Group's refinery at Curaçao, thus enabling Anglo-Saxon to use its own tankers to carry Curaçao product to Fall River and to export from Houston and the West Coast an amount equal to the imports. When this arrangement was curtailed late in 1930 and abandoned for good in 1932, the tanker market was extremely depressed, so that Shell found it possible to charter vessels at extremely low cost for the next few years. By 1934, however, the charter market had started to move up again. It was apparent that the company would have to make more satisfactory arrangements if it were not to be hopelessly non-competitive.

Long-term charters were never approved by the Maritime Commission, so the company decided to go into contracts of affreightment. Such arrangements were simple: a carrier would agree to provide shipment for so many barrels of oil over a specified period at a given rate. His charge, at a fixed rate over a long period, could be expected to be somewhat lower than the cost of spot-chartering because full-time employment would be guaranteed his vessels. The first of these long-term contracts of affreightment was negotiated by Shell with the Pennsylvania Shipping Company, headed by Charles Kurz of Philadelphia, whose vessels Shell had chartered in the years just previous. The contract went into effect January 1, 1934, for a period of five years.[38]

This arrangement worked out satisfactorily for both parties, and insured Shell stable tanker arrangements at reasonable cost. In 1935, a similar contract of affreightment was signed by Shell and Charles Kurz & Company and in 1937 contracts with Kurz's companies were extended to handle tanker transportation on the West Coast, with the exception of the voyage to Hawaii. (Because of the small quantities involved, the Hawaiian run could be handled more cheaply by competitors' vessels.) Some 70% of the company's Atlantic Coast tanker requirements were supplied by these fixed-rate contracts of affreightment in the eight-year period ending with 1941. In five of the eight years, this arrangement also made possible rates below the going tanker market, and protected the company against sudden, sharp rises in transportation costs.

These flat-rate contracts were not wholly equable: in times of depressed tanker rates, Shell's expense for ocean freight would be higher than if the company were chartering on the open market; in times of high rates, especially if they were accompanied by high operating expenses, Shell would be at a definite advantage but Kurz would be realizing too small a return on his vessels. As early as 1931, mention of a cost-plus-fixed-fee arrangement had been made. During 1937, the idea was revived and became the subject of serious conversations between Shell and Kurz. As a result of these discussions, it was proposed that to take care of Shell's growing needs Kurz would enlarge his fleet by building two new tankers. Shell would sign a 15-year contract of affreightment that would guarantee him full-time employment for these vessels or others of similar capacity. The rates paid would be Kurz's actual costs plus a fee for his operating profit.

The problem of how to provide funds for building these vessels was not quite so easy to solve. Kurz did not have funds sufficient for so large an undertaking and Shell could not lend him the money, or act as co-signer or surety for him, without the risk of such a loan being interpreted as evidence of indirect ownership of the vessels. The Merchant Marine Act of 1920 stipulated that vessels engaged in intercoastal trade must be owned at least 75% by citizens of the United States, so Shell could at best lend or guarantee only 25% of the total amount required. With his 15-year contract of affreightment as security (a contract long enough to completely pay out the cost of the vessels), Kurz turned to the banks in his attempt to borrow the remaining 75%. The banks said they were, as a matter of policy, opposed to lending money for a period of longer than five years. Insurance companies were interested in the investment possibility of a 15-year loan, but the ones who expressed interest were mutual companies, owned by their policyholders. For them to attempt to satisfy the Maritime Commission (which must approve the transaction) of the nationality of each individual policyholder would have been an overwhelming task. Kurz was about to give up the search, when unexpected assistance came from one of Shell's chief competitors.

At the request of the Maritime Commission, which was acting on behalf of the Navy, Standard Oil of New Jersey had signed a contract with the Maritime Commission, on January 3, 1938, agreeing to build twelve "defense type" tankers. These vessels were to be constructed and owned by private capital, with the understanding that certain so-called "defense features" would be built into them, chiefly greater speed (5 to 6 knots faster than ordinary tankers) and greater structural strength so as to permit the installation of gun mounts if they should ever be necessary. In case of war, the tankers would be turned over to the government for use as Navy fueling vessels; in return, the Maritime Commission agreed to foot the bill for the defense features, about a third of the vessel's total cost of $2,250,000 each. The Jersey company did not want all twelve tankers for its own use, and was anxious to have other tanker owners participate in this contract that had been signed with the government. Kurz approached them, and when no other tanker operators came forward with offers to participate, the Jersey people offered to help Kurz buy two of the twelve tankers. In February 1938, Standard of Jersey agreed to lend Kurz 50% of the cost of the vessels at 4½% interest, secured by a first mortgage. To obtain another 25%, Kurz resorted to a five-year bank loan secured by a second mortgage on the tankers. The remaining 25% could, as mentioned, be a direct loan from Shell or a loan guaranteed by the company. These two 18,000-ton tankers, named the *Seakay* and *Markay* (from initials of members of the Kurz family) were placed in service in March and May, 1939.

In September of that year, war broke out in Europe and the Maritime Commission began negotiating for the construction of another twelve tankers with Navy defense features, similar to those built by Jersey but slightly smaller. Kurz, backed by the assurance of long-term contracts of affreightment from Shell, contracted with the Maritime Commission to build five of these tankers. Socony-Vacuum contracted for six and the twelfth was never built. These vessels were financed 25% by a loan from Shell and 75% by two New York banks, Irving Trust Company and the Central Hanover Bank & Trust Company. Shell, by offering long-term contracts of affreightment to Kurz, thus made possible construction of 7 of the 23, or 30%, of the "defense features" tankers which were built.

Kurz was able to repay the loans much sooner than anticipated. The *Seakay* was purchased by the government in October 1940 and the *Markay* in June 1941 for conversion into "baby flat top" aircraft carriers named, respectively, the *Santee* and the *Swanee*.* The other five vessels were taken over by the Navy as rapidly as they were completed.

For Shell's immediate needs, these cost-plus-fixed-fee arrangements were of little use prewar, and during the war all shipping was under the direction of the government. These developments of the late Thirties were important, however, for they established the pattern to which Shell would revert in the years following the war. The company's ocean transport requirements have since 1945 been put almost entirely on this cost-plus basis, giving Shell ocean transport costs as low as it can hope to enjoy without actually owning a fleet.

---

* Kurz ordered replacements for these vessels from Sun Shipbuilding & Dry Dock Company. They were named for their predecessors, *Seakay* and *Markay*. The second *Seakay* was sunk during the war.

More Crude Oil

"WE STILL have our troubles," Godber had written Alexander Mackay back in 1920, "one of which is lack of crude." [39] To both men this lack of balance between Roxana's own-produced crude and the demands of its refineries probably seemed temporary, something which would right itself once a few more oil fields had been discovered. And no doubt such would have been the case, had not the increase in gasoline demand all during the Twenties more than kept pace with the rate of Roxana's discoveries of new crude oil reserves. In 1920, when Godber had lamented the company's shortage of crude, Roxana had been forced to purchase 147,000 barrels of oil from other producers in order to meet its refining demands. Nine years later in 1929 the company, now owning five refineries instead of one, found it necessary to purchase more than 13,000,000 barrels of crude from outside sources! With the widespread adoption of proration and unit operation plans in the early Thirties, the amount the company could produce from its own wells was greatly curtailed, and its purchases had to be increased commensurately. During 1930, Shell's purchases in the Mid-Continent were 23,300,000 barrels, a figure which by 1937 had risen to 35,650,000 barrels, 58% of Shell Petroleum's total crude oil requirements.

During the earlier years of the Thirties, this high percentage of purchases, while a source of serious concern, had not been a cause for outright alarm, because crude oil was then selling at unprecedented lows. During the second half of the Thirties, however, the price of crude got back to respectable levels. From 1935 to 1940 the average national price ranged between $1.02 and $1.18 a barrel, a price nearly as high as that of the late Twenties, while product prices remained well below the levels of the Twenties. This improvement in crude prices was chiefly the result of increased demand, rather than of curtailed production. Total U. S. crude oil production in each of the years between 1935 and 1940 exceeded one billion barrels, a figure attained only once before, in the boom year of 1929.

As a corollary to the efforts the Shell organization was making to better its position in the transportation and distribution ends of its business, there was an earnest and sustained effort during this period to improve the ratio of Shell Petroleum's own-produced to purchased crude. A primary goal was to convert the ratio of 1937—58% purchased, 42% own-produced—to at least a reversal of these percentages, and obtain 60 barrels of oil from company wells for every 40 barrels purchased. The program to accomplish this goal called for intensive exploration for new oil fields, searching for deeper producing zones in existing fields, developing cheaper drilling techniques, purchase and exchange of proven oil properties, construction of new crude oil pipe lines, and a general overhaul of pipe line operating practice to reduce costs.

As mentioned in the preceding chapter, the company's exploration efforts were largely abandoned during the early Thirties. Where lease obligations made it necessary to drill, an attempt was usually made to farm out the acreage to another operator in return for a small overriding royalty; failing this, the leases were in many cases surrendered to avoid the expense of drilling. Only in the areas where the chances of striking oil seemed exceptionally promising did the company drill.

Then, in 1934, chiefly to meet lease obligations, drilling was started up again on a larger scale. In East Texas, Shell Petroleum that year drilled 103 wells in addition to the 540 wells it already had there.† Also during 1934, the company discovered a new field in the Roanoke area, twenty miles east of Iowa, Louisiana—a field which had been discovered by another company in 1931, with Shell holding a substantial amount of favorably located acreage. The 1934 drilling activity increased Shell Union's total shut-in production by almost 45% but, because of proration, the actual rate of the company's production increased by only about 1%.

With 1935 came the first of a new series of large expenditures for exploration. Exploratory drilling was stepped up, and Shell Petroleum turned every penny it could spare into exploratory work. During 1935, a new deep zone was opened in the Oxford, Kansas, pool where Shell Petroleum already held a majority of the acreage. A new field was also discovered in the Turon district of Kansas. Drilling in East Texas continued extremely active; during 1935 alone, the company had to complete no less than 247 new wells there to protect its competitive position. Producing wells were completed during the year in the Hobbs field of eastern New Mexico.

During 1936, a number of small properties were brought into

---

† Of these wells, Shell Petroleum had drilled 371 and farmed out 169.

production in western Kansas, and the limits of old fields in Kansas and Oklahoma were extended. Shell Petroleum drilled a discovery well in the Lucien-Hayward (Oklahoma) area, and the West Billings field discovered late in 1935 was developed. There was also a discovery on the Texas Gulf Coast, the Nome field near the Louisiana border.

The year 1937 brought several more discovery wells. In February, an extremely successful test well was completed in Terrebonne Parish, Louisiana, in what is now called the Gibson field, where Shell Petroleum owned about 10,000 acres. In August, Shell Petroleum brought in the discovery well on a 5,000-acre block which it owned in the Howley field of western Kansas. In December, the discovery well was completed in the Clam Lake field, in Jefferson County on the Gulf Coast of Texas, where Shell held a 50% undivided interest in leases covering the entire area.[40]

Southern Illinois

During the summer of 1937, the company drilled its first well, a dry hole, in one of the new Illinois Basin fields. Late in December 1937 a shallow producing well was completed in Shell's block of acreage near Centralia, Illinois. During 1938 what can probably be called the last of the old-time oil booms got under way in the country adjoining Centralia. Speculators, promoters, and shoestring operators poured in on Centralia and nearby Salem just as they had converged on Titusville, Spindletop, Smackover, and the dozens of other oil boom towns since 1859. It was a "poor-boy" oil field, with oil spread over a fairly large area, located at shallow depths, and situated near to market—in a state with no production-restricting legislation.‡ At Centralia wells were only 1,300 to 1,400 feet deep. Any man with

‡ Illinois had signed the original Interstate Oil Compact agreement in 1935, but had been unable to secure the enactment of the necessary state conservation laws called for in the Interstate Compact. Once new production had been discovered in the state, a vociferous minority, composed largely of royalty owners and independent refiners, used every means at their disposal to block passage of any law which would limit their immediate incomes by reducing the production of gas or oil. As a result, these new pools were developed with reckless abandon; reservoir energy was rapidly dissipated, and the new Illinois production, reaching a peak in 1940, fell off rapidly thereafter. In the fields around Salem, gas wastage was particularly distressing. During 1939, 134 billion cubic feet of gas, more than the state's entire consumption that year, was flared in the fields, with the burning torches visible at night for fifty miles.[41] It was a maddening example of how men will refuse to learn, even from experience: the very same thing had occurred in the same area with the same results only a generation before.

a few dollars' credit and a makeshift drilling rig could get down to the oil-bearing formation.

Shell had been exploring the southern Illinois area since late 1935. In October 1937, it set up a production area office at Centralia under E. G. Robinson and began drilling with portable rigs just west of Centralia. Within a year, 38 Shell wells had been completed at depths of 1,300 to 1,400 feet, with an average daily production of 53 barrels. As there was not enough pressure to lift the oil, the Centralia wells had to be put on the pump immediately.

In August 1938, a large new field was discovered at Salem, a few miles east of Centralia. There and at other nearby locations such as Benton, Dale-Hoodville, Rural Hill, and Mt. Carmel, Shell developed substantial production in the last years of the Thirties, the total of its Illinois Basin production during these years rising to between 40,000 and 50,000 barrels a day. Since all of this oil was shallow, flush production, Shell Petroleum did not consider it worth while to build a pipe line to the area. Instead, the company sold its Illinois oil or arranged trades with companies who already had pipe lines running through the region, the chief of these being Ohio Oil Company.[42]

Ten Section

On the Pacific Coast, important additions were made to Shell Oil Company's reserves during this period. The limits of the Ventura field were extended by new discoveries in 1934. The same year shallow production was discovered in the Edison field and Shell Oil resumed production in the Capitan field which had been discovered in 1930 but had been kept shut in because of lack of demand. During 1935, the limits of the Round Mountain, Mountain View, Mt. Poso, and Edison fields were extended, and in 1936 a really outstanding discovery was made in the floor of the San Joaquin Valley. This flat region had never been susceptible to surface geology, but Shell Oil put the reflection seismograph to work with good effect on an area which hitherto had been thought to hold no oil.

The drilling of the Ten Section discovery well was completed on June 2, 1936, and was regarded by Shell men on the Coast as their most important strike since Signal Hill, fifteen years earlier. All the land was in the hands of a single owner, the Kern County Land Company, which years earlier had fenced in a 10-section tract in the area, giving rise to the name. Shell's leases from the Kern County

Land Company, when finally completed, came to just over 10 sections in total area, some 6,433 acres.[43]

Two years later, in 1938, Shell Oil brought in its first productive well in the Canal field, near Ten Section, with initial production of 2,200 barrels a day.

Buying Producing Properties

In addition to acquiring oil by discovery and drilling up proven property, Shell Petroleum undertook to better its position by buying and trading oil-producing properties. The first large purchase of this nature was the acquisition in 1934 of 252 acres of producing property in the East Texas field from the Lion Oil & Refining Company for $1,425,000 in cash and oil. Shell Petroleum's East Texas acreage was further enlarged in 1938 and 1939 by purchases from the Bennett Petroleum Corporation and R. G. Trippett totalling 124 acres for approximately $1,120,000.[44]

On the Pacific Coast, even larger purchases had been made and at an earlier date. In 1931, the interests of Getty-Babcock-Armstrong in the Kettleman North Dome Association comprising some 232 acres had been acquired for more than $2½ million. Four years later, in 1935, the interest of the Pacific Western Oil Company in the same field, amounting to some 306 acres, was acquired for nearly $4 million. At the same time Shell in partnership with Standard of California purchased Pacific Western's interest in the Inglewood field, 38.6 acres for approximately $1½ million.[45] A large number of smaller properties were also purchased during this period. In each case, the nearness of prospective purchases to other Shell properties or to company-owned trunk pipe lines was a major consideration in evaluating the attractiveness of a proposed deal.

Trading oil-producing properties in fields which had begun to decline, or in fields remote from company-owned pipe lines, for newer production or properties nearer to a pipe line connection was actively pursued during this period. Late in 1938, Shell Petroleum traded its leases in the Burbank field to Phillips Petroleum Company in exchange for Phillips' interest in two leases in the Churchill, Kansas, field, another in Udall, Kansas, and other leases at Avant, Oklahoma. In March 1939, Shell turned over its relatively small holdings in the Seminole District of Oklahoma to Carter Oil Company, in exchange for the latter's leases at Healdton and Wildcat Jim, Oklahoma. In the summer of the same year, Shell's famous old Cushing leases, the Linda and Maley Yarhola, were deeded to Sinclair, the latter company giving in exchange its interest in the North Lucien, Oklahoma, unitized field which Shell operated, a substantial lease in the Tonkawa field, and other properties in the Ploog, Chase, Hafermann, and Lorraine unitized pools, all of them in Kansas.[46]

Portable Rigs and "Slim-Hole" Drilling

With the resumption of extensive drilling about 1934, Shell's production engineers turned their attention to the development of cheaper drilling methods. Exploratory drilling, which so often ended in failure anyhow, was a particularly fertile field for economy. By the late Thirties, two developments in the interest of cheaper exploratory wells had been put to fairly general use: portable rigs and "slim-hole" drilling.

About 1930, Shell in California had begun using portable rigs in the Bakersfield area. In reality, this rig consisted of a lightweight standard derrick and engine works mounted on skids or wheels so that it could be moved from one well location to another without the expense or lost time involved in dismantling and reassembling the derrick and accompanying machinery. The second idea, that of using a smaller-diameter drill stem, also received an early trial in California in the Ten Section field.

Neither portable rigs nor slim-hole drilling were Shell developments,* but in the Mid-Continent where Shell Petroleum had a large amount of drilling to be done, these techniques received a thorough trial and further refinement under the active encouragement of H. Bloemgarten, former assistant to Van der Linden at The Hague, who had been made vice president in charge of production at St. Louis during 1935. Slim holes, i.e., smaller holes of even diameter from top to bottom, had been part and parcel of the "poor-boy" drilling outfits common in the East Texas field during the early Thirties. Traditional drilling methods used two, three, or more sizes of bits, drill stem, and casing, but many East Texas operators resorted to the short cut of drilling the entire well with the smallest size of bit and drill stem because the smaller sizes cost less to buy.

---

* Portable rigs have a venerable history. Matador had used them, 1917–1919, while drilling on the Colony Creek structure in Wyoming; other companies had used portable equipment at earlier dates. The Thirties witnessed the adoption of modern portable drilling equipment.

Shell Petroleum began experimenting with slim-hole equipment and by 1938 was using it for shallow drilling in Oklahoma and western Kansas. Going one step further, the company tried dispensing with drill pipe altogether and using instead the cheaper casing pipe, previously used to line the hole after the well had been completed. To complete a well in this fashion, the drill bit was removed and the casing which had been used as drill stem was cemented in place.

With lighter drill stems, drilling rigs did not need to be so heavy. Working with the Franks Manufacturing Corporation of Tulsa, Shell Petroleum engineers developed a truck-mounted portable rig, sturdy enough to drill to 4,000 feet through hard formations. A smaller bit was used, a smaller hole drilled, and the standard 7-inch casing was replaced by lighter and cheaper 4½-inch casing. This new equipment reduced by one-third the per-foot cost of drilling a well, and was used extensively by Shell for the shallow drilling in southern Illinois during the late Thirties.

The portable derrick did away with the capital cost of a permanent derrick, which customarily had been left on each well site after completion of the well. For well-servicing operations (clean-outs, work-overs, etc.), satisfactory truck-mounted derricks were soon developed. In ensuing years, portable derricks were built strong enough to drill deep wells, but the usefulness of slim holes seemed to be confined to shallow fields.[47]

These cheaper drilling practices made possible more exploratory drilling for a given amount of money, and in proven fields helped bring about the reduced drilling costs which had become mandatory as a result of proration; for with reduced output, it took much longer to pay out a well's drilling expense.

The Bakersfield Line, New Pipe Line Practices

In both the Mid-Continent and on the Pacific Coast, new pipe line construction was undertaken to furnish transportation for the increased supplies of crude oil. In California, the desirability of extending the Valley Pipe Line southward to the Bakersfield area had been visualized for some time, but the volume of Shell's own production there had not justified it. In the decade following Shell's entry into the Bakersfield area, the company's oil had been transported by Union Oil pipe lines to San Luis Obispo and thence by Union tankers to Shell refineries. Finally by early 1936, Shell's production and purchases in the Mt. Poso, Round Mountain, Kern River, Kern Front, Mountain View, Edison, Buena Vista, and Midway fields had reached sufficient volume to make a line from Bakersfield to Martinez practicable. Construction was authorized in the spring of 1936 and by early summer, when the new Ten Section field was discovered, work was well under way. The Ten Section field would have made the new line necessary, so that it was fortunate indeed that it was already building.

A new right-of-way from Bakersfield to Caliola (the southernmost end of the old Valley line) was acquired and a 10-inch line laid. From Caliola north to Martinez, the company was able to use the second-line rights acquired back in 1914. The old line consisted of alternate stretches of 8- and 10-inch pipe. These were now disconnected from each other, and the gaps in each filled in to make two lines on the old Valley Pipe right-of-way, one an 8-inch line for light oils, the other a 10-inch line for heavy oil. The heavy oil line employed heat in the pumping stations, to reduce viscosity and make pumping easier.

Four construction crews went to work on different segments of the new Bakersfield–Martinez line simultaneously. The result was a remarkably speedy construction job: the first weld was made on July 22, 1936, and the last on October 21, just three months later. The new line, 258 miles long, had been tested, dedicated, and put into operation by late December. It cost $4,500,000 and, together with the old line, could deliver 48,000 barrels of crude a day to the Martinez refinery. Some measure of the progress in reducing pipe line construction costs may be had from the fact that, in spite of a 65% increase in industrial construction costs between 1915 and 1936, the new Bakersfield–Martinez line in 1936 cost $7,467 a mile against $6,450 a mile for the Valley line in 1915, an increase of only 15%.[48]

In the Mid-Continent, the parallel line from Cushing to Wood River, which the Salmon committee had recommended, was completed and put into operation during 1937. In keeping with common practice in the pipe line business, this line had been "looped" at the time of the building of the East Chicago refinery in the mid-Twenties. "Looping" refers to the laying of a parallel line part way between each station to augment capacity by increasing the ease of pumping. By 1937, this looping was so extensive that it was necessary to lay only 72 miles of new pipe to complete the gaps in the "loops," and obtain a second line running parallel to the first over the Cushing-to-Wood River right-of-way. Additional pumping equipment was, of course, necessary.

During this period a great deal of attention was directed towards reducing pipe line operating costs and increasing transportation efficiency. One of the most spectacular of the operating economies was the inauguration by Shell Pipe Line Corporation of a pipe line air patrol in June 1939. For years, pipe line walkers had covered the pipe line right-of-way on foot, looking for signs of leaks and for breaks in the pipe line telephone and telegraph wires which are strung along the right-of-way.§ C. B. McMahan of the Mississippi River Fuel Corporation, a gas transmission company, had for a decade been patrolling his company's pipe line by air, and had demonstrated that it could be done safely. Shell was the first oil company to adopt his cheaper method. Two airplanes were engaged to patrol some two-thirds of Shell Pipe Line's total mileage. By flying at low altitudes (300 to 500 feet), the pilots could spot the dark patches on the ground that indicated leaks and see breaks in the telephone wires. In a single hour, one air-borne inspector could cover more ground than the old pipe line walker could walk in a week, and at about half the cost.[49]

Another important saving in pipe line operation was the elimination of most of the possibilities for evaporation. As much as possible, the oil was kept confined to the pipe line or to gas-tight tanks; the number of float-tanks on the line was cut to a minimum. The saving from decreased evaporation losses amounted to about 1% of the crude handled, or some $700,000 annually for the amount Shell Pipe Line transported.[50]

Around $10,000,000 a year had been budgeted by Shell Petroleum for exploration during the years 1935 to 1940. This was a lot of money in depression years, but the expenditure did enable Shell Petroleum to arrest, and then reverse, the trend of its crude oil pur-

§ Shell has a company-owned telephone and telegraph system, using wires following the pipe line right-of-way, both in the Mid-Continent and on the Pacific Coast. In California, the "pipe line system" connects the Shell Building in San Francisco with the Shell Building in Los Angeles, the production and marketing offices at Sacramento, the Long Beach, Ventura, and Bakersfield production offices, and the refineries at Martinez and Wilmington. In the Mid-Continent, similar circuits stretch from the Wood River refinery and the St. Louis Shell Building to the Houston Shell Building and Houston refinery, going by way of West Texas; leased lines tie the St. Louis end to head office in New York. Radio circuits have supplemented wires in recent years.

chases. By 1940, the company had nearly reached, and during 1941 it exceeded, its goal of producing at least 60% of its refineries' needs.

SHELL PETROLEUM CORPORATION CRUDE OIL SOURCES, 1937–1941

	Own Production (Barrels)	Purchased Oil (Barrels)	Produced By Company
1937	26,265,000	35,645,000	42.5%
1938	24,992,000	28,643,000	46.6%
1939	29,607,000	28,130,000	51.3%
1940	33,210,000	25,115,000	57.0%
1941	36,217,000	20,404,000	64.0%

8

New Finance

DURING the late Thirties, the prudent debt-management policies begun by Shell Union early in the depression were continued. In 1936, the two remaining 5% bond issues dating from the late 1920's were retired from the receipts of a new $60,000,000 3½% bond issue sold to investors in March 1936. After paying off the earlier bond issues, the balance of the receipts from the new issue amounted to some $11,500,000 in new money. This was augmented at the same time by the receipt of about $6,600,000 from the sale of the Shell Union's interest in The Flintkote Company.

The purchase of a half-interest in Flintkote, large manufacturers of asphalt roofing and liquid asphalt products, had been made at the height of the expansionist Twenties, when every company, Shell included, seemed bent on acquiring companies that performed related or by-product operations.* Flintkote's prosperity had been based on

---

* Flintkote, organized in New Jersey in 1901, had by the late Twenties become a large consumer of asphalt in the manufacture of shingles, roll roofing, and building paper. It had also acquired the Kirschbraun-Belknap patents for impregnating paper and paperboard with clay-base asphalt emulsions. This latter aspect of Flintkote's business appealed to the Shell Group, for Shell in London had in the mid-Twenties bought up a series of British patents for making soap-base cold-asphalt emulsions. These emulsions, called "Colas" (cold asphalt), could have widespread application, the Shell people felt, for resurfacing partially worn roads. The Kirschbraun-Belknap patents, joined to the Colas patents, would give Shell a good position in the industrial asphalt field. Primarily with this in mind, Adrian Corbett, representing the Group, conducted negotiations in London with Chester E. Rahr, Flintkote president, during the summer of 1928, resulting in an agreement (August 30, 1928) between Anglo-

the building boom of the Twenties which collapsed with the onset of the depression. Thereafter much of the company's plant capacity was forced to lie idle, with a resultant effect on earnings. Early in 1932, the Shell interests exercised their rights under the purchase contract to replace Flintkote president Chester E. Rahr with John H. Plunkett, the able manager of Flintkote's Los Angeles plant. By dint of judicious pruning and hard work, Plunkett, guided by the Shell Union management, put the company's affairs in order during his brief presidency. He died in February 1934 and was succeeded by I. J. Harvey, Jr., a former Shell man who had been a Flintkote vice president since 1931. Harvey started production of a more diversified line of products and by 1935 he was able to report a profit of $1,300,000.

Unfortunately, each new move toward diversification carried Flintkote that much farther away from Shell. It was not difficult to see that the Flintkote operation would soon become entirely alien to oil men accustomed to thinking of manufacturing and selling bulk quantities of petroleum products. Besides, Flintkote had in August 1934 sold to the Royal Dutch-Shell companies in Europe its holdings in the Colas-Flintkote companies abroad, and it was this cold-asphalt emulsion end of the business which had chiefly interested Shell.

For these reasons, it was decided late in 1935 to find a purchaser for the Shell half-interest in The Flintkote Company. The New York brokerage firm of Lehman Brothers agreed to purchase the interest outright, and early in 1936 the stock transfer took place. Lehman's paid Shell Union $44.50 a share for stock which had cost the company $29.50 some six years before. To Shell Union, this sale brought the return of the principal it had invested in 1929, plus a profit of $15 a share which after taxes amounted to $2,840,000.[52]

The proceeds from the bond issue, sale of the Flintkote stock, and improved earnings during the mid-Thirties supplied the cash needed

---

Saxon and Flintkote. The Shell Group agreed to assign Flintkote all of its future patents in the asphalt field, to supply $8,200,000 of new capital (equal to the balance-sheet value of Flintkote at the time), and receive in exchange new shares of common stock that carried the right to elect a majority of the board of directors. Shell Union took half of these new shares when they were issued early in 1929, paying $4,367,500 cash, or $29.50 a share; the remainder was subscribed by Bataafsche. Later the same year, Flintkote acquired the Colas patents from the Group and set about organizing Colas-Flintkote subsidiaries in 18 foreign countries to make and market Colas emulsions for road-building purposes. Flintkote sold these subsidiaries to the Shell Group in August 1934. In the United States, Colas emulsions were manufactured by Flintkote but sold by the asphalt salesmen of the Shell oil companies, an arrangement which has continued since the 1936 sale of Shell's interest in Flintkote.[51]

during the second half of the Thirties for an accelerated program of capital expenditures. During these years, Shell Union companies once again began to lay out substantial amounts, particularly in exploration and production activity.

SHELL UNION OIL CORPORATION CAPITAL EXPENDITURES, 1935–1940

1935	$36,000,000
1936	36,500,000
1937	44,100,000
1938	36,800,000
1939	41,780,000
1940	37,989,000

A chief source of funds for capital investment is the annual deduction made from current income to cover depreciation. When this amount is insufficient to cover contemplated expenditures, earnings retained for reinvestment in the business generally make up the difference. This was the case in 1935 and 1936, although in both years there were also supplementary funds provided by outside sources. In 1937, however, the depreciation write-off of $37,518,000 and the retention from earnings of $5,771,000 were not enough to meet contemplated new capital expenses of $44,100,000, and so Shell Union borrowed $3,500,000 from Bataafsche at rates equivalent to bank interest.[53]

During 1938, with business taking a turn for the worse, it was desirable to keep a good cash position. The depreciation allowance for the year was enough to cover contemplated new capital expenses, but cash position, at $15,967,000, was the lowest in years. Primarily to bolster cash position, a $25,000,000 loan was arranged with Equitable Life in June 1938. Shell Union 15-year bonds bearing interest at 3⅝% were issued to the insurance company.

On July 1, 1939, the $60,000,000 worth of 3½% bonds issued in 1936 and the $25,000,000 worth of 3⅝% bonds issued the previous year were refinanced by a new issue of $85,000,000 at 2½%, a full percentage point lower. Despite having to pay penalties for the early redemption of these recent issues, the long-term saving in interest made such refinancing well worth while.

Depreciation write-offs in 1939 just about equalled capital expenditures. This additional financing, plus the improvement in the company's cash position, made it possible for Shell Union to undertake $38,000,000 worth of new capital expenditure in 1940 without additional outside financing.

Shell Union had paid no dividends on its common stock since mid-1930, and no dividends on the preferred since October 1931. Improved financial results permitted resumption of the preferred stock dividend in July 1936, and full payment of preferred arrears, amounting to $26.12 per share, was made in December 1936. At the same time, a small dividend, 25 cents a share, was paid to the patient holders of the common stock. Since that time, common stock dividends have continued without interruption. In June 1940, the common stock, which had been without par value, was assigned a nominal value of $15 a share.

The preferred stock was paying a fixed dividend of 5½% per year, which in 1929 was a reasonable enough rate for interest. A decade later, however, it was far too much. By late 1940, the number of shares of preferred stock outstanding, originally 400,000, had been reduced by purchase and retirement to 331,225 shares. To redeem them would cost some $35,535,000. Early in 1941, the company sold $15,000,000 of 20-year bonds carrying interest at 2¾%, and $10,000,000 worth of serial notes, scheduled to fall due between 1942 and 1953 and bearing interest at rates running from ⅜% to 2½%. These funds, together with some $11,000,000 from the Shell Union treasury, were used to retire the preferred stock issue in its entirety early in 1941.

These refinancing transactions cut in half the expense of carrying the company's debt, and in addition provided several millions of dollars of new money for much-needed capital expansion. By 1941, the funded debt again stood at more than $100,000,000, double the amount of late 1935. But nearly $40,000,000 of new money for capital expenditure had been provided by this means in the years since 1935, and the company's cash position had been enhanced by another $40,000,000.

Investigations and Lawsuits

THE period of the late 1930's brought a new and far from welcome development—almost constant investigation and legal harassment of the oil industry, and individual companies within it, by various departments of the Federal government. Without doubt, some of this activity stemmed from an honest desire to enforce the law or secure information that would be of use and profit to some operation of the government. But it was hard to escape the conclusion that a large part of this activity was undertaken purely to persecute and bedevil business, especially "big business." An excellent example of this bedevilment of the oil industry was offered by the so-called Madison Case. Here the country was treated to the remarkable spectacle of one department of the government bringing criminal action against the oil companies for doing what another department of the same government had suggested and approved.

The Madison Case

During the days preceding the N.R.A., prices received for gasoline were, as already mentioned, extremely low. Refiner after refiner dumped gasoline on the market for less than the cost of the crude. Under the N.R.A., Tank Car Stabilization Committees were formed at the request of Secretary of the Interior Harold L. Ickes, administrator of the Petroleum Code. Arrangements were made in the major refining areas for the larger oil companies to buy a part of the small refiners' "distress" gasoline, rather than let it be dumped on an already depressed market. It was hoped that this arrangement would help stabilize the wholesale price of gasoline (a commendable objective in the days of N.R.A.) and give the independent refiners a better chance of breaking even. Generally, each major company was assigned one or more of these independents, from whom the major company was expected to buy distress gasoline as it was offered. These refiners were jocularly referred to as "dancing partners" of the larger company. There was nothing secret or clandestine about the buying arrangements thus set up; they were officially encouraged, published in detail, and well understood throughout the oil trade.

Whether or not the buying arrangements resulted in an improvement in the price of gasoline is debatable. At the time the arrangements were first set up, the Shell management had expressed opposition to the idea in the annual report for 1933: "There is still too great an inclination to look for palliatives rather than to strike at the root of the evil. For instance, both in the East and on the Pacific Coast, plans have been adopted to create gasoline buying pools, the financing of which is to be undertaken by the major units in the industry. The object of these pools is to purchase distress gasoline from smaller refiners. Your Directors hold the view that while such measures, under certain conditions, may possibly serve a desirable purpose if the crude supply has been properly balanced with demand, so long as this is not the case such pools can only encourage the overproduction of gasoline rather than discourage it." However, despite their opposition to the arrangement, the Shell companies were obliged to go along when the plan was made a part of the N.R.A. code for the petroleum industry.

In May 1935, the National Industrial Recovery Act, on which the N.R.A. was based, was invalidated by the Supreme Court. A buying arrangement similar to the one which had been in effect during the N.R.A. days was continued with, the oil men understood, the express approval of Secretary Ickes. In mid-June, only a few weeks after the death of the N.R.A., a group of disgruntled jobbers met in Washington and appointed a committee to call upon the Attorney General and request an investigation into whether or not there were secret agreements among the refiners for the purpose of fixing jobber margins.† On August 1, the Attorney General announced to the newspapers that an anti-trust investigation of the oil business was under way, and soon F.B.I. men began popping up around the country to question jobbers about their relations with their sources of supply.

In April 1936, the Justice Department announced that a Federal grand jury would be impanelled to conduct an investigation, and that the jury would sit at Madison, Wisconsin. This choice of a location from which the grand jurors would be chosen could not but provoke comment, for Wisconsin was not an oil-producing or oil-refining state; it was not even an especially large center of oil consumption. Those who feared the worst were quick to point out

† These jobbers (a very small portion of the jobbing trade) were disgruntled because the major companies were buying up the "distress gasoline" which had previously given the jobbers the dirt-cheap products they used in price wars. These cut-rate marketers felt little concern over the independent refiner's plight; in fact, the greater the refiner's distress, the better it was for them. The only real complaint of this jobber group, never publicly expressed, was that the majors, in buying up distress gasoline at a decent price, were keeping the ammunition for price wars out of the hands of the cut-throat marketers.

that Wisconsin was, however, a known home of the Progressive movement and that the average Wisconsin voter, who had for much of his life been a follower of the La Follettes, could be counted on to look at big business with a suspicious eye.

The grand jury met at Madison on May 4, 1936, sat until mid-June, and late in July returned a criminal indictment charging 23 oil companies, three trade publications, and 58 individuals with conspiracy to fix the tank car prices of gasoline in the Midwestern states commonly referred to as "Standard of Indiana territory." Among the oil company defendants Shell Petroleum Corporation was included; and among the individuals two Shell Petroleum officials, Fraser and Lakin. In early November, the grand jury handed down a second indictment charging 24 oil companies and 46 individuals, most of them the same companies and people as in the first indictment, with agreeing to fix margins and adopting uniform jobber contracts. A technical flaw was found in the constitution of the grand jury, so it was dismissed, another jury impanelled, and the two indictments handed down anew by the new grand jury in December 1936. The trial of the first indictment was set to begin at Madison, before a jury, on October 4, 1937.

From the outset, the government's case did not seem strong. Certainly there had been no "conspiracy," for anything the oil companies had done had been openly arrived at and widely publicized. Furthermore, they had done it, they maintained, at the suggestion of and with the express consent of the government, as represented by Secretary Ickes. And even if these buying arrangements had been organized to limit the free movement of prices (as any "stabilization" move admittedly is), how could the government hope to prove "unreasonable" restraint of trade, the criterion in anti-trust cases, when the prices of gasoline in the Mid-Continent were still at such shocking lows?

But there were two factors which were to weigh heavily against the oil companies on trial at Madison. The first was a turn of events which they had not contemplated. The judge quite properly refused to admit as evidence certain letters from Ickes, unless Ickes would appear in court to acknowledge that they were his instructions and approval as a government official, and not just an expression of personal opinion. Ickes understandably refused to appear as a voluntary witness and embarrass the administration of which he was a member. The oil companies, equally understandably, did not wish to force him to appear under subpoena, for a man who delighted in calling himself "The Old Curmudgeon" could be a dangerous and tricky witness if forced to appear against his will.‡ Thus the companies were deprived of their most valuable defense.

The other factor which worked against the oil companies at Madison was, in part at least, of their own making. In a small city where their every move was observed and recorded, some of the men on trial made the serious mistake of affecting grandeur, or what passed for grandeur. Whether the initiative came from Madison residents who saw a chance to make some extra money, or whether it was the idea of the oil men themselves makes little difference. The fact remains that a leading hotel, a country club, and many of the largest private homes were rented to the oil men and their lawyers for their exclusive occupancy for the duration of the trial. To top it off, the defendants engaged a spectacular array of legal counsel, headed by Col. William J. (Wild Bill) Donovan. For a conference room and offices, the lawyers—more than fifty in number—rented the premises of a closed-up bank. The local newspapers promptly dubbed this meeting place the "Oil Barons' Marble Hall," and wrote extensively of the "luxurious homes" which the defendants were occupying. An editorial in a Sheboygan newspaper entitled "Lavish Spending in Madison" was deemed by the judge so prejudicial to the defendants' case that prospective jurors who had read it were excused from serving. With this sort of public ill-feeling against the men on trial, a jury was impanelled and the trial started.

During the trial, the indictments against the three trade papers and some of the oil companies and individuals were dismissed, leaving when the trial ended on January 22, 1938, sixteen oil companies and thirty individuals as defendants. After nine hours' deliberation, the jury returned a verdict of guilty. The defendants were adjudged to have committed a misdemeanor under the Sherman Act of 1890 and were fined $5,000 each. Following the verdict, new trials were granted to three oil companies and fifteen individuals and in the case of one company and ten individuals the judge set aside the verdict and entered a different judgment. This reduced the number of active defendants to twelve oil companies and five individuals, among whom Shell Petroleum and Lakin were included.

These defendants appealed to a higher court, and in July 1939

‡ In *The Secret Diaries of Harold L. Ickes,* Vol. II, New York, Simon & Schuster, 1954, Ickes acknowledges the unfairness of the case against the oil men. He also reveals that originally the Justice Department was determined to press for jail sentences if the defendants were found guilty.

the Circuit Court of Appeals at Chicago reversed the convictions and granted new trials to all concerned. The Department of Justice, however, carried the case to the United States Supreme Court, which upheld the government lawyers and reversed the Circuit Court in a decision handed down May 6, 1940. Justice Douglas in delivering the majority opinion ruled out the element of "reasonableness," hitherto an important consideration in anti-trust cases, and held that any combination which tampers with price structures is in itself unlawful. There was no doubt that the High Court's decision was politically expedient, but whether it was fair treatment was another matter. The New York *Times* commented editorially:[54]

> The evidence seems clear, not only in the whole record of the Government-approved N.R.A. codes but in correspondence and reports of the Secretary of the Interior, for example, that price "stabilization" operations of the oil companies were undertaken with the knowledge, approval, and encouragement of Federal officials. The Supreme Court majority does not deny this.
>
> The charge of which the twelve oil corporations and five persons were found guilty was of forming a concerted movement to buy "distress gasoline" from independent refiners in 1935 and 1936. But the Federal Surplus Commodities Corporation is a branch of the government set up for the very purpose of buying up so-called surplus farm commodities to remove gluts and support prices, and this is considered highly patriotic work. As if that were not enough, farmers are induced by tempting cash offers from the Government to combine to bring about a pro-rata restriction of acreage. The Government does still more to hold up farm prices by extending "non-recourse" loans to farmers and, if necessary, keeping the equivalent of an entire year's crop off the market to raise prices. Milk farmers, again, are permitted and encouraged under various laws to combine to form "bargaining agencies" to get better prices.
>
> It is impossible to detect in all this any consistent or well-thought-through set of principles.

The second indictment in the Madison Case, charging that the oil companies had conspired to limit jobber margins and write uniform jobber contracts, never came to trial. In June 1938, the defendants, feeling that the decision in the first indictment had prejudged the rest of their case, pleaded *nolo contendere* and paid fines and court costs aggregating $385,000.

A surprising and little-publicized aspect of the Madison Case was the trial of the civil suits for treble damages brought by several of the aggrieved jobbers, following the Supreme Court decision of 1940. The forms and terms of the contracts brought into court in these civil cases showed great variations in jobber contracts. It is interesting to note that in these civil suits (despite the fact that the Supreme Court had already declared the defendants guilty of conspiracy), the suing jobbers were unable to offer convincing evidence of injury to themselves, and all of their cases failed.[55] The Madison Case was, however, a smarting defeat which made a deep impression in oil trade circles. "The prosecution of the case," in the words of a competent observer, "left the industry, rightly or wrongly, with an abiding feeling of distrust." [56]

Divorcement Agitation

In April 1938, attack upon the industry came from a new quarter as Senator Guy Gillette introduced a bill in Congress which would compel the separation of the marketing end of the business from other branches of the petroleum industry.[57] No "integrated" company such as Shell would be permitted to engage in any marketing activity and must immediately divest itself of all its marketing properties. Many of the same jobbers who had thought the Madison trial a good idea rallied to the support of Senator Gillette's Divorcement Bill, as it was called.

In almost every line of business there had been since 1920 a concerted effort to cut the costs of distribution. Now it was apparent to many, in Congress and out, that deliberately to hand the business of oil marketing over to the middlemen would hardly be a step in this direction. Senator Borah proposed as an amendment to the Gillette bill an idea which had been suggested several times during the past half century: that pipe lines be divorced from oil company ownership.§ The Divorcement Bill was dropped for the moment only to be revived later on several occasions, for it remained for many years a favorite project of Senator Gillette's.

Advocates of divorcement continue to argue that major integrated

§ The idea that independent pipe lines would somehow provide cheaper products and more advantageous transportation rates has long been an obsession with many who have not bothered to think the matter all the way through. George S. Wolbert, Jr., in his extremely able book *American Pipe Lines* (Norman, University of Oklahoma Press, 1952, pp. 99-104) shows how pipe line divorcement would discourage wildcatting, delay extension of pipe lines to new fields, encourage early abandonment of stripper wells, increase pipe line rates, and fail to bring a flood of cheap gasoline from independent refineries, as some jobbers have hoped. The only sure result of such action would be increased prices to the consumer.

companies have an "unfair" advantage over their smaller, non-integrated competitors in that profits of one department of the business, such as pipe line transportation or refining, can be used to "subsidize" another end of the business, generally marketing. Actually this argument, when stripped of its verbiage and lofty principle, boils down to the fact that the smaller companies object to the integrated companies being in a position to pass on some of their distribution economies in the form of lower prices.[58]

Other Investigations, The T.N.E.C. Hearings

By November 1938, the company was also hearing from Thurman Arnold, Assistant Attorney General, asking, on behalf of the Department of Justice, detailed data on Shell Union's exchanges and purchases of finished motor fuel. The same month, Garland Ferguson, chairman of the Federal Trade Commission, as part of an attempt to prove the "subsidization" mentioned above, was writing Belither for detailed information on the profit or loss sustained on the marketing of each of the company's products over a period of several years. By early 1938, Arnold had taken another tack and was asking, by means of a questionnaire sent to every refinery in the country, details of their ownership, products they manufactured and sold, and their throughput for the years 1931 to 1938. He laid particular stress on the kinds of cracking patents used, from whom they were licensed, and the rate and amount of royalty paid. A year later, he was requesting copies of all cracking-patent licensing agreements then in force.[59]

But the grandest of all the investigations was the T.N.E.C. The Temporary National Economic Committee was created by Congress in June 1938, in response to a message from the White House urging a "need for a thorough study of the concentration of economic power and its detrimental consequences."[60] Senator Joseph C. O'Mahoney was made chairman of the committee, which had Leon Henderson as executive secretary and included representatives of the Department of Justice, the Securities and Exchange Commission, the Federal Trade Commission, and the Departments of Labor, Commerce, and the Treasury, and was therefore not a purely Congressional committee. The T.N.E.C. hearings started on December 1, 1938, and ran through April 3, 1941, covering the whole field of American "big business." The verbatim testimony filled 37 closely printed volumes, from which an additional 43 volumes of monographs were prepared and published by the committee. Almost every question to which there was an answer (and many another to which there was, indeed, no answer) was propounded by the eager questioners.

The oil industry was before the committee nearly a month, from September 25 to October 20, 1939. During this time a great many witnesses associated with the industry were called upon to testify. The hearings were opened by a series of papers, delivered by nine men associated with the industry, each well acquainted with his field. To present the paper on employment and working conditions within the industry, Anderson, at the time vice president of Shell Petroleum in charge of personnel, was selected. These nine papers, together with a digest of T.N.E.C. testimony pertaining to the oil industry, were published in book form by the American Petroleum Institute, and constitute a valuable source book of the industry.[61]

The "Mother Hubbard" Suit

The questionnaires, investigations, legislation, and attempts at legislation of the late Thirties were brought to a crashing climax in 1940, when on September 30 the Attorney General in the U. S. District Court for the District of Columbia filed an all-embracing anti-trust suit against dozens of smaller oil companies and twenty-two major companies, including Shell. The bill of complaint covered every department of the business, a total of 69 charges in all. Among the many charges were: that the companies had conspired to maintain uniform prices for crude oil, that they controlled practically all of the crude oil available for refining, that they were restricting the production of crude with the collusion of the American Petroleum Institute, that common-carrier pipe lines owned by oil companies charged unreasonably high rates to preclude their use by outside shippers, that the oil companies' ownership of barges, tankers, and tank cars made for oppressively high rates for independent companies, that the oil companies distributed their products only through wholesale and retail outlets whose policies they could control, and a list of other alleged practices that constituted a catalog of almost every conceivable offense an oil company could commit.[62] Because the complaint covered everything, the case soon became known as the "Mother Hubbard" suit, in honor of that all-enveloping feminine garment. During the war years, the suit was laid aside by the government, but it was revived after the cessation of hostilities and remained

in the courts until June 1951, when government attorneys finally
moved for its dismissal.

The Elkins Act Consent Decree

At the same time that it brought the "Mother Hubbard" suit, the
government also instituted suits claiming that company-owned pipe
lines were violating the Elkins Act of 1903. This law forbade a
common carrier to grant rebates in any form to any shipper. In its
suit, the government contended that the oil companies who owned
common-carrier pipe lines were in effect granting rebates to themselves, for the dividends which the pipe line companies paid their oil
company owners, the government said, served to reduce in a roundabout way the cost of the owner's shipment.* In December 1941,
the action under the Elkins Act was settled when the government
attorneys and 79 oil company and pipe line company defendants,
including Shell, consented to a judgment without trial. This "consent
decree" provided that common-carrier pipe lines owned by oil companies might not pay their owners annual dividends of more than 7%
of the value of the pipe line property. Any excess of earnings over
this 7% was to be retained in the pipe line company's surplus account,
where it could be used for new capital outlay or to retire prior
indebtedness, providing the indebtedness had been contracted for
the purpose of capital expenditure.[64]

If a compromise between the oil companies and those who were
crying for the divorcement of pipe line ownership was necessary,
the consent decree was probably as fair a compromise as could have
been hoped for. It left the oil companies in possession of their pipe
lines and permitted a moderate annual return on their investment.
At the same time, it should have effectively demolished any public
suspicion that pipe lines owned by oil companies might be charging
rates that were too high. If they were, they certainly could not hope
to benefit, as all of the pipe line's profit (over the small amount
permitted for dividends) would be impounded.

That these suspicions were ill-founded was borne out by the later
course of events. The Elkins Act consent decree went into effect on
January 1, 1942. During the following decade, oil companies were

---

* The government preferred to ignore the point that a dividend is a return upon
capital invested, and that in this instance the oil companies most certainly had millions
of dollars invested in pipe lines. Competent legal minds, considering the question
fairly, cannot see how pipe line dividends could be considered rebates, as long as the
rates charged for transportation were reasonable.[63]

more active than ever before in the building of pipe lines. This activity is more potent than any legal argument in support of the companies' contention that they build pipe lines for their own convenience and not to discommode competitors, as many associated with the government case seemed to think. The reason why oil companies have continued to build pipe lines is that pipe lines provide the cheapest form of overland transportation for oil and oil products. Few groups of independent capitalists have come forward and offered to build oil pipe lines. Consequently, if the companies are to enjoy the cheapest and most efficient means of transport, they must build the lines themselves.

This brief mention of some of the investigations and lawsuits of the late Thirties shows that an oil company executive of the period had his hands full merely to comply with almost endless government requests and defend his company from attack. If he was also able to attend to everyday business, it was proof of extraordinary powers of concentration. That the Shell management was able to handle all these things and in addition accomplish a sizeable amount of reorganization was evidence of an unusual capacity for hard work.

10

Labor Relations, The Benefit Plans

GENERALLY speaking, the years of the mid-Thirties were turbulent ones in labor relations. The oil industry, because it was already paying wages above the average, providing good working conditions, and—most important of all in depression times—supplying continuity of employment far above the average, escaped this period of turmoil with only a few scratches. In his paper before the T.N.E.C. in 1939, Anderson, with a good deal of pride, told of the traditionally friendly relationships between the oil companies and men who worked for them. "These achievements of the industry in harmonious relations," he said, "have come from the simple expedient of recognizing through the years—without pressure—the right of labor to a fair share of the proceeds of the business." In proof, he cited the Bureau of Labor Statistics strike figures for the latest five-year period then available, 1933–1937. During these years, there had been 1,995 strikes in the textile industry, 441 in the machinery group, 427 in iron and steel, 221 in the automotive industry, 212 in bituminous coal, and only 18 in petroleum refining.[65]

Two of these 18 strikes occurred, unhappily, at Shell Petroleum refineries. The first was at Wood River, where for the first time since the opening of the refinery in 1918, operations were interrupted by a labor dispute. A key union, the operating engineers, went on strike July 12, 1936, over the refusal of the company to rehire one of their members who had been discharged when he was found asleep on the job. The strike lasted until mid-August when officials of thirteen non-striking unions, whose members had been thrown out of work by the strike, interceded and offered to act as arbitrators. The operating engineers then agreed to go back to work. As always, the strike was a loss to all concerned. The striking and non-striking employees lost a month's pay. Shell Petroleum suffered a direct loss of more than $400,000, for the strike came at the height of the summer motoring season and the company had to buy large amounts of gasoline from other refiners to meet its commitments to customers.[66]

At Wood River, the refinery workers had been organized by American Federation of Labor craft unions. At East Chicago, Arkansas City, and Houston, the C.I.O. Oil Workers Union became the recognized bargaining agent for unionized employees. It was at Houston that the other strike took place, connected somewhat with developments at East Chicago. In the fall of 1937, the East Chicago refinery management was negotiating a contract with the union local there, when the Houston local also presented its demands for a new contract. The union's national officers proposed that Shell Petroleum agree to a single contract covering all three refineries, with the East Chicago wage scale applicable to Houston. The company replied that it would not be willing to begin negotiations at Houston until an agreement had been reached at East Chicago. To force the company to comply, the union threatened to strike and when that did not change the company's position, a general strike was ordered to begin at Houston on November 19, 1937. It lasted five weeks, until December 23, 1937, when the men went back to work. Negotiations for a contract began early in January 1938.

On the Pacific Coast, the late Thirties saw the discard of the famous M.O.T., the Memorandum of Terms that had served as a satisfactory contract between employer and employees all during the Twenties.

From 1933 to 1935, no satisfactory form of agreement existed, chiefly because of disputes over who was entitled to represent the employees. The last of the M.O.T.'s was signed in May 1935 to run one year. At its expiration in 1936, difficulties again developed over the proper bargaining agents, with the unions maintaining that they represented all the employees and the company insisting, in certain locations where union representation had little popularity, that employees should be allowed to continue selection of their delegates in the traditional manner.

This confusion was settled by two developments. First, the National Labor Relations Board ordered the company in May 1937 to "desist from refusing to bargain" with five unions who claimed to be the exclusive representatives of all Shell employees in California. Next, the N.L.R.B. held a series of elections during 1938, a separate election for each of the groups claimed by the five unions. The general and machinists' groups voted for representation by the Oil Workers International Union (C.I.O.), the electrical group for representation by the International Brotherhood of Electrical Workers (A.F.L.), and the blacksmiths and boilermakers voted for no representation. A contract with the Oil Workers Union was concluded early in 1939 and revised in 1940, and one with the electrical union was signed in 1939. Surprisingly enough, although arrived at by different representatives, these contracts differed little in their fundamentals from the old memoranda of terms.[67]

The Shell Pension Plan

During the second half of the Thirties, public attention began to focus on social security measures, such as pension plans. The Federal government's social security law providing for old age pensions, unemployment insurance, and other benefits was enacted in August 1935. Before this, there had been private pension plans but their development had been gradual. In 1900, there were less than 100 such plans in the United States, by 1920 there were approximately 300 company plans, and by 1930 their number had increased to 500. The depression years generated great concern over job security; by 1938, approximately 1,000 company pension plans were in operation throughout the country.[68]

Deterding had opposed pensions, regarding them as "a dole" and maintaining instead that the Provident Fund was the best way to provide for an employee's future.[69] Because of this outspoken opposition to company pensions, it was not until after Deterding's retirement from the management that the Shell companies began to discuss pension plans. Late in 1937, the Shell Union companies appointed a committee to inquire into the probable costs of a "joint contributory" pension plan. The weekend before they were scheduled to meet in New York to discuss their recommendations, in February 1938, a pension plan adopted by the European Shell companies was announced in London, retroactive to January 1 of that year.[70] Immediately thereafter, Shell Union engaged an outside actuary to develop a comparable plan for the Shell companies in the United States and Canada. On August 8, 1938, a pension plan for the United States and Canada was announced in broad outline, although some of the details were still to be worked out. The agreement creating the Shell Pension Trust was adopted just before Christmas 1938, the whole made retroactive to January 1, 1938.[71]

The Shell Pension Plan provided that an employee with twenty years' service could retire upon reaching the age of sixty (fifty-five in the case of women) and receive a monthly pension check for the rest of his life.† The pension would be 40% of his "average final compensation," a figure determined by averaging compensation received during the last five years of employment. The plan was non-contributory, the company bearing the entire expense without contributions from the employees. All employees were eligible, unlike the Provident Fund which at that time was open only to monthly-salaried, or "staff," employees. When a pensioned employee had also been a member of the Provident Fund, a deduction from his pension was made on that account.‡ After age sixty-five, amounts a pensioner was entitled to receive from Federal social security were deducted from the Shell pension. Beneficiary options were provided for those who might wish to make provision for a widow or other dependent. By electing to draw a reduced pension during his own lifetime, a retiring employee could arrange matters so that upon his death his beneficiary would be paid a pension for life or a lump-sum cash

† Age qualification modified as of December 15, 1955, to permit a male employee to elect to remain, with the company's concurrence, until sixty-five (sixty for women).

‡ On an annual basis, this deduction was 4% (since reduced to 2½%) of the amount (principal plus interest) of the company's contributions to the employee's Provident Fund.

payment, or both. For those who wished to retire early and for those who might be obliged to retire because of physical disability, there were other provisions; and a proportionate pension was provided for those who reached the age of sixty before they had accumulated twenty years of service with the company.[72]

Early in February 1939, William P. West, janitor at the Drumright production office, became the first Shell employee in the United States to receive a pension check, made retroactive to the date of his retirement, January 1, 1938. By the end of 1955, a total of 3,826 Shell employees in the United States had retired on pension.[73]

The American Provident Fund

Shell employees in the United States belonging to the Provident Fund were members of the world-wide fund set up at The Hague in 1912. Their contributions, in accordance with the terms of that fund, could be made either in Dutch guilders or British pounds. The American Shell companies had elected to make their remittances by purchasing pounds at prevailing rates of exchange. With the monetary fluctuations of the early Thirties, this buying of pounds worked sometimes to the advantage and sometimes to the disadvantage of employees who were contributing. In addition, currency fluctuations made it difficult for the directors of the Fund to invest, as they would have liked, in American securities having attractive investment possibilities.

To overcome these difficulties, the American Shell companies in 1936 began to consider creating a separate Provident Fund kept in dollars and invested in dollar securities. Outbreak of the war in Europe made such a move imperative. Early in October 1939, a new Provident Fund, wholly independent of the fund at The Hague, was established in New York. All Provident Fund members in the United States and Canada were notified of the creation of this new dollar fund, and were invited to contribute to it. Some 8,700 of them, or 92%, elected to do so. Balances which they had already accumulated remained in the sterling fund, but contributions to the new fund were kept in dollars and invested in American securities.

With this combined Pension Plan and Provident Fund, employees retiring from the service of any of the Shell companies were admirably provided for. The cash "road-stake" provided by the Provident Fund amounted to approximately one-fifth an employee's total Shell earnings, plus interest, a substantial sum—enough to buy a home, a farm, or a small business. And the monthly pension check provided regular income to help defray essential living expenses.

It should be mentioned that the terms of the Provident Fund were changed late in 1943 to enable all employees to participate, regardless of whether they were paid by the hour or by the month. This enlargement of the plan greatly increased the amount of money which the employing companies had to contribute, so the percentages which employees might contribute during the early years were scaled down. Instead of being eligible to contribute 10% after one year's service, as under the old plan, an employee from 1944 onwards began by contributing 2½% of his salary during his second and third years of service, 5% during the fourth, fifth, and sixth years, and 10% thereafter. As before, the plan was optional. No one was obliged to join, but once an employee had begun participation in the fund, he could not withdraw. The money he had paid in, plus the company's matching contribution, plus compound interest, was available to him when he left the company. If he left before he had put in five years of service, he was entitled to his own contribution and the interest on it; after five years, the entire amount was his. Employees previously not eligible jumped at the chance to join, and in the few weeks preceding January 1, 1944, when the new Provident Fund went into effect, more than 90% of those eligible signed up.[74]

In addition to the Provident Fund and the pension plan, the American Shell companies had other benefit plans. The chief of these were insurance plans, group life insurance, and insurance against loss of income in case of illness or accident. These plans, varying considerably with each Shell company, were put into effect during 1927, and have operated in a variety of forms since that time. Because of the group nature of this insurance, it was available to employees at a cost much lower than on the open market.§

§ In the case of employees not eligible for Provident Fund participation, provision was generally made for a certain amount of free life insurance, the premiums on which were paid entirely by the company. This feature was discontinued with the adoption of liberalized Provident Fund participation.

Corporate Simplification

As A final move in the streamlining operation of the Thirties, Shell Union undertook to consolidate its chief operating subsidiaries into a single company. The first move in this direction came in 1931, when the joint owners of Comar, Continental Oil Company (which had absorbed the old Marland Oil Company) and Shell Petroleum, dissolved Comar and thereafter operated its properties on a partnership basis. In 1936, another step toward simplifying the corporate set-up was made when Shell's interest in The Flintkote Company was sold. The same year also saw a change in Shell Eastern Petroleum Products, Inc. Late in October that company was dissolved and on October 31, 1936, its assets taken over by its sole stockholder, Shell Union. In day-to-day operations, this corporate change did not affect Shell Eastern's organization to any marked degree. Shell Union took over intact the entire Shell Eastern organization and set it up as a division of Shell Union Oil Corporation.

In 1937 and 1938, steps were taken to dissolve the Wolverine Petroleum Corporation. Wolverine held only a relatively small amount of oil property, all of it in Oklahoma. After several years of active production, its properties had started the inevitable decline and earnings had fallen off to a point where there was no reason for continuing the corporation as a separate entity. It probably would have been dissolved earlier had there not been a minority stock interest. There were 180,000 shares of Wolverine common stock, of which slightly more than two-thirds were owned by Shell Union. In June 1937, F. J. Lewis, of Chicago, the chief minority stockholder, sold his holding of nearly 37,000 shares to Shell Petroleum which immediately set about acquiring the balance of the minority interest. By early November 1938, Shell Union and Shell Petroleum between them owned all of the outstanding Wolverine stock except 45 shares in the hands of a "hold-out" stockholder who eventually consented to sell. Shell Union transferred its shares to Shell Petroleum and the latter company, as chief shareholder of Wolverine, then promulgated a plan of dissolution, which contemplated transfer to Shell Petroleum Corporation of all Wolverine assets. By the end of December 1938, the Wolverine properties had become a part of the holdings of Shell Petroleum Corporation.

The biggest move in the consolidation of the Shell operating companies came in the spring of 1939. Late in March, the Shell Oil Company in San Francisco and the Shell Petroleum Corporation in St. Louis agreed on a proposal for a merger. The Shell Oil Company would be merged into the Shell Petroleum Corporation, and the name of the new combined organization would be Shell Oil Company, Incorporated. Beginning April 1, 1939, the new name and corporation were in effect. Two months later, on May 31, Shell Union turned over the properties of its Shell Eastern division to the new corporation. From the first of June 1939, the entire operation of producing, refining, and marketing oil and oil products was conducted by one nation-wide operating company, Shell Oil Company, Inc. As it had owned all the shares of all three companies, Shell Union was the sole stockholder of the merged company. The Shell Pipe Line Corporation, legally a common carrier, was best kept a separate company; and the Shell Development and Shell Chemical companies, along with the Shell Oil Company of Canada, could not be consolidated because Shell Union owned only a half interest in each of them.

For the moment, this corporate consolidation did not bring sweeping changes in operating policies or in personnel. Only the top elective officers were affected. Fraser, who had been president of the St. Louis company, was made president of the new Shell Oil Company, Inc.; Belither, who had been president of the San Francisco company, became executive vice president and chairman of the board; Kittinger, who had been executive vice president of the Shell Eastern Division of Shell Union, was made vice president in charge of marketing at New York; F. A. C. Guépin, who had been executive vice president at San Francisco since 1937, became general vice president at St. Louis; and Bloemgarten, who had been general vice president at San Francisco since the previous summer, returned to Holland.* Other vice presidents in the San Francisco and St. Louis offices were continued without change, and day-to-day operations remained on much the same basis as before.

It was a full year before the corporate consolidation of 1939 had any tangible effect upon the ordinary employee. By April 1940, it was generally agreed between the executive groups in New York

---

* Eleven years later, in 1948, Bloemgarten was elected a managing director of the Royal Dutch Company; during the same year he was appointed a managing director of the Group's main operating companies. He retired from these positions in 1956.

and St. Louis that continuance of both these offices was neither economical nor desirable from an administrative point of view. The question of the city best fitted to be head office for the East-of-the-Rockies area was thoroughly discussed. Guépin prepared a special report that clinched the matter. In the end, the consideration which won out was the same as that which had prompted the move from Tulsa twenty years before. In 1919, Tulsa had been on the western edge of the territory in which Roxana was operating; in 1940, St. Louis was near the western boundary of the marketing area which the company had recently chosen for itself. There were, of course, other considerations. New York was more and more becoming a head office city, and departments of the company which had to have daily contact with other large concerns could function more effectively in New York.

The decision to move to New York was made with extreme reluctance. Such a move meant uprooting a large number of native St. Louisans who knew their city as a pleasant place to work and live; Shell had in St. Louis a company-owned office building which could provide office space at lower cost than rented space in New York; and, of no small importance, the company disliked leaving a town which had been so hospitable a home for two decades. Regretfully, the decision to move was finally made, and announced to employees late in the spring of 1940. Guépin and Anderson for the next few months devoted their attention to the necessary reorganization which such a move entailed and finally to the actual details of the move itself.

More accurately, the proposed move was a dispersal of the St. Louis staff in several directions. Not all were to go to New York. A large number composing the St. Louis marketing division would remain in St. Louis to continue the sales activity of the westernmost portion of Shell's midwestern area. The work of 86 other employees was decentralized and the employees transferred to marketing divisions and refineries. The exploration and production group at St. Louis and the head office of Shell Pipe Line Corporation (some 65 persons in all) were moved in a body to Houston where they could be closer to the scene of operations. To make the move to New York, 320 employees were selected; another group, numbering 308, were notified that their services would be terminated on September 1. One of the objects of the consolidation of offices had been to cut head-office overhead by reducing staff. The people thus eliminated in St.

Louis were engaged chiefly in doing those things which were already being done in New York: accounting, stenographic, and clerical work.

Company officers, Fraser particularly, were deeply concerned over those scheduled to be dismissed. Only a few days after the impending move had been announced, Fraser appointed Glenn Byers, Shell's oldest personnel hand in the Mid-Continent, to head up a special placement office to help find jobs for these people. Byers' placement office called on some 800 firms in the St. Louis area with whom Shell had close business connections, and left with them summary sketches outlining the capabilities of each of these individuals. Whenever news of a job came in, those who seemed qualified to fill it were dispatched to apply for it, carrying the recommendation of the company. All during the summer months of 1940, employees affected by the lay-off were permitted to take as much time as they wished to hunt for new jobs. Each was given a card of introduction from Shell, directed to the prospective employer. The placement bureau remained behind in St. Louis after the move to New York, and by January 1941, 278 of the 308 laid off—a full 90%—had new jobs that were as good as, or even better than, the positions they had held with Shell.[75]

The new office space in New York was an enlargement of the quarters occupied by Shell Union and Shell Eastern in the R.C.A. Building, Rockefeller Center, since 1934. Additional floors were engaged and the offices completely reconstructed during the summer to make room for the combined organization. On August 24, the big move began and over Labor Day weekend a New York Central passenger train, followed by a 47-car freight train, transported most of Shell's St. Louis people with their personal and business effects to the new headquarters. On September 3, 1940, the day after Labor Day, the new combined office was in operation.[76]

On the executive level, the move brought several changes. R. P. Bascom, who had been with Shell Pipe Line Corporation from the beginning and who was now president of the pipe line company, took this opportunity to retire and T. E. Swigart, who had been vice president in charge of exploration and production at Houston, became president of the pipe line company, succeeding Bascom. Galloway, who had filled in for Swigart during the latter's absence on special assignment in 1938–1939, now became vice president of exploration and production at Houston, and in addition head of

Welding the last joint of the Bakersfield-Martinez pipe line, October 16, 1936. *Left to right*, W. P. Durkee, Jr., marketing vice president; Sidney Belither, president; G. H. van Senden, manufacturing vice president; and F. B. Simms, pipe line superintendent.

Dispatcher's control board, ingenious feature that made possible accurate control of many products shipped, one after the other, through the same pipe line. Paper tapes, a different color for each product, are moved through the slot of this scale board, duplicating the actual product movement. Wood River-Lima products pipe line was completed in 1938.

This 4,200-gallon semi-trailer, first of Shell's "Clipper" trucks, appeared on the scene in 1936; its larger capacity and longer range spelled the end of the old sub-depot.

Looks like an old-time oil boom, which it was: Southern Illinois, 1939–40. This muddy road near Shell leases at Salem was once good black-top.

One of the Franks portable drilling rigs, developed by Shell e n g i n e e r s and the Franks Manufacturing Company. Such rigs were widely used in Illinois fields. This one is at Centralia, 1941.

all exploration and production activities east of the Rockies. Both Swigart and Galloway made their offices in Houston. Anderson, shortly after the move to New York was completed, left for Houston to become vice president and general manager of the pipe line company. Guépin was given the new title of senior vice president, located in New York.

In the case of some of the St. Louis departments which had no counterparts in New York, such as the manufacturing department, there were no changes. The New York head office was primarily a marketing organization, and it was in this department that the most severe dislocations occurred. Kittinger in New York became the company's vice president in charge of marketing east of the Rockies; Lakin, who had been marketing vice president at St. Louis, was made regional vice president at Chicago with general supervisory duties over company operations in the Midwest. Since there were parallel sub-departments in both the St. Louis and New York marketing organizations, one manager in each case had to give way. In some cases another job of equal rank and responsibility was found elsewhere in the company for the manager thus displaced; in other cases he became assistant manager of the department, with the result that both former assistant managers were now without title. The total number affected by these dislocations was comparatively small.

This new office in New York was the head office for all Shell Oil Company operations east of the Rockies.† The position of the San Francisco office would for another decade continue unchanged, with Belither for all practical purposes continuing to direct West Coast operations as before. Duplicate sets of departments and departmental subdivisions, with their vice presidents and managers, were maintained in both San Francisco and New York, although consultation to assure uniformity in matters of nation-wide import was henceforth more frequent.

At the start of Shell operations in America, the California company had been the first to develop into a successful, full-scale, integrated company. Its position among the Shell companies in the United States was, for that reason, foremost. The growth of the Mid-Continent

---

† The company continued to operate the St. Louis Shell Building until January 1948, when it was sold to a group of realty investors organized as 1221 Locust Corporation. The name of the building was not changed and the St. Louis marketing division continued to make its headquarters at the old address.

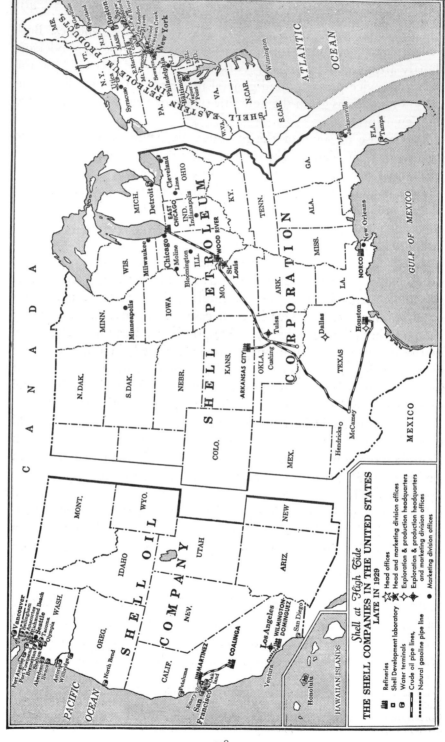

Shell at High Tide

THE SHELL COMPANIES IN THE UNITED STATES
LATE IN 1929

☆ Head offices
☆ Head and marketing division offices
◇ Exploration & production headquarters
◈ Exploration & production headquarters and marketing division offices
● Marketing division offices

⛽ Refineries
⛽ Shell Development laboratory
⛽ Water terminals
Crude oil pipe lines
Natural gasoline pipe line

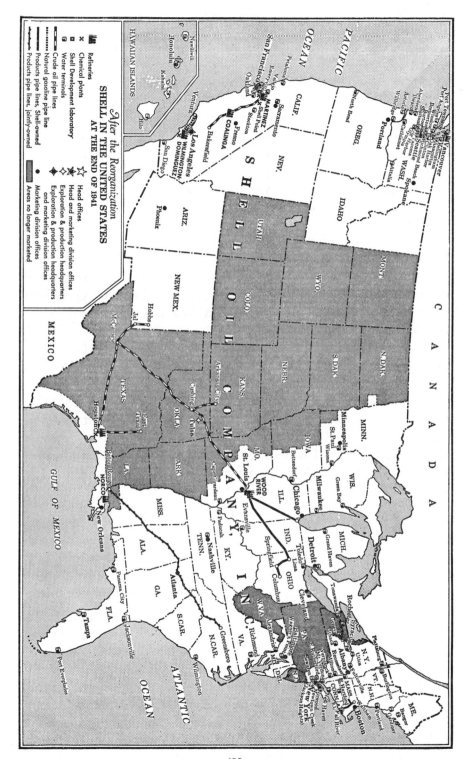

After the Reorganization
SHELL IN THE UNITED STATES
AT THE END OF 1941

Refineries
× Chemical plants
▢ Shell Development laboratory
⊛ Water terminals
Crude oil pipe lines
Natural gasoline pipe line
Products pipe lines, Shell-owned
Products pipe lines, jointly-owned

☆ Head offices
◇ Head and marketing division offices
◆ Exploration & marketing division headquarters
  and marketing division offices
• Marketing division offices
▨ Areas no longer marketed

company was slow at first, but gradually it had overtaken and then passed the West Coast company in size. The crude oil production figures of the two organizations accurately reflected this change:

CRUDE OIL PRODUCTION COMPARED, 1920–1940

	Shell Pacific Coast (Barrels)	Shell East of the Rockies (Barrels)
1920	6,146,000	3,065,000
1930	16,060,000	16,876,000
1940	17,843,000	33,210,000

In 1920, the crude oil production of the Shell Company of California had exceeded that of the Roxana company in the Mid-Continent by about two to one, and the California company's voice in Shell councils carried greater weight in just about that proportion. Ten years later, after a decade of extremely active development, the importance of the Mid-Continent organization had increased proportionately. By 1940, the ratio had been reversed, with the East-of-the-Rockies segment of the company playing henceforth an increasingly dominant role in Shell affairs.

But no one could forget that the California company's contributions in money and in men had helped make this state of affairs possible. The profits of Shell of California, before and during the Twenties, were a chief source of new capital for building the Roxana organization; and during the depression years, West Coast earnings helped offset the St. Louis company's large losses. Equally important to the successful growth of the East-of-the-Rockies organization were the scores of able men—Van Eck, Duhig, Swigart, Anderson, Kittinger, Lakin, Watson, to mention only a few who come readily to mind—contributed by the California company to the staffs of Shell Union, Shell Petroleum, and Shell Eastern.

By 1940, it was apparent to the men in charge of Shell's operations that the extensive reorganization work which they had undertaken was paying off. Efforts to acquire more crude oil reserves and production were succeeding handsomely; new pipe lines had been built to lower the cost of shipping both crude and products; new arrangements for both inland waterway and deep sea transport had opened the way to lower rates; elimination of marketing depots and more intensive use of the new trucks had cut distributing costs; existing indebtedness had been refinanced at much lower carrying charges and new money for capital expenditure obtained at attractive rates. Organizationally, the company had been streamlined, its management decentralized to give the men in the field more authority, the offices combined to reduce overhead, and excess corporate structure eliminated.

On top of all this, Shell Union was able to show a cash balance of more than $57,000,000 at the end of 1940, enough to undertake any foreseeable program of plant expansion. It was fortunate that the company had taken this opportunity to put its house in order, for the healthy state of its affairs would prove an immense advantage in the war years just ahead.

CHAPTER IX

A Venture in Chemicals

1928–1940

O N MORE than one occasion, the Shell companies' European parentage had stood them in good stead. Sound financing methods, a thorough understanding of the money markets, ultra-conservative accounting policies—each of these was European in inspiration, and each had proved of excellent service to the American Shell companies during the long, trying period of the depression. In yet another aspect of the business, this European heritage was at work—and had been since the late Twenties. Disapproval of waste in any form, a thoroughly Dutch characteristic, had led to the creation in America of two new Shell companies which were by 1940 beginning to assume considerable importance in over-all operations. They were the Shell Development and Shell Chemical companies, organized in an attempt to make profitable use of the tremendous amounts of oilfield and refinery waste gases which had up to then been flared into the air or, at best, burned for boiler fuel.

The Shell companies in the United States had attacked the problem of oilfield gas wastage much earlier than most of their competitors. They had done their best to recover from oil-well gas all the saleable light hydrocarbons. They had, during the Twenties, further extended the market for these natural gasoline fractions by developing successful stabilizing processes which made long-distance shipment of natural gasoline economically feasible. They had, in the late Twenties, turned their gasoline plants to the manufacture of "Shellane," a mixture of propane and butane. They had attempted, with particular success in California, to find a market for the "dry" gas which emerged from these natural gasoline plants. And finally, the Shell companies had attacked gas wastage from the other end by urging conservation methods which would drastically curtail the amounts of gas produced in oil fields.

The Shell companies had, however, done very little about utilization of the waste gases produced in refineries as a by-product of cracking. The quantities of these gases were at first insignificant, but with the rapid expansion of cracking facilities in the second half of the Twenties, the volume of cracking gases became enormous. They could be put to use as refinery fuel, and in a few favored industrial areas, such as East Chicago, sold to public utilities who resold them for fuel to neighboring plants and factories. For the most part, however, cracking gases that could not be burned for refinery fuel were flared as waste—a practice excusable enough in the early days of cracking when frequent interruptions and shut-downs made cracking units an undependable source of gas supply. But with the advent of more dependable and more extensive cracking operations, the volume of these cracked gases became too large and too steady to ignore.

The solution of what to do with these gases would obviously not come from the men who were occupied with the daily operation of refineries. They were absorbed in developing and further perfecting their cracking processes and in obtaining maximum gasoline yields. They were, in truth, too near the problem and too busy with other matters to worry much about waste gases. The worrying took place in Holland, where the frugal Dutch saw only too clearly that large amounts of potentially valuable materials were being produced in cracking, and asked themselves if somehow these gases couldn't be turned to account.

On the management level, J. B. Aug. Kessler, the younger, concerned himself with these problems from 1925 onwards [1] and the present Shell Development and Shell Chemical companies owe much to his vision and perseverance during their trial period—as much, indeed, as the Royal Dutch owes to the elder Kessler for his perseverance and vision during the period of that company's establishment and early growth. Kessler had an intense interest in the scientific aspects of the business and an appreciation of what scientific investigation might do for Shell's business. Together with Sir Robert Waley Cohen, he had been instrumental in getting the Group to continue underwriting Sir Harry Ricardo's anti-knock research all during the Twenties.[2] Kessler's election as a Royal Dutch managing director in 1924 was, therefore, a milestone in the history of the Shell Group's research activity. Within a very few years, big plans involving sizeable expenditures began to be put forward. While the inspiration of the new ventures was clearly European, their successful execution was to take place in America. To launch these new enterprises in the United States, the logical choice was Pyzel, already the "grand old man" of the technical end of Shell's business. For the first decade, Pyzel's guiding hand was to be all-important.

It was easy to see that an almost new industry, producing useful products from cracking-plant waste gases, would require a foundation of new research and development work, for which special laboratory facilities would have to be provided. Research into hydrocarbon chemistry and processing techniques was not a new thing for the Royal Dutch-Shell Group; in fact, it antedated the formation of the Group.

As far back as 1902, the Royal Dutch Company, then still an operating organization, had opened a laboratory in connection with its Charlois (Rotterdam) gasoline redistilling plant. It was a control laboratory, testing the plant's raw material and products and running incidental tests on paints and other materials for the company's purchasing department. After the creation of the Asiatic Petroleum Company in 1903 as a joint marketing agency for Royal Dutch and Shell Transport & Trading Company, the Royal Dutch became interested in some of the problems connected with products made from the Shell company's Borneo crude oil. The Borneo oil contained a high percentage of aromatic hydrocarbons which were, in accordance with gasoline specifications of the day, highly undesirable. The aromatics also affected the burning properties of kerosene made from this oil.[3]

The Charlois laboratory was too small to handle these problems, and had no room in which to enlarge. As a result, a temporary laboratory was set up at Schiedam, Holland, across the river from Charlois, in a building that had once been a gin distillery. W. C. Knoops, a young chemical engineer who was placed in charge, devised a method for removing from the Borneo gasoline two of its most bothersome aromatics, benzene and toluene. His process was installed on a commercial scale in a plant built by the Group in 1907 at Reisholz, Germany. The plant at Charlois, using bubble columns copied from alcohol distilling, prepared a gasoline cut rich in toluene, or benzene, as the case might be.* These fractions were shipped to the Reisholz plant where they were treated with nitric acid (nitrated). The toluene (or benzene) separated out and combined with the nitric

---

* Benzene and toluene were treated in the same manner.

acid to form mono-nitro-toluene (or mono-nitro-benzene). The process did more than produce an aromatic-free gasoline; the mono-nitro-toluene and mono-nitro-benzene were of high purity and were eagerly bought for use as raw materials by German aniline dye producers.

Further intensive nitration would convert mono-nitro-toluene into the famous explosive, tri-nitro-toluene (T.N.T.). The experience gained with the Reisholz nitration plant enabled the Shell Group to build T.N.T. plants in England and France during the First World War, for production of large quantities of this desperately needed explosive. This nitration of Borneo gasoline was the Group's first step towards producing chemical products from petroleum.

The Schiedam laboratory was shut down in 1909, leaving only the Charlois testing laboratory. Meanwhile, supervision of the production and refining aspects of the Royal Dutch and Shell companies' businesses had been concentrated in Bataafsche Petroleum Maatschappij, organized in Holland at the time of the Royal Dutch-Shell amalgamation in 1907. Testing and control of ever-increasing quantities of materials ordered for oil fields and refineries abroad, as well as control and standardization of products manufactured by the refineries, obviously would require a larger installation than the small laboratory attached to the distillation plant at Charlois. To meet this need, a central laboratory, owned and operated by Bataafsche and independent of any manufacturing operation, was opened at Amsterdam in 1914 with a staff of about 25 men.

In addition to routine testing and control operations, the Amsterdam laboratory developed new methods of analysis and standardized testing procedures. The Group's first volume of standard test methods was published in 1920. By that year, the Amsterdam laboratory had grown to a point where its staff numbered some 120 persons, a large laboratory at that time for any oil company. Most of this staff worked on research and development directly connected with refinery products, processes, and processing equipment. Until 1927, very little work was done in the direction of converting petroleum raw materials into chemical products by chemical processes. As a first step in this direction, a chemical department was set up at Amsterdam in 1927 under A. J. van Peski to devote itself entirely to chemical research.

Prior to this move, the prospects of chemicals based on petroleum had been studied and discussed in the years 1925–1927 by Kessler, his fellow managing director De Kok, Pyzel, and Knoops, who had done the early nitration work at Schiedam and now headed the new chemical department at The Hague. Before embarking on any enterprise, three questions, they felt, had to be answered: (1) What raw materials are available that are suitable for chemical manufacture? (2) What products can be made from them? (3) Will there be a market for these products?

The best raw materials for the present were natural gas and by-product gases from cracking. The latter were particularly promising since they contained chemical unsaturates, suitable for use as chemical "building-blocks." To have these "building-block" gases in pure form was important, for the presence of other compounds led to undesirable side-reactions that multiplied the difficulties of chemical processing. Here some of the earlier work done at Amsterdam proved an important advantage. The pressure distillation work done by J. H. C. de Brey during the years 1918–1924 in the course of developing his stabilizer and the elaborate mathematical calculations for distilling-column design undertaken by Dr. W. J. D. van Dyck had given the Shell Group a knowledge of column design that was, in general, far ahead of that possessed by its chief competitors. Shell's ability to design and build columns capable of sharp fractionation meant that raw materials suitable for chemical manufacture could be delivered in pure form.

As to products, the large body of chemical research carried on during the previous seventy-five years pointed to a great many hydrocarbon derivatives that could, on a laboratory scale at least, be prepared from the raw materials available.

The most important question, the availability of markets for these products, could be answered favorably. Newly developed processes for making fibers, films, and lacquers from synthetic materials required as solvents ever-increasing quantities of specialized alcohols and ketones, the demand for which could not be met from existing sources of supply. By happy coincidence, many of these solvents could be made from the by-product gases of petroleum cracking.

It was therefore a question of applying known chemistry to develop laboratory reactions into full-scale commercial processes that could produce saleable products cheaply and efficiently. This would require costly and extensive research with no guarantee of ultimate success. But the answers to the three big questions seemed favorable enough to warrant taking the risk. At a meeting held in The Hague on April 5, 1927, and attended by Kessler, De Kok, Pyzel, and Knoops, it was decided that the Shell Group should enter the chemical business immediately via the manufacture of synthetic ammonia, using processes already known. Before other products could be made, a great deal of new knowledge would have to be acquired. For this dual program, chemical manufacture and fundamental research, an expenditure of $10,000,000 was recommended. Investigation, it was confidently expected, would show the way to new products and new processes. But no one knew for sure where these new enterprises would lead, or whether they could ever be made to yield a profit.

Here, then, was adventure in oil—high-priced adventure it would sometimes seem during the depths of the depression. The difficulties to be overcome were immense. A chemical reaction might be known and well understood in the laboratory; to reproduce it on a commercial scale with commercial equipment and get commercially feasible results was quite another matter. It was the difference between theory and practice. In the brand-new petroleum chemical industry of 1927, the gulf between theory and practice could have seemed impassable. "You could not," Pyzel remarked later, "buy a book and look up how to build an acetone plant. You had to find out for yourself." [4]

Despite these apparent obstacles, the prevailing mood in The Hague was one of high optimism, a frame of mind that befitted adventure into the unknown. Kessler in a letter to his good friend De Kok wrote: "We should have confidence, energy, and courage enough to develop this new chemical part of our business even if it does not give profits to start with. . . . The main thing is to find the right people for this work. . . . Do not let us be frightened by some preliminary cost calculations which show that we may not make money in the beginning. I do not expect to make any money; on the contrary, I expect it will cost a good deal of money before we shall actually produce on a more or less large scale. The only thing we need is scientific knowledge and I do not see why we should not be able to get that." [5]

The Success of the Chemists

THE scientific knowledge which the Shell companies now had to acquire lay in the field of organic chemistry, a development almost entirely of the past hundred years. Organic chemistry, applied to industrial problems, had brought scores of astonishing advances in manufacturing. Perhaps it will be well to inquire briefly into this new science which in itself represented an achievement of the human brain as remarkable as any of its practical applications.[6]

Ordinary, or "inorganic," chemistry had gradually evolved from the alchemy of the Middle Ages. By 1800, the chemistry of non-carbonaceous compounds was fairly well understood and the theory of irreducible elements was generally accepted. To take a simple example, it had been determined that water was composed of two of these irreducible elements—hydrogen two parts and oxygen one part. A chemical shorthand had been developed in which "H" stood for hydrogen and "O" for oxygen.† Water could thus be written, in accordance with its chemical composition, H_2O. Further, a great deal had been learned about *synthesizing* a more complicated compound from two or more simpler components, as well as *analyzing*, or breaking a compound down to determine the identity of these components.

In synthesizing and analyzing compounds, a highly useful discovery had been made. The shorthand formulae representing chemical compounds could be added or subtracted mathematically to show, with a fair degree of accuracy, what went on in a chemical reaction. Thus, the preparation of sulphuric acid, H_2SO_4, could be expressed on paper:

$$H_2O \quad + \quad SO_3 \quad \longrightarrow \quad H_2SO_4$$

H_2O	$+$	SO_3		H_2SO_4
(water)	(plus)	(sulphur) (trioxide)	(yields)	(sulphuric acid)

Around this type of chemical knowledge, modest businesses had grown up through the centuries—the manufacture of simple acids,

---

† The present system of chemical notation, using Roman letters in upper and lower case, was developed about 1814 by the Swedish chemist Baron Jöns Jakob Berzelius. It represented a simplification of the undecipherable symbols that had been utilized by medieval alchemists, partly for reasons of economy in writing but more particularly to guarantee secrecy.[7]

caustics, pharmaceuticals, and other similar compounds. Important as these businesses were, they did not become major industries, for the substances in greatest demand by industry (leather, textiles, dyes, etc.) were *organic*, of animal or vegetable origin. These organic materials were far less simple; they were intricate mixtures of complicated compounds and existing chemical knowledge could not unravel the mystery of their composition. Accordingly, it was postulated by chemists of the Eighteenth and early Nineteenth Centuries that organic substances contained some mysterious "vital force" which ruled out the possibility of their ever being produced artificially by synthesis.

An ever-present ingredient of all these complicated and useful "organic" substances was carbon—that mysterious element which can appear, even in its pure state, as lampblack, pencil "lead," or a crystal-clear diamond. A big difficulty with carbon compounds, and a chief source of their mystery, was the fact that several radically different compounds might all have the same percentage composition, and therefore the same over-all chemical formula. For instance, methyl ether, a gas, and ethyl alcohol, an intoxicating liquid, had the identical composition, two atoms of carbon, six of hydrogen, and one of oxygen. For both, the chemical formula C_2H_6O was the same. Yet they were far from identical: one was a gas at room temperature and insoluble in water, the other boiled at $78°$ C. and was soluble in water. To this disturbing phenomenon the chemists gave the name *isomerism* (from Greek words meaning "equal parts"); two substances with identical formulae were said to be *isomers* of each other. As the number of carbon atoms in a molecule increased, the number of possible isomers increased unbelievably. Soon, chemists were able to calculate with mathematical precision the isomers in the methane (or paraffin) series, simplest of the hydrocarbon compounds. The series began with simple gases such as methane, CH_4, and ethane, C_2H_6, which had no isomers, and progressed to substances like eicosane, $C_{20}H_{42}$, a waxy material that had, according to calculations, 366,319 possible isomers, or tetracontane, $C_{40}H_{82}$, calculated to have 63,491,178,805,831 possible isomeric forms.[8] Needless to say, no one has ever attempted to isolate these 63 trillion separate compounds, nor do we actually know that they exist.

In the face of such complexities, the difficulties of dealing with carbon compounds remained unsolved for a great many years. Then, in the mid-Nineteenth Century came the molecular theory of matter, which was soon adopted by physicists and chemists everywhere. As a sequel to the molecular hypothesis, the theory of linkages was proposed, offering for the first time a plausible explanation of the phenomenon of isomerism.

According to the molecular theory, the smallest obtainable particles of a given substance were called *molecules*. Molecules, in turn, consisted of *atoms* of the various chemical elements. In this fashion, a molecule of water (H_2O) consisted of two atoms of hydrogen joined to a single atom of oxygen. What held these atoms together? No one knew but it was postulated that perhaps these atoms were held together by invisible bonds, and that the atoms of some elements had more "arms" available for combination than atoms of other elements. If such a theory were valid, the single oxygen atom in water would have two "arms," the hydrogen atoms one each. A structural formula was invented to express this relationship, and water became thereby:

$$H-O-H$$

Further investigation hit upon the valence (the number of arms, or bonds, available for combination) of carbon as four. With the aid of this theory of linkages and the structural formula, it was possible to indicate the difference between methyl ether and ethyl alcohol, for their formulae could be written in two different ways to show that they were separate substances. In this manner, methyl ether was shown to have one structure

$$\begin{array}{ccc} H & & H \\ | & & | \\ H-C-O-C-H \\ | & & | \\ H & & H \end{array}$$

while ethyl alcohol had a separate and distinct form

$$\begin{array}{cc} H & H \\ | & | \\ H-C-C-O-H \\ | & | \\ H & H \end{array}$$

This ability to explain by structural formulae the nature of the isomers of carbon compounds was the key to a whole new science, the chemistry of carbon compounds known as "organic chemistry." ‡ Armed with organic chemistry, industrial chemists developed a brand-new, almost startling industry in western Europe during the second half of the Nineteenth Century. The gas-lit cities of that era and the newly organized steel industry required tremendous amounts of gas and coke, produced by the destructive distillation of soft coal in gas retorts and "coke ovens." As a by-product, this distillation yielded large quantities of "coal tar," a viscous liquid for which there was little use.

It was to this coal tar, a cheap and abundant source of hydrogen and carbon, that the new organic chemists turned their attention. The first successful chemical products made from coal tar were aniline dyes, which offered a much greater variety of colors and were much cheaper than dyes made from roots, tree leaves, bark, insects, clay, and other time-honored sources of natural pigment. Better dyes followed, synthesized from heavier coal-tar fractions, and other new products from coal tar made their appearance: explosives, and new pharmaceuticals such as aspirin. Some of these new products, the dyes for instance, replaced less satisfactory or more costly natural products; others (aspirin and other coal-tar drugs) represented new combinations of properties and enriched the world by making possible wholly new products.

The medieval alchemists had spent fruitless lifetimes in their search for a "philosopher's stone" which would transmute base metals into gold. Their Nineteenth Century successors in the field of organic chemistry did much better; theirs was a wonderful new world where new products could be made to order from the waste products of gas and coke manufacture. The Germans, because they were willing to devote time, money, and endless patience to research which was not immediately productive of commercial results, took an early lead in the manufacture of coal-tar chemicals.§

In Germany, as in other countries, this new industry based upon organic chemistry and coal tar was, almost without exception, in

‡ The successful synthesis of organic chemicals disproved the old idea that organic materials constituted a separate class of substances, and thus eliminated the earlier concepts of "organic" and "inorganic" chemistry. The old term has, however, been retained as a convenient way of expressing the longer and more cumbersome phrase "chemistry of carbon compounds."

§ In 1913, the last year before World War I, Germany produced some 80% of the world's dyestuffs, Switzerland 5%, United States 2%, Great Britain 1¼%, France 1%, other countries the rest.

the hands of newly organized groups of men and not the gas and coal companies who produced the raw materials. Some of the German firms grew to large size, competing fiercely with each other, not only commercially but also in research and patent positions. In 1925, these German firms amalgamated to form the huge I. G. Farben-industrie, the German dye and chemical trust. In England, a somewhat similar course of development resulted (1926) in the formation of Imperial Chemical Industries, Ltd., the chemical giant of that country. In America, the chemical industry did not follow this pattern of development. Aside from The Barrett Company,* the producers of coal-tar chemicals in America prior to World War I were of small importance. During that war, the shortage of dyestuffs throughout the Allied world brought many new producers into the field. One of them, E. I. du Pont de Nemours & Company, already more than a century old and grown to giant size through activities in the gunpowder and explosives field, began the manufacture of synthetic dyestuffs and organic chemicals in 1917.

In all three countries it is important to note that the coal companies, the gas companies, and the steel companies with coke ovens had almost without exception missed the boat as far as this new chemical business was concerned. Absorbed in the production and marketing of large amounts of basic commodities, they probably regarded chemical manufacture as too trifling in size and too far afield to bother with it. For a long while it looked as though this neglect of the chemical business would be repeated by the oil companies.

Ever since Professor Silliman's analysis of petroleum back in 1854, five years before the Drake well was brought in, men had known that except for minor impurities petroleum consisted wholly of hydrocarbons. In addition, petroleum occurred in liquid and even gaseous states, a distinct advantage over coal which, before it could be processed chemically, had to be converted from its solid form. Best of all, the by-product gases from cracking that offered a starting point for an oil-based chemical industry were simple in their chemical and physical structure. This was an advantage from the chemist's point of view, for it meant he could expect to process these simpler ingredients with a minimum of trouble from disturbing side-reactions.

Oil, then, offered an admirable starting point for a chemical in-

* Now a division of Allied Chemical & Dye Corp., formed in 1920 by the merger of several coal-tar chemical companies.

dustry. Would the oil companies be the ones to reap the profit by utilizing their own wastes, or would they by default allow others to move into this promising field? Certainly the latter was more than a remote possibility. A company outside the oil business had been one of the first to put petroleum to use as a source of chemicals. The Union Carbide & Carbon Corporation, which already manufactured chemicals from other materials, in 1920 organized a new subsidiary, the Carbide & Carbon Chemicals Corporation, to manufacture from petroleum gases a liquefied propane fuel gas (marketed as "Pyrofax") and ethylene glycol for manufacture into explosives, and later on, for use as an automobile antifreeze under the trade name "Prestone." For gases, Carbide relied in part on natural-gas wells in West Virginia, and in part upon refinery waste gases, early contracting for a substantial part of Standard of Indiana's gas output at Whiting.[9]

Then, at about this same time an oil company, Standard of New Jersey, decided to attempt the manufacture of isopropyl alcohol from petroleum. In 1920, the Jersey company bought a large batch of patents covering numerous aspects of cracking and also alcohol manufacture, from Carleton Ellis, a well-known practicing chemist.[10] The following year, the Jersey people began the manufacture of isopropyl alcohol from propylene, but they were at this early date doomed to encounter sizeable difficulties. No oil company of the day, Jersey included, had enough background in research to jump feet-first into chemical processing. A chief cause of Jersey's difficulty was that raw cracked gases, mixed with each other, were immediately subjected to the first processing step on the road to alcohol. This failure to start with a pure raw material resulted in an end product that was a mixture of isopropyl alcohol, several other kinds of alcohol, and a dark tarry liquid. To separate these various products and obtain a saleable isopropyl alcohol was a very difficult task. Silent witness to Jersey's troubles was a long string of patents covering processes for purifying impure isopropyl alcohol. Later on, when pure raw materials were available, these would not be necessary. It is little wonder that such experiences tended to dampen Jersey's enthusiasm for the chemical business. A separate organization for research work, the Standard Oil Development Company,† was set up in 1927, but it was primarily to develop promising new oil processes; in an agreement with the I. G. Farben interests as late as 1929, Jersey agreed to turn over to the

---

† The earlier Standard Development Company, organized in 1922, was purely a patent-licensing organization.[11]

I. G. any chemical developments not closely related to the oil business. [12]

This, in brief, was the state of affairs in the chemical and oil fields in 1927.‡ The successful growth of the coal-tar chemical business seemed to indicate a similar lucrative future for petroleum chemicals. Large amounts of gas were being put to no use at all, and new fractionation methods now made it possible to separate these waste gases into chemical raw materials of high purity. In America, Shell's chief competitor had already essayed the chemical business and, although Standard was now temporarily disenchanted, the experience of Union Carbide in the same field pointed to the eventual success of petroleum-based chemicals. In Germany, the I. G. Farben was beginning to tread perilously close to Shell's normal business, the manufacture and supply of motor fuels. The Bergius patents,§ which were purchased by the I. G. Farben in 1927, and the competing Fischer-Tropsch process, devised by Ruhrchemie A. G., were on their way to producing (as they did seven years later) a successful synthetic gasoline from coal or coal derivatives, air, and water.[13] For Shell to capitalize on its own waste products, to keep even with Standard of New Jersey, its chief competitor, to be in a position to strike back at the I. G. in that company's own field, synthetic ammonia and organic chemicals—all these made the chemical business an attractive proposition. And so the fateful step was taken. The Shell companies in Europe and America embarked upon the business of manufacturing and selling chemicals, a business of which they still had much to learn.

‡ To indicate that it has not been overlooked, the author feels it necessary to point out that a predecessor of the present Cities Service Company was producing chemicals from petroleum in Oklahoma prior to 1920. General opinion in the industry, however, is that the circumstances surrounding this production were such as to make it purely fortuitous. Cities Service was then, as now, a large producer and transporter of natural gas. Air mixed with the gas caused pipe line corrosion and the company, trying to remove the causes of the corrosion, found that the air could be removed by passing the gas-air mixture over certain kinds of catalysts. Quite incidentally, this catalytic reaction produced small quantities of methyl alcohol and formaldehyde, which were extracted and sold. Cities Service did not attempt to exploit its discovery further, either by enlarging the production of these by-product chemicals or by trying to make related products.

§ The Royal Dutch-Shell Group for several years following World War I financed hydrogenation experiments by the famous German chemist, Dr. Friedrich Bergius, who attempted to convert heavy oils into saleable light products by means of his hydrogenation process. In the mid-Twenties, the Group abandoned this effort as being intrinsically too expensive. The validity of the Group's conclusion was later verified by Standard of New Jersey, which did experimental work on hydrogenating heavy oils in the early Thirties after it had bought American rights to the Bergius and other I. G. patents.

The Need to Know More: Emeryville

THE gases from which the Shell organization now proposed to manufacture chemicals were, as we have seen, of two kinds.

The first were oilfield gases, natural gas from gas wells and gas
produced by flowing oil wells. These gases were composed of highly
stable, "saturated" hydrocarbons, which meant that they were unreactive chemically. Under certain conditions, up to 85% of their
volume was pure methane which could be a prolific, cheap raw
material for making the pure hydrogen needed to manufacture ammonia. These unreactive oilfield gases would, at least at the start, be
of use chiefly in the manufacture of synthetic ammonia and ammonia
fertilizers.

By-product gases from cracking provided the other source of
abundant cheap gas. A barrel of cracking feed stock yielded some
500 cubic feet of waste gases, composed for the most part of the
same stable hydrocarbons encountered in oilfield gas. However, there
was one important difference: from 15% to 20% of the volume of
the refinery waste gases consisted of hydrocarbons which were chemical unsaturates, and therefore highly reactive. These gases—ethylene
(C_2H_4), propylene (C_3H_6), the butylenes (C_4H_8), and the amylenes
(C_5H_{10})—offered the greatest immediate promise as chemical building-blocks. Ethylene, propylene, and the butylenes could, on paper
at least, be converted into ethyl alcohol, isopropyl alcohol, and the
butyl alcohols by the simple addition of water.

There was still much to be learned about them. Thus far, in pointing up the similarities between coal tar and petroleum as sources of
hydrocarbons, we have omitted mention of their differences. A
fundamental difference was the nature of the molecules themselves.
Because coal tar is the product of a high-temperature process, it
consists largely of molecules which have good stability under high
heat. The characteristic coal tar molecule was represented structurally
as a ring, in marked contrast to the long, straight-chain molecules of
many petroleum compounds. These straight-chain, or aliphatic,
molecules had been studied academically, but very few industrial
laboratories had thus far made excursions into aliphatic chemistry.

Shell promptly set out to do so. The ethylene, propylene, butylene,
and amylene gases were not available in Holland from natural sources,

but butane was, in the form of "bottled gas." This bottled butane could be cracked to produce ethylene and propylene. Using these gases for experimentation, the Amsterdam laboratory began gas research in the mid-Twenties. With the creation in 1927 of a new department charged solely with chemical research, this work was greatly intensified.[14] This research was fruitful in that it helped to give Shell some firsthand knowledge of aliphatic chemistry and served to indicate the wide range of products which could be made from refinery waste gases. Amsterdam was not, however, an ideal center for cracking-gas research. Far away from cracking installations, it would always have to employ homemade gases for experimentation, and these gases did not exhibit the peculiarities of the gases actually produced by cracking units. This and other considerations led Pyzel to urge the establishment of a separate research center in the United States.

At the meeting in The Hague in April 1927, his proposal was fully discussed. It was suggested that the old Simplex organization could be used as a nucleus of the new American research organization; and Pyzel was asked to investigate the operating procedures of other concerns which had set up their research departments as separate companies.

The lesson of the Group's early laboratories in Holland had not been lost. From the start, it was planned to set up the new American research organization in such a manner that it could not possibly degenerate into the testing department of a refinery. It would be separate and apart from the existing Shell companies in America; would employ the best academic scientists it could find, put them under competent direction, and leave them alone to work in an atmosphere of complete freedom. It would need to be located near a good university so that its staff could utilize the university's scientific library and have daily contact with fellow scientists in the academic world. Also, the new organization should be located near a source of natural gas, should be near enough to a refinery to receive the supplies of cracked gases and other materials which would be needed for experimentation, and near enough to one of the company's main offices to take advantage of its administrative facilities.[15]

The St. Louis and San Francisco areas both met these specifications, but the California location was the favorite from the first. In his search for a location for the new laboratory, Pyzel first considered Palo Alto, the home of Stanford University, and reasonably near

Shell of California's head office at San Francisco and refinery at Martinez.[16] This choice was soon abandoned for Emeryville, a small industrial community on the eastern shore of San Francisco Bay, directly opposite that city and adjoining Berkeley, home of the University of California. In addition to being nearer to both San Francisco and Martinez, Emeryville had the additional advantage of being zoned exclusively for industry and this meant that pilot-plant installations could be erected without restriction. Four acres of property in Emeryville were purchased late in 1927.

Meanwhile, the new research company was being provided with a corporate organization. As the reader will recall, the Simplex Refining Company and its Trumble patents had been excluded from the Shell-Union merger in 1922. Simplex had in the meantime been owned by Asiatic of New York; and in 1926, that company had rechartered Simplex as a Delaware corporation. The new Simplex company's chief assets were the old Trumble patents, most all of which had expired or were on the point of expiration. The Simplex refinery design and engineering sections under N. W. (Skip) Thompson had seen the period of their greatest usefulness, for Shell's American refineries were now built and had their own engineering departments. It was decided that the new research company could be provided by winding up the design end of the Simplex business, and converting Simplex into a patent-licensing and research company.

Early in 1927, Simplex's name was changed to Shell Development Company and its corporate purpose thereafter became "active experimental and research work with the natural commercial desire to get tangible financial results at the earliest stage compatible with the nature of the work." [17] A year later, the company's charter was enlarged in line with these objectives. Thus the Trumble patents, which fifteen years before had represented the American Shell companies' first venture into improved processing, fittingly became the foundation of Shell's new industrial research organization.

Ownership of the reconstituted Shell Development Company was shared equally by Shell Union and Bataafsche. On June 15, 1928, headquarters were transferred from New York to San Francisco. Pyzel, who had little patience with the mechanics of business organization, asked that someone other than he be made the new company's chief executive. Accordingly, H. R. Gallagher, who had ably headed the West Coast marketing operations since 1912, was made president of Shell Development Company. Pyzel assumed the less burdensome title of vice president, although it was understood from the outset that he would have charge of the new company's technical affairs. G. C. Noble and John Lauder, who were, respectively, secretary and treasurer of Shell Oil in San Francisco, filled these posts for Shell Development. The new company, which had only modest requirements for office space, moved into the Russ Building at 235 Montgomery Street.

Of paramount importance at this point was the selection of a qualified research director who would be responsible for getting the laboratory built and staffed, and who would direct the actual research. Selection of this research director was entrusted to Waley Cohen, himself a chemistry graduate from Cambridge. In his choice, Waley Cohen pointed up the fact that he clearly understood the difference between basic research, which Emeryville would be conducting, and the applied research of refinery laboratories. He reached outside the Group's organization—and the field of petroleum technology, as well—to pick Dr. E. Clifford Williams, only thirty-five, a brilliant chemist and proven administrator. Williams was well acquainted with the coal-tar field, having spent several years with the British Dyestuffs Corporation. He had then returned to the academic world to start the first chemical engineering curriculum in England, and at the time of his selection as director of research for the Shell Development Company was dean of the science faculty at University College, London.

Arriving in California in May 1928, Williams at the start gave a hint of his versatility by dispensing with an architect and designing the new Emeryville laboratory himself. The main structure, built to accommodate an initial staff of 40 to 45 scientific workers, was a plain affair of steel and reinforced concrete, innocent of ornamentation. It was two stories high, with a three-story center section. In anticipation of future expansion, the upright supporting girders were run through the roof and all utility lines (water, steam, drains, etc.) were carried up to that level.[18]

An unusual feature of Williams' building was that the outside walls and two rows of columns along the center hall supported the entire weight of the floors and inside walls. The utility lines providing gas, water, electricity, compressed air, vacuum, steam, drainage, and vent connections were run around the outside walls with outlets at standard ten-foot intervals. This made it possible for the interior walls, which carried no structural weight or service connections, to be taken down at will and rearranged to provide working space of any size desired—an excellent precaution in a laboratory where it was difficult to foresee the size to which some experiments might eventually grow. Gone were the old, heavy, expensive workbenches which had been a familiar fixture of the chemical laboratory for a half century and more. Matching the laboratory, the furniture was of Spartan simplicity and consisted of basic movable units which could be combined to make work areas of any size desired.

As another measure for simplicity's sake, no storage space was provided in the laboratory rooms. Instead, the Emeryville laboratory had a central storeroom department designed to deliver supplies of materials and clean apparatus so speedily that old-fashioned storage arrangements were no longer necessary, and highly trained scientists would not be obliged to spend a large part of their time "doing dishes."

The new Emeryville laboratory was built and equipped in just four months, and cost, complete, $200,000. Williams and the first of his staff moved in late in October 1928. By the end of the year, the staff totalled 35; it continued to grow year after year throughout the depression, until by 1939 the number at work in the Emeryville laboratories exceeded 500. The accomplishments of these eleven years were in keeping with the laboratories' physical growth.

4

Synthetic Ammonia from Natural Gas

FROM discoveries made in the laboratories at Emeryville and Amsterdam, the whole of Shell's chemical business was to evolve. The chief exception to this was the ammonia business. It had been decided at the outset that, to gain experience in the business, the Shell Group would build a synthetic ammonia plant in Holland, based on the gases from steel-mill coke ovens. This experience could then be utilized in the design and construction of a second plant which would utilize natural gas to make ammonia.

A likely source of this coke-oven gas in Holland was the Royal Dutch Blast Furnaces and Steel Works, at Ymuiden.* Arrangements

* Not connected with the Royal Dutch Petroleum Company.

were made with this company to organize a jointly owned concern called N. V. Maatschappij tot Exploitatie van Kooksovengassen ("Mekog" for short) to build and operate a synthetic ammonia plant at Ymuiden.

As for the process to be employed, several were already in successful operation. The simplest, cheapest, and quickest method would be to license an existing process. Perhaps the best known was the Haber-Bosch method of nitrogen fixation, the pioneer synthetic ammonia process, which had gone into production in Germany in 1913. The rights to the Haber-Bosch process, however, were owned by the I. G. Farben companies and the Shell Group had no wish to approach the I. G. for a license. Instead, Pyzel went to Westphalia in the summer of 1927 to report on the rival Mont Cenis ammonia synthesis process, controlled by Gasverarbeitungs G.m.b.H., or "Gaveg," as it was called. A preliminary license agreement covering the Mont Cenis process was signed with Gaveg in October 1927, and in April 1928 a world-wide contract was negotiated between Gaveg and B.P.M., giving Bataafsche and its nominees the rights to the Mont Cenis process in every country except Germany.[19]

The Haber-Bosch and Mont Cenis processes utilized different methods to carry out the same general steps. Nitrogen (which comprises about 80% of the earth's atmosphere) was extracted from the air and reacted with pure hydrogen to get ammonia (NH_3). This pure ammonia boiled at 33° C. below zero, so it was a gas at normal temperatures. To overcome ammonia's unmanageable nature, it was usually reacted with sulphuric acid to get ammonium sulphate, a stable, granular compound which could be easily applied to land under cultivation. The fertilizing element of ammonium sulphate was the nitrogen which had been recovered from the air.

At Ymuiden, a plant capable of "fixing" twenty tons a day of atmospheric nitrogen was built by Mekog and put into operation in September 1929.[20] It was actually two plants, for a complete duplicate installation had been provided as insurance against mechanical failures.

By this time, plans for the second ammonia plant, to operate on natural gases, were beginning to take shape. Pyzel was placed in charge of the project, and was given a world-wide choice of plant location.[21] No location was as promising as the California market. Large quantities of petroleum gases were an essential consideration, as was also the proximity of a ready market for commercial fertilizers. In both respects, California was eminently qualified.

Of all the agricultural regions in the United States, California with its ten-month growing season was far and away the leading producer of intensively cultivated, high-value crops. Orchard, vineyard, and truck-garden harvests brought cash returns greater than the fodder and grain crops of the Midwest, or the cotton, soybean, and peanuts of the South. The grower of these high-value crops was obviously a more willing customer for expensive synthetic fertilizers. To make the California location even more attractive, there were no synthetic ammonia plants of any size in the western part of the United States.† Freight charges from the East would provide the new plant with a certain amount of protection, as would the sizeable duty on imported fertilizer in effect since 1890.‡ In addition to the California market, there were other likely customers for synthetic fertilizers in Hawaii and the Pacific Northwest, areas which could be easily reached by cheap water transportation.

To own and operate the ammonia plant and any subsequent ventures into chemical manufacture, a separate company seemed best. On February 18, 1929, a corporation called Shell Chemical Company was chartered under the laws of Delaware; for the time being, its stock was held by Shell Development and its officers were the same as that company's.

The first choice for a plant site was the Los Angeles area, with its plentiful supply of natural gas. Kessler and Gallagher, however, preferred a deep-water location in the San Francisco Bay area, which would also be much nearer to Martinez, Emeryville, and the San Francisco office. In June 1930, Shell Chemical gave up the idea of a Los Angeles location and for $400,000 acquired a 636-acre site on a promontory near Pittsburg, California, some 15 miles east of Martinez. This neck of land jutting out into the bay was promptly christened Shell Point, and the new plant was known by that name even before it was finished.

Shell Point, it was planned, would utilize the Mont Cenis process under the license agreement previously negotiated by Bataafsche.§

† A synthetic ammonia plant, following the German plan and using coal as a source of hydrogen, had been built at Syracuse, N.Y., in 1921, by the Atmospheric Nitrogen Corp., a subsidiary of Allied Chemical & Dye. Later in the Twenties, similar plants had been built by a few other Eastern chemical companies.

‡ $4 to $7.50 per ton, depending on degree of concentration.[22]

§ Royalties of $100,000 a year were paid by Shell Chemical to Asiatic of New York, which held American rights to the Mont Cenis license on behalf of B.P.M. In February 1934, B.P.M. arranged with Gaveg to buy a paid-up license; the Shell Chemical royalty payments continued until 1939.[23]

Nitrogen would be supplied, as at Ymuiden, by compressing air to its liquid state and fractionating it under high pressures. The German Linde company had furnished the low-temperature air-fractionation apparatus for Ymuiden. An order was placed with them for similar equipment for Shell Point. The synthesis phase of the process, where the nitrogen was reacted with hydrogen in the presence of a catalyst to form gaseous ammonia, would also remain about the same. The chief difference between the Shell Point plant and its predecessor at Ymuiden would be in the manner of obtaining the hydrogen.

The Shell Point plant was to be the first in the world to use natural gas to make ammonia, so it would have to work out its own methods for preparing pure hydrogen from natural gas. The simplest method would be to obtain the required hydrogen from methane, the simplest of hydrocarbons, which had four atoms of hydrogen to one of carbon. "Wet" gas from oil wells contained some 37% of methane, but "dry" gas, such as that being sold by the public utilities, contained methane in percentages as high as 85%. These public utilities had themselves already done a great deal of experimental work which might be of use.

Because California contained no coal, the state's utility companies had several years earlier generated gas from an oil fraction called "gas oil," produced as a by-product in refining kerosene. Like coal gas, gas generated from oil had a heat content of about 500 British thermal units per thousand cubic feet. When natural gas had become available in California in quantities, the utilities replaced part of the gas they were generating from oil with natural gas which was cheaper. Since natural gas contained about 1,000 B.T.U. per thousand cubic feet, it had been necessary for several years to "reform" the natural gas to bring it down to the heat level of the manufactured gas, so that the two could be mixed without difficulty. Later on, during the Twenties, the utility companies had converted entirely to natural gas, making it possible to eliminate the reforming step. The older installations for reforming natural gas and for manufacturing gas from oil were kept on a stand-by basis by most utility companies as an auxiliary source of supply during winter months.

Several of these companies now freely tendered their experience to Pyzel's two sons—Fred, chief engineer of Shell Development Company, and Ewald, superintendent of the Shell Point plant. They had been assigned to develop a gas-reforming process to supply the hydrogen needed by the new ammonia plant. On every side, information and assistance were offered to the younger Pyzels, and the Southern

California Gas Company in Los Angeles even went so far as to put a full-scale gas-reforming unit and an experienced operating crew at their disposal.[24]

The test runs in this unit provided the kind of operating data which Shell needed to have on the production of hydrogen from natural gas. The utility company's generosity made possible a great saving in time by allowing use of their equipment as a pilot plant. Operation was simplified and hydrogen yields increased by using temperatures higher than those normally employed by the utility companies. As a result of this careful study at the Southern California Gas Company's plant, the gas reformers ordered for Shell Point embodied several important changes in construction and flow design.

The gas-reform section at Shell Point was completed and installed by April 1931, several months ahead of the rest of the equipment. This interval was used for training operators. As there was no source of natural gas near Shell Point and the cost of running a gas line from one of Shell's fields such as Ventura would have been prohibitive, Shell Oil arranged to have gas delivered to Shell Point by one of the public utilities to whom it normally sold gas.[25]

Finally, in August 1931, the chemists, engineers, and operating supervisors who had been in virtually constant attendance during several weeks of trial runs folded their cots and began to draw up normal working schedules. The gas-reform plant was functioning smoothly, delivering a steady stream of hydrogen; the Linde liquid-air plant, wrapped in heavy layers of insulation and encrusted with ice wherever the sample lines emerged, supplied the nitrogen. From "the dollar line," a pipe in the synthesis plant that hopeful operators had painted with dollar signs, ammonia was at last emerging.[26]

5

Hard Times at Shell Point

THE optimism for the new ammonia plant was purely technological. Shell Chemical, made up of oil men, was launched upon the unfamiliar seas of the chemical industry. The new company would not for some time encounter smooth sailing. The trouble was not with the plant behind the "dollar line," but with the market conditions this side of it: 1931 was a poor year to launch a new business of any kind.

During 1929, nitrogen fertilizers sold for $40 to $46 a ton, but with the advent of the depression world markets for synthetic fertilizers fell apart. Efforts to support the market were made by some of the large European producers during 1930, but like most such efforts they were of little use and serious price wars broke out during 1931. Even before Shell Point had come into operation, suggestions were being made in Holland that manufacture of ammonium sulphate be discontinued at Ymuiden and the plant converted to the hydrogenation of oil. Late in August 1931, with Shell Point barely in production, the Group's chemical department at The Hague was suggesting to San Francisco that Shell Point be closed. The reasons for this deep pessimism were not far to seek. Shell Chemical during 1931–1932 found itself realizing from its ammonium sulphate as little as $16.50 a ton, while its own manufacturing costs amounted to about $30 a ton.[27]

The new venture was fortunate, however, in three respects: deficits in the beginning had been fully expected and therefore came as no surprise; the friends of the enterprise among top management did not waver in their faith; and the Shell Development and Shell Chemical companies at this point received a new president who would do much to see them through their trying initial period.

The few months of operation during 1931 cost Shell Chemical a net loss of $243,000; in 1932, this figure rose to more than a million dollars; and the following three years resulted in additional, though slightly smaller, operating losses. In its first five years, Shell Chemical cost its backers a net of $6,231,000 in deficit, loans, and stock subscriptions. Deficit alone totalled $2,813,000, a sizeable figure representing nearly half of Shell Chemical's gross sales during the same period. One need not be a professional accountant to realize how great must have been the temptation during the early Thirties to curtail or wholly abandon operations of this new company which seemed to offer nothing but another way of losing money.

The Shell Point plant had cost more than five million dollars to build; to cover operating losses and new capital expenditures, more and more money was advanced until the original $10,000,000 appropriation for research and chemical manufacture was approached, and then exceeded. The size of this sum must be viewed against the background of the darkest days of the depression, when no one had as yet made a real success of petroleum chemicals, when most all the

Shell companies in America were losing money, and economy committees were hunting for ways in which to save not millions but even a few thousands of dollars. Pyzel, as a founder of both companies, was called upon more than once to protect them from the economy axe; in these efforts he was strongly backed by Kessler and De Kok on the Royal Dutch side and Sir Robert Waley Cohen of Shell Transport & Trading. These three were, Pyzel recalled later, never-failing friends of this investment in the future.[28]

In February 1931, before the Shell Point plant had been completed, the Shell Development and Shell Chemical companies received a new president, Cornelius B. de Bruyn, a Hollander who had risen through the marketing end of the business to become general manager of Astra Romana, the Group's chief company in Romania. De Bruyn was a man of cautious and deliberate temperament, the very opposite of a plunger; yet once he had convinced himself of the fundamental soundness of the new chemical enterprise, he became one of its strongest champions. The period of his presidency, 1931–1941, was a most critical one for the new enterprise and De Bruyn must be given a large measure of credit for the vigorous action he took to put the company on its feet.*

During September, De Bruyn convinced the Group's management that Shell Point should "in any event work through to the spring of 1932 for the purpose of collecting data on profitability and the distribution of costs." [29] During this period of operation and for several months thereafter, the plant was operated as designed, except that much of the ammonia production was not sulphated. Sulphate brought prices so abysmally low that the plant's losses could at least be cut by not sulphating some of the ammonia it manufactured. Shell Chemical sold some of its ammonia in liquefied form to Hercules Powder Company's nearby explosives factory, where it was converted into nitric acid.[30]

Those first months of operation showed costs which on occasion were nearly double the proceeds realized from the sale of sulphate.

---

* Late in 1929, as soon as the Shell Development Company had been successfully launched, Gallagher had returned to his former position, marketing vice president of Shell Oil in San Francisco. In the interim, from late 1929 until De Bruyn's election in 1931, Legh-Jones filled the office of president of Shell Development, and J. E. F. de Kok, managing director of the Royal Dutch Company charged chiefly with technical affairs, served as president of Shell Chemical. These interim presidencies were little more than nominal, for both men had heavy duties in other connections. Pyzel as vice president of both companies was regarded as their actual operating head, despite his distaste for administrative work.

It is not surprising, then, that De Bruyn began a determined attack upon production expense, with Pyzel supplying as he had for twenty years the technical genius and imagination needed to effect great improvements in manufacturing methods. In two directions, their efforts were a spectacular success. They succeeded in getting more production out of the plant, and they greatly reduced the cost of one of their chief raw materials, sulphuric acid.

The sulphuric acid with which ammonia was reacted to form ammonium sulphate was, as previously mentioned, of no particular value as a fertilizing agent. It was merely a means of "packaging" gaseous ammonia in manageable form. It was expensive packing material, too, for nearly three pounds of sulphuric acid were needed to sulphate a pound of ammonia. At the same time, Shell refineries were discarding as useless large quantities of sulphuric acid which had become contaminated in treating processes.

Ideas to use this black, evil-smelling waste acid in the manufacture of ammonium sulphate were by no means new. Dr. Abraham Gesner, the original refiner of kerosene, had suggested it in 1861, and there were patent applications on the subject as far back as 1868 and as recent as 1920. The Scotch shale-oil refiners of the Nineteenth Century had derived considerable profit from sulphate manufacture. But similar attempts by petroleum refiners had produced a sulphate that was dark-colored, sticky, and bad-smelling. Most sulphate manufacturers despaired of ever using waste acid successfully. These previous failures did not discourage Pyzel. In May 1932, he set Dr. Jan Ruys and his staff in the Shell Point laboratory to work on ways of utilizing sulphuric acid sludge.[31]

There was pressing need for cutting Shell Point's cost of sulphate manufacture. Well aware of this, Ruys and his staff worked around the clock, day after day, for many weeks until finally they had favorable results to report. By August 1932, they had developed the principles of a process for making acceptable clean sulphate from black, smelly waste acid and the new process moved into the pilot plant stage. Then followed a year of bad smells, gummed equipment, sulphate as black as tar, or caked in stone-hard clinkers. But by September 1933, the process could be declared a success: they were using acid sludge from the refineries to make ammonium sulphate, without the addition of new acid. The sulphate made by this method was only slightly colored when compared to sulphate made from fresh acid, and in one respect at least it was superior. It was more free-running, an important property in any fertilizer applied by mechanical equipment. A full-scale sulphating plant using the new process was built and put into operation at Shell Point in December 1933. Tank cars of acid sludge began to arrive from the refineries, and purchases of new acid fell off.[32]

From the refineries' point of view, this profitable utilization of acid sludge had salutary effects. Disposal of acid sludge had hitherto been a time- and fuel-consuming nuisance. Now Shell Chemical would pay fifty cents to a dollar a ton for the privilege of taking it off a refiner's hands. The refinery operation was improved, for now that the refineries could sell their spent acid, they were inclined to introduce fresh acid earlier, and this improved their treating processes. In preparing the acid sludge for use in the sulphating process, the black, tarry compounds which had originally discolored the acid were separated from it. Since they were heavy oil fractions, they made a satisfactory, although smelly, boiler fuel.[33]

Of even greater effect upon costs at Shell Point was a large increase in output made possible by the introduction of "double operation," suggested by the plant superintendent, Ewald Pyzel. With European caution, the plant at Ymuiden had been provided with a large number of stand-by units. The same course had been followed by The Hague office when it ordered equipment for Shell Point. Beyond a doubt, it was a good idea. In the event of a breakdown, or of removing a unit from operation for repairs or a clean-out, the stand-by units could be brought into operation and daily production continued without interruption. It was also a wise precaution for a plant employing, as Shell Point did, European equipment for which spare parts could not easily be had in California. But sound as these precautions might be, they were also dreadfully expensive. Ewald Pyzel figured that he had standing idle at Shell Point some 80% to 85% of a "second" plant. The plant had been designed to produce 40 tons a day; why not supply the missing 15% to 20% of equipment and run at least part of the time at double capacity? It meant of course taking some chances. Instead of a single plant with a very safe margin of stand-by equipment, they would have two plants without any spare equipment at all. To De Bruyn it was a chance that must be taken: "We have to run 'both plants', or we'll never make any money." [34]

Most of the large, expensive parts of this "second plant"—the Linde air fractionating equipment, the Linde hydrogen purification equipment, the catalytic synthesis plant, and five of the six heavy compressors required—were already installed. The chief additional need was an extension to the gas reforming plant and a sixth air compressor; these were purchased and installed during 1934 at a cost of some $125,000. Other pieces of equipment brought the outlay to $200,000. With these relatively modest additions, the Shell Point plant was able to begin "double operation" in December 1934. It was, De Bruyn wrote in his annual report in 1934, a complete success and "proved that we can obtain a production of 81 tons of ammonia daily when running full speed under favorable conditions. Of course, this cannot be done every day of the year, but we can expect a very large increase in our production during 1935." Gradually production, as a result of double operation and closer control of operating techniques, rose from 40 tons a day in 1934 to 59 tons in 1935, to 66 tons in 1936, and 71 tons in 1937.[35]

Important improvements such as double operation and the use of waste acid in sulphate manufacture helped make a success of De Bruyn's program to pare operating expenses. Shell Chemical's costs for finished ammonium sulphate declined steadily, and meanwhile the market gradually improved. By late 1934, Shell Point could at last show a profit margin on its ammonium sulphate, and this figure improved considerably during 1935, the first full year of double operation.[36]

Credit for putting Shell Chemical's ammonia operation into the black was due primarily to the two developments just described. However, two other developments, soon to be of importance, had their origin during this period when every attempt was being made to cut costs. One was aimed at obtaining extra revenue from the sale of a by-product, the other at further reducing costs by eliminating the necessity for converting all of the plant's production into ammonium sulphate.

By-product pure carbon was produced in the gas-cracking operation. Pure, or nearly pure, carbon had been produced for a number of years in a variety of manners and a considerable market existed for it under the commercial names "lampblack" and "carbon black." The cheaper lampblack served as a pigment in inks and paints and as "filler" in soft rubber articles. The more expensive carbon black was used in enormous quantities as a coloring and strengthening agent for rubber, especially the rubber for automobile tires. The Shell Chem-

Shell Development Company's original laboratory, Emeryville, California, 1928.

New four-story addition to Emeryville laboratory, built in 1938.
Original laboratory, with a third story added, is at far left.

Shell Chemical's synthetic ammonia plant, at Shell Point, near Pittsburg, California, is shown here under construction, late in 1930.

Synthetic glycerine pilot plant at Emeryville laboratory, late 1930's.

Shell Chemical's Houston plant under construction, summer 1941. In background is Shell Oil's Houston refinery and, in the distance, the Houston Ship Channel.

ical sales department had not had much success in disposing of the company's by-product carbon, for it had to compete on the market with cheap lampblack carbon from many other sources. Shell Point's carbon was, however, of high purity and therefore excellent for metallurgical uses. In 1936, facilities were installed at Shell Point for drying the plant's carbon production and making it into briquettes for use in metallurgy. With its appearance in this easier-to-handle form, Shell carbon found a ready sale, chiefly to the new West Coast steel industry. By 1940, it was also being sold in pellet, pulverized, and screened-powder form to the rubber industry.[37]

The other development of this period was the pioneering by Shell Chemical of a wholly new method of applying ammonia fertilizers to land under cultivation. Most of the California land on which ammonium sulphate was used was also under irrigation. Gaseous ammonia (NH_3) dissolves readily in water to form aqua ammonia, or ammonia water. De Bruyn suggested that Shell Chemical's gaseous ammonia might be introduced directly into irrigation water. Several interested technologists, working in cooperation, set out to find a practicable way of doing it. Ludwig Rosenstein, chief chemist of Shell Chemical, and Felix Kortlandt, also of the chemical company, worked with Dean D. Waynick and F. H. Leavitt, of the Association Laboratory, an independent agricultural testing laboratory, and Paul Greening, of the Greening-Smith Co. In the years following 1932, Shell Point engineers developed apparatus for metering liquid ammonia from pressure cylinders directly into the flowing waters of an irrigation ditch.[38]

This system, which Shell Chemical later christened "Nitrogation," was a tremendous step forward. The company was saved the expense of converting ammonia into ammonium sulphate; the weight of the fertilizer was greatly reduced which meant lower shipping and handling charges for everybody concerned; the irrigation water carried the ammonia evenly through the farmer's fields, wholly relieving him of the labor of spreading fertilizer; and the nitrogen in the ammonia gave more efficient service as a fertilizing agent. This technique was not, of course, perfected all at once; it took many months of experimentation to determine the optimum amounts of ammonia—a maximum of 109 parts of ammonia to one million parts of water, 50 to 70 parts for the average commercial application.[39]

The farmer, accustomed since time immemorial to spreading a bulk fertilizer on his soil, had to be shown that this painless new method would really work. Leavitt, who had several ideas on sales techniques, resigned his former connection and went to work for Shell Chemical. Primarily as a result of his efforts, the chemical company developed a "Nitrogation" service to treat the farmer's soil with "Shell NH_3" (the trademark adopted for Shell Chemical's anhydrous ammonia). The company supplied the equipment, furnished the ammonia, and charged only for actual quantities used—and did it at rates competitive with the price of ammonium sulphate. The farmer was relieved not only of the work of applying fertilizer, but also of buying, storing, and handling ammonium sulphate. Growth of the Nitrogation service was slow but perceptible: by 1937, some 12%, or one-eighth, of Shell Point's total ammonia production was going to Nitrogation.[40]

Nitrogation was adapted only to areas regularly under irrigation. Equally desirable, but more difficult, was development of a similar method for use in dry-farming country. A method for injecting ammonia gas directly into the soil was developed by Leavitt during 1939–1940. The new method, called Nitrojection, combined fertilizer application and cultivation in one operation. It employed a patented cultivator with injection pipes on the backs of the cultivator teeth; these pipes were connected by hoses to an ammonia cylinder mounted on the cultivator.[41]

Nitrogation and Nitrojection were trade-marked names for services performed by agricultural distributors with equipment approved, and in many cases furnished, by Shell Chemical. These methods of applying fertilizer were in ensuing years widely adopted in the Central Valley of California and the Pacific Northwest. More recently they have been used in connection with lower-value crops such as rice on the Gulf Coast and corn in the Midwest.

By 1940, Shell Point's production of ammonia had levelled off at some 55 million pounds a year, of which roughly one-half was being converted into ammonium sulphate. That year sulphate prices were $32 a ton, double the price of the early Thirties, so some million and a half dollars were realized from its sale—the Pacific Coast market taking two-thirds, and the rest going to the Philippines. The other half of Shell Point's ammonia production (51%) was sold as anhydrous and aqua ammonia to industrial users in tank cars and drums, and a substantial part of the anhydrous ammonia was shipped in cylinders. Most of the cylinder ammonia went into irrigation water as fertilizer; smaller amounts were sold to commercial refrigerator plants in the United States and some dozen countries in Central and South America, the Pacific Islands, and the Far East.[42]

6

Alcohols, Ketones, and Iso-Octane

THE Shell Development Company had been organized to do fundamental research. At the start, at least, the plans called for this research to be directed toward developing commercially feasible processes for making chemicals from petroleum waste gases.

As Shell's entry into ammonia manufacture was to be made by way of established processes, the new Emeryville laboratory turned its attention at once to chemicals which could be made from refinery waste gases. These waste gases, as we have just seen, contained some 15% to 20% of "unsaturated" hydrocarbons—ethylene (C_2H_4), propylene (C_3H_6), mixed butylenes (C_4H_8), and amylenes (C_5H_{10}). These unsaturates lacked the two atoms of hydrogen needed to make them stable compounds. The natural tendency was for them to seek to acquire these missing atoms by combining with another chemical compound. This tendency to combine made unsaturated gases highly reactive, and therefore very attractive starting materials for chemical manufacture.

Ethylene, the simplest of these unsaturates, was for various reasons considered to be not the most attractive subject for study. The amylenes, with five atoms of carbon, presented greater chemical problems because of their more complicated structures; in addition, they represented desirable gasoline constituents which raised the question of whether they should be classified as "waste" gases at all. It was, therefore, on propylene and the butylenes that Shell Development was to concentrate its research effort for the next decade.

Within a remarkably short time the laboratory at Emeryville developed and had in pilot plant operation a process for making secondary butyl alcohol. In its essence, this process was the chemical combination of water with normal butylene to get secondary butyl alcohol (C_4H_9OH). In reality, however, it was not this simple. Water and butylene gas do not readily react with each other at normal pressures and temperatures, so a more roundabout method had to be adopted for adding the water. Butylene gas could be absorbed in sulphuric acid to produce an intermediate, butyl hydrogen sulphate. Water could then be added to this intermediate compound to split it apart (or "hydrolize" it) into sulphuric acid and secondary butyl alcohol.

Complicated as this circuitous method of adding water may sound to the layman, it was relatively simple to the chemist. The real difficulty of the process lay in the separation of the butylene isomers which were mixed with butanes in the so-called "C_4 cut." The gases which made up this C_4 cut—normal butane, isobutane, normal butylenes, and isobutylene—were too near each other in boiling point to be separated by existing fractionation methods. Research at Emeryville, based on earlier work done at Amsterdam, finally came up with a successful separation method.

The key to this separation process was the fact that isobutylene can be absorbed in a 65% solution of sulphuric acid, whereas normal butylenes will not be easily absorbed unless the acid is of a much higher concentration.[43] By reacting the C_4 fractions first with a 65% solution of sulphuric acid and then with an 85%–95% solution, the butylenes were selectively removed by absorption, leaving a mixture of butane and isobutane. This absorption process was important in that it made possible the sharp separation of gases previously inextricable. Emeryville's quick success was very largely due to the Shell Group's extensive experience with absorption and extraction processes, for it is safe to say that the Group had a backlog of knowledge in this field more extensive than that of its chief competitors.

In the development of continuous processing techniques, the new petroleum chemical industry was to differ markedly from the coal-tar chemical business. Most of the process equipment of the orthodox chemical industry was merely a magnification to plant size of laboratory "batch" equipment. But the oil men, accustomed to continuous processing in their refineries, were not content with batch methods when they entered the chemical business. Their introduction of continuous methods had a lasting effect not only on their own but upon all chemical processing, and without doubt made possible cheaper chemicals than would have otherwise been the case.

Secondary Butyl Alcohol

Shell Chemical acquired a small site adjoining the Martinez refinery, from which it was to draw its supply of cracking gases. Under the supervision of S. C. Carney and R. Z. Moravec, small semi-commercial plants for the separation of the butane-butylene cut and the manufacture of secondary butyl alcohol were built late in 1930.[†] This alcohol could now be manufactured for about 50¢ a gallon, but the market for it was not yet large. During 1931 Shell Chemical sold 5,000 pounds of secondary butyl alcohol, much of it to chemical laboratories, industrial and academic, who ordered small quantities for experimental use. It found some use as a solvent for enamels and lacquers and as a constituent of hydraulic brake fluids and of flotation agents used in ore recovery, but the chief importance of Shell Chemical's new secondary butyl alcohol was that it provided an intermediate for the manufacture of a much more versatile chemical, methyl ethyl ketone.[45]

Methyl Ethyl Ketone

By removing two atoms of hydrogen from a secondary alcohol, a corresponding ketone can be formed. This dehydrogenation of secondary butyl alcohol yielded methyl ethyl ketone, a highly useful solvent for the surface coating industry. MEK, as the trade has since called it, had been available up to this time only as "light acetone oil," a by-product made when wood was distilled to produce alcohol. This circumstance was a barrier to any widespread use of MEK. Since it was a by-product, the amounts produced were limited, and because it was produced in wood distillation the quality was subject to wide variation. Shell's pure methyl ethyl ketone was of stable quality and could be produced in quantity at reasonable prices. It was an excellent material for the perfume industry which could make a violet scent from it; it could also be converted into diacetyl compounds used to give margarine its butter-like taste. MEK was an excellent solvent for almost all organic materials: nitrocellulose lacquers, cellulose nitrate, cellulose acetate, ethyl cellulose, to mention only a few. Other uses could no doubt be developed for it, and soon were: it made excellent paint-, lacquer-, and varnish-removers; it was used as an intermediate for processing into insecticides, artificial leather, adhesives, industrial cleaning compounds, and printing inks; and it proved an excellent agent for use in extractive processes such as the dewaxing of lubricating oils.[46]

[†] Because they were experimental in nature, these early alcohol plants at Martinez were actually operated by Shell Development Company, with Shell Chemical reimbursing the Development company for its expenses. This arrangement continued until September 1, 1932, when Shell Chemical assumed control of operations.[44]

Using a catalyst developed by Martin de Simo of Shell Development, a semi-scale MEK plant was built on the laboratory grounds at Emeryville. During 1931 and 1932, this plant dehydrogenated much of the secondary butyl alcohol produced at Martinez. Eleven thousand pounds of MEK produced in this manner were sold by Shell Chemical during 1931, and 81,000 pounds in 1932. In December 1933, a full-scale MEK plant was put into operation at Martinez. Total production of MEK that year from the old semi-scale plant and the new commercial unit was more than a million pounds, making it the company's most important product after ammonia.[47]

Tertiary Butyl Alcohol

Both secondary butyl alcohol and methyl ethyl ketone had their origin in the normal butylenes, as they are called to distinguish them from their isomer, isobutylene. Isobutylene could be made to yield another alcohol by the same process of acid treatment and hydrolysis. This tertiary butyl alcohol produced from isobutylene found a place in the manufacture of artificial musks for perfumes, in the preparation of cleaning compounds, as a blending agent in insecticides and disinfectants (it was in itself toxic to weevils, moths, and their larvae), as a denaturant for ethyl alcohol, as an alkylating agent to introduce the tertiary butyl group, and as a secondary solvent in the dewaxing of lubricating oils. Shell Chemical sold small quantities of tertiary butyl alcohol during 1932, and in April 1933 put in operation a semi-commercial plant for its manufacture at Martinez.[48]

Iso-Octane

Separation of isobutylene from normal butylene was, as we have seen, accomplished by absorbing these gases in sulphuric acid of differing degrees of concentration. Isobutylene, the more reactive of the two gases, could be absorbed in a 65% concentration of cold sulphuric acid. Sometimes, instead of hydrolizing this mixture of isobutylene and sulphuric acid to produce tertiary butyl alcohol as described in the preceding paragraph, it was desired merely to separate the acid from the isobutylene. In this process of recovering the isobutylene from sulphuric acid, the acid and butylene mixture was heated, and this led to a reaction whose effects were to be felt far beyond the field of the chemical industry.

The molecules of isobutylene, C_4H_8, combined with each other to form a new molecule having double the number of carbon and hydrogen atoms. Polymerization, as chemists call this union of like molecules, yielded di-isobutylene, C_8H_{16}. This was coming very close to iso-octane, C_8H_{18}, the compound which had for nearly a decade been considered the "perfect" anti-knock fuel, rated "100" on the octane rating scale. Because di-isobutylene was an unsaturated compound, the addition of two atoms of hydrogen could be accomplished readily to get a pure iso-octane.[49]

Here was news of the very first importance to Shell Oil. Iso-octane, previously a chemical manufactured for laboratory use at a cost of about $20 a gallon,[50] might conceivably be made synthetically at prices low enough to allow it to be used in commercial fuel. Work was pushed on this new Shell polymerization process at Emeryville, and a pilot plant erected. The hydrogenation step, also devised at the laboratory, took place over a finely divided nickel catalyst. Early in 1934, the Army Air Corps placed an order with Shell Chemical for 1,000 gallons of iso-octane.

The finished iso-octane to fill this order came from a two-part plant. The di-isobutylene was produced at the Martinez chemical plant, where the mixtures of isobutylene and sulphuric acid were available as by-products of alcohol manufacture. Hydrogenation of the di-isobutylene to iso-octane took place at Shell Point, where a stream of pure hydrogen was available from the gas-reforming units. The Shell Point operating staff were already familiar with hydrogenation, and were able to build a small liquid-phase hydrogenation plant from spare parts of the ammonia plant and get it in operation in little more than a week's time.[51]

At the end of April 1934, the first quantities of this iso-octane were shipped to the Air Corps Matériel Command, at Wright Field, Dayton, Ohio. During the remaining months of 1934, Shell Chemical sold 18,750 gallons of iso-octane at an average price of 71¢ a gallon, roughly double its cost. In its annual report for that year, the company modestly noted, "In April we started making iso-octane in a small plant. As far as we know, the Shell Chemical was the first company selling iso-octane in car loads."[52]

Further development of iso-octane was soon after turned over to Shell Chemical's oil-company sisters. Other more efficient processes followed in rapid succession in the years following 1935, opening the way to large-volume production of 100-octane gasoline during the war years. These developments are discussed at greater length in the chapter covering the war years.

Isopropyl Alcohol and Acetone

The chemical products discussed so far—secondary butyl alcohol, methyl ethyl ketone, tertiary butyl alcohol, and synthetic iso-octane—all had their origin in the butylene gases. The next lightest gas, propylene, could be converted into isopropyl alcohol by processes very similar to those used to make the butylenes into secondary and tertiary butyl alcohols. Isopropyl alcohol ("IPA") was a versatile and highly useful solvent; both Standard Oil of New Jersey and Carbide & Carbon Chemicals had begun its manufacture during the Twenties. It had been quickly adopted by industrial users as a substitute for ethyl alcohol, which was then hedged about with restrictions arising from the national Prohibition law. William Haynes, author of an exhaustive history of the chemical business, regards this early IPA production as a milestone in petroleum-based chemicals, "the first fruit of deliberate scientific exploration of petroleum as a chemical raw material." [53] In 1922, some 37,500 gallons of isopropyl alcohol were synthesized from propylene; nine years later, annual production from the same source was 1,500,000 gallons.[54]

Isopropyl alcohol found a ready market as "rubbing alcohol"; it was an almost universal solvent for industrial applications (many substances insoluble in water dissolve readily in alcohol); it was used as antifreeze in automobile radiators; it became a component of lacquers, thinners, pharmaceuticals, and disinfectants; and it filled most of the large gap caused by the disappearance of industrial ethyl alcohol. Best of all, acetone, an equally versatile substance, could be prepared from IPA by simple dehydrogenation. Quite extensive plant capacity for the manufacture of isopropyl alcohol and acetone was already in existence at the time of Shell's entry into the chemical field. It was, no doubt, the existence of this plant capacity which made Shell Chemical decide to concentrate at first on the less common derivatives of butylene.

By the mid-Thirties, however, the extreme purity of Shell Chemical's alcohols had become a convincing sales argument. Despite competition, there was a place on the market for a high-purity isopropyl alcohol and an acetone of equal purity. Plants to process propylene into IPA and make acetone from the isopropyl alcohol were built at Martinez during 1934 and put into operation in January 1935.[55] These new plants marked a turning point in the commercial history of Shell Chemical. The markets for both IPA and acetone were already developed, and as a result these chemicals could be put into quantity production at once.

Alcohol prices generally were low in the mid-Thirties, so at the start all of Shell Chemical's IPA production at Martinez was converted into acetone, which promptly became the bread-and-butter mainstay of the chemical company's business. Shell Chemical's ability to furnish a product with guaranteed purity of better than 99% could not help making a hit with the countless industrial processors who used acetone in one or more of their operations. As a result, acetone sales were not only profitable but provided an excellent advertisement for the new chemical company and led to acceptance by the trade of some of its relatively untried products.

Most waxes, oils, fats, greases, dyes, synthetic resins, and similar materials are soluble in acetone, a circumstance which has led to its becoming "one of the chemical workhorses of industry." [56] It is an ideal component of auto finishes and other sprayed paints; of nail polish, artificial leather, and photographic film; and an indispensable solvent for the spinning solution used in rayon mills. These are but a few of the most important uses of acetone. It is also widely used as a raw material for the manufacture of other chemicals.

The Dominguez Plant

The manufacture and sale of acetone was the first impressive success in Shell Chemical's program to put the by-product gases of cracking to profitable utilization. During 1935, plans got under way to build a larger and more efficient series of chemical plants adjoining the Dominguez refinery. The Martinez units, although full-scale plants, had been experimental in that several of them were trail blazers in their fields. Out of the knowledge gained from them, new and more efficient units could be designed to process the much larger supply of cracking gases available at the Wilmington-Dominguez refinery. Construction of new chemical units at Dominguez began late in 1935. Facilities were provided for the manufacture of all products then made at Martinez, except tertiary butyl alcohol. The new Dominguez chemical plant was completed and the first of its units put into operation during June 1936.[57]

Very soon, small plants were erected at the Dominguez installation for the manufacture of other derivatives of these alcohols and ketones. During 1937, a new unit at Dominguez began the manufacture of diacetone alcohol, a solvent for lacquers and artificial leather components and an ingredient of hydraulic brake fluids. In 1938, two other new products went into production at Dominguez: mesityl oxide, a solvent for lacquers and thinners; and methyl isobutyl ketone, solvent for a wide range of materials, component of rubber cements, and a denaturant for ethyl alcohol. The production and sales volume of these three new products were destined for the next several years to remain small in comparison with the company's more widely known products such as acetone.[58]

Sales volume of many of the earlier chemicals continued small. Because of limited demand, no unit for the manufacture of tertiary butyl alcohol was provided at the new Dominguez plant. Then, in 1937, the Martinez plant stopped making secondary butyl alcohol and methyl ethyl ketone because the new Dominguez plant could do it cheaper. By this time, Dominguez was outproducing Martinez by more than three to one; it was in fact running in excess of anticipated capacity and at a rate sufficient to supply Shell Chemical's entire requirements of alcohols and ketones. As a result, the Martinez plant, which had the higher unit costs, was closed down from August 1938 until July 1939.[59]

Selling the Shell Chemicals

The sale of these new chemicals was far from easy. A few of the older ones, like isopropyl alcohol and acetone, were already known in the trades which had a use for them; in such cases Shell Chemical's production of them could be rapidly absorbed by the existing market. But these conditions did not prevail for most of the new Shell chemicals. The majority were new products, relatively unavailable until now, with strange new names and unexplored properties. The Shell Development and Shell Chemical people could see multitudes of uses for their new products. The problem was to create among the groups who offered a potential market, first, an awareness of these new chemicals, and, second, a willingness to try them. Further, it was desirable to do this at an early date before large sums were spent to erect plants which quite conceivably might prove unprofitable.

No ordinary sales department could be expected to handle such an assignment. This was exploratory work. It needed to be done before the decision to build the plant was made, and it had to be in the hands of experts. All these considerations led Shell Development Company in 1932 to institute a market development department as a logical part of its operations. This department, under Leo V. Steck, ten years later to become Shell Chemical's vice president in charge of sales, employed trained scientific men with an enthusiasm for new ideas to explore and develop the sales potential of proposed new products. The new department's efforts were concentrated in the beginning on developing a market for methyl ethyl ketone which had not previously been available in commercial quantities and pure form. In this attempt, Steck and his staff were highly successful. Market development has continued to be an important part of Shell Development's work and a very necessary preliminary to construction of new chemical plants.

Sales of the new chemicals, once the plants had been built and put in operation, were in the hands of the Shell Chemical sales department at San Francisco under S. S. Lawrence, chosen primarily for his familiarity with the nitrogen-fertilizer field. Lawrence's department was small, as Shell Chemical had decided that, during the initial years at least, commission agents could handle its relatively small volume more cheaply than a large, full-time, salaried sales force. Lawrence's men served primarily as sales supervisors and experts.

Original plans, as we have seen, had contemplated that the sale of Shell Chemical's nitrogen fertilizers would be confined to the Pacific Coast. Sales of the ammonia fertilizers in this area were placed in the hands of The Barrett Company, which had for some years past acted as sales agent for ammonium sulphate produced by steel manufacturers in other sections of the country. R. W. Greeff & Co., sales agents for the Dutch quinine interests, were commissioned to handle Shell Chemical's alcohols and ketones east of the Rockies. Export sales of these solvents had by 1937 assumed considerable importance; that year some 10¼ million pounds, about one-quarter of the company's total solvent sales, were marketed in 25 countries abroad. This percentage continued to increase until the outbreak of the Second World War interrupted exports.[60]

Now, at last, in the mid-Thirties, the confidence that Kessler and Waley Cohen had displayed a decade earlier began to be justified by results. Shell Chemical's million-dollar deficit of 1932 was the low point; losses were gradually cut during the ensuing years. Then, in 1936, with "double operation" of the ammonia plant in full swing, with ammonia fertilizer prices improving, and with a second, much larger solvents plant in operation at Dominguez, Shell Chemical was able to pay its first dividend, $290,000 for the year, a figure which would increase gradually as the company's capacity and markets grew.

Expansion at Emeryville

The research facilities at Emeryville continued to expand, even during the darkest periods of the Thirties. Initially, Williams and his staff had as a first order of business the discovery and development of commercially feasible processes for the manufacture of chemicals from refinery waste gases. With several Shell Chemical plants successfully making a variety of alcohols and ketones, this period was now past. Attention could at last be turned to some of the other facets of basic research which had been contemplated since the beginning.

The first of these new fields of research was oil-refining technology. In 1933, Shell Development set up a new department at Emeryville to explore basic problems in the refining field. S. Tymstra, who had long been associated with refining operations in various parts of the world, was placed in charge of this new section and given the title of associate director of research. A year later, Emeryville set up a new department of physical research under O. A. Beeck. In 1935, two additional departments were created: oil-production research under Albert G. Loomis; and research on the application of chemical products under W. J. Hund.[61]

This increased activity enlarged the staff at Emeryville beyond the capacity of the original building. A third story had been added to the original laboratory in 1933, but it was still not enough. Staff at Emeryville now totalled 250, with fifty more—clerks, stenographers, patent attorneys—in the San Francisco head office.[62] More space would be needed soon, and during 1935 additional acreage was acquired adjoining the original laboratory. This permitted much-needed expansion of Emeryville's pilot-plant installation, and the construction during 1937 of an engine-testing laboratory. To accommodate the fast-growing staff, a large new four-story laboratory and administration building, connected to the original structure, was erected in 1938.[63]

In the beginning, the Chemical and Development companies had been as inextricably mixed as the hydrocarbons in which they dealt. Now they were growing up and acquiring complete staffs of their own. They would in the future be less closely connected. The first sign of this impending maturity came at the end of 1935. Pyzel and De Bruyn, who had held identical offices in both companies, resigned their connection with Shell Development, and henceforth gave their full attention to Shell Chemical. The new president of Shell Development was J. F. M. Taylor, who had helped develop low-level cracking at Dominguez in the Twenties, and who had since 1932 been Shell Petroleum's vice president in charge of manufacturing at St. Louis.

7

Synthetic Glycerine from Propylene

RESPONSIBLE for the rapid physical growth of Shell Development were the many projects already mentioned—plus an extremely important new one, substitutive chlorination. This unorthodox chemical reaction was to open up a whole new field of industrial chemicals, the allyl derivatives, which up to now had been in the realm of laboratory chemicals. Around substitutive chlorination and the processes derived from it, Shell Chemical was to make the bulk of its new plant expenditures during the next ten years. Credit for the perfection of the discovery rightly belongs to Emeryville; and the publication of the process in detail in 1940 constitutes one of Shell Development's outstanding contributions to scientific knowledge.

During the early Thirties, Williams delighted in asking his newly hired chemists what would happen if they added chlorine (which like hydrogen has a valence of one) to propylene. Invariably they answered as they had been taught: that the chlorine atoms would attach themselves to the propylene molecule at the double bond, its point of structural weakness. And, true enough, this is what did happen when the reaction occurred *cold*.

ADDITIVE CHLORINATION

$$
\begin{array}{c}
\text{H} \quad \text{H} \quad \text{H} \\
| \qquad | \qquad | \\
\text{H}-\text{C}=\text{C}-\text{C}-\text{H} \\
| \\
\text{H}
\end{array}
\; + \; \text{Cl}-\text{Cl} \; \xrightarrow{\text{Cold}} \;
\begin{array}{c}
\text{H} \quad \text{H} \quad \text{H} \\
| \qquad | \qquad | \\
\text{H}-\text{C}-\text{C}-\text{C}-\text{H} \\
| \qquad | \qquad | \\
\text{Cl} \quad \text{Cl} \quad \text{H}
\end{array}
$$

propylene, C_3H_6 chlorine, Cl_2 dichloropropane, $C_3H_6Cl_2$

Now, what if the same ingredients were combined at high heat— say 500° C.? Not the same reaction, for this is where the phenomenon of substitutive chlorination came into play. Williams and his colleagues had not been the first to note the reaction; it had been observed at ordinary temperatures with isobutylene by a Russian, M. Scheschukow, who had published his findings in 1883–1884.[64] Little attention had been paid to this work in the half-century following. Now Shell Development was to make a thorough study of the reactions of hydrocarbons with chlorine, and emerge with some startling results.

Briefly, this is what happened in substitutive chlorination. At very high temperatures (about 500° Centigrade) the chlorine atoms, instead of attacking the double bond to form dichloropropane as shown above, left the double bond intact. One of the hydrogen atoms of the propylene was displaced by a chlorine atom to form allyl chloride, an unsaturated molecule; the other chlorine atom combined with the displaced hydrogen atom to form hydrochloric acid which could then be separated from the allyl chloride.

SUBSTITUTIVE CHLORINATION

$$
\underset{\text{propylene, } C_3H_6}{\overset{\overset{\displaystyle H \quad H \quad H}{\displaystyle | \quad | \quad |}}{H-C=C-C-H}} + \underset{\text{chlorine, } Cl_2}{Cl-Cl} \xrightarrow{500°C.} \underset{\text{allyl chloride, } C_3H_5Cl}{\overset{\overset{\displaystyle H \quad H \quad H}{\displaystyle | \quad | \quad |}}{H-C=C-C-H}} + \underset{\text{hydrochloric acid}}{HCl}
$$

This allyl chloride was a valuable chemical raw material, for it was an unsaturated molecule and therefore combined easily with other chemicals to yield a variety of highly useful products. On paper, this high-temperature chlorination of propylene to give allyl chloride is similar to the reaction Scheschukow discovered with isobutylene. However, the mechanism of the two reactions is completely different, which probably explains why the substitutive chlorination of propylene had lain undiscovered and, indeed, unattainable.[65]

One of the products that conceivably could be made from allyl chloride was glycerine—a colorless, odorless, sweet-tasting liquid normally produced as a by-product of soap manufacture. Since its discovery in 1779 by Karl Wilhelm Scheele (the Swedish chemist who also discovered oxygen, chlorine, ammonia, manganese, and barium), glycerine had been put to an increasing number of uses, and would perhaps have gone into many more products had only its price been more stable. The main supplier of glycerine was the soap industry which relied upon vegetable oils and upon the meat industry for its fats; glycerine prices, like those of meat, were always changing. This state of affairs made glycerine subject to sweeping market fluctuations; its price went up and down, from lows of 10 cents a pound to highs of 60 and 70 cents a pound. The increase in consumption of glycerine (62 million pounds in 1920, 170 million in 1936) indicated existence of a healthy market demand; the supposition was that this market might be far larger with a stable price. Beyond doubt, many potential glycerine users held back rather than risk adopting a raw material whose price could rise and fall to such an alarming degree.[66]

The first large-scale use for glycerine had been as a component of nitroglycerine and dynamite. Here price was not all-important for, under stress of war, manufacturers of explosives would pay high prices for glycerine. But during the Twenties, new peacetime uses for glycerine had appeared. Alkyd resins, made from glycerine, formed the basis of a superior new series of enamels, ideal for applications where a hard, lasting finish on metal was required, such as on automobiles and electric refrigerators. Other millions of pounds of glycerine annually were going into the new Du Pont wrapping, Cellophane, of which 17% was glycerine. Another important user was the tobacco industry which had discovered that glycerine made an ideal humectant, helping to keep cigars and cigarettes fresh and moist. None of these new users of glycerine could stand violent fluctuations in the price of their raw materials and still stay in business. When the price of glycerine got too high, they would have to raise the price of their products unduly, thereby suffering a loss in sales, or else shift over to less expensive, less desirable substitute materials.

Reasoning that these and other manufacturers who had never used glycerine because of the instability of its price might welcome a synthetic product at a stable price, Shell Development started work on a synthetic glycerine process in 1936. Substitutive chlorination was already being employed by Shell Development in the production of methallyl chloride, which had proceeded to a semi-plant scale during 1935, and in the first semi-scale production of allyl chloride and allyl alcohol which had been achieved during 1936. From here on, it was a problem not of how to proceed to glycerine but by which route. Answers were furnished by extensive research carried on at Emeryville under the direction of H. P. A. Groll.[67]

Of the six feasible routes, two were the most promising: from propylene by high-temperature substitutive chlorination to allyl chloride, from allyl chloride to allyl alcohol by hydrolysis, from allyl alcohol to chlorohydrins by reaction with hypochlorous acid, and thence to glycerine by hydrolysis. The other main route was to allyl chloride as before, then by chlorohydrination to dichlorohydrin, and from dichlorohydrin to glycerine by hydrolysis. Both of these routes were tested extensively and found satisfactory. By 1937, the synthetic glycerine process had been carried through pilot-plant operation—so satisfactorily that the following year Shell felt it was ready to announce the new process.

At the American Petroleum Institute's annual meeting in Chicago in November 1938, Williams, in an address innocently entitled "Modern Petroleum Research," startled the industry with his news.[68] He opened by observing:

> The oil industry in comparatively recent years has changed from a rather crude art, by which an abundant raw material was converted by the simplest processes into a few products which would burn or slip, into one of the great scientific industries of the day. That, incidentally, has enormous consequences in the realm of higher management. Commercial, financial, and political acumen alone are no longer sufficient foundation for the direction of this industry. The days when oil, like coal, might be . . . produced, graded, and sold into a receptive market, have gone, and with each year that passes the industry takes its place more and more in that company of scientific industries whose success depends on the ability and vision of our research workers and on the highly scientific control of the industrial operations themselves. There are unpleasant shocks awaiting those charged with the conduct of our industry who either are not well-informed on, or are unreceptive to, what is going on in several of the leading research laboratories of today.

To illustrate just how unpleasant these shocks could be, Williams went on to outline Shell Development's process for producing from petroleum a high-quality glycerine in abundance and at prices equal to or below those of the natural product. Concluding this summary, he pointed out:

> The value of synthesizing glycerine from petroleum, therefore, lies in the possibility it gives of stabilizing prices of a universally used commodity. It would not be anybody's intention to compete with existing supplies to the extent of reducing prices to unprofitable levels, but we have a process which, if necessary, could produce the

whole world requirements of glycerine from petroleum gases. This is sure to exercise a stabilizing influence on a fluctuating commodity.

At the same time, if the capacity of existing sources should fall below requirements, the petroleum industry could quickly step into the breach.

But if the existence of Shell's synthetic glycerine process acted as a brake on the manufacturers of natural glycerine, so, conversely, did low prices of natural glycerine stand in the way of a new plant to utilize the synthetic process. When Shell Development had been set up it had been agreed that any process, once it reached the commercial stage, would be turned over to Shell Oil if it were a refining process, or to Shell Chemical if it were in the realm of chemical manufacture. Shell Chemical now began a careful estimation of the costs which the glycerine process would entail, balancing them against anticipated receipts.

These calculations were not encouraging. At prevailing prices, the margin of profit would be far too low to warrant the construction of an expensive new plant. Heretofore, Shell Chemical had dealt in processes which could be started in a relatively modest way and then expanded as demand for the product increased. With glycerine it was quite a different story. A small plant could not hope to operate economically. It had to be a large plant or none at all. Having just escaped six years of deficit operation—and, to be truthful, not quite sure that the days of deficits were yet over—Shell Chemical was chary of undertaking additional large expenditures which might put it right back in the red.

The only hope for a glycerine plant at this juncture would be a long-term contract, if one could be arranged, to dispose of a large percentage of the proposed plant's annual output. Pyzel (who still retained his connection with Shell Chemical, although he had come to New York as vice president of Shell Union in 1937) looked over the field to see if he couldn't find such a customer. It wasn't a far search to pick out Du Pont, one of America's largest manufacturers of the things that used glycerine in large amounts—nitroglycerine, dynamite, cellophane, and the large line of Duco paints and lacquers. Surely, it would be in Du Pont's interest to have an abundant supply of glycerine at stable prices.

Pyzel went to see the Du Pont people and found them very much interested. They suggested that Shell put up a plant. Pyzel pointed out that it wasn't quite that simple, that Shell Chemical would need large supplies of chlorine which it did not produce. The Du Pont people then mentioned a plant of theirs in New Jersey that had an overproduction of chlorine, and suggested that Shell could erect a glycerine plant nearby. But Shell Chemical had no manufacturing operations east of the Rockies and Shell Oil none east of Wood River. Pyzel knew it would be hard to persuade the Shell management to build a plant in the East, especially one which would take part of its raw material from, and sell all of its finished product to, a single customer. Since a stable supply of glycerine was in Du Pont's interest and since Du Pont already had the necessary chlorine, Shell at this point countered with a suggestion that Du Pont build the plant, using the Shell process under a license arrangement. Here the Du Pont people hesitated, and here the matter was to rest for a full decade.[69]

In the war years which came so soon afterward, both Shell and Du Pont were to wish many times that this plant had been built. But for the moment, the new glycerine process remained in the role Williams had forecast for it—a brake upon the price of natural glycerine, and a guarantee of ample production if at any time the soap industry could not meet the demand. Eventually, it was just such a long-term contract from Du Pont and thirteen other companies that helped the glycerine plant get started at Houston in 1948, after the long delays and interruptions occasioned by war.

Houston Plant

These discussions with Du Pont had served to highlight Shell Chemical's need for plant facilities east of the Rockies. Proverbially, the chemical industry is one which "takes in its own washing." Most chemical companies depend upon other chemical companies both as a source of raw materials and a customer for finished products. This fact did not operate in Shell Chemical's favor, for a great percentage of the American chemical industry was concentrated in the industrial areas of the Atlantic Seaboard. Because Shell Oil had no refinery on the Atlantic Coast, the company could not, of course, build a plant in this area, unless it proposed to purchase its raw materials (refinery gases) from refiners other than Shell. It could, however, do the next best thing: build a plant at Houston, adjoining the large Shell refinery there. By-product gases were available there from the refinery's cracking units, and products could be shipped to the Atlantic Seaboard by water transportation.

During 1940, construction of a new chemical plant got under way on a site immediately south of the Houston refinery. It was designed to produce in large quantities the chemicals with which Shell Chemical had experienced such success, isopropyl alcohol and acetone. This large, new plant went quietly into operation late in November 1941 and during its first year more than doubled Shell Chemical's acetone output.[70]

The second part of the new Houston plant was of far greater current interest. It got under way in September 1941, the first in the United States to make butadiene on a commercial scale.[71] Its story, however, is properly a part of the chapter on the war years.

8

Other Research, Other Laboratories

To PRESENT a fair account of the activities of Shell Development and Shell Chemical during the Thirties is the work of a full-length book, instead of a single chapter. It should be noted, then, that mention has been omitted of less spectacular but equally important work done by the Development company's oil production section under Loomis: successful acid-solvent treatment of oil wells (1936), development of improved water-base drilling fluids (1936), improved methods for analyzing drill cores (1938), and new knowledge of oilfield flow (1938). Or the extensive work done both at Emeryville and Amsterdam on separation processes and the design of fractionation columns, work which helped make the Shell organization outstanding in both those fields.

Important to the research work done by the various Shell companies were (1) some sort of arrangement to provide for free exchange of technical information, and (2) a clear understanding as to responsibility for taking out and licensing patents. These arrangements were formalized in the so-called Simplex agreement, a patent-licensing and information-exchange contract between the Shell companies in America and those in Europe, signed in April 1932 and made retroactive to January 1, 1929. All signatories to the agreement received paid-up licenses under the old Trumble patents owned by Simplex, and it was agreed that henceforth all patents (except for ammonia manufacture) acquired by any of the Shell companies should be the property of Shell Development in North America and of B. P. M. in the rest of the world. Shell Union would receive a free license for the use of its subsidiaries. The Simplex agreement was important in that it established the broad outlines of patent policy and information-exchange arrangements among the various Shell companies.[72]

Exchange of information was more difficult in practice than it sounded on paper. Responsibility for corrective measures fell to Tydeman, who had been transferred from his post in St. Louis to Shell Development Company late in 1932. In this capacity, Tydeman did considerable work in standardizing report forms and laboratory classifications; and he prevailed upon the Amsterdam laboratory to prepare its reports in English, for most Dutch scientists wrote easily in English. His job was also to find out what the refinery laboratories were doing, and in this connection he and Van Senden instituted in 1936 the Shell Oil-Shell Development meetings which in the beginning were held at intervals of every six weeks. In these meetings, a distinction was made between *research*, which implied fresh investigation, and *development* which was improvement of current operation.[73]

In this latter field, improvement of current operation, groups had grown up in both the San Francisco and St. Louis manufacturing departments which proved of immense help in coordinating research. They were the nuclei of what later became the product application departments. A. G. Marshall headed the San Francisco group; A. B. Culbertson the one in St. Louis (located after 1940 in New York).

The manufacturing departments had laboratories of their own and an account of Shell research activity is not complete without some mention of them. Previously conducted on a small scale, these refinery laboratories were expanded during the Thirties to keep pace with the new, more complicated processes and processing equipment. All these laboratories were engaged in *applied* research, as distinguished from *fundamental* research being carried on by Shell Development at Emeryville.

Martinez Laboratory

The first of the refinery laboratories was, of course, the one connected with Martinez. Before that refinery was even completed, Dr. Alphonse W. Jurrissen, the young Dutch chemist who had come over to take charge of the refinery laboratory, had set himself up in the laboratory of the American Oriental Company's refinery on Bull's

Head, Martinez, the installation which Shell had rented pending completion of its own Martinez plant. There Jurrissen and a small staff made up the first Shell laboratory in America. Soon after the new Martinez refinery started up in 1916, this staff moved into a new laboratory on the refinery grounds. In addition to routine analytical work, the Martinez laboratory undertook several experimental projects during 1916: investigations, among other things, into kerosene treating to remove aromatics and the possibility of making medicinal petrolatums from California crude oil.[74]

The old Trumble converter was also part of this laboratory at Martinez and work was continued on it sporadically for several years. Another early experiment, treatment of lubricating oils with clay, had progressed to such a point by 1919 that plant-sized trials of it began in that year. In 1922, a separate building to house the investigational work was built and the following year, Dr. G. P. Koch, formerly a chemist with a Philadelphia pharmaceutical house, was placed in charge of it. The new laboratory's first project was the removal of sulphur and gum from pressure distillate.[75]

The continuing development of automobile engines called for different performance characteristics in gasoline. In order to keep the refinery abreast in this respect, Van Senden in 1921 hired G. A. Kramer, a mechanical engineer engaged in engine research for the U. S. Bureau of Mines, and set him up in a motor laboratory which at the start consisted of a four-cylinder Continental engine equipped with a dynamometer. Later, during 1924–1926, Kramer did valuable work on high-vacuum distillation of lubricating oils and took out several patents.[76] With the advent of the depression, research at Martinez slowed down to a standstill and was not expanded until the late Thirties.

Wood River Laboratory

At Wood River, the development of the refinery laboratory took a roughly parallel course, although it differed in detail. A control laboratory was set up when the refinery went on stream in 1918 and was in charge of Ralph R. Mathews,‡ who had been a member of Jurrissen's first staff. During the early Twenties, the Wood River laboratory did a mixture of analytical and experimental work with

‡ Later executive vice president of the Battenfeld Grease & Oil Corp., Kansas City.

the analytical work predominating. Then, in 1927, a Ricardo engine was brought from England (the first variable-compression engine in the United States) and put in charge of T. B. Rendel, a relative of Ricardo. This early engine work was in the nature of testing rather than research. During 1928, product performance research started at Wood River when four chemists, Dr. E. R. P. E. Retailliau, Dr. G. H. von Fuchs, Dr. N. J. G. Alozerÿ, and E. G. Travis, were hired and put to work on gasoline treating and lubricants manufacture. In 1933, their work and Rendel's engine work were separated from the refinery control laboratory and set up as a separate research laboratory.[77]

By 1935, the engine-testing section of the Wood River laboratory had acquired a variety of test engines and in 1938 a new building was erected to house this section, along with the chemical section which by now had been greatly enlarged. Generally speaking, the subsequent work of the Wood River laboratory was concentrated on product development and product performance, with the evolution of processes and processing equipment being left to other Shell laboratories.

With Shell's entry into the manufacture of 100-octane gasoline, Doolittle arranged for fuel laboratories throughout the oil industry to purchase 70,000 gallons of iso-octane to test aviation fuels for antiknock rating. Shell and Standard of New Jersey each produced one-half of this original batch; after that, Shell supplied the whole quantity of this pure iso-octane, known as S-Reference Fuel. It was made at the Wood River laboratory. About 1933, work done at the Wood River laboratory resulted in the adoption of a cetane-number system for rating Diesel-engine fuels in a fashion somewhat similar to the octane-number system used for automobile engines. The Wood River laboratory undertook to make and supply this Diesel reference fuel to the laboratories of the whole industry, a practice which still continued in 1956.[78]

By the end of the Thirties, Wood River had a large and well-equipped laboratory. It had done much to improve the techniques of testing, had developed new products such as anti-rust steam turbine oil, and had added immeasurably to the company's reputation among manufacturers of automotive, aircraft, and Diesel engines.

Wilmington Laboratory

The newer refineries in Southern California and Houston also had research laboratories. Since both refineries were volume producers of a comparatively few petroleum products, it was only natural that their research should revolve about processes and process equipment. Experiments on clay-treating of gasoline were conducted at Wilmington, 1924–1927; and considerable pioneer work on fractional distillation and column design, 1927–1931. This work was not done in a formal laboratory devoted to research but was conducted by the refinery's technological department. One noteworthy product, the Super-Shell gasoline put on the market in California in 1930, was developed at Wilmington 1929–1930. During the Thirties investigative efforts at Wilmington were confined almost entirely to process research.[79]

Houston Refinery Laboratory

Refinery research at Houston began in 1933, when Dr. Ivan Cliff was assigned to cracking problems and Dr. J. D. Long to fractionating problems. Cliff was provided with a thermal cracking pilot plant and began a long series of runs to evaluate the cracking characteristics of a large variety of crude oils. For Long's work on fractionation, a 100-plate, 100-foot-tall column was built, capable of fractionation precise enough to take a one-quart fraction from a 100-barrel charge.[80] By 1934, the number of these experimental columns had increased to eight. Five years later in 1939, under the managership of Dr. Harold Gershinowitz,§ a laboratory building was erected for the Houston refinery research group and the thermal cracking and fractionation pilot plants were moved to a location adjoining the building. To these two important refining processes, cracking and fractionation, the Houston laboratory has devoted almost all its efforts.

Geophysical Laboratory

The geophysical laboratory, built by Shell Petroleum at Houston in the mid-Thirties, could trace its origins back to the company's first use of the torsion balance in 1922. These early instruments, like the long procession of geophysical tools that followed them, were in constant need of expert adjustment and repair. Because this work was delicate and highly specialized, the company found it necessary from the beginning to maintain a seismic workshop to keep existing instruments in repair and manufacture new or modified instruments as the

§ Later (1945) to head Shell's exploration and production research center at Houston, and still later (1953) to become over-all head of Shell research activity as president of Shell Development Company.

occasion arose. This seismic workshop led a wandering existence during the late Twenties and early Thirties, being located for short periods of time at Houston (two locations), Dallas, and then Houston again.

Soon after Bloemgarten became vice president in charge of exploration and production at St. Louis in 1935, he encouraged the establishment of a permanent geophysical center which would be more than a workshop and have facilities for geophysical research, as well. A site was purchased on Bellaire Boulevard just south of the Houston city limits and there a modern laboratory building was completed in July 1936. A nucleus of highly trained technical men was assembled under Frank Goldstone, chief geophysicist, and much new design work was done on improved geophysical instruments. By 1938, the staff numbered forty people.

During these years, the workshop facilities at the Houston geophysical laboratory, which were under the supervision of Dr. Eugen Merten, manufactured an ever-increasing number of seismic instruments for the use of Shell companies in the United States and also for sale to associated companies abroad. Until the war interrupted exchange of personnel, the Houston laboratory also served as a training center for Shell geophysicists from other countries. Following the war, the new exploration and production research center was built on adjoining land.[81]

Sewaren Oil Burner Research

Another research group that had been working away since 1930 was insignificant in size, but important for the results it was later to produce. As noted in an earlier chapter, range oil burners and domestic furnace burners had made their appearance in the New England states during the Twenties. The New England Oil Refining Company had begun some investigation of the fuels for these burners, and one of that company's sales engineers, E. B. Glendenning, was assigned to range and oil burner fuel. His activities were continued by the new Shell Eastern company, and in the fall of 1930, W. A. Sullivan, Jr., and L. H. Ventres were assigned to fuel and oil burner research in a small laboratory set up at the Sewaren, New Jersey, terminal. There a variety of fuel blends were burned under simulated operating conditions to give Shell a wealth of data on the peformance of various fuels, a field in which few oil companies were doing research. Sullivan and Ventres were joined by Glendenning in the mid-Thirties and in the years following 1940 they were able to announce several important developments.[82]

This, then, was the complexion of Shell research from 1930 to 1940. In laboratories ranging in size from the five hundred at Emeryville to the two men at Sewaren, competent graduates of America's technical schools were at work on many phases of petroleum research. They were involved in fundamental research such as determining the nature of friction or the qualities of a lubricant. They were developing new products to be made from former wastes, thus launching their company into the new chemical business. They were improving older products, adding new properties that would better serve the customer's needs. They were cooperating constantly with the manufacturers of automotive, aircraft, and Diesel engines, of oil burners and other petroleum-consuming equipment, in an attempt to anticipate requirements. They were, in a word, applying inquisitive minds to any course that gave promise of doing a job better or cheaper, always with an ultimate goal in mind: to utilize in the most profitable manner every possible fraction of a barrel of crude oil. For years the meat packers had boasted that they used everything of a pig except his squeal; by the late Thirties a lot of oil men were beginning to feel the same way. But wiser heads among them suspected it was only the beginning.

CHAPTER X

United for the War Effort

1941–1945

Bʏ 1942, the Second World War had spread from Europe to engulf hundreds of millions of the earth's population on every continent. It was a new kind of war, of enormous size and amazing speed, a war of movement carried on by mechanized armies supported by staggering quantites of matériel.

Military mechanization, begun hesitantly during the 1914–1918 conflict, was now complete. Every foot soldier in the field was preceded by fast-moving motor tanks, flanked by motorized artillery, and supported by a never-ending stream of motor trucks, command cars, jeeps, and other specialized vehicles. A typical division in World War I had employed mechanized equipment to the extent of 4,000 horsepower; its counterpart twenty-five years later averaged 187,000 horsepower, an increase of nearly 5,000%.[1] In the sky overhead, a genuine revolution had occurred. Clouds of fast new reconnaissance and fighter planes sped through the air, a sharp contrast to the few lumbering old crates of World War I. And bombers, brand-new aerial weapons of ever-increasing speed and range, carried their loads of destruction deep into enemy territory. The naval war was waged not only on the surface of the sea, but in the air above and the depths below.

It was a war of machines, complicated, fantastically expensive machines, machines with a voracious appetite for supplies of all kinds, but particularly of petroleum. Every one of these war machines needed oil—gasoline for tanks and trucks and jeeps; a superior grade of it for fighter planes and bombers; oil fuels for transports, submarines, and battleships; and lubricants for them all. From beginning to end, World War II was a war of oil. Oil must get through, and in sufficient quantity. Without it, every military operation would stop. In the military camp, oil was heat and light; in the field, it was electricity for radios and telephones; it supplied the cooking fires for Army kitchens, the refrigeration for blood plasma. It was the margin between life and death, success and failure. Without oil, all military operations must halt.

Between December 1941 and August 1945 the Allied war machine used almost seven billion barrels of oil, a quantity that transcends imagination. The United States was called upon to supply nearly six of these seven billion barrels, some 85% of the total, an amount equal to more than a quarter of all the oil produced in America from the time of Drake's original well in 1859 up to the beginning of 1941. Some idea of the vastness of these supplies may be gathered from the shipping needed to transport it. Oil accounted for more than half of all the cargo shipped overseas during the war, and in several invasions it comprised more than 65% of the total tonnage.[2] To undertake a supply program of such magnitude and vital importance was a fearful responsibility. To meet these requirements promptly and fully, without the familiar "too little, too late" of wartime was indeed a remarkable achievement. "At no time," wrote the Army-Navy Petroleum Board at the end of the war, "did the Services lack for oil in the proper quantities, in the proper kinds, and at the proper places. . . . Not a single operation was delayed or impeded because of lack of petroleum products. No Government agency and no branch of American industry achieved a prouder war record."[3]

Tremendous as it was, this achievement was not all. Essential civilian requirements, more than double in volume the needs of the military,[4] were successfully met, and in two other major departments of the war effort, the American oil industry played an important role by furnishing materials for synthetic rubber and explosives. Deprived of normal rubber supplies by the fall of Malaya and the East Indies, the country was confronted with a critical shortage of rubber which could have delayed Allied military operations by one to two years. Such a disaster was averted by the untiring, single-minded cooperation of all who had a hand in the manufacture of synthetic rubber. Foremost among these were the oil companies, who were able to make from petroleum two-thirds of the nation's requirements of butadiene, the most important ingredient of synthetic rubber.

In the manufacture of explosives and munitions, oil went not to fill a deficiency, as it did in the case of synthetic rubber, but to augment supplies from regular sources which proved inadequate to the full load of wartime demand. One of the most spectacular explosives of both World Wars was T.N.T. used in "blockbusting" aerial bombs, depth charges, naval and land mines. How the oil industry helped fill this gap was another heartening wartime production story.

Equally heartening—at least to those inside the oil industry—was the discovery that dozens of hotly competing oil companies could drop their mutual antagonisms and cooperate without stint, exchanging with each other their valued technical information, trade secrets, and "know-how," lending highly trained personnel to competitors, and even making available to the rest of the industry, without charge, patents that were very valuable business properties. A quarter of a century earlier, during World War I, another generation of oil men had made the pleasant discovery that they could work together harmoniously for the common good. But two decades of hard-fighting competition and the retirement from the business of virtually all of the older generation of oil men had pretty effectively erased memories of this earlier wartime cooperation.

The industry (or parts of it) had during the early Thirties cooperated in the N.R.A. and, slightly later, in the formulation of the conservation laws. Memories of these experiences were often far from pleasant. Frequently the oil men had found themselves in sharp conflict with each other and with Secretary of the Interior Ickes, who had acted as Petroleum Administrator under the N.R.A. code. Next followed a period of several years when Ickes had pressed for, and the industry successfully resisted, Federal control of oil conservation. Then came the Madison Trial in the late Thirties, with several members of the Industry being prosecuted in court for carrying out what they maintained were Secretary Ickes' instructions, and Ickes refusing to appear as a witness at their trial. It was small wonder, then, that few could foresee anything but bad times ahead when, late in May 1941, the President set up a new agency, the Office of Petroleum Coordinator for National Defense, and appointed Ickes to head it. This appointment followed by one day the President's declaration on May 27, 1941, of an "unlimited national emergency." The duties of the new agency were (1) to determine the increased amounts of petroleum products that would be needed for rearmament, and (2) to make specific recommendations for fulfilling these requirements.[5]

The new agency had no powers of compulsion, so from the start Secretary Ickes adopted a conciliatory course. This change of attitude was first manifested early in June 1941 when Ickes appointed a lifelong oil man and sales executive of Standard of California, Ralph K.

Davies, to the position of deputy coordinator with authority equal to Ickes' own. This pleasant surprise was an earnest of the changed climate in Washington. Only a little earlier one could have expected to see such an agency staffed with doctrinaire economists armed with directives, intent upon remaking the world and regulating the oil business to their hearts' content. But now that the government was in dead earnest, it called upon the oil industry for the very reasons which had seemed "crimes" to many New Dealers only months before—the industry's bigness, the size and efficiency of the large units within it, its ingenuity and self-reliance in matters such as transportation.

The new Petroleum Coordinator and his deputy proposed to organize their agency along the same lines used in the oil business— exploration, production, transportation, refining, etc.—and to invite in to run these departments the most experienced operating oil men they could find. They would try to keep orders and regulations to a minimum, relying on the industry to achieve the desired goals through voluntary action, and they suggested that the industry create a com- mittee organization to assist the government in these matters.

This forthright and intelligent approach had the effect intended. A few days after Davies' appointment, a meeting was called in Washing- ton and there Ickes and Davies outlined their proposals for a "govern- ment-industry team" based not upon coercion but upon voluntary cooperation. They described the organization they had in mind: a small Washington staff and five district operating divisions, organized on a business basis and managed by people of recognized ability and long experience in the oil business. They appealed to the oil men for their complete cooperation and asked that the industry proceed at once to set up committees for each of these five districts. These com- mittees, the first of which were set up in July 1941, were called simply "Petroleum Industry Committee for District No. 1," "Petroleum In- dustry Committee for District No. 2," etc. The five districts were No. 1 (office in New York, territory Eastern Seaboard, Maine to Florida), No. 2 (office in Chicago, territory the Mid-Continent from Ohio to Oklahoma), No. 3 (the Gulf-Southwest from Alabama to New Mexico with headquarters in Houston), No. 4 (the Rocky Mountain states, office at Denver), and No. 5 (office in Los Angeles) covering the Pacific Coast states, Alaska, and Hawaii.[6]

The voluntary industry committees for each of these O.P.C. dis- tricts were composed of a general over-all committee and divisional subcommittees for marketing, refining, production, transportation, and so on. The members were active oil men, appointed by the Office of the Petroleum Coordinator, and they served without pay. They collected the data upon which supply and demand estimates were based, attended to the physical execution of policies established by the official government oil agency, and acted as liaison on the local level between the government agency and the industry. The expense of these district offices was met by contributions of the individual oil companies.[7]

These district industry committees did such valuable work that the O.P.C. decided late in 1941 to create a similar national committee, made up of the leaders of the industry, to meet periodically in Washington. The government agency asked 79 industry leaders to serve on this committee, which was called the Petroleum Industry War Council (P.I.W.C.). It held its first meeting in Washington on December 8, 1941, the day the United States entered the war. The P.I.W.C. met on the average of once a month thereafter all during the war.[8] This group, comprising as it did the pick of the country's oil executives, offered the government oil agency an excellent audience for its views and, conversely, provided the government agency with an almost instant means of obtaining "the industry view" of any proposed course of action. The harmonious government-industry partnership in oil affairs throughout the war was in great measure a direct result of the mutual trust and understanding developed in these P.I.W.C. and industry district committee meetings.

In April 1942, the Office of Petroleum Coordinator for National Defense changed its name to Office of Petroleum Coordinator for War, but it was not until December 1942 that a successor agency, the Petroleum Administration for War (P.A.W.) was created with full wartime powers, retaining the staff and policies of its predecessor organization. For a full year and a half the industry had been honoring the formal "recommendations" of the Petroleum Coordinator so faithfully that no one could detect the difference when these recommendations became legally enforceable orders of the Petroleum Administration for War. Unlike other war agencies, the P.A.W. never found it necessary to create a "compliance division" to handle the enforcement of its directives and orders. And the actual number of orders issued was very small—only 50, and not all of these were in effect at one time.[9]

For staff, the P.A.W. and its predecessors turned to the oil companies, asking for qualified executives of long experience familiar with every aspect of the business. Since these men were also the top management talent of the companies employing them, the question might well have arisen: Can they be spared? But it did not. Through meeting places such as the P.I.W.C., the companies were convinced of the necessity for supplying the government with the very best assistance available. Top executives and highly trained technical personnel were encouraged to serve their turn when called upon, even though it meant a substantial financial sacrifice for most of them.

As a result, the P.A.W. avoided the blunders, large staffs, and constant confusion that were characteristic of many another wartime production agency. At its peak, in mid-1943, the P.A.W. had less than 1,500 employees counting the Washington organization and the employees of its five district offices at New York, Chicago, Houston, Denver, and Los Angeles. A further index of the efficiency of this business management in government was the cost of operating the P.A.W. and its predecessor agencies. For the entire period, from May 1941 until May 1946, total operating expense was less than $19,000,000 —certainly the cheapest of the major wartime agencies.[10]

The story of the war period is above all else the story of a cooperative effort, with contributions being made not by one company, or even by a handful of companies, but by the whole of the oil industry. To disentangle the story of Shell's particular contributions to this joint effort is, therefore, not always possible; and, where possible, not always fair, because equally important contributions were made by others. From the first, the Shell Union companies joined every cooperative effort without hesitation. In some of these efforts, they took the lead. In all of them, they played a substantial and highly creditable part. Outstanding were Shell's roles in the manufacture of 100-octane aviation gasoline, in the supply of butadiene for synthetic rubber, in the production of toluene for explosives, in the creation of the military portable pipe line. These developments will be discussed in this order.

Development of 100-Octane

THE manufacture of 100-octane gasoline was one of the important production stories of the war. To appreciate it, the reader will need to know, at least roughly, what 100-octane is and how it is made on a commercial scale.

The commercial iso-octane, which Shell shipped to the Army Air Corps at Wright Field in April 1934, was "100-octane" in that it rated 100 on the octane scale. But no one proposed that iso-octane be used as a finished fuel. Foreseeable supplies of it promised to be too limited for that; it was, even at Shell's new low price, too expensive for fuel; and it lacked many desirable fuel properties, such as volatility needed for cold-weather starting. Wright Field blended these first quantities of Shell iso-octane with a high-quality aviation gasoline from California and added enough tetraethyl lead to bring the octane-rating of the mixture up to 100. The cost of such a blend was less than half the cost of pure iso-octane, and it had in addition necessary fuel properties such as volatility.[11]

From this point onward, blending became standard practice in the production of premium-grade aviation fuels. The base of the blend would be a good, high-grade gasoline produced from selected crudes by straight-run refining methods. To this would be added nearly as much commercial iso-octane, and then smaller quantities of other high-antiknock hydrocarbons. This mixture of "base stock" and high-antiknock hydrocarbons generally rated somewhere about 90 on the octane scale. Enough tetraethyl lead (between 3 and 4 cubic centimeters per gallon) was then added to bring the rating of the blend up to 100.[12] This blend was 100-octane gasoline, the fuel of which America would hear so much during the next decade.

Once 100-octane had made its initial appearance, interested oil technologists turned their efforts toward improving the yield and lowering the price of first one, and then the other of the components which went into the 100-octane blend. During the remainder of the 1930's the high-antiknock components received the lion's share of the attention.

It was success in the manufacture of a high-antiknock hydrocarbon, iso-octane, that had made the first 100-octane gasoline a reality. How Shell first produced this once-expensive hydrocarbon on a commercial scale has been mentioned in the preceding chapter. How the company next proceeded, in the depths of the depression, to invest heavily in new plant capacity for producing iso-octane is an even more creditable story. Actual production, on a large scale, was needed to demonstrate that 100-octane gasoline could be made generally available and that the price could be reduced to a reasonable level. Unless this convincing practical demonstration had been made, there would have been little further development of 100-octane manufacturing methods—and little, if any, improvement in aircraft engines to take advantage of the new fuel.

For his highly intelligent efforts in selling the Air Corps and the management of his own company on the desirability of 100-octane fuel and the necessity of building on faith large-scale plants to make it, Doolittle deservedly receives a large measure of credit. Within the Shell executive group there was general appreciation of, and belief in, the future of aviation; this attitude counted in Doolittle's favor and did much to ease his job. Ever since Shell in London had begun under-writing Ricardo's fuel experimentation some twenty years earlier, the Shell Group had on a number of occasions undertaken surprisingly large expenditures in the long-term interest of developing the aviation market. The results of this policy were clearly visible: during this twenty-year period, the Shell companies all over the world had managed to stay out ahead of their chief competitors in most matters pertaining to aviation. It was therefore not surprising that Shell Oil and Shell Petroleum should decide to take a gamble on new plant construction for aviation gasoline at a time when economy and cost cutting were chief considerations in every department of the business.

During 1935, they built and put into operation three large-scale iso-octane plants, one each at the Martinez, Houston, and Wood River refineries. By June 1936, these three plants were capable of producing 6,000,000 gallons of iso-octane a year. Their chief competition was from Standard Oil of New Jersey which had installed its first iso-octane plant (100 barrels a day) at Baton Rouge in September 1935. During the second half of 1935, the Air Corps bought 900,000 gallons of 100-octane gasoline, 600,000 gallons from Shell, the balance from Standard of New Jersey. This volume production and sale had the anticipated effect upon price; by June 1936, 100-octane gasoline was selling for 18¢ to 20¢ a gallon, against 50¢ a year earlier. Shell's 100-octane blends at this time were 42% iso-octane, so the company's iso-octane production at this point was enough to make 14,500,000 gallons of 100-octane gasoline a year, half again as much as Doolittle's total estimate of Army and Navy requirements for the year ending June 30, 1937.[13]

In his book *Development of Aviation Fuels*, S. D. Heron, a leading independent expert associated with aircraft engine and fuel development for more than thirty years, tells the course events took at this point: "J. H. Doolittle (later Lt. General, USAAF), then Aviation Manager of Shell, in particular risked his future by persuading Shell to go heavily into plant expansion for the production of 100-octane fuel. The risk taken by Doolittle was shown when the Wright Field plans for service test of 100-octane fuel were opposed by the Army General Staff, and for some time the purchases by the Army were not sufficient to keep the plants newly installed by the oil industry operating at anything like capacity. The Army General Staff was slow to appreciate the advantages of 100-octane fuel and, in addition, was disturbed about the possibility of insufficient supply in time of emergency. Wright Field battled the General Staff for about two years over the question of standardizing 100-octane fuel for all combat aircraft. . . . Had the General Staff been able to foresee that the daily consumption of 100-octane fuel . . . would be about 20,000,000 gallons by the combat forces of the United States alone during World War II, Wright Field would doubtless have lost the argument."[14] On the other hand, Heron adds, had the General Staff been able to foresee that the oil industry would be able to meet this staggering demand, and at the low price of approximately 16¢ a gallon, there probably would have been no argument in the first place.

Confronted with the necessity for planning fuel supply for a wide range of motorized equipment amid the confusion and hurry of war, the Army General Staff had adopted one of those theoretically perfect ideas: it wanted all engines from motorcycles to bomber planes designed so that they could utilize a single fuel and thus simplify supply problems in wartime. The Air Corps Matériel Command at Wright Field, Dayton, Ohio, responsible for research and development for the Air Corps, promptly proceeded to demolish the General Staff's position. Tests conducted at Wright Field during 1934 with 100-octane gasoline, made from Shell iso-octane, had given excellent results. Even with existing engines, 100-octane gave increases in power output of 15% to 30% over the power obtainable with 75-octane gasoline. In its campaign against what it considered the inertia of the

War Department, Wright Field in the spring of 1935 took the highly unorthodox step of publishing its research data.[15]

This information had an immediate effect upon the aircraft engine industry. Wright Aeronautical at once began to design an 8-to-1 compression-ratio engine, capable of utilizing the power and economy of 100-octane. Test results of this new engine, made public early in 1936, were another landmark in the development of modern aviation. Not only did the Wright engine make possible substantial increases in power: it also reported fuel savings of at least 15%, opening up a vista of long-range military aircraft. These and many other points were thoroughly aired at a hearing held at Wright Field in November 1936. As a result, the Army committee finally recommended the adoption of 100-octane fuel for combat, and ordered that all Air Corps engines (except those of training planes) be designed for 100-octane fuel after January 1, 1938.[16]

Meanwhile, Shell built additional iso-octane manufacturing facilities at the Wilmington refinery, completed in July 1936. With the existing plants at Martinez, Houston, and Wood River, the company's total investment in this risky new business now stood at $2,000,000.[17] For the nation it was a worth-while investment, for early large-scale production of iso-octane from these plants gave aircraft engine manufacturers an opportunity to design and build more powerful high-compression engines then, in the mid-Thirties, instead of having to wait until the country was in the midst of a war. For this initial advantage, the Air Corps—and the public—could thank the Shell polymerization processes, and the men who risked the money to put them into full-scale operation.

How did companies like Shell, Jersey Standard, and Phillips, all active developers of 100-octane gasoline manufacture during the Thirties, justify such long-range gambles to their shareholders? They usually couldn't on a strict profit-and-loss basis. Heron, who worked closely with them during this period, wrote: "This commercial competition was a result of the profit motive, but was far from profitable . . . and was really competition for technical prestige. Technical prestige in the case of aviation often punishes the corporate balance sheet but may be said to be profitable in the sense that a company engaged in any branch of the aviation business goes out of business sooner or later if technical prestige is lacking." [18]

Shell's organized research and technology, described in the previous chapter, had by the outbreak of the war grown into a tremendously large technical organization—how large we realize when we try to apportion credit for developments such as 100-octane gasoline. Merely to mention by name those who played an important part in this development would require the compilation of long and, for the reader, tedious lists of Shell Oil, Shell Development, and Shell Chemical engineers and chemists, to say nothing of their counterparts simultaneously at work in B.P.M.'s huge laboratories at Amsterdam. In a like manner, it is almost equally difficult for any one company, or nationality, to establish exclusive claims to these complicated technological developments. Organized research has brought hundreds of parallel discoveries—developments so similar that disinterested writers are often baffled by company claims that seem conflicting, or even identical. Few of these flat claims will stand up under scrutiny; indeed, it will usually develop that such claims were originated not by the company's research men but by lay members of the staff who were unfamiliar with the full complexity of the subject.

In the case of 100-octane, almost every oil company laboratory made contributions—some, it is true, more important than others. The sum total of these parallel and complementary discoveries, plus the equally important operating techniques developed by the few firms with commercial units, comprised the patents and "know-how" that made possible large-scale manufacture of 100-octane during the war.

With these cautionary words firmly in mind, we will now mention briefly the few processes that were most important to 100-octane manufacture. Of first importance chronologically were the Shell polymerization processes, employed in the five plants installed by the company between 1935 and 1937.

The Polymerization Processes

Polymerization—combining two unsaturated molecules with each other, usually by catalytic action, to form a third, larger molecule— was not new as a chemical reaction, having been known and practiced in organic chemistry laboratories at least since the 1870's. The unsaturated gases produced in petroleum cracking and in the coal tar industry offered the organic chemist a prolific source of materials for use in polymerization. Many besides Shell (among others the Universal Oil Products Company, of Chicago, Anglo-Iranian Oil Company in England, the I. G. Farbenindustrie in Germany, and Imperial Chemical Industries, Ltd., in England) had by the mid-Thirties investigated polymerization of one or another of these unsaturated gases, using various catalysts, and had taken out a number of patents.[19]

Standard of New Jersey had since 1929 made by small-scale polymerization methods a di-isobutylene that the Ethyl Corporation hydrogenated into chemically pure iso-octane and sold to motor-testing laboratories who used it as the basis of the octane-rating scale.[20] In spite of this early start, it apparently did not occur to either of these companies that iso-octane cheap enough for use as a gasoline component might be produced in a similar manner. Shell's achievement was to see this possibility, to do the research necessary for the development of an inexpensive process, and to succeed—accomplishments more difficult than they sound.

The first process, developed at Emeryville and installed full-scale during 1935 at the Martinez, Houston, and Wood River refineries, was called cold-acid polymerization. The C_4 gas fraction (butanes, butylenes, and isobutylenes) was contacted with sulphuric acid of 65% concentration at room temperature. The acid, at this strength and temperature, absorbed up to 90% of the highly reactive isobutylenes. In this manner, the isobutylenes were separated from the butanes and normal butylenes with which they had been mixed. Next, this mixture of sulphuric acid and isobutylene was heated to 212°F. and held there for about a minute. The resulting chemical reaction produced a product containing about 75% di-isobutylene. This "polymer" product was then separated from the acid, washed with caustic, and distilled.[21] The next step in the process was the addition of hydrogen, using a Shell-owned low-pressure hydrogenation process. The finished product was commercially pure iso-octane, suitable for blending with base stock to make 100-octane gasoline.

Although the Shell cold-acid polymerization process worked well and produced a remarkably pure product, no one in the Shell organization was content to rest with it. To lower the price, yields needed to be increased by every method available. Of the C_4 gases (butanes, butylenes, and isobutylenes), the cold-acid process utilized only iso-butylene, and not all of that. Counting losses during polymerization, purification, and hydrogenation, only about two-thirds of the isobutylene charge stock eventually wound up as iso-octane. Emeryville set to work to see if another process could be devised capable of utilizing a greater portion of the available feed stocks.

In remarkably short time, the Shell hot-acid polymerization process was announced. By using a hot sulphuric acid solution (140°–194°F.)

of the same 65% concentration, and by carefully elevating the temperature, Emeryville was able to absorb all of the isobutylene feed stock plus a good part of the normal butylenes. Then, manipulating the temperature with great care, the acid and hydrocarbon mixture was gradually raised about 20° and held for 10 to 15 minutes in two "time tanks" where it was allowed to simmer. This difference in processing minimized the tendency of isobutylene to combine with itself and promoted instead the combination of an isobutylene molecule with one of butylene. The new method, called "copolymerization," nearly doubled the yield; the hot-acid process was able to utilize two-thirds of the available unsaturates as against one-third with the cold-acid process. This copolymerization, a self-combination (polymerization) of isobutylene, accompanied by a simultaneous combination of isobutylene and butylene, gave a mixed product which Shell called "mixed octylenes," or "hot-acid octylenes." Hydrogenated in the same manner that the di-isobutylene had been, it gave not one but a mixture of iso-octanes, which Shell called hot-acid, or H. A., octanes.* The octane number of these H. A. octanes was very near 100 (98.8 to 99.2 depending on the temperature of the copolymerization process) and the slight impairment in octane number was more than compensated for by the greatly increased yield.

Shell promptly installed the new hot-acid process in its refineries to supersede or supplement the cold-acid process which had been in operation only a few months. By the spring of 1936, the Shell Petroleum management was proposing to close down its Houston polymerization plant and convert it, just for the sake of experiment, into a phosphoric-acid polymerization process which Universal Oil Products was developing.[22] A reading of the correspondence of these years shows that the Shell executives responsible for the company's manufacturing program were willing at a moment's notice to drop existing methods of their own development in favor of any process which promised lower manufacturing costs. Their willingness to continue making iso-octane, putting it in storage all during 1936 when there were almost no orders for it, is also pleasant evidence of a disposition to bet on the future.[23]

---

* Strictly speaking, "iso-octane" is a name that can be applied to any of the 17 isomers of octane, for the iso-prefix is, by definition, used to designate isomeric forms. The particular iso-octane adopted for the octane-rating scale, called by the chemists 2-2-4 trimethyl pentane, is by arbitrary definition "100" and is the one oil men have in mind when they say "iso-octane."

Alkylation

An item of cost which constantly came up for discussion was the expense of hydrogenation. Although Shell had its own hydrogenation process and was thus spared the necessity of paying royalties, the cost of this extra step still ran high. In the spring of 1936, the company's out-of-pocket cost for a gallon of iso-octane at Wood River was 14½¢, of which 2.3¢ was for hydrogenation; at Houston the cost was 18¢ a gallon, of which 4¢ went for hydrogenation.[24]

There was a way open to circumvent the necessity for hydrogenation. If butane, C_4H_{10}, could be made to combine with butylene, C_4H_8, the product would be C_8H_{18}, an octane. Moreover, by-product butane was much more plentiful than the butylenes in the refinery by-product gases. Such a process should yield a much cheaper product, and in supply large enough to meet any anticipated requirement. The difficulty was with butane; it was a saturated hydrocarbon, extremely stable, and therefore a difficult raw material for the chemist. One of the butanes, isobutane, was more reactive than normal butane and for this reason held out more hope. To combine it with normal butylene was easy enough on paper, and a number of oil companies had been investigating this reaction, called alkylation,† for some years —among them Anglo-Iranian, Texaco, Jersey Standard, and Shell companies both in the United States and abroad.

The Shell Group had begun work on alkylation at the Amsterdam laboratory in the 1920's, and Shell in the United States had undertaken other alkylation researches in the early Thirties, independently at Emeryville and in cooperation with Universal Oil Products at Chicago.[25] Because it was in full-scale production of 100-octane ingredients, Shell perhaps realized more clearly than others the value of a successful alkylation process. By 1936–1937, the main problems of alkylation seemed well on their way to solution.

In the Shell alkylation process, isobutane and butylene were mixed with strong sulphuric acid; the acid was then drawn off, and the remaining traces of acid were removed by neutralization with caustic soda. The resulting "alkylate" was separated from the unreacted hydrocarbons by distillation, and these fractions were returned to the process along with incoming feed stock. The Shell alkylate was

† Originally of more specialized meaning, the term *alkylation* has been broadened in recent years to include a reaction in which an *alkyl*, or straight-chain hydrocarbon, is substituted for the hydrogen in another hydrocarbon compound.

split into two parts: a low-boiling fraction with an octane number of 95, and a heavy alkylate with an octane rating of 80–85.[26]

Shell was not alone in developing an alkylation method. Patent applications of several companies, describing parts of more or less similar processes using other catalysts, other temperatures, or different pressures, were filed during the late Thirties. The Patent Office held that several of these applications were "in interference" of the others. Here were the beginnings of a legal snarl which very possibly might lead to patent litigation worse than any of the cracking-patent cases of the 1920's. Most of the oil companies now filing alkylation patents had been through the tedious cracking suits of the Twenties, the last of which had not been settled until December 1937. All of them were resolved to prevent a recurrence of similar legal difficulties. During 1939, attorneys representing Shell, Anglo-Iranian, Jersey Standard, Texaco, and, soon after, Universal Oil Products, undertook discussions to see if some means could be devised for averting litigation over this new process. The lawyers were successful, and arranged cross-licenses to permit each patentee to use the other's alkylation patents.[27] This arrangement allowed development work on alkylation to go forward unhampered by claims and counterclaims, and made it possible for the process to be licensed without difficulty to all refiners who desired to use it.‡

As soon as the patent situation had been cleared up, construction of the new units got under way. Both Shell and Jersey had plans drawn for extensive construction of alkylation units; now there was a race to get them built. Shell's plans in May 1939 called for a 1,500-barrel-a-day alkylation plant at Wood River, another of like capacity at Houston, a 600-barrel unit at Wilmington, and a 300-barrel plant at Martinez. These plants totalled 3,900 barrels a day capacity; the next month saw this goal increased to 4,535 barrels a day, 27.6% of the total alkylation capacity under construction by the industry, and the largest amount of any individual company.[29]

A close second in planned alkylation capacity was Standard Oil of

‡ This patent-pooling arrangement received the sanction of government approval in December 1941 when the P.A.W. issued Recommendation 23, inviting owners of alkylation patents to make them freely available. Each of the companies mentioned above subscribed to these arrangements, and reduced their royalty requirements from 1¢ a gallon (42¢ a barrel) to 15¢ a barrel for product designed for government purchase; by late in the war, this latter figure had been further reduced to 10½¢ a barrel, or ¼¢ a gallon. Alkylation royalties, after deduction of expenses, were divided 24.6% to Shell, 24.6% to Texaco, 32.8% split between Standard of Jersey and Anglo-Iranian, and 18.7% to U.O.P. The M. W. Kellogg Company, which had done a good deal of practical engineering work on the process, collected a commission as licensing agent.[28]

New Jersey. In September 1938, the Jersey company completed conversion of an idle cold-acid polymerization plant at Humble's Baytown, Texas, refinery into a commercial-size alkylation unit; to this plant goes the credit of being the country's first. The alkylation plant at Shell's Martinez refinery, the second in the country, was completed and put on stream August 18, 1939. The Wilmington alkylation plant (September 12, 1939), the Houston plant (October 25, 1939), and the Wood River plant (January 17, 1940) followed in a matter of weeks. The plant at Norco, undertaken after the others were well under way, was completed in September 1940, the last of Shell's prewar alkylation units.[30]

The advent of alkylation was, beyond doubt, the most important single step in the advancement of 100-octane manufacture, for it made possible virtually unlimited quantities of high-antiknock components for 100-octane fuel. The mixed octanes produced by alkylation, generally called "alkylate" for convenience, had an anti-knock value comparable to iso-octane, and could be produced in great abundance at a fraction of the cost of commercial iso-octane. "If any single process of refining," wrote Heron in his history of aviation fuels, "can be said to have been the keystone of production of 100-octane fuels during World War II, alkylation would unquestionably merit the title." [31]

Isomerization

Next most important to alkylation were the isomerization processes. To make the quantities of alkylate required for the war, available supplies of isobutane would have been inadequate. This difficulty, happily, was solved in advance of requirements by the development of "isomerization" processes to convert the more abundant normal butane into isobutane. Shell's first butane isomerization plant, using a Shell-developed vapor-phase isomerization process, was built and put into operation in June 1941. Other isomerization processes were developed by U.O.P. and Standard of Indiana. Isomerization processes were responsible for supplying other aviation gasoline ingredients during the war, notably isopentane which would have been in extremely short supply had it not been possible to isomerize it from pentane. In addition to the vapor-phase isomerization process, used for making isobutane from butane, Shell had a liquid-phase isomerization process useful for converting butane, pentane, and hexane into their corresponding isomers. It was one of the ironies of war that Shell men found themselves installing this latter process not in their own plants, where the isopentane supply situation was considered satisfactory, but in the plants of competitors.[32]

One after the other, the C_4 gases from refinery cracking had been put to use to make high-antiknock components for 100-octane aviation gasoline. First isobutylene, relatively the scarcest, had been converted by the cold-acid polymerization process and hydrogenation into commercial iso-octane. Next, a large part of the normal butylenes and all of the isobutylene were utilized by the hot-acid polymerization process which, again by hydrogenation, yielded more abundant and cheaper "hot-acid octanes." Then came alkylation which eliminated hydrogenation and converted the butylenes along with isobutane into high-antiknock "mixed octanes." Last of all came butane isomerization to transform the remaining, and most abundant, C_4 hydrocarbon into a form suitable for alkylation. In this manner, all of the C_4 gases, isobutylene, butylenes, isobutane, and butane—flared as refinery waste only a few years earlier—were at last fully utilized. Shell could declare, as it did in a magazine advertisement, "The torch that blazed for 15 years is out."[33]

Catalytic Cracking

During these early years of 100-octane manufacture, the chemists, technologists, and research men were occupied almost wholly with processes that would produce more and better high-antiknock components. This was eminently sensible, for without these high-antiknock components (commercial iso-octane, H. A. octanes, and alkylate), large-scale production of 100-octane gasoline could not have been inaugurated. Processes to make aviation base stocks of higher octane rating and in greater quantity were the next to receive attention.

A decided quality improvement in the gasolines called "aviation base-stock" had taken place in the years since 1930. The improvements were not, however, undertaken for the effect they would have on aviation gasoline; they were a result of the "octane race" in the motor gasoline field. This quality race, continuing throughout the Thirties, spurred development of a new method of cracking which in turn brought sharp improvements in the gasolines used for aviation base-stock.

Credit for commercial development of modern catalytic cracking goes to Eugene J. Houdry, of France. Working with the financial backing of the Socony-Vacuum and Sun oil companies, Houdry completed his process and announced it to the industry in 1937. The

Houdry process combined vapor-phase cracking with catalytic cracking, a little-used method developed twenty years earlier by A. M. McAfee and installed by Gulf Oil in 1915. In Houdry's process, the catalyst did the work done by temperature and time in the thermal processes; the new process could, therefore, operate at greatly reduced pressures and temperatures. The gasoline produced by catalytic cracking had a much higher octane number and a much lower sulphur content than the fuels produced by thermal cracking. Omitting consideration of sulphur's deleterious effects, this lowered sulphur content was desirable because a high-sulphur gasoline was less susceptible to improvement through the addition of tetraethyl lead. The initial high octane numbers of catalytically cracked gasoline plus its high degree of "lead susceptibility" made the new Houdry gasoline a good bet for the octane race then in progress.[34]

During 1939, Socony-Vacuum and Sun began large-scale construction of Houdry units, posing a clear threat to their chief competitors. With the new process, Sun and Socony could make motor gasoline 3 to 4 octane numbers better than the rest of the industry. Equally important, they were, for the moment at least, spared the expense of installing alkylation units, for by using this high-octane Houdry gasoline as base stock, Sun and Socony could make a high-octane aviation fuel without the use of alkylate.[35]

What was the best course open to Shell and the other companies who had already made large investments in units to produce high-quality blending components? They could, for a time anyhow, continue to meet quality competition in the motor gasoline field § by adjusting their refining processes upward and adding more tetraethyl lead. This would mean slightly increased manufacturing costs, but would avoid the huge outlays entailed in building catalytic cracking units. The Houdry units were of enormous physical dimensions, and the cost of an individual unit ran not to thousands but millions of dollars. The process was not continuous in the sense that Dubbs cracking was; there was every possibility that improvements in the near future would bring a continuous process completely superseding this expensive equipment.* On top of this, royalties for the Houdry process were high. For Shell, it seemed the course of wisdom not to

§ Using Houdry components, Sun had introduced a 73-octane "regular" gasoline in November 1939.[36]

* This proved to be the case. Socony turned its attention to a continuous process and in 1942 announced the Thermofor (T.C.C.) process which has since displaced the early Houdry units entirely. The Houdry installations could not be converted and had only salvage value.

install Houdry units but to attempt to develop a catalytic process of its own.

In this course, the company was to be greatly assisted by Standard Oil of New Jersey. The Jersey company had negotiated for the Houdry process during 1937, had given the project up as too expensive,† and had decided instead to develop its own catalytic method. To help in the development work, Jersey enlisted the aid of the M. W. Kellogg Company, designers and builders of refinery equipment, and of the I. G. Farbenindustrie, which had extensive knowledge of the chemical nature of catalysts. Standard of Indiana joined this catalytic research project during 1938, and within the next twelve months a number of other oil companies also became interested: Texaco, Anglo-Iranian, Universal Oil Products, and the Royal Dutch-Shell Group. Each of these companies undertook fresh research on some aspect of catalytic cracking. By the early years of the war, a new catalytic cracking process had been developed that promised to be more economical than Houdry's.[38]

The largest contribution to the new process was made by Standard of New Jersey. During 1940, that company discovered a "fluid" catalyst, a finely divided powder (chemically, a complex of alumina and silica compounds) that would, when aerated and kept at high velocities, exhibit the flow characteristics of a liquid. The possibilities of such a "fluid" catalyst were immense. It could be made to flow through the pipes and chambers of cracking equipment, mixing intimately with the vapors of the incoming charge stock. In this suspended state, cracking could occur until coke deposits on the individual catalyst particles had made them chemically inactive. The mixture of catalyst and cracked vapors could then be separated, the vapors condensed into products, and the catalyst "regenerated" by burning off the accumulated coke. The continuous flow and catalyst regeneration features of the "fluid process" were ingenious pieces of engineering and offered outstanding operating advantages.

As far as octane number was concerned, Dubbs and other existing methods of thermal cracking could not hope to compete with the new fluid catalytic process. However, the Dubbs process would continue to be useful, for it was one of the few methods capable of using heavy residues as feed stock. The fluid process could take a wide cut of gas oils as feed stock, but it could not handle oils containing asphalt or

† For a paid-up license, the Houdry people are said to have asked Jersey $50,000,000.[37]

sludge, for they coked the catalyst much too quickly. In the matter of feed stocks, the Dubbs and fluid processes complemented each other.[39]

In the absence of wartime conditions, it would probably have required a much longer time for the new fluid catalytic cracking to be adopted generally.‡ The fluid units were tremendously expensive because of their overpowering size—some fifteen stories high, with

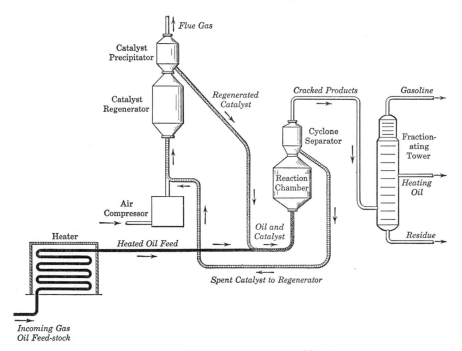

FLUID CATALYTIC CRACKING

Highly simplified drawing showing how "fluid" catalyst, because of its flow properties, permitted the development of a continuous system.

dimensions equally massive in other respects. Most refiners would no doubt have postponed building them for several years to come. But by 1942, when the first full-scale unit was completed, a war was on in earnest. Every available method for making high-octane aviation gasoline components was being examined and evaluated. Fluid cata-

‡ Patents covering the fluid catalytic cracking method were pooled in response to P.A.W. Recommendation 41, issued in July 1942, an arrangement quite similar to that covering the alkylation patents. Royalty was 5¢ a barrel on all products produced by fluid catalytic cracking, and went one-half to Standard of Jersey, which had made the heaviest contributions; the other half was shared by Anglo-Iranian, Texaco, Shell, M. W. Kellogg, and U.O.P.[40]

lytic cracking was one of the most promising, for it could produce enormous quantities of high-octane base stock. So, in spite of cost, most of the nation's large refiners turned at once to construction of the new fluid cracking units.

3

Wartime Production of 100-Octane

WHEN America entered the war in December 1941, the country was producing about 40,000 barrels of aviation gasoline a day, less than 7% of the amount it would be turning out at the end of the war.[41] In the long months between December 1941 and August 1945, the back-breaking job confronting the oil industry was to make up this huge deficit in production.

It was a rare piece of good fortune for the country and its allies that the oil companies, by a happy junction of circumstances, were in a position to meet the enormous demand suddenly thrust upon them. Alkylation and catalytic cracking, excellent new processes for making high-antiknock components and aviation base-stock on an almost unlimited scale, were ready for large-scale expansion. Not every oil company was familiar with them, but the companies that had led in the development of these processes had mastered their intricacies and would, for the duration of the war, gladly share their operational "know-how" with the fiercest of competitors. Thus, the potentialities for rapid expansion of aviation gasoline manufacture were good. On top of this was an already sizeable production, admittedly far short of wartime needs, but nevertheless at the rate of 600,000,000 gallons a year on December 7, 1941—far more than the country had any right to expect.

From the beginning, the oil companies had been obliged to supply their own incentives for manufacturing 100-octane gasoline. In such an atmosphere it was not surprising that only a few of the largest companies had undertaken to make high-octane fuel on a commercial scale before 1939. At Doolittle's instance, Shell Petroleum in May 1939 began to prepare a monthly report showing not only its own but all of its competitors' facilities for the manufacture of 100-octane. The first of these reports showed facilities totalling in capacity 5,790 barrels a day; of this Jersey Standard accounted for 48.3%, Shell 25.3%, and four other companies (Standard of California, Gulf, Phillips, and Socony) the remainder. During the next six months, several of these companies—Shell foremost among them—continued to enlarge their production facilities. By November 1939, total national capacity had doubled and Shell's share, primarily as the result of the company's construction of new alkylation plants, had risen to 40.3% of the total, against Jersey's 25.2% and 11.3% for The Texas Company which had just entered the field.[42]

Following the outbreak of hostilities in Europe in the fall of 1939, facilities for making 100-octane continued to double about every twelve months. By October 1940, capacity had reached 20,000 barrels a day, and of the actual production that month (17,050 barrels a day), Shell produced 25.5%, Standard of New Jersey 27.5%. By the end of 1941, at the time of America's entry into the war, daily capacity was 40,000 barrels a day. Of this total, Shell accounted for 22.5%, Standard of New Jersey 25.2%. From these figures it will be seen that Jersey Standard and Shell were the largest prewar suppliers of 100-octane fuel. They continued to occupy a leading position in 100-octane manufacture all during the war years, although expansion by other refiners reduced their percentage of the total.

"EQUIVALENT PRODUCTION" OF 100-OCTANE GASOLINE, 1942–1945 [43]

	Percentages by Companies			
	1942	*1943*	*1944*	*Jan.-July 1945*
Standard of New Jersey[§]	25.2	26.2	19.8	14.8
Shell Oil	22.5	12.8	11.0	9.5
Socony-Vacuum	10.5	8.9	7.9	7.3
Standard of California	10.9	7.4	5.4	6.1
Texaco	7.1	6.5	6.5	6.9
Sinclair	2.8	5.4	5.7	5.8
Sun	8.0	4.2	3.9	3.9
Phillips	5.3	6.4	5.1	4.6
Standard of Indiana	.2	1.3	4.9	5.0
Gulf	.9	3.5	2.4	1.7
Atlantic Refining	—	3.9	2.1	1.9
Cities Service	—	.7	3.2	4.1
All Others	6.6	12.8	22.1	38.4

§ Includes production of Jersey's Aruba refinery which averaged between a quarter and a sixth of that company's total, and transfers from others which accounted for another 10%. Shell's contributions to these totals are impressive against the background of the two companies' prewar domestic refining capacities; Jersey's refinery intake was 163,770,000 barrels in 1941, double Shell's 81,450,000 barrels.

Shell's total production of 100-octane or better during the period of the war (January 1942 through July 1945) was 1,890,000,000 gallons, 13.1% of the national total—an enviable record for a company having 6% of the nation's refining capacity.[44]

Shell Petroleum's closing down of the Arkansas City and East Chicago refineries in the late Thirties and subsequent erection of new facilities at Wood River had been undertaken chiefly for economic reasons. However, a secondary factor which received considerable attention at the time was that new refining processes, such as polymerization and alkylation, required large concentrations of by-product gases at a single refinery. Shell's action in concentrating the capacities of three refineries at Wood River had an important effect upon the size of its wartime contributions to aviation gasoline manufacture.

Beginnings of the Government-Industry Program

In June 1940, the President set up the Advisory Commission to the Council of National Defense. Dr. Robert E. Wilson of Standard Oil of Indiana was appointed to head up the section dealing with petroleum products. Wilson at once became concerned over the inadequacy of the armed services' 100-octane estimates. Early in September 1940, at the height of the Battle of Britain, he submitted a report estimating wartime 100-octane requirements of the Army and Navy at 71,300 barrels a day, on the basis of an air force of less than 13,000 planes. Three months later, the Joint Aeronautical Board, representing both services, put total requirements for the period July 1, 1941 to July 1, 1942 at 33,492 barrels a day, less than half Dr. Wilson's estimate.[45]

These estimates contemplated the needs of the air force then extant, or soon to be built. During 1940, President Roosevelt announced a new goal for the nation, 50,000 planes. When Wilson submitted an estimate for this force of 3,000,000 gallons (more than 190,000 barrels) a day, it was, Heron wrote, "received almost with derision. The suggestion . . . was regarded by intermediate and high level military staffs in Washington as an attempt by the oil industry to feather its nest." [46] This skepticism was due, in part at least, to the fact that the oil industry had never bothered to explain its manufacturing problems. "The rapidity with which the oil industry (and particularly Shell and Jersey) had met the Army request for 100-octane fuel had served to confirm the previously held opinion." [47] There were also a number of other considerations. A good many people still thought we would not get into the war; others, who feared we might, opposed preparedness measures on the grounds that such measures would only carry us that much nearer to war; most believed that President Roosevelt's call for 50,000 airplanes was mainly rhetoric; and a surprisingly large number of those in authority clung to the belief that "gasoline is gasoline," that military demands could be met simply by shutting off the flow of gasoline to civilians.[48]

In mid-1941, the President's Advisory Commission to the Council of National Defense (which after many changes and shufflings was to become the War Production Board) ceased to be responsible for petroleum products and Dr. Wilson returned to private industry "with a lively sense of defeat." [49] His work had not been in vain, however, for Ickes and Ralph Davies in their newly established Office of the Petroleum Coordinator took up where he had left off. They took the President's call for 50,000 airplanes seriously, and began surveys to determine the fuel requirements of such an air armada. They concluded that existing capacity should at least be doubled right away and late in September 1941, after several months of nagging, experienced their first victory when James V. Forrestal, then Under Secretary of the Navy, recommended a doubling of capacity.[50] Government support of any major plant construction program was by this time necessary, for materials were under allocation and new refinery units could not be built without government certification. The difficulty of getting the required certificates was greatly increased in the case of aviation gasoline, for there was at the time no shortage, but in fact a comfortable surplus of production over domestic demand. As a result, materials allocations were withheld and no sizeable new construction of aviation gasoline facilities took place during 1941.

Ickes and Davies gave a convincing demonstration of their courage and foresight all during the late months of 1941. They continued in their conversations with government officials to hammer away at the fact that, in the event of war, new production of aviation gasoline could not be had immediately because construction of the necessary new units would require nine to eighteen months under the most favorable of circumstances. At the same time, they turned to the oil men and in confidential conversations explained the gravity of the situation and asked the industry's support in devising methods to increase aviation gasoline production immediately in the event of hostilities. The wholehearted response they received from oil men spoke well for the companies' willingness to devote themselves to a program that was in the national interest, without asking for government favors or guarantees or worrying about the effect that this large-scale expansion might have on their peacetime aviation gasoline business.

Squeezing It Out of a Hat

Immediately after Pearl Harbor Day, everyone was willing to admit the wisdom of the discussions that had been going on between Ickes, Davies, and the industry during the fall of 1941. The day after America entered the war, the services, at the first meeting of the Petroleum Industry War Council, announced that they must have as much 100-octane as possible right away and 150,000 barrels a day by mid-1943, a demand which Ickes, Davies, and their industry group had already anticipated and laid plans to supply. F. S. Clulow, who had become Shell manufacturing vice president on the West Coast at the time of Van Senden's retirement in 1938, remembers that he and one of his senior assistants, M. E. Spaght, were on their way from San Francisco to attend this meeting in Washington at the time the news of Pearl Harbor was announced. At the December 8 meeting, Clulow recalls, representatives of the armed services asked that the current aviation gasoline production of 40,000 barrels a day be increased to 80,000 barrels at once, but could not begin to visualize the quantities that would eventually be needed—their 150,000-barrel-per-day projection demand was only a quarter of the 600,000 barrels a day the industry would be turning out by the end of the war.[51]

It was apparent to everybody that the really critical phase of 100-octane production would be the period immediately ahead. Construction of sizeable new manufacturing facilities would require upwards of a year and a half. Meanwhile, if America and its allies were not to lose the war in the skies, production of 100-octane must be greatly increased—almost wholly from existing facilities. It was an exercise in ingenuity entirely unlike anything the American refiner had ever faced before; but the combined efforts of the refiners, and their able and intelligent helpers in the government petroleum agency, not only rescued the services from their supply predicament but actually exceeded the goal. By July 1, 1943, production of 100-octane was well in excess of 200,000 barrels a day. Even in a day when production "miracles" had become commonplace, such outstanding performance could not but excite enthusiasm and admiration. The oil industry's outstanding performance during these months was noted with particular appreciation by the very same government groups that had been responsible for the inadequate estimates. An Army general in the North African campaign summed up this feeling in a conversation with Ickes late in 1942: "The job which has been done with 100-octane . . . is one of the most amazing things I have ever witnessed. It is almost unbelievable. They have virtually squeezed it out of a hat." [52]

The general was almost literally correct. Following plans submitted by the P.A.W.* in November 1941, several changes were put into effect in the weeks immediately following Pearl Harbor. The result was an increase of 40% in 100-octane production at the time it was most needed. The first of these measures involved making specific operating changes (often minor) at specific plants; in the aggregate, these changes resulted in an increase of 6,000 barrels a day, or 15%.

A second beneficial change was to increase the permissible tetraethyl lead content from 3 to 4 cubic centimeters per gallon. Lead gives flexibility to the operations of a refiner of high-octane gasoline, for the addition or omission of relatively small quantities of tetraethyl lead will permit him to swing up and down the octane scale at will. Added to a gallon of 70-octane straight-run base stock, 1 c.c. of lead will raise the anti-knock rating of the fuel to 81-octane; 3 c.c.'s will raise it to 88-octane; and 4 c.c.'s will bring a further increase to 90-octane. Every increase in octane number which could be effected in this manner meant a saving of scarce alkylate and other blending agents, and every such saving meant a greater total production of finished 100-octane. Prewar, the services had generally held that 3 c.c.'s of tetraethyl lead were the maximum that could be safely added to a gallon of gasoline. But when the production advantages of 4 c.c.'s were pointed out, the Army readily consented to the increase, which was authorized within a week of Pearl Harbor Day. This increased lead content made it possible to spread the available alkylate; the result was an immediate jump of 25% in 100-octane production. [53]

Many oil men and several members of the P.A.W. felt that the permissible tetraethyl lead content could be increased yet again and production raised still further. But the Army Air Force objected; spark-plug fouling on long missions would be fatal, and even at

---

* The Petroleum Administration for War, as noted earlier in this chapter, was not created until December 1942, but the Office of Petroleum Coordinator for National Defense and its successor, the Office of Petroleum Coordinator for War, and finally the Petroleum Administration for War all had the same staff and same objectives. For simplicity, they are here considered identical and called by the P.A.W. name.

shorter range would mean unnecessary engine maintenance. Finally, after a year and a half of argument, the Air Force gave in. After July 1943, 4.6 c.c.'s of tetraethyl lead were added to 100-octane. This further increase in lead content accounted for $3\frac{1}{2}\%$ of the total production increase 1942–1943, even though it was in effect only during the last quarter of that period.

Another feature of the "quick 100-octane program," promoted by the P.A.W. during the early months of the war, placed emphasis upon maximum efficiency in blending. Often the base stocks and high-anti-knock hydrocarbons available at a given refinery were a poor combination when used with each other. The ideal procedure would be to bring together the components that could "do the most for each other" by way of increasing anti-knock value. This the P.A.W. decided to do despite the additional expense of rail shipments and likelihood of adding to the already congested freight situation. This shuffling of components to produce a larger total of finished 100-octane was accomplished by means of monthly blending schedules issued to every refiner producing 100-octane components. The schedule told him what to blend, where to obtain his components, and to whom he should ship other components at his disposal.

Among these components was a new catalytically cracked base stock, which by early 1942 was beginning to be produced in some quantity as a result of the conversion of Houdry units. Just before Pearl Harbor, in November 1941, the Sun Oil Company voluntarily offered to withdraw its Houdry equipment from the manufacture of motor gasoline and instead to make upwards of 10,000 barrels a day of 100-octane at a price to be set by the P.A.W. Socony-Vacuum and other owners of Houdry units followed suit. The immediate value of the catalytically cracked material was (as in the case of increased lead content) a higher octane number, reducing the amount of alkylate needed in blending. With "cat-cracked" instead of straight-run base stock, a given amount of alkylate made nearly twice as much finished 100-octane. Conversion of Houdry units to the manufacture of aviation base-stock was responsible during 1942-1943 for another 15% of the total increase in production.[54]

Of primary importance in drawing up the blending schedules responsible for these increases was a small group of oil company manu-facturing executives appointed in October 1942 by the P.A.W. and known as the Aviation Gasoline Advisory Committee. The members of the committee, each thoroughly conversant with his own company's operations, met frequently throughout the war and exchanged informally the information which later materialized as P.A.W. operating schedules.[55]

During early 1942, "rich-mixture performance," the importance of which was originally emphasized by research work of Shell companies in England and Holland, became prominent in the discussions of American airmen. In war, how a fuel performed "at rich mixture," with the throttle wide open, could be all-important. A fuel of high rating under rich-mixture conditions could give a fighter pilot the sudden surge of quick power he needed to overtake the enemy, or provide the lifting energy to get a heavily laden bomber off the runway. The services announced that after July 1, 1942, they would require a fuel with a rich-mixture rating of better than 100-octane.† This announcement followed the successful demonstration of a new Shell-developed wartime process for making a rich-mixture additive.

Cumene

To obtain the desired rich-mixture characteristics by adding more alkylate or tetraethyl lead would have meant an over-all decrease in 100-octane production. The best way to get 100+ rich-mixture rating without sacrificing volume was, as the British had already demonstrated, to add aromatics—ring-type hydrocarbons, of which benzene and toluene were perhaps the best-known. Aromatics were abundant in coal-tar compounds and were also found in smaller quantities in petroleum. One of the best aromatics for gasoline enrichment was cumene (otherwise known as isopropyl benzene) which had, by the motor method, an anti-knock value of 99.3 octane and in rich-mixture blending a "performance number" of 124. As a booster of rich-mixture performance, cumene was under the circumstances preferable to either toluene or benzene, both of which had been used by the British for rich-mixture blending.‡ During the Battle of Britain, the

---

† These numbers over 100-octane are expressed by "performance numbers," and both lean- and rich-mixture ratings are generally indicated. Thus the expression "100/130 grade" refers to a fuel which at lean mixtures (cruising conditions) gives 100-octane performance but at full throttle will give 1.3 times, or 130%, of the energy of 100-octane. Performance numbers, like octane numbers, do not indicate the fuel's composition but its response to given conditions. In general, however, it could be said that a gallon of 100-octane fuel plus 1 c.c. of tetraethyl lead gives a "performance number" of about 125.

‡ Toluene was slightly better than cumene as a rich-mixture additive, but all available toluene was needed at this time for T.N.T. manufacture. Benzene was not as good as cumene, because in quantities sufficient to provide the desired rich-mixture rating it tended to cause freezing of gasoline lines at high altitudes.

aromatics used for this blending were a mixture of natural benzene and toluene, produced by the Edeleanu extraction process from high-aromatic Borneo and Venezuelan crudes. The Group, with its long experience in Edeleanu extraction, produced most of this aromatic blending material. A quite natural result was that the Shell companies in America should be more alert than most of their competitors to the rich-mixture possibilities of these aromatic compounds.[56]

American crudes were not as rich in aromatics as oils from many foreign fields, and as a result relatively little extraction capacity had been built in America to remove them. Natural sources were, consequently, out of the question. Shell Development set itself the task of producing a synthetic aromatic, choosing cumene because of its high performance value. The project was hedged in by two important restrictions: a workable process must use existing refinery equipment and an easily obtained catalyst.

Emeryville's success in this project was easily the outstanding achievement of the "quick 100-octane program." By February 1942, Shell was able to inform the P.A.W. that it had developed a process for alkylating coal-tar benzene with propylene gas from refinery cracking to produce a synthetic cumene. Polymerization equipment built earlier could be converted to cumene manufacture with only minor modifications. For a catalyst, the new process would use the same phosphoric acid employed in the U.O.P. "selective polymerization" process. The only drawback was a supply of coal-tar benzene. It was already used as a gasoline blending agent and as a raw material for synthetic rubber manufacture, and was in critically short supply. Could it be spared for cumene manufacture?

The Shell representatives succeeded in convincing the P.A.W. that coal-tar benzene going into cumene manufacture would be of greater over-all benefit than the quantities of benzene then being used for aviation gasoline blending. In April 1942, Shell obtained the P.A.W. and W.P.B. approvals necessary to convert a trial plant. Three weeks later, the Norco polymerization unit had been converted, and on May 5, 1942, it turned out its first quantities of synthetic cumene. Similar conversion work went ahead full-speed at Wood River, and by June cumene production was under way there.

This production of cumene was of high importance. Cumene was, first of all, a highly desirable rich-mixture additive; with it, a gasoline rated as 100/130 grade could be easily manufactured. Equally important, cumene was also a high-antiknock additive. Its availability on a substantial scale reduced the requirements for other high-antiknock blending components such as alkylate, and spread the supplies of alkylate to make possible additional over-all increases in aviation gasoline production.

Shell offered its new cumene process free to all competitors, and the conversion to cumene manufacture got under way at once. Within four months, enough units had been converted to bring total cumene production to more than a quarter of a million gallons daily. During the following year, additional conversions took place and by the end of 1943, there were 19 plants using the Shell cumene process, 17 in the United States and two in Canada. The cumene from these plants was, next to construction of new facilities, the most important source of increased production during the two years of the quick 100-octane program. Official P.A.W. figures showed a 225% increase in 100-octane production during these two years, from less than 80,000 barrels a day early in 1942 to more than 260,000 barrels daily at the end of 1943.[57]

SOURCES OF INCREASED 100-OCTANE PRODUCTION, 1942–1943 [58]

New Facilities (second half of 1943)	79.8%	
Use of Cumene as a Blending Agent	51.2%	(Shell Innovation)
Minor Improvements, Rearrangements	31.5%	
Conversion of Houdry Units	31.2%	(Sun and Socony)
Use of Codimer as Blending Agent	20.5%	(Jersey Innovation)
Increasing Lead from 4 to 4.6 c.c./gal.	7.9%	
Use of Toluene and Other Blending Agents	2.9%	
	225.0%	

Avaro

Early in the war, the Shell Group's long-standing interest in aromatics had led to the production of "Avaro" at the Group's Curaçao refinery. Avaro (a shorthand expression for *aviation aromatics*) was a mixture of benzene, toluene, cumene, and other aromatics of the same boiling range as gasoline. Avaro was not as effective for rich-mixture blending as cumene, but its production came at a time when every aromatic additive was desperately needed, and it could be manufactured without interfering with other wartime refining programs. Charge stock for the Avaro process consisted of cuts of straight-run gasoline and naphthas, "spare-part" fractions left over from the manufacture of products such as toluene. This charge stock was subject to high temperature cracking (or "reforming") in thermal cracking units made idle by the lessened production of civilian gasoline. Twice-through cracking of this light charge-stock yielded a mixture of aromatics suitable, because of their boiling range, for blending into aviation gasoline. The process was installed at Wood River and Houston during 1943, where it made possible the production of the first thermally cracked material suitable for use in 100+ gasoline. Although it was not adopted by other refiners, the Avaro process offered an excellent illustration of the way Shell strained every effort to produce a maximum yield of 100-octane while avoiding construction that would use new materials.[59]

Xylidine

During 1943, Shell Chemical undertook construction of facilities to produce yet another aromatic, xylidine—called in the language of wartime secrecy "Specification C.S." (The letters stood for "cumene substitute.") Adding 3% of this "C.S." to a gallon of 100/130-grade fuel, along with another 1.4 c.c. of lead, raised the rich-mixture rating of the fuel to 150 performance number. The resultant "super-fuel," called Grade 100/150, had initially been made in England by adding monomethyl aniline to 100/130-grade fuel and raising the lead content from 4.6 to 6 c.c. per gallon. Shell in England had taken a leading part in the production of this new super-fuel for the R.A.F., so it was only natural that Shell Development should explore the possibilities of a similar fuel for the U. S. Air Force.

The Army was impressed by the performance of this 100/150-grade fuel which made it possible to increase power at full throttle by another 15%, giving British fighter planes the emergency power they needed to intercept German "buzz bombs." [60] Its manufacture would, however, present serious problems, for monomethyl aniline was derived from coal-tar benzene, already in critically short supply. As a result of extensive engine testing at Emeryville, Shell Development suggested xylidine which could be made from much more abundant materials and would give nearly identical results.

At Army request, Shell Chemical in June 1943 agreed to design and build a large-scale plant to manufacture xylidine from nitroxylenes. To save construction time, the Army Ordnance Department suggested that the company utilize the Cactus Ordnance Works, a partially built ammonia plant in the Texas Panhandle. By exercising considerable ingenuity in improvisation and designing a process to fit the available equipment, the Shell engineers on the job converted the Army's ammonia works into a xylidine plant of 2,800 barrels a day capacity in exactly seven months. It began operating late in January 1944.[61]

The xylidine plant was a short-term project. The military wanted and needed the best obtainable rich-mixture fuels for the invasion of Europe in the summer of 1944. Fuels made with xylidine proved admirably adapted to short-range interception just before and immediately following the invasion. With the invasion past, combat conditions altered. In the Pacific, emphasis was on lean-mixture fuels to lengthen cruising range. By late 1944, pressing need for xylidine had passed and the Army ordered Shell Chemical to close down the Cactus plant at the end of 1944.

Building the "Cat Crackers"

To the average bystander, these aspects of the aviation gasoline program were not even known. The most impressive feature of the wartime 100-octane program was the construction of new facilities. By the second half of 1943, the first of the new units began to come on stream and by early 1944, the "quick 100-octane program" might be said to have run its course. From this point onward, new plants went into production one after the other and accounted for an overwhelming percentage of the huge increase in production during the next fifteen months—600,000 barrels a day by March 1945, double the rate of January 1944.

Building this amount of new plant capacity in wartime was frequently a disheartening affair. The only authoritative gauge of future requirements were the estimates of the Army and Navy and, during the early days of the war, these estimates were consistently too low. The P.A.W. was constantly faced with the difficult problem of trying to convince the War Production Board and the services that they would need more gasoline than they thought they would. Even with additional expansion approved and priorities granted, the battle had just begun for, in the words of the wartime Washington wisecrack, "a priority is only a hunting license." For the first eighteen months of the war, the priorities given 100-octane projects were generally far too low to command the necessary attention from material suppliers and equipment fabricators. The synthetic rubber program had been given precedence over 100-octane, a particularly maddening state of affairs to the P.A.W., for the rubber program was looking to 100-octane manufacture for a large percentage of the butylenes it would use as feed stock. Finally, in July 1943, the W.P.B. assigned the 100-octane facilities scheduled for completion that year the highest W.P.B. priority rating. From this point onward the 100-octane program's priority troubles were less serious, although supplies never came easily; the materials required for a 100-octane plant—steel plate, valves, pumps, instruments, electric motors, and special alloys—were remarkably similar to those used in the construction of Naval war vessels.[62]

A complete 100-octane installation consisted of an alkylation plant to supply high-antiknock components and a catalytic cracking unit for the manufacture of high-octane base-stock, together with necessary auxiliary treating units. Because alkylate was in very short supply, and because the alkylation plants required smaller amounts of critical materials, they were put up first, some months ahead of the catalytic cracking units. All told, 30 alkylation plants were built by the industry during the war years. The Shell Union companies had already built alkylation plants at five of their refineries during 1939–1940, so they did not need new alkylation facilities except at Wilmington and Wood River, where catalytic cracking plants were under construction. At each of these refineries, a new alkylation plant was built during 1943 to process the gas from the new "cat crackers."

Construction of the catalytic cracking installations had started early in the war. To save materials and to make procurement easier, the W.P.B. and P.A.W. adopted a standard design for each type of catalytic cracking unit. Not every refiner who wished to build a cracking plant was permitted to do so. Only 31 of the fluid process units were authorized, and the government agencies had to satisfy themselves on several points before granting the necessary construction authority. To win approval, a refinery needed to be strategically located both as to feed stocks and transportation, and preference was given to refineries that would require a minimum amount of new auxiliary facilities. In February 1942, Shell obtained authorization to build two fluid catalytic cracking units at Wood River, and in June 1942 authority for a third unit at Wilmington. Permission to erect a fourth unit at Houston was withheld until after the end of the war.

The Wilmington "cat cracker" was ready for operation in November 1943, the first of the fluid cracking units to be completed under the wartime construction program. At Wood River, construction proceeded more slowly; the refinery's twin catalytic cracking units got into operation early in 1944, one in February, the other in March. These fluid catalytic cracking plants were the largest units ever built in a Shell refinery; they towered fifteen stories into the air and dramatized for all who saw them the immense volume of the company's wartime production. The Wilmington plant, because it was the first of the wartime fluid units to be completed, became a training ground for competitors' employees who would later operate fluid cracking plants that were still under construction. Shell gladly assisted in this work and even prepared a manual of "cat cracker" operation that was widely used throughout the industry in plants employing the fluid cracking process.[63]

It was now just ten years since Shell had shipped its first 100-octane to the Air Corps in 1934. To celebrate this tenth anniversary, mark the official opening of the new twin "cat crackers" at Wood River, and remind Shell people everywhere of the important job still ahead of them, the company held a 100-octane birthday party at the refinery on Sunday, April 30. The P.A.W. proclaimed "National 100-Octane Week"; the Army sent exhibits of captured German, Italian, and Japanese matériel, along with the newest in American weapons; Robert P. Patterson, Under Secretary of War and one of the staunchest friends of the 100-octane program, came to speak; the "Army Hour" broadcast the ceremonies around the world; a voice especially close to Shell people, that of Lieut. Gen. James H. Doolittle, was piped in from London; and the New York *Times* took note of the occasion in an editorial:[64]

> Ten years ago today, 1,000 gallons of 100-octane gasoline, the first ever to be produced in commercial quantities, was delivered by the Shell Oil Company to the Army Air Corps at Wright Field. The company commemorates that anniversary by opening its new twin catalytic cracking plant for the manufacture of high-octane gasoline at Wood River, Illinois, and the Petroleum Administration for War, the Army and the Navy will inaugurate tomorrow the national celebration of 100-Octane Week. There can be little question that fuel of 100-octane or better rating, set down in huge quantities for our Air Force and Navy fliers around the world, has been one of the vital underlying factors in our superiority over the enemy. The margin in speed and performance provided by such gasoline has heavily weighted the odds in our favor and saved hundreds of lives.
>
> Many details of the wartime advances in petroleum technology, especially in relation to high-octane, must still remain on the confi-

dential list, but it is a matter of record and a tribute to the petroleum industry that constant improvement in quality and reduction in price have accompanied the development. The first 1,000-gallon shipment delivered from California to Ohio ten years ago cost $2.40 a gallon. Today the price to the air services in bulk is less than the motorist pays for his day-by-day fuel at the roadside pump. Many companies and individuals have shared in the achievement represented by our dominance in high-octane fuel. It should not be forgotten, however, that among the many debts which American airpower owes to Lieutenant General Doolittle is his insistence a decade ago, when, as a civilian, he was in charge of the aviation development of Shell, that his company carry on energetically research in 100-octane gasoline.

4

Synthetic Rubber

THE fall of Singapore and the capture of Java, both within three months of Pearl Harbor, deprived the United States of 90% of its normal rubber supply and precipitated the most critical materials shortage of the war. Supplies of rubber on hand had to be made to last until a new synthetic rubber industry could be built and put into operation. How these supplies were stretched beyond all expectation and how a new industry was built from scratch in two years were outstanding chapters in a war crammed full of exciting production stories.[65]

One reason why synthetic rubber could be put into full-scale production so rapidly was that it was by no means new, although most members of the American public seemed to believe so at the time. Rubber had, in fact, been one of the first synthetic materials produced by organic chemists in their laboratories. As far back as 1860, the British chemist Charles G. Williams had discovered that the decomposition of rubber yielded isoprene, C_5H_8, a colorless liquid that, exposed to light and air, would form a rubber-like mass. Later chemists theorized that isoprene combined with itself (polymerized) to form the large complex molecules which gave rubber its useful properties such as elasticity. In natural rubber, this polymerization had somehow been accomplished by nature. The fluid called "latex" which flows under the bark of a rubber tree is a watery emulsion of isoprene. Could not compounds similar to isoprene be reacted with themselves to yield a synthetic rubber that would perhaps be superior in some respects to the natural product? German chemists, who did not flinch in the face of difficult problems, went to work on synthetic rubber around the turn of the century.

The Start of Synthetic Rubber

Their first rubber, called methyl rubber, was made in 1901 from dimethyl butadiene, a hydrocarbon closely akin to isoprene. In 1906, the Bayer firm (one of the concerns which later went into the I. G. Farben combine) produced butadiene, a close relative of isoprene, from the common chemical acetylene. During the First World War, the Germans turned out several tons per day of a serviceable synthetic called Buna, made by polymerizing butadiene with sodium.§ The decade following World War I was a time of wildly fluctuating natural rubber prices ($1.12 a pound in 1925, 3¢ a pound in 1932–1933) with the result that, except in a few specialized applications, synthetic rubber could not hope to compete with the natural product. In America two oil-resistant synthetic rubbers made their appearance in these years. Thiokol, invented in 1922 by Dr. J. C. Patrick, of Kansas City, was first produced commercially in 1930. Neoprene, the invention of Father Julius Nieuwland of Notre Dame, was purchased by Du Pont who began small-scale production of Neoprene in 1933. Because of their special properties, these two synthetic rubbers found a small but steady market.

The only country with any real incentive for developing an all-purpose synthetic rubber was Germany, where in the early 1930's a militaristic new government came to power. Germany was far removed from sources of natural rubber, and remembered all too clearly how serious the interruption of the rubber imports had been in the 1914–1918 war. With the German government underwriting the expense, the I. G. Farben attacked its Buna rubbers with renewed vigor.

By introducing to the butadiene chain about 25% of styrene, a relatively cheap chemical made from benzene and alcohol, the I. G. came up with a Buna variant called Buna-S (the "S" for styrene), patented in 1934. In many general-purpose applications, Buna-S showed considerable promise. But there were still formidable barriers

§ The name Buna is from the initial syllables of *bu*tadiene and *na*trium (sodium).

in its way: it cost more than natural rubber, and it was difficult to fabricate on machines built to handle natural rubber.

Standard of New Jersey, which held American patent rights to the I. G.'s Buna rubbers, managed to interest two tire companies, Firestone and United States Rubber, in undertaking research into the difficulties of fabricating synthetic rubber. Two other large rubber companies, Goodrich and Goodyear, were convinced that they could develop synthetics free of the German patents and continued their own independent research. During 1940, Goodrich actually made and sold several thousand tires having a natural rubber carcass and a tread of Goodrich synthetic rubber. Goodyear erected a one-ton-per-day pilot plant in 1939 to turn out its own synthetic.

Meanwhile, the Jersey people met with moderate success in the introduction of Buna-N, or Perbunan, a specialty rubber developed by I. G. Farben during 1935. It was made from butadiene and acrylonitrile and had a high resistance to oil. Buna-N was introduced to the American market during 1937 at $1 to $1.20 a pound, and proved well suited to uses such as the manufacture of gasoline hose.

Tightening of Rubber Supplies

The year 1940 was a time of decision for the rubber business. With France fallen, the Low Countries invaded, and the Battle of Britain raging in the skies over England, it was apparent to many Americans that their own country was daily drawing nearer the European conflict. Even if America should manage to avoid actual participation in the war, it must expect interruption in supplies of raw materials that came from faraway lands by tenuous lines of supply. There was no telling when these lines might be cut, or for how long.

During June 1940, a bill was passed by Congress to permit the government to enter directly into the business of buying and accumulating "national stockpiles" of several key commodities. On June 28, the Rubber Reserve Company, a subsidiary of the Reconstruction Finance Corporation, was set up to do the buying necessary for the rubber stockpiling program. This piece of prudent foresight was offset by failure to limit rubber consumption. Automobile production continued at a high level all during 1941 and 775,000 tons of natural rubber were used by the United States that year, most of it for new automobile tires.

Attempts to create a national synthetic rubber industry had met with little success. Late in the summer of 1940, the whole problem was dumped into the ample lap of Jesse Jones, who as R.F.C. Chairman had over-all supervision of the rubber stockpiling program. The rubber industry and members of the Advisory Defense Committee (predecessor of the War Production Board) were urging an estimated $100,000,000 expenditure by the government to put up plants capable of turning out 100,000 tons a year of Buna-S. Some of the committee members had already carried their ambitious plan to the White House, where it had been turned down. Now they came to Jones, and after a series of conferences scaled down the program to four 10,000-ton plants which, with the butadiene and styrene facilities to supply them, could be built for about $25,000,000. This more modest program received the President's approval.

But this action, promising as it was, did not build the necessary plants. They were still "on paper" when America entered the war in December 1941. The synthetic program had been made to seem less urgent by the success of the stockpiling effort; there was reluctance to jeopardize friendly trade relations with nations supplying natural rubber; and the technological difficulties of building a full-scale new industry were not to be treated lightly. The process of reacting butadiene and styrene to produce raw Buna-S rubber was relatively uncomplicated. The larger technical difficulties lay before and after this point.

A big problem was to compound the raw Buna-S with carbon black and other "fillers" so that it would resemble natural rubber closely enough to be used in existing tire-making machinery. This was a problem for the rubber companies.

The other consideration was raw material supply. Styrene was then being produced on a modest scale by only one manufacturer, the Dow Chemical Company. It could be made from coal-tar benzene and ethylene gas from petroleum sources. Details had still to be worked out, but there was little doubt that sufficient quantities of styrene could be supplied. That was a problem for the chemical industry.

The big question mark was butadiene, which composed some 75% of Buna-S rubber. Here the question was not whether butadiene could be made, but from what sources, by what methods, and in what quantities. Butadiene could be made from almost any organic compound, if one were willing to go to the expense of elaborate processing. Indeed, at this time more than 80 distinct classes of organic compounds were known to have been converted into butadiene.[66] To produce it by a simple process, from materials that were available in abundance, seemed a problem for the oil companies because they had cheap sources of hydrocarbon gases.

The Germans were making their butadiene from acetylene gas, produced by burning coal and limestone together in an electric furnace. Standard of New Jersey succeeded in making acetylene by cracking natural gas with an electric arc, but the cost of the electric power made it too expensive to be a cheap source of butadiene. In the years just before the war the Jersey people experimented with other, cheaper hydrocarbons.

The Shell Butadiene Process

Meanwhile, Shell Development Company, spurred on by the small-volume but attractive businesses in Buna-N and other specialized rubbers, increased its efforts to develop a synthetic specialty rubber of its own. During their extensive investigation of substitutive chlorination, Williams and his staff had noted that chlorination of normal butylenes at moderate temperatures yielded dichlorobutane, $C_4H_8Cl_2$. By removing two molecules of hydrochloric acid, this dichlorobutane could be converted into butadiene, C_4H_6.[67]

As early as 1935, Shell Development was making butadiene by this method in the laboratory. Now work began to convert this laboratory reaction into a cheap and efficient industrial process. By 1938, a pilot plant capable of producing up to one ton a day of butadiene was in operation at Emeryville. This small unit, originally looking only toward small-scale manufacture of a specialized synthetic, assumed a larger importance during late 1939 and early 1940. With manufacture of an all-purpose synthetic rubber under serious consideration, any dependable source of butadiene was needed. The Emeryville pilot plant was kept in steady production throughout 1939, 1940, and 1941. In addition to proving the workability of Shell's butadiene process, it supplied badly needed raw butadiene to the rubber companies who were experimenting with the compounding and fabrication of synthetic rubber.[68]

Shell Chemical was planning to erect a new plant adjoining the Shell Oil refinery at Houston. Early in 1941, the chemical company decided to build a commercial-size butadiene unit as part of this new plant. The butadiene unit was given priority; despite growing shortages of materials, work on it was pushed ahead at maximum speed all during the spring and summer months of 1941. In September 1941, various units of the plant were able to go on stream for experi-

A. E. Lacomblé was Shell Development's president, 1943–48; board chairman, 1949–50.

Jan Oostermeyer headed Shell Chemical from 1942 until his retirement in 1953.

President Roosevelt presenting Congressional Medal of Honor to Brig.-Gen. James H. Doolittle for his part in the famous raid over Tokyo, April 18, 1942. Looking on are Gen. H. H. Arnold, Mrs. Doolittle, and Army Chief of Staff Gen. George C. Marshall.

Wood River's twin catalytic cracking units tower 15 stories in the air, 1944.

This plant at Norco was first to produce cumene for aviation gasoline, 1942.

mental runs. By November, the "bugs" had been ironed out of this first butadiene-from-butylene plant and it went into commercial production a few weeks before Pearl Harbor.[69]

The completion of the Shell Chemical butadiene plant was a bright spot in a year otherwise full of cheerless prospects for the future of synthetic rubber. At a cost of $2,000,000 of its own money, Shell had gone ahead and built a full-scale plant that offered little hope of immediate profit. During 1942, this little Houston plant was the towering giant of the American synthetic rubber industry. By the end of that year, it had produced 4,000 tons of butadiene, enough to make 5,300 tons of Buna-S rubber, sufficient for well over a million average-size automobile tires.[70]

The Shell management made no comment on the Houston plant's operating losses, some half-million dollars at the end of 1942. It was a small price to pay for a plant that in an hour of need turned out a full one-third of the nation's butadiene. In each of the ensuing two years, the Houston plant increased its output greatly; during 1944 it produced at double the rate of 1942. The Shell butadiene process, originally intended for manufacture of small-volume specialty rubbers, was not adaptable to the larger plants the government had set about building. Because of wartime shortages, the Houston plant had difficulty in getting supplies of chlorine so the Shell butadiene process, whatever its merits, could not be safely relied upon for large-scale production of synthetic rubber.*

The Government Rubber Plants

With the outbreak of actual hostilities, the synthetic rubber program became a much more urgent affair. The week after Pearl Harbor, the owners of patents covering various processes for the manufacture of synthetic rubber met in Washington and on December 19, 1941, signed an agreement permitting each signatory company to use the others' patents on a royalty-free basis. They also agreed to a free exchange of technical information on manufacturing techniques, an important concession on the part of the rubber companies whose individual skills in compounding crude rubber had hitherto been considered trade secrets.

The government, through the Reconstruction Finance Corporation

---

* This operating experience with a chlorination plant, while not financially successful at the time, proved useful to the Shell organization following the war, when Shell Chemical erected a plant to produce glycerine, also by chlorination.

and its subsidiaries, proposed to build and own all facilities for the manufacture of synthetic rubber, and for the production of the raw materials, styrene and butadiene. The synthetics manufactured would be the all-purpose Buna-S (rechristened "GR-S," for "Government Rubber-Styrene") and a much smaller quantity of Buna-N, which was likewise rechristened "GR-N." Purchase of plant sites, design and construction of individual plants, and subsequent operation of the plants would be placed in the hands of companies of demonstrated experience. The Defense Plant Corporation, a subsidiary of the R.F.C., would take legal title to the plants and lease them for $1 a year to the companies who were entrusted with their management. The plants would be run for the account of the Rubber Reserve Company, another R.F.C. subsidiary, with the private operators receiving a modest management fee.

Jan Oostermeyer, new president of Shell Chemical † succeeding De Bruyn who had retired at the end of 1941, participated in the rubber meetings on Shell's behalf and helped negotiate the agreement that was signed on February 5, 1942, to cover the manufacture of butadiene. The signatories to the butadiene agreement—three Shell companies, four affiliates of Standard of New Jersey, Phillips Petroleum, The B. F. Goodrich Company and a subsidiary, Carbide and Carbon Chemicals Corporation, The Koppers Company, Dow Chemical Company, Celanese Corporation, United Gas Improvement Company, Houdry Process Corporation, The Lummus Company, and Universal Oil Products Company—agreed to share their patents, technical information, and "know-how" to make raw butadiene in accordance with the plan which had been evolved calling for government ownership and operation, with private companies acting as managers.

The Rubber Reserve broke up the rubber program into its component parts and parcelled them out to the companies best fitted by skill, manpower, and experience to do the job. The plants which would combine the butadiene and styrene to produce raw synthetic rubber (copolymerization plants, they were called) were placed in the hands of the rubber companies. Recognized chemical companies (Carbide, Koppers, Dow, Monsanto) undertook to build and operate the

† Oostermeyer had held responsible positions in Group marketing companies in China and Chile. In 1939, he had come to San Francisco to be De Bruyn's assistant, and two years later was elected vice president of Shell Chemical. Oostermeyer's eleven-year presidency was a highly important period in the chemical company's history; by the time of his retirement in 1953, Shell Chemical had long since ceased to be a marginal operation and become a sizeable and profitable part of Shell's business.

necessary styrene facilities. Butadiene, the material that would be needed in largest quantity, would come from two sources: alcohol and petroleum.

At the request of the Rubber Reserve, seven individual oil companies (Shell, Standard of New Jersey and its subsidiaries, Phillips, Cities Service, Sinclair, Sun, Standard of California) and a joint corporation owned by five other oil companies operating in the area of Baytown, Texas (Atlantic Refining, Gulf, Pure, Socony-Vacuum, and Texaco) undertook the construction of petroleum-based butadiene plants. Plants totalling about two-thirds of the petroleum-based butadiene capacity would use a process developed by Standard Oil of New Jersey to produce butadiene by the catalytic dehydrogenation of butylene. The other petroleum-based butadiene plants would employ either the Phillips or Houdry two-step processes. Both of these processes started with butane, dehydrogenated it to produce butylene, and then dehydrogenated the butylene to make butadiene.

Butadiene could also be produced from ethyl alcohol, and although alcohol was in heavy demand in wartime, plants to make it could be erected rapidly and the Carbide & Carbon Chemicals Corporation had developed an efficient, two-step process to convert it into butadiene. Alcohol-based butadiene would cost more to produce, but the Rubber Reserve did not want to put all its eggs in one basket and accordingly authorized construction of three large plants employing the Carbide process. Two of these plants were to be built and operated by Carbide, the third by Koppers. Together, they had a designed capacity of 242,000 tons a year, or one-third of the total anticipated butadiene production. The rubber program at this point, in the late spring of 1942, contemplated facilities for a total production of 805,000 tons per annum of synthetic rubber, seven-eighths of it the all-purpose "GR-S."

The companies selected to build and operate plants for making butadiene, either from petroleum gases or alcohol, were given contracts and instructed to proceed with all possible speed. The petroleum-based plants would take a year or more to build, the alcohol-based plants not so long. Meanwhile, until these plants could commence operation in late 1943 and early 1944, the country would have to get along on the raw natural rubber in the national stockpile and the "reclaim rubber" that could be salvaged. Even more important than these reserves of rubber was the "rolling stockpile" of tires already on the public's automobiles. These had to be made to last, probably for the duration of the war.[71] Primarily to conserve existing rubber, strict gasoline rationing was inaugurated. Motorists were also required to turn in surplus tires, and a nation-wide scrap rubber drive accumulated a large stock of reclaim rubber.

The Torrance Plant

During the months the butadiene program was being parceled out, Shell Chemical had, at the request of the Rubber Reserve, prepared and submitted no fewer than seventeen plans, many of them calling for processes which would not use butylene. Finally, the company was asked in the fall of 1942 to build a sizeable plant in the Los Angeles area, capable of turning out 25,000 tons a year of butadiene. It was to use the one-step butylene dehydrogenation process developed by Standard of New Jersey and draw its butylene supply from refineries nearby. The purification facilities of this plant would be made large enough to accommodate the output of a "quickie" plant being built by the Southern California Gas Company.[72]

Torrance, south of Los Angeles and convenient to several refineries and to the Southern California Gas Company plant, was selected as the site for the government butadiene plant which Shell Chemical had agreed to build and operate. The Southern California Gas Company plant would crack naphtha and other light distillates at intense heat (a method known as "regenerative stove cracking") to produce a stream of C_4 hydrocarbon gases which contained some 40% of crude butadiene along with other usable gases such as butylene. The output of both plants was to be brought together and purified at Torrance, so purification facilities were designed sufficient to handle a total annual output of 55,000 tons of butadiene.

Because the gas company's "stove cracking" process would use a good deal of existing equipment, it could be completed at an early date. Shell Chemical concentrated on completing the purification facilities of the Torrance plant first and on July 27, 1943, it began operation, only eight months after government approval of the final plans. During its first twenty-four hours of operation, 75 tons of specification butadiene (98½% pure) were produced, a record for this type of installation. Operators of similar plants had, and would continue to have, a great deal of difficulty with purity during the initial months of operation.[73]

Construction of catalytic dehydrogenation facilities, the remainder of the Torrance plant, went ahead briskly. On April 20, 1944, the Torrance dehydrogenation plant turned out its first butadiene from butylene. During 1944, the combined operation at Torrance produced 39,240 tons of specification butadiene, enough for 10,000,000 average automobile tires.[74]

The butylene for Torrance's operation was collected from several refineries, each with a little gas to spare. No single refiner was thus called upon to furnish the plant's full requirements, which probably would have interfered with the aviation gasoline program. Shell's Wilmington-Dominguez refinery traded butylene to the Torrance plant in exchange for isobutylene which Torrance received in the stream from the Southern California Gas plant. Aside from this, materials for the Torrance plant came from companies other than Shell.[75]

On several occasions during ensuing months, the Torrance plant exceeded its designed capacity. Frequent difficulties at the Southern California Gas Company plant interrupted the stream of butadiene gases from that source, and Shell Chemical's experience with gas cracking at Shell Point made it possible for Shell engineers to come to the assistance of the Southern California company, thus repaying in part the courtesies which this company had extended to Shell Development in the late 1920's. Eventually the chief problems of regenerative stove cracking were ironed out. To derive maximum use from the Torrance purification facilities, the Rubber Reserve early adopted the policy of shipping impure butadiene from all over the United States to Torrance for recycling. In its first year of operation, the Torrance plant, in addition to its own production, processed more than 10,000 tons of low-quality butadiene from other manufacturers.[76]

The only other West Coast facility for the manufacture of butadiene was at El Segundo, a plant of much smaller capacity built for the government by Standard Oil of California. It employed the two-step Houdry process for converting butane into butylene, and thence to butadiene. It did not run smoothly, and quantities of its partially processed gases were piped from El Segundo to the Torrance plant where they could be mixed with the gases that were arriving from the Southern California Gas Company's plant.[77] The butadiene from the Shell-operated plant at Torrance was delivered by pipe line to a nearby copolymer plant operated by Goodyear; there it was converted into GR-S rubber. On adjacent property, Dow Chemical erected and operated on behalf of the government a plant to furnish the necessary styrene. This aggregation of plants, all near together and operating as a unit, comprised the West Coast synthetic rubber industry.

Because Shell had more experience in the manufacture of butadiene than any of its neighbors, Shell Chemical and Shell Development were constantly called upon for technical assistance, and at times had as many as 100 highly trained research men helping the operators of other government rubber plants.[78] In any cooperative effort, it is difficult to single out for praise a particular company or individual. Shell had, however, made a few distinct contributions, as Bradley Dewey, Rubber Director, noted in a letter to Oostermeyer in 1944: [79]

> Before leaving Washington, I would like to express my appreciation to your company for the contributions which it has made to the success of the Synthetic Rubber Program. Your early work with butadiene at Houston has been of great assistance in the development of the Government program and your design and construction of the large unit at Torrance has been a major factor in the West Coast synthetic rubber program.
>
> Most particularly, I would like to express my appreciation for the way in which both your company and Shell Development Company cooperated in a satisfactory solution of the manufacture and purification of butadiene by regenerative stove cracking. The problems in this field have been many, but with the cooperation of the various operators, it is now possible to produce butadiene in large quantities and of satisfactory quality.

By the end of 1944, the rubber shortage was over. Synthetic rubber plants throughout the country were turning out more rubber than the fabricators could handle. By late 1945, the country's synthetic rubber industry was producing 600,000 tons of all-purpose rubber annually, two thirds of it from petroleum sources. The three large grain-alcohol butadiene plants had done yeoman service and continued to run considerably above their designed capacity all during 1944 and for several months of 1945. But with alcohol at 90¢ a gallon, they were a high-cost source. As soon as the war had ended, the Rubber Reserve closed them down. Butylene-based rubber, on the other hand, even with the prospect of renewed competition from natural rubber, seemed to have a chance. Butadiene could be made from butylene at an average cost of 7¢ a pound.[80] This meant that synthetic rubber, once considered an impossibility because of price competition, could look forward to an interesting and profitable future.

5

Oil is Ammunition

THE First World War had introduced T.N.T. (tri-nitro-toluene), a devastatingly destructive explosive for the demolition ordnance of modern warfare—torpedoes, land and sea mines, aerial bombs, shells for long-range artillery. One of T.N.T.'s chief components was toluene, a ring-type hydrocarbon obtained as a by-product of coke manufacture. During World War I, the Royal Dutch-Shell Group had shown the Allies how to overcome their toluene shortage by extracting toluene from petroleum.‡ In World War II, with its "blockbusting" bombs, toluene would be needed in enormous quantities. With the outbreak of hostilities in Europe in the fall of 1939, the Army Ordnance Department prepared new estimates of its toluene requirements and concluded that there would be a severe shortage of toluene in the event of war. In December 1939, the Ordnance Department addressed a letter to several oil companies, Shell included, inquiring whether any of the oil companies had, or could propose, a satisfactory process for making toluene from petroleum.

For economic reasons, Shell Development passed over the extraction-by-nitration process used by the Group in World War I, as well as the possibility of using the Edeleanu process which extracted aromatics with sulphur dioxide. Turning instead to phenol (carbolic acid) as an extractant, Shell Development came up with a process for recovering toluene of "nitration grade" (99+% purity) from petroleum. The process consisted of two steps: (1) prefractionation to produce a toluene concentrate, and (2) extractive distillation of this concentrate, using phenol as the solvent.

During the summer of 1940, construction of a unit embodying the Shell toluene recovery process was begun at the Houston refinery. It was completed on December 2, 1940, and got into operation on a small scale before the end of that month. By mid-April 1941, all operating difficulties incident to starting up a new process had been ironed out, and the Houston toluene plant was in full production. This plant, the first in the United States to produce toluene from petroleum on a commercial scale, processed 7,500 barrels a day of light fractions to produce 120 to 140 barrels a day of one-degree-

‡ See pages 100-101, 504-505.

boiling-range toluene. It operated on products made from the "sweet" (non-sulphurous) crude of East Texas. A second unit to extract toluene from the "sour," sulphur-bearing oils of West Texas was built during the next few months, and put in operation early in November 1941. This second unit had a capacity of 200 barrels a day, making a total for the two units of some 13,000 gallons of toluene a day.[81]

The other sizeable producer of toluene was, as in the case of aviation gasoline and synthetic rubber ingredients, Standard Oil of New Jersey. Jersey, Indiana Standard, and M. W. Kellogg had been responsible for the development of Hydroforming, a modification of hydrogenation in which the oil was contacted in a hydrogen atmosphere with a metal oxide catalyst. Hydroforming converted a large part of the naphthenes and some of the paraffins into aromatics. Among these aromatics was toluene. The problem was to extract it. Jersey's subsidiary, the Humble Oil & Refining Company, decided to attempt this extraction with the Edeleanu method, and late in 1940 made a proposal to the Army for the construction of a government-owned toluene plant adjoining Humble's Baytown, Texas, refinery. This plant, completed in the fall of 1941, and known as the Baytown Ordnance Works, was designed with enough capacity to supply a large part of the Army's anticipated toluene requirements. The Hydroforming process produced ample supplies of light fractions rich in toluene, but the SO_2 recovery process encountered difficulty at first in producing a toluene of nitration grade, and the Baytown plant did not operate at designed capacity until well into the spring of 1942. From then on, the Baytown plant was the largest single producer of toluene in the country, and during the war period accounted for roughly one-half of all the toluene produced from petroleum.[82]

This Baytown toluene was "synthetic" in that the Hydroforming process had produced it by chemical conversion of other hydrocarbons. A serious limiting factor of toluene plants such as Shell's Houston installation was that the amount of natural toluene to be recovered was small, even in the richest toluene-containing fractions. The yield of Shell's Houston units on total volume processed was only about 1 ½ %.[83]

Shell Development had anticipated this shortcoming, and all during 1941 Emeryville worked hard to develop a synthetic process capable of converting other hydrocarbons into toluene. This work resulted in a catalytic dehydrogenation process, which removed six atoms of hydrogen from methyl cyclohexane to yield toluene. Before announcing its process, Shell Development took steps to augment the available supplies of methyl cyclohexane by devising an isomerization process capable of making methyl cyclohexane from dimethyl cyclopentane. The Shell synthetic toluene process as finally announced was a combination of isomerization and catalytic dehydrogenation. The separation method was the same phenol extraction which Shell was already using for natural toluene.

During 1942, Shell Oil began construction of two large plants embodying the new Shell synthetic toluene process, one at the Dominguez refinery, the other at Wood River where a large toluene extraction unit meanwhile had been erected and put into operation early in May 1942. The Dominguez synthetic toluene plant went into operation during December 1942. It was a large plant and drew its feed stocks not only from the Wilmington-Dominguez refinery but also from Martinez, where two prefractionator columns to make a toluene concentrate were built and put into operation in September 1942. The Wood River synthetic toluene plant went on stream in mid-January 1943.[84]

From the beginning of 1943 onwards, Shell Oil had an impressive array of facilities for producing toluene. There were two units at Houston for the extraction of natural toluene, each costing over half a million dollars; the Martinez prefractionator, which cost the same amount; and the large installations at Dominguez and Wood River, each costing well over four million dollars to build—a total expenditure for toluene facilities of some $10,570,000, with all funds supplied by the company.[85]

The government-owned Baytown Ordnance Works, operated by Humble, accounted for almost exactly one-half of the total toluene produced from oil. A large share of the remaining production was turned out by Shell in facilities it had built and paid for itself. Few other companies expressed a wish to risk their own funds on toluene facilities, for it was anticipated that there would be little or no postwar market for petroleum toluene. As in the case of aviation gasoline and butadiene, Shell's great contribution to toluene manufacture was in starting manufacture early, in having practicable processes and full-scale plant equipment, and in being willing to take the financial risk involved in going ahead. As in the other instances, this fortunate state of affairs was of considerable assistance during the first, most perilous days of the war.

LEADING MANUFACTURERS OF PETROLEUM TOLUENE [86]
(THOUSANDS OF GALLONS)

	Total Petroleum Toluene	Baytown Ordnance Works	Per cent by Baytown	Shell (Private Funds)	Per cent by Shell
1940	52	–	–	small	–
1941	4,084	2,427	59.4%	1,410	34.5%
1942	55,560	49,736	89.5%	5,764	10.4%
1943	123,405	66,797	54.1%	25,026	20.3%
1944	168,363	69,632	41.4%	22,425	13.3%
1945	132,818	50,690	38.2%	18,110	13.6%
	484,282	239,282	49.4%	72,735	15.0%

The Baytown Ordnance Works, as already noted, employed Hydroforming to manufacture synthetic toluene and sulphur dioxide extraction to extract it. Other refiners who built synthetic toluene units generally adopted Hydroforming in conjunction with the Shell toluene recovery process. Shell's phenol extraction method was installed during 1943 by Standard of Indiana, Pan American, Gulf, Continental, Sinclair, Texas, and Pure Oil.[87]

6

Wartime Pipe Lines

EVEN before America entered the war, parts of the country had a preview of wartime petroleum shortages. In April 1941, the British, who had lost a substantial part of their tanker fleet, asked for American assistance in transporting petroleum products across the Atlantic. The Neutrality Act stood in the way of direct transportation to England by American vessels. To provide assistance and yet keep within the law, the Maritime Commission at the direction of the President asked that a "shuttle service" be set up to carry oil products from Gulf Coast and Caribbean refineries to New York and Halifax, there to be transshipped into waiting British tankers. Fifty American tankers were removed from their regular runs and put into this shuttle service, which cut two weeks off trans-Atlantic crossings of the British tankers and made possible a substantial increase in supplies to England.[88]

With the carrying capacity of 50 tankers diverted to this shuttle service, the East Coast very shortly began to feel the pinch, for these tankers had been transporting a fifth of the total petroleum requirements of the area. How to prevent a severe shortage of petroleum products on the East Coast was a pressing problem presented by Ickes and Davies to the first meeting of the new petroleum agency in June 1941.

Several expedients were suggested. The one most productive of immediate results was a suggestion for large-scale reversion to long-distance rail transportation. For Gulf-to-East Coast shipments, railroad tank car was ten times as expensive as ocean tanker; and to handle receipt of whole trainloads of products, most Atlantic Seaboard companies had to build large unloading-rack installations. This method was admittedly very expensive, and Ickes and Davies were unable to promise the oil men either increased prices or reimbursement for the extra expense. It is to the credit of the companies that they went ahead anyway, with the assistance of the railroads, who reduced their rates and did everything possible to expedite shipments.§ By the early fall of 1941, rail movements of petroleum products into the Atlantic Seaboard area had increased 30-fold. So smoothly was this impending shortage forestalled that some of the press and public, annoyed at Ickes' request for voluntary "gasless Sundays," were quick to brand it a "phoney shortage." [89]

For the oil men, the experience was anything but phoney. It offered a sobering illustration of the trouble that could be expected from any prolonged interruption of tanker service between Gulf Coast refineries and Atlantic Seaboard consuming centers. During 1941, suggestions for pipe line facilities to connect these two areas were discussed. National Defense Pipe Lines, Inc., a company set up for the purpose by several leading oil companies, proposed a products line from the Houston-Beaumont refining area to New York City. The line was to be 20 inches in diameter and cost an estimated $70,000,000. The same group also drew up plans for a large-diameter crude oil line. Plans for the crude line were completed in September 1941, but the government Supply, Priorities and Allocation Board rejected the

§ Later in the war, the companies were reimbursed by the government for most of this extra transportation expense.

request for materials, as well as the Petroleum Administration's subsequent request for reconsideration.[90]

Pearl Harbor Day renewed the urgency for long-distance pipe line projects, even though some in government could not yet see the value of these lines. In February 1942, the projected large-diameter crude line was turned down once again by the priorities board. During the months immediately following Pearl Harbor, the entire domestic oil transportation situation was under constant survey by the best-qualified members of the industry. On March 23, 1942, nearly a hundred leading figures in the pipe line business assembled at Tulsa, stayed in continuous session for three days and nights, and drew up a 10-point proposal that became, with slight modifications, the nation's pipe line program for the duration of the war.[91]

The "Big Inch" and "Little Big Inch"

Of prime importance in this program were the two large-diameter pipe lines proposed a year earlier, both to run from Texas to the New York City area. Like many other wartime facilities, these lines were to be financed by the Reconstruction Finance Corporation, and owned by its subsidiary, the Defense Plant Corporation. As in the case of the synthetic rubber plants, the government needed experienced pipe line people to design, build, and operate these government-owned facilities. Companies who had been advocating these two lines stepped into the breach. Eleven major oil companies,* or their pipe line affiliates, joined to organize War Emergency Pipe Lines, Inc., a non-profit corporation to build and operate the "Big Inch" and "Little Big Inch," as they were already being called. W. Alton Jones, president of Cities Service, served as president; Burt Hull, president of Texaco's pipe line company, agreed to superintend construction; and W. R. Finney, of Jersey Standard, took charge of over-all design. The industry made available without charge the aerial surveys and plans which had been drawn up the previous summer.

T. E. Swigart, president of Shell Pipe Line, prepared the economic report which was used by Secretary Ickes in his fight to obtain Congressional support for the first segment, the 24-inch crude oil line from Longview, Texas, to Norris City, Illinois. This construction was finally authorized by the War Production Board in June 1942; subsequent approvals came more easily. The first pipe was laid early in

---

* Atlantic Refining Company, Cities Service, Gulf, Pan American, Shell, Sinclair, Socony, Standard of New Jersey, Sun, Texaco, and Tide Water.

August, and on the last day of December 1942, oil was being pumped into the Texas end of the Big Inch line even though the first leg was not yet finished. The segment from Norris City, Illinois, to the New Jersey terminus was finished in August 1943.[92]

Meanwhile, the 20-inch products pipe line, nicknamed the "Little Big Inch," was authorized in February 1943. It closely followed the designs the industry had prepared in the summer of 1941. It ran from the Houston-Beaumont refining area to Linden, N. J., near New York City, and was completed in a year. The Big Inch line was 1,478 miles long and the Little Big Inch line was 1,714 miles in length. Together they cost $148,000,000, approximately as much as two battleships, but in the successful prosecution of the war these lines were equal to a whole fleet of battleships. The Big Inch alone replaced 60 to 75 tankers, or 30,000 railroad tank cars.

"There was," the P.A.W. history remarks, "a magic about the Big Inch which captured the imaginations of everyone—the government and the oil industry, the newspapers and the public, and even the hard-bitten pipe liners who built it." The progress of its construction was followed with a degree of public interest rarely exhibited in a project of this sort. It required the best efforts of nearly every pipe line construction company in the country, working under the direction of the most competent pipe line people from the oil companies. "They did the job," continues the P.A.W. history, "in far less time than ever was hoped for, and they did it at an expenditure of many millions of dollars less than was estimated and provided." And once in operation the Big Inch and its companion, the Little Big Inch, more than came up to advance expectations. Together, they transported more than half a million barrels daily, one-third the East Coast pre-war demand. From their completion to the end of the war, the two lines actually delivered 380,000,000 barrels of crude oil and products from Texas to the Atlantic Seaboard, well over half of it military supplies.[93]

Reversing the East Texas Line

A great many private pipe line systems were tied into the Big and Little Big Inch lines. The Big Inch was fed by crude oil lines of several oil companies. Shell Pipe Line Corporation's 10-inch East Texas-to-Houston line, built twelve years earlier, was one of these. Its direction of flow was reversed. From July 1943 to the end of September 1945, Shell's East Texas line pumped crude from southwest Texas north to join the main stream of the Big Inch at Longview, a total of 35,000,000 barrels in all.[94]

Ventura-Wilmington Crude Line

Other shorter pipe lines, less dramatic than the Big Inch and Little Big Inch, helped in their own areas to relieve the congestion of wartime transportation. One of these was Shell Oil's Ventura–Wilmington crude oil line, built during the summer of 1941, in the last few hurried months before the war. It was 86 miles long, 10¾ inches in diameter, was laid over rough terrain in 52 days, and cost $2,500,000.[95] The new line promptly freed for other use the equivalent of two tankers formerly needed to carry Ventura oil to the Martinez and Wilmington refineries. In addition, it had spare capacity which made possible a further release of tankers.

Plantation Products Line

Another line of considerable importance to the war effort was that of the Plantation Pipe Line Company, built during 1941–1942. The Plantation line was projected during 1940 as a commercial venture owned 49% by Standard of New Jersey, 27% by Standard of Kentucky, and 24% by Shell. It was planned as a products pipe line some 812 miles long, stretching from Baton Rouge to Greensboro, North Carolina, running through the heart of the Deep South, with branches to Birmingham and Montgomery, Alabama; Chattanooga and Knoxville, Tennessee; and Macon and Columbus, Georgia. The designs called for 12-inch pipe for the first 450 miles, 10-inch pipe for the rest of the way, 8-inch line on the branch to Chattanooga and Knoxville, and 4-inch pipe on the other branches—altogether some 1,261 miles of pipe, making the Plantation line not only the largest products system but the largest and longest pipe line undertaken up to that time.[96]

The route had been surveyed and the work of acquiring the right-of-way begun when, early in 1941, railroads who stood to lose a substantial amount of business threw a serious obstacle in the way of the project. Plantation's applications to 24 railroads asking for permits to cross their tracks were refused in all except one instance. Matters thus ground to a halt in the spring of 1941, at the very time an East Coast shortage threatened because of the diversion of tankers to the shuttle service. Completion of the Plantation line would, it was calculated, release six tankers, not to mention a sizeable number of barges. The test case came in Georgia, where the Southeastern Pipe

Line Company (owned by Gulf and Pure) was building a products line from Port St. Joe, Florida, to Chattanooga, Tennessee. The Southeastern people had a bill introduced in the Georgia legislature to convey upon the pipe line company the right of eminent domain and enable it to bring condemnation proceedings against landowners unwilling to sell. This measure, opposed by the railroads and rail unions, was defeated by the Georgia legislature in March 1941. Despite appeals from President Roosevelt, Secretary Ickes, and Secretary of the Navy Frank Knox, the Georgia legislature adjourned without reconsidering its action.[97]

At this point, Representative Cole of Maryland introduced in Congress a bill to permit interstate pipe line companies to exercise the right of eminent domain if, in the opinion of the President, such action was "in the interests of national defense." The Cole bill, strongly urged upon Congress by the President, passed and became law on July 30, 1941. The government oil agency promptly recommended that the Plantation line, the Southeastern Line, and the Portland–Montreal crude line † be given clearance under this act. This was done late in August 1941. After months of agonizing delay, construction of the Plantation line finally began on September 1, 1941. Necessary materials had meanwhile been acquired, so the speed of the construction of the Plantation line made up in part for previous delays. By January 1, 1942, the 812 miles of main line from Baton Rouge to Greensboro were complete and in operation, and construction of the 449 miles of spur lines was well in hand. In design, the Plantation line closely followed Shell's products pipe lines in the Midwest. It was a multi-products line and up to 22 products could be handled.[98]

Further to relieve the tanker shortage, which continued to worsen during the early years of the war, the government asked Plantation to build and operate on behalf of the Defense Plant Corporation a northward extension of the line to make possible overland shipment of products all the way to Richmond, Virginia. This emergency facility, consisting of 178 miles of secondhand 8-inch pipe, was com-

---

† The Portland–Montreal line was a crude oil line conceived and built during 1941 by Standard Oil of New Jersey. It saved tankers by eliminating the long haul around Gaspé and up the St. Lawrence; more important, it made possible crude supplies to Montreal during the winter months when the river is impassable. In 1946, Jersey sold this line, which is formally known as Portland Pipe Line Corporation (American segment) and Montreal Pipe Line Company (Canadian segment), to the line's chief users. It is now owned approximately 36% by Jersey's Canadian affiliate, Imperial Oil, Limited; and 18% each by McColl-Frontenac Oil Company, Ltd. (Texaco affiliate), British American Oil Company, Ltd., and Shell Oil Company of Canada, Ltd.; and 10% by Canadian Petrofina, Ltd.

pleted in April 1943, at a cost of a little over $4,000,000. It had a daily
capacity of 30,000 barrels, enough to supply Richmond and make
available substantial amounts of product for delivery by barge in the
Chesapeake Bay area.[99]

To provide additional pumping capacity for this northward extension, Plantation during 1942 installed fourteen new stations along its
main line, raising the capacity of the main line from 60,000 to 93,000
barrels a day. The Plantation company operated the government-
owned emergency line to Richmond for the duration of the war.
With the cessation of hostilities and resumption of normal tanker
service, it was discontinued because products for the Chesapeake Bay
area could be laid down cheaper by water.

Bayou Pipe Line

The extra 30,000 barrels a day of petroleum products handled by
the temporary Greensboro–Richmond line could not be supplied at
the Baton Rouge end of the Plantation line by Standard's Baton Rouge
refinery, or by Shell at Norco. The answer, obviously, was to connect
the Baton Rouge with the Houston refining area. Shell and other
refiners in the Houston region were willing to build such a line with
their own funds. In the spring of 1942, concurrently with the start of
the emergency northward extension of the Plantation line, work began
on this new products pipe line to link Baytown, just east of Houston,
with the southern terminus of the Plantation line at Baton Rouge. Six
companies—Humble (Standard of Jersey), Pan American (Standard
of Indiana), Texaco, Pure, Crown Central, and Shell—were to furnish
the line with product, and their pipe line affiliates agreed to underwrite the line's cost, each company bearing a share of the expense
proportionate to the amount of pipe line capacity it would require.
The line, named the Bayou Pipe Line System from the terrain it had
to traverse, was a "joint venture" of these several pipe line companies
rather than a separate corporation.‡ Shell Pipe Line Corporation

‡ The Bayou line was the first to be built as a "joint venture," a system of ownership and operation that has since been quite extensively employed in connection with
the large-diameter lines, too big for any individual company, that have been built
since the war. Each participant in a joint venture owns an undivided interest in the
entire line proportionate to his percentage of participation. A single company, generally one of the participants, assumes responsibility for operating the line on a
non-profit basis and is reimbursed by the participants, again in accordance with their
percentage of participation. Each of the individual participants files tariffs for its
percentage of the line's capacity.[100]

subscribed for a 27.44% interest in the Bayou line and agreed to build and operate it as agent of the other carriers.

The building of the Bayou line epitomized the difficulties of wartime construction. New pipe was not to be had, nor were new motors, new pumps, new valves, or new tanks. The line had to be built almost entirely of secondhand materials, and this made for endless difficulties in design. Few of the obtainable pumps and motors were of the same size, age, or style. Most of the pipe available had already seen hard service in the transport of sour crude and was as a result severely pitted by corrosion and subject to flaking. The secondhand tanks available were in very poor shape, and could be used only by reassembling them to make four "new" tanks out of five old ones.

Fitting the design of the line and stations to available equipment, the Shell Pipe Line crew got to work in the summer of 1942. By mid-February 1943, the Bayou line was in operation. It consisted of 68 miles of 8-inch line from Houston to Baytown and 10-inch line for the 183 miles between Baytown and Baton Rouge. In addition, there were 51 miles of 4-, 6-, and 8-inch feeder lines to connect with the six refineries supplying product. Many of the niceties of products pipe line operation, including automatic controls, were improvised. Of the line's total cost of $8,000,000, only $1,000,000 was spent for new materials.

The Bayou line, designed for 52,000 barrels a day, was by 1945 pumping 68,000 barrels. Far from being the wartime expedient that its builders had originally conceived, the Bayou line ten years later was still operating satisfactorily at the designed capacity, even after four of the original stations had been dismantled and removed in 1947.[101]

Ohio Emergency Pipe Lines

Pipe line systems of hot competitors were as a matter of course interconnected all during the war, wherever such a joining of lines made it possible to move more oil and oil products. The industrial Northeast, heavy user of every petroleum product from gasoline to fuel oil, was hardest hit by the disappearance of tankers from domestic routes. All sorts of measures were undertaken to help tide this area over until the Little Big Inch line could be constructed and new tankers built for the Atlantic Coast run.

One of these expedients was Project 3, a scheme for reversing Sun Oil's Philadelphia–Cleveland products line and interconnecting the products lines of Standard of Indiana, Shell, and Standard of Ohio to provide feed. The Sun line was reversed in August 1942, and Ohio Emergency Pipe Lines, Inc., a non-profit corporation, was organized by Sun, Shell and Standard of Ohio to build some 111 miles of 6- and 8-inch connecting lines in the state of Ohio. Shell increased the capacity of its East products line by building a new pumping station at Muncie, Indiana, and tying the Standard of Indiana gasoline line into its own line at Zionsville, Indiana. These rearrangements and new connecting lines cost just over $2,000,000 and made available for shipment to the East Coast 20,000 barrels of gasoline a day. This mention of Project 3 is hardly calculated to fire the imagination, but it does provide a typical example of the constant reappraisal and rearrangement of pipe line capacity that continued all during the war.[102]

The Portable Pipe Line

A story with considerably more popular appeal is the development of the military portable pipe line, an innovation that materially eased the problems of supplying a highly mechanized war by taking petroleum products to the fighting fronts in bulk. Much of the credit for this ingenious line can be assigned to a single individual, S. S. (Syd) Smith, designer of Shell's Midwest products lines and manager of the company's products pipe line department.

At the outbreak of the European war in 1939, Smith began to plan an easily assembled, completely salvable pipe line that could be laid alongside roads and pumped by foolproof pumps and engines to eliminate hauling by truck the immense quantities of gasoline which would be needed at the front lines. Such a line could not be welded or screwed together as it would take too long to lay, and the pipe should be light enough to be lifted easily. Smith recalled the Victaulic couplings (rubber-lined metal semicircles fastened with a single bolt) that had been used by Roxana in the late Twenties to join temporary pipe lines built to connect portable gasoline plants with railroad sidings. These temporary lines had been buried in trenches, but Smith thought that a military line with similar couplings could be laid on top of the ground. A suitable lightweight pipe, reinforced by a spiral weld, was already being made by the Naylor Manufacturing Company, and existing Wheatley valves, Gaso pumps, and Buda gasoline engines could be assembled into a satisfactory pumping unit without much difficulty.

Encouraged by McGaw, who had recently been made vice president in charge of the company's transportation and supplies department, Smith during 1940 engaged Hanlon-Waters, Inc., of Tulsa to proceed with the construction of a pump station, using the equipment he had suggested. An important consideration was to make the line as simple and foolproof as possible, and to this end Smith thought it highly desirable that the line be automatic or nearly automatic in operation. A steady rate of off-take, as in commercial operation, could not be assured at the forward end of a military pipe line. To meet this situation, Smith designed and L. J. (Ted) Griffey, chief engineer of Hanlon-Waters, supervised the fabrication of an automatic throttle-control system actuated by the pressure in the line. If the forward end of the line were closed, the pressure inside the line would quickly rise and this increase in pressure would actuate the throttle control. One by one, the engines running the pumps would slow down, or if the circumstances required, stop completely. Opening the valve reduced the pressure, and the pressure drop had a reverse effect, causing the throttle control to start the pumps up again.

This simple series of automatic controls (the only patentable feature of Smith's portable pipe line) made it possible to operate the line from an advance base precisely as if it were a garden hose with a nozzle. Turn it off, it stopped; open the valve, it would start. Cans, drums, and vehicles could be filled with gasoline directly from a pipe line running up to the fighting front. It would not be necessary to provide large advance tank installations which, in addition to consuming precious time and materials, made excellent targets. And because the pumps started and stopped automatically, the line would not need a communications system to connect the pumping stations with each other.

The most important aspect of this portable pipe line was that it could, with expenditure of very little equipment, manpower, and fuel, transport quantities of gasoline that would otherwise require long convoys of trucks with drivers. A truck convoy heavily bombed from overhead represented a serious loss of men and equipment and could mean a major disruption of front-line activities. The portable pipe line would, of course, be vulnerable to attack from the air but, Smith argued, this would not be a serious objection if repairs to the line could be made quickly enough.

In the interest of simplicity, the line was designed around 20-foot modules. The pipe was manufactured in lengths exactly 20 feet long, gate valves to stop the flow of product in the event of a break were mounted in 20-foot sections of pipe, as were check valves for use on hills to prevent backward flow. The pumping stations were constructed so that their connections were of the same 20-foot length. This standardization of unit length made for easy and quick repair. Damaged sections of pipe, blocked off by the nearest gate valves, could be removed and replaced by new sections. Valves or stations requiring repair could in the same way be replaced by spares, and the line returned to full service in a matter of an hour or two.[103]

Proposed American use of the Burma Road to transport Lend-Lease supplies to Chiang Kai-shek stirred up the first real interest in Smith's portable pipe line. In the summer of 1941, J. K. Bausfield, general manager of the Asiatic Petroleum Company (South China), Ltd., Hong Kong, was in the United States and discussed the Burma Road with officials of China Defense Supply, Inc. Net effective transportation over the winding, mountainous 700-mile Burma Road would be only three-eighths of a truck convoy's capacity, Bausfield pointed out. The other five-eighths of the truck's capacity would be needed to carry fuel for the trip, for there were no filling stations along the Burma Road and no supplies of gasoline available in southern China. A pipe line was mentioned but discarded because of the amount of steel it would require and the time it would take to lay.

Bausfield's discussion of the problem with McGaw led the latter to suggest Smith's line, which could be laid quickly and would use a much smaller amount of steel. As a result of these discussions, a formal description of Smith's portable line, in 4- and 6-inch diameter sizes, was prepared and presented to China Defense Supply on September 17, 1941. The Chinese agency was delighted, and on the same day other copies of the presentation were delivered to Army officials who would need to approve the project, for Lend-Lease materials were legally U. S. property and their purchase had to be approved by the appropriate government agencies.

The Army was skeptical of using a portable line for long-distance transportation, and also did not believe it would prove adequate to the rugged terrain of the Burma Road. However, in October 1941, Army consent to a survey was given, and J. H. Hall, chief engineer of Shell's products pipe line department, was dispatched to make a survey of the Burma Road and report whether or not a portable pipe line would be practicable over that route. Hall arrived back in the United States in mid-February 1942, only a few days before the

British were forced to evacuate Rangoon, leaving Burma to fall to the Japanese. Hall's survey, delivered by Asiatic to China Defense Supply early in March 1942, reported favorably on a portable pipe line for the Burma Road.

In the meantime, Shell ordered a sample pumping station and 1,200 feet of portable pipe and set them up on the former refinery grounds at East Chicago. Here, in March 1942, trial demonstrations were staged for the Chinese and for representatives of the British and American Army engineers. It was apparently these demonstrations that convinced the Army. Early in April 1942, the Army engineers called Smith to Washington. He delivered to them several more copies of his specifications and blueprints. The Army Engineer Board decided to run a test on a 30-mile segment of portable pipe line over mountainous terrain at Camp Rapidan in the Shenandoah Mountains of Virginia. Smith was asked to recommend a firm to assemble four pumping stations for the test. He recommended Hanlon-Waters, who were by now thoroughly familiar with the work, and the Army took them over as suppliers, along with the other equipment-supplying contacts that Smith had developed.

Late in April 1942, without waiting for the outcome of the Virginia tests, the Army decided to go ahead and purchase some 1,200 miles of pipe line for the Burma Road. A limiting factor was the small plant capacity of the Naylor Manufacturing Company, producers of the spiral-welded pipe, so Smith made arrangements with Republic Steel to fabricate sections of thin-gauge pipe to which other suppliers welded endpieces cut from standard-weight 4-inch pipe. This pipe, strong enough to take the grooves for Victaulic couplings, and light enough (about 90 pounds) to be lifted by one man, was the so-called "invasion pipe" of which thousands of miles were eventually supplied. In October 1942, the Army placed additional orders with Hanlon-Waters, and this firm continued to manufacture the portable pumping units for the remainder of the war. Shell made Smith's designs, patents, and personal services available to the Army without charge or compensation.

The Quartermaster Corps, which was responsible for supplies, meanwhile made some attempt to develop a portable pipe line of its own. It was a unit employing a half mile of 3-inch pipe and hose and a centrifugal pump with a small gasoline engine, and was demonstrated at Army maneuvers in North Carolina. Unlike Smith's line, the Quartermaster line was not intended for pumping long distances

overland, but for unloading products into tanks, supplying airfields
that might be a few miles distant from a railroad, or unloading tankers
in areas where the shore was too marshy for heavy equipment to be
brought alongside.[104]

It was Smith's design, however, that the Army adopted with only
one modification. In his original design, Smith had placed the pumping
stations 20 miles apart and mounted them on trailer equipment for
easy portability. To reduce the weight of individual units, the Army
cut the size of the stations and designed them for placement at 10-
mile intervals. Complete with stations, the portable pipe line cost only
about $3,000 a mile.[105]

The military portable pipe line received its first real test in the
North African campaign, from late 1942 until mid-May 1943. There
seemed little likelihood of the Burma Road being retaken for some
time, so the pipe and pumping stations ordered for the Burma Road
were diverted to North Africa, and during the North African campaign four lines varying in length from 75 to 300 miles were built and
saw heavy use. When adequate manpower and transportation were
available, the portable line could be laid at rates of up to 20 miles a
day. When enough pipe was available, the line was also ideal for
transporting water. Under battle conditions, the portable pipe line
proved less vulnerable than anyone had anticipated. Painted a dull
color and laid alongside a road, it was difficult to see from the air and
even harder to hit.[106]

The same line, taken up and relaid, followed American troops as
they advanced into Sicily and Italy. On the east coast of Italy, 560
miles of line were laid from Taranto to Foggia; on the west coast a
line was built from Naples to a point 100 miles north of Rome. Other
lines, of similar construction, followed American troops through
France and into Germany. With resumption of offensive operations
in the China-Burma-India Theater, a pipe line was laid all the way
from Calcutta in India through Burma and into southern China, a
distance of 1,482 miles. Portable pipe line and portable pumping stations were used for the entire distance, with the exception of a small
amount of permanent welded line in the Calcutta area. This Burma
Road line was a few miles longer than even the Big Inch and Little
Big Inch.[107]

The 4-inch diameter pipe was the size most commonly used in
every area, and altogether some 11,000 miles of it were fabricated.
The design of the military portable pipe line remained unchanged

throughout the war, except for the Army's substitution of centrifugal pumps and smaller engines because the pumps were lighter in weight and the engines easier to come by.[108]

At the close of the North African campaign, Brig. Gen. R. F. Fowler, of the War Department's Office of the Chief of Engineers, wrote Smith a letter of appreciation: "The portable pipe line system which you designed and developed has been a material contribution to the success of our armies in the field. The aid you have given the engineers of the Supply Division in establishing manufacturing facilities and in testing the design has enabled us to deliver the equipment to the field in time to meet an urgent demand.

"The wholehearted cooperation you have given in connection with the procurement of this pipeline equipment, without financial compensation, reflects patriotism of the highest type and merits my sincere commendation." [109]

This wartime commendation was followed by recognition of a more public character. In October 1946, Smith was awarded the Medal for Merit, with a citation signed by the President praising Smith's part in "conceiving, perfecting and proving" the military portable pipe line.

7

Shell Chemical Comes of Age

DURING the war years, all of American industry developed a new appreciation of chemistry in industry. Manufacturers had an opportunity to see how hitherto unattainable properties could be supplied by chemical processing, or how products derived from chemicals could be made into satisfactory substitutes for raw materials that were no longer available. Within the Shell organization, there was a new appreciation of Shell Chemical. It was turning out an increasing variety of materials important to the war, and it had at last begun to show a respectable profit. In 1941, Shell Chemical's net earnings passed a million dollars for the first time, and during the years 1941–1945 the chemical company netted nearly $14,000,000.

The company no longer had trouble selling any of its products. Ammonia in wartime moved onto the critical list, for it was a source of nitric acid (used in the manufacture of T.N.T.), ammonium nitrate, and other explosives ingredients. Shell Chemical during 1941–1942 installed $1,300,000 worth of auxiliary facilities at Shell Point to eliminate bottlenecks and increase the plant's capacity by 25%, from 80 to 100 tons per day. Because of its important wartime uses, ammonia was on allocation and Shell Chemical could fill orders only as directed by the appropriate government agencies. In June 1942, sales of ammonia for agricultural purposes were halted at government request. However, the largest explosives plants were in areas other than the West Coast, and after meeting the requirements of nearby explosives firms, Shell Chemical during 1943 was allowed to resume sales to commercial growers and other users of agricultural ammonia. It was during this year that Leavitt's system for injecting anhydrous ammonia into the soil ("Nitrojection"), developed just prior to the war, was first put to use on a substantial scale.[110]

At Dominguez, the alcohol and ketones plants continued in full production, with chief emphasis on the manufacture of isopropyl alcohol and acetone. The I.P.A. plant, capable of producing 3,000,000 pounds a month at the outset of the war, underwent minor additions to remove bottlenecks and by the end of the war was producing at the rate of 5,000,000 pounds monthly, a two-thirds increase.[111]

Houston I.P.A. and Acetone Plants

At Houston, the new I.P.A. and acetone plants, completed late in 1941, resulted in an immediate doubling of the company's production of both these chemicals. Shell Chemical produced 42¼ million pounds of acetone in 1941, 89½ million pounds in 1942, and nearly 99 million pounds in 1943. Most of this increase came from the Houston plant, where a program of bottleneck removal had by the end of the war raised the plant's production to 9,000,000 pounds a month of I.P.A. and acetone. In 1944, for instance, production of I.P.A. at Houston was 13,313,000 pounds, half of Shell Chemical's total output, and of acetone 64,853,000 pounds, more than two-thirds the company's total acetone production.[112]

M.I.B.C. and M.I.B.K.

During 1944, an installation was erected at the Martinez chemical plant to manufacture methyl isobutyl carbinol, an alcohol, and methyl isobutyl ketone, a higher-boiling ketone, originally manufactured by Shell Chemical at Dominguez in 1938. Both these products supplemented Shell Chemical's other alcohols and ketones by offering similar solvency at higher boiling ranges. They were used chiefly as versatile solvents in the manufacture of a variety of lacquers and surface coatings. The new Martinez plant could produce some 1,200,000 pounds a month of M.I.B.C. and M.I.B.K.[113]

The Allyl Derivatives

It was also during 1944 that construction was started at Houston on a series of new units to manufacture products by chlorinating propylene. The first three of these units, completed early in 1945, made dichloropropane-dichloropropylene, marketed under the name "D-D" for use as a soil fumigant; allyl chloride, an intermediate for pharmaceuticals, anesthetics, and plastics; and allyl alcohol, a plastics intermediate. In addition to immediate war uses, these allyl products held out considerable promise for the chemical company's postwar business. With the addition of other units, additional products could be made such as acrolein, diallyl phthalate, epichlorohydrin, and glycerine dichlorohydrin. From these latter compounds, synthetic glycerine could be derived.

"D-D" mixture was put to immediate use as a soil fumigant for killing the wireworms and nematodes that feed on the roots of plants and cause large losses to growers of food crops. In Hawaii, "D-D" helped save a pineapple crop; along the Gulf Coast and Atlantic Seaboard, commercial growers of carrots, lettuce, beans, tomatoes, sugar beets, melons, potatoes, cotton, and alfalfa found "D-D" effective in controlling the "root knot" that is produced by infestations of nematodes. Subsequent experience would extend the application of "D-D" to nearly every kind of commercial crop, and make it one of the chemical company's staple products. The fumigant was injected into the soil by means of an applicator designed by R. R. Renshaw and Lester S. Hannibal of Shell Point, based on Leavitt's field work with ammonia injection.[114]

The special war projects which Shell Chemical undertook on behalf of the government have been mentioned earlier in this chapter: the design, construction, and operation of a large butadiene plant at Torrance and the conversion of the Cactus Ordnance Works to the manufacture of xylidine. The difficulties of designing, building, and staffing the Cactus plant, of patching together makeshift equipment in an inaccessible part of the country, will probably never be fully appreciated except by the men who were associated with the project.

Their long hours of hard work to convert the equipment of an ammonia plant into a new plant employing an untried catalytic hydrogenation process went without the reward of recognition accorded to plants with fine production records, for the "C.S." project was discontinued by the government during the same year that production began. This should not, however, be allowed to detract from the outstanding performance of the Shell Chemical-Shell Development-Shell Oil team responsible for redesigning and completely rebuilding the Cactus Works in the short space of seven months.[115]

During July 1943, Shell Union purchased Bataafsche's half interest in Shell Chemical Company in exchange for 400,000 shares of Shell Union common stock. Three months later, on October 1, Shell Chemical Company was dissolved and merged into Shell Union, as the Shell Chemical Division of Shell Union Oil Corporation. Oostermeyer became executive vice president of Shell Union in charge of the chemical division; otherwise, Shell Chemical's operating organization was little affected by the change in ownership.

8

Research for the War

THE industrial research man, who had for the most part worked in quiet obscurity up to now, his very expense often the subject of grumbling from economy-minded managements, was suddenly discovered in World War II to have been well worth his keep. His work, unnoticed and often unappreciated except by close associates, now became the subject of magazine and newspaper articles. The research man, like a butterfly emerging from a chrysalis, changed overnight in the public mind from a dull, plodding fellow to a glamorous figure of the first order. There was a reason for this change in attitude. World War II presented a welter of bewildering, brand-new technical questions. The great industrial research laboratories of the country demonstrated time and again that they were able to come up in a hurry with workable answers to an amazing variety of problems.

Some of the most useful and public-spirited of these laboratories were those belonging to the oil companies. The outstanding wartime contributions of the oil company laboratories were the processes they had developed, mostly during the Thirties, for use in their own business—polymerization, alkylation, catalytic cracking, and other processes important in aviation gasoline manufacture; methods for making synthetic rubber from butanes and butylenes; reforming, dehydrogenation, isomerization, extractive distillation, and other processes useful in turning out products such as toluene, cumene, and xylidine. These contributions of oil-company research served to emphasize the potential usefulness of their laboratories in the service of other causes. Even before the war had started, organizations like Shell Development were being asked to undertake research projects on behalf of one or another of the government agencies.

The large-scale research projects were channelled through the National Defense Research Council (later the Office of Scientific Research and Development), a government agency composed of some of the most prominent research scientists of the academic world. Handling of a specific project would often be given over by the N.D.R.C. to a university laboratory which would in turn farm out parts of the project to laboratories of other academic institutions or to industrial laboratories. In this manner, Shell Development was asked to undertake a great many isolated pieces of research, most of them subsidiary aspects of larger over-all projects. Other of the Shell laboratories were also asked to join in when their particular specialties and talents could be useful.

Contributions to Radar Development

The radar project, for instance, required skills and knowledge remarkably similar to those of the geophysicist. Shell's geophysical laboratory at Houston was asked to undertake part of this highly secret rush work, the manufacture and testing of pre-production models of some parts of radar equipment. The nature of the work was kept secret from the men working on it by means of breaking it into unrelated segments. Despite such handicaps, the tests were completed on schedule and the designs developed at Houston were later adopted for large-scale war production. Dr. L. A. DuBridge, later to become president of the California Institute of Technology, was during the war years director of the Radiation Laboratories at the Massachusetts Institute of Technology, which had general supervision of the project. He wrote a warm letter of appreciation to Frank Goldstone, director of Shell's geophysical laboratory: "The special skills and techniques which have been developed in the Shell laboratories have filled an especially important need in the progress of this work. We have found no other laboratory which can do these particular jobs as effectively as your Company's laboratories. Please be assured, therefore, that the efforts of your laboratory and its excellent personnel are greatly appreciated by N.D.R.C., and that the contributions which they are making to this project are of great importance and could be made by no other group of which we know." [116]

At Emeryville, the increased amount of research on behalf of the government, with no diminution in the volume of research for Shell's account, necessitated a sharp increase in personnel. In 1940, Shell Development had 490 employed at Emeryville. In 1941, the number increased to 580; in 1942, to 615; in 1943, to 833; in 1944, to 873; and in 1945 to 910, nearly double the prewar research staff. With an additional 174 persons in the San Francisco head office and the patent-licensing department at New York, Shell Development by the end of the war had 1,080 employees—a thirtyfold increase since the end of 1928. The company had during the seventeen years of operating the Emeryville laboratories spent more than $35,000,000 on basic research in petroleum. [117]

Work on Flame-Throwers

Typical of the more interesting pieces of government research undertaken by Emeryville was advance work on the flame-thrower, a project which had originated with the Standard Oil Company of New Jersey and its oil-burner manufacturing subsidiary, Gilbert & Barker. By adding a special chemical manufactured from naphthenic acid, ordinary gasoline could be converted in the field to "jellied gasoline," a material with considerable ordnance possibilities. In a gun of proper design, jellied gasoline would throw a sheet of flame, making it a devastating anti-personnel weapon. Shell Development worked at improving the design of the existing flame-thrower. A simplified control mechanism, worked out at Emeryville under the direction of R. L. Iglehart, was incorporated into the flame-thrower that was used on Sherman tanks in the Pacific during 1944 and 1945. Incendiary bombs using jellied gasoline were also developed at Emeryville and battle tests of them were made in Europe, but they were not adopted for wide-scale use. The thickening agent used in the preparation of jellied gasoline was subject to deterioration; Shell Development contributed an oxidation inhibitor which solved this difficulty. [118]

Less spectacular but of greater over-all importance was the large body of research that Emeryville continued to do on subjects such as synthetic rubber and the manufacture of aviation gasoline. A synthetic rubber laboratory was set up at Emeryville in 1940. During 1943, the company announced new separation processes and an improved catalyst for use in the government butadiene plants. During 1944, the mechanism of emulsion polymerization, important knowledge in the field of rubber and plastics, was explored in new basic research, and "Dutrex," an extender and plasticizer for rubbers, developed in 1943, was brought to the stage of commercial production.[119]

In aviation gasoline, Emeryville began large-scale testing of rich-mixture additives in 1940. This led, during 1941, to intensive studies of super-charged engine performance. From these studies came developments such as, in 1942, the Shell process for cumene synthesis, mentioned earlier. Other developments during these years were phenolic inhibitors ("Ionol") to permit long storage of aviation gasoline by combating oxidation of tetraethyl lead (1942), basic and applied studies of catalytic cracking (1942) resulting in a microspheroidal, low-attrition catalyst (1943). Improvements in the Hydroforming catalyst were made the same year. Emeryville conducted flight tests of aircraft-fuel performance, and both Emeryville and Wood River had large-scale fuel-testing laboratories, containing representative types of most aircraft and automotive engines, the engines of one laboratory in general complementing those of the other.[120]

Engine-Testing Laboratories

At the Wood River engine laboratory, engine testing was carried out for various branches of the government, in particular the Ordnance Department, which had no research set-up of its own, and the National Advisory Committee for Aeronautics, the government agency for aeronautical research. Several oil company laboratories undertook tests for the N.A.C.A. to determine lubricating oil performance under heavy loads. In cooperation with aircraft engine builders, both the Wood River and Emeryville engine laboratories undertook evaluation work on test methods for establishing lean-mixture and rich-mixture ratings, important and laborious work. As a corollary to this latter work came the establishment and evaluation of specifications to obtain the desired ratings.

Wood River was, during the early months of the war, the only laboratory in the country running rich-mixture rating tests and did this work for competitors all over the country. As the war pro-

gressed and a greater variety of materials had to be pressed into aviation gasoline manufacture, the engine laboratories also did work on
evaluating base-stocks. On occasion, the Wood River laboratory ran
tests on captured enemy petroleum products, chiefly aircraft fuels. To
help the Ordnance and Quartermaster Departments determine fuel
needs of their many types of new vehicles, the oil companies supplied
some fifty of their best engine-testing personnel to three Army proving grounds in California. Throughout the war, two or three men
from the Wood River and Martinez laboratories were generally on
loan for this work.

Pennsylvania oils had generally been considered best for aircraft
engines in the years before the war, but by 1943 Pennsylvania refiners
were finding it difficult to meet the very large demand for high-
quality aircraft lubricants. Shell, with its extensive background in extraction processes for producing lubricants, was successful in producing at Wood River an aircraft lubricating oil of Pennsylvania
quality from Mid-Continent crudes. Fundamental studies of oil behavior at Emeryville led in 1942 to the discovery of new additives for
lubricating oils, especially oils subject to the rigorous conditions of
high-performance aviation engines. These studies continued throughout the war, with constant improvements being made in the oils the
company was manufacturing.[121]

Jet Engine Laboratory

During 1944, as the jet-propulsion engine came into being, Shell set
up facilities for testing jet-propulsion fuels. The fundamentals of
these fuels were studied at Emeryville, and at Wood River a laboratory was established to study the burning of jet fuels in the jet burners then actually in use. An abandoned pump station of the old Wood
River–East Chicago crude line, situated on a remote corner of the refinery property, was used for a building. The company installed a
large compressor unit to provide the huge volumes of compressed air
needed to simulate air-borne operating conditions of a jet burner and
equipped the laboratory with a jet burner of the type then being
manufactured, plus elaborate instrumentation for observing and recording the many aspects of fuel combustion.

This jet laboratory, built and operated at Shell expense, was actually
conducted as an Air Force research project under a contract which
reimbursed Shell at the rate of $1 a year. It was the first laboratory of
its kind established by an oil company, and during the initial months
of operation, it was a highly secret affair protected by armed guards.

Its prime assignment at the outset was to study the factors that influence performance of jet fuels, such as formation of carbon, formation of gum in the fuel, the effects upon the fuel of extreme heat, and many other similar questions. In the years that have elapsed since, this pioneer jet laboratory, still operated under Air Force contract,§ has accumulated a substantial body of research data.[122]

Rust Inhibitors

New developments in corrosion inhibitors and rust preventatives were particularly appropriate to wartime. During the years between 1940 and 1945, Shell announced several new developments, most of them stemming from beginnings made in the Thirties. One of these was the use of sodium nitrite in products pipe lines to prevent rust, a technique developed in 1939 at the Emeryville corrosion laboratory, established the previous year.

In a solution of proper alkalinity, sodium nitrite protected iron and steel from attack by water and oxygen. A water-soluble, oil-soluble rust inhibitor embodying sodium nitrite was the main feature of a patented pipe line treating method developed by Shell Development and called the Shell Corrosion Inhibitor Process, or SCIP, for short. Shell Oil began using SCIP in its own products lines in the years just before the war, and reported remarkable results. Wall-pitting, a result of rapid rusting of products lines, was almost completely retarded, and rust already formed was removed by the action of the Shell additive. Less rust meant a smoother wall surface on the inside of the pipe, with resultant reduction of surface friction arising from wall-pitting. This reduced friction made possible an increase in pumping capacity that, by conservative estimates, amounted to at least 15%. Maintenance costs were cut because mechanical scrapers did not need to be run nearly as often. More important, the financial loss which had formerly resulted from the gradual dropping off in the line's capacity as the interior walls became progressively more pitted was now almost completely eliminated.[123]

Another Shell rust preventive received considerable prominence during the war as the basis of Shell's Navy "Turbo" Oil. This rust-preventing compound, now called Ionex, had its origin in a material which the Group's Amsterdam laboratory had prepared in the early Thirties by cracking the oily wax recovered in the course of purifying lubricating oil. A sample, with the information that it was very good

§ In the years following 1950, a new contract was negotiated to reimburse Shell thenceforth for its out-of-pocket operating costs.

for preventing rust, had been sent to the Wood River laboratory. There it was tried with excellent results on a piece of laboratory machinery which had been subject to frequent rusting. At about this time, Shell lubrication engineers calling upon General Electric and Westinghouse reported that these companies were troubled by rust formation in the steam turbines they manufactured for power generation. The Wood River laboratory purified and improved the Amsterdam material, and used it as the active ingredient in an anti-rust turbine oil. This oil was enormously successful in stopping turbine rust, and in the late Thirties Shell induced the Navy to try it on ships' turbines where it met with equal success. With the coming of war, any measure which would help avoid repairs or overhaul was welcomed eagerly. For the duration of the war, the Navy contracted for the company's entire output of this rust-preventing "Turbo" oil.[124]

Shell experience with rust preventives and rust-resisting additives was of good use to the services on several occasions, as new problems arose in connection with shipping and storing the machinery of war. A special piston-ring preservative oil helped eliminate spot-rusting of piston rings in storage. A coating compound protected aircraft parts during shipment. A new gun oil counteracted the tendency of microscopic rust spots to form in fingerprints. These were only a few wartime uses of rust preventives.[125]

In 1944, Shell Development Company announced a new class of vapor-phase rust inhibitors, later marketed under the trade-name "VPI." Emeryville had explored the fields of amine nitrites as rust preventives, had tested more than 150 of them, and found that one, dicyclohexyl ammonium nitrite, or "dichan" for short, could inhibit rust by entering into the water vapor of the air and preventing the oxygen of the water vapor from combining with the iron. (Rust is iron oxide; inhibiting oxidation will keep iron from rusting.) In the years immediately following the war, Shell Development licensees began manufacturing VPI-impregnated and coated paper, which proved an admirable wrapping for any machined metal in transit or storage. Shell Oil made VPI crystals which could be sprayed into stored machinery to prevent rust. VPI made possible immense savings in time and labor: an M-1 rifle, formerly shipped embedded in grease and requiring a total of three hours to unpack and clean, could now be wrapped in a boot made of VPI paper, with a total time expenditure of less than a minute.[126]

In the pipe yard at Ventura   In a production department garage

The Ladies Lend a Hand

And these two Indianapolis ladies helped keep a service station open.

Col. C. H. Chorpening, U.S. Army Engineers, on behalf of the President presents the Medal for Merit to Shell's S. S. Smith for his part in "designing, perfecting and proving" the military portable pipe line. Tulsa, October 7, 1946.

August 15, 1945, a few hours after V-J Day, gasoline rationing ended. These delivery trucks wait outside Shell's Zionsville, Ind., terminal to buy pooled gasoline.

A Penicillin Process

Emeryville's wide research experience was useful in other ways. Supplies of penicillin, the wonder drug of World War II, were limited by painfully slow methods of preparing the natural mold and by a recovery process that extracted only about half of the available penicillin, which even then was not of the purity desired. In 1944, Emeryville, because of its extensive background in solvent extraction processes, set to work to improve the method of recovering penicillin and in a matter of weeks devised a new process and built a pilot plant to test it. At the end of four months, the Shell penicillin recovery process was announced to the pharmaceutical trade. The new process made possible penicillin recoveries that were of high purity and nearly double in volume the recoveries under former processes. Five penicillin producers signed up. The success of the new method was short-lived, however. Not long afterwards another method of preparing the penicillin mold was adopted, and this radically changed the whole process.[127]

The development of an infra-red spectroscope was another contribution outside Shell Development's regular field of research. For the control of isomerization processes, a rapid and accurate analysis of practically indistinguishable hydrocarbons was necessary and normal analytical methods required several hours. As part of its research work in the field of isomerization, Emeryville in 1940 developed a spectroscopic technique of analysis that offered the desired speed, accuracy, and reproducibility of results. The new method was built around a spectro-photometer capable of measuring long-wave-length light waves beyond the visible spectrum. During 1942, this method was further refined to permit complete spectroscopic analysis of complex hydrocarbon streams containing several components. Other companies engaged in the manufacture of butadiene and aviation gasoline were eager to get instruments similar to Shell's spectroscope, because it was also useful for control of polymerization and alkylation reactions. To meet the demand, Shell Development arranged during 1943–1944 for the National Technical Laboratories of Pasadena to manufacture 75 of these spectroscopes for competitors, without royalty or profit to Shell. Shell Development also set up a three weeks' course in infra-red spectroscopy for competitors' employees who would be operating these instruments.[128]

In the line of the oil business, an improved oil-base drilling mud was developed at Emeryville in 1942, studies of paraffin wax manufacture were carried on during 1943, and the application of asphalt to uses such as canal lining was investigated during 1944. Altogether, the wartime research activities of the Shell organization were of infinite variety and highly productive of immediate results.

The executive ranks of Shell Development saw a considerable change in the years between 1940 and 1945. At the end of 1940, Tydeman, a vice president for some years, retired and Williams, vice president and director of research, resigned. Lacomblé, who had spent 1939 at The Hague organizing a research and development department, managed to escape Holland in May 1940 just ahead of the advancing Germans. He returned to the United States and in mid-1940 became chairman of Shell Development's executive committee; upon Williams' departure, he also assumed responsibility for directing research. At the end of 1942, Taylor, who had been president since 1935, went to New York to become Shell Oil's vice president in charge of manufacturing; Lacomblé succeeded to his position, at the same time retaining his duties as director of research. In May 1943, Hepner, manager of Roxana's first technical department and later secretary of Shell Development for fifteen years, retired and was succeeded by Dan M. Sheldon. Pyzel, who had resigned his official connection with Shell Development in 1935, had continued to oversee the company's patent-licensing office in New York; at the end of 1944, he retired after a long and fruitful career with the Shell organization. In preparation for this change, Hiram Norcross was appointed a vice president of Shell Development in April 1944 and placed in charge of the New York office. A. J. Johnson, in the San Francisco office of Shell Development, was elected a vice president at the same time.

9

Impact of the War on Shell's Business

GASOLINE rationing, begun in 1942 as a measure to save tires, was by the end of 1943 necessary in order to stretch available supplies. The surpluses which had haunted oil marketers all during the Thirties were gone. Instead, rationing and price ceilings were the order of the day. With this constriction in marketing, service stations were closed and boarded up. The greatly reduced volume could be supplied by fewer stations, and higher-paying war jobs and the military services beckoned to dealers and their employees. The problem now was not how to sell gasoline but how to supply the company's customers. Military requirements were always the prime consideration, but even so the quantities of petroleum products needed to keep the civilian economy going were more than double the total demands of the military.

Ration boards took over the allocation of domestic fuel oil and gasoline. To save tetraethyl lead, in short supply, the octane number of civilian motor gasoline was lowered. To make the most efficient use of trucks and available manpower, many competing bulk depots were closed and a more or less standardized "pooled" gasoline was delivered by one supplier to the stations that were nearest, regardless of the brand-signs hanging out front.

Disappearance of competition for customers brought changes in the company's advertising. In April 1941, eight months before Pearl Harbor, a series of well-prepared, full-color advertisements featuring not gasoline, but the accomplishments of Shell research, began to appear at monthly intervals in *The Saturday Evening Post, Life,* and *Collier's.* With the advent of actual wartime conditions and the disappearance of the need for product advertising, this series was continued as a logical substitute. It proved so successful that with the return of normal conditions it was continued as the company's "trademark" advertising.

Crude Oil

In exploration and production, wartime materials shortages brought changes almost equally sweeping. In December 1941, the Office of Production Management (predecessor of the W.P.B.) issued an order limiting materials for drilling new wells in proven areas to one well for every forty acres, thus decreasing the density of drilling that had plagued the industry in many of the older fields. Some of the over-drilling of the Twenties and Thirties now stood the nation in good stead. The enormous amounts of crude oil which the nation needed were supplied chiefly by opening up shut-in and cut-back production. In this way, Shell Oil raised its production from 55,639,000 barrels in 1941 to 72,395,000 barrels in 1944, an increase of 30%, while the industry nation-wide increased its total production during the same period by some 19%.

The drain upon crude oil was heaviest in California. The military requirements of the Pacific war and the high consumption rate of the

West Coast's new war industries and war workers generated a demand for products that could not be met entirely from the state's current crude oil production. Shell increased its production rate sharply in fields such as Ten Section and Ventura. Even so, these supplies were not enough and, in common with other California refiners, the company utilized crude oil shipped in by rail from the Southwest whenever tank cars could be spared.[129]

East of the Rockies, the industry's big reservoir of crude oil was West Texas, where most fields had been producing at greatly curtailed rates ever since their discovery late in the 1920's. This pent-up production was now let loose, and helped make up for the declining production rates of the older Mid-Continent fields in Kansas, Oklahoma, and Illinois. As one of the leading West Texas producers, Shell was a heavy contributor to these new supplies of crude oil.

The company's production increases during the war years were accomplished almost wholly by raising production of existing wells and drilling development wells on proven property. Shortages of materials circumscribed drilling operations, as did the even more pressing shortage of manpower. Concentrating its available men and materials on its most likely areas, Shell had a high ratio of success in the exploration wells it did drill. In July 1942, Shell discovered the Monahans field, in Ward County, West Texas, at a depth of 10,000 feet; the company held 20,000 acres of leases at Monahans. With a subsidiary of Standard of Indiana, the company discovered the Wheeler field, in Winkler County, during 1943. Other, smaller West Texas fields were discovered by Shell in 1943, 1944, and 1945. In the latter year, Shell and Cities Service jointly discovered the big T.X.L. field,* in Ector County, West Texas.[130] During 1945, the first producing well was drilled in Shell's Weeks Island field, south of New Iberia, Louisiana, a field which would become a profitable producing property despite the extreme depth of its wells.

These successes were offset by a few failures. In eastern Michigan, eight wells not of commercial proportions were drilled during the war years. In the Cape Hatteras area, some of Shell's competitors were drilling exploratory wells. Purely as insurance against the success of some of these wells, Shell felt justified in taking extensive leases in the area as protection. They were inexpensive leases and ran for a ten-year period. A land office was opened in Baltimore, and during the late

---

* The field takes its name from the ticker-tape symbol for Texas & Pacific Land Trust, on whose land the discovery well was located.

years of the war the company leased a total of about a million acres throughout the Atlantic Seaboard area. The wildcat wells then in progress proved failures, and Shell later surrendered its leases without drilling.[131]

War Profits and Renegotiation

During 1942, a War Profits Control Act was passed by Congress making all sales to the government during wartime subject to later "renegotiation" so that the government, in its wartime haste, might be protected against unduly high prices. Any company deriving a portion of its profits from sales to the government was obliged to hold itself in readiness for subsequent renegotiation of its tax settlements. The purchase of 100-octane gasoline was handled by an R.F.C. subsidiary, the Defense Supplies Corporation. During 1945–1946, renegotiation proceedings were completed between Shell Union and the R.F.C. Price Adjustment Board, with Shell Union being required to make small net cash refunds on its wartime earnings: $114,000 for 1942, $565,000 for 1943, $733,000 for 1944, and $105,000 for 1945, a total of $1,517,000.[132]

Most of these adjustments were occasioned by the increased profits of Shell Chemical, not by the wartime profits of Shell Oil, an indication that prices charged the government for products such as 100-octane were low indeed. The company contended, with proof that was hard to refute, that its improved earnings, noticeable mainly in the East-of-the-Rockies area, were a direct result of the measures taken during the late Thirties to improve the profitability of Mid-Continent operations.

Financing War Construction

One way of supplying necessary wartime manufacturing facilities was to build them at government expense and turn them over, at nominal rentals, to private companies to operate on behalf of the government. The Defense Plant Corporation, an R.F.C. subsidiary, was responsible between 1940 and 1945 for 2,300 such projects in 46 states, costing a total of $9,200,000,000. Many of these projects were undertaken by small businesses, but projects costing $3,871,000,000, or some 41% of the total, were in the hands of twenty-five of the nation's largest concerns.[133]

Most companies, at the outset of the war, adopted the view that facilities used chiefly for war production should properly be built and operated at government expense. In the oil industry, nearly all of Shell's competitors, large and small, welcomed government assistance in the construction of some of their wartime facilities, particularly the expensive, large-scale facilities for the manufacture of aviation gasoline.[134]

The Shell management did not subscribe to this thinking. In the years just before the war, the company had shown itself willing to install large-scale alkylation facilities, and with America's entry into the war, Shell continued to erect needed new facilities with its own funds. Plants for the manufacture of cumene and Avaro, toluene, and aviation gasoline were erected entirely at the company's expense. When the company began construction of the large catalytic cracking units at Wilmington and Wood River—units that, with necessary auxiliary facilities, would cost some $35,000,000—the Defense Plant Corporation offered to lend part of the cost. The company availed itself of this offer and early in 1943 borrowed $17,388,000. But before the year was out, the Shell management had decided against government loans and in December 1943 returned the entire amount of the government advances.[135] "Paying our own way" was thenceforth a point of pride with Shell executives throughout the war.†

Accelerated depreciation rates were permitted on most of these units under wartime tax law. These fast write-offs were designed to make building of wartime facilities more attractive by allowing a larger-than-normal share of their cost to be charged against current income. At the end of September 1945, when the company stopped applying accelerated depreciation, it had written off 40% of the $69,000,000 cost of its wartime plant facilities.[136] These facilities fully merited the depreciation consideration they were given, for they had been built below standard in an honest attempt to save precious material and equipment. As a result, Shell in most cases found it necessary after the war to refit and rebuild the plants erected during the war.

---

† Shell Chemical operated a Defense Plant Corporation butadiene plant, but only because the synthetic rubber program was a government monopoly. The conversion and operation of the government-owned Cactus Ordnance Works was undertaken by Shell Chemical solely to save time and materials, not money. "War Industrial Facilities Authorized, July 1940–August 1945," an alphabetical listing of individual plants published by the Civilian Production Administration, Washington, July 30, 1946, shows Shell facilities authorized with the government listed as lender of $42,-560,000. This figure does not present a fair picture for it was arrived at by adding the cost of the Torrance butadiene facilities and the Cactus Ordnance Works to the amount, mentioned above, that was borrowed and repaid by Shell during 1943.

Shell People in the War

JUST as the war altered the course of the company's affairs, so did it disrupt the personal lives of nearly every member of the organization. Within a few months of Pearl Harbor, several hundred Shell men left their jobs for the armed services and the number continued to mount as the war rolled on. For those who remained at their jobs, there was more and harder work. The pinch of a general labor shortage was felt everywhere; shipyards, aircraft factories, and ordnance works clamored for more men than were available. The lengthened work-week made its appearance and, when that was not enough, the woman war worker appeared and competently took her place beside men.

Shell, like other companies, faced a mounting volume of war orders yet had to make do with a labor force depleted by the call of the armed services. During 1942, the 36- and 40-hour weeks that had been adopted during the Thirties gave way in most Shell installations to a 6-day week of 48 hours. Overtime work on top of this further increased the hours of hundreds of individual men and women at hard-pressed installations. Women filled an interesting variety of jobs formerly held only by men. In marketing department depots, they became yard clerks and loaders; in drum-filling installations, they took on the jobs of men; they worked in service stations. In the refineries, women became truck drivers, machinists' assistants, blacksmiths' and electricians' helpers, car washers, warehouse counter "men," tank gaugers, tool room attendants, boilermakers' and welders' helpers, sample carriers, and in the refinery laboratories they practically took over from the men. At a refinery such as Martinez, women held some 20% of the jobs at the peak of the war effort, working 48 hours a week at all kinds of jobs except those requiring heavy lifting. Nation-wide, the number of Shell's male employees declined by 3,000 between 1941 and 1945, while the women on the payroll increased by a like number.[137]

The lengthened work-week affected office employees as well, although to a lesser extent. Everywhere everyone worked longer hours and much of the resulting increase in pay went into war bond purchases, which by 1943 came to 12.3% of the total payroll. Morale throughout the organization was excellent. Shell men and women, fully aware of the importance of their work, gave all their energy and ingenuity to the task at hand.

A good example of this high morale was provided by the response to a hurricane which hit the Houston refinery on July 27, 1943. The storm blew to bits the refinery's 7-story water cooler made of California redwood. Everyone knew that without cooling water, refinery operations would be halted. Even before the hurricane had abated, plans for rebuilding it were being discussed, and the refinery's chief engineer, while the storm was still raging, drove to Houston to telephone the contractors, the Fluor Corporation, of Los Angeles. Next day, most all of the refinery office force dropped their regular jobs and pitched in to help the refinery gangs clear away the debris. The P.A.W. gave the new water cooler the highest priority. Within five days the first materials began to arrive from California in freight cars hitched to passenger trains. Within three weeks the new tower was built and in operation, a job which would have taken two to three months in normal times.[138]

Long hours and excellent morale were also very much in evidence at Sewaren, Shell's marine terminal and compounding plant on the New Jersey side of New York Harbor. Early in the war, Sewaren became an important center for filling drums and cans for shipment overseas. Gasoline for American forces at Guadalcanal, and later for North Africa and Sicily, was packaged at Sewaren in the familiar 5-gallon Army "blitz" cans. With a personnel increase of 50%, most of them women, Sewaren doubled its output during these years. At peak operation, the plant loaded and shipped a 55-gallon drum every nine seconds, and for the Army it filled a total of 2,500,000 blitz cans. The filling of cans and drums for overseas shipment was also an important activity on the West Coast. At Martinez, soldiers from nearby Benicia and Port Chicago worked evenings to help fill drums; and at the Harbor Island terminal in Seattle, salesmen and accounting personnel put in nights and weekends in the drum-filling plant.

Such conscientious hard work did not go unnoticed. In January 1943, the Army-Navy "E" for excellence in war production was awarded to Shell at Wood River, the first such award to an oil refinery. A year later, in January 1944, similar awards were presented to three other Shell facilities: the Martinez refinery and the Martinez and Dominguez chemical plants. In March 1944, the National Security Award was presented to the Norco refinery.

The individual employee had an opportunity to exhibit his ingenuity in the wartime effort to stretch the supplies of critical materials by improvising and using secondhand equipment. Utilization of idle equipment received an unusual degree of attention throughout the Shell organization. At the start of the war, key people were dispatched to all parts of the country to make inventories of all unused facilities and equipment. Each item appraised was either reassigned to active use or turned in as scrap. The abandoned East Chicago refinery provided 78 railroad cars of equipment which was reassembled and used at other points around the country, often at costs of up to twice that of new equipment. Storage tanks, from the smallest up to those of 1,000,000 gallons capacity, were dismantled, shipped to other areas, and re-erected, again at costs greater than those of new tanks. Surplus tanks not needed were sold to the armed forces at nominal prices. In all cases, the objective was not money savings, but the saving of time and the conservation of critical materials.

In the construction of new units, dozens of suggestions were offered for saving materials. The building of the Wilmington "cat" cracker afforded a good example of how earnestly Shell people approached the job of stretching scarce materials. Through the use of wood and the substitution of less critical alloys, they saved on this one installation large amounts of high-priority materials: 21 tons of nickel, 34 tons of chrome, more than 3 tons of copper, 43 tons of admiralty metal, 7 tons of bronze, a ton of brass, 16 tons of lead, 25 tons of galvanized iron, 578 tons of cast iron, and 44 tons of steel.[139]

Shell also became a formidable contributor to scrap drives. During 1943 alone, the company rounded up from the oil fields, refineries, pipe lines, and marketing installations 11,000 tons of iron and steel and 125,000 tons of non-ferrous scrap. Shell supplied secondhand materials for the Big Inch and Bayou pipe lines, and the marketing department made a sizeable contribution to the collection of much-needed scrap rubber.

Early in 1942, Kittinger and his sales staff developed plans for a nation-wide rubber salvage drive to be conducted under the leadership of the oil industry. Kittinger went to Washington and presented a completely outlined program to the W.P.B. Salvage Division. The suggested program was adopted early in the summer of 1942 by the P.A.W. and P.I.W.C. The rubber drive which ensued, using the nation's service stations as collection points, brought in 454,000 tons of scrap rubber from the general public at a time when rubber was desperately short.[140]

Following this drive, which was one of the most successful salvage efforts of the war, the Shell marketing department conceived a "Save the Carcass" program, to get motorists to retread their tires before the tire carcass had worn beyond the point of usefulness. Tires then on the nation's automobiles constituted the single most valuable reserve of rubber, so conserving this rubber was of first importance. The Rubber Director and the P.I.W.C. endorsed the "Save the Carcass" program, and under P.I.W.C. sponsorship it was carried to the nation's motorists through service stations and oil company advertising.

A large number of Shell people of executive rank or specialist's qualification helped the government directly by serving in a variety of the war emergency agencies. Large numbers served with the P.A.W. and with the various oil industry district committees. Some of these services were of a temporary nature, and most of the industry district committee members served in addition to their regular jobs. For others, the period of government service was more protracted and involved personal inconvenience and financial sacrifice. Shell men served on the War Production Board, in the O.P.A., in the Army Ordnance Department, with the U. S. Air Force Matériel Command, as civilian specialists for the Navy in Panama and Iceland, with the Naval Ordnance Laboratories, as members of National Defense Research Council projects, in the War Department's Service of Supply, and even in the highly secret Office of Strategic Services.

Other Shell men served full-time on industry-sponsored, quasi-governmental agencies such as the New York Harbor Supply Terminal ("Shuttle"), the Supplies and Distribution Committee, the Industry Committee on Petroleum Barging, and the Petroleum Transport Committee of New England. Still others were lent to construction projects such as the Trans-Florida and Panama pipe lines and to contractors in charge of buying materials for butadiene plants. After the war was over, one Shell man served with the U. S. Strategic Bombing Survey, a group set up to gain firsthand information of the enemy's wartime manufacturing and supply operations, and another served with the United Nations Relief and Rehabilitation Agency.

Belither and Van der Woude became members of the highly important Petroleum Industry War Council (P.I.W.C.) at its inception, and served for the duration of the war. E. D. Cumming, who had succeeded Lacomblé as vice president of manufacturing East of the Rockies, went to P.A.W. in December 1942 to hold the important post of Director of Refining. C. E. Davis, general manager of manufacturing in New York, served on the Aviation Gasoline Advisory Committee throughout the war, and Dr. M. E. Spaght, a member of the Pacific Coast manufacturing organization, represented Shell on the A.G.A.C. in that area. Guépin, while still retaining his office and title with Shell Oil in New York, served for much of the war with the O.S.S. in the Mediterranean and Near East.‡ Kittinger, as an outgrowth of his salvage activities, was called to Washington in July 1942 to head up the Salvage Section of the Materials Division of the W.P.B. In Shell's New York office, Cumming was succeeded by Taylor, president of Shell Development, and Lakin became marketing vice president in Kittinger's stead. D. B. Hodges served as associate director of the P.A.W.'s Supply and Transportation Division, and Salmon set up the O.P.A.'s Petroleum Price Section.

With the Colors

Of the Shell people in the war, those of greatest interest to everyone were the more than 8,000 who joined the services. The company, desirous of easing the financial burdens attached to military service, made generous provisions for employees in the service of their country. The Shell military leave policy, announced in March 1942, superseded less extensive financial benefits in effect earlier. Employees, who had on Pearl Harbor Day been with the company a year, were given two months' pay at the time of their departure for service. In addition, the families of employees who were married at the time of their entry into service received a "family allowance" amounting to the difference between the employee's former Shell salary and his military pay, up to one-half the amount of his former salary. Employees who had been carrying group life insurance had this expense taken over by the company for the duration of their service. At the termination of military service, each employee was promised his old job back, or a new one of equal status and pay.[141] No mention was made of it as part of the military leave policy, but the company also endeavored wherever feasible to give returning employees better jobs to reflect advances they had made while in service. Through frequent communication, the company maintained contact with its men in service. Cards were issued to serve as an introduction to any Shell

‡ Early in 1945, Guépin returned to the service of Group companies in Europe where he subsequently played a leading role in the postwar rehabilitation of several of the Group marketing companies in Western Europe. In 1950, he was elected a managing director of the Royal Dutch Company and also a managing director of each of the Group's main operating companies.

office in the world; *Reader's Digest* subscriptions were sent by the company to men in service throughout the war; and thousands of individual employees took it upon themselves to keep in touch by letter with their Shell friends in service.

A good many of the Shell men in service attained high rank. Eaton, who had been sales manager in New York at the time of his enlistment, was up for promotion to brigadier general when he was killed in a plane crash in France; the rank was conferred upon him posthumously. Clayton M. Morrison, of the San Francisco marketing department, also attained a brigadier general's rank.

The Shell soldier of whom the world heard most was, of course, Doolittle. In October 1940, he went back into the Air Corps with the rank of major. He was assigned the problems of helping Detroit convert to war production, and by early 1942 had been advanced to the rank of lieutenant colonel. Then, on April 18, 1942, came the famous Tokyo Raid, an exploit which electrified America and once again made the Doolittle name front-page news. For leading the raid, Doolittle received the Congressional Medal of Honor and was promoted to brigadier general. His subsequent service was in Europe, where he commanded successively the 12th, 15th, and 8th Air Forces; by the end of the war, he had risen to the rank of lieutenant general. Unlike other Shell people in service, Doolittle was not on military leave but had resigned his connection with the company. It was therefore a source of great satisfaction to everyone in the company when the news was announced late in 1945 that he would be returning to Shell, as vice president and director of Shell Union Oil Corporation.[142]

Other hundreds came streaming home every week in the months following V-J Day, more than three-quarters of them returning to their old jobs at Shell. The joy of their homecoming was dampened by the memory of those who would not be back: the 184 Shell men who had died in service of their country.

CHAPTER XI

A Billion-Dollar Corporation

1945–1950

THE POSTWAR WORLD, which for many businesses was still several months in the future, burst upon the oil industry at once. On August 15, 1945, less than twenty-four hours after Japan had capitulated, rationing of gasoline and fuel oil was abolished, and motorists who for a full four years had been permitted only limited amounts of gasoline were once more able to drive into the service station and say "Fill 'er up!"

With combat activity ceased, the armed services no longer required tremendous quantities of oil products. This meant that the Petroleum Administration for War, which had controlled the oil business since 1941, was no longer needed. Ickes and Davies, true to their promise four years earlier, lost no time in winding up the agency's affairs. One month after V-J Day, 75% of the P.A.W. orders, recommendations, and directives had been rescinded. By April 1946, the P.A.W. staff, about 1,500 at peak, had dwindled to 58, and soon after the agency was abolished.[1] This prompt disappearance of production controls brought the oil industry up against the realities of postwar markets.

The nature of these postwar markets had long been of consuming interest to all businessmen. Committees had been set up and studies made in an attempt to determine whether business would be at a high level in the years following the war, or whether it would revert to the depressed levels of the 1930's. In this postwar planning, Shell was no exception. In June 1943, Fraser had set up a general planning group, under the chairmanship of Kittinger, with members representing finance, economics, and personnel; manufacturing; transportation, supplies, and distribution; and matters pertaining to Shell Development and Shell Chemical.[2] In addition, a marketing department group, headed by H. N. F. Schwall, was commissioned to make a detailed appraisal of postwar marketing potentials.

The survey of this latter group, completed in November 1943, projected anticipated increases in population, in industrial production, in the total number of automobiles, in Diesel engine use, and in number of domestic oil burners, and made an individual demand forecast for each depot and distributor. The survey assumed, correctly, that the Pacific War would end by mid-1945, and went on to project indices of industrial production, 1946–1950. As a good, conservative estimate should, these indices fell short of actuality by a small margin. Of particular interest was the forecast relative to distillate fuels: the survey predicted annual consumption for burning purposes of more than 200 million barrels. Actual annual consumption during the years 1946–1949 averaged 249 million barrels.[3]

Guided by this and other surveys, the Shell management looked forward to postwar prosperity, a view not shared by some, including government economists who continued to make pessimistic predictions as late as the summer and fall of 1945. The postwar demand for petroleum products, according to Shell's estimates, would be good, approaching by 1947–1948 the peak levels of consumption attained during World War II. However, until the automobile industry resumed large-volume production of passenger cars there would probably be a lag in the consumption of gasoline.

Shell's refinery output had been considerably enlarged during the war. Fraser feared that this increased capacity, turned loose during this interim period, might contribute to a new glut on the gasoline market. Accordingly, on August 24, 1945, ten days after the end of the war, he instructed Shell's manufacturing department to cut back the daily throughputs of the Wood River and Houston refineries by some 20%. Demand did not slacken as much as anticipated, for motorists did not scrap their cars quite as rapidly as the economists had predicted. By early 1946, Houston was again running at nearly wartime capacity; by June 1946, Wood River also was back at wartime level.[4] This unexpected market strength was a portent of what lay ahead: a phenomenal increase in demand that would lead the Shell organization to large-scale expansion in the postwar period.

While the years between 1945 and 1950 are still too recent for judicious appraisal,* it is possible to point out that they were a period of record-breaking physical activity not only for Shell and the oil industry generally, but for the whole American economy. In every depart-

---

* This remark applies with even more force to the years since 1950. The text, therefore, ends with 1950, except for passing references to a few major happenings.

ment of its business, Shell participated in this amazing growth. The company's crude oil production by the end of 1948 had passed the record levels of 1944, and yearly refinery intakes from 1947 onward were far in excess of the previous peak attained in 1944, when every oil company was straining at the seams to turn out oil products for the war. In the five years following the war, Shell's daily refinery capacity rose to 382,000 barrels a day; at the end of 1950, further extensions to refining capacity were going forward that would in the next five years push Shell's total daily refinery capacity beyond the half-million mark. The amounts of gasoline manufactured reached record highs: the 66 million barrels of 1950 was double the volume of 1935, and an increase of almost 30% over 1944. Sales, measured in dollars, increased at an even sharper rate: $915 million in 1950, nearly four times the peak year of 1929, treble 1941, and an increase of a full 100% over 1945. Beginning with 1951, the sales figure passed the billion-dollar mark, placing Shell in the top rank of American business. And in 1954, the company's assets would also pass the billion-dollar level.

This high level of sales, plus the greater degree of efficiency obtained from larger refinery and pipe line throughputs, made for lower unit handling costs. These favorable factors, plus the general improvement in prices, helped make up for some of the deficits of the Thirties. Dollar earnings for the period 1946–1950 were the best in the company's history. This record was achieved by virtue of large-scale expansion in every department of Shell's business. For this expansion, the company laid out a half billion dollars of new capital expenditure in the five years ending with 1950.

2

Money for Expansion

Long before the end of the war, it was apparent that Shell would have to be prepared to undertake unusually large capital expenditures in the first years of peace. For nearly five full years, wartime restrictions had prevented replacement of obsolete equipment. Modernization programs, begun in the late 1930's and halted by the war, would need to be continued, at much greater cost than prewar, and new facilities would be necessary to handle the increased business forecast by the surveys. In addition, the company had planned several brand-new projects in the fields of research and chemical manufacture. In anticipation of these expenditures, the company's cash position had been kept high: it finished the year 1945 with a record balance of $117,-000,000

To be able to undertake new expenditures, it was desirable to postpone redemption of the outstanding bonded indebtedness—some $81,000,000—parts of which were due in the years immediately ahead. Plans for new financing were worked out during late 1945 and early 1946, and on April 1, 1946, Shell Union issued $125,000,000 of 2½% 25-year debentures. From the proceeds of this new issue, all existing bonded indebtedness was retired, leaving a balance of some $39,000,-000 to be added to the company's working capital.

The money for the company's tremendous cash outlays during the postwar years 1945–1950 was provided by the annual depreciation write-offs, by earnings retained in the business, and by drawing on working capital (cash on hand), as can be seen from the tabulation below.[5]

CAPITAL EXPENDITURES AND SOURCES OF FUNDS, 1946–1950

	Capital Expenditures	Depreciation Write-Offs	Retained Earnings	Cash on Hand at Year-End
1946	$ 65,542,000	$ 45,686,000	$ 12,674,000	$142,388,000
1947	138,431,000	50,730,000	29,566,000	79,944,000
1948	122,717,000	60,384,000	70,984,000	88,912,000
1949	93,215,000	77,895,000	36,011,000	73,056,000
1950	86,651,000	82,969,000	49,709,000	137,168,000
	$506,556,000	$317,664,000	$198,944,000	

The total of depreciation write-offs and retained earnings for the period 1946–1950 exceeded by $10 million the total capital expenditures during the same years. Consequently, it is possible to say that, in the aggregate, the funds for Shell's postwar capital expansion came entirely from current operations. New outside financing was nevertheless desirable, particularly during the years of greatest capital commitments. Without this financing, the company probably would have hesitated to dip into cash on hand for a sum exceeding $60 million, as it did in 1947.

While the $39,000,000 realized from the 1946 bond issue was the only outside financing done by Shell Union during this period, its subsidiary, Shell Pipe Line Corporation, did arrange to borrow $22,-500,000 from banks, in exchange for serial notes guaranteed by the parent company, to help finance two large pipe line projects completed during 1949.

This is perhaps the place to mention another piece of financing which was arranged in these years, even though it did not directly affect Shell Union. In 1948, the Shell Caribbean Petroleum Company,† one of the Group's chief companies operating in Venezuela, borrowed $250,000,000 for development work from a group of American insurance companies. In order to furnish the insurance companies with adequate security, Bataafsche (which owned all of Shell Caribbean's stock) transferred to Shell Caribbean its 65% holding in Shell Union, so that Shell Caribbean could offer these shares as collateral. Because this transaction was purely for the purpose of protecting the investment of Shell Caribbean bondholders, it did not in any noticeable fashion alter existing relationships among the Shell companies involved.

3

The Continuing Search for Oil

IF there were any who had thought that oil consumption in the post-war period would return to prewar levels, they were in for a rude shock. Almost at once, increased demand made itself felt. The great volume of this increased demand can best be realized by examining the rapid increases in some of the chief oil-consuming fields. At the end of 1945 there were 31 million motor vehicles registered in the United States. By the early months of 1951 this figure had risen to 50 million, or an increase of two-thirds over 1945. In 1945, there were some 2½ million domestic oil burners in use, a figure which by the end of 1950 had risen to over 5 million, more than double. In 1945, less than 700 Diesel locomotives were on order by America's railroads; in 1950, this figure had risen to 4,400, six times as many. Use of tractors on farms rose steadily: from 2.6 million in 1945 to 4 million in 1950, an increase of more than 50%. And sales of liquefied petroleum gas

† The former Caribbean Petroleum Company. See pages 218-219.

("bottled gas") had an equally rapid growth: the 3.3 billion gallons sold in 1950 were nearly treble the sales of 1946.[6]

To meet this huge new demand, the entire oil industry had to operate at capacity. In one year in particular, 1947, demand increased at a rate faster than the companies' ability to supply it, causing temporary shortages, chiefly of distillate fuel oil. The shortage of domestic fuel oil affected several sections of the country and received a great deal of public attention. It was a shortage that had been in the making since the mid-1930's, and was due to many factors: a rapid increase in domestic oil-burner installations, the strain imposed by increased demand upon existing transportation and storage facilities, and the nature of refinery operations.

Ever since the emergence of the automobile as the refinery's chief customer, in the days before the First World War, refinery operations had been increasingly geared to the production of a maximum yield of gasoline from each barrel of crude oil. Thermal cracking processes, installed widely during the Twenties, had all been aimed at increasing the refinery yield of gasoline by reprocessing some of the distillate fuel produced in straight-run distillation of crude oil. Because it was a by-product, distillate fuel could be sold relatively cheaply, and after the first fully automatic domestic oil burners had begun to be installed in quantity in the late Twenties and early Thirties, oil fuel found increasing favor among homeowners.

By the mid-Thirties it was apparent that the low price of oil fuel and the convenience of automatic heat were causing annual increases in distillate consumption that were larger than the increases in the demand for gasoline. The 1937 Shell Union annual report had pointed this out:

> While in 1937 the domestic and export demand for gasoline increased about 9% over the year 1936, the increase for gas oil and burning oils was in the region of 20%. This trend of disproportionate increase in demand for intermediate products has during recent years been a contributing factor to an unbalanced supply and demand situation. It is an important problem similar to others which the industry has had to face during its history.

In the immediate postwar years, thousands of new houses were built, almost all of them equipped for oil heat. The price of anthracite coal, a chief competitor of oil in home heating, rose sharply because of increased wages in the coal industry. In many areas of the nation where oil heat had hitherto been substantially more costly than coal,

coal's competitive advantage now tended to disappear. In these areas, many thousands of oil burners were purchased and installed in a general conversion from coal to oil. The result was that the oil industry found itself almost overnight with hundreds of thousands of new customers. By exercising effort and ingenuity, the oil companies managed to squeak through tight supply situations during the winters of 1947 and 1948. But the disparity between the annual increases in demand for gasoline and fuel oil still remained a problem for the best minds of the industry.

While the increase in domestic fuel oil consumption occupied a paramount place in public attention, the plain fact was that oil consumption for every purpose was increasing at a tremendous rate. Oil and gas, which forty years earlier had accounted for less than one-eighth of the country's total energy production, by 1950 accounted for more than half the total motive power of the nation.[7]

UNITED STATES ENERGY SOURCES, 1910 AND 1950

	1910	*1950*
Coal	84.8%	38.3%
Oil	8.6%	40.1%
Natural gas	3.3%	16.8%
Water power	3.3%	4.8%
Oil and Natural Gas Together	*11.9%*	*56.9%*

This increase was not entirely at the expense of the coal industry: in 1950, the bituminous coal industry mined and sold some 25% more coal than it did in 1910. But oil, because of its convenience and low price, got the lion's share of the new business. All this meant that the oil industry had to continue to find new supplies of oil in large amounts to replace the oil that was being used up, and to insure an ample reserve for the years ahead.

In this connection, it is interesting to see how the traditional pattern of oil discovery once again repeated itself. Almost from the first, the oil business has been running out of oil. When the early Pennsylvania fields started to taper off, the threatened scarcity caused a rise in crude oil prices. Wildcatters, eager to cash in on the higher prices, brought in new fields in Ohio and near Bradford, Pennsylvania. Then again, around the turn of the century, with these supplies pretty well used up and demand on the rise, prices started up again. The resulting rash of new exploratory activity brought in booming new fields in Texas, California, and Oklahoma. In fact, so much new oil was found that by the onset of the First World War there were temporary depressions in many of these new oil fields. The mass production of automobiles and the demands of the war served to use up these surpluses. At the close of World War I, the industry once again found itself with short supplies and steadily rising prices. By March 1920, crude oil prices in the Mid-Continent had hit $3.50 a barrel. These high prices set wildcatters to work in record numbers, and the result was a flood of oil from new pools in California, Oklahoma, Kansas, Arkansas, and Texas.

In each of these periods of impending shortage there had been experts gloomily predicting that America's days as an oil producer were now at an end. In the 1919–1920 period of shortage, the head of the U. S. Geological Survey went so far as to predict complete exhaustion of domestic oil supplies in less than twenty years. In alarm, the Bureau of Mines sent an expert to Scotland to study methods for extracting oil from shale. It is interesting to note how closely these 1919 predictions (together with the suggested solution of producing oil from shale) paralleled some of the opinions and warnings heard during 1946 and 1947.[8] Once again, however, the alarmists had failed to consider the tremendous incentive to oil exploration that is provided by an increase in price.

In mid-1946, the O.P.A. price controls on crude oil and its principal products were removed, bringing the law of supply and demand back into operation. The price of East Texas crude (a fair barometer of crude prices) had been fixed at $1.25 a barrel all during the war years. Before 1946 was out, the East Texas price had risen to $1.70 a barrel and during 1947 it went to $2.65. The amount of exploratory activity increased immediately: in 1946, 5,700 wildcat wells were drilled; in 1950, nearly double that number. The success of this national oil-hunting program is emphasized by the fact that during each of the postwar years annual crude oil production was higher than at any time during the war years, and yet at the end of 1950 national proven reserves were 5½ billion barrels greater than at the end of 1946.

Shell's oil-hunting effort roughly paralleled that of the industry during this period. One-half of the company's total capital expenditures of the years 1946–1950 went for exploration and production, a sum slightly more than $251,000,000. This was a large expenditure but results were far from disappointing. The company drilled 27 wildcat wells in 1946, 80 in 1950—and 52 of the 80 were successful.[9]

Weeks Island

In April, 1946, the company brought into production with appropriate ceremonies the Smith-State No. 2 well in the Weeks Island, Louisiana, field, discovered by Shell a year earlier. This well, the first oil producer in the Weeks Island field, was completed at the depth of 13,770 feet, and was at the time of its completion the deepest producing oil well in the world. By the end of 1950, some 40 wells, most of them even deeper, had been completed at Weeks Island, yielding large quantities of high-quality crude oil. Despite extreme depth (by 1955, Shell had producing wells at Weeks Island in excess of 17,000 feet deep) and resultant high drilling costs, Weeks Island was one of the most prolific and profitable of the company's postwar fields.

There were other Shell finds in Louisiana during these years. In 1947, the company brought in a discovery well at Ora. In 1948, it found new production in the Section 28 Dome field of St. Martin's Parish. In 1950, deeper production was encountered in the Iowa field, a good producer for twenty years. Another Louisiana field, interesting for a different reason, was the shallow Good Hope field, located less than a mile from the Norco refinery. Although the Good Hope field was discovered by others, Shell had a large share of the acreage. Because this production was practically in the refinery's back yard, the company arranged to purchase most of the oil produced by other companies in the Good Hope field.

Offshore Oil

In common with other major companies, Shell undertook a substantial amount of exploration in offshore waters in the years following the war. During 1949, Shell began to see results from this exploratory work, when offshore wells were completed south of the Mississippi Delta in the Gulf of Mexico at a location known as Main Pass, Block 69, Plaquemines Parish. In 1950, the company brought in another Louisiana offshore field, called South Pass Block 24, in the Mississippi Delta. In the years following 1950, the South Pass Block 24 field was to prove one of the major developments in offshore oil; by late 1955, its daily production of more than 30,000 barrels made it Louisiana's largest oil field. Shell, with more than 125 wells, was the field's leading producer.[10] This new South Pass field gave every promise of developing into a memorable oil field, as important in Shell's history as landmarks like Coalinga, Signal Hill, and Tonkawa.

Elk City

In its oldest oil-producing areas, California and Oklahoma, the company continued exploration in the postwar period and further developed existing fields. In addition, Shell had the good fortune in 1947 to bring in the new Elk City field in western Oklahoma, an area that had not previously produced oil in appreciable quantities. The company's first well near Elk City had encountered gas at a depth of almost 13,000 feet but no definite indications of oil had been seen. Shell's electric well-logging expert, G. E. Archie, felt that a shallower test might prove productive. After some debate, his advice was followed. The test showed that the oil-producing formation had been penetrated and sealed off by action of the drilling mud, as had been the case at Haynesville nearly thirty years earlier. This time, though, Shell had not let its leases go, and in consequence the company became the discoverer and one of the largest leaseholders in the new Elk City field, estimated to contain more than 100,000,000 barrels of oil. The rest of the Elk City acreage was in the hands of eight other operators who agreed, late in 1950, to develop Elk City as a unitized field, with Shell as the operator.

Gasoline Plants

One of the concrete results of unit operation at Elk City was the erection during 1950–1951 of a large cycling plant to strip the natural gasoline and other desirable liquid hydrocarbons from the gas produced with the oil. This plant was built and operated by Shell, as operator of the Elk City unitized pool. After the wet gas had been stripped of its saleable liquids, the remaining dry gas was not wasted, as it would have been twenty-five years earlier. Instead, it was pumped back into the producing formation. This conservation-minded practice insured that the gas would be saved for a day when there might be a market for it. Meanwhile the gas thus pumped back served to keep up the underground pressure of the field, which in turn increased the total amount of the field's ultimate oil production.

The Elk City cycling plant was patterned on a similar plant that Shell had built five years earlier in the unitized field at Sheridan, Texas, southwest of Houston. The Sheridan field produced large quantities of gas rich in entrained liquids called "condensate." At the time, there was no gas pipe line in the area to buy this production of gas, and it would have been illegal under Texas' conservation laws (as well as against the better judgment of Shell's production department) to produce and waste this gas merely to recover the liquids in it. But the amount and nature of these entrained hydrocarbons made them well worth recovering. The company, as operator for the Sheridan unitized field (in which it held a 72% interest), designed and built a plant to process this "wet" gas and produce natural gasoline, normal butane, isobutane, isopentane, and propane. The dry gas remaining after processing was injected back into the producing formation. This cycling operation at Sheridan proved profitable from the start. During 1946–1947, the company built a 98-mile pipe line to deliver products of the Sheridan plant to the Houston refinery.

A natural gasoline plant was built in the T.X.L. field of West Texas during 1946. In the same year, a small completely automatic gasoline plant was erected at Santa Maria, California, to process the gas from Shell's old properties in that field.

Calgary

One of the most spectacular oil booms of the postwar period took place in western Alberta. In this new Canadian boom, Shell was at an initial disadvantage for it had done pioneer exploratory work in the area for several years and then abandoned its early foothold just prior to the first big discoveries.

Shell of Canada had been active in the area of western Alberta since 1940, borrowing technical and managerial personnel from Shell Oil Company's Los Angeles office. During 1944, this group brought in a gas well near Jumping Pound, some twenty miles west of Calgary. Continued efforts in this region failed to find oil. Discouraged, Shell of Canada abandoned further drilling and surrendered most of its Alberta leases outside the Jumping Pound area, which had been proved up as a gas field.

Then, a few months later, in February 1947, Imperial Oil, Ltd., the Canadian affiliate of Jersey Standard, made an important oil discovery at Leduc near Edmonton, about 150 miles north of Calgary. This discovery revived the interest of oil men in all of western Canada, and in boom proportions.

During 1948, Shell decided to re-enter the area on a substantial scale. The expense of the anticipated exploratory program would be large, too large probably to be charged against the relatively small income of Shell of Canada's refining and marketing operation. As a result, Shell of Canada's owners, Shell Oil and Shell Caribbean, decided to participate equally in Canadian exploration. Shell Oil Company, which had the necessary trained staff, was made operator.

In the spring of 1949, Shell Oil set up an exploration and production area office at Calgary and began the acquisition of leases on a large scale. Some 8,000,000 acres of exploratory leases were taken in Alberta, Saskatchewan, and Manitoba. By the spring of 1950, the company could report its first discovery, the Whitelaw field, a small producer of gas and oil in the Peace River district, some 400 miles northwest of Calgary.

The Jumping Pound gas field was retained by Shell of Canada, and managed for the latter's account by Shell Oil Company. Arrangements were made to sell the gas to a public utility in nearby Calgary, and this necessitated processing to remove impurities. For this purpose, a plant was built and put in operation in May 1951. One of the impurities removed was sulphur, readily saleable to manufacturers of sulphuric acid.[11]

Rocky Mountain Area

In mid-1943, long before the big Canadian oil boom had got under way, Shell quietly re-entered the old Rocky Mountain area, where Roxana's and Matador's efforts had been unavailing in the years between 1917 and 1922. Geologists, land men, and seismic crews from Shell's Los Angeles area office began work on a modest scale in Wyoming and Montana. In the next few years, they staked out prospects in these states and in Colorado and Utah, as well. By 1948, the size of the staff had grown sufficiently to warrant establishment of an exploration and production division office at Casper, Wyoming. During the following year, four unsuccessful wildcat wells were drilled in Wyoming, and a fifth just across the state line in southern Montana.

Instead of precipitating abandonment of the venture, these expensive failures served only to whet the company's appetite. Successes of competitors in the same area were encouraging, as were the geologic indications in several regions that were still relatively unexplored. One of the most interesting of these areas was the Williston Basin section of Montana. Here during 1950 the company obtained exploratory permits covering 150,000 acres from the Northern Pacific Railroad and 90,000 acres from the Montana-Dakota Utilities Company. These substantial tracts, added to the some 300,000 acres which the company had under lease at the beginning of 1950, plus other sizeable leases taken during the year, brought Shell's leases and options in the Rocky Mountain area to a total of some 815,000 acres at the end of 1950. Thus far, the Rocky Mountain venture had cost the company $11,-000,000 since 1943, and thus far it had yielded not a drop of oil.[12]

Our account ends with 1950, but it would be unfair to the reader not to mention that this persistence and large expenditure was at last rewarded a few months later. After thirty-four years and many millions of dollars, Shell finally brought in a successful oil well in the Rocky Mountain area—Shell Glenrock Government No. 1, in the Glenrock field, a few miles out of Casper. Then, in May 1951, the company began drilling a wildcat well near Richey, Montana, on the Williston Basin acreage acquired from Northern Pacific. A drill-stem test of this well on July 13, 1951, showed oil in commercial quantities. This discovery was reinforced by the successful completion a few months later of another Williston Basin wildcat, Shell Pine Unit No. 1, located 55 miles southeast of Richey. These discoveries were of first importance and helped focus attention of the oil world on the Williston Basin, a large potentially oil-bearing sedimentary area underlying parts of North and South Dakota, Montana, and three Canadian provinces, Alberta, Manitoba, and Saskatchewan. Amerada Petroleum had brought in a Williston Basin well in North Dakota in April 1951; Shell's two midsummer successes proved up widely separated Williston Basin areas in Montana.[13]

From this point onward, the Williston Basin oil "play" was on in earnest. In May 1953, Shell discovered the Cabin Creek field, 37 miles southeast of Glendive, and later that year Shell added South Dakota to the list of oil-producing states. It was still too early to tell whether the financial results in the Williston Basin would more closely resemble North Central Texas in 1918–1919 or East Texas in 1931 or a state like Kansas whose oil fields have been modest successes but rarely spectacular. Whatever the outcome, the company was well protected with millions of acres of leases throughout the Williston Basin area, both in the United States and Canada.

Purchased Production

Purchase of producing properties continued in the postwar period, although prices by now were well-nigh prohibitive. During 1947, Shell paid $16,500,000 cash to the Amon G. Carter Foundation for 3,000 acres of proven property with a daily production of some 5,000 barrels in the Wasson field of West Texas, where the company already had substantial production. The same year, the company made two large purchases in the Benton field of southern Illinois, acquiring a total of just over 3,000 acres of producing properties for some $5,000,000 cash. During 1948, another 3,121 acres in Oklahoma were acquired for $3,000,000 cash. In 1949, the company traded its widely scattered production in the Texas Panhandle to Phillips, in exchange for Phillips properties in the Wichita Falls area where Shell already owned other producing properties, the result of purchases during the past decade.[14]

Water-Flooding at Benton

The Benton field was typical of the shallow, flush-production fields of southern Illinois. It had been discovered in January 1941. By August of that year it had reached its peak (approximately 150 barrels per day per well) and had declined steadily thereafter. By late 1949, the Benton field had produced a total of 20 million barrels, with reservoir engineers estimating that some 6 million barrels remained to be recovered by normal pumping methods. Shell however had not purchased the Benton properties with the idea of using conventional recovery methods. The company's intention from the outset had been to conduct secondary recovery by means of water drive and thereby bring to the surface some of the oil which otherwise would have remained locked in the earth. So-called "secondary recovery methods" include repressuring by injecting excess gas back into the producing formations (the "Marietta process") and water-flooding, a process almost as old but not so widely used until recent years. It was a water-flooding project which the company had in mind for Benton.

First, Shell had to get the landowners, leaseholders, and operators in the field to consent to unitization of the Benton field, for a project of this nature needs to be operated as a single entity. Three independent operators in the field joined with Shell to finance the construction of the necessary water-supply, oil-separating and injection-pumping equipment, which together with new injection wells and field piping cost some $1,750,000. Shell was appointed operator of the unitized field and of the Benton water-flooding project which began operation in November 1949, the largest such project to be undertaken up to that time.[15]

Water-flooding is proving of great value as a secondary recovery method in old or semi-depleted fields. In the first twenty-two months under water flood, the Benton field produced a million barrels of oil more than it would have during the same period using normal recovery methods. The years since 1950 have witnessed widespread secondary-recovery activity in old producing areas such as northeast Oklahoma, where water-flooding is bringing new life to some of the state's earliest oil fields.

California

The orphan, as far as new discoveries in the postwar period were concerned, was California. In 1946, a new gas field was discovered 22 miles west of Sacramento and was quickly developed by the company. A source of gas this far north tied in admirably with Shell Chemical's raw materials needs at Shell Point. In 1950, the company discovered a new oil field of modest dimensions at North Antelope Hills, in the San Joaquin Valley. But these discoveries were small indeed compared to the increases in demand that were generated by California's spectacular postwar growth. Most of Shell's crude oil requirements on the Coast continued to come from the company's older fields. Two of the most important extensions to the company's California reserves were the result of proving up additional acreage and discovering deeper producing horizons in the Ventura and Brea fields.

For exploratory work, 1946–1950, for some 1,500 new wells drilled on proven property, and for gas-processing installations and other oil-field auxiliary equipment, the company spent a quarter billion dollars. That this large outlay brought results may be gathered by comparing two estimates of Shell's underground reserves, made by Paul Paine of Los Angeles, an authoritative and conservative appraiser of oil and gas property. On January 1, 1946, Paine estimated the company's net reserves at 745,516,000 barrels. During the ensuing five years, Shell produced from these underground reserves 357,441,000 barrels of oil.[16] Then, on January 1, 1950, Paine made another appraisal and placed the company's reserves at 833,000,000 barrels. So, despite using up half the oil with which it entered the five-year period following the war, Shell had kept abreast of the large postwar demand and added to its reserves for the future some 88,000,000 barrels of crude oil, a year's production at current rates.

4

Large-Diameter Pipe Lines

WITH the tremendous increases in consumption of the postwar period, Shell and almost every other company in the industry needed more pipe line capacity, both for crude oil and finished products. The experience of the Big and Little Big Inch lines during the war years had demonstrated the superior efficiency of large-diameter pipe lines. Large-diameter pipe lines were more economical for several reasons. A pipe 20 inches in diameter could carry, not double, but four times the volume of a 10-inch pipe. Because the larger stream encountered less friction against the walls of the pipe, pumping was easier and cheaper. To build a 20-inch pipe line required only twice the amount of pipe steel used for a 10-inch line, and proportionately fewer pumping stations were needed on the larger line. Per barrel of oil handled, both the capital costs and operating expenses of a large-diameter line were lower. A 20-inch line running at full load could move oil for 45% of the cost of pumping it through a fully loaded 10-inch line. For these reasons, the trend in pipe line construction in the postwar period was toward large-diameter lines.[17]

Because of their size, one of these new, efficient, large-diameter lines could transport more oil than was likely to be needed by a single refinery, or more oil than was available from a single company's producing fields at a particular point. Because of these factors and the additional consideration of huge construction costs, competitors with oil production and refineries in the same general areas tended to undertake large-diameter pipe lines jointly. Here again, successful wartime experience, this time with the Bayou Pipe Line System, pointed the way toward a satisfactory method of ownership and operation, the so-called joint venture.

Basin Pipe Line System

During 1946 planning got under way by several of the companies which had oil production in the Permian Basin of West Texas and refineries in the Mid-Continent. The Texas Pipe Line Company, Shell Pipe Line Corporation, Sinclair Refining Company,§ and Empire Pipe Line Company (Cities Service) agreed to join in a "limited joint-

§ Obligations and privileges under this contract later assigned to Sinclair Pipe Line Company, organized in 1951 to take over Sinclair Refining Company's pipe line operations.

ownership venture" and build a 20- and 24-inch line from Jal, New Mexico, to Cushing, Oklahoma. From Jal to Midland, the line was to be 20 inches in diameter. At Midland, where more oil would join it, the diameter of the pipe was to be increased to 22 inches. At Wichita Falls in North Texas, where still more oil would be added to the main stream, the diameter would be increased to 24 inches.

Unlike many pipe line ventures of the past, this line was undertaken with expansion built into the plans. In its initial phase, the line would have a daily capacity of 167,000 barrels. After addition of more pumping stations, it would be able to handle 195,000 barrels a day. In its third stage, when all additional stations had been added, it would be able to pump 385,000 barrels daily.

In entering this limited joint-ownership venture, each participating company contracted for a definite percentage of the line's capacity and agreed to share the same proportion of the line's construction cost. This new line was called the Basin Pipe Line System and was built and operated by The Texas Pipe Line Company, on behalf of the three other owners. The share of each company in the available capacity and in the cost of building and operating the line was Texas 44%, Shell 34%, Sinclair 13%, and Empire 9%.

The postwar steel shortage continued through most of 1946. Finally, in November 1947, enough of the specially made pipe was ready and construction began on the Basin line. By July 1948, the 20-inch segment from Jal to Midland and the 22-inch segment from Midland to Wichita Falls had been completed and put into operation with temporary pumping facilities. By June 1949, the remainder of the line to Cushing had been finished, and permanent pumping stations installed.

Ozark Pipe Line System

Participation in the Basin line met Shell's needs for additional crude-carrying capacity from West Texas to Cushing, but it did not solve the problem of getting the oil from Cushing to the Wood River refinery. The original 10-inch Cushing–Wood River line, built in 1917–1918, and the line paralleling it completed in 1937 were both crowded to capacity. It was not feasible to build the Basin line farther northwards; neither Sinclair nor Cities Service needed additional crude-carrying capacity north of Oklahoma. But Texaco, which had a pipe line terminal at Patoka, Illinois, was interested in such an extension. Accordingly, Shell Pipe Line and The Texas Pipe Line Company undertook to build a 22-inch northward extension of the Basin system on the same general basis as the Basin line. Like the Basin system, it was a "limited joint-ownership venture," with Shell supplying 55% of the capital, and acting as constructor and operator, and Texas paying the other 45% of the costs. Each company shared in this proportion in the line's capacity, initially 187,000 barrels daily and capable of expansion to 296,000 barrels a day.

This jointly owned line terminated at Wood River, and Texaco built an additional 54 miles of line to connect Wood River with Patoka. Because it went through the Ozark mountain region, the new Cushing–Wood River line was named the Ozark Pipe Line System, reviving the old name which Shell Pipe Line Corporation had discarded in 1927. As part of its Ozark line plans, Shell retired from service the 10-inch screwed line built at the time the Wood River refinery was opened. The new 22-inch line was laid along the old right-of-way, except in some of the built-up areas around St. Louis, where a new route was selected to avoid excessive land-damage payments.

In December 1948, thirteen months after construction of the Basin line got under way, Shell Pipe Line started laying the new Ozark line. It was completed, together with dual crossings* under five rivers, including the Mississippi, and put into permanent operation in July 1949. Some idea of the size of these two pipe line undertakings may be gathered from the fact that the pipe for the Ozark System alone required 85 days' continuous operation of one of the mills of the fabricators, Youngstown Sheet & Tube Company. To transport the pipe to field locations, a 60-car freight train left the Youngstown mill every 36 hours. A total of some 600 freight cars were in constant service during the period of manufacture to handle movement of the pipe. Like the Basin system, the Ozark line was equipped with electrically operated centrifugal pumps. By the end of 1950, programs were under way to expand the initial capacity of both the Basin and Ozark Systems.[18]

Coincident with the building of the Ozark line, Shell Pipe Line modernized the 10-inch line completed in 1937 by installing new electrically operated pumping equipment. The original screwed line was pulled up, and a substantial part of the pipe—still serviceable after 31 years—was reconditioned and used late in 1949 to lay a 160-mile spur line to connect the new Elk City field with the main line at Cushing.

* One of these crossings acts as a spare in case of damage to the other.

Rancho Pipe Line System

Shell participated in a third joint-ownership-venture crude line, built during 1951–1953. It was called the Rancho Pipe Line System and utilized the Shell Pipe Line right-of-way from McCamey in West Texas to Houston. The Rancho line was owned by the pipe line subsidiaries of seven companies—Shell, Sinclair, Pan American (Standard of Indiana), Phillips, Ashland, Crown Central, and Eastern States Petroleum. Shell Pipe Line Corporation, holder of 38%, the largest single interest, acted as constructor and operator. The Rancho line was 24 inches in diameter and had an initial daily capacity of 210,000 barrels when it went on stream in April 1953. Provisions were made in the design to raise the capacity to 345,000 barrels a day, when needed, by installing five additional pumping stations. Shell's old 10-inch McCamey–Houston line was no longer needed. All of it, except for a segment near the Houston end, was sold to Phillips for conversion into a natural gasoline line.

New Products Pipe Line Capacity

In the field of products pipe line transportation, there were substantial capacity increases made in each of the systems with which Shell was connected. The East products pipe line, running from Wood River to Lima, Ohio, had a capacity of 16,000 barrels a day when it was completed in 1938. Between 1939 and 1949, additional pumping stations were added to raise the capacity of the line to some 28,500 barrels a day. During the summer of 1950, a large segment of the line reached the limits to which it could be expanded by the installation of additional pumping equipment. During 1950, four completely automatic auxiliary stations went into operation, raising the capacity of the line to 32,500 barrels a day.

These stations, controlled from the products pipe line dispatching room in New York (it had been moved there with the rest of the St. Louis office in 1940) were a logical further development of the largely automatic Casey, Illinois, station, installed on the original line in 1938. The Casey station had been built so that its main items of equipment would start and stop in response to the pressure of pipe line flow. Now Shell's products pipe line department carried this idea a step further, and designed new stations that could be actuated by impulses originated by a teletype dial, which is similar to a telephone dial. These impulses could be transmitted over the pipe line's teletype circuit to start and stop the motors operating the valve-closing and pumping equipment. For completely automatic remote-control operation, the central dispatching office would need to know the meter readings that indicated speed and pressure. Working with outside concerns, Shell's products pipe line department developed equipment to report these meter readings automatically in response to a query from the teletype dial. These developments removed the chief barriers to operating fully automatic pumping stations by remote control.

On the North products pipe line, from Wood River to East Chicago, the old Diesel-driven equipment was replaced with electrically operated centrifugal pumps in 1948. During 1951–1953, the old 8-inch line was replaced by new pipe 14 inches in diameter, making possible an immediate increase in capacity from 38,500 to 85,000 barrels a day, with provision for future expansion up to 115,000 barrels daily.

The short but highly useful products pipe line system around Metropolitan Boston had its capacity increased. Shell sold a one-third interest in the segments of its line running between Waltham and Worcester to Esso, in order to allow Esso to connect a products line from its Everett refinery to Shell's line at Waltham. From Waltham, Esso could pump its products westward to Worcester using its one-third interest in the Shell line. Esso also built a new line northward from Waltham to Methuen, and Shell purchased a 25% interest in it.[19]

In Ohio, Shell's East products pipe line terminated at Lima. Since 1938, the company had rented capacity on a Standard Oil of Ohio products line in order to ship its products northward from Lima to Toledo. With expansion of the East line, the amount of capacity available to Shell on Standard's Lima–Toledo line was now not enough, but Shell did not have product movement enough between these two cities to warrant construction and operation of a separate line of its own. The southern spur of Shell's Ohio line, a 6-inch pipe running from Lima south through Springfield and terminating at Columbus, was still adequate for Shell's needs in the area. However, Standard of Ohio had built a short line from Springfield to Dayton, renting capacity on the Shell line to get its products from Lima to Springfield. Sohio's needs for capacity on the Lima-to-Springfield segment of this spur had now increased but Shell was not willing to expand capacity merely to accommodate a competitor, any more than Sohio was willing to expand its Lima–Toledo line.

Faced with these dual problems, the two companies proposed a new jointly owned pipe line company to own and operate the lines north

H. S. M. Burns
President
Shell Oil Company
1947 to date

Dr. Monroe E. Spaght
President, Shell Development, 1949–52;
Executive Vice President, Shell Oil Co.,
1953 to date

R. C. McCurdy
President
Shell Chemical Corporation
1953 to date

Dr. Harold Gershinowitz
President
Shell Development Company
1953 to date

Shell's offshore drilling in the Gulf of Mexico requires equipment like this massive drilling barge built in 1954.

Shell Pipe Line participated in large-diameter pipe line projects such as the 22-inch Ozark System from Cushing to Wood River, 1948.

and south from Lima. The new company could then make the capacity increases that were needed. During 1950, the Inland Corporation was organized for this purpose. To Inland, Shell deeded over its Lima-Springfield-Columbus spur line, and Standard of Ohio its Lima–Toledo and Springfield–Dayton lines. Inland borrowed $1,250,000 from banks and during 1950 completed the construction of a new 8-inch line, paralleling the existing line from Lima to Springfield. A new pumping station was built at Lima, capable of pumping both north and south, and two new stations were installed on the Lima–Toledo line to raise its capacity.[20]

Since the mid-Twenties, Shell had used the Great Lakes to ship products eastward from East Chicago to water terminals in Michigan and northern Ohio. This practice was continued after the completion of the Wood River–East Chicago products line in 1940. It was satisfactory except during the coldest months of winter, when the lakes froze over. To get around this difficulty and to increase its year-round carrying capacity in this area, Shell undertook to organize a jointly owned common-carrier products line. The new company, called Wolverine Pipe Line Company, was formed during 1952, owned 40% by Shell, 35% by Cities Service, and 25% by Texaco. C. S. Gentry, Shell's vice president and general counsel, retired at the end of 1952 and was made president of Wolverine. Shell Oil's products pipe line department undertook to build and operate Wolverine's 290 miles of 16-inch products line from East Chicago to Detroit and Toledo. The Wolverine line, with an initial capacity of 95,000 barrels a day, was completed and put into operation late in 1953.

During 1950, the Plantation Pipe Line Company, the important products pipe line system serving the inland sections of the South Atlantic states, began a large expansion program to increase its capacity from 95,000 to 221,000 barrels a day. A large-diameter parallel line, 432 miles of 18-inch pipe and 275 miles of 14-inch pipe, was laid alongside the earlier line from Baton Rouge to Charlotte, North Carolina. To finance this construction, the Plantation company (24% owned by Shell) sold $40,000,000 of 25-year debentures and arranged to borrow as needed an additional $15,000,000 from banks. The expanded Plantation system, with five new pumping stations, was completed during 1952.[21]

Expanding Refinery Output

THE chief problem confronting the refining end of Shell's business in the postwar period was, as during the war years, production of ever-larger quantities of petroleum products to keep up with growing market demand. Product requirements, however, differed. Now the pressure on the refineries was not for more aviation gasoline, as it had been during the war, but for much larger quantities of distillate fuels, kerosene, and automotive gasoline.

To provide the increased product yields necessary, Shell Oil in the years between 1945 and 1950 increased its refining capacity east of the Rockies by 27%. The daily distilling capacity of Wood River, 87,000 barrels at the end of the war, rose to 120,000 barrels by the end of 1950; Houston's capacity rose during the same period from 78,000 to 115,000 barrels a day; and the daily capacity of the Norco refinery went from 32,000 to 50,000 barrels. At the end of 1950, further large extensions were under way which would greatly enlarge these figures during the 1950's.

The postwar increases in Shell's refinery capacity were in some instances the result of installations of large new pieces of refinery equipment. Most of this new capacity, however, was gained from renewals, revisions, rearrangement, and enlargement of existing equipment. The extent of this program of modification and enlargement may be judged from its cost, $106,000,000, one-fifth the company's total capital expenditures for the 1946–1950 period.

The largest of the postwar refinery construction projects were at Houston. In mid-1946, a fluid catalytic cracking unit, similar to those built during the war at Wilmington and Wood River, was completed and put in operation at Houston. It was of improved design and utilized the new microspheroidal catalyst introduced by Shell Oil and Shell Development. The new catalyst, in the shape of minute globules, was expected to be much less subject to wear than the jagged-particle catalysts then in use. This expectation proved well founded, and in the years following 1946 most operators of fluid cracking units cut their catalyst losses by adopting low-attrition microspheroidal catalysts.[22]

Demand for other products, such as lubricants, continued to mount.

In 1948, a lubricating oil plant was installed at the Houston refinery, doubling the company's capacity to produce high-viscosity lubricants. Most of the output of the new Houston plant went to the Gulf Coast and Atlantic Seaboard areas. The plant was also large enough to supply the West Coast's increased needs, so instead of enlarging the Martinez lubricating oil plant, the company installed additional receiving, blending, and packaging facilities at Martinez and began to ship lubricating oil stocks from Houston to Martinez by tanker.

A by-product of lubricating oil manufacture is paraffin, recovered in the process of dewaxing the oils. The quantities of paraffin recovered in the large new lubricating oil plant at Houston, and the expanding market for paraffin as a raw material in paper carton manufacture, determined the company to essay its first venture into wax manufacture. The paraffin wax plant, completed at Houston in 1949, turned out bulk paraffin which was sold direct to large consumers, chiefly makers of paper milk bottles and similar wax-impregnated containers.

At Houston and at the other Shell refineries, a number of unspectacular but very necessary enlargement projects were undertaken and completed during the postwar years. Large numbers of new tanks were built, both for crude oil and products. New utilities were constructed for the generation of steam and electricity. New facilities were installed to furnish additional water supplies. New refinery docks and roads were built, as were new plants to make specialty products such as insecticides and spray oils. Dozens of new buildings were erected to house compounding plants, drum-filling and packaging operations, maintenance shops, and control laboratories.

In grease manufacture, the company augmented its manufacturing facilities both on the Pacific Coast and in the East-of-the-Rockies area. At Martinez, where grease had been made since the start of refinery operations, a new plant, one of the first to manufacture grease by a continuous process, was built during 1946 and put into operation early in 1947.

International Lubricant Corporation

East of the Rockies, Shell had no facilities for making grease. In June 1946, the company remedied this deficit by purchasing a small, progressive manufacturer of specialized lubricants, the International Lubricant Corporation, of New Orleans. International Lubricant had been organized in February 1929, under the name of Battenfeld Grease & Oil Company (Louisiana), Inc., to act as a wholesale outlet for the Battenfeld Grease & Oil Company, of Kansas City, which owned 51% of its stock. Four months later, the minority stockholders, E. E. Linthicum, W. H. Saunders, Jr., and associates, bought out the Battenfeld interest, changed the corporate name to the present title, engaged H. M. Fraser, a chemical engineer, and built their own grease plant.

By 1946, International was producing 25,000,000 pounds of grease annually, selling some under its own brand and packaging the rest for other companies, including Shell. For a small company, International had devoted a large amount of money and effort to research, with the result that its products were of high quality and its methods and equipment up to date. Following the purchase, International was not consolidated into Shell operations for it was turning out more product than Shell could use. International Lubricant continued as a separate entity under the management of the men who built it, W. H. Saunders, Jr., president, and H. M. Fraser, vice president. In September 1946, J. L. Webster, who had been sales manager of several Shell marketing divisions as well as assistant manager of head office lubricating oil sales, became sales manager of International Lubricant.[23]

Converting to Peacetime Operation

Reconversion was a major headache in many lines of business. For the oil refiner, it was a less serious problem. A refinery's crude-distilling units operated much the same in peace or war. Cracking units, thermal and catalytic, were without major changes adjusted to different peacetime yields—less of the light ends used in aviation gasoline and more of the distillate fuel for which there was a great postwar demand.

One of the Wood River catalytic crackers had been designed to use distillate fuel as charging stock. This unit was closed down in the postwar months because there was an urgent demand for fuel. It was restarted in 1947 after additional feed-preparation facilities had been installed to provide a different kind of feed stock.[24]

The polymerization plants that had been converted to cumene production during the war were returned to their original function of manufacturing high-antiknock "polymer" suitable for blending into automotive gasoline. The toluene plants at Wood River and Wilmington, built for war production, were for the moment made idle by the cessation of wartime demand; eventually, parts of them would be used in the production of aromatics such as xylene and benzene.

During the late 1940's, reforming (the thermal process used to transform light ends such as naphthas into mixed aromatics) underwent marked changes. A catalyst, generally platinum, was added and the new catalytic reforming was able to accomplish the manufacture of aromatics such as benzene and toluene much more efficiently. Shell adopted a Universal Oil Products platinum catalyst and late in 1950 began to convert the wartime Wood River toluene plant into a catalytic reformer, or "Platformer," as U.O.P. calls the equipment for this process. The Platforming installation was completed in the spring of 1951, and subsequently (June 1953) the Wilmington toluene plant was also converted to Platforming. The catalytic reforming process accomplished isomerization, dehydrogenation, and cyclization simultaneously. The catalyst had the virtue of a long operating cycle before it became covered with coke and had to be regenerated. Besides producing commercially saleable aromatics, catalytic reforming could also be used to convert the mixed napthenes in naphtha into a cut of mixed high-antiknock aromatics, excellent for boosting the octane number of motor fuel. Plans for brand-new Platformer installations were under way by the early 1950's. One was completed at Houston in February 1953 and a second at Martinez in June 1954.[25]

A New Refinery

By 1948, imports of crude oil by the American oil industry were beginning to assume sizeable proportions. The Shell management decided it would be prudent to select a site for a new refinery to operate on imported crude, in all probability oil from Group companies in Venezuela. This refinery, it was decided, could be located on the East Coast, near the large metropolitan centers of consumption. The company already had dockage and a substantial plant at Sewaren, just north of Perth Amboy, New Jersey. For this reason, Sewaren was selected to serve as a nucleus for the proposed refinery. During 1948, Shell bought some 600 acres of property, most of it in the town of Woodbridge, New Jersey, adjoining Sewaren.[26]

This acreage was held in reserve against the time when the company might decide to erect an East Coast refinery. For the immediate future, Shell's rapidly increasing production of crude oil in Louisiana indicated that the Atlantic Seaboard market could be more economically supplied by extending facilities of the Norco refinery. In the years following 1950, Norco's capacity was raised to 75,000 barrels a day and a catalytic cracking plant installed. This increased capacity gave Norco advantages which a Sewaren refinery could not have. The total supply of by-product gases at Norco, after this latest enlargement, was sufficient to warrant construction of a chemical plant. Further, Norco could be connected by a relatively short pipe line to the southern terminus of the Plantation line at Baton Rouge. Under this arrangement, Shell's products for the Plantation line would not have to be piped the longer distance from Houston to Baton Rouge; the excess thus made available at Houston could be shipped by tanker to the East Coast. These considerations outweighed for the immediate future the advantages of a new refinery in the area of New York Harbor.

In the years following 1950, other large-scale refinery extensions were undertaken. At Wood River, installation of a new crude-oil distilling unit and additions to catalytic cracking and alkylation facilities (1951–1954) raised the refinery's throughput by 40%. On the West Coast, where additions to refining capacity had been insignificant in the years immediately following the war, an enlargement program was undertaken during 1951. A new crude-oil distilling unit was built at Wilmington and placed in operation during November 1953. Revisions of existing facilities at Martinez, completed during 1952, had the effect of augmenting daily crude-distilling capacity by 20%.

The big problem facing Shell's California refineries in the years immediately following the war was that the company's foreseeable crude reserves in that state were only enough to supply California's rapidly expanding markets. An answer to this quandary was, happily, provided by the large new crude oil discoveries made in the late 1940's on the sparsely settled plains of western Canada. A logical market for this Canadian oil was the burgeoning Pacific Northwest, traditionally supplied from California. Here Shell decided to build a refinery, and during 1954 began construction of a 50,000-barrel-a-day refinery on an 800-acre tract at Anacortes, Washington, a peninsula location sixty miles north of Richmond Beach where the company's business had first got under way four decades earlier.

The new Anacortes refinery started up on September 21, 1955, and was in full operation by January 1956. Crude was supplied to the Northwest area by a 770-mile, 24-inch pipe line, stretching across the Canadian Rockies from Edmonton, Alberta, to Vancouver, B.C. A 16- and 20-inch spur ran from the Vancouver area southward into northwestern Washington. The line was built by Trans Mountain Oil Pipe Line Company, a Canadian corporation owned more than 60% publicly, the remainder held by five major oil companies, among them Shell of Canada.

Postwar Labor Relations

In each of the postwar years from the end of the war to 1950 (with the exception only of 1946) Shell's refineries ran at levels higher than even the periods of peak wartime production. These new highs in refining activity were achieved despite four major strikes, more than the company had experienced before in so short a time. These strikes were at Houston and other Mid-Continent locations (1945), again at Houston in 1947, on the Pacific Coast (1948), and at Wood River in 1950. All of these strikes had this in common: they arose out of differences over postwar wage adjustments.

The first strike at Houston followed immediately upon the end of the war and was part of a widespread East-of-the-Rockies strike called by the C.I.O. Oil Workers Union. With the cessation of hostilities and the disappearance of the need for overtime work, Shell in September 1945 offered all employees a general increase of 15%. The C.I.O. Oil Workers Union, rejecting this amount and similar amounts offered by other companies, asked instead for a general increase of 30%. The strike, affecting 48 oil industry plants in the Mid-Continent area, lasted from September 1945 until January 1946 when the union agreed to accept 3% in addition to the 15% increase which had been offered to and accepted by all other employees in September. In addition to Shell's Houston refinery, the 1945 strike affected the East products pipe line, the East Chicago products pipe line terminal, and two bulk depots in Detroit. For much of the period of the strike, all these facilities were in operation, for the government, exercising wartime powers that were still in effect, seized the struck facilities on October 4 and turned them over to the Navy for operation.

The 1947 strike at Houston involved the refinery and chemical plants, and lasted from March to May. It concerned other issues in addition to compensation. Three major union demands to which the company could not agree were: irrevocable check-off of union dues, payment of wages to employees on the union's negotiating committee, and granting the union virtual veto power over company-established qualifications for personnel needed to staff new units then being built at the refinery and chemical plants. In mid-May the strike was settled for a 22-cent-an-hour cost-of-living bonus, voluntary revocable check-off of union dues, and other minor concessions. The cost-of-living bonus had been offered to the union prior to the strike, and had been paid to other employees since mid-February.

The 1948 Pacific Coast strike was, like the East-of-the-Rockies strike of three years earlier, a widespread strike by the C.I.O. Oil Workers Union. In addition to Shell, the strike affected the refinery facilities of Standard Oil of California, Union, Richfield, Texaco, Tide Water, and several small refiners. During the three months' duration of this strike, many employees returned to work and some of Shell's facilities operated at partial capacity. Shell, the first to reach a settlement with the union, settled on the basis of 12½ cents per hour, the same increase offered prior to the strike. Similar settlements were later made by the other oil companies.

The month-long strike that plagued Wood River, from late August to late September 1950, grew out of failure to come to terms on renewal of contracts with the Pipefitters and Asbestos Workers Unions (both A.F. of L.). The strike spread among other unions at the refinery and was eventually settled on the basis of a 6% cost-of-living increase which the company gave to other employees in mid-September.

All of these strikes were regrettable. They caused a drop in productivity at a time when all refineries were running at capacity in an effort to keep up with demand. They cost the company large amounts of money and the men substantial losses in pay. They won little, if anything, that could not have been obtained through peaceful negotiation. To the outside observer, Shell's wage and salary policy all during the five-year period seemed more than generous. The blanket raise granted all employees in September 1945 was only the first in a series of upward adjustments to help employees meet higher living costs. The number of Shell employees remained nearly constant during this period (in 1950 there were 30,300, only 500 more than in 1946), yet the amount the company paid out for wages and salaries rose from $95 million in 1946 to $136 million in 1950, an increase of 42%—well above the rise in the consumers' price index during the same period.

Things Look Up in Marketing

FOR a full fifteen years, marketing had been the least satisfactory aspect of Shell's business. Depression, overproduction, and intense competition leading to overbuilding and resultant low unit volume had made it difficult for sales departments to show a profit. The war years, with their large-scale diversion of products to the government, accompanied by rationing of the civilian customer, had brought many of the activities of the sales department to a complete standstill. Now, in the years following 1946, the conditions necessary to sales success were once again present. There were plenty of customers; there was product enough to supply them; volume enough to permit lower unit costs; and prices firm enough to make for profitable operation.

Automobile production, halted for nearly five years, was resumed as rapidly as plants could retool. Some two million new cars reached eager customers during 1946, more than three million passenger automobiles were produced in 1947 and a like number in 1948. By 1949, the automobile industry had expanded its production facilities enough to produce more than five million new cars, the first time in twenty years that the industry had exceeded its peak production of 1929. This rate was continued, with further large increases, in succeeding years. All these new automobiles meant a brisk market for gasoline, with emphasis on improved quality to meet the demands of the new high-compression engines. As gasoline consumption climbed during the postwar years, from 30 billion gallons in 1946 to 40 billion in 1950, an increase of one-third, Shell not only kept but enlarged its share of the total market. The company manufactured 1.8 billion gallons of gasoline in 1946 and in 1950, 2.8 billion gallons, an increase of 50% during this same five-year period.

Mindful of some of the mistakes of the Twenties, the Shell marketing department did not embark upon a campaign of feverish territorial expansion. Rather, it concentrated on the expansion afforded by intensive utilization of existing markets. By increasing volume in a given area, Shell raised throughput and lowered handling costs. The sound measures inaugurated in the late Thirties—centralized distribution facilities, low-cost water and product pipe line transportation, larger deliveries from larger tank trucks—all these were continued. Marketing department distribution methods came in for thorough scrutiny of the kind that had been previously reserved for the admittedly technical ends of the business.

The Postwar Service Station

This new attention to the engineering approach was evident in the design of the company's postwar service station. Planning for the new station started during the wartime lull in sales activity. It was preceded, first of all, by a large-scale survey of motorists' preferences. Some 180,000 current and former Shell credit-card customers were asked a large number of questions, ranging from the types of goods and services they expected to find at a service station to their personal preferences in the location of the rest room.

A corner of the company's marine terminal on Newtown Creek, Brooklyn, was set aside and a full-scale model of a new station was constructed from the ground up, around two automobiles. Time and motion studies were made to eliminate the dealer's waste steps, and the "mock-up" station, built of wood, was taken apart and reassembled dozens of times during the course of its design. Leading industrial architects, such as Norman Bel Geddes and J. Gordon Carr, were retained to offer suggestions. But the project was not a one- or two-man job; it was a joint effort of the company's entire marketing organization, both east of the Rockies and on the Pacific Coast, with the lion's share of the work and planning being done by the engineering and retail departments in the New York and San Francisco marketing organizations. After a design had been tentatively adopted, a number of outstanding dealers from all over the country were brought in on several occasions to study the new station and give their opinions on its practicality.

Primary concerns were to design a station that would not be too expensive to build and that would be sufficiently productive of income to attract a high-calibre small businessman as its operator. With this in mind, the sale of goods and services received new emphasis. This meant a larger salesroom than before, more effective counter and display shelving, and, in order that the motorist might see the display window without leaving his car, a shorter gasoline pump. In cooperation with pump manufacturers, the Shell sales department evolved a shorter pump equipped with longer hose to make it easier to reach the customer's tank. To help the dealer increase his income from services such as lubrication, study was given to cutting the time required for these jobs by functional arrangement of rooms and better placement of inside equipment. To help attract and hold new customers, improved rest rooms were designed; to increase station attractiveness at night and help lower overhead expense, new and more efficient lighting was provided. This new station was unveiled to the press in October 1945 but its development continued long after that date. The station the company was building by the late 1940's had been substantially altered to give it a cleaner, more trim appearance.

Compared with the Twenties, the rate of new service station construction in the postwar period was small. High costs were a deterring factor. Exclusive of land, the new Shell station built in the years following 1946 cost anywhere from $25,000 to $50,000.[27] The rest rooms alone were often more expensive than the total cost of the old California "cracker-box" station in the 1920's. More important than new station construction was large-scale modernization of older stations. These projects generally included new lubrication equipment, lifts, new lighting and new signs, enlargement and renovation of the salesroom, and a veneer of porcelain-enamelled steel applied to the exterior surface to lend a modern appearance and eliminate the necessity for constant repainting. For service station modernization and the construction of some 300 new stations, the company spent $27,000,000 in the years 1946–1950.[28]

The trend in the postwar period was towards stations that could handle larger volumes of product, cutting the company's delivery expenses and enabling the dealer to earn a large income. As a result of weeding out small-volume outlets, Shell had 12,998 retail stations at the end of 1950, some 1,500 fewer stations than it had in 1946.† Gallonage per unit rose commensurately. A good company-owned, dealer-operated station did 10,000 gallons a month in prewar years. To be considered "good" in the postwar period, the same station had to be selling 20,000 gallons monthly. A large number of first-rate stations ran to 40,000 gallons a month or more. Even the poorer outlets (5,000 a month or less in prewar) were doing double their former business. These larger volumes and the general improvement in gasoline retail prices meant that dealers' incomes were substantially larger. In fact, many a hustling dealer had an income that was the envy of the Shell men who called on him.

---

† This figure, like other service station figures in this book, does not include stations served by jobbers. In 1950, the number of Shell-brand outlets served by jobbers was around 8,600, bringing the total number of retail outlets selling Shell gasoline to some 21,600. The reader should keep in mind similar allowances for other years.

The company encouraged its jobbers to keep abreast of the times by renovating and improving their jobber-owned retail outlets to increase volume and lower unit costs. Jobbers were urged to drop small-volume, marginal accounts; to operate training stations for the education of their new dealers; to modernize their business procedures and operating methods; to step up their advertising and sales promotional programs. The company provided real-estate guidance, merchandising assistance, a series of manuals designed to help the jobber improve his business methods, plus a large number of advertising and sales promotional materials.

The trend, started in the late Thirties, towards fewer depots serving a larger area with trucks of greater capacity continued in the postwar years and resulted in a further reduction in the number of company depots, despite the much greater volume of products sold. Company-owned depots numbered 888 in 1950, some 80 fewer than the number in 1946. During these years, many depots were enlarged substantially by the addition of new tankage and loading racks and some of the oldest depots were rebuilt completely.

Re-examining Depot Design

In the design of these new depots, the engineering approach was brought to bear in the interest of simplifying depot design to reduce capital cost and operating expense. The expense of a depot pump house was eliminated by installing weatherproof pumps which could operate out in the open. This new pumping arrangement also increased operating safety, for there was now no chance of explosive vapors collecting inside a building. There was a separate pump for each product, an arrangement which did away with the manifolds formerly used to allow a fewer number of pumps to handle, by shift-over, a variety of products. The new pumps were electrically powered and could be operated by remote control, a labor-saving feature of some importance.

The depot warehouse received a fresh examination, with the conclusion that enclosed, heated warehouse space was not needed for many products. The new warehouse, built around actual storage needs, eliminated as much enclosed space as possible and was cheaper both to build and maintain.

The depot garage was susceptible to elimination. With trucks kept in service up to twenty hours a day, it was not efficient from an engineering standpoint to provide a building in which they could be stored the few hours they were not in use. In southern climates, trucks could be parked on a corner of the depot property. Farther north, where some protection against cold was required in order to facilitate winter starting, a concrete wall was built facing the prevailing winds and the trucks parked behind it. In latitudes having a heavy annual snowfall, a roof projected outward from the wall. This protective wall was equipped with weatherproof electrical connections, so that small electric engine-warming units could be connected when necessary.[29]

As part of this scientific approach to depot design and operation, "pilot-plant" depots were created, one in each marketing division. These depots adhered carefully to all recommended procedures for stock control, truck dispatching and routing, cash and credit methods. If the recommended procedures had shortcomings, the pilot-plant depot would be quick to detect them. These selected depots also offered an ideal training ground for instructing marketing department people in the best methods of depot operation. The pilot-plant depot proved an excellent place to try out experiments in matters such as improved layout and better methods of materials handling.[30]

Depot materials-handling methods changed radically during the postwar years. Up to this point, drums and cases of packaged products had for the most part been handled entirely by hand. At best, drums had been lifted into place by hand-operated chain hoists. The fork-lift truck for mechanized handling of materials, first widely used during World War II, was in postwar years put to use in many businesses. In the depot warehouse, it found a wide variety of uses. Four 55-gallon drums could be placed end-up on a wooden skid, and the skid lifted by the fork-lift truck and stacked on top of similar pallets loaded with four drums. Pallets loaded with case goods were also handled in this manner. By the end of 1950, these methods had almost completely replaced time-consuming, back-breaking manual handling of packaged goods in Shell warehouses.

Because the newer service stations were built of impervious materials so as not to require periodic repainting, the paint and carpentry shops, which had for years been familiar adjuncts of larger depots, were closed down. Future carpentry work and paint jobs were let to outside contractors, in many instances the men who had formerly done this same work on the Shell payroll.

Large tank trucks were expensive, so every effort was made to get maximum use from them by employing additional shifts of drivers and by developing techniques such as loading them from beneath in order to cut loading time. By the end of 1950, Shell had trucks and loading pumps capable of loading at rates of up to 1,000 gallons a minute. Some idea of the improved efficiency of these new trucks may be gathered from the experience of the San Francisco depot during the month of April 1950; a single 5,280-gallon truck that month delivered more than a million gallons of gasoline—1,043,485 gallons to be exact.[31] By getting greater use out of its trucks, the company handled its much larger volume of business in 1950 with a total of 1,255 tank trucks, only 17 more than it had in 1946. Of this total, nearly one-third, or 369 trucks, were assigned exclusively to airport service.

New Water Terminals

Shell continued to build new water terminals, and in some instances to convert former railroad depots into terminals for receiving products by water. In 1947, a water terminal at Charleston, South Carolina, was purchased from Socony and new tankage installed to enlarge its capacity. During the same year, construction was begun on a new terminal on the Ohio River at Louisville, Kentucky. During 1949, a completely new lake terminal was opened at Milwaukee and two terminals were completed and put into operation in the San Francisco Bay area—one at Mills Field, San Francisco, the other at Redwood City, south of San Francisco.

In 1950, construction was started on an ocean terminal at Searsport, Maine, to replace the former barge terminal at Bangor and allow products to be unloaded directly from tankers. The same year construction of a terminal at Memphis, Tennessee, on the Mississippi was undertaken, replacing facilities which Shell had leased at that point for some years. During 1950, the first tanks of a large water terminal on the Chicago Sanitary Canal at Argo, Illinois, were installed and put in service. In addition, the Eureka, California, depot was rebuilt to allow it to receive ocean barge shipments, and work went forward on two other terminals, one at Colusa, California, the other at Kauna-kakai, Molokai, T. H. Extensive additions to tankage and pumping facilities were also made during the postwar years at six Atlantic Seaboard and three Pacific Coast ocean terminals, at 13 inland water-ways terminals, and at 12 products pipe line terminals.[32]

In mid-1946, a plant capable of producing each of the various grades of asphalt needed by Shell customers in the Northwest was put into operation at the Willbridge, Oregon, marine terminal. The new Willbridge plant made possible substantial transportation economies, for now a single grade of asphalt could be shipped in bulk by tanker from California refineries.

Division Office Reorganization

With no over-all increases being made in the company's refinery capacity on the Pacific Coast because of the small size of new crude oil discoveries, it seemed prudent to continue the prewar policy of withdrawing from marginal markets in order to supply increasing consumption in the more profitable markets. During 1947–1948, the Pacific Coast marketing department made a thorough examination of its "secondary territory." This resulted, during 1948, in a decision to vacate most of the Intermountain region—all of Montana, practically all of Wyoming, eastern Idaho, and all of Utah except the southwest corner.

Coincident with withdrawal from this area, a revision was made in the division office set-up on the Pacific Coast. The Spokane division, now no longer needed, was closed; its territory was divided between the Seattle and Portland divisions. In the San Francisco Bay area, where there had been two division offices, one at Oakland and one in San Francisco, the Oakland division was closed and its territory assigned to San Francisco. These measures helped to bring the volume of business handled by each of the Pacific Coast divisions more into line with the volume handled by the larger divisions east of the Rockies. The Fresno and Phoenix divisions were below the size normal for a Shell marketing division, so they were discontinued and their territories annexed by neighboring divisions. Fresno became a district office of the Sacramento division, and Phoenix an Arizona state office reporting to the Los Angeles division.[33]

Improved Gasoline, New Advertising

During the first few months of the postwar period, the wartime shortage of tetraethyl lead hung on, and the octane number of gasolines available only slightly exceeded those of prewar. But with the passing of the lead shortage, the octane race picked up where it had left off in the late Thirties. The race was an unconscious one at first, for many oil companies opposed further increases in octane number on the ground that only a few of the engines on the market were able to make use of substantial increases in octane rating. Such increases also added to refining costs and decreased the over-all refinery yields of motor fuel. But competition is not deterred by such arguments. By the summer of 1947, the average premium gasoline had quietly risen to 85.9 octane (as against 78–80 octane in the last prewar years) and housebrand ("regular") was averaging 80.2 octane, compared with 71–75 octane prewar. Every refiner, whether he wanted to or not, had to join the octane race or lose business.

The Shell marketing department decided during 1948 to capitalize on the substantial improvement that had been made in Shell Premium. In the fall of 1948, advertisements to promote Shell Premium were tested and proved so successful that a full-scale advertising campaign was launched during the spring and summer of 1949. The campaign centered around a catch phrase, "Activated Shell Premium—The Most Powerful Gasoline Your Car Can Use." Illustrations were humorously exaggerated cartoons showing the powerful effect of a tankful of Shell Premium.

The "Activated" campaign ran in some 500 newspapers and magazines with a total circulation of 70,000,000 and was featured in Shell's billboard advertising and carried verbally on Shell radio news programs all over the United States. At service stations, posters, banners, streamers, and advertising cards were displayed in profusion. At once dealers began to report increased sales. During 1949, Shell Premium sales went up 9.6% over the previous year, in contrast to the industry-wide increase in premium sales of one-tenth of one per cent. In 1950, the campaign, because of its success, was continued with little change. Sales increases were about equal to the previous year—up 8.2% over 1949 in the face of an over-all industry decline in premium sales. At the same time, sales of unadvertised Shell housebrand ("regular") gasoline lagged well behind the industry's average rate of increase. The "Activated" campaign was but a mild harbinger of the phenominal success that awaited marked product improvement, accompanied by vigorous advertising, in the company's "TCP" campaigns in the years following 1950.

During the war when there had been little product to advertise, the "Shell Research" series of advertisements had been started as a means of pointing out the contributions being made to the war effort by Shell's petroleum scientists. The series, run in national magazines, proved its worth in enhancing the company's reputation for scientific accomplishment and was continued on a reduced scale in the postwar period.

Sales Training

To offer suitable training to the new men who were hired in large numbers to augment the company's depleted sales force, and to provide "refresher" courses for members of the sales staff who had been out of normal selling during the war years, the prewar sales school was revived and enlarged. During 1947, a sales training school was operated at Katonah, New York, with courses lasting three weeks. In 1949, this school was shifted to Asbury Park, New Jersey.

Multi-Pump Stations

The introduction of the large-volume, multi-pump service station was another development of the postwar period. It reflected the trend, common to almost all retail merchandising, toward larger units handling larger volumes at lower unit costs. This shift in retailing was noticeable throughout the country, in larger super-markets, larger retail drug outlets, and the amazing postwar growth of suburban shopping centers—all enthusiastically patronized because they cut shopping time by providing a greater variety of merchandise under one roof and simplified the auto-age problems of ingress, egress, and parking. The "super-market" of gasoline retailing was the multi-pump station, equipped with twelve, twenty, and sometimes even more pumps.

The multi-pump idea originated with independent marketers, who, faced with higher labor costs, could no longer make price concessions that hitherto had constituted their chief sales appeal. A "gasateria," operated on the same self-service principle as a super-market, seemed to some to be the answer to rising operating costs. The large oil companies, with marketing organizations built around independent dealers, were more inclined to adopt a "wait-and-see" attitude toward the new multi-pump stations. This was particularly true of Shell, whose marketing department had devoted a good fifteen years to building a dealer organization of high-calibre, hard-working small businessmen, a large percentage of them neighborhood dealers patronized by steady customers who expected special services in exchange for steady patronage.

The multi-pump unit could not be ignored, however, for in high-volume locations it offered obvious cost advantages. At selected locations on heavily travelled highways, Shell built a few such stations. They were large, multi-pump installations featuring regular service-station service, rather than the independents' self-service. The company's first multi-pump unit was put in operation in 1948 on the East Shore Highway at Berkeley, California, and was followed by others, all in locations especially selected for their heavy traffic, at Milwaukee, Chicago, Providence, and Fort Lee, New Jersey, just across the Hudson from New York City.[34]

Public Relations

In the postwar years, members of the Shell marketing department found themselves giving increasing amounts of their time and energy to an aspect of the business that hitherto had engaged their attention very little, if at all. Before the war, they had considered it ample for their purposes if the public had a good impression of the Shell products. Now, in the postwar period, division and district managers were concerned that the public should have a good opinion not only of their products but of the company that made them and, beyond the company, an understanding and appreciation of the whole oil industry.

This change in attitude had been in the making for some ten years, and during the war the public approval which business enjoyed demonstrated better than argument that it was worth a businessman's time to keep the public on his side. Shell had set up a small public relations department in St. Louis early in 1939.[35] This department had remained small during the war years, but beginning in the fall of 1945 was enlarged considerably to provide the staff necessary to preach the company's simple public relations gospel: "Live right, and tell people about it." Practical accomplishments of the Shell public relations organization were an extensive series of documentary motion pictures, produced for the purpose of explaining the oil business to the public; a nation-wide program specifically designed to help the woman motorist; and a series of activities to promote highway safety. H. L. Curtis, who had, as assistant to the president, overseen the company's public relations activities since mid-1943, was elected vice president in charge of public relations in July 1955.

During 1946, the American Petroleum Institute began in earnest to lay the foundation for an industry-wide public relations effort. One of the country's ablest opinion-sampling organizations was engaged to survey the public's attitude toward the oil industry. Generally, it was found, the industry had good acceptance, particularly among the people who had some understanding of it. On two counts, however,

a surprisingly large segment of the public revealed serious misunder-
standings: many people said they thought gasoline prices were fixed
by collusion among the oil companies; another equally large percentage felt that the oil companies were backward about improving their
products.[36] To combat these erroneous impressions with a program of
sustained public education, to point out how competitive and progressive the industry really is, the American Petroleum Institute in
1947 set up the Oil Industry Information Committee and appropriated
a substantial budget to underwrite a campaign that included booklets,
motion pictures, and paid advertising. For personnel, the O.I.I.C.
relied chiefly on the voluntary services of oil company executives,
public relations men, and marketing department field personnel. Shell
was actively behind the O.I.I.C. effort from the beginning, and in the
years following 1947 made a heavy over-all contribution in time,
money, and men.

Things did indeed look up in marketing in the years 1946–1950.
Gone were the days of excessive oversupply, prices so poor that sales
resulted in losses instead of profits, unit volume so low that high-cost
overhead ate up such small profits as remained. As a result of the
retrenchment and reorientation of the late Thirties, Shell was on a
new, more profitable road. It was making and selling a larger
volume of products of all types—from the high-profit, low-volume
products such as specialized lubricants to the large-volume, low-
profit, bread-and-butter products, gasoline, kerosene, and fuel oil. In
specialized markets such as the sale of aviation gasoline, the company
was at last reaping the rewards of two decades of hard work; by 1950,
the aviation department could point to a host of new commercial airline contracts and announce that more passengers now flew more
miles on Shell than on any other aviation gasoline. Shell shared in the
general prosperity and by energetic merchandising increased its
total share of the market. Sales rose in proportion: $442 million in
1946, $628 million in 1947, $831 million in 1948, $817 million in
1949, $915 million in 1950, and finally, in 1951, the company at last
passed the coveted billion-dollar mark with sales that year totalling
$1,072,000,000.

Shell Chemical Corporation

DURING the war years, Shell Chemical had fully proved its usefulness and its profit-making potentialities as an important part of the American Shell organization. Wartime materials shortages had, moreover, prevented Shell Chemical from building new plants for several products that now awaited only the facilities to manufacture them. With such new facilities, the company could greatly expand its markets.

With postwar expansion in the offing, the role which Shell Chemical would play in the years ahead came in for a great deal of discussion during 1945. One point was settled without serious discussion. Everyone agreed that the chemical company needed a separate corporate organization to replace the arrangement which had existed since 1943, when Shell Union had purchased Bataafsche's 50% interest in the old Shell Chemical Company. During December 1945, a new Shell Chemical Corporation was organized to take over the business of the Shell Chemical Division of Shell Union Oil Corporation on January 1, 1946. Executive personnel of the new company was the same, except for the addition of new people. Shell Chemical's marketing activities had been under a sales department on the Pacific Coast where the bulk of its sales were made. East of the Rockies, where volume of sales was smaller, R. W. Greeff & Company, Inc., had been acting as sales agent for Shell Chemical.

Because the largest future sales potential lay in the East-of-the-Rockies area, a company-operated sales organization in this area was now clearly necessary. The arrangement with the Greeff company was terminated at the end of 1945, and a new eastern sales division of Shell Chemical was set up in January 1946, with offices at 500 Fifth Avenue, New York. Personnel to man the new sales force included some fifteen former employees of the Greeff company who had been chiefly concerned with Shell Chemical sales work. The rest were for the most part recruited from the ranks of the Shell Oil, Shell Development, and Shell Chemical organizations—men with technical and sales experience, some with both.

Shell Chemical had ambitious plans. The chemical companies who were its chief customers were clustered about the upper Atlantic Seaboard, a market to which products could be shipped by water from the Gulf Coast. Houston therefore seemed a logical choice of location for much of the chemical company's anticipated postwar expansion. The Shell Oil refinery had recently been enlarged, so more by-product gases would be available from that source; further, the Houston chemical plant could safely count on building beyond Shell Oil's ability to supply by-product gases, for the immediate area contained a number of refineries from whom gases could be purchased. In the five years from 1946 to 1950, Shell Chemical spent nearly $55,000,000 on plant expansion, the bulk of it to enlarge and diversify the chemical manufacturing facilities at Houston.

The initial phases of this big construction program got under way at Houston during 1946, but the continuing postwar shortages of materials such as steel had a dampening effect and it was not until late 1947 that construction went forward at anything approaching a normal rate. There were several facets to the Houston construction program, some of them extensions of existing facilities, others plants to manufacture brand-new products.

First on the list at Houston was a major expansion of the isopropyl alcohol plant that would more than double its capacity. In the construction of the new I.P.A. facilities, the equipment of the Houston butadiene plant, closed down in 1946, was utilized as far as possible. The increased output of I.P.A. was used chiefly for conversion to acetone, and the acetone in turn served as feed stock for two new plants. The first of these two plants, completed during 1948, converted acetone into methyl isobutyl carbinol and methyl isobutyl ketone, solvents used chiefly in the lacquer trade. The second plant, completed during 1948, used acetone as feed for making hexylene glycol, a component of hydraulic brake fluid and printing inks.

Synthetic Glycerine Plant

In September 1948, the long-awaited synthetic glycerine plant, in construction for nearly two years, went on stream at Houston and the process discovered by the Shell Development in the late 1930's became at last a manufacturing reality. Because of the world-wide shortage of fats, and the conversion of much of the soap industry to the manufacture of synthetic detergents which did not yield glycerine as a by-product, the new glycerine plant (the first of its kind in the world) found a ready market for its product among manufacturers of paints, varnishes, explosives, cellophane, and other products.[37]

Ethyl Alcohol and Ethyl Chloride

A month later, in October 1948, a plant to manufacture synthetic ethyl alcohol from ethylene gas went on stream at Houston. This plant involved construction of expensive facilities to produce pure ethylene gas, so the resultant cost, $16,000,000, was the largest single item in the chemical company's postwar budget. It was the first plant to accomplish the manufacture of ethyl alcohol by causing water to combine directly with ethylene; former processes had involved a greater number of steps. Because of high taxes on ethyl alcohol (the "drinking kind"), it had to be manufactured and shipped under close government supervision to assure that none of it escaped into beverage channels. There was no thought of selling this alcohol for eventual conversion into beverages, for Federal law requires that drinking alcohol be made from agricultural products. Shell Chemical's ethyl alcohol, manufactured in four grades, was designed for industrial uses such as the manufacture of plastics, dyestuffs, cosmetics, and printing inks. In addition, the chemical company marketed it denatured as a proprietary solvent under the trade name "Neosol."

A corollary to the ethyl alcohol plant was another new plant, opened in November 1948, for the production of ethyl chloride, using the same ethylene-producing facilities. The most important use of ethyl chloride is in the manufacture of tetraethyl lead.

Other chemical units completed at Houston during 1948 were plants for the manufacture of secondary butyl alcohol and methyl ethyl ketone, derived from it. The new units increased Shell Chemical's capacity for these two products by 150%. Both had been first manufactured by Shell Chemical back in the early 1930's, and had since become important items in the company's lacquer solvents line. By the end of 1950, plans were under way to increase the capacity of the glycerine plant by 50% (it was already turning out an amount of product equal to one-fifth the nation's prewar glycerine output) and to expand the ethyl alcohol denaturing plant to provide enough of this product to allow the company to introduce it in the Southern and Midwestern markets.

Epon Resins

Yet another plant, completed at Houston in 1950, was an outgrowth of the manufacture of synthetic glycerine. An intermediate product in glycerine manufacture is epichlorohydrin, the uses of which had been extensively investigated by Shell Development some years pre-viously. There seemed to be sufficient commercial uses for this product and a plant was built to produce it. Devoe & Raynolds, large paint manufacturers, had filed patent applications covering the manu-facture and use of epoxy resins made from epichlorohydrin and bisphenol-A. Being aware of their purchase of epichlorohydrin, Shell Chemical approached Devoe & Raynolds and negotiated a license arrangement which gave Shell Chemical exclusive rights under these epoxy resin patents, except for Devoe & Raynolds' own use of the patents. Shortly thereafter, Shell Chemical completed a new plant at Houston to turn out these epoxy resins under Shell Chemical's trade-marked name "Epon." Epon resins held great promise for surface-coating applications, as the basis of finishes that are hard but not brittle, flexible, but not soft. In adhesives, they were excellent bonding agents for sticking metal to metal, or metal to plastics.[38]

Not all the plant expansion was at Houston. At Dominguez, plant facilities for making isopropyl alcohol and acetone, which is derived from it, were increased by 50% during the years ending in 1950.

At Martinez, a revision made in 1946 to that plant's facilities for manufacturing secondary butyl alcohol and methyl ethyl ketone resulted in greatly increased production of both products. In March 1948, a new Martinez unit went on stream to manufacture ditertiary butyl peroxide, a catalyst for the manufacture of resins and plastics. During the same year, Martinez entered a fresh field, with new plants to make octyl-formol and Ionol, used by Shell and other oil companies as lubricating oil additives.

The Shell Point ammonia plant, which had been Shell Chemical's first large-scale venture, increased its capacity in the postwar years until at the end of 1950, it was producing at the rate of nearly seven times the plant's original capacity. These new extensions were carried out in three phases, and cost together some $3,500,000. During 1949, the sale of Shell Point's ammonia fertilizers, hitherto confined almost exclusively to California and the export trade, was extended to the agricultural regions of the Pacific Northwest.

In the years following 1950, the company's ammonia-producing capacity would be still further enlarged by the completion of a new ammonia plant late in 1953, located at Ventura and drawing its supplies of natural gas from Shell's Ventura field. Glycerine capacity would be likewise extended by the erection during 1954–1955 of a new $8,500,000 chlorohydrin plant adjoining the Norco refinery.

Purchase of Synthetic Rubber Plants

The government-owned butadiene plant at Torrance, which Shell Chemical had operated since 1943 for the Office of Rubber Reserve of the Reconstruction Finance Corporation, reached peak production during 1946, turning out ingredients for some 10% of the total synthetic rubber manufactured that year. As imports of natural rubber were resumed and demand for synthetics slackened, the government ordered Shell Chemical to close down the Torrance plant during 1947. It was kept on a stand-by basis with eleven Shell Chemical men in attendance to supervise maintenance. With the outbreak of the Korean War, the Rubber Reserve in August 1950 requested Shell Chemical to start the Torrance butadiene plant up again, and it returned to operation in December 1950. During 1953, Congress enacted a law to provide for the sale of the wartime synthetic rubber plants to private industry and Shell Chemical subsequently bid $30,000,000 for the Torrance butadiene plant, along with the styrene and copolymer plants which had been operated in conjunction with it. In March 1955, this bid was accepted by Congress as part of the rubber facilities disposal program.

The Move to New York

Increased emphasis on the Eastern chemical markets kept many members of the Shell Chemical head office staff at San Francisco constantly shuttling between that city and New York. The West Coast markets had been developed and put on a sound footing by nearly twenty years of constant attention. By mid-1948, it seemed the better course to move Shell Chemical's head office to New York in order to be near these newer markets. In September 1948, the move was made. Some 100 staff members, their families, and personal effects were transferred the 3,000 miles to New York and new offices opened in a building at 11 West 58th Street, overlooking Central Park.‡

At the time of the move east, a Western sales division, similar to the Eastern division established in New York at the beginning of 1946, was set up in San Francisco. Early in 1949, sales of Shell Oil's agricultural products such as spray oils, herbicides, and insecticides, formerly handled by Shell Oil special products departments in New

‡ Within a few months, space was found for Shell Chemical in the R.C.A. Building in Rockefeller Center. Most of the West 58th Street quarters were henceforth occupied by the Shell Oil purchasing department.

York and San Francisco, were turned over to Shell Chemical. Most of the Shell Oil personnel involved in this work were transferred to Shell Chemical's sales department.

Julius Hyman & Company

In 1950, Shell Chemical became exclusive U. S. sales agent for aldrin and dieldrin, two powerful insecticides made by Julius Hyman & Company, of Denver. These agricultural chemicals had been used with spectacular success to destroy boll weevils, grasshoppers, locusts, ants, wireworms and various other insects. An outstanding quality of aldrin and dieldrin was their high potency; two ounces of aldrin would kill 98% of the grasshoppers in a heavily infested acre.

After two years of successful experience in marketing the Hyman insecticides, Shell Chemical early in 1952 decided to purchase the Hyman company and its related patents. Julius Hyman & Company was operated as a subsidiary of Shell Chemical until the beginning of 1955, when the former Hyman organization was absorbed into the chemical company. In addition to the manufacturing facilities acquired, the Hyman purchase included an agricultural laboratory operated in conjunction with the plant.

In product distribution, Shell Chemical made a number of advances designed to reduce the cost of bulk shipments and speed up service to customers. With the opening of the Houston glycerine plant, a large fleet of specially built aluminum tank cars, insulated with Fiberglas, were put into service for shipping glycerine. A Shell Chemical ocean terminal for receipt of bulk chemicals shipped by water was built at Sewaren in 1946, and enlarged several times during the postwar years. Late in 1949, terminal facilities adjoining Shell Oil's new barge and pipe line terminal at Argo, Illinois, were leased by Shell Chemical from its jobber in the area, Great Lakes Solvents Corporation. This made it possible for Shell Chemical to ship products to Chicago by barge from Houston. During 1949, both the Eastern and Western sales divisions of Shell Chemical set up product distribution departments to study methods for improving transportation and packaging.

Chemical Laboratories

The basic research necessary to discover new chemical products for Shell Chemical to manufacture was being carried on by Shell Development Company, but Shell Chemical also established specialized laboratories of its own. At the Houston plant, a group was organized in 1949 to devote its time to product improvement and process development. This Houston research group was housed in a large new laboratory building built for the chemical plant's control and experimental staffs in 1947.

At Martinez, a chemical company group had until 1949 also done "technical service" work, concerned with the actual uses to which products are put by customers. Shortly after the Shell Chemical head office moved to New York, these technical service activities were transferred east to a new laboratory opened at Union, New Jersey, in 1949. At the Union laboratory, a great deal of attention was directed to the surface coating applications of Shell chemicals, particularly those used in the manufacture of lacquers and synthetic enamels. At the Union laboratory, the company's salesmen also received training in the latest applications of the products they were selling, for a chemical salesman must be a well-informed technologist.

During the postwar years, Shell Chemical's sales rose steadily, the $70 million of 1950 sales being nearly treble the $24 million of 1946. Among chemical companies, Shell Chemical was beginning to assume a position of rank and importance—so much so, in fact, that *Fortune* magazine was moved to comment, "Shell is an oil company with a very fine chemical business, not, as many Wall Streeters like to think, a specialized chemical company in the oil business." [39] For the chemical business in general, and for petroleum-based chemicals in particular, a bright future seemed to lie ahead. In spite of the imposing stature that petroleum-based chemicals had achieved by 1950, less than 1% of available crude oil and natural gas supplies was being utilized in chemical manufacture.

8

Wider Horizons in Research

WITH the end of the war, Shell management began making plans to increase the amount and extend the scope of the company's research activities. The first of these new research operations had, as a matter of fact, got under way a year before the end of the war.

In June 1944, the company purchased a 142-acre farm near Modesto, California, to be used as the site of a new agricultural research center. Two months later, Dr. Roy Hansberry, associate professor of entomology at Cornell University, was engaged as director of the new research center. During the late months of the war, the nucleus of a staff was assembled and plans drawn up for an experimental farm, laboratories, greenhouses, and service buildings. Actual construction began in September 1945, just as soon as the war was over. The buildings were complete and ready for formal dedication a year later, in September 1946. By that time, substantially all of the staff had been engaged. There were departments of entomology, nematology, horticulture, agricultural engineering, plant physiology, and plant pathology.

The buildings and other auxiliary facilities of the experimental farm occupied about six acres. The remainder of the farm was for actual raising of experimental crops. The Modesto area was irrigated, and for that reason offered a fine opportunity for simulating almost any degree of soil moisture, from the aridity of the semi-desert to the lushness of a subtropical swamp.

During 1946 and 1947, the Modesto laboratory developed new petroleum-based weed killers. Effective control of soil fungi by fumigation was demonstrated and an intensive research program into growth-regulating chemicals was undertaken. For Shell, this latter field offered considerable promise, for, compared to fertilizers and insecticides, it was a field in which comparatively little work had been done. The possibilities of growth-regulating chemicals were only partially explored. Hormone sprays, for instance, could prevent fruit crops from dropping prematurely, help produce a better quality of fruit by allowing two or three days' extra ripening, and, when applied in accordance with a schedule, simplify a fruit grower's labor problems by permitting only one section of his orchard to ripen at a time. Cotton defoliants could cause the leaves to fall off the plant while the bolls remain on, making the picking job easier when done by hand and cleaner when done mechanically. Defoliants could kill the leaves around the base of the plant, where, in humid areas, mildew has a tendency to form. A potato-plant killer could make potato tops wither and die, helping to eliminate the late-season blight which often extends underground and infects the potatoes. From oil could come fertilizers to promote growth; weed killers and defoliants to destroy undesired plants or parts of plants; regulating chemicals to control the amount or period of growth; insecticides, nematicides, and fungicides to improve the plant's vigor, productivity and chance of survival.[40]

During its first few years the Modesto laboratory was administered by the Shell Oil Company's special products department in San Francisco. Concurrent with the assignment of that department's agricultural sales activities to Shell Chemical early in 1949, the responsibility for administering the Modesto agricultural laboratory was given to Shell Development Company. In 1953, the physical assets of the Modesto research center were transferred to Shell Development.

Houston Exploration and Production Research Center

The second of the new postwar research groups was the exploration and production research center, set up at Houston late in the summer of 1945 under the direction of Dr. Harold Gershinowitz, formerly manager of the manufacturing department's research section in New York. The assignment of the new exploration and production research center was the broadest possible: to discover new ways of locating oil and to devise new or improved methods of getting the oil to the surface once it had been found. This assignment would obviously entail a great deal of new basic research, for as yet comparatively little was understood of such subjects as the underground movements of fluids. Research activities in oil production conducted by Shell Development at Emeryville were transferred to the new research center at Houston.

A carefully planned laboratory building, adjoining the site of the company's existing geophysical laboratory in the southern suburbs of Houston, was completed in December 1947. Meanwhile, much of the initial research staff had been assembled and organized into three sections: a physics department, a chemistry department, and a geological department. Each problem under consideration was broken up into its physical, chemical, and geological aspects and studied separately by each of these groups. In addition to the fundamental research activities carried on by these groups, the design and manufacture of many items of Shell's geophysical equipment continued in the old geophysical laboratory nearby. The staff of this Houston exploration and production research group numbered about 200 by the end of 1950.[41]

Postwar at Emeryville

The Shell Development laboratories at Emeryville continued to do the bulk of Shell's fundamental research. By 1946, Emeryville's original 1928 research staff of 35 persons had grown to more than 1,000 and its buildings had spread from Williams' original 2-story laboratory over an area of seven acres. In addition to Emeryville, another 200 were employed in Shell Development's head office in the San Francisco Shell Building and in the patent-licensing office at New York.[42]

With a return of peacetime operation, Emeryville could revert once more to its chief business: the accumulation of basic knowledge in the field of hydrocarbon research. Accumulation of this type of scientific knowledge, Emeryville's most important function, is not a spectacular business susceptible of easy popularization. Suffice it to say that without a tremendous backlog of fundamental knowledge, any oil company's long-term research program would soon degenerate into a multitude of short-range "practical" projects which, while useful, would not give a company technological pre-eminence in its field.

In 1949, for instance, the growing accumulation of residual fuel oil stocks at the refineries prompted fundamental research into the chemical possibilities of heavy fuel. Basic investigation of this kind was a prerequisite to development of processes for converting residuals into the more desirable lighter fractions. Because the molecules of the heavy fuels were so complex, the older tools of research were of little help on such a project. Several new research techniques had to be put to use, among them molecular distillation, selective absorption on solids, various kinds of spectroscopy (in which Emeryville had long been a leader), and extractive crystallization.

Projects that were more immediately practical continued to occupy the time of a large number of the staff. During 1949, taken as a random example, there was further work at Emeryville on the Dutrex compounds, a series of rubber "extenders" developed during the war years. Dutrex 6, valuable in "cold" synthetic rubber for tire treads, was announced that year. Plastics manufacturers witnessed full-scale demonstrations of the uses of diallyl phthalate, first announced in 1945, as a material for plastics laminates, overlays, and molding powders. Emeryville's detergent-research section announced a new material for the manufacture of household detergents. During 1949, a new laboratory unit was set up to study the cutting oils widely used in metal-working trades. Emeryville's engineering department came up with a distilling tray based upon a new concept. The new tray was placed in trial operation in five Shell refineries and chemical plants the following year. Emeryville engineers developed several mechanical extraction systems, a furnace of radically new design, and a new style of cyclone separator. And the government, well aware of Emeryville's eminence in a number of fields, awarded it several national defense research contracts. These were a few of the research highlights of a typical year at Emeryville.[43]

New Products from Research

Research such as this, much of it inaugurated several years before, enabled Shell Oil and Shell Chemical to bring out dozens of new products in the postwar years. Shell Oil in 1946 put on the market new products such as Retinax "A," a multi-purpose grease to make it unnecessary for the service station dealer to stock several greases. In 1947, a new Golden Shell motor oil with additives made its appearance, as did AeroShell "D" for light aircraft. The premium-grade "X-100" motor oil was further improved by means of additives during 1948.

Additives made possible immense improvements in motor-oil performance. Rust inhibitors helped cut tendencies toward engine rust. Anti-corrosive additives helped counteract the acid conditions responsible for much engine wear. Detergent additives kept engine sludge dispersed and helped prevent formation of varnish on piston walls. The introduction of detergent-action additives made possible the operation of gasoline and Diesel engines under severe conditions previously not feasible.

There were other products: electric transformer oils; high-speed torque-converter oils used in automatic transmissions; a variety of oils for the steel industry, such as quenching oils for tempering steel, oils for drawing stainless steels, tableway lubricants for metal working, wire rope lubricants, and steel mill roll grease. There was high-speed Diesel fuel, an all-purpose military gasoline, even an outboard motor grease. A new softening agent helped prepare deteriorated asphalt for resurfacing, another asphalt product was introduced as a penetrant for wall board manufacture. Shell Endrop "C" helped increase the yield of citrus fruits, and there was a new insecticide for truck crops important because it left no harmful residue. A new prefabricated asphalt lining for irrigation canals prevented water loss by seepage. And the U. S. Navy adopted Shell Cassis Fluid and a cleaning procedure developed by Shell for reactivation of turbines and Diesel engines. Some of these products were entirely new. Some were older products given new properties and new uses. Dozens of other products underwent a quality improvement that enabled them to do a new job, or the old one more effectively.

Work of the Specialized Laboratories

Not all the new products (Shell Oil's manufacturing department made some 30 new ones in 1948 alone) were developed entirely at Emeryville, but the basic work was usually carried out there. Product development research was carried on by the sizeable research laboratories at the Wood River and Martinez refineries.§

At Wood River, the engine-testing laboratory had grown to large dimensions in twenty years. It contained, mounted on blocks, automotive and aircraft engines of nearly every known type. Another section of the Wood River research set-up was an asphalt laboratory opened in 1948. A torque-converter laboratory, to experiment with the fluids used in the new "gearless" shifts, was established the same year. There was also a chemical section at Wood River concentrating on gasoline treating and lubricants manufacture.

The Martinez refinery laboratory, in keeping with the full range of products made at the refinery, continued to do product development work on motor oils, greases, asphalts, specialty products, and process development pertaining to them. The process for the continuous grease-manufacturing plant was largely developed at Martinez, as was the acid treatment of lubricating oils.[44]

The Houston refinery research laboratory continued to concern itself with process development. It was equipped to duplicate on small-scale equipment most refining processes, whether already in use or still in experimental stages. The Houston refinery did not have a catalytic cracker until 1946, but the refinery's laboratory had a fluid catalytic cracking pilot plant as early as 1942. Houston's lubricating-oil pilot plant was one of the most extensive in the business, and with the installation of a wax plant at Houston, the refinery laboratory installed a paraffin wax laboratory, complete with a paper-waxing machine. (The paper container industry purchased about 70% of the refinery's paraffin output.)

The Wilmington refinery's process laboratory, which earlier had done a great deal of work on process design, came more and more to duplicate the work being done at Houston. As a consequence, it was discontinued in the years following 1950.[45]

§ See pages 548-550.

Two other specialized laboratories warrant mention, not because of their size, which was very small, but because of their important accomplishments in the postwar years. At East Chicago, Indiana, a products pipe line laboratory had been set up during the war years in the basement of the old refinery office building. This "laboratory" consisted of 5,000 feet of miniature products pipe line, 2 inches in diameter, upon which actual operating conditions could be simulated. The object of this installation was to obtain more fundamental data on flow conditions within a pipe line, a subject of which little was known. One man operated the East Chicago installation; the mathematical calculations and interpretive work were done by members of the products pipe line staff in New York.

Attention was directed to the inter-facial mixing characteristics of different types of products, which flow through a products line one after the other. This work produced data from which the products pipe line department evolved a formula for predicting the exact amount of mixing that would occur between any two products under given operating conditions. This new body of accurate knowledge enabled Shell to handle a larger number of products, with a greater degree of precision, than other products pipe lines. Another development of the East Chicago laboratory was a "plug line" for loading lubricating-oil stocks, installed in postwar years on the docks of the Houston and New Orleans refineries. The plug line was a very short products pipe line, and was used to replace the dozen or so separate lines formerly required for marine loading of the various grades of lubricating oil and lubricating-oil stocks. A plug of synthetic rubber was inserted between the tenders of different grades of product to keep them from mixing.[46]

Another small laboratory of considerable value was the Sewaren oil burner laboratory, in operation since 1930.* With a staff never exceeding four men, it came up with at least three developments of importance. During 1942–1945, Sewaren developed a special combustion head for domestic oil burners to permit a burner to produce more heat from less fuel oil. The resultant savings in fuel oil averaged about 20%, and a number of oil burner manufacturers incorporated the Shell combustion head in the design of their postwar oil burners. Shell made the burner-head patents available on a royalty-free basis. In 1948, the Sewaren oil burner laboratory announced a new "smoke

* See pages 552-553.

Shell's newest refinery, opened late in 1955, is at Anacortes, Washington, a peninsula site sixty miles north of Richmond Beach, where the company first started in 1912.

The Houston exploration and production research center, opened late in 1947, seeks new methods of looking for oil and of getting it out of the ground, once discovered.

Elwood M. Payne

Shell Chemical glycerine plant, Houston, 1948, was world's first to make glycerine from petroleum.

Typical of Shell's postwar service station design is this attractive outlet built at Manchester, Vermont, in 1951 by Johnson & Dix, Shell jobbers.

meter" for the use of burner service men in measuring imperfect combustion. This meter rapidly displaced older, more expensive smoke-testing equipment. A third contribution from Sewaren was announced during 1947. It was a fuel-oil additive to prevent clogging in the filter screens of oil-burning equipment. To Shell's five refineries, this additive meant operational savings of some $250,000 a year, for it eliminated the purchase of chemicals formerly needed to treat screen-clogging. In 1949 following extensive testing in the company's own equipment, the new anti-clogging additive, named "FOA-5X," was embodied in the distillate fuel which Shell sold to homeowners.

Assistance to Colleges

During the postwar years, the Shell companies took greater notice of the assistance being rendered their business by the colleges and universities who were training future scientists. Informal assistance, previously extended to individual students, was put on a formal footing in 1947 with the creation of the Shell Fellowship Program to assist graduate students in technical universities. These fellowships carried an annual stipend of $1,200, plus $300 to the school to cover the research expenses of each fellow. The grants were made on the recommendation of the colleges concerned by the Shell Fellowship Committee, a group of senior executives representing Shell Oil, Shell Chemical, Shell Development, and Shell Pipe Line. In 1950, forty-five Shell graduate fellowships were awarded.

In 1950, a new program of research grants was inaugurated to assist the colleges and universities directly. Twelve grants of $5,000 each were made to university science departments conducting projects in basic research. The fellowships and research grants were made in fields connected with Shell's business—chemistry, chemical engineering, geology, physics, mechanical engineering—but neither the institutions nor the individual students were under any obligation to the company. During the first five years of the postwar period, Shell also joined with 22 other companies to help finance three new institutes for basic research set up at the University of Chicago.[47]

These moves pointed the way toward more extensive assistance to education in the years following 1950. In 1953, the Shell Companies' Foundation was incorporated, supported by grants from the Shell operating companies in the United States. Among the chief activities which the Foundation was designed to help was education. Programs of grants to colleges were instituted, and in 1955 a fellowship plan for the benefit of high-school science and mathematics teachers was announced. This new program was aimed at helping to alleviate the growing shortage of scientists and engineers by stimulating the teaching of chemistry, physics, and mathematics at the high-school level.[48]

Centralizing Research in Shell Development

Shell Development Company underwent several executive and organizational changes in the postwar years. In 1949, Lacomblé, president since 1943, became chairman of the board. He was succeeded as president of Shell Development by Dr. M. E. Spaght, a native Californian, graduate of Stanford and Leipzig, who had started with Shell as a research chemist at Martinez in 1933, had been manager of research and development of Shell Oil's San Francisco manufacturing department, 1940–1945, and a vice president of Shell Development Company since 1946. At the end of 1950, Lacomblé retired; he died less than two years later, in November 1952.

In June 1950, the development company's operations were reorganized by the creation of two new divisions, research and development, each headed by a vice president. All current projects were assigned to one or the other of these divisions. T. W. Evans was vice president and director of research; A. J. Johnson was vice president and director of development and engineering. A third division was responsible for service activities. During 1950, a new four-story building was erected at Emeryville, connected to the existing laboratory buildings, and in November the head office staff of Shell Development Company, located in the Shell Building, San Francisco, moved to Emeryville. This move centered all of Shell Development's personnel in one location, except for a small group concerned chiefly with patent licensing located in the New York office.

A further consolidation move came in the years following 1950. At the beginning of 1953, Spaght was made executive vice president of Shell Oil in New York; Gershinowitz succeeded him as president of Shell Development Company. At this juncture, Gershinowitz, D. M. Sheldon, secretary of Shell Development, and a few others moved to New York; the rest of the company's administrative staff remained at Emeryville.

At the same time, Shell Oil's activities in exploration and production and agricultural research were taken over by Shell Development Company. The Modesto agricultural laboratory, already operated by the development company, became the property of Shell Development, as did the newer Denver agricultural laboratory. The exploration and production research center at Houston was also turned over to Shell Development Company. In exchange for this contribution of assets, Shell Oil received new shares of stock which made it 65% owner of Shell Development, instead of 50% as formerly. Bataafsche's holding, reduced to 35%, was purchased and retired by Shell Development at the end of 1955, leaving Shell Oil the sole owner of Shell Development.

Not counting control laboratories, the American Shell organization at the end of 1955 had some 2,225 people—6% of its total employees —engaged in full-time research and development work, a guarantee, if one were needed, of technological progress in the years that lay ahead.

9

Shell Oil Company

DURING the Thirties a trend towards simpler corporate structure for the Shell companies had begun. This trend continued in the postwar years and the changes that resulted brought a number of new faces to the executive ranks.

In June 1947, Van der Woude, president of Shell Union since 1933, retired and was succeeded by Fraser, who had been president of Shell Petroleum and its successor, Shell Oil Company, Inc., for the past fourteen years. The new president of Shell Oil Company, Inc., was H. S. M. Burns, for the previous year senior vice president of Shell Oil in New York. Burns had most recently headed the Shell Company in Colombia, but most of his early experience had been with Shell of California. Starting there in 1926, Burns had worked in the exploration, manufacturing, and sales departments; later he had held positions with Shell Union and Flintkote in New York. In 1933, he had been made manager of Shell Oil's Seattle marketing division, and in 1935 he became assistant general sales manager at San Francsico. Late in 1935 he had returned to London for a year, and from there had gone to Venezuela and Colombia.

In August 1947, L. G. McLaren, marketing vice president in San Francisco for nine years, retired; he was succeeded by J. G. Jordan, for eleven years division manager at Cleveland and sales manager at San Francisco since 1945. Dr. E. F. Davis, vice president and chief geologist at Los Angeles since 1929, retired at the end of 1947; because of the reorganization of the exploration and production department then under way, no successor was named.

Consolidation of East and West

During the fall of 1948, Belither, head of Shell Oil's operations on the Pacific Coast for fourteen years, announced his intention of retiring at the end of the year. With so many in the executive ranks reaching retirement, the company proceeded to carry to a conclusion the consolidation begun in 1939. At that time Shell Oil in San Francisco, Shell Petroleum in St. Louis, and Shell Eastern in New York had merged their operations in a single company, and soon after (September 1940) the New York and St. Louis offices had been combined.§ But Shell Oil still had duplicate sets of vice presidents and department heads in New York and San Francisco. Now many of them were retiring, and this presented an opportunity for bringing together the top policy-making officials in a single office in New York.

Lakin, marketing vice president in New York, was made executive vice president of Shell Oil in San Francisco to act as Shell's senior representative on the West Coast. Jordan came to New York to replace Lakin as marketing vice president with authority over Shell marketing operations nation-wide. There were two general sales managers, one at New York, the other in San Francisco.

F. S. Clulow, vice president in charge of manufacturing at San Francisco, was transferred to New York with the same title, his sphere, like Jordan's, enlarged to embrace the whole country. C. E. Davis, formerly vice president in charge of manufacturing at New York, was named vice president in charge of refining, reporting to Clulow.

Galloway, as head of exploration and production east of the Rockies, had moved from Houston to New York in January 1948; now he was given over-all charge of Shell exploration and production activities coast to coast. Reporting to Galloway were S. F. Bowlby and E. D. Cumming, resident vice presidents in charge of exploration and production at Los Angeles and Houston.

J. H. White, vice president in charge of treasury operations at San Francisco, and A. G. Schei, treasurer of Shell Chemical, both came to

§ See pages 494-497.

New York. E. C. Peet, formerly vice president and treasurer in New York, now became vice president in over-all charge of the financial organization, with White as vice president and controller and Schei as treasurer.

This new centralization of operations at New York went into effect the first of January 1949. Changes in the legal, personnel, and purchasing departments were more gradual. C. S. Gentry, vice president and general counsel in New York, had authority over the company's legal affairs nation-wide from January 1949. A. R. Bradley, vice president in charge of legal affairs at San Francisco, continued in that capacity until his retirement at the end of 1949, at which time his position was not filled. The same held true of the purchasing and stores department: upon the retirement of S. T. Covell, general manager of the department at San Francisco, supervision of the West Coast department was turned over to W. H. Bratches, general manager of purchasing and stores in New York. At the end of May 1953, F. E. Rehm, vice president in charge of personnel and industrial relations at San Francisco, retired; E. H. Walker, vice president at New York, was thenceforth in nation-wide charge of the personnel and industrial relations organization.

The San Francisco manufacturing department, not as large as its counterpart in New York, was dissolved by transferring its members either to New York or to the refineries. McGaw, general vice president at San Francisco since late 1946, came to New York where he was put in charge of a new economic development department.* Otherwise, the changes at the beginning of 1949 involved the movement of relatively few people. For the moment, the San Francisco office remained practically unchanged in size, but during succeeding years retirements without replacement served materially to reduce the size and importance of the San Francisco office.

The final step in corporate consolidation was the elimination of the holding-company arrangement in existence between Shell Union Oil Corporation and its chief operating subsidiary, Shell Oil Company, Inc. This was accomplished in September 1949. On September 22, 1949, Shell Union stockholders met and approved a plan to merge the operating subsidiary, Shell Oil Company, Inc., into Shell Union; thereupon, Shell Union adopted a new name, Shell Oil Company. This move affected only a few Shell Union officials. Fraser, who was

---

* This department was reorganized and many of its personnel assigned to other departments after McGaw's retirement in mid-1956.

to retire within two years, became chairman of the executive committee of Shell Oil Company; Burns became president; S. W. Duhig, formerly vice president and treasurer of Shell Union and scheduled to retire in March 1950, became vice president; and F. W. Woods, secretary of Shell Union, was made secretary. Doolittle, a vice president of Shell Union, continued in the same capacity with the rechristened company and all the vice presidents of the old Shell Oil Company, Inc., assumed like positions in the newly merged concern. The old Shell Oil Company, Inc., now no longer needed, was officially dissolved in December 1949.

After 1950

In the years following 1950, other changes in Shell's executive organization took place. S. F. Bowlby and E. D. Cumming held the titles of vice president in charge of exploration and production at Los Angeles and Houston, respectively. On July 1, 1951, the managers in charge of exploration and production area offices at New Orleans, Midland, Tulsa, and Calgary were raised to the rank of vice president. Bouwe Dykstra became vice president in charge of exploration and production at New Orleans, J. T. Dickerson was made vice president at Midland, W. A. Alexander became vice president in Tulsa, and E. G. Robinson vice president at Calgary. Robinson retired in June 1952 and was succeeded by P. L. Kartzke. In August 1953 a new exploration and production area office was set up in Denver with Alexander in charge as vice president; C. P. Bristol succeeded him in Tulsa.

At the time of the July 1951 promotions, Dr. Harold Gershinowitz, then manager of the exploration and production research center at Houston, was raised to the rank of vice president; his subsequent elevation to the presidency of Shell Development Company in 1953 has been noted in the preceding section. Dr. N. D. Smith, Jr., succeeded Gershinowitz at Houston and in 1954 was made a vice president of Shell Development Company. John W. Pegg, elected a Shell Development vice president in 1950, died in February 1955 and was succeeded by J. A. Horner, who had been elected Shell Oil's corporate secretary upon the retirement of F. W. Woods in 1953; Horner held both offices.

In May 1953, Jan Oostermeyer retired as president of Shell Chemical. He was succeeded by R. C. McCurdy, twenty years with various Shell companies in exploration and production and general manager

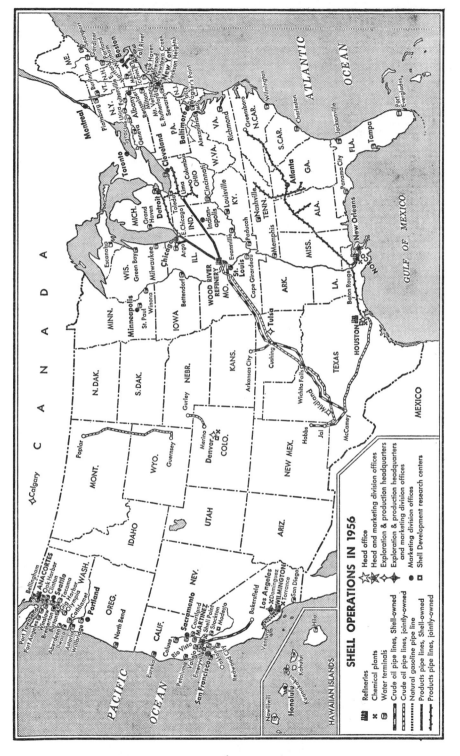

SHELL OPERATIONS IN 1956

☆ Head office
★ Head and marketing division offices
✪ Exploration & production headquarters
✪ Exploration & production headquarters and marketing division offices
● Marketing division offices
◻ Shell Development research centers

Refineries
✕ Chemical plants
⊕ Water terminals
░░░░ Crude oil pipe lines, Shell-owned
──── Crude oil pipe lines, jointly-owned
········· Natural gasoline pipe line
━━━━ Products pipe lines, Shell-owned
━━━━ Products pipe lines, jointly-owned

of the Group's operations in western Venezuela at the time of his elevation to the Shell Chemical presidency. G. R. Monkhouse, manager of Shell Chemical's Western sales division, was made a vice president of the chemical company in 1952 and was put in charge of Shell Chemical's ammonia division upon its creation in 1953. Dr. C. W. Humphreys became Shell Chemical's manufacturing vice president following the resignation of W. P. Gage in 1953.

During 1953, Peet was elected a director of The Shell Petroleum Company, Ltd., and The Anglo-Saxon Petroleum Company, Ltd., in London and assumed the position of chief financial officer of the Royal Dutch-Shell Group. Peet's position as vice president in charge of Shell Oil's financial organization was taken by J. H. White, previously vice president and controller. A. A. Buzzi was shortly thereafter elected to the office of controller.

As a result of retirements, Shell Pipe Line saw a complete change in its executive personnel. T. E. Swigart, president since 1940, retired in the fall of 1954 and was succeeded by J. T. Dickerson, vice president in charge of exploration and production at Midland. H. H. Anderson, who had retired as vice president and general manager of the pipe line company in July 1952, was succeeded by D. F. Sears. D. H. Lewis, longtime chief engineer of the pipe line company, was made a vice president in April 1952; he retired at the end of 1955. A. E. Groff, secretary, retired in February 1955 and was succeeded by W. J. Williamson. W. A. Baker, vice president and treasurer of the pipe line company, retired at the end of 1955 and was succeeded by C. C. Combs. The vacancy created at Midland by Dickerson's election to the presidency of the pipe line company was filled by J. E. Clark, who was elected vice president of exploration and production at Midland.

C. S. Gentry, vice president and general counsel, retired at the end of 1952 and was succeeded by W. F. Kenney. In the manufacturing organization, C. E. Davis, vice president in charge of refining since 1949, retired at the end of 1955; in June 1956, F. S. Clulow, vice president in charge of manufacturing, also retired. M. P. L. Love, former refinery manager at Houston, became the new vice president in charge of the manufacturing department.

In July 1951, a second general sales manager east of the Rockies was appointed. The company thenceforth had three general sales managers, one at San Francisco and two in New York: one in charge of the Midwest, the other of the Atlantic Seaboard territory. In

August 1956, each of these general sales managers was raised to the rank of vice president, continuing to report as before to Jordan, overall marketing vice president. Selwyn Eddy thus became vice president in charge of Pacific Coast marketing divisions, P. C. Thomas vice president in charge of Midwest marketing divisions, and J. L. Wadlow vice president in charge of Atlantic Seaboard marketing divisions.

The continued growth of Shell's business made organizational simplification imperative. By the mid-1950's, the American Shell companies had, after a decade of gradual change, arrived at a simple, easily understood corporate structure. Shell Pipe Line Corporation, Shell Chemical Corporation, and Shell Development Company were now all 100% subsidiaries of Shell Oil Company. Only the Canadian company, Shell Oil Company of Canada, Ltd., was not wholly owned; in it, Shell Oil held a 50% interest.† With duplicate managements and duplicate corporate structures eliminated, the major part of Shell's business was now vested in a single company, with a simple, easily remembered name, Shell Oil Company.

10

The Rise of the Shell Companies

THIS Shell Oil Company represented a culmination of more than forty years of building. The company's history during these years fell quite naturally into a few distinct periods.

The period from 1912 to 1920 saw Shell gain a toehold in a new country through a small marketing organization in the Pacific Northwest and a small oil-producing company in Oklahoma. Between 1912 and 1920, the West Coast company added the large properties of California Oilfields, Ltd., and erected a refinery at Martinez. East of the Rockies, additional crude oil producing properties were acquired and a refinery erected in the St. Louis area, some 500 miles from the Oklahoma oil fields. In 1920, the Shell companies both east and west

† In the interest of simplification, Shell Oil Company of British Columbia, Ltd., since its inception owned and managed by Shell Oil in San Francisco, had been transferred to the Shell Oil Company of Canada, Ltd., on May 1, 1945. The British Columbia company was subsequently merged with Shell of Canada on January 1, 1950.

of the Rocky Mountains had as yet to make a visible impression upon the American public.

This came during the decade of the 1920's, when the Shell companies in America expanded from relative obscurity into an organization blanketing the 48 states, operating nine refineries, producing oil or holding leases in practically every oil district of the United States, occupying two large and impressive company-owned office buildings, and having some 35,000 employees. Shell affairs were, at the end of 1929, at a high tide of expansion.

A third phase of the company's history, the painful depression years of the 1930's, witnessed a retreat from some of the beachheads established during the late Twenties. Losing money, the organization was forced to undertake a systematic appraisal of its operations and eliminate areas of unprofitability. Two refineries were closed and marketing abandoned in most of the states between the Rockies and the Mississippi, as Shell operations were reoriented around arteries of cheap transportation. The Thirties were a time of consolidation and many of the companies, started or acquired earlier, were merged into a single, large, nation-wide organization. During these inauspicious times, the basic research program of Shell Development Company, started in the late Twenties, was continued and greatly expanded, yielding results that were to be highly important to the company's future. And Shell Chemical, struggling through the difficulties of new processes and unprofitable operation, had by the late Thirties managed to place itself on a firm footing.

The fourth phase of Shell's history embraced the years of World War II. The company was able to make heavy contributions to the wartime manufacturing effort, and the technological pre-eminence of the Shell organization, the result of a quarter century of quiet innovation, was for the first time generally appreciated by the oil industry and the public in general.

The latest phase of the company's history, covering the decade following the end of World War II, was one of tremendous expansion. Like a boy who had achieved his growth and begun to "fill out" and assume a man's stature, the Shell organization, with an established framework, now matured at an unbelievably rapid pace. In every phase of activity, from exploration and production to retail marketing, Shell Oil Company now found itself in the first rank, not only of American oil companies, but of American industry. In the short space of a decade, Shell's sales trebled, its assets more than doubled, its earnings quadrupled. Its crude oil production increased by 50%, and new reserves at an even greater rate. Refining capacity doubled and manufacturing output of the chemical company nearly trebled. Because this expansion took place within the existing framework of the Shell organization, it was perhaps less spectacular than that of the Twenties, but it was far more substantial.

After forty years, the Shell companies in America had arrived at early maturity. They looked forward to an even more productive future.

Acknowledgment

A Word of Thanks to Some Helpful People

The chief sources of information available to the writer of a business history are: personal recollections of individuals who participated in building the business; correspondence, reports, account books, and corporate records of the company; and printed literature, both periodicals and books, touching upon the company and the industry of which it is a part.

During the course of writing this history, I was assisted by personal interviews with nearly two hundred individuals, most of them connected with the Shell organization, either now or in the past. Many of these generous people gave over entire days of their time to the project. Their heavy contribution is evident from even a casual perusal of the Citations of Sources, where acknowledgment is made to each of them individually.

These firsthand recollections were, of course, supplementary to the written record: old correspondence files, minute books, reports and accounting records. The task of locating and digesting this far-flung material would have been overwhelming without assistance. J. A. Abbott helped me in this work for ten months in 1948; most of our information on the company's early years in Oklahoma is the result of his energetic digging. Volunteers, who kept the historian's interest in mind, were the source of many old records which otherwise would never have come to light. W. R. Hoyt, F. E. Superior, and W. W. Yeager in the course of their work continually came across material of historical importance and were thoughtful enough to send it on. W. M. Harris provided the American Gasoline Company's original Seattle cash book; and A. L. Petterson, who had saved the original Richmond Beach log book, kindly donated it. Operating and financial statistics were scattered through forty years of records, kept in a variety of places. I am grateful to J. J. Davis for devoting most of the summer of 1948 to digging out and presenting these figures in easily understood tabular form. J. C. Thompson brought these statistics up to date and subjected them to a final check. One more word on company records: a large corporation generates an avalanche of paper, with the result that old records must constantly be reviewed and destroyed to make way for the new. Because thousands of essential financial and legal records must necessarily be retained, old correspondence suffers heavily when records are discarded. There are numerous references to old letters in the Citations of Sources; part of the reason for these references is to assist some possible future historian who may be unable to locate all of the source material that existed at the time this book was written.

The third source of information, printed matter, included old company house organs, old trade journals, newspapers, and a wide variety of technical, economic, and reference books, many of them old and difficult to come by. In the course of his research, the author of a business history becomes particularly appreciative of the value of specialized and private libraries. For their patient and imaginative assistance, I am indebted to many in this field: Miss Barbara Billings, former librarian, and Miss Ruth Jones, present librarian of the Irving Trust Company, New York; Miss Eleanor S. Cavanaugh, librarian, Standard & Poor's Corporation, New York; Miss E. Marie Becker, reference librarian, The New-York Historical Society; Miss Rose Demorest, Carnegie Library, Pittsburgh; Miss Virginia Smyth, librarian, American Petroleum Institute; Mrs. M. S. Cheever, former librarian, Asiatic Petroleum Corporation, New York, and her staff; Miss Kathleen Bannister, librarian, Shell Chemical Corporation, New York; and Mrs. Marion Minard and her excellent staff of the Shell Oil Company library, New York. My thanks are also due to the librarians and the library staffs of the National Broadcasting Company's General Library, New York; Moody's Investors' Service, New York; Netherlands Information Service, New York; Columbia University's Business School and Mining School Libraries; Chemists' Club of New York; British Information Service, New York; the Libraries of the Engineering Societies, New York; and the Science and Technology Room, the Newspaper Division, and the excellent Photostat Service of The New York Public Library. Miss Mary E. Farabaugh provided a foundation for this work by conscientiously searching and photostating complete files of the *Oil & Gas Journal* and *National Petroleum News*. S. W. Duhig and E. A. Cunningham kindly offered bound sets of the old Shell of California house organ, *Shelling The Line*. Dr. F. W. L. Tydeman donated a complete set of the old *Roxoleum*, published at Tulsa. This was only the beginning of Dr. Tydeman's generosity. He was an able student of history and from his large store of old correspondence and reports he carefully culled items likely to interest the historian; from his own capacious memory he set down his reminiscences, in long letters that must have been a chore to compose but were a delight to read; he was, in addition, a lifelong enthusiastic amateur photographer and printed up from forty-year-old negatives a large number of pictures, some of which have been used as illustrations. That he did not live to see the publication of this book is a matter of keen regret.

In addition to collecting material, I was also obliged to undertake a considerable amount of self-education as I went along, particularly in the fields of finance and technology. For their patient and cheerful explanations over the past several years, I am deeply indebted to A. A. Buzzi, D. E. Burroughs, L. C. Burroughs, O. A. Colten, J. P. Cunningham, Hugh Harvey, F. B. Hilmer, H. D. Loeb, P. M. Ludwig, E. A. Martin, J. D. Metcalfe, P. J. Morel, J. P. O'Keefe, and C. A. Rehbein. J. G. Burtt and

W. L. Hobro of Los Angeles and A. E. Groff of Houston were equally pleasant about answering questions by mail. Miss Mae Hamer and her staff of the Secretary's Office and Miss Mildred Miller and her Personnel Records staff patiently answered a long line of inquiries concerning names, dates, and places.

During the past few years, a gratifying number of academic historians have turned their attention to the oil industry. An amateur among historians, I counted myself fortunate to have the companionship and sound advice of the authors of the recent Standard Oil of New Jersey and Standard Oil of Indiana histories. Prof. N. S. B. Gras, the father of modern business history, was extremely generous with his time and good advice. The group of scholars whom he had gathered around him, Drs. Ralph W. and Muriel E. Hidy, Prof. George S. Gibb, Dr. Charles Sterling Popple, and Mrs. Evelyn H. Knowlton, all managed to arouse in me their enthusiasm for high standards of scholarship and objectivity. I owe them all a great deal. Prof. Gras read and commented on the first half of the manuscript; Dr. Muriel Hidy was of like assistance with a large section of the book; and Dr. Paul H. Giddens, well-known oil historian, author of the recent Standard Oil of Indiana history, and president of Hamline University, was also kind enough to read the early chapters of the manuscript. Mrs. Elizabeth Bricker Currier and Albert E. Haase, at work on a history of Standard Oil of California, were both helpful on more than one occasion.

When this volume was undertaken in 1947, the main objective was to assemble records and recollections while they were still available; the eventual form of publication was left undecided. After the manuscript had been completed, Shell President H. S. M. Burns appointed a History Committee to read the manuscript and make recommendations concerning publication. This committee consisted of Dr. M. E. Spaght, executive vice president of the company; Stanley W. Duhig, recently retired as vice president and treasurer of Shell Union Oil Corporation after a career covering forty-five years; W. F. Kenney, the company's vice president and general counsel; Harry Jacobs, today the company's senior employee in years of service and a key executive of the marketing organization for most of his career; and H. L. Curtis, the company's vice president in charge of public relations. Few authors, I am sure, have ever worked with a more helpful or understanding committee. Their suggestions for changes were few and were concerned not with suppression or "soft-pedalling," but with accuracy of fact and clarity of language. In the interests of accuracy, the committee suggested that various individuals who were acquainted by firsthand experience with different periods of the company's history be requested to read those portions of the manuscript which concerned them most closely.

As a result, a large number of individuals—some retired, some still active in the Shell management, some outside the company—gave generously of their time as readers of the manuscript. I am indebted to these gentlemen for their many helpful and pertinent suggestions. J. C. van Eck, who helped found the original Shell company on the Pacific Coast in 1912 and whose business career spanned almost the entire period of this history, was kind enough to read the whole manuscript. His comments, prepared, I am sure, at considerable labor to himself, were of great profit in revising the manuscript. Daniel Pyzel, one of the company's chief technological innovators and a founder of the Shell Chemical and Shell Development companies, devoted painstaking attention to the technical sections of the manuscript, making a great many material improvements. B. H. van der Linden put himself to great trouble to provide me with authoritative material on early production engineering and on the Ventura field, and carefully reviewed those parts of the manuscript.

I am also deeply indebted to a great many other busy men who took the time to read anywhere from a few pages to several chapters and comment upon events which they experienced at firsthand: H. H. Anderson, General Avery D. Andrews, the late Max W. Ball, Carl Barker, S. Belither, A. H. Boultbee, John G. Burtt, A. H. Calderwood, R. F. Carey, Admiral A. F. Carter, F. S. Clulow, D. G. Coombs, A. B. Culbertson, E. D. Cumming, H. A. Curtin, L. E. David, C. E. Davis, Dr. E. F. Davis, E. DeGolyer, G. H. Dempster, H. A. Dohrenwend, J. H. Doolittle, C. P. Dubbs, F. M. Dull, Dr. T. W. Evans, Alexander Fraser, A. J. Galloway, C. S. Gentry, Lord Godber, George E. Gordon, B. J. Gratama, L. A. Guest, John H. Harvey, the late Edward Hepner, R. B. High, W. L. Hobro, D. B. Hodges, J. A. Horner, Dr. C. W. Humphreys, A. J. Johnson, J. G. Jordan, H. R. Kemmerer, C. C. Kifer, Felix Kortlandt, P. E. Lakin, Sir George Legh-Jones, R. C. McCurdy, W. C. McDuffie, N. J. McGaw, L. G. McLaren, E. L. Miller, the late J. C. Munro, F. E. Nehr, Jan Oostermeyer, Paul Paine, A. F. H. Payne, E. C. Peet, H. W. Penterman, the late F. E. Rehm, William Reinhardt, R. C. Roberts, A. P. Ruether, J. Rysdorp, F. B. Simms, J. G. Sinclair, S. S. Smith, L. V. Steck, John R. Suman, T. E. Swigart, George P. Thomson, George Tyler, R. G. A. van der Woude, G. H. van Senden, E. H. Walker, John W. Watson, J. H. White, Forsyth Wickes, G. G. Woodruff, and F. W. Woods.

B. L. Ryan deserves special mention for volunteering to prepare a history of Shell activities in West Texas; it was a model of scholarship and accuracy. I would also like to thank Prof. R. J. Forbes of Amsterdam, co-worker of Dr. C. Gerretson on the History of the Royal Dutch, for his many courtesies over a period of years. When the manuscript was at last ready for printing, G. E. Brewer, L. G. Christie, E. A. Hugill, T. B. Rendel, and D. M. Sheldon were kind enough to read once again the parts concerned with their own specialties. G. G. Biggar read the galley proofs and offered helpful suggestions.

Photographs came from a variety of sources and credit for them is given where possible. I am particularly grateful to W. E. Feistner, B. A. Gwynn, C. C. Kifer, J. L. Seright, and the late A. E. Collins for placing at my disposal their personal collections of photographs, of which I was able to use only a few. F. H. Roberts supervised design of the jacket and endpapers; F. E. Tudor, of Manhattan Drafting Company, prepared the maps and drawings; Mrs. Ida T. Hopper, Mrs. Helene Marer, and Miss Phoebe Wilson helped make the index. Allan W. Ferrin, of Appleton-Century-Crofts, was unfailingly helpful and thoughtful. To the many others who had some part in the making of this book, my sincere thanks and appreciation for their efforts.

In the course of several years, I wearied many amiable young ladies in copying and re-copying parts of the manuscript. I would particularly like to thank Mrs. F. N. Costa for volunteering to type large sections of the manuscript in addition to her regular duties. Miss Sheila Gorman, Miss Eugenie Desbets, and W. M. Castagnetta of Shell's reproduction department lavished much care and patience on reproducing the manuscript by multilith. Mrs. Joan Marchese checked facts and figures, put in long hours typing the manuscript, read proofs, assisted in the index, and was a painstaking and willing worker in every circumstance.

Last, but hardly least, I owe a special word of thanks to my wife Polly, who cheerfully put up with the disruptions of "having a book in the house," did research, improved the manuscript, and carefully read the galley proofs.

To any whose contributions I may have neglected to acknowledge, my apologies and sincere thanks. This is a long list; it was a long book.

K. B.

New York
September 1956

Citations of Sources

The notes beginning on this page are citations of sources. Explanatory notes, enlarging upon, or qualifying some statement in the text, appear as footnotes on the same page with the statement. (This rule is violated in connection with Chapter I, in order to discuss some items of disputed scholarship.)

CHAPTER I

Big Moment of the Nineteenth Century (pages 1 to 19)

1. R. J. Forbes, *Petroleum and Bitumen in Antiquity*, Leiden, E. J. Brill, 1936. The most scholarly works available on petroleum in ancient times are those by Forbes, all of them published in Europe, and not all of them in English. One of the best accounts generally available in this country can be found in Herbert Abraham, *Asphalts and Allied Substances*, 2 vols., Fifth Edition, New York, D. Van Nostrand Co., 1945, Vol. I, pp. 1-55.

2. Forbes, *op. cit.*

3. Genesis 6:14, 11:3; Exodus 2:3.

4. Forbes, *op. cit.*; R. J. Forbes, "Fifteen Centuries of Bitumen, A.D. 300–1860," published in *Bitumen*, Berlin, January–June, 1937 (in German); Sir Boverton Redwood, *A Treatise on Petroleum*, Fourth Edition, London, Charles Griffin & Co., 1922, Vol. I, pp. 1 and 160B.

5. Forbes, *Petroleum and Bitumen in Antiquity*.

6. *Ibid.*

7. Msgr. Imbert, a Catholic missionary, 1833, quoted in Andrew Cone and Walter R. Johns, *Petrolia: A Brief History of the Pennsylvania Petroleum Region*, New York, D. Appleton & Co., 1870.

8. Forbes, *Petroleum and Bitumen in Antiquity*.

9. *Ibid.*

10. Forbes, "Fifteen Centuries of Bitumen," *supra*.

11. Forbes, *Petroleum and Bitumen in Antiquity*.

12. M. A. Symes, *An Account of an Embassy to the Kingdom of Ava . . . in the year 1795*, London, 1800; John Crawfurd, *Journal of an Embassy to the Court of Ava*, 2 vols., London, 1834, Vol. I, pp. 98-99.

13. R. J. Forbes, *Short History of the Art of Distillation*, Leiden, E. J. Brill, 1948, p. 224. Argand was granted British patent No. 1,425 on March 12, 1784, which of course means that the actual date of his invention was earlier.

14. Redwood, *op. cit.*; Vivian Byam Lewes, "Lighting," in *Encyclopaedia Britannica*, Eleventh Edition, New York, 1911, Vol. XVI, p. 651 ff.; Alexander Stuart Murray, "Lamp," *Encyclopaedia Britannica*, Chicago, 1945; F. W. Robins, *The Story of the Lamp (And the Candle)*, London, Oxford University Press, 1939. Well-rounded accounts of the development of the lamp in America are supplied by several books on American antiques; an easily available and very satisfactory one appears in Alice Winchester, *How to Know American Antiques*, New York, New American Library, 1951, pp. 149-161.

15. *Encyclopaedia Britannica*, 1911, *supra*; Abraham Gesner, *A Practical Treatise On Coal, Petroleum, and Other Distilled Oils*, New York, Ballière Bros., 1861.

16. R. J. Forbes, *Man the Maker*, New York, Henry Schuman, 1950, p. 217.

17. Abraham Gesner, M.D., *A Practical Treatise on Coal, Petroleum, and Other Distilled Oils*, Second Edition, Revised and Enlarged by George Weltden Gesner, New York, Ballière Bros., 1865, pp. 8 and 54.
18. Abraham, *op. cit.*
19. *The Engineering and Mining Journal*, February 9, 1884, p. 99. The article is unsigned, but in all probability its author was John Frederick Gesner (1839–1899), son of Dr. Gesner.
20. Gesner, *op. cit.;* for a more detailed account of Gesner's work see the author's "Dr. Gesner's Kerosene: The Start of American Oil Refining," *Business History Review*, March 1955, pp. 28-53.
21. Edwin M. Bailey, "The Dawn of Petroleum Refining," in the Institute of Petroleum *Review*, London, Vol. II (1948), p. 357; H. R. J. Conacher, "History of the Scottish Oil-Shale Industry," in *The Oilshales of the Lothians*, London, 1927, 3rd Ed., p. 240.
22. Bailey, *loc. cit.*, pp. 357, 358.
23. Contrary to what many oil historians have written, Bailey, *loc. cit.*, pp. 358-359, says that the coal mine did not cease to produce oil. Its small production (about 300 gallons a day) was too small for economic operation of a refinery. Bailey quotes letters to show that Young was still buying the mine's oil as late as 1859, and says the mine was still producing oil a year before it was closed in 1885.
24. Bailey, *op. cit.*, p. 359; Bailey, "James Young, Founder of the Mineral Oil Industry," lecture delivered before the Scottish Branch of the Institute of Petroleum, January 8, 1948, and published in the Institute of Petroleum *Review*, London, Vol. II (1948), p. 180.
25. Joshua Merrill's account in *The Derrick's Hand-Book of Petroleum*, Vol. I, Oil City, Pa., The Derrick Publishing Co., 1898, p. 889.
26. Gesner, *op. cit.*, p. 10.
27. Merrill's account, *supra*, pp. 882 and 884; Conacher, *op. cit.*, p. 241; Frederic P. Wells, *History of Newbury, Vermont*, St. Johnsbury, Vermont, The Caledonian Co., 1902.
28. Gesner (1861 edition), p. 128-129; the list is reprinted in Raymond Foss Bacon and William Allen Hamor, *The American Petroleum Industry*, New York, McGraw-Hill Book Co., 1916, Vol. I, p. 210.
29. A. C. Ferris' account, *Derrick's Hand-Book*, p. 1012 ff.; Ferris correspondence and billheads in The Bella C. Landauer Collection, New-York Historical Society.
30. This piece of inspirational journalism appeared in J. T. Henry's *The Early and Later History of Petroleum*, Philadelphia, 1873, p. 83 ff., and has been repeated with little variation by oil historians ever since. The incident is not mentioned nor is credit for the idea given Bissell in Cone and Johns' *Petrolia* (published in 1870), and Bissell thought highly enough of this book to send inscribed complimentary copies of it to his friends.

The best sources on the events leading up to the drilling of the Drake well are, as one would expect, the papers, letters, and original accounts of the chief participants in the venture. An admirable collection of these original papers, along with other relevant material, has been collected in *Pennsylvania Petroleum, 1750–1872, A Documentary History*, compiled and edited by Paul H. Giddens, and published by the Pennsylvania Historical and Museum Commission, Titusville, 1947. Next in value for the original material it contains is *The Derrick's Hand-Book of Petroleum*, cited in note 25. In it there are a number of firsthand accounts such as those of Joshua Merrill and Col. A. C. Ferris which are not printed elsewhere, and many original papers are reproduced in complete text.

Of early books about the industry, Gesner's (two editions, titles cited in notes 15 and 17) is the most objective, and contains first-class technical descriptions of oil industry practices of the time. Cone and Johns in 1870 (see note 7 for complete title) supplied the first full-length history of the industry, but their book has the earmarks of superficial investigation and hurried writing. J. T. Henry's *Early and Later History of Petroleum* published in 1873 is much more complete, and shows evidences of considerable on-the-spot investigation at a time when most of the original participants could still be interviewed.

Henry's graphic descriptions and "good stories" have caught hold of the imaginations of most subsequent oil historians with the result that his version of an event has, in general, become the accepted one.

J. J. McLaurin's *Sketches in Crude Oil*, Harrisburg, 1898, was the first of several romanticized histories which appeared during the next two decades. Finally, in 1938, Dr. Paul H. Giddens, a trained historian, brought together the events preceding and immediately following the drilling of the Drake well in *The Birth of the Oil Industry*, New York, Macmillan, 1938. Herbert Asbury, *The Golden Flood*, New York, Alfred Knopf, 1942, is another first-rate account, even though Asbury, a chronic chronicler of sin (*The Barbary Coast, The Latin Quarter, The Gangs of New York*), devotes about half his space to wild times and wickedness in the early oil boom towns.

31. "Report of the United States Revenue Commission on Petroleum as a Source of National Income," February 1866, House Executive Document, No. 51, 39th Congress, 1st Session, pp. 4-5, reprinted in *Pennsylvania Petroleum*.

32. Giddens, *The Birth of the Oil Industry*.

33. *Ibid.*

34. *Ibid.*

35. Benjamin Silliman (senior), "Notice of a Fountain of Petroleum called the Oil-spring," *American Journal of Science*, Series 1, Vol. xxiii, pp. 97-103 (1833); Benjamin Silliman, Jr., *Report on the Rock Oil, or Petroleum, from Venango Co., Pennsylvania*, New Haven, 1855, p. 19. Paul H. Giddens published this history-making report in facsimile in 1949, and the Ethyl Corporation issued a facsimile edition in 1955; the full text appears in J. T. Henry, *op. cit.*, Cone and Johns, *op. cit.*, and in Ida M. Tarbell, *The History of the Standard Oil Company*, New York, 1904.

36. Benjamin Silliman, Jr., *op. cit.*, p. 20.

37. Drake's own account, written by himself about 1870, in the Drake Museum, Titusville, and reprinted in *Pennsylvania Petroleum*, p. 64 ff.

38. Letter, Drake to W. A. Ives, New Haven, August 16, 1858, reprinted in *Pennsylvania Petroleum*, p. 144.

39. Bill from W. A. Smith to Seneca Oil Company, reprinted by J. D. Henry, *History and Romance of the Petroleum Industry*, London, 1914, p. 148.

40. From Drake's accounting, covering the period March 1 to August 31, 1859, printed in *Pennsylvania Petroleum*, p. 151, ff.; Giddens, *Birth of the Oil Industry*, p. 39; Townsend's account, p. 57, *Pennsylvania Petroleum*.

41. This is the generally accepted version, as it appears in J. T. Henry, p. 91. Henry, however, says "Saturday afternoon, August 28th"; actually Saturday fell on August 27th in 1859. Uncle Billy Smith, who drilled the well, said they struck oil on August 12th, which would have been a Friday; his son, Samuel B. Smith, placed the date at about two weeks after August 2nd, his 16th birthday. Thus, Saturday, August 13th, might well be the day. No one can say with any assurance just when the Drake well did come in. August 27th has lately been considered the official anniversary day.

42. *Pennsylvania Petroleum*, p. 184; Townsend's account, *Pennsylvania Petroleum*, p. 60; Giddens, *The Birth of the Oil Industry*, p. 35, fn.

43. *Pennsylvania Petroleum*, pp. 168 and 170-171.

44. J. T. Henry, *op. cit.*, p. 329.

45. Giddens, *The Birth of the Oil Industry*.

46. Max W. Ball, *This Fascinating Oil Business*, Indianapolis, The Bobbs-Merrill Co., 1940.

47. Averages from figures given in *The Petroleum Almanac*, New York, The National Industrial Conference Board, 1946.

48. Gesner, *op. cit.* (1861 edition), p. 128-129.

49. Giddens, *The Birth of the Oil Industry*.

50. Information on introduction of drilling to Baku, Romania, and Galicia from Redwood, *op. cit.*, Vol. I; and R. J. Forbes, "Rumania" in *The Science of Petroleum*, London, Oxford University Press, 1938.

CHAPTER II
Other Beginnings, Ten Thousand Miles Away (pages 20 to 55)

1. Unless otherwise noted, the factual material in this chapter has been taken from Volumes I and II of the monumental *Geschiedenis der 'Koninklijke'* (History of the 'Royal Dutch') by the eminent Dutch scholar, Dr. C. Gerretson. Thus far, three volumes (volume three in two parts) have been published in quarto by Joh. Enschedé en Zonen, Haarlem, 1932, 1936, and 1941; also available in a less expensive edition, small quarto, three volumes, published by A. Oosthoek, Utrecht, Volumes I and II in 1939, Volume III in 1942. These three volumes bring the story of the Royal Dutch and its affiliates up to 1914. Gerretson's history, as projected, is scheduled to be published in six volumes, of which three are yet to come.

2. *The Petroleum Handbook*, 3rd Edition, London, Shell Petroleum Company, Ltd., 1948, p. 22.

3. Letter, April 10, 1890, from the Parliamentary Secretary of the King to J. A. de Gelder. It is reproduced in Volume I of Gerretson's *History of the Royal Dutch*, and also in *The Royal Dutch Petroleum Company Diamond Jubilee Book*, The Hague, 1950.

4. *Diamond Jubilee Book*, pp. 1 and 19.

5. Letter, R. J. Forbes, Amsterdam, to the author, December 1951. The first group were hired in 1891, the others in 1892. Possibly the two Montgomery names represent a duplicate listing.

6. *Diamond Jubilee Book*, p. 71.

7. Sir Henri Deterding (as told to Stanley Naylor), *An International Oilman*, London, Harper & Bros., 1934, p. 61. These chapters, comprising the only memoir which Deterding left behind, appeared originally in serial form in *The Saturday Evening Post*.

8. Material on Rockefeller from Allan Nevins, *John D. Rockefeller, the Heroic Age of American Enterprise*, 2 volumes, New York, Chas. Scribner's Sons, 1940.

9. *An International Oilman*, pp. 9-13.

10. Material on the Samuels and their company from Gerretson; from articles in *The Shell Magazine*, London, November 1947; and from booklet "To Mark the Jubilee of The 'Shell' Transport and Trading Company Limited," London, 1947, hereafter referred to as "Shell Anniversary Booklet, 1947."

11. Dr. Paul Dvorkovitz, in *The Petroleum Review*, London, September 29, 1906, p. 178.

12. Sir Boverton Redwood, *A Treatise on Petroleum*, London, Chas. Griffin & Co., 1922, Vol. I, p. 5.

13. *Shell Magazine*, London, November 1947.

14. Letter, Hon. Peter Samuel to Alexander Fraser, June 8, 1950.

15. Said by Samuel in 1900 according to the 50th Anniversary Issue, *Petroleum Times*, London, June 17, 1949.

16. Bearsted obituary, London *Times*, January 18, 1927, p. 16.

17. Article "Fuel," in *Encyclopaedia Britannica*, 11th Edition (1910), Vol. XI, p. 277; Dr. Paul Dvorkovitz, *The Petroleum Review*, London, September 29, 1906.

18. Figures from Shell Anniversary Booklet, 1947.

19. *An International Oilman*, pp. 62-63.

20. *Id.*, p. 68.

21. This incident is recounted in the Gulf company's 50th anniversary history, *Since Spindletop*, by Craig Thompson, Pittsburgh, 1951, pp. 18-20. It is also mentioned at greater length in *Judge Mellon's Sons*, Memoirs of W. L. Mellon (in collaboration with Boyden Sparkes), Pittsburgh, 1948, pp. 276-277, where the price is given as "at the wells 20 cents a barrel." Sir Robert Waley Cohen, in an interview "Fifty Years with Shell," published in *The Shell Magazine*, London, August 1951, p. 184, recalled the price as 10 cents a barrel.

22. Shell Anniversary Booklet, 1947.

23. *An International Oilman*, p. 54.

24. Conversation, Prof. R. J. Forbes, Amsterdam, April 1952; London *Times*, February 7, 1927; Nevins, *op. cit.*, Vol. II, p. 615.

25. One of the best short summaries of the development of the automobile

will be found in Mark Sullivan's *Our Times*, Volume I, New York, Chas. Scribner's Sons, 1926. Other readable accounts are David L. Cohn, *Combustion on Wheels, An Informal History of the Automobile Age*, Boston, Houghton Mifflin Company, 1944; C. B. Glasscock, *The Gasoline Age*, Indianapolis, The Bobbs-Merrill Company, 1937; and Allan Nevins and Frank Ernest Hill, *Ford: The Times, the Man, the Company*, New York, Charles Scribner's Sons, 1954.

26. Figures for 1895 and 1905 from Sullivan, *op. cit.;* for 1910, *The Shell Magazine*, London, November 1947,

p. 163; for 1914, *The Petroleum Almanac*, National Industrial Conference Board, New York, 1946, p. 139.

27. *The Shell Magazine*, London, November 1947, p. 156.

28. Dr. Paul Dvorkovitz, *The Petroleum Review*, London, September 29, 1906, pp. 177-178.

29. *Oil & Gas Journal*, June 29, 1922, p. 74; information courtesy of C. W. Stennekes, The Hague, April 23, 1952.

30. *An International Oilman*, pp. 77-78.

31. Interview, Sir Robert Waley Cohen, "Fifty Years with Shell," *The Shell Magazine*, London, August 1951, p. 184.

CHAPTER III

Sumatra to Seattle (pages 56 to 112)

1. Details of arrival of cargoes, their amounts, the names of the vessels which brought them, and notations of first shipments to the new depots are contained in a log book kept at Richmond Beach by William Warner, superintendent at Richmond Beach for some 25 years. This book was kindly made available to the author by A. L. Petterson, an old-time employee at Richmond Beach who was still working there in 1947. "Actual Stock Book, American Gasoline Company," and "Packages Stock Book, American Gasoline Company," made available through courtesy of George N. Brennan and William Reed Hoyt, also provided much interesting material. Perhaps the most instructive of the lot was the American Gasoline Company's Seattle cashbook, 1912–1915, lent by W. M. Harris of Shell's Seattle office.

2. Interview, J. C. van Eck, New York, May 6, 1947.

3. Dr. C. Gerretson, *Geschiedenis der Koninklijke*, Vol. III, Haarlem, 1941.

4. Ida M. Tarbell, *The History of the Standard Oil Company*, Vol. II, New York, McClure, Phillips & Co., 1904.

5. Sir Henri Deterding, as told to Stanley Naylor, *An International Oilman*, London, Harper & Bro., 1934, pp. 85-87.

6. Royal Dutch Company Annual Report, 1911.

7. *The Wall Street Journal*, May 2, 1914.

8. Deterding, *op. cit.*, p. 87.

9. Gerretson says "in the first few days of 1911," but Van Eck, who was Deterding's secretary at the time, has a clear recollection of the 1910 date since the event involved him personally; Van Eck writes that Levering visited Deterding on a second trip early in 1911.

10. Gerretson, *op. cit.*, Vol. III.

11. *Ibid.*

12. Conversations, Prof. R. J. Forbes, New York, September, 1951.

13. Allan Nevins, *Study in Power: John D. Rockefeller, Industrialist and Philanthropist*, Vol. II, New York, Chas. Scribner's Sons, 1953, pp. 381-382. See also Paul H. Giddens, *Standard Oil Company (Indiana), Oil Pioneer of the Middle West*, Appleton-Century-Crofts, Inc., 1955, pp. 126-127.

14. Deterding, *op. cit.*, p. 83.

15. Memorandum of biographical material, J. C. van Eck, New York, to G. G. Biggar, January 30, 1942, and Van Eck interview (see note 2).

16. Information this and following paragraph from Van Eck interview (see note 2).

17. H. R. Gallagher, Woodside, Cali-

fornia, November 1949. Gallagher died at his home in Woodside, December 31, 1949. Before his death, he had seen and corrected the notes of this interview which he had given to C. E. Totten.

18. Interview with Ivan Hyland, attorney, Seattle, July 30, 1947; letter, J. C. van Eck to the author, December 23, 1953.

19. Ivan Hyland and Van Eck interviews.

20. Interviews, Seattle, July 30, 1947, with D. G. Fisher and Mr. and Mrs. Howard Tuckett.

21. Fisher interview, *supra*.

22. J. A. Graves, vice president, Farmers and Merchants National Bank, Los Angeles, in letter to Harris, May 5, 1911.

23. Letter, F. P. S. Harris, San Francisco, to Asiatic, London, May 4, 1911.

24. Telegram, Richmond Levering, New York, to Harris, San Francisco, May 4, 1911.

25. Corporate records and minute books. There is some indication from correspondence that there was an "American Benzine Co." which preceded this company; and indeed minutes have been found for two directors' meetings supposed to have been held at 62 Cedar Street, New York, May 10 and July 23, 1912. However, these may have very well been "lawyer's minutes" drawn up for a corporation which was never organized. According to California State records, no company of this name was ever qualified to do business in the state. (Memorandum, P. W. Harvey, San Francisco, to the author, December 11, 1951.)

26. Van Eck and Fisher interviews.

27. Seattle cashbook, American Gasoline Co., 1912–1915.

28. *Id*. Monthly receipts from sales of Havoline oil were small, generally less than $50.

29. Information on extent of early staff from interview with George E. Gordon, Redlands, California, August 29, 1947. Gordon, who was familiar with account books of this period, recalled that Gallagher was still on Indian Refining Company's payroll at the end of 1912 but neither Van

Eck nor Gallagher felt sure of this point.

30. J. C. van Eck, "Report of the Oil Market," San Francisco, August 22, 1911, cited by Gerretson, *op. cit.*, Vol. III, p. 785.

31. Van Eck interview; conversation, Ralph Hidy, New York, August 29, 1951; George Gordon interview.

32. Price, Waterhouse & Co., Audits of American Gasoline Co., 1912, 1913.

33. George Gordon interview.

34. Van Eck interview. This is no doubt the cargo that arrived aboard the S.S. *Eburna* in December 1914. The Seattle cashbook soon after shows expense account payments to H. L. Burleson, the old-time refiner from Rodeo, and in April 1915 the company bought $2,500 worth of sulphuric acid, which would have been about the amount required to acid-treat what remained of this cargo.

35. *Oil & Gas Journal*, July 17, 1913, p. 6, reprinted from *The Oil Age*, a West Coast oil trade paper.

36. The phrase is Van Eck's.

37. Information in this and preceding two paragraphs from interview with B. H. van der Linden, New York, May 22, 1947, and Gerretson, *op. cit.*, Vol. III.

38. Gerretson, *op. cit.*, Vol. III; Royal Dutch Co. Annual Report, 1913, p. 10.

39. "California's Oil," article prepared by the Petroleum Production Pioneers of Los Angeles, in American Petroleum Institute *Quarterly*, April 1948; and E. P. Bly, "Oil Pipe Lines in California," an excellent review of oil field and pipe line development in California, in Oil *Bulletin*, August, September, and October 1926.

40. Douglas G. McPhee, "The Story of Shell," *California Oil World and Petroleum Industry*, May 5, 1937.

41. Interview, Stanley W. Duhig, New York, April 8, 1948, and subsequent conversations.

42. McPhee, *loc. cit.*

43. Recalled by Eli Pedersen, Bakersfield, Calif., September 2, 1947.

44. Unnamed writer, quoted by McPhee, *supra*.

45. Several persons furnished excellent accounts of the glories of Oilfields:

W. L. Bagby, Ventura, Calif., August 18, 1947; Eli Pedersen, mentioned above; Edward Blake, San Francisco, September 19, 1947; W. E. Feistner, Long Beach, Calif., August 21, 1947; W. E. Jacobs, Hollywood, Calif., August 27, 1947; W. Fred Knief, Ventura, Calif., August 18, 1947; W. C. McDuffie, Montecito, Calif., August 30, 1947; F. E. Rehm, San Francisco, September 19, 1947, and New York, August 13, 1948; W. C. Reinhardt, Los Angeles, August 27, 1947; William Shepherd, Jr., Los Angeles, August 14, 1947; E. E. Tiffany, Long Beach, Calif., August 20, 1947; George Tyler, Los Angeles, August 28, 1947; and W. M. Vaughn, Bell Flower, Calif., August 20, 1947. An excellent account, more complete than the others, supplied by the Duhig interview mentioned in note 41.

46. W. E. Jacobs (see note 45).

47. Gerretson, *op. cit.*, Vol. III; conversation with George Tyler, Balfour, Guthrie & Co., Los Angeles, August 27, 1947. Tyler was at the time a member of Balfour's oil department.

48. Duhig interview.

49. *Oil & Gas Journal*, October 22, 1914.

50. Interview with William Brooks, Los Angeles, August 15, 1947.

51. Gallagher interview (see note 17).

52. Interview with E. P. Christie, Oakland, Calif., August 11, 1947. Mr. Christie was manager of the old Central Division, headquartered in San Francisco, from the time of its organization until his retirement in 1931. He died at the home of his son, L. G. Christie, Port Washington, Long Island, August 31, 1949.

53. Price, Waterhouse & Co., audit of Omen Oil Company, 1914; interview with E. L. Miller, San Francisco, September 17, 1947. Miller joined Shell in September 1914, and in 1928 succeeded Gallagher as vice president in charge of sales. He resigned late in 1934, and spent most of the rest of his business career as vice president of the Golden State Company, Ltd., San Francisco dairy products firm.

54. Seattle cashbook, American Gasoline Company, 1912–1914.

55. Mark Sullivan, *Our Times*, Vol. I.

56. Seattle cashbook (see note 54).

57. Interviews with David Nielsen, San Francisco, July 10, 1947, and Homer Moore, Seattle, July 29, 1947. Supporting evidence is found in the cashbook.

58. Interview, L. E. David, San Francisco, July 3, 1947; conversation, A. G. Schei, San Francisco, September 19, 1947.

59. *Oil & Gas Journal*, December 18, 1913.

60. Interview, Edward Hepner, San Francisco, July 9, 1947; letter, E. L. Miller, Lafayette, Calif., to the author, January 13, 1954; interview, L. W. Nelson, San Francisco, July 2, 1947.

61. Letter, J. C. van Eck, Santa Barbara, California, to the author, December 23, 1953.

62. A good summary of these lines is E. P. Bly article cited in note 39.

63. Interview with N. W. Thompson, San Francisco, September 9, 1947; Samuel W. Tait, Jr., *The Wildcatters, An Informal History of Oil-Hunting in America*, Princeton University Press, 1946, p. 186.

64. H. W. Crozier, "The Shell Oil Pipe Line," *Journal of Electricity, Power and Gas*, September 4, 1915; also reprinted as a booklet by Sanderson & Porter.

65. Bly, *loc. cit.*; interview, Fred B. Simms, Kernville, Calif., September 3, 1947.

66. Crozier, *loc. cit.*; interview, C. H. Beckwith, San Francisco, June 24, 1947.

67. Simms interview and subsequent correspondence.

68. Information from Daniel Pyzel, Piedmont, Calif., June 1954.

69. Walter Miller and Harold G. Osborn, "History and Development of Some Important Phases of Petroleum Refining in the United States," in *The Science of Petroleum*, Vol. II, London, Oxford University Press, 1938, p. 1466 ff:; Gerretson, *op. cit.*

70. R. J. Forbes, *Short History of the Art of Distillation*, Leiden, E. J. Brill, 1948, p. 301; conversations, R. J. Forbes, New York, October 10 and 12, 1951.

71. Interview, Erle P. Severns, Oakland, Calif., September 5, 1947.

72. A. W. Nash, "The Development of Petroleum Refining," *Journal* of the Institute of Petroleum, London, February 1940, p. 43.

73. Miller and Osborn, *loc. cit.* (note 69).

74. Arthur F. L. Bell, "Important Topping Plants of California," American Society of Mining and Metallurgical Engineers *Transactions*, 1915, p. 185.

75. Conversations, B. Gratama, New York, March 31, 1949; Eugene P. Brown, Texaco Development Corporation, New York, November 30, 1951.

76. Bell, *loc. cit.*

77. J. M. Wadsworth, *Removal of the Lighter Hydrocarbons from Petroleum by Continuous Distillation*, Washington, U. S. Bureau of Mines Bulletin 162, 1919. This is an excellent survey of the early topping plants.

78. Forbes, *Short History of the Art of Distillation*, Leiden, E. J. Brill, 1948, p. 225; Gerretson, *op. cit.*, Vol. III, pp. 167 and 684.

79. Conversation, H. E. Way, San Francisco, July 11, 1947.

80. Interviews with Daniel Pyzel, San Francisco, July 24, August 7, September 9, and September 16, 1947, and reviews of manuscript by Pyzel, 1954; also N. W. Thompson interview (note 63).

81. Letter, B. Gratama, Emeryville, Calif., to the author, July 28, 1954.

82. N. W. Thompson interview. It should be added that Pyzel, who read the manuscript of this book with great care, had not heard of this last consideration.

83. Raymond Foss Bacon and William Allen Hamor, *The American Petroleum Industry*, Vol. II, New York, McGraw-Hill Book Company, 1916, pp. 487-9; N. W. Thompson, "The Trumble Refining Process," American Society of Mechanical Engineers *Transactions*, 1917, p. 951; David T. Day, *A Handbook of the Petroleum Industry*, Vol. II, New York, John Wiley & Sons, 1922, pp. 213-218, 385-389; Sir Boverton Redwood, *A Treatise on Petroleum*, Vol. II, London, Chas. Griffin & Company, 1922, pp. 498-500; conversation, B. Gratama, New York,

October 8, 1948; quotation from Pyzel in letter, Dr. F. W. L. Tydeman, San Francisco, to the author, July 24, 1948.

84. Interview with I. M. Hemphill, Martinez, July 17, 1947.

85. Letter, J. C. van Eck, December 23, 1953; Marquis James, *The Texaco Story*, New York, 1953, pp. 42, 60.

86. Interview with Frank Coats, Martinez, July 16, 1947; Severns interview (see note 71).

87. Van Eck letter (see note 85); interviews, G. H. van Senden, Carmel, Calif., July 23, 1947, and Norman Ream, Wilmington, Calif., August 13, 1947. Ream worked at the Rodeo plant.

88. Van Senden interview; also interview with James H. Doolan, Martinez, July 16, 1947. Doolan worked at the Capitol refinery.

89. Conversation, F. E. Rehm, New York, August 13, 1948; N. W. Thompson interview; Royal Dutch Company Annual Report, 1915.

90. Reports Read at Board Meeting, Shell Company of California, April 18, 1916, p. 8; August 30, 1916, p. 7. Hereafter referred to as "Directors Report(s), San Francisco."

91. Dr. L. Edeleanu, "The Refining Process with Liquid Sulphur Dioxide," *Journal* of the Institution of Petroleum Technologists, Vol. 18, p. 900 (1932). See also Bacon and Hamor, *op. cit.*; *The Science of Petroleum*; and *The Petroleum Handbook*, London, The Shell Petroleum Company, Ltd., 1948, pp. 183-187.

92. Interview, P. E. Foster, Houston, April 14, 1948; payroll, Martinez refinery, August 15, 1916; interview, R. C. Roberts, Elgin, Ill., April 24, 1948; Van Senden interview.

93. Interview, E. R. Farley, San Francisco, July 10, 1947; Directors Report, San Francisco, January 25, 1916, p. 3, confirms this and notes that Northern division contracts had been cancelled because of the unavailability of the company's tanker, the *Silver Shell*.

94. Gallagher interview.

95. E. L. Miller interview; minute books of the Gold Shell Steamship Company, Silver Shell Steamship Company, and Pearl Shell Steamship

Company; letter, J. C. van Eck, December 23, 1953.

96. E. L. Miller interview; Directors Report, San Francisco, January 25, 1916, pp. 5-6; Royal Dutch Company Annual Report, 1916; Directors Reports, San Francisco, February 29, 1916, p. 8; July 26, 1916, p. 6; September 26, 1916, p. 9.

97. E. L. Miller interview; Royal Dutch Company Annual Report, 1919; minutes, Silver Shell Steamship Company, July, 1921; interview, W. P. O'Malley, New York, August 30, 1948; minutes, Silver Shell Steamship Company, April, 1928. All three companies were formally dissolved October 30, 1929.

98. Van Senden interview; pipe line figures from Royal Dutch Company Annual Report, 1918.

99. Redwood, *op. cit.*, Vol. II, p. 689; P. G. A. Smith, *The Shell That Hit Germany Hardest*, London, Shell Marketing Company, Ltd., 1919.

100. P. G. A. Smith, *op. cit.*

101. Memorandum, Martinez Refinery to Head Office Manufacturing Department, April 7, 1949; Severns interview.

102. Interviews with Pyzel and N. W. Thompson.

103. Report, "Function of the Service and Employment Department, Martinez Refinery, Shell Company of California," Martinez, June 6, 1921; Van Senden interview.

104. *Id.*, p. 7.

105. McDuffie interview (note 45); dates from diary kept by Stanley W. Duhig, who kindly made extracts available to the author.

106. Letter, S. W. Duhig to the author, January 23, 1954.

107. Manuscript history, "Labor Relations and Contract Negotiations," Shell Oil Company, San Francisco, 1947.

108. Price, Waterhouse & Co. audit; acreage of Guardian property from Royal Dutch Annual Report, 1915, other details from conversation with F. E. Rehm, New York, August 13, 1948.

109. Enclosure with letter, B. H. van der Linden to John R. Suman, New York, November 30, 1954.

110. Monograph on Shell Holdings in Coalinga Field, by B. H. van der Linden and D. Nolan, June 1919, quoted in attachment to Van der Linden letter to Suman, *supra*.

111. Letter from E. W. Swanson, Oil & Gas Division, Department of the Interior, published in American Petroleum Institute *Quarterly*, July, 1948.

112. Quotation in W. W. Orcutt, "Reminiscences of Early Oil Development in California," *Bulletin* of Union Oil Company of California, Los Angeles, November and December 1923; other information from "A Contribution to California Oil and Gas History," by Walter Stalder in *California Oil World*, November 12, 1941; Annual Report, California Petroleum Company, Philadelphia, 1866, copy furnished by courtesy of Paul Paine, Los Angeles. This company was one of the three organized by Scott.

113. Stalder, *loc. cit.*; Orcutt, *loc. cit.*

114. Interview, B. H. van der Linden, New York, May 22, 1947; account by Ralph B. Lloyd in *Ventura County Star-Free Press*, Ventura, Calif., September 12, 1946.

115. Manuscript history of Ventura field from files in Shell's Ventura office.

116. Quotations and other Lloyd material from Lloyd, *loc. cit.*

117. B. H. van der Linden, MS. history, "Ventura," prepared summer 1952; Van der Linden interviews; interview, F. E. Rehm, San Francisco, September 19, 1947; letter, B. H. van der Linden to the author, July 15, 1954. Actual acreage of leases totalled 12,580.29 acres.

118. Interview, C. C. Kifer, Long Beach, California, August 20, 1947.

119. Manuscript history (see note 115); Kifer interview.

120. Kifer interview.

121. *Id.*

122. Interview with Russ Harman, Ventura, August 19, 1947.

123. Manuscript history (note 115).

124. Interview, Charles Hansen, Ventura, August 19, 1947.

125. Van der Linden, March, 1950.

126. Manuscript history; Van der Linden MS.; letter, W. L. Hobro, Los Angeles, to the author, December 28, 1951; Directors Report, San Francisco, September 30, 1919.

127. Manuscript history; Van der Linden

MS.; letter, Dr. J. Th. Erb, The Hague, to Deterding, London, August 2, 1924. Both Dr. Erb and F. A. A. van Gogh, head geologist at The Hague, advised against the pro-

posed sale. The Hartman lease was quit-claimed by Shell, October 27, 1925. (Hobro letter, note 126, and Directors Reports, San Francisco, October 20 and November 17, 1925.)

CHAPTER IV

An Investment in Oklahoma (pages 113 to 170)

1. C. C. Rister, *Oil! Titan of the Southwest*, Norman, University of Oklahoma Press, 1949. The general boom atmosphere of early Oklahoma oildom is well presented in C. B. Glasscock, *Then Came Oil, the Story of the Last Frontier*, Indianapolis, The Bobbs-Merrill Company, 1938. A good short account is "Oklahoma, the State That Oil Built," an article by Russell Hogin in the July 1947 issue of American Petroleum Institute *Quarterly* and republished as a pamphlet. An account of the large fields only is given in Gerald Forbes, *Flush Production*, Norman, University of Oklahoma Press, 1942. For other background material, see note 17 below. The best account of the Texas oil fields is C. A. Warner's *Texas Oil and Gas Since 1543*, Houston, Gulf Publishing Company, 1939.

2. All information in this paragraph from Rister, *op. cit.*

3. All information about these preliminary ventures from Gerretson, *History of the Royal Dutch*, Vol. III. (See Chapter II, note 1, for full title.)

4. P. Kruisheer, "Report Respecting Oil Prospects and the Oil Industry in Oklahoma and Indian Territory," The Hague, November 10, 1909.

5. E. DeGolyer, Dallas, to the author, May 27, 1954.

6. Royal Dutch Company Annual Reports, 1920, 1929, 1935; R. J. Forbes.

7. Prospectus, The 's-Gravenhage Association, issued in June 1912. It is reprinted in full in Gerretson, *op. cit.*, Vol. III, pp. 920-924.

8. Royal Dutch Company Annual Report, 1913, p. 7; Prospectus (see note 7).

9. Gerretson, *op. cit.*, Vol. III.

10. *Ibid.*

11. Interview, J. H. Harvey, Tulsa, April 20, 1948. Details of the composition of the party were given by Harvey in a letter to J. A. Abbott, May 12, 1948.

12. Letter from Abrahams at Tulsa Hotel, Tulsa, to Deterding in London, July 28, 1912.

13. Cable, Levering, Tulsa, to Deterding, August 22, 1912.

14. Production is given in *Oil & Gas Journal*, December 5, 1912, p. 3; *Roxoleum*, January 1918, locates the leases and gives the full list of names.

15. *Oil & Gas Journal*, December 5, 1912, p. 3, gives locations of the properties; production and acreage figures from contract of September 4, 1912, between Louis C. Sands and Abrahams, quoted in minutes of first meeting, Roxana Petroleum Company of Oklahoma, October 1, 1912; details of purchase money given in Price, Waterhouse & Co., audit report, 1912.

16. Letter, J. H. Harvey, Tulsa, to the author, August 24, 1951.

17. T. D. Lyons, "Roxana," *The Commonweal*, New York, August 3, 1945, p. 380. Lyons wrote with a great deal of grace and charm, and other articles of his in the same publication (December 8, 1944, p. 190 ff.; March 23, 1945, p. 561 ff.; May 13, 1945, p. 114 ff.; August 10, 1945, p. 401 ff.; October 26, 1945, p. 47 ff.; February 8, 1946, p. 426 ff.; June 21, 1946, p. 235 ff.) give the reader a graphic idea of the Oklahoma oil business, 1905-1915. The August 10, 1945, article is also on the subject of Roxana.

18. *National Petroleum News*, October 1912, p. 21.

19. Typical of such reports was a page-long story in *Oil & Gas Journal*,

February 13, 1913, p. 2, headed "The Roxana - Waters - Pierce Refinery," and beginning "The Roxana Petroleum Company, disguised under the name of the Waters-Pierce Oil Company, has bought . . . ."

20. Robert T. Swaine, *The Cravath Firm and Its Predecessors, 1819–1948*, Vol. II, New York, 1948, pp. 75-76.

21. Roxana of Oklahoma, minutes, October 14, 1913, ratified by stockholders, October 22, 1913; minutes, June 9, 1914, October 1, 1912; Royal Dutch Company Annual Report, 1913, p. 7.

22. J. H. Harvey, Tulsa, in letter to J. A. Abbott, May 12, 1948; conversation between Harvey and the author, Tulsa, June 14, 1954.

23. "When Mrs. Abrahams and I chose the name of the Company, neither of us had any definite name in mind. Our idea was to pick a short, unusual name, whose meaning had some significance to what we were doing. Together we started checking the list of names in the back of the dictionary we had then in the office. The meaning given for Roxana was the dawn of a new day. We thought the arrival of Shell in the Mid-Continent, and the beginning of the purchase of production and leases, on a large scale, by a major interest, was such a new day for the independent interests." J. H. Harvey, Tulsa, in a letter to J. A. Abbott, May 12, 1948.

24. Deterding to Hugo Loudon, December 13, 1912.

25. Interview with Carl Barker, New York, April 3, 1951.

26. Interview, Edward Hepner, San Francisco, July 9, 1947; also much in evidence in the early correspondence of Luykx to Deterding.

27. *Oil & Gas Journal*, May 14, 1914.

28. *Ibid.*

29. *Oil & Gas Journal*, May 11, 1911.

30. Deterding to W. A. J. M. van Waterschoot van der Gracht, Tulsa, and Richard Airey, New York, January 13, 1919.

31. Craig Thompson, *Since Spindletop*, Pittsburgh, 1951, pp. 10-11.

32. Gerretson, *op. cit.*, Vol. III, pp. 810-814; and letter, C. S. Gulbenkian to Deterding, May 4, 1913, quoted by Gerretson. Gulbenkian was friendly with Deterding during these years and took a leading part in the Gulf negotiations.

33. Deterding to Van der Gracht, Tulsa, March 25, 1916.

34. Interview, Richard A. Conkling, Oklahoma City, April 21, 1948; and letter, Conkling to the author, January 19, 1952. Conkling was Roxana's chief geologist from January 1, 1915 to June 1, 1922; for some years prior to his death in 1952, he was an independent consulting geologist.

35. Article on Cushing from Oil City, Pa., *Derrick*, reprinted in *Wall Street Journal*, April 27, 1914.

36. Van H. Manning, *Yearbook of the Bureau of Mines*, Bulletin 141, Washington, 1916, pp. 122-124, quoted in George Ward Stocking, *The Oil Industry and the Competitive System: A Study in Waste*, Boston, Houghton Mifflin Co., 1925, pp. 178-179.

37. Rister, *op. cit.*, pp. 123-124, and calculations by the author.

38. There was also a Hecla Oil Company involved in the deal, its name manufactured from the initial letters of the names of five Devonian officials. Although its function has now been forgotten, it is reasonable to assume it was some sort of subsidiary of the Devonian company. This information from L. C. Ritts, long-time president of Devonian, in a letter from J. H. Harvey, Tulsa, to the author, January 23, 1952.

39. "The Yarhola Leases," article in *Roxoleum*, Roxana house organ published at Tulsa, February 1918, pp. 16-17; James McIntyre, "When Cushing Dominated the Industry," *Oil & Gas Journal*, November 11, 1926, pp. 32, 84; *Oil & Gas Journal*, May 20, 1915, p. 24.

40. "Roxana Petroleum Company of Oklahoma: Report on the Financial History of the Company from Date of Inception to December 31, 1916," Price, Waterhouse & Co., St. Louis, April 25, 1917; "A History of Devonian Oil Company, 1891–1941," quoted by J. H. Harvey, Tulsa, in letter to J. A. Abbott, May 12, 1948; *Roxoleum*, February 1918.

41. Letter, Van der Gracht, Tulsa, to

C. M. Pleyte, The Hague, July 3, 1915.

42. *Id.*

43. T. D. Lyons, "Roxana," in *The Commonweal*, August 10, 1945, p. 401-2.

44. *Oil & Gas Journal*, July 15, 1915, p. 2; letter, Van der Gracht to Pleyte, July 3, 1915; interview, J. W. Bates, Tulsa, April 20, 1948. Bates was manager of Roxana's "field department" (production) from 1915 until the end of 1925.

45. Digests of correspondence in production department files, B.P.M. head office, The Hague; letter, Van der Gracht to C. M. Pleyte, The Hague, November 11, 1915.

46. Conkling interview (note 34).

47. Palmer's early well is mentioned in Gerald Forbes, *op. cit.*, p. 12, and Rister, *op. cit.*, p. 125.

48. Roy M. Johnson, Editor, *Oklahoma History South of the Canadian*, 3 vols., Chicago, S. S. Clarke Publishing Co., 1925, Vol. III, pp. 359, 363.

49. Rister, *op. cit.*, p. 128.

50. Material on Mackay from obituary, New York *Times*, May 25, 1936, p. 19, London *Times*, May 25, 1936, p. 16, and June 3, 1936, p. 16A; Harmsworth obituary, London *Times*, January 20, 1937, p. 16.

51. Information on Watchorn from his obituary, New York *Times*, April 15, 1944, p. 11; Frank J. Taylor and Earl M. Welty, *Black Bonanza*, New York, Whittlesey House, 1950, pp. 165-168; letter, Watchorn to Van der Gracht, July 16, 1915.

52. Watchorn letter, *supra*.

53. Van der Gracht, Tulsa, to C. M. Pleyte, The Hague, November 11, 1915.

54. Royal Dutch Company Annual Reports, 1915 and 1916.

55. Minutes, directors' meeting, Roxana Petroleum Company of Oklahoma, July 3, 1916.

56. Page 107, *A History of the Shell (Roxana) Petroleum Corporation*, a 194-page manuscript by the late Walter F. Jones, St. Louis, January 5, 1932. Jones had been manager of the auditing department and was, at the time he wrote this, manager of the St. Louis personnel department and editor of *The Shell Globe* (forerunner of the present *Shell News*)

which he had started the year before. Unfortunately, his book provides little information not available elsewhere, for it was based on corporate minutes, accounting department records, and the old *Roxoleum*, all of which were, of course, thoroughly canvassed in the preparation of the present volume.

57. Minutes, directors' meeting, Roxana Petroleum Company of Oklahoma, July 29, 1916; memorandum, August 1, 1916, London office; conversation, John H. Harvey, Tulsa, June 14, 1954; interview, S. C. Carney, Tulsa, April 19, 1948.

58. Agreement June 10, 1915, with White & Sinclair, in production department files, The Hague; *Oil & Gas Journal*, January 14, 1915, p. 10.

59. Letters, Deterding to Van der Gracht, January 17, 1916, and Van der Gracht to Airey, May 31, 1916; interviews, D. Pyzel, San Francisco, July 24, August 7, September 9 and September 16, 1947.

60. Minutes, New Orleans Refining Co., June 24, 1916; letter, Airey to Luykx, April 29, 1916; title abstract memorandum, Geo. C. Schoenberger, Jr., Houston, to C. S. Gentry, St. Louis, February 20, 1936; letters, Deterding to Van der Gracht, January 17, 1916, and Airey to Deterding, April 29, 1916; minutes, New Orleans Refining Co., June 24, 1916.

61. Construction details from letters, Luykx to Deterding, November 15 and December 11, 1916; interview, Ralph B. High, Houston, December 9, 1947.

62. Letter, Van der Gracht to Airey, May 31, 1916.

63. "Oil Pipe Lines of the Yarhola Pipe Line Company," 20-page booklet, Sanderson & Porter, New York (no date), p. 4.

64. *Roxoleum*, Tulsa, May 1918, p. 6; Tulsa *Daily World*, April 8, 1917; Royal Dutch Annual Report, 1917, p. 18; Price, Waterhouse & Co. audit, 1917; interviews, Dr. F. W. L. Tydeman, San Francisco, August 4, September 8, September 10, 1947.

65. P. G. A. Smith, *The Shell That Hit Germany Hardest*, London, Shell Marketing Co., 1919, p. 39.

66. Airey obituary, *Shell Magazine*, Lon-

don, February 1948, p. 37; Smith, *op. cit.*

67. Conversation, A. S. Pentland, New York, March 3, 1950.

68. Interview, R. B. High, Houston, December 9, 1947; figures from Tydeman interview.

69. Letters, Airey to Deterding, September 27 and October 25, 1917; Tydeman interview.

70. *Roxoleum,* November 1918, p. 1; other details from Sanderson & Porter booklet (note 63).

71. Sanderson & Porter book, *supra; Roxoleum,* Tulsa, November 1918, p. 1; correspondence, F. B. Simms, Laguna Beach, Calif., June 1954.

72. Telegram, Van der Gracht to Deterding, July 10, 1918; dates and information on crossing break from a business diary kept during 1918–1919 by Dr. F. W. L. Tydeman.

73. Letter, Deterding to Van der Gracht, July 15, 1918; Royal Dutch Company Annual Reports, 1918–1920.

74. *Roxoleum,* September 1918, pp. 2-4; Tydeman interviews.

75. Figures furnished by Dr. Tydeman from records in his possession; "Wood River—Shell's Largest Refinery," *Shell Globe,* St. Louis, July-August 1932, pp. 4-7; letter, A. S. Pentland, Rockford, Illinois, to the author, February 5, 1950.

76. Letter, Deterding to Van der Gracht and Airey, August 8, 1918.

77. Interview, R. B. High, Houston, December 9, 1947; Royal Dutch Company Annual Report, 1919, p. 19.

78. This was "a real Shell 'first,'" according to letter of R. B. High to the author, July 1, 1948.

79. Later biographical material on Luykx kindly furnished by A. E. Watts, vice president, Sinclair Oil Corporation; quotation is from his memorandum of January 8, 1952.

80. Information on Lydon from interview, J. W. Watson, San Francisco, September 11, 1947, and *Shell Globe,* St. Louis, May–June 1933, p. 3.

81. "President's Letter to Employees," pages 3-4, *Roxoleum,* Tulsa, February 1918.

82. *Roxoleum,* January 1919, p. 8, August 1919, p. 12, and September 1919, inside front cover. Garrett was still signing as sales manager on September 20, 1919, so Woodruff's appointment probably came late in September. Woodruff later became the company's first vice president in charge of sales, March 1928–May 1929. He resigned his position with Roxana and later served in the same capacity with the Globe Oil & Refining Co. of Chicago. A letter, Garrett to Airey, March 11, 1919, shows that the sales manager started reporting to Tulsa at this time.

83. Information from contract, May 17, 1918, between Wm. S. Barnickel and the Tret-O-lite Corporation; letter from Edward Hepner to the author, March 3, 1948.

84. Report to Van der Gracht by Tydeman, May 16, 1918, on trial run at Healdton; *Roxoleum,* December 1918, p. 7; Jones MS. history (see note 56); letters, Dr. F. W. L. Tydeman to the author, March 23 and June 25, 1948.

85. Chart, "Wages, Hours, and Weekly Earnings of Employees . . . [of] 20 Major Oil Companies, 1914–1938," figures gathered from American Petroleum Institute special survey and submitted before hearings of the Temporary National Economic Committee, Washington, October 9–16, 1939; reproduced in *Petroleum Almanac,* National Industrial Conference Board, New York, 1946, p. 200.

86. Royal Dutch Company Annual Report for 1912, p. 16.

87. *Roxoleum,* November 1918, p. 5.

88. Their names are listed on page 10, *Roxoleum,* August 1919.

89. Letter by Van der Gracht, printed in *Roxoleum,* February 1918, p. 13.

90. Deterding to Van der Gracht, April 17, 1916.

91. Letter, Deterding to Van der Gracht and Airey, March 18, 1918.

92. *Roxoleum,* August 1919, p. 21.

93. Royal Dutch Company Annual Report, 1919.

94. Production department files, The Hague.

95. Avery D. Andrews, Semi-Monthly Report, October 31, 1921, p. 217.

96. *Roxoleum,* October 1918, p. 1; Royal Dutch Company Annual Report,

1918; interview, E. C. Peet, New York, February 27, 1948.

97. *Roxoleum,* January 1919; Royal Dutch Company Annual Report, 1919.

98. Report on Yarhola Absorption Plant by S. C. Carney, April 5, 1921.

99. Report by Van der Gracht, 1915; Rister, *op. cit.,* p. 306, gives an account of this well. On the basis of information from F. Julius Fohs, Rister blames failure of the well on Van der Gracht's selection of the drilling site.

100. Article, "The Texas Fields," *Roxoleum,* June 1918, p. 2; details and names from John G. Burtt, Los Angeles, in letter to the author, March 19, 1952, and letter, John R. Suman, New York, to the author, April 30, 1954.

101. Interview, Richard A. Conkling, Oklahoma City, April 21, 1948; *Roxoleum,* June 1918, p. 2.

102. *Roxoloeum,* May 1919, p. 17, and February 1920, p. 11; possibly this is the early East Texas well referred to in the paragraphs immediately preceding.

103. Conkling interview.

104. *Roxoleum,* January 1920; Production files, The Hague.

105. Avery D. Andrews, New York, Semi-Monthly Reports during 1920; Hague production files; Rister, *op. cit.,* pp. 215-216.

106. Hague production files; letter, John G. Burtt, Los Angeles, to the author, March 19, 1952.

107. Interviews, John G. Burtt, Los Angeles, August 22 and 25, 1947, and J. W. Bates, Tulsa, April 20, 1948.

108. Letter, H. H. Parker, treasurer of Roxana in Tulsa, to Herman Witkamp, Cheyenne, June 16, 1917; interview, Max W. Ball, Washington, May 18, 1948; correspondence between Tulsa and Cheyenne offices, 1917-1918.

109. *Roxoleum,* July 1918, p. 2-3.

110. Ball interview; *Roxoleum,* February 1918, p. 16, January 1920, p. 18, and December 1919, p. 15, which is source of quotation.

111. Letters, Deterding to Van der Gracht and Airey, July 18, 1918; Deterding to H. Colijn, September 24, 1918.

112. Balance sheet, Matador Petroleum Company, December 31, 1921; Ball interview; Andrews, Semi-Monthly Report, April 30, 1921, p. 85, and May 15, 1921.

113. Andrews, *op. cit.,* May 15 and July 15, 1921; Report Presented at Meeting of the Board of Directors, Shell Company of California, San Francisco, January 31, 1922, p. 14.

114. Letter, A. T. Schwennesen, Istanbul, Turkey, to the author, July 21, 1948.

115. Letter, Colijn to Van der Gracht, March 11, 1921; appraisal of Van der Gracht from Max Ball.

116. Conkling wrote up this trip through the Gulf and Mid-Continent in highly entertaining fashion, with pictures, in *Roxoleum,* January 1920, pp. 9-10.

117. E. L. DeGolyer, "How Men Find Oil," *Fortune,* August 1947, p. 97.

118. Interview, J. C. van Eck, New York, May 6, 1947.

119. Information on the issue of the New York shares from Royal Dutch Company Annual Report, 1916, pp. 9-12, and 1917 report, p. 32; details of the issue in New York from *Standard Corporation Records,* New York, December 1916, pp. 84-85; *Moody's Manual of Industrials,* 1950, p. 2109; New York Stock Exchange Application for Listing, No. A-15178, July 1, 1954, and press releases issued by New York Stock Exchange under date of July 20, 1954.

120. Correspondence of T. F. Lydon, secretary, to firms doing business with Roxana indicates that the actual name change took place on February 1, 1920, although the company's account books show that the change was made retroactive to October 1, 1919. *Roxoleum* for February 1920 was the first issue to carry the new name.

121. "Memorandum Re Midcontinent Organisation," London, March 5, 1919.

CHAPTER V

A Springboard to Prominence (pages 171 to 264)

1. Deterding to Van der Gracht, February 15, 1916.
2. Interview, Dr. W. van Holst Pellekaan, Beverly Hills, California, August 27, 1947; interview, George A. Macready, Los Angeles, August 25, 1947.
3. H. E. Winter, "Santa Fe Springs," in *Geologic Formations and Economic Development of the Oil and Gas Fields of California*, San Francisco, State Division of Mines, Department of Natural Resources, State of California, 1943, Bulletin 118, p. 343. Hereafter called "Bulletin 118."
4. Letters to the author from Dr. E. F. Davis, Los Angeles, July 2, 1954, and W. L. Hobro and J. G. Burtt, Los Angeles, July 2, 1954; Avery D. Andrews, Semi-Monthly Review No. 9, New York, May 15, 1921; Harry P. Stolz, "Long Beach Oil Field," p. 320 ff. of Bulletin 118.
5. Details of well from Andrews, *loc. cit.*
6. Paul Paine, Los Angeles, to the author, June 1954.
7. Recalled by C. H. Cupernell, a fireman in the Alamitos No. 1 crew, *Oil*, Los Angeles, June 20, 1946, p. 28.
8. Information in this paragraph from interview, W. E. Feistner, Long Beach, August 21, 1947.
9. Feistner, above; interview, E. E. Tiffany, Long Beach, August 20, 1947; letter, Stanley W. Duhig, Mamaroneck, N. Y., to the author, June 15, 1954.
10. Tiffany interview.
11. C. C. Kifer, Long Beach, a drilling foreman at the time, recalled several such incidents in an interview, August 20, 1947.
12. Stolz, *loc. cit.* (see note 4); interviews, W. C. McDuffie, Montecito, California, August 30, 1947, Paul Paine, Corona del Mar, California, September 1, 1947, and B. H. van der Linden, New York.
13. M. H. Soyster and Martin Van Couvering, "The Long Beach Oilfield of California," *Petroleum Times*, London, July 29, 1922, p. 158.
14. Interview, William Shepherd, Jr., Los Angeles, August 14, 1947.
15. Kifer interview; Martin Van Couvering, "Signal Hill Field Stages Comeback," *Oil & Gas Journal*, December 8, 1927, pp. 34 and 147; *Summary of Operations of California Oil Fields*, State Oil & Gas Supervisor of California, Vol. 9, No. 4, p. 16. Peak daily production came on October 24, 1923, when Signal Hill produced 259,000 barrels.
16. Drilling report, Nesa No. 1, courtesy W. L. Hobro, Los Angeles, June 11, 1954.
17. Feistner and Tiffany interviews; clippings preserved by Tiffany; and article "Saga of Signal Hill," by Martin Van Couvering, *Oil*, Los Angeles, June 20, 1946, p. 7 ff.
18. Interview with John G. Burtt, Los Angeles, August 22 and 25, 1947, and later correspondence.
19. Burtt interview; *Petroleum Facts and Figures*, 9th Ed., New York, American Petroleum Institute, 1951, p. 363.
20. Feistner interview; T. E. Swigart, Houston, to the author, July 12, 1954.
21. Feistner interview; interview, Fred B. Simms, Kernville, California, September 2, 1947; figures from Reports Read to the Board of Directors, Shell Company of California (hereafter referred to as "Directors Report(s), San Francisco"), 1922–1928.
22. *Oil*, Los Angeles, June 20, 1946, p. 14; *Petroleum Times*, London, August 4, 1923, p. 170; J. C. Van Eck, Directors Report, San Francisco, September 26, 1922.
23. Shell Union Annual Report, 1922; Directors Report, Shell Company of California, January 30, 1923; Simms interview; and interview, Erle P. Severns, Oakland, California, September 4, 1947.
24. Directors Report, San Francisco, January 30, 1923, p. 12; Shell Union Annual Reports, 1923 and 1925; interview, W. L. Hobro, Los Angeles, August 12, 1947.
25. Interview, W. Fred Knief, Ventura,

August 18, 1947; also Feistner interview.

26. Directors Report, San Francisco, December 26, 1923; Hobro interview; compilation from directors' reports for the year 1925.

27. Directors Reports, San Francisco, for months in question; Eugene L. Davis, "Torrance Oil Field," p. 298 ff., Bulletin 118; Shepherd interview.

28. Directors Reports, San Francisco, December 26, 1922, April 28, 1925, November 17, 1925, and June 15, 1926; letter, Dr. E. F. Davis, Los Angeles, to the author, July 2, 1954.

29. Glenn H. Bowes, "Seal Beach Oil Field," p. 325, Bulletin 118; letter, Paul Paine, Los Angeles, to the author, June 26, 1954.

30. Herschel L. Driver, "Inglewood Oil Field," pp. 306-309, Bulletin 118; Directors Report, San Francisco, May 26, 1925; compilation made from these reports for 1925; and Kifer interview.

31. Directors Reports, San Francisco, October 31 and December 26, 1922; March 27, 1923.

32. *Ibid.;* interviews, R. S. Tulin, Los Angeles and San Francisco, August 28 and September 10, 1947.

33. Ventura figures from brief manuscript history of Ventura field, in files of Shell's Ventura production office.

34. *Roxoleum,* April-May, 1920, p. 20; interview, A. R. May, Los Angeles, August 15, 1947; Directors Reports, San Francisco, January 31, March 28, and November 28, 1922.

35. May interview and interview with Eli Pedersen, Bakersfield, September 2, 1947; letter, Paul Paine, Los Angeles, to the author, June 26, 1954.

36. Information on Marland from John Joseph Mathews, *Life and Death of an Oilman, The Career of E. W. Marland,* Norman, University of Oklahoma Press, 1951; *Oil and Gas Development by the National Oil Scouts Association of America, Yearbook 1936,* n.p., section on Osage County (prepared by Lee A. Adams); "Continental Oil," *Fortune,* June 1939, p. 71 ff.; New York *Times,* October 4, 1941, p. 15, Marland obituary. Also other sources,

chiefly oil trade papers, mentioned in subsequent citations.

37. Marland's estimate (no doubt over-optimistic) in a letter to Kessler, May 6, 1922.

38. Marland balance sheet from *Marland Oils,* a company house organ published at Ponca City, issue of August 1921, pp. 8-11.

39. H. W. Penterman, Tulsa, to the author, May 25, 1953; copy of original agreement, furnished by Mr. Penterman; *Oil & Gas Journal,* March 25, 1921, p. 48.

40. Carl Coke Rister, *Oil! Titan of the Southwest,* Norman, University of Oklahoma Press, 1949, pp. 202-3.

41. W. F. Jones, *A History of the Shell (Roxana) Petroleum Corporation,* St. Louis, January 5, 1932, MS., pp. 135-136.

42. Letters, H. W. Penterman, Tulsa, to the author, February 29, 1952, and May 25, 1953.

43. Wallace Davis, "The Osages and Their Oil," *Oil Weekly,* December 21, 1928, p. 88 ff.

44. Figures on Tonkawa from *Marland Oils,* August 1921, p. 13; Rister, *op. cit.,* p. 203; and interview, Walter Roschke, St. Louis, April 22, 1948. Roschke was comptroller of the Comar Oil Company.

45. Ralph T. Baker, "The Greatest High Grade Oil Field," *Oil & Gas Journal,* February 22, 1923, p. 14; Rister, *op. cit.,* p. 205.

46. C. D. Lockwood, "Tonkawa Field Production by Leases," *Oil & Gas Journal,* October 15, 1925, pp. 92-94.

47. Interview, F. W. Woods, New York, May 28, 1948; C. D. Lockwood, "Braman Field to be Developed Slowly," *Oil & Gas Journal,* October 15, 1925; Davis, *loc. cit.* (note 43); Jones MS. history, p. 172.

48. Completed questionnaire submitted by Shell Union Oil Corporation to U. S. Department of Justice, June 1928.

49. Figures on number of wells and annual production in this and preceding paragraph from Department of Justice questionnaire, *supra.*

50. B. L. Ryan, "A History of Shell Oil Company's Activities in West Texas and New Mexico," Houston, August 1948, MS., p. 1; Committee on

Stock List, New York Stock Exchange, application No. A-6150, October 17, 1923; Jones, MS. history, p. 172; Rister, *op. cit.*, p. 178; C. A. Warner, *Texas Oil and Gas Since 1543*, Houston, Gulf Publishing Company, 1939, p. 168; Department of Justice questionnaire.

51. Ryan, MS. history, p. 2; conversation, L. G. Christie, New York, June 5, 1956.

52. Andrews' reports for May 15, June 15, and August 31, 1921; Department of Justice questionnaire.

53. *Id.;* calculations the author's.

54. Interview, O. D. Story, Houston, December 11, 1947. Story, then a youngster just out of school, went to Smackover to work in Roxana's early office there; got into purchasing work; went to the Dallas office at the beginning of 1925, and held various purchasing department positions in Dallas and later in the Houston office. He was in charge of Shell's oil field purchasing work in the Southwest at the time of his death, August 27, 1950.

55. Department of Justice questionnaire; *Petroleum Facts and Figures*, Tenth Edition, 1952, p. 96.

56. Department of Justice questionnaire; National Oil Scouts Yearbook, 1936, p. 266.

57. *Brass Tacks* magazine, issue not given, quoted by Mathews, *op. cit.* (see note 36).

58. E. L. DeGolyer, "Historical Notes on the Techniques of Prospecting for Petroleum," in *The Science of Petroleum*, Vol. I, London, Oxford University Press, 1938, pp. 268-275.

59. DeGolyer, *loc. cit.;* supporting correspondence is in old Roxana files.

60. DeGolyer, *loc. cit.;* Donald C. Barton, "Petroleum Geophysics," in *The Science of Petroleum*, Vol. I, p. 319 ff; letter, Prof. R. J. Forbes, Amsterdam, to the author, December 18, 1951.

61. Forbes, *supra;* letter of instructions, Dr. J. Erb to F. B. Plummer, The Hague, April 10, 1922; interviews, L. G. Christie, New York, March 28, 1951, and Walle Merritt, Los Angeles, August 28, 1947. Merritt was manager of Shell's land department on the Pacific Coast from 1929 until his retirement in 1947.

62. Christie interview; Department of Justice questionnaire.

63. E. L. DeGolyer, "How Men Find Oil," *Fortune*, August 1949, p. 100.

64. DeGolyer in *The Science of Petroleum;* Barton, *loc. cit.*

65. DeGolyer, "How Men Find Oil"; letter, E. DeGolyer, Dallas, to the author, September 2, 1954; Barton, *loc cit.*

66. DeGolyer, *The Science of Petroleum;* Barton, *loc cit.*

67. Christie interview; E. L. DeGolyer, "The Development of the Art of Prospecting," Brackett Lecture, Princeton University, December 12, 1939, published as a booklet by Princeton University Press, 1940, pp. 27-28.

68. Interview, Carl E. Lee, Houston, April 13, 1948 (Lee was a drilling superintendent in the Gulf Coast area at the time); Warner, *op. cit.*, pp. 206, 218; Ralph Arnold and William J. Kemnitzer, *Petroleum in the United States and Possessions*, New York, Harper & Brothers, 1931, p. 562; Merritt interview.

69. Conversation, L. G. Christie, New York, June 5, 1956.

70. Letter, G. E. Léonardon, Dallas, to Dr. W. van Holst Pellekaan, July 16, 1927 (Léonardon was field manager of the Schlumbergers' company, Société de Prospection Électrique); interview, T. E. Swigart, Houston, December 11, 1947.

71. Interview, General Avery D. Andrews, New York, June 24, 1952.

72. Letter, Deterding to Van der Gracht, February 5, 1916.

73. Letter, Deterding to Van der Gracht, August 28, 1918.

74. Frank J. Taylor and Earl M. Welty, *Black Bonanza*, New York, Whittlesey House, 1950, p. 165 ff.; *Oil & Gas Journal*, April 9, 1914.

75. Information courtesy of librarian, Moody's Investors' Service, New York; Taylor and Welty, *op. cit.;* listing under British Union in *Skinner's Oil and Petroleum Yearbook*, London, 1919.

76. Biographical information in this and previous paragraph from *Who's Who in America*, several editions;

Who Was Who in America, Chicago, 1942; information from old volumes of *Moody's Manual of Industrials* and *Standard Corporation Service*, supplied through courtesy of the Moody's and Standard & Poor's librarians; other details from Forsyth Wickes, who was personally acquainted with most of the Union of Delaware principals.

77. *Report of the Federal Trade Commission on Foreign Ownership in the Petroleum Industry*, Washington, Government Printing Office, February 12, 1923, pp. 70-71.

78. Conversation, Forsyth Wickes, New York, September 22, 1954; Minutes, Meeting of Board of Directors, Union Oil Company (Delaware), September 20, 1919.

79. Minutes, Union of Delaware *(supra)*.

80. Interview, Forsyth Wickes, New York, April 9, 1948.

81. *Id.*

82. Details of the offices and staff from Miss Ethel M. Scribner, New York, June 1948.

83. Deterding to Van der Gracht, January 17, 1916.

84. Minutes, Union of Delaware, October 29, 1919.

85. Minutes, Union of Delaware, January 19, January 21, and June 28, 1920.

86. Full terms of this agreement are recited in Shell Union Oil Corporation, Organization Proceedings, 1922, p. 75 ff.

87. Interviews, Miss Scribner and Forsyth Wickes; Minutes, Union of Delaware, November 17, 1920; Van Gogh's appraisal ("Union Oil Company of Delaware, Appraised as at 31st May, 1921"), p. 6, shows that Union received payment for these tankers in first five months of 1921; Board Minutes, Union of Delaware, November 15, 1920, *et seq.*

88. Minutes, Executive Committee, Union of Delaware, May 6, 1921.

89. Conversation, Forsyth Wickes, New York, September 22, 1954.

90. *Oil & Gas Journal*, March 25, 1921, p. 48.

91. Interviews, Paul Paine, Los Angeles, August 27 and September 1, 1947.

92. Van Gogh appraisal (see note 87).

93. Letter, Frederick Godber, London,

to Van der Gracht, St. Louis, September 26, 1921.

94. *Id.*

95. Letter, E. W. Marland, Ponca City, to J. B. A. Kessler, New Orleans, May 6, 1922.

96. Mathews, *op. cit.* (see note 36); *Fortune*, June 1939, p. 71 ff.

97. Cable to Union of Delaware Board, dated London, October 8, 1921, and signed by C. H. Schlacks, J. H. Brookmire, Forsyth Wickes, Colley, Paul Paine, and Henry Lockhart, Jr. (Colley was a member of Union of Delaware's auditing firm.)

98. Agreement Between Union Oil Company (Delaware) and Anglo-Saxon Petroleum Company (Ltd.), London, October 19, 1921. Full text of the agreement is printed in FTC Report (see note 77 for full title), pp. 73-78.

99. Minutes, Union of Delaware Directors, December 6, 1922; Minutes, Special Meeting of Trustees in Liquidation, Union Oil Company (Delaware), December 17, 1929.

100. Memorandum, J. C. van Eck, New York, to G. G. Biggar, January 30, 1942.

101. A good account of his career is contained in Dr. L. U. de Sitter, "In Memoriam, Mr. Dr. W. A. J. M. v. Waterschoot v. d. Gracht, D. Sc., M. E.," *Geologie en Mijnbouw*, The Hague, September-October, 1943, pp. 65-68 (in Dutch); other details can be found in *Who's Who in America*, Vol. 15 (1928-1929), p. 2106.

102. Interviews, General Avery D. Andrews, New York, September 4 and 6, 1951.

103. Letter, Deterding to Andrews, December 4, 1919.

104. Rowland & Lacy well log book, kept in ink and pencil, probably by W. E. Youle, the driller. This book was in Columbia's Brea office, and was turned over to Shell in 1922. It was made available to the author through the courtesy of W. L. Hobro of Los Angeles.

105. H. S. Botsford, "Puente Oldest Field on Coast," Los Angeles *Express*, June 23, 1921. Botsford was vice president and manager of Puente Oil Company, and this article had originally

been written by him for the May 1921 issue of *Union Oil News.*

106. E. P. Bly, "Oil Pipe Lines in California," *Oil Bulletin,* August, September, and October 1926; interview, Erle P. Severns, Oakland, California, September 4, 1947.

107. Directors Report, San Francisco, March 28, 1922; *Annual Review of California Crude Oil Production,* Conservation Committee of California Oil Producers, Los Angeles, 1951.

108. Interviews, John G. Burtt, Los Angeles, August 22 and 25, 1947.

109. *Id.;* daily production figures from Shell Union registration statement No. A-5747, New York Stock Exchange, August 1, 1922.

110. Van Gogh appraisal (see note 87); interview, Fred B. Simms, Kernville, California, September 2, 1947.

111. Jones MS., p. 157; interview, Fred W. Woods, New York, May 28, 1948. Woods joined National in 1920. He later came over to the Roxana organization, and served as secretary of Shell Union (and its successor Shell Oil Company) from 1940 until his retirement in June 1953.

112. Complete list of these companies, incorporation dates, etc., given in "Status of Subsidiaries of Central Petroleum Company," a one-sheet chart, St. Louis, December 9, 1924; Shell Union Oil Corporation, Organization Proceedings, New York, 1922, p. 98 ff.; letter, H. G. Renfro, Tulsa, to H. W. Penterman, December 23, 1953, attached to letter of same date, Penterman to the author; text of original Foster lease and list of its subsequent assignments made available through the courtesy of Penterman and Renfro, and of Herman H. Kaveler, consulting engineer, of Tulsa.

113. Contracts covering these negotiations in Shell Union Oil Corporation, Organization Proceedings, New York, 1922, pp. 75-168.

114. B. H. van der Linden, "Report on Central Petroleum Company, Oklahoma," June 30, 1922, submitted to Godber with letter of July 3, 1922; and letter, Godber, St. Louis, to Van Eck, San Francisco, July 17, 1922, which also is source of quotation.

115. Annual Report, Wolverine Petroleum Corporation, St. Louis, 1923.

116. Letter, Deterding to Van der Gracht, February 15, 1916.

117. Taylor and Welty, *op. cit.,* pp. 176-180.

118. Circular letter to the Union Oil of California stockholders, Los Angeles, October 17, 1921, and signed by twenty Los Angeles businessmen. It is reproduced verbatim on pp. 86-87 of *Report of the Federal Trade Commission on Foreign Ownership in the Petroleum Industry,* Washington, Government Printing Office, February 12, 1923.

119. Quoted at greater length by Taylor and Welty, *op. cit.,* pp. 178-180.

120. *Id.;* stock price courtesy librarian, Moody's Investors' Service, New York.

121. Memorandum, Financial Position, Shell Union Oil Corporation, August 4, 1922.

122. Senate Resolution 311, Sixty-Seventh Congress, Second Session, adopted June 29, 1922.

123. These two quotations are from Albert B. Fall's letter to Senator Lodge, dated March 21, 1921, and printed in the *Congressional Record,* April 12, 1921, pp. 166-167.

124. Avery D. Andrews, "Semi-Monthly Review," April 30, 1921, p. 89.

125. An excellent account of the Teapot Dome investigation is given in Mark Sullivan, *Our Times,* Vol. VI, New York, Charles Scribner's Sons, 1935, pp. 272-349; a briefer account will be found in Frederick Lewis Allen, *Only Yesterday,* New York, Harper & Brothers, 1931, pp. 136-149. Allen also tells of the Continental Trading Company scandal, not properly a part of the Teapot Dome case but indirectly connected with it.

126. New York *Times,* May 17, 1923, p. 1.

127. New York *Times,* March 18, 1921, p. 1; *Oil & Gas Journal,* March 22, 1923.

128. New York *Times,* March 20, 1923, p. 23.

129. *Id.,* April 18, 1923, p. 29.

130. *Id.,* May 17, 1923, p. 1.

131. *Oil & Gas Journal,* September 28, 1922, p. 84, and September 20, 1928, p. 46; Shell Union Annual Report, 1929.

132. Royal Dutch Company Annual Report, 1922, pp. 13-15.
133. This quotation from a typical Arthur Brisbane column ("Today") appearing on the front page of the New York *American,* January 19, 1928.
134. *Petroleum Times,* London, October 4, 1924, p. 526.
135. B. Silliman, Jr., "Report on the Rock Oil, or Petroleum, from Venango County, Pennsylvania," New Haven, 1855, p. 9.
136. *Id.,* p. 12.
137. Joshua Merrill's account in *The Derrick's Hand-Book of Petroleum,* Vol. I, Oil City, Pa., 1898, p. 885; U. S. Patent No. 28,246.
138. The best single summary of the thermal cracking art, particularly from a legal viewpoint, is David McKnight, Jr., *A Study of Patents on Petroleum Cracking,* Austin, University of Texas, 1938. Other important works which have been consulted in the preparation of this account are: E. Lawson Lomax, A. E. Dunstan, and F. B. Thole, "The Pyrogenesis of Hydrocarbons," paper delivered before the Seventeenth General Meeting of the Institution of Petroleum Technologists, London, November 21, 1916, and printed in the *Journal* of the Institution of Petroleum Technologists, Vol. III, pp. 36-120 (1916); Raymond F. Bacon and William Allen Hamor, *The American Petroleum Industry,* 2 volumes, New York, McGraw-Hill Book Company, 1916; Carleton Ellis and Joseph V. Meigs, *Gasoline and Other Motor Fuels,* New York, D. Van Nostrand Company, 1921 (Ellis was one of the many inventors in the field); Sir Boverton Redwood, *A Treatise on Petroleum,* 3 volumes, London, Charles Griffin & Company, 1922; David T. Day, Ed., *A Handbook of the Petroleum Industry,* 2 volumes, New York, John Wiley & Sons, 1922; Special Master's Report, U. S. v. Standard Oil Company (Indiana) et. al., in Equity No. 4131, Indianapolis, December 1, 1927 (excellent for its plain language and large clear diagrams of the early cracking processes); Russell Wiles and Horace Dawson, "Technical Reference Book to Accompany Brief of Defendant Standard Oil Company (Indiana) on the Validity of Patents," U. S. v. Standard Oil (Indiana), No. 4131, Chicago, no date, 381 pages; Roy Cross, *A Handbook of Petroleum, Asphalt and Natural Gas* (Bulletin No. 25), 832 pages, Kansas City, Mo., Kansas City Testing Laboratory, 1928 (Cross was co-inventor of the Cross process); H. S. Bell, *American Petroleum Refining,* New York, D. Van Nostrand Company, 1930 (Second Edition) and 1945 (Third Edition); Dr. W. M. Burton, "Early Days in Refinery Research," and Dr. R. E. Humphreys, "Developing First Cracking Process," in *Oil & Gas Journal,* June 2, 1927, pp. 154-158; Robert E. Wilson, "Fifteen Years of the Burton Process," *Industrial and Engineering Chemistry,* October 1928, pp. 1099-1101.
139. R. J. Forbes, "Das Bitumen in den fünfzehn Jahrhunderten vor Drake (300-1860)," *Bitumen,* Berlin, January-June, 1937.
140. William M. Burton, Address of Acceptance of the Perkin Medal of the American Chemical Society, *Journal of Industrial and Engineering Chemistry,* February 1922, pp. 162-163.
141. *Oil & Gas Journal,* August 27, 1934, p. 149.
142. Robert E. Wilson, "Pioneers in Oil Cracking," an address before the Newcomen Society, Chicago, October 29, 1946, p. 25; Burton address, *supra,* p. 163.
143. Special Master's Report, U. S. v. Standard Oil Company (Indiana), et. al., in Equity No. 4131, Indianapolis, December 1, 1927; Paul H. Giddens, *Standard Oil Company (Indiana), Oil Pioneer of the Middle West,* New York, Appleton-Century-Crofts, 1955, pp. 160-162.
144. McKnight, *op. cit.*
145. Memorandum, F. W. L. Tydeman to Van der Gracht, Tulsa, August 25, 1917; interviews, Daniel Pyzel, San Francisco, July 24, August 7, September 9, and 16, 1947.
146. Letter, Dr. F. W. L. Tydeman, San Francisco, to the author, July 24, 1948.

147. "Pioneers in Research," an official history of Universal Oil Products Company, published as a 27-page special section of *Oil & Gas Journal*, May 27, 1937.

148. Biographical sketch of C. P. Dubbs, sent with letter of H. J. Halle to J. C. van Eck, June 14, 1928.

149. Historical sketch of Universal given by Halle to the press and printed as "Development of the Dubbs Process," in *Oil & Gas Journal*, January 15, 1931; U.O.P. history (see note 147), p. U-10.

150. "Operation of Dubbs' Cracking Process Explained by Committee," report delivered at National Petroleum Association convention, *National Petroleum News*, September 24, 1919, pp. 25-26; U.O.P. history.

151. Pyzel interviews.

152. Letter, Pyzel, New York, to Van der Gracht, Tulsa, October 6, 1919.

153. Minutes, Board of Directors, Roxana Petroleum Corporation, December 29, 1919; Pyzel interviews.

154. Tydeman letter (see note 146).

155. *Id.;* interview with P. E. Foster, Houston, April 14, 1948.

156. Contract between Gasoline Products Company and Roxana, March 16, 1922; technical history of Royal Dutch-Shell, by Prof. R. J. Forbes, MS.

157. Benjamin T. Brooks, "A Brief History of Petroleum Cracking," *The Science of Petroleum*, Vol. III, London, Oxford University Press, 1938, p. 2081.

158. *Ibid.*

159. *Ibid.;* Tydeman letter.

160. Directors Report, San Francisco, September 1 and December 28, 1920; Andrews, "Semi-Monthly Review," March 15, and May 31, 1921.

161. Directors Reports, San Francisco, various dates, 1920–1921, and September 26, 1922; letter, D. Pyzel, Piedmont, Calif., to the author, December 19, 1954; McKnight, *op. cit.*

162. Directors Reports, San Francisco, May 29, 1922, and April 24, 1923.

163. Letter, D. Pyzel, Piedmont, Calif., to the author, December 19, 1954.

164. Directors Report, San Francisco, April 28, 1925, pp. 43-43A.

165. Interview, A. H. Calderwood, New York, November 30, 1954.

166. *Id;* interview, A. E. Lacomblé, San Francisco, September 11, 1947; President's Report, Shell Company of California, August 15, 1928.

167. McKnight, *op. cit.;* for a technical discussion of low-level operation, see A. L. Strout's paper "Some Developments in Commercial Cracking," delivered before the API convention, Chicago, December 4, 1929, and printed in *Petroleum Refiner*, December 1929, p. 64, ff.

168. Tydeman letter (see note 146).

169. Conversation, J. D. Metcalfe, Shell Oil Company, New York, December 5, 1952.

170. Tydeman letter.

171. Interview, A. H. Calderwood, New York, November 30, 1954.

172. Memorandum in files, dated January 1, 1929.

173. Pyzel interviews.

174. Frank A. Howard, "The Place of Cracking in Chemical Technology," *Chemical Age*, December 1922, pp. 523-525. Printed originally in *The Lamp*, Jersey company house organ, for October 1922.

175. Quoted in U.O.P. history, p. U-26.

176. McKnight, *op. cit.;* Special Master's Report (see note 143).

177. *Oil & Gas Journal*, January 15, 1931, p. 65.

178. Shell Union Oil Corporation, Executive Committee Minutes, records approval of the final terms of the settlement on November 19, 1930; U.O.P. history; recollections, Pyzel, Van Eck.

179. Pyzel interviews; interview, E. A. Martin, Shell Development Company, New York, August 11, 1948, based on information contained in corporate records.

180. Letter, C. P. Dubbs, Montecito, Calif., to the author, November 28, 1954.

181. McKnight, *op. cit.*, p. 113; Arch L. Foster, "History of Cracking Patents Shows Courts Validated Few," *National Petroleum News*, December 22, 1937, p. 19.

182. Pyzel interview.

183. Tydeman letter (see note 146).

184. U.O.P. history, p. U-16; conversations with Prof R. J. Forbes, New York, October 1951.

185. Interviews, F. M. Dull, San Francisco, June 30, 1947; Edward L. Clay, Burbank, August 26, 1947; William Shepherd, Jr., Los Angeles, August 14, 1947. Both Dull and Clay spent several years with the old Puente company.
186. Interview, George C. Rockafield, Wilmington, August 13, 1947; information also confirmed by Directors Report, Shell Company of California, April 29, 1924. Rockafield was an employee of the old Chino refinery when it was taken over by Shell; subsequently he served for many years as office manager of the Wilmington-Dominguez refinery.
187. Interview, Erle P. Severns, Oakland, September 4, 1947; written comments from D. Pyzel and G. H. van Senden; Directors Reports, San Francisco, various months of 1922 and 1923.
188. Construction at Wilmington and Mormon Island is reported upon in Directors Reports, San Francisco, January 30, March 27, April 24, May 29, October 30, and November 27, 1923; recollections, W. B. Stewart, New York.
189. Interview, J. W. Malseed, superintendent, Mormon Island Terminal, Los Angeles, August 13, 1947.
190. Roxana Petroleum Corporation, Completion Construction Report, Arkansas City Refinery, Arkansas City, Kans., March 15, 1924; contract between Arkansas City Chamber of Commerce and Roxana Petroleum Corporation, July 25, 1923.

CHAPTER VI

The Golden Era of Volume (pages 265 to 352)

1. Frederick Lewis Allen, *Only Yesterday*, New York, Harper & Brothers, 1931, p. 164.
2. *Report of the Federal Trade Commission on the Pacific Coast Petroleum Industry, Part III, Prices and Competitive Conditions*, November 28, 1921 (Washington, Government Printing Office, 1922), p. 22.
3. *Report on Prices, Profits, and Competition in the Petroleum Industry*, Federal Trade Commission, December 12, 1927 (Washington, Government Printing Office, 1928), p. 59.
4. Allen, *op. cit.*, p. 179.
5. Reprinted from *Oil Bulletin*, in *Shelling The Line*, Shell Company of California house organ, San Francisco, September 1, 1928.
6. FTC Report (see note 2).
7. Interview, E. H. Sanders, San Francisco, September 12, 1947; conversations, H. L. Curtis, New York, November 13, 1953, and George P. Thomson, San Francisco, June 2, 1954.
8. Report Presented at Meeting of the Board of Directors, Shell Company of California, San Francisco, May 29, 1922. (This series of reports referred to hereafter as "Directors Report(s), San Francisco.")
9. Letter, A. S. Pentland, Rockford, Illinois, to the author February 25, 1950. Pentland worked for the Automobile Gasoline Company from 1912 until 1929, when the company was purchased by Shell. He was the Shell marketing district manager at Rockford, Illinois, at the time of this letter.
10. FTC Report (see note 2).
11. *Ibid.*
12. *The High Cost of Gasoline and Other Petroleum Products*, Hearing of a Subcommittee of the Senate Committee on Manufacture, Senator Robert M. LaFollette (Sr.), Chairman of the Subcommittee, Washington, Government Printing Office, 1923, 2 vols.
13. Material in this and following paragraphs from an interview with Fred M. Dull, San Francisco, June 30, 1947.
14. Interviews, George P. Thomson, San Francisco, July 15, 1947, and June 2, 1954.
15. Interview, A. E. Hind, Los Angeles, August 28, 1947.

16. "Regulations Governing Operation of Shell Service Stations," two manuals of identical title, the earlier one mimeographed, the later one printed. Both are undated but internal evidence indicates 1920 and 1927. These manuals were preserved by George P. Thomson, who kindly presented them to the author.

17. Thomson interviews.

18. *Id.*

19. *Id.*

20. *The Oil Trade,* May 1926, pp. 22-25; June 1926, pp. 26-27, 60-61.

21. Sanders and Thomson interviews.

22. President's Report, Shell Oil Company, San Francisco, December 1929, p. 17. (These reports were a continuation of the series earlier called "Reports Read to Board of Directors," see note 8.)

23. Directors Report, San Francisco, September 1925; and conversation C. B. MacGlashan, San Francisco, June 1947.

24. Thomson interview; conversation, B. C. Gibson, San Francisco, July 15, 1947.

25. Interviews, E. R. Farley, San Francisco, July 3 and 10, 1947.

26. Information on dealer practices in this and succeeding two paragraphs from 1922 FTC Report (see note 2).

27. LaFollette Committee Hearings (see note 12), p. 28.

28. Information on price wars from Directors Reports, San Francisco, September 1926–May 1927.

29. Directors Report, San Francisco, June 8, 1927, p. 1.

30. Terms of both contracts given in Directors Report, San Francisco, for June 8, 1927.

31. Directors Report, San Francisco, January 19, 1926, p. 5.

32. *Id.,* April 12, 1928; President's Report, San Francisco, November 1928.

33. Directors Report, January 1928, p. 18.

34. State of California gasoline tax figures for second quarter 1928, *Shelling The Line,* September 1, 1928, p. 1.

35. President's Report, San Francisco, September 1928, p. 7.

36. *Id.,* June 14, 1928.

37. Interview, E. C. Harrison, San Francisco, July 3, 1947.

38. V. B. Guthrie, "Leasing Oil Company Stations to Operators Is Successful," *National Petroleum News,* March 20, 1929, pp. 68-74.

39. *Shelling The Line,* February 1, 1929, p. 1; President's Report, San Francisco, December 1928.

40. Interview, Earl L. Miller, San Francisco, September 17, 1947.

41. *The V. & D. Message,* Los Angeles, monthly house organ published 1929 to April 1931, when name changed to *The Message of Shell Service.* It was merged with *Shell Progress,* San Francisco, a year later.

42. Guthrie, *loc. cit.*

43. *Ibid.*

44. *Ibid.*

45. Harrison interview (note 37) and issues of *The V. & D. Message* for 1929.

46. E. L. Miller interview.

47. *Shelling The Line,* April 1, 1929, pp. 1-2; President's Reports, San Francisco, January to March 1929.

48. This and following paragraph from President's Reports, San Francisco, March to July 1929.

49. *Shelling The Line,* April 1, 1929, pp. 1-2.

50. Max K. Lakin, "Our Company Captures Utah," *Shelling The Line,* December 1, 1929, p. 5; President's Report, San Francisco, November 1929, p. 19; letter, J. W. Southworth, Detroit, to the author, November 24, 1947.

51. Interviews, David Nielsen, San Francisco, July 10, 1947, Donnell G. Fisher, Seattle, July 28, 1947, and Howard Tuckett, Seattle, July 30, 1947; Southworth letter; memorandum, Legal Department, San Francisco, March 16, 1953.

52. President's Report, San Francisco, November 1929, p. 18; interview, Homer Moore, Seattle, July 29, 1947.

53. Fisher interview.

54. *The Pipe Line,* London, October 12, 1932, p. 412. (Name changed to *The Shell Magazine* shortly thereafter.)

55. Telephone conversation, B. H. Anglin, The Texas Company, New York, September 13, 1948; details of offer in letter, Lockhart to Deterding, London, October 7, 1921.

56. Price, Waterhouse & Company audit, enclosed with letter, Godber, St.

Louis, to Adrian Corbett, London, August 3, 1922; letter, Godber to Deterding, August 30, 1922, with report covering Van Senden's and Van der Linden's appraisals; Godber, St. Louis, to Van Eck, San Francisco, July 17, 1922.

57. Shell Union Oil Corporation, Memorandum of Financial Position, August 4, 1922.

58. Interviews, A. P. Ruether, New York, May 20 and 24, 1948. Ruether left the sales department in 1931 to become manager of the crude oil supply department, a position he held until his retirement in 1954.

59. Price of new Navy 58°–60° gasoline at Mid-Continent refineries shown on summary chart published as supplement to *National Petroleum News*, March 26, 1924.

60. Letter from G. G. Woodruff, Chicago, July 23, 1948.

61. The phrase is Woodruff's, *supra*.

62. Interview, E. C. Peet, New York, February 27, 1948.

63. Minutes, Board of Directors, Roxana Petroleum Corporation, March 2, 1923; letter, Thompson, Mitchell, Thompson & Young, St. Louis, March 4, 1936, to Dillon, Read & Company, *et. al.*, New York.

64. History of the Cleveland Division, 14 pages, mimeographed, prepared by W. L. Gordon, Cleveland, 1946, based on conversations with T. W. Eysenbach, treasurer of the old Lilly White organization and later office manager of Shell's Cleveland division; memorandum, W. L. Gordon, Cleveland, to the author, February 1, 1949; correspondence and contract files, legal department, Shell Oil Company, New York.

65. History of the Cleveland Division, *supra*.

66. Walter F. Jones, *A History of the Shell (Roxana) Petroleum Corporation*, St. Louis, January 5, 1932 (manuscript), pp. 162–164; recollections, L. A. Guest, New York, July 9, 1954. Guest was assistant manager of the original Illinois division.

67. J. T. Irvine, "Hail to Central," *Shell Globe*, house organ of Shell Petroleum Corporation, St. Louis, November–December 1933, pp. 12–15. Source material on the development of Roxana's marketing during the 1920's is far from satisfactory. Many of the important records of that period were long ago destroyed, and the company moved too fast for all its acts to get into the corporate minutes; even the legal department's contract files are not complete. At this date events can be reconstructed accurately only by sifting tons of minutiae: routine correspondence, sales slips, invoices, cancelled checks, entries in cashbooks and ledgers—a staggering job which the importance of the subject does not warrant, especially since we have the story in its main outlines. Chief sources of dates have been a series of articles on the different divisions, appearing in the *Shell Globe*, St. Louis, in the early 1930's, and personnel records of the men who held key spots in the Roxana marketing organization during the 1920's.

68. *Shell Globe*, St. Louis, July–August 1933, pp. 10–13; Jones, MS. history, p. 163.

69. Jones, MS. history, p. 166; answers by Shell Union to questionnaire submitted by the Federal Bureau of Investigation, July 1928.

70. F.B.I. questionnaire, *supra*.

71. Conversation, A. F. H. Payne, New York, June 5, 1953; letter, C. C. Freeman, owner Tri-States Oil Company, Seymour, to R. J. Hall, St. Louis, April 19, 1923, stating that Roxana took over his business as of April 1, 1923; *Shell Globe*, May–June 1933, pp. 12–15.

72. Contracts and correspondence in files of Shell Oil Company legal department, New York.

73. *Oil & Gas Journal*, March 3, 1927, p. 138; F. B. I. questionnaire; interview, Harry Jacobs, New York, May 7, 1948.

74. Material on Shell American from *Shell Globe*, St. Louis, January–February 1935, pp. 14–17; *Shell News*, St. Louis, January 1939, p. 30; F.B.I. questionnaire; Jones MS. history, pp. 190–191.

75. Shell Union Annual Report, 1929, p. 4; other similar statements appeared in the oil trade press and in newspapers generally during that year.

76. Interview, E. C. Peet, New York, February 27, 1948.

77. *Shell Globe,* September - October 1932, pp. 8-11; Cleveland division history (see note 64).

78. *National Petroleum News,* September 4, 1929, p. 34; gallonage figure from Peet interview, other figures from *Shell Globe* article; Minutes, Board of Directors, Shell Petroleum Corporation, August 1929.

79. Conversation, F. H. Schlapprizzi, New York, May 15, 1953; Peet and Jacobs interviews.

80. Report on Michigan Division, Detroit, June 1939.

81. *Shell Globe,* September - October 1933, pp. 6-9; Michigan division history in company files, prepared 1940.

82. Letter, A. S. Pentland, Rockford, Illinois, to the author, February 25, 1950.

83. Files, The Hague; Peet interview; interview, A. W. Frey, New York, September 29, 1948.

84. *Shell Globe,* St. Louis, March 1933, p. 12 ff.; *National Petroleum News,* March 20, 1929, pp. 46-47; Frey interview.

85. *Shell Globe,* March 1933, p. 12 ff.

86. Letter, J. C. Munro, Biloxi, Mississippi, to the author, October 16, 1954. Mr. Munro died in November 1954.

87. Jacobs interview.

88. N. O. Fanning, "Gasoline Filling Stations Big Item," *Oil & Gas Journal,* March 20, 1924; "Compact and Trim as on Shipboard," article on model Shell station just erected in Cleveland, *National Petroleum News,* December 26, 1928, p. 75.

89. Letter, J. C. Munro, Biloxi, Mississippi, to the author, July 22, 1954.

90. Interview, J. G. Sinclair, Indianapolis, July 21, 1948. Sinclair served as a division manager for more than twenty years at Decatur, Chicago, and Indianapolis.

91. Carl R. Latowsky, "A History of the Shell Union Oil Corporation," talk before school for lubricating sales engineers, Wood River, June 2, 1930; Jacobs interview; information on Shell globes verified by E. H. Sanders who was advertising manager on the Pacific Coast during the same period.

92. Copies of the lectures covering a five-year period were preserved by Dr. F. W. L. Tydeman who presented them to the author.

93. Interview, Dr. G. P. Koch, New York, July 2, 1948.

94. Boston *Evening American,* April 19, 1929; *Oil & Gas Journal,* April 25, 1929, p. 138.

95. *Oil & Gas Journal,* August 8, 1929, p. 138.

96. Letters, Adrian Corbett, London, to George Legh-Jones, San Francisco, August 21, 1925, Richard Airey, New York, to Legh-Jones, September 9, 1925, Frederick Godber, St. Louis, to Corbett, London, October 14, 1925, and Godber, St. Louis, to Van Eck, New York, December 9, 1925.

97. "Report on the Possibilities of Developing a Market on the Atlantic Seaboard for California Gasoline," by H. R. Gallagher, November 1926.

98. Interview, Alexander Fraser, New York, March 29, 1948; conversation, J. F. Riddell, Jr., New York, September 24, 1954.

99. Interview, Admiral A. F. Carter, New York, May 27, 1948.

100. *Id.*

101. Conversations, F. A. Huestis, H. A. Curtin, New York, February 4, 1953. Both men were with the old New England organization; details of contract from *Moody's Manual of Industrials,* New York, 1921.

102. Carter interview.

103. Moody's Manual for 1921–1926; Carter interview.

104. Conversation, Henry A. Curtin, New York, February 4, 1953.

105. *Poor's Cumulative Daily Digest,* New York, January-February 1925, p. 529, March-April 1925, p. 731, November-December 1925, p. 418, October-November-December 1926, p. 379, October-November-December 1927, p. 439, January-February-March 1927, p. 507, April-May-June 1927, p. 445, July-August-September 1928, p. 417; official company circular dated February 22, 1925; *Boston News Bureau,* Boston, April 17, 1925, p. 2, November 23, 1927, January 24, 1927, p. 5, March 6, 1927, p. 11, and July 2, 1928, p. 3.

106. Carter interview.

107. *Moody's Manual of Industrials*, 1921; Carter interview; memorandum on properties of the New England Oil Refining Company, Carter to Adrian Corbett, London, January 24, 1928.
108. *Boston News Bureau,* December 31, 1926, p. 10.
109. Memorandum on the value of New England Oil Refining Company, Adrian Corbett, London, January 25, 1928.
110. Carl Barker, "Appraisal of Fixed Assets and Report on Operation, New England, Mayflower, Metropolitan, and Holden Companies," November 28, 1928; Carter memorandum (see note 107).
111. Estimate of gallonage from figures in letter, Van Eck to Kessler, December 11, 1928; property list from Carter memo.
112. Letter, Corbett, London, to Van Eck, New York, March 5, 1928.
113. *Wall Street Journal,* July 12, 1928, p. 17; *Boston News Bureau,* February 28, 1928, p. 1; conversation, Henry Curtin, February 4, 1953.
114. Letter, A. S. Debenham, director, The Asiatic Petroleum Company, Ltd., London, to New England Oil Refining Company, July 6, 1928.
115. Richard Airey, New York, to Deterding, London, October 23, 1928; Van Eck to Deterding, November 22, 1928; Airey to Deterding, October 23, 1928.
116. John J. McCloy, "Report of New England Oil Refining Company Closing," New York, February 7, 1929. McCloy, later to hold positions such as U. S. High Commissioner to Germany and chairman of the Chase Manhattan Bank, was at the time a member of the Group's New York law firm, Cravath, de Gersdorff, Swaine & Wood.
117. Letters, Airey to Van Eck, January 22, 1929, and Godber to Van Eck, January 22, 1929; telephone conversation, C. V. Beaton, New York, January 30, 1953. Beaton managed lubricant sales for Shell Eastern until 1940, at which time he went with Asiatic (New York) to manage that company's purchasing activities in the lubricants field.
118. Report, Bang Service Stations, Inc., Mt. Vernon and New York, by C.

R. Davis and L. E. Hendricks, undated but probably December 1928.
119. Price, Waterhouse & Company audits of Shell Union and subsidiaries (consolidated) for 1929 and 1930.
120. Interviews, R. M. Clough, New York, March 26, 1948, and R. F. Carey, Jackson Heights, New York, March 25, 1948; letter, Van Eck to Carter, January 31, 1929.
121. Pamphlet summarized in *National Petroleum News,* April 10, 1929, p. 37; *Oil & Gas Journal,* April 18, 1929.
122. Information on these transactions from Carey interview.
123. Carter interview; *Oil & Gas Journal,* October 17, 1929, p. 151; Clough interview; C. V. Beaton, article in *The Sign of the Shell,* New York, July 1930, p. 8.
124. Interview, G. L. Switzer, New York, December 22, 1948.
125. Carter interview.
126. Quotation from Switzer interview.
127. Article, "Mr. Jenkins and Sir Henri," *Fortune* magazine, October 1932; figures confirmed by Van Eck, May 1947, as being "substantially correct."
128. Completed questionnaire submitted to Federal Bureau of Investigation, June 1928.
129. President's Report, San Francisco, June 8, July 11, and October 11, 1927.
130. *Id.,* May 11, August 15, 1928, *et seq.*
131. Dates and figures from Shell Union Annual Report 1929, p. 3; Jones, MS. history, p. 181.
132. National Oil Scouts Yearbook, 1936, p. 270; Shell Union Annual Report, 1927, p. 2.
133. Names, dates, and figures in this and several of the following paragraphs on West Texas from "A History of Shell Oil Company's Activities in West Texas and New Mexico," a report kindly prepared for the author by B. L. Ryan, Houston, August 1948. This material was prepared with great thoroughness from firsthand sources.
134. Letter, A. E. Groff, Houston, to the author, June 26, 1953; R. P. Bascom, "Shell Has Two Types of Operation," *Oil & Gas Journal,* June 5, 1930.
135. Ryan MS.

136. Letter, T. E. Swigart, Houston, to the author, July 12, 1954; President's Reports, San Francisco, May through August 1928.

137. "Natural Gasoline is Piped 100 Miles," *Oil & Gas Journal,* August 30, 1928, pp. T-28-30; interview, Fred B. Simms, Kernville, California, September 2, 1947.

138. Interview, R. C. Roberts, Elgin, Illinois, April 24, 1948; *Shell Globe,* St. Louis, January-February 1932, p. 6; *Go-Devil,* Shell Pipe Line Corporation house organ, February 1948; F.B.I. questionnaire.

139. Roberts interview; Royal Dutch Annual Report 1927, pp. 23-24.

140. Interview, J. L. Miller, Houston, December 11, 1947 (Miller was assistant superintendent at Arkansas City at the time that refinery started operating, held the same job at East Chicago, 1928–1936, and has been superintendent of the Houston refinery since 1937); *Shell Globe,* January-February 1932, p. 6; conversation, Carl Barker.

141. Written comment, D. Pyzel, Piedmont, Calif., to the author, December 1954; conversation, C. H. Beckwith, San Francisco, June 1947. Beckwith was for more than twenty years tax manager at San Francisco, and handled real estate transactions such as the purchase of refinery sites.

142. Interview, A. E. Lacomblé, San Francisco, September 11, 1947 (Lacomblé was assistant superintendent of the Wilmington refinery at the time Dominguez was being built); Directors Report, San Francisco, September 10 and October 11, 1927.

143. This and succeeding paragraph from letter, G. H. van Senden, Carmel, California, to the author, June 10, 1954.

144. Conversation, A. B. Culbertson, New York, July 1, 1953; correspondence and conversations, 1947–1951, with Prof. R. J. Forbes and Dr. F. W. L. Tydeman; report by R. B. High, Norco, June 21, 1926; report by G. H. van Senden, Martinez, 1924.

145. Conversation, F. C. Cutting, New York, July 1, 1953; Ruether interview.

146. Interview, I. M. Hemphill, Martinez, July 17, 1947. Hemphill, manager of the Martinez refinery for several years prior to his retirement, was superintendent at Norco during 1928.

147. Correspondence files; actual price was a subject of dispute between Asiatic and Roxana for many months, and was not finally settled until December 1930.

148. General Memorandum signed by T. F. Lydon, April 20, 1929; *Shell Globe,* St. Louis, March-April 1932, pp. 4-6; dissolution certificate, signed Secretary of State, State of Louisiana, December 30, 1929; interview, A. W. Frey, New York, September 29, 1948. Frey was chief clerk of the New Orleans Refining Company's New Orleans office, and became office manager of the new Southern marketing division.

149. Conversation, E. B. Glendenning, Sewaren, January 29, 1949.

150. Public announcement dated October 10, 1928, and mailed to customers; official action not recorded in Minutes of Roxana Petroleum Corporation until October 22, 1928.

151. Article, "The Shell Building," *Shell Globe,* St. Louis, January-February 1932, p. 11.

152. Interview, George E. Gordon, Redlands, California, August 27, 1947.

153. Article, "The Shell Building, San Francisco," *Architect & Engineer,* July 1930; letter, H. H. Anderson to the author, November 1954.

154. "Survey of Operating Refineries in United States," *Oil & Gas Journal,* March 6, 1930, p. 138 ff.

155. *Shelling The Line,* January 1, 1930.

CHAPTER VII

Depression and Deficit (pages 353 to 425)

1. San Francisco *Chronicle*, April 17, 1930.
2. Material on the Great Depression and its causes from Mark Sullivan, *Our Times*, Vol. VI, New York, Charles Scribner's Sons, 1936; Frederick Lewis Allen, *Only Yesterday*, New York, Harper & Brothers, 1931; H. V. Hodson, *Slump and Recovery, 1929–1937*, London, Oxford University Press, 1938; *The Recovery Problem in the United States* (symposium), Washington, The Brookings Institution, 1936; Leonard P. Ayres, *Turning Points in Business Cycles*, New York, The Macmillan Company, 1939; Robert A. Sayre, *Consumer's Prices, 1914–1948*, New York, The National Industrial Conference Board, 1948; *The Memoirs of Herbert Hoover, The Great Depression, 1929–1941*, Vol. III, New York, The Macmillan Company, 1952; Jesse H. Jones (with Edward Angly), *Fifty Billion Dollars*, New York, The Macmillan Company, 1951.
3. Interview, E. C. Peet, New York, May 21, 1948.
4. Letter, John W. Watson, Sausalito, California, to the author, November 4, 1954. Watson was vice president and treasurer of Shell Petroleum, and later of Shell Oil Company, Inc., from 1933 to 1944; he subsequently served as treasurer of Shell Chemical until his retirement in 1948.
5. Shell Union Annual Reports.
6. Letters, H. H. Anderson, Orlando, Florida, to the author, November 1954, and J. C. van Eck, Santa Barbara, California, to the author, January 17, 1955.
7. Memorandum, Alexander Fraser to P. R. Chenoweth, October 13, 1930.
8. H. M. Fritts, New York, July 17, 1953, recalled that in some locations (chiefly along the Gulf Coast) these layoffs ran as high as 70%.
9. Information this and previous paragraph from letters, J. C. Munro, Biloxi, Mississippi, to the author, July 22 and October 16, 1954; interview, Harry Jacobs, New York, December 6, 1949; articles on the various divisions, *Shell Globe*, St. Louis, September-October and November-December 1932 and November-December 1933; conversation, F. H. Schlapprizzi, New York, July 20, 1953; and personnel records of several of the key men involved.
10. Sir Henri Deterding, as told to Stanley Naylor, *An International Oilman*, London, Harper & Brothers, 1934, p. 110.
11. *National Petroleum News*, June 19, 1935.
12. Reprinted in *Shelling The Line*, San Francisco, January 1, 1930.
13. H. S. Gibson, "Scientific Unit Control," in *The Science of Petroleum*, Vol. I, London, Oxford University Press, 1938, pp. 534-539.
14. *Ibid.*
15. Interview, B. H. van der Linden, New York, March 1950; letter, T. E. Swigart to D. V. Carter, December 11, 1947; interviews, W. C. McDuffie, Montecito, Calif., August 30, 1947 and H. H. Anderson, Houston, April 14, 1948.
16. C. E. Beecher and I. P. Parkhurst, "The Effect of Dissolved Gas Upon the Viscosity and Surface Tension of Crude Oil," *Petroleum Development and Technology*, American Institute of Mining and Metallurgical Engineers, 1926, pp. 51-69.
17. The literature on conservation is vast and voluminous, and much of it is a discouraging commentary on human greed and shortsightedness. Of first importance to the student is a file of the *Oil & Gas Journal* from 1925 to the present, for most of the major moves received more than adequate discussion in its columns. An early paper on conservation was M. L. Requa's pioneer study, "Petroleum Resources of the United States," 64th Congress, 1st Session, Senate Document 363 (March 9, 1916), although later discounted because Requa was of the "we're-running-out-of-oil" school. A few months

later was "Adequate Acreage and Oil Conservation," a paper delivered by Max W. Ball (then of the U. S. Bureau of Mines) before the 19th Annual Convention of the American Mining Congress, Chicago, November 16, 1916. A real landmark in the history of conservation is Henry L. Doherty's address, "Suggestions for the Conservation of Petroleum by Control of Production," delivered before the 131st meeting of the American Institute of Mining and Metallurgical Engineers, New York, February 18, 1925; in it Doherty sums up the "unit plan" which he had advanced the previous year, together with emendations he had made meanwhile in answer to some of the criticism directed against it. The reports of the Federal Oil Conservation Board are all of first importance: Report I (1926) dealt with the legal problems incident to production control, endorsed several of Doherty's main contentions, and recommended an Interstate Compact; Report II (1928) was an able survey of substitute motor fuels from sources other than petroleum; Report III (1929) further discussed legal problems, presenting suggested drafts of conservation laws and even a measure for compulsory unitization; Report IV (1930) presented a comprehensive survey of the supply and demand situation; Report V (1932) outlined specific proposals for an interstate oil compact, more far-reaching in many respects than the one which was finally adopted. A lively and illuminating discussion of oil industry problems of the time is contained in Samuel B. Pettengill's *Hot Oil: The Problem of Petroleum*, New York, Forum Press, 1936. Rep. Pettengill was a member of the Cole Committee which had recently conducted an extensive investigation into the oil industry's ailments; his book, written with spry good humor, presents the case for and against government control fairly, and summarizes some of the bizarre panaceas then being offered. By far the best single volume on the subject of conservation, and one which should be sufficient for all except

specialists, is the excellent symposium edited by Blakely M. Murphy, *Conservation of Oil and Gas, A Legal History, 1948*, written and published by the Section of Mineral Law of the American Bar Association, Chicago, 1949. This book is a real encyclopedia of oil conservation, written by men who were intimately associated with the conservation movement, and it contains in addition many other subjects to make it an extremely useful reference volume. *The Memoirs of Herbert Hoover*, Vols. II and III, New York, The Macmillan Company, 1952, also contain enlightening references to the oil conservation problem.

18. *Oil & Gas Journal*, August 23, 1934, p. 260; interview, A. E. Watts, New York, March, 1952. Watts was umpire of the state-sponsored proration effort at Cushing while it lasted; later he joined Harry F. Sinclair's growing organization, and has been a Sinclair vice president for some 35 years.

19. Northcutt Ely, "The Use of Federal Powers to Supplement Those of the States," in *Conservation of Oil and Gas* (see note 17 for full title). Ely was chairman of the Technical and Advisory Committee of the old Federal Oil Conservation Board.

20. B. L. Ryan, "A History of Shell Oil Company's Activities in West Texas and New Mexico," Houston, August 1948 (MS.), p. 6; C. A. Warner, *Texas Oil and Gas Since 1543*, Houston, The Gulf Publishing Co., 1939.

21. *The Memoirs of Herbert Hoover*, Vol. II, New York, The Macmillan Company, 1952, pp. 237-239.

22. *Ibid.*

23. President's Report, Shell Oil Company, San Francisco, July 1929, p. 5.

24. Interview, W. L. Hobro, Los Angeles, August 12, 1947; *Oil & Gas Journal*, June 27, 1929, p. 39; letter, Paul Paine, Los Angeles, to the author, October 8, 1954; President's Report, *supra*.

25. Interview with William Reinhardt, Los Angeles, August 26, 1947; letters, William Reinhardt, Los Angeles, to the author, November 24

and December 10, 1954; letter, T. E. Swigart, Houston, to John R. Suman, New York, October 20, 1954. Reinhardt was Shell's production vice president in Los Angeles, 1928–1931; general manager of the Kettleman North Dome Association, 1931–1937; and since 1937 vice president of the Union Pacific Railroad in charge of the railroad's oil-producing properties.

26. Warner, *op. cit.*, pp. 72 ff. and 172; Joiner obituary, New York *Times*, March 29, 1947.

27. Warner, *op. cit.*; *Oil & Gas Journal*, August 23, 1934, p. 264.

28. *Oil & Gas Journal*, August 20, 1931.

29. Blakely M. Murphy, "The Oil States Advisory Committee, a Predecessor of the Compact," *Conservation of Oil and Gas* (see note 17 for full title), p. 553.

30. Murphy, "The Formation of the Interstate Compact to Conserve Oil and Gas," *Conservation of Oil and Gas*, pp. 557-558.

31. Ely, *loc. cit.*, pp. 695-696.

32. Murphy, *loc. cit.* (note 30), pp. 558-559; Pettengill, *op. cit.*, prints pertinent extracts of Ickes' speech, pp. 251-257.

33. Murphy, *supra*, p. 595.

34. Royal Dutch Annual Report, 1923, pp. 10-12, 1931, p. 11; *National Petroleum News*, March 9, 1932, pp. 27-28; Shell Union Annual Report, 1932.

35. Article, "Mr. Jenkins and Sir Henri," *Fortune*, October 1932.

36. Prices in this paragraph from tabulation prepared by Shell Petroleum Corp., St. Louis, February 1934.

37. Interviews, E. L. Miller, San Francisco, September 19, 1947, A. P. Ruether, New York, May 20 and 24, 1948.

38. Interview, G. L. Switzer, New York, December 22, 1948.

39. *Fortune*, October 1932.

40. Shell Petroleum figures showing condition of its major retail markets, 1933.

41. Joe S. Bain, *Economics of the Pacific Coast Petroleum Industry*, Vol. II, Berkeley, University of California Press, 1944, lists those still in operation at the time his book was published.

42. Letter, P. E. Lakin, San Francisco, to the author, November 9, 1954.

43. Material on Guardian from interview with P. E. Lakin, New York, November 22, 1948; information on Guardian name from F. E. Rehm, New York, August 13, 1948.

44. Leverett S. Lyon, Paul T. Homan, Lewis L. Lorwin, George Terborgh, Charles L. Dearing, and Leon C. Marshall, *The National Recovery Administration: An Analysis and Appraisal*, Washington, The Brookings Institution, 1935.

45. Text of the Petroleum Code from *National Petroleum News*, August 23, 1933.

46. Text of Pacific Coast Petroleum Agency Agreement 1933, as amended December 1933. Prices mentioned here are for "third grade" gasoline, about which the cut-throat competition centered.

47. *National Petroleum News*, May 29, 1935.

48. *Ibid.*; Paul H. Giddens, *Standard Oil Company (Indiana), Oil Pioneer of the Middle West*, New York, Appleton-Century-Crofts, 1955, p. 549; calculation by the author.

49. *National Petroleum News*, July 3, 1935.

50. Dr. John W. Frey, member of the Petroleum Administrative Board, quoted in *National Petroleum News*, March 20, 1935.

51. *National Petroleum News*, July 10, 1935.

52. This and other information on the evolution of the oil burner from H. A. Romp, *Oil Burning*, The Hague, Martinus Nijhoff, 1937, pp. 29-36. Romp, a B.P.M. engineer, thoroughly canvassed the field and his book, though twenty years out of date, is still the best reference work in the oil burner field.

53. Article on oil burners in *Shell Globe*, St. Louis, September-October 1933, by Dr. R. T. Goodwin, manager, fuel oil sales department.

54. Walter Hill, remarks before conference of Shell aviation representatives, London, June 24, 1935. Hill headed the Group's aviation efforts for thirty-six years.

55. *Shelling The Line*, January 1, 1930, p. 7; interviews, J. H. Doolittle,

New York, June 15, 1948, A. J. M. Hamon, New York, December 7, 1948.

56. Gallonage figures from *CAA and the National Economy*, Washington, Department of Commerce, Civil Aeronautics Administration, September 1945, p. 127. As the figures quoted here are intended to show growth of air transport, sales to government agencies and aircraft manufacturers have been excluded in every case.

57. Telegram, R. M. Adamson, San Francisco, to Aviation Department, New York, September 24, 1954; Carleton Putnam, *High Journey*, New York, Charles Scribner's Sons, 1945; *Shell Globe*, St. Louis, March 1933, p. 14. Putnam, founder of C. & S., gives an excellent account of the tribulations of starting an airline and of Doolittle's personal assistance to struggling airline operators in such cases, p. 208, ff.

58. *Shelling The Line*, San Francisco, April 1, 1930; interviews with J. H. Doolittle, New York, June 15, 1948, and A. J. M. Hamon, New York, December 7, 1948.

59. Report, Tank Wagon Sales Development Program, by A. J. M. Hamon, assistant manager, aviation department, Shell Eastern Petroleum Products, Inc., New York, May 16, 1934.

60. Doolittle interview.

61. Interview, A. B. Culbertson, New York, January 5, 1949.

62. *Shelling The Line*, September 1, 1928; July 1, 1929.

63. Interview with Fred Preu, New York, January 6, 1949. Preu has been closely identified with Shell's activities in this field for twenty years.

64. Conversation, B. W. Conn, New York, January 4, 1949; interview, J. W. J. O'Dea, New York, January 7, 1949.

65. Interviews, A. P. Anderson, New York, September 30, 1954, and Boris Frolov, New York, October 6, 1954; *The Petroleum Handbook*, London, Shell Petroleum Company, Ltd., 1948, pp. 187-194; Marquis James, *The Texaco Story*, New York, The Texas Company, 1953, pp. 54, 65-66.

66. Culbertson interview; A.P.I. Library.

67. Interviews, E. Dunning, New York, January 11, 1949, and S. S. Smith, New York, January 13, 1949; Wood River Refinery, Monthly Operating Report, March 1927.

68. Dr. F. W. L. Tydeman, "Shell Introduces New Gasoline," *Shell Globe*, St. Louis, April 1931.

69. *Ibid.*; refinery operating reports; pamphlet, "Super-Shell Gasoline, What It Is and What It Does," St. Louis, Roxana Petroleum Corporation, January 1927.

70. Quotation from masthead of *Shelling The Line*; interview with Henry M. Stevens, New York, May 20, 1948; *Shelling The Line*, June 1928.

71. Harry R. Ricardo, "An Autobiography," *Mechanical Engineering*, November 1943, pp. 765-769. This is an excellent brief statement of the problems of detonation and the only authoritative account of Ricardo's early work; Ethyl Corporation history in William Haynes, *American Chemical Industry*, Vol. VI, New York, D. Van Nostrand Company, 1949, pp. 151-154, contains a good short account of the work of Midgley and Boyd.

72. Letter, R. E. Wilson, president, Standard Oil Company (Indiana), to William Haynes, March 7, 1947, quoted (Vol. IV, p. 401) by Haynes in his *American Chemical Industry*; Giddens, *op. cit.* (note 48), p. 292, says that this exclusive contract was renewed in 1929 for two more years.

73. Haynes, *op. cit.*, Vol. IV, pp. 402-403.

74. Memorandum, "Early Research at Wilmington 1924-1931," Wilmington Refinery Laboratory, April 8, 1949; date from *Shelling The Line*, June 1, 1930.

75. Conversation, T. B. Rendel, New York, March 1956; monthly operating report, Wood River refinery, January 1931; Tydeman, *loc. cit.*; work papers for 1932 Shell Union Annual Report.

76. Interview with Henry M. Stevens, New York, May 20, 1948; H. S. M. Burns, San Francisco, memorandum submitted for 1932 annual report.

77. Stevens interview.

78. Culbertson interview.

79. Interview, Alexander Fraser, New York, March 29, 1948; conversation,

A. B. Culbertson, New York, January 14, 1949.

80. Interview, E. L. Miller, San Francisco, September 17, 1947.

81. Conversation, Miss Claire E. Hoffman, New York, January 14, 1949; *The Sign of the Shell*, August 1932.

82. D. G. Coombs and L. B. Veeder, "Trends in Automotive Servicing," paper presented to 16th Annual Meeting, American Petroleum Institute, Los Angeles, November 14, 1935.

83. *V. & D. Message*, monthly house organ published in Los Angeles; *Shell Progress*, New York, March-April 1944; memorandum, H. S. M. Burns, San Francisco, February 1, 1933, in file of annual report work papers.

84. Interview, George P. Thomson, San Francisco, July 15, 1947.

85. Conversation, E. A. Cunningham, San Francisco, August 1947.

86. Information on mechanics of lease arrangements from conversation with H. L. Curtis, New York, March 2, 1954; figures from letter, Van der Woude, St. Louis, to Godber, London, November 21, 1931.

87. Curtis conversation, *supra*.

88. *Shell Globe* issues for fall of 1934.

89. John G. McLean and Robert Wm. Haigh, *The Growth of Integrated Oil Companies*, Cambridge, Harvard Graduate School of Business Administration, 1954, p. 104.

90. "On an Even Keel," manuscript reminiscences of the late R. R. Griffin, as told to H. R. Hammerman, New York, July 1945.

91. *National Petroleum News*, November 12, 1930.

92. *Oil & Gas Journal*, July 7 and July 28, 1932.

93. Conversation, A. C. Wires, New York, April 15, 1949.

94. *Oil & Gas Journal*, September 1, 1932; conversation, O. B. Roger, New York, August 27, 1956.

95. Interview, Tom Deacon, New Westminster, B. C., July 31, 1947.

96. Interview, G. L. Gardiner, superintendent, Shellburn refinery, Vancouver, July 31, 1947.

CHAPTER VIII

Competitiveness, A New Yardstick (pages 426 to 501)

1. London *Times*, February 6, 1939, p. 14.

2. Letter, J. C. van Eck, Santa Barbara, California, to the author, January 17, 1955.

3. Memorandum, N. J. McGaw, October 26, 1937, attached to letter, J. C. van Eck, London, to Alexander Fraser, St. Louis, October 28, 1937.

4. Letter, Van Eck to Fraser, March 7, 1935.

5. Letter, R. G. A. van der Woude, New York, to Fraser, St. Louis, April 2, 1935.

6. Letter, Fraser to Van der Woude, April 2, 1935.

7. Alexander Fraser, lecture delivered to manufacturing class of Harvard Business School, May 5, 1941.

8. Report, "Shell Petroleum Corporation, Report of Supply and Demand Survey, 1936," 2 vols., St. Louis, January 18, 1937. This is the formal title of the Salmon report.

9. *The Derrick's Hand-Book of Petroleum*, Vol. I, Oil City, Pa., Derrick Publishing Co., 1898, p. 562; *Oil & Gas Journal*, August 27, 1934, p. 89.

10. Interview with S. S. Smith, New York, January 15, 1951.

11. Detailed information on the products pipe line is taken chiefly from "A Confidential Report, Descriptive of the Construction and Operation of the Gasoline and Products Pipe Line (Wood River, Illinois, to Lima and Columbus, Ohio)," Shell Oil Company, Inc., St. Louis, August 1939. This report, in many ways as novel as the subject matter, is an interesting example of how lucid and attractive a report can be when prepared with care and imagination.

12. Figures courtesy of L. J. Di Miceli, New York, November 22, 1950.
13. Letter, Van Eck to Fraser, October 28, 1937.
14. Phrase used by Fraser in his Harvard Business School lecture (note 7).
15. Letter, Fraser to Van Eck, March 8, 1938.
16. Interview, R. C. Roberts, Elgin, Illinois, April 24, 1948; conversation, C. E. Davis, New York, January 29, 1951; interview, R. B. High, Houston, December 9, 1947.
17. Letter, Fraser to Van Eck, July 15, 1938.
18. Letter, Fraser to Van Eck, October 5, 1938.
19. Report, "Economics of Consolidation of East Chicago and Wood River Refinery Operations at Wood River," St. Louis, Shell Petroleum Corporation, Manufacturing Department, October 13, 1938.
20. Conversation, C. E. Davis, New York, January 29, 1951.
21. Conversation, H. E. Dischinger, New York, January 25, 1951.
22. Fraser, Harvard Business School lecture.
23. Interview, Harry Jacobs, New York, December 6, 1949; *Shell Globe,* various issues; personnel records.
24. Information in this and preceding paragraphs from report, "Shell Southern System," by N. J. McGaw and L. G. McLaren, St. Louis, March 25, 1938; minutes of management meeting held in New York to discuss the McGaw-McLaren report.
25. Letter, J. C. Van Eck, Santa Barbara, California, to the author, January 17, 1955.
26. P. E. Lakin, Vice President–Marketing, St. Louis, General Memorandum, July 20, 1940.
27. Report, "Products Pipe Line Between Fall River and Boston, Massachusetts, versus Improving Marine Facilities at Boston," by D. F. Sears and W. H. Moegelin, Shell Petroleum Corporation, St. Louis, December 23, 1938.
28. Conversations, R. F. O'Toole and L. J. Di Miceli, New York, March 26, 1951; "Massachusetts Line Completed," *Shell News,* New York, October 1941.

29. Information on Utah price structure from George P. Thomson, San Francisco, June 2, 1954.
30. Michael Silverbergh, "A History of the Rocky Mountain Division," Shell Oil Company, Los Angeles, January 1954, MS.
31. *Ibid.;* letters, Fraser to Van der Woude, February 2, 1937, and Fraser to Belither, November 25, 1939.
32. Letter, Belither to Van Eck, March 19, 1940.
33. Conversation, A. R. Boyer, New York, November 25, 1949.
34. Fraser, Harvard Business School lecture. (See note 7.)
35. *Id.*
36. Report, "Service Station Construction Policies and Costs, Mid-Continent and Eastern Areas, Shell Oil Company, Inc.," St. Louis, November 1, 1939.
37. Letter, Belither to Van Eck, September 29, 1939.
38. Information in this and following paragraphs from a report, "Tanker Transportation Survey," Shell Oil Company, Inc., New York, February 1946.
39. Letter, Frederick Godber, St. Louis, to Alexander Mackay, January 12, 1920.
40. Shell Union Annual Reports, 1934–1937.
41. W. L. Summers, "A History of Legislative Activity Relative to Conservation of Petroleum in Illinois," *Conservation of Oil & Gas, A Legal History, 1948,* Blakely M. Murphy, Ed., Section of Mineral Law, American Bar Association, Chicago, 1949, pp. 92-122.
42. Material on Centralia from interviews, J. M. MacQuarrie, New York, February 15 and 16, 1951, J. A. Horner, New York, February 16, 1951; *Oil & Gas Journal,* April 14 and September 1, 1938; articles by Harry O'Gara in *Shell News,* St. Louis, October-November 1938 and November 1939.
43. Letters to the author, F. E. Rehm, San Francisco, October 13, 1954, and W. L. Hobro, Los Angeles, July 29, 1955.
44. Memorandum from B. L. Ryan, Houston, January 26, 1949.
45. Letters from W. L. Hobro, Los

Angeles, November 4 and November 22, 1949; and F. E. Rehm, San Francisco, October 13, 1954.

46. Letter, H. W. Penterman, Tulsa, to the author, February 29, 1952.

47. Information on portable rigs and slim-hole drilling from *Oil & Gas Journal*, July 15, 1937, p. 69; conversation, R. C. McCurdy, New York, August 8, 1955; letters to the author, F. E. Rehm, San Francisco, October 13, 1954, J. W. Watson, Sausalito, Calif., November 4, 1954, Dr. E. F. Davis, Los Angeles, October 5, 1954; interviews, J. M. Mac-Quarrie, New York, February 15–16, 1951; Harry O'Gara in *Shell News*, St. Louis, October-November 1938; R. M. Dannenberg, *Shell News*, St. Louis, December 1938 and Lawrence O'Donnell, *Shell News*, St. Louis, May 1939.

48. Information on San Joaquin Pipe Line from correspondence and Shell Union Annual Report for 1936; descriptive article by F. B. Simms in *Oil & Gas Journal*, February 18, 1937, p. 42 ff.; comparative costs of pipe line construction from interviews, C. H. Beckwith, San Francisco, June 24 and September 19, 1947.

49. Glenn R. Winters in *Oil & Gas Journal*, September 21, 1939, p. 89, and *Shell News*, St. Louis, October 1939; other information on this development in letter, A. E. Groff, Houston, to the author, January 24, 1951. Material on McMahan from Wesley Price, "My Flight with a Cross-Country Hedgehopper," *The Saturday Evening Post*, March 31, 1951, p. 28.

50. Fraser, Harvard Business School lecture (see note 7); letter, A. E. Groff, *supra*.

51. Material on Flintkote from *Flintkotopics*, Morristown, N. J., July-November 1946; *Shell Globe*, St. Louis, July-August 1932, November-December 1934; *National Petroleum News*, October 31, 1928, p. 114; interview, G. K. McKenzie, secretary, The Flintkote Co., New York, September 28, 1949; and conversation, R. J. Forbes, New York, September 27, 1951.

52. Material on Flintkote sale from McKenzie interview; interview with P. M. Ludwig, New York, December 6, 1949.

53. Shell Union Annual Report, 1937.

54. The New York *Times*, May 8, 1940.

55. Material on the Madison Case in *National Petroleum News*, October 6, 1937, January 26, 1938, May 8, 1940; *Oil & Gas Journal*, June 10, October 14, November 12, November 18, 1937, January 27, April 7, July 21, 1938, and August 3, 1939.

56. Northcutt Ely, "The Government in the Exercise of the Power over Interstate Commerce," *Conservation of Oil and Gas, A Legal History, 1948*, Chicago, 1949, p. 632.

57. *Oil & Gas Journal*, April 28, 1938.

58. These sentences represent a rephrasing of arguments set forth in George S. Wolbert, Jr., *American Pipe Lines*, Norman, University of Oklahoma Press, 1952, pp. 100-121. Wolbert's book should be required reading for all advocates of divorcement.

59. Letter, Garland Ferguson to Belither, December 20, 1938; Thurman Arnold, general letters to all refineries, March 15, 1939, and July 8, 1940.

60. Dewey Anderson, executive secretary of the T.N.E.C., in foreword of "Description of Hearings and Monographs of the Temporary National Economic Committee," Washington, Government Printing Office, 1941.

61. *Petroleum Industry Hearings Before the Temporary National Economic Committee*, New York, American Petroleum Institute, 1942.

62. *Oil & Gas Journal*, October 10, 1940.

63. For discussion of this point see Wolbert, *op. cit.*, p. 145 fn.

64. Terms of consent decree signed in District of Columbia Court, December 23, 1941, by government lawyers and the oil companies' attorneys.

65. "Employment and Working Conditions in the Petroleum Industry," paper by H. H. Anderson, vice president, Shell Petroleum Corporation, p. 486 ff., in T.N.E.C. book (note 61).

66. Report, "The Wood River Strike," St. Louis, Shell Petroleum Corporation, September 30, 1936.

67. Report, "Shell Oil Company, Inc., History of Labor Relations, 1917–

1940," San Francisco, undated (c. 1947).

68. MS., "History of Shell Pension Plans," by H. A. Dohrenwend, New York.

69. Sir Henri Deterding, as told to Stanley Naylor, *An International Oilman*, Harper & Brothers, London and New York, 1934, pp. 110-111.

70. Letter, H. H. Anderson, Orlando, Florida, to the author, November 1954.

71. Dohrenwend, *supra*.

72. Booklet, "Rules and Regulations, Shell Pension Plan," Shell Pension Trust, New York, 1949.

73. Story in Tulsa *Tribune*, February 6, 1939, reprinted in *Shell News*, St.

Louis, February 1939; information from A. H. Thielker, New York, August 24, 1956.

74. Henry A. Dohrenwend, "A Short History of the Shell Provident Fund," New York, MS.; booklet, "Shell Provident Fund, Regulations and Trust Agreement, As Amended Through January 1, 1949," New York, Shell Provident Fund, 1949.

75. Harry O'Gara, "Jobs for 278 Ex-Employees," *Shell News*, New York, February 1941.

76. *Shell News*, New York, October 1940; letter, H. H. Anderson, Orlando, Florida, to the author, November 1954.

CHAPTER IX

A Venture in Chemicals (pages 502 to 553)

1. Information from manuscript history by Prof. R. J. Forbes, Amsterdam, covering the technological history of the Royal Dutch from 1890 to 1940, referred to hereafter as "Forbes, Technical History."

2. Letter, Kessler to De Kok, February 14, 1928; Harry R. Ricardo, "An Autobiography," *Mechanical Engineering*, November 1943, p. 767.

3. Information about early research activity in Holland from interviews, D. Pyzel, Piedmont, Calif., December 13 and 14, 1955, and Prof. R. J. Forbes, New York, October 10 and 12, 1951; Royal Dutch Company Diamond Jubilee Book, The Hague, 1950, p. 150; Dr. C. Gerretson, *Geshiedenis der Koninklijke* (History of the Royal Dutch), Vol. III, Haarlem, 1941, pp. 487-490.

4. Interviews, Daniel Pyzel, San Francisco, July 24, August 7, September 9 and 16, 1947.

5. Letter, Kessler to De Kok, August 25, 1927.

6. Paraphrased from James Bryant Conant, *Organic Chemistry*, New York, The Macmillan Company, 1936, p. 3. The author, who is without a technical background, found Conant's book a clear, lucid, easily understood explanation of the fun-

damentals of organic chemistry. Other works useful in the preparation of this chapter were *Hackh's Chemical Dictionary* (Third Edition by Julius Grant), Philadelphia, The Blakiston Company, 1944; and William Haynes' imposing series, *The American Chemical Industry: A History*, New York, D. Van Nostrand Company, 1945–1949.

7. Hackh, *op. cit.*, pp. 27, 122.

8. *Id.*, p. 532.

9. History of Union Carbide in Haynes, *op. cit.*, Vol. VI, pp. 429-438; *Fortune* magazine, New York, June, July, September 1941.

10. Haynes, *op. cit.*, Vol. III, p. 147.

11. Haynes, *op. cit.*, Vol. VI, p. 398.

12. *Ibid.*; Charles Sterling Popple, *Standard Oil Company (New Jersey) in World War II*, New York, Standard Oil Company (New Jersey), 1952, p. 9; text of this agreement is printed in Frank A. Howard, *Buna Rubber, the Birth of An Industry*, New York, D. Van Nostrand Company, 1947, pp. 249-251.

13. Dr. Friedrich Bergius, "The Historical Development of Hydrogenation," *The Science of Petroleum*, Vol. III, London, Oxford University Press, 1938, pp. 2130-32; R. J. Forbes, *Man the Maker, A History*

of Technology and Engineering, New York, Henry Schuman, 1950, pp. 318-19; Pyzel interviews.

14. Interview, Dr. S. L. Langedijk, Amsterdam, April 17, 1952.
15. Pyzel interviews.
16. Letter, Pyzel to Adrian Corbett, London, September 17, 1927.
17. Memorandum outlining aims of Shell Development Company, The Hague files, April 28, 1927.
18. Report, "Shell Development Company, Design of New Laboratories," by E. C. Williams, October 22, 1928.
19. Forbes, Technical History.
20. *Id.*
21. Unfinished manuscript history of Shell Chemical, prepared 1947–1948 by J. P. Cunningham, San Francisco. Its three chapters were based upon conversations with Pyzel, supplemented by Shell Chemical financial and operating records.
22. Haynes, *op. cit.*, Vol. IV, p. 442.
23. Forbes, Technical History; corporate records.
24. Cunningham MS.
25. Conversation, Felix Kortlandt, New York, October 22, 1953.
26. Cunningham MS.
27. Haynes, *op. cit.*, Vol. IV, p. 454; Forbes, Technical History; Cunningham MS.; Shell Chemical balance sheets for 1931–1932.
28. Interview, Daniel Pyzel, San Francisco, September 16, 1947; Pyzel address to Shell Development Company Service Dinner, November 17, 1951.
29. Forbes, Technical History.
30. Cunningham MS.; Shell Chemical Company, Report to Shareholders, 1934.
31. Abraham Gesner, M.D., *A Practical Treatise on Coal, Petroleum and Other Distilled Oils*, New York, Ballière Bros., 1861; Cunningham MS; Pyzel interviews; Forbes, Technical History.
32. Shell Chemical Company, Report to Shareholders, 1934, p. 11; Cunningham MS.
33. Conversation, H. D. Loeb, New York, October 1950; Pyzel interviews (note 3).
34. Cunningham MS.
35. Shell Chemical Company Report to Shareholders, 1934, San Francisco,

March 12, 1935 (mimeographed), pp. 5, 10; Shell Chemical Year Report, 1937.
36. Shell Chemical Year-End Financial Reports, 1932–1935.
37. Shell Chemical Year Reports, 1937, p. 18; 1941, p. 13.
38. Shell Chemical Corporation historical sketch, prepared by the company, in Haynes, *op. cit.*, Vol. VI, p. 380; F. H. Leavitt, "Use and Marketing of Agricultural Ammonia," *Agricultural Chemicals*, June 1953.
39. Leavitt, *loc. cit.*
40. Shell Chemical Year Report, 1937, pp. 2 and 12; calculations the author's.
41. Haynes, *op. cit.*, Vol. VI, p. 381; Leavitt, *loc. cit.*
42. Shell Chemical Year Report, 1940, pp. 13, 14.
43. Forbes, Technical History; conversation, Dr. C. W. Humphreys, New York, November 10, 1954.
44. S. C. Carney and R. Z. Moravec, Report on the Operation of the Martinez Butyl Alcohol Plant for the Month of September, 1932, quoted in memorandum, F. E. Caddy, Martinez, to L. M. Roberts, New York, November 10, 1953.
45. Haynes, *op. cit.*, Vol. VI, p. 381; Shell Chemical balance sheet December 31, 1931, shows all solvents set down for purposes of inventory at 50¢ a gallon, which must have approximated their cost; monthly financial reports, Shell Chemical Company, 1931; Forbes, Technical History.
46. *Organic Chemicals*, catalog published by Shell Chemical Corporation, New York, 1952, pp. 27-29.
47. Letter, T. W. Evans, Emeryville, to the author, November 1, 1954; memorandum, F. J. Hamerschmidt, Martinez, to Felix Kortlandt, San Francisco, March 24, 1938; figures from "Annual Sales of Products Manufactured at Martinez, Dominguez, Houston, and Emeryville," Shell Chemical Statistical Unit, New York, September 27, 1949.
48. *Organic Chemicals*, p. 38; letter, T. W. Evans, Emeryville, Calif., to the author, November 1, 1954; memo-

randum, Hamerschmidt to Kortlandt, *supra*.

49. Material on Shell's manufacture of synthetic iso-octane is contained in a brief MS. history of Shell Development Company, prepared September 1945, by Dr. Harold G. Vesper, Emeryville; E. C. Williams, "Creating Industries, 1919–1939: Petroleum," *Chemical Industries*, May 1939, p. 495; Dr. Ludwig Rosenstein, "Synthetic Chemicals from Petroleum," *Oil & Gas Journal*, November 14, 1940; Matthew Van Winkle, *Aviation Gasoline Manufacture*, New York, McGraw-Hill Book Company, 1944; *An Accounting of Shell Oil Company's Technological and Economic Contributions to the Nation's Welfare*, New York, 1944.

50. Williams, *loc. cit.*

51. Conversation, Dr. C. W. Humphreys, New York, November 10, 1954; Pyzel interviews.

52. Shell Chemical Company Report to Shareholders, 1934, pp. 11, 14.

53. Haynes, *op. cit.*, Vol. III, p. 147.

54. Carleton Ellis, *The Chemistry of Petroleum Derivatives*, Vol. I, New York, Reinhold Publishing Corp., 1934, p. 359.

55. Shell Chemical financial report, January 1935.

56. *Organic Chemicals*, pp. 12-13.

57. Shell Chemical Company Year Report, 1935; Shell Chemical monthly financial statements, June–August 1936.

58. Production figures from sales tabulation (note 47).

59. Shell Chemical Company Year Report, 1937; sales tabulation, *supra;* conversation, Dr. C. W. Humphreys, New York, November 10, 1954.

60. Shell Chemical Company Year-End Reports, 1937–1940.

61. Shell Development Company history, prepared by the company, in Haynes, *op. cit.*, Vol. VI, p. 383.

62. Account prepared for the author August 7, 1945, by Dr. Harold G. Vesper, Emeryville.

63. Haynes, *op. cit.*, Vol. VI, p. 383.

64. M. Scheschukow, "Über die Einwirkung von Chlor aus Isobutylen," *Journal* Russ. Phys. Chem. Soc., Vol. 15, p. 355 (1883); same author, "Un-

tersuchung der beim Einwirkung von Chlor auf die verschiedenen Butylenen entstehenden Produkte," *id.*, Vol. 16, pp. 178-511 (1884).

65. Letter, T. W. Evans, Emeryville, to the author, November 1, 1954.

66. E. C. Williams, "Synthetic Glycerine from Petroleum," paper delivered before meeting of American Institute of Chemical Engineers, New Orleans, December 2–4, 1940, and published in the Institute's *Transactions* for 1941.

67. *Ibid.;* Vesper, MS. history of Shell Development; letter, T. W. Evans, Emeryville, to the author, November 1, 1954.

68. E. C. Williams, "Modern Petroleum Research," paper delivered before American Petroleum Institute annual meeting, November 16, 1938, and reprinted in *Industrial and Engineering Chemistry*, News Section, December 10, 1938.

69. Pyzel interviews, 1947.

70. Shell Chemical Company Year Reports, 1941, p. 29; 1942.

71. Shell Chemical Company Year Report, 1941.

72. Text of Simplex Agreement and correspondence surrounding it, 1928–1932, in Shell Union files.

73. Memorandum, G. H. van Senden to I. M. Hemphill, Wilmington, and E. D. Cumming, Martinez, December 14, 1937; memoranda, J. F. M. Taylor to E. C. Williams, December 17, 1937, and Williams to Taylor, December 21, 1937; agenda for Shell Oil-Shell Development Meeting No. 1, January 11, 1938; interview, Dr. F. W. L. Tydeman, San Francisco, September 10, 1947, and letter, Dr. Tydeman to the author, May 21, 1949; conversation, A. B. Culbertson, New York, May 18, 1949; and letter, S. H. McAllister, Emeryville, to Culbertson, June 7, 1949.

74. Interview, Erle P. Severns, Oakland, California, September 5, 1947; memorandum, Martinez refinery to New York manufacturing department, Shell Oil Company, Inc., April 7, 1949.

75. Conversation, Dr. G. P. Koch, New York, May 16, 1949.

76. Interview, G. H. van Senden, Carmel, California, July 23, 1947, and

letter to the author, November 6, 1954.

77. Conversation, T. B. Rendel, New York, April 7, 1949.

78. Conversations, L. E. Hebl and T. B. Rendel, New York, April 6, 1949 and August 24, 1956; memorandum, Rendel to the author, July 29, 1955.

79. Memorandum, Wilmington refinery to New York manufacturing depart-

ment, Shell Oil Company, Inc., April 8, 1949.

80. Conversation, Dr. J. D. Metcalfe, New York, May 17, 1949.

81. Details from historical sketch of geophysical laboratory, Houston, May 5, 1955.

82. Conversations with E. B. Glendenning, Sewaren, and W. A. Sullivan, Jr., New York, April 5, 1949.

CHAPTER X

United for the War Effort (pages 554 to 636)

1. Figures from Max W. Ball, quoted in Harold L. Ickes, *Fightin' Oil*, New York, Alfred A. Knopf, 1943, p. 16.

2. John W. Frey and H. Chandler Ide, Ed., *A History of the Petroleum Administration for War, 1941–1945*, Washington, Government Printing Office, 1946, p. 1. This book is by far the best account of oil in the war. Also highly useful is Northcutt Ely, "The Government in the Exercise of the War Power," *Conservation of Oil & Gas, A Legal History, 1948*, Blakely M. Murphy, Ed., Chicago, Section of Mineral Law, American Bar Association, 1949, pp. 664-680. A more popular account, lavishly illustrated with photographs, is *Oil for Victory*, by the Editors of *Look*, New York, McGraw-Hill Book Company, 1946.

3. Letter read in full by Ralph K. Davies, Deputy Administrator, Petroleum Administration for War, in "A Valediction," speech before the American Petroleum Institute, Chicago, November 12, 1945, printed in the A.P.I. *Proceedings* for 1945, p. 17.

4. Shell Union Annual Report, 1945, p. 6.

5. Frey and Ide, *op. cit.*, pp. 12, 14, 374, 375.

6. Ely, *loc. cit.*, pp. 669, 671.

7. *Ibid.*; Frey and Ide, *op. cit.*, pp. 355-358. The history of the work of an individual committee is detailed in D. Thomas Curtin, *Men, Oil and War*, Chicago, Petroleum Industry Committee for District No. 2, 1946.

8. H. Chandler Ide, "Mobilizing the Oil Forces," paper presented before Special Committee to Investigate Petroleum Resources, United States Senate, November 28, 1945, and printed as part of an undated paper-covered book, *Petroleum in War and Peace*.

9. Ely, *loc. cit.*, p. 667.

10. Frey and Ide, *op. cit.*, p. 34-35.

11. Conversation, T. B. Rendel, New York, January 6, 1954; S. D. Heron, *Development of Aviation Fuels*, part two of a two-part volume entitled *Development of Aircraft Engines and Fuels*, Boston, Graduate School of Business Administration, Harvard University, 1950, p. 605. Heron's account is refreshingly unbiased and is illuminated from several viewpoints: his long years in the field of aviation fuels have been divided between the armed forces and industry, both in Britain and America.

12. Interview, J. H. Doolittle, New York, June 15, 1948.

13. Information from T. H. Green, Manufacturing Department, Shell Oil Company, New York, January 21 and February 1, 1954; memorandum, J. H. Doolittle to N. J. McGaw, June 18, 1936; C. S. Popple, *Standard Oil Company (New Jersey) in World War II*, New York, Standard Oil Company (New Jersey), 1952, p. 24; Frank Howard, *Buna Rubber*, New York, D. Van Nostrand Company, 1947, p. 53, says Jersey manufactured a small quantity of 100-octane gasoline in June 1935 (both books credit Shell with being

first); *National Petroleum News,* January 8, 1936, p. 28.

14. Heron, *op. cit.,* p. 607.
15. *Id.,* p. 605, fn.
16. *Id.,* pp. 605-606; Quentin Reynolds, *The Amazing Mr. Doolittle,* New York, Appleton-Century-Crofts, Inc., 1953, pp. 158-166, gives verbatim testimony of this hearing.
17. E. F. Zimmerman, Aviation Department, Shell Petroleum Corporation, testimony at Wright Field hearing, November 17, 1936, quoted in Reynolds, *op. cit.,* p. 163.
18. Heron, *op. cit.,* pp. 550-551.
19. Alfred W. Nash and Donald A. Howes, *The Principles of Motor Fuel Preparation and Application,* 2nd Ed., Vol. I, New York, John Wiley & Sons, 1938, pp. 457-460.
20. Popple, *op. cit.,* pp. 22-24; *Industrial and Engineering Chemistry,* January 1927, p. 146; and information courtesy E. W. Esmay, Standard Oil Company (N.J.), New York, February 24, 1954.
21. Description of process from Matthew Van Winkle, *Aviation Gasoline Manufacture,* New York, McGraw-Hill Book Company, 1944, pp. 134-136.
22. Letter, A. E. Lacomblé, St. Louis, to Godber, London, April 16, 1936.
23. Cables, Godber to Fraser, October 14, 1935, Fraser to Godber, October 23, 1935; letters, Lacomblé to Godber, April 16, April 27, and May 20, 1936; letter, H. S. M. Burns, to Fraser, June 2, 1936; memorandum, R. B. High to N. J. McGaw, June 18, 1936.
24. Cable, Lacomblé, to Godber, April 27, 1936.
25. Conversation, R. J. Forbes, New York, September 19–23, 1951; R. J. Forbes, "Technological History of Royal Dutch-Shell Group, 1890–1940," MS. (hereafter called "Forbes, Technical History").
26. *Id.*
27. Robert T. Swaine, *The Cravath Firm and Its Predecessors, 1819–1948,* Vol. II, New York, 1948, pp. 567-570.
28. Frey and Ide, *op. cit.,* p. 199; conversation, E. A. Martin, New York, January 23, 1954.
29. Hugh R. Berry, "Report on Aviation Gasoline Facilities," St. Louis, May

26, 1939 and June 1939. These survey reports were prepared monthly until November 1940.
30. Popple, *op. cit.,* p. 24; memorandum, L. C. Burroughs, New York, to the author, March 2, 1954.
31. Heron, *op. cit.,* p. 611.
32. *An Accounting of Shell Oil Company's Technological and Economic Contributions to the Nation's Welfare,* book published 1944 for use in renegotiating contracts covering the company's business for 1942 (referred to hereafter as "Renegotiation Book No. 1"); *Shell Oil Company's Research and War Production, 1943,* prepared 1944 for use in renegotiation of contracts, pp. 40-41 (hereafter referred to as "Renegotiation Book No. 2").
33. Advertisement, *The Saturday Evening Post,* April 24, 1943, pp. 54-55.
34. Information in this paragraph from conversation, Harry B. Tower, Socony-Vacuum Oil Co., New York, March 1, 1954; Benjamin P. Brooks, "A Brief History of Petroleum Cracking," *The Science of Petroleum,* Vol. III, London, Oxford University Press, 1938, p. 2086; Forbes, Technical History.
35. L. C. Burroughs, "Monthly Report on Aviation Gasoline Manufacture," St. Louis, August 1939. Burroughs took over compilation of the reports begun a few months earlier by H. R. Berry (see note 29).
36. Correspondence files between Fraser, St. Louis, and Van Eck, London, November–December, 1939.
37. Popple, *op. cit.,* p. 13.
38. *Ibid.*
39. Conversation, C. A. Rehbein, New York, March 3, 1954.
40. Conversation, E. A. Martin, New York, January 29, 1954.
41. G. C. Cunningham, "A Brief Resumé of the Story of War Time Production of 100 Octane Aviation Gasoline in the United States and the Part Played by Shell," New York, Shell Oil Company, Inc., 1946, 5 pp., mimeographed, p. 2 (hereafter referred to as "Cunningham report"); Frey and Ide, *op. cit.* "End of war" figure is July 1945.
42. Berry's report for May 1939 (see note 29), monthly report by L. C.

Burroughs, November 1939 (see note 35). Percentage calculations are the author's.

43. Cunningham report, p. 5; "equivalent production" was a term used to include actual production of 100-octane plus the potential production arising from manufacture of unblended alkylate. During the war, it was generally calculated that 100-octane gasoline required an alkylate content of some 40%; thus a manufacturer of 40,000 barrels of alkylate could say that he had a potential, or "equivalent," production of 100,000 barrels of finished 100-octane. Cumene and toluene production later became important in calculating equivalent production, for they constituted some 10% of the finished blend and in addition had the highly desirable effect of releasing about twice their volume of alkylate.

44. Shell Union Annual Report, 1945.

45. Heron, *op. cit.*, pp. 631-632; Popple, *op. cit.*, p. 31.

46. Heron, *op. cit.*, p. 633.

47. *Id.*, p. 634.

48. Frey and Ide, *op. cit.*, p. 195.

49. Heron, *op. cit.*, p. 634.

50. Frey and Ide, *op. cit.*, p. 195.

51. *Id.*, pp. 33, 194; conversation, F. S. Clulow, New York, August 15, 1955.

52. Harold L. Ickes, address before 23rd annual meeting of the American Petroleum Institute, Chicago, November 9, 1942; A.P.I. *Proceedings*, 1942, Section 1, p. 16.

53. Information this and succeeding two paragraphs from Frey and Ide, *op. cit.*, pp. 198, 199, 201.

54. Heron, *op. cit.*, p. 635; Frey and Ide, *op. cit.*, p. 201.

55. Popple, *op. cit.*; conversation, Dr. M. E. Spaght, New York, September 29, 1954; letter, Harry G. Burks, Jr., Standard Oil Company (New Jersey), New York, to the author, November 24, 1954. Dr. Burks was chairman of the Aviation Gasoline Advisory Committee throughout the war.

56. Conversation, T. B. Rendel, New York, March 12, 1954.

57. J. P. O'Donnell, "Shell-Developed Cumene Process Has Speeded Aircraft-Fuel Program," *Oil & Gas Journal*, February 24, 1944, pp. 73-75; Cunningham report, Chart No. 1.

58. Percentages calculated by author on basis of chart "100 Octane Aviation Fuel, Sources of Increased Production, January 1, 1942–December 31, 1943," Frey and Ide, *op. cit.*, p. 201.

59. Renegotiation Book No. 2, p. 44; conversation, C. A. Rehbein, New York, February 10, 1954.

60. Heron, *op. cit.*, p. 644; memorandum, T. B. Rendel, New York, to the author, August 4, 1955.

61. Interview, A. V. Caselli, New York, March 18, 1954; Shell Chemical Year Report, 1944, p. 52.

62. Frey and Ide, *op. cit.*, pp. 207-209.

63. Renegotiation Book No. 2, p. 15; dates courtesy R. S. Douglass, New York, March 23, 1954; conversation, H. D. Loeb, New York, 1951.

64. New York *Times*, Sunday, April 30, 1944, p. 8E.

65. There is a voluminous literature on the synthetic rubber program. Most of it, unfortunately for the historian, was written during the rubber crisis by people who had a point to prove or an axe to grind. The author found a helpful summary in Jesse H. Jones, with Edward Angly, *Fifty Billion Dollars, My Thirteen Years with the R.F.C., 1932-1945*, New York, The Macmillan Company, 1951, pp. 402-433, 610, 611; Frank A. Howard, *Buna Rubber, The Birth of an Industry*, New York, D. Van Nostrand Company, 1947, a well-written, interesting story of the program from beginning to end, including the early history of synthetic rubber and Jersey Standard's patent dealings with the I. G. Farbenindustrie. Howard was for many years president of the Standard Oil Development Company. Government documents with immediate bearing upon the subject include: "The Rubber Situation," House Document No. 836, 77th Congress, 2d Session, Washington, Government Printing Office, September 10, 1942 (the famous "Baruch Report"); "Report on the Rubber Program, Supplement No. 1, Year 1945," Washington, Office of Rubber Reserve, Reconstruction Finance Corporation, April

8, 1946 (listing and describing the individual plants); "Synthetic Rubber Plants and Facilities," Secondary Supplementary and Final Report of the War Assets Administration to the Congress, Washington, Surplus Property Administration, June 18, 1946; "Rubber," First Annual Report by the Secretary of Commerce, Washington, July 25, 1949; "Program for Disposal to Private Industry of Government-Owned Rubber-Producing Facilities," Washington, Reconstruction Finance Corporation, March 1, 1953; "Reconstruction Finance Corporation Program of Liquidation," Washington, November 1953. Early history of synthetic rubber is drawn from Howard's book and R. J. Forbes, *Man the Maker*, New York, Henry Schuman, 1950; details on setting up rubber program in the United States from Howard's and Jesse Jones' books and Hugh Allen, *The House of Goodyear*, Cleveland, 1949.

66. Gustav Egloff and George Hulla, "The Production of Butadiene," *Chemical Industries*, November 1943.

67. Letter, T. W. Evans, Emeryville, California, to the author, December 19, 1955.

68. *A Record of Service, Shell Chemical —1943*, San Francisco, Shell Chemical Division of Shell Union Oil Corporation, 1944, p. 43 (hereafter referred to as "Shell Chemical Renegotiation Book"); William Haynes, *The American Chemical Industry*, Vol. VI, New York, D. Van Nostrand Co., 1949, p. 384.

69. Shell Chemical Year Report, 1941, p. 29.

70. Shell Chemical Renegotiation Book, p. 53; Shell Chemical Year Report, 1942, p. 35; number of tires calculated by the author on basis of figures given in Shell Chemical Year Report, 1944.

71. Baruch Report.

72. Interview, A. W. Fleer, New York, November 30, 1953.

73. Shell Chemical Renegotiation Book, p. 45.

74. Shell Chemical Year Report, 1944, p. 48.

75. Fleer interview.

76. Shell Chemical Year Report, 1944,

p. 50; Shell Chemical Renegotiation Book, p. 45.

77. Fleer interview.

78. Shell Chemical Renegotiation Book, p. 43.

79. Letter, Bradley Dewey to Jan Oostermeyer, August 31, 1944, reproduced in Shell Chemical Renegotiation Book, p. 44.

80. "Report on the Rubber Program, Supplement No. 1, Year 1945," Washington, Office of Rubber Reserve, Reconstruction Finance Corporation, April 8, 1946, pp. 37-38, 55.

81. Memorandum, J. L. Miller, Houston refinery, to the author, April 8, 1954; letter, E. D. Cumming, St. Louis, December 31, 1940; monthly operating reports, Houston refinery, April and November 1941.

82. Forbes, Technical History; Popple, *op. cit.*, p. 107.

83. Author's calculations, based on Houston refinery monthly reports for 1941.

84. Wilmington - Dominguez refinery monthly operating report, December 1942; monthly operating report, Martinez refinery, September 1942; conversation, J. E. Marsland, New York, March 29, 1954; Wood River refinery monthly operating report, January 1942.

85. Analysis of Amortization of War Emergency Facilities, Shell Oil Company, Inc., New York, April 8, 1946.

86. Total petroleum toluene and Baytown Ordnance Works figures from Popple, *op. cit.*, p. 113; Shell figures courtesy W. A. Carnahan, Shell Oil refinery accounting department; percentage calculations by the author.

87. Conversation, J. P. Cunningham, New York, December 9, 1953; Renegotiation Book No. 2, p. 46 (see note 32).

88. Frey and Ide, *op. cit.*, p. 85; R. G. Pearson, "Petroleum Meets a Crisis," *Shell News*, New York, July-August, 1941.

89. Frey and Ide, *op. cit.*, p. 87.

90. Pearson, *loc. cit.*; Frey and Ide, *op. cit.*, p. 105.

91. Frey and Ide, *op. cit.*, pp. 102, 105.

92. Information this and following paragraph from letter, T. E. Swigart,

Houston, to the author, September 13, 1955; Frey and Ide, *op. cit.,* pp. 104-107, 417-418; T. E. Swigart, "Post-War Uses of the War Emergency Pipe Lines for Petroleum Transportation," paper delivered before the Petroleum Division of the American Institute of Mining and Metallurgical Engineers, New York, February 24, 1944.

93. Frey and Ide, *op. cit.,* pp. 104, 107.
94. Interview, H. H. Anderson, Houston, April 14, 1948.
95. Interview, F. B. Simms, Kernville, California, September 2, 1947; "Shell Completes Ventura Line," *Oil & Gas Journal,* October 30, 1941, pp. 22, 196.
96. Booklet, *The Plantation Story,* Atlanta, Plantation Pipe Line Company, 1953.
97. *Business Week,* May 31, 1941.
98. Popple, *op. cit.,* p. 147; *The Plantation Story, supra; Shell News,* March 1942, p. 9.
99. Frey and Ide, *op. cit.,* p. 417.
100. Conversation, W. F. Kenney, New York, August 15, 1955.
101. Information on building of Bayou line from Anderson interview and letter, Anderson to the author, August 1955; H. H. Anderson, C. E. Dolhonde, and L. J. Rittiner, "Bayou Attains High Capacity in War Emergency," *Oil & Gas Journal,* September 23, 1943; "Second-Hand Pipe Line," *Shell News,* September 1942.
102. Frey and Ide, *op. cit.,* pp. 417 and 420, give essential data on Ohio Emergency Pipe Lines, Inc.
103. Description of line from conversations, S. S. Smith, New York, April 14 and 16, 1954, and memorandum, M. E. Grant to Alexander Fraser, New York, March 23, 1945, with 39 pages of summarized correspondence. This summary by Grant gives a complete account of the chronology of the development of the military portable pipe line, from mid-1940 to mid-1943.
104. Description of the Quartermaster Corps line from article by J. P. O'Donnell, *Oil & Gas Journal,* October 8, 1942.
105. *Oil & Gas Journal,* August 5, 1943; "The Army's Portable Pipeline," *Na-*

tional Petroleum News, May 3, 1944, gives a good description of the line.
106. *Oil & Gas Journal,* August 5, 1943, pp. 25-26; conversations, B. C. Astrup, New York, April 22 and May 3, 1954. Astrup was a lieutenant colonel in the Army Engineers and helped operate the North African portable lines.
107. Monthly Report of Pipe Line Operation for May 1945, Headquarters, Engineer District #12, Service of Supply, India-Burma Theater.
108. Conversations, S. S. Smith, New York, April 14 and 16, 1954, and George S. Wolbert, Jr., New York, August 13, 1954. Wolbert was a pipe line instructor at Camp Claiborne, La., and later helped operate the military products line originating at Antwerp.
109. Letter, Brig. Gen. R. F. Fowler, Chief, Supply Division, Office of the Chief of Engineers, War Department, Washington, to S. S. Smith, May 29, 1943.
110. Memorandum sheets prepared by Dr. C. W. Humphreys, February 21, 1951; Shell Chemical Year Report, 1942, p. 11; F. H. Leavitt, "Use and Marketing of Agricultural Ammonia," *Agricultural Chemicals,* June 1953.
111. Humphreys memo, *supra.*
112. *Id.;* Shell Chemical Year Report, 1944; table prepared by Statistical Unit, Shell Chemical Corporation, New York, September 27, 1949.
113. Humphreys memo.
114. *Shell News,* San Francisco, July 1945, pp. 1 and 3.
115. Information from Shell Chemical records and interview, A. V. Caselli, New York, March 18, 1954.
116. Letter, L. A. DuBridge, Radiation Laboratories, Massachusetts Institute of Technology, to Frank Goldstone, Houston, October 9, 1943.
117. Figures in this paragraph from memorandum sheets prepared for the author by Dr. H. G. Vesper, Emeryville, August 7, 1945.
118. *Shell News,* San Francisco, October 1945, pp. 1-2; conversation, Hugh Harvey, New York, April 1954.
119. Memorandum prepared by Dr. H. G. Vesper, Emeryville, April 1949.

120. *Id.;* conversation, L. E. Hebl, New York, May 10, 1954.
121. Vesper memorandum, *supra;* Renegotiation Book No. 2, p. 47.
122. Conversations, H. R. Kemmerer and L. E. Hebl, New York, May 11, 1954; *Shell News,* New York, March 1945, pp. 2-3.
123. Vesper memo; conversation, R. K. Schulze, New York, May 7, 1954; Renegotiation Book No. 1.
124. Conversations, L. E. Hebl, April 6, 1949, and May 10, 1954, H. R. Kemmerer, May 11, 1954; Renegotiation Books Nos. 1 and 2.
125. Renegotiation Book No. 2, p. 46.
126. Vesper memo; conversation, E. A. Martin, New York, May 12, 1954.
127. Some details of the penicillin process are given in *Shell News,* New York, April 1945, pp. 2-6.
128. Renegotiation Book No. 1; Vesper memorandum.
129. Shell Union Annual Report, 1943; Frey and Ide, *op. cit.,* pp. 187-188, say that the total of industry crude oil shipments into California by rail reached 35,000 barrels a day just before V-J Day.
130. B. L. Ryan, "A History of Shell Oil Company's Activities in West Texas and New Mexico," MS., August 1948.
131. Letter, R. B. Roark, for Fraser, to G. Legh-Jones, London, December 12, 1945; conversations, A. J. Galloway, New York, August 8, 1955, and L. G. Christie, New York, June 5, 1956.
132. Shell Union Annual Reports, 1945, p. 2; 1946, p. 2.
133. Jones and Angly, *op. cit.,* pp. 315, 339.
134. A partial list of these government-built facilities is given by Frey and Ide, *op. cit.,* pp. 368-369.
135. Shell Union Annual Report, 1943, pp. 7-8.
136. Shell Union Annual Report, 1945, p. 3; report, "Analysis of Amortization of War Emergency Facilities, East of the Rockies and Pacific Coast Territories," New York, Accounting Department, Shell Oil Company, Inc., April 8, 1946.
137. "Shell Women at Work," *Shell News,* September 1943, pp. 8-13; interviews, I. M. Hemphill and Frank Coats, Martinez, July 16 and 17, 1947; personnel department records, courtesy W. H. Hutten, New York.
138. *Shell News,* September 1943, pp. 2-7.
139. Renegotiation Book No. 2, pp. 18-21.
140. Material on rubber drives from Renegotiation Books No. 1 and 2 and conversation, H. L. Curtis, New York, May 24, 1954.
141. "Military Leave Policy," *Shell News,* March 1942, pp. 3-4.
142. "Doolittle Returns to Shell," *Shell News,* January 1946, pp. 11-14.

CHAPTER XI

A Billion-Dollar Corporation (pages 637 to 699)

1. Figures and dates from John W. Frey and H. Chandler Ide, Ed., *A History of the Petroleum Administration for War, 1941-1945,* Washington, U. S. Government Printing Office, 1946.
2. Alexander Fraser, general memorandum, June 16, 1943.
3. "War and Postwar Markets for Petroleum Products," Marketing Department, Shell Oil Company, Inc., New York, November 1943.
4. Operating reports Wood River and Houston refineries, August 1945.
5. Figures from Shell Union Annual Reports, 1946–1948; Shell Oil Annual Reports, 1949–1950.
6. "A Report on Supply and Demand of Oil Products in 1950," New York, The Oil Industry Information Committee of the American Petroleum Institute, June 1, 1951.
7. Talk by H. S. M. Burns before New York Society of Security Analysts, March 13, 1951.
8. David White, "The Unmined Supply of Petroleum in the United States," paper before Society of Automotive Engineers, February 1919, quoted by Joseph E. Pogue,

The Economics of Petroleum, New York, John Wiley & Sons, 1921, pp. 19-21; article, "Predicts Oil's Exhaustion in 26 Years," *Roxoleum,* Tulsa, Roxana Petroleum Company of Oklahoma, June 1919; Victor Clifton Alderson, president of Colorado School of Mines, saw oil shale just around the corner in his book, *The Oil Shale Industry,* New York, Frederick A. Stokes Company, 1920.

9. Information this and subsequent paragraphs, from Shell Union and Shell Oil Annual Reports, 1946–1950, except as otherwise noted.

10. *Oil & Gas Journal,* June 18, 1956, p. 139.

11. Conversation, A. J. Galloway, New York, August 2, 1955; *Shell News of Canada,* Toronto, May 1951; conversation, B. D. Vishanoff, New York, June 4, 1951.

12. Michael Silverbergh, "A History of the Rocky Mountain Division," Los Angeles, Shell Oil Company, January, 1954, MS.

13. *Ibid.; Williston Basin Oil Review,* Bismarck, N.D., January 1954, p. 9; *Petroleum Engineer,* November 1951, p. A-49; *Oil & Gas Journal,* November 1, 1951, p. 103.

14. Memoranda, B. L. Ryan, Houston, to J. A. Abbott, January 26, 1949, and H. W. Penterman, Tulsa, to the author, January 31, 1949; *Shell Roar,* Tulsa, October 1949.

15. Booklet, *Booster for Benton,* New York, Shell Oil Company, October 1951.

16. Securities and Exchange Commission, Form A-2, Registration No. 2-6269, filed by Shell Union Oil Corporation, April 16, 1946, pp. 14, 17, gives 1946 figure; 1950 reserve figure from Shell Oil Company Annual Report for 1950, p. 6.

17. Letters to the author, T. E. Swigart, Houston, September 13, 1955, and H. H. Anderson, Orlando, Florida, August 1955.

18. Material on Basin and Ozark Pipe Line Systems from Shell Union Annual Report, 1948; Shell Oil Annual Report, 1950; Training Manual, Ozark Pipe Line System, Houston, Shell Pipe Line Corporation, c. 1948; Booklet, *The Basin and Ozark Pipe Line Systems,* Houston, Shell

Pipe Line Corporation, 1949; figure on top capacity of each line from letter, D. F. Sears, Houston, to the author, September 16, 1955.

19. Conversation, D. B. Hodges, New York, December 1955.

20. Conversation, L. J. Di Miceli, New York, June 27, 1951.

21. Except as otherwise noted, information on pipe line expansion from Shell Oil Company Annual Reports, 1950–1953, and *The Oil Record,* Washington, 1953.

22. Conversation, C. A. Rehbein, New York, October 4, 1954.

23. Material on International Lubricant chiefly from interview with W. H. Saunders, Jr., New Orleans, December 13, 1947.

24. Conversation, C. A. Rehbein, New York, October 5, 1954.

25. Conversation, C. A. Rehbein, New York, October 1, 1954; start-up dates courtesy manufacturing engineering department, New York.

26. Conversation, Carl Barker, New York, June 27, 1951.

27. Conversation, Harry Wearne, New York, October 15, 1954.

28. Information from H. R. Hanhart, New York, July 11, 1951, and E. Reillac, San Francisco, July 26, 1951.

29. Information on depot design from conversation, S. S. Tomlin, Jr., New York, July 13, 1951; report, S. S. Tomlin, Jr., "Suggested Layout of Warehouse, Using Scale Models," Marketing Department, Shell Oil Company, New York, June 1951.

30. Conversation, Thornton Beall, New York, March 28, 1955.

31. *Shell News,* San Francisco, May 1950, p. 1.

32. Information on terminals from W. J. Spravale, New York, April 20, 1951; and memorandum, J. H. Sembower, San Francisco, to the author, May 24, 1951.

33. Conversations, D. E. Burroughs, New York, November 9, 1949, and July 11, 1951.

34. *Shell News,* July 1951.

35. General memorandum, Alexander Fraser, St. Louis, January 6, 1939.

36. Printed report, "Those Who Know You Well Think Well of You," Opinion Research Corporation, 1946.

37. Paper, "A New Chemical Industry

Based on Allyl Chloride," by D. L. Yabroff, Shell Development Company, and John Anderson, Shell Chemical Company, The Hague, Third World Petroleum Congress, June 1951; article, "Synthetic Glycerine, A Milestone in Petrochemical Progress," *Chemical Engineering*, October 1948.

38. Conversation, R. C. McCurdy, New York, August 8, 1955.

39. *Fortune*, August 1948, p. 74.

40. Material on Modesto from "Highlights in the Growth of the Shell Agricultural Laboratory, 1944–49," by H. G. Vesper, Shell Development Company, Emeryville, April 1949; booklet, "Better Farming Through Research," Shell Oil Company, San Francisco, 1946; article, "Darndest Farm You Ever Saw," by Frank J. Taylor, *Country Gentleman*, March 1949; and interview with Dr. Roy Hansberry, Modesto, September 3, 1947.

41. From material prepared for and reviewed by Dr. Harold Gershinowitz, Houston, April 1949.

42. Draft, "Highlights of the Growth of Shell Development Company," by H. G. Vesper, Emeryville, April 11, 1949.

43. *Shell News*, April 1950.

44. Material on Wood River and Martinez laboratories prepared for and reviewed by Manufacturing Department, Shell Oil Company, New York, April 1949.

45. Material prepared on Houston and Wilmington laboratories, Manufacturing Department, Shell Oil Company, New York, April 1949; conversation, H. R. Kemmerer, New York, April 6, 1955.

46. Material prepared on East Chicago laboratory, April 1949; conversation, R. K. Schulze, New York, July 26, 1951.

47. Conversation, J. R. Janssen, New York, July 26, 1951.

48. Conversation, W. M. Upchurch, Jr., New York, June 1956.

Some Important Dates in Shell History

1890	June 16	Royal Dutch Company organized at The Hague.
1892	February 28	First Royal Dutch refinery at Pangkalan Brandan, Lang-kat, North Sumatra, begins operation, drawing crude oil from nearby Telaga Toenggal field belonging to Royal Dutch.
	July	*Murex*, first tanker of M. Samuel & Co., London, sails for Far East through Suez Canal carrying cargo of Russian kerosene purchased from Rothschild refinery at Batum on Black Sea.
1896	July 13	H. W. A. Deterding hired as Royal Dutch Company sales manager.
1897	October 18	M. Samuel & Co. organize The "Shell" Transport & Trading Co., Ltd., to operate oil department of their business. Samuel agents in Far East contribute tank installations in exchange for stock in new company.
1901	January 25	Deterding appointed Royal Dutch managing director.
1902	June 27	Royal Dutch Co., Shell Transport & Trading Co., and Paris Rothschilds (owners of refinery at Batum) form Asiatic Petroleum Company, Ltd., as joint marketing concern for Far East. Asiatic begins business 1903.
1907		Royal Dutch Co. and Shell Transport & Trading Co. join forces in permanent alliance. Two new companies organized: The Anglo-Saxon Petroleum Company, Ltd., to own tanker fleet and large marine installations; N.V. De Bataafsche Petroleum Maatschappij (B.P.M.) to own oil fields and refineries, be in general charge of technical matters. Royal Dutch holds 60% of new companies, Shell T. & T. 40%. Marketing and commercial affairs left in hands of Asiatic Petroleum Company, Ltd., in which Royal Dutch and Shell realign their interest on 60-40 basis (Rothschild interest in Asiatic not sold until early 1930's). Royal Dutch and Shell T. & T. divest themselves of all properties, become henceforth purely holding companies. This event marks beginning of Royal Dutch-Shell Group of companies.
1909		Pieter Kruisheer, B.P.M. geologist, arrives in Oklahoma to examine oil properties offered for sale; advises against purchase.
1911	January	F. P. S. Harris and J. C. van Eck arrive in United States

		to organize marketing company on Pacific Coast to sell gasoline imported from Sumatra.
1912	July 22	Marcus S. Abrahams arrives in Oklahoma, buys six small oil producing companies on behalf of Group.
	September 3	American Gasoline Company organized to own and operate Pacific Coast marketing properties.
	September 16	First cargo of Sumatra gasoline arrives in Seattle.
	October 1	Roxana Petroleum Company of Oklahoma organized by Abrahams to take title to properties purchased in July, along with four other small oil-producing companies purchased September 4. Stock of Roxana of Oklahoma is owned by Roxana Petroleum Company (New York), organized September 13.
	October 4	First tank car of Shell gasoline shipped from American Gasoline Co. terminal at Richmond Beach, Washington.
1913	August 11	California Oilfields, Ltd., owning substantial producing properties at Coalinga, Calif., purchased for $13,000,000.
1914	April 16	Valley Pipe Line Company organized to build 170-mile line from California Oilfields' Coalinga property to Martinez, site on arm of San Francisco Bay selected for refinery.
	July 24	Name of American Gasoline Company changed to Shell Company of California, Inc.
	October	Construction of Valley Pipe Line started; completed August 11, 1915.
1915	May 15	Roxana purchases Yarhola leases in Cushing, Okla., field. Yarhola Pipe Line Company (25 miles of pipe) acquired in deal.
	July 30	Shell Company of California (no "Inc.") organized to take over business of Shell Company of California, Inc., and California Oilfields, Ltd.
	September 9	Roxana purchases extensive leases in Healdton, Okla., field.
	December	First unit of Martinez refinery in operation; balance of plant completed and put on stream during 1916. Initial capacity 5,500 barrels a day; 18,000 barrels a day by 1918.
1916	April 29	Richard Airey, representative of Shell Group, buys 363 acres of river-front property at Sellers, La., as site for tankage, docks, and future refinery; New Orleans Refining Company organized in June to take title to property.
	May	Contract let for 126-mile, 6-inch pipe line from Healdton to Cushing, Okla.
	August	Roxana starts construction of temporary refinery at Cushing. Refinery in operation March 1917; closed spring 1919.

1917	April	Roxana begins construction of refinery at Wood River, Ill., near St. Louis.
	April	Roxana establishes exploration and production office at Mineral Wells, Texas, and begins unsuccessful exploratory campaign in North Central Texas area.
	June	Roxana sets up exploratory office at Cheyenne, Wyo., to search for oil in Rocky Mountain area.
1918	August 31	First oil arrives at Wood River in new 428-mile, 10-inch Cushing-to-Wood River pipe line.
	September 23	Wood River refinery goes on stream. Approximate initial throughput 5,500 barrels a day.
1919	June	Roxana offices moved to Arcade Building, St. Louis.
	October 1	Ozark Pipe Line Corporation organized under the laws of Maryland to take over properties of Yarhola Pipe Line Company.
1920	February 1	Roxana Petroleum Corporation, organized in 1917 under laws of Virginia, takes over business of Roxana Petroleum Company of Oklahoma.
	May	Rocky Mountain venture incorporated as Matador Petroleum Company, owned jointly by Roxana and Shell Company of California. Abandoned as unsuccessful in 1922.
	May 8	Norco Refinery (then called Good Hope) begins operation; initial capacity, about 5,000 barrels a day.
1921	March	Roxana, first licensee of Dubbs cracking process, begins operation of Dubbs unit at Wood River.
	June 25	Shell of California brings in Alamitos No. 1, discovery well of prolific Signal Hill (Long Beach) field.
	September 19	Roxana acquires from Marland Oil Company half interest in Comar Oil Company, owner of substantial leases in Tonkawa (Okla.) field, discovered three months earlier. After profitable career, Comar dissolved 1931.
	October 19	After several months of negotiation, Royal Dutch-Shell Group signs agreement to acquire properties of Union Oil Company (Delaware).
1922	February 8	Shell Union Oil Corporation organized under Delaware law as holding company to own former Union of Delaware properties, Shell Company of California, Roxana Petroleum Corporation, Ozark Pipe Line Corporation. Stock issued 28% to Union of Delaware, 6.3% to Dundee Corporation (former minority partner in Roxana), 65.7% to Royal Dutch-Shell Group. Union of Delaware properties divided between Shell of California and Roxana.
	March 7	Gosnell No. 3, discovery well of Ventura, California, oil field brought in by Shell of California after nearly 6 years of drilling and expenditure of $2½ million; field develops into one of Shell's most profitable holdings.

	October	Shell Union exercises option acquired in Shell-Union deal, purchases during following year two-thirds interest in Oklahoma producer, Central Petroleum Company, rechristens it Wolverine Petroleum Corporation. Wolverine dissolved December 1938.
1923	February 12	Roxana purchases Lilly White Oil Company, large jobber of Lima, Ohio.
	April 1	Roxana purchases Tri-States Oil Company, small jobber of Seymour, Ind., and begins first retail sale of Shell-branded gasoline in Midwest. Sets up Illinois, St. Louis, and Chicago marketing divisions during month of April.
	September 25	Wilmington refinery of Shell Company of California begins operation. Initial capacity, 25,000 barrels per day.
	December 15	Roxana completes refinery at Arkansas City, Kansas. Initial capacity, 12,000 to 14,000 barrels a day.
1924	June	Roxana establishes central exploration and production office at Dallas, begins leasing activity in West Texas and Louisiana. Company explores with torsion balance, introduced to United States by Roxana during 1922.
1925	September	McCamey field (West Texas) discovered with Roxana holding extensive acreage.
1926	January 1	Roxana offices move into new Shell Building, St. Louis.
	July	Hendricks field (West Texas) discovered; Roxana acquires extensive acreage.
	October	Roxana buys half interest in Great American Gasoline Co., Kokomo, Ind., jobber; rechristened Shell American Petroleum Company and operated as separate company until end of 1955 when remaining stock interest acquired by Shell.
	October	Yates field (West Texas) discovered with Roxana holding acreage. McCamey, Hendricks, and Yates, all prolific producers, but not developed immediately owing to distance from markets and lack of pipe line facilities.
1927	March	Roxana opens East Chicago, Ind., refinery, drawing crude oil through 249-mile, 8-inch pipe line connecting with northern terminus of existing line at Wood River. East Chicago initial capacity, 15,000 barrels a day.
	April 1	Shell Company of California begins operation of 100-mile, 4- and 6-inch gasoline pipe line to transport natural gasoline from Ventura field to Wilmington refinery.
	September 1	Dominguez refinery of Shell Company of California put in operation. Dominguez, located near Wilmington, essentially cracking plant extension of Wilmington refinery; two operate as unit from beginning.
	October 25	Ozark Pipe Line Corporation changes name to Shell

<table>
<tr><td></td><td></td><td>Pipe Line Corporation; begins building 10-inch, 481-mile line to connect Cushing with McCamey, West Texas. Completed March 1928.</td></tr>
<tr><td>1928</td><td>August 30</td><td>Royal Dutch-Shell Group and Shell Union jointly agree to purchase half interest in The Flintkote Company, manufacturers of asphalt shingles, for $8,200,000; Shell given privilege of nominating majority of Flintkote directors. Shell's Flintkote holding sold early in 1936.</td></tr>
<tr><td></td><td>October</td><td>Shell Development Company, organized to do basic hydrocarbon research, moves into new laboratory at Emeryville, Calif.</td></tr>
<tr><td></td><td>October 22</td><td>Roxana stockholders vote to change company name to Shell Petroleum Corporation.</td></tr>
<tr><td>1929</td><td>January 1</td><td>Name of Shell Company of California changed to Shell Oil Company.</td></tr>
<tr><td></td><td>January</td><td>Shell-owned service stations on Pacific Coast leased to Van Fleet-Durkee, Inc.; V. & D. sublet stations to dealers, introduce new merchandising methods, sell out to Shell in March 1932.</td></tr>
<tr><td></td><td>February 4-5</td><td>Shell Union purchases marketing properties, Fall River refinery, and inventories of bankrupt New England Oil Refining Company for slightly more than $6,000,000. Refinery closed and converted into ocean terminal; marketing properties and marketing personnel become nucleus of new Shell organization on Atlantic Seaboard, Shell Eastern Petroleum Products, Inc., organized January 2.</td></tr>
<tr><td></td><td>February 18</td><td>Shell Chemical Corporation organized to manufacture chemicals from petroleum by-products, utilizing processes originated by Shell Development research.</td></tr>
<tr><td></td><td>March</td><td>New Orleans Refining Company, owner of refinery at Norco, La., purchased by Shell Petroleum Corporation. Shell Petroleum uses Norco product to enter Deep South market, opens marketing division offices at New Orleans and Jacksonville.</td></tr>
<tr><td></td><td>August 13</td><td>Shell Petroleum refinery on Houston Ship Channel begins operation; initial throughput 20,000 barrels a day. Product destined for Atlantic Coast market. Crude supplied by 446-mile, 10-inch pipe line, completed from McCamey (West Texas) to Houston refinery, April 1929.</td></tr>
<tr><td></td><td>September 1</td><td>Shell Petroleum purchases Western Oil Refining Company and Columbus Oil Company, large jobbers and retailers of Indianapolis and Columbus, Ohio, for $6,600,000. On same day new marketing divisions set up at Detroit and Cleveland.</td></tr>
<tr><td></td><td>December</td><td>Shell Eastern begins marketing in the District of Columbia; Shell is now coast to coast, in all 48 states and Hawaii.</td></tr>
</table>

1930	April 16	New 29-story Shell building in San Francisco dedicated by Sir Henri Deterding.
	July 1	Shell Union, losing money, omits dividend on common stock; not resumed until July 1, 1936.
	September	Shell Chemical plant to produce secondary butyl alcohol from refinery waste gases goes into operation at Martinez.
1931	January 6	Holders of chief process patents in thermal cracking field sign agreement ending fifteen years of litigation. Patents assigned to Universal Oil Products Co., which is purchased by Shell and four other oil companies.
	March 11	Shell Union acquires 50% interest in Shell Company of Canada which (Aug. 26) changes name to Shell Oil Company of Canada, Ltd.
	August	Shell Chemical plant, first to make synthetic ammonia from natural gas, goes into operation at Pittsburg, Calif.; initial designed capacity, 40 tons per day.
	September	191-mile, 10-inch pipe line completed to transport Shell's East Texas production to Houston refinery.
	December 31	Shell Union closes year with net loss of $27,000,000; intensive program of cost-cutting and retrenchment throughout organization.
1932	July 1	All salaries cut 10%; 15,000 employees laid off 1931–1932. Several Midwest marketing divisions consolidated, 1930–1932, in drive to cut overhead.
	December	Dallas exploration and production office closed; headquarters for Gulf-Southwest oilfield activity moved to Houston.
1933	April 8	Shell Petroleum launches highly successful "Super-Shell for Price of Regular" campaign, flagging sales revive.
	April	Shell Chemical begins manufacture of tertiary butyl alcohol at Martinez.
	December	Shell Chemical puts in operation at Martinez its first full-scale plant for production of methyl ethyl ketone.
1934	April 30	Shell ships to U. S. Army Air Corps first commercial quantities of iso-octane, used to manufacture 100-octane gasoline for Air Corps planes; company builds extensive aviation gasoline manufacturing facilities during next three years.
1935	January	Shell Chemical puts in operation at Martinez plant to produce isopropyl alcohol and acetone.
	December 31	Shell Union reports net income of $6,800,000, ending prolonged period of deficit.
1936	March	Shell Union sells $60,000,000 bond issue at lowered interest rates to provide money for expansion, retire high-interest indebtedness.
	April	Shell Petroleum sets up committee of economists to

chart company's operation for ensuing five years; exhaustive report, rendered January 1937, recommends sweeping revisions in Shell Petroleum operations.

June
: Shell Chemical completes new plant at Dominguez for manufacture of alcohols and ketones.

June 2
: Shell discovers Ten Section field in San Joaquin Valley, Calif.

October
: Shell Eastern Petroleum Products, Inc., becomes Shell Eastern Division of Shell Union Oil Corporation; organization overhauled and rejuvenated by addition of West Coast marketing executives.

December
: 258-mile, 10-inch crude pipe line completed from Bakersfield, Calif., to Martinez following old right-of-way from Coalinga northward.

1937 September
: Construction starts on products pipe line, running east from Wood River refinery through heart of Illinois and Indiana. Main 8-inch line completed to Lima, Ohio, June 1938; 6-inch spur to Columbus finished in 1939; over-all length 450 miles. Line materially reduces Shell's freight costs, permits more profitable operation.

1938 June
: Obsolescent Arkansas City refinery, serving area of marginal profitability, closed down and dismantled; Shell Petroleum begins process of withdrawing from marketing in most of area between Rocky Mountains and Mississippi River.

1939 March 31
: Shell Oil Company, San Francisco, merged into Shell Petroleum Corporation, St. Louis, to form new operating company, Shell Oil Company, Inc., which a month later also takes over Shell Eastern properties.

August 18
: Alkylation plant, second in country, built at Martinez refinery, embodying new process for low-cost production of high-antiknock aviation gasoline components. During next six months, Shell puts three additional alkylation plants in operation, providing valuable manufacturing capacity in advance of wartime needs.

1940 March
: East Chicago refinery, in need of rebuilding, closed down; new equipment installed instead at Wood River. Former East Chicago-to-Wood River crude oil pipe line converted to products service for Chicago and Great Lakes area. Addition of new capacity at Wood River makes possible economic utilization of refinery waste gases for manufacture of aviation gasoline components.

September 1
: St. Louis and New York executive offices of Shell Oil Company, Inc., combined at New York.

December 2
: Toluene recovery unit, using Shell-developed process, completed at Houston refinery.

1941 September
: As part of new plant at Houston, Shell Chemical completes plant to make butadiene from petroleum gases,

first commercial-scale butadiene installation based on petroleum.

December — Shell producing 22½% of U. S. aviation gasoline at outbreak of war.

1942   January 1 — Plantation Products Pipe Line System, 10- and 12-inch multi-products line, goes into operation from Baton Rouge, La., to Greensboro, N. C. Main line 812 miles long with 449 miles of spur lines to Birmingham, Montgomery, Chattanooga, Knoxville, Macon, and Columbus, Ga. System owned 24% by Shell.

April — Army orders initial manufacture of military portable pipe line, designed and developed by Shell products pipe line department. Military line used extensively in North Africa, Italy, France, and China-Burma-India Theater.

May 5 — Polymerization unit at Norco refinery, converted in three weeks to manufacture of cumene, goes into operation. Cumene process, developed by Shell, installed in 17 U. S. and 2 Canadian refineries, makes possible 23% increase in aviation gasoline production during 1942–1943.

July — Shell discovers Monahans field (West Texas).

1943   January — Wood River refinery wins Army-Navy "E" for war production, first such award to oil refinery. Similar awards won by Martinez refinery, Shell Chemical Martinez and Dominguez plants in January 1944.

February — Bayou Pipe Line System, 27% owned by Shell, completed between Houston refining area and Baton Rouge, to feed Plantation Pipe Line System. Shell Pipe Line Corporation acts as contractor, builds line almost entirely of secondhand materials.

July 27 — Start of operation of butadiene plant at Torrance, Calif., built and operated for government by Shell as part of wartime synthetic rubber program.

October 1 — Shell Union acquires 100% interest in Shell Chemical Company which becomes Shell Chemical Division of Shell Union Oil Corporation.

November — Catalytic cracking unit at Wilmington refinery, first of fluid cracking units completed under wartime aviation gasoline program, goes into operation.

1944   January — Xylidine ("C.S.") plant completed by Shell Chemical for government in Texas Panhandle, using Shell-developed processes. Xylidine makes possible production of rich-mixture fuel of better than 100-octane rating, highly useful during months of European invasion; plant discontinued November 1944.

April 30 — Wood River refinery celebrates tenth anniversary of 100-octane gasoline, inaugurates two catalytic cracking units, one completed in February, the other in March.

1945	August	By war's end Shell, with 6% of nation's refining capacity, has produced more than 13% of total wartime aviation gasoline.
1946	January 1	Shell Chemical, a division of Shell Union since October 1943, reconstituted as Shell Chemical Corporation; postwar expansion of chemical company begins with creation of sales offices east of Rockies.
	April	Shell brings in first oil-producing well in Weeks Island, Louisiana, field at depth of nearly 14,000 feet; field proves profitable despite extreme depths of wells.
	April	Shell Union borrows $125,000,000 to provide for postwar expansion, retire existing higher-rate indebtedness.
	June	Shell buys International Lubricant Corporation, grease manufacturer of New Orleans.
	September	Catalytic cracking unit, using Shell-developed microspheroidal catalyst, put in operation at Houston refinery.
	September	Agricultural research center opened at Modesto, California.
	November	Territory served by Houston exploration and production area office divided; new area offices created at Midland and New Orleans.
1947	November	Shell discovers Elk City field in western Oklahoma.
	November	Start of construction, Basin Pipe Line System, 20- and 24-inch joint-venture crude oil pipe line from Jal, N. Mex., to Cushing, Okla., 34% owned by Shell; completed June 1949.
	December 7	New exploration and production research center opened at Houston.
1948	September	Synthetic glycerine plant, using process developed at Emeryville during 1930's, goes into operation at Houston plant of Shell Chemical Corporation; world's first plant to make glycerine from petroleum.
	September	Shell Chemical head office moved from San Francisco to New York.
	October	Plant to manufacture ethyl alcohol goes into operation at Shell Chemical's Houston installation, first to make alcohol by direct hydration of ethylene.
	December	Construction starts on Ozark Pipe Line System, 22-inch joint-venture crude line from Cushing, Okla., to Wood River, Ill., 55% owned by Shell Pipe Line Corp., contractor and operator; completed July 1949.
1949	January 1	Shell Oil New York and San Francisco executive offices combined, top policy-making officials move to New York.
	April	Exploration and production area office set up at Calgary, Alberta, to handle company's participation in new Canadian oil fields.

	September 22	Shell Union Oil Corporation absorbs Shell Oil Company, Inc., changes Shell Union name to Shell Oil Company.
1950	April	Shell discovers South Pass Block 24 field in Mississippi Delta, major offshore oil field that by 1956 was Louisiana's largest producer.
	May	Shell Development head office moves from San Francisco to Emeryville; laboratories enlarged by completion of new building.
	November	Shell Chemical begins manufacture of Epon resins at Houston.
1951	July 13	Shell brings in successful well at Richey, Montana, extending Williston Basin producing area.
	December 31	Shell's annual sales for first time exceed billion-dollar mark.
1952	April 30	Shell Chemical buys Julius Hyman & Co., Denver, manufacturer of high-potency insecticides. Hyman organization absorbed into Shell Chemical January 1, 1955.
1953	April	Completion of Rancho Pipe Line System, 24-inch joint-venture crude line from McCamey to Houston. Shell Pipe Line, 38% owner, acts as constructor and operator.
	November	Wolverine Pipe Line Company begins operation of 290-mile, 16-inch products line, from East Chicago through Michigan to Toledo. Shell, 40% owner of Wolverine stock, acts as constructor and operator.
1954	January 1	Exploration and production area office opened in Denver to oversee company's oilfield operations in Rocky Mountain region.
	August 11	Shell discovers South Pass Block 27 field, important offshore field in Mississippi Delta.
	December 31	Company assets pass billion-dollar mark.
1955	March	Government accepts Shell Chemical's $30,000,000 bid for Torrance, Calif., synthetic rubber facilities.
	September 21	First crude oil charged to stills in new Anacortes, Wash., refinery; full operation by early 1956. Initial capacity, 50,000 barrels a day.
	December	Butte Pipe Line Company, 60% owned by Shell, completes 509-mile crude oil pipe line from Poplar, Mont., to Guernsey, Wyo., connecting with eastbound common-carrier pipe lines.

Officers of the Shell Companies

Following is a list of the elective officers of the chief Shell companies in America from the time of their organization up to the present. Smaller subsidiaries such as Wolverine, Comar, Lilly White, Shell Oil Company of British Columbia, Ltd., and several others are not listed. In general, officers of the parent companies served as officers of these subsidiaries.

The companies are set forth in this order: (1) The American Gasoline Company and its successors on the Pacific Coast; (2) The Roxana companies and their successors east of the Rockies; (3) Shell Eastern; (4) Shell Pipe Line Corporation and its predecessor companies; (5) Shell Development Company; (6) Shell Chemical Corporation and its predecessors; (7) Shell Union Oil Corporation and its successor, Shell Oil Company; and (8) a listing of directors of Shell Union and its successor, Shell Oil Company. This information has been taken from the minute books of the companies concerned, supplemented where necessary by dates from personnel department files.

Persons who held office for organizational purposes only (generally members of the companies' outside legal counsel) are not included in this listing, nor are persons holding the offices of assistant secretary and assistant treasurer.

Ret. in parenthesis following a name indicates that the official so designated retired from Shell's employ on the date last shown; (*Res.*) indicates that he resigned from the company's service at this time; (*D.*) that he died while still in the company's service.

1. The Pacific Coast Companies

AMERICAN GASOLINE COMPANY, 1912–1914
SHELL COMPANY OF CALIFORNIA, INC., 1914–1916
SHELL COMPANY OF CALIFORNIA, 1915–1929
SHELL OIL COMPANY, 1929–1939
SHELL OIL COMPANY, INCORPORATED
(Pacific Coast Territory), 1939–1949

The American Gasoline Company was organized under the laws of the State of New York on September 3, 1912, and on June 24, 1914, changed its name to Shell Company of California, Inc. It owned and operated the company's early marketing facilities on the Pacific Coast. On July 30, 1915, a new Shell Company of California was chartered under the laws of the State of California and late in 1915 took over the properties of Shell Company of California, Inc., and California Oilfields, Ltd. Shell Company of California, Inc., was dissolved June 27, 1916. The Shell Company of California changed its name to Shell Oil Company on January 1, 1929; it was for a quarter century the chief Shell operating subsidiary on the Pacific Coast. On March 31, 1939, it was merged into Shell Petroleum Corporation to form Shell Oil Company, Inc. The president, secretary, and treasurer of the San Francisco company assumed new titles at the time of this 1939 merger. Functions of other West Coast officials continued with little change until January 1, 1949, when the Pacific Coast and East-of-Rockies managements were combined into one nation-wide management headquartered in New York.

President:

J. C. van Eck	November 19, 1912—August 5, 1914
W. Meischke-Smith	August 5, 1914—October 11, 1915
J. C. van Eck	October 11, 1915—January 13, 1916
W. Meischke-Smith	January 13, 1916—April 30, 1919
J. C. van Eck	June 9, 1919—January 1, 1923
George Legh-Jones	January 1, 1923—August 5, 1934
Sidney Belither [1]	August 6, 1934—December 31, 1948 (Ret.)

Executive Vice President:

F. A. C. Guépin	November 18, 1937—March 31, 1939
P. E. Lakin	January 1, 1949—to dissolution of company

General Vice President:

J. C. van Eck	{August 5, 1914—October 11, 1915 {January 13, 1916—June 9, 1919
W. Gould	March 14, 1932—June 26, 1933

---

[1] On April 1, 1939, with the merger of Shell Oil and Shell Petroleum to form Shell Oil Company, Inc., Belither assumed the title of executive vice president of the latter company; to this title was added Chairman of the Board, Shell Oil Company, Inc., on June 23 of same year.

Sidney Belither	June 26, 1933—August 5, 1934
H. Bloemgarten	July 6, 1938—March 31, 1939
Charles E. Mott	July 1, 1939—April 6, 1942
David Heggie	June 1, 1944—January 1, 1945 (Ret.)†
N. J. McGaw	November 1, 1946—November 16, 1948

Vice President—Marketing:

H. R. Gallagher *	⎰October 6, 1914—October 4, 1928 ⎱April 12, 1929—February 29, 1932 (Res.)
E. L. Miller	⎰October 1, 1928—April 15, 1929 ⎱November 16, 1930—December 1934 (Res.)
W. P. Durkee, Jr.	November 27, 1934—May 31, 1938 (Res.)
L. G. McLaren	June 1, 1938—August 31, 1947 (Ret.)
J. G. Jordan	September 1, 1947—(to N.Y. at end of 1948)

Vice President—Production (Los Angeles):

Paul Paine	June 15, 1922—June 15, 1923 (Res.)
W. C. McDuffie	June 16, 1923—July 1, 1926
Wm. Reinhardt	January 1, 1928—March 15, 1931 (Res.)
J. U. Stair	March 17, 1931—October 22, 1939 (D.)
Dr. E. F. Davis	March 26, 1940—September 15, 1944
E. D. Cumming	September 15, 1944—August 31, 1946
S. F. Bowlby	August 1, 1946—to dissolution of company

Vice President—Geology (Los Angeles):

| Dr. E. F. Davis[2] | January 2, 1929—December 31, 1947 (Ret.) |

Vice President—Manufacturing:

G. H. van Senden	⎰January 2, 1930—September 15, 1933 ⎱March 26, 1935—August 31, 1938 (Ret.)
A. E. Lacomblé	October 1, 1933—March 15, 1935
F. S. Clulow	September 1, 1938—(to N.Y. at end of 1948)

Vice President—Treasury:

John Lauder	December 28, 1920—July 31, 1933 (Ret.)
David Heggie	August 1, 1933—May 31, 1944
J. H. White	June 1, 1944—(to N.Y. at end of 1948)

Vice President—Law:

| A. R. Bradley | June 1, 1944—to dissolution of company |

------

* Was general vice president with duties of later marketing vice presidents.

† Died June 8, 1946.

[2] Title was "vice president and chief consulting geologist for entire United States" from September 15, 1944, to retirement December 31, 1947.

Vice President—Industrial Relations:

F. E. Rehm   July 11, 1944—to dissolution of company

Secretary:

E. de G. Birch	November 19, 1912—November 11, 1914
R. A. Lewin	November 11, 1914—April 20, 1926 (Res.)
G. C. Noble	April 20, 1926—December 18, 1928 (Res.)
A. R. Bradley [3]	January 2, 1929—to dissolution of company

Treasurer:

E. de G. Birch	November 19, 1912—November 11, 1914
John Lauder	November 11, 1914—July 31, 1933 (Ret.)
David Heggie [4]	August 1, 1933—May 31, 1944
J. H. White [5]	June 1, 1944—(to N.Y. at end of 1948)

---

[3] Title after April 1, 1939, was "assistant secretary and head of legal department." Died May 12, 1950.

[4] Title was "assistant treasurer" after April 1, 1939.

[5] Title was "assistant treasurer."

2. The East-of-the-Rockies Companies

ROXANA PETROLEUM COMPANY OF OKLAHOMA, 1912–1919
ROXANA PETROLEUM CORPORATION, 1919–1928
SHELL PETROLEUM CORPORATION, 1928–1939
SHELL OIL COMPANY, INCORPORATED
(East of Rockies Territory), 1939–1949

Roxana Petroleum Company of Oklahoma was chartered under the laws of the State of Oklahoma on October 1, 1912. In 1917, a new Roxana Petroleum Corporation was organized under the laws of the State of Virginia to take over the assets of Roxana of Oklahoma; this transfer took place on or about February 1, 1920, retroactive to October 1, 1919. The Roxana Petroleum Corporation in October 1928 changed its name to Shell Petroleum Corporation. As of March 31, 1939, Shell Oil Company, San Francisco, was merged into Shell Petroleum Corporation and the new company called Shell Oil Company, Incorporated. As of May 1, 1939, Shell Eastern Petroleum Products Division of Shell Union Oil Corporation was also merged into the new Shell Oil Company, Incorporated. Head Office was moved from Tulsa to St. Louis in 1919, from St. Louis to New York in 1940. On September 22, 1949, Shell Union Oil Corporation, 100% owner of Shell Oil Company, Inc., voted to absorb the latter company and changed the Shell Union name to Shell Oil Company. Properties of Shell Oil Company, Inc., were transferred to its parent on September 30, 1949; Shell Oil Company, Inc., was dissolved on December 29, 1949.

President:

Clinton D. Martin	October 3, 1912—March 1, 1913 (Res.)
N. G. M. Luykx	March 1, 1913—March 1, 1917 (Res.)
W. A. J. M. van Water-schoot van der Gracht	March 1, 1917—January 30, 1922 (Res.)
Frederick Godber	January 30, 1922—October 1, 1928
U. de B. Daly	October 1, 1928—April 11, 1931 (Res.)
R. G. A. van der Woude	July 1, 1931—September 5, 1933
Alexander Fraser	September 5, 1933—July 1, 1947
H. S. M. Burns	July 1, 1947—(serving at dissolution of company September 1949)

General Vice Presidents:

N. G. M. Luykx	October 4, 1912—March 1, 1913
Benjamin F. Rice	March 1, 1913—April 16, 1917 (Res.)
Richard Airey	April 16, 1917—June 25, 1935
Frederick Godber	February 13, 1920—January 30, 1922
Adrian Corbett	January 30, 1922—July 28, 1922
R. G. A. van der Woude	July 29, 1922—January 28, 1924
T. F. Lydon	July 29, 1922—June 4, 1933 (D.)
U. de B. Daly	March 29, 1928—October 1, 1928
Alexander Fraser	November 19, 1930—September 5, 1933
W. Gould	November 19, 1930—March 31, 1932
H. H. Anderson	⎰November 9, 1932—December 31, 1934 ⎱July 1, 1935—December 31, 1936

R. P. Bascom   June 19, 1933—July 20, 1939
J. W. Watson   October 11, 1933—September 16, 1940
A. J. Galloway   {October 10, 1934—April 20, 1936
                        {April 1, 1939—September 16, 1940
T. E. Swigart   March 22, 1938—April 1, 1939
S. W. Duhig   March 25, 1939—June 29, 1939
F. A. C. Guépin   April 1, 1939—September 16, 1940
L. T. Kittinger [6]   July 27, 1943—December 31, 1948 (Ret.)
N. J. McGaw   March 26, 1946—November 22, 1946

Senior Vice President:

F. A. C. Guépin   September 16, 1940—January 1, 1945
H. S. M. Burns   November 1, 1946—July 1, 1947

Vice President—Exploration:

Dr. W. van Holst
Pellekaan   March 29, 1928—November 11, 1938 (Ret.)

Vice President—Production:

G. S. Rollin (St. Louis)   March 29, 1928—November 9, 1932
H. Bloemgarten (St. Louis)   September 24, 1935—November 11, 1938
H. Bloemgarten (New York)   February 9, 1943—December 31, 1947
A. J. Galloway (New York) [7] January 1, 1948—to dissolution

Vice President—Production: Texas-Gulf Area (Houston):

T. E. Swigart   November 9, 1932—March 22, 1938
A. J. Galloway   March 22, 1938—April 1, 1939
T. E. Swigart   April 1, 1939—September 1, 1940
A. J. Galloway [8]   September 16, 1940—December 31, 1947
E. D. Cumming   January 1, 1948—to dissolution

Vice President—Production: Mid-Continent Area (Tulsa):

G. S. Rollin   November 9, 1932—April 20, 1936 (Res.)
A. J. Galloway   April 20, 1936—March 22, 1938
R. B. Roark   October 21, 1937—July 31, 1947 (Ret.)

Vice President—Manufacturing:

Dr. F. W. L. Tydeman   January 2, 1930—December 31, 1932
J. F. M. Taylor   October 11, 1933—November 8, 1935
A. E. Lacomblé   November 8, 1935—March 25, 1939
E. D. Cumming   April 1, 1939—February 9, 1943

---

[6] Served as vice president, Washington, D.C., from May 9, 1947, until retirement December 31, 1948. Died February 11, 1955.

[7] Authority over exploration and production for entire U. S. after January 1, 1949.

[8] In charge of exploration and production East of the Rockies.

J. F. M. Taylor	February 9, 1943—July 19, 1945 (Res.)
C. E. Davis	July 19, 1945—January 1, 1949
F. S. Clulow *	January 1, 1949—to dissolution of company

Vice President—Refining:

| C. E. Davis | January 1, 1949—to dissolution of company |

Vice President—Personnel and Industrial Relations:

| H. H. Anderson [9] | January 1, 1937—May 12, 1941 |
| E. H. Walker | November 17, 1948—to dissolution of company |

Vice President—Sales (Marketing):

G. G. Woodruff	March 29, 1928—May 1, 1929 (Res.)
E. L. Miller [10]	June 19, 1929—November 15, 1930
L. van Eeghen	October 1, 1930—April 20, 1936
P. E. Lakin [11]	April 20, 1936—September 16, 1940
L. T. Kittinger [12]	April 26, 1939—July 27, 1943
P. E. Lakin	July 27, 1943—December 31, 1948
J. G. Jordan *	January 1, 1949—to dissolution of company

Vice President—Transportation and Supplies:

H. H. Anderson	January 1, 1935—June 30, 1935
N. J. McGaw	April 26, 1939—March 26, 1946
D. B. Hodges	January 1, 1947—to dissolution of company

Vice President—Shipping and Supplies (New York):

| R. R. Griffin | April 26, 1939—September 15, 1940 |

Vice President—Marine Transportation:

| R. R. Griffin | September 16, 1940—July 31, 1946 (Ret.)[13] |

Vice President—Law (Vice President and General Counsel):

| C. S. Gentry * | May 8, 1944—to dissolution of company |

Vice President—Economic Development:

| N. J. McGaw | January 1, 1949—to dissolution of company |

---

* Authority over entire U. S. from January 1, 1949.

[9] Title was vice president in charge of personnel.

[10] Export Sales after October 1, 1930.

[11] Served as regional vice president, Chicago, September 16, 1940 to July 27, 1943.

[12] Vice President—Sales, Atlantic Coast Territory, April 26, 1939, to Sept. 16, 1940.

[13] Marine Transportation made part of Transportation and Supplies upon Griffin's retirement. Griffin died October 22, 1946, shortly after retirement.

Vice President—Financial Organization:

E. C. Peet *   January 1, 1949—to dissolution of company

Vice President and Controller:

J. H. White *   January 1, 1949—to dissolution of company

Secretary:

John H. Harvey	October 1, 1912—October 11, 1913
H. H. Parker	October 11, 1913—July 3, 1914
John H. Harvey	July 3, 1914—November 18, 1916 (Res.)
T. F. Lydon	November 18, 1916—July 29, 1922
P. R. Chenoweth	July 29, 1922—January 28, 1936 (Res.)
C. S. Gentry	January 28, 1936—March 23, 1937
J. T. Dickerson	March 23, 1937—September 16, 1940
C. S. Gentry	September 16, 1940—January 1, 1949
J. A. Horner	January 1, 1949—to dissolution of company

Treasurer:

John H. Harvey	October 1, 1912—October 11, 1913
G. Harry Dann	October 11, 1913—August 21, 1914 (Res.)
C. B. Singleton (asst. treas.)	August 21, 1914—May 1, 1916
H. H. Parker	May 1, 1916—July 8, 1918 [14]
T. F. Lydon [15]	July 8, 1918 [14]—June 4, 1933 (D.)
J. W. Watson [16]	June 19, 1933—May 8, 1944
E. C. Peet [17]	May 8, 1944—December 31, 1948
A. G. Schei *	January 1, 1949—to dissolution of company

---

* Authority over entire U. S. from January 1, 1949.

[14] Parker was still treasurer of Roxana of Oklahoma at this time; Lydon was treasurer of Roxana Petroleum Corporation (Va.) from March 8, 1917.

[15] Also vice president from July 29, 1922.

[16] Vice president from October 11, 1933.

[17] Vice president and treasurer.

3.   Shell Eastern Petroleum Products, Inc., 1929-1936

Organized under laws of Delaware, January 22, 1929, as a 100% subsidiary of Shell Union. On November 2, 1936, Shell Eastern was taken over by Shell Union and operated as Shell Eastern Petroleum Products Division of Shell Union Oil Corporation until May 1, 1939, at which time its properties and organization were merged into Shell Oil Company, Inc.

President:

A. F. Carter	February 6, 1929—September 1, 1933 (Res.)
W. Gould	September 14, 1933—to dissolution of company

Vice Presidents:

W. J. Filer	January 23, 1929—August 25, 1936
E. de Gray Birch	February 10, 1932—February 2, 1933
O. H. Bond	May 18, 1933—to dissolution of company
T. R. Kurtz	May 18, 1933—to dissolution of company
W. Gould	June 28, 1933—September 14, 1933
L. T. Kittinger	August 25, 1936—to dissolution of company

Secretary:

U. F. O'Brien	February 26, 1929—January 16, 1932 (Res.)
J. L. Sweetin	May 19, 1932—to dissolution of company

Treasurer:

U. F. O'Brien	February 6, 1929—January 16, 1932 (Res.)
E. de Gray Birch	February 10, 1932—February 2, 1933
O. H. Bond	May 18, 1933—to dissolution of company

4. Shell Pipe Line Corporation and Predecessors

YARHOLA PIPE LINE COMPANY, 1914–1919
OZARK PIPE LINE CORPORATION, 1919–1927
SHELL PIPE LINE CORPORATION, 1927 to date

The predecessor of Shell Pipe Line Corporation was the Yarhola Pipe Line Company, an Oklahoma corporation, which held its first meeting June 30, 1914. A year later it was purchased by Roxana along with the Yarhola leases, and on July 19, 1915, the first officers representing the new Shell ownership were elected. The Yarhola Pipe Line Company built the Healdton–Cushing line, and the first Shell pipe line from Cushing to Wood River. On October 9, 1919 officers were elected for the new Ozark Pipe Line Corporation, chartered in Maryland, which had on October 1, 1919, taken over all of Yarhola's assets; the Yarhola company was legally dissolved November 22, 1922. On October 25, 1927 Ozark Pipe Line Corporation changed its name to the present Shell Pipe Line Corporation.

President:

J. H. Evans [18]	June 30, 1914—July 13, 1914
A. W. Leonard [18]	July 14, 1914—July 19, 1915
N. G. M. Luykx	July 19, 1915—March 1, 1917 (Res.)
W. A. J. M. van Water-schoot van der Gracht	March 1, 1917—December 15, 1921 (Res.)
Frederick Godber	January 30, 1922—September 19, 1928
U. de B. Daly	September 19, 1928—April 11, 1931 (Res.)
R. G. A. van der Woude	July 1, 1931—October 11, 1933
Alexander Fraser	October 11, 1933—July 20, 1939
R. P. Bascom	July 20, 1939—August 31, 1940 (Ret.)
T. E. Swigart	September 1, 1940—September 30, 1954 (Ret.)
J. T. Dickerson	October 1, 1954—to date

Vice Presidents:

Benjamin F. Rice	July 19, 1915—April 16, 1917 (Res.)
Richard Airey	April 16, 1917—June 25, 1935
Frederick Godber	February 13, 1920—January 30, 1922
Adrian Corbett	January 30, 1922—July 28, 1922
R. G. A. van der Woude	July 28, 1922—January 28, 1924
T. F. Lydon	July 28, 1922—June 4, 1933 (D.)
R. P. Bascom	January 11, 1928—July 20, 1939
Alexander Fraser	June 19, 1933—October 11, 1933
R. B. High	July 20, 1939—June 25, 1941
H. H. Anderson	May 13, 1941—July 31, 1952 (Ret.)
P. H. Swinchatt	March 17, 1942—to date

---

[18] Officer prior to Shell's purchase of Yarhola.

W. A. Baker   October 4, 1946—December 31, 1955 (Ret.)
D. H. Lewis   April 24, 1952—December 31, 1955 (Ret.)
D. F. Sears   August 1, 1952—to date
C. C. Combs   January 1, 1956—to date

Treasurer:

W. H. Albro [19]   June 30, 1914—July 13, 1914
R. E. Fuller [19]   July 14, 1914—July 19, 1915
John H. Harvey   July 19, 1915—November 18, 1916 (Res.)
T. F. Lydon   November 18, 1916—June 4, 1933 (D.)
J. W. Watson   June 19, 1933—July 20, 1939
W. A. Baker   July 20, 1939—August 31, 1940
E. H. Mueller   September 1, 1940—October 4, 1946
W. A. Baker   October 4, 1946—December 31, 1955 (Ret.)
C. C. Combs   January 1, 1956—to date

Secretary:

W. H. Albro [19]   June 30, 1914—July 13, 1914
R. E. Fuller [19]   July 14, 1914—July 19, 1915
John H. Harvey   July 19, 1915—November 18, 1916 (Res.)
T. F. Lydon   November 18, 1916—July 28, 1922
P. R. Chenoweth   July 28, 1922—January 28, 1936 (Res.)
C. S. Gentry   January 28, 1936—March 23, 1937
J. T. Dickerson   March 23, 1937—July 20, 1939
J. D. Watkins   July 20, 1939—August 31, 1940
A. E. Groff   September 1, 1940—February 28, 1955 (Ret.)
W. J. Williamson   March 1, 1955—to date

---

[19] Officer prior to Shell's purchase of Yarhola.

5. Shell Development Company

In 1926, the Simplex Oil Refining Company was organized in Delaware to act as a successor in patent-licensing matters to the old Simplex Refining Company. With the decision in the late 1920's to spend several million dollars in new research, the Simplex name was changed (February 1927) to Shell Development Company. Shell Development became an active research concern on June 15, 1928, when its offices were transferred from New York to San Francisco. From the start of its research career until 1953, Shell Development Company was owned 50% by Bataafsche; from 1953 to the end of 1955, Shell Oil Company owned 65% of the Development Company's stock. As of December 31, 1955, Shell Development purchased and retired its stock held by Bataafsche and became henceforth a wholly owned subsidiary of Shell Oil. Concurrent with this move, the office of Chairman of the Board was eliminated.

Chairman of the Board:

Avery D. Andrews	February 18, 1927—June 15, 1928
George Legh-Jones	June 26, 1928—October 22, 1929
J. C. van Eck	October 22, 1929—May 3, 1937
R. G. A. van der Woude	June 24, 1937—July 1, 1947 (Ret.)
Alexander Fraser	September 4, 1947—December 31, 1948
A. E. Lacomblé	January 1, 1949—December 31, 1950 (Ret.)[20]
H. Bloemgarten	January 1, 1951—December 31, 1955

President:

Richard Airey	February 18, 1927—June 15, 1928
Herbert R. Gallagher	June 15, 1928—October 22, 1929
George Legh-Jones	October 22, 1929—November 2, 1931
Cornelius B. de Bruyn	November 2, 1931—December 31, 1935
Jack F. M. Taylor	December 31, 1935—December 31, 1942
A. E. Lacomblé	January 1, 1943—December 31, 1948
Monroe E. Spaght	January 1, 1949—December 31, 1952
Harold Gershinowitz	January 1, 1953—to date

Vice Presidents:

Alexander Fraser	February 18, 1927—June 15, 1928
Daniel Pyzel	June 15, 1928—December 31, 1935
John Lauder	October 22, 1929—October 5, 1933
C. B. de Bruyn	February 16, 1931—November 2, 1931
David Heggie	October 5, 1933—May 19, 1944
Dr. E. C. Williams	December 22, 1936—December 31, 1940 (Res.)
Dr. F. W. L. Tydeman	July 15, 1938—December 31, 1940 (Ret.)[21]
Hiram Norcross	April 1, 1944—August 26, 1949 (D.)
Ava J. Johnson	April 1, 1944—to date

---

[20] Died November 5, 1952.

[21] Died November 23, 1952.

J. Howard White	May 19, 1944—December 30, 1950
Dan M. Sheldon	June 18, 1945—May 11, 1949
Monroe E. Spaght	May 1, 1946—December 31, 1948
John W. Pegg	December 1, 1950—February 23, 1955 (D.)
T. W. Evans	December 1, 1950—to date
N. D. Smith, Jr.	July 1, 1954—to date
J. A. Horner	April 15, 1955—to date

Treasurer:

A. M. Houston	February 18, 1927—June 15, 1928
John Lauder	June 15, 1928—October 5, 1933
David Heggie	October 5, 1933—May 19, 1944
J. Howard White	May 19, 1944—December 31, 1950
W. R. Balfour	January 1, 1951—March 12, 1953
A. G. Schei	March 13, 1953—to date

Controller:

| J. H. White | March 13, 1953—December 1, 1954 |
| A. A. Buzzi | December 1, 1954—to date |

Secretary:

Alexander Fraser	February 18, 1927—June 15, 1928
G. C. Noble	June 15, 1928—October 5, 1928
Edward Hepner	October 5, 1928—October 22, 1929
E. de Gray Birch	October 22, 1929—November 2, 1931
Edward Hepner	November 2, 1931—May 25, 1943 (Ret.) †
Dan M. Sheldon	May 25, 1943—to date

---

† Died January 4, 1956.

6.   Shell Chemical

SHELL CHEMICAL COMPANY, 1929–1943
SHELL CHEMICAL DIVISION OF SHELL UNION OIL
   CORPORATION, 1943–1945
SHELL CHEMICAL CORPORATION, 1946 to date

Shell Chemical Company was organized February 18, 1929, under the laws of Delaware, its stock originally held entirely by Shell Development Company. During 1931, this ownership arrangement was changed so that Shell Development's owners, Shell Union and Bataafsche, each became 50% owner of Shell Chemical. On July 31, 1943, Shell Union acquired Bataafsche's interest in Shell Chemical Company, and as of October 1, 1943, the latter company became the Shell Chemical Division of Shell Union Oil Corporation. Late in 1945, a new company, Shell Chemical Corporation, was organized under Delaware laws and the assets of the chemical division were transferred to it as of January 1, 1946. Shell Chemical Corporation is wholly owned by Shell Oil Company.

Chairman of the Board:

G. Legh-Jones	March 27, 1929—October 22, 1929
J. B. Aug. Kessler	October 22, 1929—October 1, 1943
F. A. C. Guépin	November 30, 1950—March 7, 1956

President:

H. R. Gallagher	March 29, 1929—October 22, 1929
J. E. F. de Kok	October 22, 1929—February 16, 1931
C. B. de Bruyn	February 16, 1931—December 31, 1941 (Ret.)
J. Oostermeyer [22]	January 1, 1942—May 31, 1953 (Ret.)
R. C. McCurdy	June 1, 1953—to date

Vice Presidents:

D. Pyzel	March 29, 1929—October 1, 1943
John Lauder	October 23, 1929—October 2, 1933
B. Engelsman	October 22, 1929—February 16, 1931
David Heggie	October 2, 1933—October 1, 1943
M. W. Holtrop	May 8, 1936—May 1, 1939
J. Oostermeyer	May 6, 1941—December 31, 1941
W. P. Gage [23]	December 1, 1941—January 31, 1953 (Res.)
L. V. Steck [23]	May 19, 1942—to date
J. W. Watson	January 1, 1947—July 1, 1948 (Ret.)
G. R. Monkhouse	January 1, 1952—to date
C. W. Humphreys	October 15, 1953—to date

---

[22] Was executive vice president in charge of the Chemical Division, Shell Union, October 1, 1943—December 31, 1945.

[23] Served as vice presidents of Shell Union during period chemical company was division of Shell Union, October 1, 1943—December 31, 1945.

Treasurer:

John Lauder	March 27, 1929—October 2, 1933
David Heggie [24]	October 2, 1933—October 1, 1943
J. W. Watson	January 1, 1946—July 1, 1948 (Ret.)
A. G. Schei	July 1, 1948—to date

Secretary:

Edward Hepner	March 27, 1929—May 25, 1943 (Ret.)
E. Reillac [24]	May 25, 1943—October 1, 1943
J. Rysdorp	January 1, 1946—September 1, 1948
G. E. Brewer	September 1, 1948—to date

Controller:

J. H. White	March 15, 1949—November 15, 1954
A. A. Buzzi	November 15, 1954—to date

---

[24] There was no office of treasurer or secretary during period October 1, 1943-December 31, 1945, when Shell Chemical operated as a division of Shell Union.

7. Parent Company

SHELL UNION OIL CORPORATION, 1922–September 1949
SHELL OIL COMPANY, September 1949 to date

Shell Union was organized in Delaware, February 7, 1922, and functioned chiefly as a holding company until September 22, 1949, when the stockholders voted to absorb the chief operating subsidiary, Shell Oil Company, Inc., and rename the surviving organization Shell Oil Company. The transfer of properties took place on September 30, 1949, and the old Shell Oil Company, Inc., was dissolved December 29, 1949.

Chairman of the Board:

Sir Henri W. A. Deterding	May 15, 1924—December 23, 1936 (Ret.)
Sir Frederick Godber	February 5, 1937—July 30, 1946
Sir George Legh-Jones	July 30, 1946—June 30, 1951 (Ret.)
Sir Francis Hopwood	July 5, 1951—to date

Vice Chairman of the Board:

J. C. van Eck	October 11, 1933—February 5, 1937

Chairman of the Executive Committee:

Alexander Fraser	September 22, 1949—March 31, 1951 (Ret.)
H. S. M. Burns	April 26, 1951—to date

President:

Avery D. Andrews	February 8, 1922—May 5, 1922
William H. Allen	May 5, 1922—November 8, 1922
Sir Henri W. A. Deterding	November 8, 1922—May 15, 1924
J. C. van Eck	May 15, 1924—October 11, 1933
R. G. A. van der Woude	October 11, 1933—July 1, 1947 (Ret.)
Alexander Fraser	July 1, 1947—September 22, 1949
H. S. M. Burns	September 22, 1949—to date

Executive Vice President:

Jan Oostermeyer [25]	October 1, 1943—December 31, 1945
M. E. Spaght	January 1, 1953—to date

Vice Presidents:

Richard Airey	March 4, 1922—May 5, 1922
Adrian Corbett	May 5, 1922—March 14, 1923
J. C. van Eck	November 16, 1922—May 15, 1924
G. H. van Senden	October 11, 1933—February 7, 1936

---

[25] Served as head of Shell Chemical Division of Shell Union Oil Corporation.

W. P. Durkee, Jr.	October 11, 1933—February 7, 1936
L. T. Kittinger [26]	October 27, 1936—May 1, 1939
R. R. Griffin	{May 26, 1936—August 26, 1936
	{October 27, 1936—May 1, 1939
D. Pyzel	February 5, 1937—December 31, 1944 (Ret.)
S. W. Duhig	January 31, 1938—March 31, 1950 (Ret.)
W. P. Gage [27]	October 1, 1943—December 31, 1945
L. V. Steck [27]	October 1, 1943—December 31, 1945
J. H. Doolittle	January 1, 1946—to date
A. S. C. Hulton	March 23, 1951—March 6, 1953
* P. E. Lakin	September 22, 1949—March 31, 1954 (Ret.)
* A. J. Galloway (Explor. & Prod.—New York)	September 22, 1949—to date
* S. F. Bowlby (Explor. & Prod.—Los Angeles)	September 22, 1949—to date
* E. D. Cumming (Explor. & Prod.—Houston)	September 22, 1949—to date
* F. S. Clulow (Manufacturing)	September 22, 1949—June 30, 1956 (Ret.)
M. P. L. Love (Manufacturing)	July 1, 1956—to date
* C. E. Davis (Refining)	September 22, 1949—December 31, 1955 (Ret.)
* D. B. Hodges (Trans. & Supp.)	September 22, 1949—to date
* J. G. Jordan (Marketing)	September 22, 1949—to date
Selwyn Eddy (Pacific Coast Marketing Divs.)	August 23, 1956—to date
P. C. Thomas (Midwest Marketing Divisions)	August 23, 1956—to date
J. L. Wadlow (East Coast Marketing Divisions)	August 23, 1956—to date
* E. C. Peet (Financial Org.)	September 22, 1949—November 15, 1954
(General V.P.)	November 15, 1954—August 27, 1956
* J. H. White (V.P. & Contr.)	September 22, 1949—November 15, 1954
(V.P. in Charge of Finance)	November 15, 1954—to date
* C. S. Gentry (V.P. & General Counsel)	September 22, 1949—December 31, 1952 (Ret.)
* A. R. Bradley (V.P., Asst. Genl. Counsel, S.F.)	September 22, 1949—December 31, 1949 (Ret.)
W. F. Kenney (V.P. & Genl. Counsel)	January 1, 1953—to date
* N. J. McGaw (Economic Development)	September 22, 1949—June 30, 1956 (Ret.)
* E. H. Walker (Personnel & Ind. Relations, N.Y.)	September 22, 1949—to date

---

[26] Served as chief operating executive, Shell Eastern Petroleum Products Division of Shell Union.

[27] Were vice presidents of Shell Chemical while it was division of Shell Union.

* Had been officer of similar capacity, Shell Oil Co., Inc., on September 22, 1949, when Shell Union and Shell Oil were merged. See sections 1 and 2 of this appendix.

* F. E. Rehm (Personnel &   September 22, 1949—May 31, 1953 (Ret.)[28]
   Ind. Relations, S.F.)
E. G. Robinson (Explor. &   June 28, 1951—June 30, 1952 (Ret.)
   Production—Calgary)[29]
P. L. Kartzke (Explor. &   November 24, 1952—to date
   Production—Calgary)
J. T. Dickerson (Explor. &   June 28, 1951—October 1, 1954
   Production—Midland)[29]
J. E. Clark (Explor. & Pro-   October 1, 1954—to date
   duction—Midland)
B. Dykstra (Explor. & Pro-   June 28, 1951—to date
   duction—New Orleans)[29]
W. A. Alexander (Explor.   June 28, 1951—August 1, 1953
   & Production—Tulsa)[29]
        (—Denver)   August 1, 1953—to date
C. P. Bristol (Explor. &   January 1, 1954—to date
   Prod.—Tulsa)
Dr. H. Gershinowitz (Re-   June 28, 1951—December 31, 1952
   search & Tech. Services—
   Houston)[29]
H. L. Curtis (Public Rela-   July 11, 1955—to date
   tions)

Treasurer:

Alexander Fraser   February 8, 1922—May 5, 1922
James H. Brookmire   May 5, 1922—May 15, 1930
Stanley W. Duhig   May 15, 1930—September 22, 1949
A. G. Schei   September 22, 1949—to date

Controller:

J. H. White   September 22, 1949—November 15, 1954
A. A. Buzzi   November 15, 1954—to date

Secretary:

Alexander Fraser   February 8, 1922—May 5, 1922
James H. Brookmire   May 5, 1922—May 15, 1930
Stanley W. Duhig   May 15, 1930—January 31, 1938
C. S. Gentry   January 31, 1938—August 27, 1940
F. W. Woods   August 27, 1940—April 23, 1953 (Ret. June 30,
                                  1953)
J. A. Horner   April 23, 1953—to date

---

* Had been officer of similar capacity, Shell Oil Co., Inc., on September 22, 1949, when Shell Union and Shell Oil were merged. See sections 1 and 2 of this appendix.

[28] Died November 27, 1955.

[29] Represents reorganization Exploration and Production Department, July 1, 1951.

8. Directors

SHELL UNION OIL CORPORATION

(name changed to SHELL OIL COMPANY September 22, 1949)

Indicates members of original board

* Avery D. Andrews	February 8, 1922—November 8, 1933
* Richard Airey	February 8, 1922—April 20, 1936
* William H. Allen	February 8, 1922—November 8, 1922
* James H. Brookmire	February 8, 1922—May 16, 1935
* Adrian Corbett	February 8, 1922—November 16, 1922
* Frederick Godber	February 8, 1922—July 30, 1946
(Knighted 1942; created Baron Godber 1956)	
* J. C. van Eck	February 8, 1922—December 31, 1946
* Frederic W. Allen	February 11, 1922—December 15, 1933
* Lewis L. Clarke	February 11, 1922—to date
* Bayard Dominick	February 11, 1922—December 23, 1936
* Charles Hayden	February 11, 1922—February 7, 1937
* Henry Lockhart, Jr.	February 11, 1922—April 14, 1943
* T. W. Phillips, Jr.	February 11, 1922—November 21, 1934
* Samuel F. Pryor	February 11, 1922—November 21, 1934
* Charles H. Sabin	February 11, 1922—October 11, 1933
* Samuel M. Vauclain	February 11, 1922—January 9, 1929
* E. P. Whitcomb	February 11, 1922—August 13, 1925
* William W. Woods	February 11, 1922—July 12, 1922
Sir Henri W. A. Deterding	November 8, 1922—December 23, 1936
J. B. Aug. Kessler	{November 8, 1922—May 17, 1934 {February 11, 1941—June 30, 1948
Alexander Mackay	November 8, 1922—May 26, 1936
Dr. Aug. Philips	November 8, 1922—May 21, 1925
Hon. Walter H. Samuel	November 8, 1922—May 17, 1934
(Became The Rt. Hon. Viscount Bearsted in 1927)	
Sir Robert Waley Cohen	November 8, 1932—May 18, 1933
George Legh-Jones	{May 21, 1925—September 12, 1934 {May 26, 1936—June 30, 1951
(Knighted 1952)	
U. de B. Daly	September 19, 1928—April 22, 1931
J. E. F. de Kok	March 13, 1929—October 28, 1940
R. G. A. van der Woude	May 21, 1931—June 30, 1947
Arthur O. Choate	May 19, 1932—April 10, 1935
Ernest Sturm	May 17, 1934—December 23, 1936
Alexander Fraser	{May 21, 1936—June 27, 1939 {July 1, 1947—March 31, 1951
S. Belither	February 8, 1937—June 27, 1939
Bernard M. Culver	February 5, 1937—December 6, 1950
Gayer G. Dominick	{February 5, 1937—June 27, 1939 {January 1, 1945—to date
D. Pyzel	February 5, 1937—December 31, 1944

779

Lewis E. Pierson	June 27, 1939—November 10, 1954
H. Wilkinson	{June 27, 1939—January 2, 1942 {July 1, 1945—February 20, 1953
Forsyth Wickes	April 18, 1940—to date
Francis Hopwood (Knighted 1953)	{April 15, 1943—June 30, 1945 {July 30, 1946—to date
Thomas A. Morgan	February 8, 1944—to date
James H. Doolittle	April 18, 1946—to date
Jerome C. Hunsaker	April 25, 1946—to date
B. Th. W. van Hasselt	January 28, 1947—December 31, 1951
J. H. Loudon	{July 29, 1948—February 20, 1953 {August 23, 1956—to date
H. Bloemgarten	April 21, 1949—August 23, 1956
J. W. Boyle	April 21, 1949—February 6, 1950
Cason J. Callaway	April 21, 1949—to date
Stanley W. Duhig	April 21, 1949—March 31, 1950
H. S. M. Burns	September 22, 1949—to date
P. E. Lakin	September 22, 1949—March 31, 1954
J. W. Platt	February 6, 1950—February 20, 1953
James B. Black	June 23, 1950—to date
F. A. C. Guépin	April 5, 1951—February 20, 1953
F. J. Stephens	September 27, 1951—February 20, 1953
L. Schepers	April 3, 1952—February 20, 1953
A. J. Galloway	February 20, 1953—to date
M. E. Spaght	February 20, 1953—to date
E. C. Peet	April 22, 1954—to date
R. C. McCurdy	February 24, 1955—to date

Statistical Tables

The following tables present consolidated financial and operating data for the American Shell companies for the years 1912–1955. This information was prepared by Shell Oil Company head office accounting department from financial statements, audits of Price, Waterhouse & Company, stockholders' annual reports, and Securities and Exchange Commission registration statements.

Information obtained from other sources is indicated by appropriate footnotes.

The tables are arranged in the following order:

I. SALES IN DOLLARS

Shell Oil Company and Predecessor Companies

(Figures do not equal total, for several minor subsidiaries are here omitted)

Year	Total	Shell Pacific Coast	Shell Mid-Continent	Shell Atlantic Seaboard	Shell Pipe Line & Predecessor Cos.[a]	Shell Chemical
1912	$ 398,200	$ 48,935	$ 349,265			
1913	1,334,481	465,714	868,767			
1914	1,782,047	1,383,103	398,944			
1915	2,863,977	1,723,000	1,140,977			
1916	11,254,607	7,180,907	4,073,700			
1917	16,475,919	9,832,063	6,643,856			
1918	23,442,196	14,567,175	8,875,021			
1919	23,744,573	14,509,962	9,234,611			
1920	38,687,400	22,186,380	16,501,020			
1921	28,312,913	17,776,729	10,536,184			
1922	45,735,301	28,456,285	17,233,336		$ 45,680	
1923	74,274,426	45,882,579	26,055,550		31,888	
1924	93,244,776	53,295,894	38,840,514			
1925	111,351,392	55,711,286	54,213,588			
1926	149,438,692	71,832,794	73,514,920			
1927	140,325,813	71,347,153	66,004,229			
1928	179,195,392	89,879,668	85,975,852			
1929	240,398,877	98,446,086	115,963,990	$23,112,148		
1930	236,435,528	83,037,666	102,260,533	50,902,167		
1931	174,532,533	57,414,218	69,738,038	46,643,196	638,068	134,761[c]
1932	158,616,917	50,014,093	61,356,059	46,494,423	586,730	634,175[c]
1933	165,049,752	49,695,085	64,223,809	50,576,722	324,449	1,485,697[c]
1934	186,707,730	54,002,816	80,343,494	51,688,016	274,670	1,429,845[c]
1935	202,169,218	59,047,849	90,065,621	52,354,938	191,331	2,638,797[c]
1936	231,698,034	70,290,672	103,872,123	56,578,506	351,675	3,540,313[c]
1937	260,307,699	80,968,745	116,350,697	62,514,061	370,054	4,608,296[c]
1938	252,831,764	82,928,582	113,945,743	55,632,954	251,276	4,208,297[c]
1939	248,402,482	78,728,860	111,579,270	57,901,869	192,483	4,991,137[c]
1940	254,103,591	78,948,962	175,138,056		16,573	6,437,562[c]
1941	300,053,408	89,492,017	210,537,921		23,470	8,326,195[c]
1942	329,031,776	101,555,808	227,382,584		93,384	13,857,182[c]
1943	408,034,171	127,110,882	262,120,265		689,747	18,113,277
1944	490,478,204	142,908,366	319,951,934		1,625,120	20,742,656
1945	476,709,195	151,722,074	303,743,667		1,160,123	20,083,331
1946	442,487,450	132,910,340	284,170,603		107,589	23,016,799
1947	628,105,211	161,975,878	432,564,762		794,113	28,547,035
1948	831,221,137	193,668,765	593,889,870		779,926	37,722,571
1949	817,935,586	764,533,287[b]			1,508,052	48,081,174
1950	915,329,056	836,381,102			3,845,031	70,473,516
1951	1,072,433,548	969,349,827			4,544,602	97,522,447
1952	1,142,631,978	1,037,283,690			6,486,363	97,762,713
1953	1,269,551,079	1,139,851,498			2,930,224	125,811,257
1954	1,312,059,959	1,171,146,351			2,104,583	138,809,025
1955	1,484,069,013	1,288,433,874			1,774,678	193,860,461

[a] Transportation income after eliminating receipts from Shell companies.
[b] Pacific Coast and East of Rockies consolidated from 1949 on.
[c] Sales receipts less commissions, freight, and cost of containers.

II. NET INCOME

Shell Oil Company and Predecessor Companies

(Figures do not equal total, for some subsidiaries are here omitted)

Year	Total	Shell Pacific Coast	Shell Mid-Continent	Shell Atlantic Seaboard	Shell Pipe Line & Predecessor Cos.
1912	$ 133,265	$ (11,000)	$ 144,265		
1913	220,730	(26,983)	261,687		
1914	140,289	57,000	88,669		
1915	536,543	38,000	502,706		$ (3,941)
1916	2,430,600	580,000	1,849,077		1,536
1917	866,162	589,000	126,365		150,797
1918	2,274,096	1,689,000	875,455		(290,359)
1919	4,384,137	3,344,000	1,146,711		(106,574)
1920	8,830,872	5,891,000	2,454,745		485,127
1921	4,842,571	3,281,000	465,563		1,096,008
1922	9,596,351	4,798,729	1,990,213		1,183,904
1923	*16,859,156	9,744,821	2,438,928		3,044,447
1924	*18,562,738	10,854,032	2,406,539		3,828,636
1925	*20,415,960	7,591,359	6,050,447		4,237,911
1926	*31,518,966	12,795,834	10,330,663		4,921,232
1927	11,344,915	12,397,783	(7,810,728)		4,938,961
1928	20,395,021	13,905,393	(4,176,460)		9,495,317
1929	17,573,249	11,707,964	(9,203,990)	$(1,598,125)	13,695,107
1930	(5,095,574)	6,773,179	(28,570,762)	(2,968,481)	15,177,792
1931	(27,008,310)	(1,748,528)	(33,852,511)	(6,274,720)	14,791,934
1932	660,076	2,565,555	(16,161,610)	(2,482,924)	11,648,358
1933	(4,240,965)	1,126,659	(13,367,197)	(1,950,863)	10,540,848
1934	(1,353,901)	2,494,419	(11,766,404)	(1,476,127)	7,946,839
1935	6,812,835	3,479,421	(1,375,374)	101,121	5,550,171
1936	22,494,364	10,659,635	3,259,103	(1,029,286)	6,600,735
1937	20,668,880	15,270,255	1,176,393		5,985,752
1938	11,318,423	13,880,400	(6,458,615)		5,825,816
1939	11,805,713	8,768,261	(606,120)		4,613,360
1940	15,654,678	9,082,928	2,635,244		4,233,115
1941	17,334,214	7,527,560	6,454,484		4,313,057
1942	17,732,191	4,931,987	12,072,207		2,822,185
1943	26,196,525	13,231,409	12,564,164		3,003,969
1944	30,341,390	12,257,238	12,168,811		3,077,429
1945	30,821,315	21,106,654	7,079,058		2,108,987
1946	34,697,034	16,010,227	16,678,020		2,716,617
1947	61,432,505	17,145,177	14,815,369		2,457,807
1948	113,793,427	26,793,867	83,428,045		2,396,980
1949	80,399,726	78,066,083			3,976,951
1950	94,185,727	85,011,355			4,064,545
1951	97,020,194	84,485,056			4,421,466
1952	90,872,834	84,865,555			5,033,837
1953	115,406,585	105,455,091			4,745,706
1954	121,126,546	105,710,560			5,730,171
1955	125,531,950	102,527,293			6,797,627

---

* These figures are net after setting aside special reserve fund.

( ) Indicates deficit.

III. NET CRUDE OIL PRODUCTION
Shell Oil Company and Predecessor Companies
(Barrels)

Year	Total	Shell Pacific Coast	Roxana Petroleum & Successor Cos.	Comar Oil Company [a]	Wolverine Petroleum Corporation [b]
1912	443,000		443,000		
1913	723,000		723,000		
1914	505,000	4,268,000[e]	505,000		
1915	5,704,000	3,104,000	2,600,000		
1916	8,836,000	4,752,000	4,084,000		
1917	9,279,000	6,293,000	2,986,000		
1918	9,503,000	6,788,000	2,715,000		
1919	9,157,000	6,695,000	2,462,000		
1920	9,211,000	6,146,000	3,065,000		
1921	7,893,000	4,889,000	3,004,000		
1922	16,644,000	10,980,000[d]	5,664,000[d]		
1923	33,700,000	21,699,000	4,648,000	5,523,000	1,830,000
1924	33,828,000	21,580,000	5,520,000	4,863,000	1,865,000
1925	34,576,000	19,565,000	7,886,000	5,902,000	1,223,000
1926	35,562,000	20,581,000	8,468,000	5,530,000	983,000
1927	36,618,000	19,209,000	13,767,000	2,750,000	892,000
1928	47,788,000	22,624,000	22,651,000	1,698,000	815,000
1929	46,791,000	23,702,000	21,020,000	1,332,000	737,000
1930	34,599,000	16,060,000	16,876,000	994,000	669,000
1931	31,058,000	13,532,000	16,226,000	709,000[e]	591,000
1932	30,999,000	14,921,000	15,517,000		561,000[f]
1933	35,032,000	14,054,000	20,466,000		512,000[f]
1934	35,307,000	14,226,000	20,585,000		496,000[f]
1935	43,278,000	18,796,000	23,994,000		488,000
1936	46,218,000	21,230,000	24,526,000		462,000
1937	48,653,000	21,945,000	26,265,000		443,000
1938	46,214,000	21,222,000	24,992,000		[g]
1939	47,826,000	18,219,000	29,607,000		
1940	51,053,000	17,843,000	33,210,000		
1941	55,639,000	19,422,000	36,217,000		
1942	60,041,000	23,956,000	36,085,000		
1943	67,708,000	28,855,000	38,853,000		
1944	72,395,000	28,115,000	44,280,000		
1945	69,275,000	26,470,000	42,805,000		
1946	65,224,000	22,679,000	42,545,000		
1947	71,356,000	21,591,000	49,765,000		
1948	78,550,000	21,712,000	56,838,000		
1949	70,095,000	22,537,000	47,558,000		
1950	72,216,000	20,699,000	51,517,000		
1951	86,221,000	25,021,000	61,200,000		
1952	96,099,000	30,864,000	65,235,000		
1953	104,268,000	36,437,000	67,831,000		
1954	97,694,000	34,102,000	63,592,000		
1955	101,581,000	30,765,000	70,816,000		

[a] Figures shown are Roxana's half share of Comar's production, net.
[b] Figure is Wolverine total net production which Roxana was entitled to purchase.
[c] Includes last four months of 1913.
[d] Estimated from Royal Dutch annual report, 1922.
[e] Comar dissolved December 31, 1931.
[f] From annual reports, Wolverine Petroleum Corporation.
[g] Wolverine dissolved end of 1938.

IV. CRUDE OIL PURCHASES

Shell Oil Company and Predecessor Companies

(In net barrels—all purchases, including royalty oil, less sales of crude)

Year	Total	Shell Pacific Coast	Shell Mid-Continent
1912			
1913			
1914			
1915	(1,672,000)	(1,672,000)	
1916	164,000	164,000	
1917	163,000	(157,000)	320,000
1918	1,580,000	1,460,000	120,000
1919	1,380,000	1,243,000	137,000
1920	538,000	391,000	147,000
1921	531,000	70,000	461,000
1922	610,000	(484,000)	1,094,000
1923	2,431,000	(1,796,000)	4,227,000
1924	5,317,000	(2,127,000)	7,444,000
1925	13,204,000	2,978,000	10,226,000
1926	12,783,000	2,744,000	10,039,000
1927	16,129,000	6,339,000	9,790,000
1928	18,880,000	7,923,000	10,957,000
1929	24,835,000	11,809,000	13,026,000
1930	35,943,000	12,620,000	23,323,000
1931	28,455,000	7,038,000	21,417,000
1932	28,470,000	8,751,000	19,719,000
1933	33,682,000	9,815,000	23,867,000
1934	30,592,000	6,841,000	23,751,000
1935	34,504,000	6,941,000	27,563,000
1936	36,115,000	4,227,000	31,888,000
1937	41,485,000	5,840,000	35,645,000
1938	34,627,000	5,984,000	28,643,000
1939	34,137,000	6,007,000	28,130,000
1940	32,062,000	6,947,000	25,115,000
1941	29,587,000	9,183,000	20,404,000
1942	33,384,000	9,612,000	23,772,000
1943	34,117,000	9,128,000	24,989,000
1944	37,482,000	10,874,000	26,608,000
1945	39,654,000	14,427,000	25,227,000
1946	38,897,000	11,939,000	26,958,000
1947	35,917,000	12,350,000	23,567,000
1948	44,103,000	12,028,000	32,075,000
1949	56,085,000	15,772,000	40,313,000
1950	57,963,000	14,087,000	43,876,000
1951	60,249,000	15,685,000	44,564,000
1952	47,245,000	12,946,000	34,299,000
1953	52,442,000	11,798,000	40,644,000
1954	65,703,000	15,158,000	50,545,000
1955	75,532,000	17,985,000	57,547,000

( ) Excess of sales over purchases.

V. REFINERY CAPACITY

Shell Oil Company and Predecessor Companies

(Daily capacity at end of year in barrels)

Year	Total	Shell Pacific Coast	Roxana Petroleum and Successor Companies
1912			
1913			
1914	(No refining operations prior to years first shown)		
1915			
1916	13,000	13,000	
1917	26,500	19,000	7,500
1918	28,500	21,000	7,500
1919	27,500	20,000	7,500
1920	36,000	21,000	15,000
1921	29,000	14,000	15,000
1922[a]	60,000	27,000	33,000
1923	95,000	43,000	52,000
1924	95,000	54,000	41,000
1925	105,000	56,000	49,000
1926	180,000	72,000	108,000
1927	220,000	87,000	133,000
1928	240,000	93,000	147,000
1929	290,000	109,000	181,000
1930	299,000	107,000	192,000
1931	298,500	89,000	209,500
1932	290,300	90,000	200,300
1933	290,000	83,000	207,000
1934	285,000	71,000	214,000
1935	308,200	83,000	225,200
1936	296,300	96,000	200,300
1937	313,600	108,000	205,600
1938	291,700	104,000	187,700
1939	245,900	90,000	155,900
1940	255,200	82,000	173,200
1941	255,500	90,000	165,500
1942	253,600	111,000	142,600
1943	267,000	120,000	147,000
1944	286,800	133,000	153,800
1945	282,700	138,000	144,700
1946	314,700	109,000	205,700
1947	341,700	107,000	234,700
1948	355,700	103,700	252,000
1949	367,000	97,000	270,000
1950	382,000	97,000	285,000
1951	397,000	97,000	300,000
1952	429,000	119,000	310,000
1953	479,000	134,000	345,000
1954	504,000	134,000	370,000
1955	561,000	184,000	377,000

[a] Figures for Pacific Coast from 1922 on are by subtraction.

VI. REFINERY CRUDE OIL INTAKES FOR YEAR

Shell Oil Company and Predecessor Companies

(Barrels)

Year	Total	Shell Pacific Coast	Roxana Petroleum and Successor Companies
1912			
1913			
1914	(No refining operations prior to years first shown)		
1915			
1916	4,881,000	4,881,000	
1917	8,459,000	6,928,000	1,531,000
1918	10,239,000	7,728,000	2,511,000
1919	9,750,000	7,150,000	2,600,000
1920	10,662,000	7,522,000	3,140,000
1921	8,160,000	4,996,000	3,164,000
1922[a]	15,018,000	9,688,000	5,330,000
1923	25,824,000	15,748,000	10,076,000
1924	32,864,000	19,901,000	12,963,000
1925	36,220,000	20,441,000	15,779,000
1926	45,163,000	26,144,000	19,019,000
1927	53,536,000	31,176,000	22,360,000
1928	60,209,000	31,459,000	28,750,000
1929	75,476,000	36,285,000	39,191,000
1930	67,300,000	28,205,000	39,095,000
1931	62,072,000	21,504,000	40,568,000
1932	59,525,000	23,354,000	36,171,000
1933	65,882,000	24,230,000	41,652,000
1934	65,459,000	18,990,000	46,469,000
1935	75,292,000	22,540,000	52,752,000
1936	81,413,000	23,641,000	57,772,000
1937	82,522,000	23,529,000	58,993,000
1938	81,867,000	23,451,000	58,416,000
1939	80,801,000	23,016,000	57,785,000
1940	80,612,000	24,107,000	56,505,000
1941	81,453,000	25,203,000	56,250,000
1942	85,201,000	27,147,000	58,054,000
1943	90,269,000	30,452,000	59,817,000
1944	102,453,000	33,557,000	68,896,000
1945	102,540,000	35,525,000	67,015,000
1946	99,403,000	29,659,000	69,744,000
1947	102,934,000	29,581,000	73,353,000
1948	116,258,000	28,968,000	87,290,000
1949	119,356,000	32,459,000	86,897,000
1950	125,215,000	31,021,000	94,194,000
1951	142,083,000	35,812,000	106,271,000
1952	139,632,000	38,567,000	101,065,000
1953	150,371,000	41,641,000	108,730,000
1954	157,262,000	42,635,000	114,627,000
1955	168,896,000	41,881,000	127,015,000

---

[a] Figures for Pacific Coast from 1922 on are by subtraction.

VII. GASOLINE MANUFACTURED

Shell Oil Company and Predecessor Companies

(Barrels)

Year	Total	Shell Pacific Coast	Roxana Petroleum and Successor Companies
1912			
1913			
1914	(No refining operations prior to years first shown)		
1915			
1916	195,000	195,000	
1917	453,000	254,000	199,000
1918	645,000	283,000	362,000
1919	851,000	419,000	432,000
1920	1,572,000	734,000	838,000
1921	1,444,000	557,000	887,000
1922	2,729,000	1,462,000	1,267,000
1923	6,865,000	4,112,000	2,753,000
1924	9,419,000	4,282,000	5,137,000
1925	11,931,000	4,907,000	7,024,000
1926	17,395,000	8,073,000	9,322,000
1927	20,675,000	10,178,000	10,497,000
1928	25,596,000	12,369,000	13,227,000
1929	31,213,000	15,374,000	15,839,000
1930	32,477,000	13,616,000	18,861,000
1931	30,366,000	10,916,000	19,450,000
1932	29,447,000	11,607,000	17,840,000
1933	28,562,000	10,469,000	18,093,000
1934[a]	28,101,000	9,088,000	19,013,000
1935	33,666,000	10,759,000	22,907,000
1936	38,165,000	12,342,000	25,823,000
1937	39,571,000	12,945,000	26,626,000
1938	40,594,000	12,564,000	28,030,000
1939	40,949,000	11,916,000	29,033,000
1940	39,484,000	11,113,000	28,371,000
1941	42,309,000	12,494,000	29,815,000
1942	41,614,000	13,797,000	27,817,000
1943	42,901,000	15,273,000	27,628,000
1944	51,367,000	16,785,000	34,582,000
1945	51,005,000	16,985,000	34,020,000
1946	43,826,000	13,788,000	30,038,000
1947	48,110,000	14,058,000	34,052,000
1948	55,736,000	13,535,000	42,201,000
1949	63,003,000	16,658,000	46,345,000
1950	66,332,000	16,058,000	50,274,000
1951	74,591,000	18,916,000	55,675,000
1952	74,005,000	19,978,000	54,027,000
1953	81,375,000	22,206,000	59,169,000
1954	84,220,000	21,699,000	62,521,000
1955	91,631,000	21,077,000	70,554,000

[a] Figures for Pacific Coast from 1934 on are by subtraction.

VIII. MILEAGE OF TRUNK PIPE LINES

Shell Oil Company, Shell Pipe Line Corporation, and Predecessor Companies

(*Note:* It should be called to the reader's attention that pipe line mileage figures are not as indicative as they might at first glance seem. "Trunk line" and "gathering line" have been subject to continual redefinition, with the result that much so-called trunk line of earlier years was later reclassified as gathering line. Another difficulty arises from the trend in recent years towards large pipe lines owned jointly by several companies. The problem of showing this ownership as miles of pipe line has been arbitrarily solved here by including the total lengths of such lines, and indicating by a footnote the lengths included and Shell's percentage interest in each. A more serious problem cannot be overcome: some of the new 20-inch diameter lines will transport roughly four times the volume of the old 8- and 10-inch lines; this extra carrying capacity cannot be shown in any chart of miles. This should be particularly borne in mind when examining figures from 1949 onward.)

	CRUDE OIL TRUNK LINES			Product and Natural Gasoline Lines (Total)
Year	Total	Pacific Coast	East of Rockies	
1915	194[a]	169[a]	25[a]	
1916	194[a]	169[a]	25[a]	
1917	295[a]	169[a]	126[a]	
1918	723[a]	169[a]	554[a]	
1919	723[a]	169[a]	554[a]	
1920	723[a]	169[a]	554[a]	
1921	751	169	582	
1922	804	169	635	
1923	968	215	753[b]	
1924	1165	226	939	16[c]
1925	1299	264	1035	16
1926	1514	282	1232	16
1927	2064	394	1670	129
1928	3085	399	2686	139
1929	3683	412	3271	149
1930	3746	412	3334	149
1931	3808	428	3380	151
1932	3833	467	3366	151
1933	3843	467	3376	150
1934	3845	473	3372	150
1935	3922	511	3411	150

[a] Figures for years 1915–1920 calculated as follows: Valley Pipe Line, built 1915, 169 miles; Healdton to Cushing line, built 1917, 126 miles; Cushing to Wood River line, put in operation 1918, 428 miles. The old Yarhola Pipe Line Company, purchased in 1915, had some 25 miles of pipe, classified as gathering line from 1917 onward.

[b] By subtraction.

[c] Figures in this column, 1924–1937, represent natural gasoline lines on the Pacific Coast; first Shell products pipe line, from Wood River to Lima, Ohio, was put in service during 1938.

MILEAGE OF TRUNK PIPE LINES (*continued*)

| Year | CRUDE OIL TRUNK LINES | | | Product and Natural Gasoline Lines (Total) |
	Total	Pacific Coast	East of Rockies	
1936	4308	657	3651	150
1937	4570	670	3900	156
1938	4604	667	3937	672
1939	4654	684	3970	713
1940	4344	687	3657	963
1941	4506	685	3821	1835[d]
1942	3775	661	3114	2281[e]
1943	3813	689	3124	2566[f]
1944	3800	693	3107	2566
1945	3806	678	3128	2587
1946	3845	680	3165	2587
1947	3836	683	3153	2718
1948	4236	688	3548[g]	2719
1949	4912	689	4223[h]	2709
1950	4645	693	3952[i]	2965[j]
1951	4686	694	3992	3609[k]
1952	4644	694	3950	3587
1953	4788	700	4088[l]	3986[m]
1954	4828	713	4115	4023[n]
1955	5331	716	4615[p]	4343[q]

[d] Includes 812-mile trunk line of Plantation Pipe Line Company built during 1941. From 1941 to 1949, 23.3% of Plantation's stock was held by Shell.

[e] Includes 449 miles of Plantation spur line completed during 1942.

[f] Addition during 1943 of 303 miles of Bayou Pipe Line System, 27.44% owned by Shell.

[g] Includes 341 miles of Basin Pipe Line System, 34% Shell-owned, then under construction.

[h] Basin System mileage included, 515 miles; 433 miles of Ozark Pipe Line System, 55% Shell-owned.

[i] From this point onward, Basin System, 524 miles; Ozark System, 440 miles.

[j] Includes 273 miles Inland Corporation line; Inland stock, 1950–54, owned 50% by Shell.

[k] Plantation Line, under expansion, now 1968 miles long and Shell ownership increased to 24.04%.

[l] Includes 460-mile Rancho Pipe Line System, 44% owned by Shell, and 89 miles of Sterling Pipe Line System, one-third Shell-owned. Sterling mileage 98 miles in 1954, 126 miles in 1955.

[m] Expanded Plantation System now 2051 miles long; Inland line 295 miles; also includes 295-mile Wolverine Pipe Line, stock held 40% by Shell.

[n] Inland lines included, 333 miles.

[p] Includes 509-mile line of Butte Pipe Line Company, stock held 60% by Shell.

[q] Includes 587 miles of line owned by Inland Corporation, whose stock is now held 30% by Shell.

IX. TANK CARS AND TANK TRUCKS

Shell Oil Company and Predecessor Companies

| | RAILROAD TANK CARS | | | | TANK TRUCKS OWNED BY COMPANY | | |
| | Pacific Coast Owned | East of Rockies | | | | | |
Year	Total	& Leased	Owned	Leased	Total	Pacific Coast [c]	East of Rockies
1912	7	7			15	15	
1913	28	28			33	33	
1914	28	28			43	43	
1915	38	38			64	64	
1916	88	38	50		75	75	
1917	400	170	230		101	101	
1918	964	161	553	250	114	114	
1919	1109	201	658	250	130	130	
1920	1202	196	756	250	147	147	
1921	1323	170	903	250	203	203	
1922	1492	189	930	373	325	325	
1923	2548	407	1614	527[a]	744	638	106
1924	3255	412	1907	936[a]	943	664	279
1925	3518	410	1899	1209[a]	1084	754	330
1926	4398	416	2266	1716[a]	1166	772	394
1927	5127	442	2336	2349[a]	1242	781	461
1928	5725	437	2335	2953[a]	1310	877	433
1929	7544	473	3135	3936	1806	1000	806
1930	6801	551	3354	2896	2131	992	1139
1931	5888	607	3354	1927	2061	931	1130
1932	5223	601	3354	1268	2038	895	1143
1933	5469	589	3353	1527	1978	822	1156
1934	5364	591	3350	1423	1745	697	1048
1935	5211	626	3346	1239	1729	703	1026
1936	4922	643	3342	937	1639	755	884
1937	5295	755	3334	1206	1511	690	821
1938	5150	735	3327	1088	1489	700	789
1939	4778	658	3316	804	1439	708	731
1940	4979	658	3298	1023	1415	693	722
1941	4950	706	3265	979	1269	721	548
1942	5272	706	3261	1305	1244	738	506
1943	5403	723	3231	1449	1211	729	482
1944	4655	684	3174	797	1135	671	464
1945	4555	652	3151	752	1135	684	451
1946	4067	858	2296	913	1238	728	510
1947	4451	991	1819	1641	1382	761	621
1948	4745	610	4135[a]		1251	1251	
1949	4591	591	4000[a]		1266	1266	
1950	3795	578	3217[a]		1255	1255	
1951	4233	883	3350[a]		1264[a]	1264[a]	
1952	4378	958	3420[a]		1223[a]	1223[a]	
1953	4620	1155[b]	3465[a]		1157[a]	1157[a]	
1954	4644	969	3675[a]		1136[a]	1136[a]	
1955	4426	876	3550[a]		1209[a]	1209[a]	

[a] Estimated.

[b] Movement of Montana crude oil by tank car.

[c] Figures for early years include tank wagons.

X. WATER TERMINALS, DEPOTS, AND SERVICE STATIONS
Shell Oil Company and Predecessor Companies
(Service stations estimated; do not include stations served by jobbers)

APPROXIMATE NUMBER OF
RETAIL OUTLETS, ALL TYPES

Year	Pacific Coast	East of Rockies	Atlantic Seaboard	Total Retail Outlets	BULK DEPOTS Pacific Coast	BULK DEPOTS East of Rockies	BULK DEPOTS Total Depots	Ocean Terminals
1912	25			25	6		6	
1913	100			100	12		12	
1914	208			208	18		18	
1915	308			308	31		31	
1916	510			510	32		32	
1917	712			712	32		32	
1918	913			913	32		32	
1919	1,014			1,014	32		32	
1920	1,317			1,317	32		32	
1921	1,523			1,523	39		39	
1922	1,841			1,841	77		77	
1923	2,184	1,069[a]		2,235	146	58	204	
1924	2,556	1,575[a]		2,686	152	88	240	
1925	2,913	2,487[a]		3,438	191	109	300	
1926	3,259	3,080[a]		4,048	189	151	340	
1927	3,593	3,957[a]		5,150	221	219	440	
1928	4,012	[b]		6,309	414	258	672	
1929	4,366	6,966		11,332	469	549	1,018	7
1930	4,338	8,774	400	13,512	565	660	1,225	8
1931	4,156	8,754	532	13,442	569	624	1,193	8
1932	5,199	7,631	555	13,385	589	578	1,167	8
1933	5,467	8,036	822	14,325	596	637	1,233	8
1934	5,441	10,051	746	16,238	531	652	1,183	9
1935	5,762	14,607[c]		20,369	537	668	1,205	9
1936	5,696	14,543		20,239	551	670	1,221	9
1937	5,554	13,868		19,422	541	695	1,236	9
1938	5,345	13,999		19,344	532	702	1,234	10
1939	5,536	13,609		19,145	529	668	1,197	10
1940	6,150	13,247		19,397	523	554	1,077	10
1941	5,974	11,720		17,694	514	510	1,024	10
1942	4,971	10,282		15,253	516	450	966	10
1943	4,471	9,104		13,575	516	445	961	10
1944	4,116	8,869		12,985	463	459	922	10
1945	4,470	8,682		13,152	465	472	937	10
1946	4,753	9,835		14,588	474	487	961	10
1947	5,055	9,706		14,761	475	486	961	9
1948	4,882	9,174		14,056	472	499	971	9
1949	4,654	9,040		13,694	410	501	911	9
1950	4,553	8,445		12,998	408	480	888	9
1951	4,492	7,466		11,958	401	437	838	10
1952	3,974	6,837		10,811	402	424	826	10
1953	3,516	6,557		10,073	396	411	807	9
1954	3,473	6,448		9,921	398	405	803	9
1955	3,532	6,542		10,074	395	426	821	9

[a] Information supplied in answer to government questionnaire, June 1928.
[b] Accurate figure unavailable.
[c] Atlantic Seaboard stations included in East of Rockies after 1934.

Index

Citations of sources are indexed where they provide significant additional information: 716 (44) refers to page 716, citation 44. Halftone illustrations are indicated in this manner: *f.* 144, meaning following page 144. Maps and line drawings are indicated by italicized page numbers; *n* refers to footnote on page mentioned.

Wolbert, G. S., Jr., 483*n*, 746(108)
Wolverine Petroleum Corp., *f.* 208, 223-26, 353, 493
Wolverine Pipe Line Co., 657
Wood River laboratory, 549-50, 621-23, 624, 638, 687
Wood River, Ill., refinery, 142-47, *f.* 144, 166, *f.* 208, 244-47, 252-53, 300, 302, 314, 328, 343, 349, 367, 407, 409, 410-12, 415, 433-34, 435, 445-47, 488, 561, 565, 568-69, 576, 582, 584, 601, 630, 632, 638, 658, 660-64; catalytic crackers, 586-87, *f.* 592, 630, 660; hot-acid polymerization, 566
Woodruff, G. G., 150, 300, 301, 313, 349, 717(82), 767
Woods, F. W., 694, 723(111), 778
Woods, W. W., 779
Woodward, H. B., 120
Work, Hubert, 232-33
World-Powell, Tex., field, 334
World War I: fuel oil in, 99-101; labor in, 104, 144, 152-54; Martinez refinery and, 99, 101-102; oil industry and, 99-104; Royal Dutch-Shell Group and, 100-101; tankers in, 100, *f.* 112; toluene in, 100
World War II: chemical production, 615-18; crude oil production, 627-29, 644; financing in, 629-30; marketing and, 626-30; military leave policy, 635-36; oil industry and, 555-59; oil needs in, 554-55, 627; personnel and, 631-36; pipe lines and, 602-16; rationing, 626-27; research and, 618-26; salvage drives, 633-34; service sta-

tions and, 626; Shell Chemical Co. and, 615-18; Shell companies and, 559; Shell people in wartime agencies, 634-35; synthetic rubber and, 588-98; tankers and, 464, 602-603, 606-607; toluene, 599-602; women workers, *f.* 624, 631-32
Wrightsman Petroleum Co., 196
Wyoming: exploration in, 162-64, 648-49; marketing, 297, 455, 671

"X-100" motor oil, 686
Xylene, 660
Xylidine ("C. S."), 584-85, 617-18

Yale, Okla., field, 139, 156, 159
Yankee Filling Stations, Inc., 323
Yankee Filling Stations of New Haven, Inc., 323
Yarhola absorption plant, 158-59
Yarhola leases, Okla., 132-33, 134, 470
Yarhola, Linda and Maley, 132
Yarhola Pipe Line Co., 132, 145, 169
Yates, Tex., field, 335, 337, 380, 383, 413
Ymuiden, Holland, ammonia plant, 520-22, 524, 527
Youle, W. E., 220
Young, James, 8-9, 235
Youngstown Sheet & Tube Co., 83, 144, 654
Yowell, O. P., 178, 181

Zijlker, Aeilco Janz, 20-24, 33-34, *f.* 48
Zoroaster, 40
Zulver, Cornelius, 100

Set in Linotype Janson and printed by
THE HADDON CRAFTSMEN, INC., *Scranton,*
Pennsylvania, on paper manufactured
by the S. D. WARREN COMPANY, *Boston.*